Short Story Criticism

Guide to Gale Literary Criticism Series

For criticism on	Consult these Gale series
Authors now living or who died after December 31, 1959	*CONTEMPORARY LITERARY CRITICISM (CLC)*
Authors who died between 1900 and 1959	*TWENTIETH-CENTURY LITERARY CRITICISM (TCLC)*
Authors who died between 1800 and 1899	*NINETEENTH-CENTURY LITERATURE CRITICISM (NCLC)*
Authors who died between 1400 and 1799	*LITERATURE CRITICISM FROM 1400 TO 1800 (LC)* *SHAKESPEAREAN CRITICISM (SC)*
Authors who died before 1400	*CLASSICAL AND MEDIEVAL LITERATURE CRITICISM (CMLC)*
Authors of books for children and young adults	*CHILDREN'S LITERATURE REVIEW (CLR)*
Dramatists	*DRAMA CRITICISM (DC)*
Poets	*POETRY CRITICISM (PC)*
Short story writers	*SHORT STORY CRITICISM (SSC)*
Black writers of the past two hundred years	*BLACK LITERATURE CRITICISM (BLC)*
Hispanic writers of the late nineteenth and twentieth centuries	*HISPANIC LITERATURE CRITICISM (HLC)*
Native North American writers and orators of the eighteenth, nineteenth, and twentieth centuries	*NATIVE NORTH AMERICAN LITERATURE (NNAL)*
Major authors from the Renaissance to the present	*WORLD LITERATURE CRITICISM, 1500 TO THE PRESENT (WLC)*

ISSN 0895-9439

Volume 29

Short Story Criticism

Excerpts from Criticism of the Works of Short Fiction Writers

Anna J. Sheets
Lawrence J. Trudeau
Editors

GALE

DETROIT · NEW YORK · LONDON

STAFF

Anna J. Sheets, Lawrence J. Trudeau *Editors*

Debra A. Wells, *Assistant Editor*

Susan Trosky, *Permissions Manager*

Kimberly F. Smilay, *Permissions Specialist*
Sarah Chesney, *Permissions Associate*
Stephen Cusack, Kelly Quin, *Permissions Assistants*

Victoria B. Cariappa, *Research Manager*

Michele P. LaMeau, *Research Specialist*
Julie C. Daniel, Tamara C. Nott, Tracie A. Richardson,
Norma Sawaya, Cheryl L. Warnock,
Research Associates

Mary Beth Trimper, *Production Director*
Deborah Milliken, *Production Assistant*

C. J. Jonik, *Desktop Publisher*
Randy Bassett, *Image Database Supervisor*
Michael Ansari, Robert Duncan, *Scanner Operator*
Pamela Reed, *Photography Coordinator*

Library of Congress Catalog Card Number 88-641014
ISBN 0-7876-2052-1
ISSN 0895-9439

Printed in the United States of America

10 9 8 7 6 5 4 3 2 1

Contents

Preface vii

Acknowledgments xi

Preface

A Comprehensive Information Source on World Short Fiction

hort Story Criticism (SSC) presents significant passages from criticism of the world's greatest short story writers and provides supplementary biographical and bibliographical materials to guide the interested reader to a greater understanding of the authors of short fiction. This series was developed in response to suggestions from librarians serving high school, college, and public library patrons, who had noted a considerable number of requests for critical material on short story writers. Although major short story writers are covered in such Gale series as *Contemporary Literary Criticism (CLC)*, *Twentieth-Century Literary Criticism (TCLC)*, *Nineteenth-Century Literature Criticism (NCLC)*, and *Literature Criticism from 1400 to 1800 (LC)*, librarians perceived the need for a series devoted solely to writers of the short story genre.

Coverage

SSC is designed to serve as an introduction to major short story writers of all eras and nationalities. Since these authors have inspired a great deal of relevant critical material, *SSC* is necessarily selective, and the editors have chosen the most important published criticism to aid readers and students in their research.

Approximately eight to ten authors are included in each volume, and each entry presents a historical survey of the critical response to that author's work. The length of an entry is intended to reflect the amount of critical attention the author has received from critics writing in English and from foreign critics in translation. Every attempt has been made to identify and include excerpts from the most significant essays on each author's work. In order to provide these important critical pieces, the editors sometimes reprint essays that have appeared elsewhere in Gale's Literary Criticism Series. Such duplication, however, never exceeds twenty percent of an *SSC* volume.

Organization

An *SSC* author entry consists of the following elements:

■ The **Author Heading** cites the name under which the author most commonly wrote, followed by birth and death dates. If the author wrote consistently under a pseudonym, the pseudonym will be listed in the author heading and the author's actual name given in parentheses on the first line of the biographical and critical introduction.

■ The **Biographical and Critical Introduction** contains background information designed to introduce a reader to the author and the critical debates surrounding his or her work.

■ A **Portrait of the Author** is included when available. Many entries also contain illustrations of materials pertinent to an author's career, including holographs of manuscript pages, title pages, dust jackets, letters, or representations of important people, places, and events in the author's life.

■ The list of **Principal Works** is chronological by date of first publication and lists the most importantworks by the author. The first section comprises short story collections, novellas, and novella collections. The second section gives information on other major works by the author. For foreign authors, the editors have provided original foreign-language publication information and have selected what are considered the best and most complete English-language editions of their works.

■ **Criticism** is arranged chronologically in each author entry to provide a useful perspective on changes in critical evaluation over the years. All short story, novella, and collection titles by the author featured in the entry are printed in boldface type to enable a reader to ascertain without difficulty the works discussed. Also for purposes of easier identification, the critic's name and the publication date of the essay are given at the beginning of each piece of criticism. Unsigned criticism is preceded by the title of the journal in which it appeared.

- Critical essays are prefaced with **Explanatory Notes** as an additional aid to students and readers using SSC. An explanatory note may provide useful information of several types, including: the reputation of the critic, the intent or scope of the critical essay, and the orientation of the criticism (biographical, psychoanalytic, structuralist, etc.).

- A complete **Bibliographical Citation,** designed to help the interested reader locate the original essay or book, precedes each piece of criticism.

- The **Further Reading List** appearing at the end of each author entry suggests additional materials on the author. In some cases it includes essays for which the editors could not obtain reprint rights. Boxed material following the further reading list provides references to other biographical and critical sources on the author in series published by Gale.

Beginning with volume six, SSC contains two additional features designed to enhance the reader's understanding of short fiction writers and their works:

- Each SSC entry now includes, when available, **Comments by the Author** that illuminate his or her own works or the short story genre in general. These statements are set within boxes or bold rules to distinguish them from the criticism.

- A **Select Bibliography of General Sources on Short Fiction** is included as an appendix. This listing of materials for further research provides readers with a selection of the best available general studies of the short story genre.

Other Features

A **Cumulative Author Index** lists all the authors who have appeared in SSC, CLC, TCLC, NCLC, LC, and Classical and Medieval Literature Criticism (CMLC), as well as cross-references to other Gale series. Users will welcome this cumulated index as a useful tool for locating an author within the Literary Criticism Series.

A **Cumulative Nationality Index** lists all authors featured in SSC by nationality, followed by the number of the SSC volume in which their entry appears.

A **Cumulative Title Index** lists in alphabetical order all short story, novella, and collection titles contained in the SSC series. Titles of short story collections, separately published novellas, and novella collections are printed in italics, while titles of individual short stories are printed in roman type with quotation marks. Each title is followed by the author's name and corresponding volume and page numbers where commentary on the work is located. English-language translations of original foreign-language titles are cross-referenced to the foreign titles so that all references to discussion of a work are combined in one listing.

Citing Short Story Criticism

When writing papers, students who quote directly from any volume in the Literary Criticism Series may use the following general forms to footnote reprinted criticism. The first example pertains to material drawn from periodicals, the second to material reprinted from books:

[1]Henry James, Jr., "Honoré de Balzac," The Galaxy 20 (December 1875), 814-36; excerpted and reprinted in Short Story Criticism, Vol. 5, ed. Thomas Votteler (Detroit: Gale Research, 1990), pp. 8-11.

[2]F. R. Leavis, D. H. Lawrence: Novelist (Alfred A. Knopf, 1956); excerpted and reprinted in Short Story Criticism, Vol. 4, ed. Thomas Votteler (Detroit: Gale Research, 1990), pp. 202-06.

Comments

Readers who wish to suggest authors to appear in future volumes, or who have other suggestions, are invited to contact the editors by writing to Gale Research, Literary Criticism Division, 835 Penobscot Building, Detroit, MI 48226-4094.

Acknowledgments

The editors wish to thank the copyright holders of the excerpted criticism included in this volume and the permissions managers of many book and magazine publishing companies for assisting us in securing reproduction rights. We are also grateful to the staffs of the Detroit Public Library, the Library of Congress, the University of Detroit Mercy Library, Wayne State University Purdy/Kresge Library Complex, and the University of Michigan Libraries for making their resources available to us. Following is a list of the copyright holders who have granted us permission to reproduce material in this volume of *SSC*. Every effort has been made to trace copyright, but if omissions have been made, please let us know.

COPYRIGHTED EXCERPTS IN *SSC*, VOLUME 29, WERE REPRODUCED FROM THE FOLLOWING PERIODICALS:

American Imago, v. 55, Winter, 1978. Copyright © 1978 by Johns Hopkins University press. Reproduced by permission of The Johns Hopkins University Press.—*American Literature*, v. XXVIII, November, 1956; v. XXVIII, November, 1962; v. XXVIII, November, 1963; v. XXXVII, January, 1966; v. XLI, January, 1970. Copyright © 1956, renewed 1973; 1962, renewed 1990;1963, renewed 1991; 1966, 1970 Duke University Press, Durham, NC. All reproduced by permission.—*Book World—The Washington Post*, v. X, November 2, 1980; v. 12, October 24, 1982. Copyright © 1980, 1982 Washington Post Book World Service/Washington Post Writers Group. Both reproduced with permission.— *Colby Library Quarterly*, v. IX, December, 1971. Reproduced by permission of the publisher.—*Commonweal*, v. XLIX, March 11, 1949; v. LXXVIII, July 12, 1963; v. LXXXVI, August 25, 1967. Copyright 1949, © 1963, 1967 Commonweal Publishing Co., Inc. All reproduced by permission of Commonweal Foundation.—*Extrapolation*, v. 22, 1981; v. 27, Winter, 1986; v. 35, Summer, 1994. Copyright © 1981, 1986, 1994 by Kent State University Press. All reproduced by permission.—*German Life and Letters*, v. 24, July, 1971. Reproduced by permission of Blackwell Publishers Limited.—*Germanic Notes and Reviews*, v. 24, Spring, 1993. Reproduced by permission.—*Jack London Newsletter*, v. 10, May-August, 1977 for "Jesse Stuart's Use of Local Legends" by Mary Washington Clarke. Reproduced by permission.—*JEGP (Journal of English and Germanic Philology*, v. LXXIV, July 1975. Reproduced by permission of University of Illinois Press.—*Journal of Popular Culture*, v. 5, Spring, 1972. Reproduced by permission.—*Modern Fiction Studies*, v. 27, Spring, 1981. Copyright (c)1981. Reproduced by permission of The Johns Hopkins University Press.—*Neophilologus*, v. 78, January, 1994 for "Preconceived and Fixed Ideas: Self Fulfilling Prophesies in 'Der tolle Invalide auf dem Fort Ratonneau'" by Sheila Dickson. Reproduced by permission of the publisher and the author.— *Partisan Review*, Vol. XVI, July, 1949. Reproduced by permission.—*Publishers Weekly*, September 22, 1997. Copyright 1997 by Reed Publishing USA. Reproduced from Publishers Weekly, published by the Bowker Magazine Group of Cahners Publishing Co., a division of Reed Publishing USA. Reproduced by permission.—*Quarterly Review of Literature*, v. 2, 1945. Reproduced by permission.—*Renascence: A Critical Journal of Letters*, XVII, Summer, 1964. Copyright © 1964, Catholic Renascence Society, Inc. Reproduced by permission.—*Slavic and East European Journal*, v. 16, Spring, 1972. Reproduced by permission.—*Slavic Review*, v. 33, June, 1974. Reproduced by permission.—*South Atlantic Review*, v. 55, January, 1990. Copyright © 1990 by the South Atlantic Modern Language Association. Reproduced by permission.—*Southern Humanities Review*, v. XII, Winter, 1978 for "Politics in Graham Greene's 'The Destructors'" by Jesse F. McCartney. Copyright © 1978 by Auburn University. Reproduced by permission of the author.—*Studies in Short Fiction*, v. III, Fall, 1965; v. III, Spring, 1966; v. VIII, Fall, 1971; v. XI, Spring, 1974; v. XII, Winter, 1975; v. 14, Winter, 1977. Copyright © 1965, 1966, 1971, 1974, 1975, 1977 by Newberry College. All reproduced by permission.—*The Atlantic Monthly*, v. 209, June, 1962 for "Master Craftsman" by William Barrett. Copyright © renewed February 20, 1990 by The Atlantic Monthly Company. Reproduced by permission of the author.— *The CEA Critic*, v. 33, March, 1971. Reproduced by permission.—*The Explicator*, v. XXVIII, December, 1969; v. XXIX, January, 1971. Copyright © 1969, 1971 Helen Dwight Reid Educational Foundation. Both reproduced with permission of the Helen Dwight Reid Educational Foundation, published by Heldref Publications, 1319 18th Street, NW, Washington, DC 20036-1802.—*The German Quarterly*, v. XXXVII, 1964; v. XLII, May, 1969; v. XLVI, March, 1973; Both reproduced by permission.—*The Germanic Review*, v. LVII, Winter, 1983 for "Achim von Arnim and the Romantic Grotesque" by Kari E. Locke. Copyright © 1983 Helen Dwight Reid Educational Foundation. Published by Heldref Publications, 1319 18th Street, NW, Washington, DC 20036-1802.—*The Journal of General Education*, v. XXVIII, Spring, 1976. Copyright © 1976 by The Pennsylvania State University. Reproduced by permission of The Pennsylvania State University Press.—*The Journal of Narrative Technique*, v. 12, Fall, 1982 for "Narrative Structure and Theme in 'Young Goodman Brown'" by Norman H. Hostetler. Reproduced by permission of the publisher and the author.—*The Nathaniel Hawthorne Journal*, 1973 for "The Woe That Is Madness: Goodman Brown and the Face of the Fire" by Robert E. Morsberger; 1973 for "'Young Goodman Brown' as Historical Allegory" by Barton Levi St. Armond; 1975 for "The Reader in 'Young Goodman Brown'" by Sheldon W. Liebman; 1978 for "'Young Goodman Brown': Haw-

COPYRIGHTED EXCERPTS IN *SSC*, VOLUME 29, WERE REPRODUCED FROM THE FOLLOWING BOOKS:

Achim von Arnim
1781-1831

(Full name Ludwig Joachim von Arnim) German novella and short story writer, poet, novelist, dramatist, essayist, editor, and critic.

INTRODUCTION

An influential figure in the German Romantic movement, Arnim inspired among his contemporaries a renewed interest in their national literature and culture. His unfinished novel, *Die Kronenwächter,* was Germany's first historical novel, and is considered important to the development of that genre in German literature. He is also known for his collection of folktales and lyrics, *Des Knaben Wunderhorn,* which he compiled with Clemens Brentano, and which prompted a significant revival of interest in German folklore. He is best remembered, however, for his numerous novellas, including *Isabella von Ägypten, Der tolle Invalide auf dem Fort Ratonneau,* and *Die Majoratsherren.* In these works Arnim blended folkloric motifs with Romantic sensibility, seeking to reveal a higher historical truth and to invigorate the German national spirit.

Biographical Information

A descendant of Prussian nobility, Arnim was born in Berlin and raised there by his maternal grandmother. He attended the university of Halle, where he pursued studies in the sciences, particularly experimental physics. While attending Halle, Arnim published several articles in scientific journals. In 1800 he entered the University of Göttingen, where he met Brentano, his later collaborator and lifelong friend. Brentano encouraged Arnim to abandon his scientific studies and concentrate his talents on writing. While travelling through western Europe and England between 1801 and 1804, Arnim published his first novel, *Hollins Liebeleben.* Modeled closely on Johann Wolfgang von Goethe's *The Sorrows of Young Werther,* the novel received little critical attention. Arnim eventually settled in Heidelberg, where he organized and became a leader of the Heidelberg Romantics. There he published *Des Knaben Wunderhorn,* which brought him the recognition he sought. Goethe, especially, encouraged his literary efforts, and Arnim looked to him as a mentor. Although Goethe approved of Arnim's style, he could not support the younger man's preoccupation with German medievalism, and the relationship deteriorated. Arnim's literary concerns were shared, however, by such figures as Brentano, the brothers Jakob and Wilhelm Grimm, and Joseph Görres, and together this group edited the short-lived journal *Zeitschrift für Einsiedler,* which encouraged the study of German folklore. It was discontinued after five months

but was published in book form as *Tröst-Einsamkeit,* Stirred by the wars of liberation against Napoleon, the Heidelberg Romantics then concentrated on more realistic and historical depictions of Germany, composing patriotic war songs and producing nationalist propaganda. In 1809 Arnim returned to Prussia, where he developed the mature writing style characteristic of his later work, particularly his novellas. In 1811 he married Brentano's sister, Bettina, and the following year he published his best-known novella collection (commonly known as *Novellensammlung 1812*). Arnim returned to his family estate in Wiepersdorf, forty miles south of Berlin, in 1814, and he remained there until his death of a stroke in 1831.

Major Works of Short Fiction

The novellas *Isabella von Ägypten, Der tolle Invalide auf dem Fort Ratonneau,* and *Die Majoratsherren* are regarded as three of Arnim's finest efforts, and they were quite popular in nineteenth-century Germany. In these works, Arnim successfully blends a historical picture of Germany with elements of the fantastic and grotesque. *Isabella von*

Ägypten pairs the historical Holy Roman Emperor Charles V with such fictional and mythic figures as the gypsy princess Isabella, a golem, and a mandrake root that becomes the dwarf Cornelius. Arnim employs these figures in an historical allegory depicting the fall of the Hapsburg dynasty. In *Die Majoratsherren* religious figures, such as Adam, Eve, and the Angel of Death, are featured in a critique of French decadence prior to the Revolution. *Der tolle Invalide* is considered by many to be his most accomplished work. In addition to skillfully combining the realistic and the fantastic in this story of a man's madness, Arnim also conveys a psychological awareness and moral insight not found in any of his other compositions.

Critical Reception

Although Arnim is generally given a minor position in the German Romantic movement, he is recognized for his part in inspiring a renewed interest in German folklore. Despite the initial popularity of Arnim's works, critics long censured them as confusing and poorly organized conglomerations of history and myth, elevated themes and grotesque imagery, and Romantic aesthetics and political commentary. Recent commentators, however, have found unifying patterns of imagery unifying Arnim's novellas, and they have observed consistent and coherent applications of the author's aesthetic, moral, and political views in the works. Increasingly, they have come to regard Arnim's novellas as his most successful creative works. In this shorter form, critics agree, Arnim overcame his predilection for extraneous detail and his tendency toward diffuseness which mar his longer works. Vickie L. Ziegler's comments on the collection *Der Wintergarten* can be applied to many of Arnim's novellas: "*Wintergarten* was not simply a futile literary exercise from a man who read too much; it was Arnim's attempt to advance his own deeply held beliefs about the interdependent role of literature, political action, and religious belief."

PRINCIPAL WORKS

Short Fiction

Der Wintergarten: Novellen (novella collection) 1809
**Isabella von Aegypten, Kaiser Karl des Fünften erste Jugenliebe: Eine Erzälung; Melück Maria Balinville, die Hausprophetin aus Arabien: Eine Anekdote; Die drei liebreichen Schwestern und der glückliche Färber: Ein Sittengemälde; Angelika, die Genueserin, und Comus, der Seilspringer: Eine Novelle* (novella collection) 1812
Die Majoratsherren (novella) 1820
Landhausleben (miscellaneous short fiction) 1826
†*Sechs Erzälungen: Nachlass von L. Achim von Arnim* (novella collection) 1835

Other Major Works

Hollins Liebeleben: Roman (novel) 1802
Des Knaben Wunderhorn. 3 vols. [with Clemens Brentano] (folktales and lyrics) 1806-08
Armuth, Reichthum, Schuld und Buss der Gräfin Dolores: Eine wahre Geshichte zur lehrreichen Unterhaltung armer Fräulein aufgeschrieben (novel) 1810
Halle und Jerusalem: Studentspiel und Pilgerabenteuer (drama) 1811
Die Kronenwächter (unfinished novel) 1817
Ludwig Achim von Arnim's sämmtliche Werke. 22 vols. (collected works) 1839-57

* This collection is often referred to as *Novellensammlung 1812.*

† This posthumous publication includes *Frau von Saverne; Die Einquartierung im Pfarrhause; Die Weihnachts-Austellung; Juvenis; Fürst Ganzgott und Sänger Halbgott;* and *Der tolle Invalide auf dem Fort Ratonneau.*

CRITICISM

Lawrence M. Washington and Ida H. Washington (essay date 1964)

SOURCE: "The Several Aspects of Fire in Achim von Arnim's *Der tolle Invalide,*" in *German Quarterly,* Vol. XXXVII, No. 4, November, 1964, pp. 498-505.

[*In the following essay, the Washingtons trace the fire imagery in* Der tolle Invalide, *noting that Arnim presents both "[n]atural and supernatural aspects of fire" in the novella.*]

In reading Achim von Arnim's Novelle, **Der tolle Invalide,** one is soon aware of the frequent occurrence of the word "Feuer" and related expressions. This seems at first to be merely clever word play, but a closer inspection shows that the various aspects of fire are so intimately connected with the events and characters of the story that they reflect the basic structure of the Novelle.

Fire is an unusually complex motif because it is so rich in connotative associations. From the earliest mention in primitive mythology, man has endowed fire with both natural and supernatural significance. He has sought it for its positive creative potentialities and has, at the same time, feared its destructive powers. Fire has thus come to represent symbolically things as various as home, love, heavenly grace, and on the other hand, war, hatred, and eternal damnation.

Arnim's awareness of the basic complexity of his motif is evident in the opening scene of the narrative. Count Dürande, the elderly commander of disabled veterans at Marseilles, is shown complaining of two kinds of coldness. The penetrating dampness of the October air makes him shiver physically, while the thoughtless gaiety of people in the street on their way to a ball chills him psychologically with a sense of being left out of social affairs ("einsam frierend"). To overcome his physical discomfort, the old commander shoves fuel onto the fire on his hearth, using his wooden leg as a poker. In addition to its warming effect, the fire also inspires his imagination by calling to mind his favorite hobby, fireworks. Dürande becomes so absorbed in daydreams that he forgets the danger inherent in the flames and fails to notice when his wooden leg catches fire: "In der Freude des Gelingens, wie er schon alles strahlen, sausen, prasseln, dann wieder alles in stiller Grösse leuchten sah, hatte er . . . nicht bemerkt, dass sein hölzernes Bein Feuer gefangen hatte und schon um ein Dritteil abgebrannt war."

At this point, a young woman who has been waiting to speak to Dürande rushes forward and tries to smother his flaming leg with her apron, but this also ignites. The commander's shouts bring help, and the fires are quickly put out with a bucket of water.

Though fire has played a multiple role in this first incident, its activity has been concentrated on a natural plane. It has shown itself a physical and psychological comforter, but at the same time dangerous as a seductive fascinator and potential destroyer when out of control. Fire in its physical manifestation is opposed by a natural enemy, water, which extinguishes it.

A further significance of fire is suggested in Arnim's charming description of olive leaves burning like love-sick hearts in the hearth: "Die knisternde Flamme ist mit dem grünen Laube wie durchflochten, halb brennend, halb grünend erscheinen die Blätter wie verliebte Herzen." This is the inner fire of love and has a dual potentiality: it is either life-giving ("grünend") or destructive ("brennend"). The two-fold significance of love is reiterated in the young woman's story. Rosalie opens her plea for understanding of her wounded husband Francoeur by stating that her love is the cause of all his trouble: "Meine Liebe trägt die Schuld von allem dem Unglück, -ich habe meinen Mann unglücklich gemacht und nicht jene Wunde; meine Liebe hat den Teufel in ihn gebracht und plagt ihn und verwirrt seine Sinne." By linking her love with the devil's influence, Arnim extends the scope of fire into the realm of the supernatural.

It is a characteristic of supernatural realities that they can be perceived in the realm of ordinary experience only by their outward and visible effects. Fire and light are such visible signs for Arnim, who uses them to show the presence of the invisible forces of evil and good.

Fire is used to indicate supernatural evil where Rosalie describes her meeting with Francoeur and her mother's subsequent discovery of their affection. Her mother curses them and appears to emit flame with her words: "als ob eine Flamme aus ihrem Halse brenne." When Rosalie laughs hysterically, her mother exults: "Hörst du, der Teufel lacht schon aus dir!" The devil, the man of fire and personification of evil, takes possession of Rosalie and her life at this time. When Francoeur and Rosalie are married,

the priest exhorts him to share the burden of her troubles, even her mother's curse, and Rosalie notices that the effect of the curse is then half lost. Shortly thereafter, Francoeur begins to experience an aversion to the church and to all religious matters and reports an inexplicable compulsion to curse them, "einen so heftigen Zorn und Widerwillen gegen Geistliche, Kirchen und heilige Bilder . . . , dass er ihnen fluchen müsse, und wisse nicht, warum." He seeks to dispel his blasphemous thoughts through wild activity, but his pranks and conflict with authority only emphasize more clearly the abnormal condition of his mind and spirit. This continues even after Rosalie is freed from the devil's influence through the birth of her child. She becomes the constant opponent of evil, meeting wild behavior with calmness, hatred and jealousy with love and constancy.

Though Rosalie has grown up in the midst of immorality, she is untouched by her sordid surroundings, and she seems to Francoeur in the hospital to be wearing a halo, "Heiligenschein," about her head. When she tries to explain this as the effect of her bonnet, he responds that the halo comes from her eyes.

The term "Teufel" has quite different significance for Rosalie and Count Dürande. For her, the devil is a real being whose power over her husband is responsible for his wildness and her misery. The count, however, is sure that Rosalie, as a German girl, could not possibly understand a Frenchman, for the French are all by nature somewhat devilish: "Die Frau liebt ihn, aber sie ist eine Deutsche und versteht keinen Franzosen; ein Franzose hat immer den Teufel im Leibe!" Thus, for Count Dürande, "Teufel" may be essentially synonymous with rascal, a person of extraordinary mischief and inventiveness; "Ein Teufelskerl" is his exclamation on first hearing of Francoeur's attack on the retreating general. The two interpretations lead to basically different ways of dealing with Francoeur's aberrations in behavior. While Rosalie shudders at each new deed of her husband, the count is delighted with his daring and entrusts him with responsibility for explosives and dangerous weapons. Dürande doubts his interpretation of Francoeur's behavior only for an instant, when he asks him: "Aber Euch plagt doch nicht der Teufel, und Ihr stiftet mir Unheil?" To this question, Francoeur gives an evasive answer, which could be regarded as admitting rather than denying the devil's presence: "Man darf den Teufel nicht an die Wand malen, sonst hat man ihn im Spiegel." Because of his preconceived judgment, however, Count Dürande feels reassured by Francoeur's words and turns over the command of the fort to him without further hesitation.

Francoeur is particularly fascinated by fire and all fiery things: even his speech is embellished with references to fire. Greeting Rosalie after her meeting with Count Dürande, Francoeur cries, "Du riechst nach dem trojanischen Brande, ich habe dich wieder, schöne Helena!" In subsequent conversation with the count, Francoeur reveals that he has long been a fireworks enthusiast, a "leidenschaftlicher Feuerkünstler, der seinem Regimente schon alle Arten Feuerwerke ausgearbeitet hatte," and he enters into Dürande's plans for the king's birthday celebration "mit funkelnder Begeisterung." When he takes over Fort Ratonneau in the harbor of Marseilles, Francoeur exclaims, "Ich will mir lieber die Zunge verbrennen, ehe ich zugebe, dass unsre Feinde Marseille einäschern oder wir sie fürchten müssen."

Francoeur's preoccupation with fiery things is particularly evident after he assumes control of the fort. His first attention is given to the preparation of fireworks and to readying the fort for a possible attack by the English. He sets one of the two soldiers assigned to his command to preparing the fireworks, while the other paints the cannons black, the devil's color. The feverish activity of the first days at the fort seems to relieve Francoeur of his wildness: "Bei dieser Thätigkeit liessen ihn seine Grillen ruhen, er war hastig, aber alles zu einem festen Ziele, und Rosalie segnete den Tag, der ihn in diese höhere Luftregion gebracht, wo der Teufel keine Macht über ihn zu haben schien." After this brief respite, however, Francoeur's diabolical tendencies are awakened to even greater intensity by a remark of a former military comrade, Basset. Basset, now Count Dürande's servant, has overheard his master speak of Francoeur's possession by the devil. In an effort to help his old friend, Basset invites a priest, Father Philipp, to visit the fort and exorcise the devil in Francoeur. This information, with its implication that he has been betrayed to the count by his wife, arouses Francoeur's anger and jealousy, and his eye flashes fire: "Francoeur hatte etwas Furchtbares in seinem Wesen, sein dunkles Auge befeuerte sich, sein Kopf erhob sich, seine Lippen drängten sich vor." When Father Philipp appears, Francoeur seizes him and hurls him over the gate.

At this point Rosalie appears, "erhitzt vom Feuer," but this "Feuer" is not a destructive or supernatural, but a natural and desirable kind, the flame of the home hearth. Her hospitable efforts to give their guest the most generous portions of food are misinterpreted by Francoeur and inflame his jealousy still further. He banishes Rosalie and the others from the fort and locks himself in the ammunition tower.

Proclaiming the presence of Satan within himself, Francoeur orders his two soldiers to carry Rosalie's belongings to Count Dürande with the words: "Sagt: das schicke ihr Satanas." He further threatens them with his devilish power: "In mir ist der König aller Könige dieser Welt, in mir ist der Teufel, und im Name des Teufels sage ich euch, redet kein Wort, sonst zerschmettere ich euch!"

Francoeur's bravado now reaches a peak, as does also his demonstration of skill with fireworks: "Welch ein Anblick! An allen Enden des Forts eröffneten die Kanonen ihren feurigen Rachen, die Kugeln sausten durch die Luft, . . . mit hellem Lichte schoss Francoeur einen Bündel Raketen aus einer Haubitze in die Luft, und einen Bündel Leuchtkugeln aus einem Mörser, denen er aus Gewehren unzählige andre nachsandte." This daring experiment of shooting fireworks from the weapons of the fort creates such a magnificent spectacle that Count Dürande asserts that for this display alone Francoeur's treason should be pardoned.

Natural and supernatural aspects of fire are combined in Francoeur's siege of Marseilles, and with diabolical ingenuity he thwarts every attempt to divert the threat to the city. But just at the point where these destructive forces show their greatest power, Arnim inserts an incident in which fire plays a curiously different role. Dazed by the shock of her husband's behavior, Rosalie has taken a wrong path in her flight from the fort and comes to the bank of the river where she enters a small boat and floats downstream. Night falls, and she sinks into troubled sleep. In the dark she is almost run down by a ship in the harbor, but the light from rockets fired by her husband reveals her presence and effects her rescue. Momentarily, the usual roles of fire and water are reversed: water is the threatening element, fire the saving. Just as in the opening scene the warming fire of the hearth is shown to have also a destructive side, now the basically negative force of fire is turned to a positive effect.

While she lies in the small boat, Rosalie dreams of her mother and sees her burning with the fire of the curse she has uttered, a torment from which only Rosalie can save her: "Rosalie sah im Traume ihre Mutter von innerlichen Flammen durchleuchtet und verzehrt und fragte sie, warum sie so leide? Da war's, als ob eine laute Stimme ihr in die Ohren rief: 'Mein Fluch brennt mich wie dich, und kannst du ihn nicht lösen, so bleib' ich eigen allem Bösen.'" This experience brings Rosalie to a recognition and acceptance of her mission as the combatant of fire and the evil it represents.

She reminds Count Dürande of his original promise to forgive Francoeur three misdeeds, but he feels these actions by Francoeur are too serious to be considered under the agreement. Finally, after three days, he announces his intention of storming the fort. In a final plea, Rosalie wins clemency for Francoeur on condition that she deliver over the fort without bloodshed.

In the most dramatic scene of the Novelle, Rosalie climbs the path to the fort in the face of the guns manned by her crazed husband. She shows no fear when Francoeur threatens her, but asserts calmly, "Nicht Tod, nicht Teufel trennen mich mehr von dir." Her steady advance causes a terrible struggle within Francoeur. Perspiration appears on his brow and cheeks. He tears off coat and vest and in a final gesture of desperation grasps a handful of hair and rips it from his head, His old battle wound is opened, and blood flows out, combining with his tears to fall on the fuse of the cannon and extinguish it. The mixture of blood and tears which puts out the smoldering fuse is a long step from the simple bucket of water used to extinguish the fire in Rosalie's apron and Dürande's wooden leg and accompanies an increased depth and complexity in the Novelle. The awakening of Francoeur's feelings, stirred by Rosalie's love, have produced the tears. His life blood, flowing in answer to her proffered sacrifice, unites with his tears to destroy the threat of the cannon. A sudden wind, reminiscent of the original pentacostal "rushing wind" described in the Bible [Acts 2:2] and hence symbolic of heavenly grace, completes the purification by blowing gunpowder from the holes of the cannons and the devil's flag from the tower. Francoeur describes his experience of release from the devil's influence as the departure of a chimney sweep from the chimney: "Der Schornsteinfeger macht sich Platz, er schreit zum Schornstein hinaus!" This sweep may be the devil himself beating a hasty retreat in the face of the forces of good, or it may represent the cleansing of the spirit after the devil's fire has been extinguished, just as a chimney is cleaned after the fire at the base is put out. Francoeur recognizes that the removal of the diabolical fire makes room for the fire of love and says to Rosalie, "Der schwarze Bergmann hat sich durchgearbeitet, es strahlt wieder Licht in meinen Kopf, und Luft zieht hindurch, und die Liebe soll wieder ein Feuer zünden, dass uns nicht mehr friert."

Heavenly grace now descends on the couple in the guise of two doves, frequent symbols for the Holy Spirit, who carry in their bills green leaves, i.e. new life. Green leaves and flowers appear again in the wreaths which are presented to Rosalie and Francoeur by the people. They remind the reader of the olive leaves on Count Dürande's hearth at the beginning of the narrative, but while these were threatened and consumed by fire, the leaves at the close of the story represent the triumph of life over destruction, of love and faith over the devil and his fiery powers. In the couplet which concludes the Novelle, "Gnade löst den Fluch der Sünde, / Liebe treibt den Teufel aus," Arnim summarizes the victory of the Holy Spirit and love over the devil and his earthly manifestations.

The motif of fire has thus developed with the development of the story. It first appears on the physical level of burning branches on Count Dürande's hearth, flames which warm him but endanger his life as they are transferred to his wooden leg. Rosalie's plea for her deranged husband introduces a different level of fire, the supernatural with its superstitious accompaniments. This is fire from outside ordinary human experience, holy fire in the "Heiligenschein" about Rosalie's head in the field hospital, the flames of hell in Francoeur's diabolical behavior. The intensity of the demonic fire increases with the tension in the narrative until it breaks back into the physical level as Francoeur trains his guns on the city of Marseilles. As if to remind his reader that fire is not necessarily an evil force, Arnim introduces it twice in positive ways close to the climax of the story, in the hospitable hearth flames of the fort kitchen and at the rescue of Rosalie by the light from fireworks. Then in a grand finale, all aspects of fire appear at once. Rosalie's holy faith opposes Francoeur's demonic evil; the flames of his insanity are extinguished, the "chimney" of his mind is cleansed, and the Holy Spirit descends on them both with the promise of the beginning of a new life symbolized in green leaves and flowers.

Hermann F. Weiss (essay date 1969)

SOURCE: "The Use of the Leitmotif in Achim von Arnim's Stories," in *German Quarterly,* Vol. XLII, No. 3, May, 1969, pp. 343-51.

[*In the essay below, Weiss argues that recurring motifs serve to unify a number of Arnim's seemingly loosely constructed stories and novellas.*]

Achim von Arnim's tales have repeatedly been censured for lack of structural unity and only a few, for instance *Der tolle Invalide* and *Frau von Saverne,* have escaped such criticism. However, attempts have been made recently to reevaluate Arnim's narrative art. In his penetrating study on *Die Majoratsherren* Heinrich Henel has demonstrated the surprisingly coherent structure of this seemingly confused story. Basing his interpretation on several short narratives by Arnim, Wolfdietrich Rasch has tried to defend the author against his critics on the grounds that such features as the loose plot contruction and sudden transitions of his tales resemble the techniques of an improvising oral storyteller. While Rasch's approach helps us to appreciate a number of Arnim's stories, among them *Angelika, die Genueserin und Cosmus, der Seilspringer,* it fails to account for the existence of an interesting unifying device in several of his tales, namely the leitmotif. To be sure, unsophisticated leitmotifs like the recurring Homeric epithet are part of the tradition of the oral epic. But Arnim's use of complex leitmotifs in *Die drei liebreichen Schwestern und der glückliche Färber* or *Owen Tudor,* for instance, goes far beyond the range of an improvising narrator and implies a considerable amount of deliberation and planning. In order to demonstrate the scope of Arnim's leitmotif techniques I shall progress from a discussion of simple devices, namely the repeated emphasis on certain phrases, gestures, and physical features, to an analysis of more complicated forms.

Stock phrases and gestures, which Arnim employs sparingly, came to be used widely during the nineteenth century in the works of such authors as Otto Ludwig, Raabe, and Fontane. Apollonius in *Zwischen Himmel und Erde,* for example, often wipes the dust off his jacket, and by this trait Otto Ludwig, probably inspired by his studies of Dickens, who used similar devices, expresses the scrupulousness of this character. In three of Arnim's tales stock phrases tell us something about the persons who use them. "Werde Er kein Narr"—with this or a similarly curt sentence Lenchen in *Die drei liebreichen Schwestern* several times tries to check Golno's real or imagined extravagance. This recurring phrase brings out Lenchen's wry didacticism, her "Übermacht der Verständlichkeit," which saves her from the foolish mistakes the people around her fall prey to. Time and time again Rennwagen, one of several comically one-sided figures in the posthumously published tale *Die Ehenschmiede,* refers to himself as "ein Mann ohne Vorurteile," thus insistently setting himself up as the objective scientist. This technique, which involves using a stock phrase indiscriminately in all kinds of situations, lends itself to humorous effects and it had, of course, been a part of the comical tradition for centuries. Arnim himself must have been aware of this when he gleefully adopted the constantly repeated phrase "der Tebel hol mer" from Reuter's *Schelmuffsky* in his own story **"Die drei Erznarren,"** which is contained in *Der Wintergarten.*

The leitmotif in Arnim's *Die Kirchenordnung* goes beyond a stock phrase since it helps to characterize the choleric temper of the captain through an ironic combination of words and actions. Threats like "Soll ich Euch den Spiess durch den Leib rennen?" occur often and sometimes the captain actually clutches his lance. Even though this quick-tempered man considers his words a mere figure of speech, he fulfills them in the end by unwittingly piercing Diaz, whom he had persecuted in earlier years on account of the latter's fratricide.

A somewhat more extended and inventive use of the figure-related leitmotif occurs in Arnim's posthumously published fragment **"Martin Martir."** Martir's habit of shutting and opening his eyes is definitely related to the central theme, the development of the court chaplain from fanatic to fool, and as such goes beyond a physiognomic characteristic. The very first sentence, which tells of Martir's preaching against the "indecent" dresses of the ladies at the duke's court, gives us an idea of his hysterical suspicion of the weaker sex. As always during a sermon, he closes his eyes because he wants to overcome his shyness and lack of concentration; but soon we see him literally closing his eyes to the world in other critical situations as well. When Mariella misplaces his manuscripts, he makes his characteristic response while commending himself to heaven, "indem er tun wolle, wie ihm der Geist gebiete." Without questioning this kind of inspiration, he beats the girl and, upon opening his eyes, is shocked to find her unconscious. Only now does he realize that she is identical with the princess who had attracted him earlier that day and, as a result, he gets involved in the painful process of self-recognition: "es war die böse mir selbst lang versteckte Glut, die mich hier zur Raserei eines gewaltsamen Angriffs gegen die Geliebte brachte . . . es war die schreckliche irdische Lust im Bunde mit Tod und Sünde, die alle Lehren, allen Willen, nur nicht den Abscheu gegen die Sünde in mir unterdrückte."

Here for the first time Martir comes to distrust his "Glut," to which he had ascribed all his good qualities earlier and which had long seemed suspect to the people around him. Nevertheless, he cannot for a while liberate himself from his former attitudes: He shuts his eyes when cursing Faust for withholding information on Mariella's state of health and he also yields to his "Geist" as he recognizes Faust's kindness to him: "Er drückte die Augen ein, wollte wieder den Geist in sich walten lassen um den Dank in heftiger Ergiessung der Worte auszusprudeln. . . ." Primarily his own experiences force him to face the world, but Faust, too, has an important role to play in this process. In fact, he reminds us of a psychiatrist, with Martir lying on a bed and revealing his shortcomings while Faust provides a corrective frame of reference: "Nich Auge zu, um Gottes Willn, Teufel drückt dir die Auge zu und sprickt aus dir, Aug in Aug dat mus sick sehn, so hat böse Feind keine Macht."

Already the duke had linked Martir's fanaticism with the works of the Devil, but it is only now that the chaplain fully realizes the influence of Satan: "ja musste er sich nicht selbst wie einen vom bösen Geist lange Besessenen scheuen." After Faust has cured him physically and mentally, Martir is ordered to leave the court in order to become minister of a poor parish. There one of his parishioners responds harshly to his request for the tithe, and his reaction proves that he has become more humble and mature: "Diese Rede hätte sonst den Geist in ihm völlig empört, auch drückte er unwillkürlich die Augen zu. . . . Gleich öffnete er die Augen." At the conclusion of this interesting fragment Martir, the righteous fanatic, has turned into a humble penitent who resolutely discards the pretensions of his former life and no longer relapses into his defense mechanism. Martir now decides to play the fool in order to attain a new sense of freedom.

While the leitmotif in **"Martin Martir"** reinforces the theme of the story, it lacks the richness of association which distinguishes the the leitmotifs in *Fürst Ganzgott und Sänger Halbgott, Owen Tudor, Der tolle Invalide,* and *Die drei liebreichen Schwestern.* As opposed to the three other tales, the leitmotif in the good-humored narrative *Fürst Ganzgott und Sänger Halbgott* (1818) is linked to the development of one person, the German prince Ganzgott. However, it is also far removed from Martir's stereotyped response, because two contrasting sets of recurring motifs, which are not related to Ganzgott's appearance, constitute a leitmotif complex: stone and petrifactions on the one hand, bursting or removed stone on the other. How do such references to geology express the theme of the story?

Boredom afflicts Ganzgott and his court until a tenor named Halbgott gradually succeeds in extricating the prince from his dull routine. After removing a mineral collection in which Ganzgott had significantly never taken any interest, Halbgott dissuades him from drinking at the Karlsbad spa. This development is symbolically underscored by a little natural disaster: "Und wie sie einander die Hand gaben, krachte es in der Tiefe des Töpelflusses. 'Die Sprudelschale ist geborsten!' riefen viele Leute. . . . 'Ein gutes Zeichen für uns,' rief Halbgott, 'dass wir statt des Wassers guten Kaffee trinken sollen'." Later on the prince twice refers to this event metaphorically, each time at an important junction in the tale. The first instance occurs when Ganzgott, already grown more independent, decides that something drastic must be done to alter the course of his rigid life: "wir tauschen die Rollen, aus dem Scherz wird Ernst, sonst kann ich die Steinschale nicht mehr sprengen." During this exchange of roles the prince excels as a tenor and regains the favor of his wife through the mediation of Halbgott, whereupon Ganzgott declares his reeducation completed: "die steinerne Schale fürstlicher Angewöhnung ist mir gesprengt; hat doch selbst der Sprudel seine schwere Steinschale . . . gesprengt, als wir Karlsbad verlassen. . . ." Through exploiting this disaster metaphorically, Arnim leaves no doubt as to its relation to the theme of Ganzgott's redemption.

In the passages just quoted, bursting stone has come to symbolize the prince's endeavor to free himself from a stultifying life while references to petrifactions underline the boredom and rigidity of his former existence. Arnim adds another leitmotif variant by associating this dullness with the folktale about Hans Heilig, which explains the origin of a group of cliffs near Karlsbad. According to this tale, Heilig, aroused by jealousy, transformed his bride and the wedding-guests into stone. Provoked by the tiresome account of a guide, Halbgott playfully distorts this version through a pun linking boredom and petrifaction: "Halbgott behauptete: es sei Hans Langweilig gewesen, der auf dem Wege schon seiner Braut und all den Seinen so viel Langeweile gemacht, dass sie eingeschlafen und so gewissermassen versteinert wären." From then on Ganzgott repeatedly calls himself "versteinert" and "Hans Langweilig" until he can finally announce: "ich bin nicht mehr Hans Langweilig."

When a complete study is made of the leitmotif in nineteenth-century prose works, Arnim will occupy an important position in it as an early master of the complex theme-related leitmotif.

—Hermann F. Weiss

As opposed to **"Martin Martir"** and *Fürst Ganzgott und Sänger Halbgott, Owen Tudor* is unified by a leitmotif completely dissociated from any figure. The frame plot of this narrative involves the reunion of a Welshwoman with her lover and the experiences of her traveling companions on their trip to Wales. Since the Welshwoman's tale about Owen Tudor and Queen Catherine likewise deals with the reunion of lovers, a strong thematic connection exists between frame and story. This link is strengthened by the leitmotif of dancing. In fact, Owen's superb dancing first makes him attractive to Catherine, and it is while dancing that she declares her love for him. Similarly, the old gentleman in the frame first met his wife at a ball. In addition, dancing as a simple expression of joy occurs in both story and frame. Notwithstanding his cowl, Owens dances exuberantly upon hearing of Catherine's arrival in Wales because it offers a chance to be reunited with her. At the end of the frame story the Welshwoman, seizing the hands of her bridegroom and the narrator, dances merrily towards the shore, thus expressing happiness over her lucky escape with her lover.

In the frame Arnim refers to other forms of dancing, which are not directly linked to the love theme. The very first sentence draws the reader's attention to the leitmotif: "Die Tanzwut (Dansomanie), das himmlische neue Ballett, hielt nach der langweiligen Oper bis tief in die Nacht hinein alle Augen und Geister gefesselt, . . ." while the last sentence surprises the reader with another variant, namely a lighthearted allusion to the Dance of Death. These two passages, besides showing Arnim's desire to round off his narrative, also reflect his intent to vary his leitmotif as much as possible. Another example of this diversity is provided by the conversation in the stagecoach at the beginning of *Owen Tudor,* which moves from dance as an art form to religious dances as performed by the Jumpers. The austere Presbyterian is so violently opposed to this Welsh sect that he wants to have them all hanged, and his fellow travellers' attempts to refute his dogmatic attitude by citing precedents of former ages, such as David's dance before the Ark of the Covenant, are to no avail.

In all these variations of the dance motif a connection seems to exist between observing or taking part in the act of dancing and an enthusiastic and stimulated state of mind, be it the growing involvement of the Jumpers in their religious exercises or the narrator's exultation over the ballet performance. But Arnim guides the reader in the search for a meaning which might unify the various aspects of dancing. In a discussion preceding the visit of the coach party to the service of the Jumpers, the young traveller reveals the metaphysical foundations of the dance motif. According to him, "alle Wege lebendiger Tätigkeit" help us to transcend this chaotic world and reach "die himmlische Einheit, die alles Leben durchdringt und heiligt"—a phrase which echoes the Romantic craving for synthesis. Singling out two activities relevant to the tale, the young man mentions the love of innocent people like Owen and Catherine and the elevating experience of religious dancing. Although he does not refer to other aspects of dancing, they, too, lead to a sense of unity since any vigorous activity is supposed to achieve this result. In all its various manifestations the dance motif in *Owen Tudor* can be regarded as a symbol of harmony and as such it is well suited to accompany the theme of the reunification of lovers.

In *Die drei liebreichen Schwestern* a nonvisual leitmotif, the number three, is woven into the fabric of the story. Often a connection seems to exist between this number and a propitious course of events. Both in the title and in the text people appear in groups of three. When Golno, the hero, is expelled from Stettin by the jealous Wigand's gang, three of the men kindheartedly console him and propose three foreign countries as possible places of refuge. Through a stroke of luck three sailors come his way shortly afterwards and take him to a schooner bound for Holland, one of the countries suggested. Following the reunion of the three sisters, Golno gets engaged to Charlotte, the youngest, and Arnim emphatically describes how the affections of these three young women sustain the hero: "er bemerkte nicht, wie nahe die drei Schwestern ihm standen, wie sie ihn alle drei umfassten und küssten; doch wenige Augenblicke, in denen kein Wort gesprochen wurde, genügten ihm zur Überzeugung, dass sein Glück fest begründet sei in drei treuen Herzen." Later in the story Charlotte reports overhearing a conversation of three earth spirits bent on harming Golno. Paradoxically, it is this very threat that helps to save him because, as a result, Charlotte is so alert that she immediately perceives Golno lying unconscious on the ground.

Remarkably often in this narrative, spans of time stretch over periods ranging from three days to three years. According to Lenchen's account the hermit is fortunate enough to meet her three days after he has buried his own child, and later she remains with his body for three days. Three years after his separation from Lenchen and, significantly, in the spring, Golno is finally able to choose a wife, and his wedding with Charlotte lasts three days. Three months after her encounter with the spirits, Charlotte departs from her boarding school, just in time to pass the spot near Berlin where Golno lies unconscious.

Golno's social rise, which is but one aspect of his amazing luck, is also linked to the number three. Relying on his intuition, he finishes dyeing a huge supply of black cloth just at the time when there is great demand for it because of the funeral of Frederick I of Prussia. With three wagons full of this material he travels to Berlin, where he makes such a fortune that he becomes an associate of the new king. Even though his rapid climb from artisan to an intimate of Prussian aristocrats is set in early eighteenth-century Dutch and Prussian cities, it reminds us of the trials and eventual good fortune of many fairy-tale heroes, whose fates Röhrich sums up aptly as follows: "Die Frage nach dem Glück ist ein ganz zentraler Gedanke des Märchens . . . das Thema 'Glück' im Märchen bedeutet nämlich, dass es immer auch Unglück gibt: Nicht mühelos erringen die Helden den Erfolg, sondern dieser fällt ihnen erst nach einer Bewährung zu. . . ."

A consideration of the various links between *Die drei Schwestern* and the fairy-tale tradition will help us towards a better understanding of the number motif. Significantly, the keyword "Glück," which signals the importance of this theme, occurs very frequently. As in many fairy tales all good characters are eventually rewarded, but not before enduring hardships. Thus it is only after years of painful bachelorhood that Golno meets a suitable partner. Both Lenchen, who experienced a harsh childhood, and Susanna, who suffered from unrequited love for Golno, finally achieve contentment through establishing an orphan home. On the other hand, the impact of evil figures is gradually removed. For example, brutal Wigand is jailed because he has threatened Golno's life, and with the death of Lenchen's callous stepfather his blighting influence comes to an end.

The most obvious link to the fairy-tale tradition is, of course, the fact that Arnim worked a fairy tale proper into his story. Anyone familiar with the *Kinder- und Hausmärchen* will realize that Lenchen's account of her childhood is a free adaptation of the *Sterntaler* tale. In order to connect it with Golno's life Arnim introduces the Virgin Mary and her Son, and just before Lenchen receives the treasure from the stars the Virgin promises her: "es ist dein Herr, der Sohn Gottes, der dir Glück wird bringen und jedem, den du liebst und der an ihn glaubt." At the beginning of the story Lenchen hands over her treasure to Golno and thus lays the foundation of his good luck. During his life Mary's promise is plentifully fulfilled since he loves Lenchen and remains a fervent believer. In his simple trust, Arnim's hero resembles a specific fairy-tale hero, the so-called "Dümmling." Like him, Golno is not really stupid, even though the people around him may think so. Thus he pays far too much for Mr. Schnaphan's yellowing linen, but he makes a huge profit when selling the dyed

cloth at the king's funeral. Furthermore, it is only through literally believing a lottery advertisement that he wins a lot of additional money. Following "seiner unbewussten Ahnung" rather than reason, simple-minded Golno turns out to be luckier than anybody else.

Just as the hero, the theme, and the structure of *Die drei liebreichen Schwestern* are linked to the fairy-tale tradition, so is Arnim's use of the leitmotif. Significantly, the number three first occurs in the interpolated fairy tale, but only a few times and rather unobtrusively, merely referring to time spans and Lenchen's stepsisters. Arnim's friendship with the Grimm brothers as well as his own thorough knowledge of folk literature must have made him aware of the frequent use of three in fairy tales. Undoubtedly he recognized that this number is often associated with the central theme of this genre, namely the successful, if not entirely smooth, pursuit of happiness. For instance, frequently a sequence of three trials, all of which the hero undergoes with success, leads to a happy ending, as in *Die drei Federn*. Through continuing the use of three beyond the interpolated account Arnim signals to the reader that the fairy-tale atmosphere is not confined to that part alone. In fact, this recurring number carries all the associations of that genre, such as miracles and the hero's eventual good fortune, over into Golno's eighteenth-century world.

Not only does Arnim's story *Die drei liebreichen Schwestern* contain a fairy tale, but it also bears a thematic resemblance to this genre, and the author has, in addition, transformed a traditional number motif into a leitmotif accompanying and reinforcing this theme. When a complete study is made of the leitmotif in nineteenth-century prose works, Arnim will occupy an important position in it as an early master of the complex theme-related leitmotif—a technique which was to be explored more fully by other authors later in the nineteenth century.

J. Edward W. Mornin (essay date 1971)

SOURCE: "National Subjects in the Works of Achim von Arnim," in *German Life and Letters,* Vol. 24, No. 4, July, 1971, pp. 316-27.

[In the excerpt below, Mornin examines the use of old German stories in the pieces in Der Wintergarten *and in the novella* Isabella von Ägypten. *The critic argues that Arnim used these materials in order to "purify and morally regenerate the Germans" through his works.]*

Achim von Arnim's political activities in the years 1806-13, his publication of German folk-songs in *Des Knaben Wunderhorn* (1806-8), and his literary exploitation of German historical subjects and of old German traditions, legends and literature have caused him to be regarded as a typical representative of the patriotic and national trend discernible in German Romanticism in the early years of the nineteenth century. Despite this, little attention has been paid to fundamental aspects of the relationship between the national subject matter of his works and their patriotic value. Biographical studies and Arnim's published correspondence make it clear, indeed, that his employment of material derived from German history and folk-tradition and from old German literature was politically motivated, but textual investigations have thrown little light either on the psychological effect which he sought to achieve through his literary nationalism or on the purpose of his distinctive treatment of national subjects. Through an examination of some typical works, the present study will attempt to relate Arnim's patriotism specifically to his treatment of subject matter drawn from history, folk-lore and old German literature.

From when he first became conscious of the forces shaping his age, Arnim saw that the 'Kleinstaaterei' which had characterized Germany's political structure since 1648 would make it impossible for individual German states to withstand the attack which he knew would be launched against them sooner or later as a consequence of the belligerent foreign policy pursued by the young French Republic, and later by Napoleonic France. In a Germany divided at the beginning of the nineteenth century into over three hundred petty states and split, too, between allegiance and hostility to France, German patriotism, as distinct from local patriotism, had no single person or centre capable of claiming its loyalty. The German language, however, and a literature based on a peculiarly German tradition were among the few common denominators in this confusion. As a consequence, writers were uniquely suited to assist in the establishment of a common German front, which Arnim believed was necessary as a defence against the French and for a secure future. He expresses an awareness of this as early as 1802, in a letter written to Brentano. He considers it the poet's duty to educate society, and reveals a scheme for founding a printing press for the people, the proceeds of which will go towards opening 'Sängerherbergen' in cities and a 'Schule der Dichtkunst' in Schloss Laufen near the Falls of the Rhine. It is implied that the literary productions which such undertakings will encourage will be typically German in character; and the result of disseminating these works will be a strengthening of the bond between the German states:

> Dies giebt den Deutschen einen Ton und eine enge Verbindung, jeder Streit zwischen ihren Fürsten muss sich selbst verzehren, weil der Deutsche gegen seine Brüder nicht zu Felde zieht . . .

Arnim's plan was never realized, but its underlying idea became the inspiration for many of his writings as well as for *Des Knaben Wunderhorn*, the first volume of which appeared in 1806, a year which saw Arnim's worst fears for Germany realized through the dissolution of the Holy Roman Empire, the foundation of the Federation of the Rhine as a French protectorate, and the humiliating overthrow of Prussia at Jena and Auerstedt. . . .

Der Wintergarten (1809) is a collection of short-stories which are based for the most part on seventeenth-century German prose works. It has a Novelle framework in the tradition established by Boccaccio and followed by Goethe in his *Unterhaltungen deutscher Ausgewanderten* (1795). A group of people in a country house tell stories to pass the long winter, which—it is expressly indicated that winter is an allegory—is symbolic of Germany under French occupation, as the imagery of Arnim's formulation unmistakably indicates: 'Alles besetze und bewachte dieser traurige Winter mit seiner langweiligen Heerschaar'. . . . The professed purpose of the stories was

> . . . nichts Bestimmtes von den Begebenheiten der Zeit zu reden und dafür allerlei Geschichten aus andern Zeiten und Ländern zu sammeln, die dann gemeinschaftlich genossen [werden sollten] . . .

They are, ostensibly, meant to entertain and to provide an escape for the reader; but in reality they are of considerable contemporary political interest and are motivated by patriotic concern.

Arnim has treated the old German sources of *Der Wintergarten* artistically, not academically. He has shortened some and, less commonly, expanded others as he pleased, and on occasion he has even combined works by different authors—as in **'Philander unter den streifenden Soldaten und Zigeunern im Dreissigjährigen Kriege',** which is composed of excerpts from the *Wunderliche und wahrhaßtige Gesichte Philanders von Sittewald* (1643) by Johann Michael Moshcherosch and from Grimmelshausen's *Springinsfeld* (1670). He has also abandoned the frequent scholarly digressions and lengthy quotations from classical authors to be found in his originals, and has omitted coarse and sensational elements common in seventeenth-century novels. His purpose was to make palatable to a modern reading public old works which were typically German in character and which he considered, therefore, of patriotic value.

'Das wiedergefundene Paradies' provides a good example of Arnim's treatment of his source material in *Der Wintergarten*. The tale is derived principally from episodes in the novel *Die Insel Felsenburg* (1731-43) by Johann Gottfried Schnabel. Arnim has, however, made a short story out of a lengthy novel by retaining only those parts of the novel which are pertinent to his central design—which is to depict characters whom he considered typically German—while he has interwoven these with incidents from the life of the German general Graf Hans Ulrich von Schaffgotsch (1595-1635), who does not figure in Schnabel's work but whom Arnim regarded as an outstanding example of German manhood. Though Arnim basically re-tells the plot of Schnabel's novel in his own words, he sometimes keeps close to the original—for instance, in the following passage, where a hermit foretells the hero's future:

> (a) 'Verwegener Jüngling, warum willst Du Dich unterstehen, die Wohnung zu verschütten, woran ich so viele Jahre gearbeitet, ehe sie zu meiner Bequemlichkeit gut genug war. Meinst Du etwa, das Verhängniss habe Dich von ungefähr in den Graben gestossen und vor die Thür meiner Höhle geführt? Nein, keinesweges!

sondern, weil ich mit meinen Händen acht Personen auf dieser Insel aus christlicher Liebe begraben habe, so bist Du auserkoren, meinem vermoderten Körper einen gleichen Liebesdienst zu erweisen. . . . Wisse auch, dass der Himmel etwas besonderes mit Dir vorhat. Deine Glückseligkeit aber wird nicht eher anfangen, bis Du zwei besondere Unglücksfälle erlitten, und diesem Deinem Schlafgesellen zur bestimmten Zeit den Lohn seiner Sünden gegeben hast.'

(b) 'Verwegner, Du willst verschütten, was ich in vielen Jahren ausgearbeitet; kein Ungefähr hat Dich in diese Höhle geführt, denn wie ich acht Menschen auf diese Insel begraben habe, so bist Du auserkoren den letzten Liebesdienst zu erweisen. Wisse, dass der Himmel etwas Besonderes mit Dir vorhat, doch wird Dein Glück erst nach zweien Unglücksfällen anheben; Du aber wirst Deinem Schlafgesellen den Lohn seiner Sünden geben.'

It is significant that this passage relates to the German hero's killing of the French villain and suggests, therefore, that Arnim's contemporaries, too, might avenge themselves on the French for their misdeeds. Far from being escapist, Arnim's tale is, despite its fantastic plot and exotic setting, of great contemporary interest, for it contrasts sharply the German national character with the French character. The villain Lemelie is 'aus edlem Geschlechte in Frankreich', while the Graf von Schaffgotsch in particular, who becomes in Arnim's version of Schnabel's story the patron of the hero Albert, is characterized by his simplicity, uprightness and loyalty—virtues which, it is implied, are typically German.

> The old German stories of *Der Wintergarten* have, in general, no explicit political moral, for Arnim believed that the essential feature of a national education was the exposure of the Germans less to propaganda than to works of literature which revealed aspects of the German character.
>
> —*J. Edward W. Mornin*

The value of a tale like **'Das wiedergefundene Paradies'** is indicated in the framework of the third 'Winterabend' of the collection. Here a former German ambassador first speaks against those Germans who allow themselves to be abused and, while in foreign (i.e. French) service, even oppress their own countrymen. He then suggests that an end might be put to this through an educational reform, and he sharply criticizes the Pestalozzian method of education: 'Einen Menschen zum Menschen erziehen zu wollen ist eitel menschlicher Kram, zum Menschen ist er von Gott geschaffen . . .' He advocates that children should receive a national education and be brought up in the

tradition of the fatherland. Writings like **'Das wiedergefundene Paradies'**, by inculcating an awareness of the German national character, may be regarded as Arnim's contribution to the education of his compatriots—and not only to the children among them, one assumes.

The old German stories of *Der Wintergarten* have, in general, no explicit political moral, for Arnim believed that the essential feature of a national education was the exposure of the Germans less to propaganda than to works of literature which revealed aspects of the German character. **'Abrogast von Andelon und Elisa von Portugal, Albrecht von Werdenberg und Amisa von Ponazari'**, for instance, is taken more or less word for word from a 1761 edition of the *Alte Schwäbische Geschichten* of the medieval chronicler Thomas Lirer, and has no express political message. Yet it clearly serves Arnim's political ends, for in it the Germans are shown to be respected throughout Europe, and they are described as virtuous, enterprising, faithful and brave. Here Arnim's patriotism is the inspiration for his publication of a work which has preserved features of the national character. His intention was to purify and morally regenerate the Germans through such works, as he indicates, in the words of the Ritter von Thurn, in the introduction to *Der Wintergarten*:

> Überaus ein edel und hübsche Meinung ist's, sich in dem Spiegel der alten Historien, die uns von den Vorältern verlassen sind, zu besehen, uns dadurch zum Guten zu wenden, das Uble zu fliehen, Herzen und Gedanken in den Dienst des Allmächtigen zu richten.

The collection was intended to bring about a national rebirth such as is symbolized at the end of the work: the winter's ice on the river is broken up, and from an ice-floe which comes drifting downstream people rescue a child in a cradle—emblematical of new life.

Of the Novellen published in 1812 *Isabella von Aegypten* is most typical of Arnim in the use made of subject matter drawn from German folk-lore sources, which have been treated with characteristic freedom and imagination. The manner in which the heroine of the tale obtains the mandragora root (*Alraun*) of German folk-lore is specified in detail, Arnim following in its essentials the procedure indicated by Grimmelshausen in his *Simplicissimi Galgen-Männlin oder Ausfürlicher Bericht, woher man die so genannte Allräungen oder Geldmännlin bekommt* (1673). Once the 'Alraun' has been acquired, however, Arnim endows it with a human personality and involves it in adventures of his own invention. He introduces him, for instance, to another German folk-lore figure, Bärnhäuter, which he knew from Grimmelshausen's *Der erste Beernhäuter* (1670). Arnim's Bärnhäuter is, however, apart from his hirsute appearance, his wealth and, of course, his name, Arnim's own creation. These motifs are woven together in whimsical fashion and are further embroidered by being incorporated in a fictitious myth of the gypsies. Arnim blatently disregards the facts of German legend by indulging in a grotesque pun and having a 'Springwurzel'—which in German folk-tradition opens all doors—make the 'Alraun' jump; and by analogy with his 'Springwurzel' he invents a 'Sprechwurzel' to make him talk. Legend and history—the story is set in the early sixteenth century—are also intermingled freely. Isabella, a fictitious gypsy princess, is in duty bound to lead her people back to Egypt, from which they had been banished for refusing shelter to Mary and Joseph on their flight from Israel. According to legend, a son whom she will bear to the (historical) Erzherzog Karl of the Netherlands will succeed in the centuries-old task and lead the gypsies home. To obtain the wealth which would facilitate her access to Karl, Isabella procures a mandrake which finds many treasures for her, including that of Bärnhäuter, who then becomes the mandrake's slave. The mandrake falls in love with Isabella and, to rid himself of this troublesome rival, Karl, who also loves her, has a golem (of Jewish tradition) made in her image, which he then tries to foist on to the mandrake. So alluring is the golem, however, that Karl himself becomes enamoured of her and escapes from her clutches only with difficulty. Though in love with Karl and pregnant with his child, Isabella is faithful to her people and to her destiny and sets out for Egypt with her followers. This tale is intended to be entertaining, which it certainly is; but it is much more than that, for it also has a message meant especially for the Germany of Arnim's day.

Isabella von Aegypten mirrors Arnim's attitude towards certain contemporary social and political problems, and at the same time suggests a solution to them. Karl, who later became German Emperor and would have protected the gypsies had Isabella become his permanent mistress, represents the Emperor Napoleon, who might have brought a measure of stability and justice to all of Germany—as he did to the German states of the Rheinbund—at the price of German independence. There can be little doubt, in spite of what a recent critic writes, that the golem reflects the anti-Semitic side of Arnim's nationalism. She has been made out of clay by a learned Jew, and her temporary enslavement of Karl, which might have brought disaster upon everyone, is a veiled allusion to what Arnim considered the consequences of Napoleon's emancipation and protection of the Jews. Isabella, finally, provides an example for the Germans to follow. Through her selfless devotion to her people she overcomes both the stratagems of the golem and her love for Karl, which would have kept her in the Netherlands and would have prevented the gypsies from returning to their homeland and fulfilling their national destiny. The Germans, Arnim implies through this, should likewise act for what they know to be the long-term good of their nation, lest it fall into the power of their enemies.

Through his depiction of the gypsy way of life as a whole, Arnim also sought to teach the Germans that it was only through the faithful observance of ancient traditions—as exemplified by their will to return to Egypt and by the ritual funeral feast which Isabella prepares for her father—that the gypsies had not been absorbed by other peoples but had remained intact as a nation. He meant that the Germans, too, should cultivate their traditions in the interests of national survival; and it was to give them a notion of what these traditions were that he couched this moral in a tale which is rich in German folk-lore themes. . . .

Reference has already been made to the liberties which Arnim took in remodelling the sources of his national works. Though it is not possible to give here a more complete account of the instances in which he has deviated either radically or slightly from his originals, it is appropriate to close with a brief consideration of the reasons for these deviations.

Arnim's belief in the sovereignty of the artist over his creation, which he shared with all the Romantics, doubtless encouraged him to exercise complete freedom in the treatment of his sources. No less contributory, however, must have been the fact that the aims which he pursued through his writings were essentially political. The contemporary political effectiveness of his writings meant more to him than either their scholarly accuracy or their lasting aesthetic appeal; and his objectives, he thought, could be obtained more readily through a proliferation of appropriate themes than by a refinement of any one of them. By making known as much material as possible derived from German folk-songs and folk-tales and from old German novels and histories, it was his intention to instill into his readers an awareness of and pride in the German spirit dormant in these writings. His ultimate purpose, which was sometimes underscored by the moral of a work, was to create among Germans a community spirit, which would, he believed, provide a significant contribution to solving the problem of Germany's political subjugation to France and provide a meaningful basis for Germany's political development.

Paul F. Casey (essay date 1980)

SOURCE: "Images of Birds in Arnim's *Majoratsherren,*" in *German Life and Letters,* Vol. XXXIII, No. 3, April, 1980, pp. 190-98.

[*In the essay below, Casey argues that Arnim's novella "exhibits a detailed and extended avian imagery which lends an intricate coherence to the story."*]

About the genesis of Ludwig Achim von Arnim's novella *Die Majoratsherren* we are certain only that it first appeared in the *Taschenbuch zum geselligen Vergnügen auf das Jahr 1820* and was later, in 1839, included in the second volume of Wilhelm Grimm's edition of Arnim's collected works. Walther Migge, the editor of the most authoritative edition of Arnim's work, finds, somewhat vaguely formulated, stimulus for its creation in the '. . . nach 1815 einsetzende allgemeine Interesse für Magnetismus und Somnambulismus.'

The story has met with very little critical approval. Arnim's friends, Brentano, Görres and the Brothers Grimm, had expressed themselves less than enthusiastically on his earlier collection *Vier Novellen* (1812) and on his novel *Die Kronenwächter* (1817). Possibly as a consequence, '. . . äusserte sich Arnim später in Briefen nur noch wenig über seine literarischen Arbeiten', and thus we have little to go on as to his objectives in this story.

The feeling among his friends seems to have been that Arnim allowed his tales to run on at length without any strict observance of form, a cardinal virtue among literary men of the time. As Jacob Grimm wrote to Arnim:

Du bist Dir immer in Deiner Eigenthümlichkeit gleich geblieben . . . Ich nenne diesen Fehler unpraktische oder unnatürliche Ueberladung und Verwickelung.

In reference to Arnim's *Die Majoratsherren,* Grimm wrote further, on 3 November 1819, about the

. . . wunderliche und unnatürliche Übergänge, welche die wahre, lebendige Poesie, die Dir zu Theil geworden ist, launenhaft treiben und beeinträchtigen.

And on the same date, Grimm also wrote to Karl von Savigny about Arnim:

In der Unnatur und fast sündlichen Verwirrung seiner Pläne vergehen die schönsten Gaben aller seiner reichen Poesie.

Die Majoratsherren has, through the years, continued to elicit similar responses from critics. Ralph Tymms [in *German Romantic Literature,* 1955] observes that 'more than anywhere else in Arnim's writing one is oppressed by what almost appears to be wilful disregard for form and economy.' The thrust of the criticism of *Die Majoratsherren* shows that the greatest problem for most commentators is Arnim's inability to structure his stories coherently: 'Goethe dubbed Achim von Arnim a loose-hooped barrel, and most other critics agree that his artistic form does not hold' [Bruce Duncan, 'Some Correspondences between Arnim's *Majoratsherren* and Fichte's Concept of the *Ich,*' *Monatshefte* 68, 1976]. So firmly established is this belief that the small body of criticism surrounding the story tends to disregard any details of the work that run counter to this conclusion. *Die Majoratsherren,* traditionally found wanting in form, has thus had its fate resolutely sealed.

Yet Heinrich Henel, in his commentary on the story, demonstrates that in *Die Majoratsherren*:

behält der Dichter die Zügel fest in der Hand, ja er arbeitet nach einem von vornherein festliegenden Plan. Die Stimmigkeit zahlreicher Einzelheiten, die anfänglich willkürlich scheinen, lässt sich nicht anders erklären.

Henel points out the necessity of a repeated and attentive reading, whereas 'Grimm urteilte nach einmaligem Lesen, und da springt allerdings fast nur das Traumhafte und Koboldartige von Arnims Dichtungen in die Augen.' In addition, Arnim's *Die Majoratsherren,* despite its purported lack of form, had considerable influence on Edgar Allan Poe's *The Fall of the House of Usher,* perhaps more than E. T. A. Hoffmann's *Das Majorat,* which is usually credited with providing Poe's inspiration. The 'Maskenball' scene, in which Esther is observed by the Majoratsherr ministering to a grotesque assortment of imaginary

guests, also bears a marked resemblance to Poe's story *The Masque of the Red Death.* It would thus seem somewhat ironic that Poe, the master of form and strong proponent of the 'single-effect' theory of the short story, should have chosen as his model the supposedly formless Arnim, repeatedly chastised for his failure to adhere to any recognizable and clearly defined structure. Similarly, the grotesque elements, which are immediately noticeable in Arnim's story, have led to its being termed ' . . . eine der grössten grotesken Erzählungen . . . in deutscher Sprache überhaupt.'

The imagery of *Die Majoratsherren* has, however, not attracted the attention of critics that its form and its grotesque aspects have. Even the casual reader will have noticed the unusually large number of different birds and poultry which are mentioned in the course of the novella: at least fourteen birds are specifically and repeatedly named. In addition, abundant reference is made to bird-related objects, such as feathers, wings, nests, etc. All of these references are moulded by the author into a fairly clear pattern: the bird images form clusters that are inextricably woven into the characterizations of the four main figures in the tale. They provide the reader with a framework of symbolic reference and allusion that supports Henel's contention that beneath the convoluted structure of the story, a clearly conceived pattern is discernible, one which attests Arnim's having all the artistic threads in his hand.

Die Majoratsherren introduces us first to the 'Vetter' or 'Leutnant'. As a relative of the Majoratsherr he is entrusted, in the latter's continual absence, with the supervision of the ancestral home, the 'Majoratshaus'. Commencing with a minor reference to his punctuality (people are said to be able to set their 'Kuckuckuhren' by his movements), Arnim increasingly associates the Vetter with one bird, the cock. The Majoratsherr takes up residence in the Vetter's modest house, an abode which itself is a direct result of the Vetter's association with birds and poultry:

Nebenher war es eine Liebhaberei von ihm, Truthähne und andres Federvieh zu mästen, und Raubtauben über die Stadt auszusenden, die immer mit einigen Überfliegenden in die geheime Öffnung seines Daches heimkehrten . . . Von dem Erworbenen hatte er sich ein elendes finsteres Haus im schlechtesten Teile der Stadt, neben der Judengasse, und vielerlei alten Kram gekauft, ...

The house in which the Majoratsherr chooses to reside, and from which he is to observe Esther in her house across the Judengasse, has thus been paid for by the receipts of the Vetter's questionable trade in 'Truthähne und andres Federvieh'. The Vetter's gait is repeatedly characterized as his . . . 'geckenhaften, schöntuenden Hahnentritt und Stutzerlauf . . . , der ihn in das Haus hineinzutreiben drohte, während ihm dabei der Degen, den er nach alter Art durch die Rocktasche gesteckt hatte, zwischen die Beine schlenkerte.'

The Hofdame, in actuality the Majoratsherr's natural mother, is the object of the Vetter's amorous attentions, and she, too, visualizes him as a cock. In speaking to the

Majoratsherr, she describes 'wie er da täglich unter schielenden Seitenblicken der Alten, und mit Hohnlachen der Gassenbuben in lächerlichen Hahnentritten vor meinem Fenster vorübertrippelt. In his dress, as well, he still demonstrates a penchant for 'rote Kragen' and copper-red buttons: 'Gleiche Farbe zeigte auch der fuchsrote dreieckige Militärhut mit der wollenen Feder'. In addition to walking like a cock with its tail-feathers between its legs, he resembles one in outer appearance as well, an indication of his overweening self-pride.

After his marriage to the Hofdame, who thereby avenges herself for the Vetter's having killed her lover years ago, 'er trug die physische Angst in seinem Herzen, wie ein gebissener Hahn, der einmal vor seinem Gegner flüchtig geworden ist'. As a result of this marriage, the Vetter literally goes to the dogs, for the Hofdame has him tending her pets—but not just any dogs, for these, too, are specified:

> Auch hatte er zum Spazierengehen nun so wenig Zeit übrig, seit ihm die Frau eine Anzahl junger Hühnerhunde und Hetzhunde zum Abrichten übergeben hatte.

The Majoratsherr himself, a fanciful young man who sees the real world only through the fantastic creations of his mind, spends his nights in mystical studies and phantasmagoric reveries. 'Davon kommt der Geisterspuk im Kopfe', reports the Vetter: 'er lebt ja wie die Nachteulen'. On seeing the doctor's carriage, the Majoratsherr is convinced, 'der Tod sitzt auf dem Bocke, Hunger und Schmerz zwischen den Pferden; einbeinige und einarmige Geister fliegen um den Wagen'. The Vetter explains that this is surely a trick of the Majoratsherr's imagination, for 'es ist unser bester Arzt und Chirurgus; . . . sein Kutscher ist freilich mager, und seine Pferde abgetrieben, aber die den Wagen umflattern, sind Sperlinge. . . .' A propensity of the Majoratsherr gradually becomes evident in the story. Although the Majoratsherr tends to see birds as 'Geister' almost everywhere, he himself becomes most closely associated with the swallow, an identification established by the extended image which might be termed the 'Schwalbenepisode'.

After a particularly restless night spent with his books, the Majoratsherr longs for the day and tranquillity:

> Endlich wurde es Tag; die grossen Schatten der Häuser lagerten sich unter dem hellen Himmel, die Mägde sprangen frisch geschuht, als ob sie sich an diesem Tage durchaus nicht beschmutzen wollten, von einem trocknen Stein zum andern, die Schwalben dagegen kreuzten hin zu dem köstlichen Baumörtel, der ihnen der gestrige Regen bereitet hatte, und füllten damit alle Lücken der menschlichen Architektur. Auch an dem Fenster, das zu Esther blickte, hatten sich heute zwei von den zwitschernden Grauröcken eingefunden, und wollten ihr Nest gerade da ankleben, wo er durch die einzige helle Scheibe zu Esther hinblickte. Da stand der Majoratsherr zweifelnd, ob er sie stören, ob er alles abwarten solle, was ihm so bedeutend schien. Seine Sinnesart überwog für das Abwarten. Nun ihm Esther verborgen, konnte er sich an den lieben Ge-

schöpfen, an ihrer Lust, an ihrem Fleisse nicht satt sehen, es war ihm zu Mute, als ob er sich selbst da anbaue, als hänge sein Glück davon ab, dass sie fertig würden, . . .

In keeping with his personality, the Majoratsherr is, of course, unable to take any resolute action to remove the birds, although they obstruct his view of Esther. He is not at all sure he even wants to, for he now associates the swallows with his own predicament. He comes to connect his happiness with their progress in constructing the nest at his window. Indeed, he celebrates their industry by composing a song, and comes to think of the swallows as a premonition of his fate:

> Die Sonne scheinet an die Wand,
> Die Schwalbe baut daran;
> O Sonne, halt nur heute Stand,
> Dass sie recht bauen kann.
> Es ward ihr Nest so oft zerstört,
> Noch eh' es fertig war,
> Und dennoch baut sie wie betört;
> Die Sonne scheint so klar!
> So süss und töricht ist der Sinn,
> Der hier ein Haus sich baut;—
> Im hohen Flug ist kein Gewinn,
> Der fern aus Lüften schaut,
> Und ging er auch zur Ewigkeit
> Er passt nicht in die Zeit,
> Er ist von ihrer Freudigkeit
> Verschieden himmelweit.

When he awakens in the evening, having as usual slept through the day, the Vetter has a surprise ready for him: not only has his study been newly furnished with sofa, chairs, commodes and tables, 'aber die Schwalben waren herabgestossen'. The Majoratsherr's first thoughts are ominous: 'Meine guten schützenden Engel sind vertrieben. . . . Ich soll sie sehen, meinen Todesengel, soll den ganzen Traum durchleben, der mich plagte; . . .'

Esther, throughout the story, is consistently associated with the dove, an image that expands towards the end of the narrative into the 'geflügelte Seele' which she symbolizes for the Majoratsherr. The first mention of the doves in the story, other than those led home by the 'Raubtauben' of the Vetter, has an almost religious significance. Confused by his hallucinations of what he sees as a 'Maskenball' in Esther's room, the Majoratsherr loses his way in his hurry to reach her and enters the Vetter's poultry room:

> Er blickt umher in dem Raume, und still umsitzen ihn heilige Gestalten, fromme Symbole, weisse Tauben; und das Gefühl, wie er zwischen Himmel und Hölle wohne, und die Sehnsucht nach dem himmlischen Frieden, dessen Sinnbilder ihn umgaben, stillte wie Öl die Sturmeswellen, die ihn durchbebten, und eine Ahnung, dass er ihm nahe, dass es seiner auf Erden nicht mehr bedürfe, drängte seine aufglimmende Tätigkeit für Esther weider zurück.

Esther, peace and the dove are all inextricably related. His failure to find his way to her indicates his inability to find the middle way in life. The 'Truthähne' appear as 'höllische Geister' and the doves as 'heilige Gestalten', which puts the Majoratsherr in a position 'zwischen Himmel und Hölle'. The Vetter, finding him in the poultry room, admonishes him: 'Kommen Sie in Ihr Zimmer zurück . . . sonst verlassen die Tauben ihre Eier'. The consequence of the Majoratsherr's fascination with Esther, as this warning suggests, is his destruction.

The doves recur when the Majoratsherr hears of Esther's death, in this instance a 'Scheintod', but his indecisiveness is most apparent:

> Der Majoratsherr allein, während alles lief um zu schauen, blieb erstarrt in seiner Fensterecke liegen, bis die Tauben heimkehrend es mit lautem Flügel umflogen, und die Aufwärterin sagte: 'Ach Gott! da haben sie wieder eine mitgebracht; wer weiss, welchem armen Menschen sie gehört hat, und wie viele sich darum grämen!'

The Vetter's 'Raubtauben' have brought home a dove which the Majoratsherr immediately associates with Esther: 'Sie ist's' rief der Majoratsherr, 'die himmlische Taube. . . .' The 'armer Mensch' to whom it belonged is symbolically the Majoratsherr himself, and he reflects that he will not be long in joining her: '. . . ich werde nicht lange um sie weinen'.

The relationship between Esther, the rightful heir to the Majoratshaus whose place has been usurped by the Majoratsherr, and her ugly stepmother is reflected in the image of 'die arme Taube' and 'der grimmige Geier'. The Majoratsherr observes, from his window, the stepmother's entry into Esther's room:

> . . . sie erschien nicht wie ein menschliches Wesen, sondern wie ein Geier, der lange von Gottes Sonne gnädig beschienen, mit der gesammelten Glut auf eine Taube niederstösst.

Vasthi, the stepmother, is associated consistently with predatory birds. Henel remarks that in removing the picture of Adam and Eve from Esther's death chamber, Vasthi is acting as 'Geier Gottes' and takes on Esther's share of original sin.

Besides the 'Geier' image which occurs repeatedly, Vasthi is described as 'ein grimmig Judenweib, mit einer Nase wie ein Adler'. Her physical description is enhanced through use of yet a further bird image:

> Der Majoratsherr . . . blickte sich um, erschrak aber, dass die Jüdin einen schwarzen Raben auf dem Kopfe trug, . . . er fragte, wer die grimmige Alte mit dem Raben auf dem Kopfe gewesen?

In his eyes, she even squawks like the raven: 'und nun erschallte hinter ihm ein fürchterliches Rabengekrächze aus dem Munde der alten Jüdin'.

Occasionally, other bird images occur in the story, such as in the description of the guests at Esther's wedding:

Eben so fremdartig waren alle Zeichen der Lustigkeit unter den Zuschauern, welche Nachtigallen und Wachteln künstlich nachmachten, einander zwickten und Gesichter schnitten. . . .

But the major associations are of the 'Hahn' with the Vetter, the 'Schwalbe' with the Majoratsherr, the 'Taube' with Esther, and the 'Geier' and 'Rabe' with Vasthi, for these are the four main characters in the tale.

The various bird associations physically and spiritually characterize the figures with whom they are connected: Esther's innocence stands in sharp contrast to the vulture-like qualities of Vasthi. The Vetter, in marrying the Hofdame, loses his pride and all the cock-like qualities he possessed and is thoroughly emasculated.

—Paul F. Casey

The various bird associations physically and spiritually characterize the figures with whom they are connected: Esther's innocence stands in sharp contrast to the vulture-like qualities of Vasthi. The Vetter, in marrying the Hofdame, loses his pride and all the cock-like qualities he possessed and is thoroughly emasculated: 'Dem Hochzeitstage zu Ehren wurde alles Geflügel geschlachtet.' And Vasthi, in keeping with her greedy, predatory role, comes to acquire, 'für eine Kleinigkeit', the Majoratshaus itself.

The image the Majoratsherr has of himself as the swallow and Esther as the dove may have yet further echoes. The swallow, besides being the sacred bird of Venus, the goddess of love, is not infrequently an image of Spring and of cyclical rejuvenation. This would seem to be in keeping with Arnim's employment of the image. In the 'Schwalbenlied' the Majoratsherr composes about the bird, it is once more trying to construct a new home against the onslaughts of nature and time. The Majoratsherr views himself as in much the same predicament, attempting to construct a new life, and he is fascinated by the bird's industry, something he himself lacks. When the swallow is driven away, it is a sign to the Majoratsherr of his own imminent failure. The swallow suggests rejuvenation and self-renewal; it returns each year in the spring to pick up the pieces and to work again at survival. The nest the swallow builds of worthless 'Baumörtel' is only a temporary dwelling and reminds the reader (and the Majoratsherr?) of the transitory housing provided by the human body for the soul. The swallow's nest echoes the message of 2 Corinthians 5, 1:

> Wir wissen ja, wenn unser irdisches Haus abgebrochen wird, erhalten wir einen festen Bau von Gott, ein ewiges Haus im Himmel.

The nineteenth-century writer de la Bouillerie has interpreted swallows and their nests in just this way, as suggestive of the body/soul relationship:

> Nehmen wir uns die Schwalbe zum Vorbild: Lassen wir das Nest zerfallen und denken wir vielmehr an unsre Flügel! Erinnern wir uns, dass unsre ewige Wohnung nicht aus irdischer Materie besteht, sondern dass wir für den Himmel geschaffen sind.

In addition, German Romantic poets have frequently employed the swallow as an image of steadfastness in change and of the cyclical nature of time. One thinks most readily of Brentano's 'Auf dem Rhein' and Chamisso's 'Lebe wohl'. The swallow as an image for the Majoratsherr is, however, more akin to Friedrich Rückert's use of the bird in 'Aus der Jugendzeit':

> Wohl die Schwalbe kehrt, wohl die Schwalbe kehrt,
> Und der leere kasten schwoll,
> Ist das Herz geleert, ist das Herz geleert,
> Wird's nie mehr voll.

> Keine Schwalbe bringt, keine Schwalbe bringt
> Dir zurück, wonach du weinst;
> Doch die Schwalbe singt, doch die Schwalbe singt
> Im Dorf wie einst.

The Majoratsherr longs to emulate the swallow, but lacks totally its industry, purpose, and decisiveness. It is clear from the 'Schwalbenlied' that he himself realizes this. In that it reflects a number of the aspects of his ambiguous longings, the swallow is a well-chosen image for the Majoratsherr's spiritual crisis.

Esther's identification with the dove, besides conveying the quality of innocence and purity, likewise associates her with the human spirit. The dove as symbolic of man's soul was a common motif in Visigothic and Romanesque art, and a Slavic belief is that, at death, the soul turns into a dove. This is not so far removed from the dove as a symbol of the Holy Spirit. The description of Esther's death, as witnessed by the Majoratsherr, adds to this sense: the dove image becomes expanded into the 'geflügelte Seele', in some respects reminiscent of Goethe's 'schöne Seele' image. Earlier on, as a premonition, the Majoratsherr cried: 'Wo ist die geflügelte Seele, der ich mich einst in reiner Umgebung zu nahen hoffte?' And as the 'geflügelte Seele' folds her hands towards heaven and disappears with the Todesengel, we are informed in 'Sperrdruck':

> . . . es schien überall durch den Bau dieser Welt eine höhere, welche den Sinnen nur in der Phantasie, die zwischen beiden Welten als Vermittlerin steht, . . . vergeistigt, indem sie das Höhere verkörpert.

Arnim's tale thus exhibits a detailed and extended avian imagery which lends an intricate coherence to the story. The conflict in the narration between the material and the spiritual is pointed up in this imagery, especially in the 'Schwalbenepisode'. Such a highly developed pattern suggests an attentiveness to detail and the existence of a carefully conceived plan of operation. Henel points out that Arnim's art is 'dass er alles Schwere in die Luft spielt wie Federbälle', and this is nowhere more aptly illustrated than in the avian imagery of *Die Majoratsherren,* in which the characterizations, motivations, and interrelationships of the four main figures are skilfully reflected.

Kari E. Lokke   (essay date 1983)

SOURCE: "Achim von Arnim and the Romantic Grotesque," in *The Germanic Review,* Vol. LVIII, No. 1, Winter, 1983, pp. 21-32.

[*In the following excerpt, Lokke contends that Arnim's use of the grostesque in* Isabella von Ägypten *"represents an attack upon early nineteenth-century aesthetic expectations, rational thought and social norms through its intermingling of incongruous elements and its juxtaposition and fusion of opposites."*]

A side from André Breton's assertion [in his introduction to *Contes Bizarres,* 1933] that Achim von Arnim's *contes bizarres* are the finest works of prose fiction produced by either the eighteenth or the nineteenth century, critical appreciation of Arnim's fantastic tales has been virtually nonexistent until recently. This striking fact has represented an obligatory point of departure for contemporary Arnim research and has resulted in numerous surveys and summaries of negative critical response to Arnim's work. The charges aimed at Arnim are twofold and closely related: 1) that his works are aesthetically anarchical and lacking in formal coherence 2) that they represent an insult to both the historical and the fantastic by indiscriminately and grotesquely mixing these two incompatible realms.

It is certainly true that Arnim delights in a rather playful intermingling of fact and fiction. The "once upon a time" of Goethe, Tieck, Wackenroder and Brentano's *Märchen* is not for him; Napoleon's defeat and occupation of Arnim's beloved Prussia made aloofness from political and historical realities an impossibility for him. Thus Arnim abandons timelessness and universality for a specific historical and cultural situation. His *Isabella von Ägypten: Karl des Fünften erste Jugendliebe,* for example, is set in sixteenth-century Holland and is the story of the fictional gypsy princess Isabella and her love affair with the actual historical figure Charles V, Holy Roman Emperor from 1515 to 1555. Arnim even goes so far as to explain a historical fact—Charles' political failure, his premature forfeiture of the throne and withdrawal to an isolated cloister in St. Juste—as the result of Charles' guilt over his sacrifice of his first love, Isabella, to greed and worldly ambition.

It is also true that Arnim's work abounds in seemingly incongruous and irreconcilable elements. *Isabella von Ägypten,* for example, contains, in addition to the title figure, the poverty stricken gypsy princess and savior of her people: 1) a mandrake man, Cornelius Nepos, conjured up by Isabella from the "tears" of her unjustly hanged father and named after a second rate Roman writer who glorified the exploits of Hannibal. Cornelius is greedy, pugnacious, and ambitious; he has great rhetorical gifts and the ability to ferret out hidden money. As Charles' Minister of Finance, he is pronounced "die Seele des Staates." 2) the *Bärnhäuter,* a man who made a pact with the devil, agreeing to wear a bear skin and to refrain from talking, praying and washing for seven years in exchange for all the money he wants and the hand of the Pope's illegitimate daughter. As punishment for his greed, he is doomed to keep eternal watch over his money and is brought back from the grave when Cornelius discovers his wealth. 3) a Golem Bella, an exact double of Isabella, minus the soul, formed from clay through magical incantation, who is totally greedy and materialistic.

Such richness of imagination is clearly too much for most people, who instead of looking for the order behind the apparent chaos of Arnim's work, simply declare it excessive and undisciplined. Even the English translators of the work, Pierce and Schreiber [in *Fiction and Fantasy of German Romance,* 1927], presumably sympathetic to a work they chose to translate, reveal their lack of understanding by deleting the *Bärnhäuter* episode as well as the conclusion of the novella, dismissing them as "too wildly romantic." By truncating the novella, they unwittingly throw its careful structure into relief, for without Isabella's apotheosis in the final utopian funeral scene, the work loses much of its force and the oppositions around which it is built—matter/spirit, fact/fantasy, comedy/tragedy, life/death—are not properly resolved or highlighted.

Any interpretation of Arnim's work must come to terms with both his bizarre, seemingly anarchical imagination and his strong sense of history. It must inquire into the meaning of his "fantastic historicity," his need to give his supernatural tales "einen festen Boden in der Aussenwelt," as he himself puts it. It is Arnim's idealist philosophy which will in fact provide the key to an understanding of his intermingling of the supernatural, the wildly fictional and the factual in a grotesque style appreciated until recently only by the surrealists. In his introduction to the *Novellensammlung* containing **Isabella von Ägypten,** Arnim describes the poet as a rider of Pegasus, divine inspiration, a rider who has the choice either to restrain or to give free rein to this force, the creative imagination, mediator between the human and the divine. Only those who give Pegasus freedom reach Olympus. Those who wish to dominate Pegasus, instead of simply riding, are doomed to reincarnation as the Pegasus of other writers, who will direct and control them in turn, instead of allowing them their freedom. "Nur die wenigen, die sich der Begeisterung frei überlassen haben, ohne sie beherrschen zu wollen, die bleiben unverwandelt, und kommen ohne ein solches Leiden zum Urquell des höhern Lichtes, . . ." This ideal poetic source is also the transcendent spirit behind history, the divine order and meaning behind historical fact which Arnim describes in his beautiful introduction to *Die Kronenwächter.* Only poetry, Arnim says, can truly reveal the mysteries of history which can never be bound into a

system by human reason. Thus it is not personal whim which leads Arnim to describe historical events in a bizarre and fantastic manner, but rather his desire to show that their source and meaning are beyond human rationality. And only the poet with the historical perspective can express this divine spirit behind history, this "Heimlichkeit der Welt":

> Die Geschicke der Erde, Gott wird sie lenken zu einem ewigen Ziele, . . . Es gab zu all Zeiten eine Heimlichkeit der Welt, die mehr wert in Höhe und Tiefe der Weisheit und Lust, als alles, was in der Geschichte laut geworden. Sie liegt der Eigenheit des Menschen zu nahe, als sie den Zeitgenossen deutlich würde, aber die Geschichte in ihrer höchsten Wahrheit gibt den Nachkommen ahndungreiche Bilder und wie die Eindrücke der Finger an harten Felsen im Volke die Ahndung einer seltsamen Urzeit erwecken, so tritt uns aus jenen Zeichen in der Geschichte das vergessene Wirken der Geister, die der Erde einst menschlich angehörten, in einzelnen, erleuchteten Betrachtungen, nie in der vollständigen Übersicht eines ganzen Horizonts vor unsre innere Anschauung. Wir nennen diese Einsicht, wenn sie sich mitteilen lässt, Dichtung, sie ist aus der Vergangenheit in Gegenwart, aus Geist und Wahrheit geboren.

The poet, Arnim says, is a seer who sees truth in the crystal ball of history.

The poet, Arnim says, is a seer who sees truth in the crystal ball of history.

—*Kari E. Lokke*

Like the poet, the historical figure as well should seek attunement and surrender to this "Heimlichkeit der Welt," this transcendent historical spirit. In fact, escape from the historical moment is impossible for the individual: "Der Einzelne achtet sich reicher an Vertrauen als seine Zeit, und achtet sich gross, sich ihr zu entziehen. Aber keiner vermag es, seiner Zeit zu entfliehen, wie noch keiner seine Mutter verleugnen konnte, ehe er geboren." Depending upon one's point of view, this surrender to history can be seen either as the complete suppression of all individuality, "radikalste Verurteilung des Einzelnen," as Gerhard Rudolf calls it, or as true fulfillment of the individual through understanding of one's specific role in a suprapersonal order. The latter interpretation is, I think, more truly consonant with Arnim's work as a whole and with **Isabella von Ägypten** in particular. For if one examines the tale carefully, one sees that it is the story of Karl and Isabella's simultaneous and diametrically opposed personal decisions, decisions which in fact determine their fates. Whereas Isabella refuses to succumb to her attraction to Cornelius, Karl is seduced by Golem Bella. He furthermore refuses to marry Isabella (symbol of his poverty stricken but noble people) even though she is pregnant with his son, instead submitting her to a mock marriage with the avaricious, pugnacious Cornelius (symbol of the acquisitive spirit of capitalism).

Just as Karl decides to sacrifice both Isabella and the welfare of his people to his greed and lust for power, so Isabella chooses to leave him and unite her destiny with that of her people. On the night of this fateful decision, the gypsy people gather under the window of the room where she is staying with Karl. Torn between her people and the sleeping prince, Bella draws near him and he pushes her away:

> Sie nahete sich im innern Kampfe dem Bette des Erzherzogs, sie küsste ihn; wäre er erwacht, sie hätte nicht von ihm lassen können; aber er stiess sie im Schlaf von sich; ihm träumte, als ob die goldne Kette, worin er die Völker führte, ihm selbst, der sie hielt, immer enger um den Fuss wickelte, dass er dadurch zu fallen fürchtete; darum stiess er sie von sich.

Thus Karl falls victim to his own desire for power and wealth, symbolized by the golden chains which Cornelius procures for him in his dream, chains which enable him to command legions of soldiers in a campaign against the Spanish, but which eventually ensnare him and lead to his political ruin. Isabella, on the other hand, realizes her mission of leading the gypsy people back to their homeland Egypt, where she founds a utopian realm of peace and love. The narrator's apostrophe: "Deine Liebe ist nicht untergegangen in ihrer Verschmähung, der eine sollte sie nicht begreifen, nicht würdigen, nicht bewahren, dass sie übergehe zu einem Volke, welches in Deiner Liebe sich befreite." At a crucial moment, then, individual will and conscious choice unite with the will of God to determine the fate of Karl and Isabella; whereas Karl allows personal desire to rule him, Isabella understands her role in a historical process larger than herself. Arnim's conception of the role of the individual in history can, in fact, be seen as the idealist prototype of the Marxist dictum that freedom comes through attunement to historical forces and that the hero is not the person who can "stop or change the natural course of things" but rather the human being whose "activities are the conscious and free expression of this inevitable and unconscious course" [George Plekhanov, *The Role of the Individual in History,* 1967].

As we turn from Arnim's idealist *Geschichtsphilosophie* to his means of expressing this world view in a much-maligned and misunderstood style, the question of the appropriateness of the grotesque as a means of conveying Arnim's fantastic historicity arises. A brief discussion of romantic and contemporary theories of the grotesque will perhaps help illuminate the aesthetic background of Arnim's own bizarre and eccentric style, at the same time that a close look at Arnim's unique grotesque should help elucidate the history and meaning of this problematical literary term. In Friedrich Schlegel's *Gespräch über die Poesie* the character Antonio reveals the crucial role which historical consciousness plays in the romantic appreciation of the grotesque. In his discussion of the novels of Jean Paul Richter, a discussion which is also highly appli-

cable to Arnim's art, Antonio defends Richter's works against the accusation that they are nothing but "ein buntes Allerlei von kränklichem Witz" by admitting the accuracy of this description and stating that "solche Grotesque und Bekenntnisse noch die einzigen romantischen Erzeugnisse unsers unromantischen Zeitalters sind." According to Antonio, the present historical era is so lacking in imagination, so inimical to the production of great poetry, that grotesque art is the "Naturprodukt," the "Naturpoesie" of such an epoch: "Wir dürfen nun einmal die Forderungen . . . an die Menschen der jetzigen Zeit nicht zu hoch spannen, und was in so kränklichen Verhältnissen aufgewachsen ist, kann selbst natürlicherweise nicht anders als kränklich sein." And at the same time that Antonio sees "Phantasie" and "das Phantastische" as the essence of romantic poetry, he also emphasizes that "wahre Geschichte das Fundament aller romantischen Dichtung sei," that "die romantische Poesie . . . ruht . . . ganz auf historischem Grunde, weit mehr als man es weiss und glaubt." And it is, in fact, a historical event—the French Revolution—which for Schlegel is the ultimate embodiment of the grotesque in his time. Schlegel describes this all-important event in his *Kritische Fragmente* as "die furchtbarste Groteske des Zeitalters, wo die tiefsinnigsten Vorurteile und die gewaltsamsten Ahndungen desselben zu ein graues Chaos gemischt zu einer ungeheuren Tragikomödie der Menschheit verwebt sind." Thus Schlegel's aesthetic of the grotesque is developed against the background of the French Revolution, a cataclysmic political and social event followed by profound disorientation. Similarly, Friedrich Dürrenmatt sees the predominance of the grotesque and the tragicomic in twentieth-century literature as directly and immediately related to two specific political and social disasters: "the sellout of the white race" and the atomic bomb. . . .

For both Schlegel and Dürrenmatt, the grotesque is seen as the only possible aesthetic response to the social turmoil and malaise of their times. Similarly, there is no serene and balanced beauty in Arnim's works because such classical beauty would be a lie for him. Arnim furthermore repeatedly expresses his strong belief in the deep connection that binds every artist to his time as well as his equally strong fear that his own age is incapable of true poetry. Thus, in Arnim's *Der Wintergarten* the beautiful artificial garden is destroyed by one gust of winter air, symbolizing the reality which the friends and compatriots have tried to exclude from their gathering. This reality is the occupation of Berlin by the figure of Winter "mit seiner langweiligen Heerschar," the Napoleonic troops. Suddenly, the morning light in the mural framing the garden becomes the harsh light of political reality, "die Höllenflammen unsres Weltteils": "Der Morgen, seht, der hinter jenen Bergen hinüber scheint, das sind die Höllenflammen unsres Weltteils, wie ist die Kunst zu schwach, den Abgrund zu bedecken mit schönem Schein, doch diese Kunst ist schrecklich, die betrügt, die rechte Kunst ist wahr, sie heuchelt nicht den Frieden, wo sie ihn nicht geben kann."

The Napoleonic campaign, is, however, for Arnim less a cause than a symptom of the sickness of his age, which he sees as the rise of the middle class after the defeat of the aristocracy in the French Revolution. As Alain Faure neatly puts it, Arnim's political attitude is neither revolutionary nor counterrevolutionary but rather postrevolutionary. Like so much romantic literature, Wordsworth's *Prelude* and Hölderlin's *Hyperion,* to cite just two examples, Arnim's entire oeuvre can be seen as a reaction to the excesses of the French Revolution and its failure to reach its proposed goals of "Liberté, Egalité, Fraternité." Arnim's postrevolutionary stance takes the form of an explicit attack upon the bourgeoisie, a class which Arnim identifies with greed and materialism. The avaricious, self-seeking characters in *Isabella von Ägypten*—Braka, who is Isabella's manipulative guardian, Golem Bella, the Bärnhäuter and Cornelius, Karl's Finance Minister—are all embodiments of the bourgeois capitalistic spirit. These characters prevent the permanent union of Karl and Isabella, symbol of Arnim's political ideal, both medievalistic and proto-socialist in its exclusion of the bourgeoisie, the union of aristocracy and people. As Reinhold Schneider states in his *Vom Geschichtsbewusstsein der Romantik,* Arnim saw that the French Revolution had put an end to the privileges of the nobility and that the aristocracy henceforth must give themselves to those they once ruled:

> Was bisher den adligen Häusern eigen war, das soll nun aller Eigentum werden: es gilt "alle Welt zu adeln"; der Geist des Rittertums soll des Volkes Geist werden. Es sollte die neue Bestimmung, die Rettung des Adels sein, dass er sich unbedingt hingab an das Ganze und den Geist, der ihn geprägt in die Sinnesart des Volkes einmünden liess; konnte Adel nicht mehr sein wie bisher, so musste das Volk adlig werden; denn auf das Ritterliche kann die Welt nicht verzichten. Das alte Rittertum sei untergegangen, schrieb Arnim an Brentano nach der Schlacht von Auerstadt (17. November 1806); ein neues möge beginnen.

If the noble, the individual, the poet, has much to give the people, they have even more, in the form of their own vital culture, to give in return.

—*Kari E. Lokke*

But if the noble, the individual, the poet, has much to give the people, they have even more, in the form of their own vital culture, to give in return. And who should better understand the treasures of German folk culture than the editor of *Des Knaben Wunderhorn?* Arnim's essay *Von Volksliedern,* published with *Des Knaben Wunderhorn* makes it clear that his hopes for the future of German language and literature, like his political hopes, lie with the common people and not with the middle class which he considered to be "ganz unfähig der Poesie." This essay also expresses his hope that German literature will someday regain the vitality, freedom and natural beauty embodied in the folk literature of the past. He speaks of the

"Freiheit alter Sprache" as opposed to "die Starrheit der heutigen," and in a statement reminiscent of Schiller's *Naive und sentimentalische Dichtung,* reveals a nostalgia of the sick for the healthy, nostalgia for that naive love of life which the romantic poets found in folk literature.

> Mit wehmütiger Freude überkommt uns das alte Gefühl des Lebens, von dem wir nicht wissen, wo es gelebt, wie es gelebt, was wir der Kindheit gern zuschreiben möchten, was aber früher als Kindheit zu sein scheint, und alles, was an uns ist, bindet und löst zu einer Einheit der Freude. Es ist, als hätten wir lange nach der Musik etwas gesucht und fänden endlich die Musik, die uns suchte!—

Here Arnim's idealization of the past is clear; he wants to go beyond his own childhood, beyond the childhood of his people to an absolute childhood, an absolute purity and unity of being. It is as if he were once again searching for the spiritual source of all music—"die Heimlichkeit der Welt"—in order to give himself up to it. Arnim's desire to infuse his tales with the spirit of folk literature is particularly evident in *Isabella von Ägypten.* The most strikingly grotesque characters—the mandrake man, the golem and the *Bärnhäuter*—all enter the tale from the world of folk culture, the mandrake from the mainstream of European folklore, the golem from the Jewish tradition, and the *Bärnhäuter,* by way of Grimmelshausen, from Germanic lore.

This intimate connection between the grotesque and folk culture—so evident in Arnim's work—is the focal point of Mikhail Bakhtin's discussion of the aesthetics of the grotesque in his *Rabelais and His World.* According to Bakhtin, the grotesque of alienation and absurdity as described by Schlegel and Dürrenmatt, represents a modern conception of the term, prevalent only since the romantic era. He sees the older, original grotesque, which he terms grotesque realism, as a celebration of the fullness and variety of life and traces the history of this aesthetic back to medieval carnivals and festivals of the people. In these festivals a great sense of liberation was created through the suspension of normal class and rank distinctions and through the disregard for normal behavioral codes. These carnivals

> . . . celebrated temporary liberation from the prevailing truth and from the established order; they marked the suspension of all hierarchical rank, privileges, norms, and prohibitions. Carnival was the true feast of time, the feast of becoming, change and renewal. It was hostile to all that was immortalized and completed.

There is a joyous sense of change, flux and movement. "All the symbols of the carnival idiom are filled with this pathos of change and renewal, with the sense of the gay relativity of prevailing truths and authorities." In light of Bakhtin's theory, it is particularly appropriate in *Isabella von Ägypten* that the union of Karl and Isabella, the union of indigent gypsy and aristocrat, which produces the future ruler of the gypsy people, should occur during a folk festival and that Karl's presence at this event should be described as "eine Herablassung, die ohne Beispiel war," in other words, as an action which violates previously established standards.

According to Bakhtin, all sense of alienation ceases in these festivals as the people feel themselves part of one united body in a physical, social and even cosmic sense; the individual and body are not separate from other humans or from the rest of reality, as they are in modern times.

> In grotesque realism, therefore, the bodily element is deeply positive. It is presented not in a private, egotistic form, severed from the other spheres of life, but as something universal, representing all the people. As such it is opposed to severance from the material and bodily roots of the world; it makes no pretense to renunciation of the earthy, or independence of the earth and the body.

Even death itself is not seen as final or entirely negative, for death is the return to the earth, the source of new life. Hence the grotesque is ambivalent; it reveals human weakness, impermanence and flux at the same time that it celebrates these qualities; for change may mean growing old and dying, but it also means regeneration and rebirth in a very concrete and physical sense. The downward movement of the wheel of fortune is always followed by a corresponding movement upward.

Arnim's grotesque characters—Golem Bella, the *Bärnhäuter* who returns from the grave so filthy that parsley is growing from his bearskin, the phallic *Wurzelmännlein* Cornelius and the two old women, Braka and Frau Nietken—clearly represent this grotesque conception of the body. The Golem, the *Bärnhäuter* and the mandrake man all exist in a netherworld which links the human to the animal, vegetable and mineral; Golem Bella is part clay, the *Bärnhäuter* part animal and Cornelius part plant. And the old women, Braka and Frau Nietken, are truly symbols of life's spontaneous regenerative powers; age in no way inhibits their enthusiasm for life. When Bella and her entourage arrive at Frau Nietken's and find her kneeling in prayer, Bella and the *Bärnhäuter* join her. Not so Braka; she asks her friend if she's praying for deliverance from the hiccups brought on by overindulgence in alcohol. She then takes a pitcher of beer and drinks, Arnim says with obvious appreciation, for everybody. When Frau Nietken rises from her prayers, she too gives proof of her liveliness by dancing so vigorously that her astounded audience breaks out into howls of laughter. These old women's nicknames for each other—"alte Vettel," "tolles, altes Trompetengesichte"—reveal Arnim's own fondness for them. Their mixture of decrepitude and vigor, their warts, wrinkles and whiskers bring to mind Bakhtin's analysis of the role played by the aged in grotesque realism. Bakhtin considers the Medieval and Renaissance depiction of bodily protuberances in old people as symbolic of burgeoning, unceasing life. In particular Bakhtin describes a group of figurines in the Leningrad museum which represent aged women who are grotesquely pregnant and hideously laughing. This intermingling of death

and life is, for Bakhtin, the essence of the grotesque conception of the body:

> Contrary to modern canons, the grotesque body is not separated from the rest of the world. It is not a closed, completed unit; it is unfinished, outgrows itself, transgresses its own limits. The stress is laid on those parts of the body that are open to the outside world, that is, the parts through which the world enters the body or emerges from it, or through which the body itself goes out to meet the world. This means that the emphasis is on the apertures or the convexities, or on various ramifications and offshoots: the open mouth, the genital organs, the breasts, the phallus, the pot belly, the nose. The body discloses its essence as a principle of growth which exceeds its own limits only in copulation, pregnancy, childbirth, the throes of death, eating, drinking or defecation. This is the ever unfinished, ever creating body, . . . The unfinished and open body (dying, bringing forth and being born) is not separated from the world by clearly defined boundaries; it is blended with the world, with animals, with objects. It is cosmic, it represents the entire material bodily world in all its elements. It is an incarnation of this world at the absolute lower stratum, as the swallowing up and generating principle, as the bodily grave and bosom, as a field which has been sown and in which new shoots are preparing to sprout.

Interestingly enough, the same terms which Bakhtin employs in praise of grotesque realism—spontaneity, brimming-over abundance of life, protuberance, excretion, unfinished and open body—are precisely the terms which are used in deprecation of Arnim's style and form. Arnim's close friend Wilhelm Grimm, for example, can compare Arnim's work to an overflowing goblet, an ever-revolving kaleidoscope, a multi-limbed and faced Indian deity, and a partially framed picture, without seeing the strange beauty and fascination of these images. Even Alain Faure, clearly sympathetic to the symbolism, thematics and content of Arnim's work, suggests that analysis of its formal elements must have recourse to "notions plus ou moins suspectes: celles de 'digression,' 'd'excroissance' ou de 'protubérance.' Le terme de 'Auswüchse' devient indispensable, les éléments rebelles étant mis au compte de l'ironie romantique, de la liberté souveraine de l'artiste par rapport à son oeuvre."

The joyously irreverent grotesque of popular culture is, according to Bakhtin, the true grotesque which degenerates with the development of bourgeois culture and its emphasis upon the isolated individual. Existence—biological, social and cosmic—is then divided up into separate units which are fixed and isolated, instead of constantly growing, changing and merging with one another. With the arrival of German Romanticism, a new grotesque emerges, the grotesque of Friedrich Schlegel and Jean Paul Richter:

> Unlike the medieval and Renaissance grotesque, which was directly related to folk culture and thus belonged to all the people, the Romantic genre acquired a private "chamber" character. It became, as it were, an individual carnival, marked by a vivid sense of isolation.

The carnival spirit was transposed into a subjective, idealistic philosophy. It ceased to be the concrete (one might say bodily) experience of the one, inexhaustible being, as it was in the Middle Ages and the Renaissance [Bakhtin].

The humor loses its gaiety and joyousness and becomes sombre, ironic and sarcastic like the black humor of *Die Nachtwachen des Bonaventura.* The modern grotesque of twentieth-century surrealism, of Kafka, Mann, Dürrenmatt and Beckett has its roots, Bakhtin suggests, in this romantic grotesque of subjective isolation and alienation.

I have dwelt so long on Bakhtin's theory of the grotesque partly because it provides a valuable historical corrective for Wolfgang Kayser's well-known ahistorical analysis [*Das Groteske: Seine Gestaltung in Malerei und Dichtung,* 1957], but more essentially because it provides an excellent picture of the spirit of folk culture which Arnim admired and sought to recapture in his *Isabella von Ägypten.* Clearly, as Gerhard Rudolf states, *das Volk* represents for Arnim "jener Bereich, der noch den Ursprüngen des Lebens nahe steht, dem regenerierende Kraft zukommt." And like the grotesque as characterized by Bakhtin, so the popular culture which is its source is seen by Arnim as a source of regeneration, rejuvenation and liberation. "Mir gefällt auch das Freieste, auch das Burleskeste," Arnim says, thus bringing to mind the liberating power of the grotesque.

It is, however, impossible for the Romantic poet like Arnim to return to the simplicity and freshness of folk culture and literature. Eating from the tree of the knowledge of good and evil is, as Schiller states in his *Über naive und sentimentalische Dichtung,* an irreversible act. And Arnim is the nineteenth-century heir to seven centuries of Prussian aristocratic tradition, rather than a sixteenth-century peasant. The exuberant, irreverent and joyful celebration of the unity of all people and all life becomes an ideal—like "die Heimlichkeit der Welt" and "die Musik die uns suchte"—which Arnim longs for rather than the palpable reality it constitutes in folk culture. Arnim never became the *Volksdichter* he dreamed of being; instead he was perhaps the least widely read of all major Romantic writers.

Thus the inclusion of folk motifs and characters in *Isabella von Ägypten* does not produce "grotesque realism" in Bakhtin's sense, but rather a unique romantic grotesque which might be said to telescope the entire historical development of the grotesque into itself. Placed as it is between the medieval and Renaissance folk grotesque and the modern grotesque as described by Schlegel and Dürrenmatt—the dark, abysmal grotesque taken by Kayser as the ahistorical essence of the term—, Arnim's work embodies elements of these two aspects of the grotesque as well as a third type which Bakhtin calls the romantic grotesque. In its pure romantic form, the grotesque is valued as indicator of an ideal transcendent order. Hugo's *Préface de Cromwell,* for example, justifies the use of the grotesque in religious terms by asserting that modern literature, literature born of Christianity (Hugo follows the Schlegels' equation of the romantic, the modern and the

Christian) expresses the real rather than the beautiful; it must contain both the sublime and its opposite, the grotesque:

> . . . le réel résulte de la combinaison toute naturelle de deux types, le sublime et le grotesque, qui se croisent dans le drame, comme ils se croisent dans la vie et la création. Car la poésie vraie, la poésie complète, est dans l'harmonie des contraires.

Christianity is both the source and the justification of Hugo's aesthetic of the grotesque; art must reflect the harmony of opposites in God's creation. Thus the grotesque, which creates "le difforme et l'horrible" as well as "le comique et le bouffon" has the essentially positive function of giving poetry a new wholeness and fullness.

The grotesque is a sign of vitality and vigor, not sickness, decadence and alienation.

> Et comme il est libre et franc dans son allure, comme il fait hardiment saillir toutes ces formes bizarres que l'âge précédent avait si timidement enveloppées de langes. . . . Nous dirons seulement ici, que comme objectif auprès du sublime, comme moyen de contraste, le grotesque est, selon nous, la plus riche source que la nature puisse ouvrir à l'art. . . . Le contact du difforme a donné au sublime moderne quelque chose de plus pur, de plus grand, de plus sublime enfin que le beau antique; et cela doit être.

Kayser suggests that Hugo emphasizes the contrast between the sublime and the grotesque in order to indicate that inhuman forces have invaded the familiar world, that the grotesque consists in the contrasts which refuse reconciliation. Kayser's interpretation, however, is a distortion of Hugo's text. For even if humans are not always able to comprehend the significance of the grotesque, harmony and reconciliation still exist for Hugo at the level of God's creation as a whole: "Ce que nous appelons le laid, . . . est un détail d'un grand ensemble qui nous échappe, et qui s'harmonise, non avec l'homme, mais avec la création tout entière." Like Arnim, then, Hugo not only asserts the primacy of the real over the beautiful, but he also sees the grotesque as indicator of a suprapersonal order beyond the comprehension of human reason. The grotesque of both Arnim and Hugo thus throws the sublime into relief. Just as Quasimodo's physical ugliness highlights his spiritual beauty and generosity, so the crass materialism and physicality of the grotesque characters in Arnim's tale throw Isabella's purity and goodness into relief. Ironically it is not Arnim's sublime Isabella who has the most presence and power in the tale, but rather the grotesque incarnations of bourgeois greed and aggression—Cornelius, Braka, the Golem and the *Bärnhäuter*—who seem to hold center stage till the very end of the tale. As Jacob Grimm says of Cornelius, the *Wurzelmännlein,* "überhaupt ist es mit seinem Wesen und Eingreifen das Gelungenste in der Erzählung und die Hauptfigur." The force of Arnim's grotesque creations is perhaps vivid testimony to the inevitable ascendancy of the class they represent, just as Isabella's ethereal, ghostlike presence reflects the frailty of the utopian ideal she symbolizes. It is indicative of Arnim's complex and transitional historical position that he, as aristocrat, creates from folklore motifs centuries old, powerful symbols of bourgeois greed and materialism.

Arnim's grotesque is, I think, a reflection of reality in a multi-faceted mirror, a mirror which has, in fact, been cracked and even shattered, perhaps in the attempt to penetrate beyond the surface of the real. The alternation of the Medieval-Renaissance, the romantic and the modern grotesque as defined by Bakhtin creates an unsettling and provocative shifting of perspectives which intensifies the difficulties any form of the grotesque seems to present to many readers. At one moment the tale seems a celebration of Cornelius as an embodiment of the earthiness, irreverence and indefatigability of human will and desire which overshadows the pale, deathlike Isabella. At other times, it is the clarity and sublimity of Isabella's goal which shines forth. And at still others Arnim's grotesque seems modern in its pessimism and nihilism, in its capacity to instill, as Kayser says, not a fear of death, but a fear of life. This is particularly evident in the characterization of Cornelius as an almost demonic embodiment of the connection between capitalism, militarism and male libido. Before Cornelius becomes Karl's Minister of Finance, and "die Seele des Staates," his aggressive nature longs for a glorious military career. The intensity of his ambitions is matched only by his complete lack of self-awareness which renders him incapable of perceiving the unsuitability of his three-foot frame for such a career. (Cornelius is, of course, a relative of Napoleon.) One of the judges whom he asks to certify him as a human being suggests that he might be very effective on the battlefield making surprise attacks on the enemy from the pants pockets of larger soldiers!

The grotesque in all its manifestations in *Isabella von Ägypten* represents an attack upon early nineteenth-century aesthetic expectations, rational thought and social norms through its intermingling of incongruous elements and its juxtaposition and fusion of opposites. In particular the oppositions fact/fiction, matter/spirit, comedy/tragedy, and death/life are challenged consistently from beginning to end of the tale. As Arnim writes in a letter to Jacob Grimm objecting to Grimm's distinction between *Natur-* and *Kunstpoesie:* "Nach dieser meiner Überzeugung wirst Du es in mir begreiflich finden, dass ich sowohl in der Poesie wie in der Historie und im Leben überhaupt alle Gegensätze, wie sie die Philosophie unsrer Tage zu schaffen beliebt hat, durchaus und allgemein ableugne. . . ." When this refusal of analysis and neat categorization breaks down false societal and ideological barriers to expose the truth of life's unpredictability and spontaneity in order to celebrate the unity and power of that life, then Bakhtin's grotesque realism results. When, on the other hand, the reader is shocked into a realization of the fundamental absurdity and frightening disorder of the universe, then one finds the modern grotesque as described by Kayser. And finally, when the interplay of apparent opposites is used dialectically to reveal an ideal transcendent order, the romantic grotesque appears. The following detailed analysis of *Isabella von Ägypten* will reveal the presence

of all three tendencies and seek to understand their fusion in a unique romantic grotesque. The analysis will concentrate upon the four previously mentioned pairs of oppositions whose interplay creates the aesthetic structure of the work.

Even the most abstract and least obvious of these oppositions—that between fact and fiction—is present throughout *Isabella von Ägypten* in a striking manner. Arnim's novella beautifully exemplifies the historical quality which Friedrich Schlegel terms the essence of romantic poetry; as emphasized earlier in this essay, Schlegel suggests that romantic poetry must have a basis in historical reality, whereas classical literature excludes historical material. In fact, the distinction between fiction and "reality" loses its validity in romantic art: "Es ist gar keine Rücksicht genommen auf den Unterschied von Schein und Wahrheit, von Spiel und Ernst." Not only does Arnim place the historical figure Charles V side by side with the fictional gypsy queen Isabella. He also turns the historical fact of the persecution of the gypsies (itself justified by the myth of their cruelty to Mary and the Christ child) into the tale of their redemption through Isabella and the son she bears as a savior to her people. And at the end of the tale Arnim explains a historical fact—Charles' forfeiture of the throne and withdrawal into religious meditation—by means of the fictional Isabella and the ever-present mandrake root. This little *Männlein,* in his self-immolation through anger, takes one step deeper into fictionality by being transformed into the ghost of a mandrake root, who haunts Charles and reminds him of his sins until Charles is forced to abandon the political world "um in heiligem Leben, in Busse und Gebet jeden bösen Wunsch zu bannen." The source of Charles' greatest remorse is, of course, his treatment of Isabella whom he sacrificed to greed and worldly ambition. In their old age, however, both choose to die on the same day and are reunited for eternity. Arnim attributes his beautiful description of Isabella's death to Taurinius, the author of an existing travelogue, thus in the final scene giving Isabella's existence the appearance of historical veracity.

> **Arnim's use of folklore reflects his refusal to draw an absolute distinction between the real and the imaginary.**
>
> —*Kari E. Lokke*

This mixture of historical fact and pure fiction allows Arnim the expression of his utopian political visions. He unites a king and a poverty-stricken gypsy, not in a gesture of ridiculous sentimentality, but in an attempt to destroy the boundaries between two irreconcilable social groups. He also envisages the salvation of the gypsies, a people whom he loved and whose persecution he deplored. Thus Arnim's free play with fact and fiction which so offended the Grimm brothers serves the utopian function which Bakhtin sees as fundamental to the grotesque. And by giving his visions "einen festen Boden in der Aussenwelt," Arnim stresses the contrast between what is and what ought to be at the same time that he gives his ideals the quality of potential realities.

Like his intermingling of fact and fiction, Arnim's use of folklore also reflects his refusal to draw an absolute distinction between the real and the imaginary. All three folklore characters, the *Alraun,* the golem and the *Bärnhäuter,* represent the power of the human imagination to create fictions which take on autonomous existence. This is most obvious with the *Bärnhäuter* who appears at the exact moment Braka finishes relating his tale to Bella and Cornelius. Thus the *Bärnhäuter*'s imaginary presence in the minds of Bella, Cornelius and Braka evokes his real entrance into their lives. The magical evocations of the mandrake root and the golem parallel the *Bärnhäuter*'s genesis. The golem comes into existence as a result of the Prince's desire to deceive Cornelius so that he can have the real Bella all to himself. Golem Bella is thus a reflection of the Prince's desirous, possessive and deceitful side. She is also a reflection of her Jewish maker's inner being: "nämlich Hochmut, Wollust und Geiz." Aside from revealing Arnim's painfully obvious anti-Semitism, the golem, like the *Alraun* and the *Bärnhäuter,* illustrates one of the novella's recurrent themes: inner and outer worlds can never remain totally distinct, imaginative creations are reflections of inner visions which, when projected onto the outer world, can become so powerful that they escape control and lead an autonomous existence.

Similarly, Cornelius Nepos, "das kleine Ungeheuer," also symbolizes the power of the mind's creations to take on a life of their own, Frankenstein fashion. Although Isabella is at first charmed and fascinated by the life she has created, Cornelius' nasty, willful petulance soon disturbs her and makes her wish she could do away with him. Arnim suggests a parallel between Isabella's creation of the mandrake man and God's creation of humanity: "So fröhlich und ernstlich zugleich begann sie dies Werk, ein Wesen zu schaffen, das wie der Mensch seinen Schöpfer, bis an sein Ende sie betrüben sollte; selbstzufrieden wie ein junger Künstler, dem alles über Erwartung glückt, besah sie ihr kleines, unförmliches Ungeheuer." Just as humanity seems unworthy of divine origin, so little Cornelius appears unworthy of Isabella:

> Was wundern wir uns über ihre sonderbare Neigung zu der halbmenschlichen Gestalt, nachdem sie zu dem schönsten Fürstensohne so ausschliessliche Neigung gezeigt hatte; es ist das Heiligste, diese Anhänglichkeit an alles, was wir schaffen, und ruft uns, während wir vor den Hässlichkeiten der Welt und unsren eignen erschrecken, die Worte der Bibel in die Seele: 'Also hat Gott die von ihm geschaffene Welt geliebet, dass er ihr seinen eingeborenen Sohn gesendet hat.' O Welt, bilde dich schöner aus, dass du dieser Gnade würdig werdest.

This parallel between human creativity and God's creation of the world shows just how real the products of the imagination are for Arnim, just how much power he plac-

es in the hands of the artist. Certainly this theme also expresses Arnim's own fear of his strange and powerful imagination which created not only beautiful utopian visions but also sub-human monsters.

Isabella's love for her creation is holy, "das Heiligste," because it is a love for divine creativity itself—the source of all life. Yet the mandrake root and his counterparts seem less expressions of the life force than perversions of it. They are all grossly materialistic and completely lacking in spirituality. All are subhuman embodiments of matter gone mad; the golem is clay, the mandrake root a plant and the *Bärnhäuter* part animal. We have thus come to a second fundamental opposition which these three freaks highlight: that between the spiritual and the material.

Cornelius is, of course, a personification of greed. His *raison d'être* is to supply "Geld und was ein weltliches Herz sonst begehre, mit stehlender, untrüglicher Listigkeit." The old gypsy woman Braka makes it clear to him that "er müsse Schätze graben und sich um weiter gar nichts bekümmern"; providing riches is his sole purpose in life. When his affinity for riches finally brings him to the position of Minister of Finance to Charles, Chievre, Charles' Machiavellian advisor, perceives the unmistakable value of the greedy little fellow's talents:

> Gott segne Ihre Hoheit mit einem Finanzminister in der kleinen Person dieses Alrauns, der Ihre künftige Grösse fest begründen kann; unabhängig von den Launen der Stände schaff er Euer Hoheit künftig die Mittel, jede Tätigkeit für sich zu benutzen. Er wird die Seele des Staates; sein Genie wird göttliche Rechte und menschliche Wünsche, die ewig einander widersprechen ausgleichen können. Lange lebe der Erzherzog und sein Reichsalraun!

With this beautifully hypocritical speech Arnim's political satire is clear as he reveals his awareness of the allpowerfulness of capital in the sixteenth-century world. More importantly, however, Arnim's satire is a critique of his own age and its tendency, so well described by Heine in his *Die romantische Schule,* to replace religion with commercialism and to deify money:

> Besteht nun die heutige Religion in der Geldwerdung Gottes oder in der Gottwerdung Geldes? Genug, die Leute glauben nur an Geld; nur dem gemünzten Metall, den silbernen und goldenen Hostien, schreiben sie eine Wunderkraft zu; das Geld ist der Anfang und das Ende aller ihrer Werke.

The *Bärnhäuter,* for example, sold his soul to the devil during his lifetime and became so enamoured of his wealth that he was condemned to stand watch over it after his death. He agreed to the pact with the devil and was willing to don a bear's skin and to refrain from praying, and washing for seven years. "Haar und Bart waren ihm dermassen gewachsen und verfilzt, dass er von Gottes Ebenbildlichkeit wenig mehr übrigbehielt; Petersilie war ihm auf seiner Haut gewachsen, das sah gar erschrecklich aus." He spent so little time with people that he nearly lost his capacity for speech—a symbol of his loss of humanity. The *Bärnhäuter*'s utter lack of spirituality is symbolized by his grotesquely unkempt appearance and by his degeneration from "Gottes Ebenbild" to the level of the animal and vegetable. Like the equation of dirtiness with ungodliness, the *Bärnhäuter*'s marriage to the Pope's illegitimate daughter is a protestant symbol for the perversion of spirituality.

Similarly, Golem Bella is a body without a soul, a personification of loveless lust and ugly greed. She wheedles pearls from the Prince and drives the hungry and exhausted Isabella from her door for fear that Bella will cost her money. After making love to the golem, the Prince

> . . . konnte . . . nicht begreifen, was ihm mitten im Genusse gefehlt hatte; sein ganzes Herz war traurig und schwer, weil es nicht jubeln konnte, wie damals, als er sich von Bella in Buik trennte; ja, es war ihm, als sei es ein andres Wesen gewesen, das bei ihm geschlummert, und wäre sie nicht früher fortgeschlichen gewesen, er hätte sicher die dunkeln Locken von der Stirn erhoben, um das Wort des Todes zu entdecken.

Though unaware that he has been victimized by his own treachery, desire and deceit, the Prince nevertheless feels that his beloved has been replaced by a being of crude sexuality: "Gewiss ist jene verloren, die ich liebte, die im Tor meines Lebens wie die zarte Morgenröte vor der hellen Sonne verschwunden ist; statt des Götterbilds habe ich eine irdische Gestalt umarmt, die mich in niederer Glut an sich zieht, und vor der mein Herz zurückweicht." Despite his vow to stay away from this new Isabella whom he does not love, he soon feels "eine unwiderstehliche Begierde zu diesem Golem" and begins to doubt the reality of spirituality and to value lust over love because it seems more real to him:

> Es war ein Drang andrer Art, als er geahnt, aber er konnte ihn doch nicht abstreiten, nicht zurückweisen; auch konnte er nicht leugnen, dass diese Empfindung etwas Bestimmtes, etwas Mögliches forderte, während jene sich vielleicht ins Unendliche traumartig ausblühte; ja in diesem Zwiespalte seines Gemütes schien ihm das Wesenlose, das Ungewisse in jenen hohen Freuden leer und verachtlich gegen diesen erkannten Sieg seiner Sinne.

After the golem's destruction, the Prince washes his hands and face "um jede Spur dieser falschen Berührung mit der Erde zu tilgen," but neither he nor Bella can forget the betrayal and be as they had been. Thus Golem Bella's soulless sensuality highlights Isabella's spirituality and otherworldliness just as the *Bärnhäuter*'s bodily and monetary filth shows us by contrast her purity and Cornelius' egoism throws Isabella's selflessness into relief. Bella does not belong with the company she keeps and is often ashamed of them. Similarly her sensitivity makes her shy away from "das rauhe Volk"—the gypsy people. This emphasis upon Isabella's isolation and spirituality is clearly far removed from the Medieval and Renaissance grotesque celebration of the body and the unity of all people; the opposition between Isabella's sublimity and the crudeness of her aged guardian and her monster entourage is a manifestation of the grotesque as defined by Hugo, the grotesque which Bakhtin calls the romantic grotesque.

Whereas Arnim's absolute opposition of the material and the spiritual represents the essence of the romantic grotesque as defined by Hugo and Bakhtin, Arnim's humor seems to vacillate between the earthy-irreverent and the chillingly demonic-macabre. The humorous and the tragic are so closely interwoven as to be inseparable in this tale. Once again Schlegel's description of romantic poetry comes to mind: "Es ist darin gar keine Rücksicht genommen auf den Unterschied von Schein und Wahrheit, von Spiel und Ernst." Even the saddest events are tinged with comedy. When Bella, for example, leaps into the swiftly flowing river to embrace her father's corpse, Simson, the ferocious black dog, holds her skirts tightly in his jaws to prevent her from being carried downstream with her father's body. Braka can only laugh when she comes upon this strange scene, so intensely still it seems petrified: "Die Alte musste nach ihrer Art lachen, weil es etwas so seltsames war, ungeachtet es ihr sehr zu Herzen ging und sie nicht von Herzen sondern nur mit dem dürren Munde wie ein hungernder lachen musste." This Kafkaesque gallows humor is but one variety of the mixture of comic and tragic to be found in *Isabella von Ägypten*. The burlesque also intrudes upon the most serious and touching moments in this unpredictable tale. While Isabella is weeping over the Prince's betrayal, the *Bärnhäuter* takes her in his arms and waxes poetic over the simple happiness of a worm in a rotten plum at the same time that he naively wonders about the worm's motives for soiling its home with its droppings and thus spoiling its own "Lebensgenuss." Unexpectedly Arnim summarizes his attitude towards greed and the hoarding of money in a comparison which Freud would have loved: "Der einfältige Kerl dachte nicht, dass sein eignes Sammeln im Leben nichts anders gewesen war, als was die Maden in der edlen Frucht anhaufen."

It is, of course, Cornelius who is the comic hero of the tale. The *Alraun*'s obtrusive little presence makes a comic perspective inevitable and prevents the reader from totally identifying with the events of the tale. He embodies the essence of grotesque humor as described by Gilbert Muller in his book on Flannery O'Connor [*Nightmares and Visions: Flannery O'Connor and the Catholic Grotesque*, 1972]:

> The grotesque character is a comic figure. It is impossible to sympathize with him, despite his agonies, because we view him from a detached perspective, and when we are not emotionally involved in his suffering, we are amused. . . .
>
> As with the grotesque character the entire technique of the grotesque is also essentially comic, for we always view the grotesque from a vantage point. To be certain, the subject matter of the grotesque—the raw material which creates the vision—is always potentially horrible, but the treatment of this material is comic: this explains the peculiar complexity of tone, combining both horror and the ludicrous, which characterizes the grotesque as an art form.

As a ridiculous representation of pure libido and male ego, Cornelius seems a truly self-conscious, modern symbol. He appears both infantile and aged: "sein gelbfaltiges Gesicht schien entgegengesetzte Menschenalter zu vereinigen." "Zwar sah er aus wie ein altes Männlein, das zum Kinde zusammengeschrumpft war, aber es hatte noch alle Unarten der kleinsten Kinder dabei." According to the folk myth the mandrake root has its seed in the sperm of a hanged man. Arnim may have cleaned up the myth in the name of "Decenz" as Jacob Grimm suggested by attributing the origin of the mandrake to Herzog Michael's tears. Nevertheless the original myth remains in the reader's mind just as the phallic shape is obvious.

Significant parallels exist between Cornelius' life story and that of the Prince so that, in effect, Cornelius' existence runs alongside the Prince's providing a constant comic commentary upon it. Cornelius, for example, is Charles' rival for Isabella's affection, and the Prince's unreasonable jealousy of the little freak seems almost more ludicrous than Cornelius' reaction to him. The mandrake man is born on Charles' birthday, a product of Isabella's longing for the Prince. Soon, however, Isabella seems to forget the Prince and to fall in love with her creation just as Charles is seduced by the golem. Yet whereas Isabella eventually perceives the true nature of the *Wurzelmännlein,* the Prince is deceived by the golem, makes love to her and thus destroys his relationship with Isabella. As previously suggested, the Alraun represents Charles' lust for power; in arranging the mock marriage between Cornelius and Isabella, Charles is sacrificing her to this part of himself. When Bella leaves Charles she also leaves Cornelius who is disconsolate until he shapes the clay remaining from the golem into a second double of Bella whom he much prefers to the real thing. Charles, of course, also likes Cornelius' creation and steals it from him, causing him to burst with anger. With this strangely comic death, all humor leaves the tale and Cornelius is internalized into Charles as the symbol of his evil deeds and guilty conscience.

We have here arrived at the final and perhaps most fundamental opposition in *Isabella von Ägypten,* the opposition between life and death. The tale opens with the death of Isabella's father which coincides with the birth of the *Alraun* and the birth of Isabella's love for the Prince. And the novella ends with the death of Isabella and Charles to the world and their rebirth into eternal life. Countless details reveal Arnim's fascination with the interpenetration of life and death: the meal Bella eats in honor of her father's corpse, the black dog who greedily devours his store of bones before his death in the magic ritual which conjures up the mandrake man, the dance of the peasants under the gallows as Bella and her companions ride by.

The characters often seem more dead than alive; Arnim truly is, as Heine declared, "ein Dichter des Todes." Isabella is so pale and ghostlike that she frightens people, so pure and spiritual that she does not belong in this world. In order to avoid persecution, she goes out only at night. She is even taken for a corpse and nearly thrown into the river by two men who find her sleeping on her journey home after her abandonment by the Prince. Only when these two men are distracted by the sight of a body being removed from the gallows is she saved from this fate. Braka and Frau Nietken have one foot in the grave figuratively speaking and the *Bärnhäuter* literally so. After his return from the grave, he eats so much that his body begins to come alive again:

> ... auch erhob sich zuweilen ein solcher Streit, zwischen dem lebenden und verstorbenen Körper in ihm, dass es ihm über der ganzen Haut zuckte und juckte. Ebensolcher Zwiespalt war in seiner Meinung von der Herrschaft: sein verstorbener Leib rechnete sich zu Herrn Cornelius, sein neulebender war ganz der Frau Braka und schönen Bella ergeben und achtete den Herrn nicht mehr als einen Glückspilz.

It is the dead part of the *Bärnhäuter* which Cornelius rules, for Cornelius is himself dead in his materialism. Similarly, the golem is an automaton without a soul who loses even the appearance of life when the syllable *ae* from the word *Aemaeth* (truth) is erased from her forehead and the word *Maeth* (death) remains. Such characters and images lend both life and death a menacing quality. One feels far from the spontaneous, irreverent celebration of the rhythms of life and death which Bakhtin describes and much closer to the fear of life's chaos and absurdity which Kayser sees as the essence of the grotesque.

Such efforts to categorize *Isabella von Ägypten* make it clear that no theory of the grotesque can fully explore such a complex and ambivalent work. If the tale is allowed to speak for itself, however, one sees that the dark and threatening tone which predominates in the early part of the work gradually gives way to the expressions of hope and faith with which the novella ends; there is a movement from the demonic to the spiritual and transcendent. The work opens with tragicomic black humor in the funeral of Isabella's father. Cornelius, frighteningly modern embodiment of the absurdity and chaos of human libido, greed and desire, dominates the main body of the work. After the death of Cornelius the tone changes radically and the final double funeral of Charles and Isabella is a comedic conclusion in its representation of the lovers' reconciliation and marriage in death. Furthermore, the closing pages of the novella are filled with symbols of the continuity of life and death; both Isabella and Charles *choose* to die on the same day and are placed living into their coffins. Charles dies blissfully with the image of Isabella before him. And Isabella dies, not only with faith in an afterlife, but also with the awareness of her people's love and gratitude to her. The visions of her dying moment are not merely images of the paradise awaiting her, but also visions of her people's future on earth, for she has begun the task of uniting her people which her son will continue. Thus Arnim unites the romantic grotesque with the more realistic tradition which emphasizes the continuity of life on earth. This union of the romantic and the realistic tradition is evident in Arnim's concrete detailed description and praise of the funeral celebrations which honor Charles and Isabella:

Jenes Leichenbegängnis Karls muss uns nicht wie eine wunderliche Schauspielerei erschrecken. . . . Unsre eitle Zeit verachtet jede Leichenfeier, bei unsern frommen Voreltern war oft ein anständiges Leichentuch einzige Mitgabe der Braut und ein prachtvoller Sarg schloss ein bescheidnes Leben. Wer wagt das Sonderbarkeit zu schelten? Es war Nebenäusserung jener Einheit, die uns in aller ihrer Geschichte anspricht. . . . Welche Einheit und Ausgleichung aller Verhältnisse, wie fest begründet alles an der Erde und doch dem Himmel eigne, zum Himmel führend, an seiner Grenze am herrlichsten und prachtvollsten geschlossen.

Isabella von Ägypten is but one example of the legacy of unique fantastic tales, superbly grotesque satire and beautiful utopian visions which Arnim bequeathed to his literary and cultural descendants when he died at the relatively early age of fifty.

Vickie L. Ziegler (essay date 1991)

SOURCE: "Achim von Arnim's *Der Wintergarten:* Introduction," in *Bending the Frame in the German Cyclical Narrative: Achim von Arnim's* Der Wintergarten *&* E. T. A. Hoffmann's Die Serapionsbrüder, The Catholic University of America Press, 1991, pp. 9-24.

[*In the following excerpt, Ziegler presents a broad over-view of* Der Wintergarten, *discussing the work's connections to Arnim's aesthetic philosophy, to German folklore, and to the social and political events of the author's time. Ziegler also examines the relation of the frame narrative to the individual tales in the work.*]

> Es müsste sonderbar in ihren Winter hinein blühen,
>   wenn ihnen so der
> Sinn für das Grosse eines Volks aufgehen sollte und
>   für sein Bedürfnis.
>   —"Von Volksliedern," 1805

> "Things would have to flower remarkably in their
>   winter, if for them
> the sense of the greatness of a people and its needs
>   were to open up."
>   —"On Folk Songs," 1805

While the works of Achim von Arnim often seem like the forlorn stepchildren of German Romantic literature, even within a mistreated family, one child may suffer more from misunderstanding and neglect than the others. The condescending dismissal that *Der Wintergarten* has suffered is probably due in large part to the dependence of the work on sources, which is initially its most striking characteristic. With the exception of Wulf Segebrecht, most critics have not been willing to look more deeply at this narrative.

Wintergarten deserves a better fate than an airy dismissal as a badly seasoned rehash of older material, not only because it was important to Arnim's own development as

a writer, but also because Arnim had to examine problems similar to the post-World War II German political situation. In both cases, Germans had experienced the capitulation of their country in the face of a devastating defeat as well as the total collapse and decay of value systems in the personal and political spheres. Seen as a linchpin in Arnim's early development, *Wintergarten* takes on added significance. *Wintergarten* was not simply a futile literary exercise from a man who read too much; it was Arnim's attempt to advance his own deeply held beliefs about the interdependent role of literature, political action, and religious belief.

In 1808, when Arnim began collecting materials for this cycle, he had already immersed himself for years in the study of older German literature, the first fruits of which were the *Wunderhorn*. There are two main streams apparent in this pursuit: the belief, which was with him from the very first, that art is a means for all sorts and conditions of men to come together and the didactic, exemplary value of older literary works.

Because of this didactic tendency, Arnim's goals differed from those of the philologically inclined literati. Johann Friedrich Voss, for example, the renowned Homer translator, blasted Arnim for the liberties taken with original texts. Clemens Brentano wanted to restore an old folksong; Arnim wanted to change the points of emphasis. The purpose of this new version was to make material from the past accessible to his contemporaries so that it could have the desired exemplary effect. Arnim believed that it was the mission of art to present this material in such a way that those in a different age understood it and learned the necessary lessons.

Drawing the appropriate conclusion from the past to affect one's behavior in the present seemed particularly crucial to Arnim in the early years of the nineteenth century as Napoleon stormed through Europe. His concern with the fate of his countrymen was already apparent in the important essay. "On Folk Songs," written in 1805. This work contains numerous passages lamenting the spiritual decline of Germany from its earlier greatness, implying the existence of a more propitious period in Germany history. The belief in a Golden Age was one that Arnim had in common with other Romantics; Möllers notes that he agreed with Grimm's concept of a paradisical time which marked the beginning of human history, when God's will and man's were identical. Arnim's own adaptation of these ideas differed from those of other Romantics. Unlike Novalis, who projected human wishes into the past, Arnim believed in the continual presence of this primordial time in human history. Another passage from the folk song essay bears this belief out: "Und als ich dieses feste Fundament noch unter den Wellen, die alten Strassen und Plätze der versunkenen Stadt noch durchschimmern sah, . . ." ["And as I saw, still under the waves, this firm foundation, the old streets and squares of the sunken city still gleaming through the water . . ."].

If the primordial time still exists buried in the events of the day, then a way must be found to bring it to view in the present. Like other Romantic writers, Arnim saw art as an intermediary between different worlds, but he connected it with other purposes. Novalis saw art as a passport to the past that never was, while E. T. A. Hoffmann used literature as a means to explore the mysterious demimondes of the subconscious existence. But for Arnim, art was to be the midwife to a rebirth of the best of the German spirit into a present which sorely needed it.

Even in the poem "Zueignung" (Dedication), which appears at the very beginning of the work and which dedicates *Wintergarten* to Bettina, Arnim brought in the theme of preservation of the inspirational. (Bettina Brentano, whom Arnim would later marry, was the sister of Clemens Brentano.) The setting of the poem was an orangerie in Aschaffenburg in mid-September, 1808, where Arnim and Bettina parted and where he watched the stagecoach disappear. Arnim uses the real situation to introduce an artistic allegory grafted onto the orange tree, which bears blossoms and fruit at the same time. Just before he introduces the picture of the gardener picking the flowers and the fruit, he says of the spirit: "Der Geist sich offenbart in Frucht und Blüte" ["The spirit reveals itself in fruit and blossom"], while the fruit of the orange tree is "schöner Künste Frucht" ["The fruit of beautiful arts"]. The gardener lets the fruit that spills out of the rusty helmet fall, since he has an abundance, but as it falls, it hits a tambourine lying in the grass and produces music:

Ich fand das Tamburin mit Wohlgefallen,
Das unten lag, worauf sie (Frucht vz) tönend fiel,
Das Schöne ist auf Erden unverloren,
Es klingt zur rechten Zeit, den rechten Ohren.

With joy I found the tambourine which lay below, on which the fruit fell with a ringing sound. Beauty is not lost on earth if it resounds at the proper time to the right ears.

These lines could be read as an announcement of Arnim's plans for *Der Wintergarten*: He would like to ensure both that the fruits are not lost and that the appropriate ears hear the sounds. In both cases, in the orangerie and in the *Wintergarten,* the garden does serve as a sort of refuge where art may fulfill its role.

While the image of the helmet in the poem is problematical, the description of it implies a positive disposition towards it on the part of the author:

Es war ein Helm von altem, rost'gen Eisen,
Worin der Gärtner seine Frucht gepflückt,
Manch schwerer Hieb liess sich darauf noch weisen,
Doch schwerer hat ihn schöne Frucht gedrückt;
So musst der Helm vor meinen Augen reissen,
Der fest geschmiedet schien und reich beglückt:
Der alten Waffen schwer errungner Segen,
Und schöner Künste Frucht, lässt sich nicht hegen.

It was a helmet made of rusty old iron, which the gardener used for picking fruit, many a heavy blow had left a mark which still remained, yet beautiful fruit had weighed down more heavily upon it; so before my very eyes, the helmet had to split, which seemed so strongly forged and richly graced: The hard-won blessing of the old weapon and the fruit of beautiful arts cannot be contained together.

The helmet could well be a symbol for Prussia: the battle scars, the appearance of strength and wealth, the advantages that were won with old weapons. Yet this helmet cannot hold the fruits of art, which could be a disguised call on Arnim's part for a Germany that could learn from the fruits of the spirit.

Arnim's intent to hunt for such fruits is apparent at the very beginning of *Wintergarten,* when he cites Ritter von Thurn, a figure out of French didactic narrative, in an idyllic and idealistic introduction, linking the records of the past with service to God and their relationship to the present. This quiet prelude contrasts sharply in form and content with the reference to current events which comes immediately after the remarks of Ritter von Thurn:

Diese guten Worte eines alten Ritters mögen in diesem verdriesslichen, immer wiederkehrenden Winter, wo allen schönen Kindern Zeit und Weile lang wird, *wohl zur rechten Zeit wiederholt werden; doch keinem geziemen sie besser, als der nun zerstreuten, übellaunigen Wintergesellschaft,* zu deren Unterhaltung die folgenden Geschichten zusammengebracht wurden, *die sehr unzufrieden mit der ganzen Welt,* doch immer etwas Neues von ihr wünschte, endlich aber mit allem, was bloss erzählt und nicht geschehen, ganz nachsichtig, aufmunternd, wohlwollend und zufrieden schien. (emphasis mine)

These good-natured words from an aged knight could certainly be repeated at an appropriate time in this vexatious winter, which keeps returning, where for all handsome children time and leisure seem long; yet for no one are they more suited than for the distracted, illhumored winter gathering, for whose entertainment the following stories were collected, people who were very dissatisfied with the entire world yet who always wanted something new from it, who however seemed finally forebearing, well disposed, indulgent, and satisfied towards everything that was merely told and did not occur.

The stormy style of this description reflects the miserable morale of the Prussians in their winter of discontent, a situation to which Arnim alludes when he introduces the only rule for the stories, namely to make no specific references to current events, but rather to collect stories from other times and countries.

The majority of these inner stories deal with the manner in which the individual, faced with a personal or political crisis, behaves; it must have seemed particularly crucial to Arnim in 1808 to improve the present by analyzing the past. Prussia had capitulated to Napoleon's forces during the campaign of 1807 and lost territory west of the Elbe. Frustrated by the prostration of his country, Arnim had no ready outlet for his overwhelming desire to help. Military service as well as the bureaucracy were out of the question, the latter partly because of Arnim's ideas about a new social order.

> **The majority of the stories in *Der Wintergarten* deal with the manner in which the individual, faced with 2 personal crisis, behaves; it must have seemed particularly crucial to Arnim in 1808 to improve the present by analyzing the past.**
>
> —*Vickie L. Ziegler*

In addition to urging the citizenry to defend their country in his short-lived periodical "Der Preusse" "The Prussian," Arnim also wrote political articles and essays. One of the most famous, "Was soll geschehen im Glücke" ("What should happen with a fortunate turn of fate") contains valuable insights into Arnim's ideas about Napoleon as well as thematic parallels with some of the *Wintergarten* material. The opening lines of the essay reveal Arnim's ideas about Napoleon's place in history and the formation of a new nobility through education. The problem with Napoleon, as Arnim saw it, was that he had betrayed the goals of the French Revolution; however, because the uprising was a movement of the people, the death of Napoleon would not end it. Arnim's solution to the issues raised by the French Revolution was a radical one and would not have been much appreciated by the ruling classes of this time: "Das ganze Volk muss aus einem Zustande der Unterdrückung durch den Adel zum Adel erhoben werden" ["The entire nation must be elevated by the aristocracy from a condition of oppression to nobility"]. Behind these remarks stands Arnim's love for and almost messianic belief in the value of older literature in forming this new chivalric order.

The onslaught of the current national catastrophe brought on by the French caused Arnim's earlier ideas about the didactic value of art and its connection with religion, history, and politics to express themselves in *Der Wintergarten.* The preceding discussion has shown that *Wintergarten* had to be didactic and had to depend heavily on sources for Arnim to achieve the goals most dear to him. Many of these sources were, as Göres points out, not originally moral stories per se, but Arnim changed their focus in his adaptation and made them exempla for the characters in the frame. This process is at work in the story of the first evening, **"Die Liebesgeschichte des Kanzlers Schlick und der schönen Sienerin" ("The love story of Chancellor Schlick and the beautiful Sienese")**, which Arnim changed from a rollicking and bawdy Renaissance novella into a more idealized love story. In it he analyzes the importance of faithfulness and the effect of European politics on love; both of these themes relate to the situation of the lady of the country house, madly in love with a French officer.

Arnim chose the frame story genre because it offered several advantages, such as introducing material from widely different sources. Another attraction for him was that the gathering of a group of people listening to someone else provides a setting that lends itself to didactic purposes, a tendency that becomes apparent as the guests are mustered in the initial frame. The meeting of well-bred friends and strangers in an isolated house was already well known to Arnim through Boccaccio and Goethe. However, although the country houses in Boccaccio and Goethe are places of refuge either from the plague or from the French Revolution, Arnim does not intend for his Germans to enjoy the privileges of class and position; leisure and solitude available to them in this house should make it easier for them to receive the lessons of the stories, so that they, as they do at the end, can make their contributions to rebuilding German society.

The plague that threatens the *Wintergarten* guests is neither bubonic nor revolutionary, but a disease of the soul. Arnim's guests have no names, but this anonymity does not serve to flatten them out into mere stereotypes or to mint them as coinage of representative ideas. This namelessness rather serves to emphasize the connection between these people and Arnim's readers, particularly when it becomes a matter of the lessons that Arnim wants to convey. The inner stories function either as positive, negative, or analogical examples that can work directly on the guests and Arnim's readers.

The only figure who does not fit the description of the frame characters as outlined is the first one to appear, the half-allegorical, half-real Winter. We see him at the beginning and at the end as a bent, gray, aged man and, in between, as a season. Arnim's integration of Winter in these two guises into the narrative is as pervasive as the snow that Winter brings along. As Migge points out, Arnim loved to let allegorical or mythical figures assume a real shape in his stories, with enough of their transcendental nature showing to disquiet the other characters. He uses this procedure with Winter; although we first see him as a freezing gray old man in need of a ride, the narrator himself seems to doubt his existence as a real person. Rather, he encourages the reader to believe that the character symbolizes the frozen passiveness of Prussia after the departure of the victorious French troops:

> So zog also der Winter ein, wo die Feinde ausgezogen, und meine frohen Erwartungen und Gedanken erstarrten wie der lebendige Strom, der durch die Strasse floss. Alles besetzte und bewachte dieser traurige Winter mit seiner langweiligen Heerschar, selbst wo die kaufmännischen und adligen Häuser ihre hohen Stirnen, mit mancherlei Bildwerk gekrönt, erheben, hing er seinen weissen Glanzteppich auf, und selbst an dem Boden knirschten die gejagten Füsse noch unwillig, dass auch der treue Boden, den selbst die Feinde mussten stehen lassen, seine Farbe angenommen.

> Thus the winter moved in, where the enemies had evacuated, and my joyful expectations and thoughts grew stiff like the lively stream which flowed through the streets. With his tedious legion, this dismal winter

occupied and guarded everything. Even where the h ouses of the merchants and the aristocracy raise their high foreheads, crowned with various kinds of sculpture, he hung up his glistening white carpet, and even on the ground the driven feet crunched resentfully, because the faithful earth, which even the enemies had to leave alone, had also taken on his color.

The narrator continues with this militaristic tone in the frame of the second evening, but after that, there is only one reference to winter. It comes in a comparison of avalanches with people's moods in the seventh evening, before the reappearance of Winter as the fiancé of the lady of the house in the eighth evening. When Winter returns in human form, the first signs of spring, warmth, and light, also arrive. This appearance of the sun parallels the inner story of Jacob Böhme and Aurora, with the emphasis on the dawning of God's revelation to him. Since it is the lady of the house who will eventually see the error in her choice of lovers, it is she who has preoccupied herself with the study of Böhme and who in some way serves as the model reader Arnim wished to have. Well educated, sensitive, and sensible, she needs only exposure and help to understand.

The central position of the lady of the house in this cycle reveals itself immediately in the narrative. After Winter is introduced, she appears in the unusual guise of a motionless statue covered with snow, who runs in alarm at the narrator's unexpected arrival. Her position and the fact that she appears blanketed in snow underscore her central role in the novella in the frame and foreshadow her engagement to Winter. Hopelessly in love with the French officer, the lady accepts Winter's suit out of resignation and despair.

The narrator entreats the inhabitants of the country house to let him in and, as he arrives on the scene of their future evenings, several elements appear in the description that are of significance to the major themes of the story. The room to which he is led has been redone in the Gothic manner, indicating the importance of an older period in German history, as well as the interest of the estate's owner in this time. The first object he sees upon entering the room is the painting of the French officer, standing in a place of honor with flowers before it; that, plus the sighing of a flute clock, indicate that there is a melancholy aspect surrounding the picture. The lady of the house confirms this impression in saying that her nerves are on edge because she has suffered greatly and that the snow covers many painful memories. Because of her misguided choice of admirers, she has no real sense of direction and purpose, since personal inclination and national loyalty do not coincide. However, she has in her personality those traits that make change possible, and she likes the older periods of German art, which pleases the narrator.

The succession of other guests and members of the group follows much more briskly, without the lingering attention that Arnim devotes to the lady. Her sister, an intelligent, sensible woman who has never fallen in love, spends most of her time embroidering and pouring tea.

The young invalid with a wooden leg attracts the reader's attention immediately; his character description is perhaps the most positive of any in the group. The invalid, unlike the others present, has suffered in the service of his country; for this reason, Arnim assigns him a didactic role vis-à-vis the others in the group, with special attention paid to his assault on the lady's misplaced affections. This role comes quickly to the fore in the frame for the first evening, as the invalid tells the love story of the Chancellor Schlick and the beautiful Sienese, relating it to her love for the French officer. While his overriding interest lies in winning the lady for himself (and thereby for their country), he also exemplifies the sort of self-sacrificing bravery that should inspire some other members of the circle (the narrator clearly describes this function at the beginning of the fourth evening, which deals with war). In the frame of the sixth evening, the envoy tries to induce the invalid to write his memoirs, ". . . Warum lassen Sie untergehen was Sie allein berichtigen können?" ["Why do you let perish what you alone could correct?"] since memoirs are the most valuable kind of history.

The envoy, unemployed due to the German defeat, is the next guest to make his appearance. He remains a shadowy figure until the third evening's frame, where the reader initially sees him in an unimportant role. The invalid and the narrator, mentally lamed by the cold, begin to dissect the personalities of the colony members in such a way that they distort reality. Yet the first appearance of the envoy in center stage reveals its importance, as the narrator's preface implied that it would. The envoy makes an elegant, eloquent, and forceful speech, reflecting many of Arnim's own ideas about the connection between blood revenge and piety, the German's adulation for anything foreign, and the ensuing inability to sacrifice for the common good. Because of his experience abroad and his proximity to the government, he sees his countrymen both as individuals and as citizens of the state. The envoy performs an extremely important function in the frame, providing an intellectual counterweight to the invalid, whose long-standing passion for the lady of the house often softens his sharp mind or sinks him into the sloughs of despond. The envoy's return to the diplomatic service of his country provides an example to the other members of the circle, such as the *Geniale,* who comes with him, and the readers.

Both the invalid and the envoy have served their country in their respective spheres. For this reason, each of them operates some of the time in a different didatic role, functions that set them apart from the other frame characters. While the invalid can bring home to the hearers the real dimensions of military courage and the cruelty of war, the envoy can teach the guests about the essence of history and the value of the past for the present. Because he is an envoy, he has an important double perspective: he sees himself not only as a German among Germans, but also as an observer of Germans abroad.

Neither the actress who accompanies the envoy nor the sister of the lady of the house plays a real role in the frame. However, the last three women to appear figure in several evenings: the *Geniale* (the ingenious woman), the *Gesunde* (the healthy woman), and the *Kranke* (the sick woman). The *Geniale,* who makes her entrance by graciously pressing snowballs into the hands of her acquaintances, reappears in the seventh frame, *Winterlaunen* (Winter moods), which offers a light-hearted pause between the stories about Jacob Böhme and Prince Charles. The pause, **"Die drei Erznarren"** (**"The three notorious fools"**), is intended to drive away the depressing mood of the *Winterlaunen,* caused by the depressing situation in which they find themselves. Although many of the frames deal with the intellectual problems confronting the Prussians because of Napoleon, this one concentrates on the group's mood and emotion. No member of the company registers mood changes as quickly as the mercurial *Geniale.* Her perverse humors call forth all sorts of criticism from the others, which she takes to heart. She ends the story by going off with the envoy to help her country.

The *Gesunde* and the *Kranke* appear as a pair in the introduction and in the fifth frame. One immediately senses some of the liberated woman in the *Gesunde,* a quality reinforced during her major appearance as a sort of Amazon in the fifth frame. Her vigor manifests itself in a kind of aggressiveness. The *Kranke,* on the other hand, participates in only passive activities. A gossip, she introduces the fifth frame **"Mistris Lee"** story, saying the English lord entertained her with it. The balancing of these two opposites in the fifth frame, their only major appearance, shows a certain deftness in Arnim, not only because of their opposite natures, but also because **"Mistris Lee"** has qualities in common with both of them.

As he develops the story about the lady of the house and the French officer in his description of the frame society, Arnim gives definite hints as to how he intends to apply the examples of the inner stories to the characters in the country house. Naturally, Arnim did not intend to reach only those Prussian women in love with French officers, but all those less devoted to their nation than they could be.

Arnim's choice of a cyclical frame as the vehicle to present his lessons from older literature enables him to bring his intelligent and sensitive countrymen right into the country house, where they may feel affinities with certain characters and expose themselves to the benefits of the stories as well. The conventions found in the *Decameron*—the isolated society in which each individual tells a story and the rule which forbids reference to the events of the day— these Arnim retained as had Goethe before him. He kept as well something much more important from Goethe, something which characterizes the German cyclical narratives: the interaction between the inner stories and the frame. Like Arnim, Goethe depended heavily on sources for his inner stories. Unlike Arnim, the novellas that Goethe took from sources have often been exhaustively and exhaustingly analyzed, while in Arnim's case, most critics have ignored his adaptations and the reasons for them. Most of Arnim's inner stories were not originally intended to function in the specific, applied manner for which Arnim used them. He cut them loose from their literary moorings, not because he was insensitive to the artistic unity of

the original, but because he saw in that original what Göres refers to as the "verdeutlichende Exempel" (elucidating model).

In order to understand more fully how Arnim developed the network of relationships between the frame and the inner stories, one must examine the technical aspects of various elements of the frame and inner story as they appear in the **Wintergarten.** The frame itself was not a means to ban threatening forces from a group escaping from the current crisis. While that was true in the *Decameron,* and partially true in Goethe's *Unterhaltungen* (*Conversations*), it is not the case with **Wintergarten,** though it may seem that the ban on stories of the present places it in this category. The rule serves two functions: it creates an oasis, and banishes the distracting present with its nefarious tendency to preoccupy totally the minds of the audience. The rule serves not to provide the opiate of oblivion, but of offer mental space for those lessons from the past helpful in coping with the present. Arnim's use of the frame structure for mastery of a situation rather than for escapism has an antecedent in *Unterhaltungen;* we find a similar function in Hoffmann's *Die Serapionsbrüder,* particularly in those stories dealing with madness.

Unlike Goethe and Hoffmann, Arnim uses a first-person narrator, who has many apparent similarities with himself. Like Arnim, the narrator has been on a research trip looking for old songs and he enjoys older art as much as his creator. In his introduction to the Concordia story, he refers to his writing it down on the basis of other stories. The frame of the eighth evening contains the narrator's account of his own interest in Böhme and his collection of Böhme materials. Arnim chose a first-person narrator very like himself because of his deep, personal involvement with the major themes of the work, the degree of intimacy that such a narrator brings, and the added realism in the reproduction of an oral narrative situation. In addition, the narrator, who is part of the colony, yet outside it, can stand aside and comment on events in a more impartial way than some members of the group.

In Goethe's *Unterhaltungen,* the inner stories fall into thematic groups, a convention that probably came from Boccaccio, who had a subject for each day. Since **Wintergarten** has never been taken seriously as a successor to *Unterhaltungen,* the existence of a definite thematic pattern has not received the attention it deserves. . . .

[The] most important narrators are the invalid, the envoy, and the narrator. . . .

The invalid, the envoy, and the narrator reveal their worries about the spiritual state of the German people, concerns that appear in the frame as well as in the older exemplary material. The inner stories circle round the interrelated themes of national history, love, and the inner man.

The Schlick story portrays the hopeless conflicts engendered when adulterous love runs afoul of national and political allegiance. **"Albert und Concordia"** and **"Altdeutsche Landsleute"** (**"Compatriots from an earlier** age") describe marital love in the context of constancy to ethical and religious norms of conduct. In each, the love story takes place against the backdrop of a political situation: in **"Albert und Concordia,"** the formation of an ideal society in the wilderness; in **"Altdeutsche Landsleute,"** against the fidelity of Germans to each other in occasionally hostile foreign courts.

The theme of war, begun in **"Altdeutsche Landsleute,"** reaches a peak in the fourth evening. Here the invalid's rules for soldiers in the frame and the Philander story from the Thirty Years' War appear, as well as the discovery of Ariel sleeping on the desecrated *Viktoria* monument. Affairs of state predominate in the Jean Froissart chronicle of the sixth evening, as they do also in the account of Charles Stuart in the ninth. However, **"Mistris Lee,"** the middle story and frame five, concentrates on right and wrong behavior, particularly in the person of Mistris Lee, the enigmatic "neue Amazone" ("new Amazon"). Negative and positive examples also appeared in the stories of the second and third evenings, but always in conjunction with general or abstract themes, such as the ideal society or the conduct of war.

The Schelmuffsky story forms a pleasant interlude before the dawning of a new day, heralded in the eighth evening, which is devoted mostly to Böhme. The inspirational quality of Böhme's life can, as Arnim presents it, herald the beginning of a new dawn for Germany; attendant on the advent of this time of light is the death of Winter, announced in the frame, a death that occurs on several levels.

Sheila Dickson (essay date 1994)

SOURCE: "Preconceived and Fixed Ideas: Self-Fulfilling Prophesies in *Der tolle Invalide auf dem Fort Ratonneau*," in *Neophilologus,* Vol. 78, No. 1, January, 1994, pp. 109-18.

[*In the following essay, Dickson analyzes not only Francoeur's madness but the behavior of various other characters in* Der tolle Invalide *in terms of the psychological theories of Arnim's day.*]

Achim von Arnim's generation witnessed an expansion of scientific and pseudo-scientific interest in unconscious and pathological states of mind, which came to be regarded as providing the deepest insights into the psyche. Looking inwards at the processes of the mind led concomitantly to an appreciation of the extrinsic influences brought to bear on the intrinsic perspective. Man was often perceived as under threat from these influences and as unable to control his own destiny.

This would seem to represent the general consensus of opinion expressed in **Der tolle Invalide auf dem Fort Ratonneau,** in particular with respect to the main protagonist. The characters offer theories to explain Francoeur's present mental state, based primarily on Rosalie's account

of past events. Each of their interpretations in its own way depicts the individual at the mercy of external forces.

Rosalie herself is convinced that her husband has been afflicted by the curse put on her by her mother. Her interpretation reflects a belief in supernatural powers impinging on the individual mind and a fatalistic presupposition that these powers cannot be overcome.

The Commandant, however, having heard Rosalie's version and then having met Francoeur himself, puts another complexion on events with the opinion "die Frau liebt ihn, aber sie ist eine Deutsche und versteht keinen Franzosen; ein Franzose hat immer den Teufel im Leibe!" His interpretation is that Rosalie's view is inadequate, even insensitive, and that any notion of a curse must be understood figuratively, as the manifestation of a particular national characteristic. His reading substitutes superstitious fatalism with the equally overwhelming force of racial determinism.

Like Rosalie, the next person to hear the story, the servant Basset, takes the concept of possession literally, but he does so in a more conventionally religious sense, and, unlike Rosalie, he asserts the power of institutionalised Christianity to combat evil spirits. According to his understanding man is no more than a battleground for these opposing forces.

At the end of the story the Commandant officially pardons Francoeur on the grounds that "seine Wunde ihn des Verstandes beraubt gehabt." The same diagnosis, made by an army doctor, had in fact been the original reason for sending Francoeur to Marseille, and it is confirmed by the surgeon who examines Francoeur at this point and explains his behaviour as symptomatic of a splinter of bone working its way to the surface inside his head. Had Francoeur not literally reopened his wound, according to the surgeon, madness would have been inevitable and incurable. This explanation also presents man in a passive role.

It can be suggested, however, that the characters advance unjustifiably deterministic hypotheses. Critics have pointed to the fact that the actual outbreak of Francoeur's madness, which occurs within the story, is motivated by a series of incidents which provide the reader with a certain amount of background material on which to base an analysis of its causes: Francoeur learns through Basset that his wife has been discussing him behind his back with the Commandant, that he is thought to be possessed by the devil, and that arrangements have been made, again behind his back, to exorcise him. So in effect what puts Francoeur over the edge are the actions and reactions of other people. Francoeur himself perceives these as external agencies attempting to control his life.

The characters' implicit assumption that man can be reduced to a willess automaton, controlled from without, would render pointless any further attempt at character analysis, as such an individual would not be responsible for his or her actions. It would follow, therefore, that the manifestations of Francoeur's madness could provide no information on his emotional make-up. But this postulate can also be challenged. Significantly, it is not Basset's information in itself that is the trigger for Francoeur's breakdown and the catalyst for his declaration of war, but the relative size of portion he and Basset are offered when Rosalie dishes up her *Eierkuchen*. The central importance of this incident lies in its very triviality. It illustrates neatly the particular way in which Francoeur's perspective is distorted: his behaviour is an over-reaction symptomatic of impulsiveness, immaturity, insecurity, jealousy and hurt pride. Within the context of Francoeur's past and present behaviour, this forms part of a consistent pattern. Rosalie and Basset (who knew Francoeur previously) are terrified but not surprised at his outburst, and both realise immediately what his intention is on entering the tower; not because of their *a priori* knowledge of any curse, but because of their *a posteriori* familiarity with Francoeur's character. And the Commandant, contrary to his public pronouncement—which merely fulfils a promise to Rosalie—actually considers and rejects loss of responsibility through madness as a possible line of defence for Francoeur as, he concludes, "es ist zu viel Einsicht, Vorsicht, und Klugheit in der ganzen Art, wie er sich nimmt." He sees clear evidence, in other words, that Francoeur is still acting in line with his own intellect and personality.

Thus the characters' theories are disproved by their own anecdotal evidence. On the basis of this narrative hearsay we can draw two conclusions. Firstly; that while Francoeur's outburst is indeed provoked by extrinsic pressures, these pressures are human and social, not anonymous and paranormal, and while they affect his behaviour, there is no reason to believe that they determine it: rather than the source of his madness they are the final straw. Secondly; that any illness Francoeur suffers does not cause a change of personality, which could be attributed to an external agent imposing a certain pattern of behaviour, it merely exaggerates certain traits of character that have always been present, and which therefore bear witness to the particular way in which Francoeur experiences the world.

Clearly the opinions held by the characters misrepresent the nature of the influences to which the individual is exposed, and the measure of freedom that individual has in their response to these influences. To understand the relationship between these causes and effects we must disregard simplistic theories of mind-control, whether transcendental, genealogical or physiological, and turn our attention instead to the much more subtle and complex area of human intercourse, where certain external, contingent events within the context of human experience trigger an individual reaction from a particular character.

Seen in these terms Francoeur's situation, far from posing an exception, exemplifies a general principle of contemporary philosophical thought, which defined reality as a personal response rather than a given state, and which understood this personal response in terms of the mind conferring meaning on the world through a cumulative process of collecting, interpreting and storing sensual, intellectual and emotional data. According to this under-

standing the individual has to react to an objectively existing world but does so subjectively; a proposition which locates his conduct between determinism and free-will, and can understand new experience only within his or her own pre-set parameters; a process which entails inevitable subjective moulding of reality, varying only in degree.

If we employ this line of argument to investigate why all the characters in *Der tolle Invalide* misinterpret in the particular way they do, we find that, while Francoeur's perspective provides an extreme example of distortion, the perspectives of all characters exhibit significant bias.

> **Francoeur's situation, far from posing an exception, exemplifies a general principle of contemporary philosophical thought, which defined reality as a personal response rather than a given state.**
>
> —*Sheila Dickson*

It can be demonstrated, for instance, that Rosalie is as guilty as Francoeur of jumping to conclusions. From the beginning her relationship with her husband is marred by a lack of openness, due to her expectations of how he would react to her feeling that she is possessed by the devil. She invents a series of excuses to explain her frequent tears, because she is convinced he would no longer love her if he knew "the truth". This reflects a deep-rooted sense of insecurity on her part. Where Rosalie does display security, however, is in her unshakeable belief in the power of evil spirits. Her conviction that her love has passed on the curse to Francoeur, but that he remains unaware of this and must consequently be protected from himself, leads her to disregard any other possible explanation for his behaviour, such as that offered by medical diagnosis. Her conclusions presuppose the existence of the curse, and cannot be tested due to her refusal to approach Francoeur directly.

From the retired Commandant's point of view Francoeur's behaviour corresponds to a bellicose model of soldiery, and a patriotic ideal of nationality. This leads him to pass the light-hearted, even facile judgement that Francoeur's devil is no more than his French nature and that Rosalie is unable to understand his character because she is German. Such simplistic limitation of character to generalised behavioural stereotypes is a clear instance of prejudice and indicates that he is arguing from a (questionable) foregone conclusion, based on his own fantasies.

Basset's interpretation is the product of a naively Christian belief in diabolic possession. His conclusion that Francoeur should be confronted with his demon is, however, not based on a genuine conviction that this is necessary, nor on a belief in the real supremacy of the Church over the devil, but on the desire of the lower orders for the entertainment provided by an exorcism. In order to gratify this desire he makes the situation fit this interpretation; in other words he argues from an expedient conclusion which he subsequently makes the facts fit.

The most striking example of interpretation on the basis of preconception, however, is provided by the *Eierkuchen* episode. Due to his sensitive and passionate nature Francoeur misinterprets others' behaviour, particularly Rosalie's, and then uses this misinterpretation to justify the feelings aroused in him by Basset's confession, to which he is then entitled, in his own judgement, to give full rein. When he decides in advance how he will interpret Rosalie's behaviour in dividing up the food, he is consciously and deliberately pre-establishing a conclusion. He makes it clear to Basset that he knows what will happen, and so by passing judgement in advance he endows his highly subjective opinion with the authority of objective proof. However this reasoning is based on the logical fallacy of *post hoc, ergo propter hoc*. So in their attempts to justify their own beliefs all characters have in fact created, with varying degrees of self-awareness, their own personal self-fulfilling prophecies.

If, within the period of Arnim's writing, distortion was increasingly recognised as an unavoidable consequence of the subjective process of mediating reality, the (pseudo-) scientific analysis of extreme cases illustrated how the misinterpretations which arise from this could become pathological. In the contemporary medical debate on madness and abnormal psychology the concept of the fixed idea (*idée fixe*) was identified as a force directing thought within both the conscious and the unconscious mind. The fixed idea describes the capacity of the mind to convince itself, or become convinced, of what it wants to believe in, which is often based on a distorted view of the actual state of affairs, and to consistently engineer situations that will inevitably result in a confirmation of this distorted view; in other words, to set up fallacious self-fulfilling prophecies. In this way prejudices can develop into obsessions.

In *Der tolle Invalide* it can be argued that certain pathological beliefs and behaviour exhibited by both Francoeur and Rosalie spring from their own particular obsession, which is based on the kind of prejudiced beliefs already reviewed, and which relates most obviously to their experience of the curse. Having dismissed the characters' options of a supernatural agency, a national trait and a physiological condition, there remains strong evidence in the text that the curse is in fact the manifestation of a fixed idea in the minds of the two main characters; a distortion which arises from their individual reaction to an idea suggested to them by an external authority. By applying the same dialectic of cause and effect as above, the extraneous forces which bring the curse itself into being can also be revealed as personal and social rather than anonymous and superhuman, and the curse's manifestations distinguished as the characters' own individual misinterpretations of external data rather than as a comprehensive imposed programme of behaviour.

The very disturbing experience Rosalie undergoes would be expected to leave a lasting effect upon any individual, but the extent of the effect depends on her response to it. A sensitive, immature individual, Rosalie is particularly susceptible to influence and lacks the emotional strength to put the experience behind her. This, coupled with her fatalistic world view, leads her to become convinced that she must be possessed. Her conviction is not borne out by diabolic visions or evil thoughts, however, but solely by the vivid picture of her mother cursing her, which she cannot get out of her mind:

> Aber immer musste ich der Mutter denken, wenn seine (Francoeurs) Lebendigkeit im Erzählen mich nicht zerstreute; die Mutter erschien mir schwarz mit flammenden Augen, immer fluchend vor meinen inneren Augen und ich konnte sie nicht los werden.

What torments Rosalie is not the curse, but the memory of the curse being passed; it is the idea of the curse rather than its actuality. If Rosalie is cursed it is because she takes her mother's words at face value, due to the literal nature of her own religious and superstitious beliefs and her childlike acceptance of her mother's authority; in other words, it is because she accepts, quite consciously, the judgement passed on her by another person. The origin of the fixed idea in Rosalie's mind can, therefore, be traced back to the external influence of suggestion coupled with the internal processes of her own interpretation of this data, which lead her to live up to the idea put in her mind, confirming with her opinions and actions the expectations it arouses. Her curse is man-made, not supernatural: it is an extreme illustration of the power one human being can have over another and, more particularly, of the influence of upbringing on personal development.

The assertion that the power of the curse lies only in the individual's belief in it is supported by the way in which Rosalie overcomes it. It has been argued by Colin Butler, among others, that Rosalie's personality develops in the course of the story, in that she learns to take responsibility for herself and her actions [Butler, "Psychology and Faith in Arnim's *Der tolle Invalide*," *Studies in Romanticism* 17, 1978]. A key stage in this development is her dream while asleep in the boat. Her mind is once again filled with a vision of her mother, but the picture has changed significantly:

> Rosalie sah im Traume ihre Mutter von innerlichen Flammen durchleuchtet und verzehrt und fragte sie: Warum sie so leide? Da war's als ob eine laute Stimme ihr in die Ohren rief: "Mein Fluch brennt mich wie dich, und kannst du ihn nicht lösen, so bleib ich eigen allem Bösen."

Rather than torture Rosalie this picture brings home to her the torture experienced in the mind which invoked the curse. Whether interpreted literally as demonic persecution or figuratively as psychological distress, the torment is internal and personal. Butler interprets this development in terms of Rosalie having gained insight into her mother's condition. If this is the case then this insight is, surely, the realisation that the curse exists within her mother and that she and her mother are suffering as a direct result of the latter's actions ("*mein* Fluch" (my emphasis)). Refocussing her attention from the devil on to her mother humanizes the curse for Rosalie, and as a result, for the first time, the possibility of defeating the curse through individual action can be raised. That this depends solely on Rosalie's personal response gives her a sense of purpose which engenders increased self-confidence (a reaction reminiscent of her sudden assertiveness when faced with the wounded Francoeur's helplessness). She comes to believe that she can overcome the curse, and this belief makes her able to confront Francoeur, in so doing explicitly demonstrating this conviction.

As she approaches the fort the townsfolk curse Rosalie as the source of their misfortune. At this stage, however, she does not let herself be influenced in this way: "Viele fluchten auf Rosalien, weil sie Francoeurs Frau war, aber dieser Fluch berührte sie nicht." Further evidence that a curse can only affect someone who believes in it and takes it on board. This curse is powerless to influence her because she does not let it influence her.

The individual's autonomy in a moment of strength is, however, as deceptive as his impotence in a moment of weakness. Rosalie's newly developed confidence that she can break the curse is, once again, a thought put into her mind by an external source—indeed by the same source that originally suggested to her the idea of the curse—and Rosalie herself subsequently refers to an "innerliche Stimme" guiding her actions. For this reason one must be careful of arguing for any real change in Rosalie's character. She remains susceptible to external influence: but responds freely to these influences in each situation.

When one considers Francoeur's suffering as a result of the curse it is important to realise that Rosalie's request to the Commandant to keep their conversation secret and her account of her attempts to conceal from her husband "the truth" about the curse are misleading. It becomes clear from her narrative that Francoeur is perfectly well aware of the curse and of its implications for him. Rosalie describes the following incident at their wedding:

> Ein alter Geistlicher hielt eine feierliche Rede, in der er meinem Francoeur alles ans Herz legte, was ich für ihn getan, wie ich ihm Vaterland, Wohlstand und Freundschaft zum Opfer gebracht, selbst den mütterlichen Fluch auf mich geladen, alle diese Not müsse er mit mir teilen, alles Unglück gemeinsam tragen.

Rosalie's silence is neither necessary nor effective. Francoeur has already been presented with the particular interpretation of the situation Rosalie herself believes, and this in a particularly brutal fashion: in public by a third party. The priest demands that Francoeur take responsibility for the sacrifices Rosalie has had to make for him, and for the curse itself. He refers specifically to the curse, so it is obviously common knowledge, and he effectively pronounces Francoeur's guilt. By telling Francoeur that he

must share all Rosalie's suffering the priest is in a sense wishing the feeling of being cursed on Francoeur.

The sight of Rosalie's mother calling down a curse on her daughter, an event to which he was witness, greatly upset Francoeur (". . . auf den der Vorfall schlimm gewirkt hatte"), and this reiteration of the situation (a very subjective one) could only reinforce the impression. So, like Rosalie, Francoeur is subjected to a very disturbing experience. Like Rosalie he too is a sensitive, immature individual, vulnerable to external influence; and so, for the same reasons, Francoeur's mind also becomes tormented by the memory or idea of the curse. But there is an important distinction: while he too accepts the judgment passed on him by an external source (in his case the priest—also a human being, not a supernatural agency), he does so only on a subconscious level, due to the fact that his character will not admit Rosalie's literal and superstitious beliefs. His conscious mind suppresses the memory as too painful to bear, but the repressed feelings of guilt and responsibility are a constant pressure. This is reflected in his subsequent behaviour:

> Bald aber klagte er, dass jener Prediger in seinem schwarzen Kleide ihm immer vor Augen stehe und ihm drohe, dass er dadurch einen so heftigen Zorn und Widerwillen gegen Geistliche, Kirchen und heilige Bilder empfinde, dass er ihnen fluchen müsse und wisse nicht warum, und um sich diesen Gedanken zu entschlagen, überlasse er sich jedem Einfall, er tanze und trinke und so in dem Umtriebe des Bluts werde ihm besser.

This image of a picture which constantly obtrudes on his thoughts suggests a state of mind similar to Rosalie's, as described by herself. It motivates Francoeur's odd behaviour in pulling faces and engaging in mindless activity; these are not manifestations of a curse, but attempts to exhaust his mental and physical energies in order to take his mind off an obsession, a fixed idea which has been put in his mind, which he does not question nor even fully acknowledge, and which he therefore cannot dismiss. Rosalie herself tells the Commandant "er trommelte tagelang, *um sich zu zerstreuen*" (my emphasis). This also explains why Francoeur seems so much better at the fort as, due to the many things that have to be done and the genuine interest Francoeur has in the task he has been set, he has a meaningful outlet for these energies. Francoeur at leisure, on the other hand, had to create his own distractions, and this led him (at this point and not when he is at the fort) to act out of character. Consider the two explanations contained in the description of the latter period in Francoeur's life:

> Bei dieser Tätigkeit liessen ihn seine Grillen ruhen; er war hastig, aber alles zu einem festen Ziele, und Rosalie segnete den Tag, der ihn in diese höhere Luftregion gebracht, wo der Teufel keine Macht über ihn zu haben schien.

The narrator attributes the improvement specifically to the fact that he is kept busy, while Rosalie persists in her belief in diabolic possession, which she links here to geo-graphical location (at high altitude Francoeur is nearer God than the devil). In spite of her insight with respect to her own mental state that the anguish can be temporarily alleviated when her attention is focussed elsewhere, namely on Francoeur's stories (which are her *Zerstreuung,*) and in spite of her literal belief that they share everything, Rosa-lie remains incapable of perceiving the similarities be-tween her own situation and that of her husband.

The fact that Francoeur chooses to believe in Rosalie's infidelity is a sign of his distorted, even pathological perspective, but far from being insane, his reaction is understandable as, in a way, it provides relief from the guilt he feels.

—Sheila Dickson

The events at the wedding also put Francoeur's reaction to Basset's priest friend into perspective. His dislike of priests springs from the fact that in truth it was a priest who cursed him, in the sense that a priest put the sugges-tion of guilt into his head, or reinforced feelings already present by putting them into words. Philipp approaches Francoeur just as Basset has told him that he is believed to be possessed by the devil. With this revelation occupy-ing his mind Francoeur does not even see Philipp; his thoughts are fixed on the priest who married him. The narrator provides insight into Francoeur's mental process-es at this point: "er sah wieder den schwarzen Geistlichen vor Augen, wie die vom tollen Hunde Gebissenen den Hund immer zu sehen meinen, da trat Vater Philipp in den Garten . . ." This simile confirms the impression gained from Francoeur's own description of his state of mind, as reported by Rosalie, of Francoeur being the victim of an attack, and as tormented subsequently by the indelible and wholly personal memory of this attack: an identical expe-rience to that of Rosalie. Basset's remarks and Philipp's appearance are the external stimuli which at this point recall to Francoeur's mind his own particular torture, name-ly his feelings of guilt and responsibility, and bring the idea of the curse into the open between Rosalie and Fran-coeur for the first time.

When Rosalie told the Commandant "mein Mann kommt von Sinnen, wenn er die Geschichte hört," the implication behind this statement was that Francoeur's madness would only surface with a knowledge of the curse. The same idea was expressed by Francoeur himself in his glib reply to the Commandant's direct enquiry as to whether he was afflicted by demons: "Man darf den Teufel nicht an die Wand malen, sonst hat man ihn im Spiegel." And this is in effect what happens. The final outbreak of Francoeur's madness is the direct and immediate result of his being

told that he is considered to be possessed by the devil: it is his reaction to this suggestion.

The fact that Francoeur chooses to believe in Rosalie's infidelity is a sign of his distorted, even pathological perspective, but far from being insane, his reaction is understandable as, in a way, it provides relief from the guilt he feels. His belief that Rosalie has betrayed him leads him to the conclusion, logical in the circumstances he posits: "sie hat unendlich viel für mich getan und gelitten, sie hat mir unendlich weh getan, ich bin ihr nichts mehr schuldig, wir sind geschieden!" He uses the clandestine meeting with the Commandant as a means of calling quits in his relationship with Rosalie. Now that he has been made conscious of his own suffering he makes her betrayal cancel out her sacrifices so that he may be free of any further responsibility and guilt. He then pro-ceeds, quite consciously and deliberately, to promote this self-fulfilling prophecy by playing the part into which he has been cast. Unlike Rosalie, however, Francoeur does not truly believe in devils and curses, this is purely an external suggestion. The fact that he accepts this role, while lacking any real conviction, underlines his imma-turity and suggestibility.

Francoeur's part in breaking the curse and curing his madness again follows a familiar pattern. Like Rosalie he gains clearer insight and, like Rosalie, this causes him to take action. In his case Rosalie's march towards the fort, confronting him with evidence of her love for him, is the external stimulus. This triggers a response not dictated by the part he is acting, nor by any preconceived ideas con-cerning their relationship, but which represents the first genuine expression of his true feelings. His personality too, therefore, develops and matures in the course of the story, and he now literally tears out the inner distortion of his perspective with his own hand. Like Rosalie in the same situation, however, Francoeur is still reacting to external influence, rather than taking sovereign, autono-mous action; a fact which is confirmed by the surgeon's final explanation of Francoeur's recovery as depending equally on the strength of his individual personality ("die gewaltige Natur Francoeurs") and external, contingent events ("äussere Gewalt").

In the final analysis, then, the curse in *Der tolle Invalide* is what the characters make it. Rosalie, Francoeur, and indeed Rosalie's mother, create their own curse as a per-sonal response to a particular experience. Theirs is a patho-logical distortion, but one which is rooted in the concep-tual distortion inherent in all subjective ideas and beliefs. The characters are neither fully in control of their actions, in that they are responding to contingencies, nor are they entirely passive, as their response reflects their own be-liefs and prejudices. And so, the alternative explanations offered for Francoeur's madness—the devil, literal or met-aphorical, and the splinter of bone—are in truth equally misleading and irrelevant. In advancing these theories the characters are victims of their own and other people's ideas. They are attempting to rationalise the seemingly mysterious within their own particular *Weltbild*, and in so doing offer the reader the chance to explore the real mysteries of the complex personal and social dynamics which underpin such human behaviour.

FURTHER READING

Bonfiglio, Thomas Paul. "Electric Affinities: Arnim and Schelling's *Naturphilosophie.*" *Euphorion* 81, No. 3 (1987): 217-39.

> Examines *Isabella von Ägypten* for evidence of the "fundamental electromagnetic cosmology" that informs Arnim's work.

———. *Achim von Arnim's* Novellensammlung 1812: *Balance and Mediation.* New York: Peter Lang, 1987, 225 p.

> Analysis that contends Arnim's 1812 collection of novellas "is indeed a coherent opus that diagnoses a socio-historical problem, describes its genesis, and offers a prognosis together with an ideal program for its solution." Bonfiglio finds the novellas organized and unified around a structure of polarities.

Butler, Colin. "Psychology and Faith in Arnim's *Der tolle Invalide.*" *Studies in Romanticism* 17, No. 1 (Spring 1978): 149-62.

> Maintains that in this novella Arnim achieved a perfect blend of religious and psychological themes and illustrated "the possibility of faith from the character of human experience."

Duncan, Bruce. "Some Correspondences between Arnim's *Majoratsherren* and Fichte's Concept of the *Ich.*" *Monatschefte* LXVIII, No. 1 (Spring 1976): 51-9.

> Contends that Johann Gottlieb Fichte's philosophy regarding self and consciousness "serves as a unifying principle of [*Die Majoratsherren*], that it becomes a paradigm for, not an explanation of, the characters' development."

———. "Fate and Coincidence in Arnim's *Seltsames Begegnen und Wiedersehen.*" *Seminar* 15, No. 3 (September 1979): 181-89.

> Argues that the coincidences in the novella, while seemingly contrived, "invite the reader to speculate on the causal relationships at work in the historical world and thus to gain insight into the higher reality that ultimately determines our destinies."

Frye, Lawrence O. "Mesmerism and Masks: Images of Union in Achim von Arnim's *Hollins Liebeleben* and *Die Majoratsherren.*" *Euphorion* 76, Nos. 1-2 (1982): 82-99.

> Discusses Arnim's treatment in two of his works of the belief in mesmerism and "the invisible magnetic fluid which inhabits all forms of existence in our universe."

Hoermann, Roland. "Symbolism and Mediation in Arnim's View of Romantic Phantasy." *Monatashefte* LIV, No. 4 (April-May 1962): 201-15.

> Explores the influence of Romantic beliefs concerning fantasy on Arnim's perception of reality as demonstrated in his major works.

Lösel, Franz. "Psychology, Religion and Myth in Arnim's *Der tolle Invalide auf dem Fort Ratonneau. New German Studies* 5, No. 2 (Summer 1977): 75-90.

> Asserts that *Der tolle Invalide,* commonly considered atypical among Arnim's works, actually reveals techniques and concerns characteristic of the author.

———. "Allusions and Word-Play in Arnim's *Fürst Ganzgott und Sänger Halbgott.*" *German Life and Letters* 41, No. 3 (April 1988): 213-26.

> Uncovers a rich pattern of references to contemporary cultural events in Arnim's novella.

Whiton, John. "Crisis and Commitment in Achim von Arnim's *Der tolle Invalide auf dem Fort Ratonneau.*" In *Crisis and Commitment: Studies in German and Russian Literature in Honour of J. W. Dyck,* edited by John Whiton and Harry Loewen, pp. 221-36. Waterloo, Ontario: University of Waterloo Press, 1983.

> Argues that Rosalie's "change from insecurity and lack of trust in Francoeur's integrity and love for her to complete self-confidence and utter and resolute faith in him and his love" brings about her husband's cure.

Ray Bradbury
1920-

(Also wrote under the pseudonyms of Douglas Spaulding and Leonard Spaulding) American short story writer, novelist, scriptwriter, poet, dramatist, nonfiction writer, editor, and author of children's books.

INTRODUCTION

Regarded as an important figure in the development of science fiction, even though he does not write primarily in that genre, Bradbury was among the first authors to combine the concepts of science fiction with a sophisticated prose style. Often described as economical yet poetic, Bradbury's fiction conveys a vivid sense of place in which everyday events are transformed into unusual, sometimes sinister situations. In a career which has spanned more than fifty years, Bradbury has written fantasies, crime and mystery stories, supernatural tales, and mainstream literature, as well as science fiction. In all of his work, Bradbury emphasizes basic human values and cautions against unthinking acceptance of technological progress. His persistent optimism, evident even in his darkest work, has led some critics to label him as sentimental or naive. Bradbury, however, perceives life, even at its most mundane, with a childlike wonder and awe, which charges his work with a fervent affirmation of humanity.

Biographical Information

Bradbury was born on August 22, 1920, in Waukegan, Illinois, a small town that frequently emerges as the setting in his stories. In the mid-1930s Bradbury's family moved to southern California, where he graduated from Los Angeles High School in 1938. Determined to become a writer, Bradbury created his own science fiction magazine called *Futuria Fantasia,* although he produced only four volumes. Bradbury worked as a newsboy in Los Angeles from 1940 to 1943, to support his writing. His first published story, "Pendulum" (with Henry Hasse), surfaced in *Super Science Stories* in 1941. Shortly thereafter, Bradbury's macabre tales regularly appeared in such pulp magazines as *Black Mask, Amazing Stories,* and *Weird Tales.* The latter magazine served to showcase the works of such fantasy writers as H. P. Lovecraft, Clark Ashton Smith, and August Derleth. Derleth, who founded Arkham House, a publishing company specializing in fantasy literature, accepted one of Bradbury's stories for *Who Knocks?,* an anthology published by his firm. Derleth subsequently suggested that Bradbury compile a volume of his own stories; the resulting book, *Dark Carnival* (1947), collects Bradbury's early fantasy tales. Due to the success of this first collection, in addition to publication of his stories in

The Best American Short Stories of 1946 and the *O. Henry Prize Stories of 1947,* Bradbury's stories were soon published in such mainstream periodicals as *Collier's, The Saturday Evening Post,* and *The New Yorker,* where they reached a wider audience. A prolific author, Bradbury has published numerous short story collections since, earning a reputation as an authority of fantasy literature in the process.

Major Works of Short Fiction

Although he has produced volumes of work in many genres, Bradbury is essentially a short story writer. Sometimes his works cross genres. For example, the novels *The Martian Chronicles* (1950), *Fahrenheit 451* (1953), and *Dandelion Wine* (1957) are frequently treated by critics as short story collections, in which chapters are connected by a simple framing device. The stories in *The Martian Chronicles,* for example are linked by the theme of human settlement on Mars. Another significant collection of short stories, *The Illustrated Man* (1951), also uses a framing device, basing the stories on the tattoos of the title character. Bradbury's earlier stories—particularly those collected in *Dark Carnival, The Martian Chronicles,* and *The October Country* (1970)—have been compared to those of Edgar Allan Poe because of their grotesque and sometimes horrific story lines. "Skeleton," in *Dark Carnival,* for example, is about a man who grows so repulsed by his own skeleton that he has it removed, consequently becoming "a human jellyfish." "The Third Expedition" (first published in 1948 as "Mars Is Heaven" in *Planet Stories* and later collected in *The Martian Chronicles*) is about Americans who travel to Mars where they become reunited with their deceased relatives, who, in actuality, are hostile beings whose human faces melt away in the night as they murder the Americans in their sleep. The futuristic and sometimes morbid themes of Bradbury's early collections rarely surface in his more recent works. *Driving Blind* (1997), for example, only contains four traditional science fiction stories. The majority, though bizarre, are more nostalgic, optimistic, and romantic. They tend to deal with the everyday. All of Bradbury's fiction, from *Dark Carnival* to *Driving Blind,* is issue-oriented, as he frequently addresses such themes as racism, censorship, religion, and technology, often infusing the text with authorial commentary.

Critical Reception

While Bradbury's popularity is acknowledged even by his detractors, many critics find the reasons for his success difficult to pinpoint. Some critics were aggravated that Bradbury's futuristic stories, which are often labeled as a science fiction, most often reflect poor scientific knowledge and, at times, an aversion toward technology. Among his defenders was Russel Kirk, who called Bradbury "a moralist," adding that he "is interested not in the precise mechanism of rockets, but in the mentality and the morals of fallible human beings who make and use rockets." Willis E. McNelly concurred, stating that Bradbury "is a visionary who writes not of the impediments of science, but of its effects upon men." Some of Bradbury's detractors have likewise pointed to inconsistencies within Bradbury's text. Thomas M. Disch argued that Bradbury's "dry-ice machine covers the bare stage of his story with a fog of breathy approximations." More forgiving critics have excused any oddities in Bradbury's short stories as imaginative and inventive. Christopher Isherwood wrote that Bradbury's "brilliant, shameless fantasy makes, and needs, no excuses for its wild jumps from the possible to the impossible." Yet by far the greatest complaint of Bradbury is that his fiction is overly sentimental and didactic. Commenting on *The Martian Chronicles,* Kent Forrester observed that "Bradbury's ideas are so violently drawn . . . that the stories are weakened unless we are as enthusiastic about his ideas as he is." One enthusiastic reviewer, Damon Knight, wrote, "Bradbury's strength lies in the fact that he writes about the things that are really important to us . . . the fundamental prerational fears and longings and desires." Content aside, most critics have expressed appreciation for Bradbury's poetic prose. Forrester concluded that although Bradbury's "prose is occasionally over-

cooked it is still, in small chunks, superior to any other prose in science fiction. It is prose, like good poetry, that sticks in the mind."

PRINCIPAL WORKS

Short Fiction

Dark Carnival 1947
*The Martian Chronicles 1950
The Illustrated Man 1951
*Fahrenheit 451 1953
The Golden Apples of the Sun 1953
The October Country 1955
*Dandelion Wine 1957
A Medicine for Melancholy 1959
The Meadow 1960
The Ghoul Keepers 1962
†R is for Rocket 1962
The Small Assassin 1962
The Machineries of Joy 1964
The Autumn People 1965
The Vintage Bradbury 1965
†S is for Space 1966
Tomorrow Midnight 1966
‡Twice Twenty-Two 1966
Bloch and Bradbury: Ten Masterpieces of Science Fiction [with Robert Bloch] 1969
I Sing the Body Electric! 1969
Whispers from Beyond [with Bloch] 1972
Selected Stories 1975
The Best of Bradbury 1976
Long After Midnight 1976
To Sing Strange Songs 1979
The Ghosts of Forever (story, essay, and poetry) 1980
The Stories of Ray Bradbury 1980
Dinosaur Tales 1983
The Love Affair (story and poetry) 1983
*Something Wicked This Way Comes 1983
A Memory of Murder 1984
The Toynbee Convector 1988
Quicker Than the Eye 1996
Driving Blind 1997

Other Major Works

NOVELS

Something Wicked This Way Comes 1962
Death Is a Lonely Business 1985
A Graveyard for Lunatics 1990
Green Shadows, White Whale 1992
Yestermorrows; Obvious Answers to Impossible Futures 1993

PLAYS

Something Wicked This Way Comes [adaptor; from his novel of the same title] 1962

Way in the Middle of the Air   1962
The Anthem Sprinters, and Other Antics   1963
The World of Ray Bradbury   1964
The Day It Rained Forever   1966
Leviathan 99   1966
The Pedestrian   1966
Dandelion Wine   [adaptor; from his short story collection
   of the same title]   1967
Christus Apollo   1969
Madrigals for the Space Age   1972
The Wonderful Ice-Cream Suit and Other Plays   1972
Pillar of Fire and Other Plays for Today, Tomorrow, and
   Beyond Tomorrow   1975
That Ghost, That Bride of Time: Excerpts from a Play-in-
   Progress   1976
The Martian Chronicles   [adaptor; from his short story
   collection of the same title]   1977
Fahrenheit 451   [adaptor; from his short story collection
   of the same title]   1979
A Device Out of Time   1986
Falling Upward   1988
The Day It Rained Forever / 6610   1991

POETRY

Old Ahab's Friend, and Friend to Noah, Speaks His Piece:
   A Celebration   1971
When Elephants Last in the Dooryard Bloomed:
   Celebrations for Almost Any Day in the Year   1973
That Son of Richard III: A Birth Announcement   1974
Where Robot Mice and Robot Men Run Round in Robot
   Towns   1977
The Bike Repairman   1978
Twin Hieroglyphs That Swim the River Dust   1978
The Aqueduct   1979
The Author Considers His Resources   1979
This Attic Where the Meadow Greens   1979
The Last Circus   1980
The Haunted Computer and the Android People   1981
The Complete Poems of Ray Bradbury   1982
Forever and the Earth   1984
Death Has Lost Its Charm For Me   1987
Dogs Think Everyday is Christmas   1997
With Cat for Comforter   [With Louise Max]   1997

SCREENPLAYS

It Came from Outer Space   1953
The Beast from 20,000 Fathoms   [adaptor; from his story
   "The Foghorn"]   1953
Moby Dick   [adaptor; from the novel Moby Dick by
   Herman Melville]   1956
Icarus Montgolfier Wright   [with George C. Johnson]   1962
An American Journey   [author of narration]   1964
Picasso Summer   [under pseudonym Douglas Spaulding;
   with Ed Weinberger]   1972

JUVENILIA

Switch on the Night   1955
The Halloween Tree   1972
The April Witch   1987

Fever Dream   1987
The Foghorn   1987
The Other Foot   1987
The Veldt   1987

NONFICTION

Zen and the Art of Writing   1973
The Mummies of Guanajuato   1978
Beyond 1984: Rememberance of Things Future   1979

* These titles are sometimes considered novels.

† These titles are intended for children.

‡ This title contains *The Golden Apples of the Sun* and *Medicine for Melancholy*

CRITICISM

Christopher Isherwood   (review date 1950)

SOURCE: A review of *The Martian Chronicles, Tomorrow*, Vol. X, No. 2, October, 1950, pp. 56-8.

[*In the following assessment of* The Martian Chronicles—*the first major review of any Bradbury work—Isherwood considers Bradbury an author of fantasy literature in the tradition of Edgar Allan Poe, rather than an author of science fiction.*]

In February 1999, the first rocketship from Earth will land on Mars. Its two crew members will immediately be shot dead by a Mr. Yll K, with a gun which fires bees. Six months later, the crew of a second rocket will be subjected to a mercy killing by Mr. Xxx, a psychologist, in the belief that his victims must be incurable lunatics. In April 2000, the crew of a third rocket will likewise be murdered, while under a deep hypnosis which persuades them that they are visiting their dead relatives and their childhood homes on Earth. But the fourth expedition, in 2001, will be successful, because almost the entire Martian population will have succumbed, in the meanwhile, to an unfamiliar disease carried by the Earthman—chicken pox.

After this, the process of colonization will go forward rapidly for the next four years, bringing the total number of settlers up to 90,000. Then, in November 2005, atomic war will break out on Earth and nearly all of them will return home, leaving the planet practically deserted until October 2026—the date of the arrival of the Thomas and Edwards families, two parties of war refugees escaping on hoarded rockets. These will form the nucleus of a new settlement; and no doubt, in time, others will follow them. Here Mr. Bradbury's **Chronicles** end.

It is easy to understand why science fiction, and more particularly space-travel-fiction, should be enjoying a revival of popularity at the present time. Faced by probable destruction in a third world war, we turn naturally to dreams of escape from this age and this threatened planet. But that is not the whole of the explanation. For, while the "realistic" two-fisted action-story is going through a phase of imaginative bankruptcy, the science-fiction story grows more prodigious, more ideologically daring. Instead of the grunts of cowboys and the fuddled sexual musings of half-plastered private detectives, we are offered adult speculation about the dangers of galactic imperialism and the future of technocratic man. The best of this new generation of science-fiction writers are highly sensitive and intelligent. They are under no illusions about the prospective blessings of a machine-age utopia. They do not gape at gadgets with adoring wonder. Their approach to the inhabitants of other worlds is anthropological and nonviolent. They owe more to Aldous Huxley than to Jules Verne or H. G. Wells. Insofar as the reading public is turning to them and forsaking the cops and the cowboys, the public is growing up.

This is not to suggest, however, that Ray Bradbury can be classified simply as a science-fiction writer, even a superlatively good one. *Dark Carnival,* his earlier book of stories, showed that his talents can function equally well within comparatively realistic settings. If one must attach labels, I suppose he might be called a writer of fantasy, and his stories "tales of the grotesque and arabesque" in the sense in which those words are used by Poe. Poe's name comes up, almost inevitably, in any discussion of Mr. Bradbury's work; not because Mr. Bradbury is an imitator (though he is certainly a disciple) but because he already deserves to be measured against the greatest master of his particular genre.

It may even be argued that *The Martian Chronicles* are not, strictly speaking, science fiction at all. The most firmly established convention of science fiction is that its writers shall use all their art to convince us that their stories *could* happen. The extraordinary must grow from roots in the ordinary. The scientific "explanations" must have an authoritative air. (There are, as a matter of fact, some science-fiction writers whose work is so full of abstruse technicalities that only connoisseurs can read it.) Such is not Mr. Bradbury's practice. His brilliant, shameless fantasy makes, and needs, no excuses for its wild jumps from the possible to the impossible. His interest in machines seems to be limited to their symbolic and aesthetic aspects. I doubt if he could pilot a rocketship, much less design one.

"The rockets were American," he remarks, with characteristically casual implausibility, "and the men were American and it stayed that way." In other words, he had decided, quite arbitrarily, to tell the story of a purely American immigration and doesn't want to confuse the issue by cluttering up Mars with a lot of foreigners. I think this decision has been entirely justified. For the impact of an immigration gains enormously in violence and drama when the immigrants all belong to the same cultural group.

Through the interstellar spaces, now, as once over the great plains—headed for Mars instead of California and Oregon—the Americans come. First the pioneers; rough,

simple, uninhibited men who celebrate their arrival by shooting off their guns, shouting and dancing and getting drunk; later, they build the first crude noisy mining towns. Then the settlers and their womenfolk; city people, merchants, middlemen, bringing trade with them and respectability and tidiness and church religion. Then a great wave of Negroes from the southern states, looking for a new free life. Then the sophisticates; tourists, planners, reformers, interferers, sociologists, shoppers; amateurs of "atmosphere" and eccentrics like Mr. William Stendahl, who erects a replica of the House of Usher in order to mete out a literally Poetic justice to the Society for the Prevention of Fantasy. Then, last of all, the old, "the dried-apricot people," who wish merely to end their days somewhere else, amidst fresh sights and surroundings.

Mr. Bradbury contrasts his very earthy Earthmen with the weird, beautiful, remote Martians; fair, brown-skinned creatures who have eyes like gold coins. They live in houses of crystal, amidst groves of wine-bearing trees; they paint pictures with chemical fire and make books sing by stroking them, like harps, with their six-fingered hands. They wear masks when they wish to hide their feelings. Their children play with golden spiders. Their race is already dying out and most of their cities are uninhabited by the time the first rocketships arrive; but they have accepted their fate calmly, with a philosophy which resembles Taoism. When the chicken pox plague nearly annihilates them, the few survivors hover around the Earth-settlements in ghostly impotence. One, who tries in his loneliness to attach himself to the Earthmen, telepathically takes on the forms of their lost children and friends. He dies of exhaustion, being unable to satisfy everybody at once.

The immigration fails because, with its hot-dog stands and neon lights and gin and hymn singing and automobiles, it remains too obstinately American; it renames the mountains and the forests and the rivers, but it never takes true possession of the planet; its settlement is only a camping party, not a real home. A few realize this. The first of them is Jeff Spender, an archaeologist attached to the Fourth Expedition. Foreseeing the vandalism and crass materialism which will follow their occupation, he turns crazy, believes himself to be a chosen avenger of the Martians, and kills several of his companions. His warning and his death are in vain. The Americans do their ugly stupid will and depart, lured by homesickness to their own destruction in Earth's atomic war. And then, at length, after many years, comes Mr. Thomas. He, unlike all his predecessors, has made a complete act of immigration. He blows up his rocket and burns his old papers; and when his children ask to see the Martians he shows them their own reflections, in the water of a canal. Such, as I understand it, is the moral of this book.

The Martian Chronicles is episodic; a collection of formal short stories interspersed with bridge-passages which are written in the style of prose-poems, only a few paragraphs long. It has been impossible for me, in this small space, to convey more than a hint of the vital imagination, anger, humor and pity which Mr. Bradbury has brought to his work. Two of his best stories I have not even referred to; I must mention them now. The first of them is about Mr. Hathaway, one of the very few settlers who remains on Mars after the outbreak of the war on Earth. When his wife and his three children die, he makes four robots to resemble them. He lives with these robots, happy after a fashion, and sometimes even forgetting that they are not human. He grows old. They do not change. Then, one morning, a rocketship lands on its way back from a twenty-year voyage to Jupiter, Saturn and Neptune; it is the same ship of which Hathaway was a crew member on the Fourth Martian Expedition. Hathaway dies of a heart attack brought on by his excitement. When his old friend, the Captain, breaks the news to the robot-wife, she explains that Hathaway has never taught her, or the children, how to feel sad. "He didn't want us to know. He said it was the worst thing that could happen to a man to know how to be lonely and know how to be sad and then cry." So the Captain and his men take off again, for Earth, leaving the robots to their uncanny mimic life. ". . . and in that hut, as the wind roars by and the dust whirls and the cold stars burn, are four figures, a woman, two daughters, a son, tending a low fire for no reason and talking and laughing." They probably won't wear out for two hundred years.

The other story is set in the war-devastated California of 2026. It is about a marvelous mechanical house; a house which cleans itself, cooks its own meals, waters its own garden, wakes its inmates in the morning and reads aloud to them in the evening. But the inmates are no longer there. All that remains of them are their silhouettes, scorched into the wall of the west face by an atomic blast. The house goes on functioning, hour by hour, day by day. This story simply describes its automatic motions, from dawn till ten o'clock on an August evening, when the wind blows a tree bough through the kitchen window, knocking over a bottle of cleaning solvent and starting a fire. The house makes horribly human attempts to save itself, but it fails. "In the last instant under the fire avalanche, other choruses, oblivious, could be heard announcing the time, playing music, cutting the lawn by remote-control mower, or setting an umbrella frantically out and in the slamming and opening front door . . . a few last cleaning mice darting bravely out to carry the horrid ashes away!" And so our lopsided, labor-saving, thought-destroying mechanistic culture symbolically dies.

Have I made this book sound depressing? It is not—despite its dreadfully timely theme, and one's knowledge that the worst part of its prophecy may well come true, not in 2005 but this very next year. Only the second-rate artist depresses his readers. In work such as this, the sheer lift and power of a truly original imagination exhilarates you, almost in spite of yourself. So I urge even the squeamish to try Mr. Bradbury. His is a very great and unusual talent.

Gilbert Highet (essay date 1965)

SOURCE: "Introduction," in *The Vintage Bradbury*, Vintage Books, 1965, pp. vii-x.

[In the essay below, Highet comments on the originality of Bradbury's short fiction.]

One of the most difficult things to achieve in writing fiction is individuality. Hundreds of novels, thousands of short stories are produced every year. Most of them differ from one another only in the locality of their settings, the credibility of their plots, and the atrocity of their sexual and sadistic episodes. Few indeed are those authors whose style and intelligence and interpretation of life are so intense, so distinguished, that their work can be instantly recognized by any sensitive reader, and once recognized can never be forgotten. The fact has been described in a fine antithesis by Truman Capote, himself a highly original author: he is reported to have said of some current novel, "That's not writing, that's typewriting."

Ray Bradbury is one of the most original living American authors: all his work is stamped with the inimitable mark of individuality. No one else could possibly have written his stories. He himself would be utterly incapable of turning out those huge masses of literary meatballs and fictional frankfurters which pour from the publishing kitchens to glut even the most avid reader.

Take his style. A curious mixture of poetry and colloquialism, it is so brisk and economical that it never becomes cloying, so full of unexpected quirks that it is never boring. Occasionally I find it a little too intense and breathless. Ray himself sometimes looks and talks like an enthusiastic teen-ager who has just discovered his own strength, pulled the Sword from the Stone, and believes that he can cope with the world. But there is not a shadow of doubt that it is his own creation, and that it communicates his own clear vision both of the real and of the unreal.

Next, take his subjects. Whatever they are, they are not realistic. But they are human. Real life presses in upon us all the time—usually in the form of crowds or machines. Most of the bad fiction written today, as novels, short stories, and TV and motion-picture plays, is painfully realistic, in that it shows men and women more as objects than as subjects, conditioned and dominated by machines and crowds rather than living genuine lives of their own. With this kind of realism Ray Bradbury has nothing to do. His stories take place in the world of the spirit. He would have written stories equally disconcerting and equally distinguished if he had been born, not in 1920, but in 1820, or 1520, or 20 A.D. Whatever the qualities may be for which future generations will admire him—and they will—we can be sure that he will not be studied as a mirror of external American life in the mid-twentieth century.

What does he write about? Magic. Ghosts. Dreams turning out true, truth dissolving into dreams. The world, which seems dully solid to grownups, transformed into exciting and sometimes appalling fantasy in the minds of children. The future—which we are trying to mold, but which (he knows) will prove to be startlingly different from our plans and our dreams, even our fears. Aristotle said that in making a story it was better to have it impossible and probable, than unconvincing and possible. Most of Ray's stories are impossible—so far; but they are certainly convincing.

He has been misunderstood. He has been underestimated. He will gain a wider and more thoughtful public than he had at first; and his work will last. But he has been misinterpreted. He has often been described as a writer of "science fiction." This is a mistake. He knows little about science; he cares even less. He is a visionary. Technology he scarcely admires and scarcely uses. If it occupies his mind at all, it is not as a convenience or a source of extra muscle-power, but as a possible extension of the abilities of the human spirit. The idea that he can pick up a small machine in California and talk to someone in New York does not excite him. But he once told me that he would be truly enthralled by the invention of a machine which could recover the sounds of the distant past. If we can detect those impossibly distant objects called quasars, why cannot we recapture the sounds of Gettysburg, the words of the first performance of *Hamlet,* the speeches at the trial of Socrates?

Ray Bradbury is not a science-fiction writer. He is an author of tales of fantasy. His American predecessor is Edgar Allan Poe. His French predecessor is Villiers de l'Isle-Adam. His German predecessor is the author of the Tales of Hoffmann. His English predecessors are (in part, though not wholly) Wells and Kipling. His Greek predecessors are Lucian, and (before him) the creator of Cloud-Cuckoo-Land, Aristophanes.

Fantasy detached from machinery is rare nowadays. Fantasy which enlarges rather than degrades human life has been rare at all times. Franz Kafka was a fantast like Ray Bradbury; but he was a bitter and hopeless pessimist, in whose world everyone struggled and was defeated and did not even glimpse a glory in the mind. Ray Bradbury is both a pessimist and an optimist. The man who is freed from his own hateful skeleton to become as flat and fluid as a mollusc; the explorer of space who, while being burnt to death, becomes a shooting star; the playroom where, out of the imaginations of two quiet bored children, are born horrific monsters; the automated house which survives the death of its occupants and the end of the world—these and other conceptions of Ray Bradbury's are horrors. They are not so foul, not so bestial as the horrors which fill our hospitals and prisons; but they are horrors. Beside them, he puts puzzles. Peter Pan, the boy who would not grow up—is he a hero, or a horror? J. M. Barrie made him a lovable fairy, usually acted by mature women so slender that they can (with the help of complex mechanisms) fly. Ray Bradbury makes him a real boy, who cannot grow up, but cannot fly: one who suffers both the torments of youth and the tortures of age. And beside both horrors and puzzles, he puts beautiful and moving fantasies of a future world where we may be as happy as we all wish to be, and memories of a boyhood universe where even the worst monsters can be overcome by energy and confidence—the same sort of energy and confidence which have transformed him from an eager self-taught tale-spinner into a distinguished American author.

Damon Knight   (essay date 1967)

SOURCE: "When I Was in Kneepants: Ray Bradbury," in *In Search of Wonder: Essays on Modern Science Fiction,* Advent Publishers, pp. 108-13.

[*In the following essay, Knight presents a brief overview of Bradbury's early short fiction, noting that his principal subject is childhood.*]

Ray Bradbury began writing professionally at the flood-tide of the cerebral story in science fiction—in 1940, when John Campbell was revolutionizing the field with a new respect for facts, and a wholly justified contempt for the overblown emotional values of the thirties. Bradbury, who had nothing but emotion to offer, couldn't sell Campbell.

Bradbury didn't care. He adapted his work just enough to meet the standards of the lesser markets—he filled it with the secondhand furniture of contemporary science fiction and fantasy—and went on writing what he chose.

It's curious to look back now on those first Bradbury stories and reflect how far they have brought their author. Not many of them are stories at all; most are intensely realized fragments, padded out with any handy straw. The substance of **"The Next in Line,"** for one especially vivid example, is in a two-page description of some Mexican mummies, as relentlessly and embarrassingly horrible as any tourist photograph. The remainder—the two American visitors, the car trouble, the hotel room, the magazines—is not relevant, it merely plumps out the skeleton enough to get it into a conventional suit of clothes.

On a story-a-week schedule, Bradbury sold prodigiously to *Weird Tales, Planet Stories, Thrilling Wonder.* One day we awoke to discover that he had leapfrogged over John Campbell's head, outside our microcosm altogether: his work was beginning to appear in *Harper's;* in *Mademoiselle;* in the *O. Henry Prize Stories;* on the radio; in *Esquire, Collier's, The Saturday Evening Post.*

Outside the huge, brightly-colored bubble he had blown around himself, "serious" critics reacted with rapture:

> . . . the sheer lift and power of a truly original imagination exhilarates . . . His is a very great and unusual talent.
>
> —Christopher Isherwood

Inside the bubble, we get at once a clearer and a more distorted view of Bradbury. Although he has a large following among science fiction readers, there is at least an equally large contingent of people who cannot stomach his work at all; they say he has no respect for the medium; that he does not even trouble to make his scientific double-talk convincing; that—worst crime of all—he fears and distrusts science.

. . . All of which is true, and—for our present purposes, anyhow—irrelevant. The purists are right in saying that he does not write science fiction, and never has.

To Bradbury, as to most people, radar and rocket ships and atomic power are big, frightening, meaningless names: a fact which, no doubt, has something to do with his popular success, but which does not touch the root of the matter. Bradbury's strength lies in the fact that he writes about the things that are really important to us—not the things we pretend we are interested in—science, marriage, sports, politics, crime—but the fundamental prerational fears and longings and desires: the rage at being born; the will to be loved; the longing to communicate; the hatred of parents and siblings, the fear of things that are not self. . . .

People who talk about Bradbury's imagination miss the point. His imagination is mediocre; he borrows nearly all his backgrounds and props, and distorts them badly; wherever he is required to invent anything—a planet, a Martian, a machine—the image is flat and unconvincing. Bradbury's Mars, where it is not as bare as a Chinese stage-setting, is a mass of inconsistency; his spaceships are a joke; his people have no faces. The vivid images in his work are not imagined; they are remembered.

Here is the shock of birth, in **"No Particular Night or Morning"**:

"Have you talked about this to the psychiatrist?"

"So he could try to mortar up the gaps for me, fill in the gulfs with noise and warm water and words and hands touching me . . . ?"

And the death-wish, Bradbury's most recurrent theme:

. . . When I was living I was jealous of you, Lespere . . . Women frightened me and I went into space, always wanting them and jealous of you for having them, and money, and as much happiness as you could have in your own wild way. But now, falling here, with everything over, I'm not jealous of you any more, because it's over for you as it is for me, and right now it's like it never was.

("Kaleidoscope")

Forty-five thousand people killed every year on this continent . . . made into jelly right in the can, as it were, in the automobiles. Red blood jelly, with white marrow bones like sudden thoughts . . . The cars roll up in tight sardine rolls—all sauce, all silence.

. . . You look out your window and see two people lying atop each other in friendly fashion who, a moment ago, had never met before, dead. . . .

("The Concrete Mixer")

The gulf between Bradbury and the science fiction writers is nowhere more clearly evident than in the lavish similes and metaphors that are his trademarks:

The first concussion cut the rocket up the side with a giant can opener. The men were thrown into space like a dozen wriggling silverfish.

("Kaleidoscope")

. . . And here were the lions now . . . so feverishly and startlingly real that you could feel the prickling fur on your hand, and your mouth was stuffed with the dusty upholstery smell of their heated pelts. . . .

("The Veldt")

The aim of science-fantasy, more and more as it becomes what it has always tried to be—adult fiction—is to expand the imagination, stretch it to include things never before seen or dreamed of. Bradbury's subject is childhood and the buried child-in-man; his aim is to narrow the focus, not to widen it; to shrink all the big frightening things to the compass of the familiar: a spaceship to a tin can; a Fourth of July rocket to a brass kettle; a lion to a Teddy bear.

There is so much to say about Bradbury's meaning that perhaps too little has been said about his technique. He is a superb craftsman, a man who has a great gift and has spent fifteen years laboriously and with love teaching himself to use it. "For here was a kind of writing of which there is never much in any one time—a style at once delicate, economical and unobtrusively firm, sharp enough to cut but without rancor, and clear as water or air." That's Stephen Vincent Benét, writing in 1938 about Robert Nathan; the same words, all but the next to last phrase, might have been written with equal justice of Bradbury. His imagery is luminous and penetrating, continually lighting up familiar corners with unexpected words. He never lets an idea go until he has squeezed it dry, and never wastes one. I well remember my own popeyed admiration when I read his story about a woman who gave birth to a small blue pyramid; this is exactly the sort of thing that might occur to any imaginative writer in a manic or drunken moment; but Bradbury wrote it and sold it.

Why Bradbury's world-line and that of the animated cartoon have never intersected, I do not know; perhaps because the result would necessarily scare the American theater-going public out of its underpants; but clearly, in such stories as **"Jack-in-the-Box,"** Bradbury is writing for no other medium. The gaudy colors and plush textures, the dream-swift or dream-slow motion, the sudden dartings into unsuspected depths of perspective, or contrariwise, the ballooning of a face into the foreground—these are all distinctive techniques of the animated cartoon, and Bradbury uses them all.

As for the rancor, the underlying motif of much early Bradbury, the newer stories show little of it; this might be taken as a sign that Bradbury is mellowing in his thirties, and perhaps he is; I have the feeling that he is rather trying to mellow—deliberately searching for something equally strong, equally individual, less antagonistic toward the universe that buys his stories. I don't think he has yet found it. There's the wry, earthy humor of **"En la Noche,"** the pure fancy of **"The Golden Kite, The Silver Wind"**; these are neutral stories, anyone might have written them. There are the moralistic tales; if you find the moral palatable, as I do in **"The Big Black and White Game"** and **"Way in the Middle of the Air,"** these are sincere and moving; if you don't, as I don't in **"Powerhouse"** or **"The**

Fire Balloons," there is a pious flatness about them. Then there is sentiment; and since Bradbury does nothing by halves, it is sentiment that threatens continually to slop over into sentimentality. At its precarious peak, it is a moving and vital thing: when it slops, it is—no other word will do—sickening.

It has been said of Bradbury that, like H. P. Lovecraft, he was born a century or so too late. I think he would have been a castaway in any age; if he would like to destroy airplanes, television sets, automatic washing machines, it's not because they make loud noises or because they have no faces or even because some of them kill people, but because they are grown-up things; because they symbolize the big, loud, faceless, violent, unromantic world of adults.

Childhood is after all Bradbury's one subject. When he writes of grown-up explorers visiting the sun or the Jurassic jungles, they are palpably children playing at spacemen or time-travelers. He writes feelingly and with sharp perception of young women and of old people—because, I think, he finds them childlike. But it's only when the theme becomes explicit that his song sings truest:

> The boys were playing on the green park diamond when he came by. He stood a little while among the oak-tree shadows, watching them hurl the white, snowy baseball into the warm summer air, saw the baseball shadow fly like a dark bird over the grass, saw their hands open in mouths to catch this swift piece of summer that now seemed most especially important to hold onto. . . .

> How tall they stood to the sun. In the last few months it seemed the sun had passed a hand above their heads, beckoned, and they were warm metal drawn melting upwards; they were golden taffy pulled by an immense gravity to the sky, thirteen, fourteen years old, looking down upon Willie, smiling, but already beginning to neglect him. . . .

Learned opinion to the contrary, Bradbury is not the heir of Poe, Irving or Hawthorne; his voice is the voice (a little shriller) of Christopher Morley and Robert Nathan and J. D. Salinger. As his talent expands, some of his stories become pointed social commentary; some are surprisingly effective religious tracts, disguised as science fiction; others still are nostalgic vignettes; but under it all is still Bradbury the poet of 20th-century neurosis, Bradbury the isolated spark of consciousness, awake and alone at midnight; Bradbury the grown-up child who still remembers, still believes.

The young Ray Bradbury wrote a story called **"Skeleton,"** about a man obsessed by the fact that he carries a horrid, white, grinning skeleton inside him. The story was raw, exuberant, gauche, pretentious, insulting to the intellect, and unforgettable. *Weird Tales* published it, and later it appeared in Bradbury's first collection, ***Dark Carnival.***

The story did not soothe its readers' anxieties nor pamper their prejudices, nor provide vicarious adventure in a ro-

mantic setting. Far from solving his problem by his own courage and resourcefulness, the hero let it be solved for him by a strange little man named Munigant, who crawled down his throat, gnawed, crunched and munched away the bones which had so annoyed him, and left him lying on his carpet, a human jellyfish.

Time passed; Bradbury got a little older, stopped running quite so hard. His stories acquired depth, smoothness, polish. Little by little he stopped writing about corpses, vampires, cemeteries, things in jars; instead, he wrote about civil rights, religion and good home cooking. The slicks, which had begun buying him as a curiosity when he was horrid, kept on buying him as a staple when he turned syrupy.

Dandelion Wine consists of sixteen loosely connected tales without a ghost or a goblin in them; they are familiar in tone and rhythm, but these stories are no longer what we mean by fantasy; they are what Hollywood means by fantasy. The setting is an imaginary Midwestern town, seen through the wrong end of a rose-colored glass. The period is as vague as the place; Bradbury calls it 1928, but it has no feeling of genuine recollection; most of the time it is like second-hand 1910.

Childhood is Bradbury's one subject, but you will not find real childhood here, Bradbury's least of all. What he has had to say about it has always been expressed obliquely, in symbol and allusion, and always with the tension of the outsider—the ex-child, the lonely one. In giving up this tension, in diving with arms spread into the glutinous pool of sentimentality that has always been waiting for him, Bradbury has renounced the one thing that made him worth reading.

All the rest is still here: the vivid images, the bombardment of tastes and sounds and smells; the clipped, faceless prose; the heavy nostalgia, the cuteness, the lurking impudence. The phrases, as before, are poignant ("with the little gray toad of a heart flopping weakly here or there in his chest") or silly to the point of self-parody ("lemon-smelling men's room"). The characters are as lifelike as Bradbury's characters ever were: bright, pert, peppermint-stick people, epicene, with cotton-candy hair and sugar smiles.

Maybe Bradbury, like his own protagonist in **"Skeleton,"** grew uneasy about the macabre forces in himself: or maybe success, that nemesis of American writers, was Bradbury's M. Munigant. Whatever the reason, the skeleton has vanished; what's left is recognizable but limp.

Russell Kirk (essay date 1969)

SOURCE: "Fantasy: The World of Ray Bradbury," in *Enemies of the Permanent Things: Observations of Abnormality in Literature and Politics,* Arlington House, 1969, pp. 109-24.

[In the essay below, Kirk alleges that it is Bradbury's preoccupation with the "moral imagination," rather than science and technology, that distinguishes him from other writers of science fiction.]

To commence as a writer for the pulp-magazines is no advantage; nor is writing screen-plays in Hollywood, decade after decade, generally to be recommended for those who would be men of letters. Such was Ray Bradbury's background. He had the advantage, however, of never attending college—which salutary neglect preserved him from many winds of doctrine, insured that his talents would not be spoilt by Creative Writing 201, and gave him leisure and appetite to read good books innumerable, the love of which suffuses Bradbury story after Bradbury story.

Hollywood writer though he is, Bradbury has had only one of his stories made into a film, and that in England: *Fahrenheit 451,* a passionate and tender and terrifying description of a democratic despotism not necessarily very far distant in the future, in which all books are burnt because they are disturbing influences in an egalitarian and sensate culture. It is something of a pity that Bradbury did not write the screen-play himself, for he is as good a dramatist as he is a writer of stories. His three short plays, under the general title *The World of Ray Bradbury,* ran for nearly a year in Los Angeles—but closed after a few days in Manhattan.

The rising generation in Los Angeles (of whom Bradbury is the chief hero) loved those three plays—*The Veldt, To the Chicago Abyss,* and *The Pedestrians.* Yet the New York play-reviewers were more ferocious with Ray Bradbury than with any other man of mark in my memory, and they succeeded promptly in preventing anyone in New York from perceiving those truths which are best revealed by fable and parable. The rising generation of Manhattan was left with such plays as *The Toilet* for ethical instruction.

Bradbury (who thinks of himself, so far as he has any politics, as something of a revolutionary) was assailed by the New York critics as a "romantic reactionary." Charitably, Bradbury later remarked to me that perhaps the Manhattan critics merely had been waiting to gun him down once he should ride out of his western fastness. But there was more than that to their vituperative detestation. They perceived that Bradbury is a moralist, which they could not abide; that he has no truck with the obscene, which omission they found unpardonable; that he is no complacent liberal, because he knows the Spirit of the Age to be monstrous—for which let him be anathema; that he is one of the last surviving masters of eloquence and glowing description, which ought to be prohibited; that, with Pascal, he understands how the Heart has reasons which the Reason cannot know—so to the Logicalist lamp-post with him.

Thus the champions of decadence and deliquescence, the enemies of the permanent things, accurately discerned in Ray Bradbury a man of moral imagination, who must be put down promptly. For like Lewis, like Tolkien, like other talented fabulists, Ray Bradbury has drawn the sword against the dreary and corrupting materialism of this cen

tury; against society as producer-and-consumer equation, against the hideousness in modern life, against mindless power, against sexual obsession, against sham intellectuality, against the perversion of right reason into the mentality of the television-viewer. His Martians, spectres, and witches are not diverting entertainment only: they become, in their eerie manner, the defenders of truth and beauty.

Consider those three short plays attacked by the Manhattan reviewers. *The Veldt* is a story of children abandoned by modern parents to the desolation of the Screen—and of how thwarted imagination takes its vengeance, the predators of the mind growing literally red in tooth and claw. *To the Chicago Abyss* is a picture of the evocative power of tender trifles, restoring the rudiments of order after the Bomb has fallen. *The Pedestrians* has to do with two men flung into prison for preferring nocturnal strolls to the compulsive TV screen. Alive with pity and terror, such plays cannot be tolerated by any Logicalist.

Some librarians, too, have taken alarm. Bradbury's stories are *disturbing!* No disturbances can be permitted in this perfect American culture of ours. In error, a company which distributes educational books included among a consignment of books for children one copy of *Fahrenheit 451.* A female librarian detected this work of heresy, and fired off a letter of furious protest to the wholesaler. How dared they send such a dreadful book? "I took it right out in back and burned it." Tomorrow is already here.

Some paragraphs ago, I mentioned that Bradbury has been injudiciously described as the world's greatest living science-fiction writer. Now he does, indeed, look forward to man's exploration of the planets, although not to the gloating "conquest" of space. But for science and technology, *per se,* he has no more taste than did C. S. Lewis. H. G. Wells expected man to become godlike through applied science; yet Wells' interior world was dry, unloving, and egotistical. Bradbury (who never drives, never flies in planes if he can help it, and detests most gadgets) thinks it more probable that man may spoil everything, in this planet and in others, by the misapplication of science to avaricious ends—the Baconian and Hobbesian employment of science as power. And Bradbury's interior world is fertile, illuminated by love for the permanent things, warm with generous impulse.

That man may replenish the universe for the greater glory of God, Bradbury would have man fling himself to the most distant worlds. But this is an ambition far different from the arrogance of Wells and his kind—who, in the phrases of Robert Jungk, aspire to the throne of God, and who exhort man "to occupy God's place, to recreate and organize a man-made cosmos according to man-made laws of reason, foresight, and efficiency."

Through nearly all of Bradbury's "science-fiction" tales run forebodings like those of Jungk. Bradbury knows of modern technology, in the phrase of Henry Adams, that we are "monkeys monkeying with a loaded shell." He is interested not in the precise mechanism of rockets, but in the mentality and the morals of fallible human beings who make and use rockets. He is a man of fable and parable.

Every one of us, Bradbury says in a letter to me, has "a private keep somewhere in the upper part of the head where, from time to time, of midnights, the beast can be heard raving. To control that, to the end of life, to stay contemplative, sane, good-humored, is our entire work, in the midst of cities that tempt us to inhumanity, and passions that threaten to drive through the skin with invisible spikes." The author of three hundred tales of the fantastic knows the permanent things as well as did the poet of the Waste Land.

Bradbury is not writing about the gadgets of conquest; his real concerns are the soul and the moral imagination. When the boy-hero of *Dandelion Wine,* in an abrupt mystical experience, is seized almost bodily by the glowing consciousness that he is really *alive,* we glimpse that mystery the soul. When, in *Something Wicked This Way Comes,* the lightning-rod salesman is reduced magically to an idiot dwarf because all his life he had fled from perilous responsibility, we know the moral imagination.

"Soul," a word much out of fashion nowadays, signifies a man's animating entity. That flaming spark the soul is the real space-traveller of Bradbury's stories. "I'm alive!"— that exclamation is heard from Waukegan to Mars and beyond, in Bradbury's fables. Life is its own end—if one has a soul to tell him so.

The moral imagination is the principal possession that man does not share with the beasts. It is man's power to perceive ethical truth, abiding law, in the seeming chaos of many events. Without the moral imagination, man would live merely from day to day, or rather moment to moment, as dogs do. It is the strange faculty—inexplicable if men are assumed to have an animal nature only—of discerning greatness, justice, and order, beyond the bars of appetite and self-interest. And the moral imagination, which shows us what we ought to be, primarily is what distinguishes Bradbury's tales from the futurism of Wells' fancy. For Bradbury, the meaning of life is here and now, in our every action; we live amidst immortality; it is here, not in some future domination like that of Wells' *The Sleeper Awakens,* that we must find our happiness.

So it will not do to treat of Ray Bradbury, despite his abhorrence of much in the modern world and despite his distrust of man armed for the conquest of space, as if he were a prophet of the coming doom. For no recent writer is more buoyed up by the ebullient spirit of youth, and none more popular with intelligent young readers. Probably no one ever has written so understandingly of twelve- and thirteen-year-old boys as Bradbury does repeatedly, particularly in *Dandelion Wine,* with its prosaic-romantic setting of Waukegan, Illinois (Bradbury's birthplace) and a thousand other American towns about 1928. Perpetual youth, and therefore perpetual hope, defy in Bradbury's pages the fatigue of this century and the ambitions of exploiting scientism.

If spirits in prison, still we are spirits; if able to besmirch ourselves, still only we men are capable of moral choices. Life and technology are what we make of them, and the failure of man to live in harmony with nature is the failure of moral imagination. That failure is not inevitable. To understand Bradbury's disquietude and his high hopes, we may look at his book about the tragic human conquest of Mars, *The Martian Chronicles*; and at his book about the wonder and terror behind the facade of any little town, *Something Wicked This Way Comes.*

Steven Dimeo (essay date 1972)

SOURCE: "Man and Apollo: A Look at Religion in the Science Fantasies of Ray Bradbury," in *Journal of Popular Culture,* Vol. 5, No. 4, Spring, 1972, pp. 970-78.

[*In the essay below, Dimeo uncovers moralism in Bradbury's short fiction.*]

Although religious thinking in the space age has been largely dominated by Nietzschean apostasy, science fiction itself seems to be giving more and more attention to man's relationship with the divine. Religious themes have long been treated in the genre but the first to give it serious and even literary consideration was C. S. Lewis in his trilogy *Out of the Silent Planet* (1938), *Perelandra* (1944), and *That Hideous Strength* (1945) which lofted the Christian mythology complete with angels and devils into tangible planetary realms. Since then the more notable examples of science fiction with more innovative religious implications have included Gore Vidal's *Messiah* (1954), James Blish's *A Case of Conscience* (1958), Walter

M. Miller, Jr.'s *A Canticle for Leibowitz* (1960), Robert Heinlein's *Stranger in a Strange Land* (1961), Frank Herbert's *Dune* (1965) and *Dune Messiah* (1969), and Michael Moorcock's *In His Image* (1968). Four of those works have won the Hugo award, the field's highest annual honor for fiction. In the opinion of science-fiction historian and biographer Sam Moskowitz it was however, Ray Bradbury with his short stories **"The Man"** (1949) and **"The Fire Balloons"** (1951) in particular who "provided the bridge between C. S. Lewis and the main body of science fiction in the magazines" [*Seekers of Tomorrow*, 1967]. Baptized a Baptist, Bradbury grew to be a self-confessed agnostic in his teens. But he has since recognized the significant role religious concerns have played in his life and his writings. As he explained with only some degree of levity in our interview, "I realize very late in life now that I could have made a fine priest or minister" [Unpublished, 1969].

Certainly his moral awareness suggests some truth to the claim. Having called himself in fact "a writer of moral fairy tales," he defends his moralistic strain when he says in another interview, "Touch any s-f writer working today and you will, nine times out of ten, touch a moralist" ["A Portrait of a Genius," *Show*, December, 1964]. Two other science-fiction writers have noted this aspect of Bradbury's work. Henry Kuttner writes [in "Ray Bradbury's Themes" *Ray Bradbury Review*, 1952], for instance, "The converse of James Branch Cabell, Bradbury deals realistically with a romantic theme: the value of faith." Chad Oliver, speaking of the tone of **The Martian Chronicles** (1950) in particular, explains further, "Bradbury's faith in the essential dignity of the common man prevented him from falling into the hopelessness of T. S. Eliot, but he is nonetheless a religious man and there are echoes of 'The Waste Land' and 'The Hollow Men' in his work." Since those observations were made, Bradbury has published the novel *Something Wicked This Way Comes* (1962), a heavy-handed allegory in which two 13-year-old boys, Jim Nightshade and Will Halloway, led by Will's father Charles (modeled after Bradbury's own father), defeat Death and Evil in the form of a carnival and its proprietor Mr. Dark. At his worst, as a matter of fact, Bradbury has belabored morality to death. Charles Halloway, who discourses lengthily on Good and Evil in that novel, epitomizes this self-conscious moralizing. It is apparent in *Fahrenheit 451* (1953) when the ex-English teacher Faber condemns the future-present for having abandoned the reality and dreams of books, when the old man in **"To the Chicago Abyss"** (1963) eulogizes the forgotten trivia like cigarettes and candy bars of the world before the nuclear war erased all but the memory, or when the robot grandmother in **"I Sing the Body Electric!"** elaborates too much on the perfection of machines and the more-than-mortal love she symbolizes.

But Bradbury has elsewhere simplified his conception of morality in a way that suggests the broader nature of that faith in man which Oliver refers to: "Light is good. Dark is evil. Life is good. Death is evil. Man, representing this good of light and life, moves against death and universal darkness" ["Remembrances of Things Future," *Playboy*,

January 1965]. Only when Bradbury puts aside his penchant for homily to focus on the teleology and hierology implicit in this mortal effort to wade through darkness does he transcend a superficial didacticism. His literary interest in religion is thus at its best not a concern for morality but rather for mortality and immortality. Upon understanding Bradbury's opinion of the interrelationship between science and religion and man and god in the age of space, the Christian, divine, and transcendental allusions in his stories can be seen to underline the symbolic implications of his fictional pilgrimages into space itself.

Bradbury calls attention to the similarity of science and religion in especial. "This whole talk about science and religion being two ways of thinking or two separate things is ridiculous," he says. "They're both the same thing. . . . Science provides tools, insights, theories. So does religion. And religion relates us to the universe at the same moment that science is trying to relate us to that same universe. But whereas science provides us with working theories that are relevant to tools at hand, three-dimensional tools that we can pick and change the environment with, religion simply says where tools are no longer usable or the information is not available, then you've got to go on faith. . . . From this point on, you need someone who will make you easy with the unknowable and the mystical side of life. And you've got to have it, that's all. If you don't have it on my level, you're going to have it on the half-assed level of the astrologers." Bradbury looks askance at the younger generation's belief in these pseudo-sciences, political fanaticism or hero worship of one sort or another but sees it as inevitable in the light of the century's relative religious vacuum. He has suggested, however, that present scientific aspirations can fill that void. "As the years went by," he explains, "I found myself getting more and more interested in just the whole universe—you know, who we are, what we're doing here, where we're going, what our plans are for the next billion years. That's a long time and space is one of our ways of planning. The more we get into space, the more religious we've got to become. We're going to be meeting more mysteries." It is no surprise then that Bradbury described his following the first satellite across the night sky as "'an absolutely religious experience'" ["The Magic World of Ray Bradbury," *Los Angeles Magazine*, March 1962]. For more than ever before science has put man closer to the heavens he had formerly considered the territory of the gods.

Since man's ascension into space has clearly brought the dreams of a god-like flight to fruition, Bradbury predictably places man at the center of the universe in the romantic and Renaissance tradition. As he explains it [in Kitte Turmell's "Predicting the Future is an art as Old as Plato," *Youth*, January 17, 1965], "I feel that in the Space Age each person must look on himself as a god, that is, a living part of the universe, a moving intelligence. If God lives, he lives in us." In an essay he writes, too,

> But now very late in the scroll of earth, phoenix man, who lives by burning, a true furnace of energy, stoking himself with chemistries, must stand as God. Not

represent Him, not *pretend* to be Him, not deny Him, but simply nobly, and frighteningly *be* Him.

["Remembrance of Things Future"]

His concept is clearly pantheistic as he suggests in another essay that even delineates an eternal purpose of self-discovery to man's scientific aspirations:

> We may take some comfort in daring to think that perhaps we are part of some Divine stir and per-ambulation, a vast blind itch of a God universe to touch, taste, see, hear, know itself.
>
> If all the universe is God, then on the instant are we not extrusions of dumb, miraculous matter put in motion to protest unknowingness, to combat darkness, to willfully expunge Death, to long for immortality, to cherish Being, and with our own extrusions, our metal machineries of joy and confusion begot in testpit and factory, to go off in search of yet finer miracles basking under far-journeying suns?

["Cry the Cosmos," *Life*, 53]

The egoistic pantheism echoes the very same "Thou Art God" philosophy the Martian-trained Valentine Michael Smith martyrs himself for in Heinlein's *Stranger in a Strange Land*. The view of course is not original but derives out of what William H. Whyte in *The Organization Man* has called the Protestant rather than the Social Ethic, and echoes in fact the doctrine of self-reliance advocated by the 19th century ex-Unitarian minister Ralph Waldo Emerson. Though not particularly new to science fiction in the twentieth century, it has never been analyzed in such terms. Perhaps the individual, more than ever before, has once again become to writers like Bradbury or Heinlein the single standard in a scientific society dominated by the relativity and uncertainty of Einstein and Heisenberg or the very power of the atom and the computer.

In any case, while Bradbury conceives of man in general as a kind of god today, he also has recognized his own divine pretensions as a fundamental human truth. Speaking of **"The Miracles of Jamie,"** a story he has not had reprinted since its publication when he was 26, he explains it was "about a little boy who thought he was the reincarnation of Christ. And when his sister is dying, he goes into the bedroom, unbeknownst to his parents, and commands her to live and it doesn't work. And that's a big disillusionment. Not that this ever happened in my life. But every Christian boy is full of ideas about the Second Coming. . . . Well, I imagine [even] every Jewish boy thinks he's a Messiah or maybe knows it. So I think the only disillusionment I might have had, on just a secret level and not a big thing that I can tell about, is that whole thing of the Christ image when I was very young. I'm not even sure about that. But the fact that I wrote a story about it, I think, proves there was some interest in the legend when I was 11 going on 12."

He has since then, however, vicariously resurrected the illusion, for he sometimes imputes Christ-like qualities to his characters. For instance in **"El Dia de Muerte"** (1947), a story that smacks of Hemingway from the gory descrip-tion of a bullfight to the name Villalta for the matador, the little boy Raimundo who is killed by a car corresponds to the Mexican imitating Christ who falls from the cross. The psychiatrist Dr. Immanuel Brokaw in **"The Man in the Rorschach Shirt"** (1966) embodies spiritual leaders and ultimately Christ, too. The narrator describes the doctor's disappearance as a kind of reverse visitation: "So the giant who had been Gandhi-Moses-Christ-Buddha-Freud all layered in one incredible American dessert had dropped through a hole in the clouds." And when ten years later the narrator meets the man again, Dr. Brokaw "Reared up like God manifest, bearded, benevolent, pontifical, erudite, merry, accepting, forgiving, messianic, tutorial, forever and eternal. . . ." Brokaw himself relates the personal revelation of his prior imperfections in terms of Moses on Mt. Sinai:

> 'Holy Moses, Brokaw, I cried, all these years down from the Mount, the world of God like a flea in your ear. And now, late in the day, old wise one, you think to consult your lightning-scribbled stones. And find your Laws, your Tables, different!'

And when the narrator sees Brokaw go out amongst the multitude on the beach, he sees another Christ metaphorically walking on water: "He seemed to tread lightly upon a water of people. The last I saw of him, he was still gloriously afloat." It seems significant, too, that Harry Smith in the more recent **"Henry the Ninth"** (1969) becomes the incarnation of England's famous real and fictional men of history on Christmas Eve.

But the divine qualities are often more universal than Christian. On the artistic level, to begin with, Edgar Allan Poe in **"The Exiles"** (1949) tells his fellow authors who have been banished to Mars, "'I am a god, Mr. Dickens, even as you are a god, even as we all are gods. . . . '" The special effects artist Terwilliger who sculptures a miniature dinosaur in **"Tyrannosaurus Rex"** (1962) similarly thinks of himself as a god when he considers, "I feel . . . quite simply that there stands my Garden and these my animal creations which I love on this Sixth Day, and tomorrow, the Seventh, I must rest." It also takes Bodoni in **"The Rocket"** (1950) seven days to remodel his otherwise useless ship into a world of illusion that simulates for him and his children a journey to Mars they haven't the money to take in reality. Perhaps, too, it is no accident that the charlatan who originally sells the rocket to Bodoni for $2,000 is named Mathews, Hebrew for "gift from Jehovah."

When the references do not metaphorically enhance the labors of mortal creators, they depict man in one way or another trying to transcend the confines of his body and commune with a kind of Over-Soul in the Zen tradition. In **"The Homecoming,"** which won an O. Henry Memorial award in 1947, the boy Timothy's frustrated desire to assume the supernatural dimensions of his relatives in effect reflects the more general human aspirations to shuffle off the mortal coils. Cecy, reappearing in **"The April Witch"** (1952), actually demonstrates divine powers in her ability to become one with an amoeba, a water droplet, or even a mortal like Ann Leary in whose body she comes to know human love. On an even grander scale, Hollis and his crew, scattered apart from the explosion of their rocket in **"Kaleidoscope"** (1949), unite with God Himself, as this passage implies: "There were only the great diamonds and sapphires and emerald mists and velvet inks of space, with God's voice mingling among the crystal fires. . . . Their [the crew's] voices had died like echoes of the words of God spoken and vibrating in the starred deep." Certainly—perhaps even too obviously—the heroine of **"Powerhouse,"** a story which in 1948 also won the O. Henry award, becomes one with a pantheistic world when she literally becomes the electricity that links all of mankind. Before this mystical experience; she hasn't faith enough to accept her mother's imminent death. But the powerhouse where she and her husband stay that night proves to be a kind of church that provides the faith, for afterwards electric sparks are "like saints and choruses, haloed now yellow, now red, now green and a massed singing beat along the roof hollows and echoed down in endless hymns and chants." The next morning after the night rain has ceased, she looks out under the clear desert sky and sees now that she is still a part of all humanity, a part of a divine design in the world:

> And she could see the far mountains; there was no blur nor a running-of-color to things. All was solid stone touching stone, and stone touching sand, and sand touching wild flower, and wild flower touching the sky in one continuous clear flow, everything definite and of a piece.

This impulse to discover God in oneself is not as implicit in these tales of what *Time* [in "Poet of the Pulps," March 23, 1963] has called "infinite interfusion" so much as it is in Bradbury's fictional pilgrimages. And there is no Last Judgment, no discrimination implied in his personal eschatology. Man's projected odyssey into infinity is itself aiming at the eternity of the empyrean. We are striving for the stars, as Bradbury puts it, "Because we love life and fear death. Man craves immortality. . . . Once man is continuous from Mars to Pluto to the Coalsack Nebula, and the threat of racial death banished, the questions about annihilation will be meaningless." Inevitably then in **"The Machineries of Joy"** (1962) Father Brian, who begins to face the religious crisis inherent in the space age, realizes that the leap into space is simply another Genesis for mankind. He suggests as much at the story's conclusion when he awaits the televised launch and "the voice that would teach a silly, a strange, a wild and miraculous thing: How to count back, ever backward . . . to zero."

The nature of the goal receives symbolic treatment in **"The Golden Apples of the Sun"** (1953), a title taken aptly from the lines of Yeats' "The Song of Wandering Aengus." In this story a rocket named alternately Copa de Oro ("Cup of Gold"), Prometheus, and Icarus heads directly for the sun to catch a part of the ultimate dream of mankind, the gold at the end of the rainbow, a reference the story itself makes. But the golden apples are not wealth alone. They are immortality as well, for the fire plucked from the sun is "a gift of fire that might burn forever."

They are spirituality, for the sun is described as "the bodiless body and the fleshless flesh." They are finally the wisdom of a god as suggested by the captain's burning tree simile for the sun. For the image recalls not only the Tree of Knowledge but also Moses' vision of God as the burning bush. What the rocket's Cup scoops up is not merely part of the sun, then, but

> a bit of the flesh of God, the blood of the universe, the blazing thought, the blinding philosophy that set out and mothered a galaxy, that idled and swept planets in their fields and summoned or laid to rest lies and livelihoods.

In **"The Man"** the trip to the stars becomes even more clearly an archetypal search for the Holy Grail. Before Capt. Hart and Lt. Martin discover Christ has just visited the planet they have landed on, they discuss man's purpose in space:

> 'Why do we do it, Martin? This space travel, I mean. Always on the go, Always searching. Our insides always tight, never any rest.'

> 'Maybe we're looking for peace and quiet. Certainly there's none on Earth,' said Martin.

> 'No, there's not, is there? . . . Not since Darwin, eh? Not since everything went by the board, everything we used to believe in, eh? Divine power and all that. And so maybe that's why we're going out to the stars, eh, Martin? Looking for our lost souls, is that it? Trying to get away from our evil planet to a good one?'

> 'Perhaps, sir. Certainly we're looking for something.'

On discovering Christ has brought peace to the nearby city, Martin is content with His effect. But the nervous, ambitious Capt. Hart ignores the probable futility and takes off in the rocket to pursue the cause, Christ Himself. The title of the story seems doubly ironic in the final analysis, for Christ to Capt. Hart represents man successfully transcending his own limitations. Perhaps, too, the Man here is actually Capt. Hart himself who comes to epitomize man's driving discontent.

Unlike Capt. Hart, Father Peregrine in **"The Fire Balloons"** appears to discover what he sets out looking for. The pilgrim that his name implies, he searches for a bit of Beauty more lasting than the Fourth of July balloons in the Illinois town of his youth. Only after his ridiculous effort to 'convert' the Martians does he believe his search has ended with these blue and sentient globes. Once men like him, they have evolved out of mortality altogether. As man's freed and sinless soul and intellect, they are finally happy and at peace.

But has this discovery subsequently set the priest's own mind at ease? Admittedly the Martians that he finally calls "the fireworks of the pure soul" represent more of a constant than the transient fire balloons in his past that "dwindled, forever gone . . ."; the Martians are "fixed, gaseous, miraculous, forever." But Father Peregrine's reactions there in the hills counterpose Christ's in the wilderness. The priest enjoys succumbing to mortal temptations when he plummets from a cliff or fires three bullets at himself only to be saved by the "blue round dreams." Despite yet because of the discovery, he seems by his very actions to despair of that chimerical immortality before his eyes.

The changes in his character and in Father Stone's offer the key to understanding what the end of the quest really signifies. Father Peregrine attempts at first to proselyte the Martians, then realizes that he must finally learn from them instead. After understanding what the Martians are, Father Stone, who was formerly more interested in recognizing "the inhuman in the human" rather than "the human in the inhuman," regrets that they can only descend out of the hills to First Town "'to handle our own kind.'" He believes the round glass model they have constructed is not just a sign but Christ after all. But there will be Christs on the other worlds, too, and only when they can be apprehended as a whole will the "Big Truth" be known. For now both the priests must walk "down out of the hills toward the new town"—back to mortal reality. But they intend to climb again, as this passage indicates:

> 'May I'—cried Father Peregrine, not daring to ask, eyes closed—'may I come again, someday, that I may learn from you?'
>
> The blue fires blazed. The air trembled.
>
> Yes. Someday he might come again. Someday.

The search that seemed over for Father Peregrine has actually just begun. Despite Bradbury's previous protestations, man in his space odyssey remains only an inchoate god.

But can such a pilgrimage ever really be over? The achievements that Bradbury depicts are either partial or ephemeral. Other stories which more subtly evince this apparently pervasive preoccupation with man's Daedelus-like aspirations, bear out the same principle. In **"The Fox and the Forest"** (1950), to take one example, William and Susan Travis—the assumed name may mean to suggest the travellers that they are—jump back in time from the imminently destructive world of 2155 A. D. to the festive peacefulness of Mexico in 1938 A. D. Their real patronym "Kristen" implies that they are in fact Christian pilgrims turning away from what they consider to be an evil society. But the policing Searchers foil their plan and the couple inevitably return to their obligations in the future. Perhaps Bradbury suggests the fantastic, irreparably romantic nature of such pilgrimages when he explains ["Ray Bradbury Keeping an Eye on Cloud IX," *Los Angeles Times*, March 15, 1970],

> 'I love my work and love the world with all its nonsense and hydrogen bombs. I'm not a blind optimist—I see the evil. I circumvent it when I can and warn people where I can warn them.'

> 'But I don't know how to cure morons, the only thing I can do is be honest—and take a trip on my imagination when it seizes me and says, "Run away."'

Probably unconsciously, then, Bradbury has provided a fictional testimony for the disillusioning truth in Oscar Wilde's apothegm, "Never to achieve—that is the true ideal." Not that man will ever stop looking. Carl Jung in his study *Flying Saucers: A Modern Myth of Things Seen in the Skies* (1959) concluded that the saucers in their mystically circular perfection temporarily became modern man's visionary surrogate for God. Bradbury has simply seen God in NASA's Saturns and Apollos. The apotheosis seems particularly despairing now that the Nixon administration is cutting away at their priority and intimidating them with questions of rationale. Yet Bradbury's tendency may be almost inevitable now that existentialism has seen through the institutionalized illusions of religion in the past and left a Weltanschauung that forces us to face a life of meaningless absurdities. By means of a genre that has been both utopian and dystopian, fantastic and realistic, Bradbury at least and perhaps science fiction itself are helping the pendulum swing again from that void to one beyond the gravity of the brutal truth.

Kent Forrester (essay date 1976)

SOURCE: "The Dangers of Being Earnest: Ray Bradbury and the Martian Chronicles," in *The Journal of General Education*, Vol. XXVIII, No. 1, Spring, 1976, pp. 50-4.

[*In the following essay, Forrester cites a number of literary flaws in the stories collected in* The Martian Chronicles, *chief among which is Bradbury's tendency to lecture the reader at the expense of his narrative. Even so, the critic lauds Bradbury's more imaginative prose, asserting that it is "superior to any other prose in science fiction."*]

I read my first Ray Bradbury story when I was about ten, and it was love at first sight: prose as rich as the cream filling of the Twinkies I loved, creatures bizarre enough to please a ten year old palate, machinery and rockets abundant enough to satisfy a boy living in those pre-Romantic 1950s.

I drifted away from science fiction and Bradbury about fifteen years ago. But I never forgot Bradbury's stories. I remembered the blue triangle baby in **"Tomorrow's Child,"** the writhing pictures on the skin of the Illustrated Man, the Martian's crystal homes in *The Martian Chronicles*. When my interest in science fiction was reawakened about three years ago, I especially relished the thought of rereading Bradbury's stories, whose images had stuck in my memory for over a decade. However, when I reread Bradbury, I found disquieting elements that I hadn't noticed when I was younger. There was, for instance, a shrill devotion to ideas at the expense of his narratives.

Few people love their ideas as much as Ray Bradbury loves his. He overstates them in newspaper interviews, he forces them into the mouths of his heroes, who then try to harangue us into right reason, and he sometimes stops his narration to lecture us. I'm reminded of Wells, who eventually became more fond of his role as lecturer-moralist than of his role as a storyteller.

Bradbury once estimated that he had turned out almost three million words of fiction before he made his first sale [*Ray Bradbury, All Our Yesterdays,* 1969]. Those three million words taught Bradbury how to handle prose rhythms and lush description, but they didn't teach him cold-blooded revision.

Never has an author asked so much of his readers. Bradbury's nostalgia for a golden age, his hatred of "glitter-eyed psychiatrists, clever sociologists, resentful educationalists, antiseptic parents," and his anti-materialistic biases occasionally seduce him into artistic lapses [*"The Exiles,"* in *The Illustrated Man,* 1952]. Once an advocate of Technocracy, Bradbury has turned on his previous love with a passion.

In **"—And the Moon Be Still as Bright,"** for instance, the sensitive Jeff Spender likes wood instead of chemical fires, castigates Americans because they love Chicago plumbing too much, quotes Byron, and knows that "living is life." All well and good. However, when Spender shoots to death six fellow crew members because they are materialistic philistines, Bradbury continues to justify Spender's behavior. "How would you feel," Spender asks rhetorically, "if a Martian vomited stale liquor on the White House floor?"

Moreover, Captain Wilder, Bradbury's spokesman for the *via media,* sides with the mass murderer. Wilder secretly hopes that Spender will escape, he almost shoots Parkhill in the back when that entrepreneur charges after Spender, and he demands of his men that Spender be shot "cleanly." Finally, Wilder gives Spender a hero's funeral when he buries him in a Martian sarcophagus. The last we see of Spender is his "peaceful face."

It would seem that readers who are not blinded by Spender's noble sentiments would be fed up with him by the time he kills six people. Bradbury asks too much of us when he comes just short of justifying Spender's behavior on the grounds that he doesn't want to see the golden houses and tile floors desecrated. That is, Bradbury put sullied flesh on an idea and then asked us to admire the flesh along with the idea.

Bradbury's ideas are so violently drawn in *The Martian Chronicles* that the stories are weakened unless we are as enthusiastic about his ideas as he is. Bradbury can't resist, for instance, forcing his characters onto soap boxes, where they spend their time lecturing us on Rousseauian primitivism, the pleasures of the imagination, and the crassness of American society. At least a fourth of **"—And the Moon Be Still as Bright"** consists of Spender's lectures on ecology and aesthetics; and Stendahl in **"Usher II"**

and Dad in the **"Million Year Picnic"** are as preachy as Spender. Bradbury lacks either the inclination or the skill to weave these sentiments into his plot.

In an article in *Extrapolation,* Robert Reilly, infatuated by Bradbury's "neo-humanism," suggests that the Martians of *The Martian Chronicles* are well-defined and consistent when he calls them a "courteous," "reserved" and gentle race ["The Artistry of Ray Bradbury," *Extrapolation,* Vol. 13, December, 1971]. And it is true that in the fourth expedition Wilder calls the Martians a "graceful, beautiful, and philosophical people." Later, in the story **"The Off Season,"** we see the Martians behaving as kindly as Wilder tells us they behave when, after Sam Parkhill murders a few of them, they turn their cheeks and give Sam Parkhill their land.

Yet these same Martians, under the exigencies of Bradbury's plots, are quite a different people. When Bradbury needs the first Earth expedition murdered, he uses a Martian, one of those "gentle" creatures, as the murderer (**"Ylla"**). Ylla's husband, who lives in that crystal-pillared house built by a race that knows how to blend "religion, art, and science," becomes a cold-blooded killer when his jealousy is aroused. The second expedition is wiped out by a Martian psychologist who thinks they are Martian madmen, and we find out that there are an incredible number of Martian madmen among a population that is supposed to be so reasonable and philosophical. Finally, the seventeen members of the third expedition are murdered in their beds by these Martians that we are told by Bradbury to admire. Under the influence of Bradbury's plots, the Martians kill. Under the influence of his "neo-humanism," we are *told* that the Martians are cleaner and nicer than we are.

Bradbury also occasionally becomes so enamored with his prose that he forgets to ask himself if his descriptions fit his stories. For instance, the conclusion to **"The Third Expedition"** contains the kind of evocative tableau—with its brass band, coffins, and mourners—that Bradbury is so fond of. However, it is so implausible that it should jar any reader who is not completely caught up in Bradbury's prose. Never have the Martians been pictured as whimsical humorists, yet here they are participating in an American burial after they have killed the American visitors. The "mayor" makes a speech, the "mourners" cry, and the brass band plays "Columbia, the Gem of the Ocean." What are we to think of all this? Until this time, the Martians have shown no sentimental attachment to humans, no traces of whimsy, and no interest in psycho-drama. Yet there they are, still dressed in Earth clothes and Earth faces, forced to act in an implausible scene because the author loves to describe a nostalgic burial and is unable to stop his pen. As an isolated tableau, the burial scene is a masterpiece. It has the power of pleasing our taste for the unexpected and sensational. But the scene doesn't satisfy our need for a well-made plot and internal consistency. That Bradbury is writing fantasy science fiction is no excuse. The world that a fantasy author creates—like the worlds created by medieval theologians—must be internally consistent.

But enough of this. Despite their literary "flaws," I remembered Bradbury's stories, when I had forgotten most of the others. So I reexamined his stories in a search for what made his stories memorable. My first discovery was that I—perhaps we—can forgive an author his shortcomings if he can make up for them in other ways. Daniel Defoe didn't know when to stop a story, but we easily forgive him. We remember Crusoe's island adventures and forget his boring overland trip back to England from Portugal. We can forgive Alexander Pope his personal attacks on his various enemies because of his sustained inventiveness and cleverness. So despite his shortcomings, Bradbury's strengths make his books memorable.

Although his prose is occasionally overcooked it is still, in small chunks, superior to any other prose in science fiction. It is prose, like good poetry, that sticks in the mind. Let me point to a single example out of *The Martian Chronicles*. It's hard to forget those dormant robots waiting in the cellar in **"Usher II,"** because Bradbury's prose rhythms are appropriate to the action and because he is master of the small, sensuous detail that captures our imagination:

> Full grown without memory, the robots waited. In green silks the color of forest pools, in silks the color of frog and fern, they waited. In yellow hair the color of sun and sand, the robots waited. Oiled, with tube bones cut from bronze and sunk in gelatin, the robots lay. In coffins for the not dead and not alive, in planked boxes, the Metronomes waited to be set in motion. There was a smell of lubrication and lathed brass. . . . And now there was a vast screaming of yanked nails. Now there was a lifting of lids.

Bradbury has more to offer than prose: his imagination is inventive and vivid. I don't agree with Damon Knight that Bradbury has a "mediocre" imagination [*In Search of Wonder*, 1967]. Bradbury does not work like Hal Clement, whose controlled visions construct coherent extraterrestrial environments and then people them with believable and appropriate creatures. Bradbury's mind creates the outlandish (stealing a cup of gold from the sun, blue triangle babies, etc.); and when his prose is working, he carries it off. His visions of the Martians and their environment in *The Martian Chronicles* may be contradictory, but they are aesthetically pleasing and richly imaginative. Crystal homes, blue-sailed sandships, coffined robots, singing books, rockets that turn the winter landscape into summer—these details go a long way toward compensating for other artistic lapses.

Let me list a few images out of Bradbury's stories and see if you don't remember the same ones I remember: the scurrying metal mice in **"There Will Come Soft Rains"** who are used as miniature vacuum cleaners, and who continue to work feverishly as their house burns down; the mechanical coffin in **"Wake for the Living"** that embalms the brother and then digs his grave and covers it behind him; the children's nursery in **"The Veldt,"** with electronic walls that fill the room with the smells and sounds of African lions; the crushed butterfly on the boots of the time traveler in **"A Sound of Thunder."** And always the running children in tennis shoes, the rockets belching flames, the old-fashioned burials.

But most of all, Bradbury deserves our praise for those stories that deal with, in Damon Knight's words, our "fundamental prerational fears and longings and desires" [*In Search of Wonder*]. Bradbury knows, as all good writers know, how to touch that residue of ancient images that we carry around with us: lost Edens (which come in the form of small American towns of the 1920s), new green beginnings for the pioneers on Mars, nostalgia for universally lost childhoods, the fear of the wicked that this way comes. Bradbury—thank goodness—never tires of touching these strings.

Do these strengths of Bradbury overcome his weaknesses? I think they do. In that one thing that is, to my mind, important to most science fiction—an artist's ability to engage us in that world of oiled robots, strange beings, time paradoxes, other worlds, and bizarre futures—Bradbury is *very* good. And that's why I remembered Ray Bradbury.

Willis E. McNelly (essay date 1976)

SOURCE: "Two Views: Ray Bradbury—Past, Present, and Future," in *Voices for the Future: Essays on Major Science Fiction Writers*, Bowling Green University Popular Press, 1976, pp. 167-75.

[*In the following excerpt, McNelly purports that Bradbury's short fiction is thematically tied to mainstream American tradition.*]

Ray Bradbury, hailed as a stylist and a visionary by critics such as Gilbert Highet and authors such as Aldous Huxley and Christopher Isherwood, remained for years the darling, almost the house pet, of a literary establishment otherwise unwilling to admit any quality in the technological and scientific projections known as science fiction. Within the field of science fiction itself, Bradbury's star zoomed like the *Leviathan '99* comet he later celebrated in a significant but ill-fated dramatic adaptation of the *Moby-Dick* myth. Fans pointed to Bradbury with ill-concealed pride, as if to prove that, at least with him, science fiction had come of age and deserved major critical attention.

Certainly America's best-known science fiction writer, Bradbury has been anthologized in over 300 different collections. His own individual works number in the dozens and have been translated into even more languages. After some ten million words—his own estimate—he feels almost physically ill unless he can spend four hours a day at the typewriter. His aim is to work successfully in virtually every written medium before he changes his last typewriter ribbon. His plays have been successfully produced both in Los Angeles and off Broadway. He is currently researching the history of Halloween for a TV special, and he still collects his share of rejection slips for short stories, novellas, or movie scripts, with a larger share of acceptances.

Bradbury's major themes transform the past, present, and future into a constantly shifting kaleidoscope whose brilliance shades into pastels or transforms language into coruscant vibrations through his verbal magic. Contemporary literature to reflect its age, he believes, must depict man existing in an increasingly technological era, and the ability to fantasize thus becomes the ability to survive. He himself is a living evocation of his own theory—a sport, a throwback to an earlier age when life was simpler. Resident of a city, Los Angeles, where the automobile is god and the freeway its prophet, Bradbury steadfastly refuses to drive a car. He has no simplistic anti-machine phobia; rather his reliance on taxicabs or buses springs from the hegira his family made from Waukegan, Illinois, to Los Angeles during the depths of the Depression when he was 14. The roads, he recalls, were strewn with the hulks of broken cars. Since that time his continual concern has been the life of man, not the death of machines. Man must be the master of the machine, not its slave or robot. Bradbury's art, in other words, like that of W. B. Yeats, whom he greatly admires, is deeply dependent upon life. Like Yeats in "The Circus Animals' Desertion." Bradbury must ". . . lie down where all the ladders start, / in the foul rag-and-bone shop of the heart."

If Bradbury's ladders lead to Mars, whose chronicler he has become, or to the apocalyptic future of *Fahrenheit 451*, the change is simply one of direction, not of intensity. He is a visionary who writes not of the impediments of science, but of its effects upon man. *Fahrenheit 451*, after all, is not a novel about the technology of the future, and is only secondarily concerned with censorship or book-burning. In actuality it is the story of Bradbury, disguised as Montag, and his lifelong love affair with books. If the love of a man and a woman is worth notarizing in conventional fiction, so also is the love of a man and an idea. A man may have a wife or a mistress or two in his lifetime, and the situation may become the valuable seedstuff of literature. However, that same man may in the same lifetime have an endless series of affairs with books, and the offspring can become great literature. For that reason, Bradbury feels that Truffaut was quite successful in translating the spirit of the novel, and the viewer who expects futuristic hardware or science fiction gimmickry will be disappointed in the motion picture. "Look at it through the eyes of the French impressionists," Bradbury suggests. "See the poetic romantic vision of Pissaro, Monet, Renoir, Seurat, or Manet that Truffaut evokes in the film, and then remember that this method was his metaphor to capture the metaphor in my novel."

"Metaphor" is an important word to Bradbury. He uses it generically to describe a method of comprehending one reality and then expressing that same reality so that the reader will see it with the intensity of the writer. His use of the term, in fact, strongly resembles T. S. Eliot's view of the objective correlative. Bradbury's metaphor in *Fahrenheit 451* is the burning of books; in *The Illustrated Man,* a moving tattoo; and pervading all of his work, the

metaphor becomes a generalized nostalgia that can best be described as a nostalgia for the future.

Another overwhelming metaphor in his writing is one derived from Jules Verne and Herman Melville—the cylindrical shape of the submarine, the whale, or the space ship. It becomes a mandala, a graphic symbol of Bradbury's view of the universe, a space-phallus. Bradbury achieved his first "mainstream" fame with his adaptation of Melville's novel for the screen, after Verne had aroused his interest in science fiction. *Moby-Dick* may forever remain uncapturable in another medium, but Bradbury's screenplay was generally accepted as being the best thing about an otherwise ordinary motion picture. John Huston's vision was perhaps more confining than Ray Bradbury's.

Bradbury's own view of his writing shows a critical self-awareness. He describes himself essentially as a short story writer, not a novelist, whose stories seize him, shake him, and emerge after a two or three hour tussle.

—*Willis E. McNelly*

Essentially a romantic, Bradbury belongs to the great frontier tradition. He is an exemplar of the Turner thesis, and the blunt opposition between a tradition-bound Eastern establishment and Western vitality finds itself mirrored in his writing. The metaphors may change, but the conflict in Bradbury is ultimately between human vitality and the machine, between the expanding individual and the confining group, between the capacity for wonder and the stultification of conformity. These tensions are a continual source for him, whether the collection is named *The Golden Apples of the Sun, Dandelion Wine,* or *The Martian Chronicles.* Thus, to use his own terminology, nostalgia for either the past or future is a basic metaphor utilized to express these tensions. Science fiction is the vehicle.

Ironic detachment combined with emotional involvement— these are the recurring tones in Bradbury's work, and they find their expression in the metaphor of "wilderness." To Bradbury, America is a wilderness country and hers a wilderness people. There was first the wilderness of the sea, he maintains. Man conquered that when he discovered this country and is still conquering it today. Then came the wilderness of the land. He quotes, with obvious approval, Fitzgerald's evocation at the end of *The Great Gatsby:* ". . . the fresh, green breast of the new world . . . for a transitory enchanted moment man must have held his breath in the presence of this continent . . . face to face for the last time in history with something commensurate to his capacity for wonder."

For Bradbury the final, inexhaustible wilderness is the wilderness of space. In that wilderness, man will find himself, renew himself. There, in space, as atoms of God, mankind will live forever. Ultimately, then, the conquest of space becomes a religious quest. The religious theme in his writing is sounded directly only on occasion, in such stories as **"The Fire Balloons,"** where two priests try to decide if some blue fire-balls on Mars have souls, or **"The Man,"** where Christ leaves a far planet the day before an Earth rocket lands. Ultimately the religious theme is the end product of Bradbury's vision of man; the theme is implicit in man's nature.

Bradbury's own view of his writing shows a critical self-awareness. He describes himself essentially as a short story writer, not a novelist, whose stories seize him, shake him, and emerge after a two or three hour tussle. It is an emotional experience, not an intellectual one; the intellectualization comes later when he edits. To be sure, Bradbury does not lack the artistic vision for large conception or creation. The novel form is simply not his normal medium. Rather he aims to objectify or universalize the particular. He pivots upon an individual, a specific object, or particular act, and then shows it from a different perspective or a new viewpoint. The result can become a striking insight into the ordinary, sometimes an ironic comment on our limited vision.

An early short story, **"The Highway,"** illustrates this awareness of irony. A Mexican peasant wonders at the frantic, hurtling stream of traffic flowing north. He is told by an American who stops for water that the end of the world has come with the out-break of the atom war. Untouched in his demi-Eden, Hernando calls out to his burro as he plows the rain-fresh land below the green jungle, above the deep river. "What do they mean 'the world?'" he asks himself, and continues plowing.

Debate over whether or not Bradbury is, in the end, a science fiction writer, is fruitless when one considers this story or dozens like it. The only "science" in the story is the "atom war" somewhere far to the north, away from the ribbon of concrete. All other artifacts of man in the story—the automobile, a hubcap, a tire—provide successive ironies to the notion that while civilization may corrupt, it does not do so absolutely. A blownout tire may have brought death to the driver of a car, but it now provides Hernando with sandals; a shattered hubcap becomes a cooking pan. Hernando and his wife and child live in a prelapsarian world utilizing the gifts of the machine in primitive simplicity. These people recall the Noble Savage myth; they form a primary group possessing the idyllic oneness of true community. The strength of Hernando, then, is derived from the myth of the frontier; the quality and vigor of life derive from, indeed are dependent upon, the existence of the frontier.

Yet irony piles on irony: the highway—any highway—leads in two directions. The Americans in this fable form a seemingly endless flowing stream of men and vehicles. They ride northward toward cold destruction, leaving the tropical warmth of the new Eden behind them. Can we recreate the past, as Gatsby wondered. Perhaps, suggests Bradbury, if we re-incarnate the dreams of our youth and

reaffirm the social ethic of passionate involvement. And nowhere does he make this moral quite as clear as in *Fahrenheit 451.*

Originally cast as a short story, **"The Fireman,"** *Fahrenheit 451* underwent a number of transmutations before finding its final form. From the short story it became an unpublished novella, **"Fire, Fire, Burn Books!"** and was again transformed by twenty days of high speed writing into the novel. An examination of a photocopy of the original first draft of **"The Fireman,"** reveals how carefully Bradbury works. His certainty with words makes for extremely clean copy: three or four revisions on the first page; none on the second. He adds an adverb, "silently"; cuts an unnecessary sentence; sharpens the verb "spoke" to "whispered"; eliminates another sentence; anglicizes a noun. Nothing more. Yet the artistry is there, the clean-limbed expressive prose, the immediacy of the situation heightened by the terseness of the dialogue, the compounded adjectives, the brevity and condensation everywhere evident.

Inspection of his rewrite of the same page shows some further small but significant changes, changes that give Bradbury's prose its evocative poetic quality. Note the modifications in the following sentences: "Mr. Montag sat among the other Fire Men in the Fire House, and he heard the voice tell the time of morning, the hour, the day, the year, and he shivered." This becomes sharper, more intense: "Mr. Montag sat stiffly among the other Fire Men in the Fire House, heard the voice-clock mourn out the cold hour and the cold year, and shivered." The voice now "mourns," not "tells," and the appeal to the senses is clarified, the general made specific as "some night jet-planes . . . flying" becomes "five hundred jet-planes screamed." These changes may be minor, to be sure, but they indicate the method of the writer at work. Titles which Bradbury provided to successive drafts indicate something of the way his mind moves: **"The Fireman," "The Hearth and the Salamander," "The Son of Icarus," "Burning Bright," "Find Me in Fire," "Fire, Fire, Burn Books!"** These metamorphosed into *Fahrenheit 451,* as anguished a plea for the freedom to read as the mid-twentieth century has produced.

Yet even *Fahrenheit 451* illustrates his major themes: the freedom of the mind; the evocation of the past; the desire for Eden; the integrity of the individual; the allurements and traps of the future. At the end of the novel, Montag's mind has been purified, refined by fire, and phoenix-like, Montag—hence mankind—rises from the ashes of the destructive, self-destroying civilization. "'Never liked cities,' said the man who was Plato," as Bradbury hammers home his message at the end of the novel. "'Always felt that cities owned men, that was all, and used men to keep themselves going, to keep the machines oiled and dusted'" (**"The Fireman"**).

The leader of the book-memorizers at the end of the novel is significantly named Granger, a farmer, a shepherd guiding his flock of books along the road to a new future, a new Eden. "Our way is simpler," Granger says, "and better and the thing we wish to do is keep the knowledge intact and safe and not to anger or excite anyone, for then if we are destroyed the knowledge is most certainly dead. . . . So we wait quietly for the day when the machines are dented junk and then we hope to walk by and say, here we are, to those who survive this war, and we'll say Have you come to your senses now? Perhaps a few books will do you some good."

This vision of the future which Bradbury provides at the end of *Fahrenheit 451* shows his essentially optimistic character. In fact, Bradbury seized upon the hatreds abroad in 1953 when the book was written, and shows that hatred, war, desecration of the individual are all self-destructive. Bradbury's 1953 vision of hatred becomes extrapolated to a fire which consumes minds, spirits, men, ideas, books. Out of the ashes and rubble revealed by this projected vision. Bradbury reveals one final elegiac redemptive clash of past, present, and future:

> Montag looked at the mens' faces, old all of them, in the firelight, and certainly tired. Perhaps he was looking for a brightness, a resolve, a triumph over tomorrow that wasn't really there, perhaps he expected these men to be proud with the knowledge they carried, to glow with the wisdom as lanterns glow with the fire they contain. But all the light came from the campfire here, and these men seemed no different than any other man who has run a long run, searched a long search, seen precious things destroyed, seen old friends die, and now, very late in time, were gathered together to watch the machines die, or hope they might die, even while cherishing a last paradoxical love for those very machines which could spin out a material with happiness in the warp and terror in the woof, so interblended that a man might go insane trying to tell the design to himself and his place in it. They weren't at all certain that what they carried in their heads might make every future dawn brighter, they were sure of nothing save that the books were on file behind their solemn eyes and that if man put his mind to them properly something of dignity and happiness might be regained.

What has been Ray Bradbury's contribution to science fiction? The question might well be rephrased: What has been Ray Bradbury's contribution to mid-twentieth century American literature? Neither question is easy to answer without risking the dangers of over-generalization. From the viewpoint of science fiction, Bradbury has proved that quality writing is possible in that much-maligned genre. Bradbury is obviously a careful craftsman, an ardent wordsmith whose attention to the niceties of language and its poetic cadences would have marked him as significant even if he had never written a word about Mars.

His themes, however, place him squarely in the middle of the mainstream of American life and tradition. His eyes are set firmly on the horizon-Frontier where dream fathers mission and action mirrors illusion. And if Bradbury's eyes lift from the horizon to the stars, the act is merely an extension of the vision all Americans share. His voice is that of the poet raised against the mechanization of mankind. Perhaps, in the end, he can provide his own best summary:

The machines themselves are empty gloves. And the hand that fills them is always the hand of man. This hand can be good or evil. Today we stand on the rim of Space, and man, in his immense tidal motion is about to flow out toward far new worlds, but man must conquer the seed of his own self-destruction. Man is half-idealist, half-destroyer, and the real and terrible thing is that he can still destroy himself before reaching the stars. I see man's self-destructive half, the blind spider fiddling in the venomous dark, dreaming mushroom-cloud whispers, shaking a handful of atoms like a necklace of dark beads. We are now in the greatest age of history, capable of leaving our home planet behind us, of going off into space on a tremendous voyage of survival. Nothing must be allowed to stop this voyage, our last great wilderness trek.

> [William F. Nolan, "Bradbury: Prose Poet in an Age of Space," *F&SF*, May 1963]

A. James Stupple (essay date 1976)

SOURCE: "Two Views: The Past, the Future, and Ray Bradbury," in *Voices for the Future: Essays on Major Science Fiction Writers*, Bowling Green University Popular Press, 1976, pp. 175-84.

[*In the excerpt that follows, Stupple explores the relationship between the past and the future in Bradbury's short stories.*]

Anyone who has ever watched those classic "Flash Gordon" serials must have been puzzled by the incongruous meeting of the past and the future which runs through them. Planet Mongo is filled with marvelous technological advancements. Yet, at the same time, it is a world which is hopelessly feudal, filled with endless sword play and courtly intrigues. It is as if we travel deep within the future only to meet instead the remote and archaic past. This is not, however, a special effect peculiar to adolescent space operas. On the contrary, this overlapping of past and future is one of the most common features of science fiction. It is found, for example, in such highly acclaimed works as Frank Herbert's *Dune* and Ursula LeGuin's *The Left Hand of Darkness*, futuristic novels whose settings are decidedly "medieval." A similar effect is also created in such philosophical science fiction novels as Isaac Asimov's *Foundation* trilogy, Walter Miller's *A Canticle for Leibowitz*, and Anthony Burgess' *The Wanting Seed*. In each of these works a future setting allows the novelist an opportunity to engage in an historiographical analysis; in each the future provides the distance needed for a study of the patterns of the past. But of all the writers of science fiction who have dealt with this meeting of the past and the future, it is Ray Bradbury whose treatment has been the deepest and most sophisticated. What has made Bradbury's handling of this theme distinctive is that his attitudes and interpretations have changed as he came to discover the complexities and the ambiguities inherent in it.

The horror of "Mars Is Heaven":

My first experience with real horror came at the hands of Ray Bradbury—it was an adaptation of his story **"Mars Is Heaven!"** on *Dimension* X. This would have been broadcast around 1951, which would have made me four at the time. I asked to listen, and was denied permission by my mother. "It's on too late," she said, "and it would be much too upsetting for a little boy your age." . . .

I crept down to the door to listen anyway, and she was right: it was plenty upsetting.

Space travelers land on Mars—only it isn't Mars at all. It's good old Greentown, Illinois, and it's inhabited by all the voyagers' dead friends and relatives. Their mothers are here, their sweethearts, good old Clancey the patrolman, Miss Henreys from the second grade. On Mars, Lou Gehrig is still pounding them over the fences for the Yankees.

Mars is heaven, the space travelers decide. The locals take the crew of the spaceship into their homes, where they sleep the sleep of those perfectly at peace, full of hamburgers and hotdogs and Mom's apple pie. Only one member of the crew suspects the unspeakable obscenity, and he's right. Boy, is he right! And yet even he has awakened to the realization of this deadly illusion too late . . . because in the night, these well-loved faces begin to drip and run and change. Kind, wise eyes become black tar pits of murderous hate. The rosy apple cheeks of Grandma and Grandpa lengthen and turn yellow. Noses elongate into wrinkled trunks. Mouths become gaping maws. It is a night of creeping horror, a night of hopeless screams and belated terror, because Mars isn't heaven after all. Mars is a hell of hate and deception and murder.

I didn't sleep in my bed that night; that night I slept in the doorway, where the real and rational light of the bathroom bulb could shine on my face.

Stephen King, from "Radio and the Set of Reality," Stephen King's Danse Macabre, *1981.*

Bradbury began to concentrate upon this subject early in his career in **The Martian Chronicles** (1951). In a broad sense, the past in this work is represented by the Earth—a planet doomed by nuclear warfare, a "natural" outgrowth of man's history. To flee from this past. Earthmen begin to look to a future life on Mars, a place where the course of man's development has not been irrevocably determined. But getting a foothold on Mars was no easy matter, as the deaths of the members of the first two expeditions show. To Captain Black's Third Expedition, however, Mars seems anything but an alien, inhospitable planet, for as their rocket lands in April of the year 2000, the Earthmen see what looks exactly like an early twentieth century village. Around them they see the cupolas of old Victorian mansions, neat, whitewashed bungalows, elm trees, maples and chestnuts. Initially Black is skeptical. The future cannot so closely resemble the past. Sensing that something is wrong, he refuses to leave the ship. Finally one of his crewmen argues that the similarity between this Mar-

tian scene and those of his American boyhood may indicate that there is some order to the universe after all—that perhaps there is a supreme being who actually does guide and protect mankind.

Black agrees to investigate. Setting foot on Martian soil, the Captain enters a peaceful, delightful world. It is "a beautiful spring day" filled with the scent of blossoming flowers and the songs of birds. After the flux of space travel it must have appeared to have been a timeless, unchanging world—a static piece of the past. But Black is certain that this is Mars and persists in his attempt to find a rational explanation. His logical mind, however, makes it impossible for him to accept any facile solutions. Eventually, though, despite his intellectual rigor, the Captain begins to succumb to the charms of stasis:

> In spite of himself, Captain John Black felt a great peace come over him. It had been thirty years since he had been in a small town, and the buzzing of spring bees on the air lulled and quieted him, and the fresh look of things was a balm to his soul.

As soon as he begins to weaken, he learns, from a lemonade-sipping matron, that this is the year 1926 and that the village is Green Town, Illinois, Black's own home town. The Captain now *wants* to believe in what he sees and begins to delude himself by theorizing that an unknown early twentieth century expedition came to Mars and that the colonizers, desperately homesick, created such a successful image of an Earth-like reality that they had actually begun to believe that this illusion *was* reality. Ironically, this is precisely what is done by Black and his crew. And it kills them.

Since by this time the Earthmen had become completely vulnerable to the seductiveness of this world of security and stasis, they now unreservedly accept "Grandma Lustig's" claim that "'all we know is here we are, alive again, and no questions asked. A second chance'." At this point the action moves rapidly. The remainder of the crew abandons ship and joins in a "homecoming" celebration. At first Black is furious at this breach of discipline, but soon loses his last trace of skepticism when he meets Edward, his long-dead "brother." Quickly, he is taken back to his childhood home, "the old house on Oak Knoll Avenue," where he is greeted by an archetypal set of midwestern parents: "In the doorway, Mom, pink, plump, and bright. Behind her, pepper-gray, Dad, his pipe in his hand." Joyfully the Captain runs "like a child" to meet them. But later, in the apparent security of the pennant-draped bedroom of his youth, Black's doubts arise anew. He begins to realize that all of this could be an elaborate reconstruction, culled from his psyche by some sophisticated Martian telepathy, created for the sole purpose of isolating the sixteen members of the Third Expedition. Recognizing the truth too late, the Captain is killed by his Martian brother as he leaves his boyhood "home" to return to the safety of the rocket ship.

Bradbury's point here is clear: Black and his men met their deaths because of their inability to forget, or at least resist, the past. Thus, the story of this Third Expedition acts as a metaphor for the book as a whole. Again and again the Earthmen make the fatal mistake of trying to recreate an Earth-like past rather than accept the fact that this is Mars—a different, unique new land in which they must be ready to make personal adjustments. Hauling Oregon lumber through space, then, merely to provide houses for nostalgic colonists exceeds folly; it is only one manifestation of a psychosis which leads to the destruction not only of Earth, but, with the exception of a few families, of Mars as well.

As a genre, science fiction . . . must deal with the future and with technological progress. This is its lifeblood and what gives it its distinctiveness. In order to enter the future, however, if only in a theoretical, purely speculative sense, one is forced to come to grips with the past. Change and progress call for a rejection and a sloughing off. This places a great stress upon the science fiction writer, for perhaps more than any other literary genre, science fiction is dependent upon traditions—its own conventions of character, plot, setting, "special effects," even ideas. It is as stylized an art form as one can find today in America. It is therefore ironic that such a conventionalized genre should be called upon to be concerned with the unconventional—with the unpredictability of change and process. In other words, this stasis-change conflict, besides being a function of Bradbury's own history and personality, also seems to be built into the art form itself. What distinguishes Bradbury and gives his works their depth is that he seems to be aware that a denial of the past demands a denial of that part of the self which is the past. As an examination of *I Sing the Body Electric*, his latest collection of short stories, will show, he has not been able to come to any lasting conclusion. Instead, he has come to recognize the ambiguity, the complexity, and the irony within this theme.

Of the stories in *I Sing the Body Electric* which develop the idea that the past is destructive and must be rejected before peace can be achieved, the most intense and suggestive is **"Night Call Collect."** In this grim little tale, eighty-year-old Emil Barton has been living for the past sixty years as the last man on Mars when he is shocked to receive a telephone call from, of all people, himself. In the depths of his loneliness Barton had tinkered with the possibilities of creating a disembodied voice which might autonomously carry on conversations. Now suddenly in the year 2097, long after he had forgotten about this youthful diversion, his past, in the form of his younger self, contacts him. Finding himself in a world peopled only by the permutations of his own self, the "elder" Barton tries desperately to break out of this electronic solipsism. He fails, however, and begins to feel "the past drowning him." Soon his younger self even becomes bold enough to warn him, "'All right, old man, its war! Between us. Between me'." Bradbury has obviously added a new twist to his theme. Instead of the future denying the past, it is reversed. Now the past, in order to maintain its existence, must kill off the present. Young Barton now tells his "future" self that he "'had to eliminate you some way, so I could live, if you call a transcription

living'." As the old man dies, it is obvious that Bradbury has restated his belief that the past, if held on to too tightly, can destroy. But there is an added dimension here. At the end of the story it is no longer clear which is the past, which is the present, and which is the future. Is the past the transcribed voice of the "younger" twenty-four-year-old, or is it the *old* man living at a later date in time? Or perhaps they are but two manifestations of the same temporal reality, both the "present" and the "future" being forgotten?

Of the stories in this collection one contradicts **"Night Call Collect"** by developing the idea that the past can be a positive, creative force. **"I Sing the Body Electric"** opens with the death of a mother. But, as in so many of Bradbury's writings, there is a possibility of a second chance. "Fantocinni, Ltd." offers "the first humanoid-genre minicircuited, rechargeable AC-DC Mark V Electrical Grandmother." This time the second chance succeeds: the electric grandmother is the realization of a child's fantasy. She can gratify all desires and pay everyone in the family all the attention he or she wants. Appropriately, the grandmother arrives at the house packed in a "sarcophagus," as if it were a mummy. Despite the pun, the machine is indeed a mummy, as the narrator makes clear:

> We knew that all our days were stored in her, and that any time we felt we might want to know what we said at x hour at x second at x afternoon, we just named that x and with amiable promptitude . . . she should deliver forth x incident.

The sarcophagus in which this relic was packed was covered with "hieroglyphics of the future." At first this seems to be only another of those gratuitous "special effects" for which science fiction writers are so notorious. After further consideration, however, those arcane markings can be seen a symbol for the kind of ultra-sophisticated technology of which the grandmother is an example. Thus, both the future and the past are incarnated within the body of this machine. The relationship between the two is important, for what the story seems to suggest is that what the future (here seen as technological progress) will bring is the static, familiar, secure world of the past.

There is one other story in this collection which is important because in it is found one of Bradbury's most sophisticated expositions of the subtle complexities of this theme. **"Downwind from Gettysburg"** is, once again, a tale about a second chance. Using the well-known Disneyland machine as his model, Bradbury's story concerns a mechanical reproduction of Abraham Lincoln. In itself, this Lincoln-robot is a good thing. The past has been successfully captured and the beloved President lives again, if only in facsimile. Within this limited framework, then, the "past" is a positive force. But there are complications, for just as Lincoln gets a second chance, so does his murderer. Just as John Wilkes Booth assassinated a Lincoln, so does Norman Llewellyn Booth. Thus, as Bradbury had discovered through his years of working with this theme, the past is not one-dimensional. It is at once creative and destructive. It can give comfort, and it can unsettle and threaten. Clearly, then, this story is an important one within Bradbury's canon, for it is just this set of realizations which he had been steadily coming to during two decades of writing.

Wayne L. Johnson (essay date 1978)

SOURCE: "The Invasion Stories of Ray Bradbury," in *Critical Encounters,* Frederick Ungar Publishing Company, 1978, pp. 23-40.

[*In this excerpt, Johnson discusses the principal themes of Bradbury's invasion stories, noting that they fall into one of two categories: those involving the destruction of Earthlings by Martian forces and those concerning the destruction of Martians by alien Earth creatures.*]

Seven-year-old Mink bursts into the house and begins snatching up kitchen utensils and apparently random bits of junk to be hauled outside for use in some mysterious game. "What's the name of the game?" inquires her mother. "Invasion!" the girl replies. Mink's mother goes on about her housework unaware that her daughter is telling the literal truth, and that what appears to be an innocent children's game is actually the prelude to an invasion of Earth by creatures from another world—Ray Bradbury style.

The theme of invasion is one of the oldest in science fiction. The early idea that other planets might be inhabited quite naturally suggested the possibility of eventual contact between our world and another. If the theory of evolution were correct, then it was conceivable that life forms on other planets had begun evolving thousands, even millions of years before those on Earth. Intelligent beings on Mars, for instance, might already be technologically advanced enough to visit Earth. Should they decide to do so, wouldn't their very advancement prove a threat to us?

H. G. Wells's book *The War of the Worlds* (1898) answered the question with a very dramatic yes. Wells's Martians—cold, emotionless, octopuslike horrors—fled their own dying planet and sought to conquer Earth, exterminating most of the human race in the process. The elements of the story were classic, and formed the basis for countless Earth vs. Alien tales. Science fiction pulp magazines entered a phase of greatly increased popularity during the first half of the twentieth century. The two World Wars, with their immense firepower and destructiveness, created an atmosphere quite sympathetic to stories of interplanetary invasion and warfare. In America, Orson Welles's 1938 documentary-style radio version of *The War of the Worlds* was so realistic it caused a panic, and brought the idea of interplanetary invasion to general public consciousness.

Because of the dramatic possibilities of the subject, invasion became a popular theme in science fiction film and television productions. For instance, when Bradbury's short story **"The Fog Horn"** was made into a film, it was dras-

tically altered to include an invasion motif. Thus Bradbury's rather touching story of a lonely ocean-dwelling dinosaur who mistakes a lighthouse foghorn for the cry of a long-lost mate became *The Beast from 20,000 Fathoms,* in which a typical Hollywood monster charges ashore and demolishes large sections of New York City.

Bradbury has written a number of real invasion stories, of course, and these fall into two main groups: those that involve the invasion of Earth by aliens, and those that involve the invasion of Mars by Earthmen. The story about Mink and her mother belongs in the first group. It's called **"Zero Hour,"** and comes from the collection of Bradbury's stories entitled *The Illustrated Man.* **"Zero Hour"** is essentially a suspense story. Mink's mother, Mrs. Morris, watches her daughter and the other young children in the neighborhood as they dart about playing their little game. As the day progresses, the game takes on some disturbing overtones. Mink and her friends appear to be talking to an unseen playmate in the rose bush, whom they address as Drill. When Mrs. Morris questions her daughter about this, the girl freely admits that Drill is an alien being from another dimension who is telepathically instructing the children. The aliens are teaching the children to build machines that will allow them to break through from their dimension into ours. The aliens know that no adult will take the children's game seriously until it is too late. This, of course, includes Mrs. Morris. Mink complains that some of the older boys have been teasing her and her friends: "They're so snooty, 'cause they're growing up. You'd think they'd know better. They were little only a coupla years ago. I hate them worst. We'll kill them *first.*" To this Mrs. Morris is mildly patronizing. Half jokingly she asks if parents are to be killed too. Without hesitation, Mink answers that they are: "Drill says you're dangerous. Know why? 'Cause you don't believe in Martians. They're going to let *us* run the world. Well, not just us, but kids over in the next block too. I might be queen."

Our realization that Mink means business comes early in the story. We wait to see how long it will take Mrs. Morris to catch on, but we know the mother is essentially a helpless figure. What Mink says about her and other adults is true. Even if Mrs. Morris could accept her daughter's story, we know she would not be able to convince other adults. In any case, the idea is just too fantastic. At five o'clock, the previously announced "zero hour," Mr. Morris arrives home from work. Suddenly there is a loud buzzing outside, followed by explosions. Mrs. Morris realizes the truth. She drags her astonished husband up into the attic and locks the door. Heavy footsteps mount the stairs, the lock on the attic door melts and the door swings open. A smiling Mink peers in, tall blue shadows visible behind her, and ends the story by saying "Peekaboo."

"Zero Hour" derives much of its impact from its quiet suburban setting. Mrs. Morris's life is calm, well-ordered, secure. There is considerable irony in the fact that it is not the child's imagination that dominates the scene, but rather Mrs. Morris's fantasy of her own secure suburban life. This fantasy is so strong that the mother weaves all of her daughter's increasingly threatening remarks into it. Mink is only playing a game as all children do—isn't that reassuring? Mink, on the other hand, is not imagining things at all. She sees the facts quite clearly and, at least as far as Drill allows her to, she sees through her mother's illusions.

Aliens take advantage of a quiet suburban setting again in **"Boys! Raise Giant Mushrooms in *Your* Cellar!"** from the collection *The Machineries of Joy.* This time the protagonist is one Hugh Fortnum. Fortnum looks out his window one bright Saturday morning and notices his next door neighbor, Mrs. Goodbody, spraying great clouds of insecticide in all directions. He asks her what the trouble is.

"What would you say," she asks, "if I told you I was the first line of defense concerning flying saucers?"

Fortnum humors her. "Fine . . . There'll be rockets between the worlds any year now."

"'There already *are!*' She pumped, aiming the spray under the hedge. 'There! Take that!'"

A few minutes later, a special delivery package arrives for Fortnum's son Tom. Inspired by an ad in *Popular Mechanics,* Tom had sent away for a box of "Sylvan Glade Jumbo-Giant Guaranteed Growth Raise-Them-in-Your-Cellar-for-Big-Profit Mushrooms." Almost immediately, Tom disappears down into the cellar to begin raising his crop. In a plot essentially the same as **"Zero Hour,"** it is Hugh Fortnum's fate to have an invasion plot unfold before his eyes while we wait to see if he will put the pieces of the puzzle together in time. The development of the story is more diffuse than in **"Zero Hour,"** because, for one thing, Fortnum is not alone in uncovering the invasion. There is Mrs. Goodbody—though she does not seem aware of events outside her own garden—and there is Roger Willis. Willis flags down Fortnum later in the morning when Fortnum is driving to the store. Once in the car, Willis immediately begins complaining of an unexplainable feeling he has that "something's wrong with the world." Willis has no hard evidence to pin his anxiety on: "Maybe there's something wrong with the way the wind blows these weeds there in the lot. Maybe it's the sun up on those telephone wires or the cicadas singing in the elm trees. If only we could stop, look, listen, a few days, a few nights, and compare notes."

Fortnum asks what they should be looking for, and Willis replies, "You'll know. You've got to know. Or we're done for, all of us."

By evening, Fortnum has guessed that the Earth is being invaded and that the mushrooms are somehow involved. When he tells this to his wife, she laughs. How, she asks, could mushrooms without even arms or legs take over the world? Fortnum has no answer. After his wife has gone upstairs to bed, Fortnum goes to the refrigerator for a snack: There, on a shelf in the refrigerator, is a bowl of freshly cut mushrooms. At last comes the crucial realization: The mushrooms infiltrate the human body through the stomach; once he has eaten a mushroom, a human being *becomes* an alien.

Fortnum hears his son working down in the cellar. He calls out to the boy and asks if by any chance he has eaten any of the mushrooms. In a cold, faint voice, Tom replies that he has. Tom then asks his father to come down into the cellar to view the crop. Fortnum knows that by now millions of boys have raised billions of mushrooms around the world. As he stands at the top of the cellar stairs, Fortnum struggles with the incredibility of what he knows to be true: "He looked back at the stair leading up to his wife. I suppose, he thought, I should go say goodbye to Cynthia. But why should I think that! Why, in God's name, should I think that at all? No reason, *is* there?" Fortnum then steps down into the darkened cellar, closing the door behind him.

Since **"Zero Hour"** and **"Mushrooms"** are both primarily suspense stories, they share a number of structural traits common to such stories. For instance, the secret of the invasion is revealed to the reader almost at once. Real-life invasions usually depend heavily upon the element of surprise—such as in the attack on Pearl Harbor or in the invasion of Normandy. But in a story it is difficult to sustain reader interest if the main point is concealed until the very end. By revealing the invaders' intentions at the beginning of the story, Bradbury keeps us in constant suspense, wondering if and when the protagonists will catch on. In both stories, the method of invasion is rather improbable. This is necessary because the main character must be teasingly slow in putting the pieces of the puzzle together—but without coming off as an idiot. Because the invaders' plans are quite far-fetched, we can understand it when the main characters rationalize away the threat on the basis of its incredibility and their own need to live in a safe world where such things do not happen.

Both **"Zero Hour"** and **"Mushrooms"** focus on a small area. Though the invasions are on a world-wide scale, we see little of what is happening outside the neighborhood of the main characters. An even tighter focus is maintained in the story **"Fever Dream"** from *A Medicine for Melancholy.* Here again an invasion of Earth by mysterious creatures is taking place. But this time only one person knows, and there is no way he can tell anyone else about it, for the invasion is taking place within his own body.

Thirteen-year-old Charles has been put to bed with what seems to be a bad cold. From the outside, it seems like nothing more. But Charles has begun to experience strange symptoms, which he tries to communicate to his doctor: "My *hand,* it doesn't *belong* to me any more. This morning it *changed* into something else. I want you to change it back. Doctor, Doctor!" Charles's hand shows no external signs of change, and the doctor treats the matter lightly—"You just had a little fever dream." He gives Charles a pill and leaves.

At four o'clock his other hand changed. It seemed almost to become a fever. It pulsed and shifted, cell by cell. It beat like a warm heart. The fingernails turned blue and then red. It took about an hour for it to change and when it was finished, it looked just like any ordinary hand. But it was not ordinary. It no longer was him any more.

Cut off from his disbelieving parents and the doctor, Charles tries to understand what is happening to him. He recalls how, in a book he once read, ancient trees became petrified as their wood cells were replaced by minerals. On the outside they still looked like trees, but in reality they had changed to stone.

"What would happen," Charles later asks the doctor, if "a lot of microbes got together and wanted to make a bunch, and reproduced and made *more*. . . . And they decided to *take over* a person!" Indeed, Charles has hit upon the truth, but even as he speaks his hands—possessed of a life of their own—crawl up his chest to his throat and begin to strangle him.

Later, alone again, and with his hands strapped to his legs, Charles submits to the progressive take-over of his body. He is trapped more completely than if surrounded by a whole army of soldiers. In a macabre parody of the old wives' cure for insomnia—wherein one relaxes his hands, then feet, then arms, then legs, until theoretically the entire body is relaxed—Charles's body is taken away from him bit by bit. Finally only his head is left, and in silent panic he feels his ears go deaf, his eyes go blind, and "his brain fill with a boiling mercury."

This story is a reversal of the previous stories in which the invaders were, at least in the beginning, external to the victims and brought about an internal psychological struggle. In **"Fever Dream,"** the invasion begins within one person, and after it has conquered him, it moves out into the world at large. Bradbury only touches upon this second phase as Charles, suddenly appearing well again, goes to great lengths to get into physical contact with his parents, the doctor, even his pet parakeet. We realize that Charles is now one of the invaders—a carrier—and is eagerly involved in spreading the invasion. We know too that there will be no clash of armies or weaponry, just the futile struggle of one individual after another with his or her fever dream. . . .

It will be noted that children play important roles in the stories covered so far and in several of those to follow. Bradbury's use of children in general in his stories is too large a subject to treat here. But with respect to stories about invasion, Bradbury seems to agree with the popular concept that children live in a world of their own. Though they occupy the same space as adults do, their perception of it is, in many ways, radically different. They are, in a sense, aliens in their own world. In a story (not about invasion) from the book **Dark Carnival,** Bradbury has a rather paranoid school teacher say to his class, "Sometimes I actually believe that children are invaders from another dimension. . . . You are another race entirely, your motives, your beliefs, your disobediences. You are not human. You are—children." It may not be realistic to

view the place of children in the world as in any way sinister, but in Bradbury's hands, it can certainly result in a good story.

Another common element in Bradbury's invasion stories is the theme of metamorphosis. In many stories, such as **"Mushrooms"** or **"Fever Dream,"** the victim of the invasion undergoes—or prepares to undergo—a change in which he himself becomes one of the invaders. Bradbury frequently plays off of the ambiguity of the relationship between the invader and the invaded. At the moment an invasion succeeds, the invader becomes defender—capable himself of being invaded. In some of the stories about Mars, Earthmen who have begun living on Mars are faced with the fact that they are becoming, naturally enough, Martians. In some cases, the metamorphosis is literal, as in **"Fever Dream,"** but behind this is the metaphorical truth that an invasion may be less of a change of circumstance than a change of mind.

Invasions succeed as often by the demoralization of the invaded as by the simple strength of the invaders. The means by which an invader travels can provide him with an important psychological advantage. In **"Mushrooms"** and **"Fever Dream,"** Bradbury uses covert, Trojan Horse–type devices in which the invaders arrive in disguise and are not recognized for what they are until it is too late. In other stories, involving Mars and Earth, the invasion device is usually the commonplace but inevitable rocket ship. . . .

Sometimes the mere presence of an alien force is enough to destroy a people's will to resist. In **"Perhaps We Are Going Away,"** from *The Machineries of Joy,* an Indian boy, Ho-Awi, awakens to a day that is "evil for no reason." Ho-Awi belongs to a tribe named after a bird that lives near a mountain range named after the shadows of owls. Like the birds that are featured symbolically in their myths, the Indians of the tribe are sensitive to subtle disturbances in natural events.

In the hours before dawn, Ho-Awi joins his grandfather to hunt down the cause of the ominous feeling that pervades the air. They search for evidence that something is amiss in the natural world: "They scanned the prairies, but found only the winds which played there like tribal children all day." At length they approach the shore of the great eastern ocean and Ho-Awi's grandfather catches sight of something that confirms his worst fears. He tells Ho-Awi that a great change is coming, like a change of season. Though it is just the beginning of summer, birds that cannot be seen are flying south. "I feel them pass south in my blood. Summer goes. We may go with it." Ho-Awi asks if this course of things can be stopped or reversed, but the old man, who has already spotted the first encampment of white men on the beach, knows it cannot: "Not you or me or our people can stay this weather. It is a season changed, come to live on the land for all time."

Ho-Awi then sees the white men's camp himself, and realizes his grandfather is right. Not that there is much to see, just the glint of firelight on armor, a few faces, and out on the water "a great dark canoe with things like torn clouds hung on poles over it." But the metal and the ship are evidence of a vast technological gap. So intimidating is this gap that the two Indians who have seen the modest vanguard of the white man's invasion feel their entire world vanishing. There is no warning they can give that will prepare their tribe for what is to come. Physical resistance may eventually follow, but this will be to no avail, because the psychological battle has already been lost.

Hundreds of years later, in August of 1999, the planet Mars seems enveloped by a similarly disturbing atmosphere. In **"The Summer Night,"** from *The Martian Chronicles,* strange thoughts pop into Martian heads as if from nowhere. In a theater, a Martian woman begins to sing words that are utterly alien to her: "She walks in beauty, like the night / Of cloudless climes and starry skies . . ." All over the planet, similar things occur. Children sing strange rhymes, lovers awaken humming unknown melodies. Women awake from violent nightmares and declare, "Something terrible will happen in the morning." The Martians try to reassure one another before settling into an uneasy sleep. The story ends with a lone night watchman patrolling empty streets and humming a very strange song.

Earthmen, who of course are on the way, do not appear at all in this story. But their presence has already invaded the minds of the telepathic Martians. The outcome of the coming invasion by Earthmen is not stated, but the fact that the Martians are already speaking our language, and find themselves frightened and dismayed by that fact implies that their fate will not be a happy one. The technological level of the Martians is not clear. They seem somewhat like ancient Greeks, attending concerts in marble amphitheaters while children play in torchlit alleys. There is mention of boats "as delicate as bronze flowers" drifting through canals, and of meals cooked on tables "where lava bubbled silvery and hushed." So the Martians obviously have some technological advancement. But the Martians seem to have made a decision about machinery, consigning it to a modest role in their society as an art form, a toy, and an unobtrusive support for a pastoral life style. Though it does not appear in this story, the very existence of a rocket ship en route from Earth to Mars suggests a technology out of sympathy with, and potentially destructive to, the Martian way of life.

We have come to the second major group of Ray Bradbury's invasion stories, those involving the invasion of Mars by Earthmen. Of course, in the tradition of invaders throughout history, when we are doing the invading, it is called "colonization." By having the first Earthmen arrive on Mars in a succession of solitary rockets, Bradbury is able to stage the initial contact of Earthman and Martian several times. Since many of these stories were intended to be read singly, outside the context of a book, the character of the Martians changes to suit the requirements of a particular situation. Thus sometimes the Martians are jealous and brutal, other times they are helpless and complacent. There even seem to be several different intelli-

gent life forms on Mars, each of whom responds to the invaders from Earth in a different way.

The creature in **"The One Who Waits,"** from *The Machineries of Joy,* tells its own story: "I live in a well. I live like smoke in the well. Like vapor in a stone throat . . . I am mist and moonlight and memory . . . I wait in cool silence and there will be a day when I no longer wait." This strange creature has the power, like the giant mushrooms, or the microbes of **"Fever Dream"** to take possession of other life forms. But this time we experience the story from the creature's point of view.

A rocket lands not far from the well the Martian calls home. Several men approach the well and begin testing the water. The vapor creature allows itself to be inhaled by one of the men:

> Now I know who I am.
>
> My name is Stephen Leonard Jones and I am twenty-five years old and I have just come in a rocket from a planet called Earth and I am standing with my good friends Regent and Shaw by an old well on the planet Mars.
>
> I look down at my golden fingers, tan and strong. I look at my long legs and at my silver uniform and at my friends.
>
> "What's wrong, Jones?" they say.
>
> "Nothing," I say, looking at them. "Nothing at all."

The tables have been turned; the invader has been invaded. One by one, the creature takes over the bodies and minds of the crewmen from the spaceship. It tries each one out as we might try on a new glove. It enjoys the new sensations the men provide it with of touch, taste, smell. It even has one of the crewmen it is possessing shoot himself so that it can temporarily experience death. Like the boy Charles in **"Fever Dream,"** some of the men try to resist the creature:

> I hear . . . a voice calling deep within me, tiny and afraid. And the voice cries, *Let me go, let me go,* and there is a feeling as if something is trying to get free, a pounding of labyrinthine doors, a rushing down dark corridors and up passages, echoing and screaming.

When it finally tires of its game, the creature kills the remaining crewmen by possessing all of them at once and forcing them to throw themselves into the well. The creature then resumes its post, and quietly waits for the centuries to pass.

One reason the first Earthmen are not very successful invaders is that they make no secret about their coming. There is no secret business in Martian cellars, no exploitation of Martian children. The Earthmen swoop down in noisy rocket ships in broad daylight. To make matters worse, the Martians of *The Martian Chronicles* are telepathic, so they can read the Earthmen's minds before a rocket is even sighted. Thus the Martians have plenty of time to prepare a reception. When the first rocket lands in *Chronicles,* the crew is simply shot to death by a jealous Martian who fears his wife may fall in love with an Earthman. Another expedition lands on what appears to be the outskirts of a small American town. The crew is welcomed by their own mothers, fathers, relatives, and friends—many long thought to be dead. The Martians have, of course, recreated the town and its inhabitants by reading the crewmen's minds. The crew gradually becomes separated as each member is lured off to what he believes to be his old home. Then, one by one, they are killed.

Actual warfare never does break out between men and Martians. By the time Earthmen arrive in force, most of the Martians have succumbed to diseases from Earth against which they had no immunity. The few Martians remaining abandon their cities and seek refuge in the mountains. The invasion of Mars now goes into full swing. More and more rockets arrive. Lumber and supplies are shipped in, towns are built, and roads are laid connecting them. Benjamin Driscoll, a futuristic Johnny Appleseed, stalks about the planet planting Earth trees. The plains, mountains, and canals of Mars are given new names in honor of rocket pilots, explorers, and remembered places on Earth. The first stage of the invasion is successful: A new population has settled in, and the old population has been driven out. Once the physical invasion has been completed, the more subtle invasion of culture takes place. The Earthmen, like pioneers before them, carry their art, religion, and customs with them. One of the first things an invader does once he has settled on foreign soil is to make his new environment as much like his former home as possible.

In **"The Off Season,"** from *The Martian Chronicles,* the new culture confronts the old. Sam Parkhill opens up a hot dog stand—complete with neon lights and juke box—next to a road he expects will soon be heavily travelled. Parkhill is the personification of the Ugly Earthman: loud, crude, out for the fast buck. One evening a Martian calls on Parkhill. The Martian—a fragile creature, seemingly less substantial than the glass mask and silken robes it wears—has come on a peaceful mission. But the Earthman misunderstands, believing the Martian is attempting to lay claim to the land the hot dog stand occupies. With the arrogance of the conqueror, Parkhill presents the Martian with a few facts of life:

> Look here . . . I'm from New York City. Where I come from there's ten million others just like me. You Martians are a couple dozen left, got no cities, you wander around in the hills, no leaders, no laws, and now you come tell me about this land. Well, the old got to give way to the new. That's the law of give and take. I got a gun here . . .

Before Earthmen completely settle on Mars, nuclear war breaks out on Earth. Most of the Earth people on Mars decide to return to the home planet in its time of need. In a very short time, the Earth settlements on Mars are crum-

bling ghost towns. Bradbury devotes a number of stories to the fate of the few Earthmen left behind on Mars, or the even smaller number who arrive fleeing the war on Earth. Most interesting are those in which the Earthmen undergo the inevitable metamorphosis and become Martians. The last story in *The Martian Chronicles,* **"The Million Year Picnic,"** treats this theme in a matter-of-fact way. The Thomas family—mother, father, and three sons—learn that the Earth has been all but completely destroyed. They symbolically burn a map of the Earth and, gazing at their reflections in a canal, accept their new identities as Martians.

A more poetic treatment of the metamorphosis theme is found in **"Dark They Were, and Golden Eyed,"** from *A Medicine for Melancholy.* Harry and Cora Bittering and their children Dan, Laura, and David arrive with a number of other families to set up a town on Mars. Harry immediately senses something strange about the atmosphere on Mars. "He felt submerged in a chemical that could dissolve his intellect and burn away his past." Harry expresses his misgivings to his wife: "I feel like a salt crystal in a mountain stream, being washed away. We don't belong here."

The Bitterlings and their neighbors build cottages and plant gardens. Each day the rocket from Earth brings the newspaper. Harry reassures himself that all is well: "Why in ten years there'll be a million Earthmen on Mars. Big cities, everything! They said we'd fail. Said the Martians would resent our invasion. But did we find any Martians? Not a living soul! Oh, we found their empty cities, but no one in them. Right?" News of the war on Earth reaches them, and with it the realization that there will be no more rockets for a very long time—that they are in fact trapped on Mars.

Changes slowly begin to occur. The blossoms shaken down from Bitterling's peach tree are not peach blossoms. The vegetables from the garden begin to taste subtly different. When Harry visits his friend Sam he begins to notice other things.

> "Sam," Bittering said. "Your eyes—"
>
> "What about them, Harry?"
>
> "Didn't they used to be grey?"
>
> "Well now, I don't remember."
>
> "They were, weren't they?"
>
> "Why do you ask, Harry?"
>
> "Because now they're kind of yellow-colored."
>
> "Is that so, Harry?" Sam said, casually.

Harry is experiencing a phenomenon common to invaders, that of assimilation. Invasion is not merely an intrusion, unless primarily a military operation. When one culture moves in on another, some sort of mixture will probably occur. All cultures need reinforcement to remain alive. When one population invades another and is then cut off from home, the influence of the host culture strengthens. Harry Bitterling is not the first colonial to watch his friends "go native"—but the effect rarely involves a complete transformation into the native species. But this is Mars, and Ray Bradbury's Mars at that. This is a place created by, and subject to, the laws of imagination.

Bitterling's family and friends grow taller, their eyes grow more and more golden. Though they've never been taught it, they begin to use Martian words in their conversations. Harry's son Dan declares he is changing his name to Linnl. Laura and David soon become Ttil and Werr. The transformation takes over all of them like some sweet disease. There is no force, no coercion. As they become Martians, they become more relaxed, more at peace with themselves.

Eventually the former Earthmen abandon their town and move up into the Martian hills. The former Bitterlings occupy a villa in the Pillan Mountains (formerly the Rockefeller Range, formerly the Pillan Mountains). Months later, Bitterling and his wife gaze down at the abandoned Earth settlement in the valley. "Such odd, ridiculous houses the Earth people built," says Harry. His wife answers, "They didn't know any better . . . Such ugly people. I'm glad they've gone."

So the invasion of Mars is over. Bradbury carries his theme of metamorphosis to its ultimate extreme. As in **"Fever Dream,"** and **"Boys! Raise Giant Mushrooms . . ."** the invader and his victim have become one in the same. Bradbury portrays various life forms—microbe, plant, or human being—moving out from their home worlds to fulfill the need to perpetuate themselves. But he suggests that the price of success might be an ultimate loss of identity. To survive on an alien world, the invader must unite with his victim. Both learn that in order for life to go on, any particular species is expendable, and that the invader's act of aggression may become an act of submission to the higher purpose of life itself.

Bradbury has written only one story in which Martians attempt a military invasion of Earth *à la* H. G. Wells. But the result of the invasion in **"The Concrete Mixer"** (from the collection *The Illustrated Man*) is quite a bit different from any imagined by Wells. Of course, Wells never saw American pop culture in full flower. Ettil is a peace-loving Martian who only wishes to sit home and read. His fellow Martians are getting ready to invade Earth. Ettil's father-in-law is outraged at Ettil's pacifism: "Who ever heard of a Martian *not* invading? Who!"

Ettil is thrown into prison for draft-dodging. There he is confronted with evidence that he has been reading contraband science fiction magazines from Earth. Ettil readily admits that his sole literary diet has been such fare as *Wonder Stories, Scientific Tales,* and *Fantastic Stories.* He insists that the magazines furnish proof that a Martian invasion of Earth will fail. "The Earthmen know they can't fail. It is in them like blood beating in their veins . . .

Their youth of reading just such fiction as this has given them a faith we cannot equal." Ettil is willing to be thrown into a fire along with his beloved magazines rather than join the army, but seeing the disappointment in the eyes of his son, he finally relents.

The Martians are prepared for the worst weapons the Earth might throw at them, but they are quite taken aback by the reception they actually receive. Nurtured on thousands of science fiction stories about invaders from Mars, the Earthmen regard the Martians as superstars. The first rocket to land outside Green Town, is welcomed by the Mayor, by Miss California, a former Miss America, Mr. Biggest Grapefruit in San Fernando Valley, and a brass band playing "California, Here I Come." The rout of the Martian army begins at once. Scarcely have they gotten over being violently ill following helpings of free beer, popcorn, and hot dogs, when they are whisked off to picture shows by amorous women, or pursued by evangelical preachers seeking to save their souls. Ettil is cornered by a Hollywood producer, plied with Manhattans, talked into being technical director for a science fiction film about a wildly improbable Martian invasion. Ettil sinks into a profound depression as he realizes that his fellow Martians are doomed to be lulled by the noisy pleasures of Earth until, one by one, they die in freeway accidents, or of Earth-type afflictions such as cirrhosis of the liver, bad kidneys, high blood pressure, and suicide. Worse, he realizes Earth culture will soon be exported to Mars, and that his quiet home planet will be overwhelmed with night clubs, gambling casinos, and race tracks. One can almost sympathize with poor Ettil when, having stepped into the path of a speeding car being driven by thrill-crazed teenagers, he decides not to get out of the way.

It is not surprising that Ray Bradbury should have written a number of stories about the common science fiction theme of invasion. What is notable is the consistent quality and variety his work exhibits.

Bradbury's stories, like many of his aliens, enter our minds and leave us, perhaps, subtly different from the way we were before.

Thomas M. Disch **(review date 1980)**

SOURCE: A review of *The Stories of Ray Bradbury*, in *The New York Times Book Review,* October 26, 1980, pp. 14, 32-4.

[*In the following review, Disch attacks Bradbury's collected stories as unimaginative and poorly written, asserting that "Mr. Bradbury's failures outnumber his successes."*]

Ray Bradbury is America's Official Science Fiction Writer, the one most likely to be trotted out on state occasions to give a salute to, as he puts it, "our wild future in space." In 1964 he was hired to "conceptualize" the part of the United States Pavilion at the World's Fair devoted to the

Future. From there he went on "to help plan the dreams that went into Spaceship Earth"—the latest Disney fairground now under construction. Last year a film clip of the author was the Delegate for Science Fiction at the first TABA Awards ceremony.

To those familiar with the field, Ray Bradbury's figurehead status may seem hard to account for, if only because, as he himself notes, so small a part of his output may be called science fiction. If the flagbearer's role were to be assigned to the Oldest Veteran, then by rights Jack Williamson should lead the parade. If a poll of science fiction readers were to be taken, top honors would probably go to Robert Heinlein. Even the art of self-promotion cannot account for Mr. Bradbury's eminence, for Isaac Asimov has been beating the drum of his own reputation with more vigor and persistence for decades. Yet for brand-name recognition, Mr. Bradbury has them all licked.

Could the answer be sheer literary excellence? No. Only readers who would profess Rod McKuen to be America's greatest poet, or Kahlil Gibran its noblest philosopher, could unblushingly commend Mr. Bradbury's stories as literature. If there is any difference between art and kitsch, between steak and bologna, into which category would you place the following prose specimen?

"There are a million small towns like this all over the world. Each as dark, as lonely, each as removed, as full of shuddering and wonder. The reedy playing of minor-key violins is the small towns' music, with no lights but many shadows. Oh the vast swelling loneliness of them. The secret damp ravines of them. Life is a horror lived in them at night, when at all sides sanity, marriage, children, happiness, are threatened by an ogre called Death."

That comes from **"The Night,"** the first of 100 tales collected in *The Stories of Ray Bradbury.* Though published early in his career (1946), the vein of schmaltz evident in **"The Night"** recurs in Mr. Bradbury's work as regularly as he reaches for the unattainable. Early and late are meaningless distinctions in his output. Indeed, the secret of his success may well be that, like Peter Pan, he won't grow up. What's more, he knows it. This is from his Introduction:

"I was *not* embarrassed at circuses. Some people are. Circuses are loud, vulgar, and smell in the sun. By the time many people are fourteen or fifteen, they have been divested of their loves, their ancient and intuitive tastes, one by one, until when they reach maturity there is no fun left, no zest, no gusto, no flavor. Others have criticized, and they have criticized themselves, into embarrassment."

There's the choice—love Ray Bradbury, out there beyond embarrassment, or be enrolled among those loveless, zestless critics who never go to the circus. My own experience suggests other possibilities. I've been to the circus from time to time, invariably enjoyed the show, gasped, applauded, and *even so,* my ancient and intuitive taste tells me that Ray Bradbury's stories are meretricious more often than not. Because he's risked being loud, vulgar and

smelly? No, because his imagination so regularly becomes mired in genteel gush and self-pity, because his environing clichés have made him nearly oblivious to new data from any source.

Consider this description (from **"The Night"**): "You smell roses in blossom; fallen apples lying crushed and odorous in the deep grass." Ordinarily apples don't fall when roses blossom, but in Mr. Bradbury's stories it's always Anymonth in Everywhereville. His dry-ice machine covers the bare stage of his story with a fog of breathy approximations. He means to be evocative and incantatory; he achieves vagueness and prolixity.

Perhaps it is élitist, these days, to discuss the prose style of any very popular writer. A readership in the millions proves that some sort of message is getting through. At a recent symposium of secondary-school teachers, I was assured that no s.f. writer is so teachable as Mr. Bradbury: even the least-skilled readers are able to turn his sentences into pictures in their heads. Inattentive, artless and very young readers are probably better able to construct agreeable daydreams out of Mr. Bradbury's approximative prose than if they were required to exercise their reading muscles more strenuously.

The Defense might argue that broad outlines, bright colors and stereotypical characters don't preclude the possibility of art, or at least of well-engineered amusement. Walt Disney and Norman Rockwell have endeared themselves to large audiences by such means. Indeed, there are other points of comparison even more pertinent. Like Disney, Mr. Bradbury has a knack of taming and sanitizing fairytales and myths so that even fauns and centaurs may be welcomed into the nursery. Like Rockwell, Mr. Bradbury celebrates the virtues and flavors of an idyllic, small-town American Way of Life, the myth on which a thousand suburbs have been founded.

Myths can serve various purposes: they can be decorative, a kind of literary Fourth of July bunting (as in Mr. Bradbury's **"A Scent of Sarsaparilla"**); they can be obfuscatory, a stop-gap lie to tell children before they're ready for the truth (Mr. Bradbury's tales of life in funny old warm-hearted Mexico achieve this purpose); or they can order complex emotional experience in the manner so well described by Bruno Bettelheim in his study of fairytales, "The Uses of Enchantment." Some of Mr. Bradbury's more memorable tales achieve this last and largest purpose of myth-making—offering symbolically effective ways of thinking about the unthinkable.

Even as mythmaker, however, Mr. Bradbury's failures outnumber his successes. He summons spirits from the vasty deep, but they don't come. **"The Black Ferris,"** one of only six stories collected for the first time in this volume, is representative of Mr. Bradbury at his worst.

"The Black Ferris" begins with a great gust from the fog machine—"The carnival had come to town like an October wind, like a dark bat flying over the cold lake, bones rattling in the night, mourning, sighing, whispering up the tents in the dark rain"—and goes on to recount how two small boys, Peter and Hank, discover that Mr. Cooger, the 35-year-old manager of the visiting carnival, has transformed himself into the "li'l orphan boy" who has been taken into the household of poor rich Mrs. Foley. He does this by riding the black ferris of the title 25 times in reverse. The two boys immediately apprehend the purpose of this imposture and go to Mrs. Foley to warn her:

"He's from the carnival, and he ain't a boy, he's a man, and he's planning on living with you until he finds where your money is and then run off with it some night, and people will look for him but because they'll be looking for a little ten-year-old boy they won't recognize him when he walks by a thirty-five-year-old man, named Mr. Cooger!"

Mrs. Foley refuses to heed this word to the wise, and there's nothing our little heroes can do but chase the false orphan back to the carnival. Too late to prevent him from getting back into the time-defying ferris, they assault the blind hunchback at the controls. The ferris spins, unchecked, until . . . what do you think?

"'Look,' everybody said. The policeman turned and the carnival people turned and the fishermen turned and they all looked at the occupant in the blackpainted seat at the bottom of the ride. The wind touched and moved the black wooden seat in a gentle rocking rhythm, crooning over the occupant in the dim carnival light.

"A skeleton sat there, a paper bag of money in its hands, a brown derby hat on its head."

If that tickles your sense of wonder, then there are 99 other stories in the book just as good or even better.

There can be charm in art of such systematically false naïveté, and some few writers have managed to have it both ways, writing stories that are amusing to grown-ups and exciting to children: Hans Christian Andersen, A. A. Milne, Maurice Sendak. But Mr. Bradbury is not in their league.

Orson Scott Card (review date 1980)

SOURCE: "From the Dark Carnival to the Machineries of Joy," in *The Washington Post Book World*, Vol. X, No. 44, November 2, 1980, pp. 4-5.

[*In his review of Bradbury's collected* Stories, *Card briefly discusses the author's subject matter, noting that his short fiction exceeds the boundaries of the science fiction genre.*]

Fifteen or 20 years ago, high school and college English teachers seized upon the work of Ray Bradbury. Ah! they cried in unison. Here is a science fiction writer whose work is *good*! Remarkably enough, however, the appeal of Bradbury's short stories has even survived the process

of "required reading." Bradbury is that odd thing: a mid-20th-century writer whose literary output has been almost entirely short stories. Of his so-called novels, *Dandelion Wine* and *Something Wicked This Way Comes* were cobbled together from short stories; *Fahrenheit 451* was an unfortunate expansion of a fine novelette.

In recent years Bradbury seems to have contented himself with writing unprepossessing poetry and the odd article here and there. It takes a book like *The Stories of Ray Bradbury* to remind us that in his writing career he has already given us a body of work comparable to Poe's, to O. Henry's, to de Maupassant's. What's more, rereading these hundred stories also causes me to wonder why the illusion continues, even among science fiction readers, that Ray Bradbury is or ever has been a science fiction writer.

True, his early stories first appeared in the pulps during the late 1940s. But that was not because they belonged there—Bradbury was writing neither space opera not nuts-and-bolts science fiction. In any reasonable world, the main stream of American letters would have seized instantly upon his work as a fresh voice, a new vision. Unfortunately, Bradbury began writing when the American short story establishment was already in the grip of the hardening of the arteries that would quickly lead to the paralysis we politely overlook today.

Ray Bradbury wrote about Mars, but even when he wrote the stories that later became *The Martian Chronicles* he knew that there never could be such a planet as he described. Rather he was setting his stories in the world of the dreams of a child growing up on Buck Rogers and John Carter. He was not writing science fiction. He was writing Ray Bradbury's childlike world:

It is a world of terrors, both named and nameless, that at once attract and repel.

It is a world of parents who are competent and kind, siblings who are eager to plunge into danger as long as you are close behind, tennis shoes that have miraculous powers.

It is a world where hope is the only possible philosophy, and is not disappointed.

Indeed, it is that very optimism, and not some imaginary genre, that sets off Bradbury's stories from most others. His ebullience borders on sentimentality, and if you do not read his stories in the correct frame of mind you are likely to detect cliche here and there, and mawkishness seeping through almost every tale.

For instance, the characters in **"I Sing the Body Electric"** are not particularly well-drawn. They are simply a boy and his siblings who have lost their mother. Their father arranges for them to choose a robot grandmother who is everything they want her to be. They become emotionally attached to the convincing fraud of an old lady. And then one day she, too, is "killed." This time, however, the machine they love can be resurrected easily—the faith of the children is restored, for their loved one can never be taken from them now. And more: when they are old, she will be able to come back to them and care for them as they retreat into a second childhood.

Maudlin? Yes, if you read it with emotional detachment, analyzing as you go. But Bradbury's stories resist such a reading.

It is not the characters he expects you to identify with. Rather, he means to capture you in his own voice, expects you to see through his eyes. And his eyes see, not the cliché plot, but the whole meaning of the events; not the scenes or the individual people, but yourself and your own fears and your own family and the answer, at last, to the isolation that had seemed inevitable to you. In short, if you will let him, Bradbury will give you a much better childhood than you ever had. He will name all your name-less fears and bring them home and make you like them.

In the introduction to **The Stories of Ray Bradbury,** the author states his belief that he can clearly remember all the events of his infancy, even the moment of his birth, the doctor and scalpel at his circumcision. It is perhaps too tempting to use this to explain Bradbury's unique voice: Could he not be giving us stories that see the world as an infant sees it, with unindividuated parts that cannot be named, and yet with feelings that are inextricably linked with the events that swirl around him?

Bradbury's stories do not all succeed, of course. His trib-utes to Hemingway only work if you feel toward Papa as too many people feel toward Elvis. Some of his stories are little more than an idea—what if the sea were a woman that coveted a man and regarded his wife as her rival? What, if a dinosaur were still alive in the sea and thought a fog horn was a mating call? Other stories gush too much even for me.

But where he succeeds, where his voice and his subject matter and this particular reader find harmony, I find the stories have lived in me ever since that first reading:

The hilarious story, **"Invisible Boy,"** which is the perfect expression of a parent's hopeless longing to possess a child forever.

"The Tombling Day," in which an old woman looks at the exhumed body of her old lover and learns that she is still young; another old woman in **"There Was an Old Woman"** who refuses to die and demands to have her body back.

The macabre group of people, always the same people, who endlessly gather at grisly accidents to partake of the pain and the death in **"The Crowd."**

A story of a dignified old couple who, through their sheer grace, forestall the ruin of their home in **"The Terrible Conflagration up at the Place."**

The monster children of **"The Small Assassin"** and **"To-morrow's Child."**

And most of all, the story Bradbury chose to lead off the collection of his own favorites among his work: **"The Night,"** which perhaps means so much to me because I'm just learning how much a parent is lost when a child is lost.

Indeed, that is Bradbury's magic: far more often than you will think possible, he will find the inexpressible things you most deeply know, and from then on the name of that thing will be his story. He will give you dandelion wine laced with wormwood, and you'll drink deep and regret that there are only a hundred draughts.

Hazel Pierce   (essay date 1980)

SOURCE: "Ray Bradbury and the Gothic Tradition," in *Ray Bradbury,* Paul Harris Publishing, 1980, pp. 165-85.

[*In the following examination of the stories collected in* The October Country, *Pierce connects Bradbury to the Gothic literary tradition.*]

Anyone seeking to connect a contemporary author with any established literary tradition must heed Coleridge's prefatory remarks to "Christabel" in 1798. To protect him-self from charges of "servile imitation," Coleridge came right to the point:

> For there is amongst us a set of critics, who seem to hold that every possible thought or image is traditional; who have no notion that there are such things as fountains in the world, small as well as great; and who would therefore charitably derive every rill they behold flowing, from a perforation made in some other man's tank.

Coleridge did admit an alternative when in "Kubla Khan" he described a fountain which "flung up momently the sacred river," creating a tumult in which could be heard voices. After tapping the ancient source and tossing its elements into new life, the fountain returns them, ener-gized, to enrich the original flow.

Similarly, an author can tap a literary tradition and, in playing his own variations on its themes and conventions, leave it richer for the diversion. In an interview in 1976, Ray Bradbury faced a question that touches close to that of Coleridge: are authors inventors of ideas or trappers of independent sources? [Robert Jacobs, "Bradbury," *Writ-er's Digest,* February 1976]. Bradbury rejected both the idea of invention and that of borrowing. For him, the author's purpose is to find fresh ways of presenting basic truths. In the interview Bradbury did not discuss the forms in which writers might embody these fresh insights; but close reading of certain short stories and novels reveals that he has not rejected traditional modes when they fit his purposes. . . . In these stories and novels we find Brad-bury's use of the conventions, themes, and mood of the Gothic tradition, as well as the changes he has made, thus giving it fresh energy and new range. . . .

In the early short stories, especially those collected in *The October Country,* Bradbury exercises his fancy on the grotesque. He reminds us in a short prefatory comment that most of these stories were written before he was 26 and are unique to this early period of his work. Some date back to 1943. Being close to the time of Bradbury's initial introduction to and absorption in Poe's stories, these tales could well show the influence of Poe. Certainly they exhibit a sensitive use of the Gothic mode in general.

The title, *The October Country,* immediately attracts our attention. In an epigraph Bradbury describes this *country* as gloomy, more used to fogs and mists than to sunlight, more comfortable at dusk and night than at dawn and day. There one could easily suffer a day such as Poe describes in "The Fall of the House of Usher": "a dull, dark, and soundless day in the autumn of the year, when the clouds hung oppressively low in the heavens." Bradbury's October country is compartmentalized into small dark areas, the hidden places of human deprivation and depravation. His autumn people are void of hope or optimism. Occasionally one of them rouses himself for a cruel joke or last-ditch effort. But for the most part, they live static, sterile lives.

In these early stories Bradbury has heeded, intuitively or intentionally, one of Poe's often quoted lessons to those who would write prose narratives. Poe discussed the importance of unity in a review of Hawthorne's *Twice-Told Tales,* emphasizing that the short tale which dwell on terror, passion, or horror can benefit from the "certain unique or single *effect.*" To avail himself of this "immense force derivable from totality," an author must choose his incidents with care.

Bradbury has added a footnote to Poe's advice, given not as a bit of literary credo but in the casual remark of one of his characters. In **"The Next in Line"** Marie stands looking at a pile of disjointed bones and skulls and remarks: ". . . for a thing to be horrible it has to suffer a change you can recognize." Bradbury has followed his own advice and Poe's dictum. In *The October Country* he has placed his changes against a background of familiar people, places, and activities. Many of the old Gothic conventions are present, albeit in unfamiliar guises. This perversion of accustomed twentieth-century patterns of life allow an exquisite but immense force to excite feelings of awe and dread.

[Horace] Walpole's "subterraneous" regions [in *The Castle of Otranto: A Gothic Story,* 1764] have spawned many variations: escapeways underground, dungeons, secret vaults, catacombs with their store of ancient dead. What is more natural for a couple vacationing in Mexico than to visit one of the tourist attractions, the mummies in the local catacombs? Wired to the walls of the cavernous hall are the skeletons of those whose families could not pay the fee of a conventional burial. Joseph, a stereotyped tourist, busies himself with snapping pictures and making crude remarks about Mr. Gape and Mrs. Grimace. He even tries to buy one of the skeletons from the caretaker for a few pesos. Meanwhile, his wife Marie is responding to the

---

A review of *Driving Blind*:

The 21 stories in Bradbury's new anthology are full of sweetness and humanity. Despite bizarre actions and abstract twists, all are grounded in the everyday. Here are sketches, vignettes, strange tales, colorful anecdotes, little tragedies, hilarious lies and metaphysics too. Here are a spinster's ancient love letters and the man who wrote them, wholesome small-town folk and conniving sharpsters, a moribund circus camel, a homicidal garbage disposal and a dead man searching for mourners. Much of the text is dialogue, and it works because Bradbury excels at portraying the robust textures of American speech. He is unapologetically romantic: most of the stories have love songs in them, or thunderstorms, or both, and no one seems to need to lock their door. Only four of these tales are science fiction, and one of those sneaks very cleverly out from under the genre's strictures: in the title story, Mr. Mysterious, a black-hooded stranger, is befriended by a boy whom Norman Rockwell might have painted. The reader is led to expect a supernatural change beneath the hood, but the boy has an insight of almost Philip K. Dickian subtlety about the nature of reality and memory that allows Mr. Mysterious to redeem his troubled history with both feet on the ground, while Bradbury leaps to an ecstatically optimistic ending. A few of the entries are less finished. **"Mr. Pale,"** the book's one outerspace story, leans heavily on certain tropes about the dilemmas of immortality without actually giving them substance. But in the face of Bradbury's craft and humanity, these are minor flaws.

Publishers Weekly, *September 22, 1997.*

---

human drama implicit in each "screaming" skull. When car trouble forces them to stay longer in the town, the experience works morbidly on her mind. She becomes catatonic and finally dies. Marie is a likely candidate for the "next in line." Using the familiar events of tourist travel, Bradbury has achieved low-key terror by forcing us to witness Marie's steady, seemingly inevitable disintegration into death.

Death and catacombs have become clichés in the literature of terror. Bradbury gives the cliché a fresh twist in **"The Cistern,"** evoking a romantic melancholy instead of horror. The cistern of the title is the far-flung sewer system of a town of some 30,000 people, a town large enough to allow some of its citizens to be misplaced or go unnoticed. Because the town lies near the sea, the tides and rains flow through the system. One evening a spinster muses aloud to her sister that the cistern is actually a vast underground city. A man long dead lives there, periodically enlivened by the tides, ennobled by the waters. Anna sees him joined by a woman who has died only recently, the two forever clean and loving in their watery world. When she identifies the man as her long-lost lover, we feel a deep sadness for those whom love and gentleness have passed by. That a figure should slip out of the house later in the night and that a manhole cover should slam down seems the only melancholy solution.

Atmospheric effects, which are vital to Gothic moods, take on great importance in *The October Country.* **"The Dwarf"** begins on "one of those motionless hot summer nights" and ends with "large drops of hot rain" heralding a storm. **"Touched with Fire"** glows with heat from beginning to end: 92 degrees Fahrenheit—the temperature at which the most murders occur, the heat that sunburns, drenches with sweat, and touches off ragged tempers. The thing in **"The Jar"** goes with "the noiselessness of late night, and only the crickets chirping, the frogs off sobbing in the moist swamplands." The gathering of the weird clan in **"Home-coming"** occasions a host of meteorological phenomena: lightning, thunder, clammy fog, crashing rain. When Grand-mama and Grandpapa arrive from the old country, they travel in a "probing, sucking tornado, funneling and nuzzling the moist night earth." Such aberrations, in the more placid weather one anticipates, adds to the mystery of the human turmoil taking place.

In **"The Wind,"** Bradbury works atmospheric effects in an unusual way. As a central character, the wind effectively combines ancient and modern Romance. Common sense tells us that wind blows under doors, rattles windows, and slams shutters. In a high-intensity storm it can also blow down power lines and cause great property damage and human tragedy. But Bradbury's wind is born of ancient Romance, too; it is a compendium of all the winds of the Earth, with a personality and purpose of its own.

Like Roderick Usher, "enchained by certain superstitious impressions" of his own home, in Bradbury's story Allin is enthralled by the sentience of the wind that pursues him. It laughs and whispers, then slams and crashes. It sucks and nuzzles at his house, seeking revenge on this mere mortal who dares trespass on its secret breeding and dying place in the Himalayas. Finally, it corners Allin in the house. He is isolated except for telephone contact with Herb, a rather pedestrian friend who tries to understand the situation, but cannot. When the wind turns into a feral creature with a voice compounded of the voices of the thousands killed in typhoons and hurricanes, Herb can only listen helplessly as Allin says: "It's a killer, Herb, the biggest, damnedest prehistoric killer that ever hunted prey." A primal force, the wind sucks not only at Allin's house but at his very intellect and ego.

Not all of Bradbury's houses are places in which to hide, however. Sometimes they are fragile shells to break out of. In **"Jack-in-the-Box"** a young boy lives in a four-storied house effectively sealed from the world by a natural barrier (a dense grove of trees) and an artificial barrier (a mother's unnatural fear of the world). The boy exists in this four-level universe in the company of his mother and Teacher, a bespectacled, gray-gloved person dressed in a cowled robe. From Teacher he learns a story of Creation, with a dead father as God and a future role for him as son and successor. His flight to safety is through a tunnel of trees to the strange sanctuary of the world of lampposts and friendly policemen on the beat. Only when he "dies" to his old artificial world and is "reborn" in this world of the beetles that killed Father can he throw his arms aloft and be free like the jack-in-the-box.

One refreshing difference between Bradbury's use of the Gothic mode and that of many other authors is evident in his choice of characters. When one reads a considerable number of Gothic tales, the Isabellas, Adelines, and Eleanoras tend to flow together and become that abstract entity, Beauty in Distress. She remains in our minds as a white-clothed, wraith-like figure perpetually in flight, pursued by a cruel and tyrannical male. It matters little whether his name is Manfred or Montoni, Lucifer or Death. On the other hand, Bradbury's people are personalities, believable people we can care about. Not limited by sex or age, they represent Innocence in Distress, though each is unique in his innocence.

Bradbury's people do not flee, for autumn people tend to seal themselves off until a point is reached when they must act. Often their act is so aggressive and unexpected that it tinges with dismay our sympathy for their plight. We may judge their actions, but not by any conventional moral yardstick. Instead, like Poe's prisoner in "The Pit and the Pendulum," we accept them as victims of "that surprise, or entrapment into torment, [which] formed an important portion of these dungeon deaths." Like the prisoner, Bradbury's characters suffer in the dungeons of spiritual darkness where one fights against the death of spirit. The struggle may end grotesquely, even in death, though the death is often that of the tormentor rather than the tormented.

Surprise into the grotesquerie of death? What else but surprise can we feel with 11-year-old Douglas in **"The Man Upstairs"** when he discovers that Grandma's new boarder has a collection of triangles, chains, and pyramids instead of the standard heart, lungs, and stomach? Evidently something unhuman, more used to sleeping all day in a coffin in a dark basement, now sleeps in Grandma's upper floor. A strangeness threatens the warmth of Grandma's kitchen where she teaches the basic facts of human physiology to Douglas as she deftly stuffs a fowl for the evening meal. Bradbury inveigles us into sharing the ever-expanding curiosity of the small boy, from his initial discovery to the end. Then he jolts us into ancient Romance when we find the boarder, dechained and depyramided, neatly trussed up like a Thanksgiving turkey, stuffed with six dollars and fifty cents in silver coins.

Entrapment into torment? Take Charlie of **"The Jar."** Living in a shack in the Louisiana back country, Charlie has his own personal dungeon—a narrow social group where he is ridiculed and ignored. The "thing" in the jar brings him sorely needed social attention. When his wife Thedy threatens to strip it of its mystique in front of the neighbors, Charlie is trapped by a torment; he can neither face it nor flee it. Instead, he acts decisively. Later, along with his rival, Tom Carmody, a reader may shiver as he too looks at the new thing in the jar. Grotesque though it is, we grudgingly accept Thedy's end, given the menace of her vicious tongue.

Sometimes we accomplish our dungeon deaths by our own frantic efforts. What else is hypochondria but self-entrapment into torment? We flee from our dis-ease, grabbing at any proffered relief. In **"Skeleton,"** Mr. Harris suffers acutely from aches in his bones. Gradually he becomes aware of and is then obsessed by the unwelcome skeleton that his muscles carry around day in and day out. It becomes his enemy, forcing itself out in hideous protrusions of teeth and nails. Harris's family doctor treats his problem with veiled mockery. Finally, in desperation he turns to a M. Munigant, a small dark man with glittering eyes and a sibilant voice that seems to rise in a shrill whistle. Relief at any cost, asks Mr. Harris, even that provided by M. Munigant who deftly extracts the bones from his body, leaving only a live human jellyfish.

Bradbury can turn a stock situation inside out, even invest it with a degree of humor. A standard Gothic convention is the confrontation with a supernatural force. It may be a shadowy form of a long-dead love or an ancient ancestor stepping out of his gold frame. It can appear in a mirror instead of the expected human reflection. In some tales, Satan or Death may appear in human form. With such occurrences the author is usually trying to strike a chill in the reader, as well as the character involved.

It comes as gentle relief when an author turns the tables on such apparitions. Poe did it in "Bon-Bon," when the devil rejects the soul of a gourmet-restaurateur, indicating delicately that he cannot take advantage of Bon-Bon in his drunken condition. Like Poe, Bradbury twists the classic formula. In **"There Was an Old Woman"** he gives us Aunt Tildy, a spry old lady with years of knitting left in her fingers. When a polite, dark young man with his four helpers carrying a long wicker basket come to her house, she becomes quite vexed with him. Losing the first part of the battle, she watches as they carry her body away to the mortuary. By dint of a will stronger than death, she forces her spirit to follow them to the mortuary where she commands it to merge with the body, to think, and then to force the body to sit up. Polite to the end, she leaves only after thanking the amazed mortician. With her homespun, no-nonsense mannerisms Aunt Tildy is a far cry from the emaciated Madeleine Usher inching her way from the tomb to the room where Roderick awaits her.

Robert Plank (essay date 1981)

SOURCE: "The Expedition of the Planet of Paranoia," in *Extrapolation*, Vol. 22, No. 2, 1981, pp. 171-85.

[In this excerpted essay, Plank offers a variety of interpretations of Bradbury's "April 2000: The Third Expedition," lending insight into other stories collected in The Martian Chronicles.*]*

Ray Bradbury's most famous book is not a book; *The Martian Chronicles* (1950) are chronicles in outward appearance only. Rather they are individual stories strung on a chronological line, glued together here and there with smudges of connective tissue. They were clearly written independently, and many of them were originally pub-

lished separately. The book purports to relate events that took place between January 1999 and October 2026, but many of them could have taken place—as far as they could have taken place at all—at different times and in a different sequence. This is particularly true of the first three expeditions from Earth to Mars. All three of them are wiped out, each in an unconventional manner, and each of them quite differently. Each expedition anticipates a certain type of Mars inhabitant, but there is little similarity between them.

None of the survivors, Martian or Terran, learn anything from their experience. None of these expeditions leaves a trace of itself, except that when the fourth expedition arrives fourteen months after the third, its members find a town full of Martians who have been dead ten days from chicken pox (the author's device, perhaps, to make sure they will not repeat their tricks?). It is concluded that the Martians have been infected unintentionally by members of the third expedition—"and as quickly as that it was forgotten." All that Earthmen can know, or care, is that the men of the third expedition landed on Mars and were never heard from again. Although some geographical features are named for the more eminent among them, these expeditions might as well never have taken place. Or, of course, they could have occurred in a different order. It is justified, therefore, to talk about **"April 2000: The Third Expedition"** as if it were an independent work, with not more than an occasional glance at the rest of the book.

"The Third Expedition" is a short (sixteen pages in the Bantam edition) and compact story. It observes the three classical unities of place (in and around the landed spaceship), of time (from one morning to the next), and of action. Plucking many chords of emotion, it moves deftly from utter bewilderment to revelation of conflict and swiftly to catastrophe. It is a masterpiece of its type. Later, we shall consider what that type is. The story divides itself naturally into three phases: (1) the idyll—from the landing to nightfall. The pace is leisurely, and this phase takes up the bulk of the tale, about thirteen pages. (2) the murders during the night. (3) the funeral in the morning. The last two are compressed into barely three pages.

Phase One. The spaceship is arriving on Mars. It carries a crew of seventeen, but one person has died en route. We are introduced to three of the survivors: John Black, captain; Samuel Hinkston, archaeologist; Lustig, navigator (perhaps Jews will not have first names in 2000 A.D.? No, it later turns out that it is David). The other men are neither named nor otherwise individualized. Black is eighty years old, but looks like forty—science in the second half of our century has rejuvenated him. Hinkston is forty-five; Lustig fifty. The spaceship has landed on a lawn in the middle of a town that down to the last small detail (a sheet of music entitled "Beautiful Ohio" sits on a piano) looks exactly like Green Bluff, Illinois (where Captain Black was raised), of long ago. They are later informed that the town is Green Bluff, Illinois, that it was founded in 1868, and that the year is 1926 (when Black was six years old).

The minds of the three men, understandably reeling, race through all sorts of theories to comprehend the incomprehensible. Have they, through an unexpected quirk of space travel, landed on Earth instead of Mars and thereby gone back in time? Have members of the first or second expedition survived and built—in an incredibly short time—a replica of an American town? Were space travel and the colonization of Mars secretly initiated before World War I? Has a super-clever and super-powerful psychiatrist then combatted nostalgia among the colonists by "rearranging the civilization" so that it increasingly resembles Earth, until "by some vast crowd hypnosis" he has convinced everyone that it really *is* Earth?

Naturally, none of these hypotheses seems in the least plausible. The men are left in a state of stupefied bewilderment until a shattering experience provides the straw of an explanation—each encounters some aspect from his past. Lustig sees his grandparents. Hinkston espies his old house and runs to it. Black encounters his brother Edward, who conducts him to their parents. The other men, who were left behind in the ship with orders to man the guns, have meanwhile forgotten their duty, abandoned the ship, and mingled with a crowd of Martians who have festively assembled on the lawn. "Then each member of the crew, with a mother on one arm, a father or sister on the other, was spirited off down the street into little cottages or big mansions." And so an "explanation" of the awesome mystery is offered—through the grace of God, these deceased relatives have been given a second life, in a town on Mars that exactly duplicates their environment on Earth. By implication, the space trip has been providentially arranged to grant the sixteen Earthmen a reunion with their loved ones. The men are still confused, but they readily submit to their elders' admonitions not to question the Lord's infinite wisdom and mercy. The festivities come to an end; night falls. Groggy with happiness, the men lie down to sleep.

At this point it is perhaps appropriate to interrupt the narrative for some preliminary remarks on Phase One, be it only to note several features of the story that do not quite fit into its general sweep. No discrepancies appear at first reading, but on closer scrutiny they cannot be ignored. Though they may seem minor, they turn out to have great significance. I do not mean to say that the story as such is incredible. Of course it is. What I want to point out is that even if we accept the author's premises and treat the work as though it were a credible tale, there are still some things in the natural course of events that would have gone differently. It is for this reason that one must wonder why Bradbury placed his emphases in the curious way that he did.

When Lustig meets his grandparents, who have been dead for thirty years (in other words, they died when he was twenty) he "sounded as if at any moment he might go quite insane with happiness." He "sobbed . . . turned . . . kissed . . . hugged . . . held." That the men are overjoyed is natural. But is it natural for that joy to be so all-pervasive? Would anyone, suddenly coming face to face with the dead returned to life, feel nothing else? No admixture of horror, no trace of awe? No fleeting moment of resurgent animosity, no quick pang of guilt? Would a person touch the body that he saw buried years ago, without the least hesitation? Yet, in the story as told, there is not the slightest element of ambivalence. The negative feelings are totally absent. In the events that swiftly follow, however, these pent-up feelings break out with the elemental force of murderous fury.

Though the space travelers are grown, even old, men, they do not meet dead children or wives. Their reunion is with parents, grandparents, siblings—persons who died when the spacemen were young—representing ascending rather than descending relationships. Ed Black, the only sibling whose age is given, was seven years John's senior. When he died at twenty-six, John was nineteen.

They do not even think of others who may have died, or who were left behind on Earth, except for Captain Black, who fleetingly thinks of "Marilyn" (not otherwise identified). After a brief hesitation, Ed tells him that she is out of town, but will be back in the morning. The dead have not aged. They are all exactly as they were at the moment of their deaths. The same motif occurs in an even weirder form in another of the stories, **"April 2026: The Long Years."**

There is a similar tendency to extend time backward in the description of the town. All that nostalgia would associate with a small American town of 1926 is here: an iron deer on the lawn, popular songs of the period, Victorian architecture, a robin singing in an apple tree, a grandfather clock, a brass band, front porches, and a turkey dinner. There is a "victrola," but no radio, no telephone, no automobile. It is an old-fashioned town remembered from childhood, more quintessentially so than a town ever truly was. Furthermore, we are given to understand that all the astronauts hail from places like Green Bluff, Illinois. Of course, no one knows what the distribution of the population of the United States will be in 2000. These men, however, must have been born in our own time, and we know that now some 80 percent of the population comes from cities or suburbs.

Another motif, mental influence, is only hinted at here and will be revealed in all its devastating import in Phase Two. Seeing the town, Black finds it so similar to Green Bluff that it frightens him. Then he is informed that it *is* Green Bluff. Yet, Hinkston, the archaeologist, makes the professional judgment that no artifact there is older than 1927. Two pages later, a stranger tells them that the year they have come to is 1926. Do the men discover these things because they are sharp enough to recognize the truth, or do they become true because the men think they are true? And it is Hinkston who spins out the fantastic theory about it all being the work of a master psychiatrist who influenced minds sufficiently to create an entire culture. It is the measure of Bradbury's skill that all these motifs are muted, unobtrusive. If the reader notices them at all, he does so subliminally. It also raises a question as to whether the author's skill may have operated more unconsciously than consciously.

Phase Two. Consummate skill characterizes Bradbury's transition from Phase One to Phase Two. Day and night, life and death are not in sharper contrast than these two, but one phrase bridges the abyss between them. Captain Black shares a bed with his brother Ed, the same brass bed they had shared in life, in the same room with the college pennants and such. They lie down, "side by side, as in the days how many decades ago?" They talk a little, then fall silent.

> The room was square and quiet except for their breathing.
>
> "Good night, Ed."
>
> A pause. "Good night, John."

It is that phrase, "a pause," that makes the transition. The tumbling from one joyful surprise to the next is over; the time has come to think. The shift is abrupt and complete. Phase Two has begun.

To prepare for the tremendous acceleration of his narrative, Bradbury skillfully narrows the focus. Of the sixteen men, only three are singled out for individual consideration. Then two of the three, Hinkston and Lustig drop away. The last part of Phase One is exclusively concerned with Black and his dead relatives (a residue, perhaps, of the hierarchic-patriarchic orientation so predominant in the science fiction of somewhat earlier days—if you can have the captain, why bother with lesser men?).

Phase Two consists almost entirely of Black's internal monologue. A quite new realization suddenly hits him: what if all he has lived in during this day has been a phantom world called into being by the Martians in order to destroy the invaders? That would mean that after taking all they needed to know from his mind, the Martians had conjured up the image of Green Bluff in 1926 and altered themselves to appear as the dead relatives. With their sixteen enemies safely bedded down, the Martians will spring a trap. In the night they will change back into their real selves and kill their guests.

At first Black naturally shrinks from these thoughts, but as he thinks through them, the theory becomes distressingly convincing. All the pieces fall into place, and the puzzling events assume a new, menacing meaning. He must act at once to rescue himself, for there is not a moment to lose. Unarmed, he cannot hope to subdue his pursuers, so he tries to sneak out. But what seemed to be his brother sleeping peacefully by his side has now become a Martian—wide awake, challenging him: "Captain John Black broke and ran across the room. He screamed. He screamed twice. He never reached the door." The long, leisurely spell of blissful illusion has been broken in one devastating moment. Like lightning, terrible and brief, truth has struck; it has brightly illuminated the scene, making everything clear in a flash, only to be extinguished by the stabs of death. But in what sense can we speak here of truth?

Any interpretation of an imaginative work like **"The Third Expedition"** is hazardous because it is bound to be subjective. Still, it is hard to see how anybody could read it any other way than to accept Black's last theory as the correct one; the outcome proves it. The various explanations that the men tentatively put together before they met their beloved dead are, of course, to be discarded. But even the theory that Mars is the abode of departed souls, which they dazedly accepted from their relatives, does not stand up. It was only make-believe in the purest sense of the word; the Martians made the Earthmen believe. It cannot explain why Black and his fifteen companions are murdered. Black's theory does.

To say that the theory is "correct" means that it is correct within the framework of the story. It is the premise of the story that the reunion with the dead really happened, and if we accept this, we must also accept the explanation. In other words, if we willingly accept that the astronauts landing on Mars had the experiences described in the story, then we must also accept Black's final theory. Bradbury's art has compelled us to silence the voices of critical judgment within ourselves. However, Black's theory is in fact built on several large assumptions: (1) that the Martians are able, instantaneously and without any resources but their telepathic power, to probe Black's memories, drain his mind, and know everything he has ever known; (2) that the Martians have the power to compel their victims to perceive as real an entire world around them which does not in fact exist, and to blank out most genuine reality (though they still perceive each other, they fail to perceive the bleak Martian soil where they see green lawns, etc.); (3) that though they appear as loving relatives, the Martians are, in truth, malevolent, bent on killing. These are the assumptions that form the typical world picture of the paranoiac.

Phase Three. The story could have ended with John Black never reaching the door, but instead there is a brief coda. The reader's first impression is that the conclusion is simple and fitting. The Martians have murdered the sixteen strangers, and now they bury them with appropriate rites, except that the rites are not appropriate. The only purpose of the whole phantasmagoria was to lure the Earthmen to their deaths. Having achieved this, the Martians are by themselves. There is no discernible reason for them to maintain the macabre masquerade. Yet, to some extent they do. They weep; they pretend to mourn. For what? No one is left alive whom they could want to deceive.

This "effort aimed at a void" has worried science fiction critic Jörg Hienger, who in his book *Literarische Zukunftsphantastik* [1972] devotes several pages to Phase Three. If everything on Mars that resembles Earth, he asks, is but illusion—images telepathically extracted from the minds of the astronauts and hypnotically projected back into them—who has the illusion after the men are dead? He finds the question unanswerable. Given this fact and the even weightier observation that the entire ceremony serves no purpose for the Martians—and they, after all, are the ones who have arranged it—he concludes that Bradbury here postulates an end of rationality per se, thus achieving a powerful effect of the uncanny dissolving into the comical.

Hienger's analysis has the redoubtable advantage of that rigorous logic that is the pride of German philosophy, but he applies the criterion of consistency to external events when it would be more fittingly applied to the mental processes of the author (more of that later). Bradbury may simply have felt, as his readers appear to feel, that the burial is a proper and soothing ending, with its comic relief welcome after a night of horror. Phase One offered the fulfillment in fantasy of deep longings, Phase Two of deep fears. We have come to identify with the hero, to whom these were vouchsafed; now we would want for him what we would want for ourselves should tragic death overtake us—a decent burial. How many people are there who have not drawn satisfaction from imagining their own funeral, with all those who in life offended them among the mourners—"when it's too late, you'll be sorry." This is an infinitely more banal interpretation than Hienger's, but that is no reason to reject it. The reader's first impression may not have been so far off after all.

From here there are two roads to an understanding of what **"The Third Expedition"** is all about. We can (1) analyze the mental processes in the characters as though these were actual persons, that is, as though Bradbury had written a case history, or a tale of people who could possibly exist and the situations to which they are compelled to react could possibly arise. Or, we can (2) consider the events as projections of the author's mind. We will take route 1 first.

Bradbury deals with three types of deviant mental functioning: illusions, defined as misinterpretations of actual perceptions (trivial optical illusions are the best-known examples); hallucinations, defined as perceptions subjectively experienced without appropriate objective stimulus (such as seeing somebody who is not there); and delusions, defined as false judgments without rational basis (the belief of a psychotic that he is Jesus Christ is a popular example). The hallucinating person may be aware to various degrees that his senses deceive him. The hallucination raises a question, though no answer may be forthcoming. Delusions provide answers, though there may have been no obvious question. The men, faced with the hallucinations that provide the foundation of Phase One, look frantically for an answer. In Phase Two, they find one.

The lines between these three types of malfunctioning are fluid, and there are mixed forms. There is also an infinite variety in degree of firmness and impact, from the hardly noticeable to the overpowering. In fact, illusions, hallucinations, and delusions can only be called deviations or malfunctions in the sense that an ideally operating mental apparatus would be free of them. But nobody's is. They occur fleetingly in normal life. They may be provoked in more substantial form by various kinds of illness, by drugs, or by any stress. Only in their more malignant forms do they become indicative of physical or mental illness.

Phase One is saturated with hallucinations. A web so complete that it covers the entire scene and blots out almost all normal perception does not exist in reality, so it is unavoidable that the men look for an agent beyond human experience to have caused the phenomenon. Two questions arise. Why do the men shift from their original attitude of thinking of the cause as a benevolent agent (Hinkston proclaims at an early stage that "certainly a town like this could not occur without divine intervention") to the assumption of a radically malevolent agent? And why is the "good" agent seen as supernatural ("divine intervention") while the evil one ("incredibly brilliant" Martians) is not?

In deciding that his experiences are the work of a superhuman power, Black follows, though unaware, a hoary tradition. Primitive men attributed all extraordinary events to the action of superhuman beings—spirits, demons, gods. The external appearance of these imagined beings was an unequivocal revelation of their nature; the inimical ones among them were of ghastly ugliness. We have only to look at idols that men did not adore, but rather tried to propitiate to find proof. These idols entered Christianity and the tradition of Western civilization condensed in the form of the Devil. He is still surpassingly ugly. His suspect exterior has rubbed off on literature and the arts. The villain in many popular nineteenth-century novels and plays is invariably recognizable for what he is. The young girl he wants to seduce, exploit, and ruin is incarnate innocence. Modern audiences wonder how she can be so naïve that she is not immediately warned by his black moustache and shifty eyes. But we have not always done much better. The beings that have replaced the Devil are still monsters. J.R.R. Tolkien, who consciously harks back to the Middle Ages, holds a middle line: the good are not necessarily the beautiful, but those on the side of Sauron are, as the saying has it, ugly as Hell.

Growing sophistication has wrought a fundamental change in another respect. Men, now believing that they have a soul that matters more than the body, are no longer annihilated by brute force. The frontal assault is detoured through their minds. The Devil, who in the medieval version wrung Dr. Faustus' neck as though he were killing a chicken, now works by seduction. He is not only the Prince of Darkness but also the Father of Lies. His principal "lie" is his ability to deceive his victims by setting all they desire before their eyes—by making them hallucinate. Legends are full of such instances.

It is a wide jump in time, but not much of a leap in substance from here to **"The Third Expedition."** What has happened is that the poor Devil has been secularized. In our enlightened age, we find it easier to believe in malignant octopuses on Mars than in him. God has also been secularized (in Arthur C. Clarke's *2001,* for instance, His role has been reassigned to the slabs and their masters), but not as completely. Belief in Him is still widespread and respectable. So, it does not jar that Black believes in God, but not in the Devil; that when he needs to postulate a benign influence he resorts to the idea of divine intervention, and when he needs to postulate an evil one, he turns to the Martians. But why does he have to switch from good to evil at all? Here it is instructive to consider Bradbury's immediate forerunners.

To postulate alien intelligences endowed with the hallucinogenic power that earlier ages reserved for the Devil and his cohorts is commonplace in science fiction; so much so that Hienger goes as far as to think that any alert reader versed in science fiction will have anticipated the solution long before Black proclaims it (which would be a pity, since suspense would be gone). In *Seekers of Tomorrow*, Sam Moskowitz cites two more direct precursors, both strikingly similar to Bradbury's tale: Campbell's *Brain Stealers of Mars* (1936) and especially Stanley G. Weinbaum's "A Martian Odyssey" (1934). Weinbaum's desert octopus (or whatever it is—he refers to it as "the Dream-Beast" or simply "the black horror") has undisputably the same hallucinogenic powers that make Captain Black's adversaries so formidable and uses them to similar sinister ends. It is more enlightening, though, to review the differences in Bradbury's and Weinbaum's treatment of the same motif.

Weinbaum uses it in one of many equally incredible adventures. He does not seem to know what jewel he holds in his hands, giving it away so lightly. The event remains without consequence. The loyal Martian "ostrich" protects the hero from succumbing to the lure, as in effect this intended victim remains indestructible through all his harrowing experiences. With Bradbury, the hallucinogenic power is squarely the core of the plot, and it is victorious. Resistance is impossible. Far from being inconsequential, the stratagem is decisive. The hallucination is less complete in Weinbaum's tale—the baiting apparition stands in an otherwise unaffected Martian landscape—while in Bradbury's the hallucination is all-embracing. Weinbaum has the alien power more or less reveal itself in defeat, but with Bradbury it remains, in victory, beyond perception. Its lack of shape and the absence of hints as to its nature enhance the uncanny atmosphere in **"The Third Expedition."**

There is a more fundamental difference: the role of the hallucinated person in the life of the victim. Weinbaum's character, Jarvis, thinks of Fancy Long, a New York entertainer on the as yet uninvented television, who is evidently a flirt. He may have had an affair with her, but all he will say is, "I know her pretty well—just friends, get me?" Do we get him? That was published in 1934. In any event, she clearly represents normal, conventional, adult heterosexual attraction. Things are totally different on Bradbury's Mars. Overt sexuality is absent and is kept out by the incest barrier: since all the beloved dead are blood relatives, there are no friends or "just friends." Rather, the relationship is anchored in the victim's childhood, long before adult love relationships could emerge. Moreover, the relatives are all dead, while Fancy Long is very much alive.

The comparison with Weinbaum's story makes the core of Phase One even clearer than the oddities we noted earlier. Phase One is a regression to childhood. The ambivalence of childhood was absent, having been repressed in passage to adolescence. Such ambivalence, however much of it there may have been in actual childhood, has no place in remembered childhood. Time has come to a standstill—as it always does in the unconscious. When we dream of a person we have not seen since childhood, we see him as he was then, not as we know he is now. The mental influencing, too, fits more naturally into the outlook of a child, since so much of his experience is of being manipulated by beings more powerful and of more penetrating intelligence than he is.

We are now in a position to see why the shift from the benign to the malign was unavoidable. It was the reaction to the fling beyond human limits that is embodied in Phase One. The dynamics of human development do not permit going backwards. But in Phase One the men *have* gone back, have indulged in regression. The overwhelming bliss they feel stems from their being allowed to wallow without restraint in regression. E. P. Bernabeu, author of one of the few psychological studies on science fiction stresses [in "Science Fiction: A New Mythos," *Psychoanalytic Quarterly,* 1957] this point in a passage devoted to **"The Third Expedition":** "The reliving of his 'happiest moments' is evidently in the author's plot a form of autistic gratification for which the condign punishment of the 'explorers' is their destruction." This somewhat theoretical formulation is supplemented by observation on actual behavior. People love to "go back to childhood," certainly, but it has to be a prettified childhood. Disneyland and its numberless imitations are huge successes. They reconstruct childhood fantasies. When it comes to a more real reliving of childhood, people hesitate. They shy away from psychoanalysis, but also from more mundane endeavors. The newspapers reported in June, 1977, that the inventor of Kitty Litter had developed Jones, Michigan, into a replica, as faithful as possible, of a typical town of some years ago (Green Bluff, Illinois, circa 1926?). However, the expected tourists did not come. Everything had to be auctioned off. He had invested $1,500,000 and retrieved $190,000.

The punishment for Black and his crew had to be more severe. They had "drunk the milk of paradise." Their "condign punishment" must be death. Therefore, the shift from divine intervention to the infernal machinations of Martians logically follows. It sets the tone for Phase Two. Moreover, it unifies the two very different phases. We can now take a closer look at outstanding problems that run through both phases: the subject of mental influencing and the question of the identity of the "relatives."

That somebody mistakes a person he encounters for a close relative, or sees a relative who is not there, is of course not an everyday occurrence, but it is not particularly rare. It is invariably a relative of deep emotional significance for the viewer. The experience is always surprising and often has a great impact. Many examples from both fiction and nonfiction could be given, but a few will suffice. The interest in extraordinary experiences around the moment of death has brought a spate of testimonials. Several years ago, *McCall's* related the story [Mary Ann O'Rourke, "I Have Never Again Been

Afraid of Death," November 1976] of a woman who had been given up by her doctors:

> As I lay in my bed I opened my eyes—and there, standing around my bed, were both sets of my grandparents, whom I had loved very much and who had died years before. I saw them as vividly as I am looking at you now . . . they looked just as I knew them when I was a girl. . . . I wanted to go with them . . . I felt such peace and love from their presence . . . and I have never again been afraid of death.

Winston Smith, in George Orwell's *1984* (1948), under a stress that approaches or even surpasses that of imminent death, thinks he recognizes his mother in a fellow prisoner. The idea is not as unreasonable as it may seem because his mother had disappeared many years ago, and he has no way of knowing whether she is still alive or what she might be like now. On the other hand, he has no reason to think that she would be in the same prison as he at the same time or that she would look like that other woman.

The use of this motif in literature sometimes approaches the metaphorical. Heinrich Lersch, a German pacifist poet who wrote shortly after World War I, relates in a poem how he saw a dead soldier entangled in the barbed wire in front of his trench and how from day to day he became more convinced that it was his brother (of course, he was not). Similar episodes are found in autobiographical writings of former mental patients. For example, Fritz Peters relates in *The World Next Door* (1949) how he thought, for no manifest reason, that an elderly fellow patient was his father. An encounter that does not involve clearcut mistaken identity but is relevant to our study because of the abrupt shift of feeling and roles is found in Arthur Schnitzler's *Flight into Darkness* [1972]. The protagonist develops paranoia. As his brother, who is trying to lead him back to human companionship, embraces him, the sick man feels attacked by a hostile force and stabs him through the heart.

The idea of being influenced or indeed dominated by powerful enemies who exert a mysterious influence on the mind has, of course, long been recognized as a characteristic symptom of paranoia and related conditions. Especially since Viktor Tausk's pioneering study *On the Origin of the "Influencing Machine" in Schizophrenia* (1919), the mechanism of this delusion and its role in the development of the disease have been better understood. Psychiatric practice considers it, rightly, a symptom of clear and ominous meaning.

This is not the place to discuss the lamentable phenomenon, with its overtones of credulity combined with surrender of autonomy, that nowadays more people who are not themselves paranoid will accept this special delusion than ever before. We must also forego examining whether the latest technological "progress" has in fact made such an assumption more credible than it was in earlier times. The increased willingness to believe in mental influencing is no doubt part of the general loss of certainty resulting from the fact that so much that used to be impossible has

become possible, and so it is easy to fall into the trap of thinking that everything is possible. It is also partly due to the increased empathy with the mentally ill, praiseworthy where it means greater tolerance, questionable where it tends toward apotheosis.

It is not inappropriate here, perhaps, to invoke the noble shade of the knight of the sad countenance, who has for centuries served as the paradigm of the man who lives by his illusions, hallucinations, and delusions: Don Quixote. His nobility is predicated on his world of the imagination being nobler than the shabby reality around him, and on his willingness to give everything except his honor to prove that his fantasies have a deeper reality than that of the commonplace real, and that he could live up to these standards. Can the same be said of Black and his companions?

We have now traveled along route 1 for a considerable stretch. We have come quite close to our goal, but it has proved a longwinded road. How about the second route? We will now consider the content of the story as a projection of contents in the author's mind. We can do so for a simple and basic reason: the characters in the story do not exist except in the author's mind. This is true of all fiction, though to different degrees; least of all in historical fiction, moreso in realistic fiction, and to the highest degree in tales like **"The Third Expedition."** The characters' minds have no independent existence, because the characters themselves are only creatures of the author. They see, feel, think, and act the way they do because the author makes them see, feel, think, and act in that way, not because it is their nature.

This does not mean, of course, that an author necessarily shares his characters' perceptions and emotions. No writer worth his salt is limited to portraying himself. For instance, he may describe a man committing a crime, without ever having done so himself. Nevertheless, the thought of the crime must be in the writer; his mind must encompass the potential. He may fight it within himself, and the struggle may be the very reason why he describes it. To realize this is of particular importance for understanding delusions in literature. If John Black were living in a normal world, the idea of his brother changing into a Martian and killing him would clearly be a delusion, but he lives in an abnormal world. The truth of his idea is confirmed by events, so technically it is not a delusion. But the point is irrelevant. The author knows that the world into which Black has been flung is itself but a figment. He knows that Black's theory *is* delusion.

This can perhaps be made clearer if we look at the phenomenon from a morphological viewpoint. Whatever the character's perceptions, emotions, and reasoning in relation to reality—be it genuine reality or the "reality" of the story—they are illusions, hallucinations, and delusions in *form*. And just as a move in a game derives its significance only from the rules of the game, so here the form is what matters, because the reality has been rigged by the author. He has set the rules of the game. Because an author has stacked the cards against his characters, his work is resonant with irony. Eric Rabkin misses—or ignores—

the point when in *The Fantastic in Literature* he speaks of "the sweetly lyrical romanticism of Ray Bradbury in ***The Martian Chronicles.***" The sweetness is only skin-deep. The flesh underneath writhes with horror.

The author's role may be obscured rather than elucidated by taking it for granted that **"The Third Expedition"** is science fiction, as is often done, merely because Bradbury is a science fiction writer. It is true, of course, that he is. But while it is convenient to pigeonhole an author in a specific genre, it is equally obvious that this is an over-simplification. Some of the finest science fiction stories are the work of celebrated "mainstream" writers (R. Kipling, E. M. Forster, E. B. White, and A. France come to mind), and science fiction writers have written nonscience fiction. We cannot say, "It's called science fiction, so it is science fiction." We must measure **"The Third Expedition"** against the criteria of a rational definition.

L. Sprague De Camp, in his *Science Fiction Handbook* (1953), offers this: "fiction based on scientific or pseudo-scientific assumptions (space travel, robots, telepathy, earthly immortality, etc.) or laid in a patently unreal although not supernatural setting (the future, another world, and so forth). . . ." Even though De Camp cast his net wide, works like **"The Third Expedition"** would be caught. But that was a generation ago. Since then the genre has grown, branched out, matured. Sharper differentiation has become a necessity. There is consensus nowadays that science fiction should be distinguished from such adjacent types as fantasy, weird fiction, and the Gothic story. Even utopian fiction, long in eclipse, has recovered sufficiently to claim much of the territory that by default had gone to science fiction. The classical definition that H. Bruce Franklin gave in *Future Perfect* (1966) represents the prevailing modern thinking:

> Science fiction seeks to describe reality in terms of a credible hypothetical invention—past, present, or, most usually, future—extrapolated from that reality; fantasy seeks to describe present reality in terms of an impossible alternative to that reality. . . . Science fiction views what is by projecting what not inconceivably could be; fantasy views what is by projecting what could not be.

"The Third Expedition" makes "pseudo-scientific assumptions," uses a "patently unreal setting," "projects what could not be." It is science fiction by criteria of times past, not by current criteria. This is important because it sheds light on the author's intentions, or at least on what intentions he does not have. He does not care to explore scientific developments or future human societies. He does not contribute to any of the educational or uplifting effects ascribed to science fiction: better understanding of the world we live in through better understanding of science, enthusiasm for the marvels that the future holds in store for the human race, etc. He carefully leaves such opportunities unexploited. For example, we hear next to nothing about the actual space trip, nothing about the real Mars, and nothing about the spacemen's equipment (except that they have "guns" and "atomic weapons"). More-

over, the density of oxygen in the Martian atmosphere is one-thousandth of what it is in ours. Although this was learned only through recent space probes and earlier estimates were much higher—as much as one-hundredth of ours—still, it was evident that men would not be able to breathe on Mars without special apparatus. Bradbury must have known this, yet, he chose to ignore it. He is not interested in the air the men breathe, the soil under their feet, or the ship they came in. He is interested in what goes on inside them.

The key is in his method. His technique of projecting his characters' inner life, of making it visible to his readers, is to describe events that happen in the characters' minds as though they were happening in the outside world. Obversely, what he presents as occurring on the outside—in the "reality" of his tale—is actually what goes on in the minds of his characters, and nothing else. "Out of sight, out of mind" has been reversed into "out of mind, out of sight." This method has not been much studied and does not seem to have a name yet, perhaps because it seems to be an innovation of the post-realistic era, although it is actually quite old. We find it in ancient fairy tales, in works of the Romantics, and in such modern writers as Hermann Hesse (who experimented with it brilliantly in *Demian* and *Steppenwolf*) and Franz Kafka. We are not told, for instance, that Gregor Samsa in *Metamorphosis* thinks he is a cockroach; we are told that he is changed into a cockroach (or whatever species of "vermin" best fits Kafka's description). The claim that this is the specific method of these writers, and that the Bradbury of **"The Third Expedition"** is one of them, is admittedly bold. It is based on nothing more solid than subjective impression, but it proves its worth by providing the foundation for a coherent interpretation. I know of no other approach that can.

What does the writer really do? What makes him do it? What gift does he have? These questions are of great interest to psychologists, but for a long time they were leery of tackling them. Without the concept of the unconscious, the questions could not even be approached. Freud had too much respect for the Muses to be hasty about studying them. When the collapse of the seemingly stable European civilization in World War I compelled psychology to look at problems beyond individual scope, Paul Federn, a "first generation" psychoanalyst, coined this formulation in a book published in 1919 [*Zur Psychologie der Revolution: die vaterlose Gesellschaft*]: "What we can observe in early childhood as contents of fantasies and objects of anxiety works as unconscious forces hidden in the adult, to come to light misshapen in the delusion of the ill or wellformed in the work of the artist." Much exploration has been done since then, but Federn's terse pronouncement has stood up. It fits **"The Third Expedition"** amazingly well.

Pertinent observations could, of course, be made before. When Goethe was unhappy in love and Charlotte married another man, he did not shoot himself. He wrote the story of Werther, who did. Charles Morice, a French art critic, wrote an article in 1885 ["La Semaine," *Petite Tribune*

Républicaine, April 2, 1885] reviewing the work of Odilon Redon who had produced astounding graphics, the counterpart in art of what works like *The Martian Chronicles* represent in literature (the best science fiction art is not necessarily found in illustrations of science fiction stories). Morice speaks of the double meaning of the word "dream." (Obviously it means one thing when we think of what we dreamt last night and when Martin Luther King, Jr., says, "I have a dream.") Morice says: "The meaning we must give the word "dream" is neither that of colloquial speech and prose (involuntary visions in sleep), nor the rare and poetic one (voluntary visions while awake). It is this and it is that, it is waking and sleeping. It is in truth the dream of a dream, the voluntary ordering of involuntary vision." It is this ordering of the disordered that makes the art we are dealing with what it is.

Stephen King (essay date 1981)

SOURCE: "Horror Fiction," in *Stephen King's Danse Macabre,* Berkley Books, 1981, pp. 241-360.

[*In the excerpt below, King places Bradbury's fantasy fiction in the tradition of American naturalism, adding that the early collection* Dark Carnival *contains the author's best horror stories.*]

It might be worth remembering that Theodore Dreiser, the author of *Sister Carrie* and *An American Tragedy,* was, like Bradbury, sometimes his own worst enemy . . . mostly because Dreiser never knew when to stop. "When you open your mouth, Stevie," my grandfather once said to me in despair, "all your guts fall out." I had no reply to that then, but I suppose if he were alive today, I would reply: That's 'cause I want to be Theodore Dreiser when I grow up. Well, Dreiser was a great writer, and Bradbury seems to be the fantasy genre's version of Dreiser, although Bradbury's line-by-line writing is better and his touch is lighter. Still, the two of them share a remarkable commonality.

On the minus side, both show a tendency to not so much write about a subject as to bulldoze it into the ground . . . and once so bulldozed, both have a tendency to bludgeon the subject until all signs of movement have ceased. On the plus side, both Dreiser and Bradbury are American naturalists of a dark persuasion, and in a crazy sort of way they seem to bookend Sherwood Anderson, the American champ of naturalism. Both of them wrote of American people living in the heartland (although Dreiser's heartland people come to the city while Bradbury's stay to home), of innocence coming heartbreakingly to experience (although Dreiser's people usually break, while Bradbury's people remain, although changed, whole), and both speak in voices which are uniquely, even startlingly American. Both narrate in a clear English which remains informal while mostly eschewing idiom—when Bradbury lapses occasionally into slang it startles us so much that he seems almost vulgar. Their voices are unmistakably American voices.

The easiest difference to point out, and maybe the most unimportant, is that Dreiser is called a realist while Bradbury is known as a fantasist. Even worse, Bradbury's paperback publisher insists tiresomely on calling him "The World's Greatest Living Science Fiction Writer" (making him sound like one of the freaks in the shows he writes about so often), when Bradbury has never written anything but the most nominal science fiction. Even in his space stories, he is not interested in negative-ion drives or relativity converters. There are rockets, he says in the connected stories which form *The Martian Chronicles, R Is for Rocket,* and *S Is for Space.* That is all you need to know and is, therefore, all I am going to tell you.

To this I would add that if you want to know how the rockets are going to work in any hypothetical future, turn to Larry Niven or Robert Heinlein; if you want literature—*stories,* to use Jack Finney's word—about what the future might hold, you must go to Ray Bradbury or perhaps to Kurt Vonnegut. What powers the rockets is *Popular Mechanics* stuff. The province of the writer is what powers the people. . . .

Bradbury's . . . best work, from the beginning, has been his fantasy . . . and his best fantasy has been his horror stories. . . . The best of the early Bradbury was collected in the marvelous Arkham House collection *Dark Carnival.* No easily obtainable edition of this work, the *Dubliners* of American fantasy fiction, is available. Many of the stories originally published in *Dark Carnival* can be found in a later collection, *The October Country,* which is available in paper. Included are such short Bradbury classics of gut-chilling horror as **"The Jar," "The Crowd,"** and the unforgettable **"Small Assassin."** Other Bradbury stories published in the forties were so horrible that the author now repudiates them (some were adapted as comics stories and published, with a younger Bradbury's permission, in E.C.'s *The Crypt of Terror*). One of these involves an undertaker who performs hideous but curiously moral atrocities upon his "clients"—for instance, when three old biddies who loved to gossip maliciously are killed in an accident, the undertaker chops off their heads and buries these three heads together, mouth to ear and ear to mouth, so they can enjoy a hideous *kaffeeklatsch* throughout eternity.

David Mogen (essay date 1986)

SOURCE: "Entering the Space Frontier: Quests Mundane, Profane, and Divine," in *Ray Bradbury,* Twayne Publishers, 1986, pp. 63-81.

[*In the following essay, Mogen explores mythopoetic elements in Bradbury's space-frontier fiction.*]

Bradbury's space-colonization fiction integrates two major myth systems to express the significance of mankind entering unearthly new environments: the biblical myths of the Garden and the Promised Land, and the American myth of the frontier. In fusing these myth systems Bradbury participates in an American literary tradition extending from contemporary science fiction back to initial responses to the New World of America. Since the first ambivalent Puritan accounts of their errand into the wilderness, American writing about frontier experience has evoked, explicitly or implicitly, these biblical analogies. And, given the strength of this tradition of frontier writing, it was only natural for Bradbury and other American science-fiction writers to dramatize the romance of space travel in terms of this central culture myth. Thus, American visions of the future often portray the frontier spirit revitalized by new challenges, in the fiction of scientifically oriented writers such as Robert Heinlein and Isaac Asimov as well as in Bradbury's science-fiction fables.

Paradoxically, Bradbury's treatment of the science-fiction wilderness theme struck his initial audience as original and unsettling precisely because it is so deeply traditional. Essentially, Bradbury incorporates the dominant science-fiction theme of wilderness conquest into a central mythopoeic tradition of American frontier literature, extending from ironic American Renaissance writers such as Hawthorne, Melville, and Thoreau into the present. Because of his flamboyantly metaphorical style, Bradbury's fiction makes overt the frontier analogies implicit in other magazine fiction of the forties and fifties, but he also restores the potentially theological overtones and ironies of the wilderness symbol. If the New World of Mars is imaginatively linked to earlier visions of America as a New World, both images of the "New World" can also evoke biblical images of the Garden and the Promised Land. Bradbury's characteristic irony illustrates the ambiguous implications of mankind's quest into these new "New Worlds."

Overtly integrating the prevailing science-fiction myth with this central tradition of mythopoeic American writing—a tradition at once visionary and highly ironic—Bradbury's space-colonization fiction dramatizes both the spiritual and the tragic dimensions of the theme, placing the drama of the survival quest within the larger context of a struggle to fulfill essentially religious aspirations. Fundamentally, Bradbury utilizes the ironic potential in the biblical origins of the frontier myth to warn about the tragic potential of our frontier heritage, as well as to evoke from it a stirring appeal to fulfill a manifest destiny among the stars. Though Bradbury has expressed this underlying mythos in nonfiction writing throughout his career, the first critic to articulate the full range of his meaning was Willis McNelly, who in 1969 perceived the central importance of the analogy between the myth of wilderness conquest and the myth of space colonization, and who also emphasized the spiritual dimension of Bradbury's treatment of the theme:

> For Bradbury, the final, inexhaustible wilderness is the wilderness of space. In that wilderness, man will find himself, renew himself, and there, as atoms of God, he will live forever. Ultimately, then, the conquest of space becomes a religious quest. . . . Ultimately the religious theme is the end product of Bradbury's vision of man, implicit in man's nature.
>
> ["Bradbury Revisited," *CEA Critic,*
> Vol. 31, March 1969]

Because of the ironic power of this wilderness fiction, because his irony played against the prevailing traditions of magazine fiction in the forties and fifties, Bradbury's space-colonization fiction has often been misinterpreted. A visionary who believes the human race will conquer death through spiritual rebirth in unearthly new frontiers, he has been misconstrued as a pessimist who despairs of the future. And indeed, his best fiction is filled with warnings, depicting the danger of reenacting old tragedies through ignoring the dark side of history and of human nature. If the science-fiction myth invites us back into the Garden, we must reenter with knowledge gained from the old story. For we will again encounter the serpent, in the form of the "wilderness in man himself": "Man's other half, yes the hairy mammoth, the sabre-tooth, the blind spider fiddling in the venomous dark, dreaming mushroom-cloud dreams" [**"Marvels and Miracles—Pass It On!"**, *New York Times Magazine,* March 20, 1955].

Bradbury's ambivalent wilderness imagery, evoking dreams of Paradise regained as well as of the Great Loneliness, is mirrored in his portrayal of human nature itself, which can be both the sensory consciousness of God and the spirit of the "dark brute" within, wreaking destruction with increasingly lethal machines [**"Marvels and Miracles . . ."**]. Though his visions of our future in space are charged with irony, their ambiguous implications are finally resolved through the theme of metamorphosis. For ultimately Bradbury's space-colonization fiction suggests that we will learn from our past and meet the challenges of the new frontier. Just as settlers from the Old World painfully—with tragic consequences for the natives—formed a new civilization in America, so too the struggle to make this "final, inexhaustible wilderness" home will ultimately transform earth-bound man into a being at home in its celestial dwelling places.

THE LURE OF THE SPACE FRONTIER

Bradbury's reactions to a scene in John Steinbeck's *The Red Pony* illustrate the continuity between myths of the Old West and those about the space frontier (which Bradbury helped shape). In one of Steinbeck's most moving scenes in "The Leader of the People," last story in the cycle, an old man, once a wagon-train leader, sadly explains to his grandson Jody that the spirit of "westering" that impelled him and his people across the continent has died out. There on the California coast, where the grandfather's westward quest was halted by the sea, the boy feels the sadness of the old man's vision as he reminisces about a journey "as big as God." At night Jody dreams of the heroic past, so unlike the seemingly mundane present in which he lives. Apparently unnoticed by his grandfather, however, the boy suggests that perhaps, somehow, there might be challenges as great in his own lifetime.

Steinbeck's stance in *The Red Pony* is that of the modern western, focusing on the bittersweet memories of the grandfather, who has lived beyond his time to see the westward quest trivialized and forgotten as he interminably attempts to express what made it all so grand. But Bradbury, highly moved by the scene, saw the unrealized dramatic possibilities in Jody and his ranchhand friend Billy Buck, visualizing a new kind of frontier story in which they might embody the spirit of "westering" just as the old wagon train leader did before them: "From now on there is no East and West, only up. Because the West is the westering thing, which was written of in *The Red Pony* by Steinbeck, of course, so beautifully—Billy Buck standing at the shore of the Pacific with nowhere to go. Except when I read that when I was young I said, 'Hey, Billy, I got news for you. We've got a frontier and we're gonna take it!' A lot of things were influenced by my encounter with Billy Buck and Steinbeck that year. He helped shape my thinking in *The Martian Chronicles*" [unpublished interview with the author, 1980].

Indeed, transported into the not-too-distant future, Steinbeck's yearning young boy, Jody, might well be the hero of **"King of the Grey Spaces,"** which Bradbury feels was his breakthrough story in science fiction, the story in which he first defined his distinctive approach to the subject of space. "When I made the turn from becoming an imitative writer to becoming a truly creative writer . . . I began to do stories about myself and about the kind of boy I would be if I lived in the future. I wrote stories like **'King of the Grey Spaces,'** which is no more than the story of a group of boys who want to be astronauts" [interview]. A quiet drama about adolescent boys of the future dreaming of going to the stars, the story's chief effect is to communicate the lure of the space frontier [reprinted as **"R is for Rocket,"** in *R is for Rocket*].

Though the story captures through a boy's perspective the thrill of entering the space frontier, it also emphasizes the personal sacrifice such pioneering requires. When he prepares for the frontier, the hero must relinquish his role on earth, his boyhood. The boys and their "gang" spend their free time hanging around the rocket base, conversing in space age lingo, and watching rocket launches. They all dream of being selected for astronaut training school, which selectively enlists only the brightest and most fit. When the narrator is selected his mother tells him she will adopt his best friend Ralph to take his place, news which delights the hero yet also dramatizes the poignant underside of his success, that by fulfilling his dream of space he gives up the comfort and security of his earthbound life. This effect is foreshadowed by the attitude of his teacher who, knowing he will be one of the "chosen," watches him taking an examination with "envy and admiration and pity all in one," expressing the ambiguous implications of the honor.

But if there is some sadness in the hero's success, the story nevertheless affirms that the dream he pursues is ennobling and enthralling. Though his mother is sad to lose him to the Board, she also speaks to him of his dead father, a chemist, who worked in an underground laboratory where "he never saw the stars." Thus, by pursuing the quest into space the hero not only fulfills his father's deepest dreams, he also sacrifices his personal life for all humanity to fulfill the spiritual potential of the species. The underlying analogy that informs the story is religious, as the boy's intense last talk with his mother makes clear:

"We held to each other and whispered and talked and she said many things, how good this was going to be for us, but especially for me, how fine, what an honor it was, like the old days when men fasted and took vows and joined churches and stopped up their tongues and were silent and prayed to be worthy and to live well as monks and priests of many churches in far places. . . . This was a greater priesthood, in a way, she said . . . and I was to be some small part of it. . . . I would belong to all the worlds."

"The Rocket Man" dramatizes the lure of the space frontier more painfully from a boy's perspective. The key roles in the earlier family drama are reversed: now the astronaut hero is the father; the point-of-view character, again, is a sensitive boy; and the mother, rather than a spokesman for the values of the new frontier, is cast in the more traditional role of helplessly opposing her husband's wanderlust, a role that the boy, with some reluctance, helps her play. Suspended in the middle of his parents' tragic marriage, the boy feels the emotional claims of both—of his mother and his father, of the home and of far places, of earth and of space. Like his mother, he longs for his father to remain home, and he fears for his father's life. But he also shares his father's overwhelming attraction to the mysteries of space; he is receptive to an enchanted aura about objects which have traveled to distant worlds: "And from the opened case spilled his black uniform, like a black nebula, stars glittering here or there, distantly, in the material. I kneaded the dark stuff in my warm hands; I smelled the planet Mars, an iron smell, and the planet Venus, a green ivy smell, and the planet Mercury, a scene of sulphur and fire, and I could smell the milky moon and the hardness of the stars" [*The Illustrated Man*].

Because his attraction to the space frontier is irreconcilable with his life as an earthbound family man, the rocket man's powerful loves are a source of tragedy. Like many frontier heroes before him, he is caught between two worlds, unable to reconcile their opposing claims. "Don't ever be a rocket man," he warns his son, suspecting the boy's passion for space. "Because when you're out there you want to be here, and when you're here you want to be out there." Trying to maintain a foothold in two opposing worlds, he is at home in neither.

Bradbury uses light imagery to express the emotional conflicts of **"The Rocket Man."** Within the terms of the story light is celestial and otherworldly, exercising an influence that the mother opposes with the absorbent warmth of the earth. A sympathetically portrayed though helplessly manipulative character, she cannot abide the sky. She especially fears starlight because she knows it casts a spell on her husband and son, luring them away from her. Because of the danger of her husband's job, she also perceives the night sky as a potential graveyard, so when he is gone she barricades herself behind heavy green shutters to shut out the starlight. But the news of his death establishes the final irony. He died in the sun itself, not among the stars, so she and the boy become burrowing night creatures: "The only days we ever went out to walk were the days when it was raining and there was no sun." Initially battling the lure of starlight, the mother finally must retreat even from the light of day.

In **"The Rocket Man"** light represents the overwhelming power of the myth of space, a myth whose origins are ultimately religious but which fuses a religious "sense of wonder" with an evolutionary perspective on man's destiny. **"The End of the Beginning,"** another quiet Green Town drama in which two older parents contemplate the significance of their astronaut son leaving earth, dramatizes this sweeping evolutionary perspective. As in many of these essentially philosophical space age tales, the protagonist's reverie about the meaning of space travel provides the story's climax. The theological overtones of the quest are evoked for him by words from the old spiritual, "A wheel in a wheel. Way in the middle of the air" [*A Medicine for Melancholy*]. But he also integrates his sense that the trip is essentially a holy mission with an evolutionary interpretation of its meaning. The step into space ushers in an awesome new era, not merely from a human perspective but from a cosmic perspective as well, a perspective from which all previous human history appears as merely the final stage of life's bondage to earth. Indeed, when the father thinks of manifest destiny here he identifies mankind struggling to enter space with the first seaborne life to grope onto land:

> All I know is its really the end of the beginning. The Stone Age, Bronze Age, Iron Age: from now on we'll lump all those together under one big name for when we walked on Earth and heard the birds at morning and cried with envy. Maybe we'll call it the Earth Age, or maybe the Age of Gravity. Millions of years we fought gravity. When we were amoebas and fish we struggled to get out of the sea without gravity crushing us. Once safe on the shore we fought to stand upright without breaking our new invention, the spine. . . . A billion years Gravity kept us home, mocked us with wind and clouds, cabbage moths and locusts. That's what's so god-awful big about tonight . . . it's the end of old man Gravity and the age we'll remember him by, once and for all.

The story ends by counterpoising two images—the son's rocket lights a new spot in the sky, while the father philosophically mows his lawn, caught up in the magical whirr of rotating blades and falling grass as he relishes the moment, feeling like "all mankind bathing at last in the fresh water of the fountain of youth." As this final New World image suggests, man enters the space frontier to be reborn, ultimately to be transformed by his new environment.

If Bradbury identifies man entering space with life moving from sea to land, he also dramatizes this transition through comparison to specifically American frontier experience, frequently evoking an analogy which is made manifest in an early story entitled **"The Wilderness,"** a story that is essentially a poetic reverie about the analogy itself [*The Golden Apples of the Sun*]. The plot is so simple it merely provides a vehicle with which to contemplate this central comparison between the Old West and space: a woman on Earth waits for her lover's call from

outer space and tells him she has decided to homestead with him in his new home. Most of the story consists of the woman's thoughts before and after the call, stream-of-consciousness reflections that associate the challenges posed by the new frontier with heroic myths about the frontier past.

The story's central theme is manifest in the protagonist's contemplation of the setting. The phone call takes place at a rocket base in Independence, Missouri, 2003, which establishes the initial analogy to the wagon-train era of American development. "Long, long ago, 1849" the setting was oddly similar, filled with apprehensive but hopeful settlers waiting to depart with "their wagons, their indiscriminate destinies, and their dreams." Later, she generalizes this frontier metaphor to encompass all of American history, from the initial discovery of the New World to her own destiny, emphasizing at the same time the continuity of the traditional woman's role in this mythology (a role that a new generation of writers has altered significantly)—reluctantly following her man as he pursues his dreams into the wilderness: "'1492? 1612?' Lenora sighed and the wind in the trees sighed with her, moving away. 'It's always Columbus Day or Plymouth Rock Day, and I'll be damned if I know what one woman can do about it'." And her final reflections as she falls asleep generalize the American frontier experience to an essentially cosmic perspective: "On the rim of the precipice, on the edge of the cliff of stars. In their time the smell of the buffalo, and in our time the smell of the Rocket," she reflects. "This was as it had been and would forever continue to be."

A poetic revery about the relationship between our frontier heritage and our space age future, **"The Wilderness"** anticipates a more bookish kind of story Bradbury developed in later years, in which he transports the spirits of his favorite authors out into the space frontier to witness the wonders of the new wilderness and to articulate its significance. Thus, the spirit of George Bernard Shaw speaks through a robot on board a rocket ship in **"G.B.S., Mark V,"** and in **"Forever and the Earth"** a time machine transports Thomas Wolfe from his deathbed to the future, where he composes an epic account of man's entry into space [*Long after Midnight*]. Because their protagonists so dramatically link the future to the past, such stories emphasize both the thrill of entering the unknown and the continuity of human experience.

"The Golden Apples of the Sun" develops the wilderness quest motif more actively. The kind of story that throughout Bradbury's career has generated debate about where to separate science fiction from fantasy, **"The Golden Apples of the Sun"** combines a dense fabric of mythological allusions with fanciful technology. A rocket descends to the sun's surface to retrieve a "cup" (in a mechanical scoop) of the sun's plasma, both for scientific study and simply to meet the challenge of entering the space frontier's living heart. To survive in this environment the rocket is equipped with giant refrigeration units which encase it in ice, an idea that appears to originate in boyhood memories of watching icicles melt in spring sun

[*The Golden Apples of the Sun*]. When the auxiliary pump of the refrigeration unit breaks down the captain and the crew, like frantic plumbers, fix the unit by hand in time to ward off disaster.

But if the story's technology is essentially whimsical, it is rich in mythology and literary allusions. The rocket itself has not one but three mythological names—*Capa de Oro, Prometheus,* and *Icarus*—a device through which Bradbury identifies the quest into space with heroic myths of the past, as he also does in the tripartite name titling a similarly conceived story, **"Icarus Montgolfier Wright."** Indeed, the story is a bit self-conscious about its mythological and literary origins, opening with the captain explicating to his crew the numerous literary allusions invoked by their quest—from the reference to Yeats in the story's title, to Shakespeare's "Fear no more the heat of the day," to titles of twentieth-century novels that seem to echo the theme.

The mythological center of the story is made manifest in the captain's reflections as they complete their mission: the sun's plasma is "the flesh of God, the blood of the universe" [*The Golden Apples of the Sun*]. Like their mythological ancestors, though they now possess dazzling new technologies, they enter divine realms to possess new knowledge for their tribe. As in much of Bradbury's space-frontier fiction, man's quest for excitement and knowledge serves purposes articulated only by the inspired talkers who populate his tales. The lure of the frontier in his fiction is—to adopt the words of Steinbeck's wagon-train leader—"as big as God," inspiring a "westering" impulse which, like the American frontier experience itself, brings out the best and the worst in human nature.

"The Gardens of Space": Ironies, Visions, and Transformations

In 1965 Bradbury published a credo in *Playboy* (where it was complemented by an off-color cartoon). Articulating the mythos that informs his space-frontier fiction, "Remembrances of Things Future" begins by describing the future rushing upon us, its mysteries represented in symbols we must read with "prescience" to realize our destiny. Referring to "the rockets of earthmen writing fresh Columbian history upon tideless seas," Bradbury compares the New World of space with the New World of the Americas as they first appeared to European explorers— a comparison that informs much of his fiction, especially *The Martian Chronicles.* Only by utilizing sufficient vision, he argues, can we realize our unprecedented opportunity to fulfill the goals of "three searches": the "search for national purpose," the "search for peace," and the "search for a new image of God."

As the range of motivations he alludes to suggests, Bradbury sees the "westering" impulse as a combination of various, sometimes conflicting motives, ranging from tribalism and materialism to an urge inherent in life to fulfill a spiritual destiny. Seeking larger profits, we wander into fresh pastures. And if the emphasis on the word "search"

suggests we are embarked on an epic quest, the emphasis on the "search for a new image of God" emphasizes the continuity between this fabulous future and fables of the past. Ultimately, the "westering" spirit that will take us to the stars utilizes our most advanced technologies to pursue our most ancient dreams. For we enter the new frontier seeking "wonders that will bloom for us in the gardens of space." Ironically, by leaving the world of our birth, we seek to recover Eden, where man will be "back at the center of the universe, where he once began, and from which he fell away at the beginning of knowledge, and to which he must return" ["Remembrances of Things Future"].

Though his essays unequivocally celebrate our entrance into the gardens of space, Bradbury's fiction presents more disturbing and complex images of the frontier process. Just as the biblical Garden is a complex image representing the bliss of the unfallen, the ambivalent attractions of knowledge, and the origin of evil, so Bradbury's fictional gardens are both alluring and destructive. Space itself has ambivalent associations, for as it opens up new vistas of wonder and beauty it also separates man from his roots. Thus, space appears both as a natural cathedral of God and as a void where men's souls self-destruct.

The unearthly environment of space brings out both the best and the worst in the space pioneers who enter it, as is evident in **"Kaleidoscope,"** in which the survivors of a rocket's collision with a meteor are "thrown into space like a dozen wriggling silverfish" [*The Illustrated Man*] to die slowly as their life support systems wear down. Falling through the void "as pebbles fall down wells," they remain in radio contact. In part, the story is a character study, revealing how different personality types cope with the knowledge of imminent death: one goes mad; La Spere, the most contented in life, goes to his death with spirited good will; Applegate and Hollis, after a vicious exchange, finally reconcile their differences, realizing that their meanness in the end only reflects their frustrations in life; and Stone, filled with wonder, drifts into an asteroid cloud, evoking the story's central poetic aside, which captures both the beauty and the terror of space:

> There were only the great diamonds and sapphires and emerald mists and velvet inks of space, with God's voice mingling among the crystal fires. There was a kind of wonder . . . in the thought of Stone going off in the meteor swarm, out past Mars for years and coming in toward Earth every five years, passing in and out of the planet's ken for the next million centuries. Stone and the Myrmidone cluster eternal and unending, shifting and shaping like the kaleidoscope colors when you were a child and held the long tube to the sun and gave it a twirl.

The story's title, **"Kaleidoscope,"** expresses both this central image and another underlying theme of Bradbury's space-frontier stories, the interdependent relationship between inner and outer states, between the pioneer and his environment. Just as to some extent the beauty of a kaleidoscope is in the eye of the beholder, which finds form in random patterns, so attitudes toward the space frontier shape basic perceptions. One man's garden of delight is another's desert of desolation (a theme mirroring an earlier American debate about whether the area west of the Mississippi was a new Garden or the Great American Desert). For if there is a divine presence in space in Bradbury's fiction, it is a presence paradoxically dependent upon its observer, since to Bradbury humanity in its divine aspect *is* God witnessing His creation, and "without us God would be dead another billion years or forever" [Interview].

Bradbury frequently portrays "God"—sometimes referred to as the "Life Force," a concept he adopted from George Bernard Shaw—as an interaction between an intrinsically "dead" universe and a spiritual potential embodied in man's consciousness. Thus, when the astronauts in **"Kaleidoscope"** lose radio contact their voices die out "like the echoes of the words of God spoken and vibrating in the starred deep." Interacting with the celestial environment, the crew fragments to reveal man in all his aspects, profane and divine. As they drift into oblivion they express madness, pettiness, and vengefulness, but ultimately they also express spiritual delight and a kind of innocent reverence as well. Hollis, reflecting philosophically on his wasted, fearful life, returns to his origins where he appears as a "falling star" to a small boy on Earth.

Though Bradbury's space-colonization fiction dramatizes tragedy and irony, it nevertheless projects powerful images of recovered Eden as well, which express his fervent conviction that, however problematic the process, mankind will in the end have the imagination and grace to be reborn in flesh and spirit in the "inexhaustible wilderness" of space.

—*David Mogen*

"No Particular Night or Morning" dramatizes the frightening and destructive aspects of space pioneering. The story's theme, expressed in the title, is that space travel and the frontier process itself can encourage and exacerbate escapism. Hitchcock, the central character, seeks to retreat in space from the frustrations of his life—ultimately, to retreat from reality itself. As the story opens he has already developed a psychotic logic for denying his past, visualizing his past experiences as those of corpses who no longer exist, who have nothing to do with his present self. "You're cutting yourself off that way," observes a fellow astronaut, defining a psychological strategy of withdrawal which culminates when Hitchcock launches from the rocket into space itself, where his own retreat from identity is mirrored in the void. The story develops a common motif of frontier fiction, that the frontier process attracts not only the boldest and most enterprising, but the

most desperate and unstable as well. Hitchcock is not drawn to the frontier to build anew, but precisely to lose his past and ultimately his self: "Space, thought Clemens. The space that Hitchcock loved so well. Space, with nothing on top, nothing on the bottom, a lot of empty nothings in between, and Hitchcock falling in the middle of nothing, on his way to no particular night and no particular morning . . ." [*The Illustrated Man*].

The divine aspect of space, however, is described in **"The Gift,"** a short vignette in which customs requires a couple and their young boy, launching into space on Christmas Eve, to leave their meager Christmas decorations behind. The father waits until midnight to take the disconsolate boy to a cabin with a panoramic view, where the boy looks entranced "out into space and the deep night at the burning and burning of ten billion billion white and lovely candles" while passengers sing "the old, the familiar carols" [*A Medicine for Melancholy*]. If **"No Particular Night or Morning"** dramatizes the psychic dislocation created by the frontier experience, **"The Gift"** communicates Bradbury's basic faith that we can adapt our central rituals and symbols to help make space our home, that we can rediscover old meanings in new metaphors: "I think the metaphors the Space Age has given us can transcend the old metaphors. And we take Christ along with us, we take Moses along, we take all the Old and New Testament, but we find new ways of speaking from the midst of our technologies" ["Remembrances of Things Past"].

Though space itself evokes both ironic and paradisiacal imagery in Bradbury's fiction, the phrase "gardens in space" refers even more obviously to the "new worlds" discovered there. Mars, his most fully-realized and frequently utilized setting, highlights both the diverse motives of the settlers and the ambivalent promise of a new Garden. But Bradbury's treatment of Venus emphasizes a different source of frontier tragedy—the effects of a truly inhumane environment, whose relentless rain destroys even the most hardy frontier spirits outside the protection of artificial, earthlike havens. **"The Long Rain"** submerges the reader in this Venusian atmosphere, accompanying survivors of a rocket accident on a wilderness trek as they endure the "Chinese water cure" exposure on Venus entails: "We're not made for water. You can't sleep, you can't breathe right, and you're crazy from being soggy" [*The Illustrated Man*].

Bradbury's vivid imagery generates a nightmarish atmosphere. The men themselves have become "as white as mushrooms"; a jungle storm is "a monster supported upon a thousand electric blue legs", a river "boiled out of the earth, suddenly, like a mortal wound." Counterpoised against the hallucinatory horror of the jungle is the tantalizing dream of reaching a sun-dome, one of the artificial havens men have built to survive on this world. Indeed, the story's climax simply captures the ecstasy of dry air and sunlight after torturous immersion in the endless rain.

"All Summer in a Day" presents the Hell-world of Venus from children's point of view, evoking a more subtle and poignant sense of tragedy. In a frontier schoolroom on Venus children eagerly await the sun's appearance, an event approximately equivalent in frequency to an eclipse on Earth. Bradbury's description of the children identifies them with the riotous vegetation of the planet: "The children pressed to each other like so many roses, so many weeds, intermixed, peering out for a look at the hidden sun" [*A Medicine for Melancholy*]. Starved for sunshine and open space, though they don't realize it, they romp in wild-eyed ecstasy in the sunlight, seeing clearly for the first time a landscape they cannot even recognize as alien to what they need: "It was the color of rubber and ash, this jungle, from the many years without sun. It was the color of stones and white cheeses and ink, and it was the color of the moon."

But etched in against the general tragedy implicit in the children's short-lived ecstasy in the sun is the haunting figure of Margot, whose simple poem sketches her personal tragedy: "I think the sun is a flower / That blooms for just one hour." A frail, sickly immigrant from Earth, she endures the hate of the other children because she remembers days of sunlight. Until the Venusian rains return, the children forget that they maliciously placed her in the closet when the great event began. When they return to the closet there is no sound inside. A haunting fable about the destructive side of human nature, **"All Summer in a Day"** reveals the snake from the Garden in the hearts of deprived children.

Science-fiction versions of the serpent appear in more obvious forms in other stories. In **"The One Who Waits"** [*Long after Midnight*], for instance, destructiveness is embodied (actually, disembodied) in the malevolent consciousness of an alien, a psychic entity living in a Martian "Soul Well" which possesses the bodies of a group of human visitors, destroys them one by one, then waits for new victims. **"The City"** presents another version of evil working in unexpected places. A rocket crew exploring an abandoned city on a relatively unknown planet becomes an instrument for the city's revenge. Thousands of years earlier the planet's inhabitants, betrayed and defeated in war, programmed the city to redress the injury. With a bit of surgical alteration and psychic programming, performed by the city's underground machinery, the crew is returned to earth carrying "golden bombs of disease culture" [*The Illustrated Man*] with which to infect the home planet, after which the city, animated through the centuries exclusively by this high-tech curse, enjoys "the luxury of dying." **"The Lost City of Mars"** presents a more ambiguous version of this theme, in which the live city is programmed to fulfill fantasies, rather than to exact revenge [*I Sing the Body Electric!*]. As does the carnival in *Something Wicked This Way Comes,* the story's setting reveals the inner qualities of the characters exposed to it, strengthening some and taking possession of others.

Many of Bradbury's space-colonization stories explore the ironic possibilities in the biblical and frontier analogies to the "gardens in space." But even in the tragic and ironic stories irony derives from the contrast between grim realities and the ideal images Bradbury's characters pursue. And in some stories the spiritual aspects of the quest into space are overt rather than implied. **"The Man"** treats the spiritual theme ironically, highlighting a paradox implicit in the frontier quest—that it can easily become a frantic and self-defeating pursuit of "happiness," substituting possession of external things for development of internal qualities [*The Illustrated Man*]. A somewhat comic version of Melville's Ahab, Captain Hart, initially a wheeling and dealing trader obsessed with defeating his competition, lights out in breakneck pursuit of the Saviour, "the man," when he hastily concludes he just missed his latest visitation. His crew-member Martin, the story's Ishmael-figure, visualizes the captain careening throughout the galaxy, doomed to just miss the next coming at every landing. As the captain departs, Martin and the local mayor return to the local village where He has been waiting, of course, all along. Like Ahab, Captain Hart does have moments of self-reflection, during which he almost slows down long enough to perceive the disparity between his obsessive mission and his true goals. His reflections become an ironic statement about the contradictory images that lure men into space:

> "Why do we do it, Martin? This space travel, I mean. Always on the go. Always searching. Our insides always tight, never any rest."

> "Maybe we're looking for peace and quiet. Certainly there's none on earth," said Martin.

> "No, there's not, is there?" Captain Hart was thoughtful. "Not since Darwin, eh? Not since everything went by the board, everything we used to believe in, eh? Divine power and all that. And so you think maybe that's why we're going out to the stars, eh Martin? Looking for lost souls, is that it? Try to get away from our evil planet to a good one?"

> "Perhaps, sir. Certainly we're looking for something."

Ironically, Captain Hart's decision to pursue "the Man" rather than his own profit only intensifies his obsessive superficiality. He seeks for his "lost soul" everywhere except within himself. If he ever truly encountered the Man he would request "a little—peace and quiet." But since he pursues spiritual enlightenment with the same driven avariciousness with which he pursued trading contracts, he never notices the contradiction between his methods and his ends. Nevertheless, his tragi-comic destiny illustrates the essentially spiritual origins of man's "search" in space: even the most mundane profiteers participate, however foolishly and self-destructively, in the quest for spiritual fulfillment.

Most of Bradbury's spiritual quest-figures are more humble and self-aware than Captain Hart. In its purest form—which simply generates a different system of ironies—Bradbury represents this spiritual quest through Catholic priests, who enter space eagerly seeking spiritual challenges and visitations. One of the most delightful early Mars stories, **"The Fire Balloons,"** reveals "the Man's" presence in a new form, that of the blue globes that hover in the Martian hills. Because of his somewhat suspect "flexibility," the church selects Father Peregrine, possessed of an adventurous frontier spirit eager to adapt traditional orthodoxy to new environments, to lead a group of missionaries to the wild and wooly settlements on Mars. Conceiving of their quest as a search for new forms of sin in a new environment, Father Peregrine cannot resist the greatest challenge posed by his mission—determining if the curious "fire balloons" are indeed sentient beings possessed of souls, and designing an appropriate strategy for "saving" them if they are. When he determines that the curious beings are sentient, he proceeds, in a most enlightened and unorthodox spirit of missionary dedication, to adapt the church doctrine to the native culture. In a speech that represents Bradbury's own views on how traditional symbols can be adapted to new contexts, he justifies altering the central symbols of his faith: "We deal with symbols here. Christ is no less Christ, you must admit, in being represented by a circle or a square. For centuries the cross has symbolized his love and agony. So this circle will be the Martian Christ. This is how we will bring Him to Mars" [*The Illustrated Man*].

But if Father Peregrine seeks to bring Christ to Mars, he finds instead that Mars restores to humans the living spiritual presence represented in Christian symbols. Father Peregrine's experience ironically parallels relationships between Christian missionaries and Native American cultures. And, whether or not Bradbury was consciously utilizing the parallel, Peregrine's substitution of the circle for the cross nicely resolves an historical conflict between the hierarchical models of Christianity (dividing the "saved" from the "fallen," "spirit" from "matter," etc.) and the "sacred hoop" that structures Native American ritual and belief. But just as too few Christian missionaries, perhaps, realized they were "bringing religion" to profoundly spiritual cultures, so even Father Peregrine's flexible alterations of tradition ironically miss the point, as he is the first to perceive. For when the "old ones" finally come to his new ceremony and reveal their true nature he realizes his missionary impulse in this context is not merely inappropriate but fundamentally blasphemous. The old ones do not need new symbols to represent Christ since they, in fact, *are* Him, as even the very orthodox and rather dense Father Stone comes to recognize: "Father Peregrine, that globe there—. . . . It *is* Him, after all." Having embarked on an adventurous mission to save souls, Father Peregrine returns to the frontier outpost strengthened in his true mission, knowing he has had a personal visitation from the spirit of Christ to assist in helping fallen humanity.

Other of Bradbury's overtly theological stories also dramatize conflicts inherent in adapting traditional symbols to the radically new contexts of the Space Age. "**The Messiah**" [*Long after Midnight*] presents another fervent Martian missionary whose dream of seeing "the Man" is satisfied more ambiguously. A telepathic Martian, trapped by the power of the missionary's fantasy, appears to him in his Easter devotion as the crucified Christ. Finally realizing he is fulfilling his spiritual quest by victimizing another sentient being, the priest ultimately releases the Martian after extracting a promise that he will represent Christ to him every year at Easter. Though the priest possesses admirable spiritual intensity, his "pact" parallels the ironic theme of *The Martian Chronicles,* in which settlers impose their own fantasies on their new environment, often with destructive consequences.

In "**The Machineries of Joy,**" technically a realist story, Father Vittorini outrages his Irish peers both with his flamboyant Italian personality and with his enthusiasm for speculating about the impact of rockets on their faith [*The Machineries of Joy*]. Presenting them to their dismay with Pope Pius XII's statement that "man has to make the effort to put himself in a new orientation with God and his universe," Vittorini turns an ongoing battle into a full-scale war, which ultimately is resolved when the Irish priests grudgingly accept both his colorful style and the modern age: settling down in front of a hitherto suspect television to watch the latest rocket blast-off, they contemplate whether these things are indeed God's new "machineries of joy." Pastor Sheldon, the most flexible of the Irish brethren, states the story's moral, both for spiritual leaders and for all mankind: "Why don't we climb on that rocket, father, and learn from it?"

All of Bradbury's space fiction dramatizes in some form the conflicts and possibilities created by adapting to new environments. In its purest form this adaptation process becomes metamorphosis. "**Chrysalis**" presents a literal version of this theme, in which a man overexposed to radiation is transformed physically through "delayed hereditary mutation" [*S is for Space*] into "the next evolutionary structure of man," which is biologically equipped to subsist in space. First published in *Amazing Stories* in 1946, "**Chrysalis**" is one of the few collected early stories whose melodramatic exposition illustrates Bradbury's early pulp style; but despite the awkward execution, the story does present a striking image of the metamorphosis theme implicit in much of Bradbury's more sophisticated fiction. Enclosed inside a hard shell Smith's body, like larval forms of insects in the chrysalis stage, transforms utterly, emerging finally as a being physically similar to humans but fundamentally altered. After escaping from the hospital the new man walks out under the desert sky, finishes a last cigarette which he grinds out "precisely under one heel," then gracefully soars off into his new home in space.

This metamorphosis theme is most often simply an extreme version of the adaptation process in new frontiers. In "**Dark They Were, and Golden-Eyed**" Mr. Bittering, alone among the Martian settlers, observes with horror that the frontier process has somehow reversed. Rather than adapting their environment to suit themselves, as they initially had every intention of doing, the settlers slowly transform into "Martians." Though they begin by naming their surroundings with their own names imported from Earth (the story was originally entitled "**The Naming of Names**"), they slowly revert to the old Martian names. Bickering points out indignantly that the peaches no longer look like peaches, but on one else cares. They all tan dark, their eyes turn golden, and they migrate to the hills. Finally accepting the transformation that the rest of the settlement has accepted peacefully, Bickering lies in a

Martian canal contemplating the metamorphosis process, in lines that echo the song "Full Fathom Five Thy Father Lies" in Shakespeare's *The Tempest*. Just as the underwater body changes to something "rich and strange" in the Shakespearean song, so the settlers are changed in the "river" of the Martian atmosphere:

> If I lie here long enough, he thought, the water will work and eat away my flesh until the bones show like coral. Just my skeleton left. And then the water can build on that skeleton—green things, deep water things, yellow things. Change. Change. Change. Slow deep silent change. . . .

> He saw the sky submerged above him, the sun made Martian by atmosphere and time and place.

> Up there, a big river, he thought, a Martian river, all of us lying deep in it, in our pebble houses, in our summer boulder houses, like crayfish hidden, and the water washing away our old bodies and lengthening the bones.

[*A Medicine for Melancholy*]

When new settlers come from Earth they find only natives in the hills and the abandoned frontier town. Perplexed, they begin industriously planning to transform the environment, assigning new names to their surroundings, noticing occasionally that their concentration is unaccountably distracted. . . . But as they begin work on the planet, the planet is already exercising its subtle influence on them. Though they are not aware of it, the exploitative frontier psychology that brought them there is being transformed by the idyllic atmosphere of the Garden into which they have wandered.

Implicit in all the individual tragedies and revelations in Bradbury's space-colonization stories is a central drama about the settlers' relationship to the New World, a powerful theme derived from the central frontier metaphors of American writing: in space and Mars, as in American frontier mythology, conquering new frontiers wreaks tragedy, yet ultimately shapes a distinctively new and hardy culture. If the biblical myths of Eden and the Promised Land are evoked in this drama, so too is the world-view of conquered tribal cultures here on Earth—the concept of the New World not just as property but as Mother Earth, a living presence which alternately suffers, destroys, and shapes those who come to colonize.

Bradbury's most literal treatment of this "live planet" theme, **"Here There Be Tygers,"** presents a planet that is a seductress, a conscious Garden who envelops explorers in her pastoral embrace. As in many of these stories, two characters represent the extremes of the frontier mentality, while a wise father-figure captain attempts to reconcile their opposing points of view: Chatterton, the developer, eagerly explains how men have to control planets or be controlled by them, an attitude which the captain describes as a prescription for "rape or ruin" [*R is for Rocket*]. Chatterton gives the sexual metaphor a new twist when he explains that the planet's essence, that which he must

dominate, is male, the feminine beauty only an alluring surface: "All hard underneath, all male iron, copper, uranium, black sod. Don't let cosmetics fool you." Ultimately, the planet destroys Chatterton (who is devoured by tigers) and the rest of the crew, aware that they are being seduced by a loving embrace, decide to complete their mission, then return to settle down. But as they leave the planet erupts in volcanic fury, the fury of a woman scorned, and they realize they left the Garden of their own choice, and can never return. Only Driscoll, Chatterton's opposite, remains, whistling happily as he wanders among the fine wine streams and luxurious forests, blissfully at peace, restored to the Garden by the direct simplicity of his nature.

Though Bradbury's space-colonization fiction dramatizes tragedy and irony, it nevertheless projects powerful images of recovered Eden as well, which express his fervent conviction that, however problematic the process, mankind will in the end have the imagination and grace to be reborn in flesh and spirit in the "inexhaustible wilderness" of space. With George Bernard Shaw he visualizes humanity as the Godhead realizing itself, through the very intensity of memory and desire that drives us into new frontiers. We go "beyond Eden" to discover and create new gardens. Bradbury's metaphorical theology places faith in a new model of divinity: "God. Man. Machine. A strange, but certainly not an unholy trinity." But at the end of the search, ironically, we return to our fondest myths of our origins: "Tossed out of Eden, we now go to replant our Garden on God's own lawn" ["Beyond Eden," *Omni*, April 1980].

Ray Bradbury (essay date 1987)

SOURCE: "Run Fast, Stand Still, *or* The Thing at the Top of the Stairs, *or* New Ghosts from Old Minds," in *How to Write Tales of Horror, Fantasy, & Science Fiction*, Writer's Digest Books, 1987, pp. 11-19.

[*In this essay, Bradbury explains how he wrote many of his short stories, claiming that they evolved out of personal experiences and fears.*]

Run fast, stand still. This, the lesson from lizards. For all writers. Observe almost any survival creature, you see the same. Jump, run, freeze. In the ability to flick like an eyelash, crack like a whip, vanish like steam, here this instant, gone the next—life teems the earth. And when that life is not rushing to escape, it is playing statues to do the same. See the hummingbird, there, not there. As thought arises and blinks off, so this thing of summer vapor; the clearing of a cosmic throat, the fall of a leaf. And where it was—a whisper.

What can we writers learn from lizards, lift from birds? In quickness is truth. The faster you blurt, the more swiftly you write, the more honest you are. In hesitation is thought. In delay comes the effort for a style, instead of leaping upon truth which is the *only* style worth deadfalling or tiger-trapping.

In between the scurries and flights, what? Be a chameleon, ink-blend, chromosome change with the landscape. Be a pet rock, lie with the dust, rest in the rain-water in the filled-barrel by the drainspout outside your grandparents' window long ago. Be dandelion wine in the ketchup bottle capped and placed with an inked inscription: June morn, first day of Summer, 1923. Summer 1926, Fireworks Night. 1927: Last Day of Summer. LAST OF THE DANDELIONS, Oct. 1st.

And out of all this, wind up with your first success as a writer, at $20 a story, in *Weird Tales*.

How *do* you commence to start to begin an almost new kind of writing, to terrify and scare?

You stumble into it, mostly. You don't know what you're doing, and suddenly, it's done. You don't set out to reform a certain kind of writing. It evolves out of your own life and night scares. Suddenly you look around and see that you have done something almost fresh.

The problem for any writer in any field is being circumscribed by what has gone before or what is being printed that very day in books and magazines.

I grew up reading and loving the traditional ghost stories of Dickens, Lovecraft, Poe, and later, Kuttner, Bloch, and Clark Ashton Smith. I tried to write stories heavily influenced by various of these writers, and succeeded in making quadruple-layered mudpies, all language and style, that would not float, and sank without a trace. I was too young to identify my problem, I was so busy imitating.

I almost blundered into my creative self in my last year in high school, when I wrote a kind of long remembrance of the deep ravine in my home town, and my fear of it at night. But I had no story to go with the ravine, so my discovering the true source of my future writing was put off for some few years.

I wrote at least a thousand words a day every day from the age of twelve on. For years Poe was looking over one shoulder, while Wells, Burroughs, and just about every writer in *Astounding* and *Weird Tales* looked over the other.

I loved them, and they smothered me. I hadn't learned how to look away and in the process look not at myself but at what went on behind my face.

It was only when I began to discover the treats and tricks that came with word association that I began to find some true way through the minefields of imitation. I finally figured out that if you are going to step on a live mine, make it your own. Be blown up, as it were, by your *own* delights and despairs.

I began to put down brief notes and descriptions of loves and hates. All during my twentieth and twenty-first years I circled around summer noons and October midnights, sensing that there somewhere in the bright and dark seasons must be something that was really me.

Existentialism in "The Golden Apples of the Sun":

"The Golden Apples of the Sun" is a highly mythopoetic text, invoking the myth of Prometheus, among others, in order to suggest a meaning for the mission it describes. The plot involves a handful of men, in a specially-equipped rocketship, whose mission is to bring back to earth a part of the sun which will feed all of humanity with its energy. Yet it offers, I think, irrefutable proof of Bradbury's confidence in reason and progress; for while we are meant to become intimately aware of the functioning of our childhood imagination, we are also led in this way to discover deficiencies in the dominant thought systems and literature of our society. Is there a happier world of childhood reverie dwelling within us, a world of slow and easy time waiting to be awakened? and if so, how is it possible to integrate the feelings of the child, his sense of wonder and novelty at appearances, into the complex intellectual powers of adulthood caught within the existential frame of the human condition? These are questions that Bradbury wrestles with so pertinaciously in this mythopoetic work, questions raised for him by the human drama enacted in contemporary America which was becoming history as he was responding to it.

William F. Touponce, "The Existential Fabulous:
A Reading of Ray Bradbury's 'The Golden
Apples of the Sun'," Mosiac, Vol. VIII,
Nos. 3-4, Spring/Summer, 1980.

I finally found it one afternoon when I was twenty-two years old. I wrote the title **"The Lake"** on the first page of a story that finished itself two hours later. Two hours after that I was sitting at my typewriter out on a porch in the sun, with tears running off the tip of my nose, and the hair on my neck standing up.

Why the arousal of hair and the dripping nose?

I realized I had at last written a really fine story. The first, in ten years of writing. And not only was it a fine story, but it was some sort of hybrid, something verging on the new. Not a traditional ghost story at all, but a story about love, time, remembrance, and drowning.

I sent it off to Julie Schwartz, my pulp agent, who liked it, but said it was not a traditional tale and might be hard to sell. *Weird Tales* walked around it, touched it with a ten-foot pole, and finally decided, what the hey, to publish it, even though it didn't fit their magazine. But I must promise, next time, to write a good old-fashioned ghost story! I promised. They gave me twenty dollars, and everyone was happy.

Well, some of you know the rest. **"The Lake"** has been reprinted dozens of times in the 44 years since. And it was the story that first got various editors of other magazines to sit up and notice the guy with the aroused hair and the wet nose.

Did I learn a hard, fast, or even an easy lesson from **"The Lake"**? I did not. I went back to writing the old-fashioned ghost story. For I was far too young to understand much about writing at all, and my discoveries went unnoticed by me for years. I was wandering all over the place and writing poorly much of the time.

During my early twenties, if my weird fiction was imitative, with an occasional surprise of a concept and a further surprise in execution, my science fiction writing was abysmal, and my detective fiction verged on the ludicrous. I was deeply under the influence of my loving friend, Leigh Brackett, whom I used to meet every Sunday at Muscle Beach in Santa Monica, California, there to read her superior Stark on Mars tales, or to envy and try to emulate her *Flynn's Detective* stories.

But along through those years I began to make lists of titles, to put down long lines of *nouns*. These lists were the provocations, finally, that caused my better stuff to surface. I was feeling my way toward something honest, hidden under the trap door on the top of my skull.

The lists ran something like this:

THE LAKE. THE NIGHT. THE CRICKETS. THE RAVINE. THE ATTIC. THE BASEMENT. THE TRAP DOOR. THE BABY. THE CROWD. THE NIGHT TRAIN. THE FOG HORN. THE SCYTHE. THE CARNIVAL. THE CAROUSEL. THE DWARF. THE MIRROR MAZE. THE SKELETON.

I was beginning to see a pattern in the list, in these words that I had simply flung forth on paper, trusting my subconscious to give bread, as it were, to the birds.

Glancing over the list, I discovered my old love and fright having to do with circuses and carnivals. I remembered, and then forgot, and then remembered again, how terrified I had been when my mother took me for my first ride on a merry-go-round. With the calliope screaming and the world spinning and the terrible horses leaping, I added my shrieks to the din. I did not go near the carousel again for years. When I really did, decades later, it rode me into the midst of *Something Wicked This Way Comes*.

But long before that, I went on making the lists. THE MEADOW. THE TOY CHEST. THE MONSTER. TYRANNOSAURUS REX. THE TOWN CLOCK. THE OLD MAN. THE OLD WOMAN. THE TELEPHONE. THE SIDEWALKS. THE COFFIN. THE ELECTRIC CHAIR. THE MAGICIAN.

Out on the margin of these nouns, I blundered into a science-fiction story that was not a science-fiction story. My title was "R is For Rocket." The published title was **"King of the Grey Spaces,"** the story of two boys, great friends, one elected to go off to the Space Academy, the other staying home. The tale was rejected by every science-fiction magazine because, after all, it was only a story about friendship being tested by circumstance, even though the circumstance was space travel. Mary Gnaedinger, at *Fa-*

mous Fantastic Mysteries, took one look at my story and published it. But, again, I was too young to see that **"R is For Rocket"** would be the kind of story that would make me as a science-fiction writer, admired by some, and criticized by many who observed that I was no writer of science fictions, I was a "people" writer, and to hell with that!

I went on making lists, having to do not only with night, nightmares, darkness, and objects in attics, but the toys that men play with in space, and the ideas I found in detective magazines. Most of the detective material I published in my twenty-fourth year in *Detective Tales* and *Dime Detective* is not worth rereading. Here and there, I fell over my own shoelaces and did a nearly good job of remembering Mexico, which scared me, or downtown Los Angeles during the Pachucho riots. But it would take me the better part of forty years to assimilate the detective/mystery/suspense genre and make it work for me in my latest novel, *Death Is a Lonely Business*.

But back to my lists. And *why* go back to them? Where am I leading you? Well, if you are a writer, or would hope to be one, similar lists, dredged out of the lopside of your brain, might well help you discover *you*, even as I flopped around and finally found me.

I began to run through those lists, pick a noun, and then sit down to write a long prose-poem-essay on it.

Somewhere along about the middle of the page, or perhaps on the second page, the prose poem would turn into a story. Which is to say that a character suddenly appeared and said, "That's *me*"; or, "That's an idea *I like*!" And the character would then finish the tale for me.

It began to be obvious that I was learning from my lists of nouns, and that I was further learning that my *characters* would do my work *for* me, if I let them alone, if I gave them their heads, which is to say, their fantasies, their frights.

I looked at my list, saw SKELETON, and remembered the first artworks of my childhood. I drew skeletons to scare my girl cousins. I was fascinated with those unclothed medical displays of skulls and ribs and pelvic sculptures. My favorite tune was "'Tain't No Sin, To Take Off Your Skin, and Dance Around in Your Bones."

Remembering my early artwork and my favorite tune, I ambled into my doctor's office one day with a sore throat. I touched my Adam's apple, and the tendons on each side of my neck, and asked for his medical advice.

"Know what you're suffering from?" asked the doc.

"What?"

"*Discovery* of the larynx!" he crowed. "Take some aspirin. Two dollars, please!"

Discovery of the larynx! My God, how *beautiful*! I trotted home, feeling my throat, and then my ribs, and then my medulla oblongata, and my kneecaps. Holy Moses! Why not write a story about a man who is terrified to discover that under his skin, inside his flesh, *hidden,* is a symbol of all the Gothic horrors in history—a skeleton!

The story wrote itself in a few hours.

A perfectly obvious concept, yet no one else in the history of writing weird tales had ever scribbled it down. I fell into my typewriter with it and came up with a brand-new, absolutely original tale, which had been lurking under my skin since I first drew a skull and crossbones, aged six.

I began to gain steam. The ideas came faster now, and all of them from my lists. I prowled up in my grandparents' attics and down in their basements. I listened to the middle-of-the-night locomotives wailing across the northern Illinois landscape, and that was death, a funeral train, taking my loved ones away to some far graveyard. I remembered five o'clock in the morning, pre-dawn arrivals of Ringling Brothers, Barnum and Bailey, and all the animals parading by before sunrise, heading for the empty meadows where the great tents would rise like incredible mushrooms. I remembered Mr. Electrico and his traveling electric chair. I remembered Blackstone the Magician dancing magical handkerchiefs and vanishing elephants on my hometown stage. I remembered my grandfather, my sister, and various aunts and cousins, in their coffins and gone forever in the tombyards where the butterflies settled like flowers on the graves and where the flowers blew away like butterflies over the stones. I remembered my dog, lost for days, coming home late on a winter night with snow and mud and leaves in his pelt. And the stories began to burst, to explode from those memories, hidden in the nouns, lost in the lists.

My remembrance of my dog, and his winter pelt, became **"The Emissary,"** the story of a boy, sick in bed, who sends his dog out to gather the seasons in his fur, and report back. And then, one night, the dog comes back from a journey to the graveyard, and brings "company" with him.

My listed title THE OLD WOMAN became two stories, one **"There Was an Old Woman,"** about a lady who refuses to die and demands her body back from the undertakers, defying Death, and a second tale, **"Season of Disbelief,"** about some children who refuse to believe that a very old woman was ever young, was ever a girl, a child. The first story appeared in my first collection, *Dark Carnival.* The second became part of a further word-association test I gave myself, called *Dandelion Wine.*

We can surely see now, can't we, that it is the personal observation, the odd fancy, the strange conceit, that pays off. I was fascinated by old people. I tried to solve their mystery with my eyes and young mind but was continually astounded to realize that once upon a time they had been me, and some day up ahead I would be them. Absolutely impossible! Yet there the boys and girls were, locked in old bodies, a dreadful situation, a terrible trick, right before my gaze.

Pilfering from my list, again, I seized out the title THE JAR, the result of my being stunned at an encounter with a series of embryos on display in a carnival when I was twelve and again when I was fourteen. In those long-gone days of 1932 and 1934, we children knew nothing, of course, absolutely nothing about sex and procreation. So you can imagine how astounded I was when I prowled through a free carnival exhibit and saw all those fetuses of humans and cats and dogs, displayed in labeled jars. I was shocked by the look of the unborn dead, and the new mysteries of life they caused to rise up in my head later that night and all through the years. I never mentioned the jars and the formaldehyde fetuses to my parents. I knew I had stumbled on some truths which were better not discussed.

All of this surfaced, of course, when I wrote **"The Jar,"** and the carnival and the fetal displays and all the old terrors poured out of my fingertips into my typewriter. The old mystery had finally found a resting place, in a story.

I found another title in my list, THE CROWD. And, typing furiously, I recalled a terrible concussion when I was fifteen and ran from a friend's house at the sound, to be confronted by a car that had hit an obstruction in the street and rocketed into a telephone pole. The car was split in half. Two people lay dead on the pavement, another woman died just as I reached her, her face ruined. Another man died a minute later. Still another died the next day.

I had never seen anything like it. I walked home, bumping into trees, in shock. It took me months to get over the horror of that scene.

Years later, with my list before me, I remembered a number of peculiar things about that night. The accident had occurred at an intersection surrounded on one side by empty factories and a deserted schoolyard, and on the opposite side, by a graveyard. I had come running from the nearest house, a hundred yards away, yet, within moments, it seemed, a crowd had gathered. Where had they all come from? Later on in time, I could only imagine that some came, in some strange fashion, out of the empty factories, or even more strangely, out of the graveyard. After typing for only a few minutes, it came to me that, yes, this crowd was *always* the same crowd, that it gathered at *all* accidents. These were victims from accidents years ago, doomed to come back and haunt the scene of new accidents as they occurred.

Once I hit on this idea, the story finished itself in a single afternoon.

Meanwhile, the carnival artifacts were gathering closer, their great bones starting to thrust up through my skin. I was making longer and longer prose poem excursions about circuses that arrived long after midnight. During those years, in my early twenties, prowling a Mirror Maze on the old Venice Pier with my friends Leigh Brackett and Edmond Hamilton, Ed suddenly cried, "Let's get out of here, before Ray writes a story about a dwarf who pays his way in here every night so he can stand and make himself tall in the big stretch mirror!" "That's it!" I shouted, and ran home to write **"The Dwarf."** "That'll teach me to shoot off my mouth," said Ed, when he read the story the next week.

THE BABY on that list was, of course, me.

I remembered an old nightmare. It was about being born. I remembered lying in my crib, three days old, wailing with the knowledge of being thrust out into the world; the pressure, the cold, the shrieking into life. I remembered my mother's breast. I remembered the doctor, on the fourth day of my life, bending over me with a scalpel to perform circumcision. I remembered, I remembered.

I changed the title from THE BABY to **"The Small Assassin."** That story has been anthologized dozens of times. And I had lived the story, or part of it, from my first hour of life onward, and only truly remembered and nailed it down in my twenties.

Did I write stories based on every single noun in my pages and pages of lists?

Not all. But most. THE TRAPDOOR, listed way back in 1942 or '43, didn't surface until three years ago, as a story in *Omni.*

Another story about me and my dog took more than fifty years to surface. In **"Bless Me, Father, For I Have Sinned,"** I went back in time to relive a beating I had given my dog when I was twelve, and for which I had never forgiven myself. I wrote the story to at least examine that cruel, sad boy and put his ghost, and the ghost of my much-loved dog, to rest forever. It was the same dog, incidentally, who brought "company" back from the graveyard in **"The Emissary."**

During these years, Henry Kuttner, along with Leigh, was my teacher. He suggested authors—Katherine Anne Porter, John Collier, Eudora Welty—and books—*The Lost Weekend, One Man's Meat, Rain in the Doorway*—to be read and learned from. Along the way, he gave me a copy of *Winesburg, Ohio,* by Sherwood Anderson. Finishing the book, I said to myself, "Someday I would like to write a novel laid on the planet Mars, with somewhat similar people." I immediately jotted down a list of the sorts of folks I would want to plant on Mars, to see what would happen.

I forgot *Winesburg, Ohio* and my list. Over the years, I wrote a series of stories about the Red Planet. One day, I looked up and the book was finished, the list complete, *The Martian Chronicles* on its way to publication.

So there you have it. In sum, a series of nouns, some with rare adjectives, which described a territory unknown, an undiscovered country, part of it Death, the rest Life. If I had not made up these prescriptions for Discovery I would never have become the jackdaw archaeologist or anthropologist that I am. That jackdaw who seeks bright objects, odd carapaces and misshapen femurs from the boneheaps

of junk inside my head, where lay strewn the remnants of collisions with life as well as Buck Rogers, Tarzan, John Carter, Quasimodo, and all the other creatures who made me want to live forever.

In the words of the old Mikado song, I had a little list, save it was a long one, which led me into Dandelion Wine country and helped me move the Dandelion Wine country up to Mars, and ricocheted me back into dark wine territory as Mr. Dark's night train arrived long before dawn. But the first and most important pileup of nouns was the one filled with leaves whispering along the sidewalks at three a.m. and funerals wheeling by on empty railtracks, following, and crickets that suddenly, for no reason, shut up, so you could hear your own heart, and wish you couldn't.

Which leads us to a final revelation—

One of the nouns on my list in high school was The Thing, or, better yet, The Thing at The Top of The Stairs.

When I was growing up in Waukegan, Illinois, there was only one bathroom; upstairs. You had to climb an unlit hall halfway before you could find and turn on a light. I tried to get my dad to keep the light on all night. But that was expensive stuff. The light stayed off.

Around two or three in the morning, I would have to go to the bathroom. I would lie in bed for half an hour or so, torn between the agonized need for relief, and what I knew was waiting for me in the dark hall leading up to the attic. At last, driven by pain, I would edge out of our dining room into that hall, thinking: run fast, leap up, turn on the light, but whatever you do, don't look up. If you look up before you get the light on, *It* will be there. The Thing. The terrible Thing waiting at the top of the stairs. So run, blind; don't look.

I ran, I leaped. But always, I couldn't help it, at the last moment, I blinked and stared into the awful darkness. And it was always there. And I screamed and fell back downstairs, waking my parents. My dad would groan and turn over in bed, wondering where this son of his had come from. My mother would get up, find me in a scrambled heap in the hall, and go up to turn on the light. She would wait for me to climb up to the bathroom and come back down to have my tearstained face kissed and my terrified body tucked in bed.

The next night and the next night and the night after that, the same thing happened. Driven mad by my hysteria, Dad got out the old chamber pot and shoved it under my bed.

But I was never cured. The Thing remained there forever. Only moving West when I was thirteen got me away from that terror.

What have I done, recently, about that nightmare? Well . . .

Now, very late in time, The Thing is standing up at the top of the stairs, still waiting. From 1926 to now, in the spring of 1986, is a long waiting. But at last, gleaning my ever dependable list, I have typed the noun out on paper, adding **"The Stairs,"** and I have finally faced up to the dark climb and the Arctic coldness held in place for sixty years, waiting to be asked to come down through my frozen fingertips and into your bloodstream. The story, associated out of memory, was finished this week, even as I wrote this essay.

I leave you now at the bottom of your own stair, at half after midnight, with a pad, a pen, and a list to be made. Conjure the nouns, alert the secret self, taste the darkness. Your own Thing stands waiting 'way up there in the attic shadows. If you speak softly, and write any old word that wants to jump out of your nerves onto the page . . .

Your Thing at the top of your stairs in your own private night . . . may well come *down*.

William F. Touponce (essay date 1989)

SOURCE: "Short Stories," in *Ray Bradbury*, Starmont House, 1989, pp. 83-91.

[*In the following excerpt, Touponce discusses how psychoanalytic themes, such as "psychosis, hysteria, delirium, neurosis, hypochondria, the death wish, [and] the unconscious," unify the otherwise unrelated stories collected in Bradbury's* The October Country.]

Bradbury's first collection of stories was *Dark Carnival* (1947), but . . . since the book has long been out of print (indeed it is something of a collector's item), I will not be discussing it here. We will be concerned instead with a collection of nineteen stories in the horror/weird/fantasy vein published under the title *The October Country* (1955). Fifteen of these stories are from *Dark Carnival* (which originally contained twenty-seven stories), selected, edited, and in some cases rewritten by Bradbury.

The remark made by Mr. Harris, the protagonist of the story **"Skeleton"** who is deliriously obsessed with protecting his internal organs from an attack by his own skeleton, could well serve as an epigraph for the entire volume: "How is it we never question our bodies and our being?" In reading *The October Country,* readers feel as if they were discovering their bodies for the first time as the site of the fantastic, as an unfamiliar and frightening territory full of surreal frescoes (the paintings of Dali and Picasso are several times evoked as equivalents to this experience). The body is in fact the subject (which ordinary vision obscures or even represses) and landscape of the book, that which unifies an otherwise disparate collection of stories and that by which the book represents its psychological themes of unconscious desire. Psychosis, hysteria, delirium, neurosis, hypochondria, the death wish, the unconscious—the very vocabulary of the "science" of psychoanalysis—is brought into play by these stories and deconstructed in a manner which I will indicate in a moment.

In **"The Jar"** the body is an amorphous pale thing from the wet swamps which provokes each character to project his own (sometimes murderous) fantasy. In **"The Next in Line,"** the body is a kind of mummified clay sculpted by Death into grotesque and horrifying shapes (images based on Bradbury's own visit to the cavern of the mummies of Guanajuato, Mexico) that are symbolic of the protagonist's morbid obsession with her own death. In **"The Watchful Poker Chip of Henri Matisse,"** the theme is given a parodistic treatment as an average and ordinary man slowly adds artificial parts to his body, making himself into a work of art celebrated by the avant-garde. In **"The Crowd,"** the desire to look at what happens to a body in a car accident is paranoiacally played with. In **"The Man Upstairs,"** a story which deals humorously with the facts of sexual difference, a young boy eviscerates the alien fantastic body of a vampire-like creature living in his grandmother's boarding house. In **"The Homecoming"** a girl inhabits the bodies of others, and a boy born normal into a family of supernatural freaks dreams of flying and drinking blood just like them. In **"Touched with Fire,"** a grotesquely fat woman (called Mrs. Death-Wish) is driven by a heat wave into murdering her husband. In **"The Lake,"** which deals with Freudian notion that earliest loves are the strongest and that unconsciously are never given up, only substituted for in adult life, a man visits his home town where a girl's drowned body turns up still having its golden hair (she had drowned years before but her body had never been found), which causes the man to realize that he does not love the woman he intends to marry. **"The Small Assassin"** deals with the ambivalence of a pregnancy that gives birth to a baby whose body is developed enough to enable him to kill his parents in revenge for bringing him into the world. **"Jack-in-the-Box"** records with symbolic precision the (phallic) onset of puberty, which is frightening to a boy who has always inhabited a protected Garden World and house dominated only by the presence of his dead father, whose place he is seemingly destined to take. Even his mother, masked at times as his teacher, participates in the Law of the Father, which governs this world.

As to why the themes of psychoanalysis should be the themes of a beginning fantasist, there are ample historical reasons. No one need indulge in amateur psychoanalysis of Bradbury who in any case disavows any direct influence:

> Have read little Freud or Jung. All my psychoanalytic education comes from Shakespeare's subconscious haunts that inspired and educated Freud and Jung. The creative artist always, I repeat, always precedes the analytical one. Shakespeare the father intuitionist, taught sons Freud and Jung. I always return to the original Artist. Old Will continues to teach me, late in life, along with G. B. Shaw.

> (Bradbury, personal letter to me, Aug 18, 1981)

Tzvetan Todorov points out in *The Fantastic*, which is largely confined to the nineteenth century, that in the twentieth-century psychoanalysis has replaced (and thereby made useless) the literature of the fantastic. He argues that there is no need today to resort to the devil to speak of an excessive sexual desire and none to resort to vampires to designate the attraction exerted by corpses. Psychoanalysis and the literature which is directly or indirectly inspired by it deal with these matters in undisguised terms: "The themes of fantastic literature have become, literally, the very themes of the psychological investigations of the last fifty years" [Todorov]. Despite Bradbury's disclaimer, *The October Country* can be read as an attempt to reverse this situation and to determine how the fantastic can be written after Freud.

Freud's ideas have been so widely disseminated that it need not be a question of direct influence, and Bradbury's fantasy tends to break out of psychoanalytic structures (especially Oedipal triangularity) in such books as *Something Wicked This Way Comes*. The model text for a study of this kind based on *The October Country* would be **"Jack-in-the-Box,"** where the fantastic revolves around the question of whether or not the boy will be governed by the Law and Name of the Father, taking his place with the mother, or will he break out in some fashion. But the mother/teacher mysteriously dies before the boy reaches such a decision, and like a jack-in-the-box, he springs outside of the house into a world he has been told is Death. This and other stories could be used to show that fantasy in Bradbury's texts has a complex relationship to psychoanalysis. What in fact sometimes occurs is that psychoanalysis may find itself standing before the court of fantasy; its fantasy of authority unmasked and exposed as a fiction. Two stories in particular, **"The Small Assassin"** and **"The Wonderful Death of Dudley Stone,"** are structured by the Freudian logic of ambivalence, a word prominent in both texts, a word which comes to the English language from the pen of Freud himself (and no fantasy writer *before* Freud could have used it, though of course literature may manifest its characteristics in any age), **"The Wonderful World of Dudley Stone"** dealing with the problem literary fame, fortune, and influence, always fertile ground for the psychoanalytic critic interested in a writer's anxieties. Usually, Bradbury's strategy is to include a psychoanalytic explanation of seemingly fantastic events in the story—a small child whose mother thinks it can murder, a famous writer who disappeared at the height of his powers—and then to show that the explanation is insufficient or downright wrong.

Both of these stories and **"Jack-in-the-Box"** are a bit too long for analysis here, but **"The Dwarf,"** which currently opens the collection (not part of *Dark Carnival,* originally published in *Fantastic,* 1954) is brief and interesting enough to be treated as a sort of parable about the fantasy writer's ambiguous relationship to reality. In the classical Freudian view of this relationship, to simplify and to put it very schematically, the artist is a kind of neurotic who cannot confront the frustrations of reality directly. Rather, he has a strong impulse to fantasize about himself in daydreams centering on that exalted personage Freud called "his Majesty the Ego" ["The Relation of the Poet to Daydreaming," *On Creativity and the Unconscious,* 1958]. If he also happens to have artistic talent, however, he can disguise the obviously egotistical character of these adventurous daydreams by using the formal properties of art. If readers respond in turn to these disguised wishes with their own, the writer may become famous, winning a place of fame and fortune for himself in the real world by a circuitous route.

Now, the dwarf mentioned in the title of Bradbury's story is a writer of pulp detective fiction (probably this is no accident; Bradbury himself was initially a writer of such fiction, and **"The Small Assassin"** was originally published in *Dime Mystery,* November 1946) known to the denizens of the seedy hotel he inhabits as Mr. Big! So far the dwarf's stories have not won him much recognition, but one character in the story, Aimee, at least thinks she understands his psyche. The dwarf comes every night after the crowds have dispersed to a cheap seaside carnival show to see himself in the mirror maze, in the thin mirror that makes him appear normal. Ordinarily, the mirror maze is an attraction because it offers grossly misrepresented images of the body. It is a thrill momentarily to see one's body image initially distorted and then returned to normalcy. We know it is an illusion limited by the mirror's frame. But Mr. Big's body is also distorted in reality. He is described as a "dark-eyed, dark-haired, ugly man who has been locked in a winepress, squeezed and wadded down and down, fold on fold, agony on agony, until a bleached, outraged mass is left. . . ." If the mirror distorts reality into grotesque fantasy for most people, it corrects a distorted reality for Mr. Big. It is the object around which the paradoxes of narcissism revolve in the story.

Two other characters are involved in this story, and they represent opposite attitudes toward the human need for fantasy. The owner of the mirror maze, Ralph, is completely cynical about human nature. When asked why people want to ride the roller coaster, he replies that people want to die, and the roller coaster is the handiest thing to dying there is. But Ralph is something of a voyeur, for he spies on his customers. He takes his neighbor Aimee, who runs the hoop circus and whom he has been trying to seduce, back behind a partition where they can see Mr. Big dance and pirouette and wink before the thin mirror. She, however, only feels sorry for the dwarf. And when she finds out to her surprise that he is indeed an author, she reads some passages she especially admires to Frank, who jealously responds by asking her why Mr. Big is not, then, rich and famous. This leads Aimee to speculate that perhaps what Mr. Big needs is something to boost his ego, to give him the courage to try and sell his stories to quality magazines. She speculates about what effect having a private mirror all for himself would have on Mr. Big: "A mirror for your room where you can hide away with the big reflection of yourself, shining, and write stories and stories, never going out into the world unless you had to."

Aimee wonders whether this all-of-a-piece illusion would help his writing or hurt it, and this is the story's connection with the Freudian aesthetic of fantasy. The mirror under such conditions would be an ideal place where narcissistic and pleasurable representations of the ego could be indulged in without shame or disguise, no public need for the softening of fantasy being required. However, the stories that Mr. Big currently writes, of which we are given a small sampling, are stories that have a dwarf and murderer as anti-hero, a victim of his parents' "psychosis" in having raised him in a doll's house until their death, never telling him of the real world outside in which he will be a freak. Would the ideal mirror destroy the need for such fictional disguises or increase them? This is an undecidable question, framed within a frame mirroring an abyss: are Mr. Big's stories really disguises, or are they not really displays of narcissism, since most readers do not in fact know that the author is a dwarf? In essence, the story deconstructs, through repetition and reversal, the central notions of the Freudian theory of art that links authorial fantasy through fiction to reality and the social world. What is fiction and what is reality in the mirror maze anyway? Is this the source of the dwarf's creativity?

While the story frames these questions, it provides no means to answer them, for soon, out of malicious jealousy of the dwarf's stories, which Aimee has read and interpreted to him. Frank meanly switches the thin mirror with one which makes even normal-sized people seem frightfully small. Needless to say, this is a horrible humiliation to the dwarf, who can only scream when he sees himself crushed and wadded down even further in it. His body has become unimaginably fantastic. But fiction seems to mirror reality at the end when the dwarf runs off with a gun stolen from the shooting gallery to become the murderer about which he has written. Our last glimpse of the mirror maze is paradoxically a "true" reflection of Frank grossly distorted in one of his own mirrors, "a horrid ugly little man with a pale squashed face under an ancient straw hat." Ralph, who cruelly wanted to destroy other people's illusions about themselves, is shown to himself as he really is by the illusions of his own mirror maze, an image which cannot help but remind us, incidentally, of the dwarf that sat on Zarathustra's shoulders, mocking him with the spirit of gravity (Nietzsche, *Thus Spoke Zarathustra,* trans. Kaufmann, Third Part, "On the Vision and the Riddle").

As a closing and as a kind of summary of Bradbury's fantasy, an early story of his, which is also one of the longest he has written, **"Pillar of Fire"** (in *S is for Space,* comprising forty pages, originally published in **Planet Stories,** 1948), is a good vehicle. In this story the Apollonian sun of rationality and the Dionysian dark side of the mind encounter one another again, only this time the encounter takes the form of a bitter struggle that ends in the death of the imagination. Bradbury deemed this story important enough to rework it into a successful play because of this theme, and indeed the play is something of a warning about the death of the imagination in contemporary technological society, the closest Bradbury ever comes to tragic representation. According to Bradbury, it was a rehearsal for *Fahrenheit 451* ([*Pillar of Fire and Other Plays,*] Introduction). But the protagonists are reverse images of each other, of Montag, who is trying to stop burning, and of Lantry, the last dead man "reborn" into an antiseptically clean, utopian society that has destroyed his grave (and all other graveyards on Earth), who is obsessed to the point of extreme paranoia with burning

down this society. It is more of a parallel that both stories still involve the suppression of works of fantastic fiction, but still Bradbury's protagonist in **"Pillar of Fire"** realizes only belatedly that he is the last person remembering all the old books of fantasy and imagination, and that with his death, they die also. Besides, as we will see in detail in a moment, William Lantry is essentially motivated, until almost the end of the story, by the spirit of revenge, something Nietzsche hoped to deliver man from (Nietzsche, *Thus Spoke Zarathustra,* trans. Kaufmann, Second Part, "On the Tarantulas").

The plot is fantastic in construction, made so that readers hesitate between a supernatural and a scientific explanation of the uncanny events that happen when William Lantry is reborn in the year of 2349 A.D. Is Lantry really one of the walking dead, or is he an extraordinary case of suspended animation? Appropriately, the answer to this question (the former) is set in Salem where the last graveyard had been preserved as a tourist attraction by the government as a reminder of a barbaric custom. Now this graveyard is scheduled by the government for destruction as well. The government seeks thereby to make its control over the world of darkness, death, decay (and of all writers whose imaginations are attracted to it) absolute. The society Lantry is reborn into is, therefore, an extreme Apollonian culture, as is evident from the symbolism it employs. It worships the sun of rationality, emblazoned everywhere on public buildings. The dead of this society are burned in "Incinerators," which are warm cozy temples where soothing music plays and the fear of death is abolished through ceremonies that deify fire. As Lantry watches, slowly the golden coffins of the dead roll in covered with sun symbols, and after a brief ceremony, they are cast into a flue. On the altar are written the words "We that are born of the sun return to the sun," a fantastic reversal of the words normally spoken at Christian burials.

It is these gigantic Incinerators as myths of an Apollonian culture that Lantry wants to explode, and does, killing hundreds of people in the surrounding towns. He hopes thereby to effect a revolution, to win converts to his cause by creating more walking dead. But in this rational world the dead remain dead. Because they never believed in vampires while living, they cannot be resurrected by Lantry's magical procedures later (he draws symbols of long-dead sorcerers on the floor of the makeshift morgue and chants his own formulas, to no avail). Eventually, he is picked up by the authorities and is interrogated by a man named McClure who is this century's representative of psychoanalysis and something of a detective as well. McClure tries to analyze Lantry's mortified behavior, his paleness and lack of breath, as a self-induced psychosis but is himself slowly unnerved when he finds that Lantry is the real thing, one of the walking dead. Lantry is a logical impossibility to a mind such as McClure's. Lantry is, therefore, condemned to a second death by the State, a death which is the death of every fantastic writer in history, since only Lantry remembers them. If this were a Christian fantasy in the mode of J. R. R. Tolkien or C. S. Lewis, the evident compassion of McClure for his victim would have resulted in his conversion to the imagination at the end, thereby saving it. But no, Bradbury really wants us to feel the shock of seeing the imagination die forever, and on this level of response, the story is quite effective. The second death, the death of the imagination, becomes more terrible than real death.

The ontological and linguistic paradoxes at play in the story echo Poe's "The Facts in the Case of M. Valdemar," in which the mesmerized Valdemar awakens at a certain point to proclaim "I am dead," and then quickly decomposes. In Bradbury's story, however, Lantry really *is* dead but thinks of the people who inhabit this utopia without imagination as completely dead, as deader than he ever was, because they do not know that their culture is founded on the primordial difference between light and dark, between life and death. According to Jacques Derrida, Poe's story can be read as as a deconstruction of the phenomenological notion that I am present to myself in the utterance of meaning, since the subject of the utterance "I am dead," (the "I" that says this sentence) seems to be both self-aware and unaware at the same time, or rather what Valdemar is aware of in stating the sentence is that he is dead and thus paradoxically unaware [Richard Macksey and Eugenio Donato, *The Structuralist Controversy,* 1972]. A similar argument could be made about Bradbury's story, since it plays with the idea (foremost in the structuralist study of the fantastic done by Tzvetan Todorov) that fantastic literature arises from the absence of a referent in the real world: "Labels without referents you cry! . . . Frankly, I don't believe in you either," says Lantry with scorn as he thinks of the violence done already to works of the imagination by this society, which has chosen to live without the "silly" word "vampire" and about the violence it wants to do to him.

Yet there is an intensity to this story that goes quite beyond the play of "signifires" (pun intended) and linguistic representations. The fantastic may arise from language, as Todorov argues, but **"Pillar of Fire"** also provides a good example of the ways in which Bradbury's fantasy direct investments of the social field of the sort Deleuze and Guattari describe in their book on politics and the unconscious [Gilles Deleuze and Felix Guattari, *Anti-Oedipus,* 1977]. Polemically, Deleuze and Guattari are concerned with demolishing Freud's representation of the unconscious as a private theatre of dire family secrets, which they claim is absurd, and opening it to what they call the delirium of desiring-machines as the general matrix of all social investments. According to them, this experience of delirium has two major poles of investment: a paranoiac fascisizing (*fascisant*) type that invests the formation of a central sovereignty, a State, and a second schizo-revolutionary pole that follows the lines of the escape of desire, that invests only in multiplicities or cracks in the walls of the State and that thereby causes flows to move (a perfect illustration of their thesis is the recent fantastic film, *Pink Floyd's The Wall*).

Instead of a linguistic structure, Deleuze and Guattari find the unconscious to be a kind of Nietzschean flux, manifesting astonishing oscillations from one pole of delirium to the other. In their view, it is not Oedipal structures, the

Name of the Father, which is invested by the unconscious, but every name in history ("I am every name in history," proclaimed Nietzsche in a letter written just before his collapse into madness; see *The Portable Nietzsche,* trans. Kaufmann, p. 686). Fortunately, they give many literary examples to support their argument, drawing frequently on fantasy and horror writers and on utopian novels (Bradbury is discussed, but not the story we are analyzing here). They make the interesting assertion that it is the destiny of American literature to be initially a crossing of limits and frontiers, causing deterritorialized flows of desire to circulate, only to recode this flow along the shores of moralizing, Puritan, and familialist territories. The classic case seems to be Jack Kerouac, who initially took such a nomadic voyage out (Cf. *On the Road*), but who ended by affirming the American flag (against the radicals of the 1970's such as Alan Ginsberg), the dream of a Great America, and the racial superiority of his French Breton ancestors.

However this may be and however much we may want to disagree with them about the political significance of desire in American fiction, Bradbury's **"Pillar of Fire"** clearly invests the social field in a direct manner and is constituted by a delirious oscillation between the two poles of the unconscious that Deleuze and Guattari describe. But Bradbury's fantasy goes in which a direction opposite to that which they ascribe to American literature, from paranoia to schizophrenia (these terms are not to be understood in the clinical sense, but only designate different investments of the social field). What follows is an instance of the first type, the paranoiac pole, which emerges from what they call, in their often bizarre critical vocabulary, the body without organs. The body without organs is the socius initially inhabited only by molecular desiring-machines on its surface:

> Hatred was a blood in him, it went up down around and through, up down around and through. It was a heart in him, not beating, true, but warm. He was— what? Resentment. Envy. They said he could not lie any longer in his coffin in the cemetery. He had *wanted* to. He had never had any particular desire to get up and walk around. It had been enough, all these centuries, to lie in the deep box and feel, but *not feel* the ticking of the million insect watches in the earth around, the moves of worms like so many deep thoughts in the soil.
>
> But then they had come and said, "Out you go and into the furnace!" And that is the worst thing you can say to any man. You cannot tell him what to do. . . . They had given birth to him with all their practices and ignorances.

Lantry arises from the catatonic body without organs because a fascisizing and sovereign State apparatus has selected him and subjected him to its will. His delirium, then (which intensifies in the passage I have omitted), begins as a direct investment of the social field. He was perfectly content to remain a body without organs himself, swarming with worms, bacilli, not feeling the ticking of the million insect watches (the desiring-machines) in the earth around him. But the fascisizing machine tears up the body of the earth, divides it up into new territories and structures. And so Lantry becomes a reactive paranoid, and this is exactly how Bradbury directs that the character should be played in the stage version of the story (*Pillar of Fire and Other Plays*, Introduction). Furthermore, according to Deleuze and Guattari, the political behavior of the paranoid consists in the organizing of masses and packs. He manipulates crowds; he opposes them to one another, maneuvers them. This is clearly what Lantry intends to do, hanging around the makeshift morgue where the dead bodies have been laid out in rows on the surface of the Earth, hoping to resurrect and to mobilize them into an army of the dead against the State which has banished the word dead from the language.

But in the end, when he realizes that his war machine had no hope of ever materializing and when McClure tells him that he will die of loneliness anyway because he is a freak, one of a kind, we pass to the schizophrenic pole. The passage accompanying this transfiguration is too lengthy to quote in full, but after saying that he is Poe and Bierce and a host of other fantastic creatures besides, Lantry goes on to add that

> I am a mask, a skull mask behind an oak tree on the last day of October. I am a poison apple bobbing in a water tub for child noses to bump at, for child teeth to snap . . . I am a black candle lighted before an inverted cross. I am a coffin lid, a sheet with eyes, a foot-step on a black stairwell. I am Dunsany and Machen and I am the Legend of Sleepy Hollow. I am the Monkey's Paw and I am the Phantom Rickshaw. I am the Cat and the Canary, the Gorilla, the Bat. I am the ghost of Hamlet's father on the castle wall.

The full list contains almost every name in the literary history of the fantastic, and the Name of the Father (Hamlet's father on the castle wall; Bradbury had told us how much he has learned from Shakespeare) is just another name among many. In addition, schizophrenic death affirms a host of depersonalized part-objects and intensities as well which connect the unauthorized flows of desire to organs and desiring-machines (the apple and the child's teeth which bite it). Through his masks, Lantry affirms a multiplicity of identities in the true Dionysian manner of *The Halloween Tree*. However, Lantry's desire flows outside the structures of the State with no apparent desire to return and be represented in it (as in Bradbury's *House of Haunts*). As a schizo-revolutionary, Lantry knows that escape is still possible (he had wanted to escape to Mars, where tombs still existed), even at this extreme point. Withdrawal, saying I am not of your kind, of the superior Apollonian race, but one who belongs eternally to the inferior race, the freaks, sweeps away the social covering on leaving, or at least can cause a piece of the system to get lost in the shuffle. What matters is to break through the wall, to make society *afraid* again (afraid, it seems, of the body without organs, which is, according to Deleuze and Guattari, the model of the death of the imagination, if not the experience of it). In this, Bradbury and his anti-hero, William Lantry, succeed.

FURTHER READING

Greenberg, Martin Harry, and Joseph D. Olander, eds. *Ray Bradbury.* Edinburgh: Paul Harris Publishing, 1980, 248 p.

> Collection of essays by noted critics addressing Bradbury's major works, in addition to his style, themes, influences, and attitudes concerning religion and technology.

Guffey, George R. "The Unconscious, Fantasy, and Science Fiction: Transformations in Bradbury's *Martian Chronicles* and Lem's *Solaris*." In *Bridges to Fantasy*, pp. 142-59. Carbondale: Southern Illinois University Press, 1982.

> Compares Bradbury's *Martian Chronicles* to Stanislaw Lem's *Solaris*, concluding that "both incorporate significant amounts of dreamlike and mythlike" transformations.

Huntington, John. "An Economy of Reason: The Motives of the Technocratic Hero." In *Rationalizing Genius*, pp. 69-93. London: Rutgers University Press, 1989.

> In a section entitled "Mars Is Heaven!", Huntington considers this Bradbury story atypical of the science fiction genre because of its relaxed treatment of scientific thought, but finds the story's emotional content satisfying.

Jacobs, Robert. "The Writer's Digest Interview: Bradbury." In *Writer's Digest* 56, No. 2 (February 1976): 18-25.

> Insightful interview in which Bradbury discusses why, how, and about what he writes, focusing in particular on his place in the science fiction genre.

Johnson, Wayne L. *Ray Bradbury.* New York: Frederick Ungar Publishing Co., 1980, 173 p.

> Provides a thorough thematic discussion of Bradbury's fiction.

Kagle, Steven E. "Homage to Melville: Ray Bradbury and the Nineteenth-Century American Romance." In *The Celebration of the Fantastic: Selected Papers from the Tenth Anniversary International Conference on the Fantastic in the Arts*, pp. 279-89. Westport, Conn.: Greenwood Press, 1989.

> Compares Bradbury's writing to that of Herman Melville, asserting that Bradbury's literary method of internal exploration presents a romantic view of the twentieth century.

Miller, Calvin. "Ray Bradbury: Hope in a Doubtful Age." In *Reality and the Vision*, pp. 92-101. Dallas: World Publishing, 1990.

> Noted fantasy author Calvin Miller studies the spiritual aspects of Bradbury's work within a Christian framework, and lays claim to four reasons why he reads Bradbury's short fiction: to celebrate art, to broaden our understanding, to escape the heaviness of the moment, and to believe in a better world.

Mogen, David. *Ray Bradbury.* Boston: Twayne Publishers, 1986, 186 p.

> Solid introduction to Bradbury's life, career, and major works of fiction.

Moskowitz, Sam. "Ray Bradbury." In *Seekers of Tomorrow: Masters of Modern Science Fiction,* pp. 352-73. Westport, Conn.: Hyperion Press, Inc., 1966.
Biocritical examination of Bradbury's short fiction.

Sullivan, Anita T. "Ray Bradbury and Fantasy." *English Journal* 61, No. 9 (December 1972): 1309-314.
Distinguishes between instances of horror and fantasy in Bradbury's short fiction.

Touponce, William F. "The Existential Fabulous: A Reading of Ray Bradbury's 'The Golden Apples of the Sun'." *Mosaic* VIII, No. 3-4 (Spring/Summer 1980): 203-18.
Studies mythopoetic elements in Bradbury's "The Golden Apples of the Sun," arguing that "Bradbury has given us a fable of modern consciousness which often forgets . . . its Promethean debt to the unconscious."

———. "Some Aspects of Surrealism in the Work of Ray Bradbury." *Extrapolation* 25, No. 3 (Fall 1984): 228-38.
Examines surrealist elements in Bradbury's works, particularly in "The Rocket Man."

Valis, Noël M. "*The Martian Chronicles* and Jorge Luis Borges." *Extrapolation* 20, No. 1 (Spring 1979): 50-9.
Compares Bradbury's themes of identity, personality, and time in *The Martian Chronicles* to those of modern Latin American writing as typified by Jorge Luis Borges.

Additional coverage of Bradbury's life and career is contained in the following sources published by Gale Research: *Authors & Artists for Young Adults,* **Vol. 15;** *Authors in the News,* **Vols. 1, 2;** *Concise Dictionary of American Literary Biography, 1968-1988;* *Contemporary Authors,* **Vols. 1-4R;** *Contemporary Authors New Revision Series,* **Vols. 2, 30;** *Contemporary Literary Criticism,* **Vols. 1, 3, 10, 15, 42, 98;** *Dictionary of Literary Biography,* **Vols. 2, 8;** *Discovering Authors; Discovering Authors: British; Discovering Authors: Canadian; Discovering Authors: Most-Studied Authors Module; Discovering Authors: Novelists Module; Discovering Authors: Popular Fiction and Genre Authors Module; Major 20th-Century Writers; Something about the Author,* **Vols. 11, 64;** and *World Literature Criticism.*

Janet Frame
1924-

New Zealand novelist, autobiographer, short story writer, poet, and essayist.

INTRODUCTION

One of New Zealand's best-known contemporary fiction writers, Frame is the author of numerous novels and stories that demonstrate a strong autobiographical influence. Her fiction is marked by a concern with death, poverty, and madness—matters with which Frame became familiar while growing up during the Great Depression, and later when she spent several years in a mental institution after being erroneously diagnosed as schizophrenic. In addition, Frame's works play with language, using anagrams, rhymes, puns, disrupted syntax, and other word games in order to highlight ways in which people communicate—or fail to do so.

Biographical Information

Frame was born in Dunedin, New Zealand, in 1924. As a child she began writing in an effort to liberate herself from what she has described "a background of poverty, drunkeness, attempted murder, and near-madness." During the Depression, her large family eked out a living in a rural region and endured adversity: two of her sisters drowned in separate incidents, and her younger brother suffered many epileptic seizures. Although she wanted to be a writer, Frame studied at a teacher's training college. While a student, she suffered a nervous breakdown and attempted suicide. During her subsequent hospitalization she was forced to submit to hundreds of sessions of electroshock therapy. Frame would later detail her family life and the eight years she spent in and out of mental hospitals in three volumes of autobiography. Despite her difficulties Frame continued to write, and she published her first book of short stories while still a patient. This collection, *The Lagoon*, received the Hubert Church award as New Zealand's finest prose work of 1951. After the publication of the novel *Owls Do Cry* (1957), Frame spent several years abroad, living for periods in England, Spain, and France. She returned to New Zealand upon the death of her father in 1963 and now lives near Levin. Filmmaker Jane Campion brought the story of Frame's life to the cinema in the award-winning film *An Angel at My Table* (1989).

Major Works

Frame's short stories can be grouped loosely into two categories: realistic narratives dealing with childhood or the lives of lonely and alienated adults; and symbolic tales

that employ fantastic and mythic elements in order to explore philosophical ideas and concepts. A story of the first type, "The Reservoir" is about a rite of passage from childhood. It revolves around the desire of several youths to visit a distant water reservoir that has been declared dangerous and off limits by their parents. "The Bath" treats a different phase of life, and depicts the hardships faced by a nearly invalided elderly woman for whom basic tasks such as bathing pose great challenges. She finds little joy in life except to visit the cemetery where her loved ones rest. In contrast to these stories that explore issues of everyday life, "Snowman, Snowman" is a highly fanciful piece, featuring a conversation between a snowman and a snowflake about existence and mortality. Similarly, "Two Sheep," which centers on a discussion among sheep on the way to the slaughterhouse, raises questions about death, fate, and the unexamined life.

Critical Reception

Commentators have as a rule favored Frame's more naturalistic stories over her symbolic tales. Representing the views of many critics who have found the latter to be heavy-handed, Dorothy Nyren has stated that Frame "writes her symbols large, circles around them two or three times, and, then, just to make sure, explains them." However, Judith Dell Panny, writing on "Snowman, Snowman," has applauded Frame's use of symbolism. In this story, Panny has asserted, Frame "has shaped a story of considerable complexity. Instead of endorsing a body of knowledge in the manner of traditional allegories, 'Snowman, Snowman' questions old certainties. The tale subverts our expectations, making the allegory ironical." The author's literary style has also been faulted as occasionally affected and obtrusive. Yet H. Winston Rhodes has praised "the distinctive way of seeing, the double vision, the combination of inward and outward look" that Frame demonstrates in her most successful short stories, such as "Swans," "The Reservoir," and "Keel and Kool."

PRINCIPAL WORKS

Short Fiction

The Lagoon 1951; revised as *The Lagoon and Other Stories,* 1961
***The Reservoir: Stories and Sketches* 1963
***Snowman, Snowman: Fables and Fantasies* 1963
†*You Are Now Entering the Human Heart* 1984

Other Major Works

Owls Do Cry (novel) 1957
The Edge of the Alphabet (novel) 1962
Scented Gardens for the Blind (novel) 1963
The Adaptable Man (novel) 1965
A State of Siege (novel) 1966
The Pocket Mirror (poetry) 1967
The Rainbirds (novel) 1968; also published as *Yellow Flowers in the Antipodean Room,* 1969
Daughter Buffalo (novel) 1972
To the Is-land (autobiography) 1982
An Angel at My Table (autobiography) 1984
The Envoy from Mirror City (autobiography) 1985
The Carpathians (novel) 1988

*Selections from these two volumes comprise *The Reservoir and Other Stories,* 1966.

†This volume contains eleven stories: seven reprinted from Frame's earlier collections and four previously published in periodicals.

CRITICISM

Orville Prescott (essay date 1963)

SOURCE: "Lamentations for the Woes of Life," in *The New York Times,* August 21, 1963, p. 31.

[*In the following review, Prescott finds the stories of* The Reservoir *tiringly depressing, while those of* Snowman, Snowman *he perceives to be generally unremarkable.*]

Collections of short stories proverbially sell badly. Publishers flinch and worry when novelists insist on publication of their short stories in book form. But what is a publisher to do if he admires the novelist and is betting on his future? Usually all he can do is print a small first edition and hope that the novelist's next book will be a popular smash. George Braziller, a courageous publisher who has often backed writers that he admires but the public doesn't has thought of a new approach to the problem of the novelist with a lot of short stories ready for publication. He has put them into two handsomely printed volumes enclosed in an attractive box. Surely so impressive a package must be deserved! The stories are those of Janet Frame, a New Zealand writer, whose three novels have won wide critical applause. The two volumes are called *The Reservoir* and *Snowman Snowman.*

Janet Frame has been praised by one enthusiastic critic as "the most talented writer to come out of New Zealand since Katherine Mansfield." That her talent, particularly her poetic power with words, is genuine is beyond doubt. But, far too often in these tales, she has used it only to express her own emotions—her melancholy, disillusion and despair.

Miss Frame is not interested in short stories of narrative interest, nor in the subtleties of characterization. What she really likes to do is keen shrilly over the woes of life and the misery of living. Her lamentations grow exceedingly tiresome.

The first half-dozen stories in *The Reservoir* are much the best in either of these volumes. These autobiographical reminiscences of childhood on the South Island of New Zealand possess a vitality and a feeling for normal life lacking in Miss Frame's other work. But even these stories are infused with her omnipresent gloom. Death is always lurking in her dismal world. Failure, frustration and madness prepare the way for death's final mercy.

The stories in *The Reservoir* that do not deal with children are mostly about lonely outcasts in London, a miserably untalented poet, a suicide, and three women, each of whom is a trifle crazier than the others.

Janet Frame writes about all these unfortunates with professional skill, but never with humor, drama or communicable emotion. The result is that one feels sorrier for Miss Frame than for her unfortunate characters.

The fables and fantasies in *Snowman Snowman* range in length from several of one page to one of 100 pages. Some are solemn and pretentious. Some are sardonic and satirical. All are written in a torrential poetic prose which is alternately beautiful and just fancy. They read like dreams, nightmares and fairy stories.

A few make clear, if dismal, comments on the unsatisfactory nature of human experience. Many, I presume, make the same points, but they are so obscure and ambiguous that their meaning can only be a matter of personal interpretation and guesswork.

"**Snowman Snowman,**" the title story, consists of 100 pages of conversation between a snowman, ignorant about human life, and a perpetual snowflake who tells him all about it. Needless to say, the life observed by the snowflake in a dreary London suburb is stale, flat and unprofitable—Hans Christian Andersen in reverse.

Richard M. Elman (essay date 1963)

SOURCE: "A Sense of Place," in *New York Herald Tribune,* August 25, 1963, p. 10.

[*In the following review, Elman assesses the strengths and weaknesses of Frame's writing in* The Reservoir *and* Snowman, Snowman.]

These short prose works by the New Zealand writer Janet Frame are curious mixtures of memoirs, parable, and nearly uninhibited fantasy.

In the pieces she has labelled stories [*The Reservoir*], Janet Frame uses a variety of characters to bring to our attention the private aches, fantasies and self-doubts of a particular young girl coming to maturity in rural Southern New Zealand.

In a separate volume [*Snowman, Snowman*], specifically marked "fables and fantasies," she departs from a strict narration of emotional autobiography to make what are presumably more—philosophical statements (but in a fictitious, impressionistic style) about our common mortality and our common and uncommon deformities.

Many of these pieces have appeared in national magazines in this country. The collection is handsomely designed, printed, and boxed, and Janet Frame's publishers quote from a reviewer who believes she is "the most talented writer to have come out of New Zealand since Katherine Mansfield."

What, one wonders, is such a remark supposed to mean? It is illiterate racehorse touting, not much better as journalism; as literary criticism, it is wholly irrelevant, for it tells us nothing about why we should be interested in Miss Frame's works and it takes an awful lot for granted about the work of Katherine Mansfield.

What is unique in this writing is the sense of place so painstakingly recreated by the author—the sense of place, of time past and time remembered. Few writers "down under" or elsewhere are as good as Janet Frame with particularity. Her real kinship is not with that sentimentalizing Miss Mansfield but with her arch-enemy, D. H. Lawrence.

Like Lawrence, Janet Frame can make you recall exactly every feeling of pettiness, meanness, and ignominy, every imagined deprivation as well as the truly meaningful calamities. She can also make you aware of the wonderful, terrifying, often mysterious world of Nature and of the senses and how ordinary human commerce gets between us and these experiences.

Unlike Lawrence, however, she becomes somewhat coy and perhaps just a little too chatty whenever she feels called upon to make the grand generalizations. She can be accurate and perceptive about small homely things such as why most people build illusions for themselves and why they are so anxious to assure themselves that these creations will be destroyed, or how one is reassured upon seeing one's own deformities mirrored in the lives of the famous. But when she attempts to move from these often witty, epigrammatic statements to comment on truly relevant human experience here and now, she is apt to sound like just another Katherine Mansfield—or a kind of backstreet London Sherwood Anderson—and then we come to see how remote New Zealand really has been all these years.

The most irritating problems seem to be caused by Miss Frame's deliberately "artsy" narrative techniques and her incredibly mannered prose. These are both carefully intended to give us a more intimate sense of personality, but, to a much larger extent than she may be aware, many of the verisimilitudes which she is seeking have already been discovered for us by other writers in England, Western Europe, and America. Paradoxically, it was only by a constant referral to the landscape and manners of her own country that she was able to keep this reader engrossed. But, in that same process, she often seems to attain a desperate provincialism which, after a while, enforces my feeling that the Antipodes had been more aptly named than I had ever before imagined.

Eve Auchincloss (essay date 1963)

SOURCE: "Needles & Pins," in *The New York Review of Books,* Vol. 453, October 17, 1963, pp. 5-6.

[*In the following excerpt, Auchincloss provides a mixed review of the collections* The Reservoir *and* Snowman, Snowman.]

Janet Frame's anomalous stories and fables, thirty-eight of them, come boxed and showily bound in two volumes, [*The Reservoir* and *Snowman, Snowman*], urgently suggesting that should demurrers be raised as to just *what* they are, they are at any rate Art. Leaving aside labels, what are they on their own highly individual terms? Their author is a richly gifted writer in shaky control of her gifts; in fact, the gifts have the upper hand much of the time. But when these pieces work, some of life's sad truths come smiling out of them. One gives one's consent. When they don't, the self-indulgent writing and suffocating self-absorption are too much for their diaphanous themes.

One of the best of the stories, "**The Reservoir,**" works with a childhood memory. Plotless, it flows and ripples as it will, but is always magnetized by a central ominous mystery: a place forbidden the children by the grownups.

A sense of childhood's spacious dimensions and its double-visioned consorting with the adult world rises like strong fumes from this recollection, seemingly unmediated by palpable art. Again, in **"Prizes,"** a theme is followed through a number of variations as in music. When she is firmly in command as she is in these and several other stories, she unlocks unsuspected doors.

But there is much else here that does not communicate more than an illegible suffering and surrender. She is numb to the social, historical world. Her subject is loss and death: over and over again she names all the parts of beautiful life only to conclude with the need to relinquish life itself. The monotony of the theme becomes unbearable in **"Snowman Snowman,"** a gigantic (103 pages) grabbag of blurry coyness, the *faux naïf*, rhetorical questions and exclamations straight out of a Victorian children's tract, Beautiful Meanings that recollect Richard Le Gallienne and the worst of Oscar Wilde. It happens to contain a paragraph that gives the gist of most of her stories in a nutshell:

> A man sent to a mail-order firm for a radio transmitting and receiving set. When he assembled the kit of tiny parts he found that he could send or receive only one message, S.O.S. He listened day and night, and he never found out who was sending the message or why he himself should be sending it, for he didn't need to ask for help, he was not in despair, not bankrupt or crossed in love; his life was happy. He got up one morning, washed, dressed, looked out of his window at the world, and shot himself.

The paucity of this theme in many instances drives Janet Frame to mere automatic writing. She says Death, Time, but cannot enlarge our sense of their part in our lives, any more than one can be William Blake by talking about tigers and sheep.

One should not perhaps stress the failings of so natural-born a writer, except that they obtrude in such a large part of this over-blown collection. . . . [The] best of these pieces, which are all mercurial intuition, funambulist linguistic cavortings, *moues* of witty metaphor, would have made a memorable *little* book.

Donald Hannah (essay date 1971)

SOURCE: "Janet Frame," in *Commonwealth Short Stories,* edited by Anna Rutherford and Donald Hannah, Edward Arnold, Ltd., 1971, pp. 148-50.

[*In the following essay, Hannah finds that "Two Sheep" and "A Boy's Will" are ostensibly very different but similarly convey a sense of the world as a menacing place.*]

Janet Frame, a New Zealand writer, has probably more compelling personal reasons for writing than any other author in this anthology. Having spent eight years of her life in a mental hospital she consulted yet another doctor, and 'was astonished and grateful to hear him refute all previous commandments—"Why mix, why conform? I think you need to write to survive".' And later in the same article in the New Zealand periodical *Landfall*, No. 73, she states:

> Though I began writing when I was a child and have never really stopped writing, I think I really began when my need to write was understood. . . . Freedom to write is a very narrow freedom among the many personal imprisonments suffered by those who want to write, yet it is the master key, and if a writer has determination enough to turn the key . . . then he may be able to put his dreamed works into words.

From these circumstances come some of her chief concerns as an author, which can also be traced in **"A Boy's Will"**: her preoccupation with the inner life, her absorbed interest in that very narrow border-land between fantasy and reality in which much of her work takes place, and the attempt to chart the internal processes of a personality divided between the claims of normal life and the pressing need not to mix or to conform.

'Write to survive'; but it remains at best a survival subject to constant threat from all sides. It is this awareness of undefinable menace hanging over life, waiting to strike at any moment, that both affords a major theme in her work and is the source from which it derives much of its inspiration and power. Of the **"Two Sheep"** one does indeed succeed in escaping death, but,

> if you notice him in a flock, being driven along a hot dusty road, you will be able to distinguish him by his timidity, his uncertainty, the frenzied expression in his eyes when he tries, in his condemned silence, to discover whether the sky is at last free from hawks, or whether they circle in twos and threes above him, waiting to kill him.

If Peter Cowan's story "The Tractor" is a moral fable illustrating a preconceived thesis, **"Two Sheep"** is pure fable embodying a highly personal vision of life. Several of Janet Frame's stories are cast in this form (one of her collections, *Snowman Snowman,* is subtitled *Fables and Fantasies*), and her attraction to this type of narrative goes back to her very early childhood. In the *Landfall* article she writes:

> I made my first story on the banks of the Mataura river after a meal of trout and billy tea. 'Once upon a time there was a bird. One day a hawk came out of the sky and ate the bird. The next day a big bogie came out from behind the hill and ate up the hawk for eating up the bird.' The story's not unusual told by a child of three. . . . I keep that story in mind as an example of a time in my life when I did not waste words.

"Two Sheep" is told in a bare poetic style that still, so many years later, does not waste a single word. Without a trace of sententiousness or sentimentality, it yet does much more than merely set out a simple and demonstrable moral truth. It proves nothing whatsoever, but it does constitute a whole desperate philosophy of life.

The fact that **"A Boy's Will"**, although by the same author, is so completely different in presentation serves as an illustration of the range and resources of the short-story form. Taking as its starting point Longfellow's words from his poem "My Lost Youth", 'A boy's will is the wind's will, And the thoughts of youth are long, long thoughts', the style itself develops this theme. Metaphor and imagery combine with a loose, fluid, syntactical structure to give an effect as highly poetical as Tutuola's "The Complete Gentleman". But, whereas in his case there lies a long oral folk-tradition behind it, with Janet Frame there is a distinctly literary influence, especially that of Virginia Woolf. If Tutuola in a sense is speaking aloud to an audience, Janet Frame is recording the boy's unspoken thoughts to himself. The story traces the flow of the boy's consciousness, one in which fantasy and day-dream continually mingle and run together with memories of the past and with immediate experience like coloured patterns in a kaleidoscope. Nevertheless, although the depiction of an ever-changing mood replaces the narration of a chronological sequence of events, there is still a development in the story. For, if the boy refuses to conform, and rebels against his mother's insidious tyranny, he also ultimately finds a truth in a vision of life which is not essentially dissimilar from that in the **"Two Sheep"**:

> He understood now what the television preachers meant when they insisted the skies had opened. He believed them. He saw his mother with a stone in her eyes and a bone in her throat. Stone and bone were his future.

P. D. Evans (essay date 1981)

SOURCE: "'Farthest from the Heart': The Autobiographical Parables of Janet Frame," in *Modern Fiction Studies,* Vol. 27, No. 1, Spring, 1981, pp. 31-40.

[*In the following essay, Evans discusses Frame's "tendency to write about herself and her experiences as if she were writing about other things."*]

No one approaches Janet Frame's writing for an evening of light entertainment. The atmosphere of her work is almost unrelievedly dark; its texture thick with imagery and allusion; its plots full of deceits engineered to trick the reader; its significance half-stated and often obscure, as if the process of writing has not fully released the impulses which have brought it about. It is this last quality which I wish to discuss in this essay: the sense gained by any copious reader of her work that it represents a recurring engagement with the business of writing itself, with the relationships of words and things, and with the limiting nature of the things we attempt to discuss with words, rather than being a process of steadily expressing a vision that is largely preconceived.

In discussing this, as will be evident, I have broken the rule which states that a writer's life has nothing to do with a writer's art. I break it because it does not fit the writer: Janet Frame seems to me to dictate a different critical approach because, as anyone familiar with the details of her life will know, she constantly places herself at the center of her own writing. Like the Malcolm Lowry of *Under the Volcano,* for example, Frame is an extraordinarily egocentric writer who finds herself in everything and will empathize with her environment only in order to cannibalize it, so that the flesh of others may become the substance of her fiction. Knowing this does not lessen her stature, of course, any more than it will lead us to some kind of absolute interpretation of her work. Acknowledging her fundamental egocentrism simply reveals a concealed level of meaning in her writing and helps us to understand why she writes as she does.

To begin illustrating some of these claims, I have chosen what seems at first to be one of her slightest stories, **"The Linesman."** Very little happens in this story, whose narrator describes a few moments she has spent gazing through her window at an electrical linesman who has climbed a telegraph pole to make repairs to the wires in her street. She notices certain ironies: the fact that the safety harness which prevents him from falling to his death is also holding him up against wires that could fry him to a crisp; and the contrast between this dangerous position and the surrounding lassitude of an early spring day which is being celebrated with truly suburban anonymity by women pegging out billowing washing and youths sprawled in amatory postures beneath motorcycles. There is little else to be seen, but the narrator confesses that she is unable to pull herself away from the window—because, as she reveals in the final sentence of the story, she has been hoping to see the linesman fall to his death.

On the face of it, this story appears to reveal the writer herself turning from the typewriter in boredom and admitting to a desire for a little titillation. I would suggest that there is much more to the story than this, however, and that the crucial element in it is the electricity to which the linesman is so close. Frame underwent frequent electric shock treatment herself while in psychiatric hospitals between 1947 and 1953, and she seems to have had a special fascination with electricity ever since. One thinks of the frequent references in her writing to innocuous electrical devices (such as heaters in *The Rainbirds*) and the dangers they represent; of the linesman in *Daughter Buffalo* who is burnt to death in mid-air; and, more substantially, the images of encircling fire that occur in some of the other novels. In *Owls Do Cry* the central symbol of the book, the rubbish dump with its "tickle of yellow toitoi" round its edge, is specifically related by imagery to the encircling fires of electric shock treatment; a nuclear explosion ends the fourth novel, *Scented Gardens for the Blind,* and her next, *The Edge of the Alphabet,* concludes with the killing-off of most of its characters by a falling chandelier lit to celebrate the arrival of electricity in a small English village. For this writer, electrical power is secular power, a natural force which humans use to destroy and oppress.

Watching an electrical linesman at work, then, is no straightforward thing for such a writer, who immediately sees not an artisan but herself in a symbolic situation which represents her own predicament as she sees it. The equation she appears to make is roughly as follows: the linesman like the artist has special gifts of vision, his being literal (neighbors draw their curtains in case he looks down into their houses) and hers figurative (nothing can stop her imaginative insight into the lives of other people). But both pay a price for this vision, the linesman through his proximity to a voltage which may kill him, the artist through her proximity to a voltage which, through electro-convulsive therapy, might rob her of her imagination and leave her like Daphne after her leucotomy at the end of *Owls Do Cry.* Trapped in such a predicament—the artist has even less freedom than the harnessed linesman—one may well wish occasionally for the merciful release of a sudden fall.

What Frame is doing here is done to a certain extent by all artists, who turn the surrounding world into metaphors which embody their vision. But few so distinctively focus the metaphors on their own special plight; few operate such a gravitational pull on the objects of their fictional worlds, drawing everything towards a central sensibility but refusing subsequently to force them back out again much transformed. Her tendency to do these things in her writing is present from the first collection of short stories, *The Lagoon,* which was written during her early years in a hospital. The personal nature of these stories and their subsequent tendency towards autobiographical parable can only be explained by an understanding of the importance of the events that immediately preceded her admission to a hospital in the fall of 1947.

Frame entered the hospital voluntarily, with the aim of turning herself into a professional writer. The most interesting thing she tells us about herself during this time is that she carried a copy of Rilke's *Sonnets to Orpheus* with her wherever she went. These sonnets had been written in response to the death of the daughter of a friend, a talented dancer whose sudden demise Rilke attempted to understand and to accept in a long sequence of poems about art, life, and death that were based on the classical myth of Orpheus and Eurydice. What must have fascinated Frame was the similarity of Rilke's situation to her own: just before her entry to the hospital she had lost her younger and favorite sister, Isabel, who had drowned at Picton, the beach resort home of the Frames' maternal grandparents, during a late summer holiday taken with the writer.

Rilke, then, was more than just another writer; she chose to study him because he was approaching death by means of art, and in her situation art alone offered some means of coming to terms with a tragic bereavement. Like the poet, she would dedicate her writing to understanding her loss, and it was in this mood that she began to write her first mature stories.

The reader is immediately struck by her oblique approach to her task. Although no one could deny that the stories in *The Lagoon* are insistently about death, there is an equally undeniable sense in them of the writer circling about a subject that both fascinates and repels her. The title story of the collection, for example, is set at the scene of Isabel's death, but conceals fact with a layer of fiction. The way in which this is done is worth noting. **"The Lagoon"** begins with its young female narrator returning in late adolescence to the scene of her happy childhood holidays to find that the little township as well as her favorite lagoon on the beach are far smaller and shabbier than she remembered them. She recalls her beloved grandmother, who has recently died, and especially remembers the old woman's ability to weave stories about everything in Picton except the lagoon, which "never had a proper story." Now that the old woman has gone, the girl's aunt reveals the "proper story" at last: "Your great grandmother was a murderess. She drowned her husband, pushed him in the lagoon." The girl's grandmother never mentioned the murder, as the aunt explains, because, "The reason one talks farthest from the heart is the fear that it may be hurt."

This sentence is the most crucial in the entire collection. It draws attention to the dishonesty possible in storytelling, to the ease with which writers may manipulate facts and thereby control the responses of their readers. The process of storytelling is one of the things this story is about: the grandmother's ability to tell stories about things is one of its subjects, as is the ability (conjectured by the aunt later in the story) of Dostoevsky and popular journalists to do the same. Bringing the inventedness of fiction before the reader, particularly by means of a sentence which speaks of avoidance and hurt, inevitably draws attention to the inventedness of the story itself, and it invites the reader to plunge beneath its surface in order to examine the processes of fictionalization. Aware as we are of the actual events behind the story, we are better placed than most readers to see how Frame forms life into parable. Just as the lagoon is sullied by the invading seawater, she seems to say, childhood is sullied by adult life, especially by its diminution of the transforming imaginative power we have when we are innocent. But that is not all that pollutes the lagoon of childhood: violent death, a death in the family, has contaminated it too. This is the nearest the writer comes to mentioning the incident which has hurt her heart; this, and the clear reference to the invading seawater which in fact carried her sister's life away.

This process of "talking farthest from the heart" becomes a staple of Janet Frame's fiction, a technique in which actual events, and particularly this one event (which becomes melded from time to time with the almost identical loss of her older sister, also by drowning, in 1937), are turned into fiction, but in such a way that the reader is always made aware of the fictitiousness of the fiction. In the *Lagoon* stories and others of the period, she follows a rigid system: if the location of Isabel's death is confronted—the beach—then the loss is either suffered by someone else or is less than a loss of a sister. If the doomed sister is mentioned openly (as in **"The Secret,"** where the threatened girl bears the name of Frame's older drowned sister, Myrtle), then the point of the story is that she is not going to die, after all. At no point do we find the death behind her fiction faced squarely, and at no point can we sense her retreat completely from it. Even in *Daughter Buffalo*, where she describes the drowning and the subsequent train journey from Picton with the coffin, she gives the experience to an anonymous friend of the narrator, Turnlung. She cannot avoid mentioning the topic, which is scarcely crucial to the story, yet she cannot bring herself to mention it fully. She conceals but teases, or reveals but turns away.

"The Lagoon" is the best brief example of Frame's curious behavior, but there are others that are little different. In "Swans," we again find the child narrator taking us back to the beach and again find that all is not well. Because it is the middle of the week, their father cannot come with them, and the usual crowds are not there; and these absences not only rob the place of its former magic, but they fill it with darkness and a sense of threat that is disproportionate to the events which occur. When the children find a shell that looks like a cat's eye, death enters the story at last: they are reminded of the dying cat they have left at home.

But there is a coda to this story, as in "The Lagoon," which focuses this image of death a little more sharply. As they make their way back up the beach at evening with their mother, the girls see another lagoon:

> It was dark black water, secret, and the air was filled with murmurings and rustlings, it was as if they were walking into another world that had been kept secret from everyone and now they had found it. The darkness lay massed as if you could touch it, soon it would swell and fill the earth. . . . They looked across the lagoon then and saw the swans, black and shining, as if the visiting dark tiring of its form, had changed to birds, hundreds of them resting and moving softly about on the water. Why the lagoon was filled with swans, like secret sad ships, secret and quiet. Hush-sh the water said, rush-hush, the wind passed over the top of the water, no other sound but the shaking of rushes and far away now it seemed the roar of the sea like a secret sea that had crept inside your head forever.

This is the same lagoon as before, once pleasant but now darkened by the birds which represent death; beyond it is the sound of the sea with its inescapable secret which only the writer knows.

The inevitable lagoon of "The Reservoir" is slightly different from the others in that it is man-made. The young children who are at the center of this story play frequently in their tiny local creek but are warned by their parents not to follow it inland to the reservoir which feeds it. The repetition of such warnings soon turns the reservoir into a symbol that contrasts with the innocence of the little creek: where the latter is safe, the former, as notices remind the children, is full of danger (or "ANGER," in the case of one slightly dilapidated notice). When the children decide to visit it after all, they are in effect visiting the adult life that lies ahead of each of them, but none of them is able to understand what the concrete lagoon represents, and

they return home filled with complacent bafflement at their parents' earlier warnings.

The *real* story, as in "The Lagoon," comes through implication, through the fact that the innocent mind of the child is being recreated by the experienced mind of an adult. The hidden threat of the journey to the reservoir and of the reservoir itself is revealed through images that are those of a fairy story that has gone wrong: there are "huge trees that lived with their heads in the sky, and their mazed and linked roots rubbed bare of earth, like bones with the flesh cleaned from them," and pines which make "the sound of speech at its loneliest level where the meaning is felt but never explained, and it goes on and on in a kind of despair." And the description of the reservoir has a similar feeling of inexplicable desolation:

> The fringe of young pines on the edge, like toy trees, subjected to the wind, sighed and told us their sad secrets. In the Reservoir there was an appearance of neatness which concealed a disarray too frightening to be acknowledged except, without any defence, in moments of deep sleep and dreaming. The little sparkling innocent waves shone now green, now grey, petticoats, lettuce leaves; the trees sighed, and told us to be quiet, hush-sh, as if something were sleeping and should not be disturbed—perhaps that was what the trees were always telling us, to hush-sh in case we disturbed something which must never be awakened?

The petticoat-waves are from a childhood story; the sense that they conceal something unspeakable sounds like a story from the Brothers Grimm. Here again is one of those secret seas that has crept inside the narrator's head and altered the perspective of everything she writes, making the children's final conviction that their parents have got the reservoir all wrong pathetic by contrast with the knowledge implied in the story.

Another *Lagoon* story, "Keel and Kool," makes some important developments of the parabolic method. At first, in fact, autobiography appears to have triumphed over parable, because the story openly mentions the death of a beloved sister. Once again we are at the beach, once again we are in the hands of a child-figure, but the emphasis here is on the absoluteness of death, its complete unavoidability. Instead of returning Winnie, the bereaved girl, to childhood at the end of the story, Frame sends her into a lonely pine forest where the restrained lamentation of other stories is placed in the voice of a seagull circling high above the pines, "a seagull as white as chalk, circling and crying Keel Keel Come home Kool come home Kool. And Kool would never come, ever."

Does this story show Frame coming to terms with her loss at last, able to face it after the exorcising process of art? The fact that "The Reservoir" was written after "Keel and Kool" suggests that this is unlikely and that we should continue to look at her work as parable. The key to this story, in fact, seems to be in the gull's cry, which is not only onomatopoeic but also a pun: the gull flies above the girl as an ostensible emblem of the frankness of her despair and the completeness of her loss, but, as it does, its voice draws attention to a secret loss, of someone who has been *killed and cooled*—someone dead but, so to speak, frozen in memory. Once more, then, as in **"The Lagoon"** in particular, we have an apparent story (a girl comes to terms with her loss) and a "real" or "secret" story, implied by means of a special signal.

Two factors, then, seem inextricably involved in Janet Frame's art, to judge from these early stories: first, its devotion to a single historical event, and second, the increasingly complex and subtle way in which she signals this to the reader. There is a great distance between the tell-tale words and sentences of **"The Lagoon"** and the punning of the seagull in **"Keel and Kool."** The first draw attention to themselves and are fairly readily decodable; the second seems furtive and obscure, requiring special information to be recognized, let alone understood. Generally speaking, this tendency toward obscurity becomes a dominant trait of her later writing, developing into a curious and almost neurotic desire to manipulate the reader, to treat the inventedness of fiction as a means of breaking the conventions governing the relationship of writer and audience. There is a streak of this game-playing in two of the *Lagoon* stories, **"Dossy"** and **"Jan Godfrey,"** where the reader is given a specific perspective on the stories only to be told finally that this perspective is incorrect. The replacement of apparent narrators by "real" ones becomes a staple of some of her novels (I am thinking of *Scented Gardens for the Blind* and *Daughter Buffalo,* in particular), where personae split during the course of reading and where narrators are revealed to be concoctions of other, hidden, narrators, figures who are surrogates for the author, who have been "educated" by the experience of death and who lecture the reader on the essential processes of human existence.

In many of the novels, then, Frame seems to be deliberately attempting to devalue traditional fictive methods, to baffle and to confuse the reader, and to imply the existence of qualities and values that are concealed beneath the surface of her writing; these tendencies develop directly from her short initial fiction. To do justice to a generalization like this would be impossible, but I think a fair way to conclude this essay would be to look at the single work in which most aspects of that generalization come nearest to being true. In turning to *Scented Gardens for the Blind,* I confront a novel whose considerable obscurity originates in that slight obfuscation we saw in **"The Lagoon,"** a work that is essentially a short story so encrusted with complications that it is no longer recognizable—but a work which, nevertheless, contains sufficient signals to enable the reader to decode it, to return to Frame's aboriginal "secret."

The most important character in this novel is not a human being but a black beetle which lives inside a dictionary from which it emerges through a hole between two words, *trichotomy* and *trick*. Frame is as wryly aware of the demands her writing places on her readers as anyone can be, and here she produces a parody of the reader of her own novel, caught up in a bewildering system of language from which he seeks a way out. Avid Frame readers will see immediately that the way out of *Scented Gardens for the*

Blind is to recognize that its *trick* is that its narrator, Vera Glace, is a *trichotomy* of imagined characters (herself, a husband, and a daughter) whose task is to enact the novel's themes. Recognizing Vera as the "death-educator" of the work simplifies its structure and leads us immediately back to the controlling author.

Verbal tricks like this are no different in intention from those phrases in the *Lagoon* stories which remind the reader to look below the surface of the language; they are simply more compact, revolving round single words. But it is a further trick of this novel to persuade the reader that he has only one trick to solve and that once we have identified ourselves with the literary beetle and Vera with the other main human characters our work is done. We ought to recall the untrustworthy perspective of some of those stories and ask whether Vera Glace is the "true glass" her name seems to suggest. Within her own novel she is, in the sense that she is able to see what her author believes to be "true"; semantically she is not, in that her name suggests another pun ("true ice," *via* the French) which invites our gaze outside the work in which she appears by evoking that theme of killing and cooling that has appeared before. And it is not difficult to guess where we are supposed to focus our attention, since in the same year in which she produced this novel she also produced a long story called **"Snowman, Snowman."**

There can be no doubt, I think, that the writer means us to make this unusual transition from one work to another, because the story reads like a large fragment that has somehow fallen from the novel. Its form is much the same, with the novel's long conversations between Erlene Glace and the black beetle being paralleled by those in the story between the narrating snowman and a rather garrulous snowflake. The tone of these fabulistic elements is similar; images (parachuting snowflakes which fall from story to novel, beetleskins which are shed from novel into story) are common to both; and, above all, the themes of the story—principally concerning man's false evolution away from a healing language of communion and toward the violence that has disfigured the twentieth century—are simply consummations of those of the novel.

We could say that the "successful" reader of *Scented Gardens for the Blind* becomes a sort of graduate in verbal trickery whose growing awareness of the concealing power of language has admitted him to an experience not available to all. With such awareness the opening lines of **"Snowman Snowman"** can be seen to reveal more:

> People live on earth, and animals and birds; and fish live in the sea, but we do not defeat the sea, for we are driven back to the sky, or we stay, and become what we have tried to conquer, remembering nothing except our new flowing in and out, in and out, sighing for one place, drawn to another, wild with promises to white birds and bright red fish and beaches abandoned and then longed for.
>
> I never conquered the sea. I flew at midnight to the earth, and in the morning I was made into a human shape of snow.

"Snowman, snowman," my creator said.

Here, quite openly, are the images of the first stories recreated more than a dozen years later: the beach, the unconquerable sea, the white birds above, the doomed girl (the child who makes the snowman is killed later in the story). And, more covertly, in the snowman himself are impounded further early images: wind and sea conspire to produce crystals of ice which the girl in turn conspires to turn into her snowman; two lumps of coal give it the "pine-forest eyes" that recall the dark trees that are part of the early imagery of bereavement. Containing evocations, surrounded by evocations, the snowman takes its place with Frame's other surrogates as one who has learned about mortality at first hand.

What we see at work between the novel and the story occurs perhaps a little too neatly to be wholly typical of Frame's other longer fiction, but it is the quintessence of her tendency to write about herself and her experiences as if she were writing about other things. In her other novels, the disguises vary, and the tricks of language are different; but they are still disguises and tricks, whose job is to conceal the same sensibility and experiences as before and then reveal them to a select few. However far from us in time the damaging but creative experience moves, the damaged creator seems to remain essentially the same, setting up verbal puzzles that repel the casual reader but draw the initiate down through layers of language to a truth which is always the same, to the death which, as the black beetle of *Scented Gardens for the Blind* says, is the common denominator of all things.

Pointing these things out as I have tried to do helps to explain why her writing is as it is; it does not explain away the difficulties but it explains why they are there. Knowing their origin is an unavoidable part of any approach to Janet Frame. Whether we begin at the beginning or start with her most recent novels, *Daughter Buffalo* and *Living in the Maniototo,* we must acknowledge the writer's distinctive relating of death and language in a way that yields an *oeuvre* quite unlike any other in English. It confronts us with a limiting and obsessive self-absorption as well as the liberations of a language that has been set free from the everyday. If we ignore her limitations, her liberation seems feckless and unearned; if we turn away from her linguistic gifts, we are left with darkness and self-pity. Only by seeing one as a function of the other can we see the unity of all her fiction and glimpse with sympathy the experience which constrains it.

H. Winston Rhodes   (essay date 1982)

SOURCE: "Janet Frame: A Way of Seeing in *The Lagoon and Other Stories,*" in *Critical Essays on the New Zealand Short Story,* edited by Cherry Hankin, Heinemann Publishers, 1982, pp. 112-31.

[*In the following survey, Rhodes contends that Frame's early short stories are distinguished by her treatment of perception, both of the external world and of the inner lives of characters.*]

'Yes I have a pair of eyes', replied Sam, 'and that's just it. If they wos a pair o' patent double million magnifyin' gas microscopes of hextra power, p'raps I might be able to see through a flight o' stairs and a deal door; but bein' only eyes, you see, my wision's limited.' When Janet Frame was typing her *Lagoon* stories in a glorified linen cupboard, converted into a bedroom at the boarding-house where she was working for a short period, her outward 'wision', like Sam Weller's, was also restricted. She felt, or Jan Godfrey felt, or possibly it was Alison Hendry who felt 'like Juliet lying in a vault'.

> You see there were shelves all round the walls, and
> sometimes I could feel the prickly feel of artificial
>   flowers
> that are made into wreaths and covered with a bell
>   jar, and
> put in the tomb with the dead people.

Nevertheless, in this small room without wide windows she required no optical aids of the kind described by Mr. Pickwick's servant, in order to rescue from the confusion of dream those memories of childhood and experiences of later days that constitute the raw material from which her stories were shaped. She did not need 'a pair o' patent double million magnifyin' gas microscopes' to see through the walls of the maid's retreat, because she already possessed that inward eye which is the bliss as well as the bane of solitude. Her way of seeing was both outward and inward, a form of double vision that would often disturb her readers and sometimes become a source of embarrassment to herself.

The Lagoon and Other Stories first appeared under the imprint of Caxton in 1951, at a time when Sargeson especially, but also Finlayson, Davin and Gaskell seemed by their publications to represent the post-Mansfield short story writers of New Zealand. Sargeson's collection, *Speaking for Ourselves* (1945), had helped to introduce a number of less familiar names to a wider public; and in the pages of *Landfall* which began publication two years later were to be found short stories by such writers as Ballantyne, Courage, Duggan, Cole, Middleton and Wilson. Yet Janet Frame's small volume, if it did not create any great stir among the comparatively few readers who were drawn to the Caxton imprint, was sufficiently impressive to cause the *Landfall* reviewer to speak of 'a considerable achievement' and 'a promise of future work of distinction', if the author 'should discipline her style and exercise a greater objectivity in the selection of her experience' [Patricia Guest, *Landfall,* June 1952]. No mention of a new way of seeing was made, nor perhaps could have been made, without reference to that same author's novels and short stories of more than a decade later. Yet this early volume ended in a manner that was as suggestive as it [was] enigmatic.

'**My Last Story**' is the title of the piece that fittingly concludes the collection. Janet Frame or, if you prefer, the narrator, begins with the emphatic declaration: 'I'm never going to write another story,' and confesses: 'I don't like writing stories. I don't like putting he said she said he did she did, and telling about people.' She won't write 'about the snow and the women saying how lovely every cloud has a silver lining,' about her grandmother 'sitting in a black dress at the back door and having her photo taken with Dad', about her sisters, the places where she has lived or the people she has seen. 'This is my last story,' she continues to proclaim, 'and I'm going to put three dots with my typewriter, impressively, and then I'm going to begin. . . .' These dots are not followed, however, by a new beginning until eight years later with the publication of her first novel, *Owls Do Cry.* Instead comes the sad reflection: 'I think I've got the wrong way of looking at Life.'

Such an ending both to a story and to a collection of stories should not be misinterpreted as a reluctant though ambiguous farewell to the writing of fiction. Janet Frame was conscious of the different ways of looking at life. She was caught between the outward and the inner view which to her was even a more significant reality, but required a language and a technique that seemed beyond her range. After some time had elapsed she once again attempted to deal with this dilemma in '**A Sense of Proportion**' [in *The Reservoir: Stories and Sketches*] which describes, almost in parabolic form, the inability of the youthful narrator to learn 'the tricks of the eye', a mastery of which was essential in drawing and painting. 'Notice the way the path narrows as it approaches the foothills,' she was told by her art-teacher who promptly dismissed the objection that really it was the same breadth all the way, by insisting 'You must learn to draw these tricks of the eye. You must learn to think in terms of them.' It was no use:

> I never learned to draw tricks of the eye. My paint refused to wash in the correct proportion when I was trying to fill the paper sky with sunrises, sunsets, and rainbows. My garden spades were without strength or shape; their shadows stayed unowned, apart, incredible, more like stray tatters shed from a profusion of dark remnants of objects.

Evidently she had the wrong way of looking, and consistently failed to acknowledge or reproduce on paper 'the tricks of the eye'. When asked to paint an imaginary scene, she regretfully admitted

> I had no imagination. My poverty could not even provide shadows or proportionate rainbows. The paths in my head stayed the same width right to the foothills and over the mountains which were no obstacles to vision, as mountains are agreed to be; they were transparent mountains, and there was the path, the same width as before, annihilating distance, at last disappearing only at the boundary of the picture.

She was quite unable to adjust herself to a way of seeing that depended on anything as sophisticated as perspective. She could not obey the instruction 'to draw things as they seem'. The paths in her head stayed the same width right to the foothills, and the unrecognised distinction between reality and illusion, between 'is' and 'seems', frustrated all her attempts to satisfy her teacher.

Only a few years after she had written '**A Sense of Proportion**', Janet Frame published her remarkable novel, *A State of Siege,* in which the central character, Malfred Signal, had thoroughly learnt the tricks of the eye and wanted to forget them. She had taught art for a number of years

> Pouncing on the faulty 'shadowers', trying to instil the 'sense of proportion' that in her probationary years meant persuading schoolgirls to 'match' the sides of shovels and vases, to make distant mountains distant, near faces near; but which meant to her now an attempt to rearrange her own 'view', set against the measuring standards not of the eye but of the 'room two inches behind the eyes'.

As time passed and she suddenly became free, she discovered that she was still unacquainted with herself, that her interior life, if she had any, was unfamiliar to her and had been buried beneath the weight of family responsibilities and ingrained habit. She had lacked both time and opportunity to explore whatever treasure existed in the 'room two inches behind the eyes'. The middle-aged Malfred Signal was now seeking the 'New View', the way of seeing that was not dependent on outward vision, that was not continually frustrated by the knockings from reality continuing to plague her in the refuge she had found. 'The true images were in her mind,' and

> I want only to forget the years of rigid shading, obsessional outlining and representation of objects; I want in this, still my preliminary dream, to explore beyond the object, beyond its shadow, to the ring of fire, the corona of its circumference; I want to find whether the fire is moving, leaping alive, or whether it is petrified, a burial of past fire, stone flames whose flight and dance are illusory in that they remain fixed for ever, as stone rooted to its place of being.

Malfred Signal's wish to forget the obsessional outlining and representation of objects takes the reader back through '**A Sense of Proportion**' with its 'tricks of the eye' to '**My Last Story**' and its rejection of the outward view. And so often, the stories in Janet Frame's first volume illuminate and provide an unpremeditated introduction to her later work. The way of seeing so characteristic of the author, that 'wrong way of looking at life', assumes an importance that must not be disregarded in any evaluation of her work.

Janet Frame's 'reminiscences of childhood'—a description of *The Lagoon and Other Stories* that is as inadequate as it is misleading—are unlike most sketches that attempt to recapture the age of innocence. Although, since Katherine Mansfield, the theme of 'growing up in New Zealand' has provided those who hoard their memories with an inexhaustible supply of material, the double vision of childhood has received far less attention than it deserves. Janet Frame was peculiarly qualified to enter into a world in which the borderline between fact and fantasy is not clearly marked nor, to the irritation of unimaginative and sober-minded adults, even recognised.

The game of 'make-believe' is usually associated with the happy pastimes of young children, but it is also frequently played with equal seriousness by their elders for whom an alternative truth emerges to hold them spell-bound. Waking dreams, born of desires that will not be suppressed, are prolonged until they either replace or else continue to dominate and control the ordinary truths of humdrum existence. In a number of her early stories Janet Frame tentatively explored this dual reality, attempting to reproduce a state of 'make-believe' that approaches an alternative truth. **'Miss Gibson', 'A Note on the Russian War'** and **'Treasure'** give expression to perhaps the least complex of these excursions into the wonderland of the imagination. The first of these takes the shape of a letter from an ex-pupil to her former teacher who, after reading an account of how a man had re-discovered the treasures of his boyhood in an old lumber-room, had indicated that this was the subject for the next week's essay. The girl's letter to her school-mistress begins: 'Dear Miss Gibson I was an awful liar,' for her completed essay had described a palatial home with its hundred rooms, a retinue of servants, and on the third floor a lumber-room with stained-glass, hand-painted windows. Inside this room

> I found my first reading-book, with the dear sad red and gold pictures, and I yearned for the days that were no more. I put in Tennyson here, tears idle tears I know not what they mean, O Miss Gibson you couldn't have understood how moved I was just standing there by the stained glass window, with the sun throwing a warm lingering light over the book. O Miss Gibson this was the saddest part of my essay.

The shoolgirl had allowed her imagination to carry her away until she had almost been convinced of the reality of her day-dream, of their French cook, Marie-Suzanne, of the old gardener who played the violin, of the copy of Shakespeare she had found in the lumber-room, the same copy which she had read right through at the age of six, and her watch with its three opals. Miss Gibson had written on her essay: 'Fourteen out of twenty highly improbable watch your writing,' but the ex-pupil still thought it necessary to make her confession:

> I didn't have a house with a hundred rooms, and a French cook and a gardener with a beard, I had a little place to live in. I had a mother who cooked for us and she cooked nicely too, and my father dug the garden in the week-ends, and he planted pansies, and we had cats and dogs and rabbits and a mouse in the scullery, and we had visitors sometimes who swore, and I liked being alive and I didn't care two-pence about the past it was the present that mattered, and Miss Gibson, if you really want to know, we didn't even have a lumber-room.

Neither the school-mistress in this sketch nor the youthful essay-writer herself has any illusions about an alternative

truth. One comments 'highly improbable', and the other exclaims, 'dear Miss Gibson I was an awful liar'; but **'A Note on the Russian War'** treats the game of 'make-believe' in such a way that the boundary between 'is' and 'seems' becomes a little less obvious. It begins with a scraggy sunflower that grew near the cow-byre and the potato patch, and a mother's 'sunflowers kiddies, ah sunflowers'. The sunflower soon became 'the biggest blackest sunflower in Russia' and, of course, they all became Russians and lived in the steppes. 'There are no lands outside,' the small note-writer is made to explain, 'they are fenced inside us, a fence of being and we are the world my mother told we are Russians because we have this sunflower in our garden.' This interior view of the happy child anticipates 'the room two inches behind the eyes' which so occupied the attention of the middle-aged spinster in *A State of Siege*; but if the child lives within her 'fence of being', she also lives outside. In the winter she wears great boots and

> When there was snow on the ground we went outside under the trees to sing a Russian song, it went like this, I'm singing it to myself so you can't hear, tra-tra-tra, something about sunflowers and a tall sky and the war rolling through the grass, tra-tra-tra, it was a very nice song.

Nevertheless, the external world was not far away and there were daisy-chains to be made on the lawn, and even if 'we were just Russian children on the Steppes, singing tra-tra-tra, quietly with our mother and father,' the other truth was not dispelled—'war comes whatever you sing.'

'Treasure' relates the way in which a small boy is caught between the reality and the dream, but is forced to pass from one to the other with an abruptness that is disconcerting. He knows full well that treasure is not usually found in these unexciting times beneath the floors or in the linings of chairs. He knows, or thinks he knows, the difference between fancy and fact; but the thought of those linings leads him into a dreamland of the wildest imaginings. From pretending to remember how once he had discovered fifteen five-pound notes in the side of a chair, he elaborates until the notes become rubies, pearls and diamonds that could be exchanged at the local store for cinnamon bars and striped suckers. His father spends his time cutting marbles for him from the diamonds, and the small boy's fame increases and spreads as he wins nearly every game 'because the kids were dazzled by the look of my stinkers'. Because of his fame special holidays from school become a normal occurrence, and as he passes by, jingling marbles in his pocket, he thinks he is the luckiest person alive. The waking dream is rudely shattered by a letter from the headmaster to his father, (the real father not the diamond-cutting father of his fertile imagination), who in the last line of this brief sketch 'got out the strap and said wagging it eh get those pants off and bend over.'

In *Owls Do Cry* a short exchange between Toby and Fay Chalklin refers to another strap that the children believed was used to lead the girls working at the Woollen Mills. 'Oh, that was an old story, surely you didn't believe that.

It was a child's story, and not true,' Fay protests; but Toby replies, 'child's stories are always true.' And Fay exclaims, 'Giants and fairies as well? Toby Withers!' 'Yes,' Toby stubbornly affirms, 'giants and fairies, in different shapes. There's a giant bomber and a giant loneliness.' **'Tiger, Tiger'**, one of the most successful and, at the same time, most ambiguous of the *Lagoon* stories of childhood, gives expression to two simultaneous truths that can scarcely be distinguished. It is Christmas Eve, and Jan with her little brother Dids are filled with excitement not unmixed with anxiety as they go to bed to wait for the morning. Mother had said firmly to Jan 'No, we cannot manage a tiger.' 'No the idea said Dad, no certainly not:' but Jan was quite unable to relinquish her cherished dream of possessing a real live tiger:

> It was getting nearer and nearer Christmas and I hadn't had word from Santa Claus, and I was getting worried. It had to be a tiger or life wasn't worth living. I didn't see how I had lived as long without a tiger. I couldn't think what I had thought about in days before I thought about my tiger. It had to be a tiger. So I prayed for one. Please God let Santa Claus know immediately before it is too late that I want a tiger.

Very very early on Christmas morning two small children creep into the dining-room to find and open their Christmas stockings. While Dids is unwrapping a motor-car, Jan looks everywhere for her stocking, and for a moment thinks that both God and Santa Claus have failed her; but then

> I turned round and saw my tiger. My tiger. He was curled up fast asleep. It's all right, Dids, I said, don't cry. I've got my tiger. He's brought me a tiger. I've got a tiger. Tiger, Tiger.

Are we led to believe that in order to conceal her disappointment and to comfort her little brother, Jan is merely pretending to see her tiger? Or that the intensity of her inward vision has produced to her outward gaze a real tiger, curled up and fast asleep? Although no definite answer is forthcoming, the triumphant conclusion emphasises the way in which Janet Frame attempts to penetrate the mystery of a dual reality with which the mind of a child is often familiar.

Even more remarkable is the sketch entitled **'Dossy'** with its moving account of little Dossy Park playing by herself near a convent gate. It opens with what seem to be two girls, hopping and skipping from shadow to shadow along the footpath. The bigger girl is called Dossy and her smaller companion imagines she must live in a big house,

> A big house at the end of a long long street. With a garden. And a plum tree. And a piano in the front room. And a piano-stool to go round and round on. And lollies in a blue tin on the mantel piece for father to reach up to and say have a striped one chicken, they last longer.

The two girls race each other to the convent gate, but of course Dossy wins because she is bigger; and the little girl

takes hold of Dossy's hand and asks if she can come and live with her. Dossy in her aunt's shortened dress and with dirty shoes says nothing to the little girl in her shiny new shoes and neat blue dress, and they look through the convent gates as the nuns walk up and down,

> and the little girl thought I'll be a nun some day and wear black and white and have a black and white nightie, and I'll pray all day and sit under the plum tree and perhaps God won't mind if I get hungry and eat two or three plums, and every night I'll comb out my mother's long golden hair with a gold comb and I'll have a black and white bed.

So she asks Dossy to be a nun with her, but Dossy only giggles and says 'I don't think.' Inside the gate the nuns see 'a little girl playing ball by herself on the footpath', and wonder what will become of little Dossy Park who has no mother and is always playing by herself. Only from this concluding passage does the reader discover that it is the little girl who is really called Dossy, and that her larger companion has no existence except in the imagination of the lonely, little Dossy Park.

Janet Frame's memories and evocations of childhood are by no means confined to a way of seeing that originates in an exceptionally vivid imagination. They also reproduce the timeless experience of the age of innocence to which Blake's lines have special relevance:

> To see a World in a grain of sand,
> And a Heaven in a wild flower,
> Hold Infinity in the palm of your hand,
> And Eternity in an hour.

The incidents she records may often seem trivial and scarcely significant enough for the slightest sketch, but her way of seeing and of rendering can communicate the state of rapturous contentment, of unalloyed joy, which contains Eternity in an hour, and with which the very young are familiar. Oblivious of all but the present feeling of enormous satisfaction, they may cry 'We'll live here and catch crabs and tiddlers for ever.' This excited declaration appears in **"The Lagoon,"** the first story in Janet Frame's early volume, a story that is impressive not because it relates how and why the great grandmother's husband was drowned in the lagoon, but because the children of several generations played beside it, and they

> used to skim round white stones over the water, and catch tiddlers in the little creek near by, and make sand castles on the edge, this is my castle we said, you be father I'll be mother and we'll live here and catch crabs and tiddlers for ever.

The same passage, repeated word for word, concludes **"The Lagoon,"** and with the happy cries of children the sinister tragedy that occurred so long ago is almost forgotten. Janet Frame may or may not be remembering incidents and feelings from her own early days, but here as elsewhere the story that is told is one of 'being' rather than one of 'doing'.

'Everything is always a story,' wrote Jan Godfrey, and perhaps it is not altogether an accident that her name is Jan, nor that the little girl in **'Tiger, Tiger'** is called Jan, and once again in **'Child'** it is Jan who acquires 'a best friend'. Jan and Minnie had been punished by their teacher because, sitting side by side, they had disobeyed the instruction to breathe in and out while counting up to ten. They had exceeded the limit imposed by counting up to fifteen, and thus each had found 'a best friend'. After school Jan went with Minnie to the latter's home where she lived with her grandparents, and as they ran along they repeated 'eleven, twelve, thirteen, fourteen, fifteen', laughing in conspiratorial happiness. Jan thinks

> Oh how lovely to have no mother and father and live with your grandma and grandad, to have a macrocarpa hedge instead of African Thorn, to have button-up shoes instead of lace-ups, to have a fringe and a dress with a cape collar and a skipping rope with shiny blue handles.

Everything connected with Minnie, her 'best friend', was glorious and fascinating. This is the very spirit of childhood in which feelings have little relationship to facts. Minnie's grandfather gave each of them a peppermint. They flew a kite that he had made, and they kept counting up to fifteen and giggling. A glow seemed to spread all around, and as Jan sets out for home she exclaims

> Oh, Oh. The world was good, like something to eat. There was a wind rushing over the top of the hill, and sometimes ducks flew over, dark and diamond-shaped, their wings whirring, their heads craned forward eagerly. Away on the other hill there were other birds cradled in the heaving tops of the pine trees. And down from the other hill was the place where I lived, with the African Thorn hedge, and the dahlias in the garden, and my big mother with a big blue pinny to shake at me as if it were wheat for a little chook.

'Summer' is so brief that it seems scarcely worth mentioning, except that a page and a half is enough for Janet Frame to describe the sudden change from utter despair to complete bliss, a change which she presents without waste of words. A small boy has been playing with his ball for nearly three hours, and then loses it. Darkness is falling; the rain begins; he cannot find the ball and starts to cry. The appearance of his father, a sympathetic and comforting comment, the suggestion that tomorrow the ball will easily be found, and a kind and friendly arm about his shoulder leads to the concluding sentence: 'And so we went up the stairs into the kitchen, my father and I, and I didn't care about the lost ball any more that night.' Although the sorrows and joys of childhood do not offer themes from which epics are made, their sensitive treatment in the shorter forms of narration may pleasantly activate the reader's own memories, and sometimes lead to a keener appreciation of the author's more mature work. 'Insight' is the word that is especially appropriate to Janet Frame's early as well as to her later writings, and her ability to penetrate with sympathy and understanding into the minds of her youthful characters arouses interest even

in the shortest of these brief sketches. Those simple words with which **'Summer'** concludes are highly charged with a small boy's buried feelings. They provide a minor climax that gives meaning to a child's world and to a trivial incident.

Several other stories are concerned with the wonderland of the very young. 'On the seashores of endless worlds children meet,' wrote Tagore. Thus they meet and play 'for ever' in *The Lagoon,* but also in **'My Father's Best Suit'**, in **'My Cousins Who Could Eat Cooked Turnips'**, and in **'Swans'**. The first of these recalls the days of the depression when the father of two little girls is upset because his best suit which he wears at Union meetings is torn and threadbare. The girls are sent to buy a reel of matching cotton, but return empty-handed. The right colour is unobtainable, and the suit has to be repaired with a different shade. 'Of course', the narrator recollects

> it was in the days of the depression, and that's why my father cared so much. That's why we had footnotes on our bill too, from the draper's shop at the corner, and that's why we had mince for dinner nearly every day, and specked fruit from the Chinaman's and stale cake from Dent's whenever visitors came, and I suppose that's why we wore our aunt's old clothes.

She describes these clothes in which the proportions were all wrong, but adds 'Not that we cared. We had our interests.' She does not tell us that the difficulties and worries of the parents made little entry into their consciousness, but becomes absorbed in talking about the exhilarating world of childhood.

> We got shouted to the pictures, the Jungle Mystery and the Ghost City where we cheered the goodies and booed the baddies, and we collected a piece of birthday cake every time Mickey Mouse had a birthday, and we saved up serial tickets for a bicycle and a watch and a camera and other ethereal gadgets. . . . We wrote in invisible ink with lemon, and we wrote spidery writing with green feathers, and we wrote with the blood of dahlias.

Then comes the last sentence, 'And still my father wore his light grey suit on Sundays to the Union meetings.' The contrast between the child's world and that of the adult may be a commonplace theme that has attracted many writers, but in Janet Frame's work it becomes merely an excuse for an exploration of a state of being that is exemplified in the child. These early sketches, therefore, never deteriorate into sentimental recollections. They are written, or seem to be written, by the children themselves and their voices persuade us to enter the world in which they live.

'Otherness' is a condition not easy to understand by young or by old, as **'My Cousins Who Could Eat Cooked Turnips'** amusingly illustrates. Each time three small children visited their cousins in Invercargill, they felt they were among aliens. 'It was all so sad and strange.' The cousins were

Good children, they folded up their clothes before they went to bed at night, and they put their garters on the door-knob where they could find them in the morning, and they didn't often poke a face at their father when he wasn't looking. . . . They were very clean and quiet and they spoke up when visitors came to their house, aunts and uncles I mean, and they didn't say dirty words or rhymes. They were cultured.

AND they could eat cooked turnip. Alien though everything was, Nancy who tells the story discovered to her surprise that her cousins really inhabited much the same world as herself, a child's world, not the world in which the grown-ups talk importantly, saying 'really is that so just fancy.' Yet

> For a long time I could never understand my cousins. That night they sat there in cold blood, eating cooked turnip. Perhaps it was our new nighties, perhaps it was the swing, perhaps it was the little bird that popped out to say hello, but I looked at Billy and Elsie, and Billy and Elsie looked at me, and that night we sat there too, in cold blood, eating cooked turnip.

From that moment everything seemed different, that is to say everything became the same, and in the peculiar manner of children, 'We understood.' They swung; they played house together and said 'really is that so just fancy.'

Janet Frame has told us about the first story she ever composed, a story she thought of at the age of three, and still thinks is her best: 'Once upon a time there was a bird. One day a hawk came out of the sky and ate the bird. The next day a big bogie came out from behind the hill and ate up the hawk for eating up the bird' ['Beginnings', *Landfall,* March 1965]. The words may be few and simple because her vocabulary was not extensive, nevertheless, as she suggests, she was able 'to put hawk, bird, bogie into their proper hierarchy'. She makes no comment on the theme which passes from the sinister hawk to the harmless happy bird, and then to the mysterious bogie in the hills who brings retribution by swallowing both. It is not too fantastic to discover a characteristic way of seeing in this early composition and to detect intimations of mortality in her recollections of early childhood. Life and death are close companions; and at any moment a hawk may swoop from the sky, and a bogie descend from the hills. On the first page of her novel *The Edge of the Alphabet* she writes 'Yes, outside where the hawks fly;' and in one of her longer poems ['Sunday Drive'] are the lines,

> I would stop suddenly because my mother and
>   father were dead
> and there was no one above me to bend over me,
>   there was nothing
> above me save the sky.
> Underchild, underdog, so happily under, and no one
>   now to intercept
> the hawk, the bogie, the charging bull, the glass
>   words of people . . .

Not surprisingly several stories in *The Lagoon* are wholly or partly concerned with the presence of Death in the midst of Life. The spirit whose number is 350 replies to the question, 'Any enemies?'—'Yes we all have enemies. A big black death swoops down from the skies at any moment to carry us away.' For Nini in **'The Secret'**, however, the shadow of death is scarcely a shadow. When her mother tells her the fearful secret that Nini's sister Myrtle may die at any time, Nini wouldn't and couldn't believe the doctor's pronouncement:

> Gosh we had fun together. We caught flies and fed them to spiders and we got a magnifying glass and shrivelled up the beetles in the grass . . . Myrtle couldn't die. Grandma had died, but then Grandma was old with no legs and a shrivelled up face like an old brown walnut, and Aunt Maggie had died, but Aunt Maggie was thin and she coughed all the time and said excuse me my throat, and Grandad had died but Grandad was old too, he must have been living for years and years before the beginning of the world. . . .

Myrtle couldn't possibly die because they had such fun together, and she was going to be a great actress, and for all sorts of reasons. Nor does she die in the story for in bed at night Nini hears her heart going 'Lub-dub, lub-dub, lub-dub'.

'Keel and Kool', one of the most successful of the *Lagoon* stories, immediately follows **'The Secret'** and although as the author would say the people have different names, it could be regarded as a sequel. Winnie and Eva are two sisters, but Eva had died not so very long ago, and the mother and father, together with Eva's particular friend Joan and Winnie had come for a picnic by a river. The two girls run off to play ladies by a pine tree while the mother sighed and thought 'The children were such happy little things. They didn't realise.' Yet the absent Eva is all the time in the children's minds; they continually refer to her; she haunts their games which end in a childish quarrel, all because of their love for Eva. 'The children were such happy little things. They didn't realise.'

> Winnie felt lonely staring up into the sky. Why was the pine tree so big and dark and old? Why was the seagull crying out I'm Keel I'm Keel as if it were calling for somebody who wouldn't come. Keel, Keel, come home Kool, come home Kool it cried.

The sadness, the sense of loss, the intolerable feeling of loneliness may find different forms of expression, but the child understands in its own way and from its own world. Joan had recited a new ending to Tinker, Tailor which she had learnt from Eva; and the concluding words of the unacknowledged sequel to **'The Secret'** are whispered by Winnie:

> Boots, shoes, slippers, clodhoppers . . . But there was no one to answer her. Only up in the sky there was a seagull as white as chalk, circling and crying Keel Keel. Come home Kool, come home Kool. And Kool would never come, ever.

'Swans' describes another picnic and another death. Told from the child's point of view, but by one who vividly recalls her own childhood, the day spent at 'the wrong sea' becomes a day of enormous content. Fay, Totty and their mother nearly miss the train, because the two little girls must make their pet cat comfortable in the wash-house among the slaters and earwigs and spiders. It doesn't seem well but is soon forgotten in the hurry to catch the train, in the excitement of the journey, in the different sights and sounds that claim their fascinated attention. In the train, looking at the other passengers,

> the two little girls knew for sure that never would they grow up and be people in bulgy dresses, people knitting purl and plain with the ball of wool hanging safe and clean from a neat brown bag with hollyhocks and poppies on it. Hollyhocks and poppies and a big red initial, to show that you were you and not somebody else you feared you might be, but Fay and Totty didn't worry they were going to the beach.

The wondering eyes of children, their complete absorption in their immediate surroundings, the details scarcely noticed by their elders, the intense feelings that are aroused in their explorations and games,—all provide the material from which such a sketch as 'Swans' is composed. They leave the train at the wrong station, because their mother has muddled their father's careful directions. They come to 'the wrong sea', but it doesn't matter to Fay and her sister. There are no merry-go-rounds, swings and slides; and mother may say 'Oh things are never like you think they're different and sad,' but the children feel it is 'a distinguished sea oh and a lovely one noisy in your ears and green and blue and brown where the seaweed floated. Whales? Sharks? Seals? It was the right kind of sea.' And then, coming home they saw swans on the lagoon, hundreds of them,

> Hush-sh the water said, rush-hush, the wind passed over the top of the water, no other sound but the shaking of rushes and far away now it seemed the roar of the sea like a secret sea that had crept inside your head for ever. And the swans, they were there too, inside you, peaceful and quiet watching and sleeping and watching, there was nothing but peace and warmth and calm, everything found, train and sea and mother and father and earwig and slater and spider.

Yet when they reach home, Gypsy, their cat, is dead among the earwigs and slaters and spiders. Death as well as life creeps inside your head; but it is this 'insideness', the ingathering of a store of images and impressions, the hoarding of treasure within, that so characterises Janet Frame's recollections of childhood.

In her autobiographical essay, 'Beginnings', she wrote

> As it was becoming impossible for me to reconcile 'this' and 'that' world, I decided to choose 'that' world, and one day when the Inspector was visiting my class at school I said,—Excuse me, and walked from the room and the school, from 'this' world to 'that' world where I have stayed, and where I live now.

We can only be grateful for her decision, because it resulted in establishing a way of seeing by means of which she was able to explore both worlds with startling ease. Immediately following this passage is her reference to *The Lagoon* stories which she typed slowly with one finger as she sat on her bed in the room still used as a linen cupboard. Among them are four that do not touch on the secret recesses of the minds of children, but are concerned with 'that' world, the twilight world of uncertainty, loneliness and illusion, and together become an early prologue to *Faces in the Water* and *Owls Do Cry*, to *The Edge of the Alphabet* and *Scented Gardens for the Blind*.

'Snap-dragons' describes Ruth's inward and outward farewell to prison, to the mental hospital in which she has been a patient. Sitting in the sun on the steps of the verandah and waiting for her mother to accompany her home, she watches the swaying snap-dragons and the bees being caught in their thin red throats. She knows that if you squeezed those throats the bees would 'come zooming blindly out, colliding with the sunlight, and then of course they would get their bearings and plan their course, and fly away'. Snap-dragon and bees offer a simple and effective analogy to Ruth's predicament, but have wider implications:

> If you were free did you always fly away? Or were you ever free? Were you not always blundering into some prison whose door shut fast behind you so that you cried let me out, like the bee knocking in the snap-dragon, or the people beating their hands on the walls of their ward.

She thinks of Home, the little red house far away over the hills, of her mother and father and all the others, including the dogs and cats; and she thinks of what they may think of her, and the little red house 'seemed to rock and swing, it looked like a snap-dragon'.

Janet Frame as well as Ruth could imagine herself caught in the throat of a snap-dragon, ready to collide with the sunlight and fly away home and, perhaps strangely enough, her experience of hospital life increased her capacity to build a bridge between 'this' world and 'that' world. Even in these preliminary sketches relating to memories she was unwilling and unable to suppress, both reality and dream are under the control of the author. Pathos and a lightness of touch that exclude morbidity are combined in her treatment of those who live and suffer in 'that' world. 'I don't think I'm morbid,' she murmured almost to herself in an interview, 'I just write things as they are,' and this belief is borne out in 'The Bedjacket' and 'The Park'.

With some difficulty Nan learnt from an older patient how to knit, because she wished very much to give to her favourite nurse a Christmas present that could not be bought in the nearby shops. Nan would probably never go home, for she had no home. She and Nurse Harper often walked and talked together in the grounds of the hospital, and Nan would tell the nurse that when she was allowed out in the world she would become a cook in a large hotel. Poor Nan was loud-voiced, fat and awkward, but the nurse was kind and often gave her little presents of toilet things and non-institutional underwear. So Nan learnt to knit and made a bedjacket for Nurse Harper. She loved Nurse Harper, but she also loved the bedjacket when it was finished. It was nearly Christmas when Nan suffered a relapse, and with the precious bedjacket in her arms she was placed in a single room away from the other patients. In a few days she came back to the ward, wearing the beautiful bedjacket:

> Nan sat without speaking, staring straight ahead of her. And the next afternoon, Nan who was not allowed to go shopping sent one of the patients to buy something for her, a box of soap and a face-cloth wrapped in cellophane, a Christmas present for Nurse Harper.

Such a sketch is written with sympathy and understanding. Janet Frame is able to pass from 'this' world to 'that' world and back again in a manner that disposes of any charge of morbidity. Her remark, 'I just write things as they are,' is as apt as it is true, for she is an unorthodox realist who can enter the world of fantasy and dream without losing her bearings.

This is exemplified even more powerfully and with even greater insight in **'The Park'**. Helen was expecting to leave the hospital and its surrounding park in which the patients walked up and down and round and round, the same park so well known to the narrator. Helen, however, is not allowed to go home, for she becomes sick again. In the daytime she is put in the Yard and at night in a small single room; but before long she is once again walking in the park:

> She walked in the Park all day. She walked up and down and round and round, with her bare feet on the smooth green grass . . . I watched her walking, and then I knew. There was no park really. There were no trees, nor any grass. Helen was walking up and down inside her own mind. She didn't know where she was going. She was walking round and round inside herself.

The children in **'Swans'** were fascinated by the knitting-bag with its big red initial 'to show that you were you and not somebody else you feared you might be', but Jan Godfrey in the story with that name is writing 'about a girl who is not me. I cannot prove she is not me. I can only tell you that her name is Alison Hendry.' This intimate and self-revealing sketch is a remarkable example of 'double vision', and recalls the imaginary and nameless girl whom little Dossy Park has christened Dossy. Jan is writing in the converted linen cupboard to which some reference has already been made. She describes it in detail, but wanders away from the story she has promised, at every possible point. Yet the wanderings and the seeming digressions are developed and directed to the final announcement, 'My name is Alison Hendry.' On the way to this conclusion Jan talks continually about herself and her past life, back to childhood, snippets of autobiography that are both muddled and controlled, but before long the autobiographical fragments seem to belong to another person altogether, to Alison Hendry who supposedly shares Jan's

room. It would be difficult to find in so short a space a more vivid and moving account of the state of mind of a split personality, for in 'putting a wise ear to the keyhole' of Jan Godfrey's mind the reader overcomes bewilderment to discover that Jan is not sure that she is she. Like Dossy Park and her large friend, but at another level, Jan and Alison are one, not two. From 'this' world we are brought with extraordinary tact and skill into 'that' world.

If Helen, walking up and down, round and round in the park of the hospital, didn't know where she was going but was really walking round her own mind, and if Ruth asked the question, 'Were you ever free? Were you not always blundering into some prison whose door shut fast behind you so that you cried let me out?' they were not very different from many who inhabit a more stable and conventional world. Nance in **'The Day of the Sheep'** is lost in her suburban home, almost as lost as Helen walking in the park.

> No fuss about where to live . . . but lost, look at the house look at the kitchen, and me going backwards and forwards carrying dishes and picking up newspapers and dirty clothes, muddling backwards and forwards in little irrelevant journeys, but going backwards always . . .

When Number 350 in **'Spirit'** was alive, he was wedded to Emily Barker, to meaningless routine and to habit:

> Lived in a little house, had four kids, worked at gardening, each day a round of eating and sleeping and other pleasures, pictures on the weekend, the bar on Friday nights at five for bar lunch cold fish and dead potatoes, footy in the weekend . . . every day mostly just going backwards and forwards doing this and that.

Although he admitted that he was well satisfied with three meals a day and a comfortable place in which to live, he is horrified to find that he, a human being 'in form and moving how like an angel' is to be given a nice juicy leaf as his permanent abode:

> Here is your leaf Spirit 350. Aeons and aeons of juice here. You'll be alone of course but there'll be no swooping blackbirds to bother you. You may eat and sleep and slide up and down even making a little permanent patch of your own and remember no blackbirds to bother you.

In **'Pictures'**, the woman who lives in a boarding house with her little girl ('It was awful living alone with the little girl in a boarding house') thinks and remembers and sighs, as they watch the greatest love story in the world—'Life and Love and Laughter, and Tenderness and Tears'. Waiting at the tram-stop on their return to the home that is no home, the woman stands and looks as she had sat and looked at the Pictures. 'The world was full of people and little dogs and sun; but she stands and looks and thinks about tea at the boarding house. She also thinks of going up stairs and putting the little girl to bed and then touching and looking at the daffodil in the window-box, it was a lovely daffodil. And looking about her and thinking the woman felt sad.

The tidy young man in **'A Beautiful Nature'** also lives in a boarding house where everyone thought he was 'sissy'. He was pathetically pleased if he came into the sitting room and the boarders smiled and spoke to him. Unasked, he would fetch his gramophone and play such records as *Grannie's Highland Home* until nobody was left in the room,

> so he'd turn the gramophone off and go upstairs again, and sit on his bed, and perhaps eat a piece of barley-sugar to stop himself from feeling sad.

These are the passive, unhappy inmates of a larger prison than that where Helen walked up and down or Ruth watched the snap-dragons catching the bees—the prison of Suburbia. Unlike the bees when released, they will never 'get their bearings'; they will never 'plan their course and fly away'. Sad and lonely, lost and bewildered, they rarely laugh. Only the tipsy man in **'On the Car'** laughs uproariously. 'He was very cheerful. He laughed at the people in the car and he greeted them all as old friends and he kept up a one-sided conversation with everybody.' The passengers were returning from their usual routine to their suburban homes and their usual routine. The fat man knew that 'life was a war without much time for smiling;' life was grim, and the weather was grim, 'but the drunk man didn't mind he didn't mind a bit.'

> He was awfully drunk. His shirt was grease-stained and he wore a grey felt hat, and he laughed in the wet gloom of the tram-car, he ha ha ha, he was awfully drunk.

An early reviewer of *The Lagoon and Other Stories* immediately perceived that 'the stories in this volume have a common theme, though not openly expressed as such; they are compassionate stories of the despair and the courage and the fleeting joys of 'the lost and the unhappy and the kind'. At a later date E. H. McCormick wrote [in *New Zealand Literature—A Survey*, 1959]:

> Nothing quite resembling *The Lagoon* (1951) had previously been seen in this country. Childhood reminiscences, character sketches, glimpses of city life, strange episodes that crossed the border into fantasy—all were presented in a free, colloquial, intimate prose and developed by an ostensibly casual method of association.

These comments were perceptive and, to a degree, gave adequate recognition to Janet Frame's achievement, but they took little account of the distinctive way of seeing, the double vision, the combination of the inward and outward look, which can be exemplified almost everywhere in this, her earliest production.

'The Birds Began to Sing' is a remarkable little parable with which to conclude, if only because it has relevance to 'the magical power of naming things' which is the basis for all good writing. In some ways **'The Birds Began to Sing'** may be associated with **'My Last Story'**, another attempt to determine the direction in which the author wished to travel. It is deceptive in its simplicity and, although clearly well-controlled in its development, it remains slightly enigmatic. 'The birds began to sing. There were four and twenty of them singing, and they were blackbirds.' No one should need reminding of the nursery rhyme; but only Janet Frame would be likely to ask what were the blackbirds singing when the pie was opened. For answer the birds replied 'We are singing and we have just begun, and we've a long way to sing, and we can't stop, we've got to go on and on. Singing.'

The narrator who in **'My Last Story'** had said 'I'm not going to do any more expressing' walks through the rain and over the hills, through swamps and gulleys, seeing much on the way. At last she 'stood on a hill and looked and looked'. Had she, as in **'My Last Story'**, the wrong way of looking? She wasn't singing; 'she tried to sing but couldn't think of a song.' She returns to her boarding house (the same boarding house where Jan Godfrey, where Janet Frame, lived?) and, sitting on the steps, listens with her whole being. 'The birds began to sing'—four and twenty of them. Once again she asks the name of the song, for names are important as Jan Godfrey thought:

> We cling to our names because we think they emphasise our separateness and completeness and importance, but deep down we know that we are neither separate nor complete nor very important, nor are we terribly happy.

Names are useful, even initials, as the children in **'Swans'** realised. They show that you are you 'and not the somebody else you feared you might be'.

The birds, however, are not interested in names; they were not literary. They knew nothing of the 'magical power of naming things': They stopped singing, and 'It was dark outside although the sun was shining. It was dark and there was no more singing.' Even the suggestion of an outward name for an inward feeling was enough to silence the four and twenty blackbirds, and destroy the inward and spontaneous feeling that had led to the nameless song. In *The Lagoon and Other Stories* Janet Frame knew that she was still learning the 'magical art of naming things' in the right way, by combining the outward and inward view. She was only beginning to discover the perspective that would suit her way of looking, and she was experimenting with the art of naming things in such a manner that the 'seeing' and the 'saying' would not be rendered ineffective by the 'naming'. 'We are singing and we have just begun, and we've a long way to sing, and we can't stop, we've got to go on and on. Singing.'

Fleur Adcock (essay date 1984)

SOURCE: "The Road to Independence," in *The Times Literary Supplement*, November 9, 1984, p. 1281.

[*In the following review, Adcock observes that Frame's collection* You Are Now Entering the Human Heart *mixes realism with "bizarre fantasy and semi-didactic allegory."*]

The first volume of Janet Frame's absorbing autobiography, *To the Is-Land,* told of her childhood in the South Island of New Zealand with her railwayman father, her harassed "poetic" mother who talked of books but never had time to read them, her brother, and her three sisters. The oldest sister drowned, the brother was seriously epileptic, there was never enough money; but Janet, in her skimpy home-made uniform and embarrassing home-made sanitary towels, got through High School and was accepted for training as a teacher. *An Angel at My Table* begins with her journey south from Oamaru, from a family that seemed "enveloped in doom", to the Training College in Dunedin. She was a quiet, shy student, "no trouble at all" to lecturers or landladies. Just after her twenty-first birthday, when she was in her probationary teaching year, the inspector arrived in her classroom; she excused herself politely and walked out of the school. A few weeks later she was taken to the first of several mental hospitals and diagnosed as schizophrenic.

The numbingly terrible history of the following nine years (1945 to 1954) is condensed here into some forty pages. For a fuller account of what Frame endured in Seacliff, Sunnyside, and the brutal, squalid "refractory ward" of Avondale Hospital it is necessary to read her second novel, *Faces in the Water* (in which the events described are all factual although the central character is invented), a fuller account, but not the whole story—that book, for all its horrors, omitted a good deal in order not to seem "overdramatic". The present volume makes no attempt to fill these gaps; instead it adds details of the external events which lay between the periods in hospitals—and which, as they include the drowning of her second sister and her mother's heart attack, cannot fail to have been causally related to them.

It also adds explanations. What seems to have happened is that after her first brief stay in Seacliff and the hasty, inaccurate diagnosis of schizophrenia she simply taught herself, out of books, to be what she was thought to be. As a schoolgirl and a young student she had learnt to cope with her anxieties by turning on performances—the child-poet, the clever examinee—for approval. Later, she writes, it did not occur to her "that people might be willing to help me if I maintained my ordinary timid smiling self". And anyway, great artists had always suffered from disabilities; here was hers. So for the first few months of 1946, in between working on her stories, worrying about her decaying teeth, and having "little talks" with a young psychology lecturer assigned to her as a therapist, she swotted up the symptoms of her supposed illness until she could "turn on schizophrenia" at will. When things got out of hand there was no way back: to use her grammatical metaphor, she had moved from the first person into the third—no longer "I" nor a part of "we" but "she", one of "them".

Her first book of stories, *The Lagoon,* was published while she was a committed patient, and its choice for a literary award saved her from an imminent leucotomy and led to her eventual release. But what next? "After having received over two hundred applications of unmodified E. C. T., each the equivalent, in degree of fear, to an execution" she arrived home, smiling, meek, and fearful, sure by now (from knowing genuine cases) that she was not schizophrenic, but unable to detach that largely self-affixed label. "How is Janet?" people asked in her presence. "Would she like some shortbread?"

The second part of the book records her gradual return to something like confidence. Under her superficial timidity ran the wiry thread of her determination to find her own place in the world and, above all, to write. She left her parents' dilapidated cottage and began work as a waitress in a Dunedin hotel ("I had no impatience, irritation, anger to subdue: I seemed to be a 'born' servant", she had written of an earlier, even more menial job—suspecting that she had inherited this submissiveness from her mother.) When after her six months' "probation" she was declared officially sane she celebrated by going to Auckland to visit her married sister June. There she was sought out and befriended by a benefactor who was to direct the progress-chart of her life into a firm upward curve at last. The writer Frank Sargeson, "a bearded old man in a shabby grey shirt and grey pants tied with string", was already a literary hero to her. He lived frugally in a small house with, in its vegetable garden, an army hut which he was in the habit of offering to needy protégés. He installed Janet Frame there, arranged with a friendly doctor for her to receive a sickness benefit, cooked for her, taught her to play chess, and imposed his own strict daily time-table on her. By the time she left, to travel overseas on a grant he had insisted she apply for, her first novel was finished and accepted for publication.

Throughout her schooldays she had longed to acquire imagination, which she thought of as some kind of all-purpose magical possession, absent from her competent, contrived little poems. Instead she was praised in class for being "original": different, perhaps a little peculiar. "I did not think of myself as original; I merely said what I thought" she noted afterwards. Saying what she thinks, and saying it with a fidelity to what she has seen and heard and a cool sharpness of language, is one of her great strengths as a writer. Another, of course, is imagination. Those of her short stories which rework episodes from her childhood may not have required fertile powers of invention, but they have been beautifully organized into their shapes, and her people speak and think in ways which sound like real speech; they are grim, pathetic, funny and authentic. Frame has spoken of her difficulties in creating characters, but those she has drawn from life (particularly the children) cannot be faulted.

In *You Are Now Entering the Human Heart,* her new selection of stories (chosen by herself from three earlier collections, with the addition of some hitherto unpublished work) realism alternates with bizarre fantasy and semididactic allegory. All three modes are equally natural to their author, but the mixture of flavours is startling, and it is possible to quarrel with the selection itself—a few of the briefer sketches seem too slight to have been worth including, while other, more substantial pieces may be missed. There is a great deal here to admire and enjoy, however. The childhood stories are classics of their kind, in the tradition of Katherine Mansfield but speaking with their own recognizable accent. At a time when New Zealanders were still only tentatively finding out how they spoke and behaved (as distinct from how people in English literature did), these economical, seemingly casual little pictures of small-town life were something new. Then there is another typical Janet Frame genre, the study of a lonely person in later life, perhaps a widow or widower, keeping up appearances. She is, not surprisingly, very good on isolation. If her fables and fantasies for the most part stand up less well than their neighbours in this book it is perhaps because of the contrast, or because they do not have time to establish themselves properly: Frame seems to need the spaciousness of a novel in order to engage the reader fully in her invented worlds. One exception is **"Snowman, Snowman"**, the longest piece in this collection, which just manages to overcome the cuteness of having a snowman as its narrator through the use of a deadpan, faux-naïf voice which is very much the author's own: she allows no convenient assumption and no human motive to pass unchallenged; she questions everything.

Her fictional and autobiographical writings are so closely interrelated that to read one work creates an appetite for the others; her various treatments of any subject enhance, rather than diminish, each other. Everything she presents is illuminated and thrown into sharp focus by the limpid clarity of a highly individual vision; she can be detached and passionate at the same time. The autobiography lacks the occasional flamboyance of some of her fiction—it is a deliberately subdued exercise in establishing the facts—but it is irresistibly readable, commendably honest, and, as a lesson in how courage and the will to survive defeated the effects of a ghastly mistake, inspiring.

Tom Aitken (essay date 1991)

SOURCE: "Outside the Brown Picket-Fence," in *The Times Literary Supplement,* May 31, 1991, p. 21.

[*In the following review, Aitken judges the short fiction in* The Reservoir and Other Stories *"powerful and refreshing."*]

People are sometimes admitted to psychiatric hospitals as a result of the misdemeanour of writing: this book set its author free and cancelled the leucotomy she had been about to suffer. The twenty-four stories in **The Lagoon** were written in the late 1940s when Janet Frame—in flight from

school teaching—was in and out of mental hospitals (diagnosed as schizophrenic) and worked as a domestic in hotels and hospitals. The stories were sent by a psychiatrist to Denis Glover, who placed one in the literary magazine *Landfall* and published the collection in 1951. Its obsession with childhood affronted the widespread critical assumption that New Zealand literature had put away childish things, but the book won the Hubert Church Award and rescued Frame from her well-meaning tormentors. It makes its English début, forty years on, launching Bloomsbury's new series of pocket-sized classics. If the format is self-conscious (three different styles of gold lettering in seven words), the work—albeit sometimes incompletely realized—is powerful and refreshing.

It is not surprising that commonsensical New Zealanders found Frame disturbing. She understandably disclaims identity with the characters of her fictions, but these stories, as acquaintance with her autobiographies demonstrates, show the white light of experience passing through the prism of imagination. Her personae inhabit private enclosures, understanding the world and the words which identify its parts in a partial, literal, visionary way. A small girl interprets the bigness of her retarded older friend as an emblem of comfortable circumstances and large abilities. A family visit to the seaside, made almost disastrous by the mother's incompetence, is saved by the children's accepting animal energy and scarcely formulated perception of beauty. Sisters search unavailingly for matching thread to mend their father's best trousers, fired by the quest, perceiving only dimly his need to remain respectable at union meetings during the Depression.

Frame's adult protagonists are separated by deprivation, death or madness from their fellows. There is sad comedy—a failed man and the women who distance themselves from him—and desolation: a patient knits a gift for a nurse but is destroyed by her inability to give away the object she has made; another realizes that "We were all walking inside ourselves . . . touching the brown picket-fences of our minds." Untold stories lurk behind those let out for inspection.

Authority figures—parents, teachers or psychiatrists—are stifling, threatening and often ineffectual, especially in their attempts at love. Their charges are fearfully, enviously aware of "the outside world", a phrase resonant of Eden and Apocalypse. Frame's disastrous teens and twenties would have destroyed most people, yet these pages sparkle: the prose has the sharpness of imagist poetry but its purposefulness and irony preclude mere exquisiteness; the ecstasy of the five senses is untarnished by self-pity. Often very brief, always closely focused, the stories echo the world outside the picket-fence: the popular songs, picnics, lolly scrambles, ice creams, the movies. The remote cries of gulls counterpoint the savage jealousies of little girls; the earthy taste of uncooked turnips informs the comedy of uncomprehensively refined cousins.

Frame uses repetition to thematic and musical effect. **"Snapdragons"** begins with a woman about to be taken home from an asylum watching bees apparently trapped in the throats of red flowers. Her mother arrives and she tries, unsuccessfully, to achieve rapport. The story ends: "Would she never come closer? Her little red house seemed such a long way over the hills. When the wind passed it seemed to rock and swing, it looked like a snapdragon."

The closing story announces a decision to abandon fiction while, ironically, demonstrating a rich talent for it: ". . . I'm going to put three dots with my typewriter, impressively, and then I'm going to begin . . .". This affirmation of intent to carry on is also a cry of despair: "I think I must be frozen inside with no heart to speak of. I think I've got the wrong way of looking at Life."

Judith Dell Panny (essay date 1992)

SOURCE: *"Snowman, Snowman,"* in *'I have what I gave': The Fiction of Janet Frame*, Daphne Brasell Associates Press, 1992, pp. 50-6.

[*In the following excerpt, Panny explicates the short story "Snowman, Snowman" as an allegory.*]

Whom we might meet as we pass into the "for ever" of death is one of the questions posed in *The Edge of the Alphabet*; the story **"Snowman, Snowman"** considers the nature of the destination, the "place" where one is to live "for ever and ever." . . . [**"Snowman, Snowman"** is] a skilfully composed allegory focused on fundamental human concerns. Other stories by Frame can be read as parables or fables, but the near-novella length of this one sets it apart. In **"Snowman, Snowman"** there is no emphasis on character to mask or detract from the allegorical intention: the protagonists are a snowman and a snowflake.

Published in 1963, **"Snowman, Snowman"** was the title story in the volume **Snowman, Snowman: Fables and Fantasies**. Frame's longest story, it was one of those she chose to be reprinted in the 1983 collection **You Are Now Entering the Human Heart**. It is a tale of a talking snowman who looks on the world with wondering eyes and a questioning mind. His mentor, the Perpetual Snowflake stationed on a nearby windowsill, helps him to interpret what he sees. The action is confined to part of a street that is within Snowman's range of vision, although the Perpetual Snowflake provides histories and anecdotes about neighbourhood families. The story's tension derives from the irony of Snowman's belief that he is immortal, and the reader's knowledge that he will soon melt.

If the story is read as an allegory, Snowman corresponds to man, who is thus depicted as shapeless, cold and inflexible. Ironically, humans like to see themselves as versatile, warm and distinctive. Furthermore, man's tenure on earth is scarcely more secure than that of Snowman. There is an invisible "germ cell" waiting to claim human victims: "a germ cell like a great sleeping beast lies curled upon the . . . doorstep, tethered to past centuries." The

sleeping beast, which at any moment may awaken to infect or consume, mocks human complacency. In the context of "past centuries", a man's life becomes as brief as a snowman's.

Though a critic of human self-deception, Snowman unwittingly deceives himself: "I talk of the sun but I do not believe in it." In spite of his apparent disbelief, he tries to protect himself against its heat. The Perpetual Snowflake is impatient with him: "'You are a fool of course. As self-centred as any human being. You imagine newspapers are printed to shelter you from the sun.'" But Snowman believes himself to be superior to man. Though told by a passing sparrow that he is in prison, Snowman, with specious reasoning, arrives at a conclusion he finds comfortable. He considers immobility advantageous. Instead of the danger of being whirled through the air as drifting snow, Snowman is "preserved, made safe against death." He thinks that humans, by contrast, are mortal and vanish swiftly: "I would not believe vanishing was possible if I did not observe it happening each day—around corners, into the sky, behind doors, gates, hedges." There is wit and charm in Snowman's candour. But the fixity of his perception and his limited mind and vision are recognisable as human failings.

We are amused that Snowman should consider himself "preserved" until, with a certain shock, we come to see that his attitudes mirror our own. Snowman's complacency is shared by those who consider themselves to be privileged, 'made safe', if not in this world, then in the next. Snowman asks, "I should like to know of the place where I am to live for ever and ever. Tell me." But the request is not answered. Snowman does not associate his own future dwelling-place with that of Rosemary, who died shortly after making him. The Perpetual Snowflake asserts that "the rain will treat her as earth . . . and new streams form and flow from her body to the clay and back again with circular inclusion flesh clay flesh." She survives in the memories of those who have known her: "the dead . . . drop like parachutists to the darkness of memory and survive there because they are buckled and strapped to the white imperishable strength of having known and been known." Many people, like Snowman, prefer to imagine an ideal dwelling-place.

This, however, is only one aspect of Frame's allegory. Snowman also says: "I have been made Man . . . Is it not a privilege to be made Man?" The words echo the Nicene Creed:

> Who for us men, and for our salvation came down
> from heaven, And was incarnate by the Holy Ghost of
> the Virgin Mary And was made man,

The suggestion is that Snowman is also a Christ-like figure. Christ is "as white as snow" (*Revelations* 1:14); Snowman is 'innocent'—"I am the white page." In *Revelations*, Christ "cometh with clouds." (1:7) Snowman descended to earth with other flakes that could be seen "paratrooping in clouds of silk." *Revelations* suggests that Christ's "eyes were as a flame of fire." (1:14) Snowman has "coal-black pine-forest eyes." Fire is his enemy: "I have been so afraid of fire. I did not know that I contained it within the sight of my eyes and that when I gazed upon the sun the dreaded fire would originate from myself . . . all my life I have carried fire." Dying is, indeed, an integral part of living. Snowman's words, spoken as he is melting, render ironical the earlier lines: "I have no passion. Is this why I shall live forever?" "Passion" takes on the Christian implication of suffering and death as part of a divine purpose. As he melts, Snowman discovers his own kind of suffering which bears upon him like a weight, bowing his shoulders. He is also threatened by a sharp rod-like weapon, suggesting the spear that pierced Christ's side. It is an icicle whose melting mingles with the black blood from his body. His snow bleeds from its "wounds of light." There is reference to "weeping," "thorns," a halo of light: "this bright light surrounding me." Although unaware of his identification with Christ, Snowman re-enacts a crucifixion, his adversaries being the forces of nature, the warm wind and the sun.

The significance of the link between Snowman and Christ is reinforced by the role of the Perpetual Snowflake. Snowman asks, "Who is the Perpetual Snowflake? I never knew him before, though our family is Snowflake." The Perpetual Snowflake is not mocked. His wisdom seems infinite. A "visitor from beyond the earth," he is aware of people's inner thoughts and subtle motivations. "People do not cry because it is the end. They cry because the end does not correspond with their imagination of it." At one point, Snowman announces that he no longer trusts the Perpetual Snowflake: "Since he spoke of the gap in the sky and the sun I have not trusted him." The remark casts no doubt on the integrity of the Perpetual Snowflake, but makes Snowman look foolish. The contrast between the two is sharpened by the ridiculing of Snowman through irony.

The voice of the Perpetual Snowflake is like a voice from heaven. "'Snowman, Snowman,' my creator said." These words appear on the story's first page. One assumes that they are spoken by Rosemary Dincer who, Snowman tells us, "made me to stand in her front garden." But the voice at the story's conclusion reiterating "Snowman, Snowman!" is that of the Perpetual Snowflake, implying that Snowman was called to life by the Perpetual Snowflake, his 'real' creator. The double appellation appears in the Bible when the Lord addresses a specially chosen person; "Moses, Moses" (*Exodus* 3:4) and "Samuel, Samuel" (*I Samuel* 3:10) are two examples. An allegorical parallel is suggested, therefore, between the Perpetual Snowflake and the Creator.

The image of a Perpetual Snowflake is fraught with paradox and therefore open to different interpretations. Pure (in the most literal sense) he may be transformed into a vapour. His physical presence manifests perfect order and crystalline beauty, which depends on the capacity to reflect light. Like any remarkable work of nature, a snowflake occasions wonder and respect. In addition, the Perpetual Snowflake, as old as the world itself, is an example of nature's ancient and enduring memory.

The Perpetual Snowflake is indeed immortal, since he reforms with the same beauty and perfection every winter. By mingling with the elements after he melts, Snowman too may be said to live "for ever and ever" in the form of ice, water, or cloud particles. In an ironic reversal, the photograph of Snowman that did not "turn out" shows "Solid brick, wood and stone" as "unsubstantial", while everything covered with snow becomes "strong and bold . . . capable of withstanding ordeal by season and sun." Winter snow will return season after season, but buildings will be worn away.

Like the Perpetual Snowflake, Snowman is an equivocal image. He might be viewed as a travesty of Christ. Or he could be said to mock a simplistic concept of Christ. There is a caustic edge to the statement, "You ought to be proud, Snowman, to have so changed the face of the earth, to have reduced it to such a terrible simplicity that people are blinded if they gaze upon it." The words are an obvious and innocent statement of fact, for snow can cause blindness and it does indeed transform the surface of the earth. But they almost certainly mock the way Christian beliefs, worldwide in their influence, have been reduced or modified to fit human requirements. Christ is 'made to measure' in the same way that children make snowmen to whatever size and shape they choose. "Some are seven feet tall and others are only three feet tall . . . And all have been made by children or by those whom others regard as children." A middle-aged woman named Tiny, four feet high and with the understanding of a child, makes a snowman exactly her size. When he refuses to respond as she had hoped, Tiny destroys him. Likewise, people have conceptualised Christ to fit their own expectations and have rejected him if he failed to fulfil those expectations.

Human activities provoke disparaging judgements from the Perpetual Snowflake. He mocks warmongering by likening a navy to children at play: "they press buttons which open snow-white umbrellas above the sea . . . the candy floss of death licked by small boys from the hate and fear blossoming on the tall wooden sticks." He is alluding to H-bombs and rocket-fire.

"Snowman, Snowman" examines the concept of immortality. It also re-enacts the story of Christ's death in such a way as to demand reappraisal of its significance, while allowing a range of readings. One would be that the spiritual and immortal exist, not in theological constructs and conceptions, but in the miraculous forms of nature and the energies of the changing seasons. The divine resides in the mysterious memory stored in seeds, spores and ova, and in human memory with its endless capacity for re-creation. This philosophy is reiterated in *The Carpathians*, Frame's most recent novel. Here, she describes memory as "a naked link, a point, diamond-size, seed-size, coded in a code of the world, of the human race; a passionately retained deliberate focus on all creatures and their worlds to ensure their survival." To the Perpetual Snowflake, it seems that "seed is shed also at the moment of death." The dead are part of the earth's inheritance; it draws "new forces of life from the mingled grass and sand and dead human flesh."

"Man is indeed simplicity," for it seems that he resists or misinterprets the more profound truths. Nonetheless, Janet Frame has shaped a story of considerable complexity. Instead of endorsing a body of knowledge in the manner of traditional allegories, **"Snowman, Snowman"** questions old certainties. The tale subverts our expectations, making the allegory ironical. Though he considers himself knowledgeable and competent, modern man is shown, in his "simplicity", to depend on material goods: "Coal, brass, cloth, wood." By contrast, a snowflake needs only the elements. The Perpetual Snowflake is powerful and enduring; humans, by contrast, have a brief life. The paradoxes are startling.

Anna Grazia Mattei (essay date 1992)

SOURCE: "'Two Sheep': A Fable," in *The Ring of Fire: Essays on Janet Frame,* edited by Jeanne Delbaere, Dangaroo Press, 1992, pp. 54-62.

[*In the following essay, Mattei interprets the story "Two Sheep" as an existential fable.*]

'Everything is always a story, but the loveliest ones are those that get written and are not torn up and are taken to a friend as payment for listening, for putting a wise ear to the keyhole of my mind', says the narrator-protagonist—who is, significantly, a writer—of **'Jan Godfrey'**, a story included in Janet Frame's first collection, **The Lagoon**. And the reader-friend who embarks on a story by New Zealand's most distinguished author, 'putting a wise ear to the keyhole of *her* mind', must be prepared to listen to disturbing things, things from 'that world' at the edge of the alphabet—the border-land between the imaginary and the real—often evoked in passages which strive to attain the condition of music and whose compact, contrapuntal texture dissolves in a rhythmic sequence of chromatic intervals, pure, independent sounds, cries of the soul.

The reader is immediately struck by the visionary, prophetic quality of these passages, which are almost expressionistic both in their moments of extreme dynamic tension, and in those of rapt stillness. They combine mythopoetic fantasy with rigorous logic, a taste for paradox with a passion for consistency, a bare essentiality of style with a daring use of language, resorting, to achieve this unique synthesis, to all possible linguistic and stylistic devices. While apparently employing an impersonal narrative method, this brilliant but difficult and disconcerting writer creates her own distinctive, intensely emotional world, bending, at times, the shape and structure of her work to match the inner rhythm of her vision, or, at other times, exposing beings, people and things to the light of 'a sun . . . everlastingly at noon' ['**A Sense of Proportion**'], with no chiaroscuro or shading, no concession to 'tricks of the eye', to the distortions of a perspective which does not distinguish between reality and appearance, fact and fancy. In the final analysis, however, the presumed objectivity of such moments is seen to be compromised by the lack of that 'sense of proportion' typical of someone who—like the young narrator-protagonist of the story **'A Sense of Proportion'** in *The Reservoir*—sees everything in the foreground, 'objects . . . stripped of their shadows, forced to stand in brilliant light, alone'. So, even the most pitilessly lucid vision of the torment of an unshaded world betrays that 'wrong way of looking to life' acknowledged by the narrator of **'My Last Story'** in *The Lagoon.*

It was almost inevitable that the essentially visionary quality of Janet Frame's art should find expression in parables of a faintly Kafkaesque flavour, at times inserted by the author in her novels in the form of 'a story within a story'; in Mansfield-like slices of life about the capacity of the characters, mainly children, to knit the 'unintelligible pattern of dream' (*The Lagoon*); in 'stories and sketches' (the subtitle of *The Reservoir*), characterised by a crystalline cogency of style and by great allusiveness; finally, and above all, in 'fables and fantasies' (the subtitle of *Snowman, Snowman*), apologues and allegories which contain the essence of the author's existential meditations, or which present, with an almost *fauve* technique, feverish hallucinations, landscapes of the mind menaced by an ominous sense of anguish and doom, basically the result of the perception of the cosmos as chaos.

Frame's preference for a certain kind of fiction goes back to her early childhood, as is testified by her well-known first story, 'a fable that provides the recurrent symbolism of her later work' [Jeanne Delbaere, Introduction to *The Ring of Fire: Essays on Janet Frame,* edited by Delbaere] and suggests, along with a sense of inexhaustible, primordial energy, the impending presence of Death. 'The common denominator of all fractions', as wise Uncle Blackbeetle in *Scented Gardens for the Blind* calls it, is always present in Frame's stories, short and long, which raise decidedly existentialist issues and reflect an ontological vision akin to that of Martin Heidegger. Also for Frame death is the only certain possibility of existence, the possibility which cancels all other possibilities, revealing, as it does, the contradictory nature and essential finitude of life. It is a stage in the cycle of creation, metamorphosis rather than extinction. *Death* 'as a simple darkness . . . a pure personless darkness like the original void of the universe' [*Daughter Buffalo*], 'the shrine of non-being' [Heidegger, *Vorträge und Aufsätze*], the 'nullifying nothingness' (Heidegger's 'Das Nichts nichtet') in which man, 'thrown into the world' and confronted with the ineluctability of his human predicament in an absurd universe, finds the key to the understanding of his own essence.

This *Weltanschauung* pervades also **'Two Sheep'**, a paradigmatic story which, with the unadorned simplicity of a naive painting, presents a disquieting vision of existence, subject to oppressive and destructive forces. There is no trace of sententiousness, no overindulgence in sentimentality, no complacent moralizing in this short fable, based, as is typical of Janet Frame, on the fundamental reality/ illusion antinomy—the core of her ontology—articulated in the dichotomies that occur throughout her works: true/ false, authentic/inauthentic, vision/sight, light/darkness, innocence/experience, eternity/time.

It is significant that Frame chooses as protagonists two representatives of the sacrificial animal par excellence, the symbol of patience, meekness, gregariousness, but also of proverbial stupidity. 'Two sheep were travelling to the saleyards . . .': two sheep going to their ultimate destination, the slaughterhouse at the freezing works, along 'a hot dusty valley road' that winds through rocky hills pitted with old rabbit warrens and spotted with tussocks of grass, under a burning sun. The drover rides along in his trap, leisurely, inexorably; one of his dogs sits beside him, while the other darts here and there, keeping the sheep together.

Right from the beginning of the story the author skillfully interweaves three narrative levels: the realistic, the metaphorical, and the mythic. A familiar sight in New Zealand, the flock of sheep going meekly, passively towards death suggests man's own destiny. Here the figure of the drover who takes the sheep to the slaughter recalls the mythical Hermes Psychopomp leading the souls of the dead to their final abode in the Hereafter. The landscape, too, whilst retaining certain realistic traits, assumes archetypal connotations: the *journey* in the desert, through the valley of tears along that hot dusty road which dominates expressionistically the surrounding countryside and returns like a haunting leitmotif.

Two sheep in the flock are singled out by the eye of the omniscient narrator. They are not named, they are referred to simply as 'the first' and 'the second'. This namelessness seems to reflect a conviction clearly expressed by the narrator-protagonist of **'Jan Godfrey',** when she says that although 'we cling to our names because we think they emphasize our separateness and completeness and importance', nonetheless 'deep down we know that we are neither separate nor complete nor very important, nor are we terribly happy'.

The depersonalization of the two sheep here—in accordance with a basic convention of the fable—stresses their lack of individuality, their universality, bringing into focus two distinct types: one who 'knows' and reflects on the present in the light of his knowledge of the future, and one who 'doesn't know' and, immersed in the here and now, is incapable of looking further. The 'first' sheep, in fact, who is aware of what lies at the end of the journey, lives the present to the very full, without seeing it for what it really is. Thus the burning sun for him is just pleasantly warm on the fleece, the sky is beautifully terse, the grass fresh and juicy. Clearly his love for life, his capacity to appreciate its wonders—for such seem even simple everyday pleasures—are sharpened by his awareness of approaching death. The 'second' sheep, blind to this fate, is oppressed and exasperated by the suffering and squalor of his condition: the long, hot dusty road, the intolerably heavy fleece, the threatening hawks circling overhead, waiting to seize their prey. When the prospect of death enters his mind, it is instantly removed in the name of the presumed immortality of his species, vouched for by some mysterious authority. Finally, in a climax that turns possibility into certainty, according to a highly personal logic, this reality is dismissed as 'malicious rumours', vivid dreams as terrifying as nightmares, but at bottom illusory.

The two protagonists continue their journey, one skipping nimbly and joyfully along, the other stumbling, tired and angry, accusing his companion of blindness. Once more Janet Frame uses the metaphor of blindness, of key-importance within her symbolic framework, where it represents darkness, both literal and figurative, but also prophetic insight (those punished for seeing too much are often compensated with the inner eye of the seer). Here everyone seems somehow to be condemned to this condition, since it is impossible to possess both vision and sight, gifts belonging respectively to the artist and to the ordinary, 'adaptable', man, symbolized in this story by the first and the second sheep. The former has an aesthetic relationship with reality, the latter a practical one. These two attitudes may also be seen in terms of Blake's innocence/experience dialectic, where innocence is the gift of the artist, the enlightened, 'different' individual, 'the man alone'. In fact the description of the first sheep 'gambolling like a lamb in August', underlines not only his natural disposition to sacrifice, but above all his spontaneous élan vital. 'I could walk through this valley forever, and never feel tired or hungry or thirsty', he says at a certain point. But, having to cope with the repeated complaints and accusations of his companion, he says nothing about the fate that awaits them, not so much out of compassion as to avoid confronting the truth. In an attempt to exorcize the dread of death, he gives himself up to the pleasures of the present, which, transfigured by his fantasy, becomes more and more alluring. So the filthy pen in which the flock is closed after leaving the valley road is for him 'a pleasant little house', and the lines of railway trucks, 'red caravans for our seaside holiday'. His urge to live is such that he even ignores the unjust accusations of 'a kind, elderly sheep', a chance travelling companion who tries to comfort the second sheep, weeping, so he believes, since he has been told of their true destination. In reality, the second sheep is distraught because he is imprisoned within a narrow and miserable existential condition: the fact that his fellow creatures are in the same situation does not seem to lighten his load, for, although part of the flock, the individual is an island, or—as Frame would put it— 'an I-Land', and in the end must face his destiny alone, since 'nothing can ever help' [*Owls Do Cry*]. All attempts to escape one's fate are vain; there is no stopping time, the undefeated 'impure enemy' [*Scented Gardens for the Blind*], and the changes it brings. The day of reckoning inevitably arrives, as always catching unprepared even those who, like the first sheep, were aware of its coming. 'Then suddenly he was taken by surprise and hustled out a little gate and up the ramp . . .'. The journey of the flock is now nearing its end. The sheep are jostled into the waiting truck and 'everywhere was commotion, pushing, struggling, bleating, trampling'. (The 'crescendo' of gerunds following the 'andante' of the sentence suggests effectively the increasing excitement of the moment). Suddenly faced with the tangible reality of their final destination, the two sheep seem to exchange roles. The first, brusquely forced to abandon his pleasant reflections on the beauty of life, now sees the glaring sunlight in 'its true colours': the 'gigantic burning bars', the hawks 'sizzling the sky with their wings', the pall of dust that thickens over the parched hills. In Janet Frame's universe, the sun—'the noon sun' in particular—is not only the opposite of darkness, in both a physical and a metaphorical sense, in Bergsonian terms 'intelligence' versus 'instinct', but also, in its stark, implacable fierceness, the other side, the 'lining' of death, before which 'the shadows are razed and the sun stands pitilessly at perpetual noon' ['**A Sense of Proportion**']. In this merciless moment of truth, the moment of pure vision attained, for example, by Miss Collins in '**A Sense of Proportion**', and by Turnlung in *Daughter Buffalo,* as has been noted elsewhere 'the individual merges into the Other, language into Silence, life into Death' [Jeanne Delbaere, Introduction].

The second sheep, who now 'sees' all too clearly what awaits him, becomes suddenly quite calm: after his futile complaining and grumbling, he begins to appreciate everything he has previously criticized, looking back upon it with the nostalgia that springs from the discovery of the fleetingness of life, which is valued all the more because it is soon to be lost. He acknowledges the far-sightedness of his companion, who nevertheless pays no attention to him. Face to face with death, dumbfounded 'he could hide from it no longer'. The transition from innocence to experience has been made. However much foreshadowed, the revelation of the truth always comes as a trauma to Frame's characters, a shock from which they recover either with immense difficulty, or not at all. Usually, it is the certainty of death which grants them a deeper insight into life, giving it meaning and resulting either in their annihilation, physical or spiritual, or else in madness—for Janet Frame, as for R. D. Laing [whose *Divided Self* appeared only two years after *Owls Do Cry*], a higher form of consciousness, the real authenticity of Self.

Giving up all forms of struggle and rebellion, the first sheep lies exhausted in a corner of the truck. The man responsible for unloading the sheep takes the motionless body for dead—the play on appearance and reality continues—and throws it out onto the track, to be shifted later on. 'We can't have dead sheep', he said. 'How can you kill a dead sheep?' (The implied author's detached irony, witty and at times even sardonic, is present in this story too.)

Saved from death by pure chance, the sheep struggles to his feet and trots away from the freezing works, walking warily along the railway line. Thus begins the second part of the fable, in which he remains in the foreground. He goes down one road, then another, till he finally meets up with a flock being driven in the same direction. Avoiding the watchful eye of the drover, he slips in among the other sheep in search of safety. And soon he finds himself on 'a hot dusty road through a valley where the hills leaned in a sun-scorched wilderness of rock, tussock, and old rabbit warrens'. This is clearly an echo of the description of a scene which is by now familiar to the reader. As in a refrain, the recurrence of the same words recalls the valley at the beginning of the story. Lexical repetition, with or without stylistic variations to mark the rhythm of the narration, is often employed in this short fable, and is

typical of Frame, who, in this way, underlines the obsessive return of significant themes and motifs, ultimately achieving 'what might be called a parabolic unity' [H. Winston Rhodes, 'Preludes and Parables: A Reading of Janet Frame's Novels', *Landfall*, June 1972]. The story, therefore, seems to repeat itself. We are back to the original situation, except that now the first sheep—who, previously, knew he was heading for death, and has been very close to it—takes on the attitude of the second sheep. In an attempt, which will prove illusory, to conceal his individual identity in the anonymity of the flock, he wishes, in vain, to renounce the privilege of vision and return to the reassuring ordinariness of everyday life. So he abandons himself to purely sensorial perceptions, which emphasize the harshness of reality. But as he complains of his present predicament, like his erstwhile fellow traveller, another sheep contradicts him and enthusiastically exalts the pleasures they are offered. And then it dawns on him . . . '"You mean", the first sheep replied slyly, "that your are on your way to the saleyards, and then to the freezing works to be killed"'. Wise in his experience, he recognizes the signs ('I know the code') and interprets them infallibly. But after experiencing, in the face of death, the irreconcilability of 'fact' and 'fancy', he finds himself in the infinitely precarious situation of someone 'at the edge', in a kind of twilight world, a no-man's land between being and non-being. Incapable of 'fitting in', he is no longer sure of anything, a pathetic figure, rather than a tragic one, like many of Janet Frame's characters. Uncertain of the distinction between the 'inauthentic' and the 'authentic', he does not know where truth lies. What, then, is left, except silence?

Once again the author acknowledges here the difficulty inherent in the search for truth and thus the difficulty of saying something true about the world: hence the futility of all discourse. As Vera Glace, a character associated by her very name to truth—she is, in fact, the 'mirror' of mankind (true glass) in whom words are frozen (true ice)—recognizes in *Scented Gardens for the Blind*, 'this compulsory stopping of communication is a dismal reminder of our ultimate dependence upon silence, of the fact that in the end there is really nothing to say, that silence is our true companion and partner and lover'. This awareness inevitably entails a renunciation of language, of communication—a problem of crucial importance for Frame—and therefore leads to a painful experience of alienation, which becomes, however, the root not so much of the weakness, as of the 'diversity' of one who has seen the ultimate reality and must somehow live with this terrible knowledge. This leads to the existential choice of the first sheep: 'For the rest of my life I shall not speak another word. I shall trot along the hot dusty valleys where the hills are both barren and lush with spring grass'. The subjectivity of truth is stressed here, together with the knowledge that, as Patrick White says in *The Aunt's Story,* 'there is sometimes little to choose between the reality of illusion and the illusion of reality'. Having progressed beyond the frontier of language, beyond the reach of 'the alphabet', the first sheep has no alternative: '"What shall I do but keep silent?" And so it happened . . .'.

The fable resumes its natural discursive rhythm, addressing a hypothetical reader with the final message. The tone of the authorial voice, however, does not become sententious, but remains subdued, almost muted as it traces the destiny of the protagonist of the story, that first sheep which 'over and over again . . . escaped death, and rejoined the flock of sheep who were travelling to the freezing works'. This endless wandering in circles is peculiar to Frame's characters, especially in the short stories, this 'muddling backwards and forwards in little irrelevant journeys' ['**The Day of the Sheep**'], 'mostly just going backwards and forwards doing this and that' ['**Spirit**'], 'up and down and round and round . . . up and down inside her own mind . . . round and round inside herself' ['**The Park**']. Perpetual motion, which paradoxically becomes paralysis, along the same inevitable road, as in a Dantesque circle of hunted and haunted souls. In this world, life and death are tightly interwoven, and at any moment a hawk—a familiar figure to the readers of Janet Frame, a recurrent symbol of looming cosmic danger threatening the sensitive individual—may swoop down onto its defenceless prey, or a bogie may come out from behind the hills.

In a succession of desperate attempts to escape his ultimate destination, death, the individual finds himself once more with the flock, making his way down a desolate valley at the end of which destiny lies in wait. Timid and insecure, with a delirious look in his eyes, the survivor, who has come up against his own nothingness and has shaped his life in the light or darkness, of that encounter, stands out from his fellow travellers. There is an extraordinary affinity here between this sheep and the outsider, solitary, inadequate, different, who, as such, is doomed to silence. This autobiographical character—recurring again and again in Frame's fiction—represents a paradox for the artist who claims to belong to the 'country of words' [*Beginnings*] and who is deeply aware of their beauty, danger and power, but also of their inadequacy to express the ineffable.

FURTHER READING

Craig, David. "Tanks, Trees." *New Statesman* 71 (11 March 1966): 347-48.

Applauds the naturalistic stories in *The Reservoir* but criticizes Frame's fantastic tales and her habit of "wishing sinister or apocalyptic significances onto her humdrum fabrics."

Evans, Patrick. *Janet Frame*. Boston: Twayne Publishers, 1977, 228 p.

Biocritical study that focuses primarily on Frame's novels but also discusses *The Lagoon*, *The Reservoir*, and uncollected stories.

Nyren, Dorothy. A review of *Snowman, Snowman* and *The Reservoir*. *Library Journal* 88, No. 14 (August 1963): 2926.

Summarizes the types of stories in these collections as "memories of childhood and allegorical moralities." Nyren finds Frame to be a heavy-handed author: "She writers her symbols large, circles around them two or three times, and, then, just to make sure, explains them."

"The Slipcase Syndrome." *Time* 82, No. 12 (20 September 1963): 108, 110.

Disparages *The Reservoir* and *Snowman, Snowman*: "Like her excellent . . . novel, *Faces in the Water*, the short pieces collected here deal with failure, loneliness, quiet despair, and the rubble-filled borderland between sanity and madness. But there was strength in the novel, and there is none in the stories."

"Old Girls, Young Girls." *The Times Literary Supplement* (28 April 1966): 361.

Describes the fiction in *The Reservoir and Other Stories* as uneven and objects to Frame's literary style. The critic states that "The faintly gushing intensities of the style serve well enough in the various childhood episodes . . . , but become embarrassing in the open-ended little allegories which make up a sizable part of the book."

Additional coverage of Janet Frame's life and career is contained in the following sources published by Gale Research: *Contemporary Authors*, Vols. 1-4 (rev. ed.); *Contemporary Authors New Revision Series*, Vols. 2, 36; *Contemporary Literary Criticism*, Vols. 2, 3, 6, 22, 66, 96; and *Major 20th-Century Writers*.

"The Overcoat"
Nikolai Gogol

The following entry presents criticism of Gogol's short story "Shinel'" ("The Overcoat"), first published in 1842 in *Sochinenya* (*The Works of Nikolai Gogol*). For discussion of his complete short fiction, see *SSC*, Volume 4.

INTRODUCTION

Considered one of Russia's greatest prose stylists, Gogol was an important influence on his country's literature. His short story "The Overcoat" has been deemed by many critics as the greatest story in the Russian language and a key work in the evolution of Russian literature toward realism. A quote long attributed to Fyodor Dostoevsky, that "We all come from Gogol's 'Overcoat'," has often been employed by critics to summarize the importance of this story to Russian literature. "The Overcoat" epitomizes Gogol's writing style, combining elements of realism, fantasy, comedy, and the grotesque.

Plot and Major Characters

"The Overcoat" tells the story of Akaky Akakyevich, an impoverished government clerk who lives a solitary life. One day he realizes that his winter overcoat has become worn out. He takes it to the tailor to be mended but is told that it cannot be repaired and that he will have to have a new one made. Akaky undergoes extreme deprivation in order to save money for a new overcoat. In the process, the coat begins to take a central role in his life and he begins to view the garment as the key to his future happiness. After he finally acquires the new garment, it is stolen. His calls for help and his subsequent pleas for justice go unheeded, and he falls ill with a fever and dies. After his death a ghost resembling Akaky roams the city stealing overcoats.

Major Themes

Gogol's blending of comic, grotesque, realist, and fantastic elements in "The Overcoat" has led to a wide range of opinions concerning the story's themes and the significance of its ending. The work has been interpreted variously as a story of social injustice, as tale of urban alienation and human isolation, and as a love story, with the coat serving as a metaphor for the love interest. The theme of the "little man" against "the system" was a popular one among Russian writers in the nineteenth century, and "The Overcoat" is one of many stories featuring the figure of the impoverished and mistreated government clerk. One significant way in which Gogol's story differs from others of this type, however, is its presentation of the main character. It is unclear whether the reader should feel sympa-

thy for the poor clerk—the typical response toward such characters—or whether one should regard this as ultimately a comic tale with fun being made at Akaky Akakyevich's expense. It is also not precisely clear whether Akaky is victorious against the system. Despite such ambiguity, critics have consistently noted the resonant irony and lyrical power with which Gogol invested this story.

Critical Reception

Gogol's contemporaries focused on the lyricism of "The Overcoat" and lauded what they considered the story's ground-breaking social realism which evoked sympathy for the main character (or at least for his situation). Some critics continue to hold the opinion that this is a story of social protest and that Akaky Akakyevich is the quintessential little man. Others, however, find evidence to the contrary. Early twentieth-century critics such as Boris Eichenbaum and Dmitry Chizhevsky became interested in the structure and unique narrative style of the story and in how these aspects affect the overall theme. Eichenbaum argued that Gogol's use of puns, word play, and narrative devices creates a comic and grotesque effect that makes

119

the story a mockery of a social protest. Chizhevsky, in his formalist study, found the story to be about spiritual poverty and the dangers of worldly obsessions and passions. Later scholars have viewed the story from a psychological perspective, asserting that the overcoat symbolizes a mask that enables Akaky to disguise his spiritual destitution. Others have taken a metaphysical approach, interpreting the final loss of the coat and Akaky's futile pleas for help as emblematic of humanity's spiritual desolation in an indifferent cosmos.

CRITICISM

Boris Eichenbaum (essay date 1919)

"The Structure of Gogol's 'The Overcoat,'" translated by Beth Paul and Muriel Nesbitt in *Russian Review,* Vol. 22, No. 4, October, 1963, pp. 377-99.

[*In this essay, which was first published in Russian in 1919, Eichenbaum examines the narrative devices of "The Overcoat" and discusses their relationship to the structure of the story. He argues that the comic and pathetic elements work together to create a grotesque style.*]

The structure of a short story depends in large part on the kind of role which the author's *personal tone* plays in it, *i.e.,* on whether this tone is an organizing principle, creating more or less the illusion of a narrative in the first person, or whether it serves only as a formal tying together of events, and thus occupies an auxiliary position. The primitive short story and the novel of adventure have nothing to do with the first-person narrative, nor do they need it because their whole interest and their whole movement are determined by a rapid and diverse succession of events and situations. The interlacement of motifs and their motivation—such is the organic principle of a primitive short story. This is also true as regards the comic short story—its basis is an anecdote, in itself full of comical connotations, quite apart from the first-person narrative.

Completely different does the composition become if the subject as such, the interweaving of themes supported by their motivation, ceases to play an organizing role, *i.e.,* if the narrator, in one way or another, puts himself in the foreground, as though making use of the subject only to interweave separate stylistic devices. The center of gravity is transferred from the theme (which is here reduced to a minimum) to the narrative devices, the most important comic role is given to puns, which are now restricted to a simple playing on words, now to developing small anecdotes. Comical effects are achieved by the *manner* of narration. Therefore, for the study of such a genre of composition, those very minutiae which are scattered throughout the exposition prove to be important—so that if they are removed the structure of the story disintegrates. In this connection two kinds of comic tale may be distin-

guished: (1) the narrative and (2) the creative. The first is limited to jokes, plays on meaning, and so on; the second introduces devices of verbal mimicry and gesture, inventing special comical ways of speech, sound effects, whimsical word order, etc. The first gives the impression of an even flow of speech; with the second, it is often as if an actor were concealed in back, so that the tale takes on the character of play-acting, and the composition is determined not by a simple series of jokes, but by a certain system of varied gestures mimetically articulated.

Many of Gogol's short stories or their separate parts present interesting material for an analysis of this kind of tale. Composition for Gogol is not determined by plot—plot for him is always scanty—rather, there is no plot, but only some comic situation (and sometimes even it is not *in itself* comic at all), serving, as it were, only as an impetus or pretext for the elaboration of comic devices. Thus **"The Nose"** is developed from a single anecdotal event; **"The Wedding"** and *The Inspector General* also grow out of a specific, fixed, existent situation; *Dead Souls* is put together by means of a simple accumulation of separate scenes, unified only by the travels of Chichikov. It is known that the necessity of always having something resembling a plot hampered Gogol. P. V. Annenkov tells about him: "He used to say that for the success of a tale and in general of a narrative it is enough that the author describe a room and a street which are familiar to him." In a letter to Pushkin in 1835 Gogol writes: "Do me a favor, give me a plot of some kind, *any kind, ridiculous or serious,* but a purely Russian anecdote . . . Do me a favor, give me a plot; in spirit it [*i.e.,* the work he has in hand] is to be a comedy in five acts and, I swear, funnier than the devil!" He often begs for anecdotes; thus, in a letter to Prokopovich (1837): "Ask Jules (*i.e.,* Annenkov) most particularly to write to me. He does have things to write about. Surely, some kind of anecdote must have occurred in the office."

On the other hand, Gogol was distinguished by his special skill in reading his own works, as many of his contemporaries attest. In this connection it is possible to single out two chief methods in his reading: the one—a poignant, melodious declamation; the other—a special manner of performance, a mimetic narrative, which nonetheless, as I. S. Turgenev pointed out, never passed into a theatrical reading of roles. The account of I. I. Panaev is well known, about how Gogol surprised all those present, changing directly from conversation to play-acting, so that at first his belching and the corresponding phrases were thought to be real. Prince D. A. Obolensky recalls: "Gogol read masterfully: not only did his every word come out clearly, but, often changing the intonation of his speech, he varied it and compelled the listener to assimilate the most minute shadings of thought. I remember how he began in a hollow and somehow funereal voice: 'Why depict the poverty of our life and our melancholy imperfection, . . . and here we are again in the wilderness, again we have come upon an out-of-the-way corner.' After these words Gogol raised his head, shook his hair, and continued now in a loud and triumphant voice: 'But what a wilderness and what a corner!' Here he began the magnificent description of Ten-

tenikov's village which, in Gogol's reading, came out *as if it were written in a kind of metric form* . . . I was struck most especially by the unusual harmony of his speech. Here I saw how beautifully Gogol took advantage of the local names of grasses and flowers, which he collected so carefully. *Sometimes he obviously introduced some sonorous word solely for its harmonious effect.*" I. I. Panaev describes Gogol's reading in the following manner: "Gogol read inimitably. Among contemporary men of letters Ostrovsky and Pisemsky are considered the best readers of their works; Ostrovsky reads without any dramatic affectations, with the greatest simplicity, lending meanwhile the proper shading to each character; Pisemsky reads like an actor—he, so to speak, acts out his play in reading . . . Gogol's reading was somehow a mean between these two methods. He read more dramatically than Ostrovsky, and with a great deal more simplicity than Pisemsky." Even dictation was transferred by Gogol into a special kind of declamation. Of this, P. V. Annenkov recounts: "Nicholas Vassilevich, opening his notebook in front of him, . . . would enter into it completely, and would begin to dictate regularly, solemnly, and with such feeling and fullness of expression that the chapters of the first volume of *Dead Souls* acquired a special coloration in my memory. This resembled a peaceful, evenly flowing inspiration, such as is usually produced by the profound contemplation of an object. N. V. would await my last word patiently and would continue the new sentence in the same voice, imbued with concentrated feeling and thought . . . Never yet had the pathos of dictation, I remember, reached such heights with Gogol, preserving all artistic naturalness, as in this place (the description of Plyushkin's garden). Gogol even rose from his armchair . . . *and accompanied his dictation with a proud, somewhat imperious, gesture.*"

Altogether this indicates that the basis of the Gogolian text is the first-person narrative, and that his text is composed of the presentation of live speech and verbalized emotion. Moreover: this narrative has the tendency not simply to relate, not simply to talk, but to reproduce words mimetically and by means of articulation, with sentences chosen and joined not according to the principle of logical speech alone, but rather on the principle of expressive speech, in which a special role belongs to articulation, mimicry, sound-gestures, etc. Hence the appearance in his language of the semantics of sound: the casing of the verbal sound, its acoustic characteristic becomes significant in Gogol's speech, independently of logical or factual meaning. Articulation and its acoustic effect are brought out into the foreground, as an expressive device. That is why he loves titles, surnames, given names, etc.—This gives scope for this kind of articulated play. Furthermore, his speech is often accompanied by gestures (see above) and passes into a state of creativity, which is also noticeable in its written form. The testimony of contemporaries points to these peculiarities also. D. A. Obolensky recalls: "At the station I found a book of fines and read in it a rather ridiculous grievance of some gentleman or other. Having heard it, Gogol asked me: 'Now what do you think, who is that gentleman? What are the man's habits and character?' 'Truly, I don't know,' I answered.—'Well, I will tell

you.'—And here he first started to describe in the funniest and most original way, the appearance of that gentleman, then he told me all about his career as a civil servant, even acting out certain episodes of his life. I remember, that I laughed like mad, but he went through it all with complete seriousness. Thereupon he told me that at one time he had lived with N. M. Yazikov (the poet) and in the evening, going to bed, they used to amuse themselves with descriptions of different characters and would invent suitable names for each of them." About surnames in Gogol, O. N. Smirnova reports: "He gave an extraordinary amount of attention to the names of his characters; he looked for them everywhere; they became typical; he found them on posters (the name of the hero Chichikov in volume I was found on a house—formerly there were no numbers, but

---

Gogol's characters are petrified poses. Above them, in the form of a stage manager and real hero, rules the ever merry and ever playful spirit of the artist himself.

—Boris Eichenbaum

---

only the surname of the owner), on signs; beginning the second volume of *Dead Souls,* he found the name of General Betrishchev in a book in a postal station and said to one of his friends that at the sight of that name, there appeared before him the general's figure and his grey moustache." The special attitude of Gogol to given names and surnames and his inventiveness in this sphere have already been noted in literature—for example in the book of Prof. I. Mandelshtam:

> To the period in which Gogol is still amusing himself belong, in the first place, the invention of names, composed apparently without regard to 'laughter through tears' . . . Pupopuz, Golopuz, Dovgochkhun, Golopupenko, Sverbyguza, Kizyakolupenko, Pereperchikha, Krutotryshchenko, Pecherytsia, Zakrutyguba, etc. This manner of concocting amusing names remained, however, with Gogol even later: Yaichnitsa (**'The Wedding'**) and Neuvazhai Koryto, and Belobryushkova, and Bashmachkin (**'The Overcoat'**), the last name, in addition, providing an occasion for a play on words. Sometimes he selects existing names on purpose: Akakii Akakievich, Trifilii, Dula, Varakhasiv, Pavsikakhii, Vakhtisii, and so on . . . In other instances he uses names as puns (the indicated method has been used from time immemorial by all humorous writers. Molière amuses his audience with names such as Pourceugnac, Diafoiras, Purgon, Macroton, Desfonandres, Vilebrequin; Rabelais to an infinitely greater extent uses unbelievable combinations of sounds, which provide material for laughter just because they have a remote resemblance to words, like Solmigonbinoys, Trinquamelie, Trouillogan, and so on) [*On the Character of Gogol's Style. A Chapter in the History of the Russian Literary Language,* 1902].

And so plot in Gogol has only an external significance, and because of this, is in itself static; not without reason does *The Inspector General* end with a mute scene, in relation to which everything that went before is, as it were, only a preparation. The real dynamism, and thence also the composition of his things, lies in the construction of the tale, in a playing with language. His characters are petrified poses. Above them, in the form of stage manager and real hero, rules the ever merry and ever playful spirit of the artist himself.

On the basis of these general propositions about composition and relying on the given material about Gogol, we shall try to clarify the fundamental structure stratum of **"The Overcoat."** This tale is especially interesting for this type of analysis, because in it a purely comical tale, with all the modes of verbal play peculiar to Gogol, is united with a declamation full of pathos, forming, as it were, a second stratum. This second stratum was taken by our critics as the basis, and all the complex "labyrinth of links" (L. Tolstoy's expression) resulted in a certain idea, traditionally repeated down to our own day, even in "investigations" of Gogol. Gogol might have answered such critics and scholars in the same way as L. Tolstoy answered the critics of *Anna Karenina:* "I congratulate them and can assure them boldly *qu'ils en savent plus long que moi.*"

2

First let us examine separately the basic narrative devices in **"The Overcoat,"** then let us trace the system by which they are linked.

A significant role, especially in the beginning, is played by puns of various kinds. They are constructed either on similarity of sounds, or on an etymological play on words, or on a hidden absurdity. The first sentence of the tale in the rough draft was supplied with a pun on sounds: "In the department of assessment and collections" (*sborov*)—which, incidentally, is sometimes called the department of baseness and nonsense (*zdorov*)." In the second rough redaction a note was added to this pun indicating a further play on it:

> But may the readers not think that this name was actually based on some kind of truth—not at all. Here the whole matter lies only in the etymological similarity of words. Owing to this the department of metallurgical (*gornykh*) and salt (*solianykh*) affairs is called the department of bitter (*gorkykh*) and salty (*solenykh*) affairs. Many things sometimes enter the minds of civil servants in the time left between service and whist.

This pun did not enter into the final version. Puns of the etymological variety were special favorites of Gogol and for them he often devised special surnames. Thus, the surname of Akakii Akakievich was at first Tishkevich, which was not in itself conducive to puns; next Gogol wavered between two other forms—Bashmachkevich (cf. Sobakevich) and Bashmakov—and finally settled on the form of Bashmachkin. The change from Tishkevich to Bashmachkin was prompted, of course, by the desire to create an occasion for puns, the selection of the form Bashmachkin can be explained both as a predilection for diminutive suffixes, a characteristic of the Gogolian style, and a more distinctive expressiveness (the power of imitative pronunciation) of this form, creating its own type of sound-gesture. The pun, created with the help of this surname, is complicated by comical devices, which give it the appearance of complete seriousness: "From this it can be clearly inferred that it had once upon a time originated from the Russian word *bashmak,* to wit, a shoe. But when, at what precise date, and under what circumstances the metamorphosis took place, must forever remain a mystery. His father, grandfather, and, why, *even his brother-in-law* (the pun is imperceptibly carried to absurdity—a frequent device of Gogol's), as well as all the rest of the Bashmachkins, always walked about in boots having their soles repaired no more than three times a year." The pun is, as it were, destroyed by this type of commentary—all the more so, since details which are not at all connected with it (*e.g.,* the soles) are introduced incidentally; in reality there emerges a complex, as it were, dual pun. The device of leading into absurdity or an illogical combination of words is often met with in Gogol, and it is usually masked by strictly logical syntax, giving thereby the impression that it is unintentional; thus, in the words about Petrovich, who, "in spite of the disadvantage of having only one eye and *pock marks all over his face,* carried on a rather successful trade mending the trousers and frock coats of government clerks and other gentlemen." Here the logical absurdity is further masked by an abundance of details, drawing attention aside; the pun is not put on display, but on the contrary, is concealed in every way, and thence its comical strength increases. One encounters purely etymological puns rather frequently: "calamities which beset the lives not only of titular, but also of privy, actual, court, and any other councillors, even those who *give no counsel to any man, nor take any from any one, either.*"

Such are the chief forms of Gogolian puns in **"The Overcoat."** Let us add to this another device, that of sound effects. Gogol's love of designations and names which have no meaning has been mentioned above; such "meaningless" words give scope for an original semantics of sound. *Akakii Akakievich*—that is a definite selection of sounds; not without reason was the giving of this name accompanied by a whole anecdote, and in the rough draft Gogol makes a significant remark: "Of course it might have been possible, in a certain way, to avoid the frequent juxtaposition of the letter *k,* but the circumstances were such that it was impossible to do this." In addition, the meaning of the sound in this name was prepared for by a whole series of other names, possessing also a special expressiveness of sound and evidently selected, "searched out," for this purpose; in the rough draft this selection was somewhat different:

1) Yevvul, Mokkii, Yevlogii;
2) Varakhasii, Dula, Trefilii;
   (Varadat, Farmufii)
3) Pavsikakhii, Frumentii.

In the finished form:

1) Mokii, Sossii, Khozdazat;
2) Trifilii, Dula, Varakhasii;
   (Varadat, Varukh)
3) Pavsikakhii, Vakhtisii, and Akakii

In comparison of these two tables, the second gives the impression, as far as articulation is concerned, of greater selectiveness, of an original sound-system. The comic sound effect of these names is not contained simply in their strangeness (strangeness in itself cannot be comic), but in the selection, which prepares for the comic jarring monotony of the name Akakii, which, added to Akak-ievich, sounds in this form more like a *nickname,* conceal-ing in itself the semantics of sound. The comic is further increased by the fact that the names preferred by the mother do not in any way depart from the general scheme. The result is, on the whole, an original mimicry of articulation, a sound-gesture. Interesting in this connection is still an-other passage in **"The Overcoat,"** in which a description of Akakii Akakievich's appearance is given: "And so, in *a certain department* there served *a certain clerk*—a clerk whom one could hardly style very remarkable: quite low of stature, somewhat rusty-hued of hair, even somewhat purblind, at first glance; with a bald patch over his fore-head, with wrinkles along both cheeks, and his face of that complexion which is usually called hemorrhoidal." The last word is so placed as to make its phonetic shape as-sume special emotionally expressive force and is percep-tible as a comic sound-gesture independently of meaning. It is prepared, on the one hand, by the device of rhythmic accretion, and on the other, by the concordant endings of several words, attuning the ear to the perception of sound impressions (*ryabovat—ryzhevat—podslepovat*) and there-fore it sounds grandiose, fantastic, beyond and connection with meaning. It is interesting that in the rough draft this sentence was much simpler: "and so, in this department there worked a civil servant, not very noticeable in ap-pearance, short, bald, pock-marked, ruddy, even it seemed a bit on the blind side." In the final form this sentence is not so much a *description* of appearance, as a *reproduc-tion* of it in an imitative verbal gesture: The words are chosen and placed in a certain order not on the principle of character delineation, but on the principle of sound-meaning. The internal vision remains untouched (nothing is more difficult, I think, than to draw Gogolian heroes);— from the entire sentence, there remains in memory, more than anything else, an impression of a kind of progression of sounds, ending in the rolling, and, logically, almost senseless, but in its articulative expressiveness the unusu-ally powerful word—hemorrhoidal. Here is fully applica-ble the observation of D. A. Obolensky that Gogol would sometimes "introduce a sonorous word of some kind, entirely for a harmonious effect." The whole sentence has the appearance of a complete whole, a kind of a system of sound-gestures for the realization of which the words were selected. That is why these words, like logical units, like tokens of concepts, are almost intangible—they are dis-tributed and collected anew according to the principle of the sound of speech. This is one of the remarkable effects of Gogol's language. Some of his sentences have the ef-

fect of sound-inscriptions, so much are articulation and acoustics brought out to the forefront. The most common-place word is sometimes presented by him in such a man-ner that its logical or material meaning fades away while sound-meaning is put in its place, and the simple name receives the appearance of a nickname: "He ran across a policeman on duty who, keeping his *halberd* near at hand, was shaking some tobacco from a hornlet into a calloused fist," or: "Might even while we're about it, sir, and seeing as how it's now the fashion, get a silver-plated clasp [*lap-ki pod apliké*] for the collar." The last case is an obvious game with sound-effects. (The *lpk* is repeated as *plk.*)

Gogol's speech has no median—no simple psychological or material concepts logically united into ordinary sen-tences. The distinctively imitative sound-speech is changed to a tense intonation, which shapes the sentences. His works are often constructed on this kind of change. In **"The Overcoat"** there is a vivid example of such an intonation-al influence, a declamatory period of rhetorical pathos:

> Even at those hours when all the light has faded from the grey St. Petersburg sky, and the Civil Service folk have taken their fill of food and dined each as best he could, according to his salary and his personal taste; when all have had their rest after the departmental scraping of pens, after all the rush and hustle, after their own and other people's indispensable business had been brought to a conclusion, and anything else which restless man imposes on himself of his own free will had been done, and even much more than is necessary.

An enormous sentence, building up the intonation to great tenseness at the end, is resolved with unexpected simplic-ity: ". . . in short, even while every government official in the capital was doing his best to enjoy himself, Akakii Akakievich made no attempt to woo the fair goddess of mirth and jollity." One receives the impression of a comic disparity between syntactical tenseness of intonation, be-ginning obscurely and mysteriously, and its resolution in meaning. This impression is further increased by the com-bination of words, as if expressly contradicting the syntac-tical character of the period: little hats, a pretty girl, sip-ping tea from glasses with penny biscuits; finally, the anecdote about Falkonet's monument brought up in pass-ing. This contradiction or disparity has such an effect on the words themselves that they become *strange,* enigmat-ic, sounding unusual, astonishing the ear, as if dismem-bered or thought up by Gogol for the first time. There is also in **"The Overcoat"** a different kind of declamation, penetrating unexpectedly the general punning style—sen-timentally melodramatic; it is the celebrated "humane" pas-sage which has been so fortunate in Russian criticism that from an accessory artistic device it has become the "idea" of the whole story:

> "Leave me alone, gentlemen. Why do you pester me?" And something strange was implied in the words and in the voice in which they were pronounced. In it could be heard something so pitiable that one young man . . . And for a long time afterwards, in the midst of gayest moments, there would appear before him

the little office worker with the bald spot on his brow
. . . And in these penetrating words rang other words
. . . *And he would cover his face with his hand . . . ,*

etc. The rough drafts do not contain this passage—it comes later and undoubtedly belongs to the second stratum, complicating the purely anecdotal style of the original drafts with elements of pathetic declamation.

Gogol allows his characters in **"The Overcoat"** to speak very little, and as always with him, their speech is molded in a special way, so that, in spite of individual differences, it is always stylized, and never produces the impression of everyday speech, as does, for example, Ostrovsky's dialogue. (Not without reason did Gogol read differently.) The speech of Akakii Akakievich belongs to the general system of Gogolian "sound-speech" and of mimetic articulation. It is especially constructed and furnished with a commentary: "It might be as well to explain at once that Akakii mostly talked in prepositions, adverbs, and lastly, *such parts of speech as have no meaning whatsoever.*" The speech of Petrovich, as opposed to the fragmentary articulation of Akakii Akakievich, is condensed, severe, hard, and it acts by way of contrast; there are no ordinary nuances in it—everyday intonation is not appropriate to it; it is as "contrived" and as conditional as the speech of Akakii Akakievich. As always in Gogol (cf. **"Old Fashioned Landowners," "The Tale of How . . . ,"** *Dead Souls,* and his plays) these sentences stand outside of time, outside the moment—motionless and once and for all: language in which puppets might talk. Equally contrived is Gogol's own language—his narration. In **"The Overcoat,"** this narration is stylized to resemble a special kind of careless, naive chatter. As if "unnecessary" details leapt out involuntarily: ". . . on his right stood the godfather, Ivan Ivanovich Yeroshkin, a most admirable man, who was a head clerk at the Supreme Court, and the god mother, Arina Semyonovna Byelobrushkina, the wife of the district police inspector, a most worthy woman." Or his narration acquires the character of familiar verbosity: "We really ought not to waste much time over this tailor; since, however, it is now the fashion that the character of every person in a story must be delineated fully, then by all means let us have Petrovich, too." The comic device in this instance lies in the fact that after such a declaration the "characterization" of Petrovich consists merely of the remark that he drinks every holiday indiscriminately. The same is repeated concerning his wife:

> Having mentioned his wife, we had better say a word or two about her also; but *unfortunately,* we know very little about her, except that Petrovich had a wife who wore a bonnet, and not a kerchief; there appears to be some doubt as to whether she was good-looking or not but on the whole it does not seem likely that she had very much to boast of in that respect; at any rate, only guardsmen were ever known to peer under her bonnet when meeting her in the street, twitching their moustaches and emitting a curious kind of grunt at the same time.

There is one sentence in which this style of speaking is very sharply marked. "Unfortunately we cannot say where precisely the Civil Servant who was giving the party lived. Our memory is beginning to fail us rather badly and everything in St. Petersburg, all the streets and houses, has become so blurred and mixed up in our head that we find it very difficult indeed to *get anything out of it* in proper order." If one joins to this sentence all the numerous uses of "some kind of it," "unfortunately very little is known," "nothing is known." "I do not remember," etc., then one gets an idea of the narrative method, which lends the whole story the illusion of its being a real history, told as a fact,

---

The narration is not related but acted and declaimed: not a narrator, but a performer, almost a comedian, hides behind the printed text of "The Overcoat."
—*Boris Eichenbaum*

---

but not known to the teller in every small detail. He willingly digresses from the main anecdote and introduces at intervals "they say that"; thus, in the beginning, about the petition from some district police captain ("I do not remember of what town"), thus also about Bashmachkin's ancestors, about the tail of the horse of the Falkonet statue, about the titular counselor who was made director, after which he partitioned off a special room for himself and called it "the presence chamber," etc. It is known that the story itself grew out of an "office anecdote" about a poor clerk who lost his gun, for which for a long time he had been saving money: "This anecdote was the first idea for his wonderful tale **'The Overcoat,'**" reports P. V. Annenkov. Its original title was "The Tale of a Clerk Who Stole Coats" and the general character of the narrative in the rough drafts is distinguished by an even greater stylization in the guise of careless chatter and familiarity: "Truly, I don't remember his surname," "In its essence it was a kindly beast," etc. In its final form, Gogol somewhat smoothed out this kind of device, garnished the story with puns and anecdotes, but then introduced declamation, complicating thereby the original compositional stratum. A grotesque resulted in which the mimcry of laughter is replaced by mimicry of sorrow, and both the one and the other have the appearance of a game, with a contrived alteration of gestures and intonation.

3

Let us now trace this change itself with the aim of catching the very manner of linking the separate devices. At the basis of linkage or composition lies the narration, the traits of which are defined above. It has been shown that this narration is not related but acted and declaimed: not a narrator but a performer, almost a comedian, hides behind the printed text of **"The Overcoat."** What then is the "scenario" of this role, what is its outline?

The very beginning presents in itself a collision, a break— a sharp shift in tone. The business-like introduction ("In the Department") suddenly breaks off, and the epic intonation of the narrator, which might be expected, changes to another tone—one of exaggerated irritation and sarcasm. One gets the impression of improvisation—the original composition immediately gives way to digressions of some kind. Nothing has been said as yet, but an anecdote is already there, carelessly and hastily related ("I don't remember from what town," "some kind of romantic piece of writing.") But after this, the tone noted in the beginning apparently returns. "And so in *a certain department* there served a *certain civil servant*." However, this new approach to an epic narrative is immediately replaced by the sentence which was discussed above, so contrived, so tonal through and through, that nothing whatever is left of the business-like tale. Gogol steps into his role—and, having concluded this whimsical, amazing selection of words with the grandiose-sounding and almost meaningless word "hemorrhoidal," he closes this passage with a mimetic gesture: "There is nothing we can do about it: it is all the fault of the St. Petersburg climate." A personal tone, with all the devices of Gogolian narration, definitely takes root in the story and assumes the character of a grotesque gesture or grimace. Thereby the transition is already prepared for the pun on the surname and the anecdote about Akakii Akakievich's birth and christening. The business-like sentences closing this anecdote ("It was in this way that *he came to be* called Akakii," and "Anyway, that is how *it all came to pass*") produce an impression of playing with the narrative form, and not in vain is there a slight pun concealed in them, giving them the appearance of awkward repetition. There ensues a stream of mockery—in this style the tale continues right up to the sentence: "But never a word did Akakii say to it all . . ." when the comical narrative is suddenly interrupted by a sentimentally melodramatic digression with the characteristic devices of a sentimental style. By means of this device **"The Overcoat"** is successfully raised from simple anecdote to grotesque. The sentimental and intentionally primitive content of this excerpt (in this the grotesque coincides with melodrama) is conveyed with the aid of a tensely growing intonation, having a solemn, pathetic character (the introductory "ands" and the peculiar word order: "A kind of unseen power . . . and for a long time afterwards . . . he would see . . . And in those pathetic words . . . And the poor young man used to bury his face in his hands, and many a time in his life he would shudder . . .") There results something like the device of "theatrical illusion," when an actor seems suddenly to step out of his role and begins to talk like a human being. (Cf. in *The Inspector General:* "At whom are you laughing? It's yourselves you're laughing at!" or the famous "It's a tedious world, gentlemen!" **"The Tale of How . . ."**) It is customary with us to take this passage literally—an artistic device, converting a comic short story into a grotesque and preparing a "fantastic" ending, is taken as a sincere intervention of "the soul." If such deception is "a triumph of art," in the words of Karamzin, if the naiveté of the audience may be charming, then for scholarship such naiveté is altogether not a triumph, because it reveals its helplessness. In this interpretation the entire structure of **"The Overcoat"** is destroyed, its whole artistic intent. Proceeding on the basic proposition that in a work of art, not a single sentence *can be* in itself a

simple "reflection" of the personal feelings of the author, but is always a construction and a performance, *we cannot and have no right* to see in such an excerpt anything other than a definite artistic device. The habitual manner of identifying some separate judgment with the psychological content of the author's soul is a false method for scholarship. In this sense the artist's soul, like that of a man *experiencing* various moods, always remains and must remain outside the limits of his creation. A work of art is always something made, designed, invented—not merely skilful, but also artificial in a good connotation of this word, and therefore *there neither is nor can there be* a place in it for the reflection of the empiricism of the soul. The skill and artificiality of Gogol's devices in this fragment of **"The Overcoat"** are most notably revealed in the construction of its clearly melodramatic cadence, in the shape of a primitively sentimental maxim, used by Gogol with the aim of confirming the grotesque:

> And the poor young man used to bury his face in his hands and many a time in his life he would shudder when he perceived how much inhumanity there was in man, how much savage brutality lurked beneath the most refined, cultured manners, and, dear Lord, even in the man the world regarded as upright and honourable . . .

The melodramatic episode is used as a contrast to the comic narration. The more skilful the puns, the more pathetic and stylized, of course, in the direction of sentimental primitivism, must be the device which violates the comic game. A seriously meditative form would not provide a contrast and would not be able to communicate a grotesque character to the whole composition at once. It is not surprising, therefore, that immediately after this episode, Gogol returns to what preceded it—now an artificially factual tone, now a carelessly gossipy one, with plays on words, such as: ". . . did he become aware of the fact that he was not in the middle of a line but rather in the middle of the street." Having related how Akakii Akakievich would eat and how he would stop eating when his stomach began to "bulge," Gogol again enters upon declamation, but of a somewhat different sort: "Even at those hours when . . ." etc. Here for the purpose of the same grotesque a "mute," mysteriously serious intonation is used, slowly building up in the form of a colossal *period* and resolving itself with unexpected simplicity; that which was expected, through the syntactical type of sentence, a balance in the energy of meaning between the protracted ascent ("when . . . , when . . . , when") and the cadence is not realized, for which the very selection of words and expressions has been a preparation. The lack of correspondence between the solemnly serious intonation in itself and the meaningful content is again used as a grotesque device. In place of this new "deception" of the comedian there naturally appears a new play on words concerning counselors, with which the first part of **"The Overcoat"** closes: "So passed the peaceful life of a man . . . ," etc.

This pattern, noted in the first part, in which the purely anecdotal narrative is interwoven with a melodramatic and solemn declamation, determines indeed the entire composition of **"The Overcoat"** as a grotesque. The style of the grotesque demands, in the first place, that the described situation or event be contained in a world small to the point of the fantastic, of artificial experiences (as it is both in **"Old Fashioned Landowners"** and in **"The Tale of How . . ."**) completely cut off from the large reality, from the real fullness of spiritual life, and in the second place, that this be done not with a didactic or satirical intent, but with the aim of giving scope for *a playing with reality,* for breaking up and freely displacing its elements, so that the usual correlations and connections (psychological and logical) turn out, in this newly constructed world, to be unreal, and each trifle can grow to colossal dimensions. Only against the background of such a style as this does the slightest gleam of real feeling acquire the appearance of something staggering. In the anecdote about the office worker Gogol valued just this fantastically limited, closed-in structure of thoughts, feelings and desires within the narrow boundaries of which the artist is at liberty to exaggerate details and upset the usual proportions of the world. It was on this basis that the sketch of **"The Overcoat"** was made. Here the point is certainly not in the "insignificance" of Akakii Akakievich nor in a sermon on "humaneness" to one's lowly brother, but in the fact that, having fenced off the whole realm of the story from large reality, Gogol can unite the incompatible, exaggerate the small and minimize the great. In a word, he can play with all the norms and laws of the real life of the spirit. And so indeed he does. The spiritual world of Akakii Akakievich (if only such an expression be permitted) is not insignificant (this has been introduced by our naive and sentimental historians of literature who have been mesmerized by Belinsky), but a fantasy-limited world, his own: "There, in that copying of his, he seemed to see *a multifarious (!) and pleasant world* of his own . . . Outside this copying nothing seemed to exist for him." This world has its own laws, its own proportions. The new overcoat, according to the laws of his world turns out to be a grandiose event, and Gogol provides a grotesque formula: ". . . for spiritually he was nourished well enough, since his thoughts were full of the *great idea of his future overcoat.*" And again: ". . . as though he was never alone, but some agreeable helpmate had consented to share the joys and sorrows of his life, and this sweet helpmate, this dear wife of his, was no other than the selfsame overcoat with its thick padding of cotton-wool and its strong lining . . ." The small details move to the forefront like Petrovich's toe ". . . thick and hard as the shell of a tortoise," or his snuff box—"with a portrait of some general, though which particular general it was impossible to say, for the place where the face should have been had been poked in by a finger and then pasted over with a square bit of paper." This grotesque hyperbolism unfolds as before against the background of comic narration with puns, ridiculous words and expressions, funny stories, etc.: "They did not buy marten for a fur collar, for as a matter of fact it was rather expensive, but they chose cat fur instead, the best cat they could find in the shop, cat which from a distance could always be mistaken for marten." Or: "What position the *Very Important Person* occupied and what his job actually was has never been properly ascertained and still remains unknown. Suffice it to say that *one Very Important Per-*

son had become a Very Important Person only quite recently, and that until then he was quite an unimportant person." Or again:

> The story is even told of some titular councillor who, on being made chief of some small office, immediately partitioned off a special room for himself, calling it 'the presence chamber,' and placed two commissionaires in coats with red collars and galloons at the door with instructions to take hold of the door handle and open the door to any person who came to see him, though there was hardly room in 'the presence chamber' for an ordinary writingdesk.

Along with these there are statements "from the author" in the careless tone established in the beginning, behind which a grimace seems concealed: "But perhaps he never even said anything at all to himself. How indeed is one to delve *into a man's soul* (here also is a kind of word play, if one bears in mind the general treatment of the figure of Akakii Akakievich) and find out what he is thinking about?" (a play on the anecdote, as though it were a question of reality). The death of Akakii Akakievich is related just as grotesquely as his birth—with an alternation of comic and tragic details, with the sudden "At length poor Akakii Akakievich gave up the ghost," with the immediate transition to every kind of trifle (the enumeration of the inheritance: ". . . a bundle of quills, a quire of white Government paper, three pairs of socks, a few buttons that had come off his trousers, and the *capote* with which the reader has already made his acquaintance.") and finally, with the conclusion in the ordinary style: "Who finally came into all this property, goodness only knows, and I must confess that the author of this story was not sufficiently interested to find out." And after all this—a new melodramatic declamation, as is customary, of course, after the presentation of so sad a scene, taking us back to the "humane" passage:

> And St. Petersburg carried on without Akakii, as though he had never lived there. A human being just disappeared and left no trace, a human being whom no one ever dreamed of protecting, who was not dear to anyone, whom no one thought of taking any interest in, who did not attract the attention even of a naturalist who never fails to stick a pin through an ordinary fly to examine it under the microscope . . .

The end of **"The Overcoat"** is an effective apotheosis of the grotesque, something like the mute scene in *The Inspector General.* Naive scholars, having perceived in the "humane" passage the whole point of the story, stop in perplexity before this unexpected and incomprehensible intrusion of "romanticism" into "realism." Gogol himself prompts them:

> But who could have forseen that this was not the last of Akakii Akakievich and that he was destined to be the talk of the town for a few days after his death, as though in recompense for having remained unnoticed all through his life. *But so it fell out,* and our rather poor story quite *unexpectedly* acquired a most fantastic ending.

In reality, this ending is not in the least more fantastic or "romantic" than the whole story. On the contrary, there we had a really grotesque fantasy, communicated as a playing with reality; here the story emerges into a world of more usual concepts and facts, but everything is treated in the style of a playing with fantasy. This is a new "deception," a device of the grotesque in reverse:

> . . . it [the ghost] suddenly looked round and, stopping dead in its tracks, asked, 'What do *you* want?' at the same time displaying a fist of a size that was never seen among the living. The police constable said, 'Nothing,' and turned back at once. This ghost, however, was much taller; it had a pair of huge moustachios, and walking apparently in the direction of Obukhov Bridge, it disappeared into the darkness of the night.

The anecdote, developed in the finale, leads away from the "poor history" with its melodramatic episodes. The initial, purely comic, narration returns with all its devices. Together with the moustached ghost the entire grotesquery disappears into the darkness, dissolved in laughter. Just so does Khlestakov vanish in *The Inspector General,* and the mute scene takes the audience back to the beginning of the play.

Dmitri Chizhevsky (essay date 1938)

"On Gogol's 'The Overcoat,'" translated by Priscilla Meyer and Steven Rudy, in *Dostoevsky & Gogol: Texts and Criticism,* edited by Priscilla Meyer and Steven Rudy, Ardis, 1979, pp. 137-60.

[*The excerpt below was originally published in Russian in 1938 in the journal* Sovremennye zapiski. *Here, Chizhevsky looks at the frequent use of the word* dazhe, *"even," and argues that this textual detail helps establish the narrative style and tone of the story as well as providing a key to interpreting the main theme of "The Overcoat."*]

1

Is it necessary to write more about **"The Overcoat"**? We all know Gogol's tale from our school days, and if we have later happened to read books and articles about Gogol—whether they were works following the "social approach" typical of Russian literary criticism and Russian literary history or the works of "formalists"—we always find one and the same thing in reading them: **"The Overcoat"** is one of the steps in Gogol's development as a writer in the direction of realism. Its theme, one of the "insulted and injured," the "poor clerk," is a theme cultivated in more than a hundred Russian stories and tales, for example, in *Poor Folk,* "A Faint Heart" and other early tales of Dostoevsky, by Gogol himself in **"The Diary of a Madman,"** the theme of Veinberg—

> He was a titular councillor,
> she—a general's daughter . . .

Critics usually find the central idea of **"The Overcoat"** in the famous "humane" passage, which comes immediately after the words of Akaky Akakievich, whom the clerks are teasing:

> "Leave me alone, why do you insult me?" And something strange was contained in the words and in the voice in which they were pronounced. In it resounded something so evoking of pity that one recently appointed young man who, by the example of the others, was on the verge of permitting himself to laugh at Akaky, suddenly stopped as if transfixed, and from that time on it was as if everything had changed for him and appeared in another form. Some preternatural force alienated him from the comrades he had become acquainted with, having taken them for decent, well-bred people. And long after, at the gayest moments, the short little clerk with the baldspot on top would appear to him with his penetrating words: "Leave me alone, why do you insult me?" and in these penetrating words rang other words: "I am your brother." And the poor young man would cover his face with his hands, and many times later in his life he would shudder, seeing how much inhumanity there is in man . . .

There is no doubt that this passage contains thoughts that are essential for Gogol. But isn't it strange that such a central passage stands at the very beginning of the tale, as though anticipating and making unnecessary all the subsequent development of events? But the tragic story of Akaky Akakievich only begins further on, a story which at first sight one could sooner call tragi-comic and in which such a discriminating connoisseur of the Russian classics as Dostoevsky saw mockery and derision of the hero, whose first human feeling is directed at . . . an overcoat. Did not Gogol spoil the beginning with such a continuation? Did he not weaken its effect? Did he not declare Akaky Akakievich our brother only to laugh at him spitefully later?

Such a strange disjunction in the tale's composition forces us to seek the meaning Gogol placed in it elsewhere than in the exclamation "I am your brother!"—in this thought which, with all its pathos and Christian character, smells of vulgar morality and recalls the celebrated phrase of Karamzin, "even peasants are able to feel," a phrase which we are now unable, recognizing all its justness, to read without a smile.

We will try to approach Gogol's story more closely by means of the method of "close reading," the only correct method of reading the classics, a method from which we have been weaned by newspapers, the detective novel, other "light reading," and even in school, where our own reflections on a work were made unnecessary by the explanations of textbook and teacher—yes, were we on the school bench mature enough really to understand the meaning of an artistic work?

In "close reading," in the enjoyment of Gogol's story "by bits," we notice many trifling details that seem to be insignificant features . . . Perhaps it is worthwhile to begin an analysis of **"The Overcoat"** with one of these "insignificant details." In **"The Overcoat"** one and the same insignificant little word is repeated extraordinarily often: *dazhe,* "even"! On the 32-40 pages which **"The Overcoat"** occupies in the usual editions of Gogol this little word "even" is met with neither more nor less than 73 times! Moreover, its use on several pages is particularly dense: in the space of a single page we meet it three, four, even five times! Is this an accident? Does Gogol simply repeat an unnecessary word because it happened to come to his pen?

According to everything we know about Gogol's method of work on his writings, such an explanation should seem to us hardly likely, in fact simply impossible. As is well known, Gogol endlessly polished and reworked the text of his works, reworked separate words, changing and varying them, until he achieved a final perfection, the final polish. We know from the words of S. T. Aksakov how Gogol in 1850 twice read aloud a chapter from the second part of *Dead Souls.* The Aksakovs were surprised by the second reading:

> We were struck with amazement: the chapter seemed to us even better, as if it had been written anew. The corrections were to all appearances quite insignificant: there one word was removed, here added, and there transposed—and it all came out differently.

If we had doubts about the testimony of such a judge as Aksakov,—didn't he, too much carried away with Gogol as writer, man and "prophet," overestimate him? (and, in any case, the elder Aksakov was hardly so totally captivated by Gogol as were the young Aksakovs)—there is still sufficient evidence in Gogol's published reworkings of his own works (**"The Portrait,"** *The Inspector General,* **"Taras Bulba"**) and in Gogol's manuscripts. These materials fully corroborate what Gogol himself said (in the same years), according to Berg, about his method of work as a writer:

> At first it is necessary to jot everything down as it comes to you, even if it is bad, insipid, absolutely everything, and then forget about this notebook. Then, after a month, after two, sometimes even more (this happens by itself), take what you have written and reread it: you will see that much is not what it should be, there is much that is superfluous and something that is lacking. Make corrections and marginal notes, and again discard the notebook. At the next inspection—new marginal notes—and where there is not enough room, take a separate scrap of paper and glue it in on the side. When everything is thus covered with writing, take the notebook and copy it yourself. At this point new illuminations, cuts, additions, refinements of style will appear by themselves. Between former words new ones will jump up, words which necessarily should be there but which for some reason don't appear at first. And again put the notebook down. Travel, amuse yourself, don't do anything, or at least write something else. The hour will come, the abandoned notebook will be remembered: take it, reread it, correct it in the same way, and when it is again used up, copy it in your own hand. You will notice in doing this that, together with a strengthening of style, with finishing, refinement of sentences, your hand, as it were, also

strengthens: the letters place themselves more firmly and resolutely. It is necessary to do this, in my opinion, *eight* times. For someone else, perhaps, fewer times are needed, and even more for yet another. I do it eight times. Only after the eighth copying, without fail in my own hand, does the work seem in full artistically finished, does it achieve the pearl of creation. Further corrections and revisions will perhaps spoil the matter; what artists call "overdrawing." Of course, to follow such rules constantly is impossible, difficult. I am speaking of the ideal. Another will let it go at that sooner. A man is after all a man and not a machine.

One could hardly suppose that a writer who worked in *this* way left, on account of simple mental inertia, an unnecessary little word in such excessive profusion in a work to which he assigned so important a role! Obviously, "even" has some meaning in this work, it "carries a certain function," or rather, several functions. This is always the case with Gogol: his artistic devices are many-sided, many-functional . . . Is this the role of "even" in **"The Overcoat"**? Let us consider it more closely.

2

Above all, the repetition of one and the same word characterizes, in Gogol and other writers, colloquial speech or the *skaz,* as literary historians now term it. In **"The Overcoat"**—and one should pay attention to this—the story is narrated as if not from the person of Gogol, not by Gogol himself, but by a definite narrator whom Gogol quite carefully keeps at a certain remove, at a distance from himself. Gogol is still continuing the tradition of *Evenings on a Farm Near Dikanka* and *Mirgorod* with their narrators. He emphasizes the fact that the story is being narrated by a specific, though not more closely characterized, narrator with the help of parenthetic phrases of the sort: "nothing is known about this," "I don't remember from *which* town," "Akaky Akakievich was born, if only my memory doesn't deceive me, in the early hours of March 23rd," "it's hard to say on exactly what day," "where exactly the clerk who had invited him lived, unfortunately, we cannot say: our memory begins to deceive us greatly," "what was precisely and in what consisted the duty of the *important personage,* that has remained unknown to this day," "who got all this (Akaky Akakievich's legacy) God knows; even the narrator of this tale, I admit, wasn't interested in this," and so on. Gogol uses digressions for this very aim. For example, at the very beginning of the tale: "In the department . . . ," the narrator breaks in: "But it's better not to say in which department," and there follow twenty (!) lines of digression, after which the story starts all over again: "And so, in a certain department served a certain clerk . . ." In the Ukrainian stories Gogol uses words and phrases in Ukrainian to remind the reader of the presence of a narrator. In **"The Overcoat"** and **"The Diary of a Madman"** Gogol brings his speech closest to the colloquial. In **"The Diary of a Madman"** this was simpler, the author had his hero keep a diary; Akaky Akakievich would hardly have been able to keep a diary! But the narrator is in some sense brought close to Akaky Akakievich. This approximation is achieved by the repetition of several unnecessary words, for instance, by substituting attributes which mean nothing for attributes which fill the nouns to which they refer with content: "a certain" ("a certain police inspector," "a certain director," and so on), "some sort of" ("some sort of relation," "some sort of town" and so on), "something or other," "some kind of," and so on. Gogol himself draws attention to the nature of his hero's speech:

> One should know that Akaky Akakievich expressed himself for the most part in prepositions, adverbs, and finally, in such particles as have absolutely no meaning whatever. And if the matter was very difficult, he even had the habit of not finishing the sentence at all, so that quite often, having begun a speech with the words: "That, really, is completely sort of . . . ," but then there was nothing, and he himself would forget, thinking he had already said everything.

And even the Important Personage, the tale's secondary hero,

> remained eternally in one and the same silent state, only occasionally emitting some monosyllabic sounds . . . His usual conversation with inferiors smacked of strictness and almost entirely consisted of three sentences . . .

Thus, the "impoverishment" of the narrator's speech is hardly accidental. Gogol obviously could not bring this impoverishment to the level of speech of Akaky Akakievich or of the Important Personage. If the narrator were also to "express himself . . . in prepositions, adverbs, and finally, such particles as have absolutely no meaning whatever" or "remain eternally in one and the same silent state," then there would be no story! However, Gogol does in some measure bring his narrator's speech close to the speech of his heroes: the strange "impoverishment" of language in **"The Overcoat"** serves exactly this end, though it might seem to stand in contradiction to the fundamental internal laws of any artistic work, which of necessity strives for the greatest richness and splendor within the limits of the possible. Obviously, the possibilities for richness and fullness of speech are limited here by just this peculiar "tongue-tied" quality of the narrator and heroes. . . .

3

But the numerous "even's" in **"The Overcoat"** carry not only the above-mentioned function of stylizing the story's speech as that of a *skaz;* they are connected as well with the most essential features of Gogol's humor, of the comic in Gogol.

Gogol's humor is a unique play of oppositions, of antitheses of the sensible and the senseless, a play in which the meaningful and meaningless replace each other by turns. A phrase, word or thought seems to make sense, but suddenly turns out to be an absurdity; or vice versa, what seemed nonsense turns out to be meaningful. The use of "even" relates precisely to this play of oppositions: "even" introduces an intensification, an ascent, it signifies and

marks a tension, an expectation, and if the ascent is not realized, if what is expected does not appear, we are disappointed, surprised, and Gogol has achieved a comic effect! Gogol often introduces instead of an intensification after "even" that "zero meaning" so characteristic of his work (nonsensical phrases are very frequent in Gogol's writings), and sometimes instead of an intensification we are struck by a slackening of tension. Thus the serious and the humorous alternate, and if the rising line is particularly underscored by pathetic intonation, then even simple speech seems to be nonsense: the rising line of speech, having begun to rise too high into pathos, suddenly breaks off and it all ends in nothing, in trifles or with the exact opposite of what the reader expected.

> **Gogol's humor is a unique play of oppositions, of antitheses of the sensible and the senseless, a play in which the meaningful and meaningless replace each other by turns.**
>
> **—Dmitri Chizhevsky**

In such passages one often finds the word "even." Both before and after **"The Overcoat."** Let us take an example from *Dead Souls.* Gogol is speaking about the "enlightenment" of "the town NN":

> the others were also enlightened people—those who read Karamzin, those who read *The Moscow Record,* and *even* (!) those who read nothing at all.

Or another celebrated phrase with "even" in the same role:

> (The Governor) was, however, a good-hearted fellow and *even* occasionally embroidered fancywork on tulle with his own hands.

We come across similar passages already in Pushkin's *Eugene Onegin,* a work which undoubtedly influenced Gogol (a fact which literary historians haven't gotten around to paying attention to): the portrayal of Lensky's second, Zaretsky—

> . . . a kind and simple bachelor paterfamilias, a steadfast friend, a peaceful landowner and *even* an honest man . . .

As though honesty were the rarest and most unusual mark of a man!

The function of "even" in **"The Overcoat"** is quite often the same: "even" introduces phrases and thoughts which don't stand in an expected logical connection with what precedes them, or rather, which don't have any sort of connection with the preceding at all. Examples:

The clerk's surname was Bashmachkin. By the very name it is already apparent that it at one time came from *bashmak,* shoe; but when, at what time and in what way it came from *bashmak,* nothing is known about this. The father and the grandfather and *even* the brother-in-law, and absolutely all the Bashmachkins went around in boots, only changing the soles about three times a year.

After the first logical break, the transition to the brother-in-law, who actually has no genetic tie to Akaky Akakievich, there follows yet a second break, the transition to "soles," which have nothing at all in common with the name "Bashmachkin." A whole series of similar "even's" introducing breaks in the logical train of thought are grouped around the peculiar notions of the narrator about the relation of nature and fate to the higher levels of the Russian "Table of Ranks": the Petersburg cold causes

> the foreheads of *even* those who occupy higher posts [to] ache from the frost and tears [to] come to their eyes . . .

or:

> various disasters strewn along the path of life not only of titular but even of privy, actual, court and all sorts of councillors, *even* those who don't give anyone counsel or take it from anyone themselves . . .

(a double break: "councillor" does not signify one who gives advice or counsel). When the "ghost" starts pulling the overcoats from the shoulders of Petersburg inhabitants,

> complaints came incessantly from all sides that backs and shoulders, if it were only of titular, but *even* of the most privy councillors, were subjected to absolute chills because of the
>
> nightly pulling-off of overcoats.

Another phrase in the same style:

> the mistress, preparing some fish, had filled the kitchen with so much smoke that it was impossible to see *even* the very cockroaches.

Gogol "plays" in a similar way not only with "even" but with other words as well: Petrovich the tailor

> despite his one eye and the pockmarks all over his face, engaged rather successfully in the repair of clerks' and all other sorts of trousers and tailcoats, of course, when he was in a sober state and not nourishing some other notion in his head.

And here there are plenty of parallels from Gogol's other works: such an ending concludes the contrast of Ivan Ivanovich and Ivan Nikiforovich:

> Ivan Nikiforovich, *on the other hand,* wears trouser with such ample folds that if they were blown out you

could put the whole courtyard with the barns and outhouses into them.

Or the scene from **"Taras Bulba"** in which Bulba, with several friends, takes it upon himself to sound the kettle-drums which convene a Cossack "Rada" (general assembly):

> At the sound of the drums, the first to arrive was the drummer, a tall man with one eye, *in spite of* however it being terribly bleary [from just having awakened].

Such is the technique which Gogol uses to reduce the reader to utter amazement! But often, and particularly in **"The Overcoat,"** Gogol also uses the opposite method: the reader expects something usual, understandable, positive, but instead of this Gogol startles him with something fanciful, unusual, negative. Here are some examples from **"The Overcoat"**: the names Mokkiya, Sossiya, Khozdazat are found in the Church Calendar for Akaky Akakievich, then Trifily, Duly, and Varakhisy turn up—

> "What an affliction," said the old lady, "what names they all are, I really never heard the like. At least if it were . . ."

We expect, after this "At least if it were," some fairly everyday names, but Gogol is merely setting us up for the startling:

> "At least if it were Varadat or Varukh, but Trifily and Varakhisy!"

Or:

> As he climbed the stairway to Petrovich's—which, to do it justice . . .

here the reader expects to hear something positive about the stairway, but is doubly amazed to read—

> which, to do it justice, was all soaked with water and slops and saturated through and through with that ammoniac smell which eats at the eyes and, as is well known, is inevitably present on all the backstairs of Petersburg houses . . .

Gogol's play with the word "even" belongs to precisely this technique of amazing the reader.

4

But "even" is repeated so often in the tale not merely as a technical device. "Even" is vital as well for one of the main aspects of the tale, it half opens up this aspect to us, if we are attentive enough.

We already spoke about the way in which "even" introduces an intensification, an increase, a tension which, however, Gogol goes back upon, disappointing and at the same time astounding the reader. This is a means of revealing the pettiness of the circle, of the "slice of life," depicted. What precedes "even" turns out to be pettiness, a trifle: which is to say that in this sphere of life what is insignificant, empty, what is in fact "nothing," seems meaningful and vital. It is not that easy to depict and understand "nothing"; philosophers from Hegel to Heidegger have had no small struggle with this difficulty. Gogol attempts to overcome it with his use of the word "even." The content and goals of life turn out to be insignificant, contentless; they are actually "nothing whatever."

To this sphere of the use of "even" belong those passages already cited in which Gogol gives the impression that, according to his tale's narrator, nature, fate and even the extrasensory world—a "ghost"—are oriented on the "Table of Ranks," that nature normally spares the freezing bodies, shoulders and "life paths" of clerks *of the higher ranks*.

The highest, strongest feeling of Akaky Akakievich, his passion for the new overcoat, is portrayed with the help of the same device. The clerk's feelings are presented by Gogol with a pathetic intonation, but their disclosure is rendered by insignificant, everyday trivialities. Akaky Akakievich "even" laughs or smiles, he is "even" inattentive at work, "almost" makes a slip of the pen while copying, he "even" takes notice of a pretty lady.

> At times a fire would show in his eyes, the most daring and audacious thoughts *even* flashed through his head: shouldn't he actually put marten on the collar?

But actually, Akaky Akakievich's whole life is portrayed in the same style: his devotion on the job is such that

> If they had rewarded him in proportion to effort, he, to his own amazement, perhaps might have *even* landed among the state councillors . . .

His own desires, however, are still more modest:

> and *even* if the director were to be so kind as to designate, instead of a forty ruble bonus, forty-five or fifty . . .

Only his new life task creates something akin to character in him, makes him alive, animated:

> He became somehow livelier, *even* firmer in character, like a man who has already defined and set a goal for himself.

On the street at night for the first time. Akaky Akakievich

> walked along in a gay state of mind, he was *even* suddenly, for some unknown reason, about to dart after some lady . . . However, he stopped right away and again set out very quietly as before, even wondering himself at his gallop which came from who knows where.

And after the catastrophe (and one shouldn't forget that the entire catastrophe consists of the loss of an overcoat!),

as Akaky Akakievich is struggling with death,

> finally, he was *even* foulmouthing, saying the most terrible words, so that the old lady, the landlady, *even* crossed herself, never having heard anything of the sort from him in her life, all the more since these words followed directly after the word "your Excellency."

Such is the highest possible stage of the "poor clerk's" protest!

But it is not only the basic line of plot development that is bespeckled with these "evens" which reveal the pettiness of the main hero's life and experiences. The secondary characters—the "Important Personage" to whom Akaky Akakievich brings his complaints against life and fate, Akaky Akakievich's colleagues, indeed the entire surroundings in which he lives, or rather, "exists,"—are no better. Even Akaky Akakievich's fatal invitation to the party is prompted not by the human closeness to him of his colleagues—such closeness between people may indeed arise transitorily, but it does not arise at all in **"The Overcoat"**!—

> one of the clerks, some assistant, *even,* of the head clerk, probably in order to show that he wasn't a snob in the least and *even* associated with those inferior to himself, said "So be it, I will give a party instead of Akaky Akakievich and request everyone to come to my house for tea: today, as if by plan, is my name day."

The company at the assistant's was the most brilliant: in the anteroom "hung overcoats and cloaks among which some *even* had beaver collars or velvet lapels." The characterization of the "Important Personage" is built by Gogol entirely on "even" and on "breaks." The Important Personage was "in all respects *even* no fool" and "*even* himself felt" some of his shortcomings. The scene in which Akaky Akakievich is scolded by the Important Personage is full of "evens:"

> Here he stamped his foot, raising his voice to such a loud pitch that *even* a better man than Akaky Akakievich would have been terrified;

and when Akaky Akakievich is about ready to faint,

> the important personage was satisfied that the effect had exceeded *even* his expectations, and completely intoxicated by the thought that his word could *even* deprive a man of consciousness.

The Important Personage's remorse is depicted with the help of the same device: "he *even* got to thinking about poor Akaky Akakievich" and "the thought of Akaky distressed him to such a degree that a week later (!) he *even* decided to send a clerk to find out . . . how he was." Having learned that Akaky Akakievich "had died suddenly in a fever," the important personage "was *even* left stunned, feeling pangs of conscience, and was out of sorts all day." After spending an agreeable evening with friends, he decides to visit a lady of his acquaintance, a certain Karolina Ivanovna, "a lady, it seems, of German extraction"; the appearance of the corpse drives him into "a dead fright"—manly and heroic in appearance, he

> felt such terror, that not without reason he *even* began to fear some kind of morbid attack. He *even* quickly took off his overcoat from his shoulders himself and cried to the coachman in a voice not his own: "Drive home as fast as you can!" The coachman, hearing a voice which was usually used at critical moments and would *even* be accompanied by something much the most effective . . . shot off like an arrow.

This event made such a deep impression on the important personage that "he *even* began much less often to say to his subordinates, "How dare you? Do you understand who is standing before you?"

In the fight against the dead Akaky Akakievich the police too suffer a defeat, and their heroism is characterized with the same word, "even":

> An order was given to the police to catch the corpse, no matter what, dead or alive . . . and they *even* almost succeeded in this.

But when the ghost was already in the hands of the police,

> the policeman on duty . . . burrowed just for a minute in his boot to get out a snuffbox . . . but the snuff was probably of the sort that *even* a corpse couldn't bear;

the ghost of Akaky Akakievich sneezed so violently that "he splattered all three of them right in the eye." "From that time on the policemen had such a terror of the dead that they were *even* afraid to seize the living . . ." and "the clerk-corpse began to appear *even* beyond the Kalink in Bridge."

In this aspect of "even," in the continual "breaks" of the narrative line into pettiness, into "nothingness," Gogol thus reveals the whole vain emptiness of a great love . . . for an overcoat. Thus, the pettiness of the entire surroundings of the "poor clerk," of Akaky Akakievich's colleagues, of the "Important Personage," who salves his conscience in the company of several friends "of the same rank," is revealed as well, and even the "heroism" of the police, wiped away by a pinch of vile snuff, amounts to "nothing."

5

The psychological aspect of the story is heightened by the approximation of the author to the hero. It is exactly with the goal of "approximating" himself to the hero that Gogol introduces a narrator who takes everything so seriously. Such an approximation is achieved in **"The Diary of a Madman"** by the diary form, which allows the reader a glimpse into Poprishchin's soul. Dostoevsky achieves the same result in *Poor Folk* by having his hero write letters. In the Ukrainian tales Gogol approximates his heroes with

amazing ease, even to the point of blending with them, through the mediation of his "storytellers" (Foma Grigorievich) and with the help of a mixture of two linguistic strata, the Russian literary language saturated with Ukrainianisms. But, in some cases (**"A Terrible Vengeance," "Taras Bulba," "St. John's Eve,"** etc.), the internal significance of what is narrated or, in others (**"Christmas Eve," "A May Night," "Old-World Landowners,"** etc.), the lyrical relation of the author to the "little world" *(mirok)* described by him make the author's task substantially easier. The task of approximating the hero and his internal world is much more difficult in **"The Overcoat."** As was already mentioned, it is much harder to depict the empty and the insignificant, to portray "nothingness," than it is to show the elevated or the sublime. To force Akaky Akakievich himself to tell the story of his adventures and experiences would be completely impossible, and it is not so simple to create a type of narrator close to Akaky Akakievich.

All the same, Gogol tries where possible in **"The Overcoat"** to take us into his hero's "internal world," to show us how Akaky Akakievich looks at the world. The perspective from which the world appears to Akaky Akakievich is to a significant degree revealed to us by Gogol with the help of continual repetitions of "even." "Even" points out how many things and people in the world the poor clerk sees from below. The logical sense of "even" actually consists in this: it indicates things and objects that are "high," "lofty," "significant," "inaccessible" . . . And so much belongs, for Akaky Akakievich and for the narrator of the story, to this higher sphere: overcoats with beaver collars and velvet lapels, state, court and other councillors, who are not subject to the action of those laws of nature and fate under whose power the "poor man" finds himself. Such is the world, as well, of the other characters in the tale: a new overcoat is a most unusual event not only for Akaky Akakievich, but also for his tailor.

The "little world" of the poor clerk appears to him as a great world precisely because it is full of objects which he looks at "from below"! Gogol wanted to make precisely this form of existence understandable to us, hence the innumerable "evens" characterizing the hero's internal orientation, his spiritual posture. The little world *is* the great world: in this contradiction is based the whole tale and all of its action. **"The Overcoat"** is built on oscillations between contrasting experiences. Gogol takes us into Akaky Akakievich's little world, but we are unable to remain in it, for to be reincarnated into Akaky Akakievich is not easy; therefore, our own conception of his world as a "little world" again and again destroys the illusion that we are in the "great" world experiencing a serious tragedy which decides a question of life or death for the hero. We leave Akaky Akakievich's little world, but Gogol takes us back into it again and again—to a considerable extent with the help of his "even" . . . The essence of the artistic structure of **"The Overcoat"** lies in these oscillations between evaluations of the "little," "tiny," "insignificant" (for us, for the reader) and the "huge," "great," "meaningful" (for Akaky Akakievich and for the narrator).

6

"The Overcoat" is one of the links in the development of the characteristic theme of the "poor clerk" in Russian literature. The better-known examples of this theme include, along with **"The Overcoat,"** the tales of Dostoevsky already mentioned several times, *Poor Folk, The Double,* "A Faint Heart," "Mr. Prokharchin," etc.

Gogol's plot is the most successful and effective of all the plots used in such tales, calculated by literary historians to number around 200. Later, the "social point of view" ruled exclusively in tales about the "poor clerk." Belinsky understood even Gogol's tale as social protest, a protest against the situation of "poor clerks". . . . However, if the center of Gogol's tale were actually to consist in this, in a social protest, then wouldn't it have been much more effective to portray a fully worthwhile human being of some depth trapped in a lower grade of the civil service? We shouldn't forget that Gogol himself had, in his youth, to take time from his literary works for fruitless, petty office work. . . . Of course, the understanding of Gogol's tale as a moral, "ethical" protest ("I am your brother") corresponds more to his own moralistic tendencies, but is Akaky Akakievich really a successful literary type for demonstrating this idea to the reader? One would hardly need to be a particularly proud person to refuse to see in Akaky Akakievich, with his pitiful and comic tragedy, one's "brother." Mustn't Gogol have understood that the plot of **"The Overcoat"** and the specific nature of Akaky Akakievich's psychology would sooner lead many, so many, readers to recognize Akaky Akakievich not as a brother, but rather, at best, as some sort of distant relative? Are not other tales about the "poor clerk" much more effective, for example, Dostoevsky's *Poor Folk* or "Yakov Yakovlevich," one of the best tales on this theme, by the first biographer of Gogol, P.A. Kulish?

We are unable to pause here to show in detail that the social aspect was one of the least important for Gogol himself. The idea that every human being is "our brother" was for Gogol's Christian world view an axiom which he considered it necessary to remind the reader of, in passing, at the beginning of the tale. But actually, even in this passage, if we read it without preconceived notions, the person who acts like a "man," opposing the "inhumanity" of Akaky Akakievich's colleagues, is hardly Akaky Akakievich himself, but that "young man" for whom "everything changed"! The plot of **"The Overcoat"** is more vitally connected with the problem of "one's own place" so central to Gogol's world view, a problem later vulgarized in its social aspect into the pseudo-problem of the "superfluous man." (No one noticed the remarkable—ideologically and artistically—answer of Leskov to this pseudoproblem in his story "Righteous Men," where he tried to show that there are no superfluous people.) But in connection with our analysis of **"The Overcoat"** given above, we shall now approach the tale's ideological content from a different point of view.

The source of **"The Overcoat"** is by chance known to us. It is an anecdote heard by Gogol long before the creation of the tale and related by one of Gogol's friends, Annenkov:

> Once, in Gogol's presence, someone told an office joke about some poor clerk who, by extraordinary economizing and unflagging, ceaseless work outside of his official duties, accumulated a large enough sum of money to buy a good Le Page rifle for about two hundred rubles. The first time he went out in his little boat on the Gulf of Finland to hunt, he put the precious rifle in front of him on the bow, and then, according to his own assertion, found himself in a state of oblivion; he came to his senses only upon glancing at the bow without seeing his new acquisition. The rifle had been pulled off into the water by a thick clump of rushes through which he had passed, and all his efforts to find it were unavailing. The clerk returned home, went to bed, and couldn't get up: he had come down with a fever. Only by a general subscription on the part of his comrades, who had learned of the accident and bought him a new rifle, was he restored to life, but he could never recall that terrible accident without a deathly pallor covering his face. . . . Everybody laughed at the anecdote, which was based on a true event, excepting Gogol, who listened thoughtfully and let his head sink onto his chest. . . .

What did Gogol make out of this anecdote? He replaced the object of the "noble" sport of hunting, a rifle, by a prosaic object of primary necessity. Yet all the same—no doubt, intentionally—he speaks about this object of primary necessity with the language of passion, of love, with erotic language:

> . . . he even entirely mastered going hungry in the evenings; but on the other hand he was nourished spiritually, carrying in his thoughts the idea of the future overcoat. From this time on it was as if his very existence had become somehow fuller, as if he had gotten married, as if some other person were with him, as if he were not alone, but some pleasant female life companion had agreed to travel life's road together with him—and that companion was none other than that same overcoat with the thick quilting, with the strong lining which wouldn't wear out.

> . . . but for whom all the same, albeit before the very end of his life, there had flashed a radiant quest in the form of an overcoat, which had enlivened his poor life for an instant. . . .

The reader is prepared to take such lines more as mockery directed at the poor clerk than as the expression of a real sympathy for him or as the uncovering of a consciousness of brotherhood with him. But several details in Gogol's tale become comprehensible only in terms of this "erotic" aspect. For example, the thief doesn't simply strip Akaky Akakievich of his overcoat but also says "But that's my overcoat!" Is not this night robber some sort of variation on the "strong rival" of traditional love plots? Only Akaky Akakievich's love for the overcoat awakens in him generally erotic experiences: he runs after a charming lady, looks at an erotic picture in the window of a store. . . . And the very appearance of the ghost in search of the overcoat (Gogol entitled the first draft of his story "The Tale of the

Clerk Who Stole Overcoats," which indicates that the final pages are essential and central to the work, and not merely some sort of mischievous, unnecessary ending)—is it not a unique parody of the romantic "dead lover," who leaves the grave in search of his beloved? In this sense, the plot of **"The Overcoat"** is the famous plot of Bürger's "Lenore," of Zhukovsky's "Lyudmila" and "Svetlana," the theme of stanzas from *Eugene Onegin* (VII, 11 and the variants), of Pushkin's poems ("The Incantation," etc.), of Lermontov's "A Dead Man's Love." It is the theme of the all-conquering power of love, of a love which overcomes even death.

In one sense the theme of "The Overcoat" is the theme of the all-conquering power of love, of a love which overcomes even death.

—Dmitri Chizhevsky

The fine—and, of course, forgotten—literary critic N. N. Strakhov focussed attention on the fact that Dostoevsky's *Poor Folk* is an original "retort," an answer to Gogol's **"The Overcoat."** This question has recently been beautifully illuminated by A.L. Bem. The overcoat is a meaningless, dead object, replaced in Dostoevsky's work by a live person, a girl, Varenka Dobroselova. The disinterested and timid love of the poor clerk Makar Devushkin is portrayed without a scornful glance from above, without scathing laughter, and without the slightest elements of mockery. The human honor of the "poor clerk" is restored in full!

But did Dostoevsky really understand Gogol's intention? He understood it as little as did Belinsky. As we have already stated, both the "social aspect" and the moral message ("I am your brother") are only accessory motifs in **"The Overcoat."** The Gogol who wrote **"The Overcoat"** is the very same Gogol who read the writings of the Church Fathers and the *Philokalia* [expanded in Russian as the *Dobrotoliubie*] and in whom a number of his friends saw a prophet or at least a teacher of life. It is gradually becoming clear to investigators (Zenkovsky, Gippius, Mikolaenko) what a fundamental role religious problems play in the thematics of Gogol's artistic work, and particularly the problems of "spiritual works," the feat of "spiritual combat," as presented in the writings of the Church Fathers. Gogol's letters (and not just his *Selected Passages from Correspondence with Friends,* but his actual letters—which, of course, no one reads!) are not an idle whim of "didacticism," but rather a serious, even if unsuccessful, attempt to gain a real hold on human souls, an attempt at spiritual leadership. The psychological subtlety with which the writings of the Church Fathers elaborated the problems of spiritual combat, the amazing psychological insights of the *Dobrotoliubie,* could they have remained unnoticed by Gogol? Of course not! But we don't want to

give here an interpretation of **"The Overcoat"** taking the writings of the Church Fathers as a point of departure. The immanent critical examination of **"The Overcoat"** itself brings us to the problems of "spiritual combat." Our observations are merely aimed at emphasizing, above all, that one must expect from Gogol's artistic works attempts to solve complex psychological questions and not a simple repetition of axioms ("I am your brother") and truisms ("even peasants"—and "poor clerks"—"can feel").

The theme of **"The Overcoat"** is the stirring of the human soul, its regeneration under the influence of a—granted, very peculiar—love. The possibility of the soul's stirring becomes manifest from contact with a love object, and not only with something great, elevated, or significant (an heroic exploit, one's fatherland, a live person—a friend, a loved woman, etc.), but also in meeting something everyday or prosaic. The hero's relation to the overcoat is depicted, as we have seen, with the language of eros. And a man can be ruined, led to the abyss, not only by love for something great or meaningful, but also by love for an insignificant object, if only it becomes the subject of passion, of love.

One of the central ideas of Gogol's artistic works is that each man has his own "infatuation," his own passion, something he is "carried away with." The theme is ancient: it is the theme of Horace, of the poetry of the European and Ukrainian Baroque, of one of the *virshi* of the Ukrainian mystic Grigoriya Skovoroda, a poem probably known to Gogol even if only from "Natalka Poltavka" by Kotlyarevsky (a writer from whom Gogol takes part of the epigraph to "The Fair at Sorochintsy"). Skovoroda was an exact contemporary and fellow-countryman of the compiler of the Slavonic *Dobrotoliubie,* Paisiya Velichkovsky (1722-1794). In one of his *virsha* (a spiritual song or devotional verse, sung at Ukrainian country fairs—in Gogol's time, as they still were sung at the beginning of the XXth century—by blind "lyricists"), Skovoroda begins by juxtaposing the gaudiness and sordidness of society's interests and amusements ("Every head has its mind, every heart has its love, every throat has its taste") to the "single-mindedness" of his own spiritual passion ("But I have only one thought in the world, but I alone will not lose my mind"), and concludes with the motley picture of the variety of human "infatuations," to speak in the style of Gogol. In a passage of *Dead Souls* which V. Gippius rightly recognized as one of the ideologically most important parts of the "poem," Gogol takes us back to the humorous formulation of his fellow-countryman, Skovoroda:

> Every man has his own enthusiasm: one man's enthusiasm is turned to wolf-hounds; to another it seems that he is a great lover of music and amazingly sensitive to all the profound passages therein; a third may be a great hand at putting away a huge dinner; a fourth feels that he can play a better part in this world, even though that part be but a fraction above the one assigned to him; a fifth fellow, whose aspiration is more circumscribed, sleeps and dreams of how he might promenade on a gala occasion with some aide-de-camp, showing off before his friends, his acquaintances, and even those who aren't acquainted with him. . . .

Passions, attractions, "infatuations" are here all directed (except for the love for music, but even that is actually only a "seeming" love!) toward insignificant objects. In the beginning of **"Nevsky Prospect"** Gogol depicts the "display" of the daily stroll on the Nevsky:

> One displays a smart overcoat with the best beaver on it, another—a fine Greek nose, the third—superb whiskers, the fourth—a pair of pretty eyes and a marvelous hat, the fifth—a signet ring on a jaunty finger, the sixth—a foot in a bewitching shoe. . . .

This "display" is a show of the objects of "infatuation"; what we have here are not even shadows of serious interests.

But in **"The Overcoat"** the hero's infatuation is lower than anything we come across in Gogol's prose. Nevertheless, Akaky Akakievich does have an infatuation and he puts its object, his overcoat, on display: he shows it to his colleagues, rejoices that he can, "even in the evening," show himself off in his new overcoat. Akaky Akakievich is so passionately carried away with the object of his infatuation that he can, in a way, be included among Gogol's other—serious and humorous—heroes. He has something in common not only with Gogol's "dandies," but also with his "hoarders" and with his "unhappy lovers." The type of the dandy first appears already in Gogol's Ukrainian stories:

> In the old days in Mirgorod it used to be that only the judge and the mayor went around in cloth overcoats lined with sheepskin in the winter and the whole petty bureaucracy simply wore rawhides: now both the assessor and the judge for land disputes have prepared themselves new cloth overcoats lined with astrakhan pelts. The year before last the clerk and the district scribe got dark blue crepe de chine at 60 kopeks a yard. The sexton made himself nankeen trousers for the summer and a vest of striped worsted. In a word, everyone's becoming a gentleman!
>
> **("Christmas Eve")**

But even this "infatuation" is, in the case of Akaky Akakievich, reduced to a minimum; he dreams, strictly speaking, only of a necessary bodily covering. In the process of acquiring the overcoat, Akaky Akakievich has taken the road of hoarding or acquisitiveness, thus joining the ranks of Gogol's acquisitive characters. We come across different variants of this type throughout Gogol's work, from the Ukrainian heroes (in the tradition of "buried treasure": **"A Bewitched Place," "St. John's Eve"**) to Chartkov, Chichikov, and the "gamblers." But even here Akaky Akakievich is infinitely lower than all of his fellows: his "hoarding" is hoarding with a limited, practical goal. Akaky Akakievich perishes, strictly speaking, from love; in this respect, he is a strange variant of Gogol's tragically ruined lovers, a type to which Gogol continually returns, from Peter (**"St. John's Eve"**) and Andrey (**"Taras Bulba"**) to Poprishchin and the unfortunate Piskaryov. Even Chichikov's fleeting attraction to the Governor's daughter turns out to be fatal. . . . In terms of this type Akaky Akakievich appears as a parody, a caricature, with his ardent love, overcoming death itself, for . . . an overcoat!

The meaning of this "reduction" of "passions" to the lowest possible minimum becomes clearer to us, perhaps, if we turn to Gogol's correspondence during the period when **"The Overcoat"** was written. One of the most important themes of Gogol's letters of 1840-42 is the question: is it possible to attach one's being to things of the "external world"? It is a question which Dostoevsky was also to pose to himself ("fixed ideas," a phrase which can be traced back to Pushkin's "Queen of Spades"). For Gogol it wasn't really even a question: he decides it categorically from the first. In a letter to Danilevsky of June 20, 1843, Gogol sharply contrasts the external to the internal life. One must have a "fixed anchor"; since all things of the world are doomed to destruction, a man should have an internal "center to fall back on, by which he could overcome even the very sufferings and grief of life." "The external life is opposed to the internal when a man, under the influence of passionate attractions, is carried away without struggle by the currents of life."

The "center" of which Gogol speaks is the *centrum securitatis* of Christian mysticism, God. Only in the Divine Being are certainty and firmness to be found. It is He who shows a man "his own place" (and every man has one) in the world; God is the "Supreme Commander" for whom we all work. The loss of connection with this center is the loss of one's own place in the world and of life's goal (its "command"). And the surrender of one's self to the external world by binding one's fate with the objects of this world is both the loss of one's center and, at the same time, the loss of one's self. "External life is outside of God, the internal life is in God," Gogol writes; therefore, knowledge of God (as it is traditionally in Christian mysticism) is self-knowledge:

> It is necessary to go deeply into oneself, to question oneself and learn which of our hidden sides are useful and necessary to the world, for there is no unnecessary link in all the world.

In his "Petersburg Tales" Gogol depicts people who are in the process of "losing themselves," or surrendering to the power of the external world. He himself says this about the artist Chartkov (**"The Portrait"**), who perishes from a yearning for money and fame, from a neglect of the "command" given him by God. The clerk Poprishchin (**"The Diary of a Madman"**) and the artist Piskaryov (**"Nevsky Prospect"**) perish from love for women. Akaky Akakievich perishes from "nothing"! His passionate attraction is directed at an insignificant, worthless object, and he has no center to fall back on whereby he might have opposed the world, or "overcome even the very sufferings and grief of life." A man's ruination is tragic and possible not only from grand passions, from passions directed towards the elevated, sublime or significant, but also from passions directed towards the insignificant and the petty. The whole of the world is rotten and carries man away with it into ruin by attaching onto him its existence, regardless of whether this worldly existence is in the form of something great or—an overcoat.

Even if we were to delineate (which Gogol, as we saw, does not) a "worldly" sphere limited to objects of "legitimate," "permissible" or even simply "intelligible" passions, of passions directed towards the "great" or simply the "large," even in this case Gogol's example in **"The Overcoat"** would nevertheless remain indisputable. It is probably for just this reason that Gogol chose such an extreme, paradoxical example—for us, for the "public," for the reader. In his letter to Danilevsky the question is one of grave experiences which Gogol himself takes seriously; if even in such a case Gogol considers it possible to speak about the loss of the "internal world," about a concession made to the "external world," then what is Gogol's appraisal of Akaky Akakievich! The world and the *devil* snare men not only with the great and lofty, but also with trifles, not only with ardent love for a woman, not only with a dream of unearthly happiness, not only with mountains of gold, but even with everyday trivialities, with pitiful sums saved up out of pitiful salaries, with an overcoat. If a man's entire soul becomes entangled in such details, there is no salvation for him. The plot of **"The Overcoat"** is an original treatment of the Gospel parable of "the window's mite": as a mite, a penny, can be a great sacrifice, so a trifle, an overcoat, can be a great temptation (a thought from the *Dobrotoliubie*). Not only God, but the Devil as well, values such a "mite" correspondingly.

7

The main hero of almost all Gogol's works, a hero whose name we meet in practically every work, is the *Devil*. In **"The Overcoat,"** the Devil is apparently not mentioned. But, perhaps, only "apparently." The Devil *is* mentioned several times, but only in one passage relating to Petrovich. It is Petrovich who gives Akaky Akakievich the idea of the new overcoat by refusing to mend his "housecoat" and, by the same token, puts the plot into motion. Perhaps it is only a verbal play on the word "devil" when Gogol relates that Petrovich's wife called him a "one-eyed devil" when he was drunk: "he's glutted with rotgut, the one-eyed devil." But Petrovich was sober when Akaky Akakievich came to see him, "and therefore curt, intractable and eager to demand the *devil* knows what prices." Generally, "Petrovich was subject to the whim of suddenly asking the *devil* knows what exhorbitant price. . . ." Perhaps it is also an accident that Petrovich is the owner of a snuffbox "with the portrait of some general, precisely which is not known, because the place where the face was had been punched out with a finger and then pasted over with a square scrap of paper." It is just this faceless general whom Akaky Akakievich sees at the moment when the question of the new overcoat is being decided. *The Devil is faceless!* Well-read in religious literature, a connoisseur and collector of folklore material, of folk songs and legends, Gogol of course knew that the devil appears faceless in the Christian and folklore traditions. And in-

deed, Petrovich fans the flames of passion, "the most daring and audacious thoughts" of a new overcoat, in Akaky Akakievich's soul. At Akaky Akakievich's second visit Petrovich is drunk, "but despite all this, as soon as he learned what the matter was, it was just as if the devil had given him a push. 'Impossible,' he said, 'kindly order a new one.'"

Gogol did not want merely to present Akaky Akakievich as our "brother." The main task of **"The Overcoat"** was rather to indicate the danger that is inherent even in details, in everyday trivialities, the danger, the ruin of passions, of "passionate attractions," regardless of their object, even if their object were as seemingly inconsequential as an overcoat. "Even" is for Gogol a means of emphasizing his basic idea: like an arrow, like an unrestrained passionate impulse, "even" takes our thought into the heights only so that it will fall more helplessly, descending back into everyday triviality. Akaky Akakievich's helpless impulse, directed at a worthless object, is "cast down" from an imaginary height ("even") by the Devil, who had actually set such a prosaically fantastic goal for this urge in the first place.

And that this urge, this "earthly" love of Akaky Akakievich, overcomes death itself means, for Gogol, the full loss of self, the loss even in life beyond the grave. Returning from the world beyond the grave to the cold streets of Petersburg, Akaky Akakievich by the same token demonstrates that he has found no peace beyond the grave, that he is still attached with his entire soul to his *earthly* love. . . . The sham victory of an earthly love over death is thus in reality the victory of the "killer from time immemorial," of the evil spirit, over a human soul. The Gogolian story of the "poor clerk" is hardly funny: it is terrifying.

8

We began our analysis with an obvious "detail," a verbal detail in **"The Overcoat,"** the word "even." We saw how important this "detail" is for Gogol, how it is a means of stylizing the tale as colloquial speech, as a *skaz*. We saw that Gogol adapts the same "detail" as a device in the game of his humor and that humor is for Gogol a means of fighting the "pettiness," the devilish "nothingness," of this world, a fact which it is hardly necessary to repeat. We saw that this very same verbal detail is a means of approximating the hero, of understanding him psychologically, of conveying the unique view of the tale's hero "from below." We saw, finally, that this "detail" helps us to understand the idea of the work. The further development of **"The Overcoat"** in Russian literature (Dostoevsky is reputed to have said, "we all came out of **'The Overcoat'**") could be sketched. It would involve tracing the evolution of the *skaz*, the history of "antithetical" humor, so characteristic for Gogol, the changes in the means of the naturalistic and psychological characterization of the "insignificant" hero, and finally, the evolution of the plot of the "poor clerk" tale (the vulgarization of Gogol's psychological depth into the "social tale"). But here we can only point out these various themes.

Vladimir Nabokov (essay date 1944)

"The Apotheosis of a Mask," in *Nikolai Gogol,* New Directions, 1944, 139-50.

[*A Russian-born American man of letters perhaps best known for the novels* Lolita *(1955) and* Pale Fire *(1962), Nabokov was a prolific contributor to many literary fields. He was fascinated with all aspects of the creative life: in his works, he explored the origins of creativity, the relationships of artists to their work, and the nature of invented reality. In the following essay Nabokov extols Gogol's abstract and highly stylized technique and concludes that "The Overcoat" "is a phenomenon of language and not one of ideas."*]

Gogol was a strange creature, but genius is always strange; it is only your healthy second-rater who seems to the grateful reader to be a wise old friend, nicely developing the reader's own notions of life. Great literature skirts the irrational. *Hamlet* is the wild dream of a neurotic scholar. Gogol's **"The Overcoat"** is a grotesque and grim nightmare making black holes in the dim pattern of life. The superficial reader of that story will merely see in it the heavy frolics of an extravagant buffoon; the solemn reader will take for granted that Gogol's prime intention was to denounce the horrors of Russian bureaucracy. But neither the person who wants a good laugh, nor the person who craves for books "that make one think" will understand what **"The Overcoat"** is really about. Give me the creative reader; this is a tale for him.

Steady Pushkin, matter-of-fact Tolstoy, restrained Chekhov have all had their moments of irrational insight which simultaneously blurred the sentence and disclosed a secret meaning worth the sudden focal shift. But with Gogol this shifting is the very basis of his art, so that whenever he tried to write in the round hand of literary tradition and to treat rational ideas in a logical way, he lost all trace of talent. When, as in his immortal **"The Overcoat,"** he really let himself go and pottered happily on the brink of his private abyss, he became the greatest artist that Russia has yet produced.

The sudden slanting of the rational plane of life may be accomplished of course in many ways, and every great writer has his own method. With Gogol it was a combination of two movements: a jerk and a glide. Imagine a trapdoor that opens under your feet with absurd suddenness, and a lyrical gust that sweeps you up and then lets you fall with a bump into the next traphole. The absurd was Gogol's favorite muse—but when I say "the absurd," I do not mean the quaint or the comic. The absurd has as many shades and degrees as the tragic has, and moreover, in Gogol's case, it borders upon the latter. It would be wrong to assert that Gogol placed his characters in absurd situations. You cannot place a man in an absurd situation if the whole world he lives in is absurd; you cannot do this if you mean by "absurd" something provoking a chuckle or a shrug. But if you mean the pathetic, the human condition, if you mean all such things that in less weird worlds are linked up with the loftiest aspirations, the deep-

est sufferings, the strongest passions—then of course the necessary breach is there, and a pathetic human, lost in the midst of Gogol's nightmarish, irresponsible world would be "absurd," by a kind of secondary contrast.

On the lid of the tailor's snuff-box there was "the portrait of a General; I do not know what general because the tailor's thumb had made a hole in the general's face and a square of paper had been gummed over the hole." Thus with the absurdity of Akaky Akakyevich Bashmachkin. We did not expect that, amid the whirling masks, one mask would turn out to be a real face, or at least the place where that face ought to be. The essence of mankind is irrationally derived from the chaos of fakes which form Gogol's world. Akaky Akakyevich, the hero of **"The Overcoat,"** is absurd *because* he is pathetic, *because* he is human and *because* he has been engendered by those very forces which seem to be in such contrast to him.

He is not merely human and pathetic. He is something more, just as the background is not mere burlesque. Somewhere behind the obvious contrast there is a subtle genetic link. His being discloses the same quiver and shimmer as does the dream world to which he belongs. The allusions to something else behind the crudely painted screens, are so artistically combined with the superficial texture of the narration that civic-minded Russians have missed them completely. But a creative reading of Gogol's story reveals that here and there in the most innocent descriptive passage, this or that word, sometimes a mere adverb or a preposition, for instance the word "even" or "almost," is inserted in such a way as to make the harmless sentence explode in a wild display of nightmare fireworks; or else the passage that had started in a rambling colloquial manner all of a sudden leaves the tracks and swerves into the irrational where it really belongs; or again, quite as suddenly, a door bursts open and a mighty wave of foaming poetry rushes in only to dissolve in bathos, or to turn into its own parody, or to be checked by the sentence breaking and reverting to a conjuror's patter, that patter which is such a feature of Gogol's style. It gives one the sensation of something ludicrous and at the same time stellar, lurking constantly around the corner—and one likes to recall that the difference between the comic side of things, and their cosmic side, depends upon one sibilant.

So what is that queer world, glimpses of which we keep catching through the gaps of the harmless looking sentences? It is in a way the *real* one but it looks wildly absurd to us, accustomed as we are to the stage setting that screens it. It is from these glimpses that the main character of **"The Overcoat,"** the meek little clerk, is formed, so that he embodies the spirit of that secret but real world which breaks through Gogol's style. He is, that meek little clerk, a ghost, a visitor from some tragic depths who by chance happened to assume the disguise of a petty official. Russian progressive critics sensed in him the image of the underdog and the whole story impressed them as a social protest. But it is something much more than that. The gaps and black holes in the texture of Gogol's style imply flaws in the texture of life itself. Something is very wrong and all men are mild lunatics engaged in pursuits that seem to them very important while an absurdly logical force keeps them at their futile jobs—this is the real "message" of the story. In this world of utter futility, of futile humility and futile domination, the highest degree that passion, desire, creative urge can attain is a new cloak which both tailors and customers adore on their knees. I am not speaking of the moral point or the moral lesson. There can be no moral lesson in such a world because there are no pupils and no teachers: this world *is* and it excludes everything that might destory it, so that any improvement, any struggle, any moral purpose or endeavor, are as utterly impossible as changing the course of a star. It is Gogol's world and as such wholly different from Tolstoy's world, or Pushkin's, or Chekhov's or my own. But after reading Gogol one's eyes may become gogolized and one is apt to see bits of his world in the most unexpected places. I have visited many countries, and something like Akaky Akakyevich's overcoat has been the passionate dream of this or that chance acquaintance who never had heard about Gogol.

After reading Gogol one's eyes may become gogolized and one is apt to see bits of his world in the most unexpected places.

—*Vladimir Nabokov*

The plot of **"The Overcoat"** is very simple. A poor little clerk makes a great decision and orders a new overcoat. The coat while in the making becomes the dream of his life. On the very first night that he wears it he is robbed of it on a dark street. He dies of grief and his ghost haunts the city. This is all in the way of plot, but of course the *real* plot (as always with Gogol) lies in the style, in the inner structure of this transcendental anecdote. In order to appreciate it at its true worth one must perform a kind of mental somersault so as to get rid of conventional values in literature and follow the author along the dream road of his superhuman imagination. Gogol's world is somewhat related to such conceptions of modern physics as the "Concertina Universe" or the "Explosion Universe"; it is far removed from the comfortably revolving clockwork worlds of the last century. There is a curvature in literary style as there is curvature in space,—but few are the Russian readers who do care to plunge into Gogol's magic chaos head first, with no restraint or regret. The Russian who thinks Turgenev was a great writer, and bases his notion of Pushkin upon Chaïkovsky's vile libretti, will merely paddle into the gentlest wavelets of Gogol's mysterious sea and limit his reaction to an enjoyment of what he takes to be whimsical humor and colorful quips. But the diver, the seeker for black pearls, the man who prefers the monsters of the deep to the sunshades on the beach, will find in **"The Overcoat"** shadows linking our state of existence to those other states and modes which we dimly apprehend in our rare moments of irrational perception.

The prose of Pushkin is three-dimensional; that of Gogol is four-dimensional, at least. He may be compared to his contemporary, the mathematician Lobachevsky, who blasted Euclid and discovered a century ago many of the theories which Einstein later developed. If parallel lines do not meet it is not because meet they cannot, but because they have other things to do. Gogol's art as disclosed in **"The Overcoat"** suggests that parallel lines not only may meet, but that they can wriggle and get most extravagantly entangled, just as two pillars reflected in water indulge in the most wobbly contortions if the necessary ripple is there. Gogol's genius is exactly that ripple—two and two make five, if not the square root of five, and it all happens quite naturally in Gogol's world, where neither rational mathematics nor indeed any of our pseudophysical agreements with ourselves can be seriously said to exist.

The clothing process indulged in by Akaky Akakyevich, the making and the putting on of the cloak, is really his *disrobing* and his gradual reversion to the stark nakedness of his own ghost. From the very beginning of the story he is in training for his supernaturally high jump—and such harmless looking details as his tiptoeing in the streets to spare his shoes or his not quite knowing whether he is in the middle of the street or in the middle of the sentence, these details gradually dissolve the clerk Akaky Akakyevich so that towards the end of the story his ghost seems to be the most tangible, the most real part of his being. The account of his ghost haunting the streets of St. Petersburg in search of the cloak of which he had been robbed and finally appropriating that of a high official who had refused to help him in his misfortune—this account, which to the unsophisticated may look like an ordinary ghost story, is transformed towards the end into something for which I can find no precise epithet. It is both an apotheosis and a *dégringolade*. Here it is:

> The Important Person almost died of fright. In his office and generally in the presence of subordinates he was a man of strong character, and whoever glanced at his manly appearance and shape used to imagine his kind of temper with something of a shudder; at the present moment however he (as happens in the case of many people of prodigiously powerful appearance) experienced such terror that, not without reason, he *even* expected to have a fit of some sort. He *even* threw off his cloak of his own accord and then exhorted the coachman in a wild voice to take him home and drive like mad. Upon hearing tones which were generally used at critical moments and were *even* [notice the recurrent use of this word] accompanied by something far effective, the coachman thought it wiser to draw his head in; he lashed at the horses, and the carriage sped like an arrow. Six minutes later, or a little more, [according to Gogol's special timepiece] the Important Person was already at the porch of his house. Pale, frightened and cloakless, instead of arriving at Caroline Ivanovna's [a woman he kept] he had thus come home; he staggered to his bedroom and spent an exceedingly troubled night, so that next morning, at breakfast, his daughter said to him straightaway: 'You are quite pale today, papa.' But papa kept silent and [now comes the parody of a Bible parable!] he told none of what had befallen him, nor where he had been, or whither he

had wished to go. The whole occurrence made a very strong impression on him [here begins the downhill slide, that spectacular bathos which Gogol uses for his particular needs]. Much more seldom *even* did he address to his subordinates the words 'How dare you?—Do you know to whom you are speaking?'—or at least if he did talk that way it was not till he had first listened to what they had to tell. But still more remarkable was the fact that from that time on the ghostly clerk quite ceased to appear: evidently the Important Person's overcoat fitted him well; at least no more did one hear of overcoats being snatched from people's shoulders. However, many active and vigilant persons refused to be appeased and kept asserting that in remote parts of the city the ghostly clerk still showed himself. And indeed a suburban policeman saw with his own eyes [the downward slide from the moralistic note to the grotesque is now a tumble] a ghost appear from behind a house. But being by nature somewhat of a weakling (so that once, an ordinary full-grown young pig which had rushed out of some private house knocked him off his feet to the great merriment of a group of cab drivers from whom he demanded, and obtained, as a penalty for this derision, ten coppers from each to buy himself snuff), he did not venture to stop the ghost but just kept on walking behind it in the darkness, until the ghost suddenly turned, stopped and inquired: 'What d'you want, you?'—and showed a fist of a size rarely met with *even* among the living. 'Nothing,' answered the sentinel and proceeded to go back at once. That ghost, however, was a much taller one and had a huge moustache. It was heading apparently towards Obukhov Bridge and presently disappeared completely in the darkness of the night.

The torrent of "irrelevant" details (such as the bland assumption that "full-grown young pigs" commonly occur in private houses) produces such a hypnotic effect that one almost fails to realize one simple thing (and that is the beauty of the final stroke). A piece of most important information, the main structural idea of the story is here deliberately masked by Gogol (because all reality is a mask). The man taken for Akaky Akakyevich's cloakless ghost is actually the man who stole his cloak. But Akaky Akakyevich's ghost existed solely on the strength of his lacking a cloak, whereas now the policeman, lapsing into the queerest paradox of the story, mistakes for this ghost just the very person who was its antithesis, the man who had stolen the cloak. Thus the story describes a full circle: a vicious circle as all circles are, despite their posing as apples, or planets, or human faces.

So to sum up: the story goes this way: mumble, mumble, lyrical wave, mumble, lyrical wave, mumble, lyrical wave, mumble, fantastic climax, mumble, mumble, and back into the chaos from which they all had derived. At this super-high level of art, literature is of course not concerned with pitying the underdog or cursing the upperdog. It appeals to that secret depth of the human soul where the shadows of other worlds pass like the shadows of nameless and soundless ships.

As one or two patient readers may have gathered by now, this is really the only appeal that interests me. My purpose in jotting these notes on Gogol has, I hope, become per-fectly clear. Bluntly speaking it amounts to the following; if you expect to find out something about Russia, if you are eager to know why the blistered Germans bungled their blitz, if you are interested in "ideas" and "facts" and "messages," keep away from Gogol. The awful trouble of learning Russian in order to read him will not be repaid in your kind of hard cash. Keep away, keep away. He has nothing to tell you. Keep off the tracks. High tension. Closed for the duration. Avoid, refrain, don't. I would like to have here a full list of all possible interdictions, vetoes and threats. Hardly necessary of course—as the wrong sort of reader will certainly never get as far as this. But I do welcome the right sort—my brothers, my doubles. My brother is playing the organ. My sister is reading. She is my aunt. You will first learn the alphabet, the labials, the linguals, the dentals, the letters that buzz, the drone and the bumblebee, and the Tse-tse Fly. One of the vowels will make you say "Ugh!" You will feel mentally stiff and bruised after your first declension of personal pronouns. I see however no other way of getting to Gogol (or to any other Russian writer for that matter). His work, as all great literary achievements, is a phenomenon of language and not one of ideas. "Gaw-gol," not "Go-gall." The final "l" is a soft dissolving "l" which does not exist in English. One cannot hope to understand an author if one cannot even pronounce his name. My translations of various passages are the best my poor vocabulary could afford, but even had they been as perfect as those which I hear with my innermost ear, without being able to render their intonation, they still would not replace Gogol. While trying to convey my attitude towards his art I have not produced any tangible proofs of its peculiar existence. I can only place my hand on my heart and affirm that I have not imagined Gogol. He really wrote, he really lived.

Gogol was born on the 1st of April, 1809. According to his mother (who, of course, made up the following dismal anecdote) a poem he had written at the age of five was seen by Kapnist, a well-known writer of sorts. Kapnist embraced the solemn urchin and said to the glad parents: "He will become a writer of genius if only destiny gives him a good Christian for teacher and guide." But the other thing—his having been born on the 1st of April—is true.

John Schillinger   (essay date 1972)

"Gogol's 'The Overcoat' as a Travesty of Hagiography," in *Slavic and East European Journal,* Vol. 16, No. 1, Spring, 1972, pp. 36-41.

[In this essay Schillinger asserts that "The Overcoat" is "a travesty of the saints' calendar account of St. Acacius of Sinai, and to some extent of hagiography itself."]

Does the name Akakij Akakievi in Gogol's **"The Overcoat"** indicate more than Gogol's familiar sense of humor? Quite possibly. Another origin, and this is offered by Gogol himself at Akakij Akakievič's christening, is an Eastern Orthodox calendar of saints. Among the saints in such a calendar are several Saints Acacius, one of whom, sixth-century St. Acacius of Sinai, resembles Akakij Akakievi quite closely. F. C. Driessen has written: "There is no question of chance. It would scarcely be possible to find another name which expressed so strongly the character of its bearer and at the same time embraced the nucleus of his adventures" [*Gogol as a Short Story Writer*, trans. by Ian F. Finlay, 1965]. I wish to suggest further that the **"The Overcoat"** may be read as a travesty of the saints' calendar account of St. Acacius of Sinai, and to some extent of hagiography itself.

The hagiographic account in question, available in various compilations during Gogol's time, is here translated in full from the Slavonic.

The Life of Saint Acacius of Sinai

The blessed John Climacus writes in his book about this holy monk Acacius thus: The most revered John Sabbaites informed me of this incident, truthful and worthy of hearing, saying: There was a certain elder who was very lazy and evil, whom I shall mention only and not judge, yet I shall reveal the suffering endured by this holy one. I shall tell you about this one. The elder had a young disciple named Acacius, who was simple of manner and chaste of mind and who endured so much evil that there are many who cannot believe it to be true. Not only was he tormented by the elder's humiliations and reproaches, but for days on end he was tormented by wounds inflicted by the elder. He did not endure his torment unthinkingly, for by his uncomplaining endurance and innocent sufferings he secured the grace of God which would save him from eternal torment. I saw him (said John Sabbaites to John Climacus) every day, and he looked like someone who had been bought for a slave or a captive, suffering the greatest hardships. I went on purpose to see him and asked, "How are you brother Acacius, how are you faring today?" He answered me, saying, "I am well, and God is my witness." And he showed me at times his blackened eyes, at times his neck, and at times his lacerated face. Knowing that he was a doer of good, I said to him, "Good, good, endure, brother, and you will be saved." Thus the blessed Acacius lived nine years under that harsh elder, and having been ill very little before his end, went to the Lord. They buried the deceased in a monk's sepulcher. His elder after five days went to one of the priests who was important there and said to him, "Father, brother Acacius my disciple has died." The reverend, when he heard this, answered, "I do not believe you, elder, for Acacius did not die." The elder said, "Father, if you do not believe this, then come yourself and see his grave." The most reverend father arose quickly and went with the elder to the sepulcher of that blessed toiler and spoke over Acacius' grave as if he were living, saying, "Brother Acacius, are you dead?" The wise and obedient servant even in death showed obedience and answered, "I have not died, father. He who is an obedient toiler cannot die." Having heard this, Acacius' elder became frightened, and fell prostrate to the ground in tears, and having begged the bishop for a cell near the grave and having shut himself up in it, lived a good life, cared for the salvation of his soul, and having progressed greatly, went to the Lord God, to whom glory forever, Amen.

This account is more an excerpt than a complete vita, which typically was introduced with declarations of sincerity and humility on the part of the hagiographer, emphasizing the gravity of the undertaking and setting the tone for the work. Gogol at the outset expresses his attitude toward his work, but just as Akakij Akakievi may be seen as a travesty of St. Acacius of Sinai, so the introduction to **"The Overcoat"** is instead a satirical digression: "In the department—but perhaps it is better not to say in which department. There is nothing touchier than departments, regiments, bureaus, in a word, any kind of officialdom."

> It is Akakij Akakievič's acceptance of suffering that unites him with most saints, particularly with St. Acacius of Sinai. In hagiography it sometimes happened that a saint was tormented by his brethren or by demons diguised as messengers of God. Akakij Akakievi suffered ill treatment at the hands of his fellow workers.
>
> —*John Schillinger*

Following this digression, Gogol observes the hagiographical tradition of generality, the tendency to avoid specific names and places, though here emphasized and inverted according to his humorous purposes. "In a certain department there served a certain civil servant." Subsequently, only one character other than Akakij Akakievi is mentioned by name, Petrovi the tailor. People are classified rather than referred to by name: civil servant, official, director, landlady, police inspector, Very Important Person. Geographical references are also vague. Although we know that Akakij Akakievi lives in St. Petersburg, locations within the city are obscure: "Unfortunately we cannot say exactly where the civil servant who had invited Akakij Akakievi lived. Our memory is beginning to fail us rather badly, and everything in St. Petersburg, all the streets and houses, have become so blurred and mixed up in our head that we find it very difficult to find anything up there in order." Correspondingly, the anonymous scribe who recorded the account of the life of St. Acacius of Sinai refers by name only to other hagiographers; all others are described by classification (brother, elder, holy father, bishop). Moreover, we do not know where the events occurred, only that the vita passage is taken from the Sinai paterikon (a collection of monks' lives, to be distinguished from saints' lives) which in turn were drawn from several monasteries.

Beyond these stylistic points are the many connections between Akakij Akakievi and the subject of a typical hagiography. While a saint traditionally exhibits the most noteworthy and exemplary behavior, Akakij Akakievi is "a civil servant who is impossible to describe as remarkable." His insignificant future is foreshadowed at his christening ceremony, where a saints' calendar is consulted for a name. Akakij Akakievi "began to cry and made such a grimace that it seemed he had a premonition that he would be a titular councilor."

Not infrequently a saint is born into a family of high social position. This is ironically mirrored in the description of those present at Akakij Akakievič's christening. His mother is described as "most excellent in every respect"; the godfather, a head clerk, as a "most admirable man"; and the godmother, the wife of the district police inspector, as a "most worthy woman." Akakij Akakievič's rank as titular councilor qualifies him, marginally, as nobility and is roughly equivalent to a captaincy in the military. It entitles him to be addressed as "your honor." But only a young man could be proud of this title; a man of Akakij Akakievič's years should have advanced to a higher rank. St. Acacius of Melitina, on the other hand, became a bishop, and was instrumental in the ousting of Nestor at the third ecumenical council in Ephesus in 431, while St. Acacius of Sinai was apparently significant enough to have had his likeness rendered in an ikon by Theophanes.

The tasks daily performed by a monk such as St. Acacius of Sinai and by Akakij Akakievič are identical. Akakij Akakievi "was seen in exactly the same place, in exactly the same position, doing exactly the same kind of work, as a copier of documents." Traditionally, the chief occupation of Orthodox monks was the copying of church documents. We find here a travesty of the monk who praises God by his humble service, for Akakij Akakievič is devoted to the act of copying itself. Bolting down whatever food was placed before him (flies and all) Akakij Akakievič would "get up from the table, take out his inkwell, and start copying the papers he brought home with him. If, however, there were no more papers to copy, he would make another copy for his own pleasure."

It is Akakij Akakievič's acceptance of suffering that unites him with most saints, particularly with St. Acacius of Sinai. In hagiography it sometimes happened that a saint was tormented by his brethren or by demons disguised as messengers of God. Akakij Akakievič suffered ill treatment at the hands of his fellow workers: "The young clerks laughed and cracked jokes about him. . . . They told made-up stories about him in his presence. . . . They showered bits of paper on his head and called it snow. But never a word did Akakij Akakievič say to this, as if there were no one there." St. Acacius of Sinai showed this same quiet perseverance under the cruel torments of his elder. However, as we noted in his vita, "He did not endure his torment unthinkingly, for by his uncomplaining endurance and innocent sufferings he secured the grace of God which would save him from eternal torment." Akakij Akakievič, on the other hand, did not persevere because of an exalted idea. He is an insignificant man performing a small task with no thought as to why he does so. "It would be hard to find a person who lived his job as much as he. That's not all: he served ardently—nay, with love." Indeed, he saw a varied and pleasant world in his copying, so much so that he had certain favorite letters.

Although no philosophy underlay Akakij Akakievič's diligence, he ultimately had the same effect upon certain of his tormentors as did St. Acacius of Sinai upon the cruel elder. A new clerk, attempting to have some fun at Akakij Akakievič's expense, desisted suddenly ("as though pierced through the heart") upon hearing the latter's mild plea, "Leave me alone, why do you pester me?" "And from that time on everything changed for him and took on a different appearance. A kind of unnatural force repelled him from his colleagues, whom he had taken for decent, well-bred men." Moreover, Akakij Akakievič's pathetic plea becomes a Christian message, for in it the young clerk thought he heard the words, "I am your brother." And as the words of St. Acacius of Sinai from the grave caused his elder to prostrate himself in tears, Akakij Akakievič's specter made a "deep impression" on the Very Important Person. To be sure, Akakij Akakievič's "conversions" were on a lower level: it was not his example that led others onto the righteous path, but rather their realization that they had taken advantage of a pathetic nonentity.

In his clothing Akakij Akakievič resembles a monk. Yet travesty is in evidence here also, since he did not neglect his clothing for ascetic reasons. His tattered clothes simply reflect his meager salary, which in turn reflects his capabilities.

In hagiography, a saint shunned the activities of his contemporaries and occupied himself with spiritual pursuits. Akakij Akakievič "had not once in his life paid attention to what goes on every day in the street." Gogol emphasizes the introverted and inconsequential nature of Akakij Akakievič's thoughts, contrasted to the elevated thoughts of a saint, with the following example: "If a horse's muzzle, appearing from some unknown place, came to rest on his shoulder and blew a gale on his cheek from its nostrils, only then did he notice that he was not in the middle of a line, but rather in the middle of the street."

The hagiographer frequently places an eloquent prayer on the lips of a saint in an attempt to illustrate the saint's spiritual elevation. Akakij Akakievič, however, "for the most part expressed himself in prepositions, adverbs, and such particles as have decidedly no meaning whatsoever." Rather than illustrating a lofty mind, Akakij Akakievič's words bear witness to an empty mind. The words of St. Acacius of Sinai, on the other hand, are those of one who has consciously accepted suffering and regards it as one of the most important steps toward his goal.

Only when Akakij Akakievič is provided with a definite goal (which, it should be noted, was not of his own choosing, but a matter of necessity) do his acts begin to approximate the conscious ascetic conduct of a monk. The overcoat becomes for Akakij Akakievič an object of veneration worthy of great personal sacrifices. For the overcoat he cuts down his already minimal expenses, omits his evening tea, does away with candles and walks carefully to avoid wearing out his shoes. "He even got used to going hungry in the evenings, for he was nourished spiritually, ever bearing in his thoughts the idea of his future overcoat." Akakij Akakievič's character at this point becomes more fully delineated along the lines of a saint: "His whole existence seemed now somehow to have become fuller, as if he had gotten married. . . . He became more lively, and even firmer in character, like a man who had already defined and set himself a goal. Doubt vanished from his face and his actions as did indecision, and so did all of his vague and vacillating characteristics. At times a gleam would appear in his eyes. . . ."

Five days after his burial in the monastery, St. Acacius of Sinai spoke from beyond the grave, causing his elder to fall prostrate in tears, repenting his cruel treatment of his disciple, and to devote himself to the salvation of his soul. A few days after his interment in the municipal cementery, Akakij Akakievič appears in the streets of St. Petersburg, disappearing only after he has stolen an overcoat from the Very Important Person, a symbolic divestment which frightens the latter out of his wits and causes him to become much more considerate of his subordinates. Akakij Akakievič's "miracle" is immediately undercut with the following: "The police were given orders to catch the dead man at all costs, dead or alive, and to punish him most severely as an example to others." The events themselves, however, provide perhaps the most structurally significant link between Akakij Akakievič Bašmačkin and St. Acacius of Sinai: without them we would not have the miracle which is required for sainthood. Furthermore, the treatment of them by Gogol is consistent with the intent to travesty which it has been the purpose of this paper to demonstrate.

Elizabeth C. Shepard (essay date 1974)

"Pavlov's 'Demon' and Gogol's 'Overcoat'," in *Slavic Review,* Vol. 33, No. 2, June, 1974, pp. 288-301.

[*Below, Shepard postulates that "The Demon" by N. F. Pavlov inspired "The Overcoat" and that in some ways Gogol's story is a response to Pavlov's.*]

On Sunday, February 24, 1852, the epilogue to the tragicomedy which was N. V. Gogol's life was played out in the University Chapel in Moscow. Curiosity seekers, government officials, members of high society—"people who had not wanted to know Gogol during his lifetime," Khomiakov bitterly remarked later—thronged the final rites performed over the writer's emaciated body. Among the crowd in the chapel was Gogol's old acquaintance, N. F. Pavlov (1803-64), a former serf, actor, university student, law clerk, and journalist who had made his way into Moscow's *beau monde* and had married a wealthy heiress. Several days after the funeral, Pavlov set down his reaction to it in a letter to A. V. Venevitinov:

> He was buried with due respect and with all possible honors. . . . The deceased's body was brought to the university chapel. Students stood watch day and night. Zakrevsky [the governor general of Moscow] came to the funeral service with his ribbon on. In farewell, a laurel wreath was torn to bits; everyone wanted some

of it, if only a leaf, as a keepsake. Khomiakov and those of his mind were displeased; they had opposed holding the funeral service in the university chapel, asserting that it was too much like a salon, that the class of people which Gogol had most esteemed would not enter it, and that this funeral was a civil, not a religious act. All the others and I were of a completely opposite opinion. Gogol's funeral should have had the social character which it did. The beggars, footmen, and tradespeople whom they [Khomiakov et al.] wanted would not have come even to a parish church, because to appreciate a writer one has to be literate, and anyway that class of people has always preferred an affected literature to a literature of genius. Count Zakrevsky hasn't read Gogol, but he came to the funeral, whereas the Moscow merchants, who also haven't read him and who consequently have the same rights, did not come. . . . Most curious and striking of all was the gossip among the populace during the service. There was a swarm of anecdotes. They all were trying to find out what the rank of the deceased had been. The policemen speculated that he was some kind of important count or prince. No one could imagine that it was a writer whose funeral was being held. One cart driver finally assured them that it was the chief clerk at the university who had died; that is, not the one who makes copies, but the one who knows how to address each person in writing—the sovereign, some general or other, whomsoever.

Witty, urbane, even cynical, Pavlov must have enjoyed embriodering upon a basic situation which offered such an opportunity to poke fun at the Slavophile enthusiasms of his Muscovite friends and to indulge in a bit of discreet irony at "their" writer's expense: the rumors, the speculation, and the confusion, the policemen and the driver, and the ironic *pointe* of the boldly asserted mistaken identity—a clerk. What could be a more fitting encomium to the creator of Akakii Akakievich? But perhaps a deeper irony was intended.

In 1835, while Gogol was privately complaining about the slow sales of his *Arabesques* and *Mirgorod,* Pavlov's first collection of stories, *Three Stories,* was sold out within a few weeks of its publication, and Pavlov was riding the crest of a literary notoriety which shortly was enhanced by official censure of the book. Amidst a welter of travel accounts, philosophic, fantastic, historical, and neosentimental stories, and tales with Caucasian, Eastern, and Ukrainian settings, Pavlov's stories struck their readers as refreshingly contemporary, a quality which was all the more titillating in view of their evident dependence on the most recent French models. Frequently compared with Balzac, of whose works he was the first Russian translator, Pavlov shared with his great French contemporary a piercing insight into the mechanisms of social power and an overriding interest in the themes of money and social mobility. A pragmatist whose later political thought would owe a debt to English utilitarianism, Pavlov conceived of human nature in terms of self-interest. In his society stories, vanity (*samoliubie*), as both an innate and an acquired trait, was exposed as the major moving force in human events. Starting from the premise that by masking self-interest with idealism people are consciously or unconsciously dishonest with themselves and with others, Pavlov probed the quality of that dishonesty, and dramatized its consequences. The tsar and Count Uvarov were not alone among Pavlov's contemporaries in finding this viewpoint offensive. S. P. Shevyrev, for example, found Pavlov's unidealized treatment of his female protagonists "impermissible." And V. G. Belinsky, although he included Pavlov on the list he compiled in 1835 of the six writers who constituted the "full circle of the history of the Russian short story," was suspicious of the kind of "truth" which he found in Pavlov's stories, and which he contrasted by implication with the truth embodied in Gogol's works.

Pavlov's second volume of three stories, *New Stories,* appeared in 1839. Here, in "The Masquerade" and "A Million," Pavlov continued his investigation of high society and its "domestic secrets." But in "The Demon" Pavlov focused on a plebeian protagonist who was increasingly commanding the attention of Russian writers—the "unfortunate petty clerk" (*bednyi chinovnik*).

Andrei Ivanovich, the middle-aged hero of "The Demon," is a clerk of unspecified rank who works in an unnamed department of the immense imperial bureaucracy in St. Petersburg. The one incongruous note in his modest existence is his wife, a nineteen-year-old beauty whose taste for luxury he indulges insofar as he is able, but from whom he is in fact as estranged as he is from his fellow workers and society at large. Andrei Ivanovich's tedious work as a copyist had colored his entire existence: "the regular flow of his life, and his habitual regularity, formality and sense of order had saved him from developing unrealizable desires, and from making dangerous comparisons between himself and others." But late one night, as he sits gazing out over the "enchanted" capital, "incorporeal inspiration, like an invisible sprite" descends upon him, and he is "re-born." Invested with demonic vision, he suddenly perceives the disparity between the haves and the have-nots, and questions why this must be so. The following night he conceives a plan (which is not revealed to the reader), and falteringly writes out a petition. Early the next morning he calls at the office a General, where, by means of a bribe, he succeeds in having the document accepted. He returns several days later, and after a prolonged wait is admitted into that inner sanctum of bureaucratic power, the private office of a General. Here, the story's climactic confrontation between the Little Man and the System takes place. Tongue-tied by years of silent humility, Andrei Ivanovich gropingly describes his lifelong devotion to duty, and at last blurts out the reason for his visit: the General has "offended" him by stealing his wife's affections, he claims. Outraged, the General orders him to leave. But Andrei Ivanovich's plan works as he knew it would. After several minutes, the General summons a clerk and casually obtains the information that Andrei Ivanovich's wife is indeed beautiful. Sometime later, Andrei Ivanovich is discovered in a new apartment, with a servant in attendance, a carriage and pair at the door, and an Anna (the Order of Saint Anne) around his neck. No longer obliged to go to the office, he receives callers and affably responds to their admiration of his

success: "True, true, my dear fellow. Where there's a will, there's a way."

This brief précis does not begin to convey the thoroughness with which the Petersburg thematic complex is exploited in "The Demon." As is typical of Pavlov's technique, the relatively uneventful plot is heavily overlaid with descriptive and psychological detail. But the précis does suggest an important way in which Pavlov's treatment of the unfortunate petty clerk ran counter to the prevailing mode of that figure's portrayal in Russian fiction of the time. While apparently responding to the advent of what Belinsky had announced to be the "popular" era in Russian literature, Pavlov retained in "The Demon" the detached and skeptical narrative tone of the "urbane" (*svetskii*) persona which had informed his society stories. And it is evident that such a narrative tone violated the existing generic norms of the *chinovnik* story. Indeed, in the opinion of a Soviet scholar, this is the chief difference between the two story forms: "But the most important difference of the *chinovnik* story [from the society story]—its basic pathos—consists of the author's palpitating sympathy for the little man . . ." [M. A. Belkina, "'Svetskaia povest'' 30-kh godov i 'Kniaginia Ligovskaia' Lermontova," *Zhizn' i tvorchestvo M. Iu. Lermontova,* 1941]. This sympathy may be evidenced in interpolated authorial commentary, and in the weighting of descriptive detail to evoke compassion for the protagonist. The narrative's central conflict may be structured around a collision of the Individual and the State. The more modest the Little Man's attempt to extract any benefit from the System, the more pathetic his failure to do so may be made to appear. The inevitability of his failure is a central premise. An ethical evaluation may therefore be implicit in the outcome of the narrative: although he is defeated, the clerk-protagonist wins a moral victory, since by the very fact of his inability to confront the System on its terms, he demonstrates his moral superiority to it.

Elaborated during the 1820s and early 1830s, the conventions of the *chinovnik* story were authoritatively established in the mid-1830s by Gogol's **"Notes of a Madman"** (1835) and Pushkin's "The Bronze Horseman" (1837). But the exemplary *chinovnik* story in Russian fiction is Gogol's **"The Overcoat"** (1842). It is a story which is curiously reminiscent of Pavlov's "The Demon." At the end of September 1839, Gogol arrived in Russia after spending over three years abroad. He brought sketches for **"The Overcoat"** with him. His arrival thus coincided with the time when interest in Pavlov's *New Stories* was at its height. These considerations suggest the possibility that, as at least two of their contemporaries seem to have thought (see below), Pavlov's story may have contributed in some way to the creation of Gogol's masterpiece. What can be discovered that might link Gogol's writing of **"The Overcoat"** with a knowledge of "The Demon"? What interactions between the two texts point to "The Demon" as a putative source for **"The Overcoat,"** and what might have motivated this hypothetical relationship?

Scholars have concluded that Gogol began work on **"The Overcoat"** in July 1839, while in Marienbad. M. P. Pogodin arrived in Marienbad on July 9, and sometime during the month he spent there he took down the preliminary sketch from Gogol's dictation. Gogol resumed work on it a month later in Vienna, where he spent the better part of August and September, leaving for Moscow with Pogodin (who had rejoined him) on September 22. This second sketch represents a reworking of the beginning of the story, plus the addition of the episode concerning the clerk's birth and an outline of his visit to the tailor. Thus when Gogol returned to Russia, the story was still in a very fragmentary state (in print the fragment amounts to three pages of a quarto volume).

Several clues to the genesis of **"The Overcoat"** have been cited by literary historians, who have been especially inclined to entertain any plausible evidence concerning the sources of Gogol's works, since his chronic inability to think up story ideas is well attested. One of these clues is Annenkov's well-known statement about the *chinovnik* anecdote, which he says Gogol heard sometime in the mid-1830s. Another is the suggestion offered by the editors of the Academy edition of Gogol's works (but not repeated in subsequent editions), that Gogol was intrigued by one or more anecdotes told by a companion in Marienbad. A third clue, which is frequently cited, is contained in a letter Gogol wrote to his mother in 1830, in which he relates how, for lack of funds, he had to make do that winter with his summer overcoat. But what about "The Demon"? Could Gogol have been acquainted with it before he began work on **"The Overcoat"**? Or could his subsequent reading of "The Demon" have had some effect on the way the initial story idea was elaborated?

Initially, the first suggestion seems unlikely. Not only is it doubtful that Gogol (who had been abroad since the summer of 1836) could have heard anything substantive about "The Demon," but also, in view of the fact that *New Stories* could not have appeared before the end of June 1839 (and probably not until the second half of July), a copy could not have reached him until well after he had begun **"The Overcoat."** But there was another, indirect route by which the story could have reached him. It is only natural to assume that when Pogodin arrived in Marienbad, Gogol would have been anxious to hear news of his old circle of Moscow acquaintances and their literary activities. The imminent publication of a volume by one of Gogol's "close friends" would surely have been interesting to him. All the more so since one story in the book, "The Demon," represented an incursion into the territory of Gogol's own writing. Pogodin not only knew of the stories, but, as his diary shows, he had already read them.

Gogol and Pogodin arrived in Moscow on September 26, just before *New Stories* became available there. A month later Gogol left for St. Petersburg, traveling with S. T. Aksakov, who reports that Gogol read Pavlov's new volume at this time, and reread it shortly thereafter—that is, at the time when he resumed work on **"The Overcoat."** Thus, not only could Gogol have known Pavlov's story before he began **"The Overcoat,"** but he certainly knew it well before more than a few pages of his story were written.

The two stories present similar structural profiles. Of the same length (some thirty-one pages of a crown octavo volume), they include casts of characters who fulfill similar plot functions: the clerks; the wife ("The Demon"), the tailor and his wife (**"The Overcoat"**); the Generals; various episodic clerks and functionaries; and the *fantastic* city itself. The events of "The Demon" are distributed among five chapters, a narrative schema with which the events of **"The Overcoat"** can be made to coincide, as it were, fortuitously.

> **Not only could Gogol have known Pavlov's story before he began "The Overcoat," but he certainly knew it well before more than a few pages of his story were written.**
>
> —*Elizabeth C. Shepard*

Both narratives open with a portrait of the clerk-protagonist whose monotonous existence is depicted against a background of the bustling life of his department and the surrounding city. Middle-aged copy clerks (Andrei is forty-five, Akakii over fifty), they are superannuated fixtures in the offices where they have served for decades. . . .

Their offices are filled with much younger men who either ignore them or occasionally tease them, and neither Andrei nor Akakii choose to participate in the limited social life available to them, which in both stories includes going to clerks' parties, eating in restaurants, and looking in shop windows (a particularly dangerous activity, associated with sexual fantasies). The city itself is hostile territory where inimical forces lie in wait for Andrei and Akakii. This perilous passage, which must be braved twice a day, links office with home, public with private life, and work with leisure. But these two sectors are barely distinguishable, since they encompass the same activity—copying. . . .

Thus the chief mode of existence for both clerks is isolation—a state of nearly total social exclusion which in both stories is conveyed through an inability to communicate verbally (a handicap which Andrei finally overcomes, but which Akakii only overcomes in afterlife). The "calm flow" of their isolated lives is not, however, destined to last. External reality intrudes on their closed worlds, introducing the necessity for change: Andrei realizes that his wife's material wants outstrip his ability to provide for them, and Akakii realizes that his overcoat is inadequate to withstand the rigors of the Petersburg winter. Both face the problem of money; and, for both, what the money is needed for becomes an obsession.

Ensuing events involve fantasy, through the association of the protagonists' new material concerns with supernatural (diabolic) forces. This association is realized in the following sections of both works: in "The Demon" in the nocturnal scene during which Andrei is possessed by the demonic spirit of his newly raised consciousness, and in **"The Overcoat"** in Akakii's dealings with the tailor.

Having "awakened" to reality, the two clerks have acquired a new purposefulness, which is then tested in confrontations with the city and with the bureaucracy. Carrying his petition, Pavlov's clerk makes his harrowing trip across Petersburg, assaulted from all sides by the sights and sounds of "egotism" and "greed." Reaching the General's residence, he has his initial encounter with the System. Clothed in his new overcoat, Gogol's clerk makes *his* trip across Petersburg, and is assaulted by robbers who take his coat. He also seeks official redress for a wrong, and, like Andrei, finds that his way to the authorities is momentarily blocked by an equivocating underling.

These preliminary encounters are followed by the climactic scene of the interview between the clerk and the General (the rank of Gogol's Very Important Person is revealed once). Gogol's treatment of this scene closely parallels Pavlov's: the wait in the antechamber, the clerk's tongue-tied state, the General's sense of power, the hyperbolization of the distance separating the adversaries, the General's taking offense at a mild verbal impropriety, and the enraged order to leave, uttered in a shout. The epilogues of the two narratives reflect their opposite resolution of the Little Man's confrontation with the System. His obsession fulfilled by means of a fictitious injury, Andrei Ivanovich emerges into the daytime world of the capital and sheds his nocturnal aspect, his "spirit" self. The fulfillment of his obsession thwarted by a very real injury, Akakii Akakievich dies, and reappears to haunt the Petersburg nights as a "phantom."

Although these similarities are suggestive of a relationship between "The Demon" and **"The Overcoat"** which goes beyond their generic kinship, the present argument would be strengthened if their equally obvious differences were discovered to correlate with their similarities. In short, what in Pavlov's story might have prompted a response from Gogol?

It is apparent that Pavlov's resolution of the confrontation between the Little Man and the System is unconventional and, furthermore, is predicated on a cynical view of human nature and society (Reality) which is the antithesis of the idealist world view embodied in the conventions of the *chinovnik* story. Pavlov's clerk is the image of self-interest, and this petty demon triumphs through his accommodation to, and masterful manipulation of, the System and its values. "The Demon" is a travesty of the *chinovnik* story, a comic *quid pro quo* which mocks the reader's expectations of philanthropic pathos. Just as in Pavlov's society stories, where stereotypes of upper-class characters such as the Byronic Hero and the Idealized Heroine are unmasked (cf. in particular the companion pieces of "The Demon" in *New Stories.* "The Masquerade" and "A Million"), in "The Demon" Pavlov offers a critique of the stereotyped features then coalescing in the figure of the unfortunate petty clerk.

Pavlov's satiric intent is signaled in the opening paragraph of the story: "Andrei Ivanovich was either not educated or not rich enough to use a wax candle, but at the same time he clearly had such nobility of soul that he did not spare tallow. A small room served as his study. It was cleaner than any clerk's study in the whole rest of Russia." Having pointed the joke with Gogolian hyperbole, Pavlov continues in the same vein with a description of the room's modest accessories:

> Moreover, several objects demonstrated that the owner [of the room] was not always swimming in ink, was not always occupied with work, but permitted himself to enjoy life, to diversify his interests, and was sensible to the need of enlightenment and thirsted for poetry. It was particularly evident that, fortunately, he did not read foreign languages, but nourished himself solely on the works of his native land. Consequently, he was in the fortunate position of the Turk who does not see other men's wives. A nice little Alexandrine column made of bronze, several lithographs of Russian manufacture, one issue of some journal or other, two or three volumes of some sorts of stories, and a nightingale in a cage satisfied the whims of mind and heart. . . . I almost forgot the room's most important ornament— a pile of business papers.

> Thus, wherever Andrei Ivanovich might turn, he was confronted with the familiar, with the native: a book by a Russian writer, a picture by a Russian artist, a case from a Russian court, and a nightingale from a Russian grove.

At this point, certain of Pavlov's Muscovite friends must have begun to suspect that in this portrait of "patriarchal custom" their witty friend was preparing a trap for their proto-Slavophile sensibilities. They would have been right. For while "The Demon" is a demonstration of the universality of human self-interestedness, its protagonist is not simply Everyman, he is emphatically a Russian Everyman. Andrei Ivanovich, the quintessentially Russian Little Man, the "sleepy, patient, useful, virtuous" clerk, will "awaken" to life as it really is, and will demand his share. Most significantly, in terms of the developing controversies between Slavophiles and Westernizers, the rebellion of the clerk is pointedly not the result of contagion by foreign notions. Rather, Pavlov's story implies that the true foreign notions are those which are projected on the Little Man by the idealistic Russian intelligentsia.

The thrust of Pavlov's argument did not escape his informed contemporaries, progressives and conservatives alike. Ivan Panaev, Belinsky's close companion at the time, asserted in 1839 that "owing to the strained quality of its content . . . 'The Demon' had to be told *in the most extremely strained manner,* thereby exposing its author's most unpleasant view of life." That *unpleasantness*—a worldly, morally detached skepticism—also provoked Shevyrev. An erstwhile intimate of Pavlov who in the 1840s had become almost a "disciple" of Gogol, Shevyrev commented in 1846: "In an outburst of irritable satire . . . Pavlov described in 'The Demon' the total moral abasement to which that victim [the *chinovnik*] of social conditions could descend. . . . Perhaps 'The Demon' gave rise to Gogol's **'The Overcoat.'"** Shevyrev's comments clearly spring from a consideration of the moral action of the respective stories, and it is evident that from this point of view **"The Overcoat"** can be read as a direct reply to "The Demon," as a refutation of Pavlov's view of human, or at least Russian, nature.

Pavlov's story presents a harsh picture of human nature as innately and incorrigibly materialistic. Gogol's story, on the other hand, seems to offer the assurance that although human nature and the world itself are tainted with corruption, they are, to some degree at least, perfectible.

—*Elizabeth C. Shepard*

Pavlov's story presents a harsh picture of human nature as innately and incorrigibly materialistic, and of life as an unceasing round of deception and "oppression of one's neighbors" in the struggle for advantages—"money, power, women"—which are distributed by the "injustice of fate." Gogol's story, on the other hand, seems to offer the assurance that although human nature and the world itself are tainted with corruption, they are, to some degree at least, perfectible. Where Gogol's narrative holds out the hope of a higher moral law, or otherworldly retribution, Pavlov's narrative is thoroughly secular, and he notes only that the efficacy of moral restraints imposed by traditional religious beliefs is subverted by hypocrisy. Pavlov's General gains the favors of a young mistress. Nothing occurs which would alter his relations with others; indeed, his vanity and sense of power have been enhanced. Gogol's General, accosted by Akakii's ghost, abandons his plan to visit his mistress, and rushes home to his family. From then on he thinks twice before shouting at his subordinates. Pavlov's clerk, who has deliberately gone about losing his wife, is recompensed for this loss by a large share of life's advantages: a spacious apartment in the fashionable quarter of the city, servants, new status, and leisure. His former coworkers gape admiringly at his success, as totally undisconcerted as he himself is by the means of its accomplishment. Gogol's clerk, whose coat was torn from him, dies brokenhearted and delirious, and is shoved into a pine coffin. He leaves an estate of quill pens, copy paper, socks, buttons, and a threadbare garment. His death is almost overlooked by his coworkers, and within a week another faceless clerk sits in his place.

Andrei Ivanovich's success is assured by the discovery he makes in the antechamber to the General's office, where he "corrects the false opinions" that he had held of others. He sees that self-interest and obsequiousness before superior rank are concealed beneath the polished exteriors of all those who had formerly seemed so worldly and pow-

erful; he sees that they are all the "same sorts of Andrei Ivanoviches"; and he therefore "recognizes his neighbors *as his brothers*" (italics added). But Gogol's reader is led through pathos to a different discovery. For although there can be no denying that "savage coarseness . . . is even to be discovered in the man whom the world considers noble and honorable," this falls away at the sudden recognition of the communality of humankind:

> "Leave me alone. Why do you insult me?" And there was a strange ring in those words and in the voice in which they were uttered. In that voice could be heard something that moved one to compassion—so much so that one young man, recently appointed, who followed the example set by the rest and permitted himself to ridicule him, suddenly stopped as though pierced to the quick, and from that time on, everything seemed to change for him and to appear in a different light; some unknown force seemed to repel him from the comrades with whom he had become acquainted because he thought they were decent, well-bred men. And for a long time afterward, during his happiest moments, he could visualize the little clerk with the bald spot on his forehead, and hear his heartrending words: "Leave me alone! Why do you insult me?" And in those heartrending words, he caught the ringing sound of others: *"I am your brother"* (italics added).

Pavlov's *chinovnik* story breaks with convention most markedly in its avoidance of pathos, in its view of the Little Man as a shrewd opportunist rather than as a helpless victim. Pavlov's uncompromising rejection of the philanthropism and neosentimentalism which are prominent in popular Russian fiction at the close of the romantic era was yet another "impermissible" act on his part:

> For example, compare **"The Overcoat"** with a story that has a basic situation which is almost identical to it—"The Demon," by the talented writer N. F. Pavlov. Just compare the scene with the superior officer in each man's story! And by the way, reading "The Demon" you cannot help but acknowledge that talent is clearly present here, that the analysis here is extraordinarily deep. Perhaps it is precisely because the analysis tries too hard to be deep that the talent takes the monsters of its fantastically attuned imagination for real, living creations, and the sufferings of poor Andrei Petrovich [*sic*], who has been possessed by the idea that a poor existence will wear out the life of his pretty little better half, grow to unbelievably colossal proportions, and what is strange is that the more they try to grow, the less capable you become of *sympathizing* with them, and the whole of the author's *pathos* is wasted. On the other hand, how simply told is the clerks' behavior with Akakii Akakievich, and his grief at the loss of his overcoat. *Your heart is wrung,* and at the same time, in a transport of ecstasy, you revel in that *truthful* artistic analysis [Apollon Grigor'ev, *Literaturnaia kritika,* 1967; italics added].

Thus, in the nationalistically oriented mainstream of post-1840 Russian criticism, **"The Overcoat"** could be viewed as a standard against which works by writers such as Pavlov could be measured in the continuing process of discrediting elitism, cosmopolitanism, and lack of "truth" in Russian prose fiction. But Gogol himself appears to reveal a polemical lining in his garment when he implies at the outset of **"The Overcoat"** that he is coming to the defense of the *chinovnik,* "a person who, as everyone knows, has been sneered at and joked about at will by various writers who have the praiseworthy habit of setting upon those who cannot stand up for themselves." For whom besides N. F. Pavlov could this gibe have been tailor-made?

Simon Karlinsky (essay date 1976)

The Sexual Labyrinth of Nikolai Gogol, Harvard University Press, 1976, 333 p.

[*In this thematic study the critic argues that Gogol's story is a romantic tale with the overcoat representing the love interest.*]

The single most famous short story in the whole of Russian literature, **"The Overcoat"** is also the most widely misunderstood. Russian critics of the nineteenth century enveloped it in a thick fog of sentimentalization. It was credited with being the beginning of the philanthropic trend in Russian literature, the first depiction of the "insulted and injured" little man, the first realistic depiction of poverty and any number of other literary firsts, to which historically it did not have the slightest claim. The celebrated and oft-quoted maxim "We all emerged from under Gogol's overcoat," long incorrectly attributed to Dostoyevsky and ultimately traced to the turn-of-the-century French critic Melchior de Vogüé, implied that Russian realism in its totality grew out of this one story. Such a view remains widespread to this day, despite the availability of the epoch-making studies of this story by Boris Eichenbaum and Dmitry Čiževsky, who conclusively proved decades ago just how wrong and historically unfounded the traditional reputation of **"The Overcoat"** is.

Humanitarian concerns, philanthropic sympathy for the downtrodden, and concern for the "little people" had been a part of Russian literature since the Sentimentalist tales Nikolai Karamzin wrote in the 1790s; oppressed and exploited peasants were featured in comic operas with texts by Nikolev and Kniazhnin that Catherine the Great herself warmly applauded back in the 1770s. A poor, insignificant mail carrier, depicted with great sympathy and compassion, was the protagonist of Pogorelsky's "The Poppy Seed Cake Woman of Lafertovo" (1825); realistically portrayed poor and humble government clerks are found in Pushkin's "The Bronze Horseman" (1833), in Lermontov's unfinished novel *Princess Ligovskaya* (1836), and in a host of works by their lesser contemporaries. Even the archreactionary government flunky and spy Faddei Bulgarin published in the late 1820s a story about a poor and virtuous cab driver. By 1841, when **"The Overcoat"** was completed, there was absolutely nothing left to pioneer along these lines—Gogol was simply offering his own treatment of one of the most widespread themes and situations in the literature of his time.

Sociologically, what is remarkable about **"The Overcoat"** is not its portrayal of poverty, which was ordinary enough at the time, but its description of urban alienation. It is this aspect of the story that firmly places it within the context of the other stories of the St. Petersburg cycle, written some five years before it. But while the heroes of the other St. Petersburg stories chafe under the burden of loneliness and alienation, the hero of **"The Overcoat"** seems to have chosen them of his own free will as his natural mode of existence. The real literary triumph of **"The Overcoat"** is neither the rather obvious sentimentalist episode of the young man who taunts Akaky Akakievich and then realizes with dismay that he has been hurting a fellow human being nor the moving little requiem that Gogol sings after his protagonist's death, but the sympathy the story arouses in the reader for the least human and least prepossessing character in all literature, a man whom the author, furthermore, systematically undercuts and ridicules.

The very name Akaky Akakievich Bashmachkin is calculated to invite contempt and derision. The original Greek name Acacius (it occurs in Voltaire as Akakiah) means "immaculate" or "without blemish," but its Russian version sounds in pronunciation suspiciously as if it might be derived from *okakat'* or *obkakat',* "to beshit," "to cover with excrement." Russian adults, who have been familiar with **"The Overcoat"** and its hero for most of their lives, fail to perceive the connection, but Russian children who hear the name Akaky Akakievich for the first time usually giggle and look embarrassed. With his hemorrhoidal complexion, his untidy clothes always bespattered with garbage, with watermelon rinds and melon peelings clinging to his hat, and the flies in his soup he eats without noticing them, to say nothing of his excremental name, Akaky Akakievich is a character who would hardly seem calculated to arouse the reader's sympathy or to be appealing.

Gogol downgrades the man's mentality and his personal character with equal ruthlessness. An incoherent, almost mindless loner, on the verge of muteness and mental retardation, Akaky Akakievich speaks "for the most part in prepositions, adverbs, and, finally, such particles as have absolutely no meaning." He has no interest in the surrounding world, of which he takes notice only as much as is necessary to insure his bare survival. Compared to him, even the withdrawn Ivan Shponka is a model of awareness and involvement. His life is reduced to copying documents, which he does for a living at work and for his own amusement at home—a copying machine in human form that is unaware of the contents of the documents and is concerned solely with the written characters it copies. There are no other dimensions to Akaky Akakievich's character and no other interests in his life. Poprishchin in "Diary of a Madman" suffers from being at the bottom of the social and administrative ladder; Akaky Akakievich remains there by choice, stubbornly resisting all efforts to promote him to a higher rung and deliberately excluding himself from all human contact and all sociability, because this is the only way he is able to exist. In this manner he survives to the age of fifty, although his withdrawn mode of existence resembles that of a clam or an oyster more than that of a human being. All this needs to be said not in order to belittle Akaky Akakievich, which would be inhuman, but to point out, in view of the story's stubborn reputation as a paragon of compassionate humanitarianism, just who this person in the center of the story is and just what Gogol does to him and with him.

Several accounts of the origin of **"The Overcoat"** are cited in the literature about Gogol. The most frequently quoted version stems from the memoirs of Pavel Annenkov, not always the most reliable source, despite its author's one-time close association with Gogol. According to Annenkov, the story evolved from an anecdote Gogol heard about a poor civil servant who coveted a hunting rifle, got one by scraping and saving, and lost it by dropping it into the water the very first time he went duck shooting. Far more likely is the derivation of this story from a literary source, "The Demon" (1839) by Nikolai Pavlov, a prose writer whose work Gogol vastly admired and publicly championed on several recorded occasions. The connection between these two works, first pointed out by the nineteenth-century critics Stepan Shevyryov (in 1846) and Apollon Grigoryev (in 1859), has recently been conclusively demonstrated by Elizabeth C. Shepard [in "Pavlov's 'Demon' and Gogol's 'Overcoat,' *Slavic Review*, June 1974]. What unites the two stories is not only the several close textual parallels cited by Shepard in her essay, but also the basic love triangle between the poor and humble elderly government clerk, the haughty and pompous high official who is the clerk's superior, and the clerk's pretty young wife. Gogol's device of replacing the human wife with a feminine-gender object, while typical of him in general, became a highly original stroke when it was introduced into the situation borrowed from Pavlov's story. In order to make his point, Gogol had to reject the usual Russian word for overcoat, which is neuter, and name his story after a special model with a cape and fur collar, *shinel'* (this style was called a "carrick" in English, according to the findings of Vladimir Nabokov) that is feminine in gender. The textual references to the overcoat as Akaky Akakievich's "life's companion" and "the radiant guest" who shares his earthly existence are also all in the feminine gender in Russian (this very essential dimension of the story is lost in the English translations). The Soviet film based on **"The Overcoat,"** which starred Roland Bykov and was shown on American television, drove this point home still further by having Akaky Akakievich hold a lighted candle and place another next to the overcoat that is spread on his bed—a clear reference to the Orthodox wedding ceremony.

"The Overcoat" is thus in essence a love story, the most genuine, touching, and honest one in Gogol's entire *oeuvre*. This fact, although not noticed by Gogol scholars until Dmitry Čiževsky, demonstrated it in 1937, had been intuitively understood by two of Gogol's important younger contemporaries who wrote what were meant as ripostes and correctives to **"The Overcoat."** Dostoyevsky's first novel, *Poor Folk*, written in 1845 (four years after the publication of Gogol's story) and Ivan Turgenev's play *The Bachelor* (1849) both depicted elderly, poor, and lonely government clerks living in situations similar to that of Akaky Akakievich. However, instead of becoming sentimentally attached to an overcoat, Dostoyevsky's and Turgenev's characters become involved with real young women and find fulfillment in helping these women cope with the problems and difficulties they face. Dostoyevsky's protagonist (who reads **"The Overcoat"** in the course of the novel and protests vehemently that it distorts reality and slanders people like himself) loses the companionship of the young woman he befriends as heartbreakingly as Akaky Akakievich loses his overcoat. But Turgenev's kindly and resourceful elderly clerk (it was a role Turgenev wrote especially for Gogol's actor-friend Shchepkin) is actually preferred by the young woman to the superficial and heartless young man with whom she is involved at the beginning of the play. The desire on Dostoyevsky's and Turgenev's part to correct the Gogolian situation in **"The Overcoat,"** their urge to bring things closer to what is probable and possible in real life, shows their penetrating understanding of the basic mechanics of Gogol's masterpiece. But it also betrays their inability to grasp that, given his basic character, Gogol simply could not have handled the amorous involvement between an older man and a younger woman in a way that appeared normal and natural to them. **"Diary of a Madman"** was his other approach to this situation and there the man's yearning for the young woman is seen as hopeless and ridiculous. Only by making the woman an inanimate object was Gogol able to write his tender and affecting romance between a man and a garment.

> **Gogol simply could not have handled the amorous involvement between an older man and a younger woman in a way that appeared normal. Only by making the woman an inanimate object was Gogol able to write his tender and affecting romance between a man and a garment.**
>
> —*Simon Karlinsky*

The love-story dimension of **"The Overcoat,"** though semisubmerged, is nonetheless a sure-fire ingredient to which every reader of the story responds without fail. Another, equally sure-fire ingredient is the comeuppance that the character known simply as "a very important person" gets at the hands of Akaky Akakievich's ghost for having mistreated and humiliated the poor clerk when he was alive. Here, for once, Gogol deliberately undercuts the supernatural element by revealing at the very end that what the "important person" saw as a ghost was in actuality the same robber who stole Akaky Akakievich's overcoat earlier. The revenge of the ghost strikes a responsive chord in all of us, because it is always satisfactory to see the hurt underdog retaliate against his persecutor. But Gogol would not be Gogol if he did not manage to connect both the lesson taught the "important person" and the downfall of Akaky Akakievich himself with punishment for yielding to a heterosexual amorous impulse. The "important person" has his frightening encounter with the supposed ghost just as he is leaving for an evening of dalliance at the home of the German lady he keeps. Terrified by the ghost, the "important person" gives up his plans for the evening and goes straight home. As for Akaky Akakievich, his chaste amorous involvement with his overcoat gradually leads him to do something he has apparently never done in the entire half century he has spent in this world: he starts noticing real women and responding to their sexual potential. The sequence of events is gradual, but unmistakable. After acquiring his longed-for "pleasant, life-long helpmeet," his next step is to take an unprecedented interest in a painting he sees in a shop window on his way to the party his colleague gives in honor of his new overcoat: "He stopped with curiosity before a lighted shop window to look at a painting in which a beautiful woman was shown removing her shoe and thereby baring her entire leg, which did not look at all bad, while behind her back a man with sideburns and a handsome goatee was peeking at her from the door." From the woman in the painting (this same painting, incidentally, had already appeared in **"The Nose,"** where it had an entirely different function), it is but a step to involvement with real women, and this indeed happens as Akaky Akakievich is returning home from the party: "Akaky Akakievich was walking along in a cheerful state of mind; he even started running, for no discernible reason, after a lady who walked past him like a streak of lightning and every part of whose body was in extraordinary agitation."

Akaky Akakievich quickly checks his impulse, but the retribution mechanism has already been set in motion by this violently physical female by her mere presence. It is immediately after his encounter with her that he is robbed of his most precious possession, the overcoat. He is handicapped in fighting for the return of his beloved object by his sense of being tainted, which others seem to be aware of as well: when he is received by the police official to whom he wants to report the robbery, he is asked whether he had visited a bawdy house (*neporyadochnyi dom*) at the time of the robbery. "Akaky Akakievich was totally embarrassed and went out, not knowing whether the authorities were going to look into the matter of his overcoat or not." He has the humiliating encounter with the "important person," falls ill, and resorts to profanity to express his state of mind as he lies dying, mourning to the end the loss of his overcoat and, possibly, of his innocence. **"The Overcoat"** ends the way so many other love stories involving a man and a woman end in Gogol—with the death of the male participant.

"The Overcoat" is the most perfect artistic embodiment of the two constant, cardinal Gogolian themes: the lethal nature of love and the destructive potential of change—any kind of change. The happiest environments in his work are always the ones in which time stands still and each

succeeding generation follows the same familiar and patriarchal mode of existence that the earlier ones did. Such is the world of **"Hanz Küchelgarten,"** of the light opera stories in the Dikanka cycle (**"Fair at Sorochintsy," "May Night," "Christmas Eve"**), of **"Ivan Fyodorovich Shponka and His Aunt"** and of **"Old-World Landowners."** This was also the world inhabited by the protagonists of **"Terrible Vengeance," "Taras Bulba,"** and **"Viy"** until the intervention of evil forces made a shambles of their well-adjusted lives. In his reclusive, bivalvelike existence, Akaky Akakievich was perfectly adjusted and happy. "It would be hard to find a man whose life was so totally devoted to his work," we are told at the beginning of the story. "To say that he worked with zeal is not enough— no, he worked with love. There, in his copying, he discerned a whole world of his own, varied and agreeable." Fate cannot touch Akaky Akakievich until he becomes involved with his overcoat. Overcoat spells love and love brings on change, and it is at this point that Akaky Akakievich becomes just as vulnerable as the other protagonists of the St. Petersburg cycle of stories. Acquisition of the overcoat takes him out of his routine, out of his own part of town, and even threatens to take him out of the safety of his social isolation. The underlying idea is of course that safety lies only in withdrawal from current life and in lack of action, an essentially ultra-conservative idea that is basic to all of Gogol's social and political thinking. It is odd indeed that the so-called progressive Russian critics, from Belinsky and Chernyshevsky to their present-day self-styled disciples in the Soviet Union, should extol **"The Overcoat"** and deplore *Selected Passages from Correspondence with Friends* as an incomprehensible aberration on Gogol's part, for the basic philosophical idea of these two works is one and the same: the desirability of total social stasis.

Like all major masterpieces, **"The Overcoat"** is capable of conveying new and different meanings to each succeeding epoch. The sentimentalist tirades that so impressed Gogol's contemporaries can now be seen for the literary convention they are. The theme of human solitude and of urban alienation that the story so powerfully sounds can speak much more eloquently to the twentieth-century imagination than it could have to the people of Gogol's time, since we know much more about such things than the nineteenth century ever did. After Dostoyevsky's *Notes from the Underground*, Chekhov's "Heartache" and "My Life," after Kafka's *The Trial* and Nabokov's *The Defense* and *Invitation to a Beheading*, we can see that **"The Overcoat"** was the initiator of the great modern tradition of writing about the solitary and vulnerable individual human being rejected or threatened by a dehumanized collective. This theme is important and appealing on many levels of modern consciousness and it has implications for many present-day societies. Bulat Okudzhava's song "The Last Trolley" was a big underground hit in the Soviet Union at about the time when the Beatles' "Eleanor Rigby" was a big commercial success in the West. Both of these songs deal in essence with the theme that Gogol developed in his story about a lonely man's loss of his overcoat, a story which was written in 1841.

Edward Proffitt (essay date 1977)

"Gogol's 'Perfectly True' Tale: 'The Overcoat' and Its Mode of Closure," in *Studies in Short Fiction,* Vol. 14, No. 1, Winter, 1977, pp. 35-40.

[*Here, Proffitt examines the purpose of the "fantastic ending" of "The Overcoat," concluding that it was intended by the author as a parody of poetic justice.*]

Gogol's **"The Overcoat"** has recently been called "one of the most elusive as well as one of the greatest of literary creations" [Charles Bernheimer, "Cloaking the Self: The Literary Space of Gogol's 'Overcoat,'" *PMLA* 90, January, 1975]. That it is great few would deny. And that it has proven elusive none could dispute. But wherein lies its elusiveness—in the twists and turns of the text itself or in the habitual evasions of the mind of the beholder? I suggest the latter, at least when it comes to the work's "fantastic ending," as Gogol would trick us into believing.

But before we continue, it might be best to have the key facts of the ending clearly in mind. The story comes to a natural (and naturalistic) conclusion with the fact of Akaky's death, or with the belated arrival of news to that effect at his department, and the fact—presented chillingly in a short co-ordinate clause—of his mechanical replacement. Then we are plunged into a sort of coda, one which startles after so naturalistic a tale because of its seemingly fantastic goings on. We are told that rumors have spread all over St. Petersburg to the effect that "a ghost in the shape of a Government clerk had begun appearing" and that, "under the pretext of recovering this lost overcoat, [it] was stripping overcoats off the backs of all sorts of people." In fact, one of Akaky's fellow clerks, we are told, though too frightened "to get a better view of the ghost," "had seen the ghost with his own eyes and at once recognized Akaky Akakyevich." Then we hear that the police caught the ghost or corpse "by the collar," but lost hold because of its violent sneeze, and thereafter "were in such terror of the dead that they were even afraid to arrest the living."

Next, the Very Important Person is reintroduced, and we are given much seemingly tangential if not downright irrelevant information. His troubled conscience having been underscored, he is shown at a dinner with friends, at which "he drank a few glasses of champagne, which, as is generally acknowledged, is quite an excellent way of getting rid of gloomy thoughts." Leaving the dinner in good spirits, he decides to pay a visit to his mistress, who, we are informed, "was not a bit younger or better-looking than his wife." In his coach now, he gives "himself up completely to the enjoyment of his pleasant mood," though he is disturbed by a wind of "supernatural force." Then, "with a face white as snow," the ghost appears and demands the overcoat of the VIP: "Aha! So here you are! I've—er—collared you at last! . . . It's your overcoat I want, sir!" The VIP, who "nearly died of fright" and who "began, not without reason, to apprehend a heart attack," throws his coat off and shouts to the driver "in a panic-stricken voice, 'Home, quick!'" The last thing that we hear of the VIP is

that the incident had a humanizing effect on him and that subsequently he at least heard out what subordinates had to say.

Finally, there is that last paragraph, so seemingly gratuitous, but not more so, surely, than much of what we have been given about the VIP. At any rate, the ghost, Gogol tells us, "completely ceased" to appear after the theft of the VIP's coat, though some held that "the ghost of the Civil Servant was still appearing in the more outlying parts of the town." The tale concludes with one such manifestation, with the sighting by an oafish constable of a ghost "displaying a fist of a size that was never seen among the living." Terrified, the constable turns and the ghost disappears into the darkness.

Now, what are we to make of all of this? Why the startling shift from the naturalistic to the fantastic? Why the ghost? Why the final shift in the last paragraph? Most naive readers as well as many sophisticated ones write off the "fantastic ending" as fantastic: that is, it is taken to be a ghost story in which Akaky's misery is meliorated by a splurge of poetic justice. Even Leon Stilman, speaking of the tale's "paradoxical morality," holds "that Akaky Akakievich suffered injustice and that at least posthumously he found redress when the important personage in his turn became victim of a street robbery," ["Afterword" to Nikolai Gogol, *The Diary of a Madman and Other Stories,* trans. Andrew MacAndrew, 1960]. And Victor Erlich, though he qualifies himself by saying that "the satisfaction is, or ought to be, short-lived" because of the marked shift in the last paragraph, nevertheless has it that "a compassionate reader is bound to derive a measure of emotional satisfaction from the clerk's belated assertiveness and the well-deserved fright of the arrogant 'Person of Consequence'" [Victor Erlich, *Gogol,* 1969]. Finally, in his recent and brilliant study of **"The Overcoat,"** Charles Bernheimer, holding that "the nonconclusion of the story denies any notion of factuality," states that, "reabsorbed into literary freeplay after his foolhardy excursion into the material world, Akaky Akakyevich becomes the agent of what is aptly called 'poetic justice.'"

The end of "The Overcoat" is in part a parody of literary convention—specifically, that of poetic justice—and a joke at the expense of the mind that would find it.

—Edward Proffitt

To be sure, Mr. Bernheimer's "aptly" suggests that he holds such justice to be illusory with respect to Gogol's story. But I would go much further: there is not even a specter of it in the tale itself. Gogol has so shaped the end of **"The Overcoat"** as to play upon the reader's conventionality while maintaining the integrity or complete factuality of his "perfectly true" story. Indeed, the end of **"The Overcoat"** is in part a parody of literary convention—specifically, that of poetic justice—and a joke at the expense of the mind that would find it.

What kind of justice—poetic or otherwise—is it that involves "the stripping of overcoats off the backs of all sorts of people, irrespective of their rank or calling?" These surely are innocent victims themselves. Had his story been that of some other clerk, Akaky himself might have been one of them. And poetic justice, at least as I understand it, must involve grief and loss on the part of the person against whom it is directed. But the VIP, it should be noted, derives genuine benefit from the theft of his coat. Early in the story we see that he is not such a bad sort. But his notion of his position keeps him from being himself. The theft, then, frees him from his own stifling conventions and allows him to be more nearly himself. In other words, on the score of poetic justice, at least, the text is not elusive; rather, the mind of the reader is evasive, finding what it wishes where it does not really exist.

We are trapped by the conventionality of our own conventions. This Gogol conveys dramatically. He wishes us to desire poetic justice, indeed, to find it momentarily. But then we must see that the text does not allow for it, and in so seeing, feel how mere convention keeps us from reality. Should we persist in our superimposing, well the joke is on us. (In this regard one can perhaps gain insight into Nabokov's almost extravagant admiration of Gogol and **"The Overcoat"** in particular) [Vladimir Nabokov, *Nikolai Gogol,* 1944].

But it is not just on the score of poetic justice that **"The Overcoat"** concerns conventionality and its unrealities and imprisonments. Detail after detail underscores how our ingrained conventions—whether literary or social—are at odds with freedom and humanity. For example, when introducing Petrovich, the tailor, the narrator—himself a parody of convention, since he is not the reliable narrator of nineteenth-century fame—the narrator says: "We really ought not to waste much time over this tailor; since, however, it is now the fashion that the character of every person in a story must be delineated fully, then by all means let us have Petrovich, too." Realism, too, has its conventions, though they are not as readily perceived by us as those of fantasy; and too often they are in the saddle. Or take the VIP. He is a creature trapped and dehumanized by convention—in his work entirely, but in his private life as well. Thus, his mistress. Though she has nothing to offer him more than his wife, with whom he is quite content, he has one. Why? Because "he thought it right to," because he serves the conventions of his class. It is in the present context, I think, that the marvelous twists and turns of the story and its famous (at least since Nabokov) shifts of tone and texture should be placed. Such shocks as the gratuitous introduction of "Petrovich's big toe" or the "ordinary young pig, rushing out of a house" are not [as Bernheimer suggests] the vibrations of "a fluid world of shifting metamorphoses" so much as the emanations of simple factuality, or plain reality, so wonderful and various, but what we insulate ourselves against with our systems and conventions (especially, perhaps, in the modern world), what we miss because of our habitual evasions—whether those of routine or of superstition.

Most of all, the end of the story—the coda, as I have called it—in its narrative line and detail, speaks of and to our blindness and consequent vulnerability. Everything in those last few pages speaks that there is no ghost. "Under the pretext" says all. Do ghosts have collars that can be caught, and do they emit mucus? It is obvious that the "ghost" seen by the oaf at the very end is no ghost, but only the product of a superstitious mind caught in a waning rumor. With that last paragraph in mind, we must read back and recognize that there never was a ghost. The clerk who thought he saw Akaky was too petrified "to get a better view of the ghost." Surely, then, we cannot credit what he asserts to be true. He sees only what rumor and his clerky superstition would have him see. And shouldn't a ghost, bent on specific revenge, be more authoritative in its actions than to strip overcoats indiscriminately in hopes of getting the one it wants? (Here, as elsewhere, Gogol brilliantly plays on and with literary convention: he makes use of what literary convention has trained us to expect of ghosts both to underscore the conventionality of our expectation and to suggest that here we are dealing with a very substantial ghost indeed.)

As to the witness of the VIP, Gogol is careful to underpin his sighting with psychological portraiture. Thus we find the proliferation of details in the last pages concerning the VIP, details that otherwise would be irrelevant indeed. What is his state of mind when he sees the ghost of Akaky? We know that he has felt much guilt. But that is not the only underpinning that we are given for his identification. We can infer that he, like most highly routinized men, is somewhat superstitious. Then, too, the night of the theft he has had a bit too much to drink, enough, at least, to throw him off guard. Note also that he lapses into a state of free association, the only thing disturbing his vacancy being the wind, which, with "super-natural force," causes his collar to blow up and momentarily blind him. All in all, given the rumors that have been afoot, he is ready to see the ghost of Akaky. His mind is off guard, free to let guilt and superstition be acted upon by the going convention—the ghost story—to produce the ghost itself. So, chilled by the wind, which itself brings the supernatural to mind; momentarily blinded by his collar, which must bring his overcoat at least to the periphery of his thought, and thus his guilt; fearful of a heart attack, and "not without reason"—that phrase alone suggests his susceptibility; and terrified, he sees a "face . . . white as snow." But a face white as snow could hardly be unknown in Petersburg in the middle of winter. And what does this snow-blown face say? "So here you are! I've—er—collared you at last! It's your overcoat I want, sir!" Catch the melodrama of that last sentence: this is a rather stagey ghost. But it is the stammer that is triumphant. Do ghosts stammer, even ghosts of people who—like Akaky—stammered in life? Not in literature they don't, especially not when they affect such melodrama. (Again, Gogol parodies literary convention and simultaneously makes use of it, a doubleness that at least one critic holds basic to the work of the greatest

English romantics of a generation before Gogol and their quest for spontaneity and self) [Edward Duffy, "The Cunning Spontaneities of Romanticism," *The Wordsworth Circle,* Autumn 1972]. No, that is no ghost. We are dealing with nothing more than an ordinary thief, one of many, no doubt, who have found it possible to exploit the superstitious and guilt-ridden minds of their fellows and done so. Trapped by their superstitions as much as they are by their governmental modes, the law-abiding citizens of Petersburg cannot see what is before their eyes. Especially given that the police "were in such a terror of the dead that they were even afraid to arrest the living," the residents of Petersburg are easy prey, at least until that last coat is stolen. Then, of course, given how rumor spreads around Petersburg, the ghost story has run its course and come to an end for the practical purposes of thieves, though many a citizen retains his ghost long after the crime wave has ceased. Surely, too, the overcoat market of Petersburg has been surfeited in any case.

But we should not laugh too hard at the denizens of Petersburg, for the joke has proven to be on us, we who have desired poetic justice, we who have felt there to be a shift in modes at the end of the tale from the naturalistic to the fantastic. Gogol's use of the word "fantastic" is bitingly ironic. There is no shift. The end is as mundanely naturalistic as the rest of the tale, "perfectly true" (—note the adverb) from beginning to end. We have wanted ghosts, we have wanted poetic justice, and, in varying degrees, we have found both. But Gogol gives us neither. He gives us plain fact with marvelous flashes from the great reservoir of mystery—reality itself, the perfectly true. But we have preferred the poverty of our own conventional projections. Gogol is elusive only because we cannot see what is in front of us. To modify what Brenden Gill has said of Edmund Wilson, we elevate our blindness to a principle and then congratulate ourselves upon practicing it. Or perhaps one should say that Gogol is deeply elusive, with the elusiveness of reality itself. And if we don't see that, we don't because our own minds are deeply evasive.

Donald Fanger (essay date 1979)

"Epic Intentions," in *The Creation of Nikolai Gogol,* The Belknap Press of Harvard University Press, 1979, pp. 145-63.

[*In the following excerpt the critic outlines the techniques which he argues make the theme of "The Overcoat" elusive.*]

"The Overcoat" both draws on and transcends the best of Gogol's previous work. "In terms of plot," as one of his critics has observed, it is "the same sort of sentimental tale . . . as **'Old-World Landowners,'** only with a more pronounced comic coloration" [Alexander Slonimsky, "The Technique of the Comic in Gogol," in *Gogol from the Twentieth Century,* edited by Robert A. Maguire, 1974]. (The title, however, already indicates a broader symbolic intention.) In terms of setting, theme and manner, **"The**

Overcoat" clearly belongs to the world of the earlier Petersburg Tales. It extends the ironic tone of the overture to **"Nevsky Prospect,"** and in the image of Akaky Akakievich who sees only office texts before him, uncertain "whether he is in the middle of a sentence or the middle of a street," it develops the earlier image of bureaucrats so preoccupied with office matters that "instead of shop signs they see filing boxes, or the round face of the chief of their department." Like **"Diary of a Madman,"** it deals with the privations of a petty clerk and with his pathetic rebellion; like **"The Nose,"** it is filled with spurious logic and shot through with absurdity. Like all the stories, it deals with displacement.

But there is a new depth and breadth; the story is more richly problematic than any of its predecessors—and in new ways. The complex of narrative attitudes is more devious than in **"Old-World Landowners,"** the narrator himself more elusive. Where in that story he had voiced personal attitudes and claimed involvement in the events, here he is a disembodied voice, shifting levels bewilderingly, so that as a source of perspective he resembles the Petersburg wind he describes as blowing from all four directions at once. Like **"Nevsky Prospect," "The Overcoat"** is saturated with irony, but only a part of it is satirical; surveying the whole spectrum, one is struck by how much of it appears to be normless, lacking any single implied basis for judgment—which is to say any consistent rationale for the multiplicity of tones and attitudes. As in **"Diary of a Madman,"** the motif of bureaucratic formalism dominates, enclosing the solitary protagonist. But Poprishchin suffered from frustrated ambition; the opposite is the case with Akaky Akakievich, whose very name derives from the Greek for "innocuous": he is as meekly content and as fundamentally inarticulate as Poprishchin is restless and garrulous. And where Poprishchin's progress is from a kind of normality to madness, Akaky's, heavily caricatured, is from an absolutely minimal resemblance to a human being (the critic Grigoriev saw him as existing "on the very edge of nonentity") to a simply minimal degree of the same condition—and even that progress accounts for only a portion of **"The Overcoat."**

The result is a text enigmatic like that of **"The Nose,"** but differently and more fundamentally. The earlier story had involved a puffed-up officer with all-too-human desires in an absurd, surreal adventure from which he emerged unscathed and unchanged, leaving the bemused reader to ponder the question of "why authors write such stories" and what use they serve. The ultimate answer, as we have seen, is that such stories put language to luminously poetic use, making art of nonsense, playing with the reader's expectations of literature and rewarding the desirous with hints of an additional significance—satirical and psychological—which are as frosting to an already rich cake.

"The Overcoat" differs in its parable-like plot line: the reader is made to react less to the central character than to his *situation* (which, up to his death, has nothing fantastic about it). But even that reaction is unstable, because Akaky Akakievich's situation is presented now on one, now on another of three distinct levels. He is shown in the world of Petersburg, in a network of relations involving his fellow workers, his tailor, his overcoat, the Important Personage who denies him sympathy and help, his landlady, the thieves who rob him. This is the world that goes on without him "as if he had never been there," failing to perceive the disappearance of

> a creature defended by none, dear to no one, of interest to no one, who failed even to attract the attention of the naturalist-observer who doesn't overlook an ordinary fly but sticks a pin through it to observe it under a microscope; a creature who humbly submitted to office jokes and went to the grave without any particular to-do—but for whom, all the same, though it happened at the very end of his life, there appeared a bright visitant in the form of an overcoat to enliven his poor life for a moment; and on whom insupportable catastrophe then descended, as it has descended on kings and the potentates of this world.

The corrective to such neglect, however, is offered not on the level of the neglect but on the level of a comic-grotesque narration—and it depends for its realization on yet another level: that of the audience invited to reflect on the meaning of both the others. As Bakhtin summarizes the situation: "The (fictitious) event which is Akaky Akakievich's life and the event which is the actual story about him merge in the distinctive unity of the historical event which is Gogol's **'Overcoat.'** It is in precisely this way that **'The Overcoat'** entered the historical life of Russia and proved an effective factor in it" [M.M. Bakhtin, writing under the name P.N. Medvedev, *Formal'nyj metod v literaturovedenii,* 1928]. Here is one key to the elusiveness of the story: it rests on a blurring of ontological boundaries, in somewhat the way *The Inspector General* does when the Mayor's words echo as a challenge to the spectators: "What are you laughing at? You're laughing at yourselves!"

Akaky Akakievich's "life," then, is inseparable from the narrative that contains it and partakes of the radical novelty of that narrative. To call him a character is already to assume too much, just as it is to speak of the narrator as if he had a deducible "personality" or to seek the import of the story in any single perspective or stable pattern. Once more, three general discriminations can help us to grasp the special functioning of Gogol's text.

The blurring effect of assertion. This feature, which has been widely remarked, underlies the aspect of the story as comic performance. At issue in the first place are the recurrent qualifiers—the "leitmotifs of filler words," as Biely called them—that create a kind of unremovable "dotted veil" over the text: "certain," "somehow," "some," "even," "a sort of," "all the same," "it seems." To the comedy of reported events, they add the constant comedy of speech events and supply the shifts from clarity to vagueness, one of the indices of malproportion on which the grotesque effect of the story rests. (They also, incidentally, establish the license for the larger shifts that give the story its capaciousness of thematic implication, by asserting the range of narrative freedom—from nonsensical chatter to lyrical pathos, from the Bashmachkin inlaws who

only went around in boots to "the kings and potentates of this world.") As an example of the "grotesque sentence" typical of this story one critic [S.G. Bočarov] has cited the following, from the protagonist's first visit to the tailor Petrovich: "The door was open, because the lady of the house, preparing *some fish or other,* had filled the kitchen with so much smoke that you couldn't see *even* the cockroaches themselves." The whole effect is undercut, he comments, if one removes the filler words ["Puskin i Gogol," *Problemy tipologii russkogo realizma,* 1969].

There is, however, a further dimension to this blurring on the non-comic side. At the point when, through serious deprivation, Akaky Akakievich has accumulated enough money to purchase the cloth for his new overcoat, the narrator reports: "His heart, generally quite tranquil, began to beat"—a hint of a literal coming to life that was not present in an earlier draft: "Akaky Akakievich's heart, which always went on almost without any beating, began to beat more strongly." Later, when he has been robbed of his own overcoat, the terrified and conscience-stricken Important Personage undergoes a change of his own: "He even took to saying, 'How dare you? Do you understand to whom you're speaking?' much less often to subordinates; and if he did utter these words, it was not until he had first listened long enough to grasp the point."

> **The ubiquitous qualifications ("even," "perhaps," "probably," "if my memory does not deceive me," "it seemed") leave unclear exactly what is being asserted; how the narrator regards it; and how the reader is meant (or allowed) to understand what he is reading.**
>
> *—Donald Fanger*

The qualification in that last clause indicates the pitfalls of paraphrase, calling into question as it does the assertion it follows (which has already been rendered shaky by the ironic "even"). More precisely, what is called into question is the *significance* of what Gogol reports; and this question—of the inferences that the narration intends or permits—is the central critical question. The ubiquitous qualifications ("even," "perhaps," "probably," "if my memory does not deceive me," "it seemed") leave unclear exactly what is being asserted; how the narrator regards it; and how the reader is meant (or allowed) to understand what he is reading.

Relativity. The import of the story is rendered elusive not only by the ambiguous assertions or shifting tones, the "orchestra of voices" that constitutes the narration; it is grounded in a deeper relatively, since even where the pattern of presentation shows a clear connectedness, it leaves uncertain the significance of that connectedness.

This can be seen first of all in the relationship of the two principal characters, the faceless Akaky Akakievich and the nameless Important Personage (literally, "Important Face")—"the main reason for the whole disaster," as he is identified in a draft.

Akaky Akakievich is introduced as being inherently static (even at his christening he grimaces "as if he had a foreboding that he would be an eternal titular councillor")—a creature without a self, existing timelessly in the pleasant little world of his own mechanical copying:

> One director, being a good man and wishing to reward him for his long service, ordered that he be given something a little more important than ordinary copying; namely, that he be instructed to take an already prepared paper and make of it some document for another office; the job consisted only in changing the title page and changing the verbs here and there from the first person to the third. This gave him such trouble that he broke out in a sweat all over, rubbed his forehead, and finally said: "No, better let me copy something." From that time on they left him to copy forever.

It is the need to protect himself from the cold that propels him into the world of contingency; his development begins with his first exploratory visit to the tailor. Marked by a series of unprecedented events, that development is toward normality. He cries out "perhaps for the first time in his life" when told he must buy a new coat; finally reconciled to the idea, he becomes "somehow more alive." The overcoat for which he is saving is pictured as a bride-to-be, the day of its delivery "probably the most solemn day in [his] life." He goes out in the evening "for the first time in years," drinks champagne with his colleagues, feels the first stirrings of erotic attraction. After being robbed, he decides "for once in his life to show character" and demands to see the police captain; he misses work that day—"the only [such] event in his life." It is at this point that catastrophe strikes and the Important Personage is introduced—the instrument of Akaky Akakievich's only hope and so the agent of his death, which swiftly follows.

The development thus arrested appears as a touchingly "positive" one. The reader instinctively sympathizes with the increasing if derisory "fullness" of the poor clerk's life and realizes the crushing extent of his loss when the overcoat is taken from him. But though the relationship with the Important Personage is presented in moral-psychological terms, there are larger parallels that call into question this first sympathetic view, raising the suspicion that what looks like a relative liberation into selfhood may at the same time spell moral diminution. The Important Personage speaks only in formulas—a counterpart of Akaky's own tendency to stylized incoherence. He is, Gogol suggests, as much a product of position on the bureaucratic ladder as Akaky Akakievich. Just as Akaky has drunk champagne and felt sexual desire before the catastrophe, so the Important Personage, troubled by the news that Akaky has died, seeks diversion in champagne with friends and a visit to his mistress. Just as the Important Personage appears to Akaky in his delirium, so Akaky appears to the

Important Personage in his twinges of guilt. These and other parallels, in short, enforce a socially distant but unmistakable family resemblance—raising, in turn, the specter of a quite different trajectory for the poor clerk's abortive development. We have, after all, been told at the beginning that "if he had been given rewards commensurate with his zeal, [Akaky Akakievich] might even, perhaps, to his own astonishment, have found himself a State Councillor."

In this light, the overcoat appears as the symbol of false development, and its moral role in the story becomes a warning, in Victor Erlich's phrase, of the pitfalls of petty passions. Far from sympathizing with Akaky's development, then, the reader may be entitled to find it ultimately deplorable—and to find the predevelopmental Akaky, for all his apparent ludicrousness, more than preferable: ideal. As Charles Bernheimer observes:

> In true Bergsonian manner, we laugh at the unresponsive, mechanically repetitive quality of Akaky's existence, at his self-absorbed blindness and mute hesitancy, exulting thereby in our own flexibility and freedom. But the joke is really on us. We feel superior to Akaky in our adaptability to this world, but he has found a mode of being that eschews all such degrading compromises . . . [by being] undefined as an individual ["Cloaking the Self: The Literary Space of Gogol's 'Overcoat,'" *PMLA*, January 1975].

Which view of Akaky Akakievich does the narrative ultimately enforce? If we regard the question as legitimate, the answer must be neither. Both remain as presences in the text, unresolved. But the text in fact does not legitimize such a question (though it teases the reader's traditional expectation that a story should). Before we can speak of what it "ultimately" does, one final discrimination needs to be made. This concerns the progress of the narrative on the most important experiential level—that of the reader.

Dynamics: the kaleidoscope. The relativity discussed above means that on the level of theme the same ambiguity obtains as on the level of statement; and both are subsumed by the larger tendency of the narration to move on rather than to resolve. The unmotivated shifts of tone, like the undeveloped introduction of disparate themes, makes reading the story like looking through a kaleidoscope. One can identify the discrete constituents of the changing patterns but no single, dominant pattern; movement is the crux.

Nabokov emphasizes this in his own whimsical terms: "The story goes this way: mumble, mumble, lyrical wave, mumble, lyrical wave, mumble, lyrical wave, mumble, fantastic climax, mumble, mumble, and back into the chaos from which they all had derived" ["Vladimir Nabokov, *Nikolai Gogol,* 1944]. Alexander Slonimsky, in his brilliant monograph, *The Technique of the Comic in Gogol,* spells the process out in rather more useful terms, tracing the alternations of comic and serious to show how "the entire story takes on a double meaning, as it were" ["The Technique of the Comic in Gogol," in *Gogol from the Twentieth Century,* ed. by Robert A. Maguire, 1974]. But Slonimsky, alive to the novelty that allows two contrary views of the same matter to coexist in the work without canceling each other out, fails to discern the *multiplicity* of meanings that lies beyond this doubleness.

The unmotivated shifts of tone, like the undeveloped introduction of disparate themes, makes reading the story like looking through a kaleidoscope.

—Donald Fanger

These, as critics have remarked them over the years, fall into four overlapping categories: the social, the ethical, the religious, and the esthetic. The social emphasizes the pathetic side of the story, Akaky Akakievich—the quintessential little man—as victim of bureaucratic inhumanity and the indifferent city in general; it sees a realistic intent behind the story and has been the dominant view in Russia, particularly in the nineteenth century. The ethical builds on the passage where an unnamed, transitory character is haunted by the affirmation of human brotherhood he hears behind Akaky's protests at office pranks that turn into persecutions. The religious sees the main theme of the story, in Chizhevsky's words, as "the kindling of the human soul, its rebirth under the influence of love (albeit of a very special kind)" [Dmitry Chizhevsky, "About Gogol's Overcoat," in *Gogol from the Twentieth Century*, ed. by Robert A. Maguire, 1974]. (More recently, scholars have noted the presence of several Saints Acacius in the Orthodox calendar, and one in particular who was a paragon of meek service; in light of these findings, **"The Overcoat"** becomes "a travesty of hagiography" [John Schillinger, "Gogol's 'The Overcoat' as a Travesty of Hagiography," *Slavic and East European Journal*, Spring 1972].) Finally, the esthetic—which has been the main contribution of the twentieth century—sees the form of the story as at the same time the locus of value. The Formalist critic Boris Eikhenbaum identifies the work as less a story than a performance, a celebration of the artist's freedom to "violate the normal proportions of the world [and] join together what cannot be joined" ["How Gogol's 'Overcoat' is Made," in Maguire]. Building on this view the Structuralists have found still further levels of meaning in **"The Overcoat."** Sergei Bocharov has seen the structure of the story as resting on the fact that Akaky Akakievich "has no relation to life in the first person." Because he could not conceivably tell his own story, he is enclosed as an alien being within the word play of the narration, which dramatizes (beyond and apart from the events of the story) "his position in life and life's relation to him" ["Puskin i Gogol," *Problemy tipologii russkogo realizma*, 1969].

What these analyses have in common is a respect for the idiosyncrasy of the form that allows full appreciation of the capaciousness of Gogol's story, its legitimate transcendence of singleness of message—the way it "triumphantly asserts literature's independence from the repressive forces of reality and gleefully demonstrates its freedom to play with the realms of matter and spirit, life and death, to which it refers but by which it is not bound" [Charles Bernheimer, "Cloaking the Self: The Literary Space of Gogol's Overcoat," *PMLA*, January 1975].

The purpose of this selective sketch is not to give a full account of Gogol's story but to suggest how it epitomizes the new stage of his artistic practice. What is new and salient in the story is, to a large extent, also found in the novel—and both have proved unusually resistant to critical definition for similar reasons. More precisely, both have shown a tendency to serve as trampolines for critical discussions which in their very pursuit of cogency run the risk of being unfaithful to texts that manifest a very low degree of cogency in thematic terms, even as they evince the highest kind of artistic cogency in the guise of a dense and constantly eventful narrative discourse (where the events are, paradoxically, *speech* events). Such discourse uses the traditional license of comedy, for comedy offers the broadest sanctions and is, of all the artistic modes, the most nearly self-justifying. Thus the works in question are first of all performances, comic poems. But they are comic poems tending to transcendance: of Gogol's intention here, that alone is clear. His ambitious quest is to prove that "the high and the low can equally serve as means to the beautiful and good," that laughter can be serious because morally liberating.

Gogol's art at its most "Gogolian" does this with a tact unrivaled in Russian prose: the comic discourse never slips to mere instrumentality (hence the impossibility of paraphrase), but in its very authority turns problematic, prompting reflections in the reader that inevitably leave the text behind and that can never, no matter how often he returns to that text, find more than the original teasing cue. This process is itself encoded within the text of **"The Overcoat,"** through the fleeting appearance of the young newcomer who witnesses the teasing of Akaky Akakievich at work: "And long afterward, amid the gayest moments, the short little clerk with the bald spot on his forehead would appear to him with his piercing words, 'Leave me alone, why do you insult me?'—and in these piercing words there rang other words: 'I am thy brother.'" This is not, as it has so often been taken to be, a statement of the author's position but of the reader's, at one of those points when "everything, as it were, changes before him and appears in a different guise." It is an example of the way "the gay can momentarily turn into the sad if only one stand contemplating it too long, and then God knows what may not wander into your head"—of the way that, in "gay and carefree moments, another, wondrous strain of thought may suddenly and spontaneously flash by."

The verbs (wander, flash) themselves are significant: they suggest how the most significant themes make their tantalizing appearance in Gogol's text, with a recurrence that makes them more than fortuitous but less than primary. In the kaleidoscope's successive patterns we see images that prompt reflection; and in less arresting ones we may come to recognize their echoes, until each turn sets us to searching for another "key," and a growing familiarity with the separately meaningless shapes leads to a search for the perpetually elusive, constantly potential pattern that would fix them all in positions of analyzable beauty.

The metaphor is only approximate, but to the extent that it is valid it may suggest why those who claim **"The Overcoat"** is *not* about Christian charity and arbitrary authority, meekness and pride, poverty and comfort, justice, bureaucracy, city life, even literature itself—why such readers are as mistaken as those who assert that it *is* about these things. Respecting the peculiar mode of its being, it would be more accurate to say that the story is ultimately about significance and insignificance as such, in literature no less than in life. It embraces these particular instances to use them. For—as the title already indicates—the novelty of this problematic text lies in the quest it dramatizes and provokes: for serious significance, for the sense in which humble phenomena may contain it, for the criteria by which it may be identified, for the unriddling of a world. This quest is the more tantalizing because it is presented with seeming randomness, like a game of blindman's buff, the arbitrary shifts of level and perspective in the presentation symbolizing the obstacles in that search. Gogol's best art had always avoided clarity of message to pose self-regarding questions in the form of riddles. Here and in *Dead Souls* he raises the level of those riddles in line with his new conception of the comic writer as servant of the vaguest but highest ideals: ethical, moral, religious, civic, taken precisely in their ideality. **"The Overcoat,"** in its range of tones and themes, is Gogol's amplest story, manifesting in little the qualities that inform his novel. A hermeneutic challenge, endlessly evocative, intrinsically elusive, it is his monument to the capacity of art—not to "reflect" the great realities of life but to join them.

L. Michael O'Toole (essay date 1982)

"Narrative Structure," in *Structure, Style and Interpretation in the Russian Short Story,* Yale University Press, 1982, pp. 20-36.

[*In this excerpt, O'Toole examines several structural elements that he finds determining factors in the ultimate theme of the story.*]

[**'The Overcoat'** is] perhaps the most well-known and elaborately analyzed story in the whole of Russian literature. Many critics, from Belinsky onwards, have taken the theme to be similar to that which can be found on a first reading of Leskov's *The Man on Sentry Duty:* the plight of the 'little man' in the face of an impersonal and inhumane society prevailing under the autocratic rule of Nicholas I. But if an analysis of the narrative structure ultimately proved this theme inadequate in the case of Leskov's story, in the case of Gogol's it makes such a theme appear a travesty of the story's real essence.

The basic plot of 'The Overcoat' appears straightforward: a poor and pathetically limited copying clerk, Akakiy Akakiyevich, finds his old coat inadequate protection against the cold of the St Petersburg winter, skimps and saves to have a new one made, has a brief moment of triumph as the toast of his colleagues but is robbed of the prized overcoat as he makes his way home from the celebration. He summons up the confidence to ask a certain Person of Consequence to intercede with the chief of police and help to recover the stolen coat, only to be shouted at and sent packing into the street where he catches cold, goes home to bed and dies. After his death, rumours are rife about a ghost resembling Akakiy who snatches overcoats from the backs of citizens with so little respect for rank that he finally appears in the carriage of the Person of Consequence and demands back 'his' overcoat.

These bare bones yield a nicely symmetrical structure:

General Prologue:	the St Petersburg background and Akakiy's past
Special Prologue:	Akakiy's present job, private life and poverty
Complication:	the lack of a coat and gradual acquisition of the new one
Peripeteia:	the theft of the new coat
Dénouement:	attempts to recover the coat and death
Special Epilogue:	'revenge' by Akakiy's ghost
General Epilogue:	a widening circle of rumour about ghosts in St Petersburg

But such a naive narrative structure, while accounting for the socio-humanitarian theme, leaves almost completely out of the account several important elements in the story: the complex pattern of digressions, including the so-called 'lyrical digressions', the strategic importance of the Person of Consequence, the richness of Akakiy's inner life, the recurrent interventions by supernatural forces and the intricate verbal play which becomes a dynamic force in the story in its own right. We must consider each of these elements in turn before finally committing ourselves to a final statement of the narrative structure which (by definition) is a dynamic working out of the story's deep theme.

The digressions in 'The Overcoat' fulfil many functions. Moreover it is rare for any digression to have only one function. Some of them operate as elements in the narrative structure: the comment about the hero's surname, Bashmachkin, and the long anecdote about the choice of his Christian name contribute to a rather piecemeal general prologue whereby we learn some vital facts about Akakiy's past through a series of flashbacks. Vital? Well, in so far as the fate of Gogol's characters is partly determined by their names (or lack of a name, as with the Person of Consequence), the naming of Akakiy is important: as Gogol assures us, it was through this bizarre naming procedure that Akakiy 'came into being' (*Takim obrazom i prozosh-et Akakiy Akakiyevich*). So the fantastic account of how he received such a very pedestrian name turns out to be more significant than a straightforward account of significant moments in his earlier life. But this flashback is also an exercise in Shandyesque digression for its own sake, part of an elaborate effort on the part of the author to downgrade plot, narrative structure and characterization as important aspects of narrative and present the fortuitous recollection as if it were logically motivated. As many of Gogol's most brilliant critics have shown, the naming episodes are as much elaborate games with words and sounds as anything else. The rather idiotic etymological pun about the surname Bashmachkin not implying that his forefathers wore 'shoes' (*bashmaki*) prepares the way for another etymological pun whereby the narrator assures us that despite its 'recherché' (*vyiskannym*) strangeness, the name Akakiy was not 'sought' (*yego ne iskali*)—and then goes on to relate the frantic search through the calendar of saints' names which led to his 'late' mother choosing Akakiy in desperation. Even 'the late' (*pokoinit-sa*) is a rather gruesome temporal pun, since his mother is referred to as recently expired all the time she is struggling to choose. Not that the boundary between living and not living is so very clearly defined for Gogol, since this digression ends with two matching sentences where an animate masculine verb-ending only too easily slips into an inanimate neuter ending (this time a grammatical pun!): 'So this is how Akakiy Akakiyevich came about' (*Takim obrazom i proizoshel Akakiy Akakiyevich*). Then a short account of Akakiy's first signs of animation—tears and a grimace of fearful foreboding, then: 'And so this is how all this came about' (*Itak, vot kakim obrazom proizoshlo vse eto*).

We are in a grotesque world where names, puns, rumours and reputations become reality and the real is diminished, distorted or magnified to fantastic proportions. The very archaic and exotic sonority of all the alternative possible names gives way to the flat and unsonorous 'Akakiy' which manages to combine a Russian child's word for faeces, the Greek word for humility, a humbly obedient sixth-century saint, and the anguished repetition of the existential question *kak?* (How?) A detailed analysis of this infinitely rich word play of this passage would show to what extent the *kak* root, or its answer *tak* figures in the frantic search for a name:

Kakoye ona khochet vybrat' . . .
    which she wanted to choose . . .

Net, imena-to vse **tak**iye . . .
    No, the names were all *the sort* . . .

kakiye vse imena, ya, pravo,
    What sort of names they all were

nikogda ne slykhivala **tak**ikh . . .
    I really never heard *such a sort* . . .

vidno, yego **tak**aya sud'ba . . .
    obviously *such* was his fate . . .

kak i otets yego . . . **Tak**im obrazom . . .
    like his father . . . And *so*

In one digression, then, Gogol has succeeded in combining apparent plot motivation, temporality, philosophical import, etymological, lexical and grammatical puns and pure phonetic sound play, to say nothing of the syntactic rhythms and intonation curves. And these functions are not fulfilled separately. They are fused so inextricably that the verbal play becomes part of the narrative structure: life is not separable from the act of talking about life: like Akakiy himself, life is a verbal coincidence. In the same way, digressions which appear to function primarily as a mode of characterization, such as the descriptions (despite the author's intentions!) of Petrovich and his wife, of Akakiy's speech mannerisms or the family life of the Person of Consequence, or those where the prime intention appears to be the depiction of social setting, such as the vignette of how the clerks of St Petersburg spend their evening or the tale of the titular councillor who made himself a waiting-room around his desk to ape his superiors, are equally examples of verbal play in their own right. As Boris Eikhenbaum pointed out [in 'The Structure of Gogol's "The Overcoat,"' in *The Russian Review* 22, No. 4, October, 1963], there is no neutral intonation in Gogol. The description of the clerks' evening pursuits makes its impact less through the accuracy or vividness of social detail than through the fact that it is conveyed in a single sentence nearly a page long which sets up syntactic-intonational expectations which are thwarted by the bathos of the negative reference to Akakiy's way of spending his evenings: 'in a word even at the time when everything is striving to enjoy itself,—Akakiy did not give himself over to any enjoyment.'

While some of the digressions clearly serve to convey the framing elements of narrative structure, then, this is far from being their primary function. By their vigour, verbosity and virtuosity they have become more important than the story itself. . . . [T]he reader begins almost to resent the way anything as prosaic as plot distracts from the poetry of the digressions. The so-called 'lyrical digressions'—for there are at least two—are not different in kind from the other digressions in **'The Overcoat.'** Only critics (from Belinsky onwards), who feel reassured if they can find a prominent and explicit moral or political motif in a work, have given the lyrical digressions in **'The Overcoat'** a particular significance for the theme of the story. If, however, we see them as excursions into an emotional-moral dimension, comparable with the excursion into a 'sociology-of-literature' dimension of the digression with which the story opens, or the excursion into the dimension of naming rites and word-play of the digression concerning Akakiy's christening, then we may recognize that they are on a par with the other gambits Gogol uses to amuse and distract his readers. Naturally, the degree of emotionality expressed is different, but the manner in which the digressions are constructed is not. As so often, Gogol allows a phrase to generate the digression: 'something could be heard in him of the sort that inclines one to pity' and the abstract notion of something inclining one to pity inevitably brings into being a person thus inclined: 'so that one young man suddenly pulled up sharp as if pierced through . . .' This is the same mechanism as that whereby the general proposition about every private citizen considering the whole of society insulted generates a police superintendent who does feel insulted, and whereby the pun on *iskat* (to search) in *vyiskannym* (recherché) generates the desperate search for a Christian name by Akakiy's mother and godmother.

All the digressions in the story, whether 'lyrical', 'linguistic', 'sociological', or 'philosophical' contribute to the story's rich verbal texture and to the flirtatious relationship between the author/narrator and his readers.

—L. Michael O'Toole

Moreover, the stylistic mannerisms of the 'lyrical' digressions are not significantly different from those which sustain or vary the tone of the other digressions: (1) the vagueness: 'one young man who had recently been appointed' (*odin molodoi chelovek, nedavno opredelivshiisya*), 'all but permitted himself' (*pozvolil bylo*), 'as if pierced through' (*kak budto pronzennyi*), 'as if everything had changed before him' (*kak budto vse peremenilos' pered nim*), 'some kind of unnatural force' (*kakaya-to neyestestvennaya sila*); (2) hyperbole: 'suddenly' (*vdrug ostanovilsya*), 'everything' (*vse peremenilos*), 'unnatural' (*neyestestvennaya sila*), 'for a long time after at the merriest moments' (*dolgo potom, sredi samykh veselykh minut*) 'many times' (*mnogo raz sodrogalsya on potom na svoyem-veku*), 'how many' (*kak mnogo*) . . . 'and even in that man' (*kak mnogo . . . i bozhe! dazhe v tom cheloveke*). Of course, the emotional tone of the vocabulary, the inversions (*predstavlyalsya, zakryval sebya rukoyu bednyi molodoi chelovek, sodrogalsya on*) the diminutives (*nizen'kii, 's lysinkoyu*) and the exclamatory *'bozhe!'* are distinctive to the 'lyrical' digression, but our sensitive young clerk has no greater claims to credibility as representative of the author's views than the touchy captain or Akakiy's godmother. All the digressions in the story, whether 'lyrical', 'linguistic', 'sociological' or 'philosphical' contribute to the story's rich verbal texture and to the flirtatious relationship between the author/narrator and his readers; none can claim any priority as 'thematic'.

In our search for the essential theme of **'The Overcoat'** we will have to return to the narrative structure and in particular the role of the Person of Consequence in that structure. In our schematic analysis of the narrative structure we assigned the role of the Person of Consequence only to the dénouement and the special epilogue, i.e.

Akakiy's attempts to recover the coat lead him to beg the Person of Consequence to help and the latter's arrogant refusal leads Akakiy (or leaves him no option but) to catch cold and die. The threads of this injustice then get nicely tied up in the epilogue where Akakiy's ghost robs the Person of Consequence of *his* overcoat and changes his way of life and attitudes. But as Frederick Driessen pointed out in his subtle analysis of *The Overcoat*, there are important parallels between the Person of Consequence and both Petrovich and Akakiy which make his role a much more prominent one [F.C. Dreissen, *Gogol as a Short Story Writer*, 1965].

Both Petrovich and the Person of Consequence are tyrants in their own sphere who boost their own morale by browbeating and disheartening the weak and dependent like Akakiy who turn to them for help. Significantly, the same phrases are used about them: Petrovich is pleased not to have let himself down by giving in to Akakiy's pleas: 'satisfied that he had both not let himself down and had also not betrayed his tailor's art . . .' while the Person of Consequence is always held back from being sociable by the thought of 'letting down his consequence': 'he used to be pulled up sharply by the thought of whether he might through this be letting down his consequence.' And, of course, they are both much concerned with the effect their words have, as they look sideways (*iskosa*) at their hearers: 'He (Petrovich) was very fond of powerful *effects*, loved suddenly to throw a person into confusion in some way and then *glance sideways* at what sort of funny face the person would pull after such words.' 'While the Person of Consequence, satisfied that the *effect* had exceeded even his expectations . . . *glanced sideways* at his friend to discover how he viewed the matter.' Such parallelism of the syntax of these two quotations and the very words used could not be a coincidence. Moreover, Petrovich and the Person of Consequence are the only characters in the story whose early life, background and rise to their present position of authority are related (in flashbacks), and whose wives are described (accidentally, as it were, in digressions). There is even much playful discussion of the way they have acquired their present titles. Would it be too fanciful to see the general portrayed on Petrovich's snuffbox—albeit with his face pasted over with a scrap of paper—as the General of Consequence, ('face' or 'personage') the *litso* who has become 'faceless' through bureaucracy and rank? As Driessen points out, Gogol was well aware of the parallel and wished to highlight it further in his penultimate version of the story where Akakiy dreams about Petrovich making a pistol-coat which will frighten the general. Fortunately he saw that such proximity would reduce the impact of the parallel and omitted it in the story's final version.

Structurally, then, Petrovich and the Person of Consequence represent Akakiy's encounters with authority. They frame the episode of his life with his coat: his new life begins to take shape with his visits to Petrovich; it loses all shape and meaning with his visit to the Person of Consequence. Matching complication and dénouement? Yes, but while Petrovich is not changed by his encounter with Akakiy, the Person of Consequence is. For him the conversation has as far-reaching consequences as Akakiy's first visit to Petrovich had for Akakiy. The parallels and contrasts between the Person of Consequence and Akakiy are even more striking and significant.

The Person of Consequence is introduced first by one of Gogol's negative throw-away lines: 'Exactly what the Person of Consequence's official position was and what it involved has remained unknown to this day.' which is not unlike the 'Bashmachkins who always wore boots' in tone. Then by a long digression on how he acquired his title, having started as a 'Person of No Consequence'. This digression depends on some elaborate punning and morphological word-play with the word *znachitel'nyi* which, outside the set phrase *znachitel'noye litso,* means 'significant'. This is a mirror image of the digression concerning how Akakiy came by his pathetically *in*significant name. The mirror-image contrast continues with an account of the general's abuse of his supposed power at his office. Even the three phrases he uses to browbeat his subordinates: 'How dare you? Do you know with whom you are speaking? Do you realize who is standing before you?' although so different in tone, seem to echo rhythmically and in their insistence on the second person Akakiy's haunting question: 'Leave me alone, why do you insult me?' Their speech habits in general are remarkably similar: as soon as the Person of Consequence finds himself in the company of anyone just one rank below him, he is prone to lapse into a pitiful silence and utter only occasional unclear and monosyllabic noises (cf. Akakiy's reaction to anyone faintly superior when 'he would express himself mostly in prepositions, adverbs and the sort of particles which have absolutely no meaning'). Both, it is made clear, are prisoners of rank at their respective ends of the hierarchy in bearing, behaviour and speech

> Seeing Akakiy's humble look and ancient uniform, he suddenly turned to him and said: 'What do you want?' in a sharp, firm voice, that he had deliberately practised previously in his room at home, alone in front of the mirror, a whole week before he even got his present post and general's rank. Akakiy promptly experienced the appropriate shyness, got a bit embarrassed and, as best he could, insofar as his tongue would allow him, explained with the addition of the particle 'um' even more than usual, that there had been this overcoat which was quite new . . .

Two further details: as Driessen points out, Akakiy never even glances in the mirror, whereas the Person of Consequence studies himself in the mirror (almost as if Akakiy is too faint an object to have a reflection, while the general is almost nothing but reflected image, as the quotation above and the scene with his old acquaintance show); while Akakiy's entry to the office is never noticed, even by the doorkeepers, the Person of Consequence deliberately engineers meetings on the stairs. As with the mirrors, they both seem to stand on a line between reality and imagination, with Akakiy constantly trying to fade out and the Person of Consequence constantly trying to fade in.

We have needed to enumerate many details of the story here which would properly be analyzed on the level of characterization, but the parallels between these two characters are crucial for the narrative structure. (In any case, as we have pointed out, the analytical 'levels' are constructs to aid the systematic analysis: within the work itself they have no separate meaning and interact constantly.) The point is that the Person of Consequence is of considerable consequence for our interpretation of **'The Overcoat.'** I want to argue that our earlier schema of the narrative structure, the one which most commentators assume implicitly to be accurate, is in fact quite inadequate, offers only an impoverished interpretation of the theme, and fails to integrate many of the features we are considering: the digressions, the role of the Person of Consequence, the inner life of Akakiy, the role of the supernatural and, above all, the style.

'The Overcoat' falls clearly into two parallel parts, each with its own narrative structure:

	Akakiy	*Person of Consequence*
Prologue	(Underdog) Naming, background, present life	(Top dog)
Complication	Acquisition of coat	Acquisition of Akakiy's problem
Peripeteia	Loss of coat	Loss of coat
Denouement	Failure to find coat; death	Change of heart; humility
Epilogue	The supernatural takes over	

Thus the turning-point in each part of the story is the robbery of a coat, which for both Akakiy and the Person of Consequence is an object essential to their confidence and self-esteem, a buttress to their personality. What is more, the robbery takes place in both cases after a supper-party at which the central characters had drunk two glasses of champagne which make them 'merry' and when both of them were motivated by erotic plans, however subconscious: the general, though happily married, plans to visit his mistress; Akakiy, though wearing his 'life's companion', the new coat, 'even made as if to run, for no known reason, up to some lady or other who rushed past him like lightning, every part of her body filled with extraordinary movement'. Both react to the robbery by going home and shutting themselves away, greatly chastened.

By stressing all these parallels we must not, however, obscure the crucial contrasts between the two narrative structures: for the Person of Consequence status, respect from others, self-respect, family-life and a love-life on the side are real aspects of life, underwritten by the prevailing social order and social attitudes. For Akakiy all these things are temporary figments of an imagination which has been inspired by the acquisition of the overcoat, that symbol of status, companionship and love. Yet is the objective reality of the general's authority, power, family and mistress any more *real* than the subjective reality of these elements which the coat conjures up for Akakiy?

The story may divide up rather readily, as we have shown, into two distinct episodes, each with a clearly defined narrative structure. But they do relate. In terms of character, plot and setting, the two episodes are mirror images of each other. They meet in the visit of Akakiy to the Person of Consequence which resolves (however tragically) Akakiy's crisis and initiates the general's crisis. This scene, I would maintain, becomes the peripeteia of an overarching metastructure in the narrative where Akakiy's subjective reality and the general's objective reality clash. Which is more real: the live Akakiy's wraith-like figure suffering every indignity that fate and his fellow-men inflict on him or the dead Akakiy's sturdy ghost wreaking vengeance on the mighty of this world? Which is more real: a little clerk's pride and dignity in doing his chosen job to perfection, virtually *living* his sad little vocation, or a bumptious general's status and 'consequence' which depend on rehearsals in the mirror, a chain of command at the office and three fierce but meaningless phrases? Which is more real: the love Akakiy feels for his coat which raises his whole life to a new plane and even makes him capable of an erotic awareness as he gazes at a saucy painting in a shop window or glimpses a lively young woman passing, or the cynical way the Person of Consequence takes his wife and family for granted and subscribes to the prevailing morality by keeping a mistress on the side?

Reality is on the borderline between life and death, between the objective and the subjective. For that matter, it is on the borderline between the real and the supernatural. James Holquist and Victor Erlich have both demonstrated decisively the extent to which Gogol's world is balanced on a tight-rope between the real and the supernatural. Erlich puts it well: 'An Akakiy Akakiyevich-like specter starts haunting the city. At one point he seems to confront the "Person of Consequence" and brusquely to claim "his" overcoat—an experience which allegedly both frightens and chastens the overbearing official. I'm saying "seems", since we cannot be absolutely sure that this is what actually happens. So fluid is the boundary between reality and delusion in the murky world of this St Petersburg tale, so dense the fog of absurd rumors which thrive on the metropolitan muddle, that the "ghostly clerk" might well be a figment of the overbearing bureaucrat's frightened imagination, a phantom emerging from the vapors of his bad conscience' [*Gogol*, 1969]. For Gogol the supernatural is characteristically demonic in form. The devil is clearly at large in the fantastic scenes at the end of the story where a policeman in Kolomna is prevented from giving chase to a ghost by a pig which rushes out and knocks him off his feet (like the demonic pig in the story of the two Ivans which steals the deposition), and when he catches up with the ghost is threatened by a monstrous fist of inhuman size belonging to a tall figure with enormous moustaches who disappears without trace into the darkness. No doubt the wind which bothers the Person of Consequence ('suddenly springing up from God knows where and for no

earthly reason') is the same one which whistled along the streets from all four directions and blew the tonsillitis germ into Akakiy's throat. But the devil is lurking in wait for Akakiy from the very beginning. He cannot walk along the street without a chimney-sweep (from Hell?) brushing soot on him, or a builder spilling lime (for burning corpses?) on him. It is the devil that prompts Petrovich to ask such a fiendish price for a new coat, perhaps a devil who lurks in Petrovich's snuff-box with the obliterated general on the lid, for in Gogol's world snuff-boxes are coffins, sneezing really does warrant a 'God bless you!' and every lonely square is inhabited by a policeman who, despite his protective halberd, is usually caught in the act of taking snuff on his calloused fist, which, like Petrovich's tortoise-shell toe-nail, may evoke the Devil's hooves.

As Holquist sums up: 'The devil, the "unnatural power", is still at work, but he is now a symbol for the cruel, impersonal disorder of the city' ['The Devil in Mufti: The *Marchenwelt* in Gogol's Short Stories,' *PMLA* 82, October 1967]. This element is certainly present in the story, yet to make it central is once again to stress a narrowly socio-moral theme. Holquist's earlier remarks about the St Petersburg setting are far more convincing in the light of our interpretation here

> The setting is again the fantastic city Gogol called Petersburg. It is once again a place where things get lost; but this time it is not a nose, or even just an overcoat, that disappears, but the 'hero' himself. He is lost not only in the sense of losing his way (although he does this, too), but also in the sense that his very being is brought into question . . . Lest it be objected that such confusion is explainable due to the simple nature and lowly rank of Akakiy, it should be remembered that the 'exalted personage' to whom he appeals after his coat is stolen is no more secure.

The demonic setting brings us once more to our theme of the blurring of boundaries between the real and the supernatural, between the 'dead' world of bureaucratic ritual and the 'living' world of human hopes and aspirations, between 'objective' and 'subjective' views of reality, between the physical and the spiritual, between the two halves of a 'looking-glass' world.

But the boundary that Gogol blurs most brilliantly of all is that between the actual and the verbal, between what is said and the way it is said. [In his book *Nikolai Gogol*] Vladimir Nabokov has overstressed the point: 'The real plot (as always with Gogol) lies in the style', which sounds good, but ignores the notion of linear development which is essential to the plot. It would be more accurate to say that what impinges most on the reader is the verbal play, pushing the more conventional mechanisms of plot and narrative structure into the background. As we observed earlier of the digressions, so linguistic invention itself has become more important than the mere story: *histoire* turns to *discours* in a special way—the plot usually depends on some verbal association, a pun, a syntactic twist or a switch of intonation to advance at all. Nabokov again sums up the process in a memorable phrase about *Dead Souls*: 'In this dizzyingly centrifugal orgy of subordinate clauses, language is on the rampage.'

Language in Gogol's stories becomes an independent, impersonal force which takes over the personality and will of mere human beings.

—L. Michael O'Toole

Language in Gogol's stories becomes an independent, impersonal force which takes over the personality and will of mere human beings. This is made explicit in the descriptions of the two 'protagonists' of **'The Overcoat,'** Akakiy and the Person of Consequence. Akakiy is totally dominated by his inability to express himself meaningfully or even to finish a sentence he has started

> The reader should know that Akakiy expressed himself for the most part in prepositions, adverbs and, finally, the kind of particles that have absolutely no meaning. But if the subject was very difficult he even had a habit of not ending his sentences at all, so that quite often, having begun his speech with the words: 'That's really absolutely sort of . . .' there would be nothing further, and he himself would forget, thinking that he had already said everything.

A demonic force, a kind of incipient chaos, lurks in wait for Akakiy not only behind every corner of the St Petersburg labyrinth, but behind every thought that begins to shape itself in the mists of his mind. Nor does the Person of Consequence fare better with words. Despite his ability (and need) to inspire awe and obedience in all his subordinates, with a whole range of bureaucratic power gambits and three terrifying, but meaningless questions, he becomes pathetically speechless in the company of anyone below him in rank

> If he happened to be with his equals he was just as one should be, quite a decent chap and in many ways not even stupid; but as soon as he happened to be in company where there were people just one rank below him he would get quite out of control: he would fall silent and his state would arouse pity, particularly since he himself would even feel that he might have been spending the time incomparably better. Sometimes you could see in his eyes a powerful desire to join in some interesting conversation and circle, but he would be pulled up sharp by the thought: wouldn't this be just a bit much on his part, wouldn't it be too familiar, and wouldn't he be letting down through this his consequence? And as a result of these considerations he would remain all the time in the same silent state, only occasionally pronouncing some monosyllabic sounds, and thus he acquired the reputation of being the most tedious of men.

Not only the social conventions and bureaucratic hierarchies, then, but real linguistic impotence reduce both Akakiy and the Person of Consequence to a state of monosyllabic gibbering.

But they are not the only characters in **'The Overcoat'** to be dominated by language; the narrator himself seems to be as much at risk from the verbal torrent which threatens all the time to sweep away out of control his plot, his characters and his narrative structure. If Akakiy and the Person of Consequence are victims of linguistic drought, however, the narrator is a victim of sheer intoxication with words. Our last quotation provides some good examples: 1. *Balance and rhythm*: the two halves of the first sentence combine similarity and contrast: 'If he happened to be with his equals . . . ; but as soon as he happened to be in company . . .' (*Yesli yemu sluchalos' byt's rovnymi sebe . . . ; no kak tol'ko sluchalos' yemu byt'v obschestve . . .*). Similarly the three 'thoughts' that disturb the Person of Consequence in the second sentence are beautifully matched: 'wouldn't this be just a bit much on his part, wouldn't it be too familiar, and wouldn't he be letting down through this his consequence?' (*ne budet li eto uzh ochen' mnogo s yego storony, ne budet li famil'yarno, i ne uronit li on chrez to svoyego zhacheniya?*). While the conditional clause in the first sentence appears to end quite logically and appropriately, however, the main clause combines at least three features which are absolutely crucial to Gogol's style: 2. *alogism*, 3. *hyperbole*, 4. *bathos*. In this case the three are inextricably linked: the hyperbolic 'he simply got totally out of control' is not logically related to the absurd illustration of his uncontrolled state—'he kept silent'. But if we look more closely, we find a similar, if less startling play with alogism, hyperbole and bathos in the apparently logical first clause: after 'very decent' and 'in many respects' we might have expected something more positive than 'not a stupid man'. Gogol typically heightens the bathos of this alogism by throwing in the word 'even' (*dazhe*) which, as Chizhevskiy pointed out in a famous article ['On Gogol's "The Overcoat,"' in *Dostoevsky and Gogol: Texts and Criticisms*, Priscilla Meyer and Stephen Rudy, 1979] is the key word underlying a whole range of effects in **'The Overcoat'**. The tendency towards colloquialism in the narrator's choice of language—which Chizhevskiy refers to as an impoverishment but which we would rather view as an enrichment of the prevailing literary norm—is well illustrated by the particles in the phrase 'simply got totally out of control' (*prosto khot' iz ruk von*), in the self-interrogation of the free indirect questions in the second sentence quoted above. The shift in point of view signified by this increased colloquialism is, of course, made explicit by the shift to the supposed internal monologue or thoughts of the character contained within the narrative mode, but the pun with which the sentence ends involves a more typically unmotivated Gogolian shift, recalling the narrator's long digression on the word 'significant' (*znachitel'noye*), set in train by the first mention of the Person of Consequence

> What exactly the official position of the Person of Consequence was and what it involved has remained unknown to this day. The reader should know that a

certain person of consequence recently became consequential, and up to then had been a person of no consequence. However, his post even now has not been counted as of any consequence in comparison with others far more consequential. But a group of people is always to be found for whom whatever is inconsequential in others' eyes is for that reason consequential. However, he strove to bolster up his consequence by many other means . . .

Here sheer verbosity, a sort of intoxication with the endlessly expanding morphological and semantic frontiers of the pun, has driven out rational linear narrative. Language has become a demonic force in the story in its own right: it is indeed 'on the rampage'. The pun, like the alogism and the hyperbole-bathos mechanism offers a sort of verbal mirror dividing the 'real'-world of denotational meaning from the looking-glass world of infinitely receding connotations into which the reader risks falling with the narrator at every turn in the syntax. . . .

Boris Eikhenbaum, in perhaps the most famous study of **'The Overcoat,'** concluded from his analysis of . . . stylistic devices that, with the plot reduced to a minimum and the centre of gravity switched to the devices of quasioral narration (*skaz*), the personal tone becomes the organizing principle for the story. Eikhenbaum was taken to task by his fellow Formalist, Viktor Shklovsky, for his error in separating the style from the plot ['Shinel,' in *Povesti o proze* II, 1966]. The plot, says Shklovsky, is not reduced to a minimum. It is small-scale, but highly complex. The value of the *skaz* is in preserving the scale: the author uses it to examine all the details through a magnifying glass. He accepts Akakiy's thought system and at the same time never loses sight of the triviality of that system. The *skaz* discourse has the same random, alogical, spasmodic rhythm as Akakiy's thought and speech processes. Despite the somewhat tendentious socio-political conclusion this leads Shklovsky to draw, his view of the relationship between the plot and the narrative mode seems to have a richer potential.

Our own analysis of the narrative structure of **'The Overcoat'** has revealed the central shift in the story from the dead world of the living Akakiy to the lively world of his ghost; from an impersonal world which dominates the little man to a world of personalities dominated by his spirit; from a 'real' world constantly threatened by demonic forces to a world of rumours where the demon spirits have taken over. We are in the realm of the 'grotesque' which, according to [wolfgang] Kayser, is 'Not only something playfully gay and carelessly fantastic, but also something ominous and sinister in the face of a world totally different from the familiar one—a world in which the realm of inanimate things is no longer separated from those of plants, animals and human beings and where the laws of statics, symmetry and proportion are no longer valid' [*The Grotesque in Literature and Art,* 1963]. The metaphor which has presented itself time and again to describe this turning-point is the surface of a mirror. But we are never sure, ultimately, whether the original object or its reflection in the distorting glass is more real. As with narrative struc-

ture, so with plot: which are more real—the episodes which advance the action or the digressions which retard it? So with character: who is more real—Akakiy Akakiyevich, the named protagonist who acquired his name by a quirk of fate or the anonymous Person of Consequence, whose 'consequence' is constantly threatened by a pun? So with setting: which is more real—the mirage-like St Petersburg peopled by faceless bureaucrats or the rather solid city through which Akakiy's ghost pursues his vengeful course? So, finally, with narrative mode and style: which is more real—the story or the manner in which it is told, the denotational meaning of the words or their infinitely receding or demonaically interacting connotations? For in Gogol's grotesque world language is as much at risk as causality, personality and action.

R. A. Peace (essay date 1985)

"Gogol: The Greatcoat," in *The Voice of a Giant: Essays on Seven Russian Prose Classics,* edited by Roger Cockrell and David Richards, University of Exeter, 1985, pp. 27-40.

[*In this essay Peace examines the role of word play in "The Overcoat," which, he argues, elucidates Gogol's central device of having the external world act as a metaphor for the internal world of the main character.*]

"The Greatcoat" is the story of an impoverished civil service clerk, in St Petersburg, who by dint of great sacrifices manages to buy himself a new coat, but is robbed of it the very first evening he wears it. He tries to get it back by going to see a highly-placed official who gives him such a reprimand that the poor clerk falls ill and dies. Later his ghost haunts St Petersburg, stealing coats; it is only laid to rest when it has taken the greatcoat of the highly-placed official himself.

The story is often regarded as having initiated a whole tradition of Russian realism. 'We have all come out of Gogol's greatcoat' is a remark allegedly uttered by Dostoevsky (though this attribution is suspect). Yet in what sense can a story with a ghost sequence be called realistic? By realism Russian critics in the nineteenth century often meant 'critical realism', implying that a writer by portraying society 'realistically' was thereby expressing criticism of it. On the face of it the plot of **"The Greatcoat,"** as outlined, does suggest a social theme and it cannot be denied that criticism is implicit in Gogol's treatment of the police (in particular his laughter at the inept constables). Veneration of rank and the insolence of authority (the 'Important Person') are presented with implied censure. Yet, as regards his poverty, the authorities in Akakii Akakievich's own department are not responsible for his plight. The director gives him a much higher bonus than he had expected when he needs the money for his coat. Afterwards the assistant chief clerk invites him to a party, partly in honour of his coat. Nor can it be argued that the civil service has turned Akakii Akakievich into the automaton that he undoubtedly is. Indeed, he seems to have been born to his role and we learn that he had once been given more interesting work but had proved incapable of it.

Nor is it entirely true that he is portrayed sympathetically. If the other clerks poke fun at him, they do little more than the narrator of the story himself; for in spite of his strictures on those writers who mock titular councillors, he nevertheless constantly presents his own hero as a figure of fun, with a neck that reminds him of a toy plaster-kitten, and the strange ability always to find himself under a window when rubbish is being thrown out.

Moreover the poverty of Akakii Akakievich, which is the corner-stone for any social interpretation of the work, cannot be taken at its face value; it is always presented with hyperbole. In the first place, Akakii Akakievich is by no means at the bottom of the hierarchy of ranks—he is in the ninth grade, which means there were another five grades below his. Other titular councillors in Gogol do not appear to be in such financial straits. Poprishchin, for instance, in **"The Diary of a Madman"** goes to the theatre, reads the journal *The Northern Bee* and orders a new uniform. Nor in **"The Greatcoat"** itself is poverty stressed in the lives of the other minor civil servants, whose leisure time is full of theatre-going, card-playing and tea-drinking. Indeed, all their various activities are used as a contrast to set off the absolute lack of any outside activity on the part of Akakii Akakievich himself.

A contrast can also be seen in the figure of the assistant chief clerk who, if Akakii Akakievich seems incredibly poor, appears on the other hand to be exaggeratedly affluent. He is, after all, only the assistant chief clerk, yet he not only lives in the better part of St Petersburg, but occupies the best part of the house—the first floor. He has servants, is able to throw a lavish party without any difficulty and invites guests whose coats have beaver-fur collars and velvet lapels.

Akakii Akakievich has absolutely no social life and no dependents, is over fifty and has been in the department for longer than anyone can remember, yet he is apparently unable to afford something as essential as a proper coat to keep out the St Petersburg frost. It is not as though he is incompetent in monetary affairs. For every rouble which he spends he always puts half a copeck away in a money box. By this means he has already accumulated half the sum necessary for his new coat—forty roubles. According to Akakii Akakievich's system of saving, this must represent a total of eight thousand roubles which he has spent 'in the course of several years', so that, as he receives four hundred roubles per year, it represents twenty years' salary. (The actual period of saving might not be as long as this, since we know that he gets bonuses from the director.)

He is expecting a bonus for the holiday, but it is allotted in advance for other clothing:

> It was necessary to get some new trousers, to pay the bootmaker an old debt for vamping old boot-tops, and he also had to order three shirts from the seamstress,

and a couple of items of that underwear which it is unseemly to mention by name in print.

The coyness of the comic tone suggests that this is not to be taken at its face value, and indeed after his death none of this other clothing is mentioned:

> They did not seal his room, nor any of his things, because in the first place there were no heirs, and in the second place, very little inheritance had been left, to be precise—a bunch of goose quills, a quire of white official paper, three pairs of socks, two or three buttons which had dropped off his trousers, and the dressing-gown, already well known to the reader.

Yet the boots and the underclothing had earlier figured prominently in his budget, for he had resolved:

> when walking along the streets, to step on the stones and paving as lightly and carefully as possible, almost on tiptoe, so that by these means he would not wear out his soles quickly; to give his undergarments to be washed by the laundress as seldom as possible; and in order to prevent them getting too dirty from wear, to take them off every time he came home, and wear only a fustian dressing-gown, which was very ancient and had been spared even by time itself.

All this is grotesque: the poverty of Akakii Akakievich is not credible in real terms. If all the titular councillors of Tsar Nicholas I were as inexplicably indigent, he would never have had a civil service. Yet although the material poverty of Akakii Akakievich is open to question, what is not in doubt is his spiritual poverty: it is not Akakii Akakievich's lack of material resources which is striking, but the paucity of his spiritual resources. Gogol is here employing a device central to his portrayal of psychological states: the external world reflects an inner world and in Akakii Akakievich's outward indigence we have a metaphor of his inner poverty.

Akakii Akakievich's inner world is completely obsessive. He has only one passion—the copying out of words:

> One could scarcely find a man who lived so much in his job. It is not enough to say that he worked with zeal, no, he worked with love. In his copying he was aware of a world of his own which was pleasant and full of variety.

His love of writing is not merely a job; his leisure hours, spent at home, are devoted to his one great passion. Even when walking about the streets he is incapable of thinking about anything else:

> But if Akakii Akakievich looked at anything, then everywhere he saw his own clear lines, written in an even hand, and only if a horse's muzzle sprang out of nowhere, lodged itself on his shoulder and blew out through its nostrils a whole wind on to his cheek, only then would he notice that he was not in the middle of a line, but rather in the middle of the street.

This day-dream quality associated with Akakii Akakievich's copying is suggestive of 'writing' of a different order. Our hero might almost be a writer in a more fundamental sense—a man obsessed by words like Gogol himself. But Akakii Akakievich's imagination is caught not by the content and significance of words, but by their outward form; their most palpable material expression. Even in his inner world surface has ousted content.

Akakii Akakievich's obsession with words is understandable: communication is his central problem. When he is given a job which entails the alteration and the *use* of words rather than merely *copying* them, he is at a complete loss. In daily life too, communication is difficult because of his lack of words:

> It must be explained that Akakii Akakievich expressed himself for the most part in prepositions, adverbs, and ultimately in particles which had absolutely no meaning whatever. If, indeed, it were a very difficult matter, he even had the habit of leaving his phrases unfinished, so that very frequently he would begin his utterance with the words: 'It, indeed, is absolutely, and that,' and then there was just nothing else at all, and he himself would have forgotten, believing that he had already said everything.

Akakii Akakievich not only lacks words himself, he is at the mercy of the words of others, even of the rhetorical effects of Petrovich, the one-eyed tailor, who, we are told:

> . . . was very fond of powerful effects. He liked in some way or other suddenly to take people completely aback and then look sideways to see what sort of face the bewildered person would pull at such words.

The 'powerful effect' of Petrovich, the price he quotes for a new coat, is the device of hyperbole. It challenges the indigence of Akakii Akakievich on both its levels: the material and the verbal.

In all Akakii Akakievich's obsessive copying of words, what he seeks to make his own is not *beauty of style* but *communication* with someone unknown or someone important:

> . . . he would purposely take a copy for himself, for his own pleasure, particularly if the document was distinguished, not by the beauty of its style, but by the fact that it was addressed to some new or important person.

When, however, in real life he tries to communicate with a 'new and important person' (the general to whom he is advised to turn for help), he is a second time devastated by words:

> But the important person, pleased by the fact that the effect had even surpassed all expectations and completely intoxicated by the thought that a word from him could even deprive a man of his senses, glanced sideways at his friend to find out how he looked on the matter.

Here the interview with the general seems consciously to be likened to the earlier visit to the tailor: both love *effekty*, and both look sideways to see what reaction there is to their words. The interview with Petrovich ends: ' . . . and Akakii Akakievich went out, completely annihilated after such words'. With the general, however, the 'annihilation' is no longer metaphorical: after his words Akakii Akakievich takes to his bed and dies.

> **Akakii Akakievich is a character in a well-known Gogolian mould, caught between the 'visible laughter' of the outer surface and the 'unseen tears' of the inner world.**
>
> **—R. A. Peace**

Akakii Akakievich's obsession with the outer form of words, with their well-executed graphic clothing, is a mark of his desire to be master of them, and at the same time it is a sad comment on his inability to capture their content. He is thus a character in a well-known Gogolian mould, caught between the 'visible laughter' of the outer surface and the 'unseen tears' of the inner world. Yet there is one person with whom he does appear to be able to communicate. On collecting his wits in the street after his first visit to Petrovich, we are told that he:

> . . . began to converse with himself, not jerkily any more, but reasonably and frankly, as though with a sensible friend, with whom one could have a chat about something intimate and near to one's heart.

Communication which is difficult with others seems easy with himself—the one friend he has. Nevertheless there is another 'friend' who comes into his life, a friend who significantly has his own outward form—his new greatcoat. He must endure privations if he is to gain it. He must go without food. Eating for him previously had been the act of an insentient creature (he only realised that it was time to stop when he saw that his stomach had swollen) but now the idea of the coat represents a new 'spiritual' sustenance:

> He even trained himself to go without food in the evenings, but on the other hand he had spiritual food, for he bore in his thoughts the eternal idea of the future coat. From that time on it was as though his very existence had become somehow fuller, as though he had got married, as though some other person were present alongside him, as though he were not alone, as though some congenial life-long lady-friend had agreed to go together with him along life's way—and this lady-friend was none other than that very overcoat with its thick padding and strong lining that would not wear out.

The 'eternal titular councillor' has found his mate not in the 'external feminine' but in the 'eternal idea' of his new coat. A man without content has fallen in love with his new facade. The effect the coat has on his personality is remarkable:

> He became somehow livelier, even firmer in character, like a man who had determined and set himself a goal. Doubt and indecision, in a word all wavering and vague traits, disappeared of their own accord from his face and his behaviour. From time to time fire showed in his eyes, and the most daring and bold thoughts flashed through his mind: 'Should I not really put marten on the collar?'

The entertaining of 'the most daring and bold thoughts' in respect of the coat seems to be carrying on the sexual motif, and certainly the coat has replaced his old love: 'Once, when copying a document, he nearly even made a mistake, so that he exclaimed "ugh!" almost audibly and crossed himself.'

When he has enough money to buy the material for his coat, 'his heart usually quite quiet, began to beat'; and the day on which the coat was actually brought to him is given almost ceremonial importance by one of the narrator's verbal formulae:

> It was . . . it is difficult to say on what precise day, but probably on the most solemn of days in Akakii Akakievich's life, that Petrovich finally brought the coat.

This most solemn of days in the life of Akakii Akakievich might almost be a wedding. Certainly the festive occasion is linked to an awakening of feeling: 'In the meantime, Akakii Akakievich went along in the most festive disposition of all his feelings', and this new outward form has even brought him 'inner happiness'.

This sense of a special occasion is carried on in the treatment Akakii Akakievich receives at the office. It is suggested that he should throw a party that evening so that his colleagues can drink to the coat. Akakii Akakievich is saved from further embarrassment only by the intervention of the assistant chief clerk who invites everybody round to his apartment instead, as it so happens that it is his name-day:

> The whole of that day was for Akakii Akakievich just like the greatest solemn festival. He returned home in the happiest frame of mind.

His whole way of life appears to be changing:

> He dined cheerfully and after dinner he did not write anything, not a single document, but just lay like a sybarite on the bed, until it got dark.

He then puts on his greatcoat and sets out for the party.

The section which follows is one of the key sections of the story. The narrator loses his memory when he wishes to give the precise location in St Petersburg of the apartment of the assistant chief clerk. (It does not matter that he has not bothered to tell us where Akakii Akakievich lives, nor where he works.) The problem of where the assistant chief clerk lives, however, is solved by one of the narrator's verbal formulae:

> What is at least certain is that the civil servant lived in the better part of the town, therefore not at all near to Akakii Akakievich.

The formula seeks to emphasise the social distance between two worlds, but the distance is also psychological. The physical landmarks of the route, as the narrator confesses by way of excuse, are all confused in his head:

> . . . and everything that there is in St Petersburg, all the streets and the houses have become so fused and jumbled in one's head that it is difficult to get anything out of there in a decent form.

Certainly, there seems to be a parallel between what is going on in the streets of St Petersburg and what is going on in another head—that of Akakii Akakievich. His movement into greater life is not merely a physical progression, but reflects a process going on within Akakii Akakievich himself. Once more we have an example of Gogol's central device; the outer world is a metaphor for the inner:

> At first Akakii Akakievich had to pass through several desolate streets with feeble lighting, but the more he drew near to the apartment of the civil servant, the livelier the streets became, the more populated and the more powerfully illuminated.

His progress is from desolation to life—from darkness to light, and now the former automaton, who never used to notice anything in the street, seems to have his eyes open for the first time: 'He looked at all this as though it were something new.'

An even more amazing awakening seems to be taking place:

> He stopped with curiosity before the lighted window of a shop to look at a picture which depicted a beautiful woman, who was throwing off her shoe, and thus exposing her whole leg, and not a bad one at that, while behind her back a man with side whiskers and a beautiful goatee beard below his lip had stuck his head through the doorway from another room. Akakii Akakievich shook his head from side to side, grinned, and then went on his way. Why did he grin? Was it because he had encountered a thing that was completely unknown to him, but about which each one of us has retained some sort of sixth sense, or like many other civil servants, did he think the following: 'Well, those French! If they take a fancy to something like that, then it is, indeed, just as it were . . .' ? But perhaps he did not even think that—it is after all impossible to get inside the soul of another man and find out everything that he thinks.

Thus the narrator disclaims all attempt at psychological analysis. Yet his own speculations, before his assertion that it is impossible to get inside another man, not only call attention to Akakii Akakievich's state of mind, they suggest his ambiguity of response in an evocative way. A similarly effective denial of psychological insight occurs after the loss of the coat when Akakii Akakievich has returned home and gone to bed:

> . . . and how he spent the night there may be judged by those who are capable to any extent of imagining the situation of another man.

Gogol, in rejecting any possibility of getting inside his characters, is not abandoning the attempt to portray their psychology. He merely proceeds by different means. Akakii Akakievich wears his new greatcoat like a different frame of mind; his brand-new outward form is his new self. At the same time the greatcoat also has for him associations of a new relationship, a 'life-long lady-friend', so that when in his progress through the 'streets' of St Petersburg, he encounters sexual titillation, perhaps for the first time, his reactions are ambiguous—but not as ambiguous as the narrator would have us believe.

The opening paragraph of "The Greatcoat" should be a warning to the reader. It is long, involved and absolutely irrelevant to the story itself.

—*R. A. Peace*

The opening paragraph of **"The Greatcoat"** should be a warning to the reader. It is long, involved and absolutely irrelevant to the story itself. In fact the opening paragraph is a sort of verbal arabesque which goes nowhere, except back to its original starting point: from 'In one of our government departments' to '. . . a certain department.'

It is typical of Gogol to take his reader on a long aside which will go nowhere. As a form of humour it may be compared to the shaggy dog story, where the joke is not *for* the listener but *on* the listener. It is, of course, a dangerous game to play with a reader, who can always terminate the joke by putting the book down. Moreover, such a joke implies a latent hostility towards the reader. Yet if the anecdote in the opening paragraph about the police inspector has any point at all, it is to suggest quite the reverse, namely that readers (especially those in official positions) are only too prone to show hostility towards authors.

The narrator of the story is, of course, not Gogol himself. It is someone who is very naive, not at all well educated, and who as a teller of a story is incredibly inept. He re-

peatedly concentrates on inessential and often absurd details, at the expense of the plot itself—and in this sense the opening paragraph is a foretaste of what is to come. (The inept narrator is a favourite device with Gogol, and this type of tale—a story told by an illiterate narrator—is quite common in Russian literature).

But although the narrator is naive, the narrative, in effect, is not: it is full of hints, innuendoes, puns and verbal tricks of all sorts. It is through these that the tale really unfolds, and in a way which gives hidden depth to a seemingly shallow surface.

One of the great ironies of this style is that the naive narrator requires a sophisticated reader, a reader who is sensitive, not to the possibilities of personal libel, as those whom Gogol mocks in the opening paragraph, but one who is sensitive to words and tone and word-play.

Naive ambiguity is a constant feature of the narrative technique in **"The Greatcoat."** There are many puns which communicate a waywardness and playfulness of tone to the narrative, yet their contribution is not so much to the humour of the story as to the external presentation of the inner world of the central character, a man who is himself obsessed by the outward form of words, their graphic contours, only because their real content and function eludes him. The pun is precisely this: a word taken at face value which nevertheless has a hidden content beneath its deceptive surface. The verbal play has more meaning than is at first apparent, and the relationship between facade and interior is not only the central 'device' of **"The Greatcoat,"** it is the architectural principle which informs its shape.

There is a great deal of verbal play at the opening of the story, (i.e. the whole of the introductory section ending with the play on the word 'councillor'). In introducing Akakii Akakievich the narrator places exaggerated importance on the naming of his hero, whereas his formative years are merely bridged by a verbal formula: 'The child was christened. At which he began to cry and he pulled such a face as though he sensed beforehand that he would be a titular councillor.' Almost immediately after this we find him already long established in the office as a copy clerk: ' . . . so that later people became convinced that he had obviously been born into the world ready-made, in a uniform and a bald patch on his head'. His christening seems to pre-ordain his profession and his profession seems to have been entered on at birth.

This emphasis on his christening and lack of interest in his formative years suggests that his name is far more important than his life in determining his character. In particular the origin of the surname is treated with naive seriousness:

> The civil servant's name was Bashmachkin. From the very name itself one can see that at some time it had been derived from a shoe; but when, at what particular time and in what way it was derived from a shoe—nothing of this is known. Both his father and his

grandfather, and even his brother-in-law, all Bash-machkins through and through, used to walk about in boots, changing the soles only three times a year.

The whole of this explanation is patently absurd, if taken at its surface meaning. Yet, on another level, it suggests a whole train of semantic ambiguities which are picked up and developed later in the story, and in such a way as to reveal the psychological problems of Akakii Akakievich himself.

In the first place the verb 'derived' is taken quite literally, (the all important qualification 'word' which ought to precede 'shoe' is omitted) so that our hero's name appears to have come directly from an article of footwear—a shoe (just as later it will be suggested that he has almost got married to a greatcoat). Through his surname the hero is thus directly identified with a mere casing of the human body.

The narrator compounds the absurdity by asserting that all Akakii Akakievich's family wore boots, and gives the irrelevant information that they had the soles replaced only three times a year. (The saving of his soles will later figure prominently in Akakii Akakievich's economies needed to acquire the coat.) The list of Akakii Akakievich's relatives, who, according to the narrator, are all genuine Bashmachkins includes 'even a brother-in-law' (*i dazhe shurin*) despite the fact that, as this is a relationship by marriage, he could not possibly be a genuine Bashmachkin as the narrator claims. Yet the inclusion of this brother-in-law is absurd in an even more profound sense. Russian relationships by marriage are very precise, and *shurin* can only mean 'wife's brother'. For Akakii Akakievich to have a *'shurin'*, he must also have a wife, but a wife is no more in evidence than these other relatives with whom he is here credited. Akakii Akakievich is completely alone. This little verbal puzzle, therefore, tangles the 'shoe' from which his name is derived, with the relatives from whom he is actually derived (his father and his grandfather) and ties them in with a figure to whom he can only be related by a sexual bond (the brother-in-law).

The theme of the wife, who is non-existent but implied, appears again when the narrator gives examples of his 'down-trodden' existence, such as the teasing to which he is subjected at the office:

> They would relate, right in front of him, various stories concocted about him. They said about his landlady, an old woman of seventy, that she beat him, and they would ask him when their wedding would be. They would scatter paper on his head, calling it snow.

The motif of the 'shoe' is prominent in the picture which stirs a vague sexual awakening in Akakii Akakievich, and the detail seems intentional, for virtually the same picture is described at the end of **"The Nose,"** but without the mention of a shoe. At a later stage a shoe will also link this picture with his landlady. Thus the 'shoe', from which his outward identification (his name) is derived, suggests a latent sexual motif in much the same way as does that other item of apparel, his other outward form, the greatcoat.

Akakii Akakievich's progress through St Petersburg may be interpreted as a journey in self-exploration: it is certainly a progress towards light. He moves away from his own badly-lit part of the city, past the lighted window with its erotic picture to the apartment of the civil servant who has invited him; 'the assistant chief clerk lived in great style; there was a lantern shining on the staircase'.

The fact that Akakii Akakievich is at first overawed is again suggested by Gogol's external method of psychological portrayal. Akakii Akakievich is reduced to the status of an object among other objects:

> On entering the hall Akakii Akakievich saw on the floor a whole row of galoshes. Among them in the middle of the room stood a samovar, noisily emitting clouds of steam. On the walls hung nothing but greatcoats and capes, among which there were several which even had beaver collars or velvet lapels.

It seems significant that he is confronted with footwear and greatcoats. The only thing which appears to have life in this ante-room is another inanimate object—the samovar. Real life once more, it seems, is going on elsewhere: for on the other side of the wall he can hear the noise of the party. The guests have already been assembled for some time.

Nevertheless the occasion has been held partly to honour Akakii Akakievich's new coat. He is accepted by this society, and his greatcoat is rapturously admired, even though there are better ones hanging up in the hall. 'Then, of course, everybody dropped him and his coat and turned, as is the custom, to the whist-tables.' After all, Akakii Akakievich is not really at home in these surroundings. He tries to creep away, but is made to stay for supper and two festive glasses of champagne. It is after midnight when he escapes. He finds his coat, 'which, not without regret, he perceived was lying on the floor'. He carefully shakes it, and goes down to a still lighted street. Here, sexual promptings (inexplicable to the narrator) once more well up within him:

> Akakii Akakievich went along in a gay mood, and for some unknown reason he was even almost on the point of running up behind some lady or other, who went past like lightning, and every part of whose body was full of unusual movement. However, he stopped at once and went on as before very slowly, amazed himself at this unaccountable burst of speed.

His progress now, however, is away from light and conviviality towards the dark, shuttered emptiness of his own quarter of the town.

On his outward journey he had been *looking* for the first time in his life. Now, as he crosses a dark square, where a light seems 'at the world's end' and 'it is as though there is a sea around him', our explorer closes his eyes—and is robbed of his greatcoat by men with moustaches. Thus he is brutally deprived of the promise of that fuller life which had been offered to him so briefly and so tenuously.

He goes home to his landlady and the details of his return seem to reproduce in ironical terms the elements of the picture in the lighted window which had earlier aroused such strange stirrings within him:

> The old lady, the landlady of his apartment, hearing the terrible knocking at the door, hurriedly jumped out of bed and with a shoe on only one foot, ran to open the door, holding her nightshirt to her bosom out of modesty.

The landlady, as we know, has already been associated with the marital status of Akakii Akakievich by the clerks at the office, who teased him about marrying her and scattered 'snow' on his head. Now, when he comes back covered in real snow, his landlady, like the woman in the picture, confronts him with 'a shoe on one foot' and a hint of sexual titillation ('holding her nightshirt to her bosom, out of modesty'). But the 'man at the door' is not the dandy with the side whiskers and beautiful beard; it is the dishevelled Akakii Akakievich, with what little hair he has in complete disarray.

So Akakii Akakievich is thrown back on his seventy-year-old landlady, by the 'light' of whose candle he used to work in the evenings (after first having taken off his underwear to economise on laundry!). On her advice he goes to the police, but the district superintendent seems to think that the loss of the coat is in some way connected with its owner's dissolute life:

> The district superintendent received the story of the theft of the coat somehow in an exceedingly strange way. Instead of turning his attention to the main point of the matter, he began to question Akakii Akakievich as to why he was returning home so late, and hadn't he called in at some disorderly house or other?

Here, as elsewhere in the story, the significance of the coat is interpreted not in terms of the obvious, but in terms of a suggested sexual theme. The hint is present even on his death-bed, for he keeps asking his landlady to drag a coat-thief out from under his blankets.

If in the opening section of **"The Greatcoat"** verbal play is an important device for establishing motifs which are to be developed in the central section of the story, now in the final section (the ghost sequence) verbal play has a similar function. There is a recurring pun on the concepts of 'dead' and 'alive'. The police are ordered to apprehend the *'dead man* dead or alive'. One of them apparently succeeds, but loses the ghost because he pauses to take snuff of a quality 'which even a dead man couldn't stand', and from that time on the police 'got so frightened of dead men, that they were even fearful of arresting the living'. Finally, there is an 'apparition' at the end of the story, who when challenged by a policeman, shows him a huge fist 'such as you would not find on the living'.

All this seems like humour directed at the police, who throughout the story have shown themselves to be particularly inept, but there is also a serious intention behind the word-play. The ghost is first introduced as 'a dead man in the form of a civil servant' *(mertvets v vide chinovnika)*. Later he is simply referred to as the 'dead man-civil servant' *(chinovnik-mertvets)*. The verbal play on 'dead' and 'alive' is therefore a motif pointing to the artistic function of the story's fantastic ending; it raises the whole question of *'chinovnik-mertvets'*.

When he was alive, Akakii Akakievich was in reality more like a 'civil servant in the form of a dead man'. The promise of an awakening into life, flimsy though it may have been, was cruelly taken from him by men with moustaches. When he has died he returns as a 'dead man in the form of a civil servant' to avenge himself and, by one of those ironies in which the story abounds, he proves to be more effective as a dead man, than he was when alive.

It is typical of Gogol that this inversion to which the central character is subjected should also be reflected in the external world around him. When earlier Akakii Akakievich was going through the streets of St Petersburg, the narrator was insistent that everything in the city was so muddled in his head that he could not remember names; now, when his hero appears as a ghost, he is very meticulous about giving the precise location of each appearance. In the first instance a real man was going through a spiritual city; in the second a spirit man is haunting a concrete and actual city.

It is only after the ghost has robbed the 'important person' of his greatcoat that this unquiet spirit is finally laid, and the whole incident is presented with the same ironic parallelism of detail which has been noted elsewhere in the story. The important person, having just learned of the death of Akakii Akakievich, goes to a party to cheer himself up. (Akakii Akakievich had been to a party before he lost his coat.) Here (like Akakii Akakievich before him) he has two glasses of champagne. He feels in a gayer mood, and just as Akakii Akakievich had then, for some unknown reason, wanted to chase after a woman in the street, so the important person now entertains thoughts of an amorous nature:

> The champagne put him in a mood for special measures; that is he decided not to go home yet, but to call on a certain lady of his acquaintance, Karolina Ivanovna, a lady who appeared to be of German extraction, and for whom he felt an entirely friendly relationship.

Here, as in the earlier incident with Akakii Akakievich, the narrator shows himself to be naively uncomprehending about the sexual motivation of his characters.

Whereas Akakii Akakievich had been making the first tentative gestures in the direction of life, the important person has long had it firmly in his grasp. He takes an active part in the evening gathering as a man among equals; on leaving the party he is going to a real mistress; and moreover, unlike Akakii Akakievich, he also has a family:

But the important person, although he was quite content with the family affection he received at home, considered it fitting to have a lady-friend in another part of town for friendly relationships. This lady-friend was not a whit better or younger than his wife. But such puzzles do exist in the world, and it is not for us to judge them.

It seems poetic justice that the ghost should rob this 'man of substance' of his greatcoat at this precise moment. The effect is cathartic: the ghost is laid, and the general himself becomes a much better person.

The story ends with yet another ironic twist. Another ghost is seen and it is believed to be the ghost of Akakii Akakievich, but it is really an 'apparition' and when challenged by a particularly inept policeman it threatens him with a fist not unlike that of the man who had stolen Akakii Akakievich's greatcoat in the first place and had showed him a fist 'the size of a civil servant's head'. The policeman leaves the apparition alone:

> The apparition was, however, much taller and wore really enormous moustaches, and turning its steps, as it seemed, towards the Obukhov Bridge, it completely disappeared in the darkness of the night.

Even Akakii Akakievich's credibility as a ghost, it seems, is being challenged by those men with moustaches and the whole story ends on a note of darkness.

Victor Peppard (essay date 1990)

"Who Stole Whose Overcoat and Whose Text Is It?" in *South Atlantic Review*, Vol. 55, No. 1, January, 1990, pp. 63-80.

[*In the following essay, Peppard compares "The Overcoat" to stories in the supernatural genre with which Gogol was most likely familiar, in order to determine whether the conclusion is intended by Gogol to be supernatural or mundane.*]

The conclusion of **"The Overcoat"** is usually regarded as absolutely crucial to the story's whole meaning, yet there is no consensus among critics about what actually takes place at the end of the story. Indeed, one of the most fundamental questions that the conclusion poses, namely, who stole whose overcoat, remains very much in a state of doubt and dispute. There are a number of reasons for this anomalous situation. First of all, ambiguity was not only a special forte of Gogol, but an especially important feature of the romantic literature of the period in which he wrote. Specifically, Gogol's use of detail is remarkably ambiguous and filled with traps for seekers after hard facts and certain conclusions. The lack of agreement among critics and scholars over exactly what happens at the end of **"The Overcoat"** is eloquent testimony to the effectiveness of Gogol's technique.

The ending of the story has given rise to a whole range of interpretations. There are many who believe that it is truly supernatural in that Akaky Akakievich actually returns from the grave to rob the significant personage of his overcoat. As V. V. Gippius says, "in the structure of the story, a special place is occupied by the fantastic ending. (It must in fact be regarded as fantastic)" [*Gogol*, ed. and trans. by Robert A. Maguire, 1981]. From different points of view, [Dmitry] Chizhevsky, [Henri] Troyat, and [M. B.] Khrapchenko all agree [Chizhevsky, "About Gogol's 'Overcoat'," *Gogol from the Twentieth Century*, ed. and trans. by Robert A. Maguire 1974; Troyat, *Divided Soul: The Life of Gogol*, trans. Nancy Amphout, 1973; Khrapchenko, *Nikola, Gogol. Literaturngi put'. Velichie pisatelia*, 1984]. Others are absolutely convinced that the ending is in fact completely mundane; according to them, it is not Akaky Akakievich who steals the significant personage's overcoat but, rather, some thieves. In between these two radically opposed analyses there are many critics who are not entirely certain about what takes place; some lean towards the mundane view and some favor the supernatural one.

In all of the many critical analyses of **"The Overcoat"** one of the things that is most often missing is a recognition that the story, for all of its manifest brilliance and independence as a unique masterpiece, has a definite and tremendously significant relationship to the genre of the supernatural tale, particularly those tales about corpses and ghosts who have, or seem to have, returned from the dead. Therefore, in order better to understand **"The Overcoat"** it is instructive to examine it in relation to the practice of Gogol's predecessors, such as E. T. A. Hoffmann, Washington Irving, and Pushkin, as well as to Gogol's own treatment of the supernatural. In particular it is helpful to establish to what extent Gogol models his story on the generic requirements of the supernatural tale and to what extent he modifies them for his own purposes.

If some definite conclusions about the ending can be reached, a demonstration of how they reflect on some of the central questions raised by the story as a whole is in order. For example, is there a moral or a message that may be distilled from it, as is often claimed? Also, can the story be used as an instrument with which to measure the psychological and spiritual states of its author? Finally, just for whom has this text been designed, and whom has Gogol designated as the final arbiter of its meaning?

In assessing the relationship of **"The Overcoat"** to the genre of the supernatural tale it is useful to begin by noting the theories of Gary Saul Morson [as outlined his book, *The Boundaries of Genre: Dostoevsky's "Diary of a Writer" and the Traditions of Literary Utopia*, 1981] about how genres relate to one another and how they are formed and reformed. Morson's ideas are particularly relevant to those times when genres are in a state of transition, when literature is on the threshold between eras—exactly the kind of period in which **"The Overcoat"** was written. For **"The Overcoat"** (1842) appeared just at the time when Russian literature was moving from an essentially romantic depiction of character motivation to a more psychologically realistic one such as that exemplified in Lermontov's *Geroi nashego vremeni* (1840; *Hero of Our Time*, 1958). We also know that Gogol was then himself attempting, as Slonimsky puts it, to give the characters in his sequel to *Dead Souls* "lifelike, 'realistic,' fullness and richness" [Alexander Slonimsky, "The Technique of the Comic in Gogol," in *Gogol from the Twentieth Century*, ed. and trans. by Robert A. Maguire, 1974] and thereby create his own version of a psychologically realistic novel.

The first of Morson's concepts that is so illuminating with respect to **"The Overcoat"** is that of a doubly encoded text. Such a work may contain two fundamentally different texts, each of which may be for a different reader. One of the most graphic examples of this occurs frequently in children's literature, where, as happens in Lewis Carroll's *Alice in Wonderland* and *Through the Looking Glass*, one and the same story may contain such a doubly encoded structure that includes one text for the child reader and another for the adult reader. One of the reasons **"The Overcoat"** has proven so elusive and so resistant to monologizing readings is that the story is a doubly, if not multiply, encoded text.

Morson's other concept that enhances our understanding of **"The Overcoat"** is found in his description of how one may detect the presence of parody in a work of fiction. As Morson writes, "an especially common technique is the introduction of an element—an incident in the plot, let us say, or an unexpected choice of words—that is incongruous with the tone or generic conventions of the original." Here Morson is in a sense expanding the formalist critic Yury Tynianov's notion that comic motivation plays a decisive role in the creation of parody.

In light of Tynianov's and Morson's theories of parody the following passage, in which Gogol introduces an element of comedy by means of a pun, acquires special significance: "At the police station the order was given to catch the dead man (*mertvets*) at any cost, dead (*mertvogo*) or alive, and punish him as an example to others in the severest manner, and they almost even succeeded in this."

The comic tone becomes even more pronounced in a scene that could be a precursor to modern slapstick comedy when a watchman grabs hold of the (presumed) corpse, calls for help, and gets out some snuff in order to "freshen up his nose that had been frostbitten six times in his lifetime." The snuff is such strong stuff that it causes the corpse to spray the watchman in the eyes with a sneeze, at which point the corpse makes his getaway. Gogol's compilation of gestures and details may cause the reader to forget that the whole sequence of events is most improbable. Gogol resumes his play with the language when he writes, "The watchmen took such a fright of dead men (*mertvetsam*) that they were even afraid to take the living (*zhivykh*)." In this part of the story Gogol builds a network of comedy on two levels: comic gestures and plays on words. Their combined effect is to make the reader wary about this dead man who seems to have returned to haunt the living.

There is another level on which Gogol suggests that there may be an alternate reading to this apparently fantastic

tale. This is found in the extensive description of the significant personage's psychological reaction to Akaky Akakievich's death.

> Soon after the departure of the poor Akaky Akakievich, who had been severely dressed down, *a certain significant personage* began to feel something like regret. Compassion was not foreign to him; his heart was accessible to many kind movements, despite the fact that his rank very often prevented them from being manifested. . . . He even began to think about poor Akaky Akakievich. And from that time almost every day the pale Akaky Akakievich . . . would appear to him (*predstavlialsia emu*). The thought of him disturbed him to such a degree that a week later he decided even to send a clerk to him to find out what was going on and whether there was not indeed some way to help him; and when they reported to him that Akaky Akakievich had died suddenly in a fever, he was even stricken, felt pangs of conscience (*upreki sovesti*), and was out of sorts all day.

Partly in order to forget the unpleasant impression the news of Akaky Akakievich's death has made on him the significant personage goes out to a social gathering, where he drinks "a couple glasses of champagne." The narrator tells us that the champagne inspired the significant personage to visit his mistress. Before reaching her he is robbed by a man whom he recognizes as Akaky Akakievich and whose face "was white as snow and looked just like a corpse."

What is so striking in the build-up to the last act of robbery is the thorough psychological motivation provided by Gogol, whose characters are otherwise mainly known for their lack of such motivation.

—Victor Peppard

What is so striking in the build-up to this last act of robbery is the thorough psychological motivation provided by Gogol, whose characters are otherwise mainly known for their lack of such motivation. Indeed, Gogol gives all of the reasons that are necessary for the reader to conclude that it may well have been a guilty conscience that causes the significant personage to see Akaky Akakievich in his robber. Furthermore, as we shall see shortly, the device of using a character's drinking of alcohol as a stimulus for his apprehension of events as supernatural had already become well-known in the work of Pushkin and others.

For those who do not believe in the fantasticality of the conclusion of **"The Overcoat"** the description of the ghost (*prividenie*) who appears at the very end of the story is perhaps even more persuasive than the guilty conscience of the significant personage. This is, by the way, the first ghost to appear in the story, since up to that point the putative corpse (*mertvets*) of Akaky Akakievich has been the only other visitor to the city from beyond the grave. He has an "enormous moustache" and "such a fist as you won't find among the living," and consequently looks just like one of the men who robbed Akaky Akakievich, who also had a moustache and "a fist the size of a clerk's head." Since this ghost was "much taller in stature" than whoever or whatever it was that robbed the significant personage, a mundane explanation of the conclusion is that there were two thieves, exactly the two who robbed Akaky Akakievich, one of whom is tall and the other of whom is short. If this is so, it is eminently appropriate for Gogol, whose works abound in these carnivalistic pairs, such as Bobchinsky and Dobchinsky of *Revizor* (1836; *The Inspector General,* 1964) and the two Ivans of *Povest' of tom, kak possorilsia Ivan Ivanovich s Ivanom Nikiforovichem* (1834; *The Tale of How Ivan Ivanovich Quarrelled with Ivan Nikiforovich,* 1964). The two Ivans are juxtaposed to each other in approximately the same way as are the thieves of **"The Overcoat"** in that "Ivan Ivanovich is a bit thin and of tall stature; Ivan Nikiforovich is a little shorter, but to make up for it he spreads out in girth."

Yet, despite the evidence that the ending of **"The Overcoat"** may contain a spoof of a supernatural tale, many of the most serious critics of the story are not willing to deny that it is fantastic. For example, Bernheimer writes the following: "Even if one grants that the ghost seen by the frail policeman was 'really' the original thief of Akaky's overcoat, that ghost is not necessarily the same as the earlier 'corpse' which, after all, we have been explicitly told has ceased to appear" [Charles C. Bernheimer, "Cloaking the Self: The Literary Space of Gogol's 'Overcoat,'" *PMLA* 90, 1975]. Bernheimer concludes that Stilman's claim [in his Afterword to *"Diary of a Madman" and Other Stories,* trans. by Andrew R. MacAndrew, 1966] that the significant personage was robbed by the same man who robbed Akaky Akakievich "cannot be proved."

In order better to assess whether the conclusion of **"The Overcoat"** contains supernatural occurrences or simply mundane ones, it is helpful to examine how the genre of the supernatural tale had developed up to the time of the story's writing, both in Gogol and in the work of his immediate predecessors and contemporaries, and to determine to what extent Gogol is implementing the conventions of such a tale and to what extent he is altering them for his own purposes.

Ghost stories, stories about dead people who have returned to be with the living, and other supernatural tales appear in a number of different forms. In some stories events have a completely supernatural motivation. In others, fantastic apparitions and corpses only seem to take part in the events of the story, but they are in fact the product of a character's dream. There are also tales that deliberately spoof the traditional formulae of a ghost story and are designed so that only the most gullible characters and readers will believe that they are fantastic. Finally, there are stories in which it is difficult to tell whether the events are truly supernatural or only apparently supernatural. Generally speaking, it is only the first category of ghost story that is characterized by the utmost gravity in the presentation of the fantastic. The other kinds of ghost stories contain the possibility for comic and humorous twists and even outright parody of the usual fantastic motifs. It is not uncommon for a single writer to be the author of more than one type of supernatural tale. This circumstance indicates that the treatment of supernatural elements may not be so much a matter of the writer's view of the afterlife as it is of how he decides to implement literary convention.

Gogol is actually one of a very few Russian writers who is the author of fantastic tales in which events have an entirely supernatural basis. Most of the other Russian writers of this period present supernatural phenomena and occurrences either as the products of a dream or as the source of humorous situations. In Gogol's early works, such as the stories of *Vechera na khutore bliz Dikanki* (1832-1833; *Evenings on a Farm Near Dikanka,* 1964), devils freely interact with people in such a way that there is usually no doubt about their supernatural status. Yet even here, as [Yu. V.] Mann notes [in "Evoliutsiia gogolevskoi fantastiki," *K istorii russLogo romantizma,* 1973], there is a comic presentation of the fantastic in the stories **"Sorochinskaia yarmarka"** (**"The Fair at Sorochinsky"**) and **"Maiskaia noch'"** (**"A May Night"**).

Vladimir Odoevsky's story "Brigadir" (1833; "The Brigadier") is a rare example of a story by a Russian author other than Gogol in which events may be interpreted as taking place as the result of a supernatural force. In this story the narrator describes how he has been visited by the corpse of a deceased friend. Although [Delbert] Phillips has suggested that this visit is actually a dream [in *Spook or Spoof? The Structure of the Supernatural in Russian Romantic Tales,* 1982], there is no such explicit indication in the story so that the events may be apprehended as supernatural. Odoevsky's "Nasmeshka mertvetsa" (1834; "The Mockery of a Corpse," 1965) and Bestuzhev-Marlinsky's "Strashnoe gadanie" (1831; "The Terrible Divination") are stories in which dreams clearly act to rationalize what at first appears to be a supernatural return from the dead. One of the best known examples of this type of story is Pushkin's "Grobovshchik" (1831; "The Undertaker," 1983), in which Prokhorov has a reunion with some of the people he has buried. At the end of the story it turns out that it was all a drunken dream. Here, as in the case of the dream in "Pikovaia dama" (1834; "The Queen of Spades," 1983) in which the dead countess apparently visits Herman, Pushkin uses copious imbibing as a stimulus for the character's encounter with the seemingly supernatural. In "The Undertaker" what first seems to be a supernatural occurrence takes on a comic aspect when the skeletons begin to crumble and fall apart. Pushkin's humorous treatment of the skeletal remains of Prokhorov's customers serves as a parody of the serious presentation of skeletons, corpses, and specters as genuinely supernatural beings.

Comedy and humor are the means by which supernatural tales are turned into spoofs, parodies, and hoaxes. In Orest Somov's story "Prikaz s togo sveta" (1827; "An Order from the Other World") the apparently fantastic turns out to be a hoax that is played on the gullible Hohenstaufen, who wants to believe that he has been visited by his deceased ancestor (108-19). Odoevsky's "Prividenie" (1838; "The Ghost") is another story that makes fun of traditional ghost stories and people who believe in them. Here an elaborate Chinese box frame structure and an ambiguous surprise ending give the story a tone of wry humor.

In connection with stories where the borderline between the truly fantastic and the apparently fantastic is difficult to determine it is appropriate to mention E. T. A. Hoffmann, both because he is one of the most skillful and influential practitioners of fantastic tales and because he is one of the writers Gogol was brought up on. As it turns out, Hoffmann wrote only a handful of true ghost stories, and in one of these, "Eine Spukgeschichte" (1819; "A Ghost Story"), there is considerable debate among the characters over the exact nature of the apparition one of them, Adelgunde, has seen. In general the borderline between fantasy and reality in Hoffmann is extremely subtle and ambiguous, and in some cases it is possible that, as with Gogol, Hoffmann's reputation as an exponent of the fantastic leads readers to perceive mundane occurrences in a supernatural light. It is in this respect, rather than in any specific work, that Hoffmann is an important precursor to Gogol.

Two other stories deserve special attention because they treat the apparent return of people from the dead with great subtlety. Washington Irving's "The Legend of Sleepy Hollow" (1819) and Pushkin's "The Queen of Spades" both contain important models for Gogol's shift from the portrayal of clearly supernatural events to a more complex representation with psychological implications.

Irving is another of the writers Gogol was brought up on, so there is no doubt that Gogol was familiar with his stories. In "The Legend of Sleepy Hollow" Irving parodies a ghost story by providing a psychological rationale for the apparently fantastic appearance of the headless horseman. Throughout the story Irving develops the motif of Ichabod Crane's predisposition to believe in witches and ghosts, so that when Brom Bones chases him on a horse, Crane is frightened into believing that it is the legendary headless horseman who supposedly haunts Sleepy Hollow. In addition to this systematic psychological and circumstantial motivation, Irving provides details at the very end of the story that create a surprise ending—a surprise, that is, for the reader who thought he or she was reading a truly supernatural tale. For at the site of the assault on Ichabod Crane a pumpkin is found that indicates to the discerning reader that it was not the horseman who struck Crane with a skull, but Brom Bones who hit him with a pumpkin. The conclusion of **"The Overcoat"** might well be seen, therefore, as a highly concentrated variation on Irving's technique of strategically planting revealing details and clues and providing a psychological rationale for the seemingly fantastic.

"The Queen of Spades" has a particularly important point of contact with **"The Overcoat."** As Nathan Rosen has convincingly argued [in "The Magic Cards in *The Queen of Spades,*" Slavic and East European Journal 19 No. 3, 1975], the apparently supernatural in the former story has an underlying rationale in the psychology of Herman's behavior. According to Rosen, the visitation of the old Countess in a dream, her winking from her coffin at her funeral, and her appearance on the card that finally beats Herman are not fantastic occurrences or apparitions, but rather the products of Herman's unresolved guilty conscience for having caused the old Countess' death. The parallel with **"The Overcoat"** is striking. For in both stories the apparently fantastic may be only a cover for a psychological basis for the characters' behavior, which in both cases is related to a guilty conscience.

Whereas Pushkin's treatment of the supernatural is consistently ironic, Gogol, like Odoevsky, approaches the fantastic in several different ways. This is illustrated well by his stories from the middle of the 1830s. In "Vii" (1835; "Viy," 1979), Gogol's depiction of the supernatural scenes in the church at the end of the story is done in graphic and powerful detail that denies any possibility for a mundane explanation. Yet even in this story the dreams of the seminarian Homa Brut about a witch tend to blur the line between fantasy and reality and thereby introduce the possibility of a rationale for the supernatural. In the same year that "Vii" appeared Gogol published a story, **"Portret"** (1835; **"The Portrait,"** 1964), that is probably his least effective supernatural tale because its representation of the coming to life of a demonic portrait is thoroughly conventional and in no way provocative. **"The Portrait"** seems all the more anomalous by comparison with **"Nos"** (**"The Nose,"** 1964), which was published shortly after it in 1836 and which is one of Gogol's most intriguing treatments of the fantastic. Both at the beginning and at the end of the story Gogol seems to imply that the fantastic appearance of Kovalev's nose as a separate person may actually have taken place in a dream. Kovalev first discovers that his nose is missing when he wakes up one day, and the nose also reattaches itself one day when Kovalev gets up in the morning. There is no explicit indication in the story that there was a dream, however, so that **"The Nose,"** much like **"The Overcoat,"** remains wonderfully ambiguous and marvelously impervious to finalizing interpretations.

Although Gogol's treatment of the fantastic is obviously quite varied and not at all linear, the overall tendency was for it to become increasingly complex and ambiguous over the course of his career. Even the development of **"The Overcoat"** as it moved through successive drafts indicates that Gogol's technique for presenting the fantastic was still evolving as he wrote the story. Gippius finds support for his assertion that the conclusion of **"The Overcoat"** is a fantastic one in a late draft of the story. Here Akaky Akakievich threatens on his death bed to take revenge on the significant personage. Thus, the return of Akaky Akakievich's corpse in the story's final form makes good, as it were, on this threat from the earlier draft. In light of the analysis above, however, what must have taken place is that Gogol, who had already moved beyond a straightforward treatment of the supernatural, would not settle for such a conventional ending to **"The Overcoat."** It appears that sometime in the last stages of the story's composition Gogol decided to use comic absurdities and the depiction of a psychological rationale for the significant personage's behavior as means of greatly complicating the reader's apprehension of events and their significance. In the bewilderment Gogol creates for the reader one thing is certain: **"The Overcoat"** does not exemplify a continuation of a static representation of the fantastic, as has so often been assumed, but it rather signals an important new departure in Gogol's complex, mercurial employment of supernatural motifs.

Thus it may be seen that many of the motifs and techniques found in **"The Overcoat"** have precedents and that for the most part Gogol seems to be working within the traditions of the supernatural tale. It also seems clear from the foregoing that the truly supernatural tale is greatly outweighed in practice by the several kinds of spoofs and parodies of supernatural tales. In fact, it appears that the truly supernatural tale exists primarily as a theoretical model or a presumed supernatural tale, while the vast majority of stories either actively undermine that model or at the least make deviations from it. What, then, is the distinctive contribution **"The Overcoat"** makes to the tradition? Just as Pushkin and Irving do, Gogol makes the solving of the text's plot and its significance into a kind of game by planting clues and suggesting psychological rather than fantastic motivation for character behavior. But Gogol has rewritten the rules of the game to suit himself. He does this by raising the comicality inherent in parodies of supernatural tales to new heights of absurdity and incongruity with his highly developed sequence of interlocking comic gestures and play with the language that is highlighted by his sneezing corpse and the efforts of the police to punish it that "almost even succeeded."

> **Gogol takes the ambiguity characteristic of so many supernatural tales and raises it to a new level. Indeed, he creates a text that is for all intents and purposes doubly encoded, since it may be read either as a fantastic tale or a parody of one.**
>
> *—Victor Peppard*

Gogol also takes the ambiguity characteristic of so many supernatural tales and raises it to a new level. Indeed, he creates a text that is for all intents and purposes doubly encoded, since it may be read either as a fantastic tale or a parody of one. The continued lack of agreement among critics and scholars about what actually takes place in the

conclusion bears witness to the remarkable and durable success of Gogol's technique in creating this doubly encoded text.

How then does the end of the story relate to what comes before? First of all, the ending epitomizes the basic structure of the story as a whole by recapitulating the elaborate system of reversals and mutually canceling contrapuntal juxtapositions of which it consists. These reversals might be described as a kind of game of give-and-take that Gogol plays with the readers and with the characters. The model for this game is found right in the central events of the story, namely, in Gogol's "giving" Akaky Akakievich a new overcoat and then "taking" it away. In the same way, he gives the significant personage power over Akaky Akakievich only to set him up for a fall when his own coat is stolen. Gogol's *skaz* narrator engages in a similar procedure that to a large extent mirrors the story's overall structure. In some instances this narrator claims omniscience and gives away all manner of facts about the characters and events, but in others he feigns amnesia and thereby withholds information.

This system of reversals also pervades the story's basic thematics and tonality. For example, on the one hand the famous "humane passage" in which one of Akaky Akakievich's fellow clerks expresses great compassion for him cannot help but elicit sympathy from the reader. On the other hand, Akaky Akakievich's own automaton-like behavior and personality, which is signalled by his mindless copying of letters and his speech that is full of repetitive nonsense, tends to cancel, as it were, the reader's ability to sympathize fully with him. In this way the conclusion can be seen to replicate the basic structure of the story since in it Gogol gives the reader both a fantastic tale and its parodic denial.

Partly because Gogol was wrestling mightily with spiritual questions at the time he wrote **"The Overcoat,"** and partly because the story contains a stark sequence of events in its conclusion, it is often thought that the story must contain the working out of these questions in the form of a moral. Some of the most perceptive analysts of Gogol's story cannot seem to resist the temptation to reduce it to some sort of moral lesson. Chizhevsky argues convincingly that **"The Overcoat"** is a special kind of love story in which the coat takes the place of a human wife. Yet first he and later [Victor Erlich in his book *Gogol*, 1969] distill **"The Overcoat"** into a warning against becoming excessively involved with mundane, trivial, or unworthy matters, such as the acquisition of a piece of clothing.

Gogol's extended game of give-and-take poses major problems for those who are intent on attributing such moralistic meanings to **"The Overcoat."** One of the questions connected with the ending of **"The Overcoat"** concerns the reasons, if any, for which Akaky Akakievich and the significant personage are punished. Simon Karlinsky [in *The Sexual Labyrinth of Nikolai Gogol*, 1976] has made a persuasive case that Akaky Akakievich's demise and the comeuppance of the significant personage are a kind of "punishment for yielding to a heterosexual impulse." This interpretation is related to Chizhevsky's idea that **"The Overcoat"** is a special kind of love story. Before he has actually acquired his new coat Akaky Akakievich's thoughts about it make him feel as though he had been married and that the coat is his "life's companion." Then after Akaky Akakievich's death the narrator characterizes the overcoat as a "radiant guest" who had visited him. Furthermore, the acquisition of the new coat sparks in Akaky Akakievich hitherto dormant erotic impulses. First he notices the legs of a girl in a picture in a store window, and later he briefly chases after a woman he sees on the street. In Karlinsky's analysis the significant personage is also punished for an erotic impulse because he is robbed while on the way to visit his mistress.

Despite the convincing nature of Karlinsky's thesis it does not account for several important circumstances in the story. First, the situations of Akaky Akakievich and the significant personage, although deliberately juxtaposed by Gogol, are not at all identical. Akaky Akakievich's erotic experiences are both extremely limited and fleeting. The significant personage, on the other hand, has long been involved with his mistress. What is more, Gogol indicates that far from being an affair of passion this liaison is more of a longstanding routine. In fact, there is no ostensible reason why the significant personage carries on this affair, since "this lady friend was not a bit prettier or younger than his wife." It is also clear that the punishments inflicted on Akaky Akakievich and the significant personage are hardly comparable. While the significant personage loses only his overcoat. Akaky Akakievich loses both his coat and his life. In the final analysis, therefore, **"The Overcoat"** is not simply a special variant of a love story, but a grotesque parody of one.

The significant personage is sometimes thought to hold the key to the moral message Gogol is supposed to have invested in **"The Overcoat,"** particularly since the theft of his coat shocks him into repentance for his past arrogant behavior. After the theft of his overcoat he bullies people much less often with the words "How dare you, do you understand who is standing before you?" Andrew Barratt even calls this change in conduct on the part of the significant personage his "resurrection" ["Plot as Paradox: The Case of Gogol's 'Shinel'," *New England Slavonic Journal* 2, 1979]. Barratt notes that no such resurrection takes place in the case of Akaky Akakievich, but he leaves unresolved the problem of why Gogol singles out the significant personage, but not Akaky Akakievich, for salvation. Barratt believes that the story contains a "grotesque vision of the alienation and depersonalization which Gogol saw as the inevitable product not only of Russian society, but of all 'advanced' civilizations." If, as Barratt suggests, **"The Overcoat"** is primarily about a vision of society, it follows logically that Gogol should at least give some hint as to why one character is able to transcend the baleful influence of that society and reform himself, but another is not. The fact that Gogol does not give any such indication cancels in effect any moral judgements one might wish to make on the salvation or damnation of the characters.

In Gogol's game of give-and-take he often seems to imply a certain kind of moral with one hand, but he invariably subverts it with the other. This is particularly evident in the case of Akaky Akakievich, who, after receiving a dressing down from the significant personage, goes outside, catches a fever, arrives home, and dies shortly thereafter. The remarkably swift and arbitrary demise of Akaky Akakievich is echoed most poignantly in Chekhov's story "Smert' chinovnika" (1883; "The Death of a Civil Servant," 1982) in which a clerk who attempts to apologize to a superior is rebuffed, returns home, lies down on a couch, and dies. In **"The Overcoat"** Gogol even lays bare the capricious nature of Akaky Akakievich's destruction with the narrator's comment that "a proper dressing down can sometimes be that strong!"

As so often occurs with Gogol, the characters in **"The Overcoat"** do things and have things happen to them for little apparent cause. Since, as just noted, the significant personage's mistress is little different from his wife, it seems that he conducts an affair over a period of years for no apparent reason. And it is not Akaky Akakievich's culpability for his sudden death that is so striking, but rather the arbitrary manner in which it comes about. It is hard to escape the conclusion that the characters are mere pawns in the game Gogol plays with them.

Charles Bernheimer provides what at first appears to be a rejection of the tendency to draw moral conclusions from **"The Overcoat"** in his endorsement of Eichenbaum's work as an "antidote to reductive biographical and moralizing criticism." As an alternative to the reductive approach Bernheimer claims that "Gogol's text has a reflexive structure by which it insists on its purely literary status, an insistence that simultaneously operates as a defense mechanism for Gogol himself." Bernheimer concludes that the story contains an "exuberant recapture of freedom and omnipotence," but that "this omnipotence must be viewed as impotence, as self-duplicity, as an irreversible schizoid game."

Bernheimer's assertions about the literary independence and the celebration of power inherent in **"The Overcoat"** are not only most welcome as counterweights to the moralistic meanings that have regularly been ascribed to the story, but seem especially apt in relation to the story itself. In particular Gogol's game of give-and-take that he plays with both readers and characters amounts to nothing less than an assertion of his own omnipotence. And Gogol's play with, that is, his modifications and rearrangements of the literary canons of the fantastic tale found in the story's conclusion both underlines the principle of play that obtains throughout and highlights its "purely literary status."

Yet it seems that Bernheimer's characterization of Gogol's assertion of omnipotence in **"The Overcoat"** as "self-duplicity," as an "irreversible schizoid game" brings us full circle to the reductive psychobiographical school stated in up-to-date terms. At the very least it deflects focus from the story itself to the tortured spiritual and psychological state in which Gogol found himself. It also suggests that Gogol's brilliant play with compositional devices, such as the technique of *skaz* narration that places the telling of the story in the mouth of a dodgy, unreliable persona, is only a psychological avoidance mechanism and perhaps even the product of a deranged mind. The greatest danger of Bernheimer's doubling the story back onto the author, though, is that it denies the story's independent existence as a work of art.

It is time to assert emphatically that however compelling Gogol's psychological state was when he wrote **"The Overcoat,"** and however full of psychological implications the story is, it has nevertheless acquired a status that is in a vital sense not dependent on the psyche of its author for its meaning and its existence. It is time to assert that, although **"The Overcoat"** undoubtedly contains reflections of the many sexual, spiritual, and psychological obsessions and vagaries of Gogol's personality, the actual presentation of these questions in the story may be explained in purely literary terms just as well or better than it can be in psychoanalytical ones.

As his play with the conventions of the supernatural tale suggests, Gogol is responding primarily to the purely literary questions and demands posed by the genre in his shaping of the story's outcome. Whether he also manages at the same time to satisfy his own inner psychosexual and psychospiritual needs is an interesting but secondary and probably moot point. Gogol's need to remake the genre in his own fashion is at least as great as, if not greater than, his other needs, which are associated with **"The Overcoat."**

Whose text is **"The Overcoat"**? Certainly few stories contain such a multiplicity of texts. For many decades **"The Overcoat"** was viewed primarily as the outstanding example of a special genre of philanthropic tales about poor, lowly clerks. As we have seen, it is related to the love story in that it is a grotesque parody of a love story. **"The Overcoat"** is also a supernatural tale that includes a kind of co-equal parody of a supernatural tale. Gogol has given the reader a most generous helping of texts or plausible textual encodings. At the same time he has given the reader tremendous responsibility for figuring out what happens in the story and what it means. Yet in concert with the story's other assertions of omnipotence Gogol has retained control over the story's ultimate significance for himself. The doubly encoded supernatural tale/parody of a supernatural tale is therefore at once the epitome of the story's internal structure, the model of its striking multitextuality, and the most dramatic example of Gogol's retention of power over the text that makes him the final arbiter of its meaning.

Victor Brombert (essay date 1992)

"Meaning and Indeterminacy in Gogol's 'The Overcoat'," in *Literary Generations: A Festschrift in Honor of Edward D. Sullivan,* edited by Alain Toumayan, French Forum, 1992, pp. 48-54.

[*Here, the Brombert examines several possible interpretations of "The Overcoat" and argues that Gogol purposely made the story difficult to interpret because he "delighted in verbal acts as a game . . . that implied the autonomy of narrative style" from plot and meaning.*]

Akaky Akakyevich is the central character of Gogol's story **"The Overcoat."** Although Dostoevsky gave common currency to the term "anti-hero" in *Notes from Underground,* it is Gogol's Akaky Akakyevich who is the genuine, unmitigated, and seemingly unredeemable anti-hero. For Dostoevsky's antiheroic paradoxalist, afflicted with hypertrophia of the consciousness, is well-read, cerebral, incurably bookish, and talkative. Akaky Akakyevich is hardly aware, and almost inarticulate. Gogol's artistic wager was to try to articulate this inarticulateness.

The story, in its plot line, is simple. A most unremarkable copying clerk in a St. Petersburg ministry—bald, pockmarked, short-sighted, and the scapegoat of his colleagues who invent cruel ways of mocking him—discovers one day that his pathetically threadbare coat no longer protects him against the fierce winter wind. The tailor he consults categorically refuses to repair the coat which is now beyond repair, and tempts Akaky Akakyevich into having a new overcoat made, one totally beyond his means, but which by dint of enormous sacrifices, he manages to acquire and wear with a newly discovered sense of pride. But his happiness lasts only one short day. Crossing a deserted quarter at night, he is attacked by two thieves who knock him to the ground and steal his coat. Drenched, frozen, deeply upset, brutally reprimanded by a superior whose help he dared seek, Akaky develops a fever, becomes delirious, and dies.

One can hardly speak of an interesting plot line. Yet this simple story lends itself to orgies of interpretations. In fact, there may be as many interpretations as there are readers. **"The Overcoat"** can be read as a parable, a hermeneutic puzzle, an exercise in meaninglessness. But to begin with, there is the temptation to read it seriously as satire with a social and moral message. In **"The Nose,"** Gogol had already made fun of the rank-consciousness and venality of civil servants. In **"The Overcoat,"** he seems to deride systematically the parasitical, lazy, phony, world of Russian officialdom, whose members are the impotent mediators of a hierarchic and ineffectual power structure in which every subordinate fears and apes his superior. Early Russian critics, convinced that literature must have a moral message, read such a denunciatory and corrective satirical intention into the story even though it is clear that Gogol constantly shifts his tone, defends no apparent norm, and systematically ironizes any possible "serious" message.

There is of course the temptation to read **"The Overcoat"** as a tale of compassion, as a plea for brotherhood. The pathetically defenseless little clerk, taunted and persecuted by the group, remains blissfully oblivious to the cruel pranks of which he is the butt, intent on his humble copying activity. Only when the jokes become too outrageous, or interfere with his work, does he protest ever so mildly.

But here the tone of the story seems to change. For Gogol introduces a young man, recently appointed to the same office, who is on the point of sharing in the general fun, and who is suddenly struck by the strange notes in Akaky's voice which touch his heart with pity and make him suddenly see everything in a very different light. A true revelation emanating from an "unnatural" ("*neestestvennyi*") power allows him to hear other words behind Akaky's banal entreaty to be left alone. What he hears are the deeply penetrating, unspoken words echoing with poignant significance: "I am thy brother."

And with this voice from behind the voice comes the shocked awareness of how much "inhumanity" there is in human beings, how much brutality lurks in what goes as civilized society and civilized behavior. The apparent lesson in humanity given by the scapegoat victim seems, in the immediate context, to have an almost religious character, especially if one relates it to the narrator's comments, after Akaky's death, on how a man of meekness who bore the sneers and insults of his fellow human beings disappeared from this world, but who, before his agony, had a vision of the bright visitant ("*svetluy gost*"). The man of meekness, the man of sorrows, like the unspoken but clearly heard "I am thy brother," seems to have a Christian if not Christological, resonance.

But we forget Akaky's name, and that we are now allowed to do. For the patronymic appellation not only stresses the principle of repetition (Akaky's first name being exactly the same as his father's), but the funny sound repetition is even funnier because the syllable *kak* = like (*tak kak* = just as) embeds the principle of sameness in Akaky's name, determining, it would seem, his single-minded, life-long activity of copying and implicit condemnation to sameness. Regarding the many years Akaky served in the same department, Gogol observes that he "remained in exactly the same place, in exactly the same position, in exactly the same job, doing exactly the same kind of work, to wit copying official documents." But there is better (or worse) especially to Russian ears, for *kakatj* (from the Greek *cacos* = bad, evil) is children's talk for defecate, and *caca* in many languages refers to human excrement. To be afflicted with such a name clearly relates to the garbage being regularly dumped on Akaky as he walks in the street, and to his being treated with no more respect by the caretakers than a common fly. The cruel verbal fun around the syllable *kak* extends beyond the character's name, and contaminates Gogol's text. Gogol indulges in seemingly endless variations of the words *tak, kak, kakoi, kakoi-to, kak-ikh-to, vot-kak, neekak, takoi, takaya, kaknibut,* (just so, that's how, in no way, somehow, and so on) which in the translation disappear altogether. The exploitations of sound effects or sound meanings clearly correspond to a poet's fascination with the prestigious cacophonic resources of ordinary speech.

One last point about the choice of Akaky's name, specifically the Christian act of "christening": according to custom, the calendar was opened at random and several saints' names (Mokkia, Sossia) including the name of the martyr Khozdazat, were considered, only to be rejected by the mother because they sounded so strange. Akaky was chosen because that was the name of the father. But Acacius, a holy monk of Sinai, was also a saint and martyr, and we find ourselves—especially since the Greek prefix *a* (Acacius) signifies not bad, therefore good, meek, humble, obedient—back to the religious motif. If Akaky continues to copy for his own pleasure at home, this is in large part because the bliss of copying has a specifically monastic resonance. Gogol does indeed refer to his copying as a "labor of love."

Here a new temptation assails the reader. Should **"The Overcoat"** not be read as hagiography in a banal modern context, or at the very least as a parody of hagiography? A number of elements seem to lend support to such a reading of the story in or against the perspective of the traditional lives of the saints: the humble task of copying documents, reference to the theme of the martyr ("*muchenik*"), salvational terminology, sacrificial motifs of communion ("I am thy brother"), Akaky's visions and ecstasies, his own apparitions from beyond the grave. But the most telling analogy with hagiographic lore is the conversion-effect on others, first on the young man who has a revelation of a voice that is not of this world ("*svet*"), and toward the end the self-admiring, domineering, Very Important Person on whom Akaky's ghost-like apparition makes a never-to-be-forgotten impression.

> The overcoat turns out to be a form of temptation (material acquisition, vanity, pride), and the devilish tailor is the agent of this temptation just as the writer or narrator "tempts" the reader into a succession of vacuous and mutually canceling interpretations.
>
> —*Victor Brombert*

The overcoat itself can take on religious connotations because clothing, in the symbology of the Bible and orthodox liturgy, often represents righteousness and salvation. The only trouble with such an interpretation—and Gogol has written *Meditations on the Divine Liturgy* which refer to the priest's robe of righteousness as a garment of salvation—is that the coat can have an opposite symbolic significance, that of hiding the truth. Hence the traditional image of disrobing to reveal the naked self. In addition, there are many other possible meanings quite remote from the religious sphere: the metonymic displacement of the libido (the Russian word for overcoat—*shinel*—is appropriately feminine), the effects of virilization (in his new coat, Akaky surprises himself in the act of running after some woman in the street!), loss of innocence and loss of "original celibacy." The coat itself thus turns out to be a form of temptation (material acquisition, vanity, pride), and the devilish tailor is the agent of this temptation just as as the writer or narrator (who in fact is he?) "tempts" the reader into a succession of vacuous and mutually canceling interpretations.

This provocative writer-reader relationship, sustained throughout the narration, casts a special light on Akaky's fundamental activity of copying—the act of writing in its purest form. It does not take much imagination (our modern critics discover self-referentiality everywhere) to see in Akaky's copying an analogue of the writer's activity. And like the proverbially absorbed writer or scholar, he is obsessed by his writing to the point of finding himself in the middle of the street while thinking that he is in the middle of a sentence. This self-absorbed and self-referential nature of Gogol's act of writing might be seen to imply a negative attitude toward the referential world, toward all that which is not writing. Much like Flaubert, who dreamt of composing a "book about nothing," and whom contemporary critics like to view as an apostle of self-referential, intransitive literature, Gogol yearns for monastic withdrawal. Flaubert was haunted by the figures of the monk and the saint. Similarly, Gogol explained in a letter: "It is not the poet's business to worm his way into the world's marketplace. Like a silent monk, he lives in the world without belonging to it. . . ."

Pushed to a logical extreme, this sense of the radical deceptiveness of life calls into question worldly authority, and leads to a destabilizing stance that challenges the principle of authority, a subversive *gesta* of which the real hero is the artist himself. There is indeed something devilish about Gogol's narrative voice. It has already been suggested that the devil makes an appearance in the figure of the tailor who tempts Akaky into buying the coat. This caricature of the sartorial artist who quite literally is the creator of the overcoat, this ex-serf sitting with his legs crossed under him like a Turkish pasha, has diabolical earmarks: he is a "one-eyed devil" living at the end of a black staircase; he has a deformed big toenail, hard and thick as a tortoise shell; he handles a thrice referred to snuff box on which the face of a general has been effaced (the devil is faceless); he seems to be nudged by the devil and charges "the devil knows what prices."

This verbal playfulness seems to extend to the narrator himself, who undercuts his own narration in truly diabolical fashion by means of grotesque hyperbolizing, mixtures of realistic and parodistic elements, sudden shifts from the rational to the irrational, and elliptical displacements from epic triviality to unrestrained fantasy. Indulging in a game of mirages and fog-like uncertainties, the narrator subverts the logical progression of his story. Ultimately, even the ghost is debunked, and we are back in the blackness of quotidian reality. In the Russian text, these shifts in tone and textual instabilities are even more insidious, since everything seems to blur into the undifferentiated flow of seemingly endless paragraphs.

This merging of discontinuities undermines any sense of plot, undercuts the notion of subject, and suggests at every point that what is told is *another* story, thereby teasing the reader into endless interpretations that can neither be stabilized nor stopped. Some of this is the inevitable result of a mimesis of inarticulateness, a narrative style that is the imitative substitute for Akaky's manner of communicating mostly through prepositions, adverbs, and "such parts of speech as have no meaning whatsoever." But the strategy of destabilization and fragmented diction also has a deeper subversive purpose. The non sequiturs and hesitations reveal the arbitrariness of any fictional structure, and in the last analysis subvert any auctorial authority. The concluding page of **"The Nose"** represents an authorial critique of the story as incomprehensible and useless. The mediating self-negator is the fictionalized narrator identified in **"The Overcoat"** as the *"raskazyvaiushyi"*—the narrating one. And this narrator, occasionally pretending to be ignorant or semi-ignorant (like Cervantes's narrative voice as of the very first sentence of *Don Quixote*) does not know in what town, on what day, on what street the action takes place—in fact, complains of loss of memory. All this, however, only accentuates the possible importance of the unknowable and the unsayable, while protecting the protagonist's sacred privacy. The narrator clumsily speculates on what Akaky might or might not have said to himself as he stares at an erotic window display in the elegant quarter of St. Petersburg, and he concludes: "But perhaps he never even said anything at all to himself. For it is impossible to delve into a person's mind" (in Russian, literally: to creep into a person's soul).

"The Overcoat" is thus marked by conflicting and enigmatic signals, pointing to oxymoronic textures of meanings. Inversions hint at conversions. What is seemingly up is in fact seen to be down, while the reverse is equally true. The downtrodden creature turns out to be capable of heroic sacrifices, while the powerfully constituted VIP with the appearance of a *"bogatyr"* (hero) is cut down to human size by fright. On the other hand, when Akaky's fall is likened to a disaster such as destroys the czars and other great ones of this earth, one may well feel that Gogol is ironic about all heroic poses, heroic values, and heroic figures. When Akaky wears the new coat, his pulse beats faster, his bearing seems to indicate a newly discovered sense of purpose (*"tzel"*), his eyes have an audacious gleam, he appears somehow to have almost become virile. Yet the overcoat is also the emblem of false values, of trivial passion, of a silly reason for a human downfall. One might wish therefore to read a deeper significance into these mutually canceling interpretations. In English, the word *passion* is fraught with a multiple significance: in the ordinary sense, it denotes intense and even overwhelming emotion, especially of love; yet etymologically, it signifies suffering. Love and suffering are of course linked in a grotesque manner in **"The Overcoat"**. Whether such love and such suffering are commensurate with any objective reality remains unresolved in this story which seems to say that any love is great no matter what its object, that love is all-powerful; and conversely, that any passion can drag one down, that the more intense it seems, the emptier it is. Gogol's style is in itself an admirable instrument of ambivalence: enlarging trivia, and thereby trivializing what we may for a moment be tempted to take as significant.

What complicates Gogol's text for the reader is that it is not a case of simple ambivalence. It will not do to praise Gogol as a compassionate realist with an ethical message or to see him as a playful anti-realist indulging in overwrought imagery and in the reflections of distorting mirrors. The hard fact is that Gogol is a protean writer whose simultaneity of possible meanings allows for no respite and no comfortable univocal message. If the narrator is center stage, it is because ultimately he becomes a performer, a buffoonish actor mimicking incoherence itself. Intelligent readers of Gogol—Boris Eichenbaum, Vladimir Nabokov, Victor Erlich, Charles Bernheimer, Donald Fanger—have in varying degrees and with different emphases, understood that rather than indulging in a feast of ideas to be taken seriously, Gogol delighted in verbal acts as a game—a game that implied the autonomy of narrative style, a declaration of artistic independence, and a thorough deflation of *l'esprit de sérieux.*

Perhaps there is an underlying autobiographic urge in **"The Overcoat,"** and the verbal clowning and narrative pirouettes are telling a story in which the irrational takes on an exorcising and liberating virtue—much as the idiosyncrasies of Dostoevsky's *Notes from Underground* present a vehement protest against spiritually deadening rationality. What is certain is that Gogol needs to wear a mask. Haunted by the monsters born of his imagination, afraid to be unmasked, Gogol literally disappears in his writing by becoming a multiplicity of voices.

But there is a danger in depicting Gogol as an escape artist struggling against his own demons at the same time as he struggles against the repressive reality he wishes to deny. Similarly, there is the risk of considerable distortion in the determination of formalist and post-structuralist critics to draw Gogol to the camp of radical modernity by seeing him exclusively concerned with speech acts and sheer rhetoricity. Polyvalence does not mean the absence of meaning. The real problem, much as in the case of Flaubert, who complained of the plethora of subjects and inflationary overfill of meanings, is that over-abundance and multiplicity become principles of indeterminacy. Excess is related to emptiness. Similarly, Gogol seems torn between the futility of experience and the futility of writing about it, between the conviction that writing is the only salvation, yet that it is powerless to say the unsayable—aware at all points of the gulf between signifier and signified.

Nabokov may have come closest to the heart of Gogol's dark playfulness when he wrote: "The gaps and black holes in the texture of Gogol's style imply flaws in the texture of life itself . . ." [Vladimir Nabakov, *Nikolai Gogol,* 1944]. To this one might add, however, that the hollowness of the gaps, the terrifying absence, is also an absence/presence: a void that asks to be filled by the interpretive act. The dialectics of negativity, so dependent on the antiheroic mode embodied by Akaky, displace the production of meaning from the almost non-existent character and undecidable text to the creative reader.

FURTHER READING

Alissandratos, Julia. "Filling in Some Holes in Gogol's Not Wholly Unholy 'Overcoat'." *The Slavonic and East European Review* 68, No. 1 (January 1990): 22-40.
  Looks at structural and narrative similarities between "The Overcoat" and traditional Russian hagiography (idealized biographies of saints).

Bailey, James. "Some Remarks about the Structure of Gogol's 'Overcoat.'" In *Mnemozina: Studia litteraria russica in honorem Vsevolod Setchkarev,* ed. Joachim T. Baer and Norman W. Ingham, pp. 13-22. Munich: Wilhelm Fink Verlag, 1974.
  Gives a detailed structural analysis of "The Overcoat," in order to demonstrate the amount of care Gogol gave to the organization of his story.

Bernheimer, Charles C. "Cloaking the Self: The Literary Space of Gogol's 'Overcoat'." *PMLA* 90, No. 1 (January 1975): 53-61.
  Contends that the reflexive structure of "The Overcoat" serves as a defense mechanism for Gogol's fear of being annihilated by "the other."

Driessen, F. C. "The Overcoat." In *Gogol as a Short Story Writer,* trans. Ian F. Finlay, pp. 182-214. The Hague: Mouton & Co., 1965.
  Critical survey of "The Overcoat," discussing themes and stylistic techniques. Driessen reviews interpretations and analyses of other major critics while providing his own analysis.

Hippisley, Anthony. "Gogol's 'The Overcoat': A Further Interpretation." *Slavic and East European Journal* 20, No. 2 (Summer 1976): 121-29.
  Discusses the religious and spiritual aspects of "The Overcoat."

Landor, Mikhail. "'The Overcoat' and Western Story Tellers." *Soviet Literature,* No. 4 (1984): 177-85.
  Gives an overview of critiques, comments, and interpretations of "The Overcoat" by several Western writers.

Lindstrom, Thaïs S. "The Petersburg Cycle: The Overcoat (Shinel')." In *Nikolay Gogol,* pp. 88-97. New York: Twayne Publishers, 1974.
  Stylistic and thematic overview of the story.

Mills, Judith Oloskey. "Gogol's 'Overcoat': The Pathetic Passages Reconsidered." *PMLA* 89, No. 5 (October 1974): 1106-111.
  Looks at the role and personality of the narrator to elucidate the meaning of the pathetic passages in the story.

Rancour-Laferriere, Daniel. *Out from under Gogol's Overcoat: A Psychoanalytic Study.* Ann Arbor, Mich.: Ardis, 1982, 251 p.
  Examines "The Overcoat" from a Freudian perspective.

Rowe, William Woodin. "Tales: 'The Overcoat.'" In his *Through Gogol's Looking Glass: Reverse Vision, False Focus, and Precarious Logic*, pp. 113-18. New York: New York University Press, 1976.

> Examines the role of obscured vision, deceptive appearances, and clouded perception in the story.

Sloane, David. "The Name as Phonetic Icon: A Reconsideration of Onomastic Significance in Gogol's 'The Overcoat'." *Slavic and East European Journal* 35, No. 4 (Winter 1991): 473-88.

> Argues that the name of the main character of "The Overcoat" is symbolic of "a whole range of verbal behavior—from Akakij's own tongue-tiedness, to the narrator's unpredictable digressiveness, to the Important Personage's clumsy attempts to communicate."

Trahan, Elizabeth, ed. *Gogol's "Overcoat": An Anthology of Critical Essays*. Ann Arbor: Ardis, 1982, 105 p.

> Includes five essays on "The Overcoat," providing an introduction to the major critical perspectives and approaches to the story.

Additional coverage of Gogol's life and career is contained in the following sources published by Gale Research: *Discovering Authors*; *Discovering Authors: British*; *Discovering Authors: Canadian*; *Discovering Authors: Modules—Dramatists Module* **and** *Most-Studied Authors Module*; *Drama Criticism*, **Vol. 1**; *Nineteenth-Century Literature Criticism*, **Vols. 5, 15, 31**; *Short Story Criticism*, **Vol. 4**; *World Literature Criticism.*

Graham Greene
1904-1991

(Full name Graham Henry Greene) English novelist, short story writer, essayist, playwright, screenwriter, critic, autobiographer, travel writer, and poet.

INTRODUCTION

One of the most prolific and widely read English novelists of the twentieth century, Greene is known for both his best-selling suspense novels and for his more serious works of fiction, particularly the novels *Brighton Rock, The Power and the Glory,* and *The Heart of the Matter.* Greene has also been lauded for such short stories as "The Basement Room," "The Destructors," and "Under the Garden," all of which are generally considered classics in the genre. The protagonists of Greene's fiction are typically people torn by personal struggles with Roman Catholic concepts of sin and salvation, reflecting the author's concern with religious and moral questions. Greene also frequently addressed such themes as lost childhood, dreams, literature and art, and politics. In addition to writing fiction, Greene experimented with many other genres, including drama, film criticism, and travel writing. Grahame Smith has written that Greene's diverse writing career testifies "to a creative energy that . . . sought to explore the forms open to literary imagination, and to the fact that Greene [was] a writer in the deepest, as well as the widest, sense of the term."

Biographical Information

Born in Berkhamsted, a village northwest of London, Greene was one of six children. His father was the headmaster at Berkhamsted school, where Greene was educated. The regimented life and lack of privacy at the school, along with his father's constant moralizing on the sinfulness of sex, deeply affected Greene. A withdrawn child, he complained of terrible boredom, attempted suicide several times as a youth, and suffered a nervous breakdown at the age of sixteen. Despite a period of psychoanalysis in 1921, Greene attempted suicide six more times during his years as a student at Balliol College, Oxford. After graduating from Balliol in 1925, Greene worked as a subeditor on the Nottingham *Journal* and the London *Times,* later serving as a film critic and then literary editor for the *Spectator.* He married Vivien Dayrell-Browning in 1927, and the couple later had two children. While in Nottingham, Greene converted to Roman Catholicism. In his memoirs, he explains he did so partly to satisfy his wife and partly "to kill the time," but the Roman Catholic religion would later become a powerful force in both his life and literary works. Greene published his first novel, *The Man Within,* in 1929; he achieved popular success with his fourth novel, *Stamboul Train,* published as *Orient Express* in the United States. Greene separated from his wife in 1966, and shortly after he established permanent residence in Antibes on the French Riviera. Over the rest of his long and prolific career, Greene would continue to produce almost one book per year. He also traveled to such places as the Tabasco and Chiapas regions of Mexico, French Indochina, the Belgian Congo, Haiti, and Cuba during periods of social and political unrest to gather details for his works. Greene died in 1991 in Vevey, Switzerland, of leukemia.

Major Works of Short Fiction

Greene's first short story collection, *The Basement Room,* was published in 1935, but he did not receive critical attention for his short fiction until *Nineteen Stories* appeared in 1947. The pieces in this work were written between 1929 and 1948 and many originally appeared in such journals as the *New Yorker, Harper's,* and the *Commonweal.* In the preface to this collection, Greene noted:

"I am only too conscious of the defects of these stories. . . . The short story is an exacting form which I have not properly practiced: I present these tales merely as the by-products of a novelist's career." Although at the time Greene was somewhat unsure about his talents as a short story writer, this volume contains some of his best-known stories, including "The Basement Room" and "The Hint of an Explanation." "The Basement Room" centers on a seven-year-old boy, Philip Lane, who is left by his parents with Mr. and Mrs. Baines, the butler and the housekeeper. Philip comes to learn that Mr. Baines is having an affair with a young woman, and this knowledge inadvertently causes the accidental death of Mrs. Baines. Narrated by Philip sixty years after the event, "The Basement Room" addresses such themes as childhood innocence, betrayal, trust, and the nature of evil. "The Hint of an Explanation," which first appeared in the American edition of *Nineteen Stories* and was later included in *Twenty-One Stories,* is often called a moral drama because of its focus on such religious concerns as temptation, compassion, and the origins of faith. The story begins when two men meet on a train. One of the men, David, relates to the narrator of the story a childhood experience that caused him to enter the priesthood. As a young altar boy, David was persuaded by the village baker, Blacker, an atheist, to steal a consecrated communion host from his church. In return, Blacker would give him an electric train set. Although David does steal the host, he foils Blacker at the last minute by swallowing it. Another of Greene's most highly acclaimed works of short fiction, "The Destructors," appeared in *Twenty-One Stories.* Set in London's Wormsley Common, much of which was destroyed or damaged during the German bombing of World War II, this story centers on a local gang of boys. After two of its members, Trevor and Blackie, struggle for leadership of the group, the boys decide to systematically gut one of the last standing houses in the neighborhood, a building designed by famed English architect Christopher Wren. Exploring such themes as class structure, politics, creation, innocence, and depravity, "The Destructors" is considered one of Greene's most disturbing short stories. *A Sense of Reality* contains only four stories, with "Under the Garden" comprising more than half of the book. This story focuses on William Wilditch, who, suffering from lung cancer, returns to the house where he spent his boyhood holidays in order to confront a childhood memory that has obsessed him throughout his life. In this work, Greene examines lost childhood, memory, innocence, dreams, and the art of fiction writing. This collection also contains the story "A Visit to Morin," which relates the story of a man who meets a French Catholic writer whose works he admires. After their accidental meeting during mass in a village church, the two men share a drink and discuss faith and belief. *May We Borrow Your Husband?* contains twelve stories, many of which are set in the south of France and focus on marital relationships. The pieces in this collection are often described as being more humorous and playful than Greene's other short stories; Greene himself once noted they were written "in a single mood of sad hilarity." "Cheap in August," for example, relates the experiences of an English-born woman, Mary Watson, who is on vacation in Jamaica while her husband is conducting research in London for his book on James Thompson's *The Seasons.* Mary, looking for sexual adventure, has an affair with an older, overweight, and uncouth American man. "May We Borrow Your Husband?" tells the story of two homosexual interior designers, Tony and Stephen, who attempt to seduce a young husband from his wife while the couple is honeymooning in Antibes. *The Last Word,* which appeared in Britain and the United States a few weeks before Greene's death, collects works written from 1923 to 1989, with only four of the stories previously appearing in book form. This work varies greatly in subject matter and addresses such themes as corruption, disillusionment, failures of communication, and death.

Critical Reception

Greene has been the source of much contention among critics. He has been lauded as a master novelist who examined the place of religion and morality in twentieth-century society; he has also been decried as a melodramatist who relied too heavily on coincidence and metaphor. Although the majority of critics agree that Greene was an able storyteller, particularly in his delineation of setting and his skillful plot constructions, opinions vary widely concerning his ability to create believable characters and artfully communicate themes. Some of the most contentious critical debate has centered on Greene's depiction of Catholic concerns, even though Greene noted that Catholicism marked only "one period" of his career. Reaction to Greene's short fiction, which has received relatively little scholarly attention compared to his novels, reflects the general critical ambivalence toward Greene's work, with some reviewers dismissing his stories as mere preparatory sketches for his novels or simple burlesque pieces. Some have also stated that Greene used his short stories only as vehicles to work out traumatic events from his childhood or to didactically present a single theme or idea. Others, however, have called some of his short stories genuine masterpieces, and such works as "The Basement Room" and "The Destructors" have been widely anthologized and studied. Greene himself stated in the introduction to his *Collected Stories:* "I believe I have never written anything better than 'The Destructors,' 'A Chance for Mr. Lever,' 'Under the Garden,' and 'Cheap in August'." Although earlier critics tended to focus on moral themes in Greene's works and characterized him as a "Catholic writer," more recent scholars have commented on his political, social, and aesthetic themes and his use of myth, psychology, and symbolism. Recent critics have also placed more emphasis on Greene's short stories, underscoring the important role they played in the development of his writing, and have suggested they will garner wider and more serious scholarly attention in the future. Richard Kelly has concluded that Greene's short stories, "when reviewed in their entirety, . . . reveal a lifelong psychodrama that reflects his addiction to excitement, travel, and writing itself. Further, these tales reveal his persistent battle with the demons of his youth and his ability to transform them into characters and themes and later to shape them into religious, political, and social issues."

PRINCIPAL WORKS

Short Fiction

The Basement Room 1935
The Bear Fell Free 1935
Nineteen Stories 1947; also published as *Twenty-One Stories* [enlarged edition], 1954
A Sense of Reality 1963
May We Borrow Your Husband? and Other Comedies of the Sexual Life 1967
Collected Stories 1972
The Last Word, and Other Stories 1990

Other Major Works

Babbling April (poetry) 1925
The Man Within (novel) 1929
The Name of Action (novel) 1930
Rumour at Nightfall (novel) 1931
Stamboul Train (novel) 1932; published in the United States as *Orient Express,* 1933
It's a Battlefield (novel) 1934
England Made Me (novel) 1935; published in the United States as *The Shipwrecked,* 1953
A Gun for Sale (novel) 1936; published in the United States as *This Gun for Hire,* 1936
Journey without Maps (travel essays) 1936
Brighton Rock (novel) 1938; revised edition, 1947
The Confidential Agent (novel) 1939
The Lawless Roads (travel essays) 1939
The Power and the Glory (novel) 1940; published in the United States as *The Labyrinthine Ways,* 1940
The Ministry of Fear (novel) 1943
Brighton Rock (screenplay) 1946
†*The Fallen Idol* (screenplay) 1948
The Heart of the Matter (novel) 1948
The Third Man (screenplay) 1949
‡*The Third Man* (novel) 1950
The End of the Affair (novel) 1951
The Last Childhood, and Other Essays (essays) 1951
The Living Room (drama) 1953
Loser Takes All (novel) 1955
The Quiet American (novel) 1955
The Potting Shed (drama) 1957
Our Man in Havana (novel) 1958
The Complaisant Lover (drama) 1959
§*Our Man in Havana* (screenplay) 1960
A Burnt-Out Case (novel) 1961
In Search of a Character (travel essays) 1961
The Comedians (novel) 1966
#*The Comedians* (screenplay) 1967
Collected Essays (essays) 1969
Travels with My Aunt (novel) 1969
A Sort of Life (autobiography) 1971
The Pleasure-Dome: The Collected Film Criticism, 1935-40 (essays) 1972
The Honorary Consul (novel) 1973
The Human Factor (novel) 1978
Doctor Fischer of Geneva, or the Bomb Party (novel) 1980

Ways of Escape (autobiography) 1980
Monsignor Quixote (novel) 1982
Getting to Know the General (memoir) 1984
The Tenth Man (novel) 1985
The Captain and the Enemy (novel) 1988
Yours etc.: Letters to the Press, 1945-1989 (letters) 1989

*This screenplay is an adaptation of the novel *Brighton Rock.*

†This screenplay is an adaptation of the short story "The Basement Room."

‡This novel is an adaptation of the screenplay *The Third Man.*

§This screenplay is an adaptation of the novel *Our Man in Havana.*

#This screenplay is an adaptation of the novel *The Comedians.*

CRITICISM

Donald Barr (review date 1949)

SOURCE: "Graham Greene's World," in *New York Times Book Review,* February 13, 1949, pp. 3, 28-9.

[*In the following positive review of* Nineteen Stories, *Barr provides an overview of Greene's career and states that the stories in the volume reflect Greene's development as a novelist.*]

"I present these tales," says Graham Greene at the beginning of this new collection of his short stories [**Nineteen Stories**], "merely as the by-products of a novelist's career." There are eighteen stories and a fragment of an abandoned novel. Most of them are very good in themselves—two of them brilliant—but it is not only for their solid virtues as English short stories, their quietness and lucid ease, that they are important. It is also for the light they throw on one of the most interesting novelists of our generation.

The stories give us fresh glimpses of Greene's special world: the world of peeling billboards and jerry-built houses, of "dying jungles," of harassed and frightened, vainglorious and peevish, hungry and unlikable men, each with his own clumsily hidden burden of futility, damnation, or flabby love, scuttling or lounging through eternity.

Greene is now 45, and has been writing novels, "entertainments," and travel books—and these stories—for twenty years. But until the publication last year of his novel, *The Heart of the Matter,* his American readers were limited to a comparatively small coterie. Many of his books were filmed, and most of the films were bad and not Greene. In fact, *The Fallen Idol,* based on the longest of the stories in this volume, **"The Basement Room,"** and soon to be released here, is the first real Graham Greene movie: a very characteristic account of a little boy who too suddenly discovers that life means sin and responsibility and retreats from it forever.

It is easy to misunderstand Greene in either of two ways, by taking him as a superior writer of spy and murder thrillers, or as a St. Augustine condescending to the novel. Greene makes a distinction between his novels and his entertainments—a distinction the reader might find it hard to make for himself, but the author obligingly puts labels on each book: *The Confidential Agent* and *The Ministry of Fear*, for example, are entertainments. *The Power and the Glory* and *The Heart of the Matter* are novels. The next thing to know about Greene, then, is that the novels are serious studies of the human soul going about the business of eternity; they often have melodramatic plots as vehicles. The entertainments are melodramas, made tense by the cheerless Greene psychology.

Greene has been criticized on his novels (it shows what serious fiction has come to) for using coincidence too freely; in other words, for being a storyteller. Coincidence is just what the reader enjoys most directly of a plot. The entertainments, on the other hand (it shows what crime fiction has come to), have been accused of pretentiousness; and it is still rarely noticed how they have served as rehearsals for the novels.

Several of the pieces in *Nineteen Stories* are closely related to the novels in substance and spirit. **"A Drive in the Country"** is a brilliantly unpitying treatment of suicide. **"A Chance for Mr. Lever"** is a story of that choking West African forest through which Greene himself walked 350 miles without maps to look for a "seedy" (it is an important word for Greene) society nearer to our ancestral innocence than "the smart, the new, the chic and the cerebral." This trip is the basis also of **"The Other Side of the Border,"** the 1936 fragment with which the collection closes, and of the astonishing *Journey Without Maps* a travel book which records the voyage of a soul.

A few of the stories, like **"Alas, Poor Maling"** and **"When Greek Meets Greek,"** are lighter and more playful than anything else Greene has written, yet even they are peculiarly astringent.

Now why does Greene's world, this criss-cross of tired intrigue, of flickering eternal motives, fascinate us? First, it is darker and so makes us feel that we have got deeper into the human soul than the well-lighted case histories can take us. Second, the crimes seem more wicked: they are more shocking than a dozen murders in a detective story, or the cheap mechanical swaggering sadism of the Cain-Hammett school.

To some extent, these effects are tricks of an extraordinary style. Greene's style seems bare and dry, but in reality it has the rich concentration of poetry. Perhaps he strains too hard to make every adjective a fresh observation. Sometimes the mental processes of his characters are lost in new metaphors. After all, the conventionality of a metaphor saves the reader the work of abstracting its meaning. But Greene will be neither conventional nor abstract; the sharpness of his sight and sound images reminds us that he was for years a film critic. And his images not only describe but interpret; and sometimes the

reader is not sure how deep a comparison is meant to go. For instance, in his novel, *England Made Me* (1935), Anthony Farrant carried his smile "always with him as a leper carried his bell; it was a perpetual warning that he was not to be trusted." That is clear enough. But in *The Heart of the Matter,* Father Rank laughs and "swung his great empty sounding bell to and fro, ho, ho, ho, like a leper proclaiming his misery." Here we are not sure what is being said about the jovial priest; and this is a mannerism of Greene's which his readers must work to master.

Greene is a paradox. He is born a modern psychological novelist and a Roman Catholic. Catholicism, especially in the English-speaking world, has emphasized the edifying and the wholesome in literature, but Greene is preoccupied with sin. He is obsessed with the seedy, the weak and the hellish. It is difficult to express the force of that obsession. It pervades everything he writes. In his travel book, *Another Mexico,* Greene tells how, as a boy at his father's school, faith came to him—"shapelessly, without dogma, a presence above a croquet lawn, something associated with violence, cruelty, evil across the way. One began to believe in heaven because one believed in hell. . . ."

> **Greene is preoccupied with sin. He is obsessed with the seedy, the weak, and the hellish. It is difficult to express the force of that obsession. It pervades everything he writes.**
>
> *—Donald Barr*

"Literature," says Greene, "has nothing to do with edification." With Cardinal Newman, he believes that a sinless literature of sinful man is impossible. Greene is an almost unique figure in his milieu, in some ways seeming to belong to the French scene; he disturbs his co-religionists; he shows Catholics as sinful and Catholicism as difficult. He is much too unlike Chesterton. Chesterton's picture of sin was scarlet, as bright as a child's paint box; Greene's sin is black, gray—all the colors of human nature.

If being a modern psychological novelist gives an unusual tinge to Greene's Catholicism, certainly his theology accounts for much of the literary shock. It is, in fact, the key to Greene. Greene is as fully aware of social evil as any of his contemporaries; his story, **"Brother,"** written in 1936, shows that he can even feel the idealism of the Communists. He is aware of everything the Freudians are aware of; the earlier stories, like **"I Spy,"** show it. But Greene believes in Free Will and in Original Sin. He believes that human actions are caused—up to a point. And then, at that point, the will is involved. He escapes the great, softening folly of the modern psychological novel, that we are the neutral victims of our circumstances; that to understand all is to forgive all. The better we understand some of Greene's characters the more corrupt we see them to be. Pinkie, the adolescent gangster of *Brighton Rock,* one of Greene's best achievements to date, wills his own damnation; he worships evil as his Catholic parents worshiped good. The "modern" reader who cannot understand this deliberate choice of evil cannot understand Graham Greene.

There is one final difficulty about Greene's thought. But the most recent story in this collection, **"The Hint of an Explanation,"** does hint at an answer. Since *Brighton Rock* in 1938, Greene has concerned himself with the distinction between knowing good from evil and knowing right from wrong. Pinkie knows good from evil; he chooses evil. The good-natured, blowzy Ida, his Nemesis, knows only right and wrong. They are on different planes; their shadows fall on one another, but they cannot touch. Scobie, in *The Heart of the Matter,* is both a policeman, a professional distinguisher of right from wrong, and a Catholic; and he chooses sin again and again, knowing what he is doing, sure he will be damned, rather than do wrong to his wife and mistress. Is he damned? In the short story about a "free-thinker" who tries to make a little boy sell God, Greene seems to go further in explaining the relations of an evildoer and his Lord than he has yet gone.

If the reader mentally rearranges these stories in chronological order, he will find them a reflection of Greene's development as a novelist. He begins with the personal emotions, especially the emotions of family life in childhood. **"I Spy"** and **"The Man Within"** give us a boy's conflicting love and identification with his parents; later Greene turns increasingly to open didacticism as in **"The Hint of an Explanation"**; the slight, topical satires of the war years correspond to a period of silence in the larger frame. This over, with *The Heart of the Matter* he will continue to seduce us into more satanic intimacies.

David Burnham   (review date 1949)

SOURCE: A review of *Nineteen Stories,* in *The Commonweal,* Vol. XLIX, No. 1, March 11, 1949, pp. 546-47.

[*In the positive assessment of* Nineteen Stories *below, Burnham discusses stylistic and thematic elements in the short stories.*]

The variety of mood in these stories [*19 Stories*] of Graham Greene, the first of which was written in 1929 (Greene was born in 1905) and the last in 1948, will surprise readers acquainted only with Greene's best-known works, *The Heart of the Matter, The Labyrinthine Ways, Brighton Rock.* A list of American magazines in which some of the stories appeared gives a good hint of this variety: *The New Yorker, Harper's Magazine, Esquire, Tomorrow, Town and Country, The Commonweal* (*Cosmopolitan* has also printed him but, perhaps for copyright reasons, the story is not included in the American edition of *19 Stories*).

The *Esquire* story, **"When Greek Meets Greek,"** is a genial account of how two wily old frauds outsmart themselves in the attempt to outsmart one another. The *New Yorker* story, **"Men at Work,"** is a burlesque, somewhat reminiscent of early Evelyn Waugh, of wartime operations in the British Ministry of Propaganda. There are other humorous stories, in one of which, **"Alas Poor Maling,"** the humor is on the level of slapstick. The *Harper's* story, **"Proof Positive,"** and also **"The Second Death"** and to a degree **"The End of the Party,"** involve the miraculous. One of the stories, **"A Day Saved,"** is in the Kafka tradition. The remainder, more typical, deal with various degrees of moral weakness and corruption. The style varies from the succinct, packed manner of Greene's best novels to anecdotal (sometimes, with disconcerting effect, within the same story).

> Sometimes in *19 Stories* the stylistic elements become virtuosity: the compression, the vivid original metaphors, the photogenic intensification of reality, too far outrun the meaning: manner becomes mannerism.
>
> —*David Burnham*

In a note prefacing the collection, Greene acknowledges: "I am only too conscious of the defects of these stories. . . . The short story is an exacting form which I have never properly practiced: I present these tales merely as the by-products of a novelist's career." His modesty is justified by stories which exhibit him as not quite sure of himself, whereas in his novels he is always in complete mastery. Yet some of his stories are hauntingly perfect. **"The End of the Party,"** for example, a tale of identical twins whose shattering climax is followed by a climax even more shattering—a device which Greene used with like effect in *Brighton Rock* and several other of these stories: a double-twist one might say, where "twist" must be given a double meaning, the second being the twist of the knife in the wound. This, yes, is a device, but no more so than false rhymes in a poem, asymmetry in a painting. The validity of an artistic device depends upon its success and purpose. O'Henry's twist endings succeed but are usually as shallow as a practical joke; in the best of Greene, the twist provides a sudden illumination of the symbolic meaning of the whole story or novel; or else sharply intensifies the meaning, anchoring it in one's mind.

Graham Greene cannot, however, entirely be absolved of using his devices for inferior purposes. For example, his "entertainments" (thrillers) take on a special intensity from several causes, of which the significant one in this connection is his use of language and especially his syntax which causes every sentence to seem packed with meaning even when it may not be so. Several critics have complained of the monotony of his style, but this very monotony, like his monotony of atmosphere, has a cumulative force of its own and also a symbolic force: it expresses the spiritual poverty, the fear, the seediness, the obscure guilt, the disorientation of his characters better than any words of theirs could do, especially since inarticulateness or else a conscious or endemic inability to see and speak truthfully usually accompanies these qualities. Sometimes, though, the stylistic elements become virtuosity: the compression, the vivid original metaphors, the photogenic intensification of reality, too far outrun the meaning: manner becomes mannerism.

The most memorable stories in the collection have children as protagonists. This is today a hackneyed theme, but Greene gives it a deeper meaning (meanings, I should say) than the usual death-of-innocence, escapism, or routine allegory. I have already cited **"The End of the Party,"** primarily a study of fear vs. convention with overtones of adult incomprehension, the mystic bond between twins (a theme Greene treats in another of these stories and at book length in *England Made Me*): so many of these stories appear minor rehearsals for his novels), and as a final fillip, a guess about the nature of immortality. **"The Innocent,"** until its ending, is a fairly routine although unusually vivid and compressed contrast of the innocence of childhood to the heedless corruption of adulthood; the final paragraphs qualify (and yet illuminate) innocence in a manner typically Greene.

"The Basement Room," soon to appear on the screen as *The Fallen Idol,* comprises without sacrifice of central effect a remarkable variety of important and suggestive themes. On the surface it is the story of a childhood trauma which causes a boy to betray the one person he loves and to retreat forever from the terrible responsibility of involvement with other lives. The deeper meaning is suggested in Greene's story which appeared several weeks ago in this magazine. The agnostic narrator states: "Intellectually I am revolted at the whole notion of a God Who can so abandon His creatures to the enormities of Free Will." The title of the story is **"The Hint of an Explanation."** Does not this phrase perhaps offer the hint of an explanation of Greene's own obsession? Greene himself tells us (in *Another Mexico*) that he arrived at the belief in Heaven through the belief in Hell. He too, it might seem, is intellectually and also (perhaps most of all) humanly revolted by the enormities of free will. But he cannot wish free will out of existence. Terrestrial evil, his works seem to teach us (more and more explicitly), springs chiefly not from the conscious willing of evil, but from the failure to accept the basic, frightful responsibility of knowing good and evil—far more devastating than original sin because it *caused* original sin, together with all the sin which has occurred since.

Isaac Rosenfeld   (review date 1949)

SOURCE: "Twenty-Seven Stories," in *Partisan Review*, Vol. XVI, No. 7, July, 1949, pp. 753-55.

[*In the following mixed evaluation of* Nineteen Stories, *Rosenfeld praises Greene's honest depiction of childhood but faults his attempts at confessional writing.*]

Graham Greene, who writes two kinds of books, serious novels and entertainments, is never as serious or entertaining a writer as when he writes a simple story about childhood, leaving out crooks, spies, confidential agents and his own brand of Anxiety. There are several such stories in the present collection [*Nineteen Stories*] and they are the best in the volume (three of them, in fact, are good), because they were written without the intention of distilling from the steam of the pot boiler a moral critique of our age. Which is to say that Greene is at his best when he is least himself.

An unhappy childhood is a writer's gold mine, and one valuable thing Greene gets out of it is an honest basis for his stories.

—Isaac Rosenfeld

For once the perspective is immediate. We come directly to the unhappy child and his trouble without having to make the usual detour through the secondary symbol formations of flight and pursuit, etc., of the thrillers. Childhood, for Greene, is the time of the innocence and horror of sex. The innocent, in the story by that name, is the young boy capable of leaving a love message for his sweetheart in the form of a crude drawing of a man and a woman in the sex act. The grown man, returning to the scene with a prostitute for a one night stand, discovers the message still intact in its hiding place and realizes, ". . . later that night, when Lola turned away from me and fell asleep . . . the deep innocence of that drawing. I had believed I was drawing something with a meaning unique and beautiful; it was only now after thirty years of life that the picture seemed obscene." In **"The Basement Room"** (a parable of the unconscious), young Master Philip finds not a unique and beautiful meaning but something from which he spends the rest of his life in a frozen recoil; and this again is sex, now linked with murder and guilt. **"The Hint of an Explanation"** is the story of how a man found happiness and security in the Catholic Faith; which he would not have found, had he not been strongly tempted by the perverted village anti-Papist to commit a sin against the Host; which he would not have had the strength to resist, had he not had so strong a sense of sin; which he would not have had—Greene does not carry the matter so far, but there's no way out—had he not been an unhappy child. Where again, sex . . . etc.

An unhappy childhood is a writer's gold mine, and one valuable thing Greene gets out of it is an honest basis for his stories. When he faces himself, as he makes some attempt to do here in the figure of the child, he finds he can get along without antisemitism (*Orient Express*) and the rest of the vicious trash of his entertainments. Also the arrogant moralism disappears, the gratuitous (for him) Baudelairean will to damnation and the unearned Catholic eminence from which he sees Protestantism—when the Jews don't get in his way—at its demon's task of bringing sexual ease into the world. He is much better off for the chance childhood gives him to feel sorry for himself. But though childhood themes do him good as a writer, he fails to return the favor and leaves the scene bare and devoid of quality; it is reconstructed in the adult manner, and the distance between man and child is not overcome. This is the fault, it seems to me most likely, of his desire to write confession. Accordingly, his child exists only at the moment of encountering sex, and his life has meaning only as it provides the material of sin and fosters the adult's need of believing in sin. But this is confessional writing at its worst; it not only conceals, it obliterates. Only that which has been touched by guilt survives in the memory; everything else of the child's world is lost—and the loss is not even noticed by the man.

But why *confession*? It is only a man with a neurotic distaste for life who can find something to confess (in the sense distinct from telling a story) about childhood. This has made him suffer as a writer; it has robbed his scenes of richness and given his style a puckered quality, with neither warmth nor a generous rhythm. (His characteristic use of the colon, which is meant for crispness but suggests something withered, is a half stop for a pinch of alum to keep his writing wry and dry.) Save for a few unconscious lapses into vitality, Greene's whole manner is a courtship of death, and he must support himself in it only because it suits both an inherent unease of soul and an acquired one, laid on himself in a need to overcome mediocrity. He would very much like to show a depth of anguish in his work, and on his forehead the star of the damned. He succeeds in doing neither. For all his concern with morality, sin, guilt, crime, retribution and Catholicism, he remains a middlebrow with a good location—a frontage on Crisis Theology.

William Barrett (review date 1962)

SOURCE: "Master Craftsman," in *The Atlantic Monthly*, Vol. 209, No. 6, June, 1962, pp. 109-11.

[*In the following mixed review of* Twenty-One Stories, *Barrett praises Greene's craftsmanship but faults his inability to present realistic characters.*]

Graham Greene has never particularly favored the short story, yet it turns out that in his mastery of this form he is as sure and accomplished a craftsman as in the departments of drama and the novel. *Twenty-One Stories* gives us all the tales that Mr. Greene seems to want to preserve from his long and prolific career, and they bring out in very sharp relief all of his literary qualities, positive as well as negative.

The very conciseness of the short-story form, indeed, can give a greater intensity—like a harsh black-and-white drawing—to the macabre side of Mr. Greene's imagination.

In **"The Basement Room,"** a boy's glimpse into the marital tragedy of his beloved butler's life, is far more bleak and grim in its mood than the fine motion picture that was made from it some years ago by the distinguished English director Carol Reed. But the story, in its compression, has also more bite and power than the picture.

When the comic mood is upon him, Mr. Greene can be very funny, but the humor is never relaxing. **"A Chance for Mr. Lever"** tells the absurd tale of a middle-aged salesman chasing through the heart of Africa, swatting at flies and swearing at native bearers, in order to get a mining engineer's signature on a contract. He finds the engineer at last, dead of fever, and forges the signature. Does justice triumph? Of course—the once down-at-the-heels but righteous salesman, now prosperous but damned, leads the pleasant life of a *bon vivant* through all the capitals of Europe.

> The very conciseness of the short-story form can give a greater intensity—like a harsh black-and-white drawing—to the macabre side of Mr. Greene's imagination.
>
> —*William Barrett*

These stories are not evocations of mood, moment, or character, in the manner of Chekhov; they always revolve about some definite and very well plotted narrative idea. When they deal with children (as three of them do), the world of the child is never evoked; Mr. Greene is seeing the child's world through his own eyes and not through the eyes of the child. This, I think, is the clue to the final limitations of this extraordinary writer; Graham Greene never gets outside of Graham Greene, despite the range and intensity of situations and plots that his imagination can contrive. In **"A Drive in the Country"** an unemployed ne'er-do-well, hopeless for the future, proposes a suicide pact to his girl; she refuses, and while running away hears the fatal suicide shot behind her; calmly hitching a ride back to town, she steals unobserved into her father's house—the affair over. The story is absorbing; but halfway through we begin to feel uneasily that we are sitting in the dark watching upon the screen a melodrama in which the characters have their backs to us and never once turn around to show their faces as real people.

Brian Wilkie (review date 1963)

SOURCE: "Stories by Greene," in *The Commonweal*, Vol. LXXVIII, No. 6, July 12, 1963, pp. 432, 434.

[*Below, Wilkie presents a positive assessmenet of* A Sense of Reality, *discussing Greene's use of myth, fantasy, and psychology in the work.*]

In this new collection of short fiction [*A Sense of Reality*] Graham Greene does something he has not done before. In his previous work Greene has treated the world, if not his people and themes, naturalistically; his heroes have generally been morality-play figures, but his settings and plots have been matter-of-fact, circumstantially realistic. In fact, one of the most characteristic notes in Greene's serious fiction (melodrama and whimsy have always had some place in his "entertainments") has been the contrast between the sense of circumambient grace and the ridiculously shabby world in which grace operates. This literal-minded concern with dreary, commonplace reality, on which Greene seems to have hung the sign "Out of Order," has been important for him, since through the literal shabbiness of the world he has been able to attack the illusion of material well-being which men use in order to conceal from themselves the fact that they live in a fallen, evil world.

> **In Greene's myths we find the familiar broken-down, pain-filled world with which he has made us familiar: twisted bodies, obscenity, old toilet bowls.**
>
> *—Brian Wilkie*

In *A Sense of Reality,* however, two, perhaps three, of the stories lean heavily on myth, fantasy, or other forms of narrative mannerism. (The very appropriate title, incidentally, is a general one and not borrowed from one of the individual stories.) In many other authors these currently fashionable techniques might seem to have been dictated by fad or to be stridently arty. They do not seem so in this book. This is true partly because Greene does not simply translate traditional themes into contemporary terms; he takes elements from such widely varied sources as the Bible, classical mythology, psychology, and (one is tempted to suggest) personal dreams and combines them into an original, dream-like pattern. That is, the myth itself is Greene's invention, not just its application. Furthermore, Greene imprints his mythos with the familiar stamp of his own sensibility; in his myths we find the familiar broken-down, pain-filled world with which he has made us familiar: twisted bodies, obscenity, old toilet bowls.

"Under the Garden" is the longest and best of the stories. In it Greene explores once more his old theme of the "lost childhood." Wilditch, the protagonist, under a medical death sentence, returns to his early home to exorcise a haunting childhood memory, part fact and part dream, which has dominated his life. The memory concerns a sojourn in the underworld wherein he had learned about life from a subterranean dweller named Javitt (Jahweh?),

seen a wondrous treasure, and been inspired with love for Javitt's elusive and sensually beautiful daughter, whom Wilditch decides to seek in the world.

At first it seems that the old memory can be easily exorcised, for the "lake" and "island" which had been the setting for the remembered experience turn out to be little more than a puddle with a few bushes in the middle of it. But the strange discovery on the "island" of a chamber-pot which had figured in the "dream" experience convinces Wilditch that he cannot rid himself of the dream and that "there was a decision he had to make all over again." Life (or the after-life?) may have meaning after all; perhaps, after all, "Absolute reality belongs to dreams and not to life."

One cannot so briefly do justice to this complex and thematically rich story, which in ideas and techniques has a specific gravity much greater than one has learned to expect from Greene. The story is moving and acutely painful, especially in those parts which convey the adult's grotesquely shrunken world now void of the mystery of childhood wonder. And a good deal of its emotional power arises from the obscure but eerily convincing psychological myth which takes up about half its length.

The last piece in the volume, **"A Discovery in the Woods,"** is even more macabre; in it Greene takes the story of Noah and the Ark and relates it to the discovery of a wrecked transatlantic steamship high on a wooded mountainside by four stunted, pitiable children in a post-atomic age. The story can be read on a number of levels; for example, it is not only an imaginative rendering on the aftermath of atomic war, but also a kind of commentary on the Biblical story and its message.

The brief story called **"A Visit to Morin"** will undoubtedly be read as a comment by Greene on his own career and reputation. Morin is a novelist who was once in vogue because of his daring treatment of religious themes. This story is so much in Greene's familiar vein that, in its present company, one almost suspects it of being sardonic self-parody or some similar literary joke—especially when one hears Morin say, "Long after I ceased to believe myself I was a carrier of belief, as a man can be a carrier of disease without being sick." Could parody of Greene go further than that?

Hilary Corke   (review date 1963)

SOURCE: "A Strong Smell of Fish," in *The New Republic,* Vol. 149, August 31, 1963, pp. 31-3.

[*In the following mixed review of* A Sense of Reality, *Corke comments on the four stories in the volume, praising Greene's professionalism and faulting his use of paradox.*]

Although the blurb describes it as his "main occupation" during the past two years, Mr. Greene's new collection (his first since 1949) contains only [*A Sense of Reality*] 119 smallish pages and only four stories—half of which the first occupies more than half the book, so that we may not unfairly concentrate our attention upon it. **"Under The Garden"** begins with a doctor explaining to William Wilditch, in a more or less breezy impersonal way, that he has cancer of the lung. The scene is in Mr. Greene's best flat sad manner, especially appropriate for the conveying of quiet horror. Before deciding whether or not to accept the operation, Wilditch revisits the house in which he spent his boyhood holidays—it has belonged to his brother for the past thirty years but he has always hitherto avoided it, as he was disappointed that it was not left to him. Everything (surprise, surprise!) seems much smaller than he had remembered it. We are made aware that something cataclysmic happened to the boy William on an island in the lake in the garden of this house, something that determined the whole future course of his life, something that has made him now return, under the sentence of death. (The lake turns out, of course, to be a mere pond, and the few square yards of the island can be reached with a flying jump.)

At dinner the conversation conveniently turns to this "something" and his brother informs him, what he himself has forgotten, that he once wrote an account of it for his school magazine. Even more marvellously conveniently, in his bedroom is the bound volume of this magazine and from it falls a letter from his then-headmaster concerning this very story, which he finds and reads. It is couched in a *Treasure Island* style, and the mature Wilditch is outraged by its falsifications of what he remembers really to have been the case. He sits down and passes the whole sleepless night in committing the true facts to paper.

This account of his boyhood dream (for it *has* to be a dream, although he would like to believe it reality) shows how he goes down a tunnel on the island and reaches an underground cavern, in which live two timeless creatures called Javitt and Maria. Javitt has only one leg (he was born that way) and a big white beard: he sits always on a lavatory seat and engages in an endless stream of gnomic conversation—"There was a kind of reason in most of what he said, as I came to realize later." The hole under the lavatory seat goes down into the center of the earth, apparently. Maria, on the other hand, is very dusty-fusty and has no roof to her mouth and can only say "squawk, squawk." They have lived down here together for goodness knows how long, but these two ugly rogues have produced a highly glamorous daughter, one who has become a beauty-queen under the soubriquet of Miss Ramsgate.

After imbibing a great deal of Javitt's cosmic earthy half-nonsensical wisdom (the recording of which appears to be the nub of the story), the boy William escapes, taking with him "golden po" that has been lent him, out of Javitt's fabulous treasure, to do his business in. Here the written account ends, it is dawn, and the man William goes downstairs and out into the garden, where he first meets the old gardener, who has certain evident Javitt-

elements about him, and then gets onto the island. Here to his astonishment he finds evidence to support him in his wish-belief that it was not all a dream: for here, under a stump, is the golden po—a battered object with most of its yellow paint flaked off it, but a golden po all the same. His reaction—which would flabbergast one if one were not prepared for every possible assault upon one's reason and sense of fitness by Mr. Greene in his capacity of Catholic writer—is that he has been wrong to live a life without religion and that there is a definitive decision that he has to make in this department also.

It will be seen that I have to regard this tale with a mixture of qualified admiration, and puzzlement plus exasperation. Admiration—because it is well-written and professional and compelling to read. Qualified—because, as I hope to show, it is not *very* well written and because "professional" has its pejorative senses too. As to the puzzlement, there is no puzzle about that. This is, within its rather creaking mechanical frame, or frames, simply an account of a dream, and we all know the breakfast-table horror of that. So that when a *writer* takes over we expect, not just the free association of a dream, but more. Anything less is self-indulgence, not literature. What in fact, to put it with a naïveté of crudity, does Mr. Greene *mean*? Who, or what, *is* Javitt? For, if he is nothing meaningful at all, then the story is nothing meaningful at all.

I don't want to make this question a wilfully uncomprehending one. This is a story, not a treatise. Javitt can be a whole lot of things, indeed the more the merrier, and the more mixed up the merrier too. For instance, he is partly simply the old gardener, transformed by the usual alchemy of dream. He is also, as I reckon it, Mr. Samuel Whiskers, villain of Beatrix Potter's *The Roly-Poly Pudding,* known to every rightly brought-up British child. (Tom Kitten gets lost in the black chimney-flues of the old house and eventually falls into the rats' den, whereupon Mr. Samuel Whiskers screams out "Anna Maria! Anna Maria!" just as Javitt roars "Maria, Maria!" And I wonder whether this was conscious on Mr. Greene's part, or just his subconscious keeping its eye splendidly on the ball.) And we can also make other systems to accommodate Javitt. But all efforts of this sort leave so much detail artistically inexplicable that we are forced to search for some much profounder symbology than this. And here the exasperation begins.

For, if we press this question resolutely, I am afraid that we are inescapably driven to the conclusion that Javitt equals God: or more precisely, when we consider his name and his sempiternality and his beard, that Javitt equals Jehovah. It is inescapable because the detail is so arbitrary otherwise. For instance, in the tunnel, "scrawled with the simplicity of ancient man—done with a sharp tool like a chisel—was the outline of a gigantic fish." And if that doesn't place us in the catacombs, Mr. Greene is deceiving with intent. Or how about this? "[Javitt] rose on his one leg, and now that he had his arms stretched out to either wall, he reminded, me of a gigantic crucifix." And above all, this identification is the only one that doesn't make utter rubbish of the tale's conclusion.

But, if Javitt is Jehovah, then what of Maria? Alas, is she, this hideous squawking crone, the queen of heaven? And Miss Ramsgate, their child who "went upstairs," the beauty-queen for whom Wilditch says he has been searching vainly all his life? The Lamb of God? We are caught between the inexplicably arbitrary and the inexplicably squalid: and, knowing the way that Greene tends constantly to identify the deeply horrid or the deeply holy, we suppose despairingly that we must cleave to the second. And I for one, speaking as a non-religious person, find it no more than an ingenious exercise in the unnecessarily nasty. The religious on the other hand, or some of them, will doubtless find this attitude pathetically squeamish.

But no, I don't see that I have to lie down under that. It is not the nastiness that offends, it is the unnecessariness. Nor is it that, over-rational, I am offended by puzzles without solutions—*Pale Fire* is fine with me, and I'll play crosswords with the rest of them (is the hero named for his *wild itch* or because he *will ditch himself*?). But simply, I feel that here the mystery, whether consciously posed or not, is of its very nature pointlessly unpleasant. Two of the characteristics of Mr. Greene's curious mind are that it is lavatorial and that it is grossly paradoxical. This coupling of divinity and excrement here satisfies both of them.

In **"A Visit to Morin,"** paradox is rampant. This supposed interview with a Catholic writer who has lost his belief concludes with a piece of sophistry so hair-raising as to verge on the comic. (The novelist has not been to mass or confession for twenty years. As a result he has lost his belief. This proves that "the Church is right and the faith is true," for, "if a doctor prescribed you a drug and told you to take it every day for the rest of your life and you stopped obeying him and drank no more, and your health decayed, would you not have faith in your doctor all the more?" I stopped looking for fairies in the grass 38 years ago, and now I don't believe in them anymore, which doesn't, however, seem to me an altogether valid proof of their existence.)

In **"A Discovery in the Woods,"** a post-atomic fable which is much the best thing in the book, it is the Mr. Grim Grin side of things again:

> Liz tied (her skirt) up, with a knot behind just above the opening of her small plump buttocks.

> She squatted on the ground with a bare buttock on each heel.

> Anyway they wouldn't bash a girl. "Pa does," Liz said, twitching her buttocks.

> Her thighs and bottom were scratched with briars and smeared with blood the color of blackberry juice.

> She sat squatting on the thighbones of the skeleton, her naked buttocks rocking to and fro as though in the act of possession.

This brings us, space as ever pressing, to the question of professionalism.

When you peer into it more closely, Greene's writing doesn't look all that good, more a sort of slickness rubbed over cracks to conceal them.

—*Hilary Corke*

Whatever one says against Mr. Greene—and I for one have always found him aggravating and unrewarding in the light of his obvious talent—he remains compellingly readable. Why? The quick answer is that he is a professional, that he constructs well, writes clearly and employs all the age-old tricks of the story-teller's art. But recently I have begun to wonder. Professionalism can easily go stale, until it becomes the mere tired academicism that, in painting, we expect of a Royal Academician. When you peer into it more closely, the writing doesn't look all that good, more a sort of slickness rubbed over cracks to conceal them. That "buttock" series isn't merely nagging, it is also plain careless:

> He did not leave it at that or allow himself to get involved in a theological debate. He went on to indicate that. . . .

Where evidently what is meant is "He neither left it at that nor allowed himself," etc. Apparent exactness turns out to be a mere gloss of pseudo-exactness:

> The water in which he landed was only a few inches deep. . . . He sloshed ashore, the water not even penetrating his shoes.

Some shoes! Or the opening sentence of **"A Discovery in the Woods"**:

> The village lay among the great red rocks about a thousand feet up and five miles from the sea, which was reached by a path that wound along the contours of the hills.

Which leaves me wondering whether or not that five miles was as the crow flew, and how a path that winds along contours can also manage to drop a thousand feet.

We can entertain similar doubts about the constructions. The first story begins with a doctor breaking it to a patient that he has cancer, and the third story with a doctor breaking it to a patient that he has leprosy: and two out of four seems an outrageously high score for this hoary old opening. The second story employs the ancient device of the "confession to a chance-met stranger," who tells the tale—a convention from which Mr. Somerset Maugham extracted the last drop of juice years before most of us were born. The creaking mechanics of **"Under the Garden"** I have indicated in my précis of it.

As I see it, there was a time when one was prepared to overlook the superficialities and shallownesses in Mr. Greene's view of life (and for that matter in Mr. Maugham's too) because of the readability, the golden knack. But now the readability sticks in the throat, and familiarity with it gives the knack away. I do not mean that Mr. Greene is deteriorating: on the contrary. But that ever good, Greene no longer seems good enough—at the theological level, though at the thriller level I dare say it is still all right. It begins to look pompous and old-fashioned. For me the writing will no longer "carry" things like this typical sample of Javitt's wisdom:

> People are afraid of bringing May Slossom into the house. They say it's unlucky. The real reason is it smells of sex and they are afraid of sex. Why aren't they afraid of fish, then? you may rightly ask. Because when they smell fish they smell a holiday ahead and they feel safe from breeding for a short while.

—a typical gallimaufry, since most people *aren't* afraid of sex, and most sex *doesn't* smell of fish, and most people *do* "breed" on holiday like mad. (That is, if we take the text *au pied de la lettre*. If, on the other hand, we accept the malodorous *double-entendre*—as I dare say, Mr. Greene being Mr. Greene, we must—then it makes better sense, but God help us all. If that's all the smell of fish reminds him of, he'd better take a long, long dip in the sea.) Either way, I prefer to retire to the truer profundities of Tom Kitten—which are, incidentally, *really* well-written.

Carolyn D. Scott (essay date 1963)

SOURCE: "The Witch at the Corner: Notes on Graham Greene's Mythology," in *Graham Greene: Some Critical Considerations,* edited by Robert O. Evans, University of Kentucky Press, 1963, pp. 231-44.

[*In the essay below, Scott examines Greene's use of myth in his short stories, focusing in particular on his depiction of the myth of childhood within the context of African and primitive themes.*]

In the short story often lies the microcosm of an author's total vision, and for Graham Greene that medium has provided the emblem for both "the power and the glory" of his longer works. Indeed, the volume **Nineteen Stories** (1949), the best but by no means the only collection of Greene's shorter fiction, contains more than a "hint of an explanation" toward a fuller realization of his world view. Few critics, however, have perceived the significance of the short stories to the whole of Greene's work. Furthermore, those who discuss the short fiction often err in not recognizing the thick web of consciousness surrounding the hero's actions and read them as if they expressed only the conventional Christian dichotomy between good and evil. George Silveira's "Greene's 'The Basement Room,'"

[in *The Explicator* XV, December 1956] for example, searches the *Catholic Encyclopedia* to discover the relation between the Church's designation of man's seventh year for attaining the age of reason and the age of Philip when he rejects responsibility in the world. Vernon Young's review of the whole volume ["Hell on Earth: Six Versions," *Hudson Review* II, Summer 1949] practically diagnoses a sort of Augustinian neurosis as the core of Greene's creation. "His flights across the threshold of the occult, of the theological," writes Young, "are impelled by fear of physical being rather than by visions of the power and the glory." And Sean O'Faolain in *The Vanishing Hero* strongly allies Greene with "antihumanists" like Mauriac and Bernanos who encourage a return to a medieval world. In fact, nearly all Greene's works have at one time or another been considered as Christian allegories, dialogues between the body and soul, and even as Manichean tracts. But surely a man of Greene's stature, a man who most unquestionably belongs to the 20th century and not the Middle Ages, cannot wholly depend on the Baltimore Catechism for thematic structure. Like Yeats, Pound, Eliot, Faulkner, Tolkien, and even his personal favorites, Saki and de la Mare, Greene has created his own myth, one that reconstructs tradition and ritual yet speaks with the immediacy of the modern dilemma. Explicitly, Greene's central symbol is the heart of Africa, seat of our fall, and the whole myth first takes shape in his autobiographical travelogue, *Journey Without Maps*. It is continued and brought to fruition within the short stories.

> Greene found in Africa a myth of lost childhood. He wishes to find, by simply penetrating into the African heart, at what point we went astray—where man fell.
>
> —*Carolyn D. Scott*

Just as Henry James found in Europe the "thickness" and "roundness," the "fairy-tale side of life," so Greene found in Africa a myth of lost childhood, or "Pendélé," as he calls it in his latest work, *A Burnt-out Case*. He wishes to find, by simply penetrating into the African heart, at what point we went astray—where man fell. No critic can escape the childhood theme in Greene, for it is the one obsession out of which his tragedies grow. But, as in Catharine Hughes' discussion of this matter [in "Innocence Revisited," *Renascence* XII, Autumn 1959], Greene's view of childhood has been thought to include a Wordsworthian innocence. This is too simple. It cannot explain the knowledge of death that Francis Morton in **"The End of the Party"** possesses, nor Pinkie's early instinctive distaste for his parents' tawdry Saturday nights in *Brighton Rock*. These distinctly unromantic elements, however, are placed in perspective by "The Lost Childhood," an essay in which Greene both celebrates and laments his discovery of the creative endeavor in Marjorie Bowen's *The Viper of Milan.* Before this intellectual awakening, says Greene, he had lived his first fourteen years in a "wild country without a map" where his only recognition was the ancient witch Gagool of *King Solomon's Mines* whose power haunted his nursery dreams, as we shall see. But inevitably the hand must move along the bookshelf, one must grow up to the moral world, selecting a job, a taste, a death, as surely as Eve's hand moves toward the apple or Oedipus guesses the sphinx's riddle.

So in the childhood of Africa what Greene found was not a prelapsarian Eden, but Eden at the moment the apple is to be plucked: neither guilty nor innocent of the forces of evil. There the childhood of the race is indeed acquainted intimately with the devil, the witch of our dreams; yet in that intimacy it has still not lost the instinctive, ritualistic terror, the imagination which comprehends the supernatural. Thus, for Greene, our civilization has exchanged "supernatural cruelty" for a secular depravity. We have lost a creative sensitivity to witches and angels, the understanding that permits man to create and build a brave new world out of the ruin he placed on nature at the Fall. Our seedy, chrome civilization has made a Manichean sense of evil unfortunately possible.

In Africa, where there is a potential yet unrealized civilization—"the graves not opened yet for gold, the mine not broken with sledges"—Greene discovered the compelling ritual of the Liberian bush devil. These men of power govern the supernatural and natural activities of the community and with raffia skirts and carved masks, go about the countryside both terrorizing and delighting the folk. In an unconsciously erotic ritual, which Greene likens to Europa and the bull, children dance before them, courting that power who leers beneath the carved mask. These bush devils are the initiators of the young, executors of justice, and demigod priests all in one; yet in reality they may be merely the harmless village blacksmith. Greene discovered that their "power" contains that simultaneous quality of good and evil, the essence of black magic that has been lost in most of our civilized theology. He writes:

> "Devil," of course, is a word used by the English-speaking native to describe something unknown in *our* theology; it has nothing to do with evil. One might equally call these big bush devils angels—for they have the angelic properties of alacrity and invisibility—if that word contained no element of "good." In a Christian land we have grown so accustomed to the idea of a spiritual war, of God and Satan, that this supernatural world, which is neither good nor evil but simply Power, is almost beyond sympathetic comprehension. Not quite: for those witches which haunted our childhood were neither good nor evil. They terrified us with their power, but we knew all the time that we must not escape them. They simply demanded recognition: flight was a weakness.

Here Greene's myth allies itself with the archetypal recognition of evil which has absorbed the studies of Freud and Jung. In Freud this dream of the witch, which haunts Greene's heroes through several works, is part of the "ar-

chaic heritage which the child brings with him into the world, before any experience of his own, as a result of the experience of his ancestors." Indeed Freud is on Greene's mind as he leaves Africa. "Freud has made us conscious as we have never been before of those ancestral threads which still exist in our unconscious minds to lead us back." Unlike those of Freud, though, the ancestral threads which Greene has come upon are not regarded as sources of neurosis. They are rather a "dread of something outside that has got to come in." Unlike Marlow's descent into hell which culminates in "the horror" of primitive barbarism, the whole journey into the African bush confronts Greene with a "sense of disappointment with what man had made out of the primitive, what he had made out of childhood." But Greene, for all this, does not see in childhood the "clouds of glory" which surround the child of *The Prelude* who, unappalled by the drowned man's face, innocently recognizes evil from fairy tales he once read. Greene's "*something* in that early terror" is perhaps best described in Jacques Maritain's *Creative Intuition in Art and Poetry* as the "spiritual preconscious" which, unlike the "automatic Freudian unconscious" that merely embodies physical behavior or misbehavior, acknowledges the awareness of the primitive as part of the poetic activity. Thus the "something outside that has got to come in" is for Greene, as it was for James in the dream of the Gallerie d'Apollon, the comprehension, the recognition of appalling power, neither good nor evil, but a haunting, compelling synthesis of both. And thus Greene cannot espouse the conventional Christian view of the dichotomy between good and evil. In his comments on the air of evil in James's *The Turn of the Screw,* Greene says: "That story . . . belongs to the Christian, the orthodox imagination. Mine [the witches and preternatural personae of his dreams] were devils *only* in the African sense of beings who controlled power."

> **Few critics have perceived the significance of the short stories to the whole of Greene's work. Furthermore, those who discuss the short fiction often err in not recognizing the thick web of consciousness surrounding the hero's actions and read them as if they expressed only the conventional Christian dichotomy between good and evil.**
>
> —*Carolyn D. Scott*

The Christian mythos cannot be fully adequate for Greene's highly particular spiritual experience. The comment that Greene "believes in God because he believes in Satan" can only ride on the surface of his works. And so his concern, his obsessions, which, in his own words, makes "every creative writer worth our consideration," is to pursue those symbols which haunted his and all our nursery dreams: the Princess of Time, the poisoned flowers, an old Arab, Tibetan warriors, and the inevitable witch. They pursue, they persist; and his body struggles only to find they survive, not only in his own childish dreams, but also the dreams of a wailing child who cries for the dance of the bush devil. To triumph we need only to find and recognize this power; flight is weakness. This choice of triumph or weakness is the dilemma of Greene's heroes.

The struggle for and recognition of power is the theme of several of Greene's more significant short stories. After the African experience, his first descent into the spiritual underworld was **"The Basement Room,"** written in 1936 on the boat back from West Africa. In this work, a power—which is only amoral, not immoral, in fact that power which is associated with the ritual of initiation before the African bush devil—operates in child Philip's dream world to confront him with the moment of choice in what will become a moral situation. Left by his parents with the butler and housekeeper, Mr. and Mrs. Baines, Philip must choose, at the early age of seven, between the nursery and the cellar, between fruition or defeat. But he is determined not to be drawn into the adult world of secrets, love affairs, and jealousy. "For if a grown-up could behave so childishly, you were liable, too, to find yourself in their world. It was enough that it came at you in dreams: the witch at the corner, the man with a knife." However, those powers which work upon us in every situation "demand recognition," and "flight is a weakness," a weakness that Philip does not overcome.

There are two worlds in **"The Basement Room,"** which Philip must recognize and choose between, separated by a green baize door, an image Greene used elsewhere to separate the world of innocence from the world of knowledge, the world of love from the world of hate, the world of the child from the world of the adult. Cross the threshold and you have committed yourself to ruin or triumph. Greene's own fascination with this image appears later in his Mexican adventures, *The Lawless Roads,* when he recalls the baize door between his school and home, between hate and love; and again in *The Ministry of Fear* when Arthur Rowe, beginning to wake up from his dream world and amnesia, passes through the green baize door of the insane asylum to discover the source of evil that has beset him. In his nursery, Philip, burdened with Baine's secret love affair, "strained his ears for Mrs. Baines's coming, for the sound of voices, but the basement held its secrets; the green baize door shut off that world."

Philip's inadequacy also lies in his terror of the dark, of the now unfamiliar rooms of the house where dusters cover the furniture, when nurse and family are away. He too is making a journey without maps. Vivid is the terror he feels for the knock, knock, knock at the door, the bleeding head and glittering eyes of the Siberian wolves, all waiting to be recognized in his dreams. Floating up from that world is the witch, Mrs. Baines, who like the witch with Hansel, plies Philip with jam and pudding, then tricks him into telling the secret. She is like old Gagool, ancient and musty. Her very being is secret as the bush devil; she is "darkness when the night light went out," and is "flowers

gone bad." When Philip's eyes open from the dreams, the terror is real, too real for him to face. The witch with her musty hair, her breath hot, leans over his bed in an unexpected visit to ask, "Just tell me where they are." The doors and windows are wrenched open in a breath, and, wretched, he cries out, "Baines, Baines," and the witch falls in a black heap. He cannot escape on a jeweled swan as did the children of Grimm's fairy tale. Philip is not prepared to accept this violent facing of the adult world he cannot understand. He rejects loyalties and unwittingly "tells on" Baines in his reluctance to face that black heap ever again. "He'd spent it all, had been allowed no time to let it grow, no years of gradual hardening; he couldn't even scream."

Philip, in withdrawing from the dream world, surrenders the initiation to life. To use the metaphor of Greene's mythology, the secret school of the bush devil here has failed to prepare Philip for the adult, moral world. For in that primitive kindergarten which Greene once witnessed, the bush children attend lessons given by the devil for two years. They feel terror and awe for this harsh instructor, but knowledge of him prepares them for a rugged life in the bush. Failure to thrive under his fierce spell may cause one to end as a lifeless heap of clothes at the parents' door. It is best to be thrust into the power of the devil and not resist. This is an African child's baptism and rebirth. "They brought a screaming child up to the devil," writes Greene, fascinated, "and thrust him under the devil's muzzle, under the dusty raffia mane; he stiffened and screamed and tried to escape and the devil mouthed him." And so it is with Philip's own initiation under the dusty hair of Mrs. Baines, only he cannot be reborn because he resists.

The same baptism of terror is performed in **"The Hint of an Explanation"** except that here the child survives the ordeal. Acting in the role of the bush devil, Blacker, the baker, tempts and ironically instructs for the priesthood, young David by forcing a moral commitment upon him. Even though Blacker asks David to commit sacrilege, we must not interpret this request in any conventionally diabolical sense. Blacker's action betrays much the same "supernatural cruelty," the fusion of love and hate as is found in the bush devil's ritual. This reading of young David's temptation coheres with his own adult observation about the inadequacy of Satan in theology: "The word Satan is so anthropomorphic." We are instead tried by a "Thing" or power, says the priestly narrator. He hesitates to say who or what Blacker really serves. Blacker, whose intense hate becomes permeated with a curiosity close to love, is viewed by David with the awe of the supernatural similar to that of the villagers of Mosamboluhun to the local blacksmith-devil. "It is not the mask that is sacred, nor the blacksmith who is sacred; it is the two in conjunction . . . ," observes Greene. Blacker's appearance is as terrifying as the devil's mask: one wall-eye, turnip head, smears of chalk and pastry. His secret knowledge of bleeding people and opening doors in the night like the devil who says to the bush child, "I'm going to swallow you," terrifies the boy into nearly surrendering the Sacred Host. In the spell of Blacker's professed powers, David fears not to remove the Host from his mouth and place it aside. Like Mrs. Baines, Blacker is the witch who plies his victim with toys to insure his moment of success. Yet, at this moment, the full force of that power shatters into disappointment. Through Blacker's hate for, yet fascination with the Host, that recognition of power which is neither good nor evil intervenes, and the realization of this "Thing's" value for the pulp which is "God there on the chair" saves David and thus prepares him for a new, priestly life. The school of the evil has been his salvation.

This knowledge of a Thing, a power, is almost prophetic in **"The End of the Party"** when Francis Morton's dream of death comes like a big bird swooping in the darkened house. Francis has dreams which reveal to him that darkness and death are real, dreams that hold secret knowledge to which the adults are cold. These unfeeling adults, Mabel Warren and Mrs. Henne-Falcon, flutter like hens and chickens about the darkening rooms enjoying the hide-and-seek game that is a real and present terror to Francis. Like the bush villagers, the ancient joke of "frightening the child with what had frightened them" governs their unconscious actions. The spiritual terror that leads to death and a powerful realization of the essence of death are but impersonal games to the grownup, civilized world, as impersonal as the nurse's cold torch making a beam through the darkness towards Francis's death. But after death, the power of his terror, conveyed like an electric impulse to his elder twin's hand, overcomes all seedy civilization, all set programs at the birthday party. One is reminded of the significance of this in the later work, *England Made Me*, where twins also have the power of conveying their awe for death. Kate contemplating her quarrel with Tony, who unknown to her has just been killed, compares it to childhood disputes. "In childhood one had been more careful, death was closer; one hadn't this hard grip on life." Even before the African venture then, Greene in these two stories had decided that the racial childhood held understanding of the darkness of man's heart, of the surety in death. He later confirms:

> Oh, one wanted to protest, one doesn't believe, of course, in the "visionary gleam," in the trailing glory, but there was something in that early terror and the bareness of one's needs, a harp strumming behind a hut, a witch on the nursery landing, a handful of kola nuts, a masked dancer, the poisoned flowers.

In lesser works, **"I Spy,"** and **"A Drive in the Country,"** the adolescent, too, comes in contact with this power. For example, Charlie Stowe, reversing the Wordsworthian theme, finds the father "doing things in the dark which frightened him." In the second story, the young girl, disillusioned with her father's meticulous dullness, runs off in a wild ride to the dark woods with reckless Fred.'In this action she is like the child swaying in the erotic dance before the old bush devil. In her childish dream, she is courting an adult action. In the cold woodsy fog the British girl finds she must flee back to her father's cheap bolted door in terror from a suicide pact that would implicate her with a man who is damning himself. She has awakened from the dreamy dance with the devil to find

the leering eyes of an adult blacksmith beneath the painted mask. And too, the man in **"The Innocent"** discovers an obscenity he drew as a child in painful, intense desire, hidden, waiting for him in a hollow tree. It reveals the loss of that finer taste, keener pleasure, and deeper terror that must inevitably end in seedy civilization, typified by his slatternly friend, Lola.

So Evil creeps into the later dreams: "The man with the gold teeth and rubber surgical gloves; the old woman with ringworm; the man with his throat cut dragging himself across the carpet to the bed." Greene's adult heroes are struggling with the body as is Craven in **"A Little Place off the Edgware Road,"** who is reminded by a religious placard of a dream he had in which there are no worms and dissolution, the body does not decay. His only waking comfort is that it was just a nightmare. Then evil creeps in, dropping upon him the fine bloody spray from the living corpse of the "man with his throat cut" who haunted the author's own dreams. But in **"Proof Positive"** Greene reaffirms the power in the unity of the body and spirit and the rottenness in their separation when the dominant spirit, robbed of its bodily connection, "decays into whispered nonsense." Metallic civilization has created this separation of body and soul. Adult life directs what childhood instinctively knew. Religious signs are not enough. The sound of music and the drum are silent. We must go to Africa again to embrace the leper who alone can tell us of Pendélé.

Pendélé is that mysterious land of childhood which Querry, in Greene's newest work, *A Burnt-out Case*, came to Africa to seek, where in his dreams he wishes to go after death. The tawdry, seedy level of the secular, adult world has betrayed him as it betrayed Philip in **"The Basement Room."** He cannot build and create any more. His architectural skill, like Philip's Meccano set, has been stowed away somewhere. Querry goes to Africa to seek a word that falls from the lips of Deo Gratias, the leper, who whispers the secret of "Pendélé" in the darkness of the bush, very like the forest Greene stumbled through in Liberia many years before. Pendélé, a childhood place of dancing and singing, becomes the central obsession in Querry's view of his new life. Like the bush devils who speak in foreign dialects, Deo Gratias (indeed the name parody cannot be ignored) mutters all night in unintelligible mixtures of French and bush language, except for one word, "Pendélé." Dr. Colin's answer to Querry's inquiry into the meaning is a facile, unimaginative translation—"pride." This is the sort of impersonal judgment about the world which Querry has been fleeing from all his life. He insists, rather, it is this place of our childhood, where there is singing and dancing and games; where we can sleep in a single bed without the responsibilities of adults. Our mortal sins do not explain our hunger, our flight through labyrinthine ways, our exposure to evil and death.

When Querry elaborates this meaning of the word to the Superior of the hospital force, the father answers, "People have to grow up. We are called to more complicated things than that." Querry recalls the ancient initiation, ". . . surely there's something also about having to be as little children if we are to inherit. . . . We've grown-up rather badly. The complications have become too complex." For belief also belongs to the cave man; Christians do not have the corner on faith. What Querry really is looking for is at what point in our childhood we went astray; the Eden Deo Gratias cannot and will not reveal.

So intense is the impact of the metaphor about the lost childhood that later Querry, figuratively, translates his questioning life into a fairy tale about a country boy and a king. Mme. Rycker, his listener, says in disbelief, "You and I are much too old for fairy-stories." "Yes. That in a way *is* the story, as you'll see," Querry returns. Both have lost the way to Pendélé. The meaning to Querry's little story may be found, I think, in the lines from A. E.'s [George William Russell, 1867-1935] poem, "Germinal," often quoted by Greene: "In the lost childhood of Judas, Christ was betrayed." The little unformed face of Philip hardens, as does Querry's heart for the world.

Querry's fairy tale is not even a very good story, not so thrilling as Grimm, nor so penetrating as Perrault, but it represents Querry's coming to grips with what was missing in the civilized world, why he came down the river to the leper colony. He is too old for fairy tales, for believing that the King, or God, has sent "a bull, a shower of gold, a son." In a tawdry world where cheap statues and neo-Gothic churches abound, he can no longer cherish the ancient symbols of creativity; he can only recall and be troubled by the memory of them. He envies the unconscious devotions of his parents to the King much in the same way Greene envies the child swaying before the devil—Europa swaying before the bull, unaware of the leering adult beneath who knows of the fall, the forgetfulness.

And Querry, as he steps into the dawn, reflects on the epigram "The King is dead, long live the King." Perhaps in the new life and new country, away from the seemingly impersonal rules of the (man-made, after all) Church, he can find the King of Pendélé, the bush devil who will mouth him and dance for him.

Greene sees in primitive ritual and mythmaking something which can potentially revitalize our own civilized institutions, most of which have their origins in ancient rites.

—*Carolyn D. Scott*

Unlike Querry, Greene sees in primitive ritual and myth-making something which can potentially revitalize our own civilized institutions, most of which have their origins in ancient rites. Greene's own jungle discovery thus refreshes and fulfills his long journey as he comes to realize the relation of the whirling, demanding devil and his own

European religious longing. Suddenly recalling a childhood experience where he witnessed the ancient Jack-in-the-Green rites at a quiet crossroads, Greene writes:

> It wasn't so alien to us, this masked dance (in England too there was a time when man dressed as animals and danced), any more than the cross and the pagan emblems on the grave were alien. One had the sensation of having come home, for here one was finding associations with a personal and a racial childhood, one was being scared by the same old witches.

The search and discovery of myth seems to bring order from external or internal chaos. The fact that myth fails to distinguish the everyday act from symbolic performance encourages the modern hope that a supernatural power can permeate all things. In this realization Greene hopes for a coherent ritual not incompatible with modern institutions.

His fascination for the primitive, of course, would not exclude such an establishment as the Catholic Church. He finds for himself, as he claims for Henry James, "the treatment of supernatural evil," "the savage elementary belief" in prowling evil spirits to be adequate vehicles for expressing the "struggle between the beautiful and the treacherous." In its concept of sacrament the Church preserves those precious remnants of our childhood—the supernatural elements by which "human nature is not despicable." The life within the Catholic Church provides a quality of vision truly catholic in its absorption of the pagan and the primitive. It is not reducible to moral formulas which bind M. Rycker to his sanctimonious practices, Mme. Rycker to her spouse. The struggle for the beautiful and the treacherous in Greene's heroes and heroines requires a judge whose creative, fruitful powers of synthesis can unite the good in evil, the evil in good. Greene's myth provides that judge and judgment, and that power is God, the hound of heaven, the bush devil.

After his childhood discovery of evil, in *The Viper of Milan*, Greene remarks, "Human nature is not black and white but black and grey." It is from this assumption that Greene's mythology can take shape. In Liberia he reaffirms this basic conviction about life as he uncovers the aboriginal terror in the "grey" visage of the bush devil. Such an impact did this revelation have upon Greene that we are forced to qualify any comment we make on the seeming Manichean qualities of his fiction as well as our thinking about his concept of Hell. As R. W. B. Lewis implies, Hell does lie about Pinkie, Philip, Francis, David, and even Querry in their infancy, but the sterile, chrome, unimaginative boredom of that Hell is not found in Liberia. Rather, Hell is the civilized perversion of the primitive. With the comprehension of what the witch at the corner means to the children of Greene's fiction, with the understanding that these children are like the Liberian boy being initiated to the terror of the bush devil, we find Greene's fiction more intelligible, and even more flexible in its concept of the human act. For the myth opens up to Greene a whole spectrum of possibilities between the theological poles of good and evil, and thus it both extends the range of his ethical sympathies and sophisticates his artistic technique.

Gwenn R. Boardman (essay date 1965)

SOURCE: "Greene's 'Under the Garden': Aesthetic Explorations," in *Renascence: A Critical Journal of Letters*, Vol. XVII, No. 4, Summer, 1965, pp. 180-90, 194.

[*In the essay below, Boardman examines Greene's treatment of aesthetic concerns, including faith, belief, imagination, and moral consciousness, in "Under the Garden."*]

"Under the Garden," first published in Greene's *A Sense of Reality* (1963), might well have been written as a commentary on his own explorations, his aesthetic discoveries that have invariably been tied to actual journeys, whether to Africa, Mexico, or Indo-China. It is a mythic rendition of his recurrent themes of lost childhood, of a universal "journey without maps," and a quest for "the heart of the matter." As counterpoint to these thematic variations, there are echoes of familiar episodes, characters, and symbols from Greene's other writing.

As far back as 1936, Greene wrote of ". . . legend, figures which will dramatize the deepest personal fantasy and deepest moral consciousness of a man's time: this . . . is the only thing worth attempting." In **"Under the Garden"** he has provided his own form of legend and figures (Javitt and Maria) who do indeed dramatize both personal fantasy and moral consciousness. This fifty-nine page story could serve also as a commentary on Greene's theory and practice of the craft of fiction. At first the reader may see little evidence of the questing artist in a boy's record of exploring a dark passage with hieroglyphics on its wall. Rather than tracing a path to the creative process, Wilditch appears to discover only the way to a world smelling unpleasantly of cabbage, watched over by a dirty old woman saying "Kwawk." Moreover, the lord of this under world seems unimpressive: a big old man with a white beard sitting on a lavatory seat. Yet Javitt's words include many of Greene's own statements about the novelist's task. Like Greene, he looks at the familiar world with an unconventional eye. In addition, he and Maria are prototypes of Power, the supernatural or spiritual force whose loss from the modern world Greene has so frequently mourned.

He himself sought this ancient Power on his journey to "the heart of darkness" in 1934-35, when he followed the ancestral threads back to African "innocence." This was not a romantic journey, in spite of Greene's acknowledgement (in *In Search of a Character*) of Conrad's influence on his early work. He was not looking for the noble savage, but for the primitive, unspoiled vision: the purer pleasure and the purer terror of sharpened artistic sensibility. It was in Africa that Greene tried to discover "at what point we went astray." He emerged from his *Journey without Maps* to chart new fictional paths, beginning with *Brighton Rock*. Wilditch also "goes back"— first to the scene of his boyhood vacations, to a time before he had learned that "imagination was usually a quality to be suppressed." He too tries to discover a lost vision.

Wilditch's experience in rediscovering this lost childhood dream is a neat parable of Greene's artistic theory. Greene has written continually about the world of childhood, alluding to its cruelties and to its innocence again and again in his book reviews, novels, and film criticism. Metaphors drawn from his own schooldays recur in texts as varied as *The Heart of the Matter* and *Brighton Rock*. Repeatedly, Greene uses the phrase "lost childhood," an allusion identified in his volume of essays, where he quotes from A. E.'s [George William Russell, 1867-1935] "Germinal":

> In ancient shadows and twilights
> Where childhood had strayed,
> The world's great sorrows were born
> And its heroes were made.
> In the lost boyhood of Judas
> Christ was betrayed.

It is worth noting that this poem opens with the line, "Call not the wanderer home as yet." Its final verse suggests: "Let thy young wanderer dream on: / Call him not home. / A door opens, a breath, a voice, / From the ancient room, / Speaks to him now . . ."

The ancient room to which Wilditch wanders in **"Under the Garden"** gives new depth to Greene's theme of the artist as wanderer, explorer, map-maker. He has said, "The explorer has the same creative sickness as the writer or the artist. . . ." To fill in the map, as to fill in the characters or features of a human being, requires the urge to surrender and self-destruction. Although Greene writes, "It was plain that the young Wilditch's talents had not been for literature," the adult Wilditch is well aware that the author must "order and enrich the experience," and he examines that original experience, translating the childhood vision with the aid of his years of wandering in quest of Beauty.

The questing artist of Greene's creation is not simply a traveller and map-maker, however. He must look at the world with the eyes of childhood as well as the mind of maturity. Like the narrator of **"The Innocent,"** working out and reinterpreting a childhood memory as he lay in bed beside a pickup, Lola, Wilditch revisits the scenes of innocence, remembering and re-forming the child's experience in order to reinterpret the present. In **"The Innocent,"** the narrator recognized the distortions introduced by the cynicism of adult perception: the child's "uniquely beautiful" picture seemed momentarily more like an ugly drawing on a lavatory wall. Wilditch finds the meaning of *his* experience not in terms of a lavatory scrawl but in a tin chamberpot flecked with yellow paint. Even as he perceives its meaning, Wilditch recalls that the child found that "golden pot" uniquely beautiful, as beautiful as the drawing in **"The Innocent."**

Describing the early formative years of a writer, Greene has spoken of the "innocent eye dwelling frankly on a new unexplored world, the vistas of future experience at the end of the laurel walk." The vistas at the end of Wilditch's laurel walk eventually opened the way to his years of future experience travelling in search of Beauty (Javitt's daughter): "The purpose of life had suddenly come to me as it must have come to some future explorer when he noticed on a map for the first time an empty space in the heart of a continent."

Again, Wilditch's words clearly echo Greene's in *Journey without Maps*. Wilditch entering the heart of darkness below the tree resembles Greene, who described himself as "a complete amateur at travel in Africa . . . [with] no idea of what route to follow or the conditions he would meet." Greene even referred to his African journey as "a smash-and-grab raid into the primitive"—an amusing foreshadowing of Wilditch's experience with the treasure, which reminded him of the display in a jeweller's window. In spite of the finer artistic consciousness which Greene demonstrated after his journey, he was at first able only to see Africa in terms of such romantic adventures as *King Solomon's Mines*. The boy Wilditch also thought of "romantic explorations" and *Treasure Island* when he named the landmarks of his discovery. Yet the romantic storybook world does have something in common with actual exploration. Both belong to "the region of the imagination—the region of uncertainty, of not knowing the way about."

In the course of exploring the region of his own imagination, Greene found his way about four geographical areas that have come to serve as symbols in his artistic development. Liberia, Mexico, Indo-China, and the Congo in turn exposed new levels of artistic consciousness.

—Gwenn R. Boardman

In the course of exploring the region of his own imagination, Greene found his way about four geographical areas that have come to serve as symbols in his artistic development. Liberia, Mexico, Indo-China, and the Congo in turn exposed new levels of artistic consciousness, which Greene expressed in psychological terminology. Liberia was the world of childhood "innocence," a beginning, "before we began to go wrong." Yet these children were in a "spiritual Limbo." He then went to Mexico, where he found "adolescent" violence that yet revealed a dramatic picture of secular power superseding religious glory and suggested "the appalling mysteries of love moving through a ravaged world." After his novels of love and hate, Greene travelled to Indo-China, where he discovered the representative adult of our "chromium-plated" civilization, that cliché-ridden "innocent" American Pyle, whose "writers and lecturers made a fool of him." But he also discovered that "Under the enormous shadow of the Cross it was better to be gay." After he had been suitably gay in his delightful self-mockeries *Loser Take All, The Complai-*

sant Lover, and *Our Man in Havana,* Greene went to the Congo "In Search of a Character." Here he finally identified the character of the adult Querry—perhaps his response to Camus' view of the Absurd Man as traveller, and certainly an artist returning to life (and death). Yet the "truth" which Greene says he sought on his journeys—one he defines as "a question of style" rather than any kind of philosophical probing—is also one of "eternal values," the relation of man's soul to God. Like T. S. Eliot, Greene sees in today's lost religious sense a loss to the world of fiction, a reduction of characters to "cardboard," without the "solidity and importance of men with souls to save or lose." Unlike Wilditch, who denies that he is religious, Greene admits of his own position, "Quand on est catholique, il ne faut pas chercher à faire du 'catholicisme.' Tout ce que l'on dit ou écrit respire inevitablement le catholicisme."

Primarily, however, Wilditch expresses the problems of a writer. He learns the way to artistic truth. Entering an unknown region and determined to draw a map Wilditch, like his creator in this and many other seemingly deliberately teasing respects, is alternately attracted and repelled by the conditions of Javitt's world of mysterious Power, a world oddly touched by traces of civilization. Reading his boyhood story, a tale published six years after the original action, Wilditch is irritated by details he had omitted or altered. He wonders whether the boy had forgotten or was afraid to remember the actual experience (Greene has spoken of the novelist's need to "face his fears"). Yet Wilditch clings to the "fact" that he dreamed. Concluding, "A dream too was an experience," he begins to write an account of what he had found—or dreamed that he had found—when he first descended into the darkness under the garden.

In his essay, "Analysis of a Journey," later rephrased and incorporated into *Journey without Maps,* Greene spoke of the effect of Africa and its ancient Power upon the unconscious mind of the writer: "A quality of darkness was needed, of the inexplicable, something which has to be taken as a symbol because it has no obvious meaning for the conscious brain." He also quoted Kurt Heuser's *The Inner Journey:* "The interior: that might signify the heart of the continent, but also the heart of things, the mystery: and finally, the comprehension of himself in nature and in Time." That could be a description of Wilditch's journey, which continually echoes Greene's comparison of journey and dream. Wilditch says, recalling the details of his adventure, "Absolute reality belongs to dreams and not to life. . . . What seems is."

Wilditch travelled away from the "reality" of his mother's world, where the poetic imagination had always to be "rigidly controlled" and "speculation was discouraged." He found his own reality, as any writer must establish values for himself. His mother with her "very decided views" about any mysteries "wanted everything to be very clear." She could only tolerate "puzzles," the kind of mystery found in detective stories, where there is always an answer. But she could not approve the mysteries of imagination, of fairy stories, or of religious faith. When she wrote to the school about the "religious" feeling she was certain existed in her son's story, they responded with the comforting thought that his "little fantasy" was probably related to young Wilditch's school reading program, for the treasure of his story "is only too material, and quite at the mercy of those who break in and steal." His mother, a staunch Fabian (described in terms reminiscent of those used for Smythe in *The End of the Affair*), was not convinced; she retained a dislike for the laurel walk and the garden. Finally she hid the magazine containing the story, rather as the family for whom "God was taboo" tried to suppress the religious mystery of young James's experience in *The Potting Shed*. Yet—as this mystery was finally solved, or Sarah's hidden baptism became effective in *The End of the Affair*—the mystery of the garden could not be suppressed. Wilditch returned to the dark hidden room of his dream-reality, where the treasures of language and thought had not yet been contaminated by the clichés of popular culture or dulled by the stock responses typified in George Wilditch's lack of understanding.

George and his brother "seemed to be talking about different places and different people." George unawareness of the hidden treasure beneath his garden is an extension of his refusal to take imaginative flight. He chides Wilditch for calling the pond a lake, for referring to "treasure" in an old quarry that actually contained only "iron stuff." Although he "had been in occupation" of the house for many years, George "had no idea of what might lie underneath the garden." It remained only a problem in taxation, management, and plumbing. For George is a member of the "chromium-plated" civilization of the west that Greene continually holds responsible for the clichés of popular entertainment.

Wilditch's flight from this stifling reality leads him into the realm of darkness, without maps, where he can discover the heart of things for himself. But the boundaries of dream and reality are as uncertain as the earlier geographical frontiers. We are never quite permitted to discover the source of Wilditch's story, in spite of Greene's careful separation of adult re-creation and childhood vision by shifting from a third-person narrative to Wilditch's. For even as Artist-Wilditch separates his "corrected" version from the schoolboy fiction, he continually comments on the impossibility of separating dream from life. "A dream can only contain what one has experienced, or, if you have sufficient faith in Jung, what our ancestors have experienced." Yet even as he "explains" the story, Wilditch observes that it is no more than a pale imitation of the original action. He doubts that the boy could have been aware of the "simple facts" which keep bringing his dark experience "back to ordinary life." He cannot decide, however, whether he is dealing with child's invention, with "real" adventure, or with experiences that have "accumulated like coral around the original dream."

Thus Wilditch's story becomes an exercise in creative map-making for the reader. As Greene has said in another context, "The writer's task is the correct setting of a question." The writer must stimulate the reader to wonder, and to choose. He must create a world of sympathy (for "gray and black characters alike"); communicate a mood or atmosphere, as Wilditch communicates the cabbage odor and the strange routine of the dank underground passage; suggest moral values without ever sinking to pious homily, as Javitt's pronouncements demand re-weighing of conventional commandments. He must avoid sentimentality—hence the detachment of Wilditch's viewpoint, the repeated reminders of his "story," and the attempts to separate the primary reaction from the later judgment and rewriting of experience.

Childhood is a time of "virgin sensibility," and as Greene notes, the creative spirit is tied to innocence, the "stock of innocence" is essential for a writer.

—Gwenn R. Boardman

Thus the map metaphor is an appropriate symbolization of the artistic vision confronting the world that has been labelled (unsatisfactorily) by others, by men using the dead language of convention. By walking each path for himself, as Greene walked through Africa, and as Wilditch crawls and walks through the world below the familiar garden, the writer examines experience at first hand instead of accepting such clichés as Ida's identification of "right" and "wrong" in *Brighton Rock* or the confusion of "love" and "hate" in Bendrix's interpretation of *The End of the Affair*. Too often, as Greene observes, the popular novelist substitutes sentimental clichés and distorting commonplaces for "life as it is and life as it ought to be."

Arthur Rowe in *The Ministry of Fear* also found himself through experiences in a garden, although he too at first had "the wrong map." Like Rowe, and like the psychoanalyst of Greene's early essay, Wilditch pieces together the fragments of the past, examining these fragments in a manner that suggests the epigraph of *Journey without Maps*: "The life of an individual is in many respects like a child's dissected map. If I could live a hundred years . . . I could put the pieces together until they made a properly connected whole." Faced with death, and the vague consolation that "there's always hope," Wilditch seeks the fragments from the past of his dissected life while he attempts to answer his question.

Wilditch's question is the decision, "Whether I want my particular kind of life prolonged." He adds that he isn't a religious man and that he has "no curiosity at all about the future." He also knows that the past is "different." About the Dark Backward he is endlessly curious, although he compares himself to a Civil War leader mortally wounded and attempting to rid himself of illusions by "seeing them again with clear and moribund eyes, so that he might be quite bankrupt when death came." Instead of bankruptcy, however, he discovers the richness of restored perception:

"Curiosity was growing inside him like the cancer." The artist is alive again, as Querry was, and like Querry Wilditch is faced with death. Nevertheless, there *is* hope, for—again as in *A Burnt-Out Case*—"The man who starts looking for God has already found Him."

Wilditch's creator is Catholic and the religious overtones of the story cannot be denied. But the story is not a narrowly religious parable. Christ's injunction to the sinner wishing to enter God's kingdom to become a child, is also advice on the craft of fiction, expressed through Greene's familiar theme of "lost childhood." Greene has repeatedly praised the "admirable objectivity" of childhood—the time when we are not yet conditioned by other people's judgments. Childhood is a time of "virgin sensibility," and as Greene notes in "Herbert Read," the creative spirit is tied to innocence, the "stock of innocence" is essential for a writer. This unspoiled quality is quite different from that false innocence of Pyle, whose "writers and lecturers made a fool of him" in *The Quiet American*. "The undimmed window of the innocent eye" is the child's eye; but as noted above, in **"The Innocent"** Greene shows that the eye can only perceive the truth when it has an adult's powers of judgment.

Greene discovered the significance of "childhood innocence" in 1935, during his journey into the heart of darkness. Returning to England, he heard its loss symbolized in the cry of a tenement child—a symbol made flesh in the ensuing entertainment and novel: Raven in *This Gun for Hire* and Pinkie in *Brighton Rock*. Wilditch returns to the innocent dream of childhood, journeying back in time and in memory (again like the narrator of **"The Innocent"**), in order to re-create the myth, to restore the dulled imagination, to purge the crippling effects of his mother's response to the boy's fictional imitation of a dream action. He discovers the purpose of life, the significance of his lifelong quest, by following the dark threads of memory deep underground.

Such a dark place frequently offers enlightenment in Greene's work. The enlightenment may be religious—as in *The Power and the Glory,* where the dark prison cell brings to the whisky priest an awareness of "the convincing mystery—that we were made in God's image." Yet Greene's use of "the heart of darkness" and "the heart of the matter" is usually no more than "the hint of an explanation," phrases combined in *The Heart of the Matter* to describe the forty-day survival ordeal of a child in an open boat. Greene writes of another mystery: "J'ai toujours été préoccupé par le mystère du peché, il a toujours été à la base de mes livres." Neither God nor sinner can claim exclusive rights to this dark center, however. Like Bendrix's discovery, it may be the transformation of hate into love; or like Wilditch's, the discovery of the existence of Beauty.

"Beauty" sprung from a one-legged old man on a lavatory seat and a dumb hag in faded blue and sequins is as ambiguous a term as others in Greene's fiction. The questions raised by Greene's use of such labels as "justice" in *It's a Battlefield*, "belief" in *The Third Man,* "faith" in **"A Visit to Morin,"** or "love" in *The End of the Affair,* are asked again by Javitt. Javitt's use of language stresses the need for new words and different meanings. Not only do his riddles challenge young Wilditch. He also takes such familiar terms as "white elephant stall" at a garden fête and converts the words to "royal beasts" and man's fate—word-play that is perhaps symbolic of the linguistic traps awaiting writers. In Javitt's world, Time has "a different meaning"; the world's time is unrelated to that of the dark underground, and the ruins of time become transformed into phallic pillars. Javitt challenges Wilditch's conventional use of language with practical, cryptic, and even poetic comment, although the boy does not immediately understand. This advice is "stored in [Wilditch's] memory like a code uncracked which waits for a clue or an inspiration." Javitt, the dirty old man on a lavatory seat, is the New Muse.

Behind this role lies Javitt's resemblance to the ancient Power, which might be loosely identified with the creative force. He is also clearly associated with concepts of godhead, in spite of Wilditch's observation that Javitt resembles Darwin's carrier pigeon (reminiscent of Greene's opinion of "Darwinian materialism"). Like the Hebrew Yahweh, he has another name: one too sacred to be spoken. His symbolic value is continually hinted, whether in his knowledge of "the first name of all," his resemblance to a crucifix, or his promise of forgiveness "seventy times seven." Lest we are tempted to confuse Javitt with God Himself, however, we are told of his resemblance to an old tree-trunk, thus setting him back in the fictional world of *A Burnt-Out Case* by means of the implied resemblance to the natural man, Deo Gratias, the leper who helped to restore the dulled perceptions of the artist Querry.

Javitt challenges the boy, "Haven't I given you a kingdom here of all the treasures of the earth and all the fruits of it"—an echo of the King in Querry's parable. He adds, "You go and defy me with a spoon laid the wrong way," hinting again at the obedience demanded by God, an obedience not always understood by the suffering Catholic heroes of Greene's fiction. Wilditch writes: "For all [Javitt's] freedom of speech and range of thought, I found there were tiny rules which had to be obeyed." That these rules include the method of folding a newspaper and the placement of a spoon should not preclude their serious interpretation.

On the other hand, the satirical hints of these rules, of the golden po's "sacramental" quality, of Javitt finding portents in tea leaves, should not be taken as evidence that Greene has begun to satirize religious belief or that he is mocking the spiritual dimension of his fictional world. "Under the enormous shadow of the Cross it is better to be gay."

The parable of the Jeweller in *A Burnt-Out Case* described an artist whose treasure had been reduced from great cathedrals to golden letters of Marque. But the treasure in **"Under the Garden,"** in spite of the adult Wilditch's "skepticism of middle-age"—the comparison of the jewels with the artificial display of a cheap store window—

is a symbol of promise. It would, however, be a mistake to limit the treasure to religious meaning, in spite of its setting in an egg-shaped hall, where the swinging lamp resembles a censer, Javitt makes ceremonial preparations, and Maria dons a hat. And to dismiss these or the "sacramental" golden po as Greenean whimsy, as further examples of his too-rarely recognized sense of humor, is no more satisfactory than to read them as a religious riddle. Taken as symbols of artistic quest and discovery, however, they do contribute a number of footnotes to Greene's literary intentions. Javitt chides the boy: "You think you can just take a peek . . . and go away." This suggests a criticism of the superficial writer. It is also a precise description of the attitude of so many of Greene's critics. In the interview "Propos de table avec Graham Greene" he observed: "Quant aux incroyants, ils ne sont pas scandalisés, mais montrent une incompréhension presque totale, même les critique les plus intelligents. Ils sont si loin de toute vue chrétienne de l'homme qu'ils ne peuvent entrer dans mon univers." These critics and other writers should not be content to just "take a peek" at the varying worlds created by questing authors. Critic and reader must enter into the fictional world, encouraged by the creation of a writer who has carefully explored the mapless paths of the world about him and faced its flaws and inconsistencies, what Greene calls the "gray and black" of our existence.

The keeper of the key to Javitt's treasure, the literary inspiration, is Maria. She is Woman—"sister, wife, mother, daughter. . . . What difference does it make?" Her name places her in the complex family of Greene's recurrent character, Anne-Marie. (It is worth noting that three Christian names: Mary, Virgin or Magdaline; Anne, mother of Mary; and Rose, symbol of Christ's pain; are frequently at the center of Greene's novels.) Her appearance suggests the mysterious Power, the power Greene felt in Africa and recalled in terms of a witch that haunted his childhood. Like the witch-voiced Mrs. Baines in **"The Basement Room"** and the dark devils of Greene's African villages, Maria inspires fear in Wilditch. Yet it is her force which ultimately propels him back into the real world. She forces Wilditch back to the world where he must interpret the clues provided by the oracular Javitt.

Javitt's riddles provoke thought; Maria's actions rouse primitive instincts. Once again, Greene hints at the dual nature of the artist's inspiration. This duality is further stressed in what Wilditch calls "a strange balance"—the continual tension between fear and happiness or laughter. Most important, however, is Javitt's admonition: "Be disloyal. It's your duty to the human race. . . . Be a double agent—and never let either of the two sides know your real name. The same applies to women and God. They both respect a man they don't own, and they'll go on raising the price they are willing to offer. Didn't Christ say that very thing . . . The obedient flock didn't give the shepherd any satisfaction or the loyal son interest his father."

In spite of Greene's identification as a "Catholic" author, it is the first part of Javitt's advice that he regards as most important. When Javitt says, "Be disloyal," he might be

Greene himself sending a potential writer out into the world. In *Why Do I Write?* Greene had said that belonging to the Catholic Church would present him with grave problems as a writer if he were not "saved by my disloyalty . . . Literature presents a personal moral, and the personal morality of an individual is seldom identical with the morality of the group to which he belongs." In a second letter of this exchange of views between Greene, Elisabeth Bowen, and V. S. Pritchett, he repeated his emphasis on the "importance and the virtue of disloyalty," claiming that disloyalty encourages the writer to "roam experimentally through any human mind: it gives to the novelist the extra dimension of sympathy"—the ability to communicate a sympathetic comprehension of good and evil characters living in this world. Greene again stressed that the writer should be disloyal to the emotional and ideological clichés of his time, in order to avoid writing the sort of popular novel that substitutes cliché for truth.

Yet whatever fancies Javitt encourages in the boy, Wilditch notes that the odd adventure-dream always "kept coming back to ordinary life with simple facts." As in Greene's own works, the story should keep its characters in *this* world, its narrative set in the actual world, its plot related to "the way men really act," instead of being confined to the individual waves—the thoughts and fantasies of the cardboard characters Greene has so often attacked.

Javitt is not a sentimentalist. Whether he is discussing beauty or sex, monkeys or women, his conversation with Wilditch suggests the kind of author-reader dialogue which Greene so admires. Instead of sentimentalized sex and violence, the tired phrases of popular "entertainment," Javitt offers Beauty spawned by Maria in the dark room and the monkeys' view of death as an "accident." When he tells Wilditch, "Forget your mother and your father too," or "Forget all your schoolmasters teach you," he is again urging the fresh vision, the "disloyalty" of Greene's own creations.

There are, of course, hints of theological interpretation in Javitt's advice. The liturgical elements already noted, whether of Catholic ceremony or Christian symbol, are bound to remind any Greene reader of similar phrasing in his novels and stories. Although the experience was scarcely a religious one to the small boy, his mother had feared the worst, and the reawakened Wilditch, faced with the reality of his gold-flecked po, notes "She had reason to fear." For the whole context of this "dark mystery" is drawn from religious dialectic.

Like Javitt, Wilditch occasionally speaks with Greene's own voice, or assumes his creator's familiar mannerisms. His brother describes Wilditch as a "restless man," and adds terms reminiscent of Greene's allusions to his own restlessness and need to travel. Wilditch's curiosity about the world of darkness under the tree echoes Greene's own interest in Africa's creative heart of darkness. When Wilditch hears of Beauty he becomes like an explorer noticing a blank place on the map. When he finally becomes "achingly tired as though at the end of a long journey," he repeats Greene's experiences in *Journey without Maps,* an idea recurring in contexts as varied as *The Lawless Roads, The Man Within,* and *Our Man in Havana.*

The story suggests a myth through which Greene can express his preoccupation with the mystery of Faith, the difficulties of belief, the loss of "mystique" from today's religious life. It is difficult to avoid the suspicion that Greene's myth refers, at least obliquely, to Jung's opinion of religious failure in the West, the vision of God's underground counterpart, the nameless subterranean God. Javitt, "less interested in conversation than in the recital of some articles of belief," is indeed the ancient oracle, the guardian of the treasure. Appropriately, the jewels are hidden—even the boy must wait for the privilege of revelation—for as Green had written thirty years before in *Stamboul Train:* "We have been for a thousand years in the wilderness of a Christian world, where only the secret treasure was safe." For the author, the religious sense is important in terms of his craft. Though he does not share Jung's confidence in fantasy as a successor to Christian Faith, his personal faith is something different. The "air" of Catholicism inseparable from Greene's work or the "disloyalty" he advocates carry equal weight in the ultimate fiction, so long as the awareness of Good and Evil is there. Wilditch's growing curiosity may be a question of fiction or of faith, but it comes only after experience. His imaginative encounter with the jewels and the sources of language sends him in search of Beauty. Yet "it was only years later, after a deal of literature and learning and knowledge at second hand" that he could record a "true" version of his story. He could not remain in the underground world of darkness and sequins, canned sardines and cabbage broth, lavatory seats and old newspapers. Although his first glimpse of the treasure had made him feel that he must give up "all the riches of the world, its pursuits and enjoyments," he had to return to "the world he knew." In that world he could record for the dull George and the faithless Mother the world of mystery and imagination "**Under the Garden.**"

Walter Allen (review date 1967)

SOURCE: "Greene Thoughts in a Greene Shade," in *New York Times Book Review,* April 30, 1967, p. 5.

[*In the following mixed review of* May We Borrow Your Husband? *Allen states that the stories vary in quality but show "the author at play."*]

There is an element in writing that critics (by and large, a more serious-minded race of men than the creators whose works they discuss) give altogether too little attention. This can best be called the element of play, the writer's delight in his own cleverness and virtuosity, his ability to make bricks without straw and to do so simply for the fun it provides. It is a naive pleasure—and, for some writers, perhaps a fundamental one.

On the face of it, it is not one readily associated with Graham Greene. The great theme of his fiction has been

that of "Man's first disobedience, and the fruit of that forbidden tree." Yet no close inspection is called for to see that, from the beginning, his work has been informed by a strong element of play. It is there in his prewar "entertainments," especially in the best of them, *This Gun for Hire.* It appears, too, in his wartime "entertainment," *The Ministry of Fear.* One suspects, indeed, that these books were devised almost as much for his own enjoyment as for his readers'. But after *The Ministry of Fear* there were no more entertainments for more than a decade. Instead, there were the wholly serious novels, *The Heart of the Matter, The End of the Affair, The Quiet American,* in which he turned everything that's made into a Greene thought in a Greene shade.

Not that, in these years, Greene's will to play, his sense of virtuosity as a source of fun, was in total abeyance. It manifested itself in his admirable children's stories. In 1958, it came into full flowering in *Our Man in Havana,* surely one of the most delightful light novels of our time.

The sense of the author at play dominates his new collection of stories, ***May We Borrow Your Husband?*** For Greene, the short story has always been an occasional form, and the stories in his new volume vary greatly in merit. Two or three of them, **"The Overnight Bag," "Dr. Crombie"** and **"The Invisible Japanese Gentlemen,"** are no more than good macabre jokes. They appeared first in London weeklies and read here as though they had not quite succeeded in escaping from their original contexts. Yet in a story no longer than these, **"Beauty,"** which recounts what might be called the secret life of a prize Pekingese, a rich woman's pet, he produces a chilling parable on the theme of human vanity and mortality.

Elsewhere—and he is unlikely to take this as praise—he seems bent on showing us that he can take on Maugham at his own game and do it better. The comparison arises not merely from the fact that many of these stories are set in the south of France. It stems also from the nature of the narrator, the elderly author, his sensual appetites attenuated to the appreciation of good wine and good cheese, who observes the passing scene and records it with a sort of romantic cynicism. So, in the title story, the narrator (working out of season at Antibes on a biography of the Earl of Rochester) watches two extremely unpleasant homosexuals seduce the male half of a honeymoon couple and make all the necessary arrangements for the taking over of their lives.

One of these Antibes stories, **"Mortmain,"** which describes through the eyes and ears of the narrator—"like most writers I have the spirit of a voyeur"—the seduction of a newly deserted wife by a Lesbian, is very good indeed. Nevertheless, these first-person stories seem to me too relaxed, too undemanding of their author, to show him as the major writer he is. We are interested in them not for their own sake but because Greene wrote them. To find the real Greene in this collection we must turn to a story called **"Cheap in August."**

It relates the experience of a faculty wife, English by birth, on vacation in Jamaica while her New England husband is researching in London for his book on James Thomson's *The Seasons.* The choice of subject indicates a certain thin-bloodedness in her husband, which Greene associates with New England—and which, for him, differentiates it from the rest of America. At any rate, after 10 years of contented marriage, Mary Watson is mildly looking for sexual adventure outside it, but Jamaica in August, the cut-price season, proves anything but exciting. And then she meets Mr. Hickslaughter, a remittance man from the United States, old, fat, uncouth and terribly lonely.

He is not at all the sort of man she has dreamed of having an affair with. Indeed, "affair" is the wrong word for their brief relationship, in which her actions are prompted by pity. All the same,

> it was as though she were discovering for the first time the interior of the enormous continent on which she had elected to live. . . . Here, stretched on the bed, dressed in striped pyjamas which Brooks Brothers would have disowned, failure and fear talked to her without shame, and in an American accent. It was as though she were living in the remote future, after God knew what catastrophe.

This, wrenched out of context, will no doubt seem old, familiar Greene. In context, it isn't quite so. Pity for the human condition has always been one of his favorite subjects, but often it has seemed an abstract pity, not always united with sympathy or charity. It was this union that makes *The Power and the Glory* still, after more than 25 years, his finest book. It appears again in his most recent novel, *The Comedians,* especially in the affectionately drawn characters of Robinson and the Smiths. It suggested that *The Comedians* could mark the beginning of a new phase in Greene's development. **"Cheap in August,"** in which the accent is on purely human pity, the pity of a woman for a man on the surface grotesquely ill-suited to her, is further evidence that this may be so.

Warren Coffey (review date 1967)

SOURCE: A review of *May We Borrow Your Husband?* in *The Commonweal,* Vol. LXXXVI, No. 1, August 25, 1967, pp. 527-28.

[*In the following mixed evaluation, Coffey faults the unevenness and lack of emotional power in* May We Borrow Your Husband? *but praises five stories for their shrewdness and craftsmanship.*]

Graham Greene will be raising sixty-three this year, a remarkable old stager altogether and still doing a stint of writing every day and doing it, on the whole, very smartly, as the twelve stories in this collection [*May We Borrow Your Husband?*] show. Though three of them are skip and four are fill, that leaves five stories as shrewd and funny as any being written today. And five for twelve makes .416, and who else is hitting .400 this year?

The three skip stories are **"Beauty,"** about a rich American woman and her pekingese dog; **"The Over-night Bag,"** about a citizen who carries a dead baby back to England from France in his luggage; and **"A Shocking Accident,"** about a young man whose father is killed in the street by having a pig drop on his head. As one ready to concede that many rich American women and all pekingese dogs are deplorable, I nonetheless found **"Beauty"** over-charged with the nastiness that Greene can fall into when he starts carving up comfortable people. Stories about dead babies and about people killed by falling pigs, on the other hand, are a kind of national specialty of the English, and I was more surprised than anything else to find Greene, that most un-insular and un-English of authors, serving them up. It is a little like learning that somebody you like thinks Alfred Hitchcock is funny. But scratch an Englishman and you are likely to find something of Hitchcock, the boy who *will* tell you about the terrible and of course very droll things he has been doing to the cat.

> Several of the stories in *May We Borrow Your Husband?* have a remarkable life in them, with action and characters that move not only on the page in the reading but in the eye and mind and affections long after that.
>
> —*Warren Coffey*

The four fill stories—I call them fill because they're so flat I cannot believe Greene much believed in them and only threw them in in the Falstaffian way, "Tush, man, they'll fill a pit as well as better"—are **"The Invisible Japanese Gentlemen," "Awful When You Think of It," "Doctor Crombie,"** and **"The Root of All Evil."** The last-named of these seemed to be a parable. Of the others, I remember nothing at all. But here the body count stops because the rest of the stories have a remarkable life in them, with action and characters that move not only on the page in the reading but in the eye and mind and affections long after that.

"May We Borrow Your Husband?," though not the best of these stories, best represents the way they are put together and work. An English couple are honeymooning at Antibes. She, Poopy by name, is comely and likable but not very bright—Greene tells us that she thinks Sir Charles Snow is a writer. Her young man, Peter by name, is handsome but has more than a touch of pansy in him. Two interior decorators, Tony and Stephen, also English, undertake to steal him away from the bride, while William Harris, "*the* William Harris," a worldly-wise old author watches from the sidelines and helps the girl as much as he can.

If the girl knows what is going on, Greene writes, her story is a tragedy because of the pain of that knowledge.

If she doesn't know, it's a farce. But partly she knows, and partly she doesn't know, so the story resolves itself as a wonderfully shrewd comedy by mixing pathos and ribaldry. A lot of Greene's recent writing has used this tragedy-farce tension and got comedy from it, *The Complaisant Lover,* for example, and *Carving a Statue,* among his plays.

Greene's stories in [*May We Borrow Your Husband?*] work a number of variations on the basic pattern, the almost straight farce of **"Chagrin in Three Parts,"** for example, in which two French ladies, one widowed and one thrown over by her husband, meet for dinner and talk, sadly at first, about their lost husbands but then by wine and food and bawdy reminiscence fall into gales of Gallic laughter and go home tipsily together. **"Two Gentle People,"** on the other hand, by the pitiable mis-marriages it sketches in, arrives at something like the terror of tragedy.

"Cheap in August" touches both tragedy and farce and manages to fill up all the ground between. It's a great story. Set in Jamaica, it involves the thirty-nine-year-old wife of an American professor of English looking or half-looking for romance on her vacation. She and her husband are beautifully observed and typed, she in her sexual yearnings, he in his getting out the bumf, a book on James Thomson, to advance his career. The wife ends up in bed with a gross and sinister seventy-year-old remittance man from St. Louis who spends most of his nights crying and drinking whiskey because of his fear of dying alone in a hotel room. It's the best story in the book, by three furlongs. And **"Mortmain,"** except for some slickness in the conception and plotting, might have been almost as good.

On the whole, Greene seems in these stories to have written his way back to comic North Temperate Zone, away from the heat and the emotional intensity of his theological thrillers. He has perhaps lost something of range and emotional power along the way, but he has certainly gained in control of his matter and even in mellowness, and for knowledge of the world, who can touch this man?

A. R. Coulthard (essay date 1971)

SOURCE: "Graham Greene's 'The Hint of an Explanation': A Reinterpretation," in *Studies in Short Fiction,* Vol. VIII, No. 4, Fall, 1971, pp. 601-05.

[*In the following essay, Coulthard reexamines common interpretations of "The Hint of an Explanation," focusing on Greene's depiction of the character Blacker.*]

Good fiction, as the saying goes, lends itself to a number of interpretations. But a generation of readers brought up on irony, ambiguity, and levels of meaning has been uncharacteristically eager to accept Graham Greene's widely anthologized **"The Hint of an Explanation"** as merely a simple moral drama and enthusiastically to praise it as such.

On the surface, the story *is* simple. A chance traveling companion of a priest retells a story that the priest told him while on a train trip. There is little dramatic interplay between the priest and the narrator. The traveler's retelling of the priest's story is objective, consisting almost entirely of a restatement of the priest's own words.

The priest is as subjective as the narrator is objective, and herein lies the problem of a one-level interpretation. The cleric not only tells the story, but explains its meaning to his fellow traveler. If the reader accepts the priest's interpretation of his childhood experience, the story is elementary. Its theme is that God sends saving signs, or hints, to his chosen. These hints of God's power often come in the form of evil which, with God's help, the tempted resists and eventually thwarts.

As his name suggests, Blacker is ostensibly the embodiment of evil in the story. When the priest was a young altar boy, Blacker, by threats and bribery, persuaded him to steal a consecrated wafer from his church. Blacker supposedly wanted the wafer for evil purposes. However, just as he was about to lay hands on it, the boy found the strength and courage to foil him by swallowing it down. As a mature adult, the priest sees this event as the turning point in his life. Foiling Blacker convinced the boy of God's power to defeat evil and eventually led him into the priesthood.

The temptation is to accept the priest as Greene's spokesman and regard his interpretation as the one that the reader is supposed to share. But such a simple reading of the story raises several questions. Should the reader uncritically accept the priest's interpretation of an experience in which he is obviously quite emotionally involved—an experience which, in effect, his entire life rests upon? Is the priest, simply because he is a priest, immune from error? William E. Buckler and Arnold B. Sklare [in *Stories from Six Authors,* 1960] seem willing to take the priest at his word:

> In the priest's apologia, the hint of an explanation stems from living proof that infinite good may rise out of abysmal evil. Blacker is clearly an embodiment of black evil—he deliberately chooses to trap a child barely beyond the age of reason into sinning against himself and God. But the boy, by his capacity to resist, is for the first time able to understand good. This happiness launches him on his religious life, for he has begun to sense the power of God—how God works and the nature of life. His self-realization in the priesthood—his recognition of God—is the infinite good through God which has resulted from his encounter with the diabolical man. . . .

However, if the reader chooses to interpret for himself the meaning of the priest's story (as the traveling companion, an agnostic, seems tacitly to do), he might arrive at an explication quite different from that of the priest (and Greene himself?). First of all, there is the problem of Blacker's character. Although the obvious label name tends to stack the deck against him, the fact is that Blacker doesn't seem all that black. Even in the priest's biased account, Blacker seems at least as much sinned against as sinning. The priest admits that although Blacker was one of only two bakers in the town, "'I don't think any of the Catholics patronized him because he was a free-thinker.'" And if the priest considers the baker's "'one wall eye and a head the shape of a turnip, with the hair gone on the crown'" to be outward signs of inward evil, the gentle reader might merely deem Blacker's ugliness all the more reason to pity him. Certainly Blacker's ugliness and reputation for "free-thinking" do not justify the Catholics' excluding him from their community of worship. But the priest says, with complete aplomb, "'It would have been no good, you understand, in a little town like that, presenting himself for communion. Everybody there knew him for what he was.'" Quite opposite a demonic hatred of good, Blacker has valid reasons for disliking the Catholics of the community.

Although the obvious label name tends to stack the deck against him, the fact is that Blacker doesn't seem all that black. Even in the priest's biased account, Blacker seems at least as much sinned against as sinning.

—A. R. Coulthard

A second interpretive problem concerns Blacker's motives. The priest assumes them to have been totally and simply evil: "'That poor man was preparing to revenge himself on everything he hated—my father, the Catholics, the God whom people persisted in crediting—and that by corrupting me.'" Let us ignore the egotism of this statement for the moment and examine the possibility that the priest mistakes Blacker's motives—that Blacker, because of his ostracism, could not with self-respect express an interest in Catholicism and that what the priest regards as Blacker's diabolical scheme was really his clumsy attempt to reach out for God. Blacker was familiar with the Catholic doctrine of transubstantiation and seems to have been struggling with it. In the priest's account, Blacker feigns cynicism to the boy by saying, "'I can bake the things you eat [wafers at Mass] just as well as any Catholic can,'" but he immediately gives himself away by blurting "with sudden intensity, 'how I'd like to get one of your ones in my mouth—just to see. . . .'" It is at this point that Blacker persuades the boy to agree to steal a consecrated wafer for him. Blacker's statement, "'I want to see what your God tastes like,'" has the ring of a sincere, if grotesque, interest in communion.

As Blacker instructs his young accomplice, the boy is surprised at how well the free-thinker knows the routine of Catholic Mass. "'How carefully he had been studying the ground,'" the priest comments later. "'He must have slipped several times into Mass at the back of the church.'"

But, surprisingly, it does not occur to the priest that a knowledge of the ritual of Mass would have been of no use to Blacker in stealing a wafer and that maybe Blacker had slipped into the back of the church to worship. This interpretation is given weight by the fact that just as the boy is about to steal the wafer, he sees Blacker "watching from the back of the church. He had put on his best black Sunday clothes.'" Surely if Blacker were the blasphemer the priest makes him out to have been, he would not have felt compelled to dress appropriate before entering the church.

Later that night, Blacker furtively came to the boy's home to fetch his hard-earned wafer. Intentionally or not, Blacker is depicted in decidedly sympathetic terms in this last scene. The boy hears Blacker's whistle and opens the curtains to find him in an attitude of supplication: "'If I had reached my hand down, his fingers reaching up could almost have touched mine.'" Symbolically, Blacker is reaching out for some form of human communion, for something to cling to and dispel the meaninglessness of his life. But the boy does not reach back. Instead, in a moment of what he later considers to have been divine inspiration, he swallows the wafer in order to keep it from Blacker. Then Blacker, that archvillain and agent of the Fiend, that miscreant who had promised the boy that he would slit his throat if he failed to cooperate, "'began to weep—the tears ran lopsidedly out of the one good eye and his shoulders shook.'"

As a mature adult looking back on this incident, the priest, instead of feeling compassion for Blacker, sees the whole affair as a sort of moral allegory designed for his own benefit. "'When I think of it now, it's almost as if I had seen the Thing weeping for its inevitable defeat,'" he says. The agnostic, who serves the dual dramatic purpose of listener and, later, narrator of the priest's story, is not so sure. "'It's an interesting story,'" he tells the priest. "'I think I should have given Blacker what he wanted.'" When the agnostic wonders aloud what Blacker would have done with the wafer, the priest's response is superstitious and vague—almost, it may strike the reader, ignorant: "'I really believe that he would first of all have put it under his microscope—before he did all the other things I expect he had planned.'"

As has been suggested, the priest is so wrapped up in what the experience did for him that he virtually ignores what it did *to* Blacker. The agnostic's parting remark to the priest may be intended as an ironic suggestion. "'I suppose you think you owe a lot to Blacker,'" he says. "'Yes,'" replies the priest, "'you see I am a very happy man.'"

In attempting to explain just what Graham Greene intended to communicate in this story, two possibilities arise. The first is that, as Buckler and Sklare and other critics suggest, the priest's interpretation of the experience should be taken at face value. Implicit in this interpretation is the premise that, in effect, the priest speaks for the author and that Greene's intention and the priest's interpretation are one and the same. If this be the case, then the story is weak artistically, because it forces an interpretation upon the reader, and dialectically, because Greene asks the reader to believe that God would save one man by destroying another.

Another possibility, however, is that Greene intended for the discerning reader to weigh the priest's conclusions against the facts contained in his own account. If priest's and reader's conclusions do not agree, then the story may be seen as an understated satire on a proud, complacent priest who deigns to believe that God, for all His infinite mercy, would lead him into the priesthood by having him trod down a helpless, pitiable creature such as Blacker. In this interpretation the story is enriched by the unconscious irony of the priest's account.

Several elements in the story point to this second interpretation. Blacker lacks the power of the conventional villain, and Greene constantly plays off the priest's complacency against Blacker's helplessness. For example, juxtaposed with the pathetic picture of Blacker's abject misery over his failure to obtain the wafer is the priest's puffy statement, "'you see, *I* am a very happy man'" [my italics]. The priest's sense of superiority over Blacker pervades the story. If Greene had favored the priest's point of view, surely he would have depicted his protagonist more sympathetically. Moreover, Greene's choice of an agnostic as the priest's audience invites a skeptical look at the priest. One can't help but wonder how the priest's story strikes this uncommitted listener.

Adding to the irony of the priest's conclusions is the fact that even he seems to sense that he might have been wrong about Blacker. He admits, for example, that Blacker's nature "'did contain, perhaps, a certain furtive love.'" Recalling how Blacker, "'looking so longingly and pleadingly'" up at him, tried to coax the wafer from him by saying "'It's only a piece of bread,'" the priest muses: "'even as a child I wondered whether he could really think that, and yet desire it so much.'" But the priest has too much at stake to dwell long on such misgivings.

If Greene had intended for the reader to share the priest's interpretation of his childhood experience, would he have thrown so many obstacles in the way of that interpretation? Two inescapable facts of the story are that Blacker was a man cut off from both God and humanity and that both as a boy and as an adult, the priest responded with a singular lack of compassion. Greene's story, therefore, may be read as a "hint" to complacent Christians that one of Jesus' best known teachings, "Inasmuch as you did it to the least of these, my brethren, you did it unto me," is a two-sided coin.

Jesse F. McCartney (essay date 1978)

SOURCE: "Politics in Graham Greene's 'The Destructors'," in *Southern Humanities Review*, Vol. XII, No. 1, Winter, 1978, pp. 31-41.

[*In the following essay, McCartney discusses the political implications of "The Destructors," concluding that the story is "essentially a reflection of twentieth-century British politics."*]

Although Graham Greene's fiction has been widely praised and widely circulated, critics have focused rather narrowly on two exclusive features of it. Noting Greene's distinction between novels and "entertainments," they have provided genre studies; or, noting his Catholicism, they have discussed the religious themes in his fiction to the exclusion of other considerations. Such biases have resulted in oversights and distortions in the criticism of his work. For example, despite the genre studies just mentioned, critics have largely ignored Greene's short stories or deemed them unworthy of critical study. Greene himself relegated his short stories to an insignificant place in his canon (maintaining at most that he was a novelist who "happened to write short stories"), and scholars have taken him pretty much at his word.

In addition, their intense interest in Greene's religious theme has distracted them from a careful consideration of the social and political conflicts which are so often the source of the basic conflicts of his plots. As James L. McDonald asserts: "For far too many readers and critics, Greene is a 'Catholic' novelist." McDonald cogently argues [in "Graham Greene: A Reconsideration," *Arizona Quarterly* 27, 1971] that Greene's "deepest, most abiding concerns . . . have always been social and political, and only by recognizing them can we find a true unity and continuity in his career." Yet scholars have consistently failed to notice Greene's persistent concern with social and political issues, and the political substructure of Greene's writing remains largely unexplored.

In sum, then, scholars might have read Greene more closely, and they might have begun with his short story **"The Destructors."** It is a work rich in political implications, and Greene himself has recently said of it, "I believe I have never written anything better than **'The Destructors'**. . . ." Nevertheless, many readers of the story are puzzled by it.

Obviously, a plot which involves the paradox of the artistic destruction of a fine work of art is strange, but it is considerably less so if one places the story and the characters in a more precise political and economic context. To do so reveals the story to be essentially a reflection of twentieth-century British politics—particularly the politics of blitzed England as Greene observed it from 1945 until his writing of the story in 1954. The Wormsley Common Gang epitomizes democratic socialism in conflict with privilege and conservatism, and **"The Destructors,"** though certainly no mere political allegory, depicts a blitzed world in which the traditional values of beauty, grace, individualism, and class distinctions are succumbing to the new values of materialism, efficiency, democracy and group activity.

The story can be better understood when one recalls that the period from 1945 to 1951 witnessed the emergence of

the Labour Party and sweeping social and economic reforms which represented the culmination of the decline of
privilege. The First Reform Act of 1832 seriously called
into question the privileged status of the aristocracy. King
Edward's threat to create enough new peers to pass Lloyd
George's "People's Budget" of 1909 if the House of Lords
rejected it signaled another dramatic shift in the power
structure of England. But the *coup de grace* came in 1945.
The defeat of Churchill and the Conservatives in that year
not only resulted in the formation under Attlee of the first
majority Labour government but also marked a triumph
for democratic socialism and a stunning blow to privilege.
The nationalization of the Bank of England and other
industries and the passage of the National Health Service
Act of 1948 and other socialist programs marked a point
of no return for England which Greene and other observers noted with mixed feelings. Out of this dynamic political situation **"The Destructors"** grew and developed in
Greene's mind.

The "destructors" of the title are the members of the
Wormsley Common Gang, a group of adolescent boys who
presumably adopt a name for their gang from the geographical area of London where their activities are centered; but, of course, the name suggests both worms and
commoners. The image of worms is picked up later in the
story as Trevor explains the manner in which the gang
would destroy Mr. Thomas's house: "'We'd be like worms,
don't you see, in an apple. When we came out again there'd
be nothing there, no staircase, no panels, nothing but just
walls, and then we'd make the walls fall down—somehow.'" That the gang consists of commoners who scorn
the upper classes is apparent in the attitude of its members
toward the name and background of the newest member,
Trevor:

> When he said 'Trevor' it was a statement of fact, not
> as it would have been with the others a statement of
> shame or defiance. . . . There was every reason why
> T., as he was afterwards referred to, should have been
> an object of mockery—there was his name (and they
> substituted the initial because otherwise they had no
> excuse not to laugh at it), the fact that his father, a
> former architect and present clerk, had 'come down in
> the world' and that his mother considered herself better
> that the neighbours.

Thus, by joining the gang and, like more recent revolutionaries, changing his name, Trevor repudiates the class
system.

The gang, however, is no rag-tag band of lawless revolutionaries. Indeed, as they work from the inside destroying
Old Misery's house, they also, in many ways, conform to
establishment traditions, as did the Labour Party. For
example, though Trevor escapes the procedure somehow,
the gang apparently sometimes accepts members through
an "ignoble ceremony of initiation." Thus they follow
establishment traditions of ceremonies and inaugurations,
but these "ignoble ceremonies" parody those long-hon-
ored by the nobility. Indeed, the gang punctiliously observes its rules and operates in a decidedly democratic

fashion. Trevor is required by the "rules to state his name."
Though the gang is sceptical of Trevor's reasons for entering Old Misery's house, there is "nothing in the rules against
it." Trevor, however, while in Old Misery's house, has
missed voting on the day's activities; and Blackie informs
him, "'You can't vote now. You know the rules.'" This
observance of rules and democratic procedures—particularly of voting—is stressed thus several times in the story.

As always in politics, the question of leadership of the
party becomes crucial. Indeed, the entire first section of
the story is given over to the characterization of Trevor
and Blackie and to their struggle for leadership of the
gang. The opening line of the story appears to be an off-
hand remark that "it was on the eve of August Bank
Holiday that the latest recruit became the leader of the
Wormsley Common Gang." However, in the context of
the story, with its emphasis on the democratic rule of the
gang, the remark takes on more significance. It reveals
that Blackie's fall and Trevor's rise to power are in accord with the tenet of democracy that there is no inherent
or permanent position of rank or privilege and that even
a neophyte can rise to leadership by demonstrating skill or
charisma.

What qualities characterize Blackie's leadership? Generally, Blackie is serious, responsible, disciplined, but unimaginative. He is essentially the doer, the worker, and is
miscast as theorizer. He customarily presided when the
gang "met every morning in an impromptu car park, the
site of the last bomb of the first blitz" and proposed each
day a "plan of operations" on which the gang voted, generally such uninspired plans as snatching free bus rides
from unwary conductors. Blackie and the gang show no
awareness of the future or the need for long-range planning; similarly, they are ignorant of the past, as is evidenced by their reaction to Trevor's announcement that
Mr. Thomas's house was built by Wren. An anonymous
and representative voice of the gang responds:

> 'Who's Wren?'
>
> 'The man who built St. Paul's.'
>
> 'Who cares?' Blackie said. 'It's only Old Misery's.'

Blackie sees the house merely as property belonging to a
privileged individual, not as an emblem of the continuity
of the human race, not as a creation of artistic significance
for the heritage of England. Like the whole gang, he is cut
off from consecutive and humanistic values of the past, is
temporally isolated in a modern blitzed world to which he
responds on a day-to-day, "impromptu" basis in reaction
to the conservative values of the past.

Indeed, Blackie wishes to spurn Old Misery and everything associated with him, but he assumes his responsibility as leader when the gang is confronted by the old man.
Significantly, this confrontation is full of ambiguities,
mistrust, and failures of communication or understanding.
Old Misery accosts Mike, Blackie, and Summers as he
returns from a trip to the market:

He said glumly, 'You belong to the lot that play in the car-park?'

Mike was about to answer when Blackie stopped him. As the leader he had responsibilities. 'Suppose we are?' he said ambiguously.

'I got some chocolates,' Mr. Thomas said. 'Don't like 'em myself. Here you are. Not enough to go round, I don't suppose. There never is,' he added with sombre conviction. He handed over three packets of Smarties.

The gang was puzzled and perturbed by this action and tried to explain it away. 'Bet someone dropped them and he picked 'em up,' somebody suggested.

'Pinched 'em and then got in a bleeding funk,' another thought aloud.

'It's a bribe,' Summers said. 'He wants us to stop bouncing balls on his wall.'

'We'll show him we don't take bribes,' Blackie said, and they sacrificed the whole morning to the game of bouncing that only Mike was young enough to enjoy. There was no sign from Mr. Thomas.

In their responses, the gang members epitomize the cynicism and self-righteousness so often manifested by opponents of political conservatives. Unable to believe that Old Misery is capable of genuine charity or generosity, they suspect him of having found or stolen the candy; but as children of the blitzed world, their understanding of sleazy politics based on the cash nexus leads them to conclude that the candy is a bribe, a conclusion in which Blackie quickly acquiesces and on which he formulates his policy of demonstrating through a juvenile game an unwillingness to compromise.

The gang's suspicion of the upper classes extends to Trevor also, even after he has been accepted as one of the gang. The boys question his motives for visiting Old Misery's house, conceding that the only possible reason one might do so would be to "pinch" something. When he denies having pinched anything, they gather around him: "It was as though an impromptu court were about to form and try some case of deviation." The reference to "deviation" and the formation of a kangaroo court remind the reader of the rhetoric and the show trials of various (though not exclusively) Marxist regimes of this century.

Blackie's plodding steadiness as well as his lack of imagination is reflected in his cool response to this situation. He did not wish to exclude Trevor because of his activities: "He [Blackie] was just, he had no jealousy"; but Trevor is expected to conform to discipline, and any hint of elitism is suspect. It was Trevor's use of the word *beautiful* to describe Old Misery's house that worried Blackie; it was a word "that belonged to a class world that you could still see parodied at the Wormsley Common Empire by a man wearing a top hat and a monocle, with a haw-haw accent."

Blackie's rigidity and isolationism, however, are precisely his limitations in Trevor's mind. As political philosopher, Trevor sees that knowledge is power and defends his consorting with Mr. Thomas by saying, "I found out things." As the only member of the gang who fully understands that Mr. Thomas's beautiful house, with its spiral staircase which is two hundred years old, is the very emblem of privilege and elitism, Trevor alone conceives of the significance of destroying the house. When he explains that Old Misery will be away on the Bank Holiday and that the gang can then break into the house, one of the boys again assumes that, in their customary way of combating the establishment, they will pinch things from the house. It is against such corruption by things that Blackie and Trevor must continually fight. Blackie, ever the pragmatist, objects, saying that they want no trouble with the law. Trevor, the idealist, objects on other grounds: "'I don't want to pinch anything. . . . I've got a better idea. . . . We'll pull it down. . . . We'll destroy it.'" Again, the pragmatic Blackie objects: "'There wouldn't be time. . . . I've seen housebreakers at work.'" Trevor responds with the timeless cry of the disestablished or disenfranchised: "'We'd organize.'" He also asserts that he has the knowledge necessary for accomplishing this destruction. Having presented this challenge to Blackie's leadership, Trevor even uses British political terminology in forcing the issue: "'You can stand down, Blackie, if you'd rather. . . .'"

In the portion of the story that follows, the *dénouement* of part one, the political implications are made even clearer. Blackie is voted down; he becomes a political cast-off. At first, as the gang pays "no more attention to him than to a stranger," Blackie is angry; but his pragmatism and his fidelity to the party win out over his personal depression. He realizes that the gang just might succeed in wrecking Old Misery's house, in which case "the fame of the Wormsley Common car-park gang would surely reach around London. . . . Driven by the pure, simple and altruistic ambition of fame for the gang, Blackie came back to where T. stood in the shadow of Old Misery's wall." Moments later, "Blackie realized he had raised his hand like any ordinary member of the gang." Ultimately, Blackie resumes a position of leadership within the gang, and the democratic process comes full circle in the story as, indeed, it did in Churchill's ouster and subsequent re-election; and surely this important contemporary political event must have lurked in Greene's consciousness as a kind of model for Blackie's career, though Blackie otherwise represents Churchill's antithesis and I would again caution against an allegorical reading in favor of a symbolic one.

This scene not only portrays Blackie as the committed worker, but it also portrays Trevor once more as the political theorist, the Trotsky of the group. In addition, it demonstrates the necessity of collaboration between worker and intellectual for the success of the group's schemes. Trevor conceives of the plan in the abstract and maneuvers politically to bring about its implementation. Moreover, he is at pains to preserve the purity of the concept. He insists later in the story that no one will take anything from the house, but that it will be destroyed absolutely; and when a gang member fears that each member will have to contribute to a collection to buy tools, Trevor reveals both his naïveté and his idealism in his arch reply: "'I don't want your money. But I can't buy a sledge-hammer.'" Significantly, the pragmatic Blackie steps forward and says: "'They are working on No. 15. I know where they'll leave their stuff for Bank Holiday.'"

Section two of the story describes the beginning of the destruction of the house in such a fashion as to stress the commitment and the organization of the gang as they all share the labor of implementing their carefully-laid plan. Blackie, joining the group belatedly, "had at once the impression of organization, very different from the old happy-go-lucky ways under his leadership."

This section again reiterates the image of opposite forces working to sustain the project—i.e., the image of the pragmatic politico balanced against the party theorist. After all the other boys have left, T. discloses to Blackie a bundle of pound notes he has found in Old Misery's mattress. Immediately, Blackie asks, "'What are you going to do? Share them?'" Such a proposal seems practical and in accord with general socialist principles of sharing the wealth confiscated from the rich and privileged; but Trevor is the artist, the idealist, the theoretician, and here, at least, he thinks in terms of aesthetic rituals rather than pragmatic ends. He responds: "'We aren't thieves. . . . Nobody's going to steal anything from this house. I kept these for you and me—a celebration. . . . We'll burn them . . . one by one.'" However, Blackie cannot comprehend the intellectual theorizing of Trevor except in terms of simple vengeance. As the ash from the burning notes falls on their heads, Trevor says:

> 'I'd like to see Old Misery's face when we are through. . . .'
>
> 'You hate him a lot?' Blackie asked.
>
> 'Of course I don't hate him,' T. said. 'There'd be no fun if I hated him. . . . All this hate and love . . . it's soft, it's hooey. There's only things, Blackie,' and he looked round the room crowded with the unfamiliar shadows of half things, broken things, former things. 'I'll race you home, Blackie,' he said.

These *things,* in Trevor's mind, do not represent material wealth to be redistributed; rather they become material symbols of the established classes and of privilege, objects to be ritually destroyed in preparation for a new era.

This same emphasis on things and the absolute destruction of things as well as an emphasis on democratic procedures arises again in part three of the story when, as the boys convene for the second day of destruction, Summers protests that the activity is too much like work. Trevor responds sharply: "'You voted like the others. We are going to *destroy* this house. There won't be anything left when we've finished.'"

In this section, too, Trevor appears as the dreamer, Blackie as the worker. This characterization develops particu-larly out of the crisis which occurs when the boys discover that Old Misery is returning early from his holiday. Trevor momentarily panics as he begs for time to consider how to finish the project. As Blackie learned earlier in the story, Trevor now learns that "his authority had gone with his ambiguity. He was [now] only one of the gang."

Blackie—the doer, actor, worker—rescues the intellectual in distress. "T. stood with his back to the rubble like a boxer knocked groggy against the ropes. He had no words as his dreams shook and slid. Then Blackie acted before the gang had time to laugh, pushing Summers backward." Blackie whips the gang into line and then asks Trevor for his plan of action. Blackie "was the leader again," but now he merely implements Trevor's ideas and sees that the commands are executed.

Greene finally makes quite clear that the initial conflict has been fully resolved through collaboration. Caught up in the group enterprise, "the question of leadership no longer concerned the gang." However, Blackie's practicality remains useful; it is emphasized once again in passing in the concluding section of the story. The boys began to loosen the mortar between the bricks, but "they started too high, and it was Blackie who hit on the damp course and realized the work could be halved if they weakened the joints immediately above." Trevor is not mentioned at all in this last section of the story, his work—the planning of the destruction and the enactment of the ritualistic burning of the notes—presumably having been completed.

Scholars have consistently failed to notice Greene's persistent concern with social and political issues, and the political substructure of Greene's writing remains largely unexplored.

—*Jesse F. McCartney*

"The Destructors," however, is not merely a story about the struggle between two personality types for leadership of a gang any more than it is merely a story about the destruction of an old house by delinquent boys. That fact is made clear by the introduction of Old Misery as owner of the house that Wren built: "Old Misery—whose real name was Thomas—had once been a builder and decorator. He lived alone in the crippled house, doing for himself." The nickname given Mr. Thomas by the boys suggests not only the personal emotional state of the old man but also the unpleasant aspect of English traditions built on privilege and class distinctions—the old misery inflicted on the masses by the conservative ruling classes. Mr. Thomas's house, like the landed and hereditary houses of England, indeed the House of Lords itself, is "crippled," debilitated, and weakened: "Since the bombs fell something had gone wrong with the pipes of the house and Old

Misery was too mean to spend money on the property. He could do the decorating himself at cost price, but he had never learnt plumbing." In like manner, the Conservatives had been builders and decorators; particularly in the midst of war, Churchill and the Conservatives had stood for outer strength, appearances and form, but they failed to understand the inner problems of the nation brought about by the war and could not mend them. A man living in the blitzed world depicted by Greene was no longer capable of "doing for himself"; and the Labour Party's plans for nationalization and government assistance through democratic socialism pulled Churchill's house down around him.

Mr. Thomas, of course, never expects any accommodation with the Wormsley Common Gang. In a passage cited earlier, he approaches the gang "glumly." He voices "with sombre conviction" the conservative view that "there never is . . . enough to go round," the traditional assertion and complaint against Labour policies of providing welfare services such as those provided by the National Insurance Act of 1946 and the National Health Service instituted in 1948.

It is in section three of the story, however, that Old Misery most clearly epitomizes privilege and conservatism. The boys devise a scheme to lure Mr. Thomas to his outhouse and imprison him there so that they can complete the destruction of his house. (Incidentally, in the revised version in **Collected Stories,** Greene deliberately emphasizes the modernity of the boys by having them refer to the outhouse as the "lav" whereas Mr. Thomas consistently refers to it as the "loo"; in earlier versions, both the boys and Mr. Thomas use only the term "loo.") In leading him to the loo supposedly to rescue a boy who has gotten stuck there, the gang forces Mr. Thomas to climb his own garden wall, thus revealing to him that they have sometimes climbed it. His response is reactionary, possessive but traditionally polite, quaintly displaying the native courtesy of the privileged as well as the crotchety, authoritarian instincts which insist on deference and protocol.

> 'I'll have the wall built up,' Mr. Thomas said, 'I'll not have you boys coming over here, using my loo.' He stumbled on the path but the boy caught his elbow and supported him. 'Thank you, thank you, my boy,' he murmured automatically. . . . 'I'm not unreasonable. I don't mind you playing round the place Saturday mornings. Sometimes I like company. Only it's got to be regular. One of you asks leave and I say Yes. Sometimes I'll say No. Won't feel like it. And you come in at the front door and out at the back. No garden walls.'

The incongruity of Mr. Thomas's insistence on tradition and regular procedures at the very moment when he is about to become a political prisoner and when the final destruction of his house is going on a few yards away is overwhelming. He shares the naïveté of Churchill and other Conservatives who failed to grasp fully just how far England had come in 1945. Later, after being locked in his own loo, he "felt dithery and confused and old."

In the last scene of the story, Mr. Thomas is pictured as a pathetic old man who is outraged at the abrogation of his personal property rights. Conversely, almost everyone else in the last section views the destruction quite impersonally, including the unnamed representative of the gang who addresses the imprisoned Mr. Thomas:

> 'There's nothing personal,' the voice said. 'We want you to be comfortable tonight.'
>
> 'Tonight,' Mr. Thomas repeated increduously.
>
> 'Catch,' the voice said. 'Penny buns—we've buttered them, and sausage-rolls. We don't want you to starve, Mr. Thomas.'

The impersonal nature of this act is echoed by the lorry driver who unwittingly pulls down the house, not knowing that the boys have attached a line from the house to his lorry. After pulling down the house, the driver rescues Mr. Thomas from the loo, only to be confronted with the indignant and outraged old man who keeps reiterating "'*My* house'" (italics mine). The lorry driver apologizes for laughing at the incongruous scene of destruction as Mr. Thomas upbraids him:

> 'I'm sorry,' the driver said, making heroic efforts, but when he remembered the sudden check to his lorry, the crash of bricks falling, he became convulsed again. One moment the house had stood there with such dignity between the bomb-sites like a man in a top hat, and then, bang, crash, there wasn't anything left—not anything. He said, 'I'm sorry. I can't help it, Mr. Thomas. There's nothing personal, but you got to admit it's funny.'

Thus Trevor's prophecy that "not anything" would remain is fulfilled. The simile used to compare the dignity of the house to that of a "man in a top hat" is the final identification of the house with the privileged class, and it is, of course, the same image which comes to Blackie's mind when Trevor uses the word *beautiful* earlier in the story to describe Mr. Thomas's house. In addition, the lorry driver's echo of the nameless boy's earlier plea that "there's nothing personal" not only reflects the impersonal nature of modern life but also reinforces Trevor's earlier disdain for human emotions and his insistence that there are only "things." Thus the gang symbolically destroys not only class distinctions and privilege but also dehumanizes "itself" in the process by stressing neither beauty, individuality, love, nor grace but efficiency, democracy, collaboration, and unemotional commitment to group action.

As Mr. Thomas's house falls, the story stands—complete, unified, closely woven. Yet it remains puzzling to many readers; and in conclusion, it seems worthwhile to consider the source of this effect. I should like to suggest tentatively that the source of that puzzlement resides both in Greene's own ambiguity regarding the changing political guard and also in the distance between his own religious conservatism and the general secular liberalism of most of his readers today.

As an artist, Greene certainly must be aware that art and beauty traditionally have been the private province or concern of the aristocratic classes in Europe, and he naturally enough values the grace and elegance preserved through that conservative tradition as in Wren's architecture or other esthetic monuments. Yet as a modern intellectual very much in touch with contemporary politics, he certainly must be equally aware of the social inequities often fostered by that conservative tradition. However, the irony of that paradox is doubled, for the system which purports to correct those inequities—especially as the Labour Party attempted to correct them in England—too frequently substitutes a New Misery for an Old Misery, a blitzed, impersonal world without any esthetic sensibility or any sense of history. Thus, the ambiguous effect of the story lies partly in this double paradox inherent in the spirit of the author.

Secondly, Greene's Catholic bias tends to make him sceptical of any temporal order; and though many contemporary readers may instinctively identify with the democratic procedures and the collaborative efforts of the Wormsley Common Gang, Greene himself is much more ambivalent toward worldly reformers or revolutionaries as is evidenced in many of his works—*The Power and the Glory, Brighton Rock,* and *The Honorary Consul,* to name but three. This distance between the world-view (or other-world view) of Greene and the *Weltanschauung* of the contemporary secular reader is also, then, a source of the puzzlement often produced by **"The Destructors."**

Finally, however, the story satisfies the close reader by its perfect balance of one political viewpoint against another as the image of the spiral staircase held in suspension by "opposite forces" epitomizes the story, and these political viewpoints are much better understood when seen in the light of English politics of the decade immediately preceding the writing of the story.

John Bayley   (essay date 1990)

SOURCE: "Graham Greene: The Short Stories," in *Graham Greene: A Revaluation: New Essays,* edited by Jeffrey Meyers, The Macmillan Press, 1990, pp. 93-103.

[*In the essay below, Bayley provides a thematic and stylistic overview of Greene's short stories.*]

"The Miracle of Purun Bhagat" is a story by Kipling that comes at the end of *The Jungle Book,* and Graham Greene thought it his best. It is not hard to see why. An Indian administrator in the British Raj, of such high rank that he has had bestowed on him the rare honour of a knighthood, abandons his former way of life to become a hermit in the Himalayas. One night in the Rains the animals come past his hut, having lost all fear of men, and he realizes that a big landslide is on the way. All his old instincts of responsibility return, and he warns and saves the local villagers. For Kipling the story's moral is obvious—indeed rather glib—but as with many of the best short stores the atmo-

sphere is much more important than the anecdote, and the atmosphere in the tale is that of the Hills, and the peace and liberation they confer. There is something genuinely transcendental in the feel of it.

Greene would have felt this. In his own story **"The Hint of an Explanation,"** written in 1948, he tried for the transcendental by a rather different route, a variant on the route taken by G. K. Chesterton in the Father Brown stories. But Chesterton was coy about how he did it, in a way that Greene would never be. Greene, like a good party member, hardly ever wrote a paragraph that did not contain a statement, or at least an implication, about Catholic Truth. And this is particularly true of his stories, where, in the tradition of De Maupassant and Somerset Maugham, a point can be made, a truth about society or human nature exhibited, with essential force and economy. Greene's stories give the impression of being thrown off in the course of a busy writing life, with money as the main object, but perhaps for this reason they also seem like candles lit in church in the course of a brief routine visit.

Greene's stories give the impression of being thrown off in the course of a busy writing life, with money as the main object, but perhaps for this reason they also seem like candles lit in church in the course of a brief routine visit.

—John Bayley

Like most Greene stories **"The Hint of an Explanation"** makes no attempt to evade the time-honoured routines and conventions of the tradtional short story; in this case the long train journey, the cold, the two men huddled in their overcoats beginning to exchange conversation; the abrupt revelation in the concluding sentences. As always, Greene makes spare and economical use of these, and adds to them his own peculiar stamp of originality. As one might expect, the discomfort of the journey is emphasized, with Greene details like the stale buns bought hurriedly on the platform, the residue in its paper bag being pushed under the seat. Also stressed is the inarticulacy of the fellow-traveller, who tells the story within the story. His expository power and vocabulary are quite inadequate, as are those of most people when they start to talk about religion ("to me there seems to be a hint. That's all. A hint"), although this in itself is a convention, for naturally he tells the story well and with graphic effect.

"I had soon realised I was speaking to a Roman Catholic." The "I" who is the narrator, and who finds himself *tête à tête* with the other internal narrator, has a strong interest in the religion, from which he feels his own intelligence excludes him. As in Somerset Maugham stories, he is the persona chosen by the author, and thus partakes of at least a part of his author's nature. The Greene narrator is hungrily looking in, from outside, on some mystery that is humble, yet magical. The story quietly emphasizes, as is usual with Greene, the unredeemed and fallen nature of the world around, as it appears to the narrator and reader. The dereliction and grey contingency usual in a Greene setting here applies to an England exhausted by war ("The great useless conflict") and is stressed in details like the feeble lights in the railway carriage going out when the train rocks into a tunnel. The exclamation of Mephistophilis in Marlowe's *Doctor Faustus*—"Why, this is Hell, nor am I out of it"—applies as usual to the Greene world. In his review of a life of Rider Haggard, one of the most interesting critical things he wrote, Greene noted the story of Haggard and Kipling trout-fishing together on the Kipling estate in Sussex, and seriously agreeing together that hell was this world, and no other.

The story the second narrator tells is in a sense predictable, for Greene is too able a writer, with too shrewd a sense of effect, to try to make it striking or original. The internal narrator sticks to the point, and the paucity of information he gives about his childhood is turned to advantage, so that the story acquires the artificial simplicity of a morality play. The villain, a baker named Blacker, is desperately anxious to get the boy to steal a consecrated wafer while he is helping to serve at Mass, and tries to bribe him with the highly desirable gift of a toy electric train set. The boy agrees, and manages to leave the altar area to slip the wafer from under his tongue between the leaves of a church magazine; but when the baker calls that night he refuses to give it up, and sees the man slink off into the dark like a defeated representative of the Evil One.

The baker's motives are evil, in that he hates Catholics and wishes to discredit them, but his frantic wish to get hold of God in the wafer argues a misery and a sense of emptiness which he longs to fill. More important for the story, however, although subtly connected with this, is the way in which Greene gets across his hint of the transcendental, the thing that must have struck him in Kipling's story of Purun Bhagat. The trick of the tale comes when the internal narrator—the man within—gets up at the end of the journey.

> "Oh, well," he said vaguely, "you know for me it was an odd beginning, that affair, when you come to think of it," but I should never have known what he meant had not his coat, when he rose to take his bag from the rack, come open and disclosed the collar of a priest."

I said, "I suppose you think you owe a lot to Blacker."

"Yes," he said. "You see, I am a very happy man."

It is a good instance of how Greene's skill as a narrator works on a miniature scale. The trick of the priest's collar, although effective, is virtually predictable, but what he says is not. We may hardly have noticed, or now forgotten, the recollection of the external narrator at the beginning of the story. He had been giving his views to the other man on how the concept of God revolts him ("When you think what God—if there is a God—allows.") and the whole notion of a creator who can abandon his creation "to the enormities of Free Will." The internal narrator "listened quietly and with respect."

> He made no attempt to interrupt—he showed none of the impatience or the intellectual arrogance I have grown to expect from Catholics; when the lights of a wayside station flashed across his face which had escaped hitherto the rays of the one globe working in the compartment, I caught a glimpse suddenly of— what? I stopped speaking, so strong was the impression, I was carried back ten years, to the other side of the great useless conflict, to a small town, Gisors, in Normandy. I was again, for a moment, walking on the ancient battlements and looking down across the grey roofs, until my eyes for some reason lit on one stony "back" out of the many, where the face of a middle-aged man was presented against a window pane (I suppose that face has ceased to exist now, just as perhaps the whole town with its mediaeval memories has been reduced to rubble), I remembered saying to myself with astonishment, "That man is happy— completely happy." I looked across the compartment at my fellow-traveller, but his face was already again in shadow.

In praising Kipling's story of Purun Bhagat, Greene singled out the small embedded bits of clear description, aspects of height and space, which—at least by implication—let a new dimension of silent meaning appear in the story. In this passage something rather the same is happening, lurking behind the syntax and even the punctuation—the two "hanging" dashes for example—and emerging like the face itself in the baldness of the exclamation, "Completely happy." The rumours of the world and its activities—the battlements, the middle ages, the recent war—drop away into non-existence, and become no more important than the cleverly unemphatic propaganda unconsciously deployed by the external narrator ("he showed none of the impatience or intellectual arrogance I have grown to expect from Catholics"). The reader believes in this happiness because of its arbitrary nature, and its necessary lack of contact with the point and moral of the tale. The success of the story pinches out its propaganda, like fingers extinguishing a candle. As Blacker longs for the Host, so the external narrator thinks he once recognized this amazing state of being happy on a single face, once seen. (The story makes ingenious use here of all but invisible contrasts and incongruities: the battlements, and the idea of a "back," the gloomy dead-end view of small houses seen from a train; the face pressed to the glass like a child's to a sweet-shop window, or like Blacker's in pursuit of the Host, and yet in this case looking at nothing and with nothing to look at. Happiness is like expectation without a goal or a point.)

As in the case of "The Miracle of Purun Bhagat," the story has, so to speak, sidled past the success of its own specification, and achieved something much more difficult, but something only to be done in terms of the short-story form. Another example would be James Joyce's "The Dead," which is about life, and whose miracle of meaning celebrates the livingness of the daily moments that lead up to bed and to sleep—itself a guarantee of continued livingness. "The Dead" needs its subject, which its title declares in a manner both grave and ironic, but its epiphany transcends this subject. In **"The Hint of an Explanation"** the title leads us both away from and towards the revelation of happiness, a state which the external narrator recognizes, as Blacker the baker recognizes the mystery of the consecrated Host, and whose meaning in relation to the story can only appear through its anecdotal context.

Greene, like Kipling, and unlike Somerset Maugham, seems robustly indifferent to the quality of his tales. In his later years especially, Kipling would publish in a collection masterpieces of the genre alongside pieces merely slight or vulgar, and seemingly with no pretension to be anything else. Greene has evidently done much the same. In the Introduction to his **Collected Stories** he observes that the form bothered him when he began to practise it in the late 1920s, at the time when he was writing his first novel to be printed, *The Man Within*—"and a little bored me." He suggests, however, that it was the writing of short stories which taught him "the qualities which all my first novels so disastrously lacked—simplicity of language, the sense of life as it is lived." None the less "I remain in this field a novelist who has happened to write short stories, just as there are certain short story writers (Maupassant and Mr. V. S. Pritchett come to mind) who have happened to write novels." He also throws light on the success of a story like **"The Hint of an Explanation"** when he remarks that when it came to writing "scraps," as he called them, he knew too much about the tale before he began to write it, and hence had "days of work unrelieved by any surprise." When writing a novel "the unexpected might happen." Near the beginning of a novel, "for no reason I knew," he "would insert an incident which seemed entirely irrelevant, and sixty thousand words later, with a sense of excitement, I would realise why it was there. But in the short story I knew everything before I began to write—or so I thought."

There is indeed a sharp contrast between the "scraps," whose point was known from the beginning, and the comparatively few stories which seem to work in the same way in which Greene suggests his novels do. But, naturally enough, the stories still do things in their own way which the novels cannot, even though the technique, as the author here describes it, may be rather similar. The "surprises" inside **"The Hint of an Explanation"** are of a different order to any that come in the novels. Indeed I would say that none of the novels has a hidden subject in the sense that the story does, and that the particular effect the story achieves is remote from anything in the novels. This can be tested by comparing it with **"A Visit to Morin,"** one of the collection published in 1963 under the title *A Sense of Reality*. A narrator with a similar persona to the one in the earlier tale is greatly taken with the novels of a French Catholic writer called Morin, who sounds a bit like a real novelist such as Bernanos or Mauriac. He is distrusted by some orthodox Catholics but to others makes a strong appeal. A serious-minded bookseller in Colmar tells the narrator that he sounds even

better in German than in French, because the former language "has a better vocabulary for the profundities."

This seems the standard irony about the Church, and about spiritual matters generally, to which we are accustomed in the novels, and, however effective there, it might seem to have no place in the art of the short story. It condemns the tale to its own significance, without any escape into the unexpected and unforeseen effect which Greene in his Introduction describes (characteristically) as "cool drinks to a parched mouth." The story has something wearisomely predictable about it. The narrator encounters Morin at a Midnight Mass in a local village, where he and the writer are the only members of the congregation who do not take the sacrament. Afterwards he introduces himself and is invited back to Morin's house, where the pair drink brandy and discuss faith. Morin distinguishes it from belief, which he no longer has. The books he has written have helped to remove it. He is like a poet who writes of his feelings, "and when the poem is written he finds his love dead on the page."

Morin is a burnt-out case, with a lot of Greene in him. Like one of his characters he clings to the precisions of orthodoxy, while at the same time standing outside it. Like Greene he has used his predicament in his novels, and the self-dramatization involved has left him with a legacy of deadness and disgust. Like one of Greene's novels, the story is clever in the propaganda it makes for the Faith while seeming to reject it. Morin knows what human need is and requires. He knows that what the Church teaches is true, because he has kept away from it for twenty years, on account of a much-loved mistress, and, because he has been cut off, his belief has withered. Now his mistress is dead, but he dare not go back for fear his belief should not return. Only faith is left to him, for belief depends upon keeping the prescriptions of the Church, which he has deliberately avoided doing.

It is a nice point theologically, and it makes a nice little spiritual drama as it would in one of Greene's novels, but as a story it is a failure. It knows too well what it is about. And the little touch which ends it serves only to kill it more effectively. The non-Catholic narrator is a wine merchant, and Morin gives him a glass of excellent wine, promising to give him the grower's address before he leaves. But after Morin has described his "strange faith," which depends on the conviction that the Church must be right because his belief died when he left it, he drives the narrator back to his hotel. The narrator is rather relieved to find that Morin is not a "carrier" after all, one who infects others, without knowing he does so, with a sense of the possibility of belief. "He had forgotten to give me the address of the vineyard, but I had forgotten to ask him for it when I said good night."

Discreet as it is, the irony in those concluding sentences fails to move. Nor does the hint of a parable. At the end of Kipling's story "The Gardener," a woman at a military cemetery in Flanders asks a man working there where she can find her nephew's grave. He tells her to come with him and he will show her where her son lies. Having seen the grave she goes away, "supposing him to be the gardener." The symbolism clinches what the story has already told us: that the woman has an illegitimate son whom she has brought up as her nephew, concealing the secret from everyone in her life, almost from herself. It is still a secret when she goes away, for she has not grasped what the man said. It spite of its clever conclusion Kipling's story is moving, and does come off, because its real subject is not what is devised and constructed as an epiphany, but the horror of the cemetery itself—graphically brought home—and the sense of a perpetual, unchangeable lie which hangs over it, the lie not only of the woman but of the war and its dead. Kipling did not intend that discovery.

No doubt writers, more especially writers of Greene's calibre, take a different view of their work from the one taken by their public; but even so it is a surprise to read what Greene has written about his own stories, and the contrast they make, in his own eyes, with the novels. To his readers, I should think, they must seem just the same, only more so. With the exceptions so far noted they make the same points as his novels, in the same way. Greene speaks of himself as a "writer" in very much the way that Somerset Maugham used to, as if it were some odd and involuntary vocation, like being a priest, only of course very much more profitable. As a novelist he becomes "encrusted" with characters—Greene's very typical image is of a corpse in the Caribbean he had been told of, which came up from the sea so covered in lampreys that you could not tell it was a man's body. "A horrible image, but it is one which suits the novelist well." Is not this just what his adoring public—and Greene's public is as large and as various as Maugham's was—want to be told about their maestro? How he lives and suffers in the parts he creates from day to day, becoming his character as Flaubert developed in himself the "destructive passion" of Madame Bovary, picking up from his hero "his jealousies, his meanness, his dishonest tricks of thought, his betrayals"? Just the thing for an audience to smack their lips over, but is not it all, like so much about Graham Greene and his writing, curiously unreal, as if the writer were seen as a kind of damned soul who took upon himself the sins of his characters? No doubt the audience enjoy being told that the short story is a form of escape for this writer—"escape from having to live with another character for years on end"—but they must also enjoy the sense that their hero is just as present in his stories as in his novels, and in even more concentrated form.

The more so since his sense of release and relief, in doing a "scrap" of a story instead of toiling away on a novel, communicates itself to the reader. In many of the tales writer and reader seem to be able to be, as it were, wicked children together, let out of the grey responsibilities of school or church. Two of Greene's own favourites are "The Destructors" and "Under the Garden." In the first a gang of children under the leadership of a boy called Trevor—known as T because Trevor sounds soppy to himself and the gang—contrive to get inside an old man's house in his absence and destroy it entirely from within. The second is a long and elaborate childhood fantasy about a secret place under a garden lake, which in middle age is

found to have diminished to a pond, hardly more than a puddle. Greene's access to childhood is far more direct and more disconcerting than in the case of most writers who return to it. And the same lurking hilarity infects the stories of *May We Borrow Your Husband?*, a collection "all written during what should be the last decade of my life," which Greene would no doubt be sardonically content to see as the product of a second childhood. These "comedies of the sexual life" have the same air of release as the childhood tales, or Kipling's elaborate little farces, but many of them pass the most stringent test of a short story: they seem even better made, and reveal more, at the second or third reading. "Two Gentle People" is a story that Somerset Maugham could not have written, although Greene invokes in it, almost as if deliberately, the "guide lines" of his stories, and shows how they can be transformed into something altogether more understanding.

In his late stories Greene abdicates from his earlier personae into a relaxed good nature, no doubt designed intentionally to surprise his fans. The feeling of wariness, of a perpetual anxiety, which hangs over the earlier ones, has disappeared.

—*John Bayley*

In these late stories Greene abdicates from his earlier personae into a relaxed good nature, no doubt designed intentionally to surprise his fans. The feeling of wariness, of a perpetual anxiety, which hangs over the earlier ones, for all that they were intended to be a release from the strains of novel-writing, has disappeared. So has the itch to point a moral, or at least to make a point, the tone of propaganda which energizes and unifies all Greene's writing, even the "entertainments." It seems hardly possible that the author of "Brother," "A Drive in the Country," "Across the Bridge," and "A Chance for Mr. Lever" (another of Greene's own favourites) could much later have written some of the stories in *May We Borrow Your Husband?* But where stories were concerned Greene was a professional, getting the feel of an assignment, rather than a writer who has created a world of his own. "Brother," written in the 1930s, is almost a parody of the contemporary tale "of social significance," with a little Greene expertise and dropping of the right local place-names: *Combat*, Menilmontant. The atmosphere of the *Front Populaire* and the attack on the bourgeoisie is effortlessly conveyed, with something of that almost "camp" bravado which reminds the reader both of school stories and of the contemporary cinema, to which Greene had a strong if eccentric attachment. (In his memoirs Anthony Powell remembers Greene's film reviews in the short-lived magazine *Night and Day*, and his rhapsodies about Erich von Stroheim climbing the stairs in full uniform "to an innocent bed.") The scenarios of the early tales have the cinematic power of "focusing" on the action, while leaving the background and the minor properties of the story ignored or barely suggested. It is indeed a striking paradox that a writer as obsessed as Greene with the Catholic themes which appear—or used to appear—in almost every context of his work, has also been able to give it such a virtuosity and variety.

In one sense, but in another not. Greene the professional, like a dramatist or film-writer, always goes to the heart of his matter, ignoring everything else. The economy is a weakness as well as a strength, for oddly enough the best short stories (Greene himself refers almost wistfully to Chekhov's "The Lady with the Dog") have the air of infinite apparent leisure, as if there were room to fill in every detail of the lives presented, and find room for every irrelevance. Greene would never write a story like Chekhov's, or like Joyce's "The Dead." His stories have no place for the poetry of the supper laid out that snowy evening at the Misses Morkans, or for the water-melon of which Gurov slowly eats a slice after his seduction of the lady with the dog. These are the mysterious ingredients of the short story at its most magical. With Greene, on the other hand, every detail has to tell, and tell they do. We know that the boy in **"The Hint of an Explanation"** is tempted beyond endurance by Blacker's offer of the model railway in exchange for a wafer of the consecrated Host, because he especially covets the turntable of the little model set—"so ugly and practical and true." And in **"A Drive in the Country"** we know that the girl leaving home really loves the young man she is going with because she loves the smell of the whisky on his breath—"*his* smell."

Such touches in a Greene story are unobtrusive, but they are the signs of a master at work. A master in his late period will often make a virtue of an obvious defect—one such appears in **"May We Borrow Your Husband?,"** where the narrative contrivances of the tale—in themselves sufficiently implausible—depend on the narrator always breakfasting with the honeymoon wife, because her husband is titivating himself and regularly appears downstairs fifteen minutes after her. This processional regularity stresses the artificiality of the tale, as if it were a drawing-room comedy (Maugham again) and effectively defines the mode in which it is to work. The story, as it turns out, is all the more successful because of its impossibility: campness has taken over, and delivered through its own conventions its own kind of sour sharp insight. In these masterly tales Greene makes a positive asset of the point that he has always been "a little bored" with the short-story form. By letting the form know it, he releases a new kind of candour in the writing.

R. H. Miller (essay date 1990)

SOURCE: "Short Stories, Plays, Essays," in *Understanding Graham Greene*, University of South Carolina Press, 1990, pp. 149-76.

[*In the excerpt below, Miller analyzes three of Greene's short stories, including "The Basement Room," "The Destructors," and "Under the Garden," which the critic believes represent the themes and techniques of Greene's short fiction as a whole.*]

Graham Greene is one of the most successful short story writers of all time. Very few writers achieve the ability to rivet readers' attention to a dramatic situation, turn it into meaning through ingenious manipulations of plot, and in the end leave them astonished, breathless. His range is extensive, moving from the introspective to the bizarre to the shocking. Greene's output is contained in five collections, issued from 1935 through 1967: *The Basement Room and Other Stories* (1935), *Nineteen Stories* (1947), *Twenty-One Stories* (1954), *A Sense of Reality* (1963), and *May We Borrow Your Husband? and Other Comedies of the Sexual Life* (1967). These were subsequently brought together into one volume, *Collected Stories* (1972). In addition, several uncollected stories have appeared. Eighteen of the stories were filmed for the series *Shades of Greene,* produced by Thames Television in 1976 and shown over the Public Broadcasting System in the United States, with the simultaneous publication of a collection by that title. Three of the stories may suffice to reveal the prevailing techniques and themes of Greene's short fiction: **"The Basement Room," "The Destructors,"** and **"Under the Garden."** All three were made into films for the *Shades of Greene* series.

"The Basement Room" first appeared as the lead and title story in Greene's first published collection, in 1935. In 1948 it was released as a film, and a highly successful one, under the title *The Fallen Idol,* directed by Carol Reed, who also directed *The Third Man.* **"The Basement Room"** serves as a guide to the major themes of many of Greene's novels: the innocence of childhood and its subsequent corruption when it confronts the adult world; the insidious nature of evil and its mixture with good; the relative impotence of good in the face of evil; and, most significantly, the inevitability that trust will be rewarded with betrayal, no matter how unintended that betrayal might be.

Greene chooses to narrate this story from a third-person-limited point of view, from the vantage point of the main character Philip's deathbed, sixty years after the events of the story, and to focus subtly one's attention on the life-long impact of this episode on Philip, who has never forgotten it and who must live with its effects until his dying day. In **"The Basement Room"** the situation concerns then seven-year-old Philip and two household servants, Baines and Mrs. Baines, to whom he has been given over during "a fortnight's holiday." Philip is isolated from his parents and "between nurses," which means that he must, from the context of childhood, deal prematurely with an adult world of marital hatred, duplicity, and adultery, and must make crucial choices as to how to maintain allegiances that the adults require of him.

With its five sections the story is reminiscent of Renaissance tragedy, carrying its construct of rising action, crisis, falling action, and catastrophe, out of which a new awareness, however dim, arises for both protagonist and reader. The story focuses on one crucial event, the accidental death of Mrs. Baines, and its test of Philip's loyalty and his ability to interpret the event within the context of adult morality. The crisis occurs with the surprise return of Mrs. Baines to the house, where she catches Baines and Emmy *in flagrante*. It only remains for the catastrophe of Philip's betrayal to occur, and its result: the misinterpreting of Mrs. Baines's death by the police and the downfall of Baines and Emmy.

The focus of the story is on Philip; its narrative technique binds the readers to him, although they do not discover fully the narrative situation until the close of the story. What happened there on that day succeeded in some unconscious way of killing all Philip's innocence and destroying his childhood love of life. His innocence has no difficulty dealing with Mrs. Baines's clearly malicious nature; it fears it, while it betrays Baines both at the end of the story and earlier, when Mrs. Baines discovers the crumb of pink sugar on his lapel. Emmy, the young girl who is Baines's lover, is a great mystery to Philip throughout his life, and he dies with the question on his lips he has asked himself over and over again for the past sixty years: Who is she? The answer is that she is, like her descendant Rose in *Brighton Rock,* the potentiality for love and happiness, but she is so frail and identityless that she cannot survive in a world in which the force of evil is so strong that it traps the good (Baines) and subverts the innocent to its own cause (Philip). Philip dies an old, loveless man, never having created anything, and carrying with him the unforgettable memory of Mrs. Baines's shrill voice, a voice he could mimic with devastating effect.

The story closes with the death of innocence, the powerful sickness of the heart induced by Philip's betrayal, and foreshadows future stories to be written: *Brighton Rock* and Rose's goodness, that also of Sarah Miles in *The End of the Affair* and of Bendrix's opacity; of Scobie's innocence in *The Heart of the Matter,* and that of Pyle in *The Quiet American,* the deadliest innocent. Philip, too, as a child foreshadows all Greene's children, from the childlike Pinkie and Rose, to Coral Fellows and the Mexican boys, to the shrieking child in *The Third Man,* who almost does in Rollo Martins.

"The Destructors" first appeared serialized in two parts in *Picture Post,* July 24 and 31, 1954. Its first appearance in a collection was in *Twenty-One Stories* in 1954. Perhaps no story since Shirley Jackson's "The Lottery" appeared in *The New Yorker* in 1948 has produced such a disturbing effect on readers. Next to **"The Basement Room"** it has attracted more critical attention than any other story by Greene, and is his most frequently anthologized story. **"The Destructors"** may be Greene's best story and perhaps one of the finest in the language. It has all the qualities that have come to be expected in the short story: focus, compression, pace, and that element of surprise, that epiphany that brings one to recognizing a powerful truth. It works as both parable and allegory, parable in the sense that it is a narrative in a relatively contempo-

raneous setting that makes a clear moral point, allegorical in the sense that it "signifies" on several levels.

> "The Destructors" may be Greene's best story and perhaps one of the finest in the language. It has all the qualities that have come to be expected in the short story: focus, compression, pace, and that element of surprise, that epiphany that brings one to recognizing a powerful truth.
>
> —*R. H. Miller*

As parable the story is a mirror of experience which reflects the condition of England during the immediate postwar period, at a time when England was only gradually recovering from the destruction of the blitz and the ravages more generally of the war. The locale, Wormsley Common, has been bombed, and the house of Mr. Thomas (a.k.a. "Old Misery") sticks up like one last sound tooth in a rotten mouth. More significantly, the house symbolizes the traditions of civilization, having been designed and built by the distinguished seventeenth-century English architect Christopher Wren; yet these traditions have not been upheld over the years, and readers know that Old Misery has been sadly remiss, as have others before him, in their obligation to maintain the edifice in its proper style. The young protagonist, Trevor, or T., as he prefers to be called, sees the rude absurdity of the grand house, and he persuades his gang of boys to set themselves the task of reducing it to rubble, not by destroying it but rather by systematically gutting it and weakening its structure, so that at the close of the story it only requires the tug of the lorry at one corner of the foundation to bring the whole structure down. Old Misery, locked in his outdoor toilet, emerges to find complete destruction. It is a horrendously cruel trick to pull on an old man, but the lorry driver says at the end, "There's nothing personal, but you got to admit it's funny." The younger English generation has succeeded in extending the actions of the older to their logical conclusion, and the landscape of Wormsley Common has rational consistency now that the Wren house is gone.

At one level readers, especially older readers, with their powerful sense of the sanctity of property, react in horror to what the gang achieve. But a deeper reading of the story reveals that much more is at stake here than property; it is the loss of a work of art, the destruction not just of a building but of a wonderful idea poorly stewarded, the loss more generally of an entire culture, not to war alone but to the wanton destructiveness of a new generation who are products of that war and have no understanding of and little stake in preserving that which they do not love.

What is perhaps more appalling than the destruction is the manner in which it is carried out. T. is caught up in both a struggle for and an exercise of power and in a rejection of his heritage, of his father, a former architect, and of his mother, with her class snobbery. Politically the story is a microcosm of the acquisition and uses of power as T. succeeds in wresting control of the gang from Blackie and shapes it and motivates it to carry out his plan. What is most unsettling is that such skill and intellect are exercised by the gang in carrying out their plan. The dinnertime harangues from parents about the value of work and of dedication bear ironic fruit in their efforts.

Most powerful in the story's impact is its multilayered allegory that allows readers to see this not only as a parable on the bitter fruit of the postwar generational struggle; in a broader context it represents the death of property in a class struggle between the custodians of that property and a newer generation that sees the absurdity of that concept. On a political level it is an allegory on totalitarianism and the fruits of power, and the way in which that power, once unleashed, is difficult to control and assumes a life of its own. In another sphere it is the corruption and destruction of the good by a Manichean evil that is present in the world, ready to use those who have some small impulse toward harm and to assume a power even greater than that of those who pursue evil ends. In "The Second Coming" Yeats says, "The best lack all conviction, while the worst / Are full of passionate intensity." Greene's story is saying much the same thing here. **"The Destructors"** will remain a disturbingly powerful story and take on even more significance as time passes.

"Under the Garden" is Greene's longest story and, given its length, ought perhaps to be thought of as a novella. It first appeared in 1963 in *A Sense of Reality*. This story is as seminal a piece of Greene's fiction as any he has written. It brings together motifs of childhood and adulthood, of the meaning of literature and art, of the interplay of the conscious and unconscious life and the significance of dreams as clues to a character's nature, of the nature of myth and its meaning in real life—all major concerns in Greene's work. Additionally, it combines the strategies of three of Greene's favorite works, two of them, appropriately, children's books: the geography of *Alice in Wonderland,* the escape motif of Henry James's "The Great Good Place," one of Greene's favorite stories, and the romance of Robert Louis Stevenson's *Treasure Island*. It is at the same time one of Greene's most puzzling stories and one of his richest.

Structurally the story is multilayered. It relies on three separate narrations: that of the writer Greene, following his character William Wilditch through the trauma of learning that he has life-threatening, probably terminal lung cancer and his escape to his brother's estate, Winton Hall; that of Wilditch as a thirteen-year-old, recapturing and romanticizing a childhood dream through his story "The Treasure in the Island," printed in his school magazine *The Warburian* under the nom de plume "W. W." (for which one may surely substitute "G. G."); and that of Wilditch as an adult as he rewrites the childhood story

into a new version, the product of accretions over the fifty years since the time he had the original dream about his subterranean experience. Three separate voices, three separate stories, all drawn from one source: a dream of a most compelling kind, one that has drawn its dreamer back to it time after time, since the age of seven to the present, when he is now past fifty-seven.

The geography, taken as it is from Lewis Carroll's story, provides a parallel to the dream, for it is a journey into a new land, a timeless underground world that exists below the estate garden, accessible only by squeezing into an entrance beneath a tree root on an island in the middle of a lake. It is also an escape in the Jamesian tradition because it represents a release from the pressures of the world above, where life sucks out vitality and where, in the final version of the story, Wilditch, like his author Greene, looks back over a life of travel to escape and confront certain realities, only to wonder if he has lived at all.

In the original story—that is, the childhood story of part 1, section 5—W. W. Moves quickly through the experience to the discovery of treasure, but in his later version the treasure Wilditch discovers is of little avail. The "golden po" turns out to be an old chamber pot, painted yellow. In the second story the adventure of the cave far overshadows the treasure. The cave is inhabited by primeval parents, Javitt and Maria, both eternal but both maimed physically and symbolically, Javitt by being partially immobilized because he lacks one leg, Maria lacking the power of speech because of her lack of a palate. The one sits and speaks wisdom from his toilet seat, as Wilditch says, like a great prophet; the other races about screaming nonsense. And all this is the product of a childhood dream, written up some years later by the dreamer, mulled over during a lifetime and then rediscovered and written up again. What began as a relatively straightforward but imaginative adventure story has turned into a Freudian fable of significant proportions. Wilditch, facing what seems to be his imminent death, after a lifetime of travel in all parts of the world returns to this single experience to find meaning in it. What he discovers is that he has taken the "facts" of reality and converted them into a new reality for himself. Ernest the gardener becomes the source for much of Javitt, the garden becomes the world, and Friday's Cave and Camp Indecision become efforts on Wilditch's part, at two separate times in his life, to analyze his life and re-create that analysis as narration.

Efforts have been made to unravel this seemingly slightly disguised roman à clef, and most certainly will continue. What is more important to one's understanding of it is its way of dealing with reality and the reconstitution of reality through art. What Greene does here is remarkably similar to what one sees in the allegorical layerings of his best novels. To put it in Wilditch's own words (hence Greene's): "A puddle can contain a continent, and a clump of trees stretch in sleep to the world's edge." In other words, one can sense a truth as broad as the world in a story as confined as Wilditch's. More importantly, it is the life of art and the making of it that is most important, as the story proves its own point. Wilditch's mother, determined to kill all vestiges of the imaginative impulse in him, failed miserably, where the gardener Ernest succeeded by providing him with a character, and the pond and the little hillock provided a place for a powerful creative experience. And at the end of the story Wilditch, having returned to his island and found the old chamber pot, is overcome by a curiosity that can only be satisfied by rethinking and rewriting his story, yet again. A new understanding and new experiences demand a new narration. "Across the pond the bell rang for breakfast and he thought, 'Poor mother—she had reason to fear,' turning the tin chamber-pot on his lap".

Daniel Stern (review date 1991)

SOURCE: "Ever Greene," in *New York Times Book Review,* February 24, 1991, pp. 13-14.

[*In the following mixed review, Stern states that even though* The Last Word *does not reflect his best works of short fiction, Greene is nevertheless a masterful short story writer.*]

In the introduction to his massive 562-page *Collected Stories,* published in 1972, Graham Greene writes: "I remain in this field a novelist who has happened to write short stories, just as there are certain short story writers (Maupassant and Mr. V. S. Pritchett come to mind) who have happened to write novels."

About Maupassant and Mr. Pritchett, Mr. Greene may be right, but there is also a whole other subset of writers who are equally at home in the short story and the novel (Bernard Malamud and Flannery O'Connor come to mind). It is in this group, in spite of his demurrer, that I would place Graham Greene. So much for placement. The real trick is understanding this astonishing author at the stage of the writing life he now occupies. He is 86, has written more than 60 books—and is the world's most conspicuous nonwinner of the prize many, including this reviewer, think he clearly earned years ago, the Nobel.

From 1940 on, Graham Greene, in an unequaled display of productivity and creative originality, produced book after book that enriched our sense of what the modern novel could do in the hands of a quiet master of style and suspense (who also happened to be a tormented Roman Catholic convert and a left-wing sympathizer). That mixture produced narratives replete with irony and pity for the weak and the lost. It was the irony that saved the pity from becoming sentimental, as well as the fact that no one stood safely beyond it, not lovers, certainly not principalities and powers, not even Mr. Greene's extremely personal and ambiguous god. The result was a series of powerful novels: *The Power and the Glory, The Heart of the Matter, The End of the Affair, The Quiet American, A Burnt-Out Case, The Honorary Consul,* to select just a few. For generations Graham Greene has been a central source of the literary air all of us breathe.

In addition, there is the achievement of the "entertainments" such as *The Man Within, This Gun for Hire* and *Brighton Rock,* starting in the 1930's and continuing with *The Third Man, Our Man in Havana* and others—each reader will, undoubtedly, have his or her favorite. This distinction between "entertainments" and "serious" novels, which Mr. Greene famously invented for himself early in his career, has become less and less useful; the serious novels were all entertaining in the richest sense, and the entertainments (they were frequently subtitled as such) often have a depth many a "serious" novelist would envy.

> There is now no doubt about one thing: over the long haul, in the short story as well as the novel, Graham Greene is the Master.
>
> —*Daniel Stern*

All the while Mr. Greene was producing a steady stream of short stories, including a minor classic, **"The Basement Room"** (from which the Carol Reed film *The Fallen Idol,* starring Sir Ralph Richardson, was made). The copyright dates for his stories start in 1935 and go to 1990, lastly, *The Last Word: And Other Stories.* This is a collection of stories that, for one reason or another, the author did not wish to include in previous collections. They date from 1923 to 1989 and only four have ever appeared before in book form, none in the *Collected Stories.*

The reasons Mr. Greene gives for the original exclusions range from several of them being too derivative from some of his novels, to concern over a new generation's understanding of some World War II events. His reason for including one story dating from 1929, **"Murder for the Wrong Reason,"** was that, on rereading it 60 years later, he found he could not guess the identity of the murderer.

Only one of these additions to the canon, the last in the volume, called **"An Appointment With the General,"** reads like vintage Greene. It has all the familiar hallmarks: the bitter beauty of language that keeps doubling back on itself in irony, the despair worn like a comfortable old suit, the unsentimental scorn when dealing with the left and the right. A French journalist is sent to interview a South American general of ambiguous politics and ambitions. She leaves on the eve of her marriage's collapse, and that personal event delicately colors her interview with the general. It is a small gem. Interestingly, it is a recent work, published in 1982. Like so many of Mr. Greene's works with an exotic locale—and like his nonfiction book *Getting to Know the General*—this story may be based on direct experience, in this case Mr. Greene's regular visits to Gen. Omar Torrijos Herrera of Panama.

The vintage **"Murder for the Wrong Reason"** is interesting mainly because it prefigures Mr. Greene's enduring interest in the mystery story—but also because it contains, in miniature, every convention of that genre. Like the author, this reviewer could not tell who the murderer was until the very end. **"The News in English"** is a touching minor effort with a major backdrop; a Briton who is marooned in Germany at the war's outbreak broadcasts apparent propaganda for the Germans to the English back at home. The story is filtered through his wife's shame, an emotion altered by the revelation that something other than treason is afoot. The ending has a dying fall and Mr. Greene's voice is eloquently sustained throughout.

Less satisfying is the title tale. **"The Last Word"** is the story of the last Christian in a world in which a totalitarian proto-Communist order—in some Orwellian way—has completely eradicated the church. The hero of the story, a confused old man, turns out to be the last Pope, kept alive until the moment when even he is no longer necessary to the global regime. Though written with skill and style, this tale demonstrates the folly of second-guessing history. Since the churches of Europe have for the most part survived their former Communist oppressors, the final effect of the tale is one of a naïve, nostalgic backward look on Mr. Greene's part.

The group of stories written with a humorous, lighter effect in mind do not succeed so well here. At least they are not in a class with *May We Borrow Your Husband?*, Mr. Greene's brilliant execution of the light touch in story form. But if we follow the author's guidance (he says in his introduction to the earlier volume of *Collected Stories*: "I have never written anything better than **'The Destructors,' 'A Chance for Mr. Lever.' 'Under the Garden'** and **'Cheap in August'**") then the picture is made whole. On rereading Mr. Greene's entire *oeuvre* in this form it is clear that these stories are all worth a journey, not just a detour. Along with **"The Basement Room," "The Hint of an Explanation," "When Greek Meets Greek,"** and with his masterpiece of quiet horror. **"A Little Place Off the Edgware Road,"** in which the murderer and the corpse of his victim trade places, his short stories stake out a claim for Graham Greene that he refuses, with characteristic modesty, to make for himself—that of a genuine master of the short story.

If the stories in *The Last Word* are not examples of Mr. Greene working at the top of his form, they do give us a few new pleasures while sending us back to the often overlooked body of short stories waiting for us. There is now no doubt about one thing: over the long haul, in the short story as well as the novel, Graham Greene is the Master.

Richard Kelly (essay date 1992)

SOURCE: "Loosing the Devils," and "The Last Word" in *Graham Greene: A Study of the Short Fiction*, Twayne, 1992, pp. 3-16, 70-87.

[*In the following excerpt, Kelly examines Greene's early short stories, written during his years as a student, stating that in these works Greene worked out the "terrors and frustrations" of his youth. Kelly then discusses* The Last Word, *a work he feels "conveys a synoptic view of the stages of [Greene's] life as a writer."*]

Rarely has a writer been more obsessed with his lost childhood than has Graham Greene. In this respect he is clearly the child of the romantic period, whose poets, such as Blake and Wordsworth, celebrate the bright joys of innocence that quickly give way to the dark pains of experience. Greene also found his obsession mirrored in the novels of Charles Dickens, where Victorian society seems dead set upon destroying the bodies and souls of children. Similarly, Greene's admiration for the minor Victorian poet Arthur Hugh Clough, whom he calls the only adult poet of the age, derives from his own spiritual malaise. During Clough's years at Oxford he lost the serenity of his Christian faith and turned to writing poetry as a means of defending himself against the doubts that raged against his desire for belief in God. Like Clough, Greene's sense of dislocation from his childhood and from his Christian faith intensified during his Oxford days, and he sought to overcome his depression and to exorcise his psychic demons through his writing.

As a highly sensitive, imaginative youth, and coming from a respected, comfortable, upper-middle-class family, Greene enjoyed the opportunity to develop more exotic emotional problems than are allotted to children of the lower classes. When he first discovered that he could read, he hid this fact from his parents out of fear that they would make him enter preparatory school. He began to live a covert life, secretly reading books about adventure and mystery that his parents would not approve. As a child he also developed inordinate fears of the dark, of birds and bats, of drowning, and of the footsteps of strangers. He developed recurrent nightmares about a witch who would lurk at night near the linen cupboard in the nursery.

As a student at Berkhamsted School, where his father was headmaster, Greene's emotional problems were compounded by his sense of divided loyalties. His filial devotion was constantly challenged by his desire to be one of the boys. He was never able to resolve these conflicting loyalties, and, to make matters worse, two schoolboys, named Carter and Wheeler, sadistically exploited Greene's anxiety with cruel psychological precision. Greene has not disclosed specific details of their torment, but Norman Sherry, in his biography of Greene, has shown that these two boys, especially Carter, exercised a powerful control over Greene during a critical time in his development. More experienced in worldly matters, they took pleasure in attacking Greene's naïveté and trust. Lionel Carter not only tormented Greene for being the headmaster's son, but, after winning his confidence and discovering his secret dreams and desires, he disabused Greene of many of his romantic and chivalric ideals. As the murderer of Greene's childhood and as the arch-betrayer, Carter would appear in many guises throughout Greene's stories and novels and become one of the powerful demons Greene would spend his life as a writer attempting to exorcise. Years later Greene was to observe, "Every creative writer worth our consideration . . . is a victim: a man given over to an obsession."

In 1920 Greene's manic-depressive and suicidal behavior led his parents to send him to a psychoanalyst named Kenneth Richmond for treatment. The experience proved beneficial and Greene began self-consciously to record and analyze his dreams and feelings. It was also during this period that he began to write short stories, which served, perhaps unwittingly, to shape and help control his inchoate fears and depressions.

The short stories Greene wrote in the 1920s have been largely ignored by critics and scholars, and yet they are fundamental to an understanding of his character and his development as a writer.

—*Richard Kelly*

The short stories Greene began writing then and later during his years at Berkhamsted School and Oxford University have been largely ignored by critics and scholars, and yet they are fundamental to an understanding of his character and his development as a writer. Uncollected and not easily accessible, these stories, written during the period 1920-25, reveal the youthful obsessions that were to inform all his later work. It seems important, therefore, to examine these early creations for what they reveal about Greene the man and the writer, for, as Wordsworth says, "The child is father of the man."

Several of Greene's juvenilia, being only a page or two in length, fail to develop character, plot, or scene; rather, they sketch a mood, fear, or anxiety, usually in a self-conscious literary or allegorical form. **"The Tick of the Clock,"** for example, which was published in Greene's school magazine, the *Berkhamstedian,* in 1920, when he was only 16 years old, reveals his youthful morbidity. The story is about a lonely old lady facing death with no companion but her ticking clock. Her only wish in life was to love someone, but young men had never come her way and children now fear her. The clock attempts to console her by relating the fate of a king and a poet who unhappily died with an uneasy conscience and a failed sense of glory: "But you, you have no sin upon your conscience, you have not sought for fame or wealth, why then do you find death so hard?" When the woman replies that she cannot face death "without Love to hold me up," Fate speaks to her in Christ-like tones: "O woman of little understanding, wherefore are you sad? Do you not know that I am Fate and Fate is Death, and Death is Love Eternal? Your quest is ended, you have found that which you sought." The

next morning she is discovered dead in her bed and those who see her exclaim, "How happy she looks."

The heavy-handed allegory, the melodrama, and the unconvincing consolation offered to the old woman by Fate all mark this story as a youthful exercise. Beneath the literary posturing, however, one can detect the young Greene's concern about his own rather loveless life and the void that enhances its misery. Greene's romantic assertion that death is eternal love is a bit like whistling in the dark. It is an idea belied by his later work in which his expiring heroes and heroines are sent to anxious and uncertain fates.

In his autobiography, *A Sort of Life* (1971), Greene looks back upon **"The Tick of the Clock"** with mixed emotions. He abhors the story as literature but recalls its publication—his first—as inspiring him with confidence and a sense of glory:

> I was beginning to write the most sentimental fantasies in bad poetic prose. One abominable one, called **"The Tick of the Clock,"** about an old woman's solitary death, was published in the school magazine. I cut out the pages and posted them to the *Star,* an evening paper of the period, and for God knows what reason they published the story and sent me a check for three guineas. I took the editor's kindly letter and the complimentary copy up to the Commons and for hours I sat on the abandoned rifle butts reading the piece aloud to myself. . . . Now, I told myself, I was really a professional writer, and never again did the idea hold such excitement, pride and confidence. . . . that sunny afternoon I could detect no flaw in **"The Tick of the Clock."** The sense of glory touched me for the first and last time.

In **"The Poetry of Modern Life,"** published in the *Berkhamstedian* in 1921, Greene implicitly acknowledges Carter's disturbing effect upon his ideals. The narrator of the story is overwhelmed by a voice that declares the death of poetry in modern life: "It was just a voice in the street that I heard as I passed along, 'Poetry and Romance are dead' . . . when I heard that voice, the busy movement of the streets pressed in upon me, seeming to shut out all colour, and changing everything into a dull monotony . . . it even penetrated into my slumbers so that I seemed to be surrounded with legions of devils, all crying out, 'Poetry and Romance are dead.'" In a desperate attempt to deal with his painful disillusionment, the narrator reverts to the literary past and seeks counsel from a chivalric knight. The knight, however, merely confesses that he and his kind are dead and offers the narrator the weak consolation that there is heroic virtue in the poetry of defeat: "As long as heroic deeds are done, as long as the great world struggle between Good and Evil lasts, so long will there be poetry in life. . . . Ye know the poetry of victory, the wild enthusiasm of a people when long looked for peace arrives. But have ye yet learned the poetry of defeat?" The story concludes with this theme by describing three men dying of hunger and cold, "yet one was still striving to write some last letters to those at home, thinking in his last moments, not of himself, but of the man who had sent him and trying to save him from vain, useless regret.

Norman Sherry suggests that Greene might have been thinking of the deaths of Captain Scott and his associates Wilson and Bowers in the Antarctic, since Scott's dramatic death in the Antarctic in 1912 made him a great hero among English schoolboys. More significantly, however, Sherry connects this story by Greene with his persecution by Carter:

> Perhaps the dying man's attempt to write letters home reflects Graham's desire to write to his parents about his misery, though he could not. In the face of Carter's undermining of Greene's cherished boyhood beliefs, it is not surprising that he turned to a less romantic vision. The knight in the story offers some hope, arguing that "as long as the great world struggle between Good and Evil lasts, so long will there be poetry in life." It is possible that Carter, with his inexplicable cruelties, his nihilism, his ability to feign innocence, put Greene on to his fundamental theme, the nature of Good and Evil and the conflict between them.

In another story, **"Castles in the Air"** (1921), which earned him a first prize in a school competition, Greene reverts to the subject of disillusionment and death, heralded again by his personal devil, Lionel Carter. During the festivities at the Great Grinsted's Midsummer Fair, a grotesque piper begins to play strange music that brings an end to the noisy pleasures of the crowd and makes everyone aware of his mortal sadness. Greene's memorable description of the piper anticipates the grotesque character of the mestizo, another betrayer, in *The Power and the Glory:* "a short, hunched man, one-eyed, covered in dirt, with a great red bulbous nose protruding aggressively from his face. . . . The man grinned, disclosing great, dirty, fang-like teeth."

As the piper plays, his music conjures up in the minds of the crowd visions of beauty and romance: "to each onlooker he was different. To some he seemed a princess, with beautiful braided hair, to others as a glorious knight in shining coat of mail, but to all he was their childhood's dream of love. He was the mistress, he was the lord of those lovely twisted white marble palaces which all had constructed once, stone upon stone, in the clouds. The piper's seductive tune offers intimations of childhood immortality for all of his listeners, but then he disappears and the crowd is left in dismal silence "each with his private grief." The devil incarnate, the piper steals the very dreams of childhood love and romance he conjured up in the imaginations of his listeners.

Greene believed that his personal tormenter, Lionel Carter, destroyed his childhood joy and dreams. It is interesting to note that Greene presents the devil as a piper. The legendary piper plays music that is both seductive and destructive, thereby suggesting that Carter's imposition of his adult view of life upon Greene's youthful fantasies combines both alluring and terrifying prospects.

While he was under the psychiatric care of Kenneth Richmond, Greene wrote a story entitled **"The Creation of Beauty: A Study in Sublimation."** Unlike the other early tales, with their emphasis upon mortality and disillusionment, this one lives up to its subtitle by offering a defense against fear and unhappiness through the escapist ideal of feminine beauty. Greene's repressed sexuality—during his teens he was infatuated with several women, including a ballet student who used to visit the Richmonds—thus finds an outlet in this story about cosmic creation.

The chief architect of the universe confronts God with his misery. Following God's orders he had created man and the universe but now he is distressed that God gave man no other happiness than a woman to love. Furthermore, God has ordered the existence of darkness and sleep, which contain fear and evil dreams to torment man. All of nature, in fact, seems to conspire to harm man and defeat his work and his dreams. God answers that "because you have given him the beauty of woman, you have given him the beauty of the universe." God declares that good and evil are reconciled in man's devotion to woman:

> He will love the cold, because it is like his wayward mistress; he will love the heat, because it is as warm as her breast. He will write songs to the dark, because it is as deep, unfathomable and mysterious as love, and drowns him in the blackness of her hair. He will let himself down into sleep with a fear, because, though it bring evil dreams, yet will it also bring dreams of her for whom he lives. He will glory in the birds, for he will decorate her in their feathers.

In the midst of this lyrical celebration, Greene attributes to his femme fatale the power to assuage and reconcile many of his most profound fears: of sexuality, of the dark, of bad dreams, of drowning, and of birds. The story reads almost like a psychoanalytical exercise whereby through the sublimation of his fears into a cosmic hymn to female beauty and through the act of writing itself Greene may obtain a sense of control over his demons. Like his character God, Greene can assume the role of creator through his fiction, imposing order upon the chaos of his experience and illuminating the dark corners of his fears.

The two stories Greene published in 1922, **"The Tyranny of Realism"** and **"Magic,"** extend some of the former themes and reveal his continuing sexual repression, guilt, desire for punishment, and sense of betrayal and disappointment. Roland Wobbe was the first to note the significance of **"The Tyranny of Realism."** He sees it as a self-conscious and paradigmatic dream story important to an understanding of Greene's later work: "The story's characters reappear in a number of later variations, and its plot becomes a schematic for the conflicts in the later novels and entertainments."

"The Tyranny of Realism," published in the *Berkhamstedian* in 1922, is an allegorical fantasy that focuses upon a young boy held captive by an omnipotent tyrant named King Realism, "from whom no secrets were hid, no dark places safe." Sharing the boy's captivity and lying at the King's feet in a cold marble hall filled with the smell of a prison, corruption, and repression, is a beautiful maiden called Fantasie. The boy asks the King why his great love, Fantasie, has been stolen from him and complains that he has been robbed of his dreams and of a mystical homeland of dark caves and hidden ways, full of beauty and sweet fears. King Realism informs the boy that he is no longer imprisoned and the small room melts into rolling plains and a star-filled sky. When the boy kneels before him he discovers that the King has become God and on the throne next to him sits Fantasie, "and their lips were pressed each to each in a long passion of joy."

Wobbe's interpretation of this final scene lays the biographical framework for understanding the story:

> The final action leaves no doubt that both the God-king and the girl have betrayed the boy, and the allegorical significance of the characters begins to crystallize. The maid stands for fancy, romance, the erotic and a certain ambivalence; the God-king represents a changeable (perhaps arbitrary) authority, discipline, repression, cold, puritanical objectivity and male competition. One easily identifies the boy prisoner as the depressed young writer who feels both captive and spy in his father's school. The story contains heavy Freudian associations of repressed sexuality, guilt, and punishment.

King Realism seems to be a composite of Lionel Carter and Greene's father. Both of these figures served to undermine Greene's sense of freedom, spontaneity, and fantasy. They both exercised authority over him and demanded his loyalty. Greene's youthful dreams and chivalric eroticism, embodied in the character of Fantasie, are destroyed by the father-bully. The boy asks King Realism, "Why did you send that cold, peering slave, that Spiritualism there, to drive away my dreams, the ghosts, who used to kiss my lips and hair?" The question elucidates the psychological allegory. Berkhamsted School is the prison ruled by Mr. Greene (King Realism) and the students are the slaves "who lined the walls." Greene's father is then held responsible for destroying Greene's romantic idealism by his authoritarian rule and especially by imprisoning him with Carter, "the cold, peering slave."

The boy's release from his imprisonment turns out to be the cruelest irony, for he has been released into the larger world of adult experience where betrayal can now be recognized and innocence lamented. The boy's discovery of King Realism in an impassioned embrace with Fantasie suggests his painful role in the oedipal triangle. Greene later modifies this oedipal relationship in **"The Basement Room,"** where he has Philip discover Baines and Emmy together in a restaurant. In that story Baines is the figure associated with fantasy who betrays the boy's innocence.

Greene's next story, **"Magic,"** published in the *Weekly Westminster Gazette* six weeks after the appearance of **"The Tyranny of Realism,"** is another dream story. A writer of children's fairy stories is haunted by the spirits of children who have read his books and who are now imprisoned within his fictional fairylands. These child ghosts express their various disillusionments: one has discovered that his mythical princess is actually an old woman who wears a corset and paints her face; another has

found that the king's daughter, for whom he slew dragons, first ignores him and later runs off with someone else; and a king's daughter exclaims that the young man who rescued her from a dragon turned out to be an abusive, alcoholic husband who eats his peas with a knife.

While most of the ghostly readers bitterly complain of their disillusionment with the romantic view of life the author had instilled in them as children, one of them announces his loss of religious belief as well: "I entered the gardens of heaven to fight with the archangels, and there was nothing there save weed-grown paths. I entered the halls of God, and there was only an empty throne."

Finally, the author asks if he has given happiness to anyone and he is answered by the ghost of his own youth: "You showed me the door to happiness and I went in, and faeryland was more beautiful than any dream of yours. I went in, but they pulled me out and closed the door, and for me also there was nothing left." This young spirit, unlike the other speakers, goes on to rationalize his disillusionment be arguing that the intensity of love and beauty in fairyland is too powerful for mere mortals and that one had best settle for a life of more ordinary happiness. "Love there was like a beacon fire," he says, "here like a smouldering hearth. Yet we may warm ourselves at that hearth for a little while, you and I, and perhaps forget the beacon. It is safer so. It might have scorched us."

Besides battling his personal school demons once again in "Magic," Greene is gradually discovering the subject matter and central themes of his future fiction.

—*Richard Kelly*

Besides battling his personal school dragons once again in this story, Greene is gradually discovering the subject matter and central themes of his future fiction. His overpowering sense of fantasy, which he nourished during the covert period of his childhood by reading such books as Rider Haggard's *King Solomon's Mines*, Charlotte Yonge's *The Little Duke*, Captain Frederick Marryat's *The Children of the Forest*, the fairy stories of Andrew Lang, and the tales of Beatrix Potter, must now be counterpointed by his profound disillusionment embodied within a fiction that accommodates cruel and brutal realities. It is little wonder, then, that a novelist such as Joseph Conrad would emerge as Greene's literary hero, a man who takes the dreams and illusions of a character like Charles Marlow, in *The Heart of Darkness*, and crushes them against the savage cruelty of a figure like Mr. Kurtz.

By the time he began his studies at Oxford University, Greene had all but lost any belief in God. His undergraduate atheism derived from several causes: his psychoanal-ysis under Kenneth Richmond, which hastened his disillu-sionment with the Protestant church; his rebellion against the unquestioning faith of his parents; and the opportunity afforded him at Oxford to explore new intellectual ideas and to challenge conventional principles.

In his first story for the *Oxford Outlook,* called **"The Trial of Pan"** (1923), Greene attempts to shock the traditional members of Balliol College by describing the seductive charms of a pagan who liberates God's followers from his stern, tyrannical rule. Greene here has at least two literary antecedents: Shelley, who, as an undergraduate at Oxford proclaiming the necessity of atheism, relished his Prome-thean role in attacking symbols and figures of authority, and Swinburne who, in his early poetry, asserted the su-periority of the free and lustful pagan gods over the re-pressive and puritanical God of Christianity.

Greene's story opens on a light satirical note and estab-lishes a tone characteristic of his later comical work in *May We Borrow Your Husband?* God, in the company of his angels and his worthies, is busily judging the souls of prostitutes, murderers, robbers, and swindlers. The story then moves to Gabriel's defense of Lady Hope-Smithies against the charges that she boxed the ears of an Anglican curate, lost money playing bridge, and gave money to a cousin. Michael, however, demolishes the defense, accus-ing the defendant of always reciting "Little Annie's Death-bed" at village concerts and of keeping six pet dogs. "God summed up against her, and the jury pronounced her guilty, without leaving the box."

Greene then modulates the tone of the story to one of heavy melodrama as Pan comes before God for judgment. Greene contrasts the youthful, sexual, and energetic char-acter of Pan with the old, gloomy, and lifeless figure of God. Asked to defend himself before judgment is passed, Pan announces that he can best express himself through his music. His sensual melodies soon capture the minds and hearts of all the inhabitants of Heaven: "Never before in all Eternity had such a tune been heard in the realms of Heaven. There was not a sound in the room. The jury, the counsels, all leaned forward in a dream. And the light in their eyes changed with the changing music."

God, however, reveals himself to be out of touch with the dreams and desires of his people. He laughs at the momentary power of Pan's music and laughs at the idea of sensual pleasures set against the joys of Heaven: the cross, the sacred music, the purity, love, and peace. But as Pan's music continues to seduce the heavenly host back to a dark, primitive world of sexual pleasure and youthful freedom, God begins to feel old and weak: "He put his hand to his head. It was aching and he was feel-ing old. He felt that if the music went on much longer he would weep. There was something wrong with his nerves to-day." When the music finally ceases God realizes everyone has deserted him to follow Pan. The story ends with a description of an old, saddened, betrayed God sitting alone in the empty hall playing ticktacktoe with himself on his blotting pad.

The tale is essentially an allegory of Greene's rite of passage in which he overthrows the restrictive authority of his religious father in order to assert his sexual identity. The only segments of this heavy-handed story that point to Greene's later style are the brief satiric account of the judgment of Lady Hope-Smithies and the description of a decrepit God attempting to recall the dim past: "It was such a long, long time since he had made the world. After all, one couldn't remember everything, and it had turned out very nicely. But still he wished he could remember why he had done it all. It might be important." No other Oxford undergraduate could have written these sentences.

"The Improbable Tale of the Archbishop of Canter-bridge," published in the *Cherwell* in 1924, adds a few interesting twists to Greene's atheism. The Archbishop of Canterbridge solemnly announces to a small gathering of his peers that England and the world are doomed:

> Our cause in England, the cause of Peace and the cause of Christ, is defeated; England is doomed, she has doomed herself. A lunatic has led her dancing to dabble her feet in blood, and the notes of his mad pipings have begun to penetrate even to Europe. Gentlemen, in a month's time the world will be fighting like a pack of mad dogs. The madman with his talk of the joys of war has bewitched mankind. If it were not that this is the twentieth century I should call him Satan.

The Archbishop tells his associates he will go to the home of this incarnate devil and murder him while he is taking a bath. "I realize," he says, "that I am risking my own soul, by meeting blood with blood. But, as I have said, I do it for the good of the world."

Despite the allegorical nature of the story, the final scene is presented in graphically realistic terms that anticipate the style of Greene's later stories. After the Archbishop fires a shot he sees his victim cough up a stream of blood: "He lay still for a moment in the blood-stained water, with his head, white with soap, resting on the brass taps."

Greene then reverts to an allegorical conversation between the representative of the Church of England (Canterbridge for Canterbury) and evil incarnate. After expressing his fear that by taking justice into his own hands he might have damned his soul, the Archbishop receives a stunning revelation from his victim: "You will find no God. . . . I am God." The Archbishop asks him how he can be dying if he is God, and the story closes with the bleeding man's response: "'I made myself man,' murmured he who was once God, and sleep crept into his tones. 'A miracle . . . Very rash . . . I have done better in my day.' They were a child's eyes that twinkled up from between the H and C taps. 'Such miracles I've done. You wouldn't believe. Woods, and wars, and sheep paths, and—and you, my dear Canterbridge.' And in a bubble of bloodstained laugh-ter God died."

Despite its melodrama, bizarre theology, and allegorical characters, this story marks a significant development in Greene's thinking about the nature of good and evil. He now portrays God and Satan as one and the same. Like Dr. Jekyll and Mr. Hyde, the creator and the destroyer are paradoxically incarnate as one in the mortal body of man. The story self-consciously allegorizes Greene's own manic-depressive personality.

Long after he became a convert to Catholicism, he continued to develop this paradoxical theme through such characters as Trevor in **"The Destructors,"** Pinkie Brown in *Brighton Rock,* and Raven in *A Gun for Sale.* All three characters possess a childlike innocence and yet they all are dangerously destructive. Greene's theology is largely conditioned by his sense of a ravished childhood, thereby leading him to portray evil in rich, palpable detail that blocks out any light from the City of God. Greene's most compelling image of paradise is not based on orthodox Christian theology but instead represents his own Eden of dreamy innocence. Expelled from the Garden of Berkhamsted, Greene seeks God in the past, in the myth of his lost childhood, and not in some future paradise. The world once was bright and good, he seems to argue, but now is brutal and evil. Therefore God is Satan, the creator and the destroyer, who made the sheep paths and woods to frame humanity's innocence and then trampled it with wars and murders.

Two final stories from Greene's Oxford years, **"The New House,"** published in the *Oxford Outlook* in 1923, and **"The Lord Knows,"** published in the *Oxford Chronicle* in 1925, show him moving into his stride as a more restrained writer, abandoning heavy-handed symbolism, allegory, and fantasy for a down-to-earth dramatization of the clash between dreams and reality.

"The New House" deals with a middle-aged architect named Handry, who has long harbored a dream of designing and building a house that would harmonize with a particular tract of land. Josephs, the wealthy owner of the land, grants the architect a commission to develop the tract and build the house, but Handry soon discovers his aesthetic dream house is not what his client desires—he wants a structure that will symbolize his wealth and power, a landmark that can be seen for miles.

The conflict between dream and reality, beauty and power, overwhelms Handry and he leaves his meeting with Josephs and "dashed into the road as if from an evil spell, and yet he knew that all this struggle was in vain. He was trapped, held fast by the ropes that bind all, his wife, his family, the world. Soon he would come slinking back, mouthing embarrassing apologies, to perpetrate the betrayal."

In the denouement, years after the building is completed, two passersby comment on the monstrosity: "This used to be one of the most beautiful views in the country. That fellow Joseph's [sic] philanthropy goes too far. His architect was a fellow in the village here, with no more views on art than the average rustic. And the abomination is a waste, for Josephs never lives in it, never comes near it."

Handry, now an old man "with pathetic, puzzled eyes," who happens to be standing near the two passersby, re-

veals his corruption as he echoes the values and language of his former employer: "It is so imposing, and such a landmark. It can be seen for miles. . . . Once I disliked it, but I had queer ideas in those days. . . . Do you read Longfellow? You should. He has very inspiring ideas."

As Roland Wobbe points out, "In this story Greene brings the power of his 'devils' down to earth, as the power of wealth is equated with the economic pressure of the whole society." Throughout his life Greene retained the romantic notion that capitalism is the Satanic enemy of integrity, creativity, and art. Greene resurrects the prototype of Josephs for the character of Eric Krogh, an industrialist with dwarfed aesthetic tastes, in *England Made Me* (1935) and for the Satanic capitalist Doctor Fischer in *Doctor Fischer of Geneva or the Bomb Party* (1980).

"The Lord Knows," published in the *Oxford Chronicle* in 1925, is another tale of disillusionment. A young man who is about to get married enters a local pub to celebrate his future happiness. He is soon set upon by the local cynic and a drunk, both of whom poke fun at his sexual innocence and suggest his fiancée may not be a virgin. To make his point, the drunk lures a spider to his finger, which he has dipped into his whisky. The young man's celebration is ruined. The romance of marriage has been undermined by brutal jokes and disturbing sexual questions.

The touch of genius in this tale lies in Greene's depiction of the drunk's seduction of the spider. As the young man is discussing his forthcoming marriage with the bartender and the cynic, the drunk in the background continues to attend to the spider until he possesses it: "Off its thin scaffolding in the roof stepped delicately a spider. It swayed slowly down through space, undisturbed by the two high voices. It was very deliberate." At that moment the young man cries out in a childish voice for the men to stop spoiling things, walks out of the pub, and exclaims, "Anyway, I've won her." The drunk, however, now holds the large spider in his hand and says, "She's come, I knew she'd come; I've won her."

In reading **"The Lord Knows,"** one is again reminded of Carter's battering of Greene's dreams of chivalric romance. While at Berkhamsted Greene used to go off by himself to read the romantic poetry of Lewis Norris, whose *Epic of Hades* celebrates the loves of Helen and Cleopatra. Norman Sherry speculates that Greene may have confided his secret erotic dreams to Wheeler in the first flush of their friendship and that later Wheeler betrayed Greene by reporting the details to Carter, who cynically used them to ridicule and humiliate Greene.

As beneficial as it may have been for Greene to work out his terrors and frustrations through the psychodrama of his early fiction, most of the stories, because of their crude symbolism and abstractions, fail to connect with the experience of his readers. But Greene was learning that his personal devils might be recognized by others if they were presented in the guise of crass capitalists, cynics, and foolish drunks rather than as allegorical figures. In the future he would embody these devils in such forms as

cruel policemen, greedy smugglers, untrustworthy mesti-
zos, pious priests, and foreign dictators. As Greene matured and began traveling about the world, he discovered
his personal demons had taken up residence everywhere,
from Haiti to Indochina.

Ultimately, however, Greene's early stories serve only as
a temporary defense against his demons, sort of like whistling in the dark. Greene's sense of alienation, his fears,
and his obsession with his lost childhood continue to comprise the central themes of his fiction for the rest of his
life. Nevertheless, the compulsive act of writing served
him well in his lifelong battle with what he calls "the
panic fear which is inherent in the human condition."
Throughout most of his life he dutifully wrote a minimum
of 500 words a day. His manuscripts are filled with nota-
tions of word counts: the compulsive act of writing provided him with a sense of psychological equilibrium, but
he always had to be on guard for the next onslaught of the
demons of his youth and to defend against them with
another story, another novel, another trip to a dangerous
country to distract him from his plight. He developed an
addiction to writing: it became his drug of choice in escaping from the sense of reality he acquired under the
sinister influence of Lionel Carter, an unremarkable boy
except for his role in unwittingly helping to shape the
mind and soul of a distinguished writer.

. . . . .

The Last Word (1990) represents Greene's "last word" as
a writer of short fiction, and as such conveys a synoptic
view of the stages of his life as a writer. Many of the
stories, in fact, resemble sketches of atmosphere or character preliminary to the novels or memoirs he was writing
at the time.

The first story, **"The New House"** (1923), written during
his undergraduate days at Oxford University, is one of his
first stories to discard the heavy-handed trappings of allegory and melodrama for a realistic portrayal of an idealist
being corrupted by money. . . . **"Murder for the Wrong
Reason"** (1929) reflects Greene's interest in the dual
personality, a subject he explores in greater detail in his
retracted novel *The Man Within,* published the same year.
"The Lottery Ticket" (1938) shows Greene's engagement with the politics and violence of Mexico and anticipates his more comprehensive vision of that land in *The
Power and the Glory.* **"The News in English"** (1940) and
"The Lieutenant Died Last" (1940) reflect Greene's
patriotism and interest in espionage during the war. **"Work
Not in Progress"** (1955) and **"The Man Who Stole the
Eiffel Tower"** (1956) display his whimsical mode during
the time he was writing his comic masterpiece, *Our Man
in Havana.* **"An Appointment with the General"** (1982)
is a section of a novel abandoned in favor of a book-
length memoir, *Getting to Know the General* (1984).
Reminiscent of the melancholy comedy of the stories in
May We Borrow Your Husband?, **"The Moment of
Truth"** (1988) reflects the 83-year-old Greene's thoughts
about death. **"The Last Word"** (1988) is also about death,
but the melancholy and loneliness of the preceding story

is here replaced with a strong Christian faith that wel-
comes death as a release from a futuristic godless world.
In **"An Old Man's Memory"** (1989) Greene all but abandons the pretense of fiction to assume again the role of a
Jeremiah, predicting on a smaller scale this time, not the
end of Christianity, but the destruction of the Channel
Tunnel. Finally, in **"A Branch of the Service"** (1990), a
story published for the first time, Greene reverts to the
comic style of *Our Man in Havana* in depicting the absurdities involved in undercover operations.

"Murder for the Wrong Reason" appeared in three in-
stallments in the *Graphic* in October 1929. Although
Greene disparages and wishes he had suppressed his first
published (though third-written) novel, *The Man Within*
(1929), he has seen fit, after 60 years, to reprint the short
story he wrote at the same time, a story that embodies the
theme of the divided self he also explores in his novel.
The editor of the *Graphic* prefaces the story with the
following comment: "The young author of this story of
murder with an unusual twist in its detection won an
instantaneous success this year with his first novel, *The
Man Within,* and a brilliant future is predicted for him."

**Unlike the rather straightforward stories
he wrote during his years at Oxford,
"Murder for the Wrong Reason" is
overwritten, complex, and dependent
upon a surprise ending. It is a story that
requires at least two readings before one
can feel confident about understanding it.**

—Richard Kelly

Unlike the rather straightforward stories he wrote during
his years at Oxford, **"Murder for the Wrong Reason"** is
overwritten, complex, and dependent upon a surprise ending. It is a story that requires at least two readings before
one can feel confident about understanding it. The manner
in which the story was originally presented in the *Graphic,* with synopses of each preceding installment and with
illustrations of the various characters, significantly shaped
the readers' expectations and understanding of the action.
Both the synopses and the illustrations create, as will be
discussed shortly, plentiful red herrings that lead one to
misread the story and to have to backtrack.

Here is the synopsis that appears at the beginning of the
third installment:

> Detective Inspector Mason, entering the offices of
> Hubert Collinson with a search warrant, finds the body
> of its owner huddled in the swivel chair, with a knife
> in the heart. Mason telephones to Scotland Yard, and
> also summons a constable from a neighbouring beat.
> He tells the constable that Collinson had been a black-

mailer. Together they search for clues while awaiting the arrival of an able detective from the Yard. The constable finds a letter to the dead man signed "Arthur Callum." Mason says he knows Callum, who actually lives quite near. The constable, with visions of rapid promotion, asks his superior if they cannot pay a quick visit to Callum's flat before the arrival of the fast car from Scotland Yard. The Inspector re-reads the letter, and confronts Callum in the latter's flat. After fruitlessly interrogating him Mason leaves the flat, and on the stairs meets Rachel Mann, an ambitious actress who had become Collinson's mistress, though Callum had loved her and asked her to marry him. He tells her that the tragedy was her doing and goes into a reverie of the past. Returning to the scene of the crime he tells the constable that Callum is not the man they want, but promises him a spectacular triumph, saying that the air is full of clues. . . .

Among the five illustrations that accompany the story is a depiction of Mason's confrontation of Callum that shows the two men to be distinctly different. There is also an illustration of Mason's meeting with Rachel Mann outside Callum's flat. At the end of the story, however, the reader discovers that Rachel Mann has been dead for 10 years and that Mason's meeting with Callum and Mann occurs only in his mind and that Callum is, in fact, Mason's youthful alter-ego and not an actual character in the story. Both the synopsis and the illustrations, therefore, are red herrings designed to trick the reader, leaving him feeling cheated at the conclusion of the story.

In the final installment Greene reveals that Mason is himself the murderer. Mason melodramatically offers himself up for arrest by the constable, assuring the latter of his promotion. In retrospect, one realizes that Mason not only committed the murder but that he also set up the constable to "discover" the clues. Like Arthur Conan Doyle, Greene has Mason create the mystery and then urge the constable to solve it.

Mason/Callum could have killed Collinson years before "for the right reason"—jealousy over a woman. As it stands, he killed Collinson for "the wrong reason." As he says to the constable, "You don't see a jealous lover here, constable, only an elderly, corrupt police officer who has killed his blackmailer." Greene never makes clear why Collinson was blackmailing Mason nor how Rachel Mann died. At the beginning of the story Mason declares that "'Collinson deserved all that he got. Blackmail,' he added, 'and women.'" Clearly Mason's dealings with Collinson have involved these two separate issues, and the blackmail may have been about women, or a woman, or the death of a woman.

One of the ways in which Greene deals with the theme of the split personality is through the symbolism of a painting depicting the resurrection of Lazarus from the dead that hangs on the wall of Mason's/Callum's flat. The painting also appears in one of the illustrations. Mentioned several times throughout the story, the painting suggests the resurrection of Mason's dead, youthful self. Mason frequently speaks of his "private inquiries,"

which suggests not only his investigation into the crime but, more significantly, his introspective dialogues, his encounters with the man within. It may be that this interesting psychological subtext combined with an experimental detective story explains Greene's decision to include the story in this collection. Reading the story more than 60 years after he wrote it, Greene comments: "I found that I couldn't detect the murderer before he was disclosed. During those early years in the twenties and thirties I was much interested in the detective story (I even began *Brighton Rock* expecting it to be a detective story)."

During the winter of 1938 Greene spent five weeks in Mexico to undertake research for a book about the Mexican Revolution. Mexico was a dangerous country to visit at the time, for President Plutarco Elias Calles, in the name of his socialist revolution, was closing down the churches and exiling or murdering priests and practicing Catholics. Greene's brief visits, nevertheless, yielded three significant works: **"The Lottery Ticket"** (1938), a short story, *The Lawless Roads* (1939), an account of his travels through Chiapas and Tabasco, and *The Power and the Glory* (1940), one of his finest novels.

"The Lottery Ticket," though written in 1938, was not published until 1947, when it appeared in the *Strand Magazine* and *Cosmopolitan*. It was also included in Greene's collection, *Nineteen Stories,* which was published in England that same year. Curiously, Greene omitted the story from the American version of *Nineteen Stories* (1949) and from subsequent collections of his short fiction until the publication of **The Last Word** in 1990. Greene explains that he excluded the story from his earlier collection because "I thought then that there were too many echoes in it of *The Lawless Roads* and *The Power and the Glory*. Well, those two books today belong to an even more distant past, so I decided to give **'The Lottery Ticket'** a second chance."

Many of the details of setting and character in **"The Lottery Ticket"** are, indeed, reflected in *The Power and the Glory*: the seedy, derelict atmosphere of the Mexican towns, the omnipresent vultures waiting for another death, the roaches on the hotel walls, the banana plantations, the dentist, the fat chief of police preaching social progress, and the themes of fatalism and betrayal. Despite the evocative character of Mexico Greene develops in this story, it cannot compete with the fully realized character of the land he conjures in his novel.

Greene does not handle point of view in **"The Lottery Ticket"** with his usual skill. The story is basically told by an omniscient author. Nevertheless, Greene opens his tale with a first-person narrator who soon gives way to the omniscient author. After introducing Mr. Thriplow, an Englishman on holiday in Mexico who has just purchased a lottery ticket, the narrator comments, "I don't often believe in fate, but when I do I picture it as just such a malicious and humorous personality as would choose, out of all people in the world, Mr. Thriplow to fulfill its absurd and august purposes." There is no indication who this narrator is, and after the opening paragraph he simply recounts Mr. Thriplow's adventures.

Shortly after his arrival in a dirty and depressing village, Mr. Thriplow learns he has purchased a winning lottery ticket worth 50,000 pesos. Enjoying comfortable circumstances in England, he does not really need the money and feels ashamed at having won the lottery in the midst of so much Mexican poverty. To overcome the guilt of being a foreign exploiter and gringo, he goes to a bank and offers the money to the manager so that some good might be done with it locally. Perhaps the money could be used to establish a free library or a hospital. As he becomes involved with the Governor and the Chief of Police, however, Mr. Thriplow discovers his money will be used to "defeat reaction."

The Mexican state's view of social progress turns out to be quite different from that of Mr. Thriplow, whose British liberalism and naïveté lead to ironic consequences. It appears the money he turns over to the government is used to pay the wages of the police and the military. When Thriplow sees the government soldiers moving down the street to arrest another of the Mexican patriots, a defender of the church, he rushes to the rebel's house to warn him. The man's daughter answers the door and the dialogue that follows carries Greene's attack upon foolish British liberalism:

"It was you who gave the money, wasn't it?"

"It was, but you understand . . . no personal feeling. I am a Liberal. I cannot help sympathising with . . . progress."

"Oh, yes."

"I detest Fascism. I cannot understand how a patriot— I am sure your father is a patriot—could take arms from Germany, Italy . . ."

"What a lot you believe," she said with faint derision.

She then reveals to him that the soldiers have already carried off her father, presumably for execution.

This simple woman, a former nun, exhibits a political savvy and human understanding that overwhelms Thriplow in his moment of bitter disillusionment. Determined to make the affair easy for him, she asks for some money to help bury her father, saying, "You have done your best for us. You could go home quite happy. . . . I can see you are a kind man. Only ignorant . . . of life, I mean." With his innocence devastated, Thriplow's feelings turned to hate "for all who had so unexpectedly broken into his life, hate of the new ideas, new words. Hate increased its boundaries in his heart like an annexing army . . . and hate spread across Mr. Thriplow's Liberal consciousness, ignoring boundaries. . . . It seemed to Mr. Thriplow . . . that it was the whole condition of human life that he had begun to hate."

Like *The Power and the Glory,* this story has its clear-cut villains—the Chief of Police, the Governor, and the military—and its heroes—the executed patriot and his daughter. What complicates this story is the focus upon Mr. Thriplow. His presence diffuses the tension that should arise from the opposition between the government and the rebels, the hunters and the hunted, and shifts the reader's attention to his disillusionment. The damaged feelings of a British liberal on holiday in Mexico thus becomes more significant than the political and human fate of a nation and the Catholic church. Perhaps here is another reason why the story disappeared from the American edition of *Nineteen Stories* and failed to appear in subsequent collections until 1990.

Greene published two short stories during the war, **"The Lieutenant Died Last"** and **"The News in English,"** both of which show the British to be courageous opponents of the Germans. These tales might be read as simple morale boosters, as Greene's literary contribution to the war effort. He explains that he excluded them from *Collected Stories* not because he found them unworthy but because "Time (and with it Memory) passes with horrifying speed. How many people below the age of sixty would remember Lord Haw-Haw, whom I listened to nightly in 1940 on the radio, and understand the title and subject of '**The News in English**'? In that war, they might well ask, was it plausible for a squad of foreign soldiers to descend by parachute on an English village? None had occurred in the German war and we had been engaged in at least three conflicts since then. The questions are even more relevant today than in 1967, but I am taking the risk of reprinting them because I like the stories." For those under 60, Lord Haw-Haw was an Anglo-American named William Joyce who broadcast German propaganda in English from Berlin during the Second World War. He was captured by British soldiers in Germany in 1945, convicted of treason, and hanged.

"The Lieutenant Died Last," published in *Collier's* in 1940, is a whimsical tale about German parachute troops attacking an English village. While out poaching rabbits on Lord Drew's grounds in the small village of Potter, Bill Purves sees a small group of Germans parachute onto the field. While some of the soldiers round up the villagers and imprison them in the local tavern, Bill Purves engages the others in a gun battle and kills or wounds them. He then returns to the tavern, where the soldiers stationed there, seeing that Purves is armed, surrender to him. The narrator's conclusion to this tale displays a British pride and patriotism with a comic touch and a laconic hero. Despite his heroism, Purves is charged with poaching: "He was quite gratified: he didn't expect medals and as he said, 'I've got one back on them bloody Bojers.'"

An action-filled and humorous story, **"The Lieutenant Died Last"** also contains a brief note of seriousness. The wounded German lieutenant calls out to Purves to kill him. The narrator comments that "Old Purves always felt pity for broken animals, but he hadn't a bullet left." He then picks up the officer's revolver and kills him. Afterward he looks through the dead man's pockets and discovers a photograph of a naked baby on a hearthrug. His sense of humanity, suppressed during his battle with the Germans, overcomes him and he becomes sick to his stomach. Purves keeps this souvenir of his encounter with the Germans but never shows it to anyone. "Sometimes he took it out of a drawer and looked at it himself—uneasily. It made him—for no reason that he could understand—feel bad." The theme of pity, which became an obsessive one for Greene in his later works, surfaces even here, in this comic salute to British patriotism, and demonstrates that in Greene's mind pity transcends national boundaries.

"The News in English," published in the *Strand Magazine* in 1940, is one of Greene's earliest tales of espionage. Unlike his later spy novels, such as *Our Man in Havana* (1958), which satirizes the British Secret Service, and *The Human Factor* (1978), which makes a hero of a British traitor, **"The News in English"** celebrates the heroic patriotism of a British double agent.

Set during the Second World War, the story opens with Mrs. Bishop and her daughter-in-law, Mary, listening to a radio broadcast from Germany. The voice they hear on the radio is that of a typical English don who is proclaiming the resurgence of youth throughout the new Germany. Mrs. Bishop recognizes the voice as that of David, her son and Mary's husband. A mathematics don at Oxford, David was reported in the newspapers to have gone to Germany to evade military service, leaving his wife and mother to be bombed in England. At the time, Mary fought in vain with reporters, arguing that David must have been forced to leave England. Mrs. Bishop, however, condemns her son for his cowardice and betrayal while Mary persists in her attempt to make sense of his bizarre actions.

One evening during his broadcast David announces that somewhere back in England his wife may be listening to him: "I am a stranger to the rest of you, but she knows that I am not in the habit of lying. . . . The fact of the matter is. . . ." At that moment Mary suddenly realizes that her husband is speaking to her in code. When he was away from her on trips he employed a scheme whereby the phrase "the fact of the matter is" always meant "this is all lies, but take the initial letters which follow." Mary discovers that David is sending her details of Germany's military secrets.

Reporting this information to the War Office, Mary is told to keep David's subterfuge secret, even from his mother, otherwise his and many other lives will be lost. The War Office agrees to broadcast a message using the same code to Germany in the hope that David will hear it. The message explains how he can obtain a safe passage home.

Meanwhile, Mary must silently endure her mother-in-law's contempt for David. On his final broadcast, after reporting some military secrets, he says goodbye to his wife, indicating to her that he never received the War Office's message and that he is now lost to her forever. Mrs. Bishop exacerbates Mary's pain by commenting, "He ought never to have been born. I never wanted him. The cow-

ard," driving Mary to cry out, "if only he were a coward, if only he were. But he's a hero, a damned hero, a hero, a hero. . . ." Mary is left with an agonizing truth that she cannot reveal and looks to a future time when she can restore her husband's good reputation.

The painful note on which this story ends anticipates the conclusion of *The Human Factor,* where Castle, the British defector living in Russia, telephones his wife in England, knowing he will never be able to see her again. Castle's motivations for spying are complex and involve his loyalty to the Communists for helping to get his wife, a South African, out of her country. One of the problems with **"The News in English"** is that Greene fails to establish any motivation for David's presence in Germany. Since the War Office had no knowledge of his coded messages until Mary reported to them, David could not have been an official double agent. One can only assume that the newspaper reporters were right, that he left England to avoid military service. Once there, however, his conscience presumably led him to join the war effort by spying on the German military and hoping that his wife remembered their childish code. The story, unfortunately, does not make this very clear.

Lying behind the patriotism of this tale is Greene's obsession with the subject of divided loyalties, a subject dramatically fixed in his mind while at Berkhamsted School, where he had to deal with conflicting loyalties to his father, the school, and his peers. Greene later found a way of escaping the conflict and puts his solution forward through the character of Javitt, in **"Under the Garden":** "If you have to earn a living, boy, and the price they make you pay is loyalty, be a double-agent—and never let either of the two sides know your real name." David is Greene's first attempt to create such a character, but it would be many more years before Greene could flesh him out with complex and believable motivation.

The comic phase of Greene's career is represented in *The Last Word* by two stories that appeared in *Punch,* **"Work Not in Progress"** (1955) and **"The Man Who Stole the Eiffel Tower"** (1956). It was about this time that Greene was writing *Our Man in Havana,* a novel that captures a comic view of life that Greene, in his depressive mood, denied his previous heroes. His cocky state of well-being at the time is brilliantly embodied in the character of that novel's hero, James Wormold, a fellow with the unique sanity of the clown. Unfortunately, Greene's two pieces in *Punch* seem hollow when compared to that novel.

Conceived as a sketch for a musical comedy, **"Work Not in Progress"** offers this bizarre plot: a group of 12 Anglican bishops are kidnapped by 12 thugs who hope to steal their chasubles belonging to the Church of England. The thugs are so poorly educated they have mistaken the word "chasuble" for "chalice." After a successful kidnapping, the thugs put on the bishops' clothes. The ringleader and brains of the gang is a woman (the only woman in the cast), and she assumes the role of Archbishop of Canterbury. Meanwhile, the Archbishop of Melbourne, who has come to observe the convocation of bishops, attempts to track down the kidnappers. He locates them in Canterbury where, in the rose garden, he falls in love with the false Archbishop of Canterbury. Later the rest of the gang realize they have been betrayed by their leader and attack her. She is defended by the Bishop of Melbourne until the arrival of the true bishops in their underclothes scares away the impostors. The musical ends with the lovers singing a melodious duet and then heading off to live together in Australia.

Hardly up to the standards of W. S. Gilbert, this fantasy sketch of a musical comedy may have titillated some readers of *Punch* at the time but the piece does not hold up very well. It seems more suited now to undergraduate tastes that have come to savor the Monty Python brand of comedy. The slapstick humor of presenting 12 bishops running across the stage in their underwear and of having a female thug dress up like the Archbishop of Canterbury shows Greene shamelessly indulging in the pleasures of low comedy.

"The Man Who Stole the Eiffel Tower" opens with a riveting sentence and then lapses into disappointing frivolity: "It was not so much the theft of the Eiffel Tower which caused me difficulty; it was putting it back before anyone noticed." The narrator describes how he hired a fleet of trucks to carry the Eiffel Tower out of Paris to a quiet, flat field on the way to Chantilly. Having great affection for the structure, he is pleased to see it "after all those years of war and fog and rain and radar, in repose." Greene's anti-Americanism then surfaces as he has the narrator return to the empty site to enjoy the confusion of stupid American tourists. Finally, the narrator returns the Eiffel Tower before the employees who work there lose their wages.

The comic stories are the weakest in *The Last Word*. They are note especially funny, their humor is undergraduate and patronizing, they feature no notable characters, and their whimsy and fantasy are contrived.

—*Richard Kelly*

The comic stories are the weakest in the collection. They are not especially funny, their humor is undergraduate and patronizing, they feature no notable characters, and their whimsy and fantasy are contrived. Perhaps Greene had poured all of his comic genius into writing the novel *Our Man in Havana* (1958). In any event, one suspects he included the comic pieces in *The Last Word* to reflect what he calls his manic mood, the dynamic state of mind that gave birth to such brilliant comic characters as James Wormold (*Our Man in Havana*) and Aunt Augusta (*Travels with My Aunt*).

"An Appointment with the General" was originally published in 1982 under the title **"On the Way Back: A Work Not in Progress"** in *Firebird 1,* as part of a collection of fiction by contemporary authors. Greene's subtitle refers to the fact that this story is actually a chapter of an abortive novel that was to have been called *On the Way Back.* He conceived the idea of writing the novel in 1976, when he was invited to visit Panama as the guest of General Omar Torrijos Herrera. The invitation led to a curious friendship between the two men that lasted until the general's mysterious death in a plane crash in 1981. Greene eventually abandoned his novel *On the Way Back* in favor of writing a memoir of his friendship with Torrijos entitled *Getting to Know the General* (1984).

While being shown around Panama by the general's companion, a man named Chuchu, Greene picked up the title for his novel: "I heard Chuchu tell Captain Wong that we should see him again 'on the way back'—Captain Wong, the miraculous Christ, the Haunted House, all were promised on the way back and my projected novel with that title again emerged from the shadows. In my book the promised return would never be fulfilled—there would be no going back for my chief character." Later Greene entered a note in his diary for the new novel: "Start novel with a girl from a French left-wing weekly interviewing the General. She's escaping the pain of an unsatisfactory marriage in Paris and wants to avoid further pain. In the end she goes back to her pain and not to happiness."

Greene's note provides the outline for the surviving chapter **"An Appointment with the General,"** but in *Getting to Know the General* he tells Chuchu the plot of the rest of the novel. He believes that in telling the story to his companion he had no further need to write it: "it is a substitute for the writing." Greene's idea was to have the general assign Chuchu to show the French journalist around Panama. She and Chuchu fall in love but he is later killed by a bomb someone planted in his car. The general has the journalist flown back to Panama City by helicopter and she must see from the air all the places Chuchu promised they would enjoy on the way back.

"An Appointment with the General" opens with the French journalist, Marie-Claire Duval, awaiting her interview with Torrijos. She feels dislocated, not knowing the language and feeling threatened by the men, dressed in camouflaged uniforms and carrying revolvers, who stand around her. One of the men, Sergeant Guardián (drawn after Chuchu), announces in perfect English that the general will see her but she cannot bring her tape recorder into the interview. She thinks, "I'll have to trust to my memory, my damnable memory, the memory I hate."

The story then flashes back in time a month to the lunch she has with the editor of a left-wing French newspaper. Eager to discredit Torrijos, the editor praises Marie-Claire for her destructive interview with Helmut Schmidt and assigns her to interview the general. During the course of their conversation Greene makes it clear that the journalist will be no match for the general. She only knows French and English, knows little of geography, is dependent upon her tape recorder, and is psychologically flawed by a failing marriage. She accepts the assignment, in fact, to escape the memory of her loveless marriage.

The last section of the story focuses upon the interview, during which Guardián serves as the translator. Greene portrays the general as a wise, almost mystical figure, whose eyes are "laden with the future." In his quiet way, he undermines the destructive agenda of Marie-Claire. Her attempts to label him a Marxist or socialist are met with clever parables: "My General says the Communists are for a while traveling on the same train as he is. So are the socialists. But it is he who is driving the train. It is he who will decide at what station to stop, and not his passengers." Out of her own failed sexuality she desperately conjures up questions that would link the general's political power with sexual promiscuity: "What does he dream of? At night I mean. Does he dream of women. . . . Or does he dream of the terms he is going to make with the gringos?" "The tired and wounded eyes looked at the wall behind her," Greene writes. "She could even understand the single phrase he spoke in reply to her question. *'El Muerte.'* 'He dreams of death,' the sergeant translated unnecessarily, and I could build an article on that, she thought with self-hatred."

This story reflects Greene's own failed marriage and his hero-worshipping friendship with Torrijos. Like Marie-Claire, Greene enjoyed an exciting escape from domestic concerns upon receiving an invitation to meet with the general. It must have been an exhilarating experience for him to be taken into this leader's confidence, to be shown secret military plans, and be taken into the inner sanctum of political revolution. The character of Marie-Claire, however, not only embodies some of Greene's initial trepidations at meeting the general but serves to typify what Greene assumes are the Left's mistaken preconceived notions about Torrijos. Her vulnerability and weakness in the face of a third world savior mark her as one who, had the novel been completed, would have discovered the powerful inner resources of Greene's political hero. Ending as it does, however, the story merely sets up a straw-woman whose own decaying marriage leads her to self-hatred.

In **"The Moment of Truth,"** originally published in the *Independent Magazine* on 18, June 1988, the 83-year-old Greene turns his thoughts to the subject of death. He opens his story with a characteristically surprising simile: "The near approach of death is like a crime which one is ashamed to confess to friends or fellow workers, and yet there remains a longing to confide in someone—perhaps a stranger in the street." The hero of this story is Arthur Burton, a waiter in a London restaurant, who develops a fondness for an American couple, the Hogminsters, who, in appreciation of his solicitude, habitually sit at one of his tables.

A lonely man, Arthur lives in a small bed-sitting-room, and in the evenings enjoys a vicarious life by thinking of his various customers: dull married couples, young lovers interested only in each other, and, sometimes, married young women accompanied by older men. Arthur's sense of isolation is painfully exacerbated by his doctor's recent suspicion that he may have cancer: "the crime of death had touched him." Like a criminal, he becomes desperate to confide his illness in someone. Touched by the use of his first name and the smile of real friendship that he received from Mrs. Hogminster, he decides to make her his confidante before he returns to his doctor for the final results of his medical tests.

The next day he discloses only a small portion of his secret to her when he announces he will not be at the restaurant tomorrow because he has to go to the hospital for a checkup. The Hogminsters offer him some platitudes of reassurance and tell him they will return for another meal before they leave for America. On his day off, they add, they plan to take his earlier advice and shop at some men's stores in Jermyn Street. That night he has a dream about Mrs. Hogminster: "It was as though he had spoken to her and somehow she had given him words of sympathy which lent him courage to face his enemies, who were about to disclose the shameful truth."

The doctors inform Arthur that he does, indeed, have cancer and must be operated upon immediately. Although he is not frightened at the prospect of death, he wants "to share his knowledge and his secret with a stranger who would not be seriously affected like a wife or a child—he possessed neither—but might with a word of kindly interest share with him this criminal secret." Convinced Mrs. Hogminster is just such a woman ("he had read it in her eyes"), Arthur arranges to return to work in the hope of talking to her.

To his dismay, he discovers the manager has seated the Hogminsters at another table. When he goes over to speak with them he is disappointed at their failure to inquire about his health. All they talk about are the details of their shopping spree in Jermyn Street. Arthur excuses himself and goes into the kitchen in a state of depression: "He was going to say nothing to the manager: the next day he would simply not turn up. The hospital could inform them in due course if he were dead or alive."

Some moments later, however, the manager enters the kitchen and hands Arthur a letter from Mrs. Hogminster. Feeling immense relief, he reasons she could not discuss his secret in the restaurant for others to hear and therefore discreetly placed her inquiry and sympathy within this letter. He returns to the hospital for his operation and that night, before putting out the light over his bed, he opens and reads the letter. Mrs. Hogminster wrote: "Dear Arthur, I felt I must write you a word of thanks before we catch our plane. We have so enjoyed our visits to Chez Augustine and shall certainly return one day. And the Sales, we got such wonderful bargains—you were so right about Jermyn Street."

The droll humor of this story is reminiscent of Greene's tales in *May We Borrow Your Husband?*. And, as in the latter volume, the comic pathos is worked out within the confines of a restaurant, an establishment that Greene employs as a workshop for his imagination. The technique of a doctor giving a death sentence to his patient was employed much earlier in **"Under the Garden"** where, stirred by his diagnosis, Wilditch seeks wholeness by returning to his childhood. Now the older Greene depicts his hero's impending death as a crime, something too shameful to be told to one's family or friends, as if death were a conscious betrayal of one's communal bond, a betrayal that would inflict pain and elicit hopeless sympathy. The irony of Mrs. Hogminster's letter, however, amplifies the folly of Arthur's attempt to secure sympathy and encouragement from outside the circle of his family or friends. Greene makes it clear in his story that Arthur was in the habit of observing his customers superficially. Like the hack writer in **"The Invisible Japanese Gentlemen,"** Arthur fails to see what is really going on around him. Unlike the self-deluded writer, however, Arthur's failure to read the truth in Mrs. Hogminster's eyes leads to his utter disillusionment and desolation at the end of the story. The panic fear inherent in the human condition, from which Greene finds release through his writing, blossoms like a cancer in the moment of truth and disillusionment effected not by the doctor's diagnosis but by Mrs. Hogminster's letter.

"The Last Word," published in the *Independent Magazine* on 10 September, 1988, moves the subject of death beyond the dreary, localized confines of the preceding story to a futuristic brave new world where great spiritual heroism offers the hope of life after death. The last surviving Christian, an old man who turns out to be the last pope, has been living in a state of amnesia for the past 20 years, ever since he was shot during an assassination attempt. He is brought out of his humble apartment to meet the general of the new godless world union. He gradually recalls fragments from the past that reveal to him that he is indeed the pope, and he discovers that the general now plans to execute him.

As in *The Power and the Glory, The Comedians,* and *Monsignor Quixote,* Greene reverts to one of his favorite themes: the dramatic struggle between secular and spiritual power. Vaguely recalling Huxley's and Orwell's secular utopias, Greene's futuristic world boasts of peace through the elimination of poverty, nationalism, and Christianity. The general preserved the old man until he was sure that all of his followers were dead. On this occasion of their historical meeting, the general has the old man dressed in his formal papal robes, the clothes having been borrowed from the Museum of Myths. Over the years the old man has kept his Bible and a crucifix with one of Christ's arms broken off.

When the general tells the old man he feels sorry for his having lived so long in such dreary conditions, the man replies "They were not so dreary as you think. I had a friend with me. I could talk to him." The general, failing to understand the reference is to the broken Christ on his cross, protests that his men assured him the old man was living alone all those years. Upon learning that he will now be executed, the old man expresses his relief: "You will be sending me where I've often wanted to go during the last twenty years." "Into darkness?" asks the general.

"Oh, the darkness I have known was not death," says the old man. "You are sending me into the light. I am grateful to you."

As a symbol of final friendship between two born to be enemies, the general pours out two glasses of wine, a moment that suggests the Last Supper of Christ. The old man raises his glass as though in salute and says in a low voice some words in a language that the general cannot understand: "Corpus domini nostri. . . ." These are the words of the priest during the Communion service of the Mass. As the old man drinks his wine the general shoots and kills him. In this reenactment of the Last Supper, the old man presumably reverts to his former priestly duties and consecrates the wine as the blood of Christ. By shooting the old man (the pope, Christ's representative on earth), the general reenacts the combined roles of Judas and Pontius Pilate.

Greene adds a final paragraph to his story, however, that undermines the secular convictions of the general: "Between the pressure on the trigger and the bullet exploding a strange and frightening doubt crossed his mind: is it possible that what this man believed may be true?" This suggestion of a lingering doubt in the general's vision of a godless world seems totally unprepared for by the rest of the story. Greene seems to be reaching back a few years to *Monsignor Quixote* for his conclusion here. In that novel the representative of the Marxist state, the mayor, attends a final Mass said in pantomime by the dying Monsignor Quixote. Having no chalice or Host, Monsignor Quixote nevertheless places an imaginary wafer upon the mayor's tongue. The mayor, feeling the pressure, wonders later if he might not in fact have received Communion. Greene deftly leaves the Marxist mayor with a troubling ambiguity that suggests his capability for belief in God. The amicable relationship between the mayor and Quixote, however, is established throughout the novel, making its conclusion credible. The relationship between the general and the pope in **"The Last Word,"** on the other hand, is abstract and undeveloped, and the conclusion seems forced.

Greene would have done better to have followed the more rigid pattern of *The Power and the Glory.* Like the general of **"The Last Word,"** the lieutenant in *The Power and the Glory* has spent his life eradicating Christianity from his country. Also like the general, he is dedicated to eliminating the poverty and suffering of his people. What makes him so effective in his work is his total, unflagging belief in the rightness of his socialist program. Having brought about the capture and execution of the whisky priest, the lieutenant may miss his quarry but he entertains no misgivings about his faith in the secular state. Greene's general thus comes across as someone with an even grander accomplishment than that of the lieutenant—a worldwide socialist state—and on whose character Greene grafts the susceptibility of the genial Communist mayor from *Monsignor Quixote.* The hybrid character is not convincing.

"An Old Man's Memory" originally appeared in the *Independent Magazine* on 25 November, 1989. Although designated "a new short story by Graham Greene," the piece, less than a thousand words long, reads more like a dire warning to the English government about the potential for sabotage of the Channel Tunnel between Dover and Calais, scheduled for completion in 1994. The narrator of Greene's story, writing in the year 1995, announces that the year 1994 will never cease to horrify him: "The event of that year has a quality of nightmare about it—deaths in the darkness, in the depths of the sea, deaths by mutilation and drowning. The rotting bodies of the unrecognizable lie even today on both sides of the Channel."

The narrator (clearly no prophet) recalls Margaret Thatcher, having won her fourth electoral contest, greeting the French train as it comes up from the sea and halts at Dover to join the celebration. On the other side of the Channel the president of France awaits the British train, but it never arrives. Bombs have exploded under the Channel and the British train is destroyed along with the lives of all the people aboard it. Two years have passed since the disaster and the terrorists have not been identified or captured.

Greene borrows several details from recent terrorist activities to build his case for the dangers involved in the tunnel. Semtex appears to have been the explosive used in the tunnel and the narrator reminds us that in the late 1980s only 300 grams of Semtex were needed to blow up the Pan American plane over Lockerbie, Scotland. Now, he argues, explosives can be timed days, not hours, in advance.

The prime suspect, of course, is the IRA, but he also points to the Iranians, who had never forgiven England for its support of Salman Rushdie nor the Americans for having shot down their innocent airliner. There were, he observes, more Americans on board the train than there were English.

After noting the British and French governments' plan to reopen the tunnel by 1997, he concludes his account by predicting the public's reluctance to reenter the tunnel. Quite clearly Greene is here putting his fiction into the service of propaganda. Over the years Greene wrote hundreds of letters to newspapers and magazines in which he protested or criticized the actions of many governments and institutions. "An Old Man's Memory" is simply a more interesting form in which to cast his argument than the conventional letter to the editor. Several people in England had already pointed out the possibility that the IRA could blow up the tunnel. Greene's idea is not new, but the weight of his reputation as a novelist and his futuristic point of view perhaps give the story more political clout than a nameless activist could achieve in a television interview. But he does weaken the credibility of his narrator by having Margaret Thatcher still prime minister in 1995. The view of Westminster from Antibes had apparently grown somewhat hazy.

Published for the first time, **"A Branch of the Service"** is a comic account of an employee of a restaurant-rating association who is recruited by the Secret Service to eavesdrop on suspicious diners. Now retired, the narrator announces that he reluctantly left his profession because he lost his appetite for food.

Reminiscent of the professional eavesdroppers (and Greene himself) in the restaurants of Antibes (*May We Borrow Your Husband?*), the narrator observes his fellow diners with the analytical eye and ear of a writer. In one case his astute observation leads him to retrieve a cigarette containing some secret information of interest to the government. The cigarette leads to a new suspect, a doctor who had connections with the chemical industry, and the narrator is assigned to watch him. During the lengthy meal, however, the narrator is struck by diarrhea and after he returns from the toilet the doctor has vanished. Embarrassed by his failure, the narrator decides to retire.

Bathroom humor has a long tradition in England and Greene seems to delight in it. Years earlier in *Our Man in Havana* he drew a very funny scene in which the hero, James Wormold, is recruited into the Secret Service in a public toilet. Javitt, in **"Under the Garden,"** sits upon a filthy commode, and Beauty, the pampered Pekinese in **"Beauty,"** rolls in a clump of offal during an unscheduled spree.

FURTHER READING

Bibliographies

Cassis, A. F. *Graham Greene: An Annotated Bibliography of Criticism.* Metuchen, N.J.: Scarecrow Press, 1981, 401 p.
Thorough bibliography of works about Greene through 1979. Includes annotations and indexes.

Miller, Robert H. *Graham Greene: A Descriptive Catalog.* Lexington: University Press of Kentucky, 1979, 73 p.
Gives descriptions of the first editions of Greene's books, pamphlets, radio scripts, and letters in the collection of the University of Louisville.

Wobbe, R. A. *Graham Greene: A Bibliography and Guide to Research.* New York: Garland, 1979, 440 p.
Primary and secondary bibliography that covers publications and some manuscripts through 1976.

Biography

Sherry, Norman. *The Life of Graham Greene, Vol. 1: 1904-1939.* New York: Viking, 1989, 783 p.
Greene's authorized biography. This volume, the first volume in a projected two-volume work, details Greene's life from his birth through the beginning of World War II.

Criticism

Clarke, Peter P. "Graham Greene's 'The Destructors': An Anarchist Parable." *English Language Notes* XXIII, No. 3 (March 1986): 60-3.

    Relates historical anarchism to "The Destructors," focusing in particular on the theme of leadership in the story.

Colburn, Steven E. "Graham Greene's 'A Day Saved': A Modern Tale of Time and Identity." *Studies in Short Fiction* 29, No. 3 (Summer 1992): 377-84.

    Analysis of "A Day Saved," in which Colburn concludes that "more than in anything else he ever wrote, [this story] comes closest to dealing with the concerns of more recent novelists . . . in whose works questions of epistemology assume a central concern in the narrative structure."

Davidson, Richard Allan. "Graham Greene and L. P. Hartley: 'The Basement Room' and *The Go-Between*." *Notes and Queries* 13, No. 3 (March 1966): 101-02.

    Comparative review of L. P. Hartley's novel *The Go-Between* and Greene's "The Basement Room." Davidson states "Greene's story is thematically almost a microcosm of Hartley's novel."

Degan, James. "Memory and Automythography in Graham Greene's 'Under the Garden'." *Literature and Psychology* XXXX, Nos. 1-2 (1994): 81-107.

    Asserts "Under the Garden" is a mythic retelling of traumatic events from Greene's adolescence.

"Greene's 'The Hint of an Explanation.'" *The Explicator* XIX, No. 4 (January 1961): item 21.

    Brief commentary on "The Hint of an Explanation" in which the critic discusses the theme of evil in the story.

Farrelly, John. "Becoming Modesty." *New Republic* 120 (February 21, 1949): 25-6.

    Negative review of *Nineteen Stories* in which Farrelly calls Greene a "skilled professional entertainer" but faults his romanticism and his victimization of his characters.

Feldmann, Hans. "The Idea of History in Graham Greene's 'The Destructors'." *Studies in Short Fiction* 19, No. 3 (Summer 1982): 241-45.

    Discusses Greene's treatment of history in "The Destructors," stating that the story should be read "as a judgment on the condition of Western civilization, a judgment that reflects an unorthodox view of history."

Gorecki, J. "Graham Greene's 'The Destructors' and *Paradise Lost*." *Papers on Language and Literature* 21, No. 3 (Summer 1985): 336-40.

    Comparative analysis of "The Destructors" and John Milton's epic poem *Paradise Lost* in which Gorecki discusses the treatment of the theme of evil in each work.

Junker, Howard. "Greene's Grotesqueries." *Newsweek* 69 (May 8, 1967): 107.

    Negative review of *May We Borrow Your Husband?* Junker concludes: "What is sad about these desperate little fables is their reduction of Greene's dramatic, spacious novels, with all their melancholy music, to such tiny, tart grotesqueries."

Review of *The Last Word, and Other Stories,* by Graham Greene. *Kirkus Reviews* LVIII, No. 22 (November 15, 1990): 1556.

    Mixed review in which the critic identifies some outstanding stories in *The Last Word* but calls the rest "filler."

Kunkel, Francis L. "The Theme of Sin and Grace in Graham Greene." *Graham Greene: Some Critical Considerations,* edited by Robert O. Evans. Lexington: University of Kentucky Press, 1963, pp. 49-60.

    Examines the themes of grace, sin, and the flesh in Greene's novels and in the story "Visit to Morin."

Liberman, M. M. "The Uses of Anti-Fiction: Greene's 'Across the Bridge'." *The Georgia Review* XXVII, No. 3 (Fall 1973): 321-28.

    States "Across the Bridge" is an example of anti-fiction, a type of work in which the author interjects himself into the narrative in order to shatter illusion and comment on the writing of fiction.

Mayne, Richard. "Where God Makes the Scenery." *New Statesman* 66 (August 2, 1963): 144.

    Mixed review of *A Sense of Reality*. Mayne praises Greene's "immense power to master the reader's attention and to pervade his mind" but faults him for being too obsessive, mannered, and facile.

O'Brien, Conor Cruise. "A Funny Sort of God." *New York Review of Books* 20 (October 18, 1973): 56-8.

    Mixed review of *Collected Stories*.

O'Donoghue, Claire. "Greene's 'May We Borrow Your Hus-band?'" *The Explicator* 53, No. 3 (Spring 1995): 177-78.

    Suggests the equestrian imagery in "May We Borrow Your Husband?" reveals homosexual themes.

Pitts, Arthur W. "Greene's 'The Basement Room'." *The Explicator* XXIII, No. 2 (October 1964): item 17.

    Refutes critics who have interpreted "The Basement Room" solely as a theological tract.

Stinson, John J. "Graham Greene's 'The Destructors': Fable for a World Far East of Eden." *The American Benedictine Review* XXIV, No. 4 (December 1973): 510-18.

    Examines the elements of fable in "The Destructors," concluding the story provides "a parable-like comment on man's inborn depravity and the primacy of evil in the world."

Taylor, Marion A. and John Clark. "Further Sources for 'The Second Death' by Graham Greene." *Papers on English Language and Literature* 1 (1965): 378-80.

    Discusses biblical sources in "The Second Death," including the Gospel of St. Luke and the Gospel of St. Mark.

"Autumnal View." *Time* 84 (April 21, 1967): 104.

> Mixed review of *May We Borrow Your Husband?* that calls the stories mainly "down-to-earth escapist fare."

Wassmer, Thomas A. "Faith and Belief: A Footnote to Greene's 'Visit to Morin.'" *Renascence: A Critical Journal of Letters* XI, No. 1 (Autumn 1958): 84-8.

> Examines the speculations of character Pierre Morin on faith and belief in "Visit to Morin."

Willig, Charles L. "Greene's 'The Basement Room'." *The Explicator* XXXI, No. 6 (February 1973): item 48.

> Refutes critics who view "The Basement Room" as an examination of evil, stating that theme of the story could more accurately be described as "moral ambivalence."

Young, Vernon. Review of *Nineteen Stories,* by Graham Greene. *The Hudson Review* 2, No. 2 (Summer 1949): 311-18.

> Mixed review in which Young faults Greene's style, particularly his use of negative simile, but praises the author's depiction of English city life.

Zambrano, Ana Laura. "Greene's Visions of Childhood: 'The Basement Room' and *The Fallen Idol.*" *Literature/Film Quarterly* 2, No. 4 (Fall 1974): 324-31.

> Compares "The Basement Room" to Greene's film adaptation of the work, *The Fallen Idol.* Zambrano concludes that in the film, Greene "shifts his emphasis, making the formative pressure Philip experiences secondary to the problem of discovering truth."

Additional coverage of Greene's life and career is contained in the following sources published by Gale Research: *Concise Dictionary of British Literary Biography, 1945-1960; Contemporary Authors,* Vols. 13-16, rev. ed., 133; *Contemporary Authors New Revision Series,* Vol. 35; *Contemporary Literary Criticism,* Vols. 1, 3, 6, 9, 14, 18, 27, 37, 70, 72; *DISCovering Authors; DISCovering Authors: British; DISCovering Authors: Canadian; DISCovering Authors: Modules—Most-Studied Authors Module; DISCovering Novelists; Dictionary of Literary Biography,* Vols. 13, 15, 77, 100, 162; *Dictionary of Literary Biography Yearbook 1991; Major 20th-Century Writers; Something about the Author,* Vol. 20; and *World Literature Criticism.*

"Young Goodman Brown"
Nathaniel Hawthorne

The following entry presents criticism of Hawthorne's short story "Young Goodman Brown," first published in the April 1835 issue of *New England Magazine.* For further discussion of his complete short fiction, see *SSC,* Volume 3.

INTRODUCTION

"Young Goodman Brown" is widely regarded as one of Hawthorne's finest works. Drawing on Puritan theology and traditions of witchcraft, Hawthorne crafted a profound and complex work which has fascinated generations of readers with its portrayal of a self-deluded sinner and its ambiguous conclusion. It is typical of Hawthorne's fiction in its use of historical material, its allegorical mode, and its somber view of human nature. "Young Goodman Brown" is also important in the development of Hawthorne's fiction writing, for it prefigures many of the thematic concerns that are at the center of his novels, such as human depravity, religious doubt, secret guilt, and spiritual isolation. Critics note that this tale is integral to an understanding of Hawthorne's artistry, in that it displays the careful workmanship, rhetorical balance of style, clear narrative technique, and ambiguity of meaning which distinguish his best fiction. Although an early tale, "Young Goodman Brown" reveals the mastery which has led scholars to describe Hawthorne as one of America's most prominent and influential short fiction writers.

Plot and Major Characters

Set in seventeenth-century Salem, "Young Goodman Brown" tells the story of a naive and recently married Puritan who leaves behind his anxious wife, Faith, for a mysterious errand in the primeval forest. In a dreamlike sequence, Goodman Brown keeps an assignation with the devil, sees the shadowy figures of the colony's civil and religious leaders, and hears indistinctly the sorrowful voice of his wife. Maddened with despair at what he believes to be his wife's involvement with the devil, Brown tears through the forest and comes upon a witches' Sabbath where he finds commingled Salem's most revered saints, its most dissolute sinners, and his own wife. In this chaotic and lawless setting, the antithesis of the orderly world of daylight Salem, Goodman Brown recognizes within himself a dark propensity for evil. Urged by the devil to join the ungodly congregation, Brown at the last moment cries out to Faith to "resist the wicked one," and then finds himself alone in the cold night. At daybreak he returns to Salem a greatly changed man, convinced of the evil of others and of his own virtue for having resisted temptation. But this new understanding of his wife and neighbors only embit-

ters him, and he spends his days as a grim misanthrope. In the final paragraph, the narrator remarks that when Goodman Brown died, "they carved no hopeful verse on his tombstone; for his dying hour was gloom."

Major Themes

Hawthorne's contemporaries and modern critics have disagreed over the theme of "Young Goodman Brown" and what moral readers are to draw from their reading of the tale. Many have commented on Hawthorne's explorations of human psychology, particularly Brown's obsession with sin and guilt. According to these critics, Brown's inability to recognize his own participation in evil attests to his emotional immaturity, revealing as it does his severely limited view of human nature; even after his forest experience, he continues to deny the human potential for both good and evil. Others have focused on the sexual overtones of the story, and they interpret Brown's discovery of evil in the forest scene as his recognition and rejection of his own sexual nature. These critics point to the many sexual symbols in the tale, and they discuss the sexual implications of the devil's invitation to Brown to learn the deep mysteries of sin. Although he escapes the devil's snare and returns to Faith, with whom he begets several children, he is profoundly repulsed by his knowledge of sexual guilt; hence, he is unable to forgive Faith or the Salem villagers, whom he believes are debauched by their carnal appetites. Another group of critics have discussed "Young Goodman Brown" as a religious allegory, noting the paramount importance of Faith to Hawthorne's tale. In this reading, Brown's rejection of Faith—both his wife and his spiritual beliefs—and his subsequent fall into misanthropy reveals Hawthorne's sharp indictment of Calvinist theology. Brown, convinced that he is one of the Elect and thereby assured of salvation, discovers through his night journey the full import of Calvinist doctrine: man's natural condition is depravity, and thus all mankind deserves eternal damnation. Although critics continue to differ in their interpretation of the story's meaning, they concur that Brown's chief sins are his failure to understand the complexities of human nature and his lack of compassion for his fellow sinners.

Critical Reception

The vast number of studies (over 400) devoted to this one story attests to its popularity, but Hawthorne was himself uncertain how his tale would be received. Consequently, he passed over the tale twice when making selections for the 1837 and 1842 editions of *Twice-Told Tales,* although he did publish it in the relatively obscure *New England Magazine* in 1835. It was not until nearly twenty years after he wrote the story that he sought a wide readership for this story when he included it in *Mosses from an Old Manse* in 1846. Hawthorne's contemporaries gave the story a mixed reception; the majority of preferred the fanciful and lighter sketches in *Mosses from an Old Manse* and largely neglected the allegorical tales which Hawthorne's modern readers admire. Edgar Allan Poe, who had applauded the genius of *Twice-Told Tales,* deplored Hawthorne's reliance upon the allegorical mode in the later collection. Herman Melville, on the other hand, described "Young Goodman Brown" as a marvel, "deep as Dante." Modern criticism of the story has taken three principal directions and has varied in its response to the question of whether Goodman Brown's journey into the forest was an actual occurrence, a dream, or a Satanic trick. Early twentieth-century readers emphasized Hawthorne's treatment of the Puritan doctrines of sin and salvation, Hawthorne's obsession with evil, and the theme of sin and its blighting consequences. A second trend in interpretation of the story focused on its psychosexual elements, variously describing Brown as an Oedipal figure and Faith as representative of the ambiguity of womanhood. More recently, critics have explored Hawthorne's use of historical materials. In particular, scholars have examined Hawthorne's knowledge of and access to late seventeenth- and early eighteenth-century Puritan documents about theology, political history, and witchcraft. The most recent historical criticism of the story has noted that Hawthorne made use of details of the Puritan experience and incorporated

nineteenth-century views of gender relations as a way to examine his own culture's anxieties over theological, sexual, and moral issues. Despite these conflicting interpretations, scholars agree that "Young Goodman Brown" represents a significant achievement in Hawthorne's oeuvre and in the development of the American short story. With rare exception, critics have praised Hawthorne's mastery in exploiting his historical sources for their symbolic, psychological, and mythical possibilities. Critics continue to study "Young Goodman Brown" for its originality, its sophisticated narrative structure, its insight into the American experience, and its authentic exploration of humanity's moral condition.

CRITICISM

D. M. McKeithan (essay date 1952)

SOURCE: "Hawthorne's 'Young Goodman Brown': An Interpretation," in *Modern Language Notes,* Vol. LXVII, No. 2, February, 1952, pp. 93-6.

[*In the following essay, McKeithan observes that Hawthorne is more concerned with the demoralizing consequences of sin than with sin itself.*]

The majority of Hawthorne critics feel that **"Young Goodman Brown"** is one of the very best of Hawthorne's tales, but there is somewhat less certainty as to its meaning. The theme of the story has been variously stated as the reality of sin, the pervasiveness of evil, the secret sin and hypocrisy of all persons, the hypocrisy of Puritanism, the results of doubt or disbelief, the devastating effects of moral scepticism, or the demoralizing effects of the discovery that all men are sinners and hypocrites.

Mark Van Doren, in the fullest and most recent criticism [*Nathaniel Hawthorne,* 1949], gives a thorough analysis of the tale both as to its artistry and as to its meaning. I quote briefly from his discussion of its meaning:

> **"Young Goodman Brown"** means exactly what it says, namely that its hero left his pretty young wife one evening . . . to walk by himself in the primitive New England woods, the Devil's territory, . . . and either to dream or actually to experience (Hawthorne will not say) the discovery that evil exists in every human heart. . . . Brown is changed. He thinks there is no good on earth. . . . Brown, waking from his dream, if it was a dream, . . . sees evil even where it is not. . . . He had stumbled upon that "mystery of sin" which, rightly understood, provides the only sane and cheerful view of life there is. Understood in Brown's fashion, it darkens and sours the world, withering hope and charity, and perverting whatever is truly good until it looks like evil at its worst: like blasphemy and hypocrisy.

This survey of critical opinion is not complete, but it is all I have space for in this brief note. All of these interpretations are plausible, and a good case might be made for each. Some of them agree essentially, and the interpretation which I present below partly coincides with some of them, though it points out certain truths so obvious that I marvel at the critics' neglect of them.

At the end of Chapter VIII of *The House of the Seven Gables* Hawthorne discusses the effects on various types of mind of the discovery or suspicion that "judges, clergymen, and other characters of that eminent stamp and respectability, could really, in any single instance, be otherwise than just and upright men." But to those critics who think they have discovered in this or in similar passages the theme of **"Young Goodman Brown"** I would suggest that it would be more logical to look for the theme of **"Young Goodman Brown"** in **"Young Goodman Brown"** itself. One should carefully guard against reading into the story what is not there. Moreover, elsewhere Hawthorne frequently said that there is evil in every human heart (though evil impulses or desires may not lead to evil deeds), but he does not, in his own person, say so in this story, and that is not, I think, its meaning. The theme is Hawthorne's favorite one: sin and its blighting effects. Goodman Brown's sin is not identified, but its horrible effects are most impressively described. At the end of the story he is full of cynicism and moral scepticism; they are not his sin but merely its effects. The distinction, it seems to me, is essential to a correct interpretation of the story.

The theme of "Young Goodman Brown" is Hawthorne's favorite one: sin and its blighting effects.

—*D. M. McKeithan*

Goodman Brown is everyman of average intelligence who is striving to live the good life. For three months he had been married to a lovely young woman symbolizing religious faith. He was not loyal to Faith, though he fully expected to be loyal after just one more indulgence in sin. At some earlier time he had met Satan and had promised to meet him in the forest at night. It is doubtful that he recognized Satan at first, but he knew that his journey was an evil one, and his conscience hurt him because of his disloyalty to Faith. He had confidence in his ability to indulge in the sin—whatever it was—once more and then resist all future temptations. He did not know in advance how far into the forest he would be persuaded to go or what the results would be.

Faith urged him to postpone his journey until the next day, but he said it had to be made between sunset and sunrise. His heart smote him and he called himself a wretch to leave her on such an errand; be believed it would kill her to know what work was to be done that night—and it would have appalled him too if he had known. He thought of her as a blessed angel on earth and said, "After this one night I'll cling to her skirts and follow her to heaven." This "excellent resolve" did not prevent his making haste "on his present evil purpose." It is clear that before Brown had any suspicions concerning the sincerity of supposedly pious people—that is, before he had entered the forest—he was himself deliberately and knowingly indulging in sin, though with the intention of reforming soon.

In the body of the story Satan is the main speaker. In two disguises—first as the man with the serpent staff and second as the priest who presides at the meeting of sinners—Satan poisons the mind of Brown and destroys his belief in virtue and piety. But the reader should not make Brown's mistake: he should not suppose that Satan always speaks the truth—nor need he suppose that Satan always expresses Hawthorne's own opinions.

Satan denies the existence of virtue and piety in the world. It is a consequence and a punishment of Brown's sin that he believes Satan and thus becomes cynical. Hawthorne himself believed that evil impulses visit every human heart, but he did not believe that most men are mainly evil or that most men convert any considerable proportion of their evil impulses into evil deeds. In *Fancy's Show-Box* he said:

> It is not until the crime is accomplished that guilt clinches its grip upon the guilty heart, and claims it for its own. . . . In truth, there is no such thing in man's nature as a settled and full resolve, either for good or evil, except at the very moment of execution.

In short, Hawthorne himself does not share the black pessimism that finally came to Goodman Brown as a result of his sin. Hawthorne greatly admired many people with whom he was personally acquainted, and many good characters are pictured in his tales and romances.

Goodman Brown became cynical as a result of his sin and thought he saw evil even where none existed. This is not a story of the disillusionment that comes to a person when he discovers that many supposedly religious and virtuous people are really sinful; it is, rather, a story of a man whose sin led him to consider all other people sinful. Brown came eventually to judge others by himself: he thought them sinful and hypocritical because he was sinful and hypocritical himself. He did not judge them accurately: he misjudged them. The minister of Salem village, Deacon Gookin, Goody Cloyse, and Faith were all good in spite of what Goodman Brown eventually came to think of them.

Moreover, it is not necessary to choose between interpreting the story literally and taking it as a dream. **"Young Goodman Brown"** is an allegory—which is what Hawthorne meant when he suggested that it might have been a dream—and an allegory is a fictitious story designed to teach an abstract truth. In reality, Brown did not go into a forest at night nor did he dream that he did. What Brown did was to indulge in sin (represented by the journey into the forest at night—and of course the indulgence might have lasted much longer than a night: weeks, months, even years) under the mistaken notion that he could break off whenever he wanted to. Instead of breaking off promptly, he continued to indulge in sin longer than he had expected and suffered the consequences, which were the loss of religious faith and faith in all other human beings.

What Brown's sin was at the beginning of the story Hawthorne does not say, but it was not cynicism: at that time he was not cynical, although he was already engaged in evil dealings with Satan. Cynicism was merely the result of the sin and came later and gradually. By not identifying the sin Hawthorne gives the story a wider application. Which sin it was does not greatly matter: what Hawthorne puts the stress on is the idea that this sin had evil consequences.

Thomas E. Connolly (essay date 1956)

SOURCE: "Hawthorne's 'Young Goodman Brown': An Attack on Puritanic Calvinism," in *American Literature,* Vol. XXVIII, No. 3, November, 1956, pp. 370-75.

[*In the essay below, Connolly argues that Goodman Brown learns through his experiences that Calvinism is a faith which condemns its followers to eternal damnation.*]

It is surprising, in a way, to discover how few of the many critics who have discussed **"Young Goodman Brown"** agree on any aspect of the work except that it is an excellent short story. D. M. McKeithan [in "Hawthorne's Young Goodman Brown: An Interpretation," in *Modern Language Notes* LXVII, No. 94, February 1952] says that its theme is "sin and its blighting effects." Richard H. Fogle in ["Ambiguity and Clarity in Hawthorne's 'Young Goodman Brown,'" in *New England Quarterly* XVIII, December 1945] observes, "Hawthorne the artist refuses to limit himself to a single and doctrinaire conclusion, proceeding instead by indirection," implying, presumably, that it is inartistic to say something which can be clearly understood by the readers. Gordon and Tate assert, "Hawthorne is dealing with his favorite theme: the unhappiness which the human heart suffers as a result of its innate depravity" [Caroline Gordon and Allen Tate, eds. *The House of Fiction,* 1950]. Austin Warren [in *Nathaniel Hawthorne,* 1934] says, "His point is the devastating effect of moral scepticism." Almost all critics agree, however, that Young Goodman Brown lost his faith. Their conclusions are based, perhaps, upon the statement, "My Faith is gone!" made by Brown when he recognizes his wife's voice and ribbon. I should like to examine the story once more to show that Young Goodman Brown did not lose his faith at all. In fact, not only did he retain his faith, but during his horrible experience he actually discovered the full and frightening significance of his faith.

Mrs. Leavis comes closest to the truth in her discussion of this story in the *Sewanee Review* in which she says: "Hawthorne has imaginatively recreated for the reader that Calvinist sense of sin, that theory which did in actuality shape the early social and spiritual history of New England" [Q. D. Leavis, "Hawthorne as Poet," *Sewanee*

Review LIX, Spring, 1951]. But Mrs. Leavis seems to miss the critical implications of the story, for she goes on to say: "But in Hawthorne, by a wonderful feat of transmutation, it has no religious significance, it is a psychological state that is explored. Young Goodman Brown's Faith is not faith in Christ but faith in human beings, and losing it he is doomed to isolation forever." Those who persist in reading this story as a study of the effects of sin on Brown come roughly to this conclusion: "Goodman Brown became evil as a result of sin and thought he saw evil *where none existed*" [McKeithan]. Hawthorne's message is far more depressing and horrifying than this. The story is obviously an individual tragedy, and those who treat it as such are right, of course; but, far beyond the personal plane, it has universal implications.

> **"Young Goodman Brown" is obviously an individual tragedy, and those who treat it as such are right, of course; but, far beyond the personal plane, it has universal implications.**
>
> —*Thomas E. Connolly*

Young Goodman Brown, as a staunch Calvinist, is seen at the beginning of this allegory to be quite confident that he is going to heaven. The errand on which he is going is presented mysteriously and is usually interpreted to be a deliberate quest of sin. This may or may not be true; what is important is that he is going out to meet the devil by prearrangement. We are told by the narrator that his purpose in going is evil. When the devil meets him, he refers to the "beginning of a journey." Brown admits that he "kept covenant" by meeting the devil and hints at the evil purpose of the meeting.

Though his family has been Christian for generations, the point is made early in the story that Young Goodman Brown has been married to his Faith for only three months. Either the allegory breaks down at this point or the marriage to Faith must be looked upon as the moment of conversion to grace in which he became fairly sure of his election to heaven. That Goodman Brown is convinced he is of the elect is made clear at the beginning: ". . . and after this one night I'll cling to her skirts and follow her to heaven." In other words, at the start of his adventure, Young Goodman Brown is certain that his faith will help man get to heaven. It is in this concept that his disillusionment will come. The irony of this illusion is brought out when he explains to the devil the reason for his tardiness: "Faith kept me back awhile." That is what he thinks! By the time he gets to the meeting place he finds that his Faith is already there. Goodman Brown's disillusionment in his belief begins quickly after meeting the devil. He has asserted proudly that his ancestors "have been a race of honest men and good Christians since the days of the martyrs," and the devil turns his own words on him smartly:

Well said, Goodman Brown! I have been as well acquainted with your family as with ever a one among the Puritans; and that's no trifle to say. I helped your grandfather, the constable, when he lashed the Quaker woman so smartly through the streets of Salem; and it was I that brought your father a pitch-pine knot, kindled at my own hearth, to set fire to an Indian village, in King Philip's war. They were my good friends, both; and many a pleasant walk have we had along this path, and returned merrily after midnight. I would fain be friends with you for their sake.

Goodman Brown manages to shrug off this identification of his parental and grandparental Puritanism with the devil, but the reader should not overlook the sharp tone of criticism in Hawthorne's presentation of this speech.

When the devil presents his next argument, Brown is a little more shaken. The devil has shown him that Goody Cloyse is of his company and Brown responds: "What if a wretched old woman do choose to go to the devil when I thought she was going to heaven: is that any reason why I should quit my dear Faith and go after her?" He still believes at this point that his faith will lead him to heaven. The devil's reply, "You will think better of this by and by," is enigmatic when taken by itself, but a little earlier the narrator had made a comment which throws a great deal of light on this remark by the devil. When he recognized Goody Cloyse, Brown said, "That old woman taught me my catechism," and the narrator added, "and there was a world of meaning in this simple comment." The reader at this point should be fairly well aware of Hawthorne's criticism of Calvinism. The only way there can be a "world of meaning" in Brown's statement is that her catechism teaches the way to the devil and not the way to heaven.

From this point on Brown is rapidly convinced that his original conception about his faith is wrong. Deacon Gookin and the "good old minister," in league with Satan, finally lead the way to his recognition that this faith is diabolic rather than divine. Hawthorne points up this fact by a bit of allegorical symbolism. Immediately after he recognizes the voices of the deacon and the minister, we are told by the narrator that "Young Goodman Brown caught hold of a tree for support, being ready to sink down on the ground, faint and overburdened with the heavy sickness of his heart. He looked up to the sky, doubting whether there really was a heaven above him. Yet there was a blue arch, and the stars brightened in it." Here the doubt has begun to gnaw, but the stars are symbols of the faint hope which he is still able to cherish, and he is able to say: "With heaven above and Faith below, I will yet stand firm against the devil." But immediately a symbolic cloud hides the symbolic stars: "While he still gazed upward into the deep arch of the firmament and had lifted his hands to pray, a cloud, though no wind was stirring, hurried across the zenith and hid the brightening stars." And it is out of this black cloud of doubt that the voice of his faith reaches him and the pink ribbon of his Faith falls. It might be worthwhile to discuss Faith's pink ribbons here, for Hawthorne certainly took great pains to call them to our attention. The ribbons seem to be symbolic of his

initial illusion about the true significance of his faith, his belief that his faith will lead him to heaven. The pink ribbons on a Puritan lady's cap, signs of youth, joy, and happiness, are actually entirely out of keeping with the severity of the rest of her dress which, if not somber black, is at least gray. When the ribbon falls from his cloud of doubt, Goodman Brown cries in agony, "My Faith is gone!" and it is gone in the sense that it now means not what it once meant. He is quick to apply the logical, ultimate conclusion of Goody Cloyse's catechizing: "Come, devil; for to thee is this world given."

Lest the reader miss the ultimate implication of the doctrine of predestination, Hawthorne has the devil preach a sermon at his communion service: "Welcome, my children . . . to the communion of your race. Ye have found thus young your nature and your destiny." Calvinism teaches that man is innately depraved and that he can do nothing to merit salvation. He is saved only by the whim of God who selects some, through no deserts of their own, for heaven while the great mass of mankind is destined for hell. The devil concludes his sermon: "Evil is the nature of mankind. Evil must be your only happiness. Welcome again, my children, to the communion of your race." It is not at all insignificant that the word *race* is used several times in this passage, for it was used earlier by Goodman Brown when he said, "We have been a race of honest men and good Christians. . . ." After this sermon by the devil, Young Goodman Brown makes one last effort to retain the illusion that faith will lead him to heaven; he calls out: "Faith! Faith! . . . look up to heaven, and resist the wicked one." But we are fairly sure that he is unsuccessful, for we are immediately told: "Whether Faith obeyed he knew not."

Young Goodman Brown did not lose his faith (we are even told that his Faith survived him); he learned its full and terrible significance. This story is Hawthorne's criticism of the teachings of Puritanic-Calvinism. His implication is that the doctrine of the elect and damned is not a faith which carries man heavenward on its skirts, as Brown once believed, but, instead, condemns him to hell—bad and good alike indiscriminately—and for all intents and purposes so few escape as to make one man's chance of salvation almost disappear. It is this awakening to the full meaning of his faith which causes Young Goodman Brown to look upon his minister as a blasphemer when he teaches "the sacred truths of our religion, and of saint-like lives and triumphant deaths, and of future bliss or misery unutterable," for he has learned that according to the truths of his faith there is probably nothing but "misery unutterable" in store for him and all his congregation; it is this awakening which causes him to turn away from prayer; it is this awakening which makes appropriate the fact that "they carved no hopeful verse upon his tomb-stone."

Though much is made of the influence of Puritanism on the writings of Hawthorne, he must also be seen to be a critic of the teachings of Puritanism. Between the position of Vernon L. Parrington [in *Main Currents in American Thought*, 1927], who saw Hawthorne as retaining "much of the older Calvinistic view of life and human destiny," and that of Régis Michaud [in "How Nathaniel Hawthorne

Exorcised Hester Prynne," in *The American Novel Today,* 1928], who saw him as "an anti-puritan and prophet heralding the Freudian gospel," lies the truth about Hawthorne.

Thomas F. Walsh, Jr. (essay date 1958)

SOURCE: "The Bedeviling of Young Goodman Brown," in *Modern Language Quarterly,* Vol. XIX, No. 4, December, 1958, pp. 331-36.

[*In this essay, Walsh discusses the threefold symbolic pattern of Goodman Brown's experience in the forest which results in his surrender to despair.*]

Had Goodman Brown fallen asleep in the forest and only dreamed a wild dream of a witch-meeting?

The above question, found in the second to the last paragraph of Nathaniel Hawthorne's famous short story, **"Young Goodman Brown,"** has perhaps inspired more comment than any other sentence of the author's works. But it is futile to attempt to answer the question, especially since the author himself has intentionally avoided it. Yet most commentators have chosen between the two alternatives that Hawthorne has offered, and their choice determines the meaning they give to the short story: those who think that Goodman Brown's experience in the forest is not a dream say that he is the victim of an evil world in which he finds himself (such an interpretation makes Hawthorne more pessimistic than he is usually thought to be); those who think that Brown's experience is a dream put the responsibility for his despair, not on the world, but on him.

It is the purpose of this paper, which is more in agreement with the conclusions of the latter group, to show that Hawthorne's method in **"Young Goodman Brown"** is such that the tale's full meaning cannot be determined by the narrative itself, which would involve attempting to answer the author's question about Brown's experience in the forest. Rather, the reader must be conscious of a threefold symbolic pattern which objectifies Brown's subjective experience, thereby showing that it is he rather than the world who is responsible for his despair. The reader can never be certain about what actually happened in the forest; he can, however, be certain, not only of the nature and stages of Goodman Brown's despair, but also of its probable cause. And all this can be worked out from the symbolic pattern.

For an understanding of what happens to Goodman Brown the reader should be conscious of three sets of symbols: first, Faith, Brown's wife, represents religious faith and faith in mankind; second, Brown's journey into the forest represents an inward journey into the black, despairing depths of his soul; third, the devil represents Brown's darker, doubting side, which eventually believes that evil is the nature of mankind. The symbolic movement of the forest scenes is from the bosom of Faith to the loss of faith, which involves despair, from the village of belief to the depths of the forest of despair, and from a doubting balance of Brown's personality to the complete submergence of the brighter side into the darker side, which objectifies despair. The three sets of symbols tell the story of a man, young and naïve in the ways of the world, who, finding that men are not all good, became so convinced they are all bad that he could not remove the doubt of universal evil from his mind.

> The symbolic movement of the forest scenes is from the bosom of Faith to the loss of faith, which involves despair, from the village of belief to the depths of the forest of despair, and from a doubting balance of Brown's personality to the complete submergence of the brighter side into the darker side, which objectifies despair.
>
> —*Thomas F. Walsh, Jr.*

It is difficult to treat each set of symbols separately, so interlaced with each other are they, but first let us consider Faith, who, Hawthorne tells us, is "aptly named." Faith is symbolic of Brown's faith, which he gradually loses as he doubts more and more the existence of any goodness in man. The physical movement away from Faith, marking his own loss of faith, can be traced through the forest scene to the climax at the witches' gathering. Brown's feelings of guilt about his movement away from his wife help to underscore the psychological turmoil involved in the process. He is conscious of the dangers of the mission but is impelled onward by the thoughts of evil which hold him fascinated until it is too late to turn back to his wife and so to faith.

Tracing this symbol through, we note that as Goodman Brown enters the forest, he salves his guilty conscience with the "excellent resolve" that he will cling to Faith's skirts forever after this night. When he meets the devil, he tells him that "'Faith kept me back awhile'." As he proceeds deeper into the forest, his conscience continues to disturb him: at one point he bemoans the fact that his action will break Faith's heart, while at another point he asks himself why he should quit his Faith. But nevertheless he moves on, going deeper and deeper until his very senses play tricks on him. He tries to reassure himself against overwhelming doubts by looking to the sky; he beguiles himself that he is safe as long as he has the blue heavens and Faith.

But one cannot contemplate such thoughts about evil, which by their very nature undermine all belief, and at the same time keep one's faith. Goodman Brown tries and becomes a man who leans too far over the edge of a pit. Thus the heavens darken and the symbolic pink ribbon makes him cry out in realization, "'My Faith is gone!'," as truly it is, and he wildly laughs in his despair. The storm in his soul and in the forest rises, and he stumbles into the heart of the forest depths where there is symbolically represented the complete perversion of all that he once held dear. As Richard Harter Fogle points out, all the external manifestations of his faith are turned upside down: "The Communion of Sin is, in fact, the faithful counterpart of a grave and pious ceremony at a Puritan meetinghouse. . . . Satan resembles some grave divine, and the initiation into sin takes the form of baptism" [*Hawthorne's Fiction: The Light and the Dark,* 1952]. And as the external evidences of his religion are perverted, so, climactically, is his very faith, which is symbolized by his discovering his wife in the unholy communion. He has despaired, believing all men are depraved and religion a sham.

Second, there is the journey into the black depths of Young Goodman Brown's soul, paralleled by his journey into the dark undergrowth of the forest. When he enters the forest, we are told, "He had taken a dreary road, darkened by all the gloomiest trees of the forest, which barely stood aside to let the narrow path creep through, and closed immediately behind. It was all as lonely as could be. . . ." This act is symbolic of what he is doing: he is plunging into the road leading to despair, and the immediate closing of the trees symbolizes the shutting off of his escape. He is alone, cut off from humanity with but one companion, the devil, his own evil genius. The farther he goes, the more hopeless his plight becomes; even Brown realizes it:

> "Friend," said the other, exchanging his slow pace for a full stop, "having kept covenant by meeting thee here, it is my purpose now to *return* whence I came. I have scruples touching the matter thou wot'st of."

> "Sayest thou so?" replied he of the serpent, smiling apart. "*Let us walk on,* nevertheless, reasoning as we go; and if I convince thee not thou shalt turn back. We are but a *little way* in the forest yet."

> *"Too far! too far!"* exclaimed the goodman, *unconsciously resuming* his walk.

The italics are mine and indicate how the physical journey into the forest is related to the devil's growing power over Goodman Brown's soul and to Brown's realization of what he is doing. He knows he has gone too far, but he does not turn back. In the established pattern, he walks on, and the devil talks persuasively: "They continued to walk onward, while the elder traveller exhorted his companion to make good speed and *persevere in the path.* . . ."

It is not long until the forest is darkened by the black cloud with its attendant voices, symbolizing Brown's doubt-tortured soul as he cries in despair: "'Faith!' shouted Goodman Brown, in a voice of agony and desperation; and the echoes of the forest mocked him, crying, 'Faith! Faith!' as if bewildered wretches were seeking her all through the wilderness." Then we are told, "The road grew wilder and drearier and more faintly traced, and vanished at length, leaving him in the heart of the dark wilderness, *still rushing onward* with the instinct that guides mortal man to evil."

This scene is Hawthorne's finest bit of writing in the story, making the following scene in the heart of the forest almost anticlimactic. The point of view throughout is consistent and clear. It is Brown who sees and doubts and hears and thinks he hears. We, the readers, see both him and the innermost depths of his soul.

Third, Young Goodman Brown moves from a state of belief, in which the good and naïve side of his nature predominates, to a state of despair, in which the good side becomes submerged in the dark side, symbolized by the devil. The black man Brown meets in the forest is the dark side of his own nature objectified. What this man suggests and reveals to him are his own thoughts, which gradually possess him completely.

We are told not only that Goodman Brown looks like the devil, but that so too do his father and his grandfather. This family identification with the devil, together with the stages by which Goodman Brown comes to believe that his fellow men are evil, becomes most important to an understanding of the beginnings of the dark thoughts which eventually overpower him. The first people who are mentioned with reference to sin are his father and grandfather. Early in his journey Brown protests,

> "My father never went into the woods on such an errand, nor his father before him. We have been a race of honest men and good Christians since the days of the martyrs; and shall I be the first of the name of Brown that ever took this path and kept—"

There Brown echoes the good report he might have heard from anyone in the village; but the devil, representing the evil doubts in his mind, rejoins with,

> "I helped your grandfather, the constable, when he lashed the Quaker woman so smartly through the streets of Salem; and it was I that brought your father a pitch-pine knot, kindled at my own hearth, to set fire to an Indian village, in King Philip's war."

The facts concerning the persecution of the Quakers and the Indians Goodman Brown must certainly have known before, although in the past he might never have allowed himself to think of them in relation to sin. But what is most interesting, of all those who are mentioned and revealed by the devil, his father and grandfather have in their history that which would make one suspect that they were of the devil's party. Thus, Goodman Brown, having sinned himself or at least realizing his own potentiality for sin, makes the mistake of identifying himself, as the resemblance of three generations of Browns to the devil shows, with his ancestors in a sort of heredity of sin. Behind it all we can see the author brooding over his own ancestors, for, like Goodman Brown's father and grandfather, William Hathorne persecuted both Indians and Quakers, leading two hundred of the former into slavery after killing another eight and ordering Anne Coleman and four of her Quaker friends whipped through Salem, Boston, and Dedham.

From doubts, then, about himself and his ancestors, who show evidences of being evil, Goodman Brown moves to those whose lives are, on the surface of things, uncorrupt. But in his naïveté he begins to suspect that all men are intrinsically evil, even if they are respected members of the community, as were his father and grandfather. Doubts about his ancestors spread, until Goody Cloyse, Deacon Gookin, the parson, and finally Faith herself fall victims to his diseased mind.

The symbolic representation of such increasing doubts is given in the sequence with the devil. The devil is Brown, father, grandfather, all rolled into one, the exact counterpart of Faith, Brown's heavenly side. He is Brown's darker side, which believes that evil is the nature of man. In the forest the dark side of Brown's nature overcomes the good side. We notice that when Brown conjectures about the proximity of the devil, he appears as if he sprang from Brown's very being:

> and he glanced fearfully behind him as he added, "What if the devil himself should be at my very elbow!"

> His head being turned back, he passed a crook of the road, and, looking forward again, beheld the figure of a man, in grave and decent attire, seated at the foot of an old tree.

The devil not only looks like the Browns, but he is distinguished by a diabolic *laughter* and a *staff*. We are told that the devil discoursed "so aptly that his arguments seemed rather to spring up in the bosom of his auditor than to be suggested by himself." Brown continues on until the ribbon scene. Then the cry of despair—but note its form: "And, maddened with despair, so that he *laughed* loud and long, did Goodman Brown grasp his *staff* and set forth again, at such a rate that he seemed to fly along the forest path rather than to walk or run."

The submergence is now complete. Brown's dark nature has wholly enveloped his good. He is a devil with a devil's *laughter* and a devil's *staff*. If this were not enough, Hawthorne, describing Brown in the forest, tells us, "But he was himself the chief horror of the scene," which stresses the inward symbolic significance of Brown's experience, thereby emphasizing the fact that the cause of Brown's despair is from within, not from without. Such an interpretation is firmly clinched by the following: "The fiend in his own shape is less hideous than when he rages in the breast of man. Thus sped the demoniac on his course. . . ." And finally, we are not surprised to hear the devil say, "'Evil is the nature of mankind'," which is nothing more than an echo, in a forest of echoes, of the demon-like Brown's, "'There is no good on earth; and sin is but a name. Come, devil; for to thee is this world given'."

What actually happened in the forest must remain, as Hawthorne chose to put it, a question. What happens once Goodman Brown emerges from the forest is clear enough:

Goodman Brown lived and died an unhappy, despairing man. These clear facts imply that Brown did enter the forest. The reader, following the narrative line of the story, then asks what happened in the forest. But Hawthorne asks the same question himself, which suggests that it is futile to examine the facts of the narrative to determine the meaning of the story.

The only solution to the problem lies in the tale's complex symbolic pattern. We are sure that on the physical level Goodman Brown emerged from the dark wilderness to live the rest of his dismal life in his community. We are also sure from the threefold symbolic pattern that Brown never emerged from the forest depths of despair. And from the identification of the Brown family with the devil we can reach to the origins of that despair: we see a man who began to doubt, with some reason, the goodness of his own family, which led him to doubt the goodness of all men, until he concluded that, "Evil is the nature of mankind," words uttered by the devil, who represents the dark side of Brown's nature. Hawthorne has shown symbolically not only what happened to a man's soul, but why it happened. His handling of his symbols is expert, subtle, and brilliant enough to dispose the reader to overlook whatever narrative deficiencies there may be.

Paul W. Miller (essay date 1959)

SOURCE: "Hawthorne's 'Young Goodman Brown': Cynicism or Meliorism?" in *Nineteenth-Century Fiction,* Vol. 14, No. 1, December, 1959, pp. 255-64.

[*In the following essay, Miller contends that Goodman Brown is not meant to be representative of all humanity, and therefore Hawthorne's story is not as pessimistic as is commonly perceived.*]

Critics have agreed that Young Goodman Brown, in the course of the Hawthorne story of the same name, moves from a state of simple faith in God and his fellow man to an evil state involving damnation, or at least soul jeopardy. They have also generally implied that as well as being an individual, Young Goodman Brown is in some sense intended to be a type. They have not generally indicated, however, whether they think he is intended to typify all mankind or only one segment of it. This question is important, it seems to me, because on the answer one gives to it depends one's understanding of Hawthorne's view of man when he wrote the story, as well as one's interpretation of this enigmatic but nonetheless fascinating tale.

If, on the one hand, Young Goodman Brown is intended to represent all mankind, Hawthorne himself must be regarded, at the time of composition of this story, as a totally cynical man, obsessed with the notion that even the best of men are but whited sepulchres, unable either to save themselves or to find salvation through divine grace. But if, on the other hand, Young Goodman Brown is intended to represent only a certain segment of mankind, his creator must be viewed as much less pessimistic than the alternative interpretation would suggest.

If it is concluded that Young Goodman Brown's condition is not intended to represent that of all mankind, it remains to be considered whether such men as Brown are doomed by their nature alone to separation from God and man, or whether the kind of society in which they live is an important factor in this separation. If the latter—and if it be granted that in Hawthorne's view, the individuals who comprise society are in a measure free to alter it—it may be concluded that the story, though pessimistic so far as the fate of Young Goodman Brown is concerned, need not be so regarded as it relates to the Young Goodman Browns of the future. On the contrary, it might be regarded as melioristic in outlook, anticipating the dawning of a new and better day.

There remains to be considered an alternative to both possibilities of interpretation mentioned above. It is embodied in Henry James's conclusion that

> the magnificent little romance of *Young Goodman Brown* [sic], for instance, evidently means nothing as regards Hawthorne's own state of mind, his conviction of human depravity and his consequent melancholy; for the simple reason that if it meant anything, it would mean too much [*Hawthorne,* 1887].

This is to say, in effect, that the picture of mankind painted in **"Young Goodman Brown"** is so dark that it cannot reflect Hawthorne's view accurately. Consequently it must be viewed simply as an exercise in the free play of the imagination.

James's interpretation of Hawthorne's tale is convenient. It spares the reader the necessity of raising certain disturbing questions, such as the following: Did Hawthorne mean, in **"Young Goodman Brown,"** that the most pious-seeming of men, along with the grossest sinners, are absolutely depraved? If he did, how can his view of mankind here be squared with the views he expressed in *The Scarlet Letter,* where the scarlet letter itself becomes a symbol of natural virtue annealed by human suffering, or in *The House of The Seven Gables,* where humanity is represented by the virtuous if faltering Clifford and Hepzibah Pyncheon as well as by that melodramatic quintessence of evil, the Judge?

At the same time one is impressed with the convenience of James's approach one is led to question its correctness. For unless a story is light and frivolous, one expects the critic who finds it difficult to interpret either to discover a meaning in it, or dispraise it finally as inferior art. James, however, does neither. He is far from defining the story's tone as frivolous, he professes himself unable to find a serious meaning in it, yet he does not dispraise it. Instead he attempts to remove the story from the realm of serious art by asserting it was inspired by the "moral picturesqueness" of "the secret that we are really not by any means so good as a well-regulated society requires us to appear." James seems to mean here that Hawthorne, in writing

"Young Goodman Brown," was not interested in revealing a truth, but in achieving a poetic effect based on the paradoxical existence among men, of evil in the guise of good.

Whether or not James is right here would seem to depend on the degree of seriousness and conviction one finds in the story. If, after finishing it, one thinks of Young Goodman Brown only as a shadowy figment of the imagination, one is perhaps justified in regarding his story as a hypothetical or speculative tale. But if, like the present reader, one conceives of Brown as only a little less real than Hamlet or Othello and much more real than such characters as Hawthorne's Mrs. Bullfrog or Ethan Brand, if one shudders with Brown at the impalpable menace of the forest, and if, after finishing the story, one is drawn to dark speculation on Brown's soul state at death, one would seem obliged to take the story seriously, to try to pluck out the heart of its mystery.

Whether or not Young Goodman Brown is intended to represent all mankind would appear to depend upon whether or not the author has included in the story a representative sample of mankind, and if so, upon whether Young Goodman Brown is himself representative of that sample. If there were not a fair sample of mankind in the story, Brown would not of course be representative of all mankind, even though everyone else in the story might closely resemble him in essentials.

To put the matter specifically, if it be granted that Young Goodman Brown in the course of the story moves from a state of simple faith to an evil state, and if the story suggests—as Brown himself suspects—that the other characters of the story, as representatives of all mankind, have gone through a similar experience, it will appear that Young Goodman Brown, in the essential matters of the spirit, is representative of all mankind. But if, on the other hand, it be concluded that owing to the Devil's deluding him with false imaginings in the forest, or showing him a sample of mankind which is not truly representative, Young Goodman Brown's suspicions about the world are not justified, then it will follow that Brown himself is not representative of all mankind, but only of some vile, suspicious portion of it.

Among recent critics who conclude that **"Young Goodman Brown"** views all human nature skeptically, is Richard Fogle. He writes apropos of this tale: "Hawthorne wishes to propose, not flatly that man is primarily evil, but instead the gnawing doubt lest this should indeed be true" [*Hawthorne's Usable Truth,* 1949]. In Fogle's view, then, Brown would be representative of all mankind as well as of the other characters in the story.

[D. M. McKeithan, in "Hawthorne's 'Young Goodman Brown': An Interpretation," in *Modern Language Notes* LXVII, No. 94, February 1952] presents a view of the story very different from Fogle's. He writes:

> This is not the story of the disillusionment that comes to a person when he discovers that many supposedly religious and virtuous people are really sinful; it is,

rather, a story of a man whose sin led him to consider all other people sinful. . . . He did not judge them accurately: he misjudged them.

In other words, Young Goodman Brown does not even come near to being a representative of all mankind. Like a mirror with wavy lines in it, he perversely reflects the world as the world is not. In this view, **"Young Goodman Brown"** is the story of a warped and twisted psyche atypical of mankind in general.

One may be drawn to a conclusion very like McKeithan's without accepting all the evidence he adduces to support it. One may agree, for example, that Faith retains her virtue in the story. Even Goodman Brown, suspicious as he is, has no proof to the contrary, as the narrator makes clear: "Whether Faith obeyed [Goodman Brown's plea to 'look up to heaven, and resist the wicked one'] he knew not." And the narrator's description of Faith the next morning, "bursting into such joy at sight of him [Brown] that she skipped along the street and almost kissed her husband before the whole village," would certainly suggest that she had summoned the strength to heed her husband's plea. Joy such as Faith showed that morning would seem to be a more natural consequence of resisting temptation than yielding to it, especially with the stakes so high.

There may be some doubt in one's mind, though, whether Brown was as wrong in his judgments concerning the minister of Salem village, Deacon Gookin, and Goody Cloyse, as he was about Faith. For it appears from the story that all three, in contrast to Faith, were of Satan's party even before the forest meeting. Only Faith and Brown himself are referred to as "the converts." It is at this point that an important ambiguity arises, not of the both/and, but of the either/or variety. How do we know whether the figures Young Goodman Brown sees in the forest—the figures of the minister, the deacon, the other citizens of Salem village and of the state of Massachusetts, and Faith herself—are genuine witches, or merely specters of truly virtuous townspeople conjured up by the Devil? They cannot be both at the same time. The same sort of problem faced Hamlet when confronted by his father's ghost, but Brown, unlike Hamlet, simply ignores the problem, leaving it to haunt his interpreters.

In the absence of any final answer to this problem, I conclude that the witches Goodman Brown saw were genuine. Even Faith was a witch. . . . She had been tempted by Satan; then, yielding initially to temptation much as Brown himself had done, suffered herself to be conveyed to the Witches' Sabbath to conclude her pact. Faith's pink ribbon which Goodman Brown sees fluttering down in the forest is the confession of her initial yielding. But Faith's confession also serves as a means of grace. Openly signifying that she still delights in the beautiful things of this world, that she is still vain of her appearance, that the whiteness of her angelism is still mixed with the crimson of her passion for Young Goodman Brown, the pink ribbons keep Faith humble and honest, and thus contribute to her ultimate preservation from the Evil One. Even so, for

the duration of her stay in the forest, Faith remains a "witch."

Why do I conclude that the other figures Goodman Brown saw in the forest were also "real" witches? Principally because none of them had ever made any public confession of sin, failure to do which is a dangerous sign in any human being. The proof that they had never admitted to human frailty was Brown's trauma on discovering their guilt. In public the minister "mediate[d] his sermon," Deacon Gookin prayed "holy words," and Goody Cloyse "catechiz[ed]." None of them showed any signs of frailty corresponding to the pink ribbons of Faith, those efficacious talismans that confess one is still earthbound even though one's aspiration is heavenward. Nor did any of them confess, as Faith confessed, to "being troubled with such dreams and such thoughts that she's afeard of herself sometimes." The minister, Deacon Gookin, and Goody Cloyse were the "unco' guid, or the rigidly righteous" of Salem village, and as such were likely candidates for Satan's party.

> **Faith retains her virtue finally, and Brown is consequently wrong in continuing to view that part of humanity which Faith represents with suspicion. Brown is not representative of all mankind, and consequently the story is not totally pessimistic.**
>
> —*Paul W. Miller*

In other terms, they were pharisees, and their pharisaism led them to hypocrisy. Obeying the letter of the law, they kept from others, and perhaps themselves as well, the sobering fact that, being human, they were unable to follow perfectly the spirit of the law. They fell far short of the ideal expressed elsewhere by Hawthorne: "Be true! Be true! Be true! Show freely to the world, if not your worst, yet some trait whereby the worst may be inferred" [*The Scarlet Letter*].

To summarize, then, although one might reject some of the evidence on which McKeithan's conclusions are based, one might accept at least part of his evidence and conclusion: namely that Faith retains her virtue finally, and that Brown is consequently wrong in continuing to view that part of humanity which Faith represents with suspicion. In this view, Brown, as McKeithan asserts, is not representative of all mankind, and consequently the story is not totally pessimistic.

In apologizing for Brown's misanthropic view of mankind, one might argue that it was an easy step from the observation that all but one at the Witches' Sabbath were corrupt, to the conclusion that all at the Witches' Sabbath, indeed all mankind, were corrupt. And it would be especially easy for Brown, after discovering that some he had regarded as at least as virtuous as Faith had made a pact with the Devil, to come to the conclusion that Faith also had fallen.

At the same time one understands why Brown came to these conclusions, one must recognize that there was no valid reason for his coming to them. As long as his wife Faith gave signs of being faithful, Brown should not have despaired. Even if Faith herself had yielded to the Devil (I speak of Faith now as his wife rather than as a personified abstraction), Brown should have cast his net more widely in Salem village and beyond it in his search for virtue. He should have reckoned with the possibility that somewhere in Salem village, or at least beyond its narrow confines, there might be men neither "famous for their especial sanctity" nor "given over to all mean and filthy vice, and suspected even of horrid crimes." For it is worth noting that all of those Brown observes at the Witches' Sabbath fall into one or the other of these categories. Brown should have considered the possibility that the man who confesses his virtue is mixed with vice may possess not only humility, but true virtue as well, insofar as virtue is a plant that grows on mortal ground.

Having concluded that Brown's misanthropic view of all mankind is unjustified, and consequently that Brown, in his own devotion to evil, is not representative of all mankind, one may ask what portion of mankind he does represent.

The answer, I think, is that he represents those weaker members of a puritanical society who are traumatized, arrested in their spiritual development, and finally destroyed by the discovery that their society is full of "whited sepulchres." Others in such a society, with more strength but less moral sensitivity than Brown, recognize the power of hypocrisy to give the appearance of virtue (the *sine qua non* of success), and capitalize on this discovery to rise to the highest positions of secular and religious authority. Then there are those few hardy souls, who, like Faith, with difficulty preserve their virtue by letting a tincture of their vice be displayed on their breastplate of righteousness.

Hawthorne stands in this story, then, as an analyst and critic of the society that demands so much of a man that he can achieve what is demanded only through hypocrisy, and that blinds itself so thoroughly to the power of sin in the lives of even its best men that it denies them the ritual and balm of public confession.

Other critics have noted Hawthorne's concern with the moral rigorism of Puritanism. Vladimir Astrov, for example, comparing Hawthorne with Dostoevski writes [in "Hawthorne and Dostoevski as Explorers of the Human Conscience," in *NEQ* XV, June 1942]:

> . . . Hawthorne and Dostoevski . . . stressed the power of the irrational and the abysmal in soul and life. . . .

> Puritan rigorists had always to protect their integrity and their peace with blinds of inflexible dogmas from the impact of reality. This was the ostrich way to remain "pure" and "consistent." The security thus achieved was, of course, an illusory one. . . .

> The result was, inevitably, perpetual moral conflicts, remorse, feelings of sin and guilt.

Herbert Schneider, similarly emphasizing Hawthorne's concern with the blind, malevolent side of human nature, which no display of virtue can eradicate, writes [in *The Puritan Mind,* 1930]:

> For him [Hawthorne] sin is an obvious and conspicuous fact, to deny which is foolish. Its consequences are inevitable and to seek escape from them is childish. The only relief from sin comes from public confession. Anything private or concealed works internally until it destroys the sinner's soul.

These words shed light on the soul state of the minister of Salem, Deacon Gookin, Goody Cloyse, and Goodman Brown, as well as on that of Hester Prynne, in connection with whom they were written.

And Arthur Miller, attempting in his preface to *The Crucible* [1953] to establish a connection, long since denied by G. L. Kittredge, between the outburst of witchcraft at Salem and Puritanism, has this to say:

> The witch hunt was not, however, a mere repression. It was also, and as importantly, a long overdue opportunity for everyone so inclined to express publicly his guilt and sins, under the cover of accusations against the victims. . . . These people had no ritual for the washing away of sins. It is another trait we inherited from them, and it has helped to discipline us as well as to breed hypocrisy among us.

Finally, Hawthorne himself has in another work ["Main Street," published in *The Snow Image* III, 1900] made his criticism of Puritanism explicit:

> In truth, when the first novelty and stir of spirit had subsided,—when the new settlement [Salem] . . . had actually become a little town . . . its rigidity could not fail to cause distortions of the moral nature. Such a life was sinister to the intellect and sinister to the heart; especially when one generation had bequeathed its religious gloom and the counterfeit of its religious ardor, to the next; for these characteristics, as was inevitable, assumed the form both of hypocrisy and exaggeration, by being inherited from the example and precept of other human beings, and not from an original and spiritual source.

What better anatomy than this could be found of the kind of society that produced Young Goodman Brown?

In **"Young Goodman Brown,"** then, Hawthorne, as well as "explaining" the Salem witch trials, is pleading that what survives of Puritan rigorism in society be sloughed off, and replaced by a striving for virtue starting from the confession of common human weakness. Such a society would be based upon the firm foundation of humility and honesty rather than upon the sinking sands of human pride and the hypocrisy that accompanies it. In such a society, the soul of even a Goodman Brown might prosper. **"Young Goodman Brown"** is not so much the story of Brown's view of society as it is the story of the impact of a certain type of society on a man such as Brown.

David Levin   (essay date 1962)

SOURCE: "Shadows of Doubt: Specter Evidence in Hawthorne's 'Young Goodman Brown'," in *American Literature*, Vol. XXXIV, No. 3, November, 1962, pp. 344-52.

[*In this essay, Levin examines Hawthorne's short story from a seventeenth-century perspective and notes that Goodman Brown succumbs to despair on only spectral evidence of evil.*]

I choose for my text two statements written in the autumn of 1692, after twenty Massachusetts men and women accused of witchcraft had been executed. The first is by Increase Mather, the second by Thomas Brattle.

> . . . the Father of Lies [Mather declared] is never to be believed: He will utter twenty great truths to make way for one lie: He will accuse twenty Witches, if he can thereby bring one honest Person into trouble: He mixeth Truths with Lies, that so those truths giving credit unto lies, Men may believe both, and so be deceived [*Cases of Conscience Concerning Evil Spirits Impersonating Men*].

Brattle was astonished by the ease with which witnesses avoided a crucial distinction:

> And here I think it observable [he wrote], that often, when the afflicted [witnesses] do mean and intend only the appearance and shape of such an one, (say G[oodman]. Proctor) yet they positively swear that G. Proctor did afflict them; and they have been allowed so to do; as tho' there was no real difference between G. Proctor and the shape of G. Proctor [Letter, dated October 8, 1692].

Nathaniel Hawthorne's protagonist Goodman Brown commits the very mistakes that Brattle and Mather belatedly deplored in 1692. He lets the Devil's true statements about the mistreatment of Indians and Quakers prepare him to accept counterfeit evidence, and he fails to insist on the difference between a person and the person's "shape," or specter. Most modern critics who have discussed the story have repeated both these errors, even though Hawthorne clearly identifies the chief witness as the Devil and the setting as the Salem Village of witchcraft days. In the last decade, several articles have rightly contended that Hawthorne meant to reveal the faultiness of Goodman Brown's judgment; but the first and most cogent of these did not

prevent so distinguished a critic as Harry Levin from alluding to "the pharisaical elders" whom Goodman Brown sees "doing the devil's work while professing righteousness" [*The Power of Blackness: Hawthorne, Poe, Melville*, 1958]. And the cogent article itself insists that "it is not necessary to choose between interpreting the story literally and taking it as a dream"; that Brown neither goes into a forest nor dreams that he goes into a forest. What Brown does, says D. M. McKeithan [in "Hawthorne's 'Young Goodman Brown': An Interpretation," in *Modern Language* Notes LXVII, February 1952], is "to indulge in sin (represented by the journey . . .)."

I believe that one must first of all interpret the story literally. The forest cannot effectively represent sin, or the unconscious mind of Goodman Brown, or the heart of the dark moral wilderness, until one has understood the literal statements about the forest in regard to the literal actions that occur therein. Instead of agreeing with one recent critic [Thomas F. Walsh, Jr., in "The Bedeviling of Young Goodman Brown," *Modern Language Quarterly*, XIX, December 1958] that "the only solution to the problem" of what happens in the forest "lies in the tale's complex symbolic pattern," let us try to accept Hawthorne's explicit statements of fact. Instead of inventing a new definition of the word "witch," as another critic has done [Paul W. Miller, in "Hawthorne's 'Young Goodman Brown': Cynicism on Meliorism?" *Nineteenth-Century Fiction* XIV, December 1959], let us try to read the story in the terms that were available to Hawthorne. A proper reading of the literal action removes some of the ambiguity that it is now so fashionable to admire, but it should leave open a sufficient variety of interpretations to satisfy those who insist on multiple meanings, and it will clarify the fine skill with which Hawthorne made the historical materials dramatize his psychological insights and his allegory.

Hawthorne knew the facts and lore of the Salem witchcraft "delusion," and he used them liberally in this story as well as others. He set the story specifically, as the opening line reveals, not in his native Salem, but in Salem Village, the cantankerous hamlet (now Danvers) in which the afflictions, the accusations, and the diabolical sabbaths centered in 1692. Among the supposedly guilty are the minister of Salem Village and two women who were actually hanged in that terrible summer. Hawthorne not only cites testimony that Martha Carrier "had received the Devil's promise to be queen of hell"; he also quotes Cotton Mather's description of her as a "rampant hag," and he even violates Goodman Brown's point of view in order to introduce another actual rumor of 1692: "Some affirm that the lady of the governor was there [at the witches' sabbath]." He takes great care to emphasize the seeming presence at the witches' sabbath of the best and the worst of the community—noting with superbly appropriate vagueness, just before the climax, that the "figure" who prepares to baptize Goodman Brown "bore no slight similitude, both in garb and manner, to some grave divine of the New England churches."

There can be no doubt that Hawthorne understood clearly the importance of what was called "specter evidence" in the actual trials. This was evidence that a specter, or shape, or apparition, representing Goodman Proctor, for instance, had tormented the witness or had been present at a witches' meeting. Hawthorne knew that there had been a debate about whether the Devil could, as the saying went, "take the shape of an angel of light," and in both "Alice Doane's Appeal" and "Main Street" he explicitly mentioned the Devil's ability to impersonate innocent people. He was well aware that Cotton Mather had warned against putting too much confidence in this sort of evidence; he also knew that after the Mathers and Thomas Brattle had opposed even the admission of specter evidence (the Mathers on the ground that it was the Devil's testimony), the court had convicted almost no one and not a single convict had been executed. It seems certain, moreover, that Hawthorne had read Cotton Mather's biography of Sir William Phips, in which Mather the historian not only echoes his father's language about truths and lies, but clearly suggests that one of the Devil's purposes had been the traducing of Faith.

On the other Part [Mather wrote in 1697], there were many persons of great Judgment, Piety and Experience, who from the beginning were very much dissatisfied at these Proceedings; they feared lest the *Devil* would get so far into the *Faith* of the People, that for the sake of many *Truths,* which they might find him telling of them, they would come at length to believe all his *Lies,* whereupon what a Desolation of *Names,* yea, and of *Lives* also, would ensue, a Man might without much *Witchcraft* be able to Prognosticate; and they feared, lest in such an extraordinary Descent of *Wicked Spirits* from their *High Places* upon us, there might such *Principles* be taken up, as, when put into *Practice,* would unavoidably cause the *Righteous to perish with the Wicked,* and procure the Blood-shed of Persons like the *Gibeonites,* whom some learned Men suppose to be under a false Pretence of *Witchcraft,* by *Saul* exterminated.

[Cotton Mather, *Magnalia Christi Americana: or, The Ecclesiastical History of New England,* 1702]

If we set aside the alternative possibilities for a while and examine the story from the seventeenth-century point of view—the perception of Goodman Brown through which Hawthorne asks us to see almost all the action—we will find a perfectly clear, consistent portrayal of a spectral adventure into evil. Goodman Brown goes into the forest on an "evil" errand, promising himself that after this night he will "cling" to the skirts of his wife, Faith, "and follow her to heaven." Once in the wilderness, he himself conjures the Devil by exclaiming, "What if the Devil himself should be at my very elbow!" Immediately, he beholds "the figure of a man," and this figure quite unambiguously tells him that it has made the trip from Boston to the woods near Salem Village—at least fifteen or twenty miles—in fifteen minutes. Brown refuses the Devil's staff and announces that he is going back to Faith, but the Devil, "smiling apart," suggests that they "walk on, nevertheless, reasoning as we go."

The reasoning proceeds from this point, as the Devil tries to convince Brown that the best men are wholly evil. Most of the argument that follows corresponds to the traditional sophistry of the Devil—the kind of accusation with which Satan nearly discourages Edward Taylor's saint from joining the church in *God's Determinations Touching His Elect.* It is here that the Devil mentions true sins (the mistreatment of Indians and Quakers) in order to induce despair: men are so wicked that nothing can save them. Against this first argument Goodman Brown resists longer than some modern critics have resisted, for he sees that the alleged hypocrisy of elders and statesmen is "no rule for a simple husbandman like me." Foolishly, however, he believes the Devil's testimony (as his neighbors did in 1692), and he frankly tells him that "my wife, Faith," is the foundation of his reluctance to become a witch.

If we examine the story from the seventeenth-century point of view—the perception of Goodman Brown through which Hawthorne asks us to see almost all the action—we will find a perfectly clear, consistent portrayal of a spectral adventure into evil.

—David Levin

This admission invites the Devil to proceed, and it determines the organization of the rest of his argument. With typical subtlety he pretends to give up at once, because

". . . I would not for *twenty* old women like the one hobbling before us that Faith should come to any harm."

As he spoke he *pointed his staff at a female figure* on the path, *in whom Goodman Brown recognized* a very pious and exemplary old dame . . . [italics Levin's].

The Devil has of course conjured this "figure," which moves "with singular speed for so aged a woman," and he appears to it in "the very image"—soon afterward, "the shape"—"of old Goodman Brown, the grandfather of the silly fellow that now is." When the woman's figure has served his purpose, the Devil throws his staff "down at her feet," and she immediately disappears. Brown accepts this evidence without question, for by this time the Devil is "discoursing so aptly that his arguments [seem] rather to spring up in the bosom of his auditor than to be suggested by himself."

But Goodman Brown holds back once again, and the Devil, assuring him that "You will think better of this by and by," vanishes. Just as Brown is "applauding himself greatly," he is assaulted by another kind of airy evidence: disembodied voices. The "mingled sounds" *appear* to pass "within a few yards," and although the "figures" of the

minister and deacon "brushed the small boughs by the wayside, it could not be seen that they intercepted, even for a moment, the faint gleam from the strip of bright sky athwart which they must have passed." Brown cannot see "so much as a shadow," but "he could have sworn"—as witnesses in 1692 did indeed swear—that he recognized the deacon and the minister in "the voices, talking so strangely in the empty air."

Now, as Brown doubts that "there really [is] a heaven above him," the Devil has only to produce evidence that Faith, too, is guilty. Hearing the voice of Faith from a "black mass" of cloud that "hurried" across the sky although no wind is stirring, Brown calls out to her in agony, and the "echoes of the forest"—always under the Devil's control—mock him. Then the Devil sends his final argument, Faith's pink ribbon, as her voice fades into the far-off laughter of fiends. At the end of the story we learn that this evidence, too, was spectral, for Faith wears her ribbons when her husband returns home in the morning; but now, in the forest, Brown is convinced that his "Faith is gone," that the world belongs to the Devil. He takes up the Devil's staff and "seems to fly along the forest path rather than to walk or run, . . . rushing onward with the instinct that guides mortal man to evil."

With beautiful care Hawthorne makes his descriptive language reinforce these meanings through the rest of the horrible experience. "Flying" among the black pines, Brown finally sees the "lurid blaze" of the witch-meeting and pauses "in a lull of the tempest that had driven him onward." The verse that he hears is sung "by a chorus, not of human voices, but of all the sounds of the benighted wilderness, pealing in awful harmony together," and his own cry sounds in "unison with the cry of the desert." At the sabbath itself he sees, "quivering between gloom and splendor," *faces* belonging to the best people of the colony. A congregation shines forth, then disappears in shadow, and again grows, "as it were, *out of the darkness, peopling the heart of the solitary woods at once*" [italics Levin's]. Brown believes that he recognizes "a score" of Salem Village church members before he is "well nigh ready to swear" that he sees "the figure" of the minister, "the shape of his own dead father," "the dim features" of his mother, and "the slender form" of his wife. When he stands with the form of Faith, they are "the only [human] pair, *as it seemed,*" who hesitate "on the verge of wickedness in this dark world." It is "the shape of evil" that prepares to baptize them, and the figure that stands beside Brown is that of his "pale" wife. When he implores her to "look up to heaven and resist the wicked one," the whole communion disappears, and he cannot learn "whether Faith obeyed."

The clarification that this reading achieves for the story should remove some of the objections that have been raised against it even by its admirers. When we recognize that the Devil is consistently presenting evidence to a prospective convert who is only too willing to be convinced, we do not need to complain with F. O. Matthiessen against Hawthorne's "literal insistence on that damaging pink ribbon"; nor need we try, with R. H. Fogle, to explain the

ribbon away. One might insist that even here Hawthorne restricts his language admirably to Brown's perception, for he says that *something* fluttered lightly down through the air and that Brown, after seizing it, *beheld* a pink ribbon. Brown's sensory perception of the ribbon is no more literal or material than his perception of the Devil, his clutching of the staff, or his hearing of the Devil's statement about the fifteen-minute trip from Boston to the woods near Salem Village. But such an argument is really unnecessary. The seventeenth-century Devil could produce specters, with or without the consent of the people they resembled, and he could make cats, birds, and other familiars seem to materialize before terrified witnesses. For such a being, and with a witness overcome by "grief, rage, and terror," a ribbon posed no great difficulty.

Hawthorne's technique thus gives a clear view of his meaning. When we stop looking for what we may wish to believe about Puritans who whipped Quakers and burned Indian villages, we can recognize just what it is that Goodman Brown sees. Hawthorne does not tell us that none of the people whom Brown comes to suspect is indeed a diabolical agent, but he makes it clear that Brown has no justification for condemning any of them—and no justification for suspecting them, except for the shadowy vista that this experience has opened into his own capacity for evil. Asking whether these people were "really" evil is impertinent, for it leads us beyond the limits of fiction. The story is not about the evil of other people but about Brown's doubt, his discovery of the *possibility* of universal evil. Before reading the Devil's statements here in the light of ideas that Hawthorne suggested elsewhere, we must read them in their immediate context. At the witch-meeting, the "shape of evil" invites Goodman Brown to "the communion" of the human "race," the communion of evil, but we have no more right than Brown himself to believe the Father of Lies. Indeed, Hawthorne's brilliant success depends on this distinction. He gives us an irresistible picture of a "crisis of faith and an agony of doubt" [Harry T. Levin]; we must notice that Brown finally does exorcise the spectral meeting, but that he can never forget his view of the specters or the abandon in which he himself became "the chief horror" in the dark wilderness. He lives the rest of his life in doubt, and the literal doubt depends on his uncertainty about whether his wife and others are really evil. If he were certain that they had been present in the forest, he would not treat them even so civilly as he does during the rest of his life. It is the spectral quality of the experience—both its uncertainty and its unforgettable impression—that makes the doubt permanent.

The question, then, is not whether Faith and the others were really there, in their own persons, at the witch meeting. When Hawthorne asks whether Goodman Brown had "fallen asleep in the forest and only dreamed a wild dream of a witch meeting," and replies, "Be it so if you will," he offers an alternative possibility to the nineteenth-century reader who refuses to take devils seriously even in historical fiction. The choice lies between dream and a reality that is unquestionably spectral. Neither Hawthorne nor (at the end) even Goodman Brown suggests that the church members were present in their own persons. Brown's question is whether the Devil, when he took on their shapes, had their permission to represent them. That is why Hawthorne can say, "Be it so if you will." For the meaning remains the same even if Brown, having for some odd reason fallen asleep in the woods before the story begins, has dreamed the entire experience.

By recognizing that Hawthorne built **"Young Goodman Brown"** firmly on his historical knowledge, we perceive that the tale has a social as well as an allegorical and a psychological dimension. Hawthorne condemns that graceless perversion of true Calvinism which, in universal suspicion, actually led a community to the unjust destruction of twenty men and women. But we ought also to be reminded of some general truths about proper ways to read this wonderfully shrewd writer. We must not underestimate his use of historical materials, even when he is writing allegory; nor should we let an interest in patterns of image and symbol or an awareness that he repeatedly uses the same types of character obscure the clear literal significance of individual stories. Working over an amazingly—some critics have said, an obsessively—narrow range of types and subjects, he nevertheless achieves a remarkable variety of insights into human experience.

E. Arthur Robinson   (essay date 1963)

SOURCE: "The Vision of Goodman Brown: A Source and Interpretation," in *American Literature,* Vol. XXXV, No. 2, May, 1963, pp. 218-25.

[*In the following essay, Robinson posits that it is Goodman Brown's marital experience that has opened his eyes to the existence of evil.*]

Students of **"Young Goodman Brown"** agree in general that its main materials are drawn from Cotton Mather's *The Wonders of the Invisible World,* published the year following the Salem witchcraft trials, in which Mather describes the devil's appearing as a "small black man" to lure people to forest rendezvous where church sacraments were imitated and mocked. Hawthorne, indeed, virtually quotes Mather in placing Martha Carrier among the witches as a "rampant hag" and promised "queen of hell." I have found, however, no comment upon Hawthorne's possible use of a passage from Mather's *Magnalia Christi Americana* (1702) as a secondary source. The Puritan historian recalls Governor Winthrop's 1632 visit with the leaders of the Pilgrim settlement. "But there were at this time in *Plymouth,*" relates Mather, "two ministers, leavened so far with the humours of the *rigid separation,* that they insisted vehemently upon the unlawfulness of calling any *unregenerated man* by the name of *good-man such an one,* until by their indiscreet urging of this whimsey, the place began to be disquieted." When asked to intercede, Winthrop applied the distinction between civil and church discipline which stood him in good stead at home. Mather records the defeat of the extreme separatists:

The wiser people being troubled at these trifles, they took the opportunity of governour *Winthrop's* being *there,* to have the thing publicly propounded in the congregation; who in answer thereunto, distinguished between a *theological* and a *moral goodness;* adding, that when *Juries* were first used in *England,* it was usual for the *crier,* after the names of persons fit for that service were called over, to bid them all, *Attend, good men, and true;* whence it grew to be a *civil custom* in the *English nation,* for neighbours living by one another, to call one another *good man such an one:* and it was pity now to make a stir about a *civil custom,* so innocently introduced. And that speech of Mr. *Winthrop's* put a lasting stop to the little, idle, whimsical *conceits,* then beginning to grow obstreperous.

[*Magnalia Christi Americana: or, the Ecclesiastical History of New-England,* 2nd ed., 1820]

Obviously, this concern with calling an unregenerate man "goodman" resembles the ironic overtones in Hawthorne's story of Goodman Brown.

Without corroborating Winthrop's etymology, the *Oxford English Dictionary* offers interesting evidence upon connotations of "goodman" in colonial days. Several citations agree with Winthrop in stressing the colloquial status of the term, one entry from 1577 explaining that "goodman" is added to the surnames of yeomen "amongst their neighbours, . . . not in matters of importance or in lawe." An archaic meaning may be particularly applicable to Hawthorne's tale. After defining "goodman" as "the master or male head of a household," the *O.E.D.* cites its former application to "a husband" himself or "a householder in relation to his wife"—quoting a writer of 1593 who asks the pointed question: "Why is the husband called his wives good-manne?" Another makes the sly comment: "Little our goodmen knowes what their wiues thinkes." Hawthorne, of course, would not need to know these passages to be familiar with traditional connotations of the word.

Taken together, Mather's account and the *O.E.D.* throw a curious light upon Hawthorne's tale. Dramatizing as it does a Calvinistic concept of universal evil in mankind, **"Young Goodman Brown"** is clearly ironic in its continued stress upon the protagonist's title. Similarly the name Faith, given to Brown's wife, is played upon in such statements as "Faith kept me back a while" and "My Faith is gone." Nor is it coincidence that Brown and his wife are subjects of a common irony. Brown once calls himself by title with apparently self-conscious sarcasm: "Come witch, come wizard, come Indian powwow, come devil himself, and here comes Goodman Brown." Since this heightened realization of evil potential follows immediately upon the "goodman's" discovery that his wife has an appointment with the devil, their matrimonial situation is pertinent. In the archaic sense of "goodman" the title could mean "Young Husband Brown."

The internal evidence that the "Goodman" of the title refers in part to Brown's marital status may be subsumed briefly under three headings: 1) veiled and overt sexual references in the story, 2) the role of Brown's father and mother, 3) the significance of young Brown's dream or vision.

I

As proselytes for baptism by the devil, the most evident quality which Brown and Faith have in common is the fact that they are "but three months married." Pertinent also is the nature of the temptations presented to the devil's regular communicants. Old Goody Cloyse decided to "foot it" to the meeting, "for they tell me there is a nice young man to be taken into communion tonight." Men are attracted by the converse situation, as Goodman Brown learns upon hearing Deacon Gookin's remark to the minister, "Moreover, there is a goodly young woman to be taken into communion," and the clergyman's reply, "Mighty well, Deacon Gookin!" The dominant motivation for the secret sins revealed in Satan's speech is also sexual:

> "This night it shall be granted you to know their secret deeds: how hoary-bearded elders of the church have whispered wanton words to the young maids of their households; how many a woman, eager for widow's weeds, has given her husband a drink at bedtime and let him sleep his last sleep in her bosom; how beardless youths have made haste to inherit their fathers' wealth; and how fair damsels—blush not, sweet ones—have dug little graves in the garden, and bidden me, the sole guest, to an infant's funeral. By the sympathy of your human hearts for sin ye shall scent out all the places—whether in church, bed-chamber, street, field, or forest—where crime has been committed. . . ."

The devil's exhortation does not imply that sex is the sole origin of sin, which indeed "inexhaustibly supplies more evil impulses than human power . . . can make manifest in deeds." Satan apparently recognizes that the young couple's situation renders them particularly susceptible to allurement of the flesh. Self-knowledge, however, is not the key, since Brown is already aware of his own sinfulness. Rather, as Satan declares, the converts hitherto have retained a childlike reverence for their elders: "Ye deemed them holier than yourselves, and shrank from your own sin, contrasting it with their lives of righteousness. . . . Yet here are they all in my worshipping assembly." The verbal irony which had disturbed the congregation in Plymouth takes on a more universal cast in the mind of Brown, as one after another his more respected towns-people reveal their predilection for sin.

Clearly the climax of Brown's religious ordeal is a vision of sin in his wife Faith. Reflection suggests that mistrust of Faith is also the origin of that ordeal. For instance, why should this vision overwhelm Brown at just this time, when in his own words he is "but three months married"? The story has an "everyman" atmosphere that makes Brown, with his common name, symbolic of mankind. As a boy he had found tendencies in himself not sanctioned by the society within which he was growing up and he had blamed these upon personal weakness. His marital shock also presupposes early idealization of woman: his Faith is a "blessed angel on earth; and after this one night I'll cling

to her skirts and follow her to heaven." Brown's ordeal is to learn that his sinful longings belong to the pattern of his race, and that none are exempt, not even women.

II

The role of Brown's parents subtly reinforces the significance of sex in the story. Neither parent is living, and Brown has succeeded to his father's position. Both have been householders, but as husband, Brown insists, his father "never went into the woods on such an errand, nor his father before him." The emphasis upon succession of generations is ironic because Brown's inherited passions are the cause of these generations. Yet there is desperation in his insistence, for Satan has appeared in a guise resembling Brown so closely that the two "might have been taken for father and son." (In more modern terminology, Brown's quest for universal sin could be regarded as both a search for a father and initiation into Puritan manhood.) Goody Cloyse recognizes Satan simultaneously as the devil and the "image of my old gossip, Goodman Brown, the grandfather of the silly fellow that now is." At the witches' meeting Brown's father, far from censuring him, urges him forward to baptism in evil, "while a woman, with dim features of despair, threw out her hand to warn him back. Was it his mother?" Well may his mother warn him, for here she is, in the devil's company, unable to give her son power "to resist, even in thought," the attraction of evil. Instead she becomes another symbol of that attraction.

III

All these details in **"Young Goodman Brown"** take on a further dimension upon introduction of the dream motif near the end of the story. As usual Hawthorne leaves the degree of actuality unresolved. Has Brown, he asks, "only dreamed a wild dream of a witch-meeting? Be it so if you will. . . ." If we accept this reading of the story, much that was before objective becomes rather a manifestation of Brown's inner nature: Satan's punctilio in greeting him as "Goodman Brown," his amusement at the youth's trust in his elders, etc. Father and mother now appear only in their son's imagination. Young Brown must be conceived as simultaneously proclaiming his father's righteousness and picturing the devil's approaching him in his parent's lineaments; as revering Goody Cloyse at the same time that he imagines her scorn of him as the "silly fellow that now is" and her recognition of the devil's presence in his more experienced male ancestors. The young man's intuition is shocked by contradictory contrasts between himself and his forebears. The implication is that Brown's marital experience has awakened him to recognition of the universal role of sex, with special relevance to sin.

In short, Goodman Brown has realized that his father was a man like himself and his mother a woman like Faith. His passions and those of his wife are the product of like passions. Since Brown fights to repress this knowledge, the discovery comes subconsciously at first and then with awful awareness, emerging finally in the form of a vision.

His imagination embodies carnal appetites in all the people he has venerated from childhood—his father, the woman who taught him his catechism, the deacon, the minister, and finally and logically his mother. Against each he tests his new intuition, and in each instance he is startled anew to find that it fits. Subconsciously, the devil's speech is his own also, for the sins recounted are more in keeping with Brown's naïveté than with his image of Satanic sophistication.

The dream-hypothesis forces likewise a reassessment of Faith. The dream ends convincingly but there is no satisfactory point for it to begin, Hawthorne's technique gravitating between the traditional dream-vision and modern expressionism. Brown's opening conversation with his bride may thus be as subjective as the rest of his vision. She begins by warning her husband to sleep in his own bed this night and hints that she, too, has dreams—and yet this may be only Brown's fancy growing out of incipient doubts. The substance of his suspicion could be infidelity, since the deacon in Brown's "dream" evinces interest in Faith's initiation into evil, but the presentation of husband and wife before Satan insinuates a more pervasive doubt. Mutual discovery of guilt tends to presume a common guilt. Brown's suspicion focuses not on Faith's unfaithfulness but on the quality of their shared passion. Faced, in his imagination, with mutual recognition of their common pollution, the young husband appeals to heaven for assistance and calls on his wife to do likewise, but the vision ends before she can respond. The disillusionment is that of a bridegroom. Thereafter Brown cannot accept Faith's kisses without questioning the impulses of her nature, and he thinks of no woman as an angel on earth that will lead him to heaven.

From this point of view Faith's pink ribbons symbolize passion, and also, contrary to some critical comment, the conclusion becomes characterized by inevitability and ironic power. In the first place, doubts such as Brown's are by nature unresolved; perhaps the conviction that his wife *can* be tempted by sensuality is enough to disrupt his life. In the second place, Brown's vision ends in compromise. Through a long lifetime he shrinks at midnight "from the bosom of Faith" and scowls upon her at family prayers, but this aversion does not prevent their producing numerous offspring. Thus Brown, a middle-class Puritan yeoman, becomes no ascetic or hermit.

The significance of Brown's vision is shown in sharper relief when we see that in essence the symbolism of Faith's pink ribbons is repeated in "The Birthmark" and "Rappaccini's Daughter," first in Georgiana's flaw of complexion and then in Beatrice's poisonous plant, both of these being crimson or purple and both representative of woman's physical nature. Like Brown, Aylmer and Giovanni allow feminine imperfection to become an obsession, the one shortly after and the other shortly before marriage. Georgiana even regards her defect as one of her natural charms before her union with the idealistic Aylmer, and allegorically Hawthorne makes the servant Aminadab, who mutters, "If she were my wife, I'd never part with that birthmark," represent "man's physical nature" and Aylmer a

"type of the spiritual element" in man. Similarly Beatrice, ironically named for Dante's spiritual guide, is a paradoxical combination of a poisonous body and a soul which as "God's creature" craves "loves as its daily food." Her spirit could lead Giovanni upward, as Brown thought to follow Faith, but her physical beauty, which resembles the gorgeous but fatal plant, is deadly unless he can assimilate sufficient poison to join her upon equal terms. The moral is old and complex: woman, albeit of finer spiritual quality than man, possesses physical attributes that lure man to evil, although the evil may not be within her power or will. Beatrice's unanswered question is whose fault it is. "Oh, was there not," she asks Giovanni (speaking for her sisterhood in many Hawthorne tales), "from the first, more poison in thy nature than in mine?"

The two later stories resolve a portion of Brown's dilemma by making it clear that since woman's imperfection is physical, her spirit may triumph over "the gross fatality of earth" in heaven. Hawthorne interrupts the story of "Rappaccini's Daughter" to point out that nothing is left for Beatrice but to "bathe her hurts in some fount of Paradise . . . and *there* be well" and that Giovanni would have been wiser to attach his faith to her future purity and thus to accept the bittersweet of mortality. Lacking such a faith, Brown can neither fully accept nor fully deny his wife. Despite his compromise, however, his choice, in a way, is wiser than Aylmer's or Giovanni's. If his life is devitalized by doubt of human nature, his skepticism is restrained by a compulsion to live. He can continue in his generation only as previous generations have done, caught between the theological and marital ironies of his title "Goodman" Brown.

James W. Mathews　(essay date 1965)

SOURCE: "Antinomianism in 'Young Goodman Brown'," in *Studies in Short Fiction*, Vol. III, No. 1, Fall, 1965, pp. 73-5.

[*In the essay below, Mathews notes that Goodman Brown's fall into sin is the result of theological error.*]

Almost everyone commenting on Nathaniel Hawthorne's **"Young Goodman Brown"** has noted that its general theme is the loss of personal faith. On the specific application of certain symbols, however, there has been a good deal of disagreement. Some time ago [in "Hawthorne's 'Young Goodman Brown': An Attack on Puritanic Calvinism," *American Literature* XXVIII, November 1956] Thomas E. Connolly re-asserted the paramount allegorical significance of the character Faith and justifiably concluded that "this story is Hawthorne's criticism of the teachings of Puritanic-Calvinism," though he limited the object of Hawthorne's criticism to predestination. Giving further scrutiny to Faith can establish a more specific probability of meaning, which converts to theological terms Hawthorne's ubiquitous thesis that the most serious personal evil is retreat from reality and responsibility.

A doctrine of one group of Calvinists during the time depicted in the story was Antinomianism, which insisted that salvation was of faith, not of works. If good works existed, they came only as a secondary by-product of the mysterious divine grace; personal volition was de-emphasized, if not completely eliminated. Grace itself was contingent on the degree of the individual's faith; and a strong faith, which usually resulted in an emotional experience, was evidence enough of one's predestined salvation. According to Perry Miller [in *The New England Hind: The Seventeeth Century,* 1954], one question inherent in Antinomianism was "since the recipient of grace is assured of salvation without ever doing anything to deserve it, should he not surrender to the intoxication of certainty and give no further thought to his behavior?" Extreme Antinomians among the High Calvinists believed that "if a man was elected and predestined to salvation, no power in heaven or on earth could prevent it; and hence, no matter what the moral conduct of a man might be, his salvation was sure if he was one of the elect; the wicked actions of such a man were not sinful, and he had no occasion to confess his sins or break them off by repentance" [J. Macbride Sterret in *Encyclopaedia of Religion and Ethics,* ed., James Hastings, 1928].

> Though Brown seems to enjoy a good reputation, there is no reference to his good works. Unlike Everyman, he does not produce them as last-minute testimony to his worthiness. Only his faith exists, deluding him into passivity.
>
> —*James W. Mathews*

"Young Goodman Brown" depicts a man who is so confident in his recent union with faith that he walks superciliously into the devil's own revival without any fear whatsoever. Hawthorne tells us nothing of Goodman Brown's earlier life and acts. Though Brown seems to enjoy a good reputation, there is no reference to his good works. Unlike Everyman, he does not produce them as a last-minute testimony to his worthiness. Only his faith exists, deluding him into passivity. Faith's admonition to "put off your journey until sunrise and sleep in your own bed tonight" suggests that the influence of Faith over Brown is essentially negative. The insubstantiality of Brown's religious faith manifests itself in the pink ribbons of his wife's cap; their texture is aery and their color the pastel of infancy.

Brown is aware that his secret nocturnal journey is for an "evil purpose." He does not enter the forest ignorantly or under duress. He is prepared to witness evil and perhaps partake. But as an Antinomian, he would believe that no evil is charged against those with faith: "I'll cling to her

skirts and follow her to heaven," he cries. He is quick to exonerate himself and brand the others faithless despite his own deliberate act of keeping the evil rendezvous. He has his Faith, and the devil leads him into false confidence early when he says: "I would not for twenty old women like the one hobbling before us that Faith should come to any harm." Faith is secure at home and is Brown's supposed mystical shield against whatever may menace him. In explaining to the devil why he is late, he says that "Faith kept me back a while." Faith, thus, is temporary protection, functioning only in isolation. Her own apprehension over Brown's leaving points to her lack of remote spiritual control over her husband.

Since Brown is confident that the faith of his ancestors has protected them from the devil, he feels that he too will turn back in time or at least avoid permanent harm. As evidence of the righteousness of his people and of his righteousness, he stresses the theoretical side of religion with the practical as secondary: "We are a people of prayer, and good works to boot, and abide no such wickedness." Then amid suggestions that his own ancestors have been prone to evil notwithstanding their faith, Brown indignantly asks whether such is "any reason why I should quit my dear Faith" and join their company. Further, he asserts, "with heaven above and Faith below, I will yet stand firm against the devil." The poignant irony in Brown's show of certainty is that he lost the protection of Faith the very moment he left the confines of their cottage. Soon he hears the "voice of a young woman, uttering lamentations, yet with an uncertain sorrow, and entreating for some favor, which, perhaps, it would grieve her to obtain; and all the unseen multitude, both saints and sinners, seemed to encourage her onward." Faith is now not only a symbol of Brown's tottering assurance; she also reflects the lost hope of all who have suffered the Antinomian delusion of the abstract.

When Brown identifies this voice as that of his wife, he declares that "Faith is gone" and he becomes "maddened with despair." Now, he thinks, "there is no good on earth"; and in the sudden divestment of his old theology, his negative conclusion is understandable. Faith, who has appeared invulnerable at home removed from any encounter with sin, has become one of the devil's disciples. And as Faith is, Brown is. They stand together: ". . . the wretched man beheld his Faith, and the wife her husband, trembling before that unhallowed altar." Brown concurs with the devil's declaration that "evil is the nature of mankind." To a relativist and not a dogmatist, this recognition would be taken in stride. But the inverted Brown retreats. With one final, desperate attempt to preserve his heretofore comfortable doctrine of assurance, he urges Faith to "look up to heaven, and resist the wicked one." Here he voices the passive Antinomian means of salvation: the union of faith below and grace from above.

Though he does not see whether Faith follows his advice or not, Brown has evidence enough that passive faith is ineffectual. Hence his silent disdain of his "pious" forebears and contemporaries; in his condemnation of them he circumstantially accuses himself. He thereafter becomes "a stern, a sad, a darkly meditative, a distrustful, if not a desperate man," and he dies in "gloom." After his experience he becomes as passively cynical as he has been passively trusting. He knows that Faith has been false; but what he never fathoms is that her weakness (and the repulsive grossness of all mankind) is the result of his own theological error and is exaggerated by his continuous passivity.

Paul J. Hurley (essay date 1966)

SOURCE: "Young Goodman Brown's 'Heart of Darkness'," in *American Literature,* Vol. XXXVII, No. 4, January, 1966, pp. 410-19.

[*In this essay, Hurley discusses Goodman Brown's forest encounter with the Devil as the product of his diseased mind.*]

The critical controversy which has centered on Hawthorne's **"Young Goodman Brown"** seems to have reached an impasse. Critics have usually seen the story as an allegory embodying Hawthorne's suspicions about man's depravity. This interpretation implies that the Devil's words to Goodman Brown—"Evil is the nature of mankind. Evil must be your only happiness."—echo Hawthorne's own attitude. R. H. Fogle, for instance, writes [in *Hawthorne's Fiction: The Light and the Dark,* 1952], "Goodman Brown, a simple and pious nature, is wrecked as a result of the disappearance of the fixed poles of his belief. His orderly cosmos dissolves into chaos as church and state, the twin pillars of his society, are hinted to be rotten, with their foundations undermined." Hawthorne, Fogle says, "does not wish to propose flatly that man is primarily evil; rather he has a gnawing fear that this might be true." And Harry Levin has unequivocally stated [in *The Power of Blackness,* 1958] "The pharisaical elders . . . meeting in the benighted wilderness, are doing the devil's work while professing righteousness."

On the other hand, F. O. Matthiessen and W. B. Stein have resisted the majority consensus and suggested that it is Goodman Brown who purposely seeks for evil. Recently [in "Shadows of Doubt: Specter Evidence in Hawthorne's 'Young Goodman Brown," in *American Literature* XXXIV, November 1962] David Levin has attempted to void both points of view by insisting that Goodman Brown is misled by the Devil who conjures up apparitions to befuddle his innocent victim. The idea is comforting but not convincing. To take guilt away from human beings in order to place it on infernal powers is not a satisfactory explanation of the story. To the modern mind (and I suspect that includes Hawthorne's) either Abigail Williams and her Salem playmates were irresponsible, hysterical little liars, or Martha Carrier and Goody Proctor really were witches.

If I am correct, David Levin's contention is misleading, and we must return to the original argument. He writes, "Asking whether these people were 'really' evil is imper-

tinent, for it leads us beyond the limits of fiction." Confessing diabolical inspiration, I shall take a chance on being impertinent because I am not convinced that questions dealing with man's nature and the human heart are "beyond the limits of fiction." I believe the reader has every right to wonder if the townspeople are actually cohorts of the Devil. After all, if Young Goodman Brown did not have a nightmare or experience hallucinations, Hawthorne has created a fearful indictment of humanity. But if Goodman Brown did "dream," then the evil he saw, like the witchcraft reported in Salem in 1692, was the product of his own fancy with no reality save that supplied by his depraved imagination.

My point here is that **"Young Goodman Brown"** is a subtle work of fiction concerned with revealing a distorted mind. I believe the pervasive sense of evil in the story is not separate from or outside its protagonist; it is in and of him. His "visions" are the product of his suspicion and distrust, not the Devil's wiles. Goodman Brown's dying hour is gloomy because the evil in his own heart overflows; he sees a world darkened by the dreariness of sin. Hawthorne has given us every reason to read the story as a revelation of individual perversion (the story, after all, *is* entitled **"Young Goodman Brown"**), and speculations about man's nature or the talents of the Devil are out of place.

The tale begins with an account of Goodman Brown's departure from his home in Salem village in order to keep a strange tryst in the forest. He prepares to leave "at sunset," an hour when the world is about to be plunged into darkness. Faith, "as the wife was aptly named," begs him to "put off [his] journey till sunrise"; but he replies, "My journey, as thou callest it, forth and back again, must needs be done 'twixt now and sunrise." Like Richard Digby, the intolerant religious fanatic of "The Man of Adamant" who "plunged into the dreariest depths of the forest" and was disappointed that "the sunshine continued to fall peacefully on the cottages and fields . . . ," Goodman Brown's alliance with evil is suggested by contrasting images of light and dark which intimate a symbolic opposition between good and evil. These images of shadow, dark, and gloom become more frequent and persuasive as the story continues.

Hawthorne makes clear at once that Goodman Brown's purpose on this night is an evil one. The fact that he is aware of the sinfulness of his trip destroys any belief we may have in Goodman Brown's "simple and pious nature."

> "Poor little Faith!" thought he, for his heart smote him. "What a wretch am I to leave her on such an errand! She talks of dreams, too. Methought as she spoke there was trouble in her face, as if a dream had warned her what work is to be done to-night. But no, no; 'twould kill her to think it. Well, she's a blessed angel on earth; and after this one night I'll cling to her skirts and follow her to heaven."

Aside from the interesting emphasis on dreams, the passage is noteworthy for several reasons. Goodman Brown's conscience is troubled by his departure from Faith. He realizes that it would "kill her" if she were to know the purpose of his trip, but he assumes that his absence (his departure from faith) will be only temporary. Goodman Brown's first mistake is to imagine that faith (which, most readers are agreed, must be interpreted as faith in one's fellow men as well as religious faith) can be adopted and discarded at will. The irony of the passage resides primarily in the implication that Goodman Brown intends to get to heaven by clinging to the "skirts" of faith rather than by virtue of his own character or actions. The ironic implications become almost playful in the following sentence: "With this excellent resolve for the future, Goodman Brown felt himself justified in making more haste on his present evil purpose." Despite Fogle's concentration on the ambiguities of the story, it seems clear that Hawthorne means us to be in no doubt that Goodman Brown has already had some contact with the forces of evil and does not hesitate to renew that contact, because he feels that he will prove superior to the temptations which may assail him.

The suggestions that we are primarily concerned with the character of Goodman Brown, with some secret concerning his mind and heart, become stronger as he journeys into the forest, which functions as a symbol of withdrawal into oneself. Goodman Brown's isolation, his retreat from normal human intercourse into the strange dream world of the subconscious, is intimated by the imagery which describes his journey. He takes "a dreary road, darkened by all the gloomiest trees of the forest." Goodman Brown there encounters the man whom he has journeyed into the forest to find. The man appears to be the Devil himself, and he expects Goodman Brown.

The forest, symbol of Brown's retreat into himself, is associated with images suggestive of evil. "It was deep dark in the forest, and deepest in that part of it where these two were journeying." Hawthorne also insists on the similarity between Brown and the Devil—"the second traveller was about fifty years old, apparently in the same rank of life as Goodman Brown, and bearing a considerable resemblance to him. . . ." And we are informed that "they might have been taken for father and son." Despite David Levin's reminders of the Devil's wiles and powers, this personage is so curiously described that he is indisputably Goodman Brown's own personal devil.

Goodman Brown's faith may be "little," but it is not nonexistent. His "devil" knows, just as Goodman Brown or any contemporary criminal subconsciously knows, that belief in the morality of society must be destroyed, rationalized away, before total commitment to evil is possible. When the young man is chided by his companion for his tardiness in keeping their appointment, he replies, "Faith kept me back awhile"; but faith was not, of course, strong enough to prevent his journey. Goodman Brown's "lonely night of the soul," his pathetic struggle between good and evil, is dramatized in his dialogue with the Devil. At first he protests that he intends to return at once to the village. "'Sayest thou so?' replied he of the serpent, smiling apart." The Devil, it seems, knows his victim well. He urges the young man to walk on, insisting that they are "but a little way in the forest yet"; and Goodman Brown goes with him, not realizing how far into the forest of his own evil he has already traveled.

The Devil then begins a sly temptation of Goodman Brown, but it is a puzzling temptation because the only rewards Goodman Brown is offered are the aspersions cast on his family, his neighbors, and his church. Strangely enough, he accepts without question the words of the Father of Lies. The temptation is actually a kind of interior monologue, a debate which Goodman Brown holds with himself. He asks the Devil several questions whose purpose seems to be to keep him from evil. The questions, it is interesting to note, suggest the three institutions to which man is morally obligated: the family, society, the church. Goodman Brown asks, in effect, "What would my family think? What would the neighbors say? How would the church react?" But the Devil (or psychic rationalization) assures him that his family, his neighbors, and the leaders of his church are far more stained by the blackness of sin than he.

The Devil's temptation of Goodman Brown is actually a kind of interior monologue, a debate which Goodman Brown holds with himself.

—Paul J. Hurley

These questions are projected into vivid, concrete form in the visions which follow. As they walk on into the forest, Goodman Brown and the Devil come upon a woman whom Brown recognizes as the venerable and pious Goody Cloyse. Fearing (or pretending to fear) that she will question his being out so late in such strange company, Goodman hides himself. The Devil, however, advances on her; she recognizes him and they hold a short conversation in which the old woman reveals that she has long been on familiar terms with Satan. The young man never pauses to consider the reality of Goody's appearance, even though such consideration might be expected of any well-trained Puritan cognizant of the Devil's powers. Hawthorne's use of Goody Cloyse and her reference to Martha Carrier remind us that they were actual historical personages unjustly accused by twisted "youngsters." That Goody Cloyse's appearance is part of Goodman Brown's psychological self-justification seems clear from Hawthorne's statement in the following paragraph: "They continued to walk onward, while the elder traveller exhorted his companion to make good speed and persevere in the path, discoursing so aptly that *his arguments seemed rather to spring up in the bosom of his auditor than to be suggested by himself*" [Hurley's]. The biblical echo of the Devil's exhortation to Brown "to make good speed and persevere in the path" appears to be Hawthorne's ironic parodying of the situation since it is the path of *self*-righteousness to which Goodman Brown adheres.

When Brown finally refuses to go any further, the Devil seems entirely undisturbed by the news: "You will think better of this by and by,' said his acquaintance, composedly." Sitting by himself, Goodman Brown experiences his second "vision." He imagines that he hears the voices of the minister and Deacon Gookin, as they ride by, talking about the devilish communion which they plan to attend. Goodman's reason for believing what little evidence his senses afford him is even less good in this instance than it had been in the previous one:

> owing doubtless to the depth of the gloom at that particular spot, neither the travellers nor their steeds were visible. Though their figures brushed the small boughs by the wayside, *it could not be seen that they intercepted, even for a moment, the faint gleam from the strip of bright sky athwart which they must have passed.* Goodman Brown alternately crouched and stood on tiptoe, pulling aside the branches and thrusting forth his head as far as he durst *without discerning so much as a shadow.*

Fogle has alluded to this passage too as evidence of Hawthorne's ambiguity, but there is no ambiguity in the fact that Goodman Brown actually *saw* nothing at all. Nevertheless, he stands "doubting whether there really was a heaven above him." Goodman Brown makes one last desperate avowal of his resistance to evil: "'With heaven above and Faith below, I will yet stand firm. . . .'" But he has already departed from Faith. Goodman Brown then thinks that he hears the sound of voices: "The next moment, *so indistinct were the sounds,* he doubted whether he had heard aught but the murmur of the old forest, whispering without a wind." Hearing "one voice of a young woman," he immediately assumes it is his wife, and he cries her name. Suddenly he catches sight of an object fluttering down through the air; he clutches it and discovers it is a pink ribbon. Associating it at once with the ribbons his wife had worn that evening, he shouts: "'My *Faith* is gone!' . . . 'There is no good on earth; and sin is but a name. Come, devil; for to thee is this world given.'" Goodman Brown accepts his wife's guilt without ever having seen her.

Faith's ribbons have proved bothersome to several critics. F. O. Matthiessen objected to them because they seemed too literal and concrete; they appeared to him out of keeping with other suggestions that Brown is having an hallucination [*American Renaissance: Art and Expression in the Age of Emerson and Whitman,* 1941]. Fogle has noted that they are mentioned three times in the opening paragraphs of the story, and he feels that "if Goodman Brown is dreaming the ribbon may be taken as part and parcel of his dream." At any rate, "Its impact is merely temporary" [Fogle] (a peculiar statement in view of the fact that these ribbons appear, at last, to convince Goodman Brown of man's depravity and so "color" the rest of his life). Hawthorne concentrates so insistently on Faith's ribbons, and their effect on Goodman Brown is so devastating, that one may assume they were intended as an important symbol. If we remember that Faith is primarily an allegorical figure, an answer suggests itself. Goodman Brown, we recall, intends to get to heaven by clinging to Faith's skirts; in other words, he feels that the mere observation of ritual

will insure salvation—good works have no place in his (as they had no place in Calvinistic) theology. Faith's skirts and her ribbons fulfil somewhat the same function. The ribbons, with their suggestions of the frivolous and ornamental, represent the ritualistic trappings of religious observance. Goodman Brown, it seems, has placed his faith and his hopes of salvation in the formal observances of religious worship rather than in the purity of his own heart and soul. This interpretation is supported by the fact that what he has seen and heard of Goody Cloyse, the minister, and Deacon Gookin, even though it may condemn them as individuals, can hardly be used as a condemnation of religious faith. Goodman Brown accepts the metonymic ribbon, Faith's adornment, as reality—just as he has accepted the "skirts" of religion as a means of salvation.

Has Goodman Brown really been subjected to visions which imply the universal prevalence of evil? Has the faith of a good man been destroyed by a revelation of the world's sinfulness? It would seem not. If one accepts the fact that Hawthorne gives us no valid grounds to believe in the reality of Goodman Brown's visions and voices, he must either believe, as Fogle does, that Hawthorne feared his own knowledge of the world's evil; or he must treat those events as emanations from Brown's subconscious which intimate the corruption of Brown's own mind. Why do the young man's visions of evil concern only Goody Cloyse, the minister, Deacon Gookin, and his wife? One answer, of course, is that they represent an exceptional piety which makes their participation in evil dramatically more effective. But if Hawthorne's theme concerns the universality of human sinfulness, should we not see a wider manifestation of that evil? The only scene in which such a manifestation occurs is the Devil's communion, but that takes place *after* Goodman Brown has declared his loss of faith; and the scene of that vision, Hawthorne tells us, was "in the heart of the dark wilderness," a setting whose significance is so inescapable that Joseph Conrad would later echo Hawthorne's words (unknowingly?) in the title of one of his novels.

A more significant reason for Hawthorne's choice of those four characters occurs to us if we return to a consideration of their relationship to Goodman Brown. They are the four people in Salem village to whom he is morally responsible. Goody Cloyse "had taught him his catechism in youth, and was still his moral and spiritual advisor, jointly with the minister and Deacon Gookin." His wife is an even more important representative of the forces of morality and virtue. It seems obvious that they are the four people whose respectability must be destroyed before Goodman Brown can fully commit himself to a belief in the wickedness of the world.

The remainder of the story continues to emphasize Goodman Brown's surrender to evil. Rushing through the forest "with the instinct that guides mortal man to evil," Goodman Brown, the man who has lost faith in his fellow men, *"was himself the chief horror of the scene."* "The fiend in his own shape," Hawthorne tells us, reminding us of the similarities between Goodman Brown and the Devil, "is less hideous than when he rages in the breast of man."

The communion scene in the forest, which Roy Male finds "essentially sexual," seems to me to be entirely the product of a dream fantasy, a blasphemous parody of a religious service. In this "grave and dark-clad company" Goodman Brown, his faith totally destroyed, fancies that he sees every person he has ever known. When a call is made to bring forth the converts, "Goodman Brown stepped forth from the shadow of the trees and approached the congregation, *with whom he felt a loathful brotherhood by the sympathy of all that was wicked in his heart.*" When the converts look upon each other, Goodman Brown at last sees his wife. They are told that "Evil is the nature of mankind. Evil must be your only happiness. Welcome again, my children, to the communion of your race." But as if in denial of the Devil's assertion, just as they are about to be baptized into "the mystery of sin," Goodman Brown cries out: "'Faith! Faith!' . . . 'look up to heaven, and resist the wicked one.' Whether Faith obeyed he knew not." Goodman's cry breaks the spell of his hallucination: "He staggered against the rock, and felt it chill and damp; while a hanging twig, that had been all on fire, besprinkled his cheek with the coldest dew." That Goodman Brown has been experiencing hallucinations or dreaming seems unquestionable. The details concerning the rock and the twig are surely intended to signal Goodman Brown's return to a "rational" state of mind.

The most striking quality of the paragraph which describes Goodman Brown's return to the village of Salem is its tone. No longer are there any suggestions of the weird and incredible. The dreamlike quality of Brown's adventure in the forest is replaced by purposefully direct and forthright narration. Life proceeds in the village as it always has. Only Goodman Brown has changed. If the events of the night before had been real, or even symbolic of reality, would not Hawthorne have indicated in some way a shared knowledge between Goodman Brown and the townsfolk whom he sees? Hawthorne has told us that Brown did not know whether his wife obeyed his cry to look up to heaven. Nonetheless, he passes her without a greeting when she runs to meet him. His own distrust and suspicion have assured him that she is sinful, even though, as Hawthorne is careful to note, she is wearing the pink ribbons which Goodman Brown thought he had grasped from the air. Nor is there any change in anyone else. The minister seeks to bless Goodman Brown, but the young man shrinks from him; Deacon Gookin is praying and even though Goodman Brown can hear "the holy words of his prayer," he still thinks him a wizard. Goody Cloyse is catechizing a young girl, and Goodman Brown snatches the child from the old woman's arms. The corruption of his mind and heart is complete; Goodman Brown sees evil wherever he looks. He sees it because he wants to see it.

If Hawthorne had wished to intimate that the events of the night were real, it would hardly do to confuse us with suggestions about dreams (unless, as Fogle thinks, this was Hawthorne's method of escaping the implications of his own insight into man's depravity). A more acceptable interpretation of the ambiguity of the story is to see in it Hawthorne's suggestion that the incredible incidents in the forest were the product of an ego-induced fantasy, the self-justification of a diseased mind. It seems clear that these incidents were not experienced; they were willed. The important point, however, is that Goodman Brown has accepted them as truth; and the acceptance of evil as the final truth about man has turned him into "a stern, a sad, a darkly meditative, a distrustful" human being. Goodman Brown does not become aware of his own kinship with evil; he does not see sinfulness in himself but only in others. That, perhaps, is his most awful sin. He has lost not only faith in his fellow men but his compassion for them. And so it is that "On the Sabbath day, when the congregation were singing a holy psalm, he could not listen because an anthem of sin rushed loudly upon his ear and drowned all the blessed strain." Hawthorne never tells us that the anthem, loud and fearful as it must have been, ever reached the ears of any but young Goodman Brown.

Richard Abcarian (essay date 1966)

SOURCE: "The Ending of 'Young Goodman Brown'," in *Studies in Short Fiction,* Vol. III, No. 3, Spring, 1966, pp. 343-45.

[*In the following essay, Abcarian contradicts previous critics who state that the ending of Hawthorne's tale is anticlimactic and redundant.*]

"Young Goodman Brown" is certainly one of Hawthorne's greatest stories and arguably one of the finest short stories ever written. With the economy of genius, Hawthorne dramatizes the discovery by a young and good man "that all deified Nature absolutely paints like a harlot, whose allurements cover nothing but the charnelhouse within . . ." [Herman Melville, *Moby Dick*] and the consequences of that discovery. The story is rich and ambiguous enough to have elicited a good deal of critical comment and controversy. However various the approaches and divergent the interpretations, the most illuminating and useful studies have maintained a respectfully critical attitude toward the story. Although many critics have been puzzled and disturbed by Faith's pink ribbon and by the relationship between the daylight world of the opening and the hallucinatory world of the midnight mass, most commentators feel that the story is a successful artistic whole.

Yet alongside this criticism has run another interpretation of "Young Goodman Brown" of a curiously astigmatic sort, a criticism rendered more lamentable by its rather supercilious and complacent "modern" tone. Now this sort of thing one could easily let pass were it not for the fact that the interpretation is to be found in a popular collection of short stories for college students. The anthology is Caroline Gordon and Allen Tate's *The House of Fiction* (2nd edition). As Gordon and Tate read the story, the final paragraph is artistically damaging. Their comment upon it is as follows:

The dramatic impact would have been stronger if Hawthorne had let the incidents tell their own story: Goodman Brown's behavior to his neighbors and finally to his wife *show* us that he is a changed man. Since fiction is a kind of shorthand of human behavior and one moment may represent years in a man's life, we would have concluded that the change was to last his entire life. But Hawthorne's weakness for moralizing and his insufficient technical equipment betray him into the anticlimax of the last paragraph.

The same point is made by Wallace and Mary Stegner in their collection *Great American Short Stories:* ". . . Hawthorne was not so impeccable a craftsman as Poe; Poe would never have left this story, which up to the time of Brown's return is tight, concentrated, sensuous, sharply visualized, to end lamely with an anticlimactic appendix."

The charge is serious. In order to test its truth, we need to examine with some care the final section of the story, that is from Brown's return to the village following the midnight mass to the end of the story. This section is comprised of three paragraphs, the first describing some of the sights and sounds of Salem village and Brown's changed response to them, the second (a single sentence) in which the narrator asks the crucial question about the objective reality of Brown's experience, and the final paragraph, in which the narrator answers the question and rapidly summarizes the remainder of Brown's life.

According to Gordon and Tate (and the Stegners) the first of these paragraphs makes the final one an anticlimactic redundancy; Hawthorne's weakness for moralizing thus betrays him into violating the artistic integrity of his story.

A careful reading, I believe, will not support such a charge. The two presumably redundant paragraphs are in fact clearly different in technique and purpose, and both are vitally important to the story. The first of these paragraphs needs to be quoted in full:

> *The next morning* young Goodman Brown came *slowly into the street of Salem village,* staring around him like a bewildered man. The good old minister was taking a walk *along the graveyard* to get an appetite for breakfast and meditate his sermon, and *bestowed a blessing,* as he passed, on Goodman Brown. He shrank from the venerable saint as if to avoid an anathema. Old Deacon Gookin was at domestic worship, and the holy words of his prayer were heard through *the open window.* "What God doth the wizard pray to?" quoth Goodman Brown. Goody Cloyse, that excellent old Christian, stood in *the early sunshine at her own lattice,* catechizing a little girl *who had brought her a pint of morning's milk.* Goodman Brown snatched away the child as from the grasp of the fiend himself. Turning *the corner by the meeting-house,* he spied *the head of Faith,* with the *pink ribbons,* gazing anxiously forth, and bursting into such joy at sight of him that *she skipped along the street* and almost kissed her husband before the whole village. But Goodman Brown looked sternly and sadly into her face, and passed on without a greeting.

As the italicized phrases show, this passage is heavy with realistic specificity in both time and place, contrasting strikingly with the grotesque and timeless world of the forest. Its function is twofold: to return Brown and the reader to the daylight world of reality in which the story opened (". . . the young man pursued his way until, being about to turn *the corner by the meeting-house,* he looked back and saw *the head of Faith . . . ,*" Hawthorne writes in the opening section), and to prepare us for the final paragraph, in which the lasting and corrosive effects of the experience on Brown are revealed. To assert that the passage performs the same function as the final paragraph is either to give it a less careful reading than it deserves or retroactively to confuse the meaning of the final paragraph with this passage. In short, although the passage contains as a latent possibility what Hawthorne makes explicit in the final paragraph, without the final paragraph, the story would be inconclusive and weak. For we find the ultimate meaning of **"Young Goodman Brown"** precisely in the final paragraph, which reveals the permanent *effects* of Brown's experience. It is because the story is about the inner world of Brown rather than the world of objective fact that Hawthorne dismisses the question of objective reality (which he rightly anticipates his readers will ask) with, "Be it so if you will . . . (a sentence, we might note, which opens the "anticlimactic" final paragraph). Despite the artful ambiguity in the story that has been so often noted, by dismissing the question, Hawthorne surely could not have made clearer the central importance of the final, summarizing paragraph.

It is this final paragraph that gives such appalling power and meaning to all that has preceded it. Brown has confronted, as surely all men must at one time or another, that "great power of blackness" and is forever after dominated by its effects. Having been shown by the Devil "the whole earth one stain or guilt, one mighty blood spot," he never for a moment questions the truth of his vision. Indeed, for Brown his vision *is* reality, and it slowly consumes his heart away.

All this is revealed, and revealed *only* through the final paragraph. But this is not all it reveals. In some of the details that Hawthorne selects for the final paragraph, he seems to be suggesting that Brown, like Ethan Brand, Rappaccini, Aylmer, and Chillingworth, has become the prisoner of a partial vision that has dehumanized him, and obliterated from his mind that part of man that, according to Brown's own Christian doctrine, is made in God's image and is next to the angels in the hierarchy of being. Brown turns pale when he hears the minister speak "of saint-like lives and triumphant deaths, and of future bliss or misery unutterable" and thereby denies those qualities in man that Hawthorne so often identifies with the heart. Brown's heart, having closed the valves of its attention, disintegrates in a region of gloomy despair and distrust where the hope and affirmation offered by saintly lives and triumphant deaths cannot penetrate. The pall of Brown's denial settles upon his entire family: Faith, who lovingly asked Brown not to leave her on that fateful night, and who skipped in joy and "almost kissed her husband" on his return, Brown shrinks from; children and grandchildren bring neither joy nor innocence into his life.

Hawthorne's technical equipment, then, is superbly adequate to his purposes. If one were rash enough, as Gordon and Tate are, to suggest cuts in this fine story, surely the final paragraph would have to be the last to go. Indeed, the final paragraph bears the same relation to the entire story that the devil's address bears to the witches' meeting: both are major and indispensable climaxes. In a technical sense, the concluding paragraph is a masterful triumph of fictional narrative whereby Hawthorne turns the remainder of Brown's long life into a sharply focussed climax.

J. M. Ferguson, Jr. (essay date 1969)

SOURCE: "Hawthorne's 'Young Goodman Brown'," in *The Explicator*, Vol. XXVIII, No. 4, December, 1969, item 32.

[*In this essay, Ferguson points out the importance of color symbolism as it pertains to Faith's pink ribbons in "Young Goodman Brown."*]

Much concern has been expressed about the significance of Faith's pink ribbons in Hawthorne's **"Young Goodman Brown,"** and this commentary has perhaps been initiated in part by F. O. Matthiessen's observation that the author's "literal insistence" on them, as they first appear to Goodman Brown in the forest, damages the effect of what is otherwise portrayed as "the realm of hallucination" (*American Renaissance*, New York, 1941). More recently, Richard Harter Fogle has attempted to explain this apparent inconsistency by suggesting that the ribbons in this same instance "may be taken as part and parcel of [Brown's] dream," adding that because they vanish into their "shadowy background" their impact is "merely temporary" (*Hawthorne's Fiction: The Light and the Dark*, 1952). While these observations may help account for the concrete appearance of the ribbons, they tell us little about their meaning in the story.

To be sure, Hawthorne does "insist" on the pink ribbons—three times in the opening six paragraphs and twice thereafter at crucial points in the story—but what observers have failed to underscore is the fact that each time he mentions the ribbons Hawthorne is careful to specify that they are pink. This failure seems surprising, for it is common knowledge that color symbolism was a favorite Hawthorne device; and if we look to the color of the ribbons to yield their meaning we find an obvious interpretation for this detail which contributes to the meaning of the story perhaps more than any other single image within it. Neither scarlet nor white, but of a hue somewhere between, the ribbons suggest neither total depravity nor innocence, but a psychological state somewhere between. Tied like a label to the head of Faith, they represent the tainted innocence, the spiritual imperfection of all mankind.

As a Puritan who had been taught his catechism, Goodman Brown should have been fortified against the shock of this knowledge of the human condition. Yet, discovering the pink ribbons during his forest adventure, he cries "My Faith is gone!" It is significant that he does not refer to his faith in God, for he later dreads "lest the roof should thunder down" on the Sabbath day congregation in the meetinghouse. It is, instead, his faith in man that has been shaken, and it is in the immediate context of this piercing confession that he makes an even more terrible pronouncement: "There is no good on earth; and sin is but a name."

Hawthorne implies, however, that Goodman Brown is in error, for Faith's ribbons are still intact the next morning in Salem village as she skips to meet him, and Hawthorne "insists" they are still pink, not scarlet, as Goodman Brown would have them. Since they symbolize the condition of mankind, it is ironic that the protagonist has rejected "the communion of [his] race" and excluded himself from that condition, for in Puritan eyes he is thus guilty of the worst of all sins. It is his pride which isolates him and prevents him from seeing that he too, figuratively speaking, wears pink ribbons. This *hubris,* to use the classical term, leads to his psychological destruction and accounts for the "darkly meditative" and "distrustful" man whom Hawthorne describes at the end of the story.

Walter J. Paulits (essay date 1970)

SOURCE: "Ambivalence in 'Young Goodman Brown'," in *American Literature*, Vol. XLI, No. 4, January, 1970, pp. 577-84.

[*In the following essay, Paulits characterizes Hawthorne's tale as one in which the dominant theme is the ambivalence of the human heart when presented with a choice between good and evil.*]

My hope in this article is that a discussion of ambivalence and of its concomitants of temptation and deception may provide the still-missing clue to the interpretation of the intent of **"Young Goodman Brown."** I am distinguishing sharply between ambiguity and ambivalence. Ambiguity is concerned with intermingled meanings—the double meanings in the witches' prophecies to Macbeth or Fedallah's to Ahab, or the amphibologies in Quince's Prologue to "Pyramus and Thisbe" in *Midsummer Night's Dream* or its antecedent in *Ralph Roister Doister*. Ambivalence is concerned with opposed feelings within the same person when confronted with a value or values. **"Young Goodman Brown"** does employ ambiguity but, I think, in the service of a more pervasive theme of ambivalence.

In his fine book, *Allegory: The Theory of a Symbolic Mode*, Angus Fletcher writes: "Allegorical literature always displays toward its polar antagonisms a certain ambivalence. This much-used term does *not* mean 'mixed feelings,' unless we are willing to amend the phrase to a 'mixture of diametrically opposed feelings'." The generic names in Hawthorne's tale and the biblically allusive nature of the temptations Goodman is subjected to seem sufficient proof of Hawthorne's allegorical intent, and Hawthorne's awareness of radical ambivalence seems evident from sentences in "Rappaccini's Daughter": "It was not love . . . nor horror . . . but a wild offspring of both love and horror that had each parent in it, and burned like one and shivered like the other"; and "Blessed are all simple emotions, be they dark or bright! It is the lurid intermixture of the two that produces the illuminating blaze of the infernal regions." I believe that **"Young Goodman Brown"** is an allegorical presentation of ambivalence.

The precise ambivalence in Brown at the beginning of the tale is an attraction for the Devil conjoined with a regret at leaving Faith. Neither has Brown given himself to the Devil nor is he leaving Faith definitively: "Well, she's a blessed angel on earth; and after this one night I'll cling to her skirts and follow her to heaven." Whether this dalliance with evil makes sense theologically or socially or not seems to me to be peripheral; what is important is that Brown deserts Faith and goes into the forest to meet the Devil in a highly tentative venture. He has not firmly decided. This tentativeness is important because it springs from his emotive ambivalence—he wants two things strongly enough to be unwilling to give up either. The Devil's role is to lead him to complete evil by temptation and fall. The tale becomes in great part, thus, a record of the temptation. As Fletcher says: "The heart of moralizing actions becomes temptation, which asserts the desirability of evil."

Once in the forest and after having met the Devil, Brown almost immediately questions the emotive attraction that has drawn him there: "I have scruples touching the matter thou wot'st of." That he then "unconsciously" resumes his walk evidences the presence of the two feelings battling within him. From the time Brown shows hesitation Hawthorne casts the story into the framework of a temptation leading toward decision. The Devil's easy assumption of his role as tempter is consonant with his knowledge that the pact is not yet complete. He knows he must convince Brown of the goodness of the decision to be made. When Brown is convinced, the conflicting feelings will presumably cease, and he will become the dedicated votary a witch or warlock traditionally is.

Hawthorne, after detailing an unavailing conversation in which the Devil uses an "everybody-has-done-it" argument, constructs a major tripartite segment which has affinities with the biblical account of the triple temptation of Christ in the desert. Hawthorne's allusive use of the biblical scene is consistent with the theme of ambivalence he is working out. That Christ underwent everything that man suffered, sin excluded, is a biblical truism that Brown should have been aware of. And perhaps he is presumed to have been, because his reactions are remarkably like Christ's—up to a point. Brown is almost as stubborn as Christ. After Goody Cloyse's apparition, he says: "my mind is made up. Not another step will I budge on this errand." After he hears the Minister's and the Deacon's "voices" he cries: "With heaven above and Faith below, I will yet stand firm against the devil." But after Faith's seeming defection he appears to yield. The

yielding should be understood in its relationship to Christ's third reaction. Christ committed himself to the service of his Father: "It is the Lord your God whom you will adore" (Matt. 4:10). His decision was firm, and any feelings he might have had to the opposite of the service of the Lord (which, in terms of the biblical story, could only have been service of the Devil) dissipate, and he is at oneness with himself, and his peace is symbolized by the angels who come to minister to him. Brown should have imitated Christ. But he is deceived by the spectral evidence of the ribbon, just as he had been by the earlier apparitions, and so for a while Brown does not follow the biblical pattern. But at the initiation scene Hawthorne reverts to this important Christ-temptation scheme, and Brown *will* ultimately imitate Christ. Much, though, will have happened by then.

Brown's yielding should also be understood in its relationship to the ambivalence he suffers when he enters the forest. The Devil has not succeeded in fixing the vacillating Brown with any of the previous temptations, and until he does succeed, Brown's ambivalence will continue. It would be a mistake to read Brown's mad flight through the forest, however, as a definitive success for the Devil. After all, Brown is hurrying toward the Witches' Meeting where the initiation can actually occur, and until he arrives he is simply not an initiate. What impels him is more frenzy than rational, unimpassioned choice, and it is a standard moral dictum that passion alleviates the gravity of moral fault. Brown is "maddened with despair," he is "still rushing onward with the instinct that guides mortal men to evil," he is "the demoniac." Significantly, after Brown arrives and examines the assembly, his latent revulsion against the initiation stirs again when he does not see Faith: "'But where is Faith?' thought Goodman Brown; and, as hope came into his heart, he trembled." It seems to me that all Hawthorne can legitimately be made to say between the ribbon and the new hope is that Faith seems to have defected; but that Brown sees now the goodness of the Devil's proposal is far from evident. Thus, the great purpose of the Witches' Sabbath will be precisely to show the desirability of rationally accepting the initiation.

Therefore, Brown's state at the time of the calling-forth of the candidates is not radically different from his state when he first entered the forest: he is torn between conflicting desires. Nevertheless the flight has apparently shown him something of himself. He now knows how related he is to the entire grim group, "with whom he felt a loathful brotherhood by the sympathy of all that was wicked in his heart." He knows the instinct within him that can drive him toward evil, and he senses this same instinct in others. But the important qualification to be made here is that the brotherhood he has with the others is experienced as "loathful." The feeling is one of revulsion, and yet he does step forward for full initiation, the consequence of which will presumably be that he will become a full member of the coven. But the sense of loathing is significant, because its presence indicates that Satan's work is still unfinished. All the speeches Satan speaks prior to the aborted baptism will be directed toward one of two purposes: either Brown's final self-convincing or Brown's self-delusion. In either case the Devil's purpose will have been gained.

Hawthorne's presentation of Satan's final argument is delicate. Satan tempts the couple (really, Brown; Faith is not important in herself in the intent of the tale) with two promises, not one. The first is: "Welcome . . . to the communion of your race"; "By all the sympathy of your human hearts for sin," "It shall be yours to penetrate, in every bosom, the deep mystery of sin." This is an invitation to knowledge, to recognition of sin, first in oneself and then in others. I would suggest that, in itself, nothing is wrong with possessing this knowledge; for example, Minister Hooper's awareness of sin, while it does isolate him, paradoxically also brings him closer to his parishioners in their most critical hours, especially death. The second invitation is very different: "ye . . . shall exult to behold the whole earth one stain of guilt, one mighty blood spot"; "Evil must be your only happiness." These invitations are not directed only toward knowledge; rather they refer to values pursued and attained and to the joy one experiences in their possession. For Brown to accede to the first invitation would have been no victory for Satan. But if Brown makes evil his only good, all other goods cease to have value for him, and his ambivalence is replaced by "univalence." He will be the Devil's and a fully participating member of the coven. But the Devil's clever intermingling of the two invitations also leaves open the possibility that an uninformed "no" could still be "yes" to issues unsuspected by the simple Goodman.

Hawthorne does not allow Brown to opt for or against initiation on the terms of the second invitation. At the exactly climactic point in the tale, Brown suffuses elements of the first invitation with elements of the second. The climax does not come in terms of value and happiness but in terms of knowledge: "Herein did the shape of evil dip his hand and prepare to lay the mark of baptism upon their foreheads, that they might be partakers of the mystery of sin, more conscious of the secret guilt of others, both in deed and thought, than they could now be of their own." The entire significance of the baptism for Brown will be, then, that the two will know the sins of each other: "The husband cast one look at his pale wife, and Faith at him. What polluted wretches would the next glance show them to each other." On these terms Brown refuses the baptism violently.

The refusal is tremendously significant. In his not listening carefully to the Devil's words Brown has conflated the two promises into one meaning and has allowed the horror of the second to flow over onto the first. Value suffuses meaning in the one place in the tale where it is most necessary for Brown to recognize ambiguity, an ambiguity he more than the Devil has created because he has taken two frankly presented meanings as one and filled it with one of the feelings contending within him. Ambivalence has led Brown to the point where ambiguity can confuse him. In a revulsion against the evil, he refuses the baptism. But by this time the evil is not only evil; it is also a good—knowledge. So that when Brown rebels he rebels against knowledge of sin and does so

with all the violence of his revulsion against evil. The paradox results that an act of virtue—repelling temptation—throws him into as inhuman a state as his yielding would have done.

The definition of Brown's final state in Salem Village seems to be of critical importance for a valid reading of the tale. I cannot believe he has become "Badman Brown" on his return. After all, he has done an act of virtue, even though he does not recognize the error he had allowed to enter and never will. His stance becomes, therefore, that of the man who opts for the wrong by seeing the wrong as right. And the decision does not remove ambivalence, because all the rest of his life is spent in pursuing the knowledge he has denied himself. He habitually ascribes to others what he suspects they are guilty of (here is his evil: he does not forgive nor sympathize, but then how could he?—he is not *sure*). His state becomes one of doubt, a concomitant of ambivalence.

But the elements of the ambivalence have changed. In the beginning Brown was torn between Faith and the Devil. Now the ambivalence is rarefied and psychologized. Its object is Faith and all the other human beings in the village. He can never know their evil, and yet he is drawn toward them; he judges, but always on doubt. Fletcher describes the state:

> This "chronic coexistence of love and hatred, both directed towards the same person," becomes something more subtle when it is transferred to the sphere of doubt and certainty. Along with the emotions that are ambivalent, when this coexistence is in full force, there are likely to be intellectual equivalents in the form of extreme doubt as to the good and/or evil of the loved object.

The terrible thing about Brown is that his customary spirit is that of the "hanging-judge," but never with assurance; he vacillates and in his vacillation suffers. Drawn toward wife and fellowmen, he can be only a begetter of children rather than real husband and father, and he is never a companionable fellow among fellows. He is always searching, scrutinizing, judging, condemning. The "loathful brotherhood" can never become a loving brotherhood, either in evil or in charity, because his suspicion isolates him. He had refused knowledge of sin because he had thought its possession was evil, and his lifelong imperception then casts him into a second ambivalence more harrowing than the first, because he lives in it in a state of righteousness concerning himself and of condemnation of others—but always agonizing because never complete.

Hawthorne's allegory presents a common human situation which occurs when a man is in possession of only partial knowledge and is torn between opposing goods and feelings. He can—and in **"Young Goodman Brown"** does—choose wrongly, either knowingly or not. In either case he must pay the price. If the choice was a mistake, the price can cause the spectator to complain: "But it really wasn't his fault! He was trying to do right." No matter. The intolerance of the whole rests on the shoulders of each. That is why I do not read Hawthorne as completely condemning Brown or completely approving him. Brown is Everyman on his uncertain pilgrimage, wanting both good and evil at the same time and not being alert enough to keep them from getting confused. He pays the price in his own unhappy life. In other words, **"Young Goodman Brown"** is an artistic presentation of an ambivalence all human hearts and heads may be subject to and that some, probably many, fall prey to.

Reginald Cook **(essay date 1970)**

SOURCE: "The Forest of Goodman Brown's Night: A Reading of Hawthorne's 'Young Goodman Brown'," in *The New England Quarterly,* Vol. XLIII, No. 3, September, 1970, pp. 473-81.

[*In the essay below, Cook provides a psychoanalytic interpretation of Hawthorne's short story, observing that Goodman Brown's compulsive pact with evil is caused by his masochistic desire to punish himself.*]

> "Thou wouldst not think how ill all's here about my heart . . ."
>
> *Hamlet* v. 2, 220

I

In a literary epoch when the dominant field of action was the frontier settlement, the forest, and the fort, Hawthorne focussed on the world of moral imagination. His **"Young Goodman Brown"** is a paradigm of this particular world, and Brown's behavior on a fateful night in his life is the key to this haunting tale. Although the motives for Goodman Brown's behavior are ambiguous, the consequences of his compulsive acts are clear but frightening.

It is truly an enchanted forest into which Goodman Brown enters on his way to keep a tryst. "The magic forest," says Heinrich Zimmer in *The King and the Corpse,* "is always full of adventures. No one can enter it without losing his way. The forest has always been a place of initiation for there the demonic presences, the ancestral spirits, and the forces of nature reveal themselves." Brown is no exception. For in the forest he is made aware of demonic presences, ancestral spirits, and he confronts the forces of nature in their strange and fearful aspects. "The forest is the antithesis of house and heart, village and field boundary, where the household gods hold sway and where human laws and customs prevail," continues the explanatory Zimmer. "It holds the dark forbidden things—secrets, terrors, which threaten the protected life of the ordered world of common day." With one exception this is true of Brown's experience. The seat of darkness upon which the castle of Merlin stands in the forest of ancient myth is transformed in Hawthorne's tale into a Witches' Sabbath where the enchantments of primitive mythology are secularized in the dour Calvinistic scheme of universal human guilt.

"But the chosen one, the elect, who survives its [the enchanted forest's] deadly peril is," as Zimmer says, "reborn

and leaves it a changed man." Ironically, Brown's initiation and rebirth represent an inversion of the customary ritual. His survival is physical; forevermore he is spiritually spellbound, the effect of which is both bewilderment and distrustfulness. Sinking into a torpor of unredemptive guilt-consciousness, when he dies no hopeful verse is carved upon his tombstone, "for his dying hour was gloom."

The reader does not fail to see that as Brown goes from the village to the forest he passes from a conscious world to a subconscious one. Upon returning from the extraordinary forest coven to the commonplace village orthodoxy, Brown's traumatic shock leaves him a deeply suspicious man. To a reader indoctrinated in Freudian and Jungian psychology the tale gathers meaning from the modern explorations of the subconscious mind, enkindles the aesthetic sensibility by its reliance on imagination, and appeals to the antirational, which interests us in the surrealistic art of Salvador Dali, Marcel Duchamp, and Joan Miro.

We are introduced to the strange world of young Goodman Brown by its "solidity of specification." The locale is Salem Village; the time shortly after King Philip's War. Since the forest is fifteen minutes from the village, the action is significantly within the ambit of civilized society. Only the forest of the night is strange. The beginning and the end of the tale are real enough but the middle is somnambulistic. At the close Hawthorne inquires: "Had Goodman Brown fallen asleep in the forest and only dreamed a wild dream of a witch meeting?" Not to keep us waiting, Hawthorne begins the next paragraph balefully. "Be it so if you will, but, alas! it was a dream of evil omen for young Goodman Brown." If the author's "be it so if you will" is so much dust in the eyes to keep us off the target, I for one don't mind. Hawthorne's make-believe is more evocative of the heart's truths than many realist's spitting image of actuality.

II

When he leaves his three-months' wedded wife, Faith (an obvious symbol) and her pink ribbons in Salem, Brown's nocturnal journey, it is understood, cannot be postponed. It must be accomplished between sunset and sunrise. Nor is it enticing journeying. The road is dreary and narrow; the forest is gloomy. The real can hardly be distinguished from the illusory. Shadow density is accentuated. Twilight fades into dusk, dusk into gloomy night. It is scary—"as lonely as could be"; and perhaps a devilish Indian stands behind every wayside tree.

Then Brown is joined by a fellow traveler of the same rank, similarly dressed, resembling him in expression but distinguishable. He is, indeed, the Devil. Not Cotton Mather's diabolical "small black man," or Goethe's Mephisto, the tempter, or Henry James's clever Peter Quint, or Gide's *raissoneur,* or Ivan Karamazov's irritating *alter ego,* but certainly God's old Arch-Enemy—an urbane intrigant, who carries for a fetish a twisted staff that resembles a great live black snake. The diabolic fellow traveler knows all about the hereditary taint in Brown's forebears. "They were my good friends," he acknowledges familiarly. He once helped Brown's grandfather lash the Quaker women; he kindled the pitch-pine knot with which Brown's incendiary father ruthlessly set fire to an Indian village in King Philip's War. He has, to say the least, "a very general acquaintance here in New England."

Smooth, wily, taunting, facile in argument, mercurial in mood, now gravely considerate, now irrepressible in laughter, he turns aside Brown's attempts to defend the good works of his family. Subtly the Devil succeeds in infecting Brown with an apprehension of evil in his family, in his friends, in his moral and spiritual advisers, in the worthies of the community, and, not least, in his young wife. Blighting what he touches, and denigrating whomever he mentions in human society, the Devil casts a spell of profound disillusionment on Brown. First he exposes the duplicity of Goody Cloyse, moral instructress of Brown's youth, whose shadowy figure appears on the forest path in the dusk. Stubbornly Brown refuses to succumb to general suspicion on such slight circumstantial evidence. He will still trust in Faith. So the Devil to break him down confronts him with the revered minister of the village and with good old Deacon Gookin. Brown, who has stepped aside from the thread of the narrowing forest path, cannot be sure of the shadowy figures that pass along the way; only their voices are recognizable. Goody Cloyse had mumbled anticipatory remarks about seeing somewhere in the forest at "the meeting" a nice young man (Brown!). The minister and the deacon anticipate seeing a goodly young woman (Faith!) "taken into communion." Even this trying episode is not enough to overwhelm the devil-resistant Brown. He looks heavenward where the stars are "brightening." "'With heaven above and Faith below, I will yet stand firm against the devil!' cried Goodman Brown." And he does for the moment.

Brown's resolution is not shaken until he hears from an ominous dark cloud the "confused and doubtful sound of voices" of both "pious and ungodly" people. One lamenting voice is that of a young woman—apparently Faith— "yet with an uncertain sorrow, and entreating for some favor, which, perhaps, it would grieve her to obtain." This low-pitched, connotative statement is surely a stroke of Hawthorne's art when we consider the emotional plight of a baffled and bereft Brown. Shouting out Faith's name, he is mocked to the echo. Then his resolution breaks and, in his extreme dejection, the dark cloud disappears and a pink ribbon which flutters down compounds his anguish. There is no goodness he thinks; "sin is but a name." He capitulates. "Come, devil; for to thee is this world given." Abandoned, he despairs, and despairing, like Ethan Brand, he laughs hysterically loud and long. Unlike the Devil's laughter, his is not mirthful, but terrible to hear.

Brown runs madly along the wild, dreary, obscure path that takes him deeper into the heart of darkness. The night is now filled with frightful sounds and, among these, as in Mussorgsky's "A Night on Bald Mountain," there is a sound "like a distant churchbell"—the wind. Possessed by the hysteria of despair, Brown tries to outlaugh what he thinks is the scornful derision of the wilderness. In the forest of the night—that is to say, in the blackness of his

subconscious despair—"he was himself the chief horror of the scene, and shrank not from its other horrors." Devil-possessed and despairing, he runs through the haunted forest, brandishing his staff, venting horrid blasphemy, outracing the fiend who, by now, has pretty well victimized the bedeviled husbandman.

Goodman Brown's frenzied charge through the forest is halted by a lurid red light in a forest enclosure where a grave and dark-clad congregation, their several voices rolling solemnly through the wild night, worship at a Witches' Sabbath. Before the forest-hemmed group rears a pulpit rock, illumined by blazing pine tops, and among the assembled leaders of the Salem community are both the reputable and pious as well as the suspect, dissolute, and criminal. Sinners and Indian priests, heathen and Christian, are distinguishable but united. And leading the impious assembly is one of the grave New England divines.

When the cry for converts is raised, Brown is led forward by Deacon Gookin to the blazing altar where he stands with another proselyte, a veiled woman, none other than Faith. Welcomed to the loathful brotherhood of lechers, poisoners, parricides, and infanticides, the couple is exhorted to be undeceived. "Evil is the nature of mankind," they are told. "Evil must be your only happiness." Before the fiend-light of the unhallowed altar, gazed at by faces "that would be seen next day at the council board of the province, and others which, Sabbath after Sabbath, look devoutly heavenward, and benignantly over the crowded pews, from the holiest pulpits in the land," the husband and wife about to be baptized in "the mystery of sin" look upon each other and shudder. Imploring his wife to resist the devil and look to heaven, Brown breaks the spell.

The telltale disclosure of Brown's illusory nocturnal meeting is a natural fact. First he staggers against a rock which *feels* chill and damp. Then a hanging twig, which a moment before had seemed on fire, "besprinkled his cheek with the coldest dew." The tactile fact disabuses his overwrought imagination. The fiery twig is delusive. Nevertheless the nocturnal meeting will haunt him to his dying day. Next morning he is observed in Salem Village "staring around him like a bewildered man." He shrinks from the good old minister; he challenges as a recusant the old Deacon whom he overhears praying; he interferes in Goody Cloyse's religious exercises by snatching away a child being catechized, "as from the grasp of the fiend himself," and he behaves strangely to Faith who "almost kissed her husband before the whole village."

Young Goodman Brown is not the same man who at sunset the day before entered upon the errand into the wilderness with such grudging compulsion. The "fearful dream" has done its work. Somewhere in this fact and phrase is the heart of Hawthorne's message, it would seem.

III

How shall we riddle this marvellous tale? One of Hawthorne's attributions is an ability to penetrate the surface of conscious perception. In his introduction to *Psychology and Alchemy,* Jung says: "It must be admitted that the archetypal contents of the collective unconscious can often assume grotesque and horrible forms in dreams and fantasies, so that even the most hard-boiled rationalist is not immune from shattering nightmares and haunting fears." In **"Young Goodman Brown"** Hawthorne continues a lonely vigil in the dark surrealistic forest of the American mind. He reveals presciently the turbulence beneath the layers of the Puritan conscience: the form its guilt takes, the contributions of grace and election, the sense of justice, the invocation of mercy. He evokes the depth of the Puritan mind which expresses itself, not only in witches' waxen images pricked with thorns, but in the nocturnal coven and in the black man's book in which are inscribed names in blood from cut fingers. Under the spell of the dark imagination which apprehends tragic realities, Hawthorne never fails to acknowledge the community of human relationship. What Brown discovers is a terrible thing, surely; not that evil coexists with good in human nature, but that "evil is the nature of mankind." He also finds out what it means to be inducted into a mystery that makes him "more conscious of the secret of others." And he exults as he beholds "the whole earth one stain of guilt, one mighty blood spot." One mighty blood spot! To the exclusion of anything else, guilt prevails, and all things are evermore suspect.

The effect of Brown's discovery is terrible. What he should have recognized as only one of the powerful forces in "the collective unconscious" becomes *the* exclusive force. After the night of the fearful dream, Goodman Brown, of whom there are thousands resembling him as his name, sex, and age imply, is unable to accept as true of himself what is true of all men: that evil is counterbalanced by an essential good.

The dream journey is a remarkable one. The compulsion that drives him is not only inward (he doesn't, for instance, share its motive with anyone else, certainly not with Faith); it is downward. The descent is symbolized by the journey from daylight into night, from consciousness to subconsciousness, from reality to illusion, from physical to psychical, from light to dark. The chief positive factor is Brown's fidelity to the covenant, the consequences of which suggest that fidelity is not a higher virtue than intelligent exercise of will. The effect upon him is negative; he is equal to the obligation of the tryst but he is not equal to its consequences. He is forever turned darkly inward, a distrustful and despairing man.

When Brown returns from the forest, the nature of his change is as arresting as the motive for his compulsive pact with the devil is equivocal. He has been *there,* but exactly why he has had to be there is not clear. In *The Hero with a Thousand Faces,* Joseph Campbell describes the mythic hero. "A hero ventures forth from the world of common day into a region of supernatural wonder," he says; "fabulous forces are there encountered and a decisive victory is won; the hero comes back from this mysterious venture with the power to bestow honors on his fellow men." How little of Campbell's description of the hero can be applied to Hawthorne's protagonist. The world of common day is in the tale; so, too, is the region of supernatural wonders and the fabulous forces. But there is no victory, and so Brown's return from the mysterious venture is without prestigious power to bestow honors. Quite the contrary. An antihero, he rabidly infects his fellow man with the virus of his grim, inexpiable despair of human trust.

IV

What meaning does this tale have for us today? What in the story has survival value beyond the interest a reader has in the effectiveness of Hawthorne's artistic competence? How to account for Brown's malaise is really less relevant than the meaning of his actions. It would appear—and this is, I think, Hawthorne's insight—a case of psychic masochism in which Brown's compulsion is in reality the expression of the desire for self-punishment. Brown appears to do nothing wrong except to go through with a commitment that he might reasonably have rejected in the first place. Yet once having committed himself, he still might have exorcised the inner devil of suspicion. That he fails to do this is *his* particular story and *our* particular revelation. There is no forestalling self-punishment. Neither is it possible to modify the effects inflicted on others—on Faith and the community of Brown's fellowship. And this is similarly applicable to every self-destructive protagonist in literature, whether a Byronic, Melvilleian, Hardyesque, or contemporary fictional character.

The symbolic forest of the night is, in effect, young Goodman Brown's own dark soul where belief turns into doubt, faith into skepticism, and where the people encountered are the adumbrations of his daily familiars and ancestral past. This dream is symbolically true. Significantly, it underscores D. H. Lawrence's contention. "You *must* look through the surface of American art and see the inner diabolism of the symbolic meaning," said Lawrence. "Otherwise it is all mere childishness." The symbolic meaning is to be found in the stresses and conflicts, the compulsions and repressions whose compensations, as Sir Herbert Read says in *The Philosophy of Modern Art,* are found in "the physical horrors of war and persecution." The *Walpurgis Nacht* of Dachau and Buchenwald of the 1940's had its source in the conflict between the Nazis and the Jews for the extension of power in the economic system of twentieth-century Germany.

Hawthorne's tale embodies the effect of tensions applicable in the social life of a nation, a people, and individuals. **"Young Goodman Brown"** focusses on one of these archetypal stresses. The tale is, as we have noted, a paradigm. It focusses on a fearful dream that is part of our subconscious reality. Although Hawthorne's medium is fiction, he is focussing on truth as he understands it. But he has chosen to release this truth as though it were a dream fantasy. The gas ovens of the 1940's and the lurid Witches' Sabbath of the seventeenth century are equally symbolic. So symbolic, in fact, that he who runs may read, but he who runs with most deliberation may read the deepest meaning. Diabolism is quite as apparent in what others do to us by persecution as it is in what we do to ourselves when we fail in acknowledging the moral consequences of our actions.

The important point in Hawthorne's tale is not that Brown's malaise is, or seems, incurable, but that it is definitely symptomatic. Given these traits, tendencies, and impulses and the effect will be comparable. Anyone of us might be susceptible to a similar psychological predicament. The syndrome is complete. What is significant about the tale? The epiphany occurs when the reader released from the narrative's pervasive darkness is struck by Hawthorne's laser. However much Brown fails himself by stubborn will, determined pride, callow gullibility, and obsessively fixated self-centeredness, he does not, even in his frailty, fail us. As Robert Frost says: "So false it is that what we haven't we can't give." This is one of the great paradoxes in the human condition. Brown's negativism challenges us to find a means of establishing positive traits. The opposite of Brown's unendurable world of incertitude is one where the enabling virtues of compassion and pity, love and trust, fidelity, and hope are activated. Brown, one in the gallery of Hawthorne's moody men which includes Brand and Bourne, Warland and Chillingworth, is the psychological victim hung up between damnation and salvation.

In the harrowing world of incertitude in which he lives out his days Brown is psychologically sick with the fear that what he has seen in the illusory forest of the night is so, that all those hallucinatory scenes were in reality peopled by victims of sin familiar to him. When illusions are mistaken for realities the victim is caught in his own trap; is, in effect, self-betrayed. Hawthorne's climactic statement is apposite. "A stern, a sad, a darkly meditative, a distrustful, if not desperate man, did he become from the night of that fearful dream." In the forest of Brown's night only the wrath of God burns brightly. His journey into an awareness of evil brings a consciousness of guilt *without* redemption. Unable to transcend the experience through humility and compassion, he is resigned to desperation. In consequence, he symbolizes the man who is shriveled rather than tempered by the pain and suffering which accompany an encounter with evil. It can never be said of him as it is said in *Meister Eckhart:* "Not till the soul knows all that there is to be known can she pass over to the unknown good."

Hawthorne's insight is startling: that confronting us everywhere is the inescapable universal guilt, like one mighty blood spot as ineradicable as the stains on Lady Macbeth's hands and soul. The effect on Brown—and on us—is haunting. This tale reenacts an *unfortunate* fall. Brown keeps his compact, encounters a demon, and suffers an ordeal, only to be irrevocably transformed by the experience in no soul-cleansing way. "But clear Truth is a thing for salamander giants only to encounter;" says Melville, "how small the chances for the provincials then?" Small, indeed, if the provincial is like Goodman Brown who, when tested by a searing experience, proves equal to the occasion but unequal to its effect, and forever after remains a victim of a corrosive soul-torturing suspicion of general human guilt.

Wayne Dickson (essay date 1971)

SOURCE: "Hawthorne's 'Young Goodman Brown'," in *The Explicator,* Vol. XXIX, No. 5, January, 1971, item 44.

[*In the following, Dickson notes that Goodman Brown lacks charity, the greatest of the Christian virtues.*]

Nathaniel Hawthorne's **"Young Goodman Brown"** is the story of a youth's initiation into the knowledge of the universality of the evil in man's heart. The story is ambiguous on the question of whether this newfound knowledge is trustworthy or illusory, though it is perhaps significant that the only guarantor of the authenticity of Brown's experience is the Devil, himself the father of deception. Nevertheless, from the standpoint of Brown's psychology, the inherent truth of falsity of the knowledge is unimportant anyway. What matters is first that he accepts it as true, and second that, having done so, he becomes "a stern, a sad, a darkly meditative, a distrustful, if not a desperate man. . . ."

Now it is interesting that a person raised in a Puritan culture should be traumatized by the realization that evil is a universal feature of human nature. After all, that this is so is a prime tenet of the Calvinist theology. There are several possible explanations. Perhaps Brown's hitherto academic knowledge of evil had just now been personally borne home to him. Perhaps he had become convinced that evil was not just *an* ingredient of human nature, but the main ingredient. Since this still seems insufficient, I would like to suggest that at least one other factor is involved, a weakness in Brown's own character.

In *I Corinthians,* XIII, 13, the Apostle Paul establishes a hierarchy of Christian virtue: "And now abideth faith, hope, charity, these three; but the greatest of these is charity." Hawthorne seems clearly to have this verse in mind when he writes, "'But where is Faith?' thought Goodman Brown; and as hope came into his heart, he trembled." The omission of charity is conspicuous—not just its verbal omission in this passage, but also its absence in fact from Brown's life. The concept of *charity* was understood in Hawthorne's day to mean the disinterested, altruistic, forgiving love that forms the basis of Christian character. It is apparent that Brown lacks this virtue. He is unwilling to grant his neighbors the benefit of a reasonable doubt let alone the grace of forgiveness in the face of known sin. He accept at face value the experience the Devil has prepared for him, but he is unwilling to offer to even his close friends the chance to defend themselves or to explain their actions. The penalty for such a failure of charity is again hinted at by St. Paul, who says, "[If I] have not charity, I am nothing." Hawthorne puts it a little differently: ". . . they carved no hopeful verse upon his tombstone, for his dying hour was gloom."

Harry M. Campbell (essay date 1971)

SOURCE: "Freudianism, American Romanticism, and 'Young Goodman Brown'," in *The CEA Critic,* Vol. 33, No. 3, March, 1971, pp. 3-6.

[*In the essay below, Campbell rejects psychoanalytic interpretations of "Young Goodman Brown," which see the story as an allegory of the conflict caused by sexual sin.*]

Certainly Freudian criticism has made substantial contributions to the understanding of some aspects of American romanticism—in studies of the sexual symbolism in much of Whitman's best poetry, the tortured ambiguities of Melville's *Pierre* and some of his short stories, and the relation between Poe's probable impotence and his creative work, to mention only a few examples that come readily to mind. It has even been said that some of the American Romanticists themselves anticipated Freud in describing the shadowy subliminal origin of some of their images. It seems to me, however, that in the twilight area between the unconscious and the conscious of the Romanticists these vague beginnings of images which then emerged into the conscious and became full images were not pre-Freudian but were far closer to what Jacques Maritain [in *Creative Intuition in Art and Poetry,* 1955], has called creative intuition or the spiritual preconscious, of which, says Maritain, "Plato and the ancient wise men were aware, and the disregard of which in favor of the Freudian unconscious alone is a sign of the dullness of our times." Maritain says that poetic intuition is born in the unconscious but emerges from it, and the poet may be aware of it, as Bergson would have said, on the edge of the unconscious; but the Freudian unconscious is one "of blood and flesh, instincts, tendencies, complexes, repressed images and desires, traumatic memories, as constituting a closed or autonomous dynamic whole." The Freudian unconscious, then, is *automatic* or *deaf*—"deaf to the intellect, and structured into a world of its own apart from the intellect." If this description seems unfair to Freud, we must remember that even so devoted a psychoanalyst as C. G. Jung, who for several years was a follower of Freud, finally broke with him in 1913, because, in Jung's opinion, Freud's unconscious is limited to the "animal" and does not include the "divine" in man. In other words, the libido for Jung is equivalent to all psychic energy, both "human" and "divine," or, as one critic has said [Frederick J. Hoffman, in *Freudianism and the Literary Mind,* 1945], Jung's libido "is created genetically and is desexualized. . . ."

Freud's position, to say the least, is paradoxical, perhaps even contradictory. He acknowledges his indebtedness to the romantic poets and philosophers who he says discovered the unconscious before him, but at the same time Freud's philosophy is deterministic and he claims to be strictly scientific. With all his interest in literature, it constitutes for him a type of clinical study, and he considers the literary man a neurotic escapist from reality—the escape being relatively harmless unless it becomes involved with religion, which Freud regards as a dangerously harmful illusion.

The real connection, in my opinion, between Freudianism and some types of Romanticism is (1) their overemphasis on the supremacy of the individual—his boundless possibilities for realizing both pleasure and happiness, the Aristotelian distinction between pleasure and happiness becoming somewhat blurred in the process;

and (2) the tendency of both Freudianism and certain types of Romanticism to employ extravagant metaphors or symbols. The loose metaphors of the Romantic poets have been analyzed and attacked (sometimes unjustly) by the New Critics. Freud, too, is fundamentally a Romantic poet though writing in prose and concentrating on sexual metaphors or symbols that will hardly bear close logical inspection to describe the hidden motives of human thoughts and actions. The fertility of his poetic imagination applied usually to sex (sometimes to other bodily functions) reminds one of Whitman and may have its origin in ancient Dionysian or phallic rites which Whitman, it will be remembered, named as one of his many "faiths."

Freud, to be sure, does show some imaginative discrimination in the application of his theory to literature, but, perhaps flattered by their adoration of him, he lends his approval to the work of some of the most extreme among his followers—most notably perhaps Albert Mordell and Marie Bonaparte. In *The Erotic Motive in Literature,* for example, Mordell says that the source of much re-explanation of creative genius will be found "in the infantile love life of the authors." And in her *Edgar Poe, Étude Psychoanalytique,* Marie Bonaparte postulates a strong unconscious necrophilia in Poe stemming originally from his infantile sexual desire for his mother. Of course, fixation on his mother was undoubtedly one of the sources of Poe's abnormality; but, since his mother died when he was three years old, it is highly questionable whether infantile sexuality could extend that far back—such was the more reasonable conclusion of Krutch's distinguished psychoanalytical biography on this point.

If, then, there is clearly danger of excess in Freudian criticism of obviously abnormal writers like Poe, how much more caution is needed in applying such criticism to Romantic authors such as Hawthorne and Longfellow, who were not in reality sexually abnormal and for whom sex (even imaginatively) was not of primary importance as it was for Whitman.

My final illustration is concerned with the Freudian analyses of **"Young Goodman Brown,"** specifically those by Roy Male, Daniel G. Hoffman, and Frederick C. Crews. [in *The Sins of the Fathers,* 1966] says that Brown's whole forest journey is "a vicarious and lurid sexual adventure" of one whose "sexual attitude is that of a young boy rather than a normal bridegroom," and whose "fantasy experience, like that of Robin Molineux, follows the classic Oedipal pattern." Male [in *Hawthorne's Tragic Vision,* 1957] says that "almost everything in the forest scene suggests that the communion of sinners is essentially sexual. . . ." Daniel G. Hoffman [in *Form and Fable in American Fiction,* 1961] finds that "phallic and psychosexual associations are made intrinsic to the thematic development of [Hawthorne's] story. . . . Brown's whole experience is described as a penetration of a dark and lonely way through a branched forest. . . . At journey's end is the orgiastic communion amidst the leaping flames." Of the pink ribbons specifically, Male says, ". . . the pink ribbons blend with the serpentine staff in what becomes a fierce orgy of lust."

My objection to these interpretations is that they oversimplify Hawthorne by making him narrowly Freudian (or pre-Freudian). In the first place, there is nothing in the story specifically indicating the sexual blending of the ribbons referred to by Male and carried to a further extreme by Daniel Hoffman and especially by Crews. The ribbons—mentioned several times near the beginning of the story, again just before (and helping to precipitate) the climax, and again at the end (where Faith joyfully greets Brown returning from the forest)—are an important unifying symbol. They operate at the literal level to identify the young and faithful wife. The ribbon falling from the sky in the dark forest indicates that she has succumbed to temptation. Brown's perception of the falling ribbon indicates also that he has ceased to struggle against temptation ("My Faith is gone!"), and he immediately rushes to the Witches' Sabbath.

The apparent realism of the falling ribbon (to which Matthiessen objects, though not on Freudian principles) is only one aspect of the calculated ambiguity which Hawthorne achieves all through the story. His great artistry consists in his keeping the reader in the twilight zone between the fantastic or the supernatural and the realistic, with a leaning toward the former but with enough of the latter to make his treatment of "the mystery of sin" both complex and convincing. In this twilight zone the effect on the reader soon moves from an association to a fusing of the realistic and the fantastic. The realistic falling ribbon, then, soon (and almost imperceptibly) merges into the supernatural atmosphere of the preparation for the Witches' Sabbath—the same type of fusion that has been in process throughout the story.

Of course, sexual sins are mentioned in the Witches' Sabbath, but so are various other sins. For Hawthorne fornication and adultery were sins, even when (as with the lovers in *The Scarlet Letter*) there were mitigating circumstances. But for Hawthorne, as for Dante, there were far worse sins than the carnal (that of Chillingworth, for example, in *The Scarlet Letter*), and these also are in **"Young Goodman Brown."** Brown feels "a loathful brotherhood" with the congregation at the Witches' Sabbath "by the sympathy of *all* [italics mine] that was wicked in his heart"; and the Devil says in his sermon to the whole group: "It shall be yours to penetrate, in every bosom, the deep mystery of sin, the fountain of all wicked arts. . . ."

Brown's sin, then, is far worse than deserting his wife. There is no real evidence for believing, as does Crews, that the main theme of **"Young Goodman Brown"** is "Brown's horror of adulthood, his inability to accept the place of sexuality in married love." As a matter of fact, Brown has been very happily married to Faith, and the thought of this happiness almost persuades him to return to her after he has been disillusioned by discovering the wickedness of his former spiritual teacher Goody Cloyse. As he is resolving to return to Faith, these thoughts go

through his mind: "And what calm sleep would be his that very night, which was to have been spent so wickedly, but so purely and sweetly now, in the arms of Faith!" Furthermore, the melancholy of Faith at his departure and her rejoicing at his return indicate that she has been as happy in their marriage as he. The immediate cause of Brown's failure to act on his good resolution to return to Faith is the appearance in the evil forest of two others, Deacon Gookin and the minister, in both of whom Brown has trusted for spiritual guidance, but who were clearly headed for the Witches' Sabbath. Such, in Hawthorne's opinion, are the depths of "the mystery of sin" that even happily married people are often destroyed by it. Even Faith participated in the evil rites but recovered the next day and could have been happy again if Brown could also have recovered.

Crews limits Brown's "fantasy-experience" to "the classic Oedipal pattern . . . conjoined with ambiguous sexual temptation." When the Devil is reciting to Brown the sins of Brown's ancestors, Crews interprets them all as sexual. For example, the constable lashing "the Quaker woman so smartly through the streets of Salem" is, in Crews's opinion, guilty of sadistic "sexual irregularity." Following this pattern, the pitch-pine knot with which Brown's father set fire to an Indian village would have to be a phallic symbol. The "state secrets" of the church deacons, town selectmen, and members of the Great and General Court referred to by the Devil would have to be sexual in implication, for, as Crews tells us, Brown's whole forest experience "serves his private need to make lurid sexual complaints against mankind."

To repeat: The dramatic interweaving of realism with fantasy so that we willingly suspend our disbelief in the fantasy is facilitated by the pink ribbons, which are used both to maintain the realism and to unify the story. Sexual sin is present in this story, because it is part of what Hawthorne considered to be the evil in human nature, but to interpret the ribbons, the serpentine staff, the pine-knot, the constable's whip, and other objects mentioned in the story as specifically sexual symbols is to limit it to a narrowly Freudian allegory. Hawthorne was concerned, indeed almost obsessed, with what he considered to be "the deep mystery of sin, the fountain of all wicked arts," and the power of his work lies in his ability to dramatize his ideas so that they move even those who disagree with him about the nature of man.

Freudian criticism, then, can throw light on those aspects of American Romanticism which are predominantly sexual, at least in implication, but to push such analysis beyond this point is not much more helpful than, though seldom so ridiculous as, the explanation by one Freudian critic that Little Red Riding Hood's red cap is a menstrual symbol and that her whole story is an allegory of the conflict between male and female in which the young virgin outwits the ruthless, sex-hungry "wolf" [Erich Fromm, *The Forgotten Language,* 1957].

John B. Humma (essay date 1971)

SOURCE: "'Young Goodman Brown' and the Failure of Hawthorne's Ambiguity," in *Colby Library Quarterly,* Vol. IX, No. 8, December, 1971, pp. 425-31.

[In this essay, Humma argues that the ambiguous ending of "Young Goodman Brown" reveals Hawthorne's artistic failure rather than his triumph.]

Most critics of **"Young Goodman Brown"** consider it one of Hawthorne's finest short stories. Richard H. Fogle, for instance, says [in *Hawthorne's Fiction: The Light and the Dark,* 1952] that in **"Young Goodman Brown"** Hawthorne has achieved that "reconciliation of opposites which Coleridge deemed the highest art." Daniel Hoffman [in *Form and Fable in American Literature,* 1965] ranks it as "one of Hawthorne's masterpieces." To Roy Male **"Young Goodman Brown"** is nothing less than "one of the world's great short stories" [*Hawthorne's Tragic Vision,* 1957]. In spite of such accolades (or perhaps because of them), few critics are agreed as to the story's precise meaning. In general, the criticism falls into two broad categories: to the first belong such critics as Male, Fogle, and Harry Levin, who feel the story reveals Hawthorne's sentiments about the essential iniquity of mankind [Levin, *The Power of Blackness,* 1958]; to the second belong those who contend that it is not humanity at all that Hawthorne indicts, but Brown himself. For both groups, the question of whether Brown experienced or dreamed the events in the forest assumes paramount importance. Paul J. Hurley, for one, states [in "Young Goodman Brown's 'Heart of Darkness'," in *American Literature* XXXVII, January 1966] that "if Young Goodman Brown did not have a nightmare or experience hallucinations, Hawthorne has created a fearful indictment of humanity."

Mark Van Doren, on the other hand, arguing [in *Nathaniel Hawthorne,* 1949] that these events are in fact dreamed by Brown, writes that Brown "sees evil where it is not." F. O. Matthiessen and W. B. Stein also insist upon Brown's guilt, arguing with Van Doren that Brown perceives evil where is does not exist. One of the more recent apologists for this viewpoint is Hurley, who contends that the evil Brown sees is "the product of his own fancy with no reality save that supplied by his depraved imagination." Outside the pale of both groups of critics is David Levin. He argues [in "Shadows of Doubt: Specter Evidence in Hawthorne's 'Young Goodman Brown'," in *American Literature* XXXIV, November 1962] that Brown neither dreamed nor hallucinated but was instead the victim of the devil, who ingeniously conjured the apparitions, or "specters," of Brown's fellow villagers. Levin remarks that Brown commits the same error as that committed by the good Salem residents in 1692: "He lets the Devil's true statements about the maltreatment of Indians and Quakers prepare him to accept counterfeit evidence, and he fails to insist upon the difference between a person and a person's 'shape' or specter." Levin goes on to say that the majority of modern critics have fallen into the same error.

I will risk repeating their mistake (and Brown's) and argue that those elders Brown encounters in the forest are present in the flesh. The plain facts of the story warrant no other conclusion. Moreover, I would contend that the probes by Hurley and Levin are valuable for their weaknesses as well as their strengths. These weaknesses lead to an understanding of Hawthorne's real intentions in the story. After examining first Levin's article and then Hurley's, I would like to turn to the evaluation by Fogle of the story's literary merits, which he believes derive in good measure from the ambiguity in the story. Fogle argues that the ambiguity is the result of Hawthorne's reticence to express what in his heart of hearts he felt to be true of humanity, an ambiguity which Fogle says results in the "highest art." It seems to me that this ambiguity results rather in an art that is contrived and finally dishonest.

The ambiguity of "Young Goodman Brown" results in an art that is contrived and finally dishonest.

—John B. Humma

David Levin's analysis can be quickly dispensed with. He states that Hawthorne clearly recognized the significance played by "specter evidence" in the actual trials. Hawthorne, in fact, says Levin, in two stories ("Alice Doane's Appeal" and "Main Street") "explicitly mentioned the devil's ability to impersonate innocent people." But then how does Levin explain Hawthorne's failure to mention this ability in **"Young Goodman Brown"**? When Hawthorne errs it is generally in the way of overstatement, not understatement. He almost always overexposes—almost never underexposes—his tales. It seems unreasonable therefore to be asked to believe that Hawthorne would use the device of specter evidence without first establishing his intentions. Nothing else in his writings suggests he would do such a thing.

One also wonders why Hawthorne, if the reality in the story is indeed spectral, would pose the question of Brown's dreaming the event. Levin seems to feel that Hawthorne was concerned that some nineteenth-century readers might be too sophisticated "to take devils seriously even in historical fiction" and therefore felt called upon to fabricate an alternative possibility. This is a possibility, but it appears at best to be a precariously tenuous one.

According to D. Levin, the devil stage-manages the entire performance on that fateful night in the wilderness, from the moment Brown first sees Goody Cloyse until the moment at which he apparently passes out from shock. Levin's theory has the advantage of plausibly accounting for Faith's pink ribbons, a detail whose "literal existence" Matthiessen found objectionable [F. O. Matthieson, *American Renaissance,* 1941]. But it has the larger disadvantage of being unable to explain Hawthorne's treatment of the "appearances" of the minister and Deacon Gookin. Although Brown hears their voices and the sounds they make as they pass, he cannot see them. Concerning this phenomenon, Levin writes that "Brown cannot see 'so much as a shadow,' but he 'could have sworn'—as witnesses in 1692 did indeed swear—that he recognized the deacon and the minister in 'the voices talking so strangely in the empty air'." One has to ask why Hawthorne, since he gives his other specters flesh and blood embodiment, fails to do the same with the apparitions—as Levin contends they are—of the minister and the deacon. If these figures are in fact what Levin asserts they are, the devil plainly has little reason for making apparitions of apparitions. For this reason and those stated above, it seems best to go back to the original alternatives of dream and reality.

Like David Levin, Hurley believes that Hawthorne intended his story to be read as an account of a single individual's perversion and not as an indictment of the moral nature of man in general. But neither should the story be read as an account of the masterful talents of the devil: "To take guilt away from human beings in order to place it on infernal powers is not a satisfactory explanation of the story." Very true. (Levin argues, of course, that Brown is not absolved from guilt, that he should have seen through the devil's improvisations.) Yet one wonders why Hurley should feel Brown is not morally responsible in the one instance (when he is tricked by the devil) but is in the other (when he hallucinates). In both cases apparently Brown took what he saw *as* reality.

Like Levin, Hurley treads shaky ground when he argues that the passage in which Brown thinks he hears the voices of the minister and Deacon Gookin proves Brown's willingness to see what is not there. Hawthorne's passage, however, leaves little doubt that *something* is there:

> On came the hoof tramps and the voices of the riders, two grave old voices, conversing soberly as they drew near. These mingled sounds appeared to pass along the road, within a few yards of the young man's hiding place; but, owing doubtless to the depth of the gloom at that particular spot, neither the travellers nor their steeds were visible. Though their figures brushed the small boughs by the wayside, it could not be seen that they intercepted, even for a moment, the faint gleam from the strip of bright sky athwart which they must have passed. Goodman Brown alternately crouched and stood on tiptoe, pulling aside the branches and thrusting forth his head as far as he durst without discerning so much as a shadow. It vexed him the more, because he could have sworn, were such a thing possible, that he recognized the voices of the minister and Deacon Gookin, jogging along quietly, as they were wont to do, when bound to some ordination or ecclesiastical council. While yet within hearing, one of the riders stopped to pluck a switch.

Hurley writes that "Fogle has alluded to this passage too as evidence of Hawthorne's ambiguity, but there is no ambiguity in the fact that Goodman Brown actually *saw* nothing at all. Nevertheless, he stands 'doubting whether there really was a heaven above him'." There are two objections to Hurley's argument: First, there is no ambiguity about the fact that the voices Brown hears are actual voices; nor is there any ambiguity about the fact that the "figures" brush against the vegetation. Hawthorne does not after all say *seem*. Second, if Hurley's conclusions are based on the fact of the literal invisibility of the deacon and the minister, then why has he not acknowledged the literal *visibility* of the devil, Goody Cloyse, Faith's famous ribbon, Faith herself, and all those elders present at the diabolical ceremony before the stone altar?

Hurley argues further that if Hawthorne's theme had been the "universality of human sinfulness" he would have manifested a greater evidence of it: yet "the only scene in which such a manifestation occurs is the Devil's communion, but that takes place after Goodman Brown has declared his loss of faith." Perhaps Brown has made such a declaration: earlier he had proclaimed that his faith was gone, that the world was the devil's. But again, perhaps he has not: after all, his last words in the forest are "Faith! Faith! look up to heaven, and resist the wicked one." But really, what difference does it make? Why should Brown be less inclined to see evil in people while he still has his faith—and Hurley does contend that Brown is searching for evil at that point—than after he has lost it?

Hurley is convinced that had Hawthorne wanted us to believe in the literalness of the events, he would not have confused us with the dream possibility—unless (as he goes on to qualify) Fogle's theory *is* correct, and Hawthorne was attempting to escape the implications of his own suspicions about the iniquity of the human race. The latter alternative, which Hurley rejects, would appear to be more nearly the right one. But one can nonetheless turn Hurley's supposition around and ask why, if Hawthorne had wanted us to believe that Goodman Brown was dreaming, did he confuse us with the possibility that the events might be real? In actuality, there is no good reason to believe that Brown dreamed or hallucinated anything. The *only* occasion in the story when he can be observed to lose consciousness occurs *after* he has viewed the assembly at the "communion" ceremony. It is, incidentally, for this reason that Hurley is careful to hold out the possibility that Brown perhaps hallucinated instead of dreamed. Hawthorne's own reply—"Be it so if you will"—to his question as to whether Brown had "only" dreamed a wild dream certainly implies a negative response, as if he means to say, "Go ahead and believe it a dream if, for reasons of your own, that is what you must believe."

Fogle considers this ambiguity the "very essence of Hawthorne's tale." He says that Hawthorne wishes to propose, not flatly that man is primarily evil, but instead the gnawing doubt lest this should indeed be true" and concludes that the ambiguity which Hawthorne deliberately affects is integral to this purpose. I could not agree more wholeheartedly. The "multiple choice" device, as Matthiessen called it, does yeoman work in **"Young Goodman Brown."** But I must part company with Fogle when he proposes that the use of this device results in an artistic triumph, adding "depth and force to Hawthorne's thin and delicate fabric." Fogle contends that "above all, the separate instances of this 'multiple choice device' organically cohere to reproduce in the reader's mind the feel of the central ambiguity or theme, the horror of the hero's doubt. Goodman Brown, a simple and pious nature, is wrecked as a result of the disappearance of the fixed poles of his belief. His orderly cosmos dissolves into chaos as church and state, the twin pillars of his society, are hinted to be rotten, with their foundations undermined. The yearning for certainty is basic to his spirit—and he is left without the comfort even of a firm reliance in the Devil."

It should be noted that Fogle fails to consider Hawthorne's criticism of Brown—more than just implied, it seems to me—in the story's concluding paragraph. This criticism is hardly in keeping with the possibility that the events Brown witnessed were real, for if so, as even Hurley admits, Brown cannot very well be held at fault for the gloom of his later behavior. How else is he to react to such a total indictment of human nature?

In *The Catcher in the Rye,* J. D. Salinger, through the relentlessly honest eyes of Holden Caulfield, is able to impeach all those sorry details of human behavior that he—Salinger—apparently despises. Yet at the end of the novel Holden finds *himself* impeached for the damning indictments which the author has framed, with so much evident relish, in his hero's language. Is Salinger having his cake and eating it, too? It would seem that Hawthorne is attempting to both have *his* and eat it: for the multiple choice device permits Hawthorne to condemn humanity in the instance of the one possibility (the events as real), and to condemn Brown in the instance of the other (the events as figments of Brown's imagination). The question is whether such a method is art or trickery. Should we admire the story as a genuine treatment of the human condition or rather as an ingenious precursor of the O. Henry short story (*sans* the happy or wistful ending)?

Should we admire the story as a genuine treatment of the human condition or rather as an ingenious precursor of the O. Henry short story (*sans* the happy or wistful ending)?

—John B. Humma

A comparison might be helpful in this respect. Melville, in "Bartleby the Scrivener," portrays an individual who, like old Goodman Brown, lives in isolation from the rest of humanity. Like Brown's isolation, Bartleby's appears to be both willful, on the one hand, and the result of an unfortunate experience, or an accumulation of unfortunate experiences, on the other. The primary difference between the two stories lies in the authors' treatments of the protagonists' situations. In Melville's story, there is perhaps an implied criticism of Bartleby though it is difficult to know for certain. But more significantly, there is the

great—and one senses, genuine—flow of sympathy that goes out from Melville toward Bartleby and for the tragedy that this bereft man has wrought for himself. "Ah Bartleby, ah humanity," the narrator sighs at the story's end. Yet the narrator, as well as Bartleby, represents Everyman, and one can see that in spite of the pronounced differences in their situations, there is not finally so great a *distance* between them.

Although Melville sympathetically comprehends Bartleby's condition, Hawthorne on his part appears to have but little appreciation for the tragic circumstances in which Brown finds himself. Hawthorne prefers to give us after all a pair of alternate possibilities. And if, as in the one alternative, Brown actually witnessed the events in the forest, then he is faced with a situation to which he cannot possibly accommodate himself (the standard Hawthorne remedy). Hawthorne's failure to deal with the sad plight of old Goodman Brown in the light of this alternative represents nothing less than a failure of art, a failure to responsibly cope with a problem he has deliberately allowed to surface. Brown deserves not so much censure as understanding. For the reality he confronts, like that Bartleby thinks (at least) he confronts, does not for once admit of adjustment. Adjustment here for Brown would mean complicity in evil. Hawthorne's refusal, however, to confront the dilemma into which he has thrown Brown signifies more than an artistic deficiency. It also signifies a deficiency in the author of the one quality that could have brought justice to both the hero and the story: compassion. **"Young Goodman Brown"** then does not represent, as Fogle claims, the triumph of art; it represents rather the failure of the artist's vital responsibility toward his material.

Robert E. Morsberger (essay date 1973)

SOURCE: "The Woe That Is Madness: Goodman Brown and the Face of the Fire," in *The Nathaniel Hawthorne Journal 1973*, edited by C. E. Frazer Clark, Jr., Microcard Editions Books, 1973, pp. 177-82.

[*In the following essay, Morsberger contends that Goodman Brown's loss of faith in others reflects the beginnings of American political and social paranoia.*]

Hawthorne, if any one, was equipped to write the definitive novel on the Salem witchcraft delusion; but he never confronted it head on. "Alice Doane's Appeal" conjures up the victims from the graveyard, *Grandfather's Chair* and "Main Street" give the barest bones of a synopsis, "Sir William Phips" merely hints at it, and *The House of the Seven Gables* fictionalizes its heritage of guilt. But nowhere does Hawthorne give the dramatic account in depth of the trial and tragedy of Rebecca Nurse, George Burroughs, John Proctor, Giles Corey, George Jacobs and the other courageous victims, nor the damnable game of the "afflicted" girls, the admission of spectral evidence by autocratic judges, nor the sinister attempt by paranoid theocrats to maintain their power through terror. It remained for lesser writers to deal with such matters, for

Hawthorne was not so much chronicling our history as he was molding the legend of our past. Thus the wholly fictitious **"Young Goodman Brown"** is our most effective literary work in recreating the atmosphere in which the witchcraft hysteria occurred.

"Young Goodman Brown" is Hawthorne's most successful story. Here he is free from the authorial editorializing that makes some other tales excessively didactic. Nowhere does the author intrude; such moral generalizations as the story contains are spoken by the devil, who is, of course, unreliable. The reader is spared such obvious guidelines as, "and this shall be a moral unto you," that seem too contrived; and their plots are sometimes inadequate for their meaning. But in **"Young Goodman Brown,"** there are no poisoned Gothic gardens, no bosom serpents, Faustian laboratories, or other unnatural devices; the supernatural terror is not of Germany but comes from authentic American history; its folk-lore quality is not from flights of fancy but from an actual episode that has become a part of our heritage. As Hawthorne says elsewhere of the Salem burial ground, for every Bunker Hill monument in our history, there should be a Gallows Hill. As he says of democracy that it "comes from the nature of things," so does the situation in **"Young Goodman Brown"**; it is not superimposed from without but corresponds to the psychology of Puritan belief and of the Salem witchcraft delusion.

Yet the very absence of editorializing has caused considerable ambiguity. In their introductory notes to the story, Sculley Bradley, Richmond Croom Beatty, and E. Hudson Long explain its meaning as Brown's "corruption through his loss of simple faith in the goodness of mankind. . . ." This comment has stood in the widely used *The American Tradition in Literature* since 1956; but in the context both of Hawthorne's fiction and of 17th-century Puritanism, it is misleading. For Brown, as a Puritan, would have been indoctrinated with the Calvinistic concept of total depravity, according to which mankind is utterly corrupt and deserves no better than damnation. In the orthodox Calvinism of Michael Wigglesworth's doggerel "The Day of Doom," men of good works are damned to hell, and so are they

> Who dy'd in infancy,
> And never had or good or bad
>   effected pers'nally,
> But from the womb unto the tomb
>   were straightway carried. . . .

They are damned not for sins of commission but simply for their humanity in being born with "Nature/depraved and forlorn."

Accordingly, Perry Miller maintained that "It is impossible to conceive of a disillusioned Puritan; no matter what misfortune befell him, no matter how often or how tragically his fellowmen failed him, he would have been prepared for the worst, and would have expected no better" [Perry Miller and Thomas N. Johnson, *The Puritans,* 1938].

In Goodman Brown, Hawthorne did conceive of a disillusioned Puritan, but Brown's tragedy is not the loss of his simple faith; rather it is that his faith is too simple to begin with. He is, of course, aware of evil from the start, for he is concerned lest a dream have warned his wife "what work is to be done tonight" as he sets forth on "his present evil purpose." But at this stage in his development, evil is still a notion; he may believe in it intellectually as dogma, but he has not yet experienced it. So his leaving his wife for an evening of diabolical revelry at the witches' sabbath is merely an untested young man's first (and he expects final) fling. One might compare him to the youth who thinks he will just once try drugs, prostitution, or some sort of perversity—just once, to see what it's like, and never again—and who gets hooked into addiction or shocked into fanatical reaction. Goodman Brown is like the person who from perverse curiosity experiments once with LSD and has a bad trip.

His trip into the forest is indeed a bad one, so traumatic that he concludes by disbelieving in any goodness. Though he cries out to Faith to "look up to heaven, and resist the wicked one," and is whisked away from the black mass, he still believes Satan's claim that "Evil is the nature of mankind" and blights the rest of his life by acknowledging, "Come, devil; for to thee is this world given." His discovery of the hypocrisy of the catechist, clergy, ministers and magistrates of Salem has destroyed his faith in the Calvinist elect, who if they persevered anywhere should have done so in the new Zion of Massachusetts. With the participation of his wife Faith in the devil worship, there are not brands spared from the burning; the depravity is indeed total.

It is too simple to consider the story an unqualified attack on Calvinism. Though Hawthorne deplored the Puritans' grim bigotry, he respected their strength and commitment and wrote in "The Old Manse" that he preferred the warmth that their writings once had to the anemic frigidity of 19th-century liberal theology. It is true that one element of **"Young Goodman Brown"** is a criticism of Puritan self-righteousness; the devil points out to Brown that he has "a very general acquaintance here in New England" and proceeds to cite numerous instances of bigotry, persecution, and hypocrisy.

On the question of evil, the issue is more complex. Hawthorne rejected Emerson's bland dismissal of evil as mere illusion that will vanish when one rises transcendently into the world of spirit: "So fast will disagreeable appearances, swine, spiders, snakes, pests, mad-houses, prisons, enemies, vanish. . . ." But how far did Hawthorne go in the opposite direction? Melville [in "Hawthorne and His Mosses"] asked of Hawthorne "whether there really lurks in him, perhaps unknown to himself, a touch of Puritanic gloom" and concluded (later citing **"Young Goodman Brown"** as an example) "that this great power of blackness in him derives its force from its appeals to the Calvinistic sense of Innate Depravity and Original Sin, from whose visitations, in some shape or other, no deeply thinking mind is always and wholly free" and that "this black conceit pervades him [Hawthorne] through and through."

Though the lack of editorial explanation makes the story ambiguous, Goodman Brown's morbid misanthropy is not Hawthorne's. Henry James commented [in *Hawthorne,* 1879], "The magnificent little romance of **"Young Goodman Brown"** . . . evidently means nothing as regards Hawthorne's own state of mind, his conviction of human depravity and his consequent melancholy; for the simple reason that if it meant anything, it would mean too much." James further observed that the gloomy subjects of Hawthorne's tales "were not the expression of a hopeless, or even of a predominantly melancholy, feeling about the human soul."

What Goodman Brown experiences is an inversion of Jonathan Edwards' statement that it is one thing to have an opinion that God is holy and ought to be worshipped and quite another thing to have a sense of that holiness in one's heart.

—Robert E. Morsberger

To find Hawthorne's own position, we must turn to other works, for he is one author whose writings can profitably be cross-referenced. What Goodman Brown experiences is an inversion of Jonathan Edwards' statement that it is one thing to have an opinion that God is holy and ought to be worshiped and quite another thing to have a sense of that holiness in one's heart. Thus in *The Marble Faun,* explaining the pure Hilda's reaction to discovering the crime of Miriam and Donatello, Hawthorne comments on "those tears (among the most chill and forlorn that gush from human sorrow) which the innocent heart pours forth at its first actual discovery that sin is in the world. . . . They may have heard much of the evil of the world, and seem to know it, but only as an impalpable theory. In due time, some mortal, whom they reverence too highly, is commissioned by Providence to teach them this direful lesson; he perpetrates a sin; and Adam falls anew, and Paradise, heretofore in unfaded bloom is lost again, and closed forever, with the fiery swords gleaming at its gates." As a Puritan, Brown would have a knowledge of evil but a notional knowledge only until his ordeal in the forest. Then he falls into what William James [in *The Variety of Religious Experience*] calls "really insane melancholia . . . desperation absolute and complete, the whole universe coagulating about the sufferer into a material of overwhelming horror, surrounding him without opening or end. Not the conception of intellectual perception of evil, but the grisly blood-freezing heart-palsying sensation of it close upon one. . . ." Apropos of Hilda, Hawthorne explains further "that dismal certainty of the existence of evil in the world, which, though we may fancy ourselves fully assured of the sad mystery long before, never becomes a portion of our practical belief until it takes substance and reality from the sin of some guide, whom we have deeply trusted and revered, or some friend whom we have deeply

loved. When that knowledge comes, it is as if a cloud had suddenly gathered over the morning light; so dark a cloud, that there seems to be no longer any sunshine behind it or above it . . . as if the catastrophe involved the whole moral world."

Clearly Hawthorne had a perspective that Brown lacks. His own position is perhaps best seen when he describes young Phoebe Pyncheon's distress upon discovering the evil in her respectable kinsman, Judge Jaffrey Pyncheon:

> A doubt of this nature has a most disturbing influence, and . . . comes with fearful and startling effect on minds of the trim, orderly, and limit-loving class. . . . Dispositions more boldly speculative may derive a stern enjoyment from the discovery, since there must be evil in the world, that a high man is as likely to grasp his share of it as a low one. A wider scope of view, and a deeper insight, may see rank, dignity, and station, all proved illusory, so far as regards their claim to human reverence, and yet not feel as if the universe were thereby tumbled headlong into chaos.

This final view was Hawthorne's own. It is matched by Melville's statement in *Moby-Dick:* "Doubts of all things earthly, and intuitions of some things heavenly, this combination makes neither believer nor infidel, but makes a man who regards them both with equal eye."

But Goodman Brown resembles Ishmael in "The Try-Works" chapter, Melville's equivalent of a witches' sabbath, during which as helmsman Ishmael is terrified by the thought that like Brown in the dark forest, he "was not so much bound to any haven ahead as rushing from all havens astern." Recovering his senses after almost capsizing the ship, he makes a statement that can serve with uncanny accuracy as a comment on **"Young Goodman Brown."**

> Look not too long in the face of the fire, O man! . . . Tomorrow, in the natural sun, the skies will be bright; those who glared like devils in the forking flames, the morn will show in far other, at least gentler relief. . . . Nevertheless the sun hides not Virginia's Dismal Swamp nor Rome's accursed Campagna, nor wide Sahara, nor all the millions of miles of deserts and of griefs beneath the moon. The sun hides not the ocean, which is the dark side of this earth, and which is two thirds of this earth. So, therefore, that mortal man who hath more of joy than sorrow in him, that mortal man cannot be true—not true, or undeveloped. The truest of all men was the Man of Sorrows, and the truest of all books is Solomon's and Ecclesiastes is the fine hammered steel of woe. . . . But even Solomon, he says, "the man that wandereth out of the way of understanding shall remain" (*i.e.* even while living) "in the congregation of the dead."

This is what happens to Brown on his return to Salem. Ishmael therefore concludes, matching the judgment of both Melville and Hawthorne, "Give not thyself up, then, to fire, lest it invert thee, deaden thee. . . . There is a wisdom that is woe; but there is a woe that is madness." This is the woe that afflicts Brown. He has departed from

Ishmael's "insular Tahiti, full of peace and joy," into "all the horrors of the half known life"; and as Ishmael says, "Push not off from that isle, thou canst never return!"

Brown's physical return to Salem poses a number of problems. If his experience is taken literally, then everyone else who had participated in the black mass would know that he too had been there. Yet no one else appears unchanged. Is it because the others did not renounce Satan, as Brown did? Faith would know that he knows she was there, and he would know that she knows he knows. At the beginning she has a knowledge or at least a premonition of "what work is to be done tonight" and urges him to stay as much for her sake as for his own on "this night . . . of all nights in the year." Yet Faith greets him as if nothing amiss had occurred. She has not been overwhelmed with gloom; and if the rest of her days are blighted, it is because Brown's never-lifted depression turns their marriage into suttee on the psychological level.

On the other hand, if the experience is a dream, it is not clear where the dream begins, unless it does so before the story starts. The tale opens factually with Brown setting out on his journey; and while it very effectively shifts into the supernatural, there is no transition from actuality to dream. Yet the dreamlike quality of the night-journey is essential for the mystery of iniquity. Like Dante at the opening of *The Inferno,* Brown "came to myself in a dark wood where the straight way was lost. . . . I cannot rightly tell how I entered it, so full of sleep was I about the moment that I left the true way." The forest is that of the soul, and there Brown learns like Melville, that "Though in many of its aspects this visible world seems formed in love, the invisible spheres were formed in fright."

If one assumes that Brown literally drifts into a dream, other technical problems arise. Did he simply walk into the forest and fall asleep like Rip Van Winkle? Did he spend the night uncomfortably under a tree? If so, would he not realize upon waking that he had been asleep? On the level of motivation, why should he go into the forest to spend a night sleeping out, if he was not on his way to a rendezvous? The only way in which the dream version can be seen logically is for the entire story to be a dream, and such a reading still does not provide for a transition out of the dream at the end.

Yet the dream alternative is necessary for modern readers who do not believe in witches. Despite the loose ends, the final ambiguity allows for a psychological or spiritual rather than a literal experience. There was no actual witchcraft at Salem, but twenty people died there as witches, and Hawthorne's story provides the atmosphere in which such hysterical delusion could take place. As Alan Simpson states [in *Puritanism in Old and New England,* 1961], "The Puritan was always obsessed by his sense of sin. Taught to expect it everywhere, and to magnify it where he found it, he easily fell into the habit of inventing it." Though the story makes no mention of witchcraft trials, it is not difficult to imagine Goodman Brown as an accuser and prosecutor of his neighbors. In his profound suspicion of evil on the part of everyone

save himself, we see here, as Salem showed in actual history, a parable of the beginnings of American paranoia in society and politics.

Barton Levi St. Armand   (essay date 1973)

SOURCE: "'Young Goodman Brown' as Historical Allegory," in *The Nathaniel Hawthorne Journal 1973,* edited by C. E. Frazer Clark, Jr., Microcard Editions Books, 1973, pp. 183-97.

[*In the essay below, St. Armand analyzes Hawthorne's short story as "an historical parable, pure and simple."*]

In his 1964 Centenary essay, "On Hawthorne" [included in *Beyond Culture,* 1965], Lionel Trilling declared that:

> . . . in the degree that he does not dominate us, Hawthorne cannot wholly gratify us, moderns that we are. He is an exquisite artist, yet he suggests to us the limitations of art, and thus points to the stubborn core of actuality that is not to be overcome, and seems to say that the transaction between it and us is after all an unmediated one. . . . He has no great tyrant-dream in which we can take refuge, he leaves us face to face with the ultimately unmodifiable world, of which our undifferentiated human nature is a part.

Trilling's use of the word "exquisite" has heralded a new phase in the history of Hawthorne criticism and the remarkable Hawthorne revival which came to a rich culmination in the 1950's of Neo-Orthodoxy and the New Criticism. We are now in a period marked by modification and repetition, if not by absolute retrenchment, and more and more Hawthorne is being read not as a bold explorer of "a blackness ten times black" but rather as a more muddled nineteenth-century Robert Lowell. Trilling's "exquisite" means, indeed, that we are confronting a Genteel Tradition in Hawthorne scholarship, as a large territory of old ground is gone over again and the works of the Salem master seem to perform the same function as those creeds and points of early Christian doctrine endlessly refined by numberless councils of Nicaea and Trent.

All of a sudden, Hawthorne is "irrelevant." That he has no great "tyrant-dream" means, in an age just as conscious of political means and ends as the 1930's, that he can no longer move us. For how can his obtrusive didacticism jibe with the ethical relativism of the present? Trilling's final judgment of Hawthorne is that "he is not for us today, and perhaps not even tomorrow. He is, in Nietzsche's phrase, one of the spirits of yesterday—and the day after tomorrow." But, *plus ca change, plus c'est la meme chose,* for Trilling's judgment only echoes what Newton Arvin had to contend with many years ago when he replied to the standard charge that Hawthorne seemed even then somehow alien and remote. In a 1928 essay on "The Relevance of Hawthorne" [in *American Pantheon,* 1966], Arvin wrote:

For certainly, at a distance, it is difficult to see that Hawthorne is anything but a fine and attenuated voice out of the past. He was, as Mr. Mumford says, "the afterglow of the Seventeenth Century": and how unmitigably foreign to all our most urgent concerns seems that moribund and tormented Puritanism which, superficially at any rate, was the imaginative setting for his work. Compared with Emerson's gospel of self-assertion, or with Whitman's hearty empiricism, how archaic appears Hawthorne's preoccupation with the morbid "case of conscience," how dry and toneless that romantic "atmosphere" which he so sedulously exploited! What possible relevance to our own needs have these tenuous tales of ministers wearing black veils and scarecrows transformed into men of fashion, these dusky romances of hereditary guilt, of concealed crime and its retribution, of spooky "influences" and clashing "spheres"? Is this an imaginative world in which we can find ourselves ever so slightly at home? Or, to put the question in perhaps its sharpest form, is the experience of which Hawthorne's work is the product and the record an experience in which we can recognize any general and persistent representative quality? Did he celebrate an adventure that all Americans, or any large number of them, have had, and that is still, in any way, a portion of our destiny?

Like Arvin, but for different reasons, I should like to hold that Hawthorne does, indeed, chronicle "an experience in which we can recognize [a] general and persistent representative quality." The adventure which he records, I would further maintain, has precisely to do with the idea of American destiny, both national and individual, for in Hawthorne's work the forces which determine the contours of history are inseparable from those which determine the shape of the individual soul.

The short fiction which deals most prominently with the idea of destiny, as does *The Scarlet Letter* among the longer romances, is **"Young Goodman Brown"** and while its charting of the precarious state of the individual soul has often been analyzed, never to my knowledge has it been fully taken as Hawthorne first intended it to be taken: as an historical parable, pure and simple. The story was initially included as one of the author's proposed "Provincial Tales" (1829), dealing with native American themes, which were in turn raked from the ashes of a still earlier collection, *Seven Tales of My Native Land,* burned by Hawthorne in manuscript. Naturally, **"Young Goodman Brown,"** because its raw material is the Puritan mind cast in the setting of the Salem witchcraft delusion, has often been seen as a skillful exposition of the extremes of that mind itself. Yet few modern critics have explicated it as a tale of and about Hawthorne's own native land and of what can happen in and to that native land, no matter what its exact spiritual persuasion.

The particular spiritual persuasion of Puritanism remains of prime importance for the story since it provides Young Goodman Brown with the same mental set that New England Calvinism has forced on the American mind: an overwhelming sense of destiny, for either good or ill. As Robert N. Bellah has reminded us forcibly in his essay on "Civil Religion in America" [in *Daedalus: Religion in America,* Winter 1967], this sense of destiny remains with us even today and, in some respects, is an indigenous part of our political rhetoric and the way in which we think of ourselves, in spite of several recent shocks to our own self-image as Americans. Bellah writes:

> Behind the civil religion at every point lie Biblical archetypes: Exodus, Chosen People, Promised Land, New Jerusalem, Sacrificial Death and Rebirth. But it is also genuinely American and genuinely new. It has its own prophets and its own martyrs, its own sacred events and sacred places, its own solemn rituals and symbols. It is concerned that America be a society as perfectly in accord with the will of God as men can make it, and a light to all the nations.
>
> It has often been used and is being used today as a cloak for petty interests and ugly passions. It is in need—as is any living faith—of continual reformation, of being measured by universal standards. But it is not evident that it is incapable of growth and new insight.
>
> It does not make any decision for us. It does not remove us from moral ambiguity, from being, in Lincoln's fine phrase, an "almost chosen people." But it is a heritage of moral and religious experience from which we still have much to learn as we formulate the decisions that lie ahead.

We are still, then, in the same situation as is Hawthorne's Young Goodman Brown, lost in the ambiguous wood of doubt and devotion. And it is precisely his burden of Puritan belief which has been bequeathed to us, his more immediate heritage of Biblical archetypes and abiding sense of apocalyptic responsibility. The confident, even benignly bumptious inaugural addresses of a Jefferson or a Kennedy only seem to echo in their confident enthusiasms William Stoughton, the pronounced Puritan and unrecanting Chief Justice of the Salem tribunal who wrote of "New England's True Interest" in 1668 that:

> As for our advantages and privileges in a covenant state: here time and strength would fail to reckon up what we have enjoyed of this kind. If any people in the world have been lifted up to heaven as to advantages and privileges, we are the people. Name what you will under this head and we have had it. We have had Moses and Aaron to lead us; we have had teachings and instructions, line upon line and precept upon precept; we have had ordinances and Gospel dispensations, the choicest of them; we have had peace and plenty; we have had afflictions and chastisements in measure; we have had the hearts and prayers and blessings of the Lord's people everywhere; we have had the eye and hand of God; our adversaries have had their rebukes; we have had encouragements and a wall of fire around us. What could have been done more for us than hath been done?

Of course, we still have the eye and hand of God with us—on the backs of our dollar bills, where He looks over the pyramid of His republic, as we have God's name on our coinage, still hoping against hope that He trusts as much in us as we profess to trust in Him. But, even for those who feel that God has died or disappeared, Stoughton's earlier contention that "The name and interest of God, and covenant-relation to Him . . . hath been written upon us in capital letters from the beginning" holds true. Americans still cherish great expectations. The portentous outline of God's determinations remains with us, thrusting us into a gloomy state of introspection when our national election to grace is no longer rewarded by sanctifying signs or divine providences. It is then that the concluding words of Stoughton's sermon come back to torture and reprove his chosen people. "Thus it hath been with us as to grounds of divine expectation," he writes:

> And therefore let us in the fear of God learn the great truth today, and receive the instruction thereof sealed up unto all our souls: That the great God hath taken up great expectation of us, and made great promises to Himself concerning us, and this hath been—and is— New England's day and season of probation. ("New England's True Interest")

The portentous outline of America's personal expectations as a nation and the vague sense of Jehovah's promises as a God add up to exactly what Puritanical pietism left to a decadent posterity: an essentialist mind and a prevailing sense of destiny. **"Young Goodman Brown"** gets at the heart of this American dilemma of destiny, manifest or otherwise, by examining precisely the same things which television newscasters consider in their nightly dissections of the course of recent American history: the effects—the disturbingly real, physical effects—of a belief in such a destiny.

"Young Goodman Brown" gets at the heart of the American dilemma of destiny, manifest or otherwise, by examining precisely the same things which television newscasters consider in their nightly dissections of the course of recent American history: the effects—the disturbingly real, physical effects—of a belief in such a destiny.

—*Barton Levi St. Armand*

For, the knowledge of one's own destiny, be it either eternal election to God and His saints or eternal damnation to Satan and his devils, has at least certain real consequences. One acts out the part which has been assigned by the cosmic stage manager and gives him glory and praise for the grandeur of his design in spiteof any individual travail of soul. As D.H. Lawrence says for Melville's Captain Ahab [in *Studies in Classic American Literature*, 1961], "Ah, well, if my day is doomed, and I am doomed with my day, it is something greater than I who dooms me, so I accept my doom as a sign of the greatness which is more than I am." In the later history of American pietism, this particular theory that God's sovereignty gains by the indi-

vidual's "willingness to be damned" was to be known as Hopkinsian Calvinism, though it is an idea implicit in the structure of the entire theology.

One can never quite be sure even of this dismal glory, however, for the conversion may come at the penultimate second, the apocalypse may somehow—through the operation of amazing grace—be replaced by a magnificent apotheosis. What is left from all of this is the travail of soul itself—an intense watching, and listening, and waiting, and testing, an agonizing combination of "fear and trembling" and "the sickness unto death," to use Kierkegaard's terms, produced by the greater overbelief that something very definite and cosmically meaningful is going to happen.

It is just such a travail of soul which Young Goodman Brown is experiencing at the beginning of Hawthorne's story although he is reasonably sure of his own election, as he is reasonably sure of the validity of his faith—the outward evidence of an inward security of grace, of "things not seen," as Jonathan Edwards phrased it [in "Religious Affections," in *Representative Selections*, ed. Faust and Johnson, 1962]—imaged by the pious appearance of his wife and fellow townspeople. The sun of Brown's soul, however, has entered into a dusky decline for reasons Hawthorne does not bother to explain. Melville called the story "deep as Dante" and perhaps Brown, like Dante, has become entrapped in a dark wood of partial doubts and conflicting desires, the natural result of any intensely held belief such as the pietistic Calvinism I have outlined above.

Yet a vital part of that particular belief is the doctrine of original sin, and its definition by Hawthorne during the course of the tale as "the instinct that guides mortal man to evil" is enough, as a basis of belief, to account for Brown's nocturnal departure from his wife Faith and all she represents. By going into these dark woods, he is testing her as well as himself and, like Dante, undertaking a journey which could restore such "Faith" in a more genuine and strengthened form.

Such a journey is also, of course, a descent into the maw of hell itself, the hell that lies within as well as without. Hawthorne even makes it plain to us that Brown's purpose in attending the Witches' Sabbath is "evil" in nature, though whether "evil" by intent or result remains part of the ambiguities of the fable. Surely it is a dark and dangerous purpose, made even more sinister by the fact that Brown has no guide, as Dante had his Vergil, the symbol of balance and reason, to keep him from going over the brink as he loses himself more and more in this wilderness he has willfully chosen to confront alone. "He had taken a dreary road," Hawthorne writes,

> . . . darkened by all the gloomiest trees of the forest, which barely stood aside to let the narrow path creep through, and closed immediately behind. It was all as lonely as could be; and there is this peculiarity in such a solitude, that the traveller knows not who may be concealed by the innumerable trunks and the thick boughs overhead; so that with lonely footsteps he may yet be passing through an unseen multitude.

Young Goodman Brown is about to struggle with just such an unseen multitude, what Cotton Mather called the "Wonders of the Invisible World," yet at this point in his quest Brown is no more a bad Puritan than was Mather himself. His suspicions of spirits in the air reveal rather the sense of immanence and drama which composed the psychic terror of Puritan life at its most intense, a terror Mather reveals in his *Discourse on Witches,* that sermon written during the winter of 1688-1689, "after Goodwife Glover of Boston was hanged for bewitching John Goodwin's children," Mather writes,

> I am now to tell you, *That these eyes of mine have beheld all these things,* and many other more, no less amazing. Christian, there are Devils: and so many of them, too, that sometimes a Legion of them are spared for the vexation of *One Man.* The *Air* in which we breathe is full of them. Be sensible of this, you that *obey God:* There are Troops of *Tempters* on every side of thee. *Awake,* O Soul, Awake, those *Philistines* of Hell *are upon thee.* Upon the least affrightment in the dark, many simple people cry out, *The Devil! the Devil!* Alas there are Devils, thronging about thee every day. O let the thought of it make thee a careful and watchful Man. And be sensible of this, you that commit Sin: The Lord Jesus hath said of you, *Ye will do the lusts of your father the Devil.* How often do many of you make a *Mock* and a *Jeer* of the Devil, while you are drudging for him? But know, that there are dreadful *Devils* to seize upon thy forlorn, forsaken Soul at its departure hence. O become a new Man at the thought of this.

Goodman Brown indeed wants not only to be a good man but also to become as well a new man or, if already hopefully converted, at least renew his personal experience of a divine and supernatural light. Yet, Mather's preceding words to the passage I have just quoted—"is there not a Devil whose Agency must account for things that are so extravagant?"—indicates the only foundation on which Brown is prepared to judge his faith and that of others. For him, as for Mather, "The Effects are [and must be] dreadfully real" [Mather, Letter to John Richards, in *What Happened at Salem* by David Levin, 1960]. We will see that this corollary of belief has a double edge of meaning but, for the moment, it is enough to observe that Brown is forced immediately into still another doubly ponderous dilemma. Like the Salem judges and Cotton Mather, he must determine the validity of the spectral evidence which is about to unsettle and bewitch him and, like the afflicted themselves, he is about to suffer a torment so real that he cannot dismiss it as mere irrational phenomena. Once again, as Mather, writing to John Richards, said of the victims of witchcraft,

> Albeit the business of this Witchcraft be very much transacted upon the Stage of Imagination, yet we Know, that, as in treason there is an imagining which is a Capital Crime. & here also the business thus managed in Imagination yet may not be called Imaginary. The Effects are dreadfully real. Our dear neighbors are most really tormented. Really murdered, and really acquainted with hidden things, which are afterwords proved plainly to have been Realities.

In attempting to discern true witchcraft from false witchcraft, Mather and the Salem judges were confronting exactly the same problem faced by every believing Calvinist who attempted to determine which of a congregation had experienced a true conversion experience and which a false one. More than half a century later, Jonathan Edwards was to struggle with the problem in his "Treatise on Religious Affections" and come to much the same anguish and inconclusion, placing the burden of a test of faith on its behavioral effects rather than on the immeasurable inward exaltation. And almost a century after Edwards, Ralph Waldo Emerson was to announce, answering the objection of the orthodox [in *Self Reliance*], that "these impulses may be from below, not from above. They do not seem to me to be such; but if I am the Devil's Child, I will live then from the Devil." Had Emerson been a contemporary of Cotton Mather and made the same statement under the "Cross & Swift Questions" of chief examiner John Ha[w]thorne, he most assuredly would have been hanged for a witch, with little or no protest on the part of the community.

Given a *modus operandi* which puts such weight on "dreadful effects," Brown's experiment with evil in the depths of the forest is doomed to failure if we also are given the nature of the forest itself—dusky, dark, and pervaded by an uncertain light. The pragmatic insistence on concrete evidences and black or white realities allows present ambiguities to vitiate—to poison—the past. Mather had quoted Jesus to the effect that "Ye will do the lusts of your father the Devil" and had exclaimed that "Alas, we should every one of us be a *Dog* and a *Witch* too, if God should leave us to ourselves" [Mather, "A Discourse on Witchcraft"]. Thus the Devil whom Brown meets in the forest bears such a considerable resemblance to his own self that both figures together "might have been taken for father and son" and, when Brown protests that "My father never went into the woods on such an errand, nor his father before him," this satanic father-figure (who in Puritan theology is also the "Father of Lies") answers:

> I have been as well acquainted with your family as with ever a one among the Puritans; and that's no trifle to say. I helped your grandfather, the constable, when he lashed the Quaker woman so smartly through the streets of Salem; and it was I that brought your father a pitchpine knot, kindled at my own hearth, to set fire to an Indian village, in King Philip's war. They were my good friends, both; and many a pleasant walk have we had along this path, and returned merrily after midnight. I would fain be friends with you for their sake.

What occurs progressively throughout the unravelling fabric of Hawthorne's tale, then, is a systematic defamation of Brown's idealism, based as it is on a convenant theology which assumes as its first premise the integrity and good will of the Puritan founding fathers. Brown's defensive assertion that "We are a people of prayer, and good works to boot, and abide no such wickedness" is steadily enfeebled by the Devil's mustering of spectral evidences to prove his counterproposal that "I have a very general acquaintance here in New England." And so a designedly pernicious destruction of the Elders is accomplished, reaching its acme in the revelation that Goody Cloyse, whom Brown had long taken for granted as "a very pious and exemplary dame" and "who had taught him his catechism in youth, and was still his moral and spiritual advisor" is also in league with the revisionist Devil of the serpent-staff. In the unequal cross-lights of the dim forest, even she appears to be nothing more than a lecherous and hypocritical old hag, smearing herself with wolf's bane and the fat of a newborn babe in order to enjoy diabolical power in general and carnal delights in particular.

The minister of the Salem community itself and the worthy Deacon Gookin are soon added to the Devil's roster of secret sinners. But, even though "Young Goodman Brown caught hold of a tree for support, being ready to sink down on the ground, faint and over-burdened with the heavy sickness of his heart," he yet retains his "Faith" and does not slip entirely into the slough of despond. "With heaven above and Faith below" (that is, both Brown's over-belief in God's continuing and invisible covenant and "Faith," the wife of his bosom, the physical evidence or "effect" of that covenant), he exclaims, "I will yet stand firm against the devil."

Still the dark traveller with the twisted staff uses his general acquaintance to such a spectral extent that not only is Brown's faith in his ancestry subconsciously undermined but so is his general trust in governmental authority: "The deacons of many a church have drunk the communion wine with me," this Devil further reveals, "the selectmen of divers towns make me their chairman; and a majority of the Great and General Court are firm supporters of my interest. The governor and I, too—But these are state secrets." "Can this be so?" cries out the amazed Goodman Brown, expressing his confusion and sense of betrayal at the greater widening of his Puritan credibility gap.

In such a way does Brown's contention that "We have been a race of honest men and good Christians since the days of the martyrs" shatter and crumble, at the same time foreshadowing the present demoralization of America's liberal interpretation of its own history as written by the pipe and tweed historians of FDR's administration and the so-called consensus historians, who followed in their optimistic footsteps. In the dim forest of contemporary life, has not a similarly dark figure, who bears the lineaments of our founding fathers, as well as the marks of their exploitation and willful evil, pointed to a past racist history as well as to a present racist society? And has it not shaken us to repeat stubbornly, as did Young Goodman Brown, "With heaven above and Faith below, I will yet stand firm against the devil"?

Brown's own faith itself, however, cannot possibly stand against such a Walpurgisnacht of the soul. The effects are much too real, the revelation too overwhelming, when the young man sees the very wife of that soul (or at least the spectral flutter of her pink ribbons) abroad in the same dark forest of doubt and temptation. His reaction is one we have been prepared to expect: "'My Faith is gone!' cried he, after one stupefied moment. 'There is no good

on earth; and sin is but a name. Come, devil; for to thee is this world given'." If one cannot be an angel of light, or one of the shining elect, one can at least be an active devil or one of the shimmering damned. The dream of apotheosis gives way to the nightmare of apocalypse, as Brown himself becomes "the chief horror of the scene, and shrank not from its other horrors":

> "Ha! ha! ha!" roared Goodman Brown, when the wind roared at him. "Let us hear which will laugh loudest. Think not to frighten me with your deviltry. Come witch, come Indian powwow, come devil himself, and here comes Goodman Brown. You may as well fear him as he fears you."

> In truth, all through the haunted forest there could be nothing more frightful than the figure of Goodman Brown. On he flew among the black pines, brandishing his staff with frenzied gestures, now giving vent to an inspiration of horrid blasphemy, and now shouting forth such laughter as set all the echoes of the forest laughing like demons around him. The fiend in his own shape is less hideous than when he rages in the breast of man. Thus sped the demoniac on his course, until, quivering among the trees, he saw a red light before him, as when the felled trunks and branches of a clearing have been set on fire, and throw up their lurid blaze against the sky, at the hour of midnight. . . . Goodman Brown cried out, and his cry was lost to his own ear by its unison with the cry of the desert.

This is one possible reaction to the loss of Brown's Puritan dream of election: meeting madness with madness, and violence with violence—a covenant of despair rather than of hope. This nausea is not exactly existential despair, however, for the covenant is also with the devil, so that its fruition remains cosmic damnation rather than meaningless absurdity, a massive sense of failure rather than a prelude to active commitment. It is the absolute despair or sickness unto death of a Kierkegaard, the sinking of the soul as defined by that arch-Puritan apologist, Jonathan Edwards, in the sermon he entitled "Future Punishment of the Wicked":

> This is the death threatened by the law. This is dying in the highest sense of the word. This is to die sensibly; to die and know it; to be sensible of the gloom of death. This is to be undone; this is worthy of the name of destruction. This sinking of the soul under an infinite weight, which it cannot bear, is the gloom of hell. We read in Scripture of the blackness of darkness: this is it, this is the very thing. We read in Scripture of sinners being lost, and of their losing their souls: this is the thing intended; this is to lose the soul: they that are the subjects of this are utterly lost.

Most immediately, we are left once again with the effects of such a sinking of the soul, and those effects I should like to consider at the conclusion of this analysis. But, on the larger scale, what also emerges, I think, is a pattern which held true for the Puritans and still holds true for American intellectual history as a whole: in psychological terms, a manic-depressive syndrome, and, in political terms, a violent swing from elective idealism to apocalyptic pessimism. It is the change from the Kennedy years, with their unlimited sharing of a divine and supernatural light ("The torch has been passed . . .") and re-establishment of the covenant theology to the grim despair and moral intro-spection of Viet Nam, the Pentagon papers, and Water-gate, when America peered beneath the robes of its judges and seemed to find nothing but ugliness and duplicity. The gap was seen to be in both credibility and genera-tions, with the tablets shattered and the contract broken as far back as history itself could tell. This swing could just as well be, however, the change from pre-Civil War mil-lennialism to post-Civil War reconstruction, with the at-tendant rise of Naturalism in literature and Social Darwin-ism in politics.

The events differ but the terms remain the same. For, if the heavenly city is lost, history becomes a mechanism pulled by the same iron puppet-strings of environmental and hereditary law, that same "death threatened in the law" of which Edwards warned. And the reaction of men caught in the downbeat of determinism would remain much the same as that of Young Goodman Brown in Hawthorne's story—impotent rage, black despair, and an overwhelm-ing sense that the Father had somehow cheated the son of his elective birthright. The problem remains that Young Goodman Brown is a representative American even more than he is a representative Puritan. While Brown can see his former and present ideals shattered, he cannot shake off the portentous outline which is the result of those ide-als that Herman Melville, in his review of Hawthorne's "Mosses from an Old Manse," called "that Calvinistic sense of Innate Depravity and Original Sin, from whose visita-tions, in some shape or other, no deeply thinking mind is always and wholly free" [Melville "Hawthrone and His Mosses," in *The Portable Melville,* ed. Joy Leyda, 1961].

> **In abandoning the possibility of a divine and holy communion of the saints, Brown perversely proceeds to substitute absolute despair for absolute faith, being fully as Puritanical about his defection as he was about his former trustfulness.**
>
> —*Barton Levi St. Armand*

Yet in abandoning the possibility of a divine and holy communion of the saints, Brown perversely proceeds to substitute absolute despair for absolute faith, being fully as Puritanical about his defection as he was about his former trustfulness. As Chadwick Hansen [in *Witchcraft at Salem,* 1969] explains about the Puritan obsession with arriving at absolute opinions":

> What was expected was absolute consensus—discussion would proceed until opinion was unanimous, and the final product was therefore seen as a truth as absolute for the Puritan as any Papal Bull for the Catholic. If the matter were secular, or like the present one [i.e.,

witchcraft], a matter for secular decision with strong religious issues at stake, then business would proceed through normal governmental channels, with the clergy being called on for advice. Again, it was expected that final opinions and decisions would be absolute and unanimous.

In Young Goodman Brown's case, the consensus is a consensus of one, but his decision is just as absolute and just as final as any arrived at by a congregation of Puri-tans determined to achieve a perfect unanimity. Brown's conversion is a conversion in reverse to an all-or-nothing Jansenism rather than to the more immediate Puritan her-esies of either Antinomianism or Arminianism. It is ap-propriate, therefore, that the words of his diabolical bap-tism into a hellish knowledge of mankind's absolute de-pravity be spoken by the revisionist Devil, who now truly becomes his master and his father. This satanic historian re-consecrates the substance of Brown's new-found faith with the dread words "Ye have found this young nature and your destiny."

> "Lo, there ye stand, my children," said the figure in a deep and solemn tone, almost sad with despairing awfulness, as if his once angelic nature could yet mourn for our miserable race. "Depending upon one another's hearts, ye had still hoped that virtue were not all a dream. Now ye are undeceived. Evil must be your only happiness. Welcome, again, my children, to the com-munion of your race."

The millennium has been lost, so now all are doomed, all wear the black veil of sin and damnation. Young Good-man Brown has swung over to the other side of the manic-depressive syndrome and sees the entire community as damned. Yet, Brown, because of his training, his catechiz-ing at the knee of Goody Cloyse, cannot quite face the ultimate horror, which is an existential horror of pure non-being, of the void, of nothingness. He continues to be an essentialist, whose only religious possibility is the dark one of a general Day of Doom, a thundering apocalypse.

Inviting the revelation of the forest night as a test of faith, Brown finally cannot cope with the consequences of that revelation. He still clings to the idea of destiny, but the design behind that destiny is now one precisely like that which operates in Robert Frost's famous sonnet "Design": a "design of darkness to appall." To be sure, Hawthorne also suggests, like Frost, that the design is not a design at all, that it is a mere trick or conjunction of events and images, more phenomenal than metaphysical. But the Amer-ican mind has been catechized to accept a cosmic concep-tion of such design, and the obtrusive narrator's ironic query—"Had Goodman Brown fallen asleep in the forest and only dreamed a wild dream of a witch-meeting?"—disturbs too many universes with its multiplicity of answers.

Once again, we are invited only to evaluate the effects of the revelation, the physical evidences of the experience itself. This has "real" repercussions in the "real" world of men and things, for, quite specifically, Young Goodman Brown no longer acts as if he were elect, never mind the state of his soul or heart. In fact, Young Goodman Brown hardly acts at all, for he becomes afflicted with that paralysis of will which is a characteristic of what Rollo May and others have recently termed the "schizoid personality," but which Jonathan Edwards had long ago defined as the "hell within of the natural man." "So it will be with the soul in hell," he explains in the sermon already quoted ["Future Punishment of the Wicked"]:

> It will have no strength or power to deliver itself; and its torment and horror will be so great, so mighty, so vastly disproportioned to its strength, that having no strength in the least to support itself, although it be infinitely contrary to the nature and inclination of the soul to sink; yet it will sink, it will utterly and totally sink; without the least degree of remaining confort, or strength, or courage, or hope. And though it will never be annihilated, its being and perception will never be abolished, yet such will be the infinite depth of gloominess that it will sink into, that it will be in a state of death, eternal death.

The effects remain very real and very dreadful. In not acting at all, in not making religion the chief business of his life nor persisting in holy practice till the end of his days, Brown becomes an example of this paralysis of will, proving Edwards' further orthodox contention in his treatise on *Religious Affections* that "Christ is not in the heart of a saint, as in a sepulchre, or as a dead saviour, that does nothing; but as in his temple, and as one that is alive from the dead." Brown is already dead, lost in a hell of his own making, having united his heart with the Devil rather than with Christ and the persevering saints. Of the effects of Brown's dream of ill omen, if in fact it were after all a dream, Hawthorne writes in the famous conclusion:

> A stern, a sad, a darkly meditative, a distrustful, if not a desperate man did he become from the night of that fearful dream. On the Sabbath day, when the congregation were singing a holy psalm, he could not listen because an anthem of sin rushed loudly upon his ears and drowned all the blessed strain. When the minister spoke from the pulpit with power and fervid eloquence, and with his hand on the open Bible, of the sacred truths of our religion, and of saint-like lives and triumphant deaths and of future bliss or misery unutterable, then did Goodman Brown turn pale, dreading lest the roof should thunder down upon the gray blasphemer and his hearers. Often, waking suddenly at midnight, he shrank from the bosom of Faith and at morning or eventide, when the family knelt down at prayer, he scowled and muttered to himself, and gazed sternly at his wife, and turned away. And, when he had lived long, and was borne to his grave a hoary corpse, followed by Faith, an aged woman, and children and grandchildren, a goodly procession, besides neighbors not a few, they carved no hopeful verse upon his tombstone, for his dying hour was gloom.

William James might have said that Goodman Brown had somehow lost the will to believe and, with it, the possibility of belief itself, insuring that his universe become closed rather than open. What, then, are we left with at the gloomy conclusion of Hawthorne's tale, if my charting of its historical and native American themes is an acceptable one?

If Goodman Brown is even more of an American Everyman than a Calvinist Pilgrim whose progress is grievously arrested, then three distinct possibilities present themselves as means of coping with the "realities" which afflict the American consciousness. Two of them are indigenous and we have already seen both illustrated in the context of the story. One is the cheerful naiveté of believing in one's own election so securely that the dark woods of the frontier, be it the desert west of the Mississippi or the jungle north of the Mekong, pose no threats until they are deeply entered and the dusk of twilight confuses the pietistic mission which seemed so obvious and benevolent to the clear light of day. This is closely allied to an American myth which I have not considered here, yet which is just as Calvinistic in essence as any theology preached by Cotton Mather or Jonathan Edwards: the idea of applied morality, the Franklinian virtue of industrious benevolence, the bumptious confidence of Walt Disney's Davy Crockett, with his incredibly simple and incredibly appealing declaration of a national and individualistic faith—"Be sure you're right; then go ahead!" The second possibility is the manic-depressive syndrome I have sketched as the natural result of the loss of the first possibility. This is the feeling of cosmic doom, of the hand of Providence or of God being drawn away from our enterprises as a chosen people with a received tradition of supernatural history. The reaction itself takes, in turn, two forms: indiscriminate violence, a running amuck in the haunted and ambiguous forest, a sense of shame and guilt after eating the revisionist apple of unholy knowledge. And then follows the rejection of a liberal faith in any possibility at all of meritorious election—the defamation of our fathers and of "Faith" in general; the paralysis of will or isolationism which causes us to abandon all ideals and so, in not acting, act as if we were damned.

There is, of course, a third option which remains open for the American consciousness. It is the very simple way out by becoming existentialist rather than essentialist, giving up the idea of being for the idea of becoming. Walt Whitman seems to approach this in *Leaves of Grass* when he talks of the philosophy of the "Open Road" and of himself as the man with "no past at his back":

> Afoot and light-hearted I take to the open road,
> Healthy, free, the world before me,
> The long brown path before me leading wherever I choose.
>
> Henceforth I ask not good fortune, I myself am good fortune,
> Henceforth I whimper no more, postpone no more, need nothing,
> Done with indoor complaints, libraries, querelous criticisms,
> Strong and content I travel the open road.
>
> The earth, that is sufficient, . . .

Yet no one was more of a promoter and propagandist of the idea of American destiny than the good gray poet. Thus, this buoyant first section of his expansive "Song of the Open Road" ends with the qualifying parenthetical statement that:

(Still here I carry my old delicious burdens,
I carry them, men and women, I carry them with
   me, wherever I go,
I swear it is impossible for me to get rid of them,
I am fill'd with them; and I will fill them in
   return.)

Really to take to the "Open Road" would entail a pure, calm, and unflinching acceptance of the nothingness which might lie beyond it. In other words, the road might not have any end at all or it might not even be a road in itself. This heroic nothingness is at least one alternative to a cosmic conception of election or damnation—the idea of a destiny bequeathed to us by sainted or satanic fathers. Yet, for Whitman, as for Young Goodman Brown, these possibilities are somehow necessary for Americans to fill and be filled with; they are delicious but also terribly dangerous burdens.

I readily admit that in stating the American dilemma in these terms I have actually said no new thing but only explicated a text through the use of still another gospel, which generally and traditionally has been given such names as "The American Dream" or "The Mission of America." And turning to that text itself, I also confess to having read Hawthorne's **"Young Goodman Brown"** in exactly the same sense in which Edgar Allan Poe read and then summarily dismissed it: as an intolerably mystical allegory, conceived in the peculiar spirit of metaphor run mad. I could quote for some support here Thomas Connolly's observation [in his introduction to "Young Goodman Brown," 1968] that "'**Young Goodman Brown**' appears to me to come as close as a story can to being a 'perfect allegory.' It exists at all points on two levels at once without any failure on either the naturalistic or the allegorical level." I would also have to contend with him, however, that the allegory is not so much one of sexual infidelity, which welds together theological and naturalistic (i.e., sexual) levels, as it is an allegory of the uncertain pilgrimage of the American consciousness, where the infidelity violates not simply marriage vows but that covenant theology which has forced the American mind to cleave to the very idea of "Faith" itself.

In my own mind, the dilemma of the story, and the dilemma of the American Everyman which it illustrates, finally remains one of dreams. Hawthorne himself continually brings our attention to the paradoxical nature of dreams throughout the course of his tale. Faith tells Goodman Brown that she does not wish him to stray "this night . . . of all nights in the year" because "a lone woman is troubled with such dreams and such thoughts that she's afeared of herself sometimes." Brown does cast off his "Faith" but then broods that "Methought as she spoke there was trouble in her face, as if a dream had warned her what work is to be done to-night." And at the initiation ceremony of the witches' sabbath, the Devil himself reminds his two proselytes that "Depending upon one another's hearts, ye had still hoped that virtue were not all a dream."

What Hawthorne contrasts is the daydream of the future with the nightmare of the past, showing us that both are dangerous extremes which depend in too large a measure on the effects perceived in the present. Liable to be caught by the revisionist Devil, who is outside the believing community, in any part of the ambiguous forest through which he journeys, Young Goodman Brown, torch-bearer of freedom and the American Way, sooner or later must come to a point where the choice is to abandon all his dreams, or reject all specter evidence, or give up that very quest which has provided so much which is both vital and destructive in American life and American history. There is the "Open Road," but there is also the path which leads, as in Robert Frost's sonnet "Into My Own," toward "those dark trees" which stretch "away unto the edge of doom." To take that path also seems to entail an acceptance of the cosmic consequences of a belief in Providential destiny, with its corollaries of eternal damnation or eternal salvation. Frost could confidently assert, with Young Goodman Brown at the beginning of his journey, that after its completion,

They would not find me changed from him they
   knew—
Only more sure of all I thought was true.

"I do not see why I should e'er turn back," he declares, but Hawthorne has already shown us that if things go from bad to worse and keeping "Faith" at home becomes as dubious an effort as keeping "Faith" abroad, that we, too, can expect neither hopeful verses on our tombstones nor a contented posterity to read them, for the "death threatened in the law" will be already upon us.

Claudia G. Johnson   (essay date 1974)

SOURCE: "'Young Goodman Brown and Puritan Justification," in *Studies in Short Fiction*, Vol. XI, No. 2, Spring, 1974, pp. 200-03.

[*In this essay, Johnson examines "Young Goodman Brown" in terms of the Puritan doctrine of justification, in which "God might open the hearts of certain men, allowing them to descend within in order to know themselves."*]

Criticism of **"Young Goodman Brown"** has traditionally been divided into speculations about the nature of the hero's journey. Was it a dream? Or was it reality? Newton Arvin is usually cited as representative of the view that Goodman Brown received a true vision of human depravity in the woods, and F. O. Matthiessen is representative of the view that the sins witnessed by young Goodman Brown were creatures of his own making [Newton Arvin, *Hawthorne*, 1929; F. O. Matthiessen, *American Renaissance*, 1941]. Almost no modern critic supports Arvin's view, however, so the old argument rarely arises in the old way. Questions about the reality of the story and Brown's relationship to it continue to interest critics, however. A new dimension is given the problem of Goodman Brown's relation to a special kind of reality in the light of what we know and what Hawthorne knew about the Puritan doctrine of justification, a belief which has to be understood in terms of Covenant Theology. The Puritan believed that, since Adam broke the first covenant with God in the Garden of Eden, man labored under the burden of God's wrath. However, God had made a second covenant which gave man hope for some respite from God's wrath during man's life on the earth; at a time of His choosing, God might open the hearts of certain men, allowing them to descend within in order to know themselves. All things on which they had depended and all pride were mortified. Only when they had lost self in this experience would they turn to God who, subsequently, lifted the sinners up and justified them, changing their relationships to God and making their lives on earth a little easier without the burden of God's wrath.

The Puritan minister gave considerable attention not only to what justification was, but to what it was not. He knew that many sinners had convinced themselves that they had made the justifying descent when, in fact, they had not. It was the Puritan minister's duty to urge self-scrutiny in this matter. If the sinner believed that he had been completely helpless in initiating his descent and had been utterly reduced by a "sense" of sin, then he had probably known a "true" descent. If, on the other hand, he thought that he had been in some small way responsible for initiating the descent, if he had been aware of an iota of goodness within himself at the time of descent, or if he had only "known" his sins without "having a sense" of them, then his had been a false or a mock descent. He could not, therefore, expect that he would be justified.

Young Goodman Brown's journey is just such a mock descent in the Puritan tradition. Like the Puritan sinner, he begins what seems to be a journey into an inner inferno. The landscape through which he travels is but a hellish externalization of his own heart. He encounters the fiend, who also rages in his own breast, and fiend worshippers. He hears hell's "awful harmony" of inhuman sounds and perverse hymns. He sees the "lurid" red blaze against the sky. The witches' sabbath is, like Milton's picture of hell, an inverse heaven: the harmonious music of heaven is discord here; the light, unlike that of heaven, is "as one great Furnace, flam'd yet from those flames / No light, but rather darkness visible. . . ." The once-angelic company is transformed, and the gathering in **"Young Goodman Brown"** is like the gathering of the fiends in Pandemonium around the throne of Satan to discuss the fate of Adam and Eve.

As if he were in the traditional Puritan descent, Goodman Brown's various "props" or "crutches," those things on which he has depended, fall from under him. The father, the teacher, the state, the community, the church, the concept of womanhood are all challenged during his journey. But Goodman Brown's journey is far from being a genuine justifying descent. The story is, rather, similar to the Puritan minister's detailed description of the false descent, and young Goodman Brown is a paradigm for Hawthorne's negative definition of the unregenerate man whose incomplete experience with hell perverts his vision and warps his life.

Regeneration is only possible if one's sense of his own sin is as profound as that which the Puritans described in the genuine humiliation: the man in the throes of a true descent must feel that he is the most wretched creature on the earth and must know a mortification of pride in particular. To be sure, Goodman Brown knows despair and feels his own rational limitation in coping with the universe, but in no way would this hellish journey to a witches' sabbath be construed by the Puritans as a genuine descent, for Goodman Brown feels the depravity of others but not the full extent of his own.

Although the reader sees Goodman Brown as "the chief horror of the scene." Goodman Brown has no such vision of himself. In his decision to rage toward the witches' sabbath, he sees himself as choosing through pride to outdo the devil: "Let us hear which will laugh loudest. Think not to frighten me with your deviltry. Come witch, come wizard, come Indian powwow, come devil himself, and here comes Goodman Brown. You may as well fear him as he fear you'." His descent does not bring him to a vision of his own helplessness and sinfulness. Rather, from motives of despair and revenge, he initially believes that he can willingly choose to combat evil. It is Faith's sinfulness that embitters him, not his own. Furthermore, his return to the village finds him piously snatching little children from the clutches of their teachers as if he, alone, were untainted.

Momentarily he feels, with repugnance, a sense of brotherhood with the community, but that which keeps Goodman Brown in gloom is the vision given those who partake of the devil's baptism: that he would ever be "more conscious of the secret guilt of others, both in deed and thought," than he could ever be of his own. This is conclusive evidence that Goodman Brown's descent was not genuine.

The point is not that a vision of dark reality (of either himself or of others) has warped his life. What he has seen is not a true vision of others or himself. His has been a mock journey, a false vision. Though the landscape of his heart was available to him, he never saw the true extent of its terrors. Like the passengers on the Celestial Railroad, he never exposes himself to the landscape and is, thus, never sufficiently humiliated to ascend in love to a new life. The dark vision he saw was not nearly so dark as the one he should have seen but did not see. Like the stock example of the deluded, self-satisfied man of the justification sermon, young Goodman Brown stands as a negative definition of the true regenerative descent.

Edward J. Gallagher (essay date 1975)

SOURCE: "The Concluding Paragraph of 'Young Goodman Brown'," in *Studies in Short Fiction*, Vol. XII, No. 1, Winter, 1975, pp. 29-30.

[*In the essay below, Gallagher illustrates how the conclusion successfully completes the circular plot of "Young Goodman Brown."*]

In the concluding paragraph of **"Young Goodman Brown,"** Hawthorne uses the forest experience to its fullest effect, moving Brown through another series of separations to the ultimate separation, from life itself. To some critics, in fact, the concluding paragraph itself has seemed a separation, breaking the neat circularity of Hawthorne's plot, moving in linear fashion through time from Brown's figurative death at the threshold of his house to his literal death at the threshold of the grave. Yet I agree wholeheartedly with Richard Abcarian, though for different reasons, that the paragraph is not anticlimactic, a digression, an example solely of Hawthorne's penchant for heavy moralizing, or a violation of the neatly unified circular form [Abacarian, "The Ending of 'Young Goodman Brown'," *Studies in Short Fiction* III, No. 3, Spring 1966].

First, the paragraph is replete with echoes, especially verbal echoes, which tie it to incidents in the forest experience while the effect of that experience reaches its highest peak. That Goodman Brown has become permanently stern and sad as a result of his one night in the forest is linked to his stern and sad look into Faith's eyes on his return, and is further linked, ironically, to the soft and sad plea she whispered into his ear on his departure. That Brown has become "darkly meditative" contrasts his "pleasant and praiseworthy meditations" after the meeting with Goody Cloyse. The "anthem of sin" that he henceforth hears at Sabbath service in the meeting house corresponds to the "dreadful anthem" swelling out of the forest at the beginning of the Black Mass. The blessed strain of the holy psalms is "drowned" by this anthem, recalling that Faith's scream of resistance was "drowned" by laughter in the black cloud. The minister's pointed reference to "saint-like lives and triumphant deaths" suggests Brown's proud reference to his pantheon of ancestors: "We have been a race of honest men and good Christians since the days of the martyrs." Brown as a "hoary corpse," just described as shrinking from the bosom of Faith, ironically resembles the "hoary-bearded elders of the church [who] have whispered wanton words to the young maids of their households." Even death provides no escape for old Goodman Brown. He is borne to the graveyard, the site of the good old minister's morning promenade, where no hopeful verses are carved on his tomb, recalling the "verse after verse" of the lore of fiends sung in the wilderness, for his dying hour was gloom, final verification of the black man's prophecy that "Evil must be your only happiness."

Second, the concluding paragraph in a subtle way actually cements the circularity of the plot by reaching back to complete, ironically, images set forth in the introduction. Since this completion is done with irony, the paragraph satisfies a sense of achieved form by the artist without subordinating the sense of havoc wrought on the chief character. In the introduction Faith invites Brown to her bed, and in the conclusion we see him shrinking from her bosom at midnight. In the introduction Brown asks, rhetorically, if Faith doubts him; and in the conclusion, in response, we see that it is Brown who doubts her. Faith hopes that Brown will find "all well" when he returns, and, of course, he finds all evil. Brown's reply to Faith includes an admonition to "say thy prayers," but in the conclusion he continually turns away "at morning or eventide, when the family knelt down at prayer." In the beginning Brown affirms that it would kill Faith even to think of the evil in the forest, but in the end the evil in the forest has killed Brown, and it is his death that we witness. The last thing Brown says before plunging into the forest is that he will return after this one night, cling to Faith's skirts, and follow her to heaven; the last thing in the story we see is Faith following Brown, on another journey which "must needs be done," to the edge of the grave.

One image in particular, however, haunts the reader, momentarily threatening to explode the somber periodicity of the concluding sentence. After seeing Brown ignore his wife's embrace on the morning of his return and shrink from her bosom time and again later, the presence of his "children and grandchildren" here at his death inevitably suggests moments at least of consummate union with Faith. The average reader probably wants a happy ending, or at least a spark of happiness at the ending, but any expectation of that kind quickly evanesces. The suggestion really only enforces the terrible beauty of Brown's position between two worlds. The evil process in the forest has disqualified Brown from relation with the "goodly procession" which follows him. He must live in the village with the sight of the forest, till death calls him. In the symbolic terms of the story, Brown literally has no place else to go, and even death provides no escape. Hawthorne treats Brown's death neither as the time of triumph for the godly, nor as the time of the solace of annihilation for the tortured; and his sonorous but studiedly objective language here simply does not encourage emotional commitment. So, gloom inevitably has the last word.

Leo B. Levy (essay date 1975)

SOURCE: "The Problem of Faith in 'Young Goodman Brown'," in *JEGP: Journal of English and Germanic Philology*, Vol. LXXIV, No. 3, July, 1975, pp. 375-87.

[*In the following essay, Levy examines Faith as a character, an allegorical figure, and a symbol.*]

Few of Hawthorne's tales have elicited a wider range of interpretations than **"Young Goodman Brown."** The critics have been victimized by the notorious ambiguity of a tale composed of a mixture of allegory and the psychological analysis of consciousness. Many of them find the key to its meaning in a neurotic predisposition to evil; one goes so far as to compare Goodman Brown to Henry James's governess in *The Turn of the Screw* [Darrel Abel, in "Black Glove and Pink Ribbon: Hawthorne's Metonymic Symbols," in *NEQ* 42, 1969]. The psychological aspect is undeniably important, since we cannot be certain whether **"Young Goodman Brown"** is a dream-allegory that takes place in the mind and imagination of the protagonist, an allegory with fixed referents in the external world, or a combination of these that eludes our ordinary understanding of the genre itself. The story is all three: a dream vision, a conventional allegory, and finally an inquiry into the problem of faith that undermines the assumptions upon which the allegory is based.

Whether we think of the central episode of the witches' Sabbath as a dream or an hallucination, or as a nightmarish "real" experience, it must be placed in relationship to elements of the story that are outside Brown's consciousness. His point of view is in the foreground, but it must contend with the point of view of a narrator who is not identified with his perceptions. The narrator's irony and detachment, and his frequent intrusions, are measures of the distance he places between himself and a protagonist he regards with a mixture of condescension and pity. No fewer than three attitudes toward faith emerge from the story: Brown's, the view expressed in the concluding parable, and that which by implication is Hawthorne's. The elusiveness with which the narrative moves into Brown's state of mind and then outward arises from this complex view of faith, and also from the conception of Faith as a double, who "like Beatrice Rappaccini is both pure and poisonous, saint and sinner" [Roy R. Hale, *Hawthorne's Tragic Vision*, 1964]. She is at once an allegorical idea and the means by which the idea is inverted. Those celebrated pink ribbons on Faith's cap—the objects of an astonishing range of responses by critics of the story—are vital to an understanding of her metamorphosis and of Brown's desperate efforts to recover his faith.

The impression that the story hovers on the borderline between subjective and objective reality derives from Hawthorne's suggestion that Brown's experience is peculiar to him and yet broadly representative. Not until the next to last paragraph are we offered what seems to be a choice between these alternatives: Hawthorne asks, "Had Goodman Brown fallen asleep in the forest and only dreamed a wild dream of a witch-meeting?" His reply—"Be it so if you will; but alas! it was a dream of evil omen for young Goodman Brown"—is often taken to mean that we may read the story either way; but we may wonder why Hawthorne defers this question until the end. The reader may suspect that **"Young Goodman Brown"** is a tale in which reality is entirely subsumed by the consciousness of the protagonist; if so, his suspicion will be heightened when Hawthorne, in the sentence following his question and answer, less tentatively alludes to "the night of that fearful dream." And yet even this statement leaves the issue unresolved. This irresolution is not coyness on Hawthorne's part: if the dream theory were confirmed, it would have the effect of canceling a whole range of intimations that surround the dream but are not part of it. Through the dream metaphor the many hints of Brown's unconscious fascination with evil are communicated, but Hawthorne recognizes that our waking life and the life of dreams are bound up together—that life is like a dream in its revelation of terrifying truths. His point is that the truth conveyed in the dream—that faith may betray us—is also a truth of waking experience.

I

The story begins as a conventional allegory, creating the expectation that the characters will consistently exhibit the abstractions they symbolize. If Hawthorne intends Brown to be a pathological case, that intention is not evident in the early stages. The problem of man's journey into the mystery of evil is presented in the broadest possible terms. Faith Brown, the wife of three months, is simply "Faith," and Goodman Brown is Everyman. The bargain he has struck with Satan is the universal one, reinforced by such signs as the innocence with which he convinces himself that he can turn aside from his covenant and the assurances he offers himself of his good intentions. Initially, he is a naïve and immature young man who fails to understand the gravity of the step he has taken. Though Hawthorne does not provide a transitional development, he drastically alters this picture: the early indications of Brown's immaturity are succeeded by a presumably adult determination to resist his own evil impulses. His continuing willingness to join the community of sinners coexists with a reaction against that willingness. As the task of turning back becomes increasingly difficult, confronting him with one frustration after another, his struggle takes on heroic proportions.

Far from showing himself to be "a prospective convert who is only too willing to be convinced" [David Levin, "Shadows of Doubt: Specter Evidence in Hawthorne's 'Young Goodman Brown'," *American Literature* XXXIV, No. 3, November 1962]. Brown displays a mounting resistance to the Devil's enticements. No sooner does he leave Faith than "his heart smote him"; he replies to the Devil's reproach for his lateness at the appointed place, saying "Faith kept me back awhile." As the two travel into the forest the Devil observes the slowness of his companion's pace and ironically offers him his staff, thereby prompting the young man to confess, "I have scruples touching the matter thou wot'st of." He genuinely wishes to escape the Devil's snare: he withstands the revelation that the deacons and selectmen of his village, and the governor himself, have preceded him on this journey; and the discovery that Goody Cloyse, the old woman who had taught him his catechism, is a witch does not affect his determination to turn back: "What if a wretched old woman do choose to go to the Devil when I thought she was going to heaven: is that any reason why I should quit my dear Faith and go after her?" He assures himself that when he returns home he will meet the minister with a clear conscience, "nor shrink from the eye of good old Deacon Gookin"; he will sleep "so purely and sweetly now, in the arms of Faith!" It is not surprising that he is "ready to sink down to the ground, faint and overburdened with heavy sickness of his heart," when he learns that the deacon and the minister are of the Devil's company. Nevertheless, he cries out, "With Heaven above and Faith below, I will yet stand firm against the Devil!"

Beyond this point, Brown calls out three times for Faith to come to his aid, and not until he sees a pink ribbon from Faith's cap that has fluttered down from the sky and caught on the branch of a tree does he abandon hope, crying "My Faith is gone." As if to reinforce the tangible evi-

dence of Faith's desertion, Hawthorne writes that Brown "seized" and "beheld" the fateful ribbon. He now knows that Faith's voice has been mingled with the other "familiar tones, heard daily at Salem village," but now issuing from the depths of a cloud—from the company of Satan's followers sailing through the air. The most frightful episode of the tale follows: Brown becomes a "demoniac," "the chief horror" in a scene full of horrors—of terrible sounds made up of "the creaking of trees, the howling of wild beasts, and the yell of Indians." Utterly possessed by the Devil, he yields to the conviction that the world is given over to sin. But when silence falls and he enters the clearing where the assembly of the damned is gathered for the performance of its ritual, his hopes rise again because Faith, whom he expects to see, is not there. But she soon stands with him among those who are about to undergo their initiation. They are "the only pair, as it seemed, who were yet hesitating on the verge of wickedness in this dark world." They look at each other in fearful anticipation, and for the last time Brown calls out for help: "Faith! Faith! . . . look up to heaven, and resist the wicked one." But "whether Faith obeyed he knew not." The whole spectacle of the witches' Sabbath vanishes at this instant, and Brown, staggering against the rock that had formed the altar, finds hi
mself alone in the wilderness.

The withdrawal and gloom that envelop Brown after his return to the village come about not because he has yielded to the overwhelming vision of evil in the forest, but because he has repressed it.

—*Leo B. Levy*

It cannot plausibly be argued that Brown has all along been prone to the despair into which he is then plunged, since after abandoning himself to wickedness and turning himself into an image of the fiend he recovers his composure and calls upon Faith once more. He is alone among Hawthorne's many "demoniacs" in reversing the process of commiting himself to evil. Nevertheless, the sequel shows him irrevocably fallen into gloom and despair, condemned to a long life of withdrawal and suspicion. Brown has exhibited a compulsive denial of his compact with the Devil; but when his efforts to recover his former relationship with Faith collapse, he has no recourse except despair. No effort of the conscious will can save him. And yet the story is least of all a study, like "Roger Malvin's Burial," of unconscious motivation. Instead, Hawthorne seems content to emphasize Brown's helplessness. The spiritual test to which he is submitted is conducted on terms that only demonstrate the futility of his attempts to extricate himself. Even if we suppose that he unconsciously chooses to end his dream before Faith can reply, thereby condemning himself to a lifetime of faithlessness, the fact remains that Hawthorne has caught him

in a trap as diabolical as anything the Devil might invent. The psychoanalytically oriented critics interpret Goodman Brown's helplessness in terms of the projective mechanism of the dream or fantasy, which they regard as symptomatic of mental illness. The difficulty of this approach is not the contention that the presence of the Devil and his company and the rites into which Brown is drawn are projections, but that it ignores the conflict and resistance to which Hawthorne gives such explicit and emphatic attention. The projective aspect of Brown's experience is not the whole of it. His submission to evil suggests that the demands of the id have overtaken the ego; his prolonged resistance is a denial of the wishes that are the source of his projections. His conflict originates in the superego, whose task is to punish the ego for its defections and, as the voice of conscience, to repress the satisfactions of the instinctual life. Brown's recovery from the *Walpurgisnacht* episode, in which he gives way completely to the id, is made possible by the activated defense mechanisms of the ego, which cries out to be saved. If we wonder why the witches' Sabbath ends with such breathtaking abruptness, the answer might be that the ego cannot tolerate the threat of destruction that awaits it if the initiation rites take place. The sexually fraught demands of the id are put down, though at a terrible price. In psychoanalytic terms, **"Young Goodman Brown"** is about the defeat of the id by the ego and the superego. The result of this suppression is that Brown, despairing and embittered, belongs neither to the Devil's party nor to the only other life-sustaining cause he knows—that of the Puritan faith and the Puritan community. The withdrawal and gloom that envelop him after his return to the village come about not because he has yielded to the overwhelming vision of evil in the forest, but because he has repressed it. The ego forbids him to accept his evil impulses as his own; hence he projects them upon his wife, whose virtue he now distrusts, and upon the other villagers, in whose goodness he can no longer believe.

But this—or any other psychological interpretation—restricts our understanding of a story that is cast in religious and theological terms. We must move outside the limits of the dream or fantasy, beyond any view of the nature of the forest experience, and examine the ideas that structure that experience. A clue to the basic question raised by the story is provided by Henry James's complaint [in *Hawthorne*, 1879] that "if it meant anything, it would mean too much." James does not identify the specific source of his objection, but the context of his remark makes it clear that he believes that behind **"Young Goodman Brown"** is a kind of extravagance and even irrationality that gives rise to a "magnificent little romance," as he calls it, that cannot be taken seriously (James, p. 81). Evidently he found the image of a man pleading for faith and deprived of it with such arbitrariness baffling. The magical, supernatural, and mysterious connotations accompanying the disappearance of the witches' Sabbath and Brown's "awakening" may well have offended James's sense of fictional propriety as well as his sense of the writer's obligation to describe a moral crisis in rational terms. This development in the story originates in the Gothic idea of an irresistible and omnipresent evil. James, reacting against this vision, insists that the tale "evidently means nothing as regards Hawthorne's own state of mind, his conviction of human depravity and his consequent melancholy" (James, p. 81). However, it was not necessary for Hawthorne to literally subscribe to such a vision in order for his imagination to be powerfully engaged by it. The very excessiveness of his story is the source of its lasting impression upon those who have read it. Behind it is the motive that shapes such tales as "John Inglefield's Thanksgiving," "The Minister's Black Veil," and "The Christmas Banquet," among others, which are intelligible only on the principle that Hawthorne is dramatizing his feeling that once the commitment to evil has been made, its impact must prevail. There is no power strong enough to oppose it. In **"Young Goodman Brown"** the struggle is so unequal that Faith, supposedly the Devil's antagonist, is drawn into the camp of the enemy.

II

Not the least terrifying aspect of the story is the insinuation that Faith has made her own independent covenant with the Devil. There is a faint suggestion that her complicity may be prior to and deeper than Brown's. This "monstrous inversion," as Terence Martin aptly calls it [in *Nathaniel Hawthorne*, 1965]. is as sinister as anything to be found in Hawthorne's writings. This development is anticipated when Faith, imploring her husband not to leave her, says that "a lone woman is troubled with such dreams and such thoughts that she's afeard of herself sometimes," and she urges him to stay with her "this night . . . of all nights in the year." In this way, her bad dreams are linked to his, suggesting that both have prepared themselves for the same experience. However, we know nothing of the circumstances that bring her into the forest except what Brown discovers for himself. When Goody Cloyse tells the Devil that she has heard that "there is a nice young man to be taken into communion tonight," he denies the report, just as he had previously assured Brown that his Faith will not come to any harm. Brown overhears a voice like Deacon Gookin's declare that "there is a goodly young woman to be taken into communion," a statement offered not as something Brown imagines but given by one who does not know that he is listening. When the converts are brought forth, Brown approaches the congregation, "with whom he felt a loathful brotherhood by the sympathy of all that was wicked in his heart." He imagines—or sees—his father beckoning him on and his mother warning him back. Here again Hawthorne blurs the distinction between actual participants and projections. However, no such ambiguity attends the identification of "the slender form of a veiled female" brought forth by Goody Cloyse and Martha Carrier to take part in the baptismal rites: "the wretched man beheld his Faith, and the wife her husband, trembling before that unhallowed altar."

There is little agreement among critics about Faith as a character or as an allegorical figure. For some, Faith is allegorically consistent: Neal Frank Doubleday takes it as a sign of Faith's benevolence that when Brown calls upon Faith to "'resist the wicked one' . . . he is released from the witch-meeting" [Neal Frank Doubleday, *Hawthorne's Early Tales: A Critical Study,* 1972]. Even those who recognize Faith's dual character argue that she retains her allegorical identity. For Roy R. Male, "almost everything in the forest scene suggests that the communion of sinners is essentially sexual and that Brown qualifies for it by his marriage." And yet Male does not regard Faith's participation in the sexuality of marriage as an indication that she is "evil" in the sense that Brown is; one wonders why the sexual union leaves her free of the stain of original sin. Daniel Hoffman writes [in *Form and Fable in American Fiction,* 1965] that "in one sense, she *is* the forest, and Brown has qualified for admission to the witches' orgy by having carnal knowledge of her." Hoffman, too, absolves Faith of her share in the consequences of carnal knowledge: she "transcends Brown's knowledge of evil with all-encompassing love." In following Brown's corpse to the grave, "Faith remains true to him" (pp. 158, 156). But Hoffman's argument cannot resolve the paradox he himself describes: if "she *is* the forest"—if she too is guilty of carnal knowledge—how can she remain "the Devil's only antagonist in this tale," having "such faith in man that she can transcend the revelation that [Brown] is fallen?" (p. 167). After all, she too has fallen. The Devil's only antagonist, so far as the reader can tell, is Goodman Brown.

This confusion of the fictional character of Faith with the allegorical concept has its roots in the story itself. The basic thrust of the story is that faith is deficient, but the deficiency arises not from the personification of Faith as a woman and a wife but from Hawthorne's handling of the abstraction. He is not suggesting that Faith as an abstraction is susceptible to the human frailties of Everyman but somehow transcends them, even though he creates the correspondences that give rise to this misconception. His position seems to be that faith is a self-consistent principle, however unreliable and unpredictable. There is a submerged, possible unintended, but nonetheless dreadful irony in the manner in which Faith greets Brown on his return to the village, as if she had not been present in the forest and had played no part in the terrible events that take place there. She is as she was at the beginning—except that it is impossible for Brown to see her as she was. The meaning of the story arises from this discrepancy.

Faith's most conspicuous physical characteristic consists of the pink ribbons on her cap. They are the subject of many attempts to sustain an argument about her allegorical significance and to reconcile the two Faiths, one comely, almost lightsome, and the other in complicity with the powers of darkness. The ribbons provide the symbolic continuity between Faith as an ideal of religious fidelity and as a partner in a witches' Sabbath. The most obvious feature of these interpretations is their ingenuity and their diversity. To Thomas E. Connolly the ribbons "seem to be symbolic of [Brown's] initial illusion about the true significance of his faith, his belief that that his faith will lead him to heaven." Elsewhere, Connolly finds that they symbolize "illicit passion and purity." For Paul W. Miller, the ribbons "keep Faith humble and honest, and thus contribute to her ultimate preservation from the Evil One," and for E. Arthur Robinson they are "representative of woman's physical nature" and of Faith's sexual passion. Darrel Abel considers the ribbons "a badge of feminine innocence." For Paul J. Hurley, they represent "the ritualistic trappings of religious observance," and for Hyatt Waggoner they signalize Brown's immature faith. Richard H. Fogle has commented that "as an emblem of heavenly Faith their color gradually deepens into the liquid flame or blood of the baptism into sin" [Thomas E. Connolly, "Hawthorne's 'Young Goodman Brown': An Attack on Puritanic Calvinism," *AL* 27, 1956; Connolly, "Introduction," *Nathaniel Hawthorne: Young Goodman Brown,* 1968; Paul W. Miller, "Hawthorne's 'Young Goodman Brown': Cynicism or Meliorism?" *NCF* 14, 1959; E. Arthur Robinson, "The Vision of Goodman Brown: A Source and Interpretation," *AL* 35, 1963; Abel Hurley, "Young Goodman Brown's 'Heart of Darkness'"; Hyatt Waggoner, *Hawthorne: A Critical Study,* 1963; Richard H. Fogle, "Ambiguity and Clarity in Hawthorne's 'Young Goodman Brown'," *NEQ* 17, 1945]. There is no way to choose among views that differ so in their symbolic attributions; how one interprets the ribbons obviously depends upon one's prior understanding of the story.

F. O. Matthiessen [in *American Renaissance,* 1941] observes of the scene in which Brown believes he has visible proof of Faith's betrayal that "only the literal insistence on that damaging pink ribbon obtrudes the labels of a confining allegory, and short-circuits the range of association." He evidently means that the ribbon fails to work symbolically in an otherwise powerful depiction of Brown's inner experience. He contrasts Hawthorne's image of the ribbon to Melville's metaphor of "the ball of free will" held (and dropped) by Ishmael and Queequeg in *Moby-Dick,* remarking that "only by discovering such metaphors can the writer suggest the actual complexity of experience." But when Matthiessen adds that "we are bothered by the ribbon because it is an abstraction pretending to be something else," he fails to recognize that, on the contrary, it is because the ribbon is no more than a tangible object that its effect is "literal" rather than abstract, and for this reason cannot function metaphorically. It is simply a descriptive element, one of the realistic details that gives Faith such physical reality as she has. The ribbons belong to a fictional character described as "sweet," "pretty," and "little," more reminiscent of a genteel girl of Hawthorne's own day than a Puritan woman who might also have worn pink ribbons. She is the cheerful wife, one of Hawthorne's feminine figures, like Phoebe or Hilda, who serves as an emblem of steadfastness in a world of pollution.

David Levin argues that "Brown's sensory perception of the ribbons is no more literal or material than his perception of the Devil, his clutching of the staff, or his hearing of the Devil's statement about the fifteen-minute trip from Boston to the woods near Salem village." Approving this view [in *The Sins of the Fathers: Hawthorne's Psychological Themes,* 1966] Frederick Crews disputes the claim that the "tangible reality" of the pink ribbons is evidence that Faith is "really" in the forest, adding that "Brown shares Othello's fatuous concern for 'ocular proof,' and

the proof that is seized upon is no more substantial in one case than in the other." These critics do not perceive that whether we are looking at the story in psychological terms or in terms of evidence that Brown is beset by counterfeit images—spectres of real persons—conjured by the Devil, the literary relationships that give rise to these and other interpretations are still there, on the page and in the text. In this sense, it does not matter which critical perspective we choose to pursue. The ribbons are in fact an explicit link between two conceptions of Faith, connecting sweet little Faith of the village with the woman who stands at the Devil's baptismal font. We can legitimately disagree about the meaning of this duality; the fact remains that in proposing that Faith's significance is the opposite of what he had led the reader to expect, Hawthorne violates the fixed conceptual meaning associated with his character. This breaking of the allegorical mold is more than a technical violation of the genre: it turns the story in an entirely new direction, so that it is deprived of the essential feature of all allegory—the ability to derive an abstract truth from its unfolding.

Hawthorne's breaking of the allegorical mold is more than a technical violation of the genre: it turns the story in an entirely new direction, so that it is deprived of the essential feature of all allegory—the ability to derive an abstract truth from its unfolding.

—Leo B. Levy

As we have noted, Hawthorne combines the kind of allegory that depicts the interaction of characters in an external setting—a technique of "realistic" as well as allegorical narrative—with the internalization of the action in the mind of the protagonist, for the purpose of dividing the reader's perception of what is happening. The ambiguity that results has the effect of enriching the story; but when the method is applied to the ribbons, the effect is a kind of teasing. The ribbons intrude themselves upon the symbolic sphere of the story where they do not belong; they have no meaning except as a fanciful joke, a grace note woven into the solemn theme of the tale. However, they have an important dramatic function: as we see them at the beginning and end of the story, the ribbons identify the physical as distinct from the allegorical character of Faith; we have no need to see them in symbolic terms, since Faith as an abstraction is fully defined by her name alone. They are part of her adornment of dress, and they suggest, rather than symbolize, something light and playful, consistent with her anxious simplicity at the beginning and the joyful, almost childish eagerness with which she greets Brown at the end. It is only in the forest scene that the single ribbon becomes disturbing. The critics have seized upon this ribbon no less desperately than Goodman Brown himself in order to establish the continuity of the allegorical theme. But it is by means of the ribbon that Hawthorne disrupts the allegory; all that we see of Faith now is the ornament that warrants her physical presence just when her allegorical presence vanishes. The moment is dramatic in the contrast of the frivolous, fluttering piece of ribbon with the darkness, agony, and doubt that envelop the scene. It is as if Hawthorne were saying, "Yes, it is truly Faith, as you see by this ribbon, who is no longer Faith."

The psychology-oriented critics believe that they solve the problem of the ribbons by saying that they are part of Goodman Brown's dream, no more or less "real" than the rest of what his diseased mind invents out of its own necessities. This theory cannot tell us when the dream begins: does Brown dream that he bids good-bye to Faith? If so, then he may also be dreaming of his return to the village and of the despair that afflicts him, and even of his long, unhappy life and eventual death. Did he dream that he made a covenant with the Devil? Did he do so before he entered the forest to keep his appointment, waking from one dream only to fall victim to another, after a pointless evening walk? The story is constructed in such a way that questions of this kind cannot be answered; but it does make a distinction between Brown's departure and return and the period between them. We may believe that the interval is a dream, even though we cannot know when it begins. This assumption has much to be said for it; but if we follow it we must conclude that the ribbons are both in and out of the dream, that Brown is dreaming about something he is familiar with in his waking experience. It is little wonder, then, that the sight of the ribbon produces the shock that leads him to connect his dream with reality in such a devastating fashion. In emotional as well as visual terms, the world of the nightmare and the world of the Puritan community are united. This development is reinforced by the bewilderment of Brown's return to the village and its profoundly disorienting consequences. Perhaps it is not until he encounters the minister, Deacon Gookin, and Goody Cloyse, and then sees "the head of Faith, with the pink ribbons, gazing anxiously forth," that his faith is permanently shattered. The breakdown of the beliefs and assumptions that gave order and stability to his life is complete.

III

It is sometimes said that Hawthorne's purpose in **"Young Goodman Brown"** is to demonstrate the unresponsiveness of Puritanic Calvinism to the needs of the believer. However, Hawthorne's equation of the Puritan experience with the devil-worship that is its inversion is a form of dramatic hyperbole that should not be taken literally. The Puritan vision of evil was a dreadful one, and there can be no doubt that Hawthorne means to dramatize its excesses; but this is not the same thing as drawing up an indictment of Puritan faith. Hawthorne knew that witches' Sabbaths and Black Masses were not confined to Puritan New England, and he knew that the possibility of being overwhelmed by the discovery of the power of evil was universal. He reacted strongly against the bigotry, cruelty, and hypocrisy of his New England ancestors, but that

reaction does not exhaust the complex judgment he formed of them. Even the Reverend Dimmesdale, that pious hypocrite, has in his possession a larger share of the truth about the human condition—truth that derives from his faith—than the romantic and memorable rebel, Hester Prynne. Hawthorne well knew the variability of the experience of faith among the Puritans. Elsewhere he shows us that it may lead to serenity, to a dehumanizing dogmatism, or to intense suffering of spirit. Faith may also, as in **"Young Goodman Brown,"** mysteriously abandon us.

> As a form, allegory is a systmeatic organization of fixed beliefs; Hawthorne utilizes the form for the purpose of showing that the safety and security implicit in it are illusory. The meaning of the story is that its own simple definitions do not work.
>
> —Leo B. Levy

As a form, allegory is a systematic organization of fixed beliefs; Hawthorne utilizes the form for the purpose of showing that the safety and security implicit in it are illusory. The meaning of the story is that its own simple definitions do not work. Instead, we are shown that there is no necessary connection between our critical need for faith and the responsiveness of faith. This is the larger significance of **"Young Goodman Brown,"** not the comfortable parable that warns us against the sin of despair, which the moralistic tenor of the conclusion would have us believe can be avoided if only we listen attentively enough. The last paragraph turns Brown into an object lesson; but, as is often the case with Hawthorne's tales, a truer meaning is discovered before this point of constriction is reached. In his penetrating analysis of the problem of faith in Hawthorne's fiction, Taylor Stoehr, writing of "Rappaccini's Daughter" as well as **"Young Goodman Brown,"** observes that "Hawthorne seems to throw the blame on his characters, while at the same time he gives them no possible means of saving themselves." Stoehr adds that "for a man who is always complaining about his characters' lack of faith, Hawthorne himself is singularly dubious about the possibilities of life and human nature" [Taylor Stoehr, "'Young Goodman Brown' and Hawthorne's Theory of Mimesis," *NCF*, 23, 1969].

For Hawthorne, the loss of faith is always imminent, a danger that increases in proportion to our involvement in a moral reality that is always more unsettling than we like to believe. His concern in **"Young Goodman Brown,"** apart from describing the terrors of the Puritan struggle for faith, is with our inability to foresee the consequences of our choices or to judge the nature of the moral forces that press upon us. We can easily move past the point of return, and, like Goodman Brown, find that it is too late for what we want and need. Brown's last cry for Faith is the most poignant moment of the story, expressing his need to assimilate the experiences through which he has passed, and even his capacity to do so. The silence between dream and waking, or between the actuality of the witches' Sabbath and his ordinary life, is the silence of the void between spiritual need and spiritual sustenance. The reader is not less stunned than Brown himself, since he cannot easily resolve the paradox into which he has been led. He saw Brown at the outset abandon Faith; if that were all that he is meant to see, the tale would be very simple. But now the reader finds that Faith has deserted Brown—a distinction that may seem elusive but is nevertheless the crux upon which everything turns. Faith is originally the "good angel" to whose skirts Goodman Brown resolves to cling hereafter. To suggest that the good angel may turn herself into a demon is an insight that Hawthorne does not often risk, though there is also a hint of the diabolical in the transformations through which he takes Priscilla in *The Blithedale Romance.*

Hawthorne typically pays detailed attention to the costume and dress of his feminine characters as symbolic evidences of the stages through which they move. Except for her ribbons, Faith is pictorially a cipher, an abstraction for which Hawthorne refuses symbolic amplification, perhaps because of his sense of its precarious status. Therefore, Faith (or faith) becomes unresponsive, it disappears, and when it reappears it stands in the midst of all that it dreads. If, awaking at midnight, Goodman Brown shrinks from the bosom of Faith, it is because he has taken the full measure of her duplicity. "Such loss of faith is ever one of the saddest results of sin," Hawthorne says of Hester Prynne, and in *The Scarlet Letter* he castigates "the Fiend" for leaving nothing "for this poor sinner to revere." But in **"Young Goodman Brown"** it is Faith, not Satan or the sinner, whose defection is at issue.

Sheldon W. Liebman   (essay date 1975)

SOURCE: "The Reader in 'Young Goodman Brown'," in *The Nathaniel Hawthorne Journal 1975,* edited by C. E. Frazer Clark, Jr., Microcard Editions Books, 1975, pp. 156-69.

[In this essay, Liebman argues that Hawthorne's concern in "Young Goodman Brown" is to challenge the reader's own morality and to force the reader to choose between conflicting possibilities of meaning.]

Like "My Kinsman, Major Molineux" and "The Maypole of Merry Mount," **"Young Goodman Brown"** begins at dusk, and the journey on which its hero embarks is ventured among diminishing lights and growing shadows which signify a world of moral uncertainty and announce the coming of a moral crisis. In "the heart of the dark wilderness," as in so many of Hawthorne's stories, a young man is given the opportunity to see nature as it really is, illuminated by no lights other than its own and observed by his eyes only. Like Reuben Bourne, Goodman Brown

enters a "dark and gloomy" labyrinth in which the only knowledge he can gain is personal, and the only resources at his disposal are his own heart and mind. He must come to grips with the nature of things in the deep, dark, pathless wilderness of night and determine to his own satisfaction and on the basis of his own observation whether the universe is, beyond the power of his own will and desire, divine or demonic or both.

Of course Brown concludes, though only implicitly and uncertainly, that the world belongs to the devil and its inhabitants to the devil's party. As a result of his experience in the forest he turns away from Faith, his allegorical wife. He lives as if no man is to be trusted, as if no one is what he seems to be, and he dies a "darkly meditative, a distrustful, if not a desperate man." Yet what Brown has seen is never clear, as his own uncertainty suggests. He does not leave the village of his birth; he does not abandon his wife. He continues to live as a respectable member of the community despite his doubts and fears. To the very end of the story Hawthorne refuses to illuminate the facts.

There can be no doubt that young Goodman Brown is confused by the ambiguity of his experience. Perhaps more important, however, the ambiguity of the story has confused its readers as well. For this reason I intend to examine **"Young Goodman Brown"** not only in terms of Brown's relationship to the events of his life but also in terms of the reader's relationship to his experience of reading the story. In my view Hawthorne has managed his material in such a way as to challenge his reader's credulity and powers of analysis as much as Brown's, and thus the ambiguity of the tale is directed primarily at the reader, whose task it is to distinguish between appearance and reality by way of determining what happens in the story and why.

"Had Goodman Brown fallen asleep in the forest and only dreamed a wild dream of a witch-meeting?" This question raises the issues which Hawthorne always dramatizes in his best stories: what do we know and how do we know it? The critical history of **"Young Goodman Brown"** is, in relation to these questions, suggestive of the complexity of the tale, the subtlety of Hawthorne's method, and the difficulty of the reader's role: as observer, seeing through Brown's eyes, and as actor, judging the evidence as Brown must and answering the questions with which Brown must deal in the process of laying the moral foundations of his conduct.

Until recently the consensus of critical opinion held that in **"Young Goodman Brown"** Hawthorne strikes a balance between the two possible interpretations of the story. That is, he deliberately leaves the issues he raises unresolved, the questions unanswered. For many other readers, however, the ambiguity of the story is neither final nor impenetrable. What does the story mean, after all, if its data remain ambiguous? Does it mean that the facts of life are always and forever confusing? That the central feature of human existence is the irreducibility of its elements? And that therefore man cannot conduct himself in a reasonable way on the basis of his personal experience with the facts of life? With or without these questions in mind, some critics have argued that Goodman Brown actually participates in a witches' meeting, hears a priest deliver an infernal sermon, and sees his wife standing beside him ready to yield to the devil's temptation. More recently, readers have concluded that Brown merely dreams in the forest and that his experience is entirely the product of his own disturbed imagination.

The critical history of **"Young Goodman Brown"** is worth reviewing because it suggests that if recent critics are right in believing that Brown is mistaken, then Hawthorne's story has eluded its readers for more than a century. It is almost as if Hawthorne has so contrived the events in the tale, so manipulated the point of view, that readers have been led to conclusions contradicted by the facts. It seems, in short, that Hawthorne has purposely led his readers astray or has at least allowed them to go astray.

The possibility is purely conjectural of course. Yet such an interpretation rests squarely on a number of important points. First, the ambiguity of the story is real. Whatever one may conclude about the meaning of the story, one is given a choice among three possible interpretations: (1) that Brown dreamed, (2) that he did not, and (3) that it is impossible to tell one way or the other. Second, as the record of Hawthorne criticism shows, each of the three choices has been made at one time or another. Third, and most important, the reader's choices are precisely those available to Brown. And it is more than interesting that most of the story's earlier critics chose precisely as Brown chooses.

One might conclude then that Hawthorne's intention in **"Young Goodman Brown"** is to force the reader to undergo the temptations which Brown himself must endure and that he is made to see the world through Brown's eyes in order to have to make his decision with only this evidence available to him. In this way the reader is made the central character in the story, and it is *his* moral vision with which Hawthorne is concerned and *his* moral choice which Hawthorne challenges.

The reader is made the central character in the story, and it is *his* moral vision with which Hawthorne is concerned and *his* moral choice which Hawthorne challenges.

—Sheldon W. Liebman

In pursuit of this objective Hawthorne uses three principal devices: (1) diverting ambiguity, (2) dilatory exposition, and (3) dissimulated point of view. In many of his stories Hawthorne diverts the reader's attention from significant ambiguity, important events whose ambiguity derives from

a conflict between appearance and reality, by drawing the reader's attention to insignificant ambiguity, incidental events whose ambiguity derives from a conflict between the natural and the preternatural. The latter is often unresolvable, and the reader is inclined to believe that all other ambiguity is similarly unresolvable. Hawthorne frequently presents his exposition of characters in a dilatory manner. That is, he reveals the evidence very gradually and typically saves the most important information for last. Characters introduced honorifically are described pejoratively at the end, and vice-versa. As the narration continues, the initial terms of description are reversed, but the reader has already committed himself and has some difficulty extricating himself from his original view. Dissimulated point of view is Hawthorne's characteristic mode in his short fiction. The point of view shifts imperceptibly from narrator to character so that the reader sees through the character's eyes even when he thinks he is seeing through the narrator's.

This shift in perspective is accomplished in three ways. First, dialogue is presented as if it were narration. What purports to be the language of the author is really the language of the character whose point of view is dominant. Second, subjective events are presented as if they were objective. The fictional world of the story moves from the imagination of the author to that of the character, and the line between appearance and reality is blurred if not eliminated. Third, events are presented as if they were both natural (that is, of nature) and spontaneous, whereas in fact they are connected almost causally, each originating in the mind of the character, each made possible by its predecessor, and each becoming more "substantial" as the character becomes more committed to the objectivity of his subjective impressions and more accustomed to confusing concepts and percepts. In this way the "logic of compulsion" replaces the logic of nature, and, unbeknownst to the character, his thoughts take on the potency not only of events but of causes of events.

Hawthorne uses diverting ambiguity throughout **"Young Goodman Brown."** After Brown first meets the devil he (and the reader) is faced with two incidental ambiguities: the devil's staff resembles the biblical serpent, and the devil himself resembles Brown's father. "As nearly as could be discerned" the devil bears "a considerable resemblance" to Brown's father; "they might have been taken for father and son." The devil claims to have been "well acquainted" with Brown's family, especially his father and grandfather. His staff bears "the likeness" of a snake: "it might almost be seen to twist and wriggle itself like a living serpent." When the devil laughs, "his snake-like staff actually seemed to wriggle in sympathy." These ambiguities dominate the scene. Yet the real question is whether or not the devil, as a living, breathing character, is present at all. And this issue is obscured in Brown's eyes, just as the reader's attention is drawn to ambiguities which are neither important nor resolvable. The reader is tempted to conclude that this irresolution is characteristic of all of the ambiguity in the story. And he becomes accustomed to seeing through Brown's uncertain eyes on more important issues without batting an eyelash.

This device is used again in the next scene, in which Goody Cloyse appears. The old woman reminds both Brown and the reader of the devil's resemblance to one of Brown's ancestors, this time his grandfather. And Hawthorne refers to him as "the shape of old Goodman Brown." The devil touches Goody Cloyse's neck "with what seemed the serpent's tail" and leans "on his writhing stick" when he speaks to her. The real issue, of course, is whether or not Goody Cloyse actually appears, but when she vanishes Hawthorne veils the question of her appearance and disappearance with more incidental ambiguity. The devil throws his staff "down at her feet, where, perhaps, it assumed life." Hawthorne comments: "Of this fact, however, Goodman Brown cannot take cognizance. He had cast up his eyes in astonishment, and, looking down again, beheld neither Goody nor the serpentine staff, but his fellow-traveller alone, who waited for him as calmly as if nothing had happened." At the end of the story Hawthorne asks of the baptismal basin at which the priest stands, "Did it contain water, reddened by the lurid light? or was it blood? or, perchance, a liquid flame?" This too is mere question-begging since the questions assume that the forest is aflame and that "the shape of evil" stands ready to baptize Faith and Goodman Brown. These are the real ambiguities in the story though the reader is given other and not very nourishing food for thought.

Hawthorne uses dilatory exposition in his description of the devil. He is first presented as a man "in grave and decent attire." He is "as simply clad" as Brown is and "as simple in manner." He has "an indescribable air of one who knew the world." More important, he does not reveal to Brown or to the reader the full extent of his vision of despair, at least immediately. He first claims to have known Brown's family as well as any other. He helped Brown's grandfather whip a Quaker woman and helped Brown's father burn an Indian village during King Philip's war. His father and grandfather may have sinned, Brown answers, but he and his Puritan fellows "abide no such wickedness." Then the devil claims acquaintance with many deacons, selectmen, members of the General Court, and even the governor. One might acknowledge that this is so, as Brown does, however, without granting the devil too much. He simply reports that many have sinned, and Brown answers that he has nothing to do with them or they with him. Finally, the devil introduces Brown's religious instructress, the deacon of his church, and his minister. And it is only at this point that the devil suggests by his presentation of Brown's own spiritual guides that a witches' meeting is to take place and that virtually everyone will attend. That is, all men are secretly evil and worship the devil.

The priest's sermon at the height of the Black Mass is developed in the same manner. Just as the devil resembles Goodman Brown, the priest "bore no slight similitude, both in garb and manner, to some grave divine of the New England churches." And like the devil's, his message is at first by no means inconsistent with orthodox Christianity. He asks the converts, Faith and Goodman Brown, to observe those whom they have always admired and regarded as holier than themselves. They are all sinners, the priest continues, and Faith and her husband will be given an opportunity to know "their secret deeds." In addition, "by the sympathy of [their] hearts for sin," they shall be able to discover crime wherever it is being committed. This is nothing more than what Virgil promises Dante in *The Inferno,* and it reflects Hawthorne's sentiments at the end of "Fancy's Show Box": "Man must not disclaim his brotherhood, even with the guiltiest, since, though his hand be clean, his heart has surely been polluted by the flitting phantoms of iniquity." Thus, even when the priest announces that "the whole earth [is] one stain of guilt, one mighty blood spot," and grants the young couple the power "to penetrate, in every bosom, the deep mystery of sin," neither Brown nor the reader need take offense. It is not until his final words that the priest eliminates paradise from *The Divine Comedy* and deletes the hopeful lines from the last paragraph of "Fancy's Show Box": "Depending upon one another's hearts," he says, "ye had still hoped that virtue were still not all a dream. Now ye are undeceived. Evil is the nature of mankind. *Evil must be your only happiness.*"

These are no longer Hawthorne's words, of course, but the infernal rhetoric of Satan, the fallen angel, spoken in a voice "almost sad with its despairing awfulness, as if his once angelic nature could yet mourn for our miserable race." And his followers are indeed "fiend worshippers" who welcome Faith and Goodman Brown with "one cry of despair and triumph." The priest is nothing more or less than the showman in "Ethan Brand" who presents his hand to Ethan as if it were the hand of destiny, the seemingly supernatural power who beckons Reuben Bourne to expiate his sin by killing his son, and the source of Father Hooper's decision to cover his face with a black veil in order to show all men their secret sin. Yet his message is so skillfully developed that more than one reader has taken his words for Hawthorne's own, deceived as Brown is by the dilatory manner of his presentation.

Distracting and diverting as these devices are, **"Young Goodman Brown"** would still be a masterpiece of ambiguity without them. For Hawthorne's most effective and customary device of ambiguity is his manipulation of the narrative point of view, which is nowhere more powerfully in operation than in this story. The facts with which the reader must deal are complicated by the dual nature of Goodman Brown's journey. On the one hand he encounters a reality outside himself in the forest and the night. On the other hand he travels to interior domains. His experience with the world of nature is also an experience with human nature, both others' and his own. Like Wakefield, he wanders off not only into darkness but also into solitude. "It was all as lonely as could be; and there is this peculiarity in solitude," says Hawthorne: the traveler does not know what he may see or whom he may meet. To journey solitarily into darkness is to lose one's relationship to the community, and one may become thereby "an Outcast of the Universe." It is also to lose one's everyday consciousness and to enter a realm of seld ordinarily closed to those who are fearful of its depths even if they are beckoned by its temptations. As Faith tells Brown, "A lone woman is troubled with such dreams that she's afeard of herself sometimes."

Left to his own resources and entering into a deeper and deeper solitude, Brown comes closer and closer to the untrodden and undiscovered depths of his own being, a world of dreams, fantasies, and unconscious motives. He says to himself in response to Faith's warning, "She talks of dreams, too," suggesting that perhaps he too has dreamed. At the end of the story Hawthorne asks whether or not Brown had "only dreamed a wild dream of a witch-meeting?" And thus the reader is drawn into a universe in which things are half-created and half-perceived, in which appearance and reality mingle freely and disconcertingly, and in which the self discovered therein is both observer and observed.

The reader is compelled to assess and evaluate his experience of the story, particularly its language. He must deal not so much with Hawthorne's language and the events which it describes, however, but with Brown's own language and the events which it embodies. Brown's experience is ambiguous to him, and the language of ambiguity is the only appropriate medium for communication under such circumstances. He beholds, discerns, recognizes, fancies, and discovers, as well as sees and hears. Things seem and appear not only as themselves but as semblances of other things, similitudes and likenesses. And events transpire on a plane of imagination so rarified that it is only "as if" they happen. In this atmosphere of uncertain vision, thoughts become things and fears become fearful objects.

None of this would trouble the reader if Hawthorne failed to dissimulate the role of omniscient narrator. After Brown leaves Faith, however, and takes the reader into his own imaginary world, Hawthorne maintains his imposture of objective reporter. Events which appear to Brown's eyes only are recorded as if they actually happened. The devil does not appear in the forest to anyone but Brown: he "*beheld* the figure of a man . . . seated at the foot of an old tree." Nor does Goody Cloyse arrive at this unlikely spot. Brown "*recognized* a very pious and exemplary dame" in the figure pointed out to him by the devil. Deacon Gookin and the minister are not out riding in the dead of night. It is only that Brown "*heard* the tramp of horses along the road" and "two grave old voices" which "*appeared* to pass." "[H]e could have sworn, were such a thing possible, that he *recognized* the voices of the minister and Deacon Gookin." Brown "sees" a black cloud, "hears" voices come out of it, and "beholds" Faith's pink ribbon. He "sees" a fire in the distance, sees the faces of his townspeople "appear" and "disappear" in the flames, and "recognizes" many familiar faces, including Deacon Gookin's and the minister's. Finally, the priest "appears," Brown thinks he sees his father and mother, though he is not certain, and he "beholds" his Faith. In this way, the reader is given every opportunity to ignore the dominance of Brown's point of view, and he is tempted to conclude the opposite of what is obviously the case: that Brown really sees what he thinks he sees and that he is disillusioned at the end by the facts of life.

Hawthorne goes so far as to present Brown's thoughts as if they were part of his own narration. He says in his own words, after Brown has promised himself that he will return to Faith and follow her to heaven, "With this excellent resolve, Goodman Brown felt himself justified in making more haste on his present evil purpose." And he says, after Brown has once more promised to return to Faith, "And what calm sleep would be his that very night, which was to have been spent to wickedly, but so purely and sweetly now, in the arms of Faith!" That Brown's resolve is "excellent" is of course his own idea, and that his second promise is "praiseworthy" is nothing more than his own judgment.

This device is used more subtly by Hawthorne when he follows his own narrative comment with a statement by Brown which reveals that the comment is really Brown's rather than Hawthorne's. The narrator says, "[T]he traveller knows not who may be concealed by the innumerable trunks and the thick boughs overhead; so that with lonely footsteps he may yet be passing through an unseen multitude." That this is actually Brown's thought is suggested by his immediate remark: "There may be a devilish Indian behind every tree. . . . What if the devil himself should be at my very elbow!" The distinction is not very important at this point in the story, but it is very significant in a later passage. Hawthorne seems to say,

> And there they stood, the only pair, as it seemed, who were yet hesitating on the verge of wickedness in this dark world. . . . The husband cast one look at his pale wife, and Faith at him. What polluted wretches would the next glance show them to each other, shuddering alike at what they disclosed and what they saw!

Both the word *seemed* and the exclamatory tone of the passage suggest that the words might not be the narrator's. But the following statement by Brown—"Faith! Faith! . . . look up to heaven, and resist the wicked one"—also exclamatory, suggests even more impressively that the paragraph in which Hawthorne seems to regard Brown and his wife as the last pure couple on earth is actually Brown's view presented as narrative comment. Evidently, he calls on Faith to refuse communion because he is as afraid of revealing his own evil as he is of seeing hers, and he wishes to avert the "next glance."

This narrative technique is justified by the fact that the middle portion of the story, from Brown's departure to his return, is told entirely from Brown's point of view. Brown creates a devil in the guise of his father and grandfather and substantiates by the evidence of his own eyes a guilt so pervasive as to include not only his righteous forbears but also the leaders, past and present, of his own upstanding community. He conjures up his pious teacher and the foremost members of his church by a power conferred upon him by his commitment to demonic forces. With the devil's staff and laugh he becomes eventually "the chief horror of the scene." He rushes "onward with the instinct that leads mortal man to evil," the full flowering of "the guilty purpose that had brought him hither," the "evil purpose" of which he was "conscious" even at the beginning of his journey. At this point, "nothing could be more frightful than the figure of Goodman Brown," though he finds everything more frightful than himself. As Hawthorne explains, "The fiend in his own shape is less hideous than when he rages in the breast of men." In short, Brown has become a "demoniac," like Reuben Bourne and Ethan Brand, and when he approaches the congregation in the midst of the forest, he feels "a loathful brotherhood by the sympathy of all that was wicked in his heart." So far gone is he in the ways of evil that "he had no power to retreat one step, nor to resist, even in thought." Of course Brown becomes a demoniac not because he is naturally depraved or because all other men and women are but because he encounters the demons in his own heart, denies them, projects them onto others, and thereby creates an imaginary world of witches and wizards who exist in reality only as "echoes" of his own demonic cry of despair and disillusion.

Everything Brown sees in his journey into the heart of darkness is his own creation, even the darkness itself.

—*Sheldon W. Liebman*

Thus, everything Brown sees in his journey into the heart of darkness is his own creation, even the darkness itself. Having "seen" or "heard" Goody Cloyse, Deacon Gookin, and the minister discuss the evening's business, he feels "faint and overburdened with the heavy sickness of his heart." For consolation he gazes up at the sky, "*doubting* whether there really was a heaven above him." The night is clear, bright, and windless: "there was the blue arch and the stars brightening in it." Yet Brown's doubt is extreme, and despite his promise to "stand firm against the devil," because heaven is above and faith below, he "sees" contrary evidence. "While he still gazed upward into the deep arch of the firmament and had lifted his hands to pray, *a cloud, though no wind was stirring,* hurried across the zenith, and hid the brightening stars. The blue sky was still visible, except directly overhead, where *this black mass of cloud* was sweeping swiftly northward." Moving northward with the devil, this "black mass" eventually becomes a Black Mass: "Aloft in the air, *as if* from the depths of the cloud, came a *confused* and *doubtful* sound of voices." Of course the doubt and confusion are Brown's own, and the cloud emanates from his heart, just as Reuben Bourne and Father Hooper are confused and bewildered by their experience and a similarly self-created cloud darkens their respective heavens. Soon, "the dark cloud swept away, leaving the clear and silent sky above Goodman Brown"—as if the cloud, like the devil, were merely the product of Brown's morbid imagination.

The appearance of Faith's pink ribbon, to Brown the final confirmation of the powers of darkness, is simply the last in a series of sensory illusions, from seeing to hearing to touching, which deceive Brown and compel him to say, "Come, devil; for to thee is this world given." He thinks he hears Faith's voice and the cries of her pursuers, but

these are, as his own uncertain description suggests, the mocking echoes of the forest which seem to call Faith's name—"*as if* bewildered wretches were seeking her all through the wilderness." The only bewildered wretch in the forest is Brown himself, for "the *wretched* man [beholds] his Faith" and later returns to the village "staring around him like a *bewildered* man." It is Brown alone who is seeking Faith in this most unlikely of places, and it is Brown alone who is both her demonic pursuer and her devout protector. She is nowhere to be found because she exists only in his heart and can appear only after he has exorcized her—"My Faith is gone!"—and made her a demon, one of the voices of the night, intent on evil and tempting Brown to submit to powers (he thinks) not his own.

The witches' meeting itself represents the culmination of Brown's doubts and confusion. In the voices of the dark cloud, he "*fancied* that he could distinguish the accents of townspeople of his own." But "so *indistinct* were the sounds, he *doubted* whether he had heard aught but the murmur of the old forest." And then again "came a stronger swell of those familiar voices." After the appearance of Faith's pink ribbon, the objectification of Brown's fear increases. The wind tolls *like* a church bell. The echoes of the forest laugh *like* demons. It is "*as if* all nature were laughing him to scorn." A rock *resembles* an altar. The blazing pines are *like* church candles. The noise of the forest is *like* the sound of a mighty organ. Brown hears "a sound, *as if* the roaring wind, the rushing streams, the howling beasts, and every other voice of the unconcerted wilderness were mingling and according with the voice of guilty man in homage to the prince of all." Yet at the end, after Brown asserts his faith, "he found himself amid calm night and solitude, listening to a roar of the wind"—as if, like the sky which grew cloudy and clear again, the forest returns to itself, and the similitudes created by Brown's image-making mind vanish in the darkness. When he returns to the village, he finds Faith's ribbons where they were when he left, unchanged except by the power of his own self-fulfilling prophecies.

Invariably the dreamer in Hawthorne's stories becomes a madman whose demons become substantial shapes and forms actualized by the projection of self-righteously disowned feelings. The "fiends" who appear in the final pages of "My Kinsman, Major Molineux" and "Lady Eleanor's Mantle" are the ultimate expression of a pathological vision which originates in the heart of the young man whose love is shallow and understanding weak and whose encounter with the ambiguities of his experience so bewilders him that he tries to destroy the thing he loves and becomes the demon he has tried to exorcise. In these last moments the young man's vision is illuminated solely by his own demonic imagination, expressed in the torches carried by creatures marching out of his infernal depths. Like Ethan Brand he has stared so long at the fires of damnation that he sees by no other light.

Habituated to a vision both born in and nurtured by his "evil purpose," Goodman Brown sees in the forest "a red light before him"—"four blazing pines." In this typically

Hawthornesque scene, the darkness of gloom is transformed, though only fitfully, into the light of splendor. What has been denied and hesitantly resisted is now reluctantly affirmed and even desired. "As the red light rose and fell, a numerous congregation *alternately shone forth, then disappeared* in shadow, and again grew, as it were, *out of the darkness,* peopling the solitary woods at once." Brown is engaged in dialogue once again, but the terms of his internal debate are not faith and infidelity, the subject of his discourse with the devil. Brown is now caught between the infernal emotions of desire and loathing: the faces of the congregation "appear" among the flames, "quivering to and fro between gloom and splendor." Like Giovanni in "Rappaccini's Daughter," Brown is caught between hope and dread: "It is the lurid intermixture of the two that produces the illuminating blaze of the infernal regions." Nothing is clear to Brown because his heart is a battleground of conflicting forces, the demonic reflections of pity and terror. "*Either* the sudden gleams of light flashing over the obscure field *bedazzled* Goodman Brown, *or* he *recognized* a score of the church members." In these flames he "obscurely discovered" shapes and visages of horror." Only "in a sheet of flame" are the "fiend worshippers" visible. Just as Brown before *could have sworn* . . . that he *recognized* the voices of the minister and Deacon Gookin," so now he "could have well-nigh sworn that the shape of his own father beckoned him to advance." Finally, "*by the blaze of hell-kindled torches,* the wretched man beheld his Faith."

Though the reader is tempted to see as Brown sees in this episode, it is nothing more than the fantasy of a deranged man, a demoniac, dreaming a dream of horror and temptation. Any reader might be persuaded by its powerful music and dazzling lights. But just as the voices of the night fade into the sound of the dying wind, the fires of hell disappear at Brown's final invocation of Faith: "He staggered against the rock," before ablaze in "the lurid light," "and felt it chill and damp; while a hanging twig, that had been all on fire, besprinkled his cheek with the coldest dew." From the beginning of the tale, the trees have been "wet with evening dew," though they become "strangely withered and dried up as with a week's sunshine" at the devil's touch. At the end of the story everything is as it was before, except for Goodman Brown. There is no ambiguity in this pattern, and no reader need be as "bewildered" as Brown is even after his return to Salem village. This young man has been asked, and the limits and language of the choice derive from his own infidelity, to choose among the unholy trinity of false faith, loathing, and desire. He chooses loathing rather than affirm a faith in which he no longer believes and a faith which tempts him but will not take him to heaven.

If the reader has followed the process of Brown's demonization carefully, he cannot help but conclude that Brown sees nothing uncreated and untempered by his disposition. He not only takes appearances for reality; he not only peoples the wilderness with imaginary sounds and scenes; and he not only draws these voices and visions from his own mind and heart. He actually engenders from his first thought a series of events which follow inevitably upon

each other, bound by a logic of their own and linked by an adamantine chain of psychological necessity. He comes to experience with a repertoire of preconceptions, and he is utterly incapable of experiencing anything else. It is as if the ordinary conversion of impression into idea, or sensation into image, is reversed in Brown's experience. For him, thought precedes feeling (seeing, hearing, and touching) and imposes upon it categories not its own. In this way, everything follows from an event which is anterior to the moment of Brown's departure from Faith: his very conceptualization of the devil even before his meeting with him. Thus Brown *begins* by doubting his faith, and the events which succeed this thought actually derive from it. He calls forth the devil when he asks, "What if the devil himself should be at my very elbow!" He thinks of Faith and she reminds him of "his moral and spiritual adviser," Goody Cloyse. He has already thought of "that good old man, our minister," and hears the voices of "good old" Deacon Gookin and the minister. He says, "Come witch, come wizard, come Indian powwow, come devil himself, and here comes Goodman Brown." Having seen Faith's ribbon fall from the skies, he cries, "There is no good on earth; and sin is but a name. Come, devil; for to thee is this world given." And later he sees witches and wizards, Indian powwows, and the devil himself, who pronounces Brown's own sentiments in his sermon. In short, each event is prefigured in Brown's mind, each succeeding event is made possible by its predecessor, and all of the events of Brown's night journey derive from the initial confusion in his mind and heart and merely confirm the thoughts and feelings from which they derive.

In **"Young Goodman Brown"** Hawthorne plays the part of a showman with a picture-box, a role he adopts in "Main Street," displaying to the reader scenes of long ago which despite their age promise to reflect the present. Fancy's showman in another sketch displays to Mr. Smith reflections of his soul: "In every sense, however dubiously portrayed, Mr. Smith was invariably haunted by his own lineament . . . as in a dusty mirror." In **"Young Goodman Brown"** Hawthorne puts the reader in the same relation as Mr. Smith to his own fantasies. For the reader, as Hawthorne knew, comes to a story with as rich an imagination as the author possesses and with which he endows his characters. And Hawthorne knew too, as he suggests in "Fancy's Show Box," that the potential for evil as well as good, the resource of the criminal as well as the artist, is in the human heart, in the imagination. He simply asks the reader implicitly to choose between the roles of criminal and artist and to maintain, in the act of interpretation if he would choose well, the same distance from the work as exists between the author and his subject.

Thus, as if the reader himself were young Goodman Brown, as if he too journeyed with mixed motives into a world of ambiguous lights and shadows and left it dizzied and dumbfounded, he must interpret his own personal experience in the same forest through which Brown wanders and in the equally labyrinthine story which is no less mysterious and no less a test of moral insight, and through which the reader travels, like Goodman Brown, at the peril of his soul. If the reader concludes with Brown that the evidence is ultimately ambiguous, then he stands with that sadly meditative young man at the end of the tale, bewildered by the facts of his experience and uncertain of his faith. If he goes one step further and concludes that Brown has seen something unquestionably real, then the reader has heard the voice of the devil and sipped the wine of the devil's communion.

In doing everything he can to allow the reader to interpret the story in terms of his own values and moral perspective, Hawthorne is less concerned with the meaning of things than with the meaning of meaning. For the story is not so much a revelation of things as they are but of the problem of moral choice, the near inaccessibility of truth, and the power of temptation. To say this is to say nothing more than that Hawthorne was, even more profoundly than his critics have heretofore suggested, a student of Milton and a teacher of Henry James. He is the master of his subject, and his subject is almost always the reader himself, beset by all the difficulties of moral action. This is nowhere more clearly and more challengingly the case than in **"Young Goodman Brown."**

Patricia Ann Carlson (essay date 1977)

SOURCE: "Setting and Fictional Dynamics," in *Hawthorne's Functional Settings: A Study of Artistic Method,* Editions Rodopi, 1977, pp. 128-31.

[*In the essay below, Carlson discusses how Hawthorne inverts the symbolic significance of the forest and village settings to initiate the breakdown of Goodman Brown's simplistic understanding of good and evil.*]

The most obvious ambiguity in **"Young Goodman Brown"** (*New England Magazine,* April, 1835) falls under H.-J. Lang's third classification, . . . the ambiguity of external actions. Was Brown's experience in the forest real, or was it a dream? Certainly, a strong case for this ambiguity could be culled from the implications of the scenic elements, but this is not the ambiguity which I intend to discuss because, clearly, it makes little difference to the ultimate meaning which Hawthorne wished to express. To the reader who asks "[h]ad Goodman Brown fallen asleep in the forest and only dreamed a wild dream of a witch-meeting?" Hawthorne answers "[b]e it so if you will."

The ambiguity which is thematically central to the tale is the confusion of good and evil. Beginning with a clearly defined polarity of village and forest, the functional setting reflects the clearly defined separation between right and wrong in Brown's simplistic moral vision. In his uncomplicated schema Faith and Salem represent good, and the forest represents evil. But in the author's system of moral order, the relationship of good and evil is much more complex than this black-and-white paradigm by which Brown seeks to regulate his life. The tale is, therefore, a kind of initiation story in which the child-like innocence of the protagonist is exposed to the ubiquitous power of evil.

When Brown leaves Faith and Salem expecting to encounter evil in the forest, the evil he envisions is a childish concept of an unqualified wrong. Like a child who is irresistibly drawn to a forbidden fruit, Brown evinces an obsessive curiosity about the nature of evil. "[O]f all nights in the year, this one night must I tarry away from thee," he says in answer to the pleas of Faith that he remain safely at home. Yet, like a child, he thinks he can return from his escapade in the forest and take up his previous life in Salem with Faith, unscathed by his encounters in the moral wilderness. "Well, she's a blessed angel on earth; and after this one night I'll cling to her skirts and follow her to heaven.'

The events which occur during his journey, however, cause Brown's conception of good and evil to be less rigidly defined as the village becomes less distinctly separated from the forest. Gradually, everyone affiliated with the village—those who personify "good" in Brown's idealistic moral perception—are shown to be tainted with "evil" as they appear in the forest. The presentation of these persons builds in a crescendo of emotional tension for Brown as his idealism is threatened and finally destroyed. He can rationalize the implications of evil in his ancestors, the church, and the Puritan government because they are not a part of his immediate environment. The "black man of the forest" merely mentions their duplicity in order to refute the "scruples," Brown gives as an excuse for not accompanying him deeper into the wilderness. However, Brown feels much more threatened by the concrete and the immediate than by the abstract and the past. The persons presented after this are from Salem and have an intimate relationship with Brown. Consequently, the ambiguity of good and evil becomes more terrifyingly real for Brown as the village population gravitates to the forest. First, there is Goody Cloyse, who taught Brown his catechism; then there are the minister and Deacon Gookin; and finally, at the crest of the crescendo, there is Faith.

Faith's appearance in the forest represents the total breakdown of the division between village and forest, or good and evil. Since this action is a climax in the plot, the accompanying emotive context must be intensified. For this purpose, Hawthorne includes a monstrous scenic inversion which underscores the conjoining of good and evil. When his unrealistic concept of a black-and-white world is threatened by the apparent desolation of so much which he thought incorruptible, Brown searches for some stable division to which he can cling for protection and security. Seeing the night sky with the stars shining through, he thinks he has found a constant in the chaos around him and is reassured in his belief of an ordered moral system. "With heaven above and Faith below, I will yet stand firm against the devil," he says. But at exactly this moment he sees the cloud and hears Faith *above* him on her way to the witch communion.

> While he still gazed upward into the deep arch of the firmament and had lifted his hands to pray, a cloud, though no wind was stirring, hurried across the zenith and hid the brightening star. Once the listener fancied that he could distinguish the accents of townspeople

of his own, men and women both pious and ungodly, many of whom he had met at the communion-table and had seen others rioting at the tavern. . . . Then came a stronger swell of those familiar tones, heard daily in the sunshine at Salem village, but never until now from a cloud at night. There was one voice, of a young woman, uttering lamentations, yet with an uncertain sorrow, and entreating for some favor, which, perhaps, it would grieve her to obtain; and all the unseen multitude, both saints and sinners, seemed to encourage her onward.

The scenic inversion resonates through all facets of the tale, as the excerpt above illustrates. Heaven and earth, "communioners" and "taverners," saints and sinners, Salem and wilderness, Faith and Witchcraft—all are commingled in the chaotic disorder of Brown's night in the forest.

This ambiguity is continued in the inversion motif of the witch-meeting where the scenic images mingling the forest and the village metaphorically signify the merging of evil and good. The dominant image is that of a church service inverted to become a black mass. The congregation is composed of the town members; yet, instead of their faces being illuminated by the soft light of altar candles, they are grotesquely distorted by the undulations of lurid red light from four "blazing pines, their tops aflame, their stems untouched, like candles at an evening meeting" which surround a rock, "bearing some rude, natural resemblance either to an altar or a pulpit." The congregation's song reminds Brown of a hymn sung at the meeting-house, but it is "joined to words which [express] all that our nature can conceive of sin." The satanic leader of the perverse service is similar "both in garb and manner, to some grave divine of the New England churches." And the baptism will produce not grace but an intimate knowledge of the blackness in the souls of all men.

This fusion of the two dominant scenic components—the village and the forest—is reflected by less prominent constituents in the scenic presentation, thus unifying the imagery of the tale into a pattern of thematic reverberations. As an illustration, the auditory imagery of the story is rich in sounds which blends the attributes of both Man and Nature. When Brown agonizingly shouts for Faith in the forest, the mocking echoes come back to him "as if bewildered wretches were seeking her all through the wilderness." Or, at the witch communion, "with the final peal of that dreadful anthem there came a sound, as if the roaring wind, the rushing streams, the howling beasts, and every other voice of the unconcerted wilderness were mingling and according with the voice of guilty man." Or finally—reflecting the fusion in a metaphor created by a single word—the forest is described as being "peopled with frightful sounds."

This ambiguity is more than Goodman Brown can assimilate into his childishly simple view of life. Because the village cannot be the sphere of pure goodness which Brown imagined it and because Faith is not the personification of goodness as he had envisioned her, he is repulsed by them. When he would not accept evil in mankind, when he would not participate in "the communion of [his] race", Good-

man Brown lost "his hold of the magnetic chain of humanity" just as much as did Ethan Brand who had made the search for evil his life's work. In the ensemble of characters from the Hawthorne canon, these two represent opposite extremes of false perceptions and misguided attitudes toward "the power of blackness" in the human condition. Brand sees evil as a power by which he can over-reach even the mercy of God; Brown sees evil as a power which forces him to question the very existence of a God. Brown withdraws into the egocentricity of isolation, lives a life of frustration, and dies in gloom because he never accepts the fact that man lives in the forest as well as in the town.

Terence J. Matheson (essay date 1978)

"Young Goodman Brown': Hawthorne's Condemnation of Conformity," in *The Nathaniel Hawthorne Journal 1978*, edited by C. E. Frazer Clark, Jr., Gale Research Company, 1984, pp. 137-45.

[*In this essay, Matheson asserts that Goodman Brown's resistance to the Devil is based solely on his desire to conform to approved social practices and protect his public image.*]

At first glance, it might appear farfetched to see Hawthorne's Goodman Brown as the spiritual ancestor of someone like Sinclair Lewis's Babbitt. Nevertheless, there is considerable evidence that the same preoccupation with social convention, public appearance, and conformity in general that characterized Lewis's twentieth-century protagonist is behind most of the speeches and actions of Hawthorne's seventeenth-century Puritan. Indeed, if Brown does lose the battle with the Devil for his soul, a case can be made that his lack of self-reliance is the most important contributing factor in his damnation.

Virtually everything Brown says and does stems from a concern with preserving his public image in some form or other. This is first seen as he bids farewell to his "aptly-named" and obviously allegorical wife Faith. That Faith is Brown's wife, and hence "his," is symbolically just as important to the story as is her name. For this indicates that whatever can be said about her symbolic role actually applies to some aspect of Brown. They speak in a strangely ritualistic and artificial tone, as if their conversation had been rehearsed, neither Brown nor his wife really meaning what each says to the other. They give the impression of speaking not from conviction, but as if reciting lines from a prepared text. Faith's initial comment, a rather saccharine appeal to put off his journey, might appear well-intentioned enough, even though it has a lackluster ring to it. But when Brown refuses absolutely to cede to her request, brushing her off with an unconvincing speech of his own (he gives no reasons, but merely states dogmatically that he "must" go), rather than press the issue, she concludes with "'God bless you.'" This suggests, among other things, that she had not expected him to change his mind and spoke not from conviction but simply because she believed it was expected of her.

Also important is that Faith seems to know why Brown is leaving her. She is plainly aware that his journey, far from being routine and normal, involves danger and perhaps evil as well. Her reference to "this" night—probably Hallowe'en—"'of all nights in the year'," reveals her awareness that no good Puritan would venture forth from the Christian security of his home on this particular evening, unless he was up to no good. In spite of all this, we see only "melancholy" in Faith's expression (rather than sorrow, frustration, despair, or even anger) when Brown, having paid no attention to her, proceeds on his way.

Had Hawthorne wished us to see sincere efforts to dissuade Brown, surely he would have shown her persisting in her appeal. That she does not leads one to suspect the quality of Brown's religious faith generally. It certainly says a great deal about the kind of man we are dealing with, a man whose faith can provide only token guidance in a predictable and uncompelling manner. Clearly, as Brown does not take his wife's plea seriously—there is no reason why he would, so lacking in vehemence is her appeal—so he does not take faith and all that goes with it any more seriously. Religious faith is to him something "pretty" but lacking in substance or strength, something pleasant to possess but of no importance as a guide to his behavior; in a phrase, it is something to pay lip service to.

Brown's opening reply to Faith, that his journey "'must needs be done'," demonstrates his firm resolve in this matter: despite all that has been said about Brown's naiveté, it is plain that he has a reasonable notion of what he is about to do. He knows his purpose is "evil" and that he is a "'wretch'" to leave her "'on such an errand';" later, we are told his meeting with the Devil is "not wholly unexpected."

Brown then tells Faith, "'Say thy prayers . . . and go to bed at dusk, and no harm will come to thee'," advice which says much about his character. First, if he really believes that personal harm can be avoided so easily, he is more than a little naive. But more important, he assumes that all one need do to guarantee salvation is go through the motions of piety by observing a few simple precepts that pertain to superficial conduct alone. Saying prayers and retiring early are far from the most essential means whereby one attains purity of soul. That Brown believes them to be important indicates a serious deficiency in his moral sense. He is unaware that genuine virtue is an inner quality which bears at best only an incidental relationship to one's seemingly virtuous social and religious behavior.

Leaving Faith, Brown reassures himself that "'after this one night'" of sin he will "'cling to her skirts and follow her to Heaven'," an assumption even more vacuous. No intelligent Puritan would ever have maintained that salvation depended on geographical proximity to another, apparently virtuous person; on a literal level, the state of Faith's soul says nothing about the state of Brown's. But the passage also reveals that Brown thinks he can consciously perform secret acts of evil and return, unscathed,

to the fold of true virtue; that by creating only an illusion of piety in the community, while simultaneously doing evil things, he can still be virtuous and get to Heaven. Here, the true core of his morality lies only in keeping up appearances. He does not understand true, inner goodness; his only moral criterion consists in conforming to social postures of which his society approves.

> **Brown does not understand true, inner goodness; his only moral criterion consists in conforming to social postures of which his society approves.**
>
> —*Terence J. Matheson*

Brown's conversation with the Devil supports the above contention. Here, on several occasions he appears to resist the Devil, and on the surface his resistance seems to speak well of him. However, when his reasons for resistance are examined, it is plain that they do not proceed from a meaningful appreciation of the moral issues involved. For Brown's "scruples," at least initially, are only that neither his father nor grandfather ever "went into the woods on such an errand." What bothers Brown is simply that in continuing along with the Devil, he would be deviating from the "virtuous" behavior that he believes his social superiors upheld. The nonconformity and unconventionality of his journey prompt Brown's hesitation rather than any real awareness that consorting with the Devil is intrinsically sinful.

The Devil dismisses Brown's argument with a brief but revealing account of his forefathers' hypocrisies. Strictly speaking, the Devil's reply is weak and irrelevant. First, there is no proof that what he says is true. But even if it were, the evil acts of a man's ancestors could not justify his pursuit of a present evil course, as Brown will soon conclude. To anyone possessing even a modicum of moral awareness, this would be self-evident. But to Brown, for whom conformity has been the whole of his morality, the Devil's revelation and its personal implications are difficult to refute. That Brown is shocked by the eye-opening information is understandable, but that he cannot penetrate its illogic suggests his own moral shallowness and the paucity of his moral principles.

Brown doggedly proceeds in his resistance and asks how he could "'meet the eye of that good old man, our minister, at Salem village?'" As before, Brown's underlying point is his fear of the consequences of deviating from accepted social mores. What also bothers him is the possibility that he could not conceal his soon-to-be-evil, but true, identity in public, before this admired (and presumably admiring) pillar of society, the minister. In a similar vein, he adds that it would break Faith's heart, were he to cooperate with the "elder traveller." Throughout, he fears only exposure to those whose respect or admiration he craves. To underscore this fact, Hawthorne does not allow Brown to make a strong moral point anywhere in his conversation with the Devil. At no time, for example, does Brown ever touch on the intrinsic immorality of the Black Mass. Nowhere does he say, simply, that he refuses to go on because it is morally wrong to do so. Conspicuous by its absence is any mention by Brown of the evil involved in Devil worship, because Brown has no awareness as to *why* it is evil. His only concern is that to behave in such a manner would be not to conform.

That the Devil recognizes this characteristic and deals with it accordingly is seen in the all-too coincidental appearance of "Goody Cloyse," who may well be a specter conjured up to drive the young conformist to even greater distraction. Significantly, Brown, always conscious of appearances, takes "a cut through the woods" so as not to be seen behaving unconventionally. There, he is provided with evidence that would seem to put Goody clearly in the Devil's camp. In one sense what Brown hears is understandably disconcerting; a naive young man has been convinced of weaknesses and failings in a person he has hitherto respected from childhood. But, however shocking or disillusioning the experience may be, there should not be quite the "world of meaning" for Brown in his simple discovery that a respected member of the community may have an evil side or be a consummate hypocrite. Hawthorne's suggestion that Brown has been shaken to the core reinforces our awareness that his entire morality has been based on the public behavior of members of his society. Furthermore, when these behavioral models fail him, he will be left with nothing, his conscience having virtually atrophied during his social indoctrination.

Brown does appear to come close to the truth in his final exchange with the Devil:

> "Friend," said he, stubbornly, "my mind is made up. Not another step will I budge on this errand. What if a wretched old woman do choose to go to the devil, when I thought she was going to Heaven! Is that any reason why I should quit my dear Faith, and go after her?"

Although this may well represent Brown's closest proximity to the real issue, his speech is deficient, if not in the argument, at least in the manner of its presentation. First, he speaks "stubbornly" rather than from conviction. Secondly, he phrases his point as a question, suggesting doubt of the argument's worth. Surely, Brown's words are not spoken by a man firmly convinced of what he is saying. He does not put his point forcefully (for example, saying "That *is* no reason") but phrases it in an indecisive, interrogative form that seems to invite a rebuttal by the Devil.

At all events, Brown has unwittingly stumbled close enough to the central moral issue to cause the Devil to retreat temporarily, there being no satisfaction for Satan in forcing a person into Hell against his will. He retires, and Brown, flushed with smug triumph, does not think of the moral victory he appears to have won, but basks in un-

Christian self-satisfaction, complacent about what an upstanding citizen he is. His thoughts are not of how pleased God would be with him, but only with how pleasant his relationship to society has become. Hawthorne refers to Brown's meditations as "pleasant and praiseworthy," the sarcasm reminding us that his victory has been illusory.

Brown hears footsteps and again hides, having "deemed it advisable to conceal himself within the verge of the forest, conscious of the guilty purpose that had brought him thither, though now so happily turned from it." Again, Brown's appearance in the community remains more important to him than the inner state of his soul. His purity, if genuine, should have produced greater openness on his part, since, if the victory were genuine he would have nothing to hide. That he does conceal himself shows where Brown's deepest concerns still lie. Even at this moment of apparent strength, he is plainly fearful of his social superiors seeing him in a moment of unconventional behavior.

Hawthorne creates much ambiguity surrounding the encounter with "the voice like the deacon's" and "the solemn old tones of the minister" to make us question what Brown thinks he sees. But Brown, trained to emulate his elders as paragons of virtue, is disillusioned by his discovery. He despairs, "doubting whether there really was a Heaven above him," despite "the blue arch, and the stars brightening in it." There is no justification for Brown to reach such extensive and dismal conclusions; that he does so reveals again that he has no inner moral principles to fall back on. Brown reacts as if he has seen God Himself on His way to a Black Mass, and indeed in a way he has, for to the unfortunate conformist his human elders have always been his true gods.

We have seen that the only reason for Brown's reluctance to participate at the Mass is his fear of the social consequences should his participation be discovered; there is no evidence that he would not want to go if he knew he could get away with it. Could he be convinced that everyone else was behaving in a similar manner, the only major obstacle would be removed. It is doubtless for this reason that Brown seems at times to be looking for excuses to attend. Hawthorne's comment that the Devil's arguments in favor of attending seemed "to spring up in the bosom of his auditor"; Brown's readiness to believe the worst of his fellows in the light of increasingly flimsy pieces of evidence; Hawthorne's observation of Brown's "instinct that guides mortal man to evil" and his reminder that Brown "was himself the chief horror of the scene": all suggest that Brown has been looking for a way of justifying his participation, by rationalizing that everyone else has done likewise. If so, it is not surprising that Brown's next—and least convincing—vision should involve a cloud that he suspects is bearing all the townspeople to the Mass and sounds of their voices that could easily be "the murmur of the old forest." The vision concludes with the appearance of a pink ribbon out of the sky, presumably linking Faith with the Devil-worshippers. But though the ribbon is by itself no necessary proof of Faith's participation at the Mass, Brown by this point is ready—too ready—to suspect the worst of everyone, and concludes that she "'is

gone'." While this conclusion is flimsy, flimsier still is Brown's second conclusion, that "'There is no good on earth; and sin is but a name. Come, devil! for to thee is this world given'."

Brown reaches this conclusion because, having no concept of moral life as involving a personal relationship with moral values, he can conceive of it only as a social relationship with his community; in short, if others do it, to the conformist Brown it must be "right" or at least permissible. It is significant that he gives in immediately after concluding that *all* the others are on their way. His ensuing, almost eager rush to the Mass is consistent with his earlier conformity, for he is still doing what everyone else does, literally going along with the crowd, and is as oblivious to alternatives as he is to the evil involved; the voice of his conscience is nowhere to be heard. Hawthorne exposes the true weakness of the conformist's morality, by demonstrating how a man, whose every prior act has been based on the behavioral examples set by his society, behaves when he learns (or thinks he has learned) that this society regularly commits acts of evil. Having always conformed, Brown can have nothing but conformity to fall back on. Rather than see that these superiors in the community are not and never were valid models worthy of blind emulation, given the instinctively evil nature of man, and that mere conformity can never be a valid guide of action for this reason, Brown continues to conform to these same models even though he ought to realize that they are no longer worthy. Why he does so is possibly for reasons of security or habit, or because he simply "wants to." Most important, it reveals his ignorance as to how he might otherwise behave. That Brown is conforming when he rushes to the Mass is evident from Hawthorne's many suggestions that he is actually blending into the atmosphere of the evil forest and becoming indistinguishable from it: his laugh is echoed by the forest's laugh, and his cry "was lost to his own ear, by its unison with the cry of the desert." Brown has become one with his surroundings, the perfect mark of the conformist, by adapting his own behavior to that around him, in "awful harmony."

The entire spectacle of the Black Mass may well be presented by the Devil merely to confirm Brown's own belief in the ubiquity of human evil. It is interesting that despite the Devil's detailed catalogue of the vices and sins of Brown's fellows, he says nothing that Brown has not already determined on his own. For example, when Satan concludes that "'Evil is the nature of mankind. Evil must be your only happiness'," he agrees with Brown's earlier conclusion that there was no good on earth and that the world was given over to the Devil. As for Brown's witnessing of Faith at the Mass, he has already concluded that she is on her way there; doubts about his relatives have occurred very early in the tale. It is not really surprising, then, that Brown does see virtually everyone; he has already determined that he would do so. Nor is it surprising, given his conformity that Brown is initially powerless to resist. Appropriately, "the minister and good old Deacon Gookin seized his arms, and led him to the blazing rock"; as before, since they are typical of the forces determining his every act, they continue to have dominance over him.

Why, then, does Brown resist the baptism, in a final surge of apparent strength? Surely, we have been given little if any evidence that Brown has enough strength to resist. Indeed, we have every reason to doubt his sincerity and to suspect that, even if he is doing the right thing, it may be for the wrong reasons. If Brown's resistance were meant to be seen as virtuous, surely Hawthorne would have prepared us in some way to believe Brown capable of such an act. Instead, he has made every effort to demean Brown in our eyes, presenting him as utterly lacking in moral sophistication or sensitivity. Brown is not merely a naive, but basically good, man: he is superficial, cunning, and consummately hypocritical. Why then this apparent reversal?

> **Brown resists participation in the loathful brotherhood for the wrong reasons: because he is afraid of revealing himself as he actually is, not because he has seen that such participation is intrinsically evil.**
>
> —*Terence J. Matheson*

The only answer can be that no reversal has been intended by Hawthorne and that no deviation from what we have seen of Brown's character has taken place. Close examination of the passage immediately preceding Brown's resistance makes this clear: "The husband cast one look at his pale wife, and Faith at him. What polluted wretches would the next glance shew them to each other, shuddering alike *at what they disclosed* and what they saw!" (my italics). We have seen before that Brown's public image and resulting social status mean a great deal to him. Significantly, he does not resist the Devil earlier, when the Devil promises Brown that "'It shall be yours to penetrate, in every [other!] bosom, the deep mystery of sin . . .'" What bothers him is the sudden realization that such disclosure is to be mutual. It is only at this point, realizing that others will in turn see *him* as he truly is—a wretch—that he balks, and he resists not in the name of virtue but from the same fear of exposure to the public of his true nature (and the nature of his "faith") that has characterized his every previous action. Still obsessed with the need to protect his public image, even in these bizarre circumstances, Brown resists participation in the loathful brotherhood for the wrong reasons: because he is afraid of revealing himself as he actually is, not because he has seen that such participation is intrinsically evil.

He may also be dimly aware that such resistance would give him a tremendous social advantage over his fellows, for by resisting he becomes himself a pinnacle of apparent virtue, at least in his own eyes. Others may well look up to him, and certainly he will be able to derive great satisfaction from his resistance. Certain events do seem to point to this. Brown was seen before, just after his earlier "victory" over the Devil, as a self-righteous man. Moreover, Hawthorne suggests that this self-righteousness remains with him for the rest of his life, as Brown continues to regard himself as the one pure man in a community of hypocrites. As he shrinks from his wife or shudders at the minister, it is hard not to suspect that he is taking perverse satisfaction from these constant reminders of what a virtuous fellow he is in contrast with other members of his society. If the "goodly procession" of followers at his funeral is any indication, Brown has achieved his goal, having become a respected if not loved member of society. The hollowness of his achievement is, of course, underscored by Hawthorne's brief summary of his joyless life and gloomy death, the latter comment reminding us that he had essentially sold his soul for the social status he enjoyed.

Hawthorne also shows the paradoxical nature of Brown's final relationship to his society. Obsessed by the discovery that his society is unworthy of emulation, he cannot embrace "the sacred truths of our religion" or take succor from the hope offered by "saint-like lives"—true examples of virtue—because there is within his mind no room for such truths to exist, let alone grow. Obsessed with the realization that his society failed to provide adequate moral leadership, he is nonetheless so preoccupied with societal concerns to the exclusion of spiritual ones that any true sense of higher moral purpose is forever beyond him. Brown's relationship to his society, rather than his relationship to God, is still his only concern. Though he turns away from his now-reviled, former social ideals, he can conceive of no higher sphere to which he could turn that would provide him with meaningful, alternative moral knowledge; hence, his despair and gloom and his life-long obsession with his society's hypocrisy.

In a sense, **"Young Goodman Brown"** becomes as much a criticism of a rigid, conformity-ridden society as it is a portrayal of one man's lack of self-reliance. Surely, had the importance of one's public image and the consequent need to assume social postures not been so deeply impressed on Brown, and had more attention been focused on personal virtue and integrity as things of value, Brown would probably have been able to rise above the Devil's temptation to despair. That he could not is an indictment of both Brown and the society he lived in, a community where the importance of conformity has run rampant, with disastrous consequences for all concerned.

Norman H. Hostetler (essay date 1982)

SOURCE: "Narrative Structure and Theme in 'Young Goodman Brown'," in *The Journal of Narrative Technique*, Vol. 12, No. 3, Fall, 1982, pp. 221-28.

[*In the following essay, Hostetler investigates how conflict between the points of view of the title character and the narrator of "Young Goodman Brown" creates an iron-*ic *tension from which Hawthorne "develops his criticism of Brown's lack of awareness of the controlling power of the mind."*]

One of Nathaniel Hawthorne's major themes concerns conscious awareness of the reality which the mind imposes on external objects. Hawthorne's characters are repeatedly confronted by the need to establish the relationship between their imaginations and the external world. Their ability to make the epistemological distinctions between the products of their mental processes and their sense impressions of the external world frequently governs their ability to develop a sound moral relationship with other people.

"Young Goodman Brown" illustrates especially well the fatal consequences of psychological misjudgment concerning perception and reality. The problem of establishing point of view is central to developing this interpretation. Although Hawthorne's narrator exists outside the story line, the tension between the conflicting interpretations of experience provided by the narrator and Goodman Brown from their different points of view creates the basic ironic tone of the work. From this irony, Hawthorne develops his criticism of Brown's lack of awareness of the controlling power of the mind.

Recognition of this cause for Brown's behavior is essential in order to reconcile the divergent emphases that have been placed on the story. Interpretations have generally concerned themselves with the way in which Brown is deluded rather than with why Brown should make such serious errors in judgment or with why Hawthorne should so sharply and pervasively differentiate the narrator and Brown. Most critics have, of course, recognized that at least a part of Brown's experience is a "dream," "vision," or "hallucination," but they are more concerned with individual choice, often moral or theological (in which case Brown is a deluded individual), or with an introduction to knowledge, usually psychological (in which case Brown's initiation is Everyman's). Brown does destroy himself morally, as the end of the story makes clear, yet as Frederick Crews notes [in *The Sins of the Fathers: Hawthorne's Psychological Themes,* 1966], "the richness of Hawthorne's irony is such that, when Brown turns to a Gulliver-like misanthropy and spends the rest of his days shrinking from wife and neighbors, we cannot quite dismiss his attitude as unfounded." By differentiating the points of view of the narrator and Brown, Hawthorne creates the multiple perspective necessary to validate all these critical emphases.

The narrator's description of events is characterized by the ambiguity that Richard Fogle has pointed out [in *Hawthorne's Fiction: The Light and the Dark,* rev. ed., 1964]. The "uncertain light" that plays over everything obscures and confuses all appearances so that it is impossible to ascertain anything objective. Fogle, in fact, does not really go far enough in discerning ambiguities, for he restricts himself mostly to the narrator's literal expressions of doubt and alternative possibilities. He accepts as fact that Brown's conductor into the forest "is, of course, the Devil," and that Brown sees there Goody Cloyse, the minister, and Deacon Gookin, among others But the narrator never once refers to them by their names. They are always described as "figures" or "forms." Apparently, they have taken the shape of the persons whose names they use, although the evidence for this position comes only from the highly unreliable testimony of Goodman Brown and from the specters themselves—whose existence has been established only in relation to Brown's perceptions, and not the narrator's.

Brown, indeed, is the only person to whom ambiguity is an impossibility. He is absolutely certain about these identifications, despite the fact that they become progressively more ambiguous as the journey into the forest continues. The narrator first says only that Brown "beheld the figure of a man" which seems to resemble Brown's father or grandfather. But Brown, whose preceding remark ("What if the devil himself should be at my very elbow!") indicates the tenor of his thoughts, assumes at once that the figure is the devil, although he scruples against calling him such.

In the next instance, the narrator's carefully restricted construction suggests even less validity to Brown's perception. There appears a "female figure on the path, in whom Goodman Brown recognized a very pious and exemplary dame." The extent to which this figure can be identified with Brown's real "moral and spiritual adviser" is uncertain at best, but Brown immediately concludes that what he perceived is unquestionably Goody Cloyse, although as soon as he "cast up his eyes in astonishment," he no longer "beheld" her.

The minister and the deacon do not even exist as figures, but merely as disembodied voices—the conversation is supplied only by "the voice like the deacon's" and "the solemn old tones of the minister." With less evidence than before, Brown assumes that he has overheard the real "holy men." Finally, out of the rush and babble of clouds and wind, Brown fancies that he discerns the "familiar tones" of his townspeople, and particularly, "one voice, of a young woman." Yet Brown exhibits no doubt about what he assumes he has perceived passing overhead, crying "Faith!" after his wife.

At this point appears the famous "pink ribbon," which F.O. Matthiessen condemned as too jarringly literal to be accepted into the pattern of Brown's past hallucinations [*American Renaissance*, 1941]. Fogle rather lamely defends the ribbon as "part and parcel of his dream," like everything else, and, moreover, of only momentary impact. There is a sounder argument for its use, because Matthiessen's assumption of the ribbon's literal existence is contradicted by the pattern of the expanding gap between the narrator's ambiguity of description and Brown's certainty of identification. From figures to voices to clouds to wind, the objects upon which Brown projected his certainties have become more and more vague and uncertain. This incident extends the pattern, for the narrator says only that "*something* fluttered lightly down through the air, and caught on the branch of a tree" (my italics). Only

Goodman Brown "beheld a pink ribbon." Considering the quality of his past perceptions, it would be exceedingly naive to trust his eyesight at this point. The narrator, moreover, has the last word on the subject, his insistence that Faith still wears the ribbon the next morning serving as a final ironic comment on Brown's perception of the "something."

The effect of this divergence of viewpoint is to establish the credibility of the narrator's perceptions and to undermine Brown's. The reader's confidence in the narrator's point of view has been reinforced by the objectivity of the unemotional tone, reflected in the eighteenth-century rhetorical patterns, by the candor that allows him always to present Brown in terms of the latter's current evaluation of himself, and above all by the honesty that results from his refusal to commit himself to a single-minded view of an external reality that he cannot truly know.

The reader, therefore, accepts the narrator as the norm for perception against which to judge Brown, who is beset by emotional vagaries and is blind to his own motivations. Brown's expressed ideas are constantly being undercut by his situation and actions, and yet he is absolutely certain—so certain that it never occurs to him to doubt it—that he knows what constitutes external reality. This fallacious certainty and the unconscious assumption upon which it is based provide for Brown's self-destruction.

Brown's assumption is that an absolute reality actually exists, that it lies in the external world, and that it is finally knowable by man through the perception of his senses. Brown is thus an extreme Lockean in his psychology—he insists on attributing all his mental impressions to external realities which have inscribed themselves on his *tabula rasa*. It never occurs to him that the source of some of his ideas may lie within himself, in his mind and imagination. Yet through the ironic tension between Brown's ideas and the perceptions of the narrator, Hawthorne has been making clear all along that the source of Brown's only significant ideas—that is, those which actually motivate and control his actions—is Brown himself.

Brown goes into the forest in search of the source of evil (or sin, or knowledge, or whatever moral or psychological term one wishes), fully confident of finding that source in some person or place—that is, in something external to himself. Since it will be external to himself, his relation to it will be subject to his own definition, limitation, and control, as suggested by his reiterated belief that he can stop his journey and turn back whenever he wishes. From the beginning, however, Hawthorne has undercut Brown's belief through the narrator's subtle insistence that Brown has carried all his ideas of evil, and therefore all the evil of which he is capable, into the forest with him. Everybody else who enters the forest has done so, too, but Brown's psychology will not permit him to accept the analogy presented to him by his experiences, whether real or imagined. Brown's exploration of the dark forest of the mind is qualitatively indistinguishable from the one that has been experienced implicitly by all other characters in the story (including the narrator), and explicitly by Faith, who has "such dreams and such thoughts, that she's afeard of herself, sometimes." But Brown refuses to recognize that evil and knowledge and their sources are intrinsic parts of all human nature. In this sense, therefore, it is finally irrelevant whether or not Brown's experiences "really" occurred. The crucial point is that Brown asserts certainty when he ought to be raising questions and doubts.

It is finally irrelevant whether or not Brown's experiences "really" occurred. The crucial point is that Brown asserts certainty when he ought to be raising questions and doubts.

—*Norman H. Hostetler*

The narrator notes at the very beginning that all of Brown's good intentions are postulated only in the form of future actions—"With this excellent resolve for the future, Goodman Brown felt himself justified in making more haste on his present evil purpose." Brown's "companion" appears to him only after he expresses his idea that "the devil himself" might be present. Brown exclaims that he has already penetrated "too far" into the forest, but at the same time he was "unconsciously resuming his walk." The devil's arguments are so apt that they "seemed rather to spring up in the bosom of his auditor, than to be suggested by himself." While "applauding himself greatly" for determining to resist the devil, Brown hears "amidst these pleasant and praise-worthy meditations" the sounds of the minister and the deacon.

If Brown had any sense of this source of his own perceptions, he might have drawn the correct analogy with the examples of innate depravity and taken his place with Faith in the brotherhood of man. His insistent assumption that all his ideas have a reality external to himself leads him instead to the wrong conclusion. "There is no good on earth; and sin is but a name. Come, devil! for to thee is this world given." This idea obviously fills him with despair, so that he continues to the witches meeting (or unconsciously permits himself to imagine the experience), but he still has no concept of his own nature, as events at the meeting illustrate. For him, evil is still the province of the devil—that is, the source of it is external to Brown. To that error he adds his Manichaean certainty of the distinctness and absoluteness of good and evil, merely reversing his previous assumption that everybody else is good to the assumption that everybody else is bad.

Once again, however, the narrator has the last word, concluding the first portion of the story with remarks that leave no room for doubt about where the source of evil really lies. Brown rushed into the

heart of the dark wilderness . . . with the instinct that guides mortal man to evil. . . . he was himself the chief horror of the scene, and shrank not from its other horrors. . . . In truth, all through the haunted forest, there could be nothing more frightful than the figure of Goodman Brown. . . . The fiend in his own shape is less hideous, than when he rages in the breast of man.

The narrator also leaves no doubt about Brown's relationship to the rest of mankind:

The verse died heavily away, and was lengthened by a chorus, not of human voices, but of all the sounds of the benighted wilderness, pealing in awful harmony together. Goodman Brown cried out; and his cry was lost *to his own ear,* by its unison with the cry of the desert.

(my italics)

Brown does not hear his own cry for the cry around him, but the narrator hears both.

Although he does not accept the idea, Brown has already joined the congregation of evil, "with whom he felt a loathful brotherhood, by the sympathy of all that was wicked in his heart." He does not need the "baptism" to experience evil but to know its nature and the way it relates him to all people. The devil stresses this point by associating the knowledge of the catalogue of "secret deeds" with the ability "to penetrate, in *every* bosom, the deep mystery of sin, the fountain of all wicked arts, and which inexhaustibly supplies more evil impulses than human power—than my power, at its utmost!—can make manifest in deed" (my italics). *Every* bosom would include Brown's.

It would be a mistake, however, to assume that the devil is the real hero, trying his best to awaken Brown to the reality of human nature. Hawthorne's ironic ambiguities are much too complex for that. The devil is still one of Hawthorne's numerous false guides, subtly encouraging people to extend partial truths into erroneous absolutes. Although he admits the source of evil lies in the individual human, he does all in his power to foster its development and expression, as was illustrated earlier by the kinds of assistance he had offered Brown and all his friends and relations. Now he will succeed in securing Brown's damnation by encouraging him to *refuse* the baptism.

Essentially, he plays upon Brown's Manichaean conviction that everybody else is totally committed to evil. If you wish to be fully human, to join "the communion of your race," he in effect tells Brown, you too must commit yourself to evil as "your only happiness." That the devil lies when he says that "evil is *the* nature of mankind" (my italics) is established by the narrator, who makes a special point of referring to the religious activities the next morning of "the good old minister" and "that excellent old Christian," Goody Cloyse, as well as to the anxious and joyful Faith. Part of the irony of the characterizations may well be turned against the characters themselves, in view of their previous night's associations, but, in any case, their holy activities are certainly no less real than the witches' sabbath, and a great deal more plausible, given the total lack of ambiguity in the narrator's descriptions.

But Brown has already thrown the good out with the bad. Rightly convinced that a conscious commitment to the idea of total depravity would be disastrous, he naively accepts the devil's explanation, which is actually only a necessary consequence of Brown's beliefs, that a commitment to the knowledge of the moral community of human beings means the same thing. By so believing, Brown throws out forever any possibility of sympathetic identification with other people, thus cutting himself off from the only way for him to test the validity of his perceptions. His rejection of brotherhood is, therefore, equally a disaster, for it is ironically based on an unconscious commitment to the concept of total depravity. It is this commitment that allows Brown (and Brown alone, as the narrator stresses) to hear only oaths, anathemas, hypocrisy, and anthems of sin, instead of prayers, blessings, preaching, and psalms.

The narrator insists on this ironic quality by such devices as his remark that Brown is followed "to his grave" by Faith, an ironic inversion of Brown's previous belief that he would hereafter cling to Faith's skirts "and follow her to Heaven." Such a commitment would have succeeded, not because Faith was "an angel on earth" as he originally thought, but because he would be accepting humanity.

Thus the narrator carefully works out the culminating irony of the story. In seeking to cut himself off from the evil in the external world, Brown has committed himself to the evil of his own mind, without hope of understanding or correction. Seeking salvation for himself, he has committed himself to the only course that will guarantee his destruction, for only those who believe in the reality of ideas independent of sense impressions can have hope for any future except the grave. And so "his dying hour was gloom."

One of the consequences of being aware of the nature of Brown's obsession is that the critic can no longer safely dismiss Brown at the end of his analysis as merely a deluded or even deranged person. Brown, after all, clearly retains the ability to behave acceptably in his social relationships. But he has lost the ability to transcend the external forms of these relationships and thus has lost the power to create moral relationships. Hawthorne's structure and theme imply that only through moral relationships can one create a positive human existence. Brown's failure in this regard is at once more subtle than is suggested by the references to "depraved imagination" and "distorted mind" [Paul J. Hurley, "Young Goodman Brown's 'Heart of Darkness'," *American Literature* 37, 1966] and more universal than is suggested by the historical confinement of the problem to seventeenth-century Salem [as done by David Levin in "Shadows of Doubt: Specter Evidence in Hawthorne's 'Young Goodman Brown'," in *American Literature* 34, 1962] or even to Hawthorne's own mind [see Crews]. Brown's problems with perception and the products of his own imagination are potentially those of every human being. The reader dismisses the possibility of identification with Brown only at the peril of falling into Brown's obsession—another example of the complex ironies Hawthorne leaves waiting to trap the unwary reader who fails to recognize that it is precisely the contrast between the narrator's and Brown's perceptions that allows one to accept the universality of the experience while denying the validity of Brown's response to it.

Terence Martin (essay date 1983)

SOURCE: "Six Tales: 'Young Goodman Brown'," in *Nathaniel Hawthorne*, revised edition, Twayne Publishers, 1983, pp. 81-7.

[*In the following excerpt, Martin focuses on Goodman Brown's incomplete but cataclysmic initiation into evil.*]

To judge from the title, wrote Herman Melville in his review of *Mosses from an Old Manse*, one would suppose that **"Young Goodman Brown"** was "a simple little tale, intended as a supplement to 'Goody Two-Shoes.'" Whereas it is as deep as Dante." Readers since Melville's time have agreed that **"Young Goodman Brown"** is one of Hawthorne's most profound tales. In the manner of its concern with guilt and evil, it exemplifies what Melville called the "power of blackness" in Hawthorne's work. The thrust of the narrative is to move the protagonist toward a personal and climactic vision of evil which leaves in its aftermath an abiding legacy of distrust.

"Young Goodman Brown" takes in a strict if surprising sense the form of a story of initiation; ritual and ceremony dominate the central scene in which Goodman Brown is invited to become an initiate into the community of evil proclaimed by the devil. And although the ritual of initiation is perforce left incomplete, Goodman Brown is ruined for life by all that the devil shows him. In the course of one evening he is given such a monstrous perception of the scope, depth, and universality of evil that he is forever blind to the world as it normally presents itself. As David Levin reminds us in his discussion of "specter evidence" in **"Young Goodman Brown,"** however, the focus of the story remains steadily on the protagonist. The tale is not about the evil of other people in Salem village—Goody Cloyse, for example, or Deacon Gookin, or Goodman Brown's father and grandfather; it is, rather, "about Brown's doubt, his discovery of the *possibility* of universal evil" ["Shadows of Doubt: Specter Evidence in Hawthorne's 'Young Goodman Brown'," *American Literature* 34, 1962]. So corrosive is his experience that anything contrary to the vision he has seen he considers a fraud. Just as surely as if he had ascended to the heavenly choirs and achieved a mystic comprehension of the destiny of all things, he has experienced what is for him an ultimate vision.

What Goodman Brown sees in the forest persuades as well as corrodes; in a scene shuddering with woe yet stabilized by the dignity of fallen grandeur, he hears that the human race is immersed in guilt, that evil is the nature of mankind. "Welcome, my children," says the dark and majestic figure of the devil, "to the communion of your race. You have found thus young your nature and your destiny." Although at this point Goodman Brown is standing beside his wife Faith, he is unaware of her presence. In the assembly behind them, continues the devil, are all those whom they have

> reverenced from youth. . . . This night it shall be granted you to know their secret deeds. . . . [You] shall exult to behold the whole earth one stain of guilt, one mighty blood spot. Far more than this. It shall be yours to penetrate, in every bosom, the deep mystery of sin, the fountain of all wicked arts, and which inexhaustibly supplies more evil impulses than human power—than my power at its utmost—can make manifest in deeds. And now, my children look upon each other.

In such an unhallowed atmosphere Goodman Brown and Faith exchange glances, while the dark figure addresses them again in a "deep and solemn tone, almost sad with its despairing awfulness, as if his once angelic nature could yet mourn for our miserable race": you have depended upon one another's hearts, says the devil, you have hoped that "virtue were not all a dream. Now are ye undeceived. Evil is the nature of mankind. Evil must be your only happiness. Welcome, again, my children, to the communion of your race." And the assembled worshipers repeat the welcome in a cry of "despair and triumph."

There is an element of finality in the scene. Goodman Brown has traveled to the end of a journey from which he can return but never recover. He stops short of the ultimate step of infernal baptism, which would, of course, bring the story to a much different resolution. As he and Faith look at each other, they cannot make the decision which would allow each to see the hidden springs of guilt in the other: "What polluted wretches would the next glance show them to each other, shuddering alike at what they disclosed and what they saw!" Offered the power to pierce the veil that (as the Reverend Mr. Hooper knew) covers every human personality, the husband and wife cannot bear the idea of spiritual nakedness. Suddenly Goodman Brown cries out, "Faith! Faith! . . . look up to heaven and resist the Wicked One." Faith's allegorically appropriate name allows here, as elsewhere, for a masterful and open-handed ambiguity of effect. Goodman Brown is obviously addressing the image of his wife, urging her to resist the devil. At the same time he is exhorting himself to have faith, to look heavenward, to withstand the infernal eloquence of the Wicked One. And his cry has a miraculous effect; it obliterates the fiery theatrics of the scene along with the entire cast of demonic characters. "Hardly had he spoken" when he finds himself alone "amid calm night and solitude, listening to a roar of the wind, which died heavily away through the forest." At the beginning of the scene the minister and Deacon Gookin had escorted Goodman Brown to a "blazing rock." Now he staggers against the same rock and feels it "chill and damp; while a hanging twig, that had been all on fire, besprinkled his cheek with the coldest dew."

Assumed in **"Young Goodman Brown"** is a distinction between dream and reality that one must understand in the terms of Hawthorne's presentation. The question proposed to Goodman Brown is into which of these categories good and evil belong. At the outset of the story, Faith asks her husband to postpone his journey until sunrise and sleep in his own bed that night: "a lone woman," she says, "is troubled with such dreams and such thoughts that she's afeard of herself sometimes." Mulling over the guilty purpose that has brought him into the forest, Goodman Brown recalls Faith's talk of dreams; he wonders if he detected trouble in her face, "as if a dream had warned her of what work is to be done tonight." In the forest he goes through a dreamlike experience, marked by a series of abrupt transitions and sudden apparitions. The devil introduces a further notion of a dream by saying that Goodman Brown and Faith "had still hoped that virtue were not all a dream." Thus, the counterpoised terms, dream and reality, are shown to depend for their application upon one's prior attitude toward the moral nature of the world.

His spectral experience in the forest has affected Goodman Brown as the most dismal, the most horrible, and, withal, the most intransigent experience of his life. But just as the experience has been personal, so has the effect. Goodman Brown alone has changed. He alone brings the dark vision of the forest to bear on the moral life of the community.

—*Terence Martin*

And it is precisely because of Hawthorne's presentation of spectral or counterfeit evidence that such absolute distinctions founder—along with a protagonist (or reader) who would seek to apply them. For, as Levin demonstrates, the tale offers a choice "between dream and a reality that is unquestionably spectral." In the manner of witnesses at the Salem witchcraft trials in 1692, Goodman Brown fails to distinguish between the specter or shape of a person and the person himself, between appearances (fashioned by the devil) and realities (created by God). Hawthorne's language is insistent: Goodman Brown sees "figures," "shapes," "visages" that appear in the guise of those he knows. He hears the voices of invisible travelers (on invisible horses) that, "he could have sworn," sound like those of the deacon and the minister. He gazes at a cloud that hurries across the sky, although "no wind was stirring." At an early point in the journey the devil discourses "so aptly, that his arguments seemed rather to spring up in the bosom" of Goodman Brown than "to be suggested by himself." And of course that is the case if Goodman Brown has internalized the source of evil. Michael J. Colacurcio is surely right in saying that according to Hawthorne's "psychological scheme Brown's suspicion and distrust and the Devil's wiles" are two ways of describing the same phenomena ["Visible Sanctity and Spectral Evidence: The Moral World of Hawthorne's **'Young Goodman Brown'**," *Essex Institute Historical Collections* 110, 1974].

For the devil, of course, virtue must be a dream, evil the only reality. And once Goodman Brown sees the "evidence" for that idea, he can never rid himself of it. It rises within him to cast a shadow over the apparent realities of his life in Salem village that he once took as visible (and comforting) evidence of sanctity:

> On the Sabbath day, when the congregation were singing a holy psalm, he could not listen because an anthem of sin rushed loudly upon his ear and drowned all the blessed strain. When the minister spoke from the pulpit with power and fervid eloquence, and, with his hand on the open Bible, of the sacred truths of our religion, and of saint-like lives and triumphant death, and of future bliss or misery unutterable, then did Goodman Brown turn pale, dreading lest the roof should thunder down upon the gray blasphemer and his hearers. Often, awakening suddenly at midnight, he shrank from the bosom of Faith; and at morning or eventide, when the family knelt down at prayer, he scowled and muttered to himself, and gazed sternly at his wife, and turned away. And when he had lived long, and was borne to his grave a hoary corpse, followed by Faith, an aged woman, and children and grandchildren, a goodly procession, besides neighbors not a few, they carved no hopeful verse upon his tombstone, for his dying hour was gloom.

His spectral experience in the forest has affected Goodman Brown as the most dismal, the most horrible, and, withal, the most intransigent experience of his life. Since he cannot believe in Faith, no other reality can modulate the gnawing gloom of a persistent doubt. He has journeyed into the dreamworld of the forest, into the haunted mind now functioning with the full force of history, and confronted a world steeped in guilt (whether projected by his fantasies or conjured by the devil) that makes his return to the village a pilgrimage into hypocrisy. But just as the experience has been personal, so has the effect. Goodman Brown alone is changed. He alone brings the dark vision of the forest to bear on the moral life of the community. He alone, "from the night of that fearful dream," as Hawthorne says, becomes "a stern, a sad, a darkly meditative, a distrustful, if not a desperate man."

It is difficult to say precisely why Goodman Brown leaves Faith to spend his night in the forest. As we have seen, she asks him to put off his journey and tarry with her; he replies that this night of all nights in the year he must tarry away from her. He does not say what his purpose is, but conveniently uses her term: "My journey, as thou callest it, forth and back again, must needs be done 'twixt now and sunrise." And he chides her for doubting him when they are but three months married.

But he does go on his journey with a guilty conscience, leaving Faith with her pink ribbons behind. His heart tells him he is a wretch to leave Faith, "a blessed angel on earth," on "such an errand." He resolves that "after this one night" he will "cling to her skirts and follow her to heaven." Clearly, Goodman Brown wants "this one night." His journey into the forest can be defined as a kind of indeterminate allegory, representing man's irrational drive to leave faith, home, and security temporarily behind, for whatever reason, and take a chance with one (more?) adventure onto the wilder shores of experience. Our protagonist becomes an Everyman named Brown, a "young" man, who will be aged in one night by an adventure that makes everyone in this world seem a fallen idol. But our protagonist is also, and specifically, a seventeenth-century Puritan, a "young" man only three months joined to Faith, whose belief in the value of visible moral evidence becomes inverted rather than discredited. He has made a covenant to meet the devil, who has come from Boston to Salem village in fifteen minutes for the occasion. The simplicity of Goodman Brown's statements to the devil help to measure the extent of the change he will undergo in the forest. "Faith kept me back awhile," he says to explain his tardiness; "That old woman taught me my catechism," he remarks of Goody Cloyse ("and there was a world of meaning," Hawthorne writes, "in that simple comment"); finally, when he beholds a pink ribbon fluttering down from above he cries out, "My Faith is gone." At that frenzied and faithless moment he embraces the devil's premise that evil constitutes the only reality in the world.

Faith has been Goodman Brown's last resource. But the process of consigning people to the devil—or of instantly crediting reports of their wrongdoing—has its genesis in his brittle commitment to the world in which he lives. He has learned with some wonder that the devil knew his father and grandfather. With amazement he has heard the devil claim that the governor and council are firm supporters of his interest. And quickly he dissociates himself: the governor and the council have their own ways, he reasons, "and are no rule for a simple husbandman like me." That Goody Cloyse consorts with the devil—who momentarily assumes the figure of Goodman Brown's grandfather and thereby demonstrates his mastery of appearances—is a blow that strikes closer to home. Again Goodman Brown dissociates himself, this time with the vehemence necessary to cast off one who has earned his respect: "what if a wretched old woman do choose to go to the devil when I thought she was going to heaven: is that any reason why I should quit my dear Faith and go after her?" He even decides to return to Salem Village and applauds himself greatly for his resolution; then, "conscious of the guilty purpose that had brought him hither," he hides when he hears the sounds of horses approaching. The discovery that Deacon Gookin and the old minister are likewise part of the devil's brotherhood shakes him deeply, although his conviction depends on the flimsiest of aural evidence: Goodman Brown cannot see them nor discern "so much as a shadow." The point is that he immediately believes in their perfidy and looks "up at the sky, doubting whether there really was a heaven above him."

Once again, Goodman Brown dissociates himself from persons he has reverenced. Bereft now of saintly company, of father and grandfather, of governor and council, of Goody Cloyse, Deacon Gookin, and the minister, he can make one final resolution: "With Heaven above, and Faith below, I will yet stand firm against the devil." Gone is all sense of community. Already having doubted the existence of heaven, Goodman Brown stands alone, crying out "in a voice of agony and desperation" for a Faith he has deliberately left behind. At that point (let us note Hawthorne's language carefully) "something fluttered lightly down through the air, and caught on the branch of a tree. The young man seized it, and beheld a pink ribbon." From a heaven he already doubts comes "something" that this man shouting for Faith sees as a "pink ribbon." Since the pink ribbons of her cap are intact the next morning when Faith bursts into joy at the sight of Goodman Brown, what we have here is best seen as a final, Faith-testing, instance of spectral evidence. Having converted "something" to a "pink ribbon" by an ultimate projection of his guilt, our protagonist is at first "stupefied," then "maddened with despair." He speaks the obvious truth when he says his Faith is gone. He reveals his virtual solipsism when he concludes that "there is no good on earth."

As he rushes through the "haunted forest" to join the devil's congregation, Goodman Brown becomes "the chief horror of the scene." "In truth," writes Hawthorne, holding out the possibility that we might have been witnessing a specter undone by spectral evidence, "there could be nothing more frightful" in the forest "than the *figure* of Goodman Brown" (my italics). But Brown at the beginning and end of the tale is presented as a character, not a specter. He has (in a far more serious way than Wakefield) deliberately left his place in the moral universe and returned with a perspective that converts everything to evil and hypocrisy. From his dream vision or spectral adventure in the forest, he has received a paralyzing sense that the brotherhood of man is possible only under the fatherhood of the devil. His vision is absolute, unalterable; it turns his world inside out and compels him to live and die in a gloom born of his inverted sense of moral reality.

Sam B. Girgus (essay date 1990)

SOURCE: "The Law of the Fathers: Hawthorne," in *Desire and the Political Unconscious in American Literature: Eros and Ideology,* St. Martin's Press, 1990, pp. 49-78.

[*In the excerpt below, Girgus offers a psychoanalytic interpretation of Goodman Brown as a tormented neurotic who represses both his sexual desire for Faith and his doubts about his parentage.*]

On a relatively conventional level of Freudian analysis, Young Goodman Brown would appear to be an unhappy neurotic who cannot reconcile himself to his wife's carnality and cannot return or enjoy the love she represents. He cannot appreciate her natural desires: ' "Dearest heart," whispered she, softly and rather sadly, when her lips were close to his ear, "prithee put off your journey until sunrise

and sleep in your own bed to-night. A lone woman is troubled with such dreams and such thoughts that she's afraid of herself sometimes. Pray tarry with me this night, dear husband, of all nights in the year".' Possibly this is a veiled plea from the wife, one that probably was made frequently in the past, to consummate their marriage of three months. Brown, however, leaves her bed to go off into the forest, ultimately to participate in a Witches' Sabbath on All Saints' Eve, a ritual historically associated with licentiousness.

The sexual symbolism of this evening suggests that Brown succumbs to the very force of sexuality that he dreads and resists. However, the source of the resistance is important. In his behavior and beliefs he typifies some key Freudian themes regarding men's attitudes toward women and sexuality. Hawthorne writes: ' "Poor little Faith!" thought he, for his heart smote him. "What a wretch am I to leave her on such an errand! She talks of dreams, too. Methought as she spoke there was trouble in her face, as if a dream had warned her what work is to be done to-night. But, no; 'twould kill her to think it. Well, she's a blessed angel on earth; and after this one night I'll cling to her skirts and follow her to heaven".' Brown obviously idealizes his Faith as a sexual object. He exemplifies what Freud considered to be the basic ambivalence of modern men toward sexuality and toward women.

As Freud notes in a footnote of 1910 to *Three Essays on the Theory of Sexuality:* 'The most striking distinction between the erotic life of antiquity and our own no doubt lies in the fact that the ancients laid the stress upon the instinct itself, whereas we emphasize the object. The ancients glorified the instinct and were prepared on its account to honour even an inferior object; while we despise the instinctual activity in itself, and find excuses for it only in the merits of the object.' Two years later Freud proposed that such idealization incapacitates man to achieve sexual happiness and love. In 'The Most Prevalent Form of Degradation in Erotic Life,' he says, 'To ensure a fully normal attitude in love, two currents of feeling have to unite—we may describe them as the tender, affectionate feelings and the sensual feelings.' For Freud the idealization of the love object tends to guarantee the erection of severe impediments to achieving this confluence of sexuality and tenderness. Idealization prevents men from confronting the sexuality of their love objects. Such men tend to see women, including their wives, as either whores or goddesses. They prove unable to reconcile these differences. Thus, Freud says in *Group Psychology and the Analysis of Ego,* 'A man will show a sentimental enthusiasm for women whom he deeply respects but who do not excite him to sexual activities, and he will only be potent with other women whom he does not "love" and thinks little of or even despises.'

Brown typifies this division of sexual values within Western man. The method of conveying the sexual meaning of the story through metaphor and symbol sustains this division by its indirect expression of sexuality. Some examples of such symbols and metaphors are: the physical penetration of the forest; the sexuality of the Witches'

Sabbath; the pink ribbons that signify both domestic femininity and sexuality, especially as they flutter down around Brown in the forest after he hears 'a scream,' itself symbolic of penetration—'"My Faith is gone!" cried he, after one stupefied moment. "There is no good on earth; and sin is but a name. Come, devil; for to thee is this world given"'; the blatant phallic symbolism of the guide's staff—'But the only thing about him that could be fixed upon as remarkable was his staff, which bore the likeness of a great black snake, so curiously wrought that it might almost be seen to twist and wriggle itself like a living serpent'; a public ceremony marking ' "the communion of your race"' in which the young couple will find '"your nature and your destiny"'; a ceremony symbolizing the sexual act in the following way: 'And there they stood, the only pair, as it seemed, who were yet hesitating on the verge of wickedness in this dark world. A basin was hollowed, naturally, in the rock. Did it contain water, reddened by the lurid light? or was it blood? or, perchance, a liquid flame?'; the description of Brown's condition following the act of communion—'He staggered against the rock, and felt it chill and damp; while a hanging twig, that had been all on fire, besprinkled his cheek with the coldest dew.'

The indirect representation of sexuality through these symbols, metaphors and images re-enforces the psychological division in Brown that his words during the communion ceremony convey: ' "Faith! Faith!" cried the husband, "look up to heaven, and resist the wicked one".' Brown's words constitute a condemnation of her acquiescence to sexuality. Brown's idea of love places his wife in the impossible position of being both whore and madonna, of satisfying his needs while placating the demands of his obsessed conscience. Moreover, he clearly has become the so-called '"wicked one",' a man whose anxiety and conflicts turn him into a demon. 'The whole forest was peopled with frightful sounds—the creaking of the trees, the howling of wild beasts, and the yell of Indians; while sometimes the wind tolled like a distant church bell, and sometimes gave a broad roar around the traveller, as if all Nature were laughing him to scorn. But he was himself the chief horror of the scene, and shrank not from its other horrors.'

At the core of Brown's attitude towards his wife's sexuality is his resistance to his parents' sexuality and his own sexual connection to them.

—*Sam B. Girgus*

At the core of Brown's attitude towards his wife's sexuality is his resistance to his parents' sexuality and his own sexual connection to them. Brown resists the suggestion that his guide on the journey through the woods represents his father: 'Still they might have been taken for father and son.' He protests, ' "Too far! Too far!" exclaimed the

goodman, unconsciously resuming his walk. "My father never went into the woods on such an errand, nor his father before him".' However, a witch figure in the woods recognizes both men as part of the same family. She says the guide is ' "in the very image of my old gossip, Goodman Brown, the grandfather of the silly fellow that now is".' Moreover, in the communion scene Brown finds himself re-enacting in the forest the psychological turmoil of Hamlet and Oedipus when they are forced to confront their parents' sexuality and to deny their relationship to it. Thus, as Brown and Faith are called to the ceremony, Hawthorne writes, 'At the crowd, Goodman Brown stepped forth from the shadow of the trees and approached the congregation, with whom he felt a loathful brotherhood by the sympathy of all that was wicked in his heart. He could have well-nigh sworn that the shape of his own dead father beckoned him to advance, looking downward from a smoke wreath, while a woman, with dim features of despair, threw out her hand to warn him back. Was it his mother? But he had no power to retreat one step, nor to resist, even in thought, when the minister and good old Deacon Gookin seized his arms and led him to the blazing rock.'

Significantly, from a Freudian perspective Brown's thoughts undermine his intentions and raise doubts that derive from the unconscious about his parents. The problem is as much in his mind as in real external events. In addition, his inability to resolve these doubts leaves him unprepared and unable to love. His most important relationships are ruled by his neurosis. He returns from his adventure in the woods with a scowl and harshness for his wife and this remains his basic attitude toward her. Even in his sleep, he wakes before allowing himself the pleasure of indicating unconscious tenderness. 'Often, waking suddenly at midnight, he shrank from the bosom of Faith; and at morning or eventide, when the family knelt down at prayer, he scowled and muttered to himself, and gazed sternly at his wife, and turned away.' At the same time, we know that in spite of this fear of tenderness and love, Brown did not deny himself sexuality for procreation because he goes to the grave 'a hoary corpse, followed by Faith, an aged woman, and children and grandchildren.' Thus, Brown embodies a sexual ideology of repressed feelings that forces women into a restricted role and a near-total identification with family and home. Moreover, Hawthorne also suggests that the forces of repression in the unconscious that sustain this ideology have their counterpart in other ideologies as well. Thus, Young Goodman Brown's guide tells him: '"I helped your grandfather, the constable, when he lashed the Quaker woman so smartly through the streets of Salem; and it was I that brought your father a pitch-pine knot, kindled at my own hearth, to set fire to an Indian village, in King Philip's War".'

The repression of the ideologies that Hawthorne describes are attempts to deal with the chaos and instability that Brown discovers on his journey through the unconscious. The very language of the story suggests the absence of permanent meaning and of any absolute connection between appearance and reality, between the signifier and what is signified. All experience filters through the unconscious and emerges differently just as Young Goodman Brown leaves the woods a changed man. Brown learns not only to resist sexuality but also to feel the hostility of his social environment because of the ambiguity and uncertainty of the signifiers that greet him everyday. All around him he finds the distortion of signifiers of the unconscious. One scene early in the story especially dramatizes this situation of distorted signification. Hawthorne refers to the guide's staff as resembling a snake. He then adds: 'This, of course, must have been an ocular deception, assisted by the uncertain light.' In fact, the whole story rests on a form of ocular deception where things never mean what they appear to mean. The pink ribbons seem to represent soft domesticity but also symbolize the fall of Faith. The man who guides the young Puritan through the woods seems like a devil with a mission to tempt Brown, but people keep associating the man with Brown's father. Brown puts all his hope and trust in his wife Faith who turns out to be the vehicle and instrument of his downfall. The irony of her name epitomizes the breakdown of the connection between signifier and signified. Young Goodman Brown's way of dealing with this crisis of meaning constitutes his sexual poetics. His sexual poetics define his relationship to Faith, the memory of his parents and his feeling for the people of the community. Sexual poetics for Brown is how he fills in the gaps of the unconscious that separate words and things.

However, the community itself also suggests a sexual politics that brings everyone together in a kind of conspiracy against the unconscious they all share. Thus, when Goodman Brown returns in the morning from his journey in the woods, he is dumbfounded by the way all the people act as though nothing had occurred the evening before. 'The next morning young Goodman Brown came slowly into the street of Salem village, staring around him like a bewildered man. The good old minister was taking a walk along the graveyard to get an appetite for breakfast and meditate his sermon, and bestowed a blessing, as he passed, on Goodman Brown.' The other townspeople seem equally at ease and comfortable. The people of Salem evidence exactly the kind of hypocrisy that Freud felt was indispensable to keep society together. It turns out, however, that Brown's own ideology is at variance with this sexual politics of silence. The gap between his sudden appreciation of the chaos at the center of existence and their complacency exacerbates his separation from his family and alienation from the community. The frustration of Brown's own desire emphasizes that the sense of community—or consensus if you will—of Salem rests on a collective distortion of the horror of the unconscious that reveals itself at night. The story, as Claudia Johnson suggests, cannot be dismissed as simply a dream. Or, in other words, the nightmare of the story cannot be separated from the experience of waking during the day. Thus, the description of the secret life of the community suggests that Brown emerges from the woods as one of our country's first lay psychoanalysts, stricken—perhaps plagued as Freud might say—with an insight into the unconscious of the community. Hawthorne carefully documents this secret life of the community in his description of the people at the ceremony in the woods:

> Some affirm that the lady of the governor was there. At least there were high dames well known to her, and wives of honored husbands, and widows, a great multitude, and ancient maidens, all of excellent repute, and fair young girls, who trembled lest their mothers should espy them. Either the sudden gleams of light flashing over the obscure field bedazzled Goodman Brown, or he recognized a score of the church members of Salem village famous for their especial sanctity. Good old Deacon Gookin had arrived, and waited at the skirts of that venerable saint, his revered pastor. But, irreverently consorting with these grave, reputable, and pious people, these elders of the church, these chaste dames and dewy virgins, there were men of dissolute lives and women of spotted fame, wretches given over to all mean and filthy vice, and suspected even of horrid crimes. It was strange to see that the good shrank not from the wicked, nor were the sinners abashed by the saints.

The proximity of good and evil people in the crowd externalizes the inner psychological truth of the continuum of violence, love and hate in Brown's psyche. Considering the centrality of the force of the unconscious in Hawthorne's work, it is significant that the vices he lists almost all relate to sexuality:

> This night it shall be granted you to know their secret deeds: how hoary-bearded elders of the church have whispered wanton words to the young maids of their households; how many a woman, eager for widows' weeds, has given her husband a drink at bedtime and let him sleep his last sleep in her bosom; how beardless youths have made haste to inherit their fathers' wealth; and how fair damsels—blush not, sweet ones—have dug little graves in the garden, and bidden me, the sole guest to an infant's funeral. By the sympathy of your human hearts for sin ye shall scent out all the places—whether in church, bedchamber, street, field, or forest—where crime has been committed, and shall exult to behold the whole earth one stain of guilt, one mighty blood spot. Far more than this. It shall be yours to penetrate, in every bosom, the deep mystery of sin, the fountain of all wicked arts, and which inexhaustibly supplies more evil impulses than human power—than my power at its utmost—can make manifest in deeds. And now, my children, look upon each other.

Both '**Young Goodman Brown**' and 'My Kinsman, Major Molineux' concentrate on the theme of the search for a father figure. These last two speeches in '**Young Goodman Brown**' justify the sense of insecurity at the center of that search. The story's concatenation of sin condemns everyone in Salem to paternal uncertainty. Thus, both Robin and Brown repeat the plight of Oedipus. Obviously, the Oedipus story externalizes the inner insecurity in the search for identity. As Jane Gallop says [in *The Daughter's Seduction: Feminism and Psychoanalysis,* 1982], 'Paternity cannot be perceived, proven, known with certainty; it must be instituted by judgement of the mother's word.' Such uncertainty feeds Brown's anxiety and nurses his desire to impose on the society the kind of absolute authority that 'Puritans of Puritans . . . Endicott himself' forces on Merry Mount through his symbolic castration of the Maypole.

The absence of absolute connection between signifier and signified that explains the drama of language of the Oedipus complex is highlighted in the last line of **'Young Goodman Brown.'** What Elizabeth Wright takes to mean Brown's burial in an unmarked grave like Oedipus'—'they carved no hopeful verse upon his tombstone'—provides a painful symbol of the fragility of paternal and linguistic relationships. The unmarked grave stands as a silent challenge to the credibility of both law and language, a challenge that is a major theme of Hawthorne's greatest work, *The Scarlet Letter.*

James C. Keil (essay date 1996)

SOURCE: "Hawthorne's 'Young Goodman Brown': Early Nineteenth-Century and Puritan Constructions of Gender," in *The New England Quarterly,* Vol. LXIX, No. 1, March, 1996, pp. 33-55.

[*In this essay, Keil examines "Young Goodman Brown" in terms of nineteenth-century views concerning masculinity and femininity.*]

Nathaniel Hawthorne's **"Young Goodman Brown"** traditionally has been read as an examination of crises of faith, morality, and/or psychosexuality. Early readings focused on questions of theology and conduct, but since the opening years of the 1950s, a second category of readings has emphasized the psychosexual elements. Roy Male, for example, argued [in *Hawthorne's Tragic Vision,* 1957] that "the dark night in the forest is essentially a sexual experience, though it is also much more," while Frederick Crews observed [in *The Sins of the Fathers: Hawthorne's Psychological Themes,* 1966] that in his dream experience, the young, newly wed, and still oedipal Brown, fleeing from the sexuality of married love, removes himself to a place where he can voyeuristically and vicariously enjoy that which he directly shuns. The third important category of readings attempts to ground the story in the late seventeenth- and early eighteenth-century documents about witchcraft to which Hawthorne had access. Most significant of these considerations are David Levin's contention [in "Shadows of Doubt: Specter Evidence in Hawthorne's 'Young Goodman Brown'," in *American Literature* 34, 1962] that the most important topic of **"Young Goodman Brown"** is the theological and epistemological issue of "specter evidence" and Michael Colacurcio's thesis [in "Visible Sanctity and Specter Evidence: The Moral World of Hawthorne's 'Young Goodman Brown'," in *Essex Institute Historical Collections* 110, 1974] that the historical documents from which Hawthorne worked, especially those involving how you tell a saint from a witch or any other sinner, limit the scope of Hawthorne's investigation into Brown's (or his own) psyche to that made possible by the language and content of the Puritan documents. In all three of these critical categories, the authors generally assume, if they address the matter at all, that Hawthorne is concerned with late seventeenth- and early eighteenth-century issues and events surrounding American Puritan life. We must recognize, however, that—contra the assumptions that some scholars make about Hawthorne as a Puritan historian—Hawthorne could not re-create Puritan history in his historical tales; he could only construct it, basing his construction upon his readings of Puritan documents and the experience that he, as a nineteenth-century, middle-class New Englander, brought to them.

Young Goodman Brown, who has come to believe with religious fervor what he has been taught prior to marriage about the separation of male and female spheres, is disoriented by the behavioral expectations he confronts once he has entered that institution.

—James C. Keil

At least one reader suggests that part of the experience Hawthorne brought to the Puritan documents was his familiarity with contemporary documents. Frank Shuffleton [in "Nathaniel Hawthorne and the Revival Movement," in *American Transendental Quarterly* 44, Fall 1979] has pointed out convincingly that, in the climactic scene of the "witches' sabbath," Hawthorne appeared to have been working not only from Puritan archives but also from Frances Trollope's contemporary observations on the demonic aspects of evangelical tent meetings in *Domestic Manners of the Americans* (1832). Without denying the crises of faith, morality, and psychosexuality that earlier critics had discovered in **"Young Goodman Brown,"** Shuffleton notes that Hawthorne was likely to find those issues in contemporary as well as Puritan documents and events. Moreover, in recognizing that "the story's meaning has an anchor in a specific social situation in Hawthorne's nineteenth-century present, we understand the balancing power of the specific richness of the story's historical knowledge as detailed by so many scholars." If theology, morality, and psychosexuality were a devilish brew for Hawthorne's Puritan ancestors, they were no less so for Hawthorne and his contemporaries. Hawthorne places the story in the seventeenth century in order to explore the nexus of past and present in New Englanders' attitudes towards these central life experiences.

In addition to the Puritan problems of telling the saintly from the damned and the innocent from the corrupt, **"Young Goodman Brown"** takes as part of its context fundamental changes in gender and gender relations in the growing middle-class world of New England. One aspect of these changes in gender and sexuality with which the story surely is concerned is the nineteenth-century ideology of separate spheres. During the early decades of the nineteenth century, a discourse developed that sought to divide the world into public and private spheres based on gender. Men and women had lived socially, economically, and politically distinct lives in the Puritan period, but what is significant about the new, nineteenth-century gender ideology is that it constructed a "male" world that was even more and decidedly self-consciously distinct from the "female." Men should be the "sole" economic providers of the household, working, increasingly, outside of it, in the public realm. Women should provide all the other needs of the family, laboring (although it was seldom seen as such) only within the house—a structure that during this period became known as the "home" and became identified primarily with women and their children.

Of particular relevance to Hawthorne's story, however, since its concerns are with transgression as much as catechism, is that in the last two decades historians have come to understand that the clear boundaries between male/female, public/private, and work/home were blurred—that these separate spheres, essential to constructions of the middle-class world and heretofore thought rigid barriers, more accurately should be seen as thresholds through which nineteenth-century Americans frequently passed. Moreover, historians have also confirmed that the 1830s was a critical decade of change. **"Young Goodman Brown,"** probably written no earlier than the initial years of the decade and published anonymously in 1835, chronicles Hawthorne's observations about the anxieties caused by such discrepancies between ideology and behavior. Young Goodman Brown, who has come to believe with religious fervor what he has been taught prior to marriage about the separation of spheres, is disoriented by the behavioral expectations he confronts once he has entered that institution. The ideology of separate spheres was not transgressed, Hawthorne seems to suggest in **"Young Goodman Brown,"** without some psychological and moral costs.

I

Michael Colacurcio has advised that readers look for the historical contexts of early Hawthorne stories in the opening paragraphs, and that is precisely where this reading will begin. It is here in the opening paragraphs that we are introduced to both a Puritan setting and another of what Shuffleton has called Hawthorne's contemporary "anchors." The story begins with an explicit presentation of issues of gender, sexuality, and intimacy, all of which take place in the doorway between public and private.

> Young Goodman Brown came forth, at sunset, into the street of Salem village, but put his head back, after crossing the threshold, to exchange a parting kiss with his young wife. And Faith, as the wife was aptly named, thrust her own pretty head into the street, letting the wind play with the pink ribbons of her cap, while she called to Goodman Brown.

In this scene, we learn that the setting of the story is Salem village, the site of many mysterious activities in the minds of Hawthorne's contemporaries, and the time is sunset. The scene takes place in the doorway of the Browns' house, a threshold that both joins and separates not only private and public but, literally in this case, female and male. It is a threshold that both characters violate for

reasons of intimacy, although she, as we see, is clearly the more intimate of the two. About the two characters we learn that the man is young, that he is embarking on a nighttime journey, and that, apparently, he is distracted or hurried, since he fails to kiss his wife before leaving the house. Of the woman, we learn that she is married to the young man, is named Faith, is pretty, and, although she modestly wears a cap over her hair, she has adorned it with pink ribbons.

The ambiguity in the description of Faith—is or is not her name a sign of her spirituality or faithfulness? is she modest or immodest?—will recur throughout the story, and this ambiguity is the cause of Brown's great sadness and the subject of much of the scholarship on the story. Here it is important to note that the ambiguity is repeated also in her not waiting for him to return to kiss her, in her thrusting her own head through the doorway and "letting" the breeze animate the ribbons with which she has dressed her cap. Not only is the "letting" ambiguous when combined with the thrusting, "letting" is an activity that itself raises questions about who is in control of the action. Having thrust her head through the doorway in order to give her husband his goodbye kiss, Faith whispers "softly and rather sadly, when her lips were close to his ear,"

> "Dearest heart, . . . pr'y thee, put off your journey until sunrise, and sleep in your own bed to-night. A lone woman is troubled with such dreams and such thoughts, that she's afeared of herself, sometimes. Pray, tarry with me this night, dear husband, of all nights in the year!"

Surely Hawthorne means for us to think of this story as taking place in Puritan Massachusetts. Certain other factors, however—such as the threshold setting, the description of Faith, the couple's bad dreams, the implication that he has failed to sleep in his own bed on other occasions—suggest a more contemporary setting. John Demos [in *Past, Present and Personal: The Family and the Life Course in American History,* 1986] indicates that the early decades of the nineteenth century produced scads of literature on domestic life, and the "shrill tone of the new advice betrayed deep anxieties about the evolving shape and future prospects of the family." It is of course the Browns' prospects for the future about which they are most concerned. The family was changing in fundamental ways in Hawthorne's lifetime, and many New Englanders were writing and reading about the uncertainty they felt. That domestic literature was supplemented by sexual advice literature that portrayed men as sexually predatory and—a distinct difference from the Puritan construction—women as virtually passionless. Unlike the Puritan ethos, this same nineteenth-century advice literature also threatened disaster if abstinence were not the rule in all aspects of non-procreative sexuality. It is unlikely that Hawthorne was unaware of this new literature on domestic life and human sexuality, but at the very least his story betrays the same profound anxieties about contemporary family and sexual life.

Although much of Brown's anxiety later in the story involves traditional suspicions that women are especially sexual creatures, a failing of which men must beware, Faith herself may better fit an ideal of womanhood popular in the magazine literature of Hawthorne's time. According to Lois Banner [in *American Beauty,* 1983], Hawthorne "gave [this ideal] epic representation in the dovelike Hilda of *The Marble Faun* and the manipulated Priscilla of *The Blithedale Romance.*" Such a woman was known as the "steel-engraving lady" both for the "process by which she was created" and her own "moral rectitude": "When her pictorial representation is colored, her complexion is white, with a blush of pink in her cheeks." Attending a gala New York City ball in 1822, James Fenimore Cooper encountered the real-life counterparts of this American ideal: "'There is something in the bloom, delicacy, and innocence of one of these young things, that reminds you of the conceptions which poets and painters have taken of the angels.'" The ideal's delicacy and spirituality were important; later in the story, Brown will refer to Faith as a "'blessed angel on earth.'" Another characteristic of the ideal is her youth, which "underscored her purity and reflected both the nineteenth-century romanticization of childhood and its tendency to infantilize women, to view them as creatures of childlike disposition." [Banner]. Such characterizations of femininity contrast quite specifically with Puritan constructions of womanhood, which were based on Eve's seduction by the devil and her deception of Adam in the Garden of Eden.

Perhaps as the last in a series of efforts to keep Brown home this night, Faith pleads with her husband not only to stay home but to sleep with her. The young wife's desire for intimacy with her husband could not be more explicit. Brown's reply is no less direct:

> "My love and my Faith, . . . of all nights in the year, this one night must I tarry away from thee. My journey, as thou callest it, forth and back again, must needs be done 'twixt now and sunrise. What, my sweet, pretty wife, dost thou doubt me already, and we but three months married!"

In this passage Brown has deliberately conflated his wife's name with a belief system. Hawthorne's construction of Brown's speech in this manner, his association of religion with the role of wife, suggests both Puritan and contemporary possibilities. According to Edmund Morgan, for example [in *The Puritan Family: Religion and Domestic Relations in Seventeenth-Century New England,* rev. ed., 1966] Puritans feared that love of spouse could rival and interfere with love of Christ. On the other hand, in Hawthorne's lifetime women, thought to be morally superior to men, were entrusted with preparing children for Christian salvation. Nancy Cott argues that the evangelicals of the early decades "linked moral agency to female character with a supporting link to passionlessness" ["Passionlessness: An Interpretation of Victorian Sexual Ideology, 1790-1850," in *A Heritage of Her Own,* ed. Nancy F. Cott and Elizabeth H. Pleck, 1979]. If Hawthorne's concerns are as much with contemporary as Puritan gender ideology, then having a wife named Faith seems an appropriate characteristic for his main character. However, except for Brown's distrust of Faith, it is at this point in Hawthorne's

story that, although the setting seems Puritan and both periods sometimes confuse sex with "going to the devil," the gender relations begin to have more in common with nineteenth-century ideology and behavior than Puritan history.

In Brown's reply to Faith, there is an element of huffy self-importance, as if Brown were giving a prepared speech. Here we find an indication that the events of the forest are not entirely responsible for Brown's becoming a "darkly meditative, a distrustful" man; for all his youth and inexperience, Brown is already very serious, and this hyper-seriousness is part of his foolishness. In insisting that he must leave Faith this night, Brown misreads her sexual desire and fear of being alone as anxiety about his marital fidelity. Note the irony of Brown's question: he doesn't realize that it is a sexual life with her that he is running away from when he portrays himself to his young wife ("dost thou doubt me already") as a licentious stud who would take other lovers after only three months of marriage, a self-portrait that suggests nineteenth-century manhood.

Faith both conforms to and violates nineteenth-century ideology. She is pretty, modest, discreet, and her name suggests her spirituality and her devotion to her husband. At the same time, she is, within the terms of nineteenth-century ideology, aggressive in her sexuality.

—James C. Keil

In the nineteenth century, with many men away from the home for long periods of time, middle-class Americans needed a gender ideology that sanctified woman's isolation among her children. Whereas men had played important roles in the moral upbringing, education, and socialization of children in former periods, in the early nineteenth century such responsibilities all but evaporated for many middle-class men. At the same time, women's important role in the economic production that sustained the household of the eighteenth century was, at least in the discourse, eliminated. "Having required the bourgeois woman to be both elegant and nonproductive," and leaving her on her own with the children all day, Carroll Smith-Rosenberg asks [in "Domesticating 'Virtue': Coquettes and Revolutionaries in Young America," in *Literature and the Body: Essays on Populations and Persons,* edited by Elaine Scarry, 1988], "how could the bourgeois man ever trust her virtue or rest securely in the symbols of his class" (i.e., primarily, in his elegant woman and well-kept children)? What was to keep this consumer, rather than producer, of resources from straying—economically, sexually, morally, religiously? The solution was a socially redeemed image of womanhood: woman as Angel of the Home. Middle-class woman's sole province became the production of "home" life, where the values of the culture could be instilled into the items she produced, her children.

Yet Faith both conforms to and violates nineteenth-century ideology. Standing inside the doorway, she is pretty, modest, discreet, and her name suggests her spirituality and her devotion to her husband. At the same time, she is, within the terms of nineteenth-century ideology, aggressive in her sexuality. The reversal of the expected that we see Brown encounter on the threshold of his own home is probably not unprecedented. His language seems to suggest that marriage may have been a rude awakening for him. Brown's discovery of Faith's sexuality may have shattered his conception of the passivity and disinterest that women were supposed to demonstrate about sex, and this knowledge may have threatened the security of his home. The events that take place in the woods may be nothing more than his playing out of his anxious fantasies about Faith's sexuality and the ideology of separate spheres that he demonstrates in his speech and behavior at the entrance of his home.

The story's introduction, then, describes several threshold experiences, not just because it takes place in a doorway (although that too is important to our understanding of the action of the public/private discourse) but because it is this parting of Faith and Brown that defines their future intimacy. That is to say, from now on they will cross this threshold repeatedly. Intercourse is also physically and emotionally a threshold experience, and the act itself is suggested in the opening paragraphs where Faith and Brown repeatedly stick their heads in and out of a doorway graced by her pink ribbons. There is much about the physical act of sex—the orgasms, the levels of intensity, the sleeping in one's own bed—that involves thresholds, but so too does the emotional aspect, particularly the intimacy that may proceed from as well as contribute to the physical experience. Whatever we may think today, coition and orgasm were not the *sine qua non* of human sexuality in the nineteenth century; a wide range of intimate activities constituted sexuality. But notice also how those recurrent pink ribbons may have blurred Brown's whole notion of privacy, (woman's) purity, and the sanctity of the separate woman's sphere. Brown encounters these ribbons adorning the public world everywhere he goes: each time he sees Faith sticking her head out of the doorway, he notices them, and later one floats down out of the forest sky to convince him that "'There is no good on earth'" and to the devil "'is this world given'."

What happens in the woods, then, is also part of this public/private borderland, only here Brown realizes that the divisions are grotesquely blurred, and the sexual theme significantly expands to include the issues of manhood and fatherhood—much to Goodman Brown's chagrin.

II

As we follow our new husband into the woods, we notice that the image of the threshold recurs when Brown looks back at Faith before turning the corner of the meeting-house and, presumably, going out of her sight. Upon entering the woods, he finds that the "dreary road" he has chosen is "darkened by all the gloomiest trees of the forest, which barely stood aside to let the narrow path creep through, and closed immediately behind." The trees seem to cut him off effectively from his life with Faith and from Salem village. He will soon pass a "crook" in the road, which will further isolate him. Or so it would seem. His only emotions at this point are his loneliness—the same emotion his wife is, presumably, experiencing—and his guilt. However, even this guilt and loneliness, we are told on two occasions, may be occurring in the midst of "an unseen multitude". Having left the private sphere for the public as the story begins, Brown now apparently enters another sphere in which the public and private have been completely blurred.

As for Brown's thoughts of his wife and his pangs, if any, about his mission, we read:

> "Poor little Faith!" thought he, for his heart smote him. "What a wretch I am, to leave her on such an errand! . . . Methought, as she spoke, there was trouble in her face, as if a dream had warned her what work is to be done to-night. But no, no! 'twould kill her to think it. Well; she's blessed angel on earth; and after this one night, I'll cling to her skirts and follow her to Heaven."

Brown finds it impossible to believe that Faith could imagine her husband so immoral. As we soon learn, however, Faith not only can imagine Brown on such a mission, she herself takes part in one. More interesting, perhaps, is his conviction that later he will "cling to her skirts and follow her to heaven." This vision suggests the strength of Brown's *au courant* identification of his wife as a morally superior "blessed angel." But modern too is Brown's figuring of his wife as a mother to whose skirts he can cling, an image that bears witness to the difficulty Brown has in differentiating love of mother from love of wife, a dilemma with which Hawthorne and his contemporaries were not unfamiliar.

Wife came to replace mother as the moral guardian and disciplinarian of a nineteenth-century, middle-class young man's family. The move from mother's home to wife's, from child's world to man's world should not, then, be all that difficult. Of course, in reality it is far from simple, particularly because the grown son must spend half his life away from mother-wife in the world of men for which his childhood in woman's sphere has not prepared him. Many young men must have found adult life frightening and confusing. T. Walter Herbert believes that Hawthorne did: "Nathaniel maintained a 'childlike' persona because his effort to become a 'man' was complicated by the difficulties of crossing the gap between the maternal/marital sphere and the world beyond" [*Dearest Beloved: The Hawthornes and the Making of the Middle-Class Family,* 1993].

Faith has referred to what Brown is leaving home for as a "journey," but it is clear that he does not think of it as

such. He first refers to what he is about to do as an "'errand'" and two sentences later as "'work.'" There is also
no doubt that Brown is both fleeing Faith and setting out
to "go to the devil," as he phrases his errand when talking
about Goody Cloyse further on. What is it the devil can
offer him that his Faith cannot? When Brown meets up
with the devil, the gravely dressed man, mentioning the
striking of the clock on Boston's Old South Church, rep-
rimands Brown for being a "'full fifteen minutes'" late. In
this reference to the clock, the "devil's work" becomes
associated with contemporary work—labor of a modern,
rational, time-ordered sort—and thus "going to the devil"
carries the connotation of "men's business." Here also in
this encounter we notice that the devil has been expecting
Brown and knows him by name and appearance, as if the
two had met before (and we are reminded of Faith's implication that this is not the first night she has spent alone).
When to the devil's reprimand Brown replies, "'Faith kept
me back a while,'" we realize that he knows the devil well
enough to use his wife's first name with him and, further,
that he believes the devil will accept the explanation that
a woman was interfering with his ability to set to the
"errand" or "work" that is to be done.

Brown's morality is Manichean, gendered, as is his religious sensibility, which is reminiscent of the Puritans and
evangelicals. He has been catechized to believe in the
ideology of separate spheres, and his faith brooks no blurring of them. Figuring the world of wife/mother/home as
on the side of good, angels, and heaven, Brown constructs
the world of men/father/non-home as siding with evil and
the devil. Hence, we meet the devil in the shape of Brown's
father and grandfather.

Brown's new traveling companion is described as being
"about fifty years old, apparently in the same rank of life
as Goodman Brown, and bearing a considerable resemblance to him, though perhaps more in expression than
features." So similar are their appearances that "they might
have been taken for father and son"; indeed, Goody Cloyse
later recognizes the similarity immediately. But Brown does
not. Within the context of our present concerns, that lack
of recognition can be understood as reflecting middle-
class fathers' absence from the home. Middle-class mothers and children were not to cross the threshold of the
father's soiled workplace (the disaster that could result
when masculine space was invaded by the feminine is the
subject of Hawthorne's "The Birthmark"), and so increasingly sons' experiences of what fathers did and who they
were were limited to a few hours a day. Advice literature
even urged that the son's sexual education be supervised
by the mother.

Brown's failure to recognize his father and to see the world
as anything other than devil's work might also be attributed to the devil-father's magical power: "the only thing
about [the devil-father], that could be fixed upon as remarkable, was his staff, which bore the likeness of a great
black snake, so curiously wrought, that it might almost be
seen to twist and wriggle itself, like a living serpent." In
Brown's immature sensibility, in his underdeveloped sense
of fatherhood and manhood, the father has never escaped

the expression of his mature sexuality, his erect and animated phallus. It is in Brown's mind the most significant
feature about him, in fact the devil-father's
only remarkable feature.

The devil-father wishes to speed the pace of their travels
and taunts Brown, saying: "'this is a dull pace for the
beginning of a journey. Take my staff, if you are so soon
weary'." Instead of accepting the challenge, Brown gives
his companion his reasons for refusing to take up the staff:
"'having kept covenant by meeting thee here, it is my
purpose now to return whence I came. I have scruples,
touching the matter thou wot'st of'." That is to say, the
son replies to the devil-father's taunt by challenging his
moral authority by virtue of the "scruples" he learned in
the woman's sphere to which he now would return.

In this passage we also learn why the appearance of the
devil-father was not unexpected: the son had previously
agreed to the rendezvous. It is nothing other than the sight
and offering of that twisting, writhing, serpentine staff,
then, that energizes the newlywed's scruples. As he has
done more than once since he walked through the door of
his home, young Goodman Brown hesitates, pauses, looks
back. Even as he unconsciously walks on, urged forward
by the devil-father, identified in all his "evil" sexuality as
"he of the serpent," the son objects to proceeding any
further; again he renounces his "friend's" paternal relationship to him, claiming that *his* "'father never went into
the woods on such an errand, nor his father before him'."
The devil-father, smilingly reassuring young Brown that
he need not fear being "'the first of the name of Brown,
that ever took this path'," confides that "'I have been as
well acquainted with your family as with ever a one among
the Puritans. . . . They were my good friends, both. . . .
I would fain be friends with you, for their sake'." The
devil-father comforts Brown by promising him that he is
following in his father's and grandfather's footsteps (which
of course he literally is in this scene); he is fulfilling an
honorable paternal tradition, and the devil-father would
befriend Brown so that the tradition of the fathers might
be perpetuated. Of course, the foremost and essential tradition of the fathers of any multi-generational family is
the continuity of past, present, and future achieved through
the production of a family, through intercourse and sexual
intimacy, through the literal blurring of many boundaries
between the genders.

When the naive young man insists that none of the patriarchs of his family engaged in "'such wickedness'," all
being men of prayer and good works, the devil-father
replies that, wicked or not, such behavior is common among
all the patriarchs of the colony. In the midst of going
about his father's business, Brown next encounters, much
to his surprise, a woman intruding upon their forest space;
she is not just any woman, this Goody Cloyse, but Brown's
religion teacher. Hiding out of her sight, Brown overhears
an exchange between his traveling companion and his
teacher which begins with the devil-father touching her
neck with his staff and the old hag recognizing him as the
devil "'in the very image of my old gossip, Goodman
Brown, the grandfather of the silly fellow that now is'."

Despite the fact that someone has stolen her broomstick and the old woman must travel on foot, she is determined to get to the meeting because, she says, "'they tell me, there is a nice young man to be taken into communion to-night'." As he had once extended it to Brown, the devil-father now offers his staff to Goody Cloyse to aid her on her journey to the evening's assembly, and she disappears from sight.

Goody Cloyse's interest in things sexual is explicit in this encounter; this and her appearance in the woods break down the supposed barrier between male and female, public and private, work and home, husband and wife. Brown calls it a "'marvel'" to find Cloyse in the woods at night, and the narrator points out that it was Cloyse "who had taught [Brown] his catechism, in youth, and was still his moral and spiritual adviser, jointly with the minister and Deacon Gookin." After witnessing her intimacy with the devil-father, Brown reiterates that "'[t]hat old woman taught me my catechism'." Hawthorne's narrator emphasizes that "there was a world of meaning in this simple comment." Hawthorne's association of women and ministers with the religious education and spiritual welfare of the community is another characteristic of this part of the story that is more reminiscent of nineteenth-century gender relations than those of the Puritan period. Goody Cloyse's reference to Brown as that "'silly fellow'" indicates some sense on her part, too, that much of his life Brown may have had trouble distinguishing belief from practice. Moreover, Goody Cloyse, in her references to "'that silly fellow'" and the "'nice young man to be taken into communion to-night'," unwittingly has confused two aspects of Brown's identity: as child/innocent and as man/sexual creature.

As the devil-father and Brown proceed through the forest, the older man breaks off a branch of maple limb and fashions yet another walking staff. When Brown once again refuses to go any further, the devil-father suggests that he rest for a while and, before disappearing, throws the young man his staff. Brown then thinks he hears in the forest the voices of his spiritual patriarchs, his minister and Deacon Gookin, conversing about tonight's meeting. When one of them also stops to "pluck a switch," Brown overhears Deacon Gookin saying that he is looking forward to the impending ceremony, where they will find "'a goodly young woman to be taken into communion'." Shaken, Brown cannot decide whether or not what he is witnessing is real. His doubt is so great that, looking up into the night sky, he cannot make up his mind whether "there really was a Heaven above him."

Brown's belief system, his moral certainty, dependent as it seems to be on the nineteenth-century ideology of separate spheres with which he has been catechized, is quickly shattering in the heavily peopled forest. The voices of additional fellow townspeople fall on his ears, and it is obvious that all are hurrying to a late-night rendezvous. In the heart of this commotion, Brown hears "one voice, of a young woman, uttering lamentations, yet with an uncertain sorrow, and entreating for some favor, which, perhaps, it would grieve her to obtain" and for which the townspeople "both saints and sinners, seemed to encourage her onward." Brown immediately recognizes the woman's voice as Faith's. But how much more ambiguous could Faith's voice be? She both is and is not a sexual creature in this description of her cries. She both is and is not present. Faith's disembodied voice, as well as Goody Cloyse's ability to fly, to travel effortlessly, without labor, may speak to the nature of Brown's gender fantasy. One recent scholar has suggested about the ideology of separate spheres that as it "engenders and demarcates the spaces of work and personal (as opposed to working) life, both labor and women are divested of their corporeality, defined as different rather than extensive with the body" [Gillian Brown, *Domestic Individualism: Imagining Self in Nineteenth-Century America,* 1990]. Brown screams Faith's name out into the night, only to have the forest mockingly echo his "cry of grief, rage, and terror." Brown should indeed be terrorized by this experience, for he has built his entire belief system on the moral rectitude of his mother and wife—and on their rightful place nowhere but in the home.

Surely, Goody Cloyse and his Faith have no business in this forest of moral uncertainties. Brown listens in silence for a response to his cries, only to hear "a scream, drowned immediately in a loud murmur of voices, fading into far-off laughter, as the dark cloud swept" by. Something substantial floats down out of the sky, filled as it is with insubstantial voices, and Brown snatches it off of a tree limb. It is one of Faith's pink ribbons. Just as the serpentine staff is Hawthorne's synecdoche for the sexual potential of the father, this pink ribbon is, as earlier implied, his synecdoche for the sexuality of Faith. Brown cries out, "'My Faith is gone!'" It is usually argued that with this outburst, Brown proclaims his lost religious belief, but much more has been lost: his wife Faith is also literally gone; if she is present in the forest, then she cannot, according to his belief system, be who he thought her to be.

In the forest private and public spheres blur into one another; or, perhaps, the difference between public and private is nowhere as certain as Brown once thought it was.

—James C. Keil

Now Brown takes up the devil-father's staff and hurries to the communion. Along the way he encounters a forest "peopled with frightful sounds." And soon the scariest noisemaker in the forest is he: "all through the haunted forest, there could be nothing more frightful than the figure of Goodman Brown." Now deep in the heart of the forest, where no trail remains, Brown encounters "a numerous congregation . . . peopling the heart of the solitary woods." In fact, much of the adult population of Salem village has crowded into this space, both the "grave, reputable, and pious people" and "men of dissolute lives and women of spotted fame, wretches given over to all mean and filthy vice, and suspected even of horrid crimes." Most telling is the narrator's comment that it "was strange to see, that the good shrank not from the wicked, nor were the sinners abashed by the saints." Here in the forest private and public spheres blur into one another; or, perhaps, the difference between public and private is nowhere as certain as Brown once thought it was.

As Goodman Brown feels himself called forth with the rest of the converts, he "could have well-nigh sworn, that the shape of his own dead father beckoned him to advance." Indeed, he meets his spiritual fathers when his village "minister and good old Deacon Gookin seized his arms, and led him to the blazing rock" to be initiated. But this "community of men, as we have seen, includes both men and women. Even his mother seems to appear, if only, in keeping with her role as angel of the home, to throw "out her hand to warn him back." The master of ceremonies, a kind of devil-preacher, then invites his "children" to turn around and see "'all whom ye have reverenced from youth'" for their "'righteousness, and prayerful aspirations'." This night of their conversion, the children will learn of their spiritual leaders' "'secret deeds'":

> how hoary-bearded elders of the church have whispered wanton words to the young maids of their households; how many a woman, eager for widows' weeds, has given her husband a drink at bedtime, and let him sleep his last sleep in her bosom; how beardless youths have made haste to inherit their fathers' wealth; and how fair damsels—blush not, sweet ones!—have dug little graves in the garden, and bidden me, the sole guest, to an infant's funeral.

These deeds are, broadly speaking, crimes of human sexuality. Clearly Brown's devil-preacher associates sin with sexuality.

The promised knowledge of the secret deeds will give the converts the ability to determine

> "all the places—whether in church, bed-chamber, street, field, or forest—where crime has been committed, and [they] shall exult to behold the whole earth one stain of guilt, one mighty blood-spot. Far more than this! It shall be [theirs] to penetrate, in every bosom, the deep mystery of sin, the fountain of all wicked arts, and which inexhaustibly supplies more evil impulses than human power . . . can make manifest in deeds."

The language of human sexuality is omnipresent: "one mighty blood-spot," "penetrate," "bosom," "fountain," and "deep mystery." Notice also the language of unification, of the "communion of [the] race," and the way in which the devil-preacher contradicts Brown's belief in separate spheres, especially his belief that only certain wicked people, usually men, have "evil" sexual longings.

When Brown is finally face to face with his wife, just as the "Shape of Evil" prepares "to lay the mark of baptism upon their foreheads, that they might be partakers of the mystery of sin," he looks at his Faith and realizes what "polluted wretches would the next glance" mutually reveal them to be. He cries out to his wife to forego this baptism into adult sexuality and to "'[l]ook up to heaven, and resist the Wicked One'." Brown actually reverses roles here, now imagining himself leading Faith up to heaven. But it is all too late. The entire forest scene, including his wife, vanishes. He is alone because he has refused to acknowledge his wife's sexuality in this threshold experience, just as he had refused it in the doorway of his home. He has rejected the blurring of separate spheres that is the reality of adult life. Once peopled with an invisible multitude, the forest around him now is calm and quiet.

The reader is unsure what has happened to Brown, but Brown himself is quite certain that in his last words to Faith in the forest, he has resisted the devil; every inhabitant of Salem village he had formerly trusted, however, is in league with the devil or, at the very least, has secret sins of which each should be ashamed. Brown is quite right, of course, but his very lack of sin is a crime. He returns to a community in which the blurring of the separate spheres is for the first time apparent to him, and he rejects it nonetheless. Deacon Gookin is inside his home now, but his words can be heard coming through his open window. Goody Cloyse, "that excellent old Christian," stands outside her house at the latticed gate "catechising a little girl." Brown's reaction—he snatches away the "child, as from the grasp of the fiend himself"—acknowledges his fears that the little girl could be deceived as he was—not by Goody Cloyse's catechizing, because Brown still believes in what he was taught, but by the old woman's failure to live what she preached. Approaching his home, he sees "the head of Faith, with the pink ribbons, gazing anxiously forth, and bursting into such joy at sight of him, that she skipt along the street, and almost kissed her husband before the whole village." But whatever attractions Brown had to human sexuality when he left the village—as, for example, when he turned back to kiss his wife in the doorway—are now banished by the events he witnessed in the forest. So convinced is he of her sinfulness that "Goodman Brown looked sternly and sadly into her face, and passed on without a greeting."

Goodman Brown becomes a "stern, a sad, a darkly meditative, a distrustful, if not a desperate man . . . from the night of that fearful dream." Whatever huffiness and silliness Brown possessed before leaving home has been tragically transformed by his forest refusal to recognize the blurring of spheres. Brown has "a goodly procession" of children and grandchildren, but clearly there was little joy in those sexual experiences. The initiative was seldom his it seems: "Often, waking suddenly at midnight, he shrank from the bosom of Faith." And when he dies, "they carved no hopeful verse upon his tombstone, for his dying hour was gloom."

III

When we penetrate the oedipal and sexual anxieties of Hawthorne's early fiction, we tend to divorce them from the historical, and when we unearth the stories' historical concerns, we tend to separate them from the psychosexual and from Hawthorne's immediate social environment. In **"Young Goodman Brown,"** Hawthorne was not only asking his readers to imagine the synthesis of the historical and the psychosexual; he was investigating for them the relationship between Puritan anxieties about faith, morality, sexuality, and gender and his contemporaries' and his own anxieties about those subjects. A renewed interest during the 1830s in the Puritan experience and what it could offer the present probably led Hawthorne to believe that his ancestral line and his own research into Puritan history uniquely qualified him to contribute to the discourse that sought to construct a bridge between past and present New England.

In addition to recognizing Hawthorne's examination of the nexus of Puritan and contemporary experience in **"Young Goodman Brown,"** we must also consider the importance of contemporary gender issues. Nina Baym has argued [in "Thwarted Nature: Nathaniel Hawthorne as Feminist," in *American Novelists Revisited: Essays in Feminist Criticism,* edited by Fritz Fleischmann, 1982] that a sophisticated feminist criticism of Hawthorne's work "would be based on the presumption that the question of women is *the* determining motive in Hawthorne's works, driving [his female characters] as it drives Hawthorne's male characters." Recent works by T. Walter Herbert and Gillian Brown have, while throwing men into the equation, largely heeded this call. But when scholars turn their attention to issues of gender as well as other nineteenth-century contexts in Hawthorne, they tend to focus on the later works. This virtual neglect of the early material is repeated by David Leverenz, Joel Pfister, Richard H. Millington, and the above critics in their recent books focusing on Hawthorne as an observer of contemporary middle-class culture [Leverenz, *Manhood and the American Renaissance;* Pfister, *The Production of Personal Life;* and Millington, *Practicing Romance: Narrative Form and Cultural Engagement in Hawthorne's Fiction*]. It appears, then, that adequately to give Hawthorne his due, we must focus on the whole question of gender—both masculine and feminine—in *all* of his works—early and late. Such a masterful critic of human nature deserves no less than a fully comprehensive view.

FURTHER READING

Bibliography

Stanton, Robert J. "Secondary Studies on Hawthorne's 'Young Goodman Brown,' 1845-1975: A Bibliography." *Bulletin of Bibliography and Magazine Notes* XXXIII, No. 1 (1976): 32-52.

Describes over 400 studies on Hawthorne's short story.

Criticism

Abel, Darrell. "Metonymic Symbols: Black Glove and Pink Ribbon." In *The Moral Picturesque: Studies in Hawthorne's Fiction,* pp. 125-41. West Lafayette, Ind.: Purdue University Press, 1988.

An examination of the central structural symbols of "Young Goodman Brown."

Bell, Michael Davitt. "Allegory, Symbolism, and Romance: Hawthorne and Melville." In *The Development of American Romance: The Sacrifice of Relation,* pp. 126-59. Chicago: University of Chicago Press, 1980.

Discusses Young Goodman Brown as an allegorist who chooses to live according to abstract notions of good and evil rather than acknowledge his own sinful impulses.

Bunge, Nancy L. "Unreliable Artist-Narrators in Hawthorne's Short Stories." *Studies in Short Fiction* 14, No. 2 (Spring 1977): 145-50.

Examines Hawthorne's use of unreliable artist-narrators in conjunction with the theme of brotherly love.

Carpenter, Richard C. "Hawthorne's Polar Explorations: 'Young Goodman Brown' and 'My Kinsman, Major Molineux.'" *Nineteenth-Century Fiction* 24, No. 1 (June 1969): 45-56.

Regards these two tales as companion pieces and explores important parallels between them.

Clark, James W., Jr. "Hawthorne's Use of Evidence in 'Young Goodman Brown'." *Essex Institute Historical Collections* 111, No. 1 (January 1975): 12-34.

Analyzes Hawthorne's artistic manipulation of historical evidence in his writing of "Young Goodman Brown."

Cohen, B. Bernard. "*Paradise Lost* and 'Young Goodman Brown'." *Essex Institute Historical Collections* 94, No. 3 (July 1958): 282-296.

Compares John Milton's *Paradise Lost* with "Young Goodman Brown," which he describes as "a reversal of the re-birth phase of the Adamic myth."

Colacurcio, Michael J. "Visible Sanctity and Specter Evidence: The Moral World of Hawthorne's 'Young Goodman Brown'." *Essex Institute Historical Collections* 110, No. 4 (October 1974): 259-99.

Provides an extensive historicist account of Hawthorne's tale.

Connolly, Thomas, ed. *Nathaniel Hawthorne: "Young Goodman Brown."* Columbus: Charles E. Merrill Publishing Co., 1968, 143 p.

A casebook of important critical studies of the short story.

Davidson, Frank. "'Young Goodman Brown'—Hawthorne's Intent." *The Emerson Society Quarterly* 51, No. 2 (1965): 68-71.

Notes the interest of Hawthorne's story lies in its depiction of the progress of an evil thought.

Easterly, Joan Elizabeth. "Lachrymal Imagery in Hawthorne's 'Young Goodman Brown'." *Studies in Short Fiction* 28, No. 3 (Summer 1991): 339-43.

    Argues that Brown's inability to shed tears when faced with the knowledge of evil reveals his moral and spiritual immaturity.

Erisman, Fred. "'Young Goodman Brown'—Warning to Idealists." *American Transcendental Quarterly* 14, No. 4 (Spring 1972): 156-58.

    Notes that Hawthorne's story comments on the dangers of Romanticism and Transcendentalism.

Franklin, Benjamin, V. "Goodman Brown and the Puritan Catechism." *ESQ: A Journal of the American Renaissance* 40, No. 1 (1994): 67-88.

    Argues that Brown fails to assimilate the dual lessons of the Puritan catechism, that man is innately depraved but capable of attaining salvation.

Gollin, Rita K. "The Tales." In *Nathaniel Hawthorne and the Truth of Dreams,* pp. 81-139. Baton Rouge: Louisiana State University Press, 1979.

    Discusses Brown's venture into the forest as a journey into the self which ends as a nightmare of self-damnation.

Hollinger, Karen. "'Young Goodman Brown': Hawthorne's 'Devil in Manuscript': A Rebuttal." *Studies in Short Fiction* 19, No. 4 (Fall 1982): 381-84.

    Rejects the view that Hawthorne conceived of "Young Goodman Brown" as a satire and argues that the narrator recognizes humanity's capacity for both good and evil.

Jayne, Edward. "Pray Tarry With Me Young Goodman Brown." *Literature and Psychology* XXIX, No. 3 (1979): 100-13.

    A psychoanalytic study which examines Young Goodman Brown as a negative archetype and investigates Haw-thorne's use of paranoia to structure his narrative.

Jones, Madison. "Variations on a Hawthorne Theme." *Studies in Short Fiction* 15, No. 3 (Spring 1978): 277-83.

    Compares Hawthorne's use of Puritan theology in several of his best-known short stories, including "Young Goodman Brown."

Morris, Christopher D. "Deconstructing 'Young Goodman Brown'." *ATQ: American Transcendental Quarterly* n.s. 2, No. 1 (March 1988): 23-34.

    Seeks to illuminate how the reader, like Brown himself, cannot fix one meaning to the events of the story because the words and gestures lead only to uncertainty.

Mosher, Harold F., Jr. "The Sources of Ambiguity in Hawthorne's 'Young Goodman Brown': A Structuralist Approach." *ESQ: A Journal of the American Renaissance* 26, No. 1 (1980): 16-25.

    Analyzes the structure of contradictions which creates the ambiguities of Hawthorne's story.

Rohrberger, Mary. "Hawthorne's Short Stories: Analyses of Representative Works." In *Hawthorne and the Modern Short Story: A Study in Genre,* pp. 24-47. The Hague: Mouton & Co., 1966.

    Examines "Young Goodman Brown" from Freudian and archetypal perspectives.

Stoehr, Taylor. "'Young Goodman Brown' and Hawthorne's Theory of Mimesis." *Nineteenth-Century Fiction* 23, No. 4 (March 1969): 393-412.

    An analysis of Hawthorne's metaphorical style in his most celebrated short stories.

Tritt, Michael. "'Young Goodman Brown' and the Psychology of Projection." *Studies in Short Fiction* 23, No. 1 (Winter 1986): 113-17.

    Asserts that Brown projects his guilt onto Salem's inhabitants as a way to escape his knowledge of his own feelings of anxiety.

Wagenknecht, Edward. "Tales." In *Nathaniel Hawthorne: The Man, His Tales and Romances,* pp. 17-72. New York: Continuum, 1989.

    Examines the multiple levels of meaning faced by readers of "Young Goodman Brown" which make unanimity among critics impossible.

Williamson, James L. "'Young Goodman Brown': Hawthorne's 'Devil in Manuscript'." *Studies in Short Fiction* 18, No. 2 (Spring 1981): 155-62.

    Identifies Hawthorne's short story as a "hell-fired" satire of nineteenth-century conventions of authorship.

Zenna Henderson
1917-1983

American short story writer.

INTRODUCTION

Henderson is best known for her series of imaginative tales about a race of aliens, known as the People, who settled on Earth late in the nineteenth century. Although they are commonly classified as science fiction stories, Henderson's works are, by her own admission, drawn from events in her own life: "All the stories," she stated, "are based on students I have taught, places I've known, experiences I've had." Moreover, despite featuring characters who are aliens, the stories are deeply concerned with human morality and spirituality, and with "all the wonderful, slow miracles of life, growth, and being."

Biographical Information

Henderson was born September 1, 1917, in Tucson, the second of five children of Louis and Emily Chlarson. Her family was deeply religious, which had a significant impact on her later writing. She was raised in the Mormon faith but converted to Methodism as an adult. Henderson graduated from Phoenix Union High School in Phoenix and received her bachelor's degree from Arizona Teachers College (now Arizona State University) in 1940; she received her master's degree from the same institution fourteen years later. Henderson began writing in the 1940s and had her first stories published late in that decade. Henderson was a teacher throughout her adult life. During World War II she taught at the Japanese American Relocation Camp in Rivers, Arizona; from 1956 to 1958 she taught at a U.S. Air Force base in France; and from 1958 to 1959 she taught at a tuberculosis hospital in Connecticut. Most of her career, however, was spent as a grade school teacher in Eloy, Arizona. Henderson died on May 11, 1983.

Major Works

Henderson published four collections of short stories; all the pieces had previously appeared in various magazines and journals. The stories in each of the volumes *Pilgrimage: The Book of the People* and *The People: No Different Flesh* were "novelized": modified and adapted to form a unified work. These books concern the People, a race of aliens—indistinguishable from humans except for their exceptional psychic powers—who settle on Earth in the late nineteenth century. The stories explore the relationship between humans and the aliens, as the People try to adapt to their new surroundings and the frequent hostility of humans (called Outsiders by the People), while pre-serving their unique cultural identity. Henderson, employing motifs and themes drawn from the Bible, suffuses the stories with a spirituality and a faith in humanity's ability to overcome prejudice and intolerance.

Critical Reception

The fundamental goodness of many of the characters in Henderson's stories and the overriding spirituality of the tales have led some critics to call them sentimental and saccharine. Other critics, however, have found Henderson's work more complex than such labels imply. Fred Erisman, for example, has admired Henderson's treatment of universal human concerns: "Zenna Henderson's People, alien though they are and alien though they remain," he declares, "are quintessentially human in their quest for identity, and thereby provide a means for the reader to recognize and articulate his or her own yearnings, doubts, and fears." Elsewhere, Erisman has praised Henderson's employment of the myth of the American frontier, arguing that her application of the myth to the People leads "not to a new definition of what constitutes an American, but, rather, of what constitutes a human." Viewing one Henderson story from a feminist perspective, Farah Mendelson has observed an insightful analysis of gender and power roles all the more remarkable for having been written before the advent of feminism.

PRINCIPAL WORKS

Short Fiction

Pilgrimage: The Book of the People   1961
The Anything Box   1965
The People: No Different Flesh   1967
Holding Wonder   1971
Ingathering: The Complete People Stories of Zenna Henderson   1995

CRITICISM

Zenna Henderson with Paul Walker (interview date 1974)

SOURCE: Interview with Zenna Henderson, in *Speaking of Science Fiction: The Paul Walker Interviews*, by Paul Walker, Luna Press, 1978, pp. 271-80.

[*In the conversation below, which was first published in 1974, Henderson recounts her life and career, and discusses her views on the genre of science fiction.*]

What was the origin of the "People" stories? Why have you gone on writing them?

The "People" stories originated with **"Ararat."** When I first started, I planned a story about some people who crossed the Atlantic by "lifting" from their home in Transylvania—with all the concomitant stuff that goes with Transylvania. But, as usual, I found that I can't write about unpleasant people, so I changed it to interstellar refugees, and the "People" emerged.

I went on writing them because I liked them. And at a time when I was experiencing considerable unhappiness in my personal life, the stories helped occupy my thoughts.

Also the fan response was unanimously pro, and even the crank letters were mostly happy. I will probably write more of them. (You do know that each story was originally a separate novelette, don't you?)

You said you conceived each of the "People" stories as a separate novelette, but have you kept a detailed record of the characters, the events, history, etc.? You seem to have filled out the middle of the story, but have you considered an end to it?

No, I haven't compiled a history of the "People" but, this summer, a fan of mine sent me her compilation of people, ages, relationships, etc. that she used as a college paper—and I haven't even had time to read it yet! I've not considered an end. The series may expire because my interest might get engaged in other areas. As of now, I hope to write more of them.

There are certain incidents (teacher-pupil confrontation, problems of communication, etc.), themes such as loneliness, cultural isolation, alienation, the "miraculous" element in everyday life, that recur in your "People" and other stories. How autobiographical is your work?

The "People" aren't autobiographical. All of the stories are based on students I have taught, places I've known, experiences I've had, but the stories are not of any specific anything in my life. The people, places, and events are syntheses of dozens of people, places, and events plus imagination and alteration to fit the needs of the specific stories.

The miraculous in daily life I write about because I am so conscious of it all the time. Miracles go on all the time. Oh, not the wave-a-wand, *boi-oi-oing!* type of miracles, but all the wonderful, slow miracles of life, growth, and being.

There does seem to be a running theme in the stories: that of cultural isolation; of a people cut off from the mainstream of the world, fearful of cultural confronta-

tion, of misunderstanding, if not physical harm. What about this theme? And could it possibly relate to your own experiences with the Indian and Mexican children in Arizona?

Never came across it among the kids. It's only the educated adults that have coined the expression. How much Spanish culture do you think a six-year old has who was born in Eloy, and whose parents were, too? There is economic isolation when you can't afford something, but hardly anyone feels culturally isolated. The isolation I write about, and that apparently finds an answering "me, too!" from my readers, is the isolation of person from person. It's the human state. As Ogden Nash said in one of his poems—a person is never so lonely as when he tries to pretend he isn't. *Every* one is lonely. Each of us *is* an island in the last analysis. It is our reaction to this isolation that determines the type of person we are.

A multiple question. Most of your stories concern children—especially male children. And the stories in your collection, **The Anything Box,** *all seem to have a common theme, best expressed in the story,* **"Turn the Page"**: *"Believe again! You have forgotten how to believe in anything beyond your chosen treadmill. You have grown out of the fairy tale age, you say. But what have you grown into? . . . With your hopeless, scalding tears at night, and your dry-eyed misery when you waken. Do you like it?"*

Faith. The capacity for wonder, imagination, mystery, enchantment. The supreme tragedy of our growing up is our loss of the capacity for these things. And that loss results in a hollowness of being. But fortunately we have children to revive, to re-educate, us in them.

Yes, most of my stories concern children, but I quarrel with your "especially male children." I haven't conducted a head count but I'd be willing to bet that it's about six of one and a half-dozen of the other. Almost consciously I think "boy, last time—better be a girl this time."

The thing to believe in is the ultimate triumph of Good. And that God is a personal God who knows each one of us as we can't know ourselves; who has given us life for a unique function that no one else can ever perform; that we are responsible for our every action, thought, and word; and we will be held personally accountable for them when we go through Death into the presence of God. That we are never alone, never forsaken, never beyond God's love and compassion—and always as important as if we were the only mortal ever created.

Last of sermon?

Well, if you feel you are far away from God, be advised—He isn't the one who moved!

I think the feeling of futility, of emptiness, of aloneness begins to show itself in juvenile delinquency, and ends in a society that suffers as ours does now.

The major criticism of your work is that it is "sentimental." You have been accused of being a "woman's writer." How do you feel about that?

A writer is a writer is a writer. That a woman writer sounds like a woman writer is no great thing. A man writer sounds like a man writer! So? Is either of them a thing to point at either in praise or criticism? I don't consider myself "sentimental." Maybe I'm "sympathetic." I know I'm empathetic. To me a good story is a good story whether it's from a male or female. I truly don't think there is a man sound or a woman sound to a story.

Who are you?

I'm two me's. One me is just me—name, address, height, weight, place of birth. The other me is the writer. Consequently the first me has all the statistics; the writer has none. That way I can accept and enjoy the pleasant letters I get about my stories, be pleased that the writing has had the success it has had; although the business of earning a living often gets in the way of it so the writing has to go into abeyance until time permits. Still, the duality makes me very shy of meeting people who "want to meet" me. They meet the un-writing me—never the writing me.

Statistically speaking, however—I've always been mountain conscious since I was born in the foothills of Santa Catalina mountains near Tucson, Arizona. We lived mostly with Grampa and were beguiled by stories of the family being driven out of old Mexico by Pancho Villa's men. If they'd stayed they'd have had to give up their arms, which would have been suicide.

We moved a lot—twelve grade schools—but the mountains were always around somewhere. It was quite an experience to get back into the midwest—long after I was grown—and see the sky sitting down on the land full circle.

There were five of us: three girls and two boys. I'm the oldest girl, and second in the family; the only one of us who graduated from college. I was reared a Mormon—both grandfathers and great grandfathers had more than one wife—but I'm a Methodist now. One of the things about Methodism is that you can feel at home in any worship service. You may not agree with some tenets, but as long as the love of God is there, you can feel comfortable.

I graduated from Phoenix Union High School in Phoenix, Arizona; got my BA from Arizona State University (it was Arizona Teachers College, then). Got my MA at the University, too, and since graduation, about twenty-four graduate hours. Mostly languages and literature. And, yes, even with the Master's, I still teach first grade. I have no desire for the upper grades. It's more fun to count to ten for my children in English, Spanish, French, German, Japanese, and Russian.

I can get along with my Spanish, French, and German when traveling, and learned what little Japanese I have (counting and thanks) when I taught at one of the Japanese Relocation Camps during WWII. I used my French and German on an airbase in France for two years (1956-58); and I use my Spanish all the time with my kids. I think our school is about 65% Mexican. It tickles me when on Tuesdays and Thursdays we go through our "flag information" to where I say, "Another name for our flag—" and right after Old Glory, one of my boys always shrieks, "La bandera!"

Where was I? Did I mention I was married seven years; that there were no children; and that we were divorced? Or that my mother died while I was in France. My father now lives in Seattle with my stepmother. My older brother lives in Phoenix and my sister in Tucson—and Eloy is midway between—so I yo-yo back and forth on weekends. I'm claustrophobic about staying in the same place I work when I'm not working.

Right now I'm at Pinetop, Arizona, about ten miles from Show Low, and 7200 feet up in the hills. I own a summer cabin where I stay, mostly alone. For hobbies I like to do all sorts of needlework, and am currently going through a collect-quilt-patterns phase along with making afghans. I don't sew anymore, but once I made most of my dresses. I collect, too. Just about anything small that stays still long enough: thimbles, printed toys to be stuffed and sewed, old cookbooks, old needlework magazines, calendar towels. I've been through the rockhound phase, the lapidary phase, the digging for bottles phase, doll collecting. I love thrift shops and patio sales. And I like to bake, although I hate dishwashing. And I like to walk and disconcert my friends by parking way out in the parking lot of shopping centers instead of comfortably close.

About the only fiction I read any more is detective and crime stories. I don't like the tough guy stories or international intrigue, but Agatha Christie, Upfield, Ngaio Marsh, Marric, Dorothy Sayers, etc.

Hoo boy! Writer's cramp!

Now for the Writer Me—I was writing poems and stuff from the third grade up. We learned poetry in them days. Wordsworth's "I wandered lonely as a cloud" and Longfellow's (?) "There is a forest primeval / The murmuring pines etc." So I started writing poems. The first time I really tried to write for publication was in the late 40's. **"Come On, Wagon"** was my first published short story, except for a bad one in the *Christian Science Monitor*.

I haven't written a novel because I never had that much to say; nor the time to say it in; but I'm trying to get started on one this summer. Not SF or fantasy. Suspense.

You speak of two "me's": the statistical "me" (woman, teacher), and the writer "me." How does the writer "me" rank in relation to the other? Is she to be taken seriously?

The writer "me" is a person for whom I can accept praise happily, and for whose successes I can rejoice without bragging. The statistical "me" is the everyday one that, a stranger seeing, would never suspect was AN AUTHOR!; which is piquant in its own way. Perhaps the writer "me" is more nearly what I wish I were most of the time. Maybe the unexpected blossom atop, while my toes squish in the humdrum mud.

How do you work? What are your writing habits?

I write in longhand with soft leaded big primary pencils—usually leaning on one elbow on my bed or, if it's handy, sitting in an overstuffed chair with my legs over one arm and a book or magazine on my lap to write on. I write on both sides of usually yellow paper (second sheets). I type when I can no longer think up excuses, and revise as I go; then revise the rough draft, then retype the story and heave a large sigh. . . .

Science fiction, like fantasy, is adult fairy tales. It gives people who are bound tightly in conventional ruts a chance to dream.

—*Zenna Henderson*

Why do you like mysteries? Why do you feel the urge to write one? And how do the two genres, SF and mystery, compare as literatures? And I might add—do you regard SF and mysteries as literature proper, or as intellectual vices?

I don't care for the puzzle ones as much as the suspense ones. As I said, I don't care for the spy-intrigue ones, or the tough private eyes, or the ones with sex grafted on every sixth page. I like mysteries because they're easy to read. I usually read them at one sitting. The suspense ones that I like best can be re-read: Christie, Mabel Seeley, Sayers, I re-read happily. They have enough interesting story so it doesn't matter if I remember the solution ahead. And I like mysteries because often they have authentic backgrounds of various industries or professions or areas of the world that are new to me. I can fill in the gaps of my own knowledge in such stuff as mountaineering, banking, insurance adjusting, agriculture in England, the Australian Outback, etc.

As literature? I'd be inclined to believe mysteries are more nearly literature than SF is. It depends on your definition of literature. My definition is that literature reflects the life of a given period. That's rather loose but in my re-reading of mysteries reaching back into the 20's and 30's I am struck by the social attitudes that contrast with ours. The racial biases, the class distinctions, what people ate, how they dressed, what they considered good and bad. We have periods of time crystallized in these books.

SF doesn't qualify on the basis of my definition because it doesn't reflect any given period. I decided to write a

suspense novel for the same reason I decided to write SF—because I ran out of good ones to read! I started reading SF when I was about twelve, with the old *Astounding Stories* and *Amazing Stories,* and fantasy with the old *Weird Tales.* Second-hand, of course. And, from the library, the Jules Verne books. I began to write it in 1947 or thereabouts. I knew I couldn't write technical stories, so I wrote about ordinary people reacting to SF situations, or in the case of the "People," unusual people. My formula for a story is (quote from somewhere): Usual people in unusual circumstances, or unusual people in usual circumstances.

You said "SF doesn't qualify [as literature] on the basis of my definition because it doesn't reflect any given period [of history]." Then what does it do? What value is it to you?

SF, like fantasy, is adult fairy tales. It gives people who are bound so tightly in conventional ruts by their profession, or just by the cussedness of things, a chance to dream—What if so-and-so were *not* true? What would the world be like? SF presents the mind with possible or probable new frontiers, and goes on from there. SF is *fun*—or was when I used to read it a lot. And it stretches the brain and stimulates the imagination. Presupposing it is *good* SF.

You said you wrote poetry? You have a characteristic poem for me?

Poetry? Lemme go look. Oh, dear! A *characteristic* poem? They vary so, and, I might add, are much more autobiographical than my stories; even the Persona I adopt. But here's a small one:

"Sic Transit"

Because Change is the constant,
My heart its strength has spent
In sharply knowing possession
And quickly, relinquishment.

That was written in France about 1957. Oh, my! How it recalls—Well, no matter. One other kookie aspect of me that explains phrases that come back to me on galley proofs with question marks by them—maybe I mentioned it already—often, to me, movement, light, and sound are interchangeable. For instance, leaves blowing in the wind are music; lights flashing off and on are noises like a horn honking; an airplane beacon blinking chirps; bright lights blare; a sudden noise is like a shaft of light.

I can't sleep in morning buses and have trouble sleeping in boats and planes because movement is noise is light, and who can sleep in such confusion! Darkness is silence. The new moon is a high thin sustained note. A full moon fills the night with sound; music if I'm happy, cacophony if I'm in a bad mood.

Thinking it over it reminds me of something in, I think, "Turn the Page," "A part of the truth is sometimes a lie." I am as many people as there are people to react to me!

Fred Erisman (essay date 1896)

SOURCE: "Zenna Henderson's 'People' and the Quest for Self-Identity," in *Extrapolation,* Vol. 27, No. 4, Winter, 1986, pp. 320-25.

[In the following essay, Erisman declares that in her stories about the People, Henderson "takes one of the most familiar elements of science fiction, the alien encounter, and one of the most familiar elements of all literature, the quest, and makes a profoundly human document, a body of fiction that portrays a people's achieving identity."]

Few science fiction series have had the compelling appeal of Zenna Henderson's narratives of "The People." In two books and a handful of uncollected short stories published between 1952 and 1980, Henderson limns the history of an extraterrestrial civilization that, forced to flee its dying planet, finds itself on Earth. Landing in the American Southwest, late in the nineteenth century, the aliens, who call themselves simply "The People," endeavor to adapt to Terran ways and become functioning parts of human civilization. Basic survival for the People is simple, because they are humanoid in every respect, physically indistinguishable from Homo sapiens and comfortably at home in terrestrial atmosphere, gravity, and environment. Their cultural assimilation, however, is another matter entirely. Possessing a highly developed degree of cultural cohesiveness, complemented by far-reaching telepathic and psychokinetic abilities, the People discover that survival entails a struggle to preserve their race's uniqueness even as they conceal and suppress their supranormal powers.

The nature of that struggle contributes to the series' enduring appeal, for it permits the stories to operate on three levels. The initial level is one common to all popular literature, for the stories in general overtly relate the always intriguing account of a decent people slowly triumphing over adversity as they strive to endure. The second level is somewhat more subtle, for it plays upon evocative cultural archetypes. Throughout the series there is a conscious paralleling of the People's voyage with the Israelites' search for the Promised Land, a device that cannot help but evoke a sympathetic resonance.

The third level is subtler still, since it incorporates the two previous levels into a quest both archetypal and specific, a quest that, as developed in the stories, lets the particular experiences of the People parallel and illuminate suggestive elements of the American national experience. The story of the People is, simply, the story of one culture's evolution into another, an account of settlers (or colonists) slowly becoming organic parts of the land they inhabit. Thus, as she relates the vicissitudes of her aliens, Henderson goes on to demonstrate the progress of a nation's—and a People's—quest for self-identity.

That quest entails five qualities. The first of these is an awareness of one's cultural history, which historian Clinton Rossiter defines in his study of the emerging American nation [*The American Quest, 1790-1860,* 1971] as "a widespread sense of shared experiences." For the People,

this shared experience appears as a profound racial memory, preserving their sense of life generations ago on their own planet—"The Home"—and their harrowing experiences of the journey to Earth. Thus, one of Henderson's aliens, although three generations removed from the initial pilgrimage, can nevertheless recall vividly the People's origins: "It was all in my memory, the stream of remembrance that ties the People so strongly together. If I let myself I could suffer the loss, the wandering, the tedium and terror of the search for a new world . . . and I could share the bereavement, the tears, the blinding maiming agony of some of the survivors who made it to Earth . . . trying to find the best way to fit in unnoticed among the people of Earth and yet not lose our identity as the People" [*Pilgrimage: The Book of the People*]. These memories, innate in the aliens and consciously cultivated in each new generation, serve to give the People as a community the historical foundation so essential to identity.

The second component of the quest is consensus, which grows from shared adversity, for "there is nothing like an enemy, or simply a neighbor seen as unpleasantly different in political values and social arrangements, to speed a nation along the course of self-identification" [Rossiter]. The People, possessed of extra-human powers, quickly realize that terrestrial civilization, even when not actively hostile toward them, nevertheless constitutes a constant hazard, and from their efforts to seem unexceptionable comes the second stimulus toward identity. They steadfastly instill a consciousness of their differences in each new generation long after threats to their safety have vanished. Six-year-old Lala [in ***The People: No Different Flesh***], for example, is disciplined for levitating in front of a group of Outsiders (the People's term for humans), even though the witnesses are friends and aware of her powers. "Control is necessary," she says ruefully after her scolding. "Never be un-Earth away from the Group unless I'm told to." Her lesson is a vital one because many of the first generation People were persecuted as witches and the current generation is sharply aware of the shattering effect their powers can have upon an unsuspecting Outsider, though that person may be a twentieth-century sophisticate. They cannot help, therefore, seeing themselves as a people set apart, a people truly strangers in a strange land, for whom survival resides in unity.

Somewhat more complex is the third component of self-identity, interest. Interest, for an emerging nation or a people, involves the realization that "many of their vital interests as persons are linked with the purposes of the nation as a community; they show the nation the gratitude it deserves . . . by being proud of its past, loyal to its traditions, and obedient to its commands" [Rossiter]. All of these qualities characterize the People's vision of themselves. Their pride in their past is undeniable as is their loyalty to personal or family tradition, but more compelling still is their consciousness of the responsibility they owe to themselves as a distinct, cohesive society.

That social responsibility appears in many ways. One is the People's unhesitating response to the distress call, "There's need." As teenaged Karen remarks following an emergency, "When one of the People says, 'There's need,' that means Group business" (*Pilgrimage*). Another is the realization that group obedience extends even beyond emergencies; it affects every part of the People's lives, and especially that part that governs their learning to use their distinctive powers. Young Remy discovers this early on when he is expelled from a class in psychokinesis. The teacher, he complains to his parents, sees his motives as unsuitable for one of the People: "He said I don't want to be a Motiver just to be a Motiver. I want to learn to be one so I can show people up, like Father and you and the Old Ones. He says I don't want to get into Space because of any real interest in Space, but because I'm mad at The People for not telling the world they can do it right now if they want to. He says . . . he has no intention of teaching me anything as long as I only want to learn it for such childish reasons" (*People*). Angry and smarting though he is, Remy has no option: if he is to master his powers, he must accede to the will of the Group; when he does, he learns a bit about them and himself, and both grow in the process.

Even more compelling is the role of mission in the search for self-identity. If any coherent group, be it nation, race, or sect, is to attain genuine identity, it must possess an internalized sense of mission: "The belief in mission works *down and in* by encouraging each citizen of a nation to find a special meaning in his life, by telling him of one important way in which he and his compatriots are different from citizens of all other nations, and by exhorting him to labor with extra diligence and creativity lest he fail this nation that must not fail the world" [Rossiter]. The degree to which this belief informs the People's conception of their personal distinctiveness is considerable. Accepting the reality of their supranormal powers, they accept as well the difference that this reality entails. But they do not see themselves as isolated; they understand the potential of the powers they possess, and look to the time that these powers will benefit not only themselves but the world as well. "Think, *think,*" muses Bram, "what we could do if we stopped waiting and really got going. Think of Bethie, our Sensitive, in a medical center, reading the illnesses and ailments to the doctors. . . . Think of our Sorters, helping to straighten people out . . . and let healing into the suffering intricacies of the mind. . . . Hadn't Man been given dominion over Earth? Hadn't he forfeited it somewhere along the way? Couldn't we help point him back to the path again?" (*Pilgrimage*). That they have not done so at series' end does not invalidate the point: the People are conscious of what they can do, and what they may yet do, and no clearer sense of mission can be asked for.

Of all the components of self-identity, individualism is the most telling because it combines the personal with the social quest. As Rossiter notes, the degree to which a society encourages the growth of individual identity has a direct bearing upon the degree of communal identity that it achieves: "In the most stable, successful, and loyalty-commanding nations, whatever may be their pattern of social organization, the person of the individual is most respected. . . . The achievement of a sense of self-esteem

is an act of individualism; the pooling of that esteem with the similar senses of many other men is an act of community." Yet, vital as this knowledge is and inseparably linked as it is to the peculiar qualities of the People, it comes no easier to them than it does to humans.

Some difficulties arise from the very nature of the People themselves, affecting their identity and role within the particular society. In addition to the generalized powers common to all, various individuals possess other unique powers known as Gifts. All of the People, for example, can levitate, communicate telepathically, and move ordinary objects by psychokinesis. The Gifts, however, extend these powers, enabling a Sorter to explore and manipulate another's mind, and equipping a Sensitive to diagnose injuries within another's body, or giving to a Motiver psychokinetic strengths far beyond those of the ordinary People. The responsibility of a Gift, however, can often be frightening, as when Karen discovers that she is a Sorter: "I knew with a feeling of fear and pride that I was of my grandmother, that soon I would be bearing the burden and blessing of her Gift—the Gift that develops into free access to any mind . . . [and] the ability to counsel and help, to straighten tangled minds and snarled emotions. Someday I would belong to the Group as I now belonged to the family. . . . Belong to others? With an odd feeling of panic I shut the family out. I wanted to be alone—to belong just to me and no one else. I didn't *want* the Gift" (*Pilgrimage*). However, Karen ultimately makes her peace with the Gift, and as a member of the community's inner circle of leaders—the Old Ones—achieves a realization that is both personal and communal.

Still other difficulties develop as the People reveal their powers to Outsiders. The revelation, though, is often beneficial; it helps the alien person as much as the terrestrial. Thus, for example, rebellious young Francher, whose Gift lets him create audible music by mind-power alone, learns a profound lesson in individualism from his crippled teacher, an Outsider. "If you're going to be more than human you have to be thoroughly a human first," she tells him. "If you're going to be better than a human you have to be the best a human can be, first—then go on from there" (*Pilgrimage*). Pregnant Debbie, stranded by a flood in the cabin of an old mining couple, uses her powers at first to dazzle her benefactors but comes to realize her obligations to the People and Outsiders alike:

> As I had laid down the burden of Child Within only to assume the greater burden of Thann-too [her newborn baby], so also must I lay down the burden of my spoiled-brat self and take up the greater burden of my responsibility as one of The People toward Glory and Seth [the couple] and whatever the Power sent into my life. Jemmy had been right. I *wasn't* of The People. I had made myself more of an Outsider than an Outsider, even. Well, remorse is useless except insofar as it changes your way of doing things. And change I would—the Power being my helper (*People*).

For the People, as for any emerging society, preserving individual distinctiveness while reconciling it with the needs of the community is a notable and necessary achievement.

That Zenna Henderson has a quest in mind as she tells her stories of the People is obvious. The overall theme of the search for a Home (and later for the New Home) is a quest motif of the most fundamental sort, analogous to Dorothy Gale's search for the Silver Slippers or to Shane's search for a community where he can slough his gunfighter's past and start life a new. Significantly, though, Henderson is not content to make do with a generalized expression of the motif; instead, she focuses and sharpens it until she is dealing with a highly specific kind of quest, a people's search for self-identity as persons and as a society.

It is farfetched, of course, to conclude that Henderson consciously had the attributes of cultural self-identity in mind as she composed her stories. Nothing in her work or her comments upon that work suggests that she set out to write a story cycle exploring the growth of identity; if anything, she is more concerned with the sweeping question of what humankind in general might become—"what we might have had," she says in an interview, "if—like the People—we had turned to developing our latent powers instead of gadgets to do the same thing." Significantly, though, she elects to explore this question by dealing consciously with the pervasive theme of "the outcast's hunger to belong," theme that necessarily compels her to take up the issues of social, cultural, and personal identity. By thus moving from the general theme to a particular one, she gives her stories the movingly human specificity that lifts them, like the People, well out of the ordinary.

Any work of literature gains authority and credibility in direct proportion to the degree that it expresses fundamental human concerns. Zenna Henderson's People, alien though they are and alien though they remain, are quintessentially human in their quest for identity, and thereby provide a means for the reader to recognize and articulate his or her own yearnings, doubts, and fears. Every person sooner or later confronts the issue of individuality versus conformity; every person strives to find a place, however small, in the culture of the community; every person struggles to find direction, coherence, and meaning in the routines of life. So, too, do the People, and in identifying and celebrating these parallels lies Henderson's achievement. She takes one of the most familiar elements of science fiction, the alien encounter, and one of the most familiar elements of all literature, the quest, and makes a profoundly human document, a body of fiction that portrays a people's achieving identity. That her people are extraterrestrials is of no consequence; their quest is a universal one, and their carrying out of it is an undertaking that can bring meaning to them, to us, and to the generations of the future.

Farah Mendlesohn (essay date 1994)

SOURCE: "Gender, Power, and Conflict Resolution: 'Subcommittee' by Zenna Henderson," in *Extrapolation,* Vol. 35, No. 2, Summer, 1994, pp. 120-29.

[*In the essay below, Mendlesohn examines gender roles and power structures in "Subcommittee," placing the story in the context of the time it was written, before the rise of feminism.*]

Studies of gender and science fiction have remained rare despite the recent boom in gender studies. The principal reason for this is that gender remains for many a euphemism for "women." Women are gendered; men are not. The directions feminist science fiction criticism has taken have mitigated against the exploration of gender, either as an issue or a tool. Feminist criticism has instead explored a number of alternative paths, beginning from the "women in . . ." approach and the consideration of the portrayal of women in sf and moving on, in understandable desperation, to the consideration of feminist and predominantly female authors. Here I will consider briefly some of the pitfalls and potential inadequacies which both these approaches risk and suggest a move toward the exploration of gender as a historical phenomenon and as a tool for the critic employing, as an example and test case, the short story **"Subcommittee"** by Zenna Henderson.

The "women in . . ." approach to sf, exploring the portrayal of female characters rather than authors, talks of difference and stereotype, placing an emphasis on the unimaginative caricatures with which the supposedly speculative genre abounds. The difficulty this presents emerges with the very nature of "stereotype theory." Martin Barker, in *Comics: Ideology, Power and the Critics,* argues very convincingly that inherent in any discussion of stereotype are certain contradictions. Stereotype theory demands that literature and the media should "reflect" society, however, "In a society where, for example, black people are disproportionately kept in low-paid jobs and on the dole, or sent to prison, to have this simply 'reflected' in the media would cause outrage." One is then faced with the demand that only the "acceptable" face of reality be shown. Barker identifies two types of stereotype within this ideology. The first, a "deviation" from the "real world," such as suggesting that "women want sex all the time"; the second actually answers this criticism by "reflecting" the world outside. "Here, a good deal of media representation is condemned for showing women in the home, providing services to men—though of course it is in fact true that very many do."

The difficulty in challenging this, in demanding "non-stereotypical images," is further exacerbated by the tendency of the critic to be urging a hidden agenda. Ellen Seiter [quoted in Barker] suggests that the most frequent manifestation of this problem is the agenda of the "bourgeois career individual," an ideal every bit as stereotyped as that of "hearth and home." An example of how this appears in feminist sf criticism is evident in an article by Caroline Wendell [in *Extrapolation* 20, Winter 1979]. The article considers the depiction of women in the Nebula Award winners between 1965 and 1973, focusing particularly on Delany's *Babel-17* and Panshin's *Rite of Passage.*

Each of the two novels in this group has a female protagonist: Mia Havero in Alexei Panshin's *Rite of*

Passage (novel, 1968) and Rydra Wong in Delany's *Babel-17* (novel, 1966). Both heroines are tough, intellectually as well as physically. Mia can argue ethics and sports black eyes with pride; Rydra is a gifted linguist who deciphers the difficult Babel-17, and is capable of captaining a spaceship and handling herself in armed or hand-to-hand combat. Feminist criticism must centre not on the two women themselves (although they are perhaps too superpowerful to be realistic human beings), but on the male-dominated milieus in which each moves. Mia and Rydra have been taught by males and interact with males. Neither has ever had a woman figure to learn from nor are they provided with any significant female peers. Though this type of heroine is preferable to the mental defective who is totally submissive to men, neither is completely autonomous and independent because both seem to be exceptions in a world of men.

This is a classic example of attempting to have it all ways. The heroines, in fulfilling Wendell's earlier demand that female characters should not be depicted as passive, are now "too superpowerful to be realistic human beings." Clearly Wendell has her own personal perception of the limits of properly depicted independence, and speculation beyond these boundaries becomes implausible. Equally, when both Delany and Panshin depict successful women in the environment they are realistically likely to experience, they are condemned for being "exceptions in the world of men." In support of Wendell's critique it is plausible to argue that the actual difficulty is in the apparent lack of speculation in a self-declared speculative genre. Leaving aside the issue that men are rarely treated to such speculative competence either, Wendell has unfortunately already excluded this argument from her own array of weapons, in part because she herself has already set a limit of plausibility in matters of female strength; in consequence, she has set a limit on the plausibility of other areas of speculation. On Russ's "When it Changed," for example, she comments, "it [Whileaway] does not, cannot, exist. Men and women do live together and must see one another as people, not stereotypes. And that would be the best of all possible worlds."

Apart from my personal questioning of her assumption of the continued heterosexuality of the species, it appears to me that Wendell has continued to judge both "stereotyping" and "character plausibility" by her own political ideals. This is, of course, not necessarily a problem. The difficulty is caused by the placement of all value on the critic's judgment. The political agenda of the critic is neither openly acknowledged, nor does it recognize the social reality of the authors at the time of publication, for both novels are written more than ten years prior to the article and two to four years prior to the rapid development of the modern women's movement.

One mechanism by which a critic may avoid most of the above problems is specifically to target feminist sf. This has the merit—in directing itself to a study of those futures adjudged feminist, or, in the absence of such a clear dialectic or rhetoric, illustrating female perceptions of the world—of admitting, at least in theory, a multiplicity of possible female perceptions. However, as the above extract from Wendell's article demonstrates, this is not automatic, and there remains a tendency on the part of some (and I am more than willing to admit that I have been one) to adjudge plausibility of plot on the basis of political agreement. As I have suggested already, my judgment of the plausibility of Whileaway differs from Wendell's not because I believe the work any more or less challenging as literature than Wendell suggests, but because my politics make it difficult for me to believe that men are ever voluntarily going to give women anything much worth having in the way of liberation, and this includes an assumption that anything men do give—rather than that which women take—may as easily be reclaimed.

The above comments may suggest that I am arguing for academic objectivity. As I do not believe that any such thing exists, I make haste to say that such political criticism has its place. My real qualms are that so much of this type of criticism is both unhistorical and ahistorical and that neither of the two approaches detailed above actually exploit to the full the new possibilities which gender, as a tool, has opened up.

The identification of "stereotype" in any literature runs the constant risk of ahistoricism: it may remove author and text from their cultural context and require of them an awareness of the sensitivities of a 1990s academic. This is not to excuse stereotyping or a lack of speculative imagination but is merely to be aware that criticism needs to be alive to the cultural context of the author: it is difficult for any author to speculate on the inconceivable, and the interesting and innovative speculation of one generation rapidly becomes offensive to the next. An example of the ease with which nonhistorians both identify and simultaneously ignore this element is to be seen in an article by Darko Suvin and Marc Angenot, who argue that, "any literary text contains its historical epoch as a hierarchy of *significations* within the text, just as the epoch contains the text as both product and factor" [*Science Fiction Studies*, July 1979]. And yet, they are content to declare, "It is of course possible and not infrequent for readers to have a distorted perception of our common world, through ignorance, misinformation, mystification, or class interest: for them, literature will not be properly 'readable' until their interests change."

This nicely ignores the "hierarchy of significations" within the reader, of which historical epoch is only one. Feminist criticism of feminist writing, in focusing almost exclusively on a feminist subgenre, is usually able to sidestep this issue or, alternatively, march to its own inner history of which the majority of feminist readers, writers, and critics are fully aware. This does not always work, as with Sarah Lefanu's consideration of Marion Zimmer Bradley's *The Ruins of Isis* [*In the Chinks of the World Machine: Feminism and Science Fiction*, 1988]. Although both works are products of the new map laid out by the feminist movement, Lefanu, in challenging the sexual relationship at the heart of the novel, shows little awareness of the speed at which the political agenda of the women's movement changed. Consequently, she faults Zimmer Bradley for her inadequacy in answering the questions of an agenda not yet set. In turn, the temptation remains to impose upon "mainstream" sf a political context that has not in reality seeped through from the feminist subgenre. This has the effect not only of creating anachronistic negative criticism but of denying justly deserved praise where speculation around gender issues does take place, as in Delany's *Babel-17* or *The Ballad of Beta-2*.

Ultimately, feminist criticism of feminist texts, while interesting and illuminating, is a self-congratulatory circle neither reaching beyond the feminist sf community nor acknowledging and learning from the profound changes in the genre as a whole, instanced by the absence of major critical assessments of the gendered male in science fiction. As long as this remains the case, the gender debate continues to be one-sided. Gender and gender relations are subsumed beneath the study of women and of feminism in sf, something I hope both to avoid and to illustrate below.

Despite their longevity, neither of the above approaches have, as yet, allowed gender to be placed easily within a more complex matrix of identity and response. What happens when gender roles, stereotyped or otherwise, are employed by the writer to explore quite different issues? Where stereotyped and rigid gender characteristics are assumed in consequence of historical context, possibilities of speculation may actually be opened out rather than, as is conventionally assumed, restricted. I would have preferred to have turned at this point to a piece by a male author, but, anxious to employ a story I like and admire rather than one I do not, I have selected instead **"Subcommittee"** by Zenna Henderson. The story qualifies because as a piece of "pre-feminist" writing it is engaged with characters who, by a 1990s estimation, are extreme stereotypes of masculine and feminine. It would be easy to discuss this story in terms of its qualities *despite* the unfortunate stereotypes, but, by exploring what the author wrote rather than what I as a feminist might have liked her to have written, it becomes evident that the very construction of characters allows for the exploration of a complexity of issues not otherwise possible. The three issues I have selected to discuss here are gender [sic], power and conflict resolution, and the extent to which an exploration of any of these issues relies on or is supported by consideration of the others.

"Subcommittee," by Zenna Henderson, first published in 1962, is on one level a standard story of alien invasion resolved not by military victory but by understanding, friendship, and femininity—a study, in fact, of conflict resolution. Equally, however, the story is revealing as a critique of power structures and the language of power and, finally, as a study of gender.

Serena is waiting for her husband, a general, to conclude negotiations with a force of alien invaders. In order to impress upon the Earth the friendly intentions of the invaders, the aliens have suggested that all parties should bring their families to the site of the negotiations. Serena finds herself the only young mother and the only human

with a small child. As there is no communication between the humans and the aliens outside the negotiating chamber, she and her son, Splinter, are very lonely. In the meantime, negotiations are near to breakdown. The Earth generals are unable to discover the needs or desires of the aliens; there is suspicion that the presence of the aliens' families may be merely an attempt to play upon the Earth's sense of honor and to weaken a military response. And when Serena suggests a more welcoming attitude, her husband, Thorn, reverts to the language of revenge: "'Go visit! Talk!' His voice choked off. Then he calmly went on. 'Would you care to visit with the widows of our men who went to visit the friendly Linjeni? Whose ships dropped out of the sky without warning—'."

> "Subcommittee" is on one level a standard story of alien invasion resolved not by military victory but by understanding, friendship, and femininity—a study, in fact, of conflict resolution. Equally, however, the story is revealing as a critique of power structures and the language of power and, finally, as a study of gender.
>
> —*Farah Mendlesohn*

Serena, attempting to inject a more reasonable note, questions who shot first, but Thorn has by this time turned over and gone to sleep. Later conversations are no more fruitful. To Thorn the aliens are "uncommunicative" and "hostile," and Serena, isolated from the negotiations, does not know them the way he does. In this he is correct. Instead of attempting to fathom whether they want the oceans or merely the world, Serena has been sharing picnics with Mrs. Pink and her son Doovie. To her, Mrs. Pink is the nice lady next door across the fence whose son she "saved" from drowning (unnecessarily as it happens, for Doovie's feet are webbed) and with whom—having secretly learned some Linjeni—she talks "women's things," sharing skills in knitting and embroidery. Consequently, it is Serena who discovers what the aliens want: the offer of a hard-boiled egg triggers the denouement, and we discover that what the aliens so desperately need, and have come so far to find, is salt. Without it there will be no more Linjeni babies.

Were Serena male, or possibly a stronger—perhaps "feminist"—character, she would return home, tell Thorn, and wait for the generals to sort it out. Instead, she is deterred from speaking by her husband's contemptuous dismissal of her horror at the news that the negotiations are breaking down and that war is being planned. She is "idealistic" and consequently unable to contribute to the "real" world of decision making. In a show of great courage, Serena instead sneaks into the conference room the next day, springing her solution, Portia-like, upon the entire assembly.

What is it that makes this story worthy of consideration in place of any other story—of which there are many—whose fulcrum is "women's intuition"? I would argue that its importance revolves around the story's discussion of those characteristics we customarily associate with sex difference, either biological or sociological, although I do not intend to argue here whether gender is biological or sociological. In a sense, it might be considered as irrelevant to the science fiction author for whom everything, speculatively speaking, is up for grabs.

First, at no time is Serena portrayed as intuitive as such: she makes no guesses; rather, she listens and learns. Instead, Thorn and Serena are demonstrably operating from and within different social milieus. As a man, Thorn's automatic reaction to a stranger is to assess the potential challenge he—and I use this pronoun deliberately—represents. Thorn's worry is that "'We've lost a lot of the cunning that used to be necessary in dealing with other people'." What he has not lost is the belief that cunning and suspicion are the appropriate responses to the stranger. This is not necessarily bad, merely one legitimate response to a working world with a structure that requires its members constantly to defend their social status and a world in which status is determined in terms of hierarchy—a survival mechanism, if you will. Serena, on the other hand, exists within a world of morning coffee and neighborliness, with its own mores and codes of conduct. Her reaction to the stranger, therefore, is—metaphorically—to knock on the door with a cake. This is not feminine intuition or any innate feminine gentleness, but it is integral to a complex social community with its own values and demands. As an alternative to the competitive ethos of the "masculine" workplace, it has an established pattern of networking which assists in breaking down the potential for social isolation that might be the experience of the woman working in the home. Consequently, the survival skills gained by women in this early 1960s society may prove more effective in this "first contact" situation than those learned by men for use in a more combative scenario. In this story they are crucial to a peaceful resolution of the conflict, while "femininity" is revalued; presumably, the suggestion is that the masculine must work with rather than exclude the feminine in order to maximize the abilities that humans may call upon in times of need. However, this does not challenge the idea that man is always masculine or woman feminine; we are in a world of "separate spheres," and these roles are apparently fixed, a world of complementarity rather than equality, an idea that has its own validity in the history of feminist thought and retains its validity in both the "mainstream" and margins of the movement today. The clue that Henderson may see the artificial intensity of the gender divisions that she depicts rests in the names she bestows on her characters: "Thorn," hard and masculine; "Serena," gentle and peaceful. Admittedly, these may simply be conventional names of any American romance of the period, but this is arguably deliberate parody; they are just too characteristic of the romance genre to be other than tongue-in-cheek.

If Henderson's story were concerned only to show the value of femininity in the public world, **"Subcommittee"** might have ended sooner than it did. Instead, to read further is to read also an exploration and critique of power structures and the language of power. The process by which the denouement is achieved displays rather adequately the powerlessness of Serena and, inadvertently, of Mrs. Pink, the only other female character we meet in the story. Serena's attempt to offer an alternative to war is dismissed as idealistic by Thorn. Within this marriage it is made clear that her role is to listen and not criticize, a point reinforced by Serena's avowed fear of his reaction, stated toward the end of the story. Interestingly, it is made clear the next day that Mrs. Pink has had similar difficulties, for the Linjeni High Command does not appear to be aware that understanding has been reached. But then, in effect it has not, for those who have gained this understanding have no place in the hierarchy and consequently no voice. They are people to whom things happen, not men who may be actors on their own stage. Serena challenges this hierarchy when she sneaks into the conference, but she reinforces it by the very fact of this sneaking. Serena does not demand entrance nor assert to the guard that she has an important mission—usually the first method of any male hero, even if he does then resort to climbing in at a window—but instead persuades (or manipulates) the guard into allowing her to "take a look." She therefore accedes to a structure that suggests that her presence, unlike possibly that of a man on an equivalent mission, is and always remains illegitimate. One challenge to this argument is that manipulation is itself a source of power. This is to obscure the difference between the manipulation by the oppressor and the oppressed; the former is a form of coercion, the latter a means of gaining a temporary advantage by acceding to the perceptions of the powerful. While this may be a useful tactic for short-term survival, its process allows for the reinforcement rather than the undermining of extant power structures and cannot be a long-term strategy for change. Neither manipulation nor influence should be confused with power, for both rely implicitly on the consent of the subject to be manipulated, whereas power can be exercised beyond the boundaries of consent. In achieving her audience, Serena can be seen to step beyond the "feminine" and to take on the active, masculine role. However, the dynamics of power within the negotiations is not changed; the general might reasonably have had Serena removed before she were able to interrupt without fear of condemnation. That he does not is quite obviously integral to the plot, but not integral is the subsequent remarginalization of Serena. Having dropped her bombshell, Serena becomes again the hopeful idealistic female whose role is to watch and support while others work out the realities.

If Henderson's purpose is not to challenge the gender structures of her society—although she does question its values—the structure of language and the dynamic relationship of language and power are exposed. The constriction that language places on communication and the extent to which language too has a hierarchy and is gendered in its use and meaning are crucial to both the plot and to the success with which attempts are made by both human and Linjeni to resolve potential and actual conflict. Serena identifies accurately that the language and context of the conference is not conducive to conflict resolution, is not, in fact, geared to any such thing: "'What have you been talking about all this time? Guns? Battles? Casualty lists? We'll-do-this-to-you-if-you-do-that-to-us? I don't know! . . . I don't know what goes on at high level conference tables. All I know is that I've been teaching Mrs. Pink to knit and how to cut a lemon pie'."

Unsurprisingly, this induces confusion amongst the translators, culminating in their complete failure to translate "baby." As Serena contemplates, "Babies have no place in a military conference." The key to Serena's success is that she challenged the masculine culture of difference and threat in order to assert instead a culture of "neighborliness"—a term more appropriate here than "friendship," for it is deliberately inclusive and welcoming of the stranger—and the value structure of female domestic society. In addition, we also learn something of the nature of communication as a whole. Both Splinter and Serena communicate *before* either has learnt Linjeni. Splinter puts it best: "You don't have to talk to play!" Neither of course do you need to talk to war. Serena, in her turn, communicates by play acting, by mime and with food but without, interestingly, the traditional point-and-name—usually with the first reference to oneself—that has become a cliche in modern fiction, sf or otherwise. The point-and-name begins after both women have begun to learn each other's language in private and when communication—through food and through skills—has already been well established. Verbal communication becomes a gift each offers to the other rather than a necessity each wants.

Where does all this leave us? It becomes evident that a story written employing rather rigidly defined and rigidly gendered characters is offering a constructive alternative to the language of war, employing these characters in a manner humorous, but not exaggerated, in order to provide a plausible scenario. Serena employs female and feminine illustrations not merely because they are what she has at hand and is able to draw from her experience—although an exploration of how the personal becomes political might be of value here—but because the masculine language and context at hand are simply not adequate for peacemaking. The failure of the translators to keep up with Serena, their inability to find "pink" or "God" in their vocabularies, becomes a symbol of the different approaches of male and female to the process of communication. The solution suggested is not that women take over (this is not a discussion of women's rights) but that conflict resolution requires a language of its own rather than one bastardized from the language of war; it challenges the belief that such language is "neutral" yet continues to operate in a context of early 1960s ideas of the positive nature of gender difference.

That the focus of this story is on conflict resolution, rather than conflict, is in itself an early deviation from the norm of that sf concerned with war and the military. As such, to concentrate entirely on what this piece has to tell the academic reader about sf speculation on women—and to condemn it for such a lack of speculation—would be to distort the piece in terms of what it attempts to achieve and to ignore its historical specificity. However, by concentrating the discussion on conflict resolution, the manner in which gender issues are exploited *is* illuminated. Gender is not the story, but it does act both as driver and container of the plot, without which such a complex exploration of power, communication, and conflict resolution might require far greater levels of polemic than exist here. Additionally, by examining the depiction of men and women through a historical lens we learn something of the nature of Henderson's speculative abilities that enable her to exploit, rather than be confined by, contemporary social codes and conventions.

Because this is a short story, it is not possible to assess conclusively whether the resolution results in a genuine or long-lasting challenge to a value structure that places "male" survival mechanisms and social rituals above "female" or, alternatively, whether this is subsequently subsumed within an assumption of a "higher female morality," to be called on at will. My own reading that it is not is inevitably based upon my own expectations as a 1994 feminist. Should you wish to apply labels, one might term the piece "proto-feminist"; this however, to labor the point, distracts fundamentally from what the story is about.

Fred Erisman (essay date 1995)

SOURCE: "Zenna Henderson and the Not-So-Final Frontier." *Western American Literature,* Vol. XXX, No. 3, November, 1995, pp. 275-85.

[*In the following essay, Erisman analyzes Henderson's use of the myth of the American frontier in her stories of the People. Henderson applies the concept of frontier broadly, the critic contends: "She is concerned with the timeless frontier that occurs whenever an individual or a people confronts a challenge."*]

The American frontier experience has long been linked with space travel and interplanetary colonization. From at least the era of Hugo Gernsback and Edgar Rice Burroughs, the vocabulary and imagery of the frontier West have been superficially applied to the fictional exploration of space, and exploitation of the formulaic parallels between pulp Westerns and pulp science fiction has made the expression "space opera" more derogatory than "horse opera." Another kind of linkage, however, emerges from the efforts of authors to use science fiction as a deliberate means of exploring what might take place when individuals encounter an alien environment. Whether that environment is the vacuum of space or the strange reaches of a new planet, it renews the frontier encounter, providing yet another arena in which the travelers can be tested as they once were tested on the terrestrial frontier.

The synergy of science fiction and the frontier experience becomes clear in the writings of Zenna Henderson (1917-1983), who puts her western origins to good use as her work matures. Born in Arizona, raised as a Mormon (though she later became a Methodist), and educated at Arizona State University, Henderson spent more than thirty years as an elementary school teacher, working principally in the region around Eloy, Arizona. She began writing fiction in 1951, initially publishing mysteries and horror stories in the pulp magazines of the time. Then, in 1952, she published **"Ararat,"** the first of what was to become her most notable achievement, the series of stories dealing with "The People." Over the next three decades she explored in these stories the history of an extraterrestrial race, outwardly indistinguishable from human beings, who flee their dying planet to seek a new haven. Some of their number reach Earth, arriving in the American Southwest in the last years of the nineteenth century, where, like the pioneers of American myth, they set out to reconstruct a society. The aliens' efforts to adapt to a western milieu that is itself evolving enable Henderson to evoke the familiar components of Frederick Jackson Turner's analysis, yet offer a provocative new slant on the frontier synthesis [Turner, "The Significance of the Frontier in American History," *Frontier and Section: Selected Essays of Frederick Jackson Turner,* 1961].

At the heart of the frontier synthesis is the recognition that all settlers bring with them a body of well-entrenched knowledge. Material things and familiar occupations they may leave behind, but the intangibles they unconsciously retain, with the result that, as Turner points out, on the frontier "there is not *tabula rasa.*" The information, skills, attitudes, and values that accompany the settler westward constitute "the inherited ways of doing things," and the resultant tension between the old and the new becomes an element inseparable from, and essential to, the larger frontier experience. This tension is particularly acute among The People, for whom extraordinary abilities and compelling racial memories are as much a part of life as inherited attitudes and skills are for humans.

The People are set apart by powers foreign to the human race. All of them can levitate, communicate telepathically, and move commonplace objects by telekinesis. Particular individuals within the group, moreover, have special abilities, or Gifts, that extend these powers in specific ways. Motivers, for example, have telekinetic powers far stronger than those of the others. Sensitives can visualize injuries within another's body, and Sorters are able to heal a disturbed mind. Adding to their distinctiveness is a pervasive racial memory in which all share. By the time the stories end, The People have been on Earth for three-quarters of a century, yet their memories of their native planet, The Home, are as fresh and as evocative as were those of the original refugees.

Those memories retain their power into the twentieth century. They contribute to what teen-aged Karen [in **"Ararat"**] calls "the poignant sorrow that is a constant undercurrent among the People, even those of us who never actually saw the Home," and even the children of Melodye Amerson's elementary-school class in Bendo [in **"Pottage"**] evince a "homesick yearning that filled every line they had written—these unhappy exiles, three generations

removed from any physical knowledge of the Home." In some displaced societies, intellectual baggage of such magnitude might bring about estrangement, even alienation, but among The People it works to give meaning and balance to the frontier synthesis. Recognizing that they must recast their powers if they are to survive, they set out to make themselves unobtrusively functioning parts of the communities about them, and their inherited ways set the synthesis in motion.

If the inherited ways of doing things provide the raw materials for the synthesis, the energy to initiate the process comes from another source. This is the larger West into which the settlers move, where the circumstances they encounter are not those that they left, and challenge old customs and practices. As Turner puts it, "The stubborn American environment is there with its imperious summons to accept its conditions." Thus, the larger environment generates the evolutionary process. It sets the conditions within which the adaptation takes place; its components play an active role in shaping and determining the course of the synthesis; and it compels those who are to survive to accept the full extent of what it has to offer.

For Henderson's People, the "stubborn American environment" takes two forms—physical and social. The physical environment is the tangible world in which they find themselves, the larger region of the American Southwest, dotted with Hispanic place names, desert plants, and distinctive landforms such as mesas and canyons. This is a demanding, at times hostile, environment. The need for water is a constant concern, and temperature extremes can take the unaccustomed by surprise. One of the unaccustomed is Salla, who, arriving on Earth from the New Home, the distant planet settled by another party of the refugees, sets out to explore an innocent-appearing shale flat. She grievously blisters her bare feet, learning in the process that "the sun can be vicious this time of day" [**"Troubling of the Water"** and **"Jordan"**].

Though The People find hazards in the physical Southwest, they also find striking beauty. Trying to persuade Salla that Earth has wonders equal to those of the New Home, Bram takes her to a mountaintop. There the two look out

> over the vast stretches of red-to-purple-to-blue ranges
> of mountain, jutting fiercely naked or solidly forested
> or speckled with growth as far as we could see. And
> lazily, far away, a shaft of smelter smoke rose and bent
> almost at right angles as an upper current caught it and
> thinned it to haze. Below, fold after fold of the hills
> hugged protectively to themselves the tiny comings
> and goings and dwelling places of those who had lost
> themselves in the vastness.
>
> (**"Jordan"**)

Salla, overwhelmed by the sight, is brought to a moment of transcendent linkage between terrestrial experiences and The People's: "If you're lost in vast enough vastness you find yourself—a different self, a self that has only Being and the Presence to contemplate." The stubborn American environment does, indeed, carry its demands, but it can touch even an alien spirit. Salla's epiphany is no small testimony to the compelling power of the West, and hints at other discoveries to come.

Were the physical environment all that The People encounter, their story would be unexceptional as a document of the frontier. But Henderson introduces the social environment as well, and as The People endeavor over the years to adapt to the West's established, functioning society, they discover an environment that poses dangers and opportunities far greater than any found in the physical world. The greatest of the dangers is intolerance. One group of their party survives the initial passage and entry into Earth's atmosphere, only to be set upon by the rigidly God-fearing citizens of Grafton's Vow. Seeing The People's carefree levitation as witchcraft, the human settlers slaughter the entire party, justifying their actions with the biblical injunction, "Thou shalt not suffer a witch to live" (**"Angels Unawares"**). Other contingents meet a similar fate, and their history becomes a part of The People's group memory.

That history remains vivid, as Melodye Amerson, a human, discovers when she sets the Bendo community's twentieth-century schoolchildren to writing about the heritage their parents have suppressed. One child's account is heart-wrenching:

> *They found a baby under a bush. The man hit it with the wood part of his gun. He hit it and hit it and hit it. I hit scorpins [sic] like that. . . . Monster 'they yelled' evil monsters. People can't fly. People can't move things. People are the same. You aren't people. Die die die.*

> (**"Pottage"**; Henderson's italics)

The trauma of the nineteenth century leaves its mark on the twentieth; each new generation, recalling the past, learns habits of concealment, and in Bendo, these habits become repressive. But, as Melodye points out to the adults of Bendo, memories can stimulate as well as torment:

> What people *doesn't* have such a memory in larger or lesser degree? That you and your children have it more vividly should have helped, not hindered. You should have been able to figure out ways of adjusting. . . . What possible thing could all this suppression and denial yield you more precious than what you gave up?

For Henderson, social forces, even negative ones, are parts of the frontier synthesis.

A hostile people is as much an environmental determinant as a hostile place, and settlers of every ilk, if they are to survive, must adapt to both. But other people are friendly, and, for Henderson, are a determinant equally powerful. The People, from their earliest moments on Earth, meet Americans who are tolerant, compassionate, and understanding. Over and over, human families take in members of The People who are hurt or lost; Dr. Curtis, a twentieth-century human physician, allows a Sensitive to guide

him while he operates on an injured Bendo child; there even is eventual intermarriage between the two races (see, e.g., **"No Different Flesh"**; **"Angels Unawares"**; **"Pottage"**; **"Gilead"**). As they come to know the humans they encounter, they recognize the good that mankind has to offer, they gradually reveal themselves to the friendly and the tolerant, and they make no secret of their desire to learn and contribute. Dr. Curtis, having seen their powers in action, turns to Valancy and asks, "It's true what I saw . . . ? You're extraterrestrials?" Her reply is characteristic of their attitude: "At least our grandparents were. . . . But we're learning where we can fit into this world" (**"Pottage"**).

> For Henderson, social forces, even negative ones, are parts of the frontier synthesis.
>
> —*Fred Erisman*

What they learn from and about humans is important, as the adult Karen implies when she remarks to a human acquaintance, "Teachers have been our undoing—or doing according to your viewpoint." Dita, a human, is found to have powers that The People lack, giving them, as Jemmy remarks, "the third blow to our provincialism." And each new contact shrinks that provincialism further, until Karen can eventually say to Mark and Meris, a human couple, "Just because we had our roots on a different world doesn't make us of different flesh. There are no strangers in God's universe" (**"Interlude: Lea I"**; **"Wilderness"**; **"No Different Flesh"**). For The People moreso than most there can be no *tabula rasa,* but they quickly grasp what human distinctiveness can teach them as well. This awareness, too, is a part of the social frontier and it adds dimension to The People's experience.

The synthesis the frontier sets in motion leads, in Turner's analysis, to the unique traits that establish the essential American character. It is, he says, "to the frontier the American intellect owes its striking characteristics," among which are "coarseness and strength combined with acuteness and inquisitiveness . . . ; that dominant individualism, working for good and for evil, and withal that buoyancy and exuberance which comes with freedom." Henderson recognizes and accepts these traits as part of the synthetic process; because her People bring to the process attributes beyond those possessed by humans, however, she proposes a frontier synthesis that combines human and natural elements to make of The People a race of true distinction.

The crucial role the terrestrial frontier, physical *and* social, plays in the shaping of The People becomes clear late in the stories, when The People on Earth reestablish contact with the survivors who have settled the New Home. They discover, to their astonishment, that, on the New Home, there has been no synthesis. Presented with an unpopulated, virgin planet, the settlers there have used their powers physically to alter it to their needs. With no pre-existing society to stimulate adaptation and assimilation, they have overpowered the physical environment and reconstituted the home world as they knew it. They adapt the frontier, rather than adapting themselves to its conditions, and in the process forfeit the benefits of the frontier synthesis.

One of those benefits, for Henderson, is spontaneity. "We've done wonderfully well copying the vegetation and hills and valleys and streams," Salla tells Bram after seeing Earth, but "it's still a copy—nothing casual and—and thoughtless" ("**Jordan**"). Another is diversity. When Debbie returns to the New Home from Earth, she finds that its perfection quickly becomes monotony. "The precisely twenty-six trees interspersed at suitable intervals by seven clumps of underbrush" increasingly depress her, and she at last yearns passionately for even a single weed, because "at least it shows individuality" ("**Return**"). Unable, or at least unwilling to make sweeping changes in Earth's environment, The People of Cougar Canyon, Bendo, and other groups make their peace with the world as they find it, and the conditions of Earth work subtly to broaden their perceptions and their activities.

The greatest benefit of the terrestrial frontier, however, is humanity, which, for the aliens, makes the synthesis unique. The People of Earth discover that the perfection of the New Home has kept its settlers from developing qualities that they take for granted, and the result is pernicious. Bram gets a shocking demonstration of this consequence as he introduces Salla to the sights and inhabitants of Cougar Canyon. One inhabitant is the blind, armless, and legless Obla, who has been mutilated in an explosion. Bram and the others accept her deformities as a matter of course, but Salla, knowing only the New Home's perfection, recoils in disgust. Infuriated, the boy turns and snaps, "Is *that* the kind of people the Home is turning out now . . . ? Aren't you taught even common kindness and compassion?" ("**Jordan**").

Salla's shamefaced reply to his accusation speaks volumes about the role Henderson assigns to the frontier synthesis: "We don't have people like that at Home. I mean, I never saw a—an incomplete person . . . and *no* one ever stays unfinished." The New Home is undeniably a place of Edenic perfection, but its inhabitants lack the intangible attributes of tolerance, compassion, and simple humanity that The People on Earth, forced to accept the human and environmental imperfections of the living frontier, have come to possess. Unlike the stable, static life of the New Home, that on Earth, for The People as much as for humans, is a constant, evolutionary, on-going process. No single element controls, and the continuing synthesis benefits all.

Throughout her stories Henderson stresses the opportunities accruing to The People from their contact with Earth and its diversity. In contrast to that of the New Home, their life on the terrestrial frontier, even in the twentieth century, is in many ways coarse, even primitive. Yet, as

Turner postulates, they gain from that coarseness an energy and resourcefulness absent in their other-worldly kin. "This is Earth," Bram tells Salla, somewhat defensively. "We have no Healers as yet. . . . It's mostly a do-it-yourself deal with us" ("**Jordan**"). And, because the terrestrial frontier *is* "a do-it-yourself deal," The People must discover virtues and strengths where they find them, whether internal or external, social or physical, and the process makes them more fully aware of the richness of life than are the People of the New Home.

For Henderson, the complementary benefits of the synthesis are the crucial element, as her stories reveal. As The People adapt to their frontier, they recognize the part played by the western land, the regional circumstances, and the contact with humans good and evil. They see the strengths that humanity possesses, and how these strengths can complement their own abilities. As a human teacher points out to young Francher, whose powers make him chafe at Earthly constraints, "If you're going to be more than human you have to be thoroughly a human first. If you're going to be better than a human you have to be the best a human can be, first—then go on from there" ("**Captivity**"). And they come to see the continuing and beneficial challenge that Earth in all its diversity offers. A teenager from Bendo makes the point explicitly when offered the chance to go to the New Home: "We have only started to make Bendo a fit place to live in. I like beginnings. The New Home sounds finished to me" ("**Jordan**").

In this comment is the essence of Henderson's point. The People have received unique qualities from the human race. They have changed in ways that their kin on other planets have not. The change has been for the better. And the process is not, for them, at least, one that has ended in 1890, but rather one that is a perpetual beginning, allowing for still further growth. The People they remain, but they are now of Earth as well. When Bram, Earth-born and Earth-raised, is offered a chance to return to the New Home, he vacillates for a while, then realizes that for him and Salla and Obla and others among The People, the journey is but the next step in the process: "Things will happen to all three of us before Earth swells again in the portholes, but whatever happens, Earth *will* swell in the portholes again—at least for me. And *then* I will truly be coming Home" ("**Jordan**").

Throughout Henderson's stories, the synthesis that Bram voices continues apace, in telling confirmation of the power of the frontier, yet one of the great ironies is that The People must make their way in the America of the closed frontier. They arrive on Earth in 1893, the year Turner first posed his hypothesis and three years after the frontier was proclaimed closed (see "**Troubling of the Water**"), and the West they encounter is increasingly the settled West of the modern era—a region of dirt roads, ghost towns, played-out mines, rural communities, and, eventually, cities. The challenges they face and the rewards they reap, however, parallel those that the American people experienced in the decades preceding the frontier's closing. In this seeming contradiction lies perhaps Henderson's greatest contribution to the literature of the frontier and the West, for she turns her back upon the spatio-temporal frontier of historical record, and poses instead a frontier of humanity and the spirit.

Contributing to the myth of the American frontier is its role in "problems of cultural self-definition [and] the American preoccupation with defining 'Americanness.'" Because she sees these as recurring problems that extend beyond the borders of the United States, it makes no difference to Henderson that the spatio-temporal frontier of the historic West has vanished. She is concerned with the timeless frontier that occurs wherever an individual or a people confronts a challenge, the "imaginative area employed for self-definition, where the pioneer ultimately must make a new home and a new self" [David Mogen, *Wilderness Visions: The Western Theme in Science Fiction Literature,* 2nd ed., 1993]. In this respect, she echoes and even extends Henry David Thoreau's contention [in *A Week on the Concord and Merrimack Rivers,* 1849] that "the frontiers are not east or west, north or south, but wherever a man *fronts* a fact." Her concern is with the process involved in *any* "pioneering effort," rather than with the attributes of a specific physical frontier, and she develops from that concern a telling commentary upon frontiers, growth, and the human spirit (**"Jordan"**).

Zenna Henderson uses her aliens to look beyond the parochialism of the American West to a larger, even universal arena. The stories of The People are, indeed, stories of adaptation along a frontier, but they lead not to a new definition of what constitutes an American, but, rather, of what constitutes a human. As she develops her accounts of yet another encounter with the American West, she demonstrates that, so long as any individual desires to grow, there is no end to the frontier. The closing of the literal frontier is only an episode in the history of the United States, and, for those who desire it, the frontier synthesis can and will continue, in the continued definition of a new and better self. Hers is an important message for the human race, and one that establishes Henderson as a western writer for whom the themes and attributes of the American West are true universals, speaking to humans and People alike.

Additional coverage of Henderson's life and career is contained in the following sources published by Gale Research: *Contemporary Authors,* Vols. 1-4, 133; *Contemporary Authors New Revision Series,* Vol. 1; *Dictionary of Literary Biography,* Vol. 8.

"A Hunger Artist"
Franz Kafka

The following presents criticism on Kafka's short story "Ein Hungerkünstler" ("The Hunger Artist"; 1922). For an overview of Kafka's short fiction, see *SSC*, Volume 5.

INTRODUCTION

"A Hunger Artist" is often considered one of Kafka's best works and one of the most powerful and perfectly crafted short stories ever written. It was first published in the periodical *Die Neue Rundschau* in 1922 and subsequently included as the title piece in the short story collection that was the last book published by Kafka during his lifetime. "A Hunger Artist" explores the familiar Kafka themes of death, art, isolation, asceticism, spiritual poverty, futility, personal failure, and the corruption of human relationships. Some critics have argued that it is one of Kafka's most autobiographical works, viewing the story as a depiction of the isolation and alienation of the modern artist, a condition keenly felt by Kafka himself.

Plot and Major Characters

"A Hunger Artist" is told retrospectively, looking several decades back from "today," to a time when interest in the spectacle of a professional hunger artist—a person with the ability to fast for many days—was intense. It then depicts the waning of interest in such displays. The story begins with a general description of "the hunger artist" as a type of performer, and then almost imperceptibly narrows in on a single practitioner of the "art"—the protagonist. The hunger artist performed in a cage around which curious spectators crowded. He was attended by teams of watchers—usually three butchers—who ensured that he was not eating in secret. Despite such precautions, many—including some of the watchers themselves—were convinced that the hunger artist cheated. Such suspicions annoyed the hunger artist, as did the forty-day limit imposed on his fasting by his promoter, or "impresario." The impresario insisted that after forty days public sympathy for the hunger artist inevitably declined. The hunger artist, however, found the time limit irksome and arbitrary, as it prevented him from bettering his own record, from fasting indefinitely. At the end of a fast the hunger artist, amid highly theatrical fanfare, would be carried from his cage and made to eat, both of which acts he always resented.

These performances, followed by intervals of recuperation, were repeated for many years. Despite his fame, the hunger artist felt dissatisfied and misunderstood. If a spectator, observing his apparent melancholy, tried to console him, he would erupt in fury, shaking the bars of his cage.

The impresario would punish such outbursts by apologizing to the audience, pointing out that irritability was a consequence of fasting. He would then mention the hunger artist's boast that he could fast much longer than he was doing, but would show photographs of the hunger artist near death at the end of a previous fast. In this way he suggested that the hunger artist's sadness was caused by fasting, when, in the hunger artist's view, he was depressed because he was not allowed to fast more. The impresario's "perversion of the truth" further exasperated the hunger artist.

Seemingly overnight, popular tastes changed and public fasting went out of fashion. The hunger artist broke his ties with the impresario and hired himself to a circus, where he hoped to perform truly prodigious feats of fasting. No longer a main attraction, he was given a cage on the outskirts of the circus, near the animal cages. Although the site was readily accessible, and crowds thronged past on their way to see the animals, any spectators who stopped to see him created an obstruction in the flow of people on their way to the animals. At first the hunger artist looked forward to the passing of the crowds, but in time he grew irritated by the noise and disruption caused by the people, and the stench, the roaring, and the feeding of the animals depressed him. Eventually, the hunger artist was completely ignored. No one, not even the artist himself, counted the days of his fast. One day an overseer noticed the hunger artist's cage with its dirty straw. He wondered why the cage was unused; when he and the attendants inspected it, however, they found the hunger artist near death. Before he died he asked forgiveness and confessed that he should not be admired, since the reason he fasted was simply that he could not find food to his liking. The hunger artist was buried with the straw of his cage and replaced by a leopard. Spectators crowded about the leopard's cage.

Major Themes

There is a sharp division among critical interpretations of "A Hunger Artist." Most commentators concur that the story is an allegory, but they disagree as to what is represented. Some critics, pointing to the hunger artist's asceticism, regard him as a saintly or even Christ-like figure. In support of this view they emphasize the unworldliness of the protagonist, the priest-like quality of the watchers, and the traditional religious significance of the forty-day period. Other critics insist that "A Hunger Artist" is an allegory of the misunderstood artist, whose vision of transcendence and artistic excellence is rejected or ignored by the public. This interpretation is sometimes joined with a reading of the story as autobiographical. According to this view, this story, written near the end of Kafka's life, links the hunger artist with the author as an alienated artist who is dying. Whether the protagonist's striving is seen as spiritual or artistic, the leopard is regarded as the hunger artist's antithesis: satisfied and contented, the animal's corporeality stands in marked contrast to the hunger artist's ethereality. A final interpretive division surrounds the issue of whether "A Hunger Artist" is meant to be read ironically. Some critics consider the story a sympathetic depiction of a misunderstood artist who seeks to rise above the merely animal parts of human nature (represented by the leopard) and who is confronted with uncomprehending audiences. Others regard it as Kafka's ironic comment on artistic pretensions. Here the leopard signifies a positive life-affirming force opposing the hunger artist's impulse towards death.

Critical Reception

Both within and apart from the debates surrounding the thematic and allegorical significance of "A Hunger Artist," critics have explored a number of other issues. Heinz Pollitzer has observed that in order to achieve fulfillment in his art the hunger artist must die, and he links this to an overall "paradox of existence." Similarly, Claude-Edmonde Magny has seen in the hunger artist's isolation a "fundamental solitude" that is part of the human condition. Forrest L. Ingram has explored the theme of anxiety in "A Hunger Artist," finding several levels of tension in the story, and Patrick Mahony has interpreted the work

from a psychoanalytic perspective. Paulo Medeiros has pointed out that the hunger artist displays many of the symptoms of anorexia. A number of critics have examined "A Hunger Artist" in the context of Kafka's other works, and some have detected affinities to literature by other authors, including Johann Wolfgang von Goethe, Nathaniel Hawthorne, Charles Baudelaire, and others. Commentators have been nearly unanimous in their praise of the organization and structure of "A Hunger Artist" and have extolled Kafka's brilliant fusion of fantastic and realistic elements in this work.

CRITICISM

Claude-Edmonde Magny (essay date 1945)

SOURCE: "The Objective Depiction of Absurdity," in *Quarterly Review of Literature*, Vol. 2, No. 3, 1945, pp. 211-27.

[*In the following excerpt, Magny discusses the theme of "fundamental solitude" in "A Hunger Artist."*]

One must not look on Kafka merely as a spirit of denial, who ridicules all human ambitions because he cannot comprehend their nobility: he feels on the contrary very strongly the nobility of any aspiration or effort, whatever its object. The end of the ape's Report [in **"A Report to an Academy"**] is full of legitimate pride, the pride of the life that has attained exactly the goal it set and which does not admit the suggestion that "perhaps it was not worth the trouble." Kafka simply refuses to consider the ontological value of the end toward which man aspires and gives us only the most humble, and usually grotesque and vulgar, expressions of it. In Kafka our loftiest aspirations become the ambition of the ape to escape from the zoo and reach the music hall, or, better still, the ambition of K. to obtain an interview with a petty official of the Castle. His work resolves itself into a kind of mysticism without God, in which the hero seeks, almost always in vain, and by most strange and sorrowful means—at times against his will—an ecstasy which circumstance withholds from him. The most typical story in this respect is **"The Hunger-Artist,"** the story of a professional "hunger-artist" who shows himself in a cage from circus to circus, for whom fasting the longest time possible is his life purpose, an end in itself, yet with no idea of accomplishing anything else through the fast. The spectators see merely a circus stunt, a means of earning a living in which it is natural to try to cheat. The most humane among those set to watch him turn their backs, so to speak, in the night and play cards in the corner, leaving him the chance to eat on the sly. The fatality of his existence is that they never permit him to fast as long as he would like, never more than forty days, and that only in the large cities; not for medical or humane reasons, but because the interest of the public would fall off over a longer period. When they do bring him out of his cage, with great pomp, the professional faster is ready to faint, not from hunger, as the public believes, but from rage and humiliation that they will not let him fast longer. He ends by passing out of fashion and dying forgotten, without the public or anyone bothering to count the days of his fast. Here we find the theme of fundamental solitude symbolized materially by the cage (as in the story of the ape) and, morally, by the lack of understanding on the part of the public. A rejuvenation, if you wish, of the theme of the "loneliness of the artist," of the "ivory tower" or of the "Albatross," with the difference that this aloneness holds nothing poetic (it is, on the contrary, terribly vulgar, at once horrible and grotesque); it is the aloneness of the Mount of Olives with the spitting, the insults and the sponge soaked in gall; nor is it due to the public's *hostility* . . . merely to its indifference, and the inability of the crowd to understand anything; in the last analysis, it is nowhere said that this aloneness constitutes superiority: before dying, the mystic faster gives the key to the enigma: if he fasts, it is because he can do nothing else; it is a fate, not a vocation; he has never found the food he could savor; if he had, he would have gorged himself with it as all of us do. So the insatiable hunger, the divine nostalgia that possesses the mystic or artist perhaps is at bottom only some lack, something unsatisfiable, a fundamental maladjustment, the sign of an imperfect soul.

Robert W. Stallman   (essay date 1948)

SOURCE: "Kafka's Cage," in *Accent,* Vol. 8, No. 2, Winter, 1948, pp. 117-25.

[*In the essay below, Stallman investigates "A Hunger Artist" as both a metaphysical allegory portraying "the dilemma of modern man: his spiritual disunity" and a sociological allegory depicting "the dilemma of the modern artist: his dissociation from the world in which he lives."*]

"The Hunger-Artist" is one of Kafka's perfections and belongs with the greatest short stories of our time. Its theme of the corruption of inter-human relationships, as Winkler defines it, recurs throughout Kafka's work and has its perfect achievement here in this intrinsic whole.

The world of a Kafka story is one of mystery, the mysterious being obtained by a realism that is pushed to the extremes. All his details are simple and commonplace, a critic of *The Castle* points out; but Kafka subjects them "to a transmutation which makes them seem to compete with each other in enveloping us with some weighty secret." The weighty secret remains a mystification for most readers—even for Einstein. "I couldn't read it for its perversity," he is reported to have remarked upon returning a Kafka novel to Thomas Mann. "The human mind isn't complicated enough." One critic of *The Burrow* describes that story as "in itself a 'burrow' of the most complicated construction," with an ingenious system of intertwining tunnels of which he interprets the "inner fortress" alone,

"whence the whole structure can be overlooked." The present essay attempts to open up the as yet unlocked cage of **"The Hunger-Artist."**

Realism of detail within a framework of symbolism, as Max Lerner says, is Kafka's unique quality and his special gift to modern fiction. His meanings emerge at several planes at once, and the planes are interconnected. Just try to keep to Kafka's facts *as* facts! It is impossible to suppress or to minimize their allegorical overtones. For as facts—and they are not "facts" but purely imaginary phenomena—they resist a literal interpretation. Here at the literal plane, as starting-point for our analysis, are the facts of **"The Hunger-Artist"**:

> The story is about a once popular spectacle staged for the entertainment of a pleasure-seeking public: the exhibition of a professional 'hunger-artist' performing in a cage of straw his stunt of 'fasting.' His cage's sole decoration is a clock. His spectators see him as a trickster and common circus-freak and therefore they expect him to cheat, to break fast on the sly. But fasting is his sole reason for existing, his life purpose; not even under compulsion would he partake of food. For him, to fast is the easiest thing he can do; and so he says, but no one believes in him. Because the public distrusts him, he is guarded—usually by three butchers—and prevented from fasting beyond a forty-day period, not for humane reasons, but only because patronage stops after that time. His guards tempt him with food and sometimes torture him; yet they breakfast on food supplied at his expense! A great public festival celebrates his achievement, and thus he is "honored by the world." But when he is removed from his cage he collapses in a rage, not from hunger, but from having been cheated of the honor of fasting on and on and of becoming thus "the greatest hunger-artist of all time." Though emaciated almost to the point of death, he quickly recovers and after brief recuperation intervals performs again and again.

> Nowadays however he has been abandoned for other spectacles. People visit his cage in the circus-tent, but only because it is next to the stables. His spectators are fascinated by the animals. All's changed: There is no clock, and the once beautiful signs to announce the purpose of his act have been torn down. Now no tally is kept of the number of fasting days achieved. There are no guards. "And so the hunger-artist fasted on without hindrance, as he had once dreamed of doing . . . just as he had once predicted, but no one counted the days; no one, not even the hunger-artist himself, knew how great his achievement was and his heart grew heavy." Thus the world robs him of his reward. Indifference replaces admiration, and on this account he expires. He is buried with the straw of his cage and replaced by a panther, who devours fiercely the food he naturally craves. The people crowd about his cage.

Here then is the matter-of-fact account of the story stripped of interpretation. But every fact seems invested with symbolic significance. For instance, no literal meaning can be ascribed to the bizarre clock in the artist's cage. (A calendar is the logical means for reckoning the artist's fasting days.) This clock does not tick. The unclocked life of the artist outlasts centuries, and periodically he survives starvation sieges that are beyond human endurance. And so it is with all of Kafka's facts: they are symbols and they are fantasies of a dream world. The laws of physics and of biology are defied, the facts of human existence distorted. Kafka's facts ask questions which have their answer at their allegorical meaning level. The literal meaning is not complete or sufficient in its own terms, as James Burnham observes. However resolutely we try to remain at the literal in Kafka, "we always find ourselves being driven and teased and thrust beyond it. The most commonplace phrase, appearing as it will in an irreconcilable context, compels the mind to spin away. We are always walking at the edge of a cliff."

"The Hunger-Artist" at its allegorical level provides three possible interpretations: metaphysical, religious, and sociological. All three circles of meaning intersect, almost coinciding one with the other. No circle is closed, each opens onto the adjoining one and projects us into it. Hence no single self-contained system of meaning defines Kafka's intention; no single complete interpretation is possible.

"The Hunger-Artist" at its allegorical level provides three possible interpretations: metaphysical, religious, and sociological. All three circles of meaning intersect, almost coinciding one with the other. No circle is closed, each opens onto the adjoining one and projects us into it. Hence no single self-contained system of meaning defines Kafka's intention; no single complete interpretation is possible.

—Robert W. Stallman

To begin with a metaphysical interpretation, there is the double contrast between (1) the two occupants of the cage, the human and the animal, and (2) between the artist and his observers, the human beings outside who are but closed in animals uncaged. The noble body of the panther fascinates them, and this physical attraction is that which one animal has for another. For them too, their joy in living issues from their throat—and from their belly. They crave the same food and are nourished, literally, by the same sensations and appetites. What a contrast between the hunger-artist, who is no-flesh, and his spectators, who are all-flesh: the panther who consumes flesh, the butcher-guards who destroy flesh, the doctors who cure flesh! But the knife of a butcher is no release for an animal, nor is the knife of a doctor who by saving flesh saves only matter. As for the contrast between the hunger-artist and the panther, these two beings are at once wholly unlike each other and yet identical. The panther complements the hunger-artist and is parodied by him. In the portrait which opens the story the artist is portrayed as:

deathly pale, dressed in black tights, his ribs protruding powerfully, sometimes nodding politely and answering questions with a forced smile, even thrusting his arm through the bars to let them feel his emaciation, and paying attention to no one, ignoring even the striking of the clock which was the cage's sole decoration, looking straight before him with eyes almost closed, and sipping occasionally from a tiny glass of water to wet his lips.

The hunger-artist is an imitation panther. As artist he imitates life: panther-like he appears black, yet a deathly paleness reveals his true self. Time means no more to him than to the panther. And he has no use for a chair, he prefers straw. He nods his head as though beckoning to onlookers, or half-closing his eyes he stares beyond them as though intent upon some inward vision. But what a poor imitation of reality the artist presents! Protruding "powerfully" from him are ribs, only ribs, and the arm he proudly thrusts through the bars discloses not strength but emaciation. (Notice Kafka's wit here: into his parody he injects bathos.)

While the hunger-artist is a part of the sensuous world of matter, he is yet apart from it. Unlike the animal and the human, his being is spiritual and thus "free" from the claims of matter. Their "freedom," by contrast, resides somewhere in the region of their teeth, that is, in their appetite, which is to say that man as animal is never free—never free from that gnawing dissatisfaction which his purely physical appetencies create in him again and again. The hunger-artist—man as spiritual being—has that true freedom which inheres in the soul; still not even he who hungers for the claims of the divine is free from the claims of the body. He too is caged by a human being's "joy in living." One recalls the quotation from St. John of the Cross which T. S. Eliot takes as caption for his *Sweeney Agonistes:* "Hence the soul cannot be possessed of the divine union, until it has divested itself of the love of created things." In the world of **"The Hunger-Artist"** there exists a radical division between the realm of faith—the religious, the qualitative, the spiritual or the supernatural (symbolized by the mystic-faster)—and the realm of practical reason, the quantitative, the sensuous realm of physical matter (symbolized by the panther and the people). Elsewhere in his writings Kafka declares that "what we call the physical world is the evil in the spiritual one." But we do not need external evidence; the internal evidence is positive enough: In the world of **"The Hunger-Artist"** there is this dichotomy between divine and human, and this dichotomy approaches the absolute.

There is a passage in James Burnham's "Observations on Kafka" (*Partisan Review:* March, 1947) which defines Kafka's metaphysics: "His world is split by the absolute Manichaean division into Good and Evil, which is identified with the division between Light and Darkness, Spirit and Matter. . . . As with all Manichaeans, the ambivalence remains: he [Kafka] *longs for Matter, for the evil natural social world, at the same time that he denies it; he is appalled by Spirit even while he must seek it absolutely.*" (Italics mine.) Kafka's hunger-artist represents Kafka's doctrine that "There is only a spiritual world; what we call the physical world is the evil in the spiritual one, and what we call evil is only a necessary moment in our endless development." **"The Hunger-Artist"** is a kind of critique of this doctrine, for here Matter triumphs over Spirit. Though the tone of the story is one of lament for the passing of the hunger-artist, for his decline and death, none the less all the logic is weighted against his efforts at autarchy. As for our neglect of hunger-artists, our present-day practice of honoring a real panther has more to be said for it than our former-day practice of honoring a fake one. The hunger-artist seeks Spirit absolutely; he denies the "evil natural social world" at the same time that he longs for it. And this is his dilemma, even as it is ours. It is not possible for man to achieve a condition of pure spirituality, nor again is it possible for him to achieve a synthesis of spirit and matter. As the agent of divine purity the hunger-artist is a failure. His failure is signified, for instance, on the occasion when he answers the person who has explained his emaciation as being caused by a lack of food: he answers "by flying into a rage and terrifying all those around him by shaking the bars of his cage like a wild animal." This reversion to the animal divests him momentarily of the divine, and it also betrays the split-soul conflict within him. His location next to the stables serves as reminder that the claims of the animal body are necessary claims upon the soul and cannot be denied. And this is true even though matter is wholly evil (i.e., "the evil odors from the stalls," etc.); complete separation from reality can never be obtained. (Compare the idea of "complete detachment from the earth" as it figures in *The Burrow*.) Pure Spirit is as vacuous as Pure Matter.

Nowadays (to bring this history down to current times) that dualism between Spirit and Matter, which had its two-part representation in the hunger-artist and the insatiable hunger-multitude, is non-existent since one part of the dualism no longer has representation—the mystic-faster is dead. "Fasting" no longer means anything to us; nor did it in former times—except that then it was at least celebrated (albeit not without hypocrisy), honored by rituals conscientiously enacted from fast day to fast day. Everyone attended His service daily, and regular subscribers sat (as in church-pews) "before the small latticed cage for days on end." Everyone pretended to marvel at his holy feat, but not one worshiper had Faith. Yet for centuries he submitted again and again to crucifixion by these pretenders, a martyr for his cause. Because "it was the stylish thing to do," the multitude attended his "small latticed cage" as they would a confessional box. But the hunger-artist as priest hears no confession. Indeed since the multitude does not understand what faith is, it has no sin to confess. Apart from a few acolytes to His Cult, all mankind disbelieves this Christ who many times died for man's sake. And when He dies, see how the disbelievers exploit the drama of His death:

> But now there happened the thing which always happened at this point. The impressario would come, and silently—for the music rendered speech impossible—he would raise his arms over the hunger-artist as if inviting heaven to look down upon its work here upon

the straw, this pitiful martyr—and martyr the hunger-artist was, to be sure, though in an entirely different sense. Then he would grasp the hunger-artist about his frail waist, trying as he did to make it obvious by his exaggerated caution with what a fragile object he was dealing, and after surreptitiously shaking him a little and causing his legs to wobble and his body to sway uncontrollably, would turn him over to the ladies, who had meanwhile turned as pale as death.

The ladies who so cruelly sentimentalize over his martyrdom represent sympathy without understanding, a sympathy which is self-sentiment. One of them weeps, but not for him. She breaks into tears only in shame for having touched him. It is a mock lamentation these two Marys perform.

> And the entire weight of his body, light though it was, rested upon one of the ladies, who, breathless and looking about imploringly for help (she had not pictured this post of honor thus), first tried to avoid contact with the hunger-artist by stretching her neck as far as possible, and then . . . she broke into tears to the accompaniment of delighted laughter from the audience. . . .

What a difference between the theme of the Virgin mourning the loss of her Son as treated in Kafka's parody and as depicted in the famous *Avignon Pièta* or in Giotto's *Lamentation*.

It is thus that the religious and the metaphysical meanings of **"The Hunger-Artist"** coincide: (1) Christ is truly dead. Our post-Renaissance world has discarded the act of faith from its reality. (2) For the superannuated mystic there is no resurrection because today not Spirit but Matter alone is recognized. And it is recognized, this triumph of matter over spirit, even by the dying mystic, who ends a skeptic and a defeatist (not unlike Kafka himself). I had to fast, he admits, because I could find no food to my liking. Fasting is my destiny. But "'If I had found it, believe me, I should have caused no stir, I should have eaten my fill just as you do, and all the others.' Those were his last words, but in his glazed eyes there remained the firm, though no longer proud, conviction that he was still fasting." Here is the key to his enigma. So the fanatic quest of the hunger-artist, to quote Miss Magny, who has a short note on **"The Hunger-Artist"** in her critical essay "The Objective Depiction of Absurdity" (in *The Kafka Problem*), "So the insatiable hunger, the divine nostalgia that possesses the mystic or artist perhaps is at bottom only some lack, something unsatisfiable, a fundamental maladjustment, the sign of an imperfect soul."

As metaphysical allegory **"The Hunger-Artist"** portrays the dilemma of modern man: his spiritual disunity. The story is about man's search for his own meaning: what is man, Matter or Spirit? As sociological allegory **"The Hunger-Artist"** presents the dilemma of the modern artist: his dissociation from the world in which he lives. Translated into sociological terms, the division is between the artist and his society; in metaphysical terms, between the divine and the human, the soul and the body. The consequence of the corruption of the individual integrity is a corruption of inter-human relationships. There is spiritual disunity *within* the individual artist and a spiritual disunity *between* the artist and his materialistic public. (His isolation is symbolized by the cage.) The artist cannot believe in himself, nor can his public believe in him. The loneliness of the artist (in his "ivory tower"), as Miss Magny phrases it, "is the aloneness of the Mount of Olives with the spitting, the insults and the sponge soaked in gall . . ."

For his aesthetic vision the artist has to die daily and be reborn, but his artistic devotion cannot be an end in itself. The artist as poet, no less than the artist as mystic, cannot survive in isolation from society.

—Robert W. Stallman

For his aesthetic vision the artist has to die daily and be reborn, but his artistic devotion cannot be an end in itself. The artist as poet, no less than the artist as mystic, cannot survive in isolation from society. "Against this lack of understanding, this universal lack of understanding, it was impossible to fight." The division between artist and society can be bridged only by a reciprocal act of faith. But "Just try to explain the art of fasting to some one! He who has no feeling for it simply cannot comprehend it." As the initiated alone understood, "the hunger-artist would never under any circumstances, not even under compulsion, partake of any nourishment during the period of fasting. His honor as an artist forbade such a thing." The integrity of the artist is absolute, but his values are relative. His Ivory Tower is truly a cage. To point Kafka's satire, the artists of the 'Nineties, those pure aesthetes, retreated from life with a gospel of Art for Art's Sake and the disdain of Villiers de l'Isle Adam—"As for living, our servants will do that for us." But life is not irrelevant to art; the material conditions, however delimiting their influence, nourish the creative imagination. Life is at once the subject of art and its wellspring. Art and Life, Spirit and Matter—each fulfills the ever-unfulfilled appetencies of the other. Of course the artist can "fast" as no one else can do. We concede, *"in view of the peculiar nature of this art* which showed no flagging with increased age," the artist's claim of limitless capacity for fasting. But pure creativeness is nothing; the creative imagination must feed upon reality. *Art is but a vision of reality.*

True, the artist in the Renaissance and Middle Ages "lived in apparent glory, honored by the world." He had his patron, the impressario who profited from the exhibition and shared the adulatory applause; his critics, the butchers who watched over his creative activity (and always misjudged it); and his historians, the attendants who bibliographed his creative acts or achievements in works produced. An imitation panther in a cage, he was admired for his craftsmanship in imitating life, but not being distinguished from any other circus performer by "the pleasure-seeking multitude" he was taken as "no more than a source of amusement." Society exploited all his deaths and resurrections; it crucified him again and again, not by hostility but by distrust and utter indifference. Hence his despair, the issue of this universal distrust which made his act of creation so difficult for him, and which "filled [him] with a gloomy melancholy which was deepened by the fact that no one understood it." It is our glorification of the practical vision at the expense of the religious and aesthetic vision and the resultant loss of spiritual belief that is Kafka's **"Hunger-Artist"** theme. Society and the artist, each disbelieves in the other. But the artist disbelieves even in himself. It was a gnawing doubt that truly emaciated him. His unhappiness results from the dualism within himself between the aesthetic and the practical insights, the dichotomy dissociating his spiritual self from his practical being. The aesthetic soul subsists in the physical body, in the realm of matter or not at all. His denial of the realm of matter, the denial which his emaciation signifies, is only one source of his "constant state of depression." The artist is equally at fault even as the society which repudiates him, for he repudiates life itself. By his perverse denial of reality the artist's truths are *mummy truths, whereat the living mock.* His art is not *a vision of reality.* Hence the rejection of the emaciated body of art for the healthy body of life (the panther). Perhaps it wasn't his fasting to attain aesthetic perfection that made the artist so emaciated; "perhaps his emaciation came solely from his dissatisfaction with himself"—solely from dissatisfaction with the pure aesthetic vision he too fervently hungered to attain. Thus, "though longing impatiently for these visits [of the living on their way "to the eagerly-awaited barns"], *which he naturally saw as his reason for existence,* [he] couldn't help feeling at the same time a certain apprehension." He apprehends the necessity of an existence outside the cage and realizes that an absolutism of pure aestheticism is artistic and spiritual death. The people were on their way to the stables, he became convinced, "and his experience in this matter overcame even the most stubborn, almost conscious self-deception." His disillusionment is his apprehension of the fact that art has no sovereignty over life. As for his solipsistic belief that only "he who was the faster could be at the same time a completely satisfied spectator of his fasting," suppose that he had attained his illusionary ideal of artistic purity—as absolute spectator of his triumph over nature he could never comprehend his spiritual achievement without measuring it from the relative world of its physical embodiment. His death-mask conviction of final triumph is a mockery, for the triumph is an empty one.

It is the clock in the cage that triumphs over the artist. Time triumphs over the artist who denies the flux of time, which is his present reality. The clock in the cage is a mockery of the artist's faith in his *artifice of eternity*. The tragedy of Kafka's hunger-artist is not that he dies but that he fails to die into life. As he dies he seeks recognition from the world he has all his lifetime repudiated: "'I always wanted you to admire my fasting.' said the hunger-artist." It is his confession that the sovereignty of the soul (or of the aesthetic experience) is but an illusion, that spirit is nothing if isolated from matter. It is his confession that the artist must come to terms with his life, with the civilization in which he lives, with reality. "Forgive me, all of you," he whispers to the circus-manager, as though in confessional before a priest; and they forgive him—for his blasphemy against nature.

Meno Spann (essay date 1959)

SOURCE: "Franz Kafka's Leopard," in *The Germanic Review*, Vol. XXXIV, No. 2, April, 1959, pp. 85-104.

[*In the following excerpt, Spann argues that the images in "A Hunger Artist" symbolize Kafka's own personal experiences rather than abstract allegories.*]

In contrast to most of Kafka's other short narratives, **"Ein Hungerkünstler"** has a detailed, closely-knit plot which can be clearly outlined.

A hunger artist, easily the best in his field, enjoys great popularity, but nevertheless he is frustrated because neither his impresario nor the spectators properly appreciate his achievements. The impresario does not permit him to break his fasting record for business reasons; the spectators suspect the showman of trickery; and even those who know that he is an honest performer do not believe his assertion that fasting is easy for him and that he would like to fast on and on. After many gala performances, ending dramatically with music, speeches, and "lady volunteers" from the audience leading the exhausted performer to his first meal after the heroic fast, his popularity suddenly declines. The public loses interest in public fasting, and the hunger artist has to accept a position with the side show of a circus. Hardly noticed by the people who rush past his cage to see the wild animals, he now can fast as long as he wishes. But his new employers are not interested in the unbelievably high number of fasting days—they even stop recording them.

As in the majority of Kafka's works, the death of the hero is the end and climax, but in no other story excepting *Der Prozeß* has he given that climactic end such weight and importance. The entire narrative exists only for this denouement. Since much of the disagreement about this story concerns its closing paragraphs, these will have to be quoted.

> One day an overseer noticed the cage and asked the attendants why this perfectly good cage with the rotten straw inside was unoccupied. Nobody seemed to know until one of them, aided by the tablet which had listed the fasting days, remembered the hunger artist. They dug in the straw with poles and found him. 'You are still fasting?' asked the overseer. 'Aren't you ever going to stop?' 'Forgive me, all of you,' whispered the hunger artist; only the overseer, who put his ear against the bars, understood him. 'Of course,' said the overseer,

and tapped his forehead to indicate the state of the hunger artist to his men. 'We forgive you.' 'I always wanted you to admire my fasting,' said the hunger artist. 'We really do admire it,' the overseer said to humor him. 'But you must not admire it,' said the hunger artist. 'All right, then we won't admire it,' said the overseer; 'but why should we not admire it?' 'Because I must fast, I can't help it,' said the hunger artist. 'Fancy that,' said the overseer, 'and why can't you help it?' 'Because,' said the hunger artist, raising his wasted face a little and speaking with his lips pursed, as though for a kiss, directly into the ear of the overseer, so that nothing should be lost, 'because I could not find the food I liked. Had I found it, believe me, I would have eaten my fill without much ado, like you and all the others.' These were his last words, but in his glazed eyes there was still the firm, though no longer proud, conviction that he was continuing his fast.

> 'Come on now, get things in order,' said the overseer, and they buried the hunger artist along with his straw. Into the empty cage they put a leopard. It was a relief even for the least sensitive to see this wild animal bound about the cage that had so long been desolate. He lacked nothing. It was not difficult for the keepers to decide upon and bring him the food he liked. He did not seem even to miss his freedom. This noble body, filled to bursting with all it needed, seemed to carry freedom within. It seemed to be hidden somewhere between his fangs; and the joy of life came so hot and strong from his throat that it was difficult for spectators to hold their ground in front of his cage. But they crowded around in spite of this and did not want to move away.

The first interpretation of **"Ein Hungerkünstler"** appeared in H. Steinhauer's introduction to his textbook edition of 1936, the last so far in 1957. It is a four page commentary in a book by Felix Weltsch, who belonged to the inner circle of Kafka's friends and is one of his earliest interpreters. In those twenty-one years the little narrative about the professional inediant has been freely allegorized by all the commentators the author has examined. The resulting allegorical equations have been varied and sometimes mutually exclusive. The story has been interpreted as a praise—but also a criticism—of asceticism. Other commentators see in it an allegory of the suffering of the great artist, or of the sham artist, or of the relation between the artist and his public. One interpreter is "reminded" of the food shortages during the First World War and the post-war marathon craze. Some details of the story are also decoded. The lady helpers represent the ruling class which flirts with religion, or they "remind" the critic of Kafka's fiancée. The watchers with the flashlights are the conscientious critics, etc. Finally the leopard is the businessman, the philistine, sensualism, even the somber shadow of advancing German fascism. One of these commentaries, the chapter on **"Ein Hungerkünstler"** in von Wiese's book on the German Novelle, differs from those of his predecessors in length and thoroughness. Like other Kafka scholars who have written about Kafka in recent years, he criticizes commentators of the older school for their fanciful speculations. However, he believes with many of them that Kafka's style prevents to a large degree the application of traditional categories of literary criticism. In particular, the distinction between symbol and allegory seems of little use to von Wiese.

The present article, because of a basically different approach, arrives at an interpretation of Kafka's work quite different from that of von Wiese. The distinction between allegory and symbol, for example, was of great help to the author. Definitions of the two terms will follow later, but a single illustration may serve, for the present, to clarify the main difference between them. Von Wiese defines Kafka's style as follows: "Es gehört zum Wesen dieses Stiles, daß sich das Abstrakte, Geistige und Problematische nur in der gleichnishaften Bildlichkeit aussagen läßt." The *geistige Aussage,* the intellectual, the abstract conveyed by images—that is the definition of allegory. Though von Wiese does not use the term, he treats Kafka's work as an allegory. It must be stressed, however, that in his disciplined interpretation there is no room for the free associational play of the imagination that we find so often in other commentaries

---

What Kafka had to say could only be said through images. But these images are symbols expressing nothing intellectual. Most of Kafka's works seem to express how it felt to be Franz Kafka.

—Meno Spann

The author shares von Wiese's conviction that what Kafka had to say could only be said through images. But these images are in the author's opinion symbols expressing nothing intellectual. It must be said in anticipation that Kafka's **"Ein Hungerkünstler"** will be interpreted as an intimate revelation of Kafka's *Lebensgefühl.* Most of Kafka's works seem to us to express how it felt to be Franz Kafka. He himself said that much when he defined the purpose of his writing: "die Darstellung meines traumhaften inneren Lebens." Rilke's magic with symbols makes the taste of an apple and an orange an experience mediated through words, but the respective sonnets are not allegories in that they do not communicate anything abstract. The *Erlebnis* of a fruit and the *Lebensgefühl* of Kafka required symbolic, not allegorical, expression. There seems to exist in modern criticism a sometimes unconscious rationalism which prefers a thought to a feeling or experience, even if this thought—we are thinking of some of the older allegorizers of Kafka—is only trivial.

The *Aussage* which von Wiese considers to be the meaning of our story is certainly not trivial but it is a highly abstract part of an allegorical equation: "Die Vernichtung des Naturhaften—bis zum Eigensinnigen gesteigert—zeigt auf eine indirekte und zwar grotesk entstellende Weise die auf einem anderen Wege nicht mehr darstellbare, auf Askese gegründete freie geistige Existenz." According to von Wiese, this *geistige Existenz,* the life of an artist for example, suffers in the world which is absurd and animalistic, though to this world such an intellectual ascetic seems absurd. The ascetic displays himself, and he sins by priding himself on his exceptionality. But he wins the final victory, he is the superior being even when the fascination of life appears in the form of a young leopard. Does this or a similar philosophy underlie Kafka's story? Does he unequivocally take the side of the suffering spirit against the *Naturhafte?* Is the little narrative an allegory? A reexamination of the story, of Kafka's life and autobiographical statements, and an examination of **"Ein Hungerkünstler"** in relation to his other stories and to Western literature may suggest another answer.

Any experienced reader encountering Hemingway's *The Old Man and the Sea* for the first time knows that this is "more" than just a deep-sea fishing story—such as are found in *Field and Stream;* and reading Kafka's **"Ein Hungerkünstler,"** he knows that this is "more" than just a circus story in the vein of J. Tully's *Circus Parade.* In the case of writers like Hemingway and Kafka, this something "more" is taken for granted, since the reader knows the author's rank and, with that, something about the critics' opinions of his work. But, though there is seldom the *tabula rasa* required for unbiased criticism, a sensitive reader will soon discover for himself whether he is dealing with a work of art or a mere adventure yarn.

Let us assume such a reader encountering Kafka's story in *Die Neue Rundschau* without knowing anything about its author. He will notice certain accents which remove that little tale, almost at the beginning, from the category of mere circus stories. The children, e.g., as figures of contrast, are more than just part of the crowd. Then there is the importance of the hunger artist, which is raised above the level of the fame and admiration he might acquire in a naturalistic story. Correspondingly, the final degradation and neglect suffered by the showman go beyond anything possible within an actual circus. There is ultimately, throughout the story, an intensity of feeling which has nothing to do with the mere banal admiration or pity a circus character's life might provoke. This intensity of feeling calls for weighty words and expressions, as for example, "die Welt betrog ihn um seinen Lohn," "neue kommende gnädigere Zeiten," etc., which would not fit into a tale about the freak show.

The reader's interest, however, stays within the narrative and with its symbolic hero, the hunger artist, who keeps his identity and remains the center of widening, but concentric circles of meaning—to use the familiar metaphor for a symbol's effect. All through the story, his *Lebensgefühl* becomes an ever more definite experience, while the character grows in tragic significance. His fall from the height of popularity to the level of a superfluous sideshow attraction is the tragic peripeteia. The ensuing catastrophe is carefully set off and lifted above the rest of the story by a number of stylistic devices.

Up to the climax of the story, Kafka presents the hero's professional and inner life in a summary style, applying adverbs and phrases like "gewöhnlich," "oft," "kein allzu häufiger Glücksfall," all of which skip time intervals. Abruptly, the passage of epic time slows down with the phrase, "Doch vergingen wieder viele Tage," which introduces the climax. With the first appearance of direct discourse, the action slows down further to give the illusion of "real" time, in this case the last minutes before the hero's death. Through this change of tempo and through the transition from a summarizing report to the dramatic presentation of one particular, atypical scene, everything that is said and done in this scene stands out. The transition from indirect to direct discourse is all the more impressive because it is the first time that we hear the hunger artist speak. Only once before in the story has he expressed his thoughts; this was neither in direct nor indirect discourse, but in that subtle variation of the interior monologue, sometimes called *erlebte Rede* or *style indirect libre*. In this passage, his thoughts were concerned with the great grief of his life, or better, with what he then considered as such: his impresario's insistence that he end his fasting periods after forty days. And this when he, the champion performer, knew that he could fast *ad infinitum*. Now, in direct discourse, he speaks of his final and greatest grief: the realization, arrived at *in articulo mortis*, that his hunger act was a farce. With his dying words: "Verzeiht mir alle . . . immerfort wollte ich, daß ihr mein Hungern bewundert, etc." begins the climax of the story. By the word "ihr" the dying man certainly does not mean the circus roustabouts and the stupidly amused overseer. The delirious showman has a vision of the enthusiastic audiences that used to fill the halls where he was on exhibition at the height of his fame.

Any unbiased reader will listen intently to the last words of the hero, for it is a device often encountered in literature and the dramatic arts to make an important point—often to present the climax—through the words of a dying man. A reader familiar with Kafka's work will recognize the "Too late!" as he knows it from **"Vor dem Gesetz,"** *Der Prozeß*, and *Das Schloß*. Josef K. in *Der Prozeß*, too, recognizes the futility of his life a few moments before he dies "like a dog!" The hunger artist is buried like a dog with the dirty straw on which he died. His last words indicate that he has arrived at the insight that his life was built on illusion and error, and was indeed a *vie manquée*. The outstanding achievements in his profession, which had been the pride and the meaning of his existence, were of no value; they were the result of an innate deficiency. He could not eat the food others liked, and therefore was not a complete human being. This weakness, this essential lack, was, however, the foundation of his fame. The crowds came to admire the hero with the iron will who could do what no other mortal could do so well: conquer man's grimmest enemy, hunger. However, what they really saw was a sick freak.

A modern name for the life of the hunger artist would be Heidegger's "unauthentic existence." Rilke, in whose Duino Elegies Heidegger observes poetic parallels to some of his own ideas, sees in the women, the child, the so-called primitive man, the animal, "Begnadete des Seins," because they above all have authentic existence. "Women" do not appear in the story, only two "young ladies," themselves feeble, unauthentic creatures. The authentic characters appear as figures of contrast: the children with their searching, sparkling eyes approach the hunger artist with sincere admiration, while the crowds of spectators merely want to be thrilled. The primitive men are the butchers. They too approach the hunger artist with genuine feelings, sympathy in this case; and their healthy appetite contrasts favorably with the showman's fasting.

The outstanding contrast figure, however, is the leopard, Kafka's beautiful leopard, so often besmirched by his anagogizing interpreters. It seems that Steinhauer in his commentary and by referring to Kafka's leopard as a panther introduced the "denigration" of the big cat. He rendered the German word *Panther,* which is the poetic synonym for leopard, by its English cognate which is commonly understood to designate the melanistic variety of the leopard, called in German *Schwarzpanther* or *Sundapanther*. The translation "panther" is misleading, since it symbolizes to many an American and English critic all that is black and evil. They may thus even feel encouraged to think of Dante's allegorical leopard, representing wantonness and envy. Such associations make the critic impervious to the beauty of Kafka's prose poem, a beauty equal to that of Rilke's famous quatrains on the leopard and as much a votive offering to Orpheus as that poet's sonnet on the Russian stallion.

As the reader of the *Rundschau* enjoys the last tumultuous scene in which the young leopard is the hero, his understanding expands within three concentric circles. True to his symbolic, not allegorical, character, the leopard is and remains the center of these circles. The understanding of his different aspects does therefore not proceed *realiter, spiritualiter,* and *mystice;* it is an unfolding understanding, not one that moves on different disconnected planes.

The leopard is first of all a beautiful animal. Anders denies the existence of "das Schöne im Alltagssinne" in Kafka's work. He seems to mean by this questionable phrase the beautiful as it is generally understood. The leopard passage proves him wrong, as do several other passages in the writer's work to be discussed later. Kafka has created by means of his simple prose a leopard, seen of course, as Hofmannsthal said, "mit den Augen der Poesie . . . die jedes Ding jedesmal zum ersten Mal sieht, die jedes Ding mit allen Wundern seines Daseins umgibt." By its mere presence, Kafka's leopard throws everything which was humanly questionable in the story into relief: the insincerity of the impresario and the two "young ladies," the vulgarity of the overseer and the crowd, and, most important of all, the human imperfection of the professional inediant, who lacked everything. His lack of appetite had led him into a meaningless existence, deprived of dignity, joy, and freedom; but about the leopard the author says, "Ihm fehlte nichts." "He lacked nothing." He had an abundance of everything the hunger artist missed. The reader joins the people on the circus lot who crowd around the cage, fascinated by something higher than the sensational or merely aesthetic appeal of the predator. The hunger artist appears now in all his frailty and ugliness as something inimical to life, and therefore condemned by it.

> Vegetarianism was an almost religious concern for Kafka. He even compared the vegetarians to the first Christians. Once Kafka is remembered as a suffering vegetarian, the hunger artist as a symbol loses much of his mystery.
>
> —*Meno Spann*

The fascinated reader, like the crowd, does not want to move away from the cage. He is still under the influence of the leopard as he puts the *Rundschau* away. But doubts now appear. The leopard has conquered; but was his conquest not a little too easy? Nature, das *Naive* in Schiller's sense, "das Dasein nach eigenen Gesetzen, die innere Notwendigkeit, die ewige Einheit mit sich selbst," wins easy victories over man, whom Thomas Mann once defined as *das Sorgenkind des Lebens*." Another passage from Schiller's essay *Über naive und sentimentalische Dichtung* may come to the reader's mind: "Solange wir Naturkinder waren, waren wir glücklich und vollkommen; wir sind frei geworden und haben beides verloren. Daraus entspringt eine doppelte und sehr ungleiche Sehnsucht nach der Natur, eine Sehnsucht nach ihrer Glückseligkeit, eine Sehnsucht nach ihrer Vollkommenheit. Den Verlust der ersten beklagt nur der sinnliche Mensch; um den Verlust der anderen kann nur der moralische Mensch trauern." This mourning over a lost perfection accompanies the remembrance of the hunger artist; it is the last feeling the leopard evokes in the reader as a *moralischer Mensch*. He thinks of the complexity of the unfortunate man, which made the selection of food problematic for him. The modern Kafka critic might well think of Kafka himself, for whom the choice of food was a lifelong practical difficulty, and whose vegetarianism was not the result of the fad of his day, so popular among writers and thinkers. Vegetarianism was an almost religious concern for Kafka. He even compared the vegetarians to the first Christians. Once Kafka is remembered as a suffering vegetarian, the hunger artist as a symbol loses much of his mystery. Seen in this light, the disillusioned showman is still defeated by the leopard but he is not shamed by him. He is buried like a dog, dirty straw and all, but even that last indignity degrades him no more than the relegation to the trash pile did Gregor Samsa, the cockroach man, in *Die Verwandlung*.

Von Wiese, who sees in the story an allegorical tale of the conflict between *Geist* and *Natur*, comes to a different conclusion: "Wer aber dennoch unbelehrbar bleibt und dem Panther vor dem Hungerkunstler den Vorzug gibt, sich also gegen den hungernden Geist und seine Absurdität und für die Faszination des Lebens entscheidet, der hat sich damit auch in jene verfremdete, tierhafte Welt zurückbegeben, die Kafka . . . aus den Angeln zu heben versuchte." Like unimpressed by the leopard's beauty and *heile Existenz* is Felix Weltsch. In full agreement with von Wiese he interprets the last and deepest *Sinnlinie*: "Im tiefsten Grunde hungert er also aus Ekel vor dem Essen, das den Menschen geboten wird, das die Natur des Menschen verlangt und deren gesunder Repräsentant der Panther ist, dem die Fleischfetzen, . . . so herrlich munden. Und man kann—und muß wohl—den Ekel des Hungerkünstlers vor dem Essen des Menschen weiter führen bis zum Ekel vor der ganzen sinnlichen Natur des Menschen." The main part of this paper will be an argument against these misobiotic interpretations but it should be pointed out right away that Weltsch shifts the accents of the showman's last speech and thus alters the meaning of the story. The dying man does not realize that he always felt disgust for food; he realizes that he could not find the right food and that consequently his performance was meaningless. He would have preferred the ability to eat like all the rest to his questionable achievement.

One might call the end of this story a Fortinbras-end, since the relation of Fortinbras and Hamlet is one of similar ambivalence. Kafka liked this kind of finish, as its repeated occurrence in his work proves. At the conclusion of *Die Verwandlung* the parents look with pride and delight at their beautiful marriageable daughter, who will compensate for the monstrosity rotting in a pile of garbage, the noble sufferer Gregor. *Das Urteil* ends with Georg's fatal fall from the bridge, which is followed by the almost brutal statement: "In diesem Augenblick ging über die Brücke ein geradezu unendlicher Verkehr." In *Josefine, die Sängerin*, the little problematic cantatrice is quickly forgotten in *gesteigerter Erlösung*, whereas *das Volk* continues in its unbroken strength.

We left the *Rundschau*-reader contemplating the ambivalent end of the story. Will he now try to extract its "theological" or "philosophical" content? He has not yet read Brod and Muir's commentaries, nor, as a German refugee in America, the faulty translations of two key passages in Brod's biography which make a saint of Kafka. Therefore, we do not believe that he will convince himself that the story must be an allegory about the role of religion in modern society, as the first commentator called it with great assurance. As a German reader, moreover, he would not be tempted by the compound -*Künstler* in the title to think of an artist. His verbal associations would be *Zauberkünstler, Kartenkünstler, Trapezkünstler*, even *Entkleidungskünstlerin;* they would stay in the realm of the circus and variety show. We imagine the reader would put away *Die Neue Rundschau* pondering the experience of a strange *Lebensgefühl* which the symbolic language of this story had conveyed to him. The modern reader of Kafka's fiction, diaries, and letters might feel that this *Lebensgefühl* is the author's own. He ordinarily does not feel it because he also knows that he must look for allegorical equations, preferably of a religious nature, in Kafka's works.

Shortly before the composition of **"Ein Hungerkünstler,"** Kafka had spoken of a *Plan der selbstbiographischen*

Untersuchungen. Our story is the most intimate of these investigations. Kafka was, even before his illness, very conscious of his body. Throughout the tale of the hunger artist we recognize, though it is presented in grotesque exaggeration, his own *Körpergefühl*. The skeletal thinness of the showman was a physical condition the suffering author knew from personal experience. At the time he wrote **"Ein Hungerkünstler,"** Kafka weighed only 55 kg though he measured 1,81 m, hence more than six feet, a fact known from one of his frequent laments about his thinness in a letter to Milena. In those years he still detested meat, as the following scene of forced feeding in an imaginary sanatorium shows: "Was soll ich dort? Vom Chefarzt zwischen die Knie genommen werden und an den Fleischklumpen würgen, die er mir mit den Karbolfingern in den Mund stopft und dann entlang der Gurgel hinunterdrückt." Similar feelings are present in the reaction of the hunger artist led to the *Krankenmahlzeit,* which the impresario will force down his throat. Later on, in the circus, he is deeply depressed at the sight of raw pieces of meat transported past his cage.

The *Körpergefühl* of the showman is only a part, though an important one, of his *Lebensgefühl*. The dominant feeling in the earlier years of his life was frustration. The world he wanted to impress with his feat did not permit him to do his utmost. During the last weeks of his life this same world fails to realize that he is still there, though dying in the straw. The grim insight ripens in the forgotten man that his life was built on error. Behind the muted sadness and the quixotic courtesy of this pitiable bag of bones is hidden despair over a *vie manquée*. We recognize the somewhat distorted image of Kafka as he appears in the last years of his life in his letters to Milena and in the descriptions of his friends.

The literary excellence of the story lies in the organic connection of *Körpergefühl* and *Lebensgefühl,* in the interplay between food in the literal sense and food in the metaphorical sense, i.e., as the condition of *heile Existenz* as the leopard represents it. But these two aspects are inseparable, and here lies the deepest reason that any allegorical separation of the "lower" and the "higher" world destroys the very structure of the little tale. The feelings emanating from this almost real showman and this very real leopard grow in the reader into something surpassing their individual cases, but they are feelings, not ideas. The showman and the leopard remain as the core of the aesthetic experience. We do not discard them like empty husks as we do with Dante's leopard, once we have understood him *spiritualiter* as envy and wantonness, or as we discard Pharaoh's fat and lean cows, once Joseph has translated this dream allegory. Goethe defined allegory and symbol as follows: "Es ist ein großer Unterschied, ob der Dichter zum Allgemeinen das Besondere sucht oder im Besonderen das Allgemeine schaut. Aus jener Art entsteht Allegorie, wo das Besondere nur als Beispiel, als Exempel des Allgemeinen gilt; die letztere ist aber eigentlich die Natur der Poesie: sie spricht ein Besonderes aus, ohne ans Allgemeine zu denken oder darauf hinzuweisen. Wer nun dieses Besondere lebendig faßt, erhält zugleich das Allgemeine mit, ohne es gewahr zu werden, oder erst spät."

Thus the symbolic character of the story makes it impossible to "translate" the meaning of each of its individual scenes. It is the totality of details which communicates the aesthetic experience. The allegorizer must find for each of these details a corresponding interpretation unless he assumes that Kafka allowed himself some *chevilles*. None of these interpreters have been that thorough, and the allegorical equations they present for the details they selected to explain are unconvincing, sometimes fantastic.

Kafka's other works contain passages which, in their metaphors or topicality, show a relationship to *"Ein Hungerkünstler."* They all center around the idea of a *vie manquée,* of authentic and unauthentic existence, to use these anachronistic but useful terms. Georg Bendemann (**Das Urteil**) grasps—"wie ein Hungriger die Nahrung"— the bridge railing from which he is going to fall to an atoning death. Gregor Samsa (**Die Verwandlung**) tries to crawl to his violin-playing sister: "Ihm war, als zeige sich ihm der Weg zu der ersehnten unbekannten Nahrung." The vulgar scrubwoman, who announces his death and disposes unceremoniously of his remains, has the same function as the overseer in **"Ein Hungerkünstler."** Grete Samsa's epitaph in its literal and symbolic sense fits the hunger artist: "Seht nur, wie mager es war. Er hat ja auch schon so lange Zeit nichts gegessen." In *Der Bau,* the problem of food shortage is one of the animal's main problems, but here, too, the metaphorical usage of food appears: "Denn alles, was ich dort [im Bau] tue, ist gut und sättigt mich gewissermaßen." Eating and food also play an important symbolic part in *Amerika*. The horror and misery of Brunelda's world is accentuated by the disgusting way in which Robinson eats sardines and licks candy. In contrast the banquet in the nature theater in Oklahoma reflects paradisiacal conditions. And this is paradise as Kafka described it to Brod in a conversation about the novel's conclusion: "Mit rätselhaften Worten deutete Kafka lächelnd an, daß sein junger Held in diesem fast grenzenlosen Theater Beruf, Freiheit, Rückhalt, ja sogar die Heimat und die Eltern wie durch paradiesischen Zauber wiederfinden werde." Kafka defined *Rückhalt* in the same sense with a far cry from Kierkegaard: "Eine Frau haben, das hieße Halt auf allen Seiten haben, Gott haben." There is an abundance of such outcries in his diaries and Kafka's life story shows how he sought so intensely and, tragically enough, found too late, *Erlösung durch das Weib*. How could this man have glorified in his hunger artist that ascetic contempt and opposition to nature and world which the majority of the interpreters postulate?

Closely related to the quoted passages from his work are diary entries and statements in his letters that attest the autobiographical character of **"Ein Hungerkünstler."** These are to be found in all the phases of his life and culminate, so to speak, in that symbolic tale. Early in his university career he wrote: "Man beiße lieber ins Leben als in seine Zunge." Full participation in life, "engagement," would remain Kafka's ideal, but isolation was his fate. At a later time (1912), he describes himself as life's hunger artist: "Als es in meinem Organismus klar geworden war, dass das Schreiben die ergiebigste Richtung meines Wesens sei, drängte sich alles hin und ließ alle Fähigkeiten leer stehen, die sich auf die Freuden des Geschlechtes, des Essens, des Trinkens, des philosophischen Nachdenkens, der Musik zuallerest richteten. *Ich magerte nach allen diesen Richtungen ab.*" (Italics mine) This intermingling of the physical (*Organismus*) with the inner life, reaching a climax in the metaphor *abmagern,* is typical of the structure of **"Ein Hungerkünstler,"** where lack of appetite in the literal sense was fused with the *Lebensgefühl* of an unauthentic existence. Significantly enough, Kafka returns in the same diary entry to food in the literal sense. After he has once more decried his ignorance of love and music, he laments at the same pitch his frugal New Year's meal, consisting of *Schwarzwurzeln mit Spinat.* The simple food metaphor makes an occasional appearance, e.g. "Strindberg gelesen, der mich nährt." In the months preceding and following the composition of **"Ein Hungerkünstler"** (October, 1921 to March, 1922), however, it occurs frequently. "Da ich doch Mensch bin und die Wurzeln Nahrung wollen . . . weil meine Hauptnahrung von anderen Wurzeln in anderer Luft kommt, auch diese Wurzeln kläglich, doch lebensfähiger; . . . Nur vorwärts, hungriges Tier, führt der Weg zur eßbaren Nahrung, atembaren Luft, freiem Leben, sei es auch hinter dem Leben . . . Es ist die Nahrung, von der ich gedeihe, auserlesene Speisen, auserlesen gekocht. . . . Das Glück der jungen und alten Ehemänner, das einzige, an dem mich zu sättigen ich Anlage habe." The sudden increase in food metaphors is accompanied by frequent laments over his unfulfilled existence. Kafka was conscious of approaching his fortieth year, which to him as to Goethe meant a caesura in man's existence. Goethe said: "Ich will lernen und mich ausbilden, ehe ich vierzig Jahre alt werde." One of Kafka's self admonitions begins with an allusion to this Goethe passage: "Lerne (lerne Vierzigjähriger). . . ." He now condemns himself because of his wasted life as he had condemned Josef K. ten years before *nel mezzo del cammin* to the Inferno of *The Trial.* The most remarkable of these laments about his *vie manquée* was written shortly before the composition of **"Ein Hungerkünstler"**:

> Die Eltern spielten Karten; ich saß allein dabei, gänzlich fremd; der Vater sagte, ich solle mitspielen oder wenigstens zuschauen; ich redete mich irgendwie aus. Was bedeutet diese seit der Kinderzeit vielmals wiederholte Ablehnung? Das gemeinschaftliche, gewissermaßen das öffentliche Leben wurde mir durch die Einladung zugänglich gemacht . . . trotzdem lehnte ich ab. Ich habe, wenn man es danach beurteilt, unrecht, wenn ich mich beklage, daß mich der Lebensstrom niemals ergriffen hat, daß ich von Prag nie loskam, niemals auf Sport oder ein Handwerk gestoßen wurde und dergleichen.— Ich hätte das Angebot wahrscheinlich immer abgelehnt, ebenso wie die Einladung zum Spiele. Ich lehnte es aber immer ab, wohl aus allgemeiner und besonders aus Willensschwäche, ich habe das verhältnismäßig sehr spät erst begriffen. Ich hielt diese Ablehnung früher meist für ein gutes Zeichen (verführt durch die allgemeinen großen Hoffnungen, die ich auf mich setze).

The food metaphor is not used in this passage, but we find here important parallels to the inner life of the hunger artist: the unwillingness to participate in life, to partake of life's food, the reason for this unwillingness—a weakness;

the illusion that this weakness is a sign of greatness; and the late recognition of this tragic illusion.

An extraordinary man like Kafka is always on display; he must make a "show" of himself, no matter how retiring he may be. Kafka's "spectators" reacted like the hunger artist's audiences—with admiration, with concern for his literal and metaphorical *Abmagern,* with doubts of his sincerity, sometimes with open mockery.

—*Meno Spann*

An extraordinary man like Kafka is always on display; he must make a "show" of himself, no matter how retiring he may be. Kafka's "spectators" reacted like the hunger artist's audiences—with admiration, with concern for his literal and metaphorical *Abmagern,* with doubts of his sincerity, sometimes with open mockery.

In another diary entry from his last period Kafka describes in glowing colors a likewise glowing picture of Sunday boating on the Thames. His description, it seems to the author, fits Edward J. Gregory's painting "Boating on the Thames" showing a fleet of rowboats, canoes, punts, and launches near Boulter's Lock above London. They are headed for the tea gardens and picnic grounds beyond Cliveden Reach. If Kafka cannot join this sensuous festival of life, if he, the poor *Hungerleider,* has to stand aside at the shore, the reasons are his *"Abstammung, Erziehung, körperliche Ausbildung"* and not a Neo-Platonic or Christian disgust with sensuous pleasures. Yet the majority of interpreters of **"Ein Hungerkünstler"** envisage a confession of asceticism in this and many other tales of Kafka the oarsman, the swimmer, the frustrated athlete, who wanted to find delivery in a spouse's arm and before a cradle.

The ambiguity of the leopard scene has been discussed. There can be, however, no doubt that the loving description of the leopard was dictated by Kafka's sincere admiration for the animal's authentic existence even in captivity. The closest parallel in his diaries to the leopard scene is a passage written about six months before the story appeared. "Buschleben. Eifersucht auf die glückliche, unerschöpfliche und doch sichtbar aus Not (nicht anders als ich) arbeitende, aber immer alle Forderungen des Gegners erfüllende Natur. Und so leicht, so musikalisch." Symbols representing this *heile Existenz* are rare in his work, since he described the hunger he knew so well but seldom the desired food. Besides the leopard, there is the chimpanzee before he was humanized. The only human representatives are Samsa's sister (*Die Verwandlung*), the American (*Die Abweisung*), and, on a heroic level, Alexander the Great (*Der neue Advokat*).

On his deathbed Kafka read the proofs of the book **"Ein Hungerkünstler"** and events in his life which were related to the title story went through his mind. The moribund patient wrote his thoughts on slips of paper, since he had to rest his infected larynx. He describes a childhood scene, in which he, the little *Knochenbündel,* after a bath at the public swimming pool, was treated to sausage and beer by his gigantic father. He develops once more the leopard motive with allusions to the leopard scene in his story. "Mein Cousin, dieser herrliche Mensch. Wenn dieser Rob-ert . . . auf die Sophienschwimmschule kam, die Kleider mit ein paar Griffen abwarf, ins Wasser sprang *und sich dort herumwälzte mit der Kraft eines schönen wilden Tieres* (italics mine), glänzend vom Wasser, mit strahlenden Augen und gleich weit fort war gegen das Wehr zu—das war herrlich." It was the tragic irony of Kafka's last year that he, life's hunger artist, was beginning to discover the food he liked in the real and in the metaphorical sense. A child from a beloved woman, a *Heimat* without the melancholy quotes he was forced in his last years to put around that word when referring to Prague, these seemed to be within his reach when death intervened.

Kafka's influence on other writers is often pointed out, but the fact that he, too, was influenced is generally neglected, though his work is part of the tradition of Western literature. Seen against this larger background, it gains in depth and clarity of meaning. **"Ein Hungerkünstler"** is no exception; and the basic assumption of the author that it is the story of a *vie manquée* gains additional support from this viewpoint.

There is a close resemblance in both structure and content between Kafka's tale and Tolstoy's *The Death of Ivan Ilyitch,* one of Kafka's favorites among Tolstoy's writings. Kafka had reread Tolstoy's story as late as December 23, 1921, and **"Ein Hungerkünstler"** is mentioned for the first time early in 1922. There seems to be sufficient cause to assume that he wrote his story shortly after reading the Russian tale of a *vie manquée* which, as stylistic and thematic similarities indicate, had obviously inspired him. Tolstoy uses the same devices to skip time intervals already encountered in Kafka's story: "Nach siebenjähriger Amtstätigkeit in derselben Stadt" . . . "In dieser Weise gingen noch sieben Jahre hin" . . . "So war Iwan Iljitschs Leben während der siebzehn Jahre seiner Heirat gewesen." With the beginning of Ivan's fatal disease, the passage of epic time slows down from months to weeks, finally from days to the moments preceding death. Not until a few days before the final agony does the pensive sufferer arrive at the tragic insight: "Mein ganzes Leben, das bewußte Leben, ist wohl in der Tat nicht das rechte gewesen." Like the hunger artist, Ivan cannot reveal to anyone the truth his dimming eyes have seen. His insensitive wife watches him die with compassion but with as little understanding as the overseer had for the dying hunger artist. The role of the contrast figure, corresponding to Kafka's leopard, falls in Tolstoy's story to Gerassim, the young peasant lad and servant of Ivan. He is the only one living an authentic existence in that household of sham beings: "Die Kraft und Lebens-

freudigkeit Gerassims kränkten ihn nicht, ja, sie wirkten beruhigend auf Iwan Iljitsch."

Closely related to the motif of *la vie manquée* is that of *der Fahrende* as one of its representatives. The saltimbanque and the circus performer had become familiar symbols in the twentieth century of that century's growing feeling of forlornness and metaphysical wretchedness. The Saltimbanque pictures of Picasso and Rilke's fifth Duino elegy are the outstanding examples. The hunger artist has colleagues in Kafka's melancholy circus. The first of these to appear was the equestrienne in **"Auf der Galerie."** The unpitying circus director and the unfeeling spectators force the ailing equestrienne to perform on and on in the surreal circus ring. The tragedy and the sham existence of this performer are revealed to an outsider. He would like to but cannot break through this sham beauty and false front behind which a gruesome reality hides, a reality revealed in the hyena grin of Seurat's and Lautrec's circus directors. In **"Erstes Leid"** the grim revelation occurs early in the career of the showman, the trapeze artist, who realizes his *Haltlosigkeit:* "Nur diese eine Stange in den Händen, . . . wie kann ich denn leben!" To all of Kafka's showmen apply the opening lines of Rilke's Saltimbanque Elegy which appeared one year after Kafka's story:

> Wer aber sind sie, sag mir, die Fahrenden, diese ein
> wenig
> Flüchtigern noch als wir selbst, die dringend von
> früh an
> wringt ein wem—wem zuliebe
> niemals zufriedener Wille?

The germs of Kafka's circus stories, together with the basic motifs of other, yet unwritten works, appear in one of his earliest diary entries, written twelve years before **"Ein Hungerkünstler,"** further proof that these circus symbols were expressions of his own inner life. The unmarried author decries his lack of attachment to life: "Der Mann [the Kafkaesque bachelor—this and the following parenthetical insertions are mine] steht nun einmal außerhalb unseres Volkes [K. in *Das Schloß*], ausserhalb unserer Menschheit [**"Ein Hungerkünstler"**], immerfort ist er ausgenhungert [*"Ein Hungerkünstler"*], ihm gehört nur der Augenblick, der immer fortgesetzte Augenblick der Plage [**"Auf der Galerie"**], er hat . . . nur so viel Halt, als seine zwei Hände bedecken, also um so viel weniger als der Trapezkünstler im Variété [**"Erstes Leid"**]."

A few remarks should be made about the *Verfremdung* in our story. Some allegorizing interpreters consider it more fantastic than it is because certain naturalistic aspects of Kafka's showman and his life seem to them to be the author's grotesque inventions. Kafka took his subject matter for **"Ein Hungerkünstler"** from life; he was sympathetically and empathetically familiar with the world of *der Fahrende.* To illustrate the "objective correlative" for Kafka's hunger artist and to facilitate the recognition of naturalist aspects in his story, the English handbill advertising a German *Hungerkünstler* may be quoted. The showman's sobriquet is, significantly enough, Heros: "Come and see the Starvation Artist Heros; World's Champion in

1950 at the Frankfurt Zoo with 56 days of starvation; he will establish a new World Championship, 75 days without taking any food in a sealed glass box; medical care, controlled by the Red Cross Frankfurt-Main; during his time of starvation Heros will have only cigarettes and Hassia Mineral Water. . . ." The methods and accoutrements of this starvation artist are much the same as those of the fictitious one. Carbonation has been added to the plain water of Kafka's showman, he smokes cigarettes and sits in a glass box, instead of a cage, but those are simply negligible modern touches.

Other aspects of the story are also explainable in view of the particular "objective correlative". The opening sentence: "In den letzten Jahrzehnten ist das Interesse an Hungerkünstlern sehr zurückgegangen" sounds at first reading like the "Once upon a time" of an allegorical fairytale, but it is correct. The "golden age" of hunger artists was in the eighties of the nineteenth century. The American physician Dr. Henry Tanner established in 1880 a world record with forty fasting days which was broken when the Italian Merlatti endured fifty days of supervised fasting in the great hall of the Grand Hotel in Paris. That Kafka's showman feels he could go far beyond the forty day mark is believable. Heros' latest (1956) record is 93 days.

Fortunately the allegorizers, particularly the religious school, overlooked the opportunities the number forty offers to cabalistic interpretations. They missed the forty days of Christ's fast and the forty years of the Israelites in the desert. They might have considered Goethe's explanation that the figure forty is dedicated to *Beschauen, Erwarten,* above all to *Absonderung.* It is, however, unlikely, considering the realistic details of the story, that Kafka even thought of the cabalistic character of the number forty. Not the Bible but the records of Dr. Tanner, Succi, and Merlatti, well known to Kafka's generation, furnished the forty fasting days. These forty days are just as real as the protruding thorax, the black tights, the attacks of raging mania, and the final *delirium inanitionis* of his professional inediant. The only distortion, *Verfremdung,* in Kafka's story is the indifference of the circus to the fate of its unsuccessful employee. The freak of the sideshow would in reality be on the payroll and, hence, on the conscience of the circus management.

Much older than the motif of *der Fahrende* is the topos "man and the big cat," which plays such a decisive part at the end of the story. Using the concept of topos, we imply also the idea of *tradicionalidad literaria,* confident that such an approach does not make Kafka's work less original but more intelligible. The topos of man and the big cat is older than the Mycenean gate and the Homeric similies. When man was confronted with the lion, it was done to praise him or make a statement about his status. Up to the time of Goethe, man's superiority was always assumed wherever the topos was used, but that changed during the nineteenth century. At first particular human types, finally, in the twentieth century, man in general was humbled before the predators which are usually lion, leopard, and eagle. Nietzsche, the most articulate and passionate accuser

of nascent modern man, turned his metaphorical leopards loose on the drab Northern European *Herdenmenschen:* "Das du in Urwäldern / Unter buntgefleckten Raubtieren / Sündlich gesund und bunt und schön liefest." One cannot escape the melancholy observation that the praise of the "sinfully healthy" leopard in Nietzsche's and kafka's case stems from mortally sick authors.

After Nietzsche's time, the conviction spread among those concerned with literary symbols and the evaluation of man that a great metaphysical loss has been suffered, that man has been "unkinged," in Emerson's sense. The topos with its reversed evaluation of man and beast is now incorporated in the works of authors ranging from Hermann Hesse to Ernest Hemingway. The two following examples again are chosen because of their chronological proximity to Kafka's work. In the fourth of his Duino Elegies Rilke accuses man of losing his cosmic rhythm and being poisoned by an incomplete understanding of death. He concludes:

> "Und irgendwo gehn Löwen noch und wissen
> solang sie herrlich sind von keiner Ohnmacht."

Two years after Kafka's story *Der Zauberberg* appeared. In it, Thomas Mann also speaks about man, life's problem child, about his *Stand und Staat* and he, too, uses the topos in its "modern revision." A few days before his long-contemplated suicide the regal Mynheer Peeperkorn leads his "followers" on an excursion into the mountain wilderness. Here Settembrini and Naphta do their dialectical best to impress the company with a display of their counterpositions. Peeperkorn interrupts their gladiatorial oratory and points to an eagle soaring high above the group of quarreling sick men: "Der Adler, meine Herrschaften, Jupiters Vogel, der König seines Geschlechtes, der Leu der Lüfte! . . . Stoß nieder, schlag ihm mit dem Eisenschnabel auf den Kopf und in die Augen, reiß ihm den Bauch auf, dem Wesen, das dir Gott . . . Perfekt! Erledigt! After the company has settled down for one of Peeperkorn's impromptu banquets, the topos is taken up again in a way which strongly suggests **"Ein Hungerkünstler"** as a model: "Es gab Einkehr, es gab ein Essen und Trinken, ganz ausser der Zeit, jedoch mit einem Appetit, der durch das stille Gedenken an den Adler befeuert ward." If Mann's eagle was inspired by Kafka's leopard, then these passages in *Der Zauberberg* may be considered the first though indirect commentary on **"Ein Hungerkünstler"** and, in the author's opinion, a better one than many of those which followed.

The appetite that Kafka's leopard may inspire is weakened by the *stille Gedenken* the dead hunger artist deserves. When used by literary masters, the common topoi appear in subtle variations—and Kafka was a literary master. His work, we would like to emphasize in conclusion, is part of the Western tradition of literature, from which he borrowed and to which he added, for example, a beautiful leopard whom the allegorizers want to poison. For that life, among other things, we are pleading in this article.

H. M. Waidson (essay date 1960)

SOURCE: "The Starvation Artist and the Leopard," in *The Germanic Review*, Vol. XXXV, No. 4, December, 1960, pp. 262-69.

[*In the following essay, Waidson disagrees with Meno Spann's interpretation of the roles of the occupants of the cage in "A Hunger Artist" and seeks to "restore the starvation-artist to his former central position and relegate the leopard to a less exalted status."*]

In his imaginative writing Kafka gives an impression of being at an immense distance from the people and creatures he describes, and the effects of humor and controlled melancholy are intensified by this appearance of objectivity. The short story **"Ein Hungerkünstler"** in particular has attracted analysis, since the simple sequence of its events, the almost complete absence of the obviously absurd, the fact that the tale has been brought to a conclusion, that the author has restrained himself from inserting passages of elaborate argument, arouse in the reader the conviction that here Kafka is distilling his "dream-like inner life" in as concentrated and artistic a way as is likely to be found anywhere. Mr. Meno Spann's article ["Franz Kafka's Leopard," *The Germanic Review* XXXIV, No. 2, 1959] on this fascinating and elusive story is instructive in many respects, but his interpretation of the roles of the two occupants of the cage appears to me to be far from convincing. His concluding sentence commends Kafka for having added to "the Western tradition of literature" "a beautiful leopard whom the allegorizers want to poison." This is putting the cart before the horse, in other words, the leopard before the starvation-artist. At the risk of being thrown into Mr. Spann's limbo of "maimed psychoanalysts, sociologists, philosophers and theologians," I should like briefly to run through this story again as I see it, in an endeavor to restore the starvation-artist to his former central position and to relegate the leopard to a less exalted status.

"In the last decades the interest in starvation-artists has declined very much. Whereas it was formerly well worth while organizing great performances of this sort as a show of their own, today this is quite impossible. Times were different then." These opening words place the narrator a long way from his subject-matter. He is recounting events that could only have taken place decades ago, for historical reasons, and are unimaginable "today." Kafka does not explain the historical position of the starvation-artist in the world of entertainment (that has since been done by Mr. Spann); the reader will perhaps think that this career is the fabrication of a fantastic imagination, even if the bounds of everyday realism are apparently not overstepped. Mr. Spann has provided evidence of the realism of the background; the golden age of starvation-artists was the 1880's, when a world record of forty days was soon to be beaten by one of fifty, though a revival of the art has led to a new record of ninety-three days being set in Frankfurt in 1956. (Perhaps, incidentally, we live in the "new, coming, more gracious times" which Kafka's narrator sees in the "light" of the children's "observant eyes.") But why

should this evidence exclude the interpretation of the forty days in terms of the Israelites' wanderings in the desert and of Jesus Christ's fasting in the wilderness? Kafka may well have been deliberately ambivalent here.

In a number of his works Kafka happily relates events in the first person singular (e.g., **"Ein Landarzt," "Ein Bericht für eine Akademie," "Forschungen eines Hundes"**) or from the point of one man, though in the third person (*Der Prozeß, Das Schloß*). But the starvation-artist is seen both from outside and from within his own consciousness. In the first section, the account of the starvation-artist's career in prosperity, the reader is shown the starvation-artist, his relations with the public, with the butcher guardians, the manager and the chosen ladies, from the standpoint of an omniscient narrator. The period of success is followed, a few years later, by "that previously mentioned turning-point"; the second section of the story is a description of the starvation-artist's latter years, after fashion has changed and there is no room for a man of his calling except on the way to the animals. Here again we follow the starvation-artist's thought much of the time, but the narrator also records the ironical smile of the "professional colleagues" at the starvation-artist's hopes of surprising the world with his achievements even now, and describes him as being "apparently respected by the world, but with all that mostly in melancholy mood." Or the narrator himself castigates the casual charge of cheating which is made by one of the starvation-artist's later onlookers as "the most stupid lie that indifference and innate malice could invent, for it was not the starvation-artist who was deceiving, he worked honestly, but the world deceived him of his reward." These words, coming at the end of the second section of the story, are interesting as a revelation that the unknown narrator, recounting the events years after they are all over, still feels his sympathies personally involved on the starvation-artist's behalf. Kafka's narrator is reconstructing episodes from a past that most people have forgotten, but he feels so deeply for the starvation-artist that he puts in his own indignant comments on his hero's account: "Try to explain the art of fasting to somebody! To him who does not feel it, it cannot be made comprehensible."

While the starvation-artist's career in prosperity and then neglect is being described, the past tense has an imperfect meaning and dialogue is not used. As his fasting is a solitary, dedicated operation, he is essentially passive in his way of life; his work excludes him from society, though it exposes him to its gaze. After the episodes illustrating the main course of his life follow the two final paragraphs of the story. The dialogue between the circus-attendant and the starvation-artist, who is lying in the dirty straw, is full of tension; the past tense is used historically, up to the climax of the dying man's last-minute revelation. The narrator achieves a certain rhetorical pathos here, as if knowing that the death-bed confession has been worth his listeners' waiting for: "Those were the last words, but there was still in his glazed eyes the firm, even if no longer proud conviction that he would go on fasting." If the story had ended at this point, there would be no reason for doubting its completeness; the starvation-artist has died, living just long enough to be able to reveal to the circus-attendants his last reflections of repentance, explanation, and resolution.

> **Like so many of Kafka's characters the starvation-artist is between two worlds; the old, familiar life of common sense has become distasteful or unaccountably alienated, while the new world has not yet been revealed.**
>
> **—H. M. Waidson**

Apart from the last paragraph, the story is a gradual unfolding of the starvation-artist's situation and personality through characteristic episodes and through comments from the narrator. Even during the period of his international success, the starvation-artist has to reckon with being regarded as "often only a joke" by adults and with receiving unqualified admiration only from children. Elaborate precautions are taken to ensure that he does not cheat, and this depresses him, for he has nothing to fear on this account: "only the starvation-artist himself could know that, only he therefore could at the same time be the observer completely satisfied with his own fasting." One simple reason for the starvation-artist's honesty is that he finds fasting easy: "it was the easiest thing in the world." The forty-day limit to the fasting period is imposed by his manager, and is resented by the performer, who, however, endures the charade against his better judgment. The ladies who are to carry him out of his cage are his enemies because they put an ending to his fasting and lead him to food, the thought of which makes him feel nauseated. "And he looked up into the eyes of the apparently so friendly, in reality so cruel ladies . . ." Their sympathy is superficial, and based on a misconception. What appears to the mass of spectators as friendliness is from his point of view cruelty. Reality for the starvation-artist is not what it is for other people; his feet scrape on the ground as he is being carried, as if this were not the real ground, "as if they were just beginning to look for it." When feminine emotion is brought into contact with the alien world of professional fasting, it expresses itself in helpless tears "amid the delighted laughter of the spectators." K. in *Das Schloß* has to wrestle with the world of emotions represented by the various women and by their relationships with Klamm and himself; if K. wishes to fulfill his quest, he must overcome the world of Klamm and penetrate beyond. For the starvation-artist this particular barrier presents no difficulties.

In the midst of his successes the starvation-artist is melancholy but not afraid. An occasional fury of rage follows any well-meant suggestion that his melancholy may be due to his fasting, for he sees this too as an oblique reflection on the merit of his calling: ". . . to the terror of all

(he) began to shake on the iron bars like an animal." These moods do not recur in the second period, when he is neglected by the world and able to realize his ambition to carry on fasting as long as he likes: "but nobody counted the days, not even the starvation-artist himself knew how great the achievement already was, and his heart became heavy." The starvation-artist has overcome all attachment to the world, to material pleasures, human society and bourgeois normality. His quest for a second reality is, however, unfulfilled. Like so many of Kafka's characters he is between two worlds; the old, familiar life of common sense has become distasteful or unaccountably alienated, while the new world has not yet been revealed. Gregor Samsa in *Die Verwandlung* and Josef K. in *Der Prozeß* are rudely thrown out of lives of unthinking normality and plunged lost into a world where their previous values have no meaning. Gregor has an inkling of a new, higher order of experience, and the mood of his insect-state is similar to that of the starvation-artist in his later periods. The short final paragraph of "**Ein Hungerkünstler**" forms a coda introducing the leopard as new material into the story as a device for rounding it off to a satisfying conclusion. In *Die Verwandlung,* Gregor's death is followed by a comparable concluding section where the Samsa family is relieved and reinvigorated by being rid of him. They become arrogant and unjust, as in their treatment of the charwoman who has disposed of Gregor's remains, and Grete blossoms out ("at the end of their journey she stood up first and stretched her young body") into feline marriageability. Kafka had a lot of trouble with the concluding sections of his narratives (the three novels are the best known instances). If *Die Verwandlung* and "**Ein Hungerkünstler**" are in this respect artistically satisfying, while having their elements of ambiguity, Kafka was not always so successful. Emrich's analysis of *In der Strafkolonie* brings forward concrete evidence of Kafka's own dissatisfaction with its coda section to this tale. Josef K. in *Der Prozeß* in particular resists and resents being wrenched out of normality. On the other hand, K. in *Das Schloß* has chosen to come to the strange village as a surveyor, and is actively struggling to penetrate through the obstructive bureaucracy of the castle in order to realize fulfillment beyond. Josef K. is a hunted man, but K., like the starvation-artist, has taken the initiative and is unafraid. Artistic achievement may be subject to distortion through routine, showmanship, and vanity, but not through fear; for creative work is an attack on the public, even when it takes the passive form of the starvation-artist's abstract art where words, color, or music have no part, and where time is the one defining factor. The achievement of the starvation-artist has all the qualities of that of the seven dancing dogs in "**Forschungen eines Hundes**"; they do not talk or sing, they are deliberately silent, their performance is artistic and unique, they are courageous and strong, they defy nature, but yet they seem to be in need of help and arouse the watching puppy to intense wonder. "It could not be anxiety on account of success or failure that moved them so; whoever dared such things and carried them out, could no longer be afraid.—Afraid of what, then? For who was compelling them to do what they were doing here?"

The starvation-artist is unafraid; in the end he acknowledges guilt and asks for forgiveness. In these respects he has put behind him attachment to the material world in a way that Josef K. never does. The starvation-artist dies convinced of the rightness of his striving, even if aware of his own shortcomings, and does not despair of the world order and of the values of his place in it. He dies a martyr's death, not the bewildered, nearly hopeless death of Josef K. The latter persists in plans of resistance almost to the end, even when he recognizes their futility. "There was nothing heroic, if he resisted, if he now made difficulties for the gentlemen, if now in his last defence he still tried to enjoy the last glimmer of life." The "last mistake," he thinks, is on the part of the authorities, and is not his responsibility. Then the stranger leans out of the distant window and stretches out his hands; there is a possibility of sympathy and help, but Josef K. has to die "like a dog." The starvation-artist's death is by contrast one of full acceptance of his situation, based on the final insight that if the world-order is right, his life must have been wrong, or at least must have contained a serious flaw. "Forgive me, all of you," he whispers. He has attempted his mission alone, but for success he needed the co-operation of all. In **"Forschungen eines Hundes"** all dogs must use their teeth to help if the marrow from the iron bones is to become available ("But it is only an image. The marrow under discussion here is not a food, it is the opposite, is poison.") Josef K. wonders whether the man looking out of the window was "an individual" or "everybody." The starvation-artist, then, acknowledges the need for forgiveness by "all," separated from whom he has vainly carried on his life. The circus-attendant gives him a form of absolution with patronizing amusement, but the starvation-artist insists on explaining why he requires it: "I continually wanted you to admire my fasting." The motive for his action has been self-regarding, not only during the period of his success but much later too. But his fasting was no merit; he could "do no other," and his last words explain why: "Because I could not find the food that I like. If I had found it, believe me, I would have made no fuss and would have eaten my fill like you and everybody else." The starvation-artist must locate the fault within himself, in order to find conviction that his life's aim and the order of the universe are right. The last word he utters again speaks of the whole community: "everybody else," or "all." Once more **"Forschungen eines Hundes,"** which was written shortly after **"Ein Hungerkünstler"** and is close to it in its theme of food and metaphysical striving, throws light on this tale. "More and more, lately, I reflect on my life," the dog says, "I look for the decisive mistake which I have perhaps made, that has made everything go wrong, and I can't find it. And yet I must have made it, for if I had not made it, and in spite of that had not attained what I wanted through the honest labor of a long life, it would be proved that what I wanted was impossible, and complete despair would result from it." Josef K. in *Der Prozeß* refuses to admit that he has done anything wrong, refuses to acknowledge that there is any reason why he should not be allowed to go on living the care-free life of a comfortably off, unmarried bank employee. The starvation-artist has broken away from bourgeois normality and made his life into an ascetic quest. If he has failed to find the right food, he has at least realized the inadequacy of earthly food. The question of the right food is raised in many of Kafka's works, usually in the same sense as in **"Ein Hungerkünstler,"** though nowhere so insistently, nor with such serenity, as in **"Forschungen eines Hundes."** Here death is averted for the time being; the dog, having fasted until a haemorrhage brings him to the point of exhaustion, is saved by the hunting dog's music which inspires him to leap ecstatically from the "pool of blood and dirt" where he has been lying.

Mr. Spann has noted that Kafka read Tolstoy's *The Death of Ivan Ilych* on December 23, 1921. If the starvation-artist's death is to be compared with that of Ivan Ilych, the point of essential comparison seems to lie in passages such as these: "At that very moment Ivan Ilych fell through and caught sight of the light, and it was revealed to him that though his life had not been what it should have been, this could still be rectified . . . He tried to add, "forgive me," but said "forego" and waved his hand, knowing that He whose understanding mattered would understand . . . In place of death there was light."

The leopard of the final paragraph is a device to round off a story in which it has had no previous part, unless its advent was anticipated in the starvation-artist's rattling on the bars of his cage "like an animal." It is doubtful whether English usage normally ascribes any pejorative meaning to "panther" which is absent from "leopard." The *Encyclopaedia Britannica* (13th ed., 1926) says "panther" is "another name for the leopard," and describes the leopard's habits in terms which are not calculated to arouse admiration:

> In habits the leopard resembles the other large cat-like animals, yielding to none in the ferocity of its disposition. It is exceedingly quick in its movements, but seizes its prey by waiting in ambush or stealthily approaching to within springing distance, when it suddenly rushes upon it and tears it to the ground with its powerful claws and teeth. It preys upon almost any animal it can overcome, such as antelopes, deer, sheep, goats, monkeys, peafowl, and has a special liking for dogs. It not unfrequently attacks human beings in India, chiefly children and old women, but instances have been known of a leopard becoming a regular "man-eater." When favorable opportunities occur, it often kills many more victims than it can devour at once, either to gratify its propensity for killing or for the sake of their fresh blood.

The creature's presence certainly gives an ironic twist to the tale, making the reader aware of the dichotomy between mind and life, but not to the extent of asking him to abandon the sympathy aroused by the starvation-artist's life and death and suddenly to accept the leopard's as the right attitude. The circus-attendant, it is true, thinks the dying starvation-artist mad and slightly comic, but Kafka's narrator, we have already seen, certainly does not share this attitude. It is appropriate, too, that the circus visitors, previously indifferent to the starvation-artist's feats, should crowd round the leopard in appreciation, and that "the joy of life," man's animal nature, should have the last word; for the things of the mind are precarious and elusive, Kafka often implies. Benno von Wiese and Felix Weltsch may well be unimpressed by the leopard's beauty. "Ihm fehlte nichts": "It had all it wanted," "It lacked for nothing," "It was all right." Looked at as a positive statement, the implication is that the leopard is adjusted to life and society, and is without defect or frustration; that to be a healthy animal is a desirable condition. The same words, expressed in a slightly different tone of voice, imply a nausea of repulsion on the narrator's part at the crudity of natural, animal life. Any feelings of admiration that the creature may arouse are seriously qualified by the insertion three times of "seemed" in the subsequent sentence: "it did not even seem to miss freedom; this noble . . . body seemed to carry freedom too around with it; it seemed to be situated somewhere in its jaws . . ."

It is a consequence of the irony and ambivalence nearly always present in Kafka's work that the reader should be compelled to ask himself whether the hero of the story is in fact the starvation-artist or the leopard.

—H. M. Waidson

It is a consequence of the irony and ambivalence nearly always present in Kafka's work that the reader should be compelled to ask himself whether the hero of the story is in fact the starvation-artist or the leopard. The starvation-artist's name itself implies duality of purpose: fasting and artistry; the search for true food, that is, the metaphysical quest, and aesthetic achievement, that is, the artistry of fasting for its own sake. Then the word "Künstler" has the double meaning of "artist" and "artiste" which cannot be translated by one word in English: the artist is a showman, and the showman an artist; art for art's sake, without metaphysical purpose, is perhaps showmanship and not art. The starvation-artist unites in himself man's aspirations both in realms of art and of religion; the leopard represents the predatory urge of a life-force that is hostile to these spheres: "Leopards break into the temple and drink the sacrificial chalices dry; this occurs repeatedly again and again; finally it can be reckoned upon beforehand and becomes part of the ceremony" [Kafka, *Reflections on Sin*].

If the crowd and the leopard are indifferent to the starvation-artist's fate, this is no proof that Kafka wishes his readers to share this indifference. In the **"Kleine Fabel"** Kafka lets the cat have the last word and eat up the mouse; but surely we are not expected to admire the cat on this account. The starvation-artist dies with firm conviction still in his eyes; he has lost his pride, but not his sense of purpose. Josef K. in *Der Prozeß*, we have seen, has not

found in life the same purpose which the starvation-artist has, and so feels shame at dying "like a dog." But there may be hope for him; someone leans out of a window, and his clothes are neatly folded before his death. And from **"Forschungen eines Hundes"** it is clear that Kafka saw, or came to see, a quiet and moving dignity about a dog's life. Dog and starvation-artist indeed often appear, and are intended to appear, ridiculous and absurd in their struggles and misapprehensions, but it is these aspirations that can arouse Kafka's sympathies, and those of his readers, not simply ferocity of the leopard's world.

Harry Steinhauer (essay date 1962)

SOURCE: "Hunger Artist or Artist in Hungering: Kafka's 'A Hunger Artist'," in *Criticism,* Vol. IV, No. 1, Winter, 1962, pp. 28-43.

[*In the following excerpt, Steinhauer interprets "A Hunger Artist" as a religious allegory depicting "the tragedy . . . of ascetic idealism." This interpretation, he claims, "fits the text in every detail, naturally, without stretching the correspondence between symbol and thing symbolized, and it is the only one that does so."*]

Since the first wave of Kafka criticism washed over us in the thirties there has been a rising tide of interpretations of Kafka's work: theological, sociological, existentialist, ethnic, psychoanalytic, even medical. A reaction against this proliferation of readings was bound to set in; so it has become fashionable of late to decry all these abstract-learned interpretations and to argue that, since Kafka was not a philosopher but a creative artist, any attempt to derive a "philosophy" from his work is to render it too rational and therefore to falsify it. Not only is it wrong to force a general philosophy of life out of Kafka's work, but we are warned against subjecting his individual writings to a puzzle-solving treatment, against seeing in them allegories and symbols beyond the words which Kafka uses as counters of expression. The images and statements, it is contended, are in themselves the "meaning" of his work; the meaning does not lie behind the words, but in them, in their body.

That Kafka's intention is not exhausted by a one-to-one interpretation of his symbols is, of course, obvious. Goethe protested to Eckermann against the tendency of readers to look for neat ideas in works of literature and insisted that there is an "irrational" element in every writer. He meant by this, I suppose, that when we have squeezed all the rational meaning out of a poem or tale, there remains a residue of some kind that cannot be formulated in words or concepts. That residue includes the hypnotic effects produced by imagery, rhythm and verbal music, and that vague state of mystery and well-being that a good writer stirs in his reader. Even so rationalistic a writer as Thomas Mann indulges himself in effects produced by rhythmical juxtapositions, word-music, and a playful recourse to such irrational sciences as numerology.

With a writer like Kafka there is another factor that defeats a rationalist-abstract approach to his work. Like Joyce, Kafka was deeply rooted in literary naturalism. Now naturalism may be conceived as a compulsion to tell everything. It is a characteristic of non-classical literature to allow the poetic imagination to make side excursions and little exploratory tours that are their own reward and which contribute but little directly to the main economy of the work of art. In realistic writing these side excursions take the form of detailed description of milieu. Often this device is employed ostensibly for sociological reasons: to "explain" the behavior of the characters; but only too often it becomes an end in itself, satisfying the passion for fact which is the mark of sophisticated modern man.

In Kafka this love of detail is ubiquitous. A good deal of it stems from the naturalist compulsion to give the total picture, to be the camera's eye. But that is not all; there is also in him a Talmudic compulsion to modify and qualify and retract, which may be terribly distracting or deeply fascinating, depending on the temperament and literary habits of the reader.

All these concessions made, it still remains a stubborn fact that Kafka is an artist who does create allegories and parables. He does not say that Gregor Samsa awoke one morning and felt as if he were an insect. He says that Gregor Samsa awoke to find that he had turned into an insect, and then proceeds to describe his appearance and behavior as an insect in minute detail. Still, everyone knows that Kafka is depicting a state of mind and not a physiological metamorphosis.

Neider, Magny, Emrich and other students of Kafka, who denounce the allegorical interpretation of his work, having settled their account with this false approach, go on innocently to explain what the symbols "stand for." And how could it be otherwise? When Kafka writes about a mouse who is a coloratura soprano and who sings or pipes before an audience of mice, can we take him in any but an allegorical way? Or when he describes the crazy journey undertaken by the country doctor with his two fantastic horses, he must surely be talking ideas, unless he is describing wholly irrational fantasies. Since it is usually possible to derive a large measure of sense from Kafka's allegories, symbols, and parables, it seems perverse to deny anyone this path to his mental world.

The allegory or symbolism in Kafka's work appears with varying degrees of clarity from work to work. It is especially hermetic in **"A Country Doctor,"** for instance, or in the early **"Descriptions of a Battle"** or in **"The Hunter Gracchus."** On the other hand it seems fairly transparent in *The Metamorphosis* or in *Josephine the Chanteuse.* The same difference holds for the novels: *The Castle* is a difficult book, *The Trial* easy by comparison.

One of Kafka's clearest and most transparent pieces is the tale, **"A Hunger Artist."** It is so rational, so mathematically constructed in relation to some reality situation that an interpretation of it seems easy. Yet a closer reading of this beautiful story reveals many baffling problems of

detail. A review of the literature that has grown up around it shows anything but agreement on these detailed matters. But more fundamental still is the question: what does the hero "stand for"? The obvious answer is that he stands for the artist and that, in his fate, Kafka has depicted the fate of the artist in the modern world. On this Kafka criticism has been unanimous and, it seems to me, unanimously wrong.

> **While the variety of situations, problems, and crises that Kafka treats in his writings is great, it is astonishing that, among all his concerns, he seems to be almost wholly indifferent to the position of the artist in modern society.**
>
> *—Harry Steinhauer*

For while the variety of situations, problems, and crises that Kafka treats in his writings is great, it is astonishing that, among all his concerns, he seems to be almost wholly indifferent to the position of the artist in modern society, which is one of the central problems in twentieth century literature. Nor does he speculate much about the nature and mission of art. There are occasional references to music in his writings; and in the late story **"Investigations of a Dog"** music may even be regarded as a central theme. But it is quite clear from the context in which these allusions occur that Kafka, like other German writers, uses music as a loose symbol for the insubstantial, unearthly, irrational-instinctive, the ideal—as Schiller, Schopenhauer, Nietzsche and Thomas Mann have used it. When the narrator in **"Investigations of a Dog"** refers to the "air dogs" as artists and musicians, he at once nullifies this description by remarking that their artistic or musical status is an accidental one; basically they are spiritual beings and might just as well be theologians or social reformers without affecting the tale fundamentally. That Kafka had little concern for the problems of the modern artist or for the conception of the artist as a problematical being is shown by the testimony of his friends, his diaries and letters. It is true that, during one of the periods in his life when he was engaged to be married, he noted in his diary the harmful effect that marriage would have on his career as a writer. But this is clearly a specious rationalization dragged in to justify his desire to withdraw from the engagement.

The fact is that Kafka was simply not an *artiste-bohémien;* he seems to have possessed none of the prima donna qualities that we have come to associate with so many modern artists. This is not to say that he was a normal Babbitt; he had his own share of neurosis, of course, only it was not an occupational one. In another sense too he was no *artiste.* One thinks of him as one does of those Biblical writers who set out to write down the word of

God in parables and myths and turned out literary master-pieces unintentionally. For Kafka has no style and no literary diction. There is little description of nature in his work, no attempt to hold the reader's attention through sex. The fascination of his fiction lies precisely in that puzzle-solving which recent critics deplore even as they practice it.

Kafka, then, has little sympathy for the new mystique of the artist that has developed since the romantic era. He says so explicitly, as explicitly as he ever speaks, through one of his finest allegories, *Josephine the Chanteuse, or The Mouse Folk.* Here, for once, he seems to be concerning himself with the nature of the artist (though even this allegory has been interpreted in altogether different terms). His thesis seems to be that the virtuoso singing of Josephine is not different in essence from the piping or whistling practiced by the mouse folk who come to listen to her. While she is right in believing that she is especially valuable to them in times of crisis and depression through her singing, they are also right in their conviction that they lend her support which is vital to her. When Josephine asks to be relieved from the ordinary work needed for the maintenance of the community, so that she may devote herself solely to her art, the people rightly reject this as presumptuous arrogance. The story ends with a prophecy by the narrator (who is one of the mouse people and speaks from their point of view) that the day will come when the art of singing will vanish altogether because men will no longer need it. Here it seems clear that music does stand for art, not just for spirituality or the mental life, and that the allegory in general is a condemnation of artistic snobbery.

Josephine is Kafka's last story, written shortly before his death in 1924. Taken in conjunction with the negative and personal evidence presented above, it shows that we can expect no glorification of the artist from Kafka, no lament for his alienation in the world, no plea for special status among the philistines.

How then are we to account for the parable of the hunger artist, which was written at about the same time as *Josephine*? If we disregard some of the crackpot interpretations that have been suggested—that the tale is a reflection of the food shortage which prevailed in the world during and after the first world war, or of the marathon craze that swept the world in the twenties, or of the emergence of the hunger-strike as a political weapon—we may say that Kafka criticism is of one voice that **"A Hunger Artist"** depicts the crisis of the artist in modern society, the artist who has lost faith in his mission, who is torn within himself, feels himself misunderstood and unappreciated by the philistine public and cannot survive in his isolation. Recognizing that Kafka would have little sympathy with such a Bohemian conception of the artist, these commentators are forced to see the hunger artist as an unsympathetic figure. Thus R. W. Stallman, who has written the most elaborate analysis of the tale in English, finds that the hunger artist has become detached from reality and lives in his own spiritual world, symbolized by the cage, and this complete detachment from physical reality

is spiritual death. Throughout the tale Stallman sees "all the logic weighted against the hunger artist's efforts at autarchy." In his final words we are given his confession that the artist must come to terms with life, with the civilization in which he lives, with the world of total reality; he begs forgiveness for his blasphemy against nature. A German interpreter, Benno von Wiese, agrees that Kafka passes adverse judgment on his artist, and for good reason: the hunger artist has a tragic flaw that justifies his ruin. He is vain, working for fame rather than for the sake of creating beauty.

When we turn to the detailed interpretation of the allegory we find the interpreters equating the guards with critics, who live on the artist like parasites, yet are sceptical of his integrity and belittle his achievement. The impresario is the patron who, in former times, supported the artist. This seems quite untenable, for in Kafka's story the impresario is a business man who promotes the hunger artist's work for his own materialistic ends. Now this is a situation which might apply to the modern artist, but it has no meaning for the artist who depended on an aristocratic patron. Moreover, in Kafka's story, the impresario has been dismissed since the public lost interest in the performances; in reality it is the modern artist who is tied up with impresarios, critics, and art dealers. The symbolic function of the children, who are mentioned at two strategic points in the story, is not explained by these interpreters. Does it make sense to say that children are more appreciative of art and artists than adults?

But, most important of all, is it true, as Stallman argues, that all the logic is weighted against the hunger artist's efforts at autarchy? This seems to me a gross misinterpretation of the basic tone of the story. The descriptions of the guards, the impresario, the society ladies, the circus manager, and circus attendants are highly unflattering, while there is not a word of adverse criticism leveled at the hunger artist. And where is the so-called confession that Stallman speaks of? The hunger artist's last words are: "I fast because I can't do anything else, because I couldn't find the food that I like. If I had found it, I wouldn't have made a fuss but eaten my fill like you and all of you." Far from being a retraction, this is an affirmation of the justness of his position. And the narrator adds: "These were his last words, but his dimmed eyes still showed the firm, though no longer proud, conviction that he would continue to fast."

How is it possible to misread the last paragraph as a judgment of poetic justice for a life misspent? Is it not obviously a bitter comment on the obtuseness of the public, which has refused to patronize the spectacle provided by the hunger artist, but flocks to the cage in which the brutal panther prances about? This unreconciled ending is typical of Kafka, who leaves the world as he finds it—out of joint, and makes no effort to sweeten the bitter taste he has left in our mouths. And it is the outside world, not the individual at the center of the stage, that is at fault for the fate that overtakes him. In our story Kafka makes this abundantly clear. Commenting on the general indifference of the public to the exhibition of fasting and to the repeated accusations of cheating, the narrator remarks: "This was the most stupid lie that indifference and native malice could invent; for it was not the hunger artist who was deceiving, he was working honestly, but the world was cheating him of his reward."

If it is true that the hunger artist is presented sympathetically, then either Kafka is here reversing himself and supporting the modern Bohemian artist in his anti-social pose, or he is not talking about an artist at all.

In "A Hunger Artist" Kafka is not writing about an artist but about an ascetic saint.

—Harry Steinhauer

I choose the latter alternative. Kafka is not writing about an artist but about an ascetic saint. In his earlier work he had repeatedly dealt with the situation of the man who is torn between the rigorous demands of the ideal and his earthly desires. He had described how such men suffer shipwreck on this Scylla and Charybdis, not through any fault of their own but either because of environmental influences or because of the very fabric of the universe.

Perhaps the most powerful expression of man's half-way position is the unfinished tale "Investigations of a Dog," which was mentioned earlier in this paper. The dog is man—average, commonplace man, "the man from the country" (as Kafka calls him in the short parable "Before the Law"), the man who is ignorant but seeks enlightenment. An early experience, while he was groping about in the darkness, brought the dog-hero under the spell of seven musical dogs. These musical dogs are not artists, because the music that enthralls the narrator-dog emanates from their limbs and is inaudible. Music is therefore some sort of spiritual power that these seven dogs possess and that our dog-hero knows nothing about. The musical dogs vanish and the dog-hero begins to search for the meaning of life. "Where does our nourishment come from?" he asks. Science replies: from the earth. True, but the earth must first be watered and the moisture comes from above. Maybe the food itself could be obtained up there and the earth disregarded altogether. Or perhaps our nourishment comes from a union between heaven and earth. In his experiments the dog-hero tries to do without food altogether; he fasts in the hope that food may come down to him from above and "knock at his teeth for admittance." In his starvation state he hears noises (that is, music) everywhere, not only in the outside world, but within his own body too. As he listens at his own stomach, he is astonished at what he hears and smells—choice foods he had not eaten since childhood. (In Kafka, as in other writers, childhood is a symbol of innocence, purity and joy.) He becomes convinced that, if ever he eats again, he

will kill the noises and bring silence into the world. And yet he is lured into a desire for food by his memories of childhood. In this dilemma he yearns for death. But he does not die; he merely swoons and, on regaining consciousness, finds himself in the presence of a dog who sings without knowing it, who liberates our hero from his condition of despair and sets him on the road to study the science of music and its relation to food.

Here the fragment ends with a casual indication that the dog has become a common dog again and looks back to that former state of ecstasy when he judged music to be a nervous condition of hyper-excitability.

Now what would have happened if the dog had remained in his state of ecstasy, refusing food permanently, so that he might hear music? The answer to this question is supplied by the tale "A Hunger Artist."

We learn that in recent years there has been a sharp decline of interest in hunger artists. Formerly they were able to function as private entrepreneurs; for everyone was interested, and interest grew as the fasting exhibition advanced from day to day. There were even season ticket holders and night visitors. Children especially were often taken to see the hunger artist, and for them his exhibition had a special significance; they watched in naïve amazement, while for their parents the spectacle was often no more than a bit of fun in which they participated because it was fashionable to do so. The hunger artist, though not entirely oblivious of the world outside his cage, sat absorbed in his own thoughts, not even conscious of the clock which was the only piece of furniture in his cage. There were guards, usually butchers by trade, stationed outside the cage; they were selected by the people to guarantee that the hunger artist did not cheat and snatch a bite on the sly. Of course this watching was a mere formality; the initiated knew that he never ate: his professional integrity forbade his doing so. Still, the masses had to be reassured; so the guards were posted. However, even the guards did not believe in the hunger artist's integrity. Some of them were cynics, who just knew that he cheated; and to make it easier for him to cheat, they often looked the other way. Others were sincere sceptics, who watched intently all night, training their searchlights on the cage. In fact, suspicion seemed to be an integral part of hungering; no matter what precautions were taken to assure honest performance, the suspicion was there.

The result was a general dissatisfaction. The people outside the cage were dissatisfied because it was impossible to prove that the hunger artist did not cheat. The man inside the cage was unhappy because he knew that he was not cheating. For his secret was that for him hungering was not a feat, but the easiest thing in the world and something the *wanted* to do. But the more he insisted that it was easy, the more sceptical and cynical the people became.

Then there was the impresario, who was interested solely in the spectacle as a spectacle and as a business (he sold postcards to the spectators). A real Madison Avenue type he, who used the latest psychology in his manipulations; hence there was to be no fasting beyond forty days, for after that period of time public interest could not be maintained. Kafka does not say so, but we may be sure that these calculations were made for him by the Institute for Motivational Research or by the Department of Psychology at the State University. And then the celebration at the end of each fasting period: this was, of course, the crown jewel of his public relations gimmicks, and the speeches emphasized all the wrong points and the seats of honor were occupied by the wrong people.

Such was life for the hunger artist in the good old days. After the sudden change that marks the turning point in the story, when the crowds suddenly stop coming, his former existence, by comparison, does indeed deserve the epithet of "pampered" which Kafka gives it. For at least people had been interested in his exhibitions, they had at least come to them, even if for the wrong reason and in the wrong spirit. But, as usual, no sooner has Kafka made a strong statement than he begins to qualify it. Actually, he says, the change in the hunger artist's fortunes did not come as suddenly as one might suppose. Symptoms of it had long been evident to those who had eyes to see; and the reasons for the change lay deep beneath the surface. That is why no one bothered to dig for them. The fact, however, was inescapable: suddenly there is no audience to fast for. All the efforts of the impresario to revive interest in the art of fasting are futile.

The hunger artist faces up to reality, gives up his private management, and joins a great circus as one among many attractions. Such a circus can use all sorts of acts, even such an outmoded one as exhibition fasting, because of the prestige attached to the performer's name, assuming of course that he has no paranoid delusions about his own importance. And the hunger artist has no such delusions. He quietly accepts a modest place on the way to the stables. The location is not unstrategic: the crowds which swarm to see the animals must pass his cage and stop to look at him. But the advantage is more apparent than real; the beautiful dream turns into a nightmare. He finds that the dense crowds are impatient to push on to the animal stalls, those who do stop to look at him create a bottleneck, and the result is much noise and many insults. Again he discovers that those who stop before his cage do so, not from a desire to understand, but out of mere whimsicality and defiance of the pushing throngs behind them. The stragglers, who could stop and watch him at their leisure, hurry by without as much as a glance at him, so that they may miss nothing of the animal show. Only an occasional father lingers to tell his children about the old-fashioned hunger exhibitions as he remembers them from the good old days. It is in the wondering eyes of these children that the hunger artist sees some future hope of improvement in his lot.

In the meantime he lives in utter neglect; no one even bothers to change the little tablet which indicates the number of days he has already fasted. Now his great dream of being allowed to fast beyond the allotted forty days has become a reality. He can fast on and on. But how empty

is his triumph. This is one of Kafka's most masterly examples of the sport which Destiny has with man's highest aspirations. When the hunger artist had an audience, he was prevented by an external force from fulfilling himself; now that he can do so, he has no audience.

> **The neglect of the hunger artist is one of Kafka's most masterly examples of the sport which Destiny has with man's highest aspirations. When the hunger artist had an audience, he was prevented by an external force from fulfilling himself; now that he can do so, he has no audience.**
>
> *—Harry Steinhauer*

Finally the tragic dénouement comes. After many days of complete neglect, the hunger artist is noticed by the supervisor of the circus. A heartrending interrogation ensues, which shows the gross, crude misunderstanding of the hunger artist's mission by this brutish lout. The hunger artist dies in his cage of despair, but firm in his conviction about the value of his fasting. The cage is cleaned out and assigned to a panther. No fasting for him; he is for hearty meals, which are supplied to him by those attendants who ridiculed the freakish hunger artist. The panther is awesomely alive; his freedom, his *élan vital,* lies somewhere between his jaws. The crowds are terrified by him but swarm about his cage and gape.

The title of the story is significant. Kafka does not call his hero a hungering or starving artist (the German for that would be *ein hungernder Künstler*) but an artist in hungering. He probably had in mind Wilhelm Raabe's well-known novel *Der Hungerpastor*, which deals with a clergyman whose life is devoted to the pursuit of the ideal, who is a pastor of hungering. Raabe's opening paragraph reads:

> In this beautiful book I will deal with hunger, what it means, what it wants and what it can achieve. . . . To hunger, to the sacred power of genuine, true hunger I dedicate these pages.

In Raabe's novel starving is clearly a symbol of self-denial, of following the hard way rather than that of material success. Kafka repeatedly refers to the hunger artist's profession as "exhibition fasting" or just "fasting," indicating that this is his hero's main concern. We have seen that elsewhere too Kafka uses food and fasting as symbols for materialism and ascetic idealism or the supernatural. Wilhelm Emrich calls attention to the frequency of this symbol in Kafka's writings. What Kafka now tells us in **"A Hunger Artist"** is that even he who has found the way and lives by hungering has a rough time of it in our world. If Kafka were thinking essentially of the idealistic artist, his central symbol would be inept. For surely the artist is not primarily concerned with suffering and self-abnegation, but with creating works of art. In our story, however, hungering is the hero's profession.

Again, if the hunger artist is an artist, what is the role played by the impresario? In former times the impresario could only have been the patron, secular or ecclesiastical. Is it anything but peevish spleen to imply that the patron in former times was exploiting the artist for commercial purposes, or that he was generally a philistine as Kafka's impresario is? And if it is true, as Kafka assumes in his story, that the general public was at one time interested in great art, has he a right to charge that this interest was spurious? Then there is the symbol of the children. They represent unsophisticated innocence. Is Kafka seriously supporting the thesis that great art is more open to the untutored mind than to the sophisticated?

The hunger artist has always lived in a cage. Does Kafka mean to imply that the artist has always been an outsider, aloof from society, misunderstood and held in contempt? The hunger artist is today completely disregarded, says Kafka; all interest has shifted to the panther, who stands for gross entertainment. Is this even remotely true of the situation in the arts in general? One may argue that the modern artist has traded in his position of vassal to an aristocratic patron for that of business *entrepreneur* who must please the public taste at the cost of his lofty vision. But that is not the tragedy of Kafka's hero; it is rather that he has become a minor figure in a large organisation, that no one is interested in him except the few children who pass his cage. In actual fact the modern artist has, on the contrary, become a celebrity to a degree unknown to his forebears.

For these reasons it seems to me that the conventional interpretation of **"A Hunger Artist"** as an allegory of the artist's role in modern society is untenable. As I suggested above, it seems more sensible to take Kafka at his word and assume that he is describing the tragedy of hungering, that is, of ascetic idealism. In fact he seems to be giving us a phenomenology of religion as we know it from history and our own observation. This interpretation, it seems to me, fits the text in every detail, naturally, without stretching the correspondence between symbol and thing symbolized, and it is the only one that does so.

What Kafka is saying, then, is this: There were, in the past, religious ages when holiness, asceticism, spirituality, the refusal to live the worldly life were widely accepted as the true path to salvation. They were never really admired, perhaps, but at least the general public respected the external aspects of religion, the Church service, the emotional catharsis, the satisfaction of certain social needs. To the sophisticated, religion even then was a social game, an institution that must be supported for the sake of the masses, who obviously believed and could be kept in order and submission by their belief. Religion, whose essence was spirituality and unworldliness, had become organized and legalized with an army of guards to see to it that there

was no cheating. But whom were the guards watching? Who would cheat? The hunger artist of course; and here Kafka has made use of a phenomenon in the psychology of religious experience that is baffling but true. Throughout the holy Middle Ages, for instance, we find among the more sophisticated, side by side with a naïve belief in the magical powers possessed by the priests as representatives of God, a cynical scepticism about the inner lives of these holy magicians. It is a dualism of outlook, a form of "doublethink" which both stands in awe before the impressive achievement of the saint and is sceptical of its human possibility—he *must* be eating on the sly. "These suspicions," says Kafka, "were simply inseparable from the idea of fasting."

Kafka suggests that the guards or priests, those who were in constant touch with the hunger artist and most accessible to the spiritual aura that emanated from him, were most deeply affected by the canker of cynicism. For these guards, he tells us, were usually butchers or materialists, interested in meat and breakfasts and card playing. Some of them were constitutional sceptics who refused to believe that anyone could be holy because they were not holy themselves; hence there was no holiness: everyone lived like themselves, by the pleasure principle. Others among the guards were just cynics and took pleasure in the sly game they felt the hunger artist was playing behind their backs. And it was these corrupt souls who caused the hunger artist the most poignant grief.

And the impresario? He is the great diplomat churchman, the promoter of the whole enterprise and its administrator. Even he, who is closer to the hunger artist than anyone else, including the guards, does not believe in the intrinsic value of the performance which the hunger artist provides. But he is interested in assuring its external success, even at the price of destroying the idea. He has affinities with Dostoevski's Grand Inquisitor, though the analogy is not perfect. Certainly he glorifies the hunger artist, but in such a way that his achievement frightens off the potential disciples, whereas the hunger artist wants to make people believe that his art is easy, so that they may be inspired to emulate him. This is the key to the motif of admiration that runs through the allegory. The hunger artist wants to be admired, he seeks fame; this has been construed as his *hamartia* which justly brings about his downfall. But surely he seeks fame and admiration in the same spirit as God is represented in religious literature as seeking glory, honor, and praise—not because it does Him any good to be glorified, but because it is good for man to glorify something higher than himself. By glorifying God man is likely to emulate Him. The hunger artist wants glory for his art, not for his person. This is the key to the enigmatic passage at the end of the story, when the hunger artist seems to contradict himself flatly: "I always wanted you to admire my fasting," he says to the supervisor of the circus. "We do admire it," the supervisor replies. "But you should not admire it," says the hunger artist and explains that his fasting is no personal achievement, but the result of his inability to find satisfying nourishment on this earth. Clearly the emphasis is away from his person to the thing he represents. He wants admiration for the ideal of fasting, not for his personal triumph.

The cage is vital to the hunger artist as saint; his starvation is a self-imposed confinement and must always be so. For he does not want the freedom of the active man, of the materialist. Hence Kafka never reproaches him for doing without freedom, while the panther who replaces him in his cage is condemned for not missing his freedom. The panther man *should* want freedom; the saint's freedom lies in his conquest of time. That is the significance of the only object in the cage, the clock, whose ticking is so meaningful to him, not because it heralds the end of his fast, but because it reminds him that he must and can and will fast on beyond the allotted span of forty days. Surely the symbolism of the cage, the clock, and the forty-day limit lose their meaning if we think of the hunger artist as an artist.

> The symbolism of the cage, the clock, and the forty-day limit lose their meaning if we think of the hunger artist as an artist.
>
> —*Harry Steinhauer*

The tragic development which Kafka reports is the deterioration of the hunger artist's position in the world. This consists in a general decline of interest in his profession, so that he is compelled to hire himself out to a circus and take his place as one among many spectacles, and a rather minor one at that. What a clear allegory this is of the fate that has overtaken religion since about the Renaissance, when the Church ceased to be a private enterprise and a main attraction, a rival power to the state, and became a series of State Churches, or one institution among others of a secular nature. The end of our allegory is a piece of eschatology à la Dostoevski. If there is no God, says Ivan Karamazov, all is permitted. The only ethic is then the ethic of the jungle; man becomes a panther who needs no freedom, no transcendence, only meat to tear between his teeth. This reasoning, so painful to the humanist, is heard more and more in our day, and Kafka may well have subscribed to it, either to recall men to a need for God or to register his total despair. Whichever of these alternatives is the right one, the story ends without reconciliation. A good man (that is, a noble ideal) is destroyed; nothing worthwhile takes his place. For surely the satisfaction which the masses will derive from watching the antics of the panther is not a consummation that Kafka could ardently wish.

It is now necessary to consider some questions which Kafka's allegory raises. We have already discussed the problem of where Kafka's sympathy lies, with the hunger artist or with the world that is hostile to him. But it has

been suggested that there is an undercurrent of grotesque humor in the tale, directed by Kafka against his hero to show the absurdity of his ideal. Such a grotesque humor there certainly is: the holy man in the cage, bent on promoting holiness to people who can only see his activity as a stunt; the fiasco of the celebration concentrated in the horror shown by the two society ladies when they have to handle the saint's body; the alert guards; the aura of amusement in the faces of all officialdom; the patronizing air of the impresario and later on of the circus manager— all this is humor. But at whose expense? Not at that of the hunger artist, necessarily; almost certainly not in Kafka, whose hero is so often the misunderstood, maltreated victim of society or the universe. Let us not forget that Kafka is one of the early discoverers of the "absurd" universe.

A second problem: is the hunger artist a genuine saint or is he too living by the pleasure principle, except that his pleasure happens to lie in fasting? This is the traditional charge made against the ascetic by the hedonist, and Kafka seems to support it by making the hunger artist stress that it is easy to fast and by having him burst out with the words: "If I had found [the food I liked] I would have . . . eaten my fill." But is this not a characteristic touch of modesty that goes well with his role of a simple human being? How often when we praise someone for an extraordinarily difficult achievement that cost him immense labor do we hear the reply, "Oh well, I had fun doing it," when the man knows that it was anything but fun. Or again: "You admire my fasting as a triumph of renunciation. It's nothing of the sort. I fast because there is no food in this world that I can digest. If there were, believe me I would have gorged myself." Surely the emphasis is on the first part of the statement, that there is no food here to my taste. An interesting parallel is offered by a passage in *Paradise Regained* (II, 317 ff.). Jesus rejects the temptation by food which Satan offers him, but only because it is offered him by Satan:

> "How hast thou hunger then?" Satan replied,
> "Tell me if food were now before thee set,
> Wouldst thou not eat?" "Thereafter as I like
> The giver," answered Jesus.

Milton's Jesus will eat if he approves the source of the gift; Kafka's hunger artist would eat if he could find the right food. The ascetic is the man with higher tastes; here is his strength and the cause of his unpopularity with the low-tasters. It was Schiller who pointed out in his essay *On Charm and Dignity* that superhuman achievements, performed easily without effort by the genius, evoke the resentment of the many.

Is the hunger artist a vain man, as Benno von Wiese claims? Why must he exhibit himself? Why does he not fast in hiding? Why must he have an impresario? There is no evidence in the story that he seeks to convert people to his way of life. On the contrary, he even encourages the guards to eat by offering them his breakfasts. What then is his game: to show off and get applause? It is possible that we have here one of those pockets of realism that are so frequent in Kafka. Kafka may have realized that there is an element of vanity in sainthood and recorded this observation; but this need not undermine his basic admiration for sainthood. Or it may be, as suggested above, that the admiration the hunger artist craves and the exhibitions he gives are not for his selfish glorification but for the cause he stands for. In any case, exhibitions are an essential part of the faster's performance; how else can he demonstrate the beauty of his way of life? So Dostoevski's Father Zossima lives apart from the world, yet enough in the world to have an effect on those outside his cage. It is important to note that the hunger artist is realist enough to recognize the futility of seeking to convert adults, least of all the sophisticated guards. To them he gives his breakfasts—a gesture which says: since eating is all you understand, eat. He does not exhibit for these corrupt souls, but for the pure children, who may one day restore fasting to its former glory.

There remains the question of questions: is Kafka so "medieval" that he can seriously preach asceticism as a superior way of life? Well, it is a fact that Kafka has recourse to such symbols as fasting to indicate spirituality and self-denial; he represents sex as something dirty; and so he does seem to uphold medieval or early Christian asceticism as an ideal whose passing we should mourn. According to his friend Max Brod, Kafka was more than a writer; he transcended the state of art and was on the way to becoming a saint. Among the German expressionists, Kafka's contemporaries, the Dostoevskian ideal of holiness, primitive simplicity, ascetic purity was a popular literary attitude, in some cases based on genuine conviction. However, it is not necessary to press the theological commitment. Perhaps all that Kafka is saying is: even if we can conceive of a man who is all spirit and no flesh— and surely we can all admire such a man as a seven days' wonder—we shall find that his career is one of frustration; for no one ever really cared about him, and today we care even less.

Heinz Politzer (essay date 1962)

SOURCE: "Heightened Redemption: Testaments and Last Stories," in *Franz Kafka: Parable and Paradox*, Cornell, 1962, pp. 282-333.

[*In the following excerpt, Politzer praises "A Hunger Artist" as "a perfection, a fatal fulfillment" that expresses Kafka's desire for permanence.*]

[With **"A Hunger Artist"**] Kafka returns to the motif of the unknown nourishment which he had introduced in ***The Metamorphosis***. In the earlier story this image pointed quite generally to the never-to-be disclosed mystery governing man's life. Here it has been integrated in the theme of art, the Hunger Artist's art.

The tale deals with the art of fasting as well as with fasting as an art. The Hunger Artist is willing to dedicate his existence to the perfection of his craft; hence he feels justified in making all-inclusive claims in return. "Just try

to explain to anyone the art of fasting!" he exclaims at the height of his career. "Anyone who has no feeling for it cannot be made to understand it." In the original this creed of the Hunger Artist is patterned rhythmically after the words with which Goethe's Faust pronounces the superiority of his all-embracing view of the world over the petty rationalism of his entourage. Even if our artist is not a superman like Goethe's hero, he is certainly a virtuoso, a star of starvation, and his appeal, like the fascination of any romantic hero, is consciously emotional.

His desire for starvation is insatiable. He is convinced that his capacity for fasting has no limits whatever. He is inspired by the ambition to be "not only the record hunger artist of all time, which presumably he was already," but to surpass himself "by a performance beyond human imagination." This grasp for what can no longer be grasped identifies him as a Kafka hero. So does the paradox that he will have to die from starvation as soon as he succeeds in living up to his noble aim.

His impresario has imposed a forty-day limit on his fasting, a period which is measured, absurdly enough, by a clock instead of a calendar. Yet his reason for limiting the Hunger Artist's enthusiasm for perfection has nothing to do with the performer. He does not act from a realization that the Artist, too, is subject to the necessities of life. Instead, his reason—which Kafka with a touch of malice calls a "good" one—is concerned with the audience. The manager has observed that "for about forty days the interest of the public could be stimulated, . . . but after this the town began to lose interest." It is not the Artist, but the public that matters. The performer should be convinced by this argument. But his attitude toward the spectators is as paradoxical as his attitude toward himself and his art.

Not only is this Artist a man driven by the desire to achieve perfection. He is also a showman who needs spectators as he achieves his unheard-of deed. To suffer starvation by himself and for himself would not satisfy him. He depends on the acclaim, the excitement of the crowds, the military bands, the young ladies, and all the other ritual paraphernalia of a popular success. And yet this popular success forces him to interrupt his achievement long before he has come anywhere near the stage of accomplishment he feels able to reach. "His public pretended to admire him so much, why should it have so little patience with him; if he could endure fasting longer, why should not the public endure it?"

It is the public which answers this question, although in an unexpected way. For reasons unknown to Artist, impresario, and reader alike the crowds begin to disperse and his fame starts to decline. "Everywhere, as if by secret agreement, a positive revulsion from professional fasting was in evidence." Thereupon the Artist dismisses the impresario and hires himself to a circus, a big enterprise which accommodates him somewhere near the animal cages. The former star has now been moved from the center of attention to the periphery; the one-man show has degenerated to something less than a side show; the virtuoso is treated like an animal or even worse; "strictly speaking, he was only an impediment on the way to the menagerie."

Now he is able to reach perfection by starving himself to death. He is at liberty to indulge in his life's dream undisturbed. No more limits are set for him. But the audience he had hoped would watch him perform his supreme act is gone. He is left to solitude and oblivion. Time itself is suspended; the little board which used to tell his fasting days has long been showing the same number, and no more mention is made of his clock. He is breaking all records, but his achievement remains unrecorded since the public is absent.

> And when once in a time some leisurely passer-by stopped, made merry over the old figure on the board and spoke of cheating, that was in its way the stupidest lie ever invented by indifference and inborn malice, since it was not the Hunger Artist who was cheating, he was working honestly, but the world was cheating him of his reward.

The reward he has in mind is the public acknowledgment that he is reaching perfection now. Without this acknowledgment perfection will forever be imperfect.

One of Kafka's "Reflections" reads as follows: "One must not cheat anyone, not even the world of its victory." But in the case of the Hunger Artist the world has seen to it that the victory remains in its possession. Moreover, it forces the dying man to realize the contradictions inherent in his life's occupation. "Forgive me, everybody," he whispers with his last strength. If he has really been cheated by the world, why should he now ask the cheater, the world, to forgive? "I always wanted you to admire my fasting," he continues. The admiration he claimed was based on the assumption that the efforts he devoted to his task were extraordinary. He alone was able to do what he did, and more than common exertions were needed to overcome difficulties that no one but he could master. This is the very nature of records and record breaking. Yet in the same breath he says about his fasting: "But you should not admire it." Kafka has prepared us well to grasp the meaning of this blatant self-contradiction. Early in the story he informs us that this Artist's uniqueness consisted solely in the fact that "he alone knew, what no other initiate knew, how easy it was to fast." The very thought of a meal, we learn, has given him nausea. But only now, with his last words, does he betray his secret: "I have to fast, I cannot help it, . . . because I could not find the food I liked. If I had found it, believe me, I should have made no fuss and stuffed myself like you or anyone else."

The art of this Artist is a negative performance. His fasting represents a passive act, which is a paradox. Running counter to human nature, it may, at least in the minds of a curious crowd, have proved attractive, so long as it was performed as a show of self-denial and a feast of sacrifice. Our Artist, however, was cheating even when he thought that he was working honestly; he could not help starving himself; he was forced into his fanatically pursued profes-

sion by the absence of the unknown nourishment appropriate to him and his tastes. His art is produced by a deficiency, and the question whether he is at fault for not finding the right food or whether the world is to be blamed for not providing him with it, this question aims ultimately at the meaning of the role that the artist performs in any kind of human context.

The art of the Hunger Artist is a negative performance. His fasting represents a passive act, which is a paradox.

—Heinz Politzer

We are not surprised to discover that Kafka refrains from spelling out an answer to this question. He does, however, allow the Artist to die with the conviction that his performance is going to outlast his life. "In his dimming eyes remained the firm though no longer proud conviction that he was still continuing the fast." Disregarding the world and its neglect, humbled by the cognition of the deceit that was his art, he carries the paradox of his existence beyond the threshold of his life. Only there, in the beyond, is the nature of the nourishment that would have satisfied him revealed. Knowing it, he appears to be sated for the first time. He need not strive any longer; he possesses it at last. Therefore his face shows conviction without pride, firmness without the triumph of victory. It is, alas, the face of a dead man.

Previously Kafka had used many images related to food and eating to express the paradox of existence. One of the most persuasive is the following: "He gobbles up the leavings and crumbs that fall from his own table; in this way he is, of course, for a little while more thoroughly sated than all the rest, but he forgets how to eat from the table itself. In this way, however, there cease to be any crumbs and leavings." Unable to lead a fulfilled life, he depleted its very substance by doggishly feeding on its waste. Thus he never came to know the nourishment, the nurturing elements, of his own existence. The Hunger Artist, on the other hand, refuses to accept the waste—and in an act of daring revaluation he declares all ordinary food to be waste. Refusal becomes custom; custom turns into sickness, a sickness unto death. Yet from this sickness he derives fulfillment, the deadly fulfillment of his art. Literally he pays with his life for having partaken of the sublime nourishment, perfection. Kafka seems to revert here to the aesthetic philosophy pronounced in Thomas Mann's "Tonio Kröger." But what was an intellectual disquisition for Tonio Kröger and his author became a fatal reality for this Hunger Artist as well as for his creator.

The story ends with the Hunger Artist's demise and transfiguration. Although the artist's self-fulfillment is alluded to in most discreet tones, Kafka was not satisfied with this comparatively conciliatory ending. He added a more drastic finale. A great cat takes the place of the dead man. The animal, a leopard rather than a panther, is supposed to balance the art of the Artist by the uninhibited vitality of a young animal that has remained completely natural in spite of its imprisonment. "It lacked nothing," while the Artist was consumed by universal want. "The food he liked was brought him without hesitation by the attendants," whereas the impresario had to use dubious tricks to persuade the Artist to accept even a bite. The animal's "noble body, furnished almost to the bursting point with all that it needed, seemed to carry freedom around with it, too." The Artist's freedom, on the other hand, was identical with his deadly idea of perfection. Needless to say, the leopard attracts the crowds that the Artist missed when he tried to find fulfillment.

The image of this leopard is masterfully realized in a few sentences that convey a feeling of the strength which animates the animal. It is nevertheless an oversimplification. If Kafka had wanted to allegorize in his Artist the impotence of the spirit as opposed to the unbroken power of life, the leopard's *joie de vivre* would, by contrast, have revealed the intention of the story. But such a simple antithesis cannot have been Kafka's purpose. His story was meant to show that the Hunger Artist's life problem was a paradox and remained unsolved. Thus the magnificently unequivocal image of the cat was superfluous and, perhaps, even out of place.

On the other hand, Kafka uses the simplicity of the leopard to reveal the complexity with which the figure of the Artist is endowed. He has been interpreted as "a mystic, a holy man, or a priest," as an allegory of "man as a spiritual being" or as a parabolical example of the possibility of achieving a "free spiritual existence" by ascetic practices. In supplying interpretations for this figure, the critics seem to have overlooked the fact that here more than in any previous story the paradox of Kafka's own literary genius has been stated in purely artistic terms. The Hunger Artist shares with his author an insatiable desire for a spiritual security. Yet now his quest is reduced to the sphere of art, and most of the mystery of the story is vested in the artist-hero. There are, in other words, no more intermediaries confusing his dealings with the outside world. Even the impresario is "his partner in an unparalleled career. Nor is there any supreme authority who would summon him or whom he could challenge. The heaven and hell of perfection is bred in his own heart. His conflict, still metaphysical, still insoluble, has been confined to the realm of his art.

This art is fatal since it can only be perfected by the Artist's death. In view of the place it assumes in Kafka's work and the mastery of its execution, this story is a perfection, a fatal fulfillment, or at least comes very close to it. Who, after having read it, would deny the Artist a degree of permanence? One cannot help wondering whether Kafka, by stating in his will that it was to be exempted from unconditional destruction, had not suggested that he himself was willing to perish like his hero and yet harbored

the hope that he would, however conditionally, survive in the story itself. The Hunger Artist is dead; may the **"Hunger Artist"** live!

Forrest L. Ingram (essay date 1971)

SOURCE: "Franz Kafka: *Ein Hungerkünstler*," in *Representative Short Story Cycles of the Twentieth Century: Studies in a Literary Genre*, Mouton, 1971, pp. 46-105.

[*In the following excerpt, Ingram examines the theme of anxiety in "A Hunger Artist."*]

Situations which excite and heighten anxiety abound in **"A Hunger Artist"**: the fasting showman is forcibly isolated (in a cage) from the community of man. He is questing toward a goal which he is not allowed to reach. Each step toward that goal leads him closer and closer to death. The shift of interest in fasting threatens the economic security of the Impresario and the stability of the *Lebensweise* of the showman. His audience does not understand the hunger artist. Many of them suspect him of cheating. They lock him in a cage, exhibit him, and limit his freedom.

Felix Weltsch wrote that **"A Hunger Artist"** actually includes four stories in one. "Im Grunde," he says,

> besteht diese Geschichte aus vier Geschichten, vier Entwicklungslinien mit verschiedenem Sinn, die ineinander verflochten sind; die äußere Geschehen ist ihnen natürlich gemeinsam, aber der Sinn dieses Geschehens ist vielfaltig. Man braucht nur zu fragen: was ist der Sinn dieses Unternehmens, in Schaustellungen vor dem Publikum zu hungern?

Four simultaneous accurate answers can be given to that question, he says, forming four *Sinnlinien* to the story: (1) *Hungern als Sensation*—public fasting provides an outlet for the curiosity of the people; (2) *Hungern als Geschäft*—it provides security for the hunger artist and his manager; (3) *Hungern als eine Angelegenheit der Ehre*—it provides a challenge which the fasting showman is proud to prove he can meet; and (4) *Hungern aus Ekel vor dem Essen*—it is unavoidable. Each of these *Sinnlinien* supplies a convenient basis for analysis of anxiety-factors in the story.

The first, *Hungern als Sensation*, provokes anxiety superficially for the public, the hunger artist, and the Impresario, but serves at the same time to distract them from more fundamental problems. The Impresario has the constant worry of staging a good show, of keeping the audience interested and the hunger artist alive. The hunger artist's contact with the suspicious and disbelieving public; his awareness that the nature of his performance and abilities is being falsified by the manager; and his constant frustration that he can never exercise his talents fully, since he is forced to come out of his cage and take food on the fortieth day—all these cast him into melancholy. At the same time, concern for his reputation distracts him from the more fundamental issue—that if he were actually allowed to fast on and on, he would die. His discontent with the particulars of the show keep him from a too acute awareness of the freakish nature of his death-bearing life.

In the same way, the public's intense concern over the trappings of the show distract them from the normally terrifying condition of its chief actor. The show on the fortieth day of the fast is structured in such a way as to allow the public to gather in calm community before the show-stall of a man whose life is a living reminder of the approach of death. The ritual has been carefully arranged. Everything contributes toward calming the crowds: loud triumphant strains blare from the military band; pronouncements of doctors announce facts not about the health of the hunger artist, but about his physical measurements; two chosen women help the artist from his flower-bedecked cage; attendants stand ready to step in when the women's tears of discomfort cause them to relinquish their burden; the Impresario forces food through the teeth of the starving skeleton while keeping up a cheerful patter to distract the public's attention from his condition; finally, a toast is drunk not to the faster but to the public. All this, as well as the official act of watching, was arranged "zur Beruhigung der Massen."

Hungern als Geschäft evokes anxiety superficially in the public but profoundly in the hunger artist and his manager. The public is aware of the financial dimensions of the fasting showman's act; the fact that what he is doing is his business and his mode of support increases the suspicions of those members of the public who are not *Eingeweihten*. The public appoints official watchers to assure individuals (who cannot watch day and night themselves) that the hunger artist has not, indeed, taken any food for forty days. Even then, only a few ever seem really to believe that his show is real and not just a trick. They crowd around his cage day and night to satisfy themselves that they are not being cheated.

The hungering of the fasting showman provides economic security for the showman's manager, who when the shift of interest is setting in, races frantically over Europe trying to reignite the dying spark—but all in vain. He can, however, turn to another job—perhaps managing another kind of show that is in fashion. But the hunger artist is too old to change his profession. Besides he was "allzu fanatisch ergeben" to hungering to change. He still hopes to astound the world by hitherto unknown exhibitions. Never having done anything in his life, since he was so busy letting other people do things to him—he knows only one course of action: fasting on and on. Since *das Publikum* has lost interest in him, however, he has only his motive of honor to comfort him; only his knowledge that he is striving after an unreachable goal, toward unimaginable achievements in the profession of fasting. That brings us to the third *Sinnlinie, Hungern als eine Angelegenheit der Ehre.*

While the public busies itself with torchlights and the appointment of official watchers, the initiates realize that "die Ehre seiner Kunst" forbids the hunger artist from taking any food during his fasting period, and that he could

not even be forced to eat during this time. The vast majority of the population, however, could not be expected to understand this. When the hunger artist sits melancholy in his cage during the final stages of the fast, well-meaning people try to comfort him with the animadversion that anyone who had fasted so long must surely be out of spirits. This throws the hunger artist into a rage. For he has constantly boasted that he can fast much longer than forty days—indeed almost indefinitely. But the public and the Impresario would not permit this. The Impresario even tried to disprove his boast by photographs. They had robbed him of honor again and again by cutting short his fast. This, he would always contend, was the root of his melancholy. And after he had become only a "Hindernis auf dem Weg zu den Ställen" he strove, without opposition, to reach those goals he had set himself, to fast to the limits of his abilities, which he felt had "keine Grenzen." Despite the occasional remark by a passing skeptic that he was a swindle and a cheat, the hunger artist "arbeitete ehrlich, aber die Welt betrog ihm um seinen Lohn."

The hunger artist openly told his audience that fasting for him was the easiest thing in the world. Only in the final scene, however, did he dare mention to anyone (hardly even to himself) that he was helpless to do otherwise. Sitting alone in his cage, perhaps the realization of his freakish incapacity joined with his other thoughts to cause his sadness and dissatisfaction with himself—which his public attributed to his fasting too long and which he attributed to his not fasting long enough.

In the last portion of the story, the *Sinnlinie, Hungern aus Ekel vor dem Essen*, assumes centrality. The hungerer confesses at the end that he had to fast because he could not find the food he liked. During his period of isolation and silence, he has ceased to be proud of his fundamental human defect—the inability to eat. All his other passivities, arguments, boasts, and concerns had helped him to distract himself sufficiently from the important death-threatening and anxiety-provoking fact that he was unfit to live. Left alone far from the crowds, he could no longer turn his face away from the reality of his approaching death. The general public, on the other hand, could always find something else to fill the void left by the hunger artist's death. Soon enthusiastic onlookers surround his cage in which now a fresh life-loving leopard tears raw meat in his teeth.

The anxiety theme, then, is conveyed in **"A Hunger Artist"** primarily through the changes of circumstances which the passing of time brings with it. Structurally pivotal terminology of anxiety follows a different pattern than that of [**"First Sorrow"** and **"A Little Woman"**], because it is more prominently the terminology of the passing of time, of misunderstanding, and of unachieved goals. Some of the terms used earlier, however, recur here, though not necessarily at key positions in the story: *Beruhigung der Massen, das beruhigte Publikum, ruhige, Ruhepausen, quälender, störte, unzufrieden, Unzufriedenheit, befriedigt, Trost, Verdächtigungen, Urteil*, and so forth. The emphasis, however, centers on anxiety caused by being a creature of time, a creature whose life is packaged out in boxes of forty days each, a creature who dreams of fasting without limitation, but whose physical nature sets a limit on all his activities.

Richard W. Sheppard (essay date 1973)

SOURCE: "Kafka's *Ein Hungerkünstler:* A Reconsideration," in *The German Quarterly,* Vol. XLVI, No. 2, March, 1973, pp. 219-33.

[*In the following essay, Sheppard examines the role of the narrator and its relationship to the central character of "A Hunger Artist."*]

In the general attempt to say what the figure of Kafka's Hunger Artist signifies, scarcely any attention has been paid to another person in the story who is at least as important as the Hunger Artist: the narrator. On the whole, it has been assumed that the narrator is Kafka himself, if perhaps speaking in an odd voice. But this is not the case. In fact, the narrator has a distinct personality and functions as an independent character in the story.

> The narrator's personality is above all evident from his style: Außer den wechselnden Zuschauern waren auch ständige, vom Publikum gewählte Wächter da, merkwürdigerweise gewöhnlich Fleischhauer, welche, immer drei gleichzeitig, die Aufgabe hatten, Tag und Nacht den Hungerkünstler zu beobachten, damit er nicht etwa auf irgendeine heimliche Weise doch Nahrung zu sich nehme. Es war das aber lediglich eine Formalität, eingeführt zur Beruhigung der Massen, denn die Eingeweihten wußten wohl, daß der Hungerkünstler während der Hungerzeit niemals, unter keinen Umständen, selbst unter Zwang nicht, auch das geringste nur gegessen hätte; die Ehre seiner Kunst verbot dies. Freilich, nicht jeder Wächter konnte das begreifen, es fanden sich manchmal nächtliche Wachgruppen, welche die Bewachung sehr lax durchführten, absichtlich in eine ferne Ecke sich zusammensetzten und dort sich ins Kartenspiel vertieften, in der offenbaren Absicht, dem Hungerkünstler eine kleine Erfrischung zu gönnen, die er ihrer Meinung nach aus irgendwelchen geheimen Vorräten hervorholen konnte.

Important features of this passage suggest that the speaker is a professional administrator or lawyer: the relative frequency of words which include the suffix *-ig* (*ständige, merkwürdigerweise, gleichzeitig, lediglich*); the insertion of pedantic qualifications (*etwa, aber, doch, wohl, freilich*); the unnecessary repetition of virtually redundant phrases (*niemals, unter keinen Umständen, selbst unter Zwang nicht*); the vocabulary and turn of phrase reminiscent of the "amtlicher Erlaß" (*irgendeine, lediglich, eine Formalität, zur Beruhigung der Massen, unter keinen Umständen, ihrer Meinung nach*); a liking for the slightly pompous impersonal construction (*es war das . . . , es fanden sich . . .*); a preference for the formal or circumlocutory expression rather than the more colloquial expression (*damit* instead of *so dass; Nahrung zu sich nehmen* instead of *essen;* the present subjunctive *nehme* instead of the more normal *nehmen konnte; in der offen-*

baren Absicht, dem Hungerkünstler eine kleine Erfrischung zu gönnen instead of *so daß der Hungerkünstler etwas essen konnte*); a predilection for long sentences and prepositive adjectival phrases (*ständige, vom Publikum gewählte Wächter*): all this suggests that the narrator of **"Ein Hungerkünstler"** would be most at home in one of the chancelleries of *Das Schloß!*

It might be objected that this is not at all surprising, since Kafka was by profession a lawyer and would therefore be completely at home in a bureaucratic, legalistic style. This is true, but it does not follow that the narrator of **"Ein Hungerkünstler"** and Franz Kafka are the same person. In fact, Kafka detested his professional life and it would therefore be very surprising if, in his writing, an area which he always thought of as completely distinct from his office life, he should have chosen the legal style, which he once likened to the bars of a cage, as an authoritative vehicle for his own attitudes. Furthermore, we shall argue that one of the points of this story is to reveal the deficiencies in the narrative point of view, and if the force of these arguments is admitted, then it becomes impossible to maintain that Kafka's point of view is identical with that of his narrator.

Further information about the personality of the narrator is provided by a close look at the scale of values according to which he passes explicit judgment on the events of the story. Like the good administrator that he is, he hardly ever ventures an independent opinion on the fictional reality which he administers. ("Man ist zum Erzählen angestellt, also erzählt man.") He weights up the pros and cons of a situation with great conscientiousness (especially if the matter being discussed is not all that important), and he offers both sides of an argument (as he does, for instance, in the great debate about the provision of breakfasts for the guards), but he rarely passes direct judgment on the events of the story. Indeed, in the entire story, there are only five examples of direct comment by the narrator:

> . . . es fanden sich manchmal nächtliche Wachgruppen, welche die Bewachung *sehr lax* durchführten, . . .

> Als Höchstzeit für das Hungern hatte der Impresario vierzig Tage festgesetzt, darüber hinaus ließ er niemals hungern, auch in den Weltstädten nicht, *und zwar aus gutem Grund* . . . jedenfalls sah sich eines Tages der *verwöhnte* Hungerkünstler von der *vergnügungssüchtigen* Menge verlassen . . .

and, most emphatically:

> Und wenn einmal in der Zeit ein Müssiggänger stehenblieb, sich über die alte Ziffer lustig machte und von Schwindel sprach, so war das in diesem Sinn die dümmste Lüge, welche Gleichgültigkeit und eingeborene Bösartigkeit erfinden konnte, denn nicht der Hungerkünstler betrog, er arbeitete *ehrlich,* aber die Welt betrog ihn um seinen Lohn.

Because of the relative rarity of direct comment by the narrator, these five passages have a special status and require careful scrutiny. In the first, we see that although the narrator knows that the Hunger Artist would never eat anything anyway, he feels the need to censure the guards' slackness because it is in his nature to be concerned about questions of efficiency, mechanical conscientiousness, and dutifulness. In the second extract, the narrator finds it entirely reasonable that the impresario should wish to maximize profits by preventing the Hunger Artist from fasting for more than forty days. He is interested neither in the rights and wrongs of the Hunger Artist's behavior, nor in the rights and wrongs of the impresario's treatment of the Hunger Artist, he simply condones the principles of profitability and efficiency. The third example is less easy to explain. Why should the Hunger Artist, who, the narrator has told us, suffers from a profound sense of frustration, suddenly be described as "spoilt"? There is something inappropriate about this adjective and it suggests that for all the narrator's exact reporting of the Hunger Artist's plight, his sympathy for him does not run all that deep. Just when the Hunger Artist's persistent discomfort is compounded by the desertion of the general public, the narrator reveals that his own attitude toward the Hunger Artist is not free from a certain detached superiority. The fourth example involves precisely the kind of conventional assessment that might be expected from an official. The defection of the "mob" is attributed to their "addiction to pleasure" (as though this in itself were necessarily bad) and no consideration is given to the possibility that the Hunger Artist might be partly to blame for this defection. "Vergnügungssüchtig" smacks of the snap, stereotyped judgment and completely contradicts the assessment of the situation which, as will be shown, the narrator makes elsewhere.

> Considerable doubt is raised in our minds concerning the reliability of the bureaucratic narrator and his ability to deal adequately with the complex problems which face him. His judgments are unnecessary, facile, or inappropriate, and where judgment *is* called for, none is made.
>
> —*Richard W. Sheppard*

Thus, even before we arrive at the all-important fifth passage, considerable doubt has been raised in our minds concerning the reliability of the bureaucratic narrator and his ability to deal adequately with the complex problems which face him. His judgments are unnecessary, facile, or inappropriate, and where judgment *is* called for, none is made. The fifth passage quoted above completes the picture. Despite the emphasis and confidence with which judgment is passed there, the Hunger Artist reveals on the very next page that the narrator's assessment is wrong. The Hunger Artist's words towards the end of the story

have a special status because they are given directly, uncensored by the mind of the narrator, and because they amount to a deathbed confession. They must therefore surely be taken seriously. But if they are, then it is clear that the Hunger Artist has *not* been entirely honest—and this contradicts the narrator's statement: "denn nicht der Hungerkünstler betrog, er arbeitete ehrlich. . . . It is supremely ironic that at the point when the narrator most emphatically exercises his traditional right to pass judgment, he is immediately proved wrong.

The narrator also reveals his values and attitudes in less direct ways:

> Diese dem Hungerkünstler zwar wohlbekannte, immer aber von neuem ihn entnervende Verdrehung der Wahrheit war ihm zu viel. Was die Folge der vorzeitigen Beendigung des Hungerns war, stellte man hier als Ursache dar!

> Ein großer Zirkus mit seiner Unzahl von einander immer wieder ausgleichenden und ergänzenden Menschen und Tieren und Apparaten kann jeden und zu jeder Zeit gebrauchen, auch einen Hungerkünstler, bei entsprechend bescheidenen Ansprüchen natürlich, . . .

The exclamation mark in the first of these two passages indicates that the narrator is taking up an attitude towards the events and facts that he is reporting, and close inspection reveals that this reaction has been provoked not by a distortion of the truth but by a confusion of cause and effect. The narrator seems to be slightly more bothered by logical than by ethical impropriety, with the result that our faith in the validity of his judgments is further shaken. In the second extract, the rather prissy bit of officialese "bei entsprechend bescheidenen Ansprüchen" evokes the character of the petty official who has learnt to keep his head down so as not to draw attention to himself.

Other insights into the narrator's personality can be obtained by looking at the kind of thing that engages his interest, the kind of thing that he skates over rapidly, and the emotional level at which he reacts to the various events and details of the narrative. The narrator's eye is caught, for example, by the fact that it is usually butchers who are appointed to guard the Hunger Artist—"immer drei gleichzeitig." Objectively considered, this provision has something brutally monstrous and excessive about it, but the narrator's response is one of mild curiosity only: "merkwürdigerweise." This would seem to indicate that he is not able to respond appropriately to what he sees. Again, on the next page, the narrator shows an undue interest in the elaborate precautions which the authorities take in order to make sure that the Hunger Artist cannot cheat. Here again, he seems interested in these precautions primarily as an efficient administrator who appreciates efficiency in others and who is concerned to report meticulously the extent of the precautions that are taken. And, as was the case in the last example, the narrator completely fails to react emotionally to the inhumanity which characterizes these precautions. Or when the narrator deals with the ceremony which has evolved to greet the Hunger Artist's emergence from his cage on the fortieth day, we hear that there are small differences between the townspeople and the countrypeople in their ability to wait patiently for the end of the Hunger Artist's fast. We hear that the results of the medical inspection (carried out by *two* doctors) are communicated to the audience through a megaphone. We hear that the meal for the Hunger Artist is served "auf einem kleinen Tischchen." We hear that the music makes speech impossible, and so on. Wherever the reader cares to look in this passage, he will see that the narrator is concerned to record irrelevant details, and that in the process of doing so he fails to react to the sordid and exploitative aspects of the scene. Likewise, the narrator never bothers to distinguish between insignificant and significant details: early in the story, he records that the only piece of furniture in the cage is a clock, but he never asks himself what this detail might signify. He simply notes it in the same tone and with the same emphasis as he notes the fact of the two doctors or the little table.

Throughout the story, the narrator's vision is distorted by false priorities, misplaced emphases, and a quirkish perspective. He spends excessive time over incidental details and insufficient time over vitally important information.

—*Richard W. Sheppard*

Also, the narrator at one point makes the revealing remark that the Hunger Artist listens to his guards' stories: "alles nur, um sie wachzuhalten, um ihnen immer wieder zeigen zu können, daß er nichts Eßbares im Käfig hatte und daß er hungerte, wie keiner von ihnen es könnte." This is an important hint as to the nature of the Hunger Artist's guilt, his self-centeredness, but the narrator gives it in the same tone in which he had recorded the precautionary details. And he is then able, without more ado, to move on and spend an inordinate number of lines reporting with evident interest the great breakfast controversy.

Throughout the story, the narrator's vision is distorted by false priorities, misplaced emphases, and a quirkish perspective. He spends excessive time over incidental details and insufficient time over vitally important information. His emotional responses are, as often as not, inappropriate to the event in question, and when he does manage to get below the surface of the world which he beholds, he seems to do so by accident rather than by design. The efficient bureaucrat who is concerned to record as many facts as possible and to see both sides of even the most irrelevant question is unable to come to grips with the real problem of his world: the meaning of the Hunger Artist. Not surprisingly then, when he comes to make a final judgment, he gets things completely wrong. Much has been written about the distorted world of Franz Kafka, but it is always

worth asking whether the distortions exist in the world itself, in the mind of Franz Kafka, or in the mind of the person who happens to be doing the narrating.

Ingeborg Henel, in a helpful essay on **"Ein Hungerkünstler,"** overlooks the distorted vision of the narrator and writes:

> Da die Welt mit den Augen des suchenden und irrenden Helden gesehen wird, herrscht in ihr auch nicht das sonst bei Kafka übliche Dunkel, die dicke Luft oder das Schneegestöber, die zu große Nähe oder die weite Ferne, die die Dinge nur verschwommen erkennen lassen.

But, as has been indicated above, nothing could be further from the truth. The style of **"Ein Hungerkünstler"** is far from "objektiv" precisely because we are able to attach a definite personality to the narrator, locate him within space and time, and show how his vision is unreliable because of this location. For all its apparent clarity, the vision of the narrator of **"Ein Hungerkünstler"** is as dark as if it were clouded by snowstorms, because it is the product of an identifiable set of contingent circumstances. Thus, in one short story, Kafka has called into question the essential basis of nineteenth-century prose fiction, the reliability of the narrator, by the brilliant device of providing us with an ostensibly reliable narrator, who seems himself to believe in his own reliability, but is, in fact, highly unreliable. Whereas nineteenth-century prose fiction assumes that the narrator stands on an Archimedean point outside space and time, Kafka shows the impossibility of continuing to make this assumption. Whereas nineteenth-century fiction assumes that the values of the narrator, rooted in a particular and living social class, are adequate and authentic, Kafka shows us the inadequacy of a narrator who takes his identity from a hypertrophied profession. Whereas nineteenth-century fiction assumes that the narrator understood what he was looking at, Kafka shows us a narrator who fails to respond adequately to what he sees, looks without seeing and sees without understanding. Whereas nineteenth-century fiction assumes the omniscience of the narrator, Kafka shows us his narrator faced with two situations which he cannot explain. First, the narrator tells us about the change of public taste which has come about and then asks who is competent to explain this sudden swing. From the point of view of the traditional conventions of prose fiction, it is the responsibility of the narrator to do this, and it is therefore highly ironic that this particular narrator should implicitly admit that he is not up to the task which he has taken on with so much confidence. Then again, the narrator says later on in the story: "Versuche, jemandem die Hungerkunst zu erklären! Wer es nicht fühlt, dem kann man es nicht begreiflich machen." Just when the narrator ought to be helping us to understand the all-important nature of the "Hungerkunst," he abdicates his responsibility and opens the way for limitless speculation.

Thus, while Dr. Henel is justified in pointing out that the narrative technique of **"Ein Hungerkünstler"** is an unusual one for Kafka, it is more than a little misleading to suggest that this story represents a radically new departure. In this short story, Kafka says exactly the same thing about narrative unreliability as he does in his two major novels—though he says it in a different way. The unreliability of the narrator which is made clear implicitly throughout *Der Prozeß* and *Das Schloß* by having the narrator withdraw from these works to the greatest possible extent, is shown explicitly in **"Ein Hungerkünstler"** through the provision of a narrator who seems to be reliable but in fact is not. **"Ein Hungerkünstler"** can be read as the story of the struggles of a lesser K., seen through the eyes of one of the Castle officials who believes himself to be god-like, but who, like the official in K.'s dream before Bürgel, is really nothing more than a Greek god who squeals like a girl when he is pinched. Where the narrator of *Das Schloß* refuses to pass explicit judgment on K. and the world of the village because of his sense of the relativity of his own position, the narrator of **"Ein Hungerkünstler"** simply does not have enough imagination to pass relevant comments. If the narrator of *Das Schloß* holds back from his fictional world out of a sense of strength and tact, the narrator of *"Ein Hungerkünstler"* holds back from his fictional world because of his limitations. The narrator of *Das Schloß* refuses a god-like rôle, but the narrator of **"Ein Hungerkünstler"** assumes one and then rapidly reveals that he is all too human.

The effect produced in the mind of the reader when the authority of Kafka's narrator is seen to be spurious is a kind of shock. Suddenly, the reader discovers that he has been fooled by the narrator, and the shock of this realization is compounded when the reader understands that he has identified with the unreliable point of view of the narrator because it is so like his own, so like the careless way in which he himself normally deals with the world. The reader must now learn an entirely new way of reading if he is to deal with this little story. He must now keep one eye on the person of the narrator, who stands in the foreground, and one eye on the events of the narrative in the background. He discovers that he must pay as much or more attention to the details which the narrator skates over, as to those he dwells on, since this is the only way of getting past the person of the narrator and gaining a clear picture of the Hunger Artist himself.

On the whole, critics have assumed that the Hunger Artist is an allegorical figure. R. W. Stallman sees the Hunger Artist as a threefold allegory ["A Hunger Artist," *Franz Kafka Today,* 1962], Ingeborg Henel, in the essay referred to above, sees him as an allegory of the artist in general; and Harry Steinhauer sees him as an allegory of the position of religion in contemporary society ["Hunger Artist or Artist in Hungering: Kafka's *A Hunger Artist,*" *Criticism* 4, Winter 1962]. Although certain aspects of the story lend themselves to such allegorical interpretations, Kafka made (in connection with George Grosz) some penetrating remarks about allegory which we need to take into account:

> Es ist richtig, und es ist falsch. Richtig ist es nur nach einer Richtung hin. Falsch ist es, insofern es diese Teilansicht zur Gesamtansicht proklamiert. Der dicke Mann im Zylinderhut sitzt den Armen im Nacken. Das

ist richtig. Der dicke Mann ist aber der Kapitalismus, und das ist nicht mehr ganz richtig. Der dicke Mann beherrscht den armen Mann im Rahmen eines bestimmten Systems. Er ist aber nicht das System selbst. Er ist nicht einmal sein Beherrscher. Im Gegenteil: der dicke Mann trägt auch Fesseln, die in dem Bild nicht dargestellt sind. Das Bild ist nicht vollständig. Darum ist es nicht gut. Der Kapitalismus ist ein System von Abhängigkeiten, die von innen nach außen, von außen nach innen, von oben nach unten und von unten nach oben gehen. Alles ist abhängig, alles ist gefesselt. Kapitalismus ist ein Zustand der Welt und der Seele.

Clearly, the same argument can be applied to allegorical interpretations of **"Ein Hungerkünstler."** They are right and they are wrong. They are right in that one can think of many artists and divines who *are* "hunger artists," but they are wrong in that one can think of many artists and divines who are *not* "hunger artists." Even if one particularizes the allegory to the extent of saying that the Hunger Artist stands for the position of the artist or the situation of religion in *contemporary* society, the same objection applies. If the Hunger Artist is regarded as an allegory, the critic either finds himself forced into proclaiming a "Teilansicht" as the "Gesamtansicht" (in which case he probably ends up by making abstract and pretentious generalizations about the relationship of "art" and "life"), or he has to qualify his statements to make it sufficiently clear that he is talking about a particular kind of artist or divine (in which case he automatically diminishes the scope, importance, and power of Kafka's story).

> It is doubtful whether the Hunger Artist has any purpose at all, whether, despite his confession, he *has* ever looked for the right food.
>
> —*Richard W. Sheppard*

In order to avoid these pitfalls, it is probably better to regard the Hunger Artist not as an allegory of anything, but as the symbol of a psychological (or, perhaps more exactly, a meta-psychological) state which is not peculiar to artists or divines but which has undoubtedly characterized not a few artists and divines of all eras. This approach is corroborated by a passage from Kafka's *Fragmente* which suggests that Kafka himself thought of the Hunger Artist as a psychological type:

> Die Unersättlichen sind manche Asketen, sie machen Hunger-streike auf allen Gebieten des Lebens und wollen dadurch gleichzeitig folgendes erreichen:

> 1. Eine Stimme soll sagen: Genug, du hast genug gefastet, jetzt darfst du essen wie die andern und es wird nicht als Essen angerechnet werden.

2. Die gleiche Stimme soll gleichzeitig sagen: Jetzt hast du so lange unter Zwang gefastet, von jetzt an wirst du mit Freude fasten, es wird süßer als Speise sein (gleichzeitig aber wirst du auch wirklich essen).

3. Die gleiche Stimme soll gleichzeitig sagen: Du hast die Welt besiegt, ich enthebe dich ihrer, des Essens und des Fastens (gleichzeitig aber wirst du sowohl fasten als essen).

Zudem kommt noch eine seit jeher zu ihnen redende unablässige Stimme: Du fastest zwar nicht vollständig, aber du hast den guten Willen und der genügt.

The Hunger Artist is one of the "Unersättlichen" who can be found "auf allen Gebieten des Lebens" because he cannot find the right food. But, unlike the three types of ascetics to whom Kafka refers in the above passage, it is doubtful whether the Hunger Artist has any purpose at all, whether, despite his confession, he *has* ever looked for the right food. The narrator, in that tone of flat reportage which characterizes his treatment of anything important, seems to suggest this when he writes:

Warum wollte man ihn des Ruhmes berauben, weiter zu hungern, nicht nur der größte Hungerkünstler aller Zeiten zu werden, der er ja wahrscheinlich schon war, aber auch noch sich selbst zu übertreffen bis ins Unbegreifliche, denn für seine Fähigkeit zu hungern fühlte er keine Grenzen.

Because the narrator is concerned at this point simply to report the thoughts of the Hunger Artist like the good "Protokollführer" that he is, he fails to remark that the idea of "sich selbst zu übertreffen bis ins Unbegreifliche," being impossible of realization, implies doubt in the existence of "the right food," a refusal to look for it, and a love of never-ending struggle for its own sake.

Thus, even when the day of the big fasting-spectaculars is past, the Hunger Artist is too addicted to his "art," or, more exactly, to struggle, to be able to give it up, and as far as we can see from the narrator's account, this addiction to struggle is bound up with a negative impulse, an inability on the part of the Hunger Artist to accept himself for what he is. This in turn results in perpetual flight from himself:

. . . sondern er war nur so abgemagert aus Unzufriedenheit mit sich selbst. Er allein nämlich wußte, auch kein Eingeweihter sonst wusste das, wie leicht das Hungern war. Es war die leichteste Sache von der Welt.

Because the Hunger Artist is unwilling to accept the limitations of his human existence, symbolized by his refusal to eat, he resolves to flee those limitations and the self which they define, in order willfully to pursue the ideal of absolute fasting which is vacuous because it is tantamount to death. Again, without realizing the force of what he is saying, the narrator manages to suggest that such a daemonic willfulness lies at the root of the Hunger Artist's predicament when he reports:

. . . ja er behauptete sogar, er werde, wenn man ihm seinen Willen lasse, und dies versprach man ihm ohne weiteres, eigentlich erst jetzt die Welt in berechtigtes Erstaunen setzen. . . .

Most of all, the Hunger Artist desires to be left alone with his will and the fiction of greatness which he hopes to create for himself by its exercise. Thus, the Hunger Artist is in exactly the same position as Kierkegaard's "man who wills despairingly to be himself":

By the aid of this infinite form the self despairingly wills to dispose of itself or to create itself, to make itself the self it wills to be, distinguishing in the concrete self what it will and what it will not accept. The man's concrete self, or his concretion, has in fact necessity and limitations, it is this perfectly definite thing, with these faculties, dispositions, etc. But by the aid of the infinite form, the negative self, he wills first to undertake to refashion the whole thing, in order to get out of it in this way a self such as he wants to have, produced by the aid of the infinite form of the negative self—and it is thus he wills to be himself. . . . He is not willing to attire himself in himself, nor to see his task in the self given him; by the aid of being the infinite form he wills to construct it himself. . . . So the despairing self is constantly building nothing but castles in the air. . . . Just at the instant when it seems to be nearest to having the fabric finished it can arbitrarily resolve the whole thing into nothing.

Like this man, the Hunger Artist "is not willing to attire himself in himself, nor to see his task in the self given him." He "undertakes to refashion the whole thing" and constantly builds castles in the air which would be shattered by the first contact with the reality of which he is so afraid. Consequently, in his despair, the Hunger Artist is forced to exert himself ever more strenuously to escape that self which he cannot accept, and only succeeds in driving himself ever more deeply into a state of despair.

Furthermore, like "the man who wills despairingly to be himself," the Hunger Artist is, even if he himself does not realize it, infinitely close to salvation, for at the root of his striving is an unconscious desire for transcendence. This desire is legitimate enough, but the way in which the Hunger Artist tries to realize it is profoundly misguided. Camus' Sisyphus could have become a Hunger Artist, could have sought transcendence in despairingly and willfully trying to escape from the task and the condition to which he had been condemned. But because he does not try to escape and learns to accept both himself and his limitations, he transcends these and achieves a form of happiness. By contrast, Kafka's Hunger Artist is incapable of suspending the activity of his will in order to make Sisyphus' leap of faith; he confuses transcendence with self-over-coming and flees from the limitations of his humanity in order to chase the will-o'-the-wisp of absolute fasting. Whereas Sisyphus accepts his situation as a prison and transcends this prison at the moment *when* he accepts it, the Hunger Artist's willful attempt to break out of the prison of his fleshliness only imprisons him more inescapably. Thus, the narrator, without realizing the hidden force of his remarks, records that the Hunger Artist never left his cage "freiwillig," by the action of his free will, and that the only piece of furniture in his cage was a clock, the symbol of the Hunger Artist's despairing imprisonment within time. In short, the Hunger Artist's legitimate desire for transcendence becomes illegitimate because he is prepared to accept transcendence only on the terms which he himself decrees, and runs away from that self which needs to be accepted if ever it is to be overcome. The outbreaks of pathological rage to which the Hunger Artist is prone are thus the emotional symptoms of a deeply unstable personality in which will and self are disjunct. Once more, Kierkegaard's analysis of the despairing personality provides us with a direct insight into the Hunger Artist's state of soul:

> . . . he is afraid of eternity—for this reason, namely, that it might rid him of his (demoniacally understood) infinite advantage over other men, his (demoniacally understood) justification for being what he is. . . . He ranges most of all at the thought that eternity might get it into its head to take his misery from him!

Just as the Hunger Artist cannot accept himself and strives despairingly to become something that he is not, so too, it is suggested, he is unable to accept other people and strives, indirectly, to dominate them as well. Thus, he listens to the guards' stories only to prove "daß er hungerte, wie keiner von ihnen es könnte" and he yearns for the admiration of the crowds during the circus performances even though he secretly despises them. Only on his deathbed, when he begs forgiveness for having willed that people should admire him, does he realize that he had been more concerned to mystify, impress, and dominate than he had been to communicate through his art. To put it paradoxically, the man who refuses the food which the world holds out to him, who "gives thanks that he is not as other men," is completely incapable of providing the world with any food in return. Thus, early on in the story, it is said that the Hunger Artist answers questions "angestrengt lächelnd," the implication of which is that his smile, the specifically human gesture of acceptance and communication, is artificial. Consequently, one can almost hear the high of relief when, a few lines later, the Hunger Artist is permitted to sink back into himself and "bother himself with no-one." This is not an isolated action. The Hunger Artist prefers to live in the solipsistic illusion of his own excellence, rather than in the world of men, prefers to try to dominate rather than communicate. Later in the story, when the narrator records that the Hunger Artist himself was the only completely "satisfied" spectator of his fasting, he uses the German word "befriedigt," which has sexual overtones and thus suggests that the Hunger Artist's self-absorbed attempt to flee from himself and impose the fiction of his greatness upon others is tantamount to spiritual masturbation.

In view of what the narrator implies about the Hunger Artist's attitude to his world, it is surprising that he should explicitly claim that the latter had worked "honestly" and that the world had cheated him of his reward. When all is said and done, it is not really strange that the world should

remain uncomprehending towards the Hunger Artist since the Hunger Artist has provided it with nothing but the spurious glamor of spectacle. The Hunger Artist has no right to complain of being misunderstood, for the simple reason that he never seriously tried to communicate anything intelligible. It is thus hard to blame the world for its scepticism and brutality towards the Hunger Artist: by his deceptions, he has deserved the former and asked for the latter. Kafka once described sin as "das Zurückweichen vor der eigenen Sendung," and this remark applies exactly to the Hunger Artist's basic failing. His task is to be a man among men, but he refuses this and turns his back upon men out of a deep-seated sense of pride. When, however, he comes to understand what he had done and confesses when he is on the point of death, something in him breaks, the pride goes out of him and the narrator, again oblivious of the full force of his own remark, records:

> Das waren die letzten Worte, aber noch in seinen *gebrochenen* Augen war die feste, *wenn auch nicht mehr stolze Überzeugung,* dass er weiterhungere.

I do not mean to suggest that the problem of the narrator and the problem of the meaning of the figure of the Hunger Artist are two distinct problems conjoined for convenience in one story. Despite the real differences in temperament between the pragmatically official narrator and the introvertedly obsessed Hunger Artist, both men have one thing in common—a deep-seated self-centeredness. Both men have interposed a barrier of subjective prejudice, a fraudulent fiction, between themselves and the real world. The narrator tries to assimilate the complexities of the world to his legalist preconceptions, and the Hunger Artist tries to mold the world according to private fantasies of his own greatness. Both are imprisoned behind bars which they have created for themselves, and neither is able to see any of the light that may shine from behind the mundane and apparently distorted surface of the world which stands over and against them. Each in his own way condescends to the world: the narrator, like Josef K., regards the world and its inhabitants as insignificant and trivial, and the Hunger Artist, like K., assumes that the world revolves around him. Ultimately, the narrator and the central figure of **"Ein Hungerkünstler"** are not distinct, but complementary figures, a lesser K. seen through the eyes of a lesser Josef K. who is his hybristic *Doppelgänger.*

Patrick Mahony (essay date 1978)

SOURCE: "*A Hunger Artist:* Content and Form," in *American Imago,* Vol. 35, No. 4, Winter, 1978, pp. 357-74.

[In the excerpt below, Mahony analyzes Kafka's literary technique in "A Hunger Artist" and provides a psychoanalytic interpretation of the story.]

In a recent book on applied psychoanalysis, two critics have rightly said that "Kafka's **'A Hunger Artist'** is perhaps one of the most powerful, perfectly told tales ever written" [Morton Kaplan and Robert Kloss, "Fantasy of the Devouring Killer: Kafka's *A Hunger Artist*," in *The Unspoken Motive: A Guide to Psychoanalytic Criticism*, 1973]. Most of the power of Kafka's story, I would add, comes from the author's technique of broadening levels of meanings, establishing a continuum among those levels, and subjecting them to many reversals in the literary and psychoanalytic sense of the term. A clarification of Kafka's technique of inclusivity and expansiveness brings to light other dimensions affected by his utilization of reversals.

Kafka's majestic short story has attracted a great deal of stimulating criticism which according to its orientation has advanced a multitude of biographical, historical, and aesthetic perspectives. The very nature of Kafka's fiction, beset internally as it is by countless thematic balances and modifications, promotes an ever-eddying textual criticism. This notwithstanding, I still feel that much of essential importance remains to be said about the meaning and technique of **"A Hunger Artist."**

One of Kafka's principal techniques of inclusivity or broadening levels of reference lies in his structuring of vertical reference. Specifically, the hunger artist is polyvalent, occupying a mediating and Janus-faced position within the triadic hierarchy of meaning that maps out the story:

I. the religious ascetic the creative artist	the immaterial, ethereal and sublimated level
II. the hunger artist	a) the immaterializing level (hunger of itself)
	b) the worldly level (the artist's sensationalism)
III. the leopard	the physical level

The originality of this frame of reference is that it introduces an upward and downward thrust between levels, thereby departing from the uni-directional upward reference so widespread in conventional allegory. Furthermore, the levels in the above schema do not exist in absolute isolation from one another. Accordingly, Kafka has achieved a quasi-anthropomorphological description of the leopard's awareness, thus pushing the animal up towards level II, whereas the groanings and animalistic rage of the caged artist turn him down towards level III. Levels I and II are spanned by the ambiguity of "Künstler" in its double meaning of artiste and artist. The movement between levels may also be appreciated through I. A. Richards' analytical categorization of metaphor into tenor or idea and vehicle or image. When in the end, the hunger artist unimpededly extends his fasting, he literally wastes away into a diminished insignificance that must be searched out with sticks poked into a pile of straw. In other words, as the vehicle or the physical level diminishes, the tenor monopolizes the meaning and there is an upward thrust in the story; with the dwindling of the very percept, the reader himself is induced into a commentary of a radically conceptual nature. This dramatic evolution of partial allegory into near pure allegory is a rare literary achievement

and stands apart from the frequent non-dramatic presentation of allegory as a donné.

Kafka's great genius manifests itself in the choice of artist on level II. A less talented writer might conceivably have selected as protagonist an artisan of pottery who would put more "soul" into his artifacts as he improved, with the banal result that the substantiality of the artifact would be maintained till the very end. By contrast, Kafka shows his genial narrative gift in creating a type of artist who, by the literal emaciation of his body into death, becomes an inevitable and relentlessly overwhelming conceptual indicator. In this light, hunger is radically economic within the immaterial-physical hierarchy: a refined tenor succeeds a wasting body. But the very summit of narrative brilliance and suggestive reversibility is instanced by the jarring juxtaposition of the most etherealized part of the story (the death of the artist) alongside the most physical level (the rampant leopard).

> **The very summit of narrative brilliance and suggestive reversibility is instanced by the jarring juxtaposition of the most etherealized part of the story (the death of the artist) alongside the most physical level (the rampant leopard).**
>
> —*Patrick Mahony*

The three-leveled hierarchical scheme in **"A Hunger Artist"** raises the age-old question of allegory, a theoretical question ideally receiving sustained study in its own right. Be that as it may, the nature of allegory will never be fully defined without our first settling the domain of literary allusion, its techniques and properties, a domain that is even more unexplored. It would seem, at any event, that as allusion becomes less sporadic and at the same time refers to a higher "Platonic" plane of meaning, it tends to become allegorical. "Embraces" here is an indispensable qualifier of "refers to," for a mock epic, on the other hand, contains a sustained allusion to a higher level which is simultaneously rejected. Kafka's technique of poly-reference at times is rather close to that of the mock epic (as in *The Castle* and, par excellence, **Metamorphosis**). But, even if Kafka is to be associated with allegory proper, we must grant that Kafka's penchant for thematic modification, remodification, and ironical inversions breaks him off from the main allegorical tradition. Kafka's originality lies in the fact that his allegory specifically operates as a dystopia, an upside-down world where the ideal is debased or demystified and where iconoclasm is wanton, as opposed to traditional allegory in which there is a realm, immediate or distant, where the ideal remains intact.

It has been said that **"A Hunger Artist"** is strictly a literal story, but to this one may object that since a story may be coherently comprehended on the literal level, the possibility of other levels is not at all obviated. And in fact, there is allegory in Kafka's story but it is continual, not continuous. What demands even more interpretative tact is that the two more abstract domains—religious and aesthetic—are not necessarily concurrent, for at certain times they may succeed each other or just overlap. And even where there is a double reference there may not be a weight equally distributed among its individual terms, much like the distributional variability of the overdetermined dream image. In the text at hand, the artist's eventual confession that he would have eaten if he found the right food certainly applies in a critical sense more to the absolutist claims of all religions than to the Romantic artist's self-asserted mythic vocation. On the other hand, a firmer reference to aesthetic creativity is found in the statement that children inside or outside school have not been prepared for the lesson of fasting.

In the realm of religious and ascetic references, the most remarkable are those which play freely with biblical narrative and relate to Christ. First, the two lady assistants to the faltering martyr replace Simeon who helped carry the Cross, and secondly recall the two Marys present at the crucifixion, an event alluded to again in Kafka's story. The termination of the forty-day fast is announced by the impresario who is a parody of Christ's harbinger, John the Baptist. Although a herald, the impresario is untrue to his subject and does not understand him:

> The impresario came forward, without a word—for the band made speech impossible—lifted his arms in the air above the artist, as if inviting Heaven to look down upon its creature here in the straw, this sufferng martyr . . .

The passage combines the scenes of Christ as Infant laid in straw and His baptism by John. The third chapter of Matthew's gospel depicts the latter scene, rendered so familiar by religious iconography:

> And Jesus, when he was baptized, went up straightway out the water: and lo, the heavens were opened unto him.

An ironical reversal is added. In Matthew and Luke, the baptism is immediately followed by Christ's fasting for forty days, whereas in **"A Hunger Artist,"** the baptismal parody concludes the forty-day fast. Kafka's subsequent portrayal of the artist fuses iconographic representations of Christ both falling beneath the Cross and also crucified:

> . . . his head lolled on his breast as if it had landed there by chance; his body was hollowed out; his legs in a spasm of self-preservation clung close to each other at the knees, yet scraped on the ground as if it were not really solid ground, as if they were only trying to find solid ground; and the whole weight of his body, a featherweight after all, relapsed onto one of the ladies . . .

In a more general sense, the grand public did not believe in the hunger artist, living or dead. Kafka's dying protagonist who begs forgiveness is the ironic contrast of the dying Christ forgiving the spectators.

Contributing an added dimension to the ironies in the vertical technique of hierarchical inclusivity is the technique of horizontal expansion, which deftly manipulates the particular as a universal. This technique of expansion operates in two ways: the hunger artist can be both an individual and class figure; secondly, certain events centering around him, though occasional in occurrence, are softly focused so as to appear typical. More precisely, the term "hunger artist" acquires a generic dimension in occurring four times without the definite article, contrasting with over fifty occurrences with the definite article. The overall result, a stylistic coup de grâce, is the illusory union variously created between the definite and indefinite, the general and particular. After the singular and indefinite "a" in its title, the story opens with a generic statement explicitly referring to hunger artists as a class and ascribing a certain experience suffered by them all:

> During the recent decades the interest in hunger artists has lessened.

Subsequently in the first paragraph of the German version, Kafka thrice precedes "hunger artist" by the definite article, yet in each case the epithet is generic in nature:

> At one time the whole town took a lively interest in the hunger artist . . . everyone wanted to see the hunger artist at least once a day . . . and then it was the childrens' special treat to see the hunger artist . . .

Then, in the course of the second paragraph, there is a delicate shift to the *particular* hunger artist or protagonist of the story. An amateurish trait would have been to write "a hunger artist" or "the hunger artists" to designate the class. But Kafka does nothing of the kind; he deftly moves with grammatical legerdemain from the general to the particular. And yet the hunger artist is surely individualized, for not every one of his peers would sing, like to tell jokes, and so forth.

The other two occurrences of "a," in paragraphs six and eight, are limited in tonal influence. If Kafka desired indefiniteness as the predominant tone, he would have certainly employed "a" in place of "the" in the penultimate paragraph where the artist is submerged in a pile of straw. Instead, Kafka retains the major though not exclusive stress on particularity with the definite article. In this way, although the particular hunger artist is the cynosure of the story, as an allusive and inclusive force, he expands both in horizontal and vertical directions, representing other hunger artists and also those of a "higher" productivity.

Attendant with the skilful gliding between the particular artist and the artist class there is the element of the double nature, unique or occasional, and typical, of some episodes. Periodicity is surely the keynote of the hunger artist's life—his fasts are broken with small regular intervals of recuperation. Similarly, the band music and fanfare announcing the termination of his fasts is a recurrent ritualistic event ("But then there happened yet again what always happened"). In the course of this ritual, however, an episode took place which, upon second look, was by no means invariable. When the artist collapses, the two lady assistants react in their own personal ways. However, the particularization of their reactions within a cyclical chain of events fades into an impression of generalization. The detail of the nearby attendant in readiness along with the generalizing pressures of the muted style tones down the transition from the typical to the non-typical and in that manner unites the two poles. Likewise, one may see aspects of the same technique in the elaborated incident of the artist's outrage, where the typical and predictable (he raged especially when fasting a long time) dominates the particular.

In terms of point of view as well, **"A Hunger Artist"** reveals an inclusive soft focus and ultimately involves both the narrator and reader in the fabric of its reversals. In the first place, the narrator adopts a shifting partiality, favouring the hunger artist while he is alive:

> Of course there were people who argued that this breakfast was an unfair attempt to bribe the watchers, but that was going rather too far.

> . . . and never yet, after any term of fasting—this must be granted to his credit—had he left his cage of his own free will.

> And when once in a time some leisurely passer-by . . . spoke of swindling, that was in its way the stupidest lie even invented by indifference and inborn malice, since it was not the hunger artist who was cheating, he was working honestly, but the world was cheating him of his reward.

But subsequent to the artist's death, the narrator presents the bias of the circus spectators in a somewhat favorable light:

> Even the most insensitive felt it refreshing to see this wild creature leaping around that cage that had so long been dreary.

Narrative soft focus is also found in the ambiguity or doubtfulness of the narrator's omniscience. It is impossible to tell whether he is totally omniscient and therefore merely revealing the partial knowledge of the protagonists or whether he is partially omniscient and thereby participating in the partial knowledge of the protagonists. There are three outstanding instances of such ambiguity:

> Yet for other reasons he was never satisfied; it was not perhaps mere fasting that had brought him to such a skeleton thinness that many people had regretfully to keep away from his exhibitions, because the sight of him was too much for them, perhaps it was dissatisfaction with himself, that had worn him down.

> For meanwhile the aforementioned change in public interest had set in; it seemed to happen almost over-

night; there may have been profound causes for it, but who was going to bother about that.

> . . . perhaps they might even have stayed longer had not those pressing behind them in the narrow gangway . . . made it impossible . . .

A note of indefiniteness also occurs with respect to the reader-audience. Its presence is somewhat implied or felt by the narrator's use of "of course." Once, however, the audience is directly addressed—in the second person-singular and it is not clear whether the address issues from the reflecting artist, the narrator, or both:

> He might fast as much as he could, and he did so; but nothing could save him now, people passed him by. Just try to explain to anyone the art of fasting!

Briefly, the twentieth-century fascination for Kafka's works is to some degree due to their unmooring, their peculiar indefiniteness and inclusive shifting perspective which on the one hand releases from traditional stable perspectives and, on the other hand, as a result of their fragmented formal nature, command further speculation on the part of the reader.

If the traditional thrust of allegory is upward, in reference to abstractions, morality, religion, and the like, Kafkaesque allegory has a downward movement, de-idealizing abstract forces, exposing their corruption and attendantly showing their unattainability.

—Patrick Mahony

Given Kafka's technique of inclusivity and expansiveness, we are now in a better position to pursue the material which he has subjected to reversal, both in its psychoanalytical sense of defense and in the literary sense as a principle of narrative structure. As I suggested before, much of Kafka's fiction is a mixture of allegory and dystopia or upside-down utopia. If the traditional thrust of allegory is upward, in reference to abstractions, morality, religion, and the like, the Kafkaesque allegory has a downward movement, de-idealizing abstract forces, exposing their corruption and attendantly showing their unattainability. *The Trial* spectacularly testifies to such a reversed conception, and somewhat in the same category is **"A Hunger Artist"** with its various reversals, ironies; it presents no resting place or solution except death, for any other solution is inverted and begins another series of problems.

The standard analytical commentary on reversal is in Freud's metapsychological paper "Instincts and Their Vicissitudes." There, Freud lends special attention to two defenses: reversal into the opposite and turning around upon the subject's self. They are among the ego's very oldest defenses and may here be conveniently assimilated into the one rubric, reversal. In treating reversal, Freud has recourse to two pairs of component instincts (sadism and masochism, voyeurism and exhibitionism) and what he calls the total ego activity of love. Reversal may involve:

1) a change of instinctual aim, as from activity to passivity. e. g., instead of my torturing another, the other tortures me;

2) a change of object, while the instinctual aim remains the same—this is reflected by the Greek middle voice, e. g., instead of torturing another, I torture myself.

3) a reversal of content, in the one instance of love giving way to hate. In effect, writes Freud, this topic is quite complicated and he posits three opposites for love: loving-hating, love-being loved, and love and hate taken together as antithetical to unconcern or indifference.

Now, the artist is not only a simple exhibitionist (he stares into vacancy while others are looking at him) but can simultaneously be an exhibitionist-voyeur (he looks at others while they are looking at him) or then again, there's a reversal into sheer voyeurism: he triumphantly looks at the tired watchers eating after a sleepless night. The masochistic element in this voyeurism is clear, for on the other hand, the artist is depressed at seeing the meat destined for the caged animals, to which he feels inferior; similarly, he is pained by the self-asserting starers. In parallel fashion, the fasting artist is not only masochistic, but is also sadistic: he goes to great lengths to keep the watchers sleepless throughout the night, and he wants the public to maintain at considerable inconvenience their interest in his fasting past the forty-day limit.

Indeed, the story puts forth various combinations and reversals of the four component instincts: the lady assistants who, in striving for the exhibitionistic post of honor, coldly exploit the artist's exhibitionism; the spectators who sadistically delight at the distress of a lady assistant; the circus visitors that fear the leopard's roar yet in rapt voyeurism crowd around his cage to look at him; the artist's delusional madness that he can fast indefinitely, with the final result that he neglects to keep up-to-date the notice board and dwindles from sight underneath the straw, to the complete undoing of exhibitionism. And then again, concern may give way to indifference, as when the public forgets the artist; or concern may give way to a combination of both hatred and indifference as in the case of the accusation of the malicious passer-by.

The mechanism of reversal not only applies to the story's thematic elaboration of the component instincts but also the irony which Kafka uses to structure the narrative. The public would rather suppress or repress than be fully aware of its caprices, a fact brought out by the story's very last sentence which ironically reverts to the story's first sentence which sequentially complements it:

But they braced themselves, crowded round the cage, and did not want ever to move away.

During these last decades the interest in professional fasting has markedly diminished.

What is more, exhibitionistic demonstrability of the artist's fasting is ultimately self-defeating and self-punitive, for the public's voyeuristic capability is unequal to the artist's exhibitionistic powers. Only he himself can be adequate witness to his performance, but no one will believe him. Verifiability of his fasting exceeds the spectators' masochistic tolerance of inconvenience. All this adds up to the consideration that breaking a public record feeds on public acknowledgment and acclaim, and without that response, record-breaking occasions further isolation.

Hence, the artist is prisoner of his enterprise. It is possible that his very thinness is counterproductive and keeps people away; his melancholy is misunderstood as caused by fasting whereas the logical reverse was true: although he truthfully says that fasting is easy, he is accused of being modest or deceiving, and when he sings to prove he's not eating for the neglectful watchers playing cards at some distance away, they admire his hypocrisy and cleverness that much more. Even the paradoxical possibility of being intriguing because of his temporary unpopularity boomerangs against the artist:

People grew familiar with the strange idea that they could be expected, in times like these, to take an interest in a hunger artist, and with this familiarity the verdict went out against him.

The most poignant reversal, in a dramatic sense, occurs at the end of the story when the artist undergoes a change of character. He rejects the surface heroism of his past fasting as essentially an involuntary act. Though maintaining his dying decision to fast, he is no longer proud about it. This final humility from an otherwise deranged borderline character is taken as craziness itself by the overseer who continually reverses his logical position:

"Forgive me, everybody," whispered the hunger artist . . .

"Of course," said the overseer, and tapped his forehead with a finger to let the attendants know what state the man was in, "we forgive you."

"I always wanted you to admire my fasting," said the hunger artist.

"We do admire it," said the overseer, affably.

"But you shouldn't admire it," said the hunger artist.

"Well then we don't admire it," said the overseer, "but why shouldn't we admire it?"

"Because I have to fast, I can't help it," said the hunger artist.

"To me you look strange," said the overseer, "and why can't you help it?"

"Because," said the hunger artist, lifting his head a little and speaking, with his lips pursed, as if for a kiss, right into the overseer's ear, so that no syllable might be lost, "because I couldn't find the food I liked. If I had found it, believe me, I wouldn't have made any scene and would have stuffed myself like you or anyone else."

It is an ironic reversal that the artist's physical diminution is concomitant with the diminution of his fame. Ultimately visuality in all its forms fails as a compensation for orality. The narcissistic relation between eye and mouth finally collapses, to be succeeded by aurality and a quasi-osculation. The sadistic impresario gives way to the overseer who, befitting his partial role as superego, with his head turned sidewards, listens to the artist's final confession.

In Kafka's story, reversal is the creative matrix out of which the content and form are elaborated; it keynotes the gliding of levels of meaning into each other, the story's use of Biblical allusion, the dramatization of the four component instincts, and the technique of including the general in the particular and vice versa. As well, reversibility defines the story's narrative structure, whose beginning is also to be understood as following its ending. Summarily: In **"A Hunger Artist"** the aphoristic reduction of the content and imaginative structure reveals a common factor which extends in nature from an unconscious defence to some kind of counterpart in the autonomous conflict-free ego, with the latter functioning centrally in the creation of aesthetic form. The final result is a Symbolic Gestalt.

Allen Thiher (essay date 1990)

SOURCE: "A Hunger Artist," in *Franz Kafka: A Study of the Short Fiction,* Twayne Publishers, 1990, pp. 80-96.

[*In the following excerpt, Thiher examines "A Hunger Artist" in the context of Kafka's ironic commentary on the role of the artist throughout several of his works.*]

The notion of the "artist" in postromantic Germany could still conjure up the image of a creative demiurge, though Kafka's artists hardly fit this description. They are more likely to call forth a snicker. Kafka is hardly the first writer to present the artist as a laughter-provoking beast hardly worthy of serious consideration; I ask the reader to consider the following lamentation about the poet's plight by a romantic writer whom Kafka read with the greatest interest, E.T.A. Hoffmann: "Once glowed in the breast of the chosen ones the inner, holy striving to express in glorious words that which they had most deeply felt; and even those who had not been chosen had belief and devotion; they honored poets as prophets who could prophesy of a glorious unknown world full of shining riches; and they did not suppose that those who weren't elected might

be able to enter that holy realm about which poetry gave them a distant annunciation. Now everything has changed." The romantic Hoffmann thus offers at once a description of both the artist's task and the remote period when the artist could accomplish that task, all of which is couched in a complaint about the present day's fall from that glorious past. This is a familiar historical configuration. Once things were different; the poet-prophet could enter the superior realm of the sacred and the ideal. But that moment has been lost. It might appear that, as modern philosophers such as Heidegger or Derrida would have it, poets *always* find themselves as those who *once* had access to a sacred sphere, that once there was no fallenness. But in the present moment artists have "always already" undergone a fall from some moment of privileged annunciation. Or as Kafka put it in his views on our fall into history, poets are always repeating the past's decline. They live it as an eternal repetition in the present.

Hoffmann goes one step further in dramatizing this lamentation, and this is the step that interested Kafka. Hoffmann's speaker, complaining about the difference between then and now, is a dog. He is, to be sure, a rather famous dog, the Berganza that Cervantes first described in a story about his conversations with Scipion (in his *Novelas ejemplares* or *Exemplary Tales*) and whose adventures Hoffmann continued in his tale called "Nachricht von den neuesten Schicksalen des Hundes Berganza" ("Report on the latest Fate of the Dog Berganza"). The dog Berganza, like Kafka's horse Bucephalus, is well placed to report on the fall, for this canine has lived several centuries, and in his latest avatar, I think, he has become Kafka's beast artist and thinker of the twentieth century.

Reports on the fall—the fall from true humanity—are appropriately made by dogs and apes and other utterly fallen artists. We have already seen some of these fallen or degraded artists in Kafka's earlier work in which beasts are looking for knowledge and redemption, such as **"Investigations of a Dog"** (written in 1922, at the same time as the tales in *A Hunger Artist*), or, even more obliquely, in *The Metamorphosis.* One of Kafka's most remarkable portrayals of the artist as beast is found in a piece he published in **"A Country Doctor," "A Report to the Academy."** On reading this tale narrated by an ape, one immediately wants to draw analogies with James Joyce's portrait of the artist as a young man and the later portrait of the artist as a young monkey by Michel Butor, for Kafka's portrait is situated clearly in a development that leads from a view of the artist as a heroic forger of myth to one of the artist as a dealer in aping junk. But the best starting point for looking at intertextual affinities is again a romantic text, again by Hoffmann, namely his fantasy piece called "Nachricht von einem gebildeten jungen Mann" ("Report from a Cultured Young Man") which contains a letter from Milos, a well-educated ape, to his friend Pipi in North America. Hoffmann's primate has learned to ape all the mannerisms of Europeans of good education and has become a consummate artistic charlatan merely by using the instinct for imitation that causes us to laugh at apes—and which we say is the basis of our art. From the time of Aristotle to the present day Western art has constantly returned to mimesis—imitation and representation—as the basis for its existence; therefore, if the artist is an imitator, he is, as Hoffmann and, even more pointedly, Kafka show, quite literally an ape.

From the time of Aristotle to the present day Western art has constantly returned to mimesis—imitation and representation—as the basis for its existence; therefore, if the artist is an imitator, he is as Hoffmann and, even more pointedly, Kafka show, quite literally an ape.

—*Allen Thiher*

Kafka's ape narrator in **"A Report to the Academy"** is also a product of a long history, to wit, the history of the ascent of man that Darwin told in his version of the origin of the species. Kafka's ironies about art and science leave one uncertain as to whether he is presenting man as an elevated ape, or his ape as a fallen man. In any case, in Kafka's tale the well-educated ape finds that his instinct for imitation is a part of a historical process for which he must give an account; Kafka's ape is in fact reporting on his origins—the origins of a, if not the, species of ape artists—and in this respect Kafka offers the artist as a strange culmination of one of nature's more bizarre evolutionary branchings.

Beyond Darwin, Kafka's parody aims at the myth of origins itself, at that myth that would assign some end to the retrospective expansion we can create as the tale of our history. Origins are always already given by the desire to construct a limit for the distances we see behind us; or, as Kafka's ape narrator says, in pointing out the arbitrary nature of these creations: "It is now nearly five years since I was an ape, a short space of time, perhaps, according to the calendar, but an infinitely long time to gallop through at full speed, as I have done. . . ." Yet we all believe that in some sense we are still tied as apes to that long trip that took us from our origins, over evolutionary distances, to the present moment: "To put it plainly . . . your life as apes, gentlemen, insofar as something of that kind lies behind you, cannot be farther removed from you than mine is from me. Yet everyone on earth feels a tickling at the heels; the small chimpanzee and the great Achilles alike." Our animal origins remain with us, and perhaps man—or the Kafkan artist—can only exist as a beast. Kafka's ape, like all of us apparently, has become or tried to become a man by imitating what a man is. He has aped man, has followed his animal instinct for imitation, so that paradoxically he becomes a man by using his skills as an ape.

There is one noteworthy if subtle difference between Kafka the artist and his aping creation, for Kafka's correspon-

dence and diaries reveal that his greatest agony was that he could not find the freedom to be, in the simplest terms, himself, that is, the artist he longed to be. The ape who imitates man, on the other hand, claims that he did not begin imitating in order to gain his freedom once he was captured; rather, he merely wanted an *Ausweg*, a way out: "I deliberately do not use the word 'freedom' . . . may I say that all too often men are betrayed by the word freedom. And as freedom is counted among the most sublime feelings, so the corresponding disillusionment can be also sublime." For the ape has observed freedom in art and has become disillusioned:

> In variety theaters I have often watched, before my turn came on, a couple of acrobats performing on trapezes high in the roof. They swung themselves, they rocked to and fro, they sprang into the air, they floated into each other's arms, one hung by the hair from the teeth of the other. "And that too is human freedom," I thought, "self-controlled movement." What a mockery of holy Mother Nature! Were the apes to see such a spectacle, no theater walls could stand the shock of their laughter.

The ape sees our artists as practitioners in freedom, but in their human freedom they are a distortion of nature, a comic deviation that, in some sense, marks art for Kafka as a kind of derisive activity, sacred and risible at the same time.

The trapeze artist, the circus equestrienne, and the writer all use or practice freedom, but they are all deviants with regard to pure nature: freedom is a superfluous notion for a natural being. Our ape narrator, half human artist, half mimicking animal, retains a memory of a nature that asks for none of the redundant gestures of freedom, or the dubious doublings of mimesis. The natural being, like the sister at the end of *The Metamorphosis* or the panther that replaces the artist in starvation at the end of **"A Hunger Artist,"** has a body that bursts with sufficiency, that has no need of the freedom that the artists need. The caged panther, for instance, "seemed not even to miss his freedom; his noble body, furnished almost to the bursting point with all that it needed, seemed to carry freedom around with it too; somewhere in his jaws it seemed to lurk." The self-sufficiency of the natural world, like a paradise from which we are forever driven, remains in the back of our ape's mind; and once this ape has been put in his cage in Africa, the most he can desire is a way out: he decides to become an artist.

As Kafka portrays the ape in **"A Report to the Academy,"** he becomes an artist who practices Aristotle's *Poetics* by imitating what he sees about him:

> What a triumph it was . . . when one evening before a large circle of spectators—perhaps there was a celebration of some kind, a gramophone was playing, an officer was circulating among the crew—when on this evening, just as no one was looking, I took hold of a schnapps bottle that had been carelessly left standing before my cage, uncorked it in the best style, while the

company began to watch me with mounting attention, set it to my lips without hesitation, with no grimace, like a professional drinker, with rolling eyes and full throat, actually and truly drank it empty; then threw the bottle away, not this time in despair but as an artistic performer.

With this acting performance he breaks into speech and into the human community. The way out leads then from Zoological Garden to the variety stage and, on the way, leaving his apedom behind, he can reach the cultural level of the average European. Having attained this level, the ape-artist, now a comically redundant expression, can take up a proto-Kafkan position and sit by the window in his rocking chair and gaze out on that exterior world to which he is a stranger.

Kafka's ape is metamorphosed into an ironic representative of a poetic tradition that once vouchsafed the greatest philosophical seriousness to aping, and his sitting by the window figures the kind of alienation the modern artist feels in looking back on that tradition that believed imitation brought one into the realm of nature. Moreover, the tale is one of several in which Kafka seems to take pleasure in revealing that the artist is, if not a deviant, then a superfluous being whose work can just as well be done by mere imaginings, with no need for concrete realization. This minimalist strategy underlies, for example, the anticipation of conceptual art that Kafka offers in **"The City Coat of Arms,"** a later parable written two years before **"Investigations of a Dog."** This exemplary text begins by saying that all was going well in the construction of the Tower of Babel, perhaps too well, since people thought more about "guides, interpreters, accommodations for the workmen, and roads of communication" than about actually building the tower up to the heavens: "People argued in this way: The essential thing in the whole business is the idea of building a tower that will reach to heaven. In comparison with that idea everything else is secondary. The idea, once seized in its magnitude, can never vanish again. . . ."

Baukunst—or architecture, as the emblem of all arts—is reduced to a mere conceptual matter. It matters little if the edifice is ever built, since that would entail the haphazard material manifestation of the idea (every century will have its own building techniques, and usually better ones as time goes by, so why be in a hurry?). Kafka pushes the idea of mimesis to a kind of absurdly logical conclusion: if art imitates the idea or ideal, the artist need not bother with the derivative act of imitation, since the idea continues to exist independently. The idea needs no material embodiment, since, as with the concept of the Tower of Babel, it can circulate freely and traverse great historical expanses of time that, in fact, the realized work could never cross. The idea of the Tower of Babel can, for example, pop up in a parable by a German language writer living in Prague at the beginning of the twentieth century. The concept of the tower is clearly contained therein, even if the parable exists to explain the nonexistence of the material realization of the concept, which can then take on other, variant forms of nonexistence, such as the

pit of Babylon that Kafka saw as a project that one might have burrowed into existence.

If the artist's creation is at best apery, and in any case a derivative act better left undone, then the artist is thrown back upon himself to find some reason for his existence. Denied recourse to some problematic exterior realm of the ideal, he is obliged to look within himself and find the sources of art in his innards. In a sense all that is left to him is to discourse on his own condition and literally to turn himself into art—as Kafka shows in **"First Sorrow,"** and especially in his initiation into body art, **"A Hunger Artist."** Art here is the process of art, which is to say, art feeds on the mere process of the artist being an artist. Or one might say that Kafka's idea of art is minimalism with a vengeance: the artistic process is the act that can lead to the disappearance of the artist.

The first story in *A Hunger Artist* is **"First Sorrow,"** the tale of the initiation into suffering of the fanatical trapeze artist who is the story's protagonist. Swinging on a trapeze is of course a nonmimetic art and offers an ambivalent image of art as a trivial if intense process. Kafka's choice of circus artist is ambivalent in that it seems to stand for the kind of fallen status of the artist at the same time that it suggests that the artist can be found anywhere, perhaps everywhere—always already about to fall into our midsts. Living on the margins of culture, his trapeze artist is not just an acrobat who turns his body into art: he is an artist who does nothing else. Kafka is again pursuing his absurd logic to a reasonable conclusion. For if the artist is an artist only insofar as he practices his art—a proposition that Kafka entertained in several contexts—then the only way to exist as an artist is always to be an artist, that is, never to stop. So the trapeze artist never comes down from his exalted position "high in the vaulted domes of the great variety theaters." Day and night he stays on his trapeze. . . .

The hunger artist, like the trapeze artist, never stops practicing his art. He would fast for days on end, even forever, if he could. He literally uses his body for his art. And in this process of ascesis he has the capacity to symbolize every artist hero from the Christian Creator, who allowed his body to be hung up on public display, to the body artists of the sixties and seventies who, subjecting their flesh to public demonstrations of sado-masochism, proclaimed they were the art of the immediate moment. Or, from another perspective, the hunger artist looks back to these performers of degraded spectacle that were once found in the circus and the music hall, the freaks and the misfits (and historically real hunger artists) who are another double of the fallen artist who can only use his own body for his art. Kafka probably never created a character capable of generating a richer allegory, at once both specific in its description of the artist, and capable of derisively portraying the structure of most of our beliefs in artistic revelation.

Fasting, like all art, has had a historical development—and that development can only take the form of a fall. Once popular, fasting has known the fate of all art forms or movements; it has lost audience favor, and as the story progresses, the reader sees the hunger artist relegated to the periphery of our culture, finally disappearing as his art form becomes incomprehensible. Of course, the reader never *sees* that moment of great popularity that fasting once knew. This moment can only be remembered, recalled by a narrator who begins the story by saying that "During these last decades the interest in professional fasting has markedly diminished"; and then goes on to say that the art pays little today in this world that is so different from the one in which people flocked to see hunger artists. Like Hoffmann's dog recalling those days when poet prophets were honored, the narrator of **"A Hunger Artist"** remembers a time when people were not revulsed by the hunger artist, when they "understood" him and his achievement. But, the reader will ask, was there a time when art was not already a victim of misunderstanding? For this is always (and already) the meaning of the present in Kafka's work.

Kafka is giving a literal representation of the cliché about the "misunderstood artist," but with an ironic twist: this artist is truly misunderstood in that no one realizes that he cannot find the sustenance he needs, the sustenance that would free him from his miserable art.

—Allen Thiher

The narrator, like the guardian of the machine of *In the Penal Colony,* can claim to remember when the hunger artist would spend his forty days before appreciative crowds during the day, and then would be watched at night. At night, to allay suspicion that he might be eating, he would push his art even further, for "sometimes he mastered his feebleness sufficiently to sing during their watch for as long as he could keep going, to show them how unjust their suspicions were." It would seem that the hunger artist was not entirely appreciated in those past days either, for the guards would react to his song by wondering how he could sing while putting food in his mouth. In one sense Kafka is giving a literal representation of the cliché about the "misunderstood artist," but with an ironic twist: this artist is truly misunderstood in that no one realizes that he cannot find the sustenance he needs, the sustenance that would free him from his miserable art. The hunger artist would, he says later, cease fasting if he were able to find a food he liked; so he must bear the watch of those who can, like healthy animals, fling themselves in the morning with keen appetite on the breakfast that the hunger artist buys for them.

Kafka is dramatizing the most minimal art here, the art of turning a lack of substance (or sustenance) into an art form. But for the artist who cannot find the sustenance he

wants this is not a difficult task, though his audience may not wish to believe it: "For he alone knew, what no other initiate knew, how easy it was to fast. It was the easiest thing in the world. He made no secret of this, yet people did not believe him, at the best they set him down as modest, most of them, however, thought he was out for publicity or else was some kind of cheat who found it easy to fast because he had discovered a way of making it easy, and then had the impudence to admit the fact, more or less." I quote the above lines because it seems to me there is something devastating about the way Kafka, with an ironic smile, admits that starving is the easiest thing in the world. Starving is easy, and within the right framework— in a cage or a book—we can then look upon it as art. And while I do not wish to run the risk of inflating the importance of my subject—though this hardly seems possible when dealing with Kafka—Kafka appears here to be anticipating the total disarray of our current literary and artistic scene; with incomparably more irony and self-awareness than most of today's artists, he outlines the position of the artist as the fraudulent, the necessarily if haplessly fraudulent minimalist.

The changing historical understanding of art, the changing artistic fashions as it were, gives the hunger artist the opportunity to show the ease with which he fasts, though nobody is likely to be concerned with his record-setting performance. Since the hunger artist can no longer attract "today" the crowds he once did, he can no longer work alone. But a large circus agrees to take him on and places his cage near the animal cages, on a concourse that the public uses in going to and from the main attraction. He thus finds himself unwittingly in competition with the animals as a spectacle. When the way is blocked in front of his cage, people stop; fathers even remember for their children the great feats of hunger artists, but this is of little interest to the children. To increase his alienation, the hunger artist must suffer the nauseating stench of the raw meat that the keepers bring to feed the beasts of prey.

Ignored by the public, finally forgotten by the circus management, the artist fasts on and on until one day an overseer wonders why there is an empty cage standing about unused. The hunger artist has fasted himself into near invisibility. And it is at that moment that we learn that he is another of Kafka's protagonists who, for lack of sustenance, is withering away in spite of himself. As he dies he tells the overseer that he should not be admired:

> "Because I have to fast, I can't help it," said the hunger artist. "What a fellow you are," said the overseer, "and why can't you help it?" "Because," said the hunger artist, lifting his head a little and speaking, with his lips pursed, as if for a kiss, right into the overseer's ear, so that no syllable might be lost, "because I couldn't find the food I liked. If I had found it, believe me, I should have made no fuss and stuffed myself like you or anyone else." These were his last words, but in his dimming eyes remained the firm though no longer proud persuasion that he was still continuing to fast.

Like Gregor, the vermin of *The Metamorphosis,* the hunger artist falls from language into silence and then death because he cannot find the sustenance he needs. The difference between vermin and artist may appear minimal in this awful perspective, but an even more extraordinary parallel is found in their last erotic gestures—Gregor reaches up to his sister with vermin tenderness, the hunger artist purses his emaciated lips "as if for a kiss." Moreover, Kafka ends each story with an image that presents the antithesis of a withered speechless beetle or an emaciated hunger artist; he presents the image of animal self-sufficiency that the sensual sister or the sleek panther proposes. I stress this parallel because it seems to me that these two stories complement each other not only in the way they show that hunger, speechlessness, and art are parts of the same configuration, but also in the way that their final image shows that the contrary of spiritual fulfillment in Kafka is mere animal plenitude. And this is another speechless state, a natural state devoid of the sin of self-consciousness. And, finally, art stands out clearly as belonging to those who practice it as a surrogate for something they cannot name, except perhaps negatively through art.

Frederick R. Karl (essay date 1991)

SOURCE: "Modernism and Death, Kafka and Death," in *Franz Kafka: Representative Man,* Ticknor & Fields, 1991, pp. 678-81.

[*In this excerpt, Karl analyzes "A Hunger Artist" in the context of Kafka's life and times.*]

Kafka in **"A Hunger Artist"** was not merely creating emblems of the self. He was playing roles, as he had in his letters and in many other of his fictional works. The role he played out was that of a man who feared invalidation of self more than he feared death: he had to carry through in his imagination the most extreme form of art to justify himself as an artist, although his justification led to the artist's death. It was better to play such an extreme role, leading to certain death, than to chance the fact that he might live without having made that final sacrifice. Role-playing here has the typical shape of a Kafkan paradox: one seeks sure death in order to validate a life that is worth little unless it can confront final matters through some meaningful gesture.

Biographically, **"A Hunger Artist"** is a gold mine of meaning. It permitted Kafka to flout his family, by rejecting all its ideas of food, nourishment, and health, a death blow to any family and especially an upwardly mobile Jewish family in Middle Europe. Next, he could finalize a role he had played all his life, as finicky, panicked eater, vegetarian, fletcherizer. Further, the role gave him celebrity; he could use his own internal dilemmas and problems as a means of exhibiting himself and gaining fame. As an exhibition, he could gain a public by becoming a pariah, a strange object, a bizarre artifact, all the elements he had harbored in himself. Still further, as

someone already sensing his death, he could play with the edges of dying and death, approaching the end in ever finer gradations, until, with one misstep, he would be over the edge. And finally, and most importantly, all his obsessions with food, sex, and his body could be channeled into a symmetrical shape, into something he could present to the world as representing him and yet, because of its art, transcending him. It was a final act of rebellion. He located himself so far outside bourgeois society he became transformed, transcendent, even transfigured. All the earlier yearning to validate his "difference" now had a solid shape.

The hunger artist gloats over his difference; he vaunts his deprivation. His superiority lies in every moment of his indifference to what others consider life-sustaining and part of their indulgence. By not eating for more than forty days, he can demonstrate not only a record for a hunger artist, but the perfection of his art, an absolute moment that only the highest artists can achieve. In this achievement, he finds the artistic equivalent of orgasm: a perfection that transcends usual bodily enjoyment, that moment when all comes together, Kandinsky's "spiritual" moment.

The hunger artist is not past his prime. What happens as his public deserts him is that it itself, now interested only in sensational experiences, has changed. In this, Kafka has caught the shift in his part of Europe, in the early 1920s, when the countries adjoining Czechoslovakia were teetering on the edge of lawlessness, disorder, their own forms of wildness. There is a profound political message in **"A Hunger Artist."** It is not good news either for artists or for Jews. In this respect, the artist figure is a perfect symbol of the Jew and his position. Like the artist, the Jew has not fitted, has not been part of the establishment, was considered a kind of freak of nature or clown, and, as part of his fascination for the public, was exhibited. But as "tastes" changed, the Jew was not afforded that precarious position. As the public passes the hunger artist by for wilder experiences, for the jungle animals, for example, we sense their perceptions shifting; and although there is still no "leader" in view, it is clear the spectators want blood, not refinements.

In a related sense, the artist is rejected for presenting a decadent art. The Jew as artist is an equation that many nationalists and populists made to justify squashing first one and then the other. With his art judged decadent and, therefore, as corruptive of the society, the artist observes the public moving away to more wholesome exhibitions, those fitting a folk art, a folk people, a people attuned to the blood and the senses, not to the intellect. The explosion of folk art that came with the Weimar Republic and with the Bauhaus fit well into that backlash against anarchic, uncontrollable Modernism in the social and political spheres. The relationship of the hunger artist, in 1922, to these shifts in public opinion and to the way the public was manipulated cannot be neglected. Kafka may use obsession with food as his pivot, but his meanings extend well into social, political, racial, and ethnic considerations.

In this respect, Modernism itself is on trial. The artist tries to prolong the refinement of taste on which his art depends, on the qualities of intellect, will, and definition it offers to the discriminating spectator. Modernism was, after all, a fine art, and it required dedicated artists, those who, like Kafka, would commit themselves completely to their craft. When because of shifts in public tastes that was rejected (although Modernism never had a large or particularly receptive audience), then the end not only of art but as well of a kind of civilization was imminent.

> **Kafka was describing the end of things, the final moments of a civilization, the morbid directions of a new sensibility.**
>
> —*Frederick. R. Karl*

Kafka was insistent on this, as we see here and in nearly everything else he wrote in the last years of his life, including those extraordinary diary entries. . . . He was describing the end of things, the final moments of a civilization, the morbid directions of a new sensibility, all by way of manifesting these elements in himself. He was careful to demonstrate that the hunger artist is not being abandoned because he is losing his powers. His performance does not depend on age factors. When he is rejected, he is in fact refining his performance. As it turns out, the audience judges him as negating life because he is rejecting food itself; his artistry does not lie solely in negation, however, but in his assumption of a role that opens up the audience (and himself) to great mysteries, analogous to those rituals associated with the myths of life and death. The hunger artist is becoming a shaman, a clairvoyant, a seer, and if he is intense and successful enough, he will transmit his "vision" to those observing him. He has questioned the very foundation of the existence of the ordinary. He opens up questions of existential experience, of the individual edging toward the abyss, of a creature attempting to move ever closer, in asymptotic steps, toward that forbidden borderline between life and death where the ultimate mysteries lie.

What is outrageous about the artist is his lack of interest in that well-being that characterizes ordinary people and is part of ordinary life. He is tuned in to one era, they to another; and when they desert him they have relegated him to the past, to memory, elements that have no place in their new social and political sensibilities. They have put history behind them, as the German-speaking world tried to put the humiliations of the Versailles treaty behind it.

The audience seeks coarseness in its new experience, something to gratify more sensual sensibilities. The new public enjoys the smell of the menagerie and watches as raw lumps of meat are fed to the wild animals, an experience the very opposite, of course, of that offered by the refined hunger artist. It is a public associated with the bread and circuses of the late Roman Empire, to the gladiatorial fights, to orgies that left little to the imagination or intellect. With such interests, the public can gain its excitement only from sensational moments. The slow development of sensibility required by the hunger artist is a source of boredom and distaste. Also a source of distaste is the weak, frail, exhausted hunger artist—the Jew as pitiful, the artist as enervated and played out, especially when compared with the wild animal, the intense and powerful figure of the present moment.

The hunger artist becomes indistinguishable from the straw he lies in. Organic matter passes slowly into inorganic, until he is swept up as part of the garbage pile. The artist asserts he cannot find the food he likes, that if he had found it, he would have made "no fuss and stuffed myself like you or anyone else." These are his last words. But such expressions make him sound like an imposter, as though he were, as the audience has suspected, a mountebank of sorts. In the final moments, he wavers, for his denial and rejection have not depended on "taste" but on choice. The panther who has replaced him in his cage makes no such decisions. After the artist is cleared out, with the trash, the young panther eats and does not seem to mourn its loss of freedom; its noble body is sleek, bursting with energy: "His noble body, furnished almost to the bursting point with all that it needed, seemed to carry freedom around with it too; somewhere in his jaws it seemed to lurk; and the joy of life streamed with such ardent passion from his throat that for the onlookers it was not easy to stand the shock of it. But they braced themselves, crowded round the cage, and did not want ever to move away."

This Kafka panther is still young, still bursting with energy. Rilke's panther [in *Duino Elegies*] knows better. In time, it too will become enervated, as the strength implicit in its "mighty will" is slowly extinguished; and when that animal slows, the audience will desert it for some new sensation, leaving *that* panther to a deserted cage. The final lines of Rilke's poem would seem a fitting epitaph not only for panthers in captivity but for Kafka:

> *From time to time the curtain of the pupils*
> *silently parts—Then an image enters,*
> *goes through the taut stillness of the limbs,*
> *and is extinguished in the heart.*

Nearly all of Kafka's works after this are comparable expressions of farewell.

Paulo Medeiros (essay date 1992)

SOURCE: "Cannibalism and Starvation: The Parameters of Eating Disorders in Literature," in *Disorderly Eaters: Texts in Self-Empowerment,* edited by Lilian R. Furst and Peter W. Graham, The Pennsylvania State University Press, 1992, pp. 11-27.

[In the following excerpt, Medeiros asserts that Kafka's hunger artist exhibits the same characteristics as actual anorexics.]

[Kafka's Hunger Artist,] in his voluntary denial of any form of consumption . . . approximates the actual behavior of anorexics. Kafka's story, like most of his writing, hinges on a paradox and the resulting *aporia*—in this case, the confession made by the Hunger Artist, just before he expires, that he never ate "because [he] could not find the food that [he] liked." This crucial statement both questions the entire foundation for the nameless artist's existence—his capacity and wish to withstand hunger indefinitely—and negates his claim to artistic talent, because he appears to relegate all his actions to a fundamental experience of lack, the impossibility of finding food to his taste. Yet such a last denial of himself and of his art must be seen as an extension, perhaps in absolute form, of his previous practice of total denial of consumption (which brings about his death) and therefore as a final affirmation, in negative terms, of the Hunger Artist's project all along: a refusal to partake of food, parallel to the desire to set himself apart from society and even from humanity. The Hunger Artist tells his night watchers ("usually, strangely enough, butchers"), he "starved (*hungerte*) like none of them could."

To this determination to prove his superiority through his control of appetite one could add at least two other characteristics, and all are common to anorexic behavior: (1) the exhibitionism inherent in the Hunger Artist's concept of art (*Schauhunger*, "exhibition fasting"), which makes his body an object for popular marvel either as an independent curiosity show or in conjunction with a circus; and (2) the determined attempt to resist any efforts to stop the fast and the ultimate surrender to outside force, leading to his almost involuntary feeding:

> . . . finally came two young ladies . . . [who] wanted to lead the Hunger Artist down a couple of steps out of the cage, to where a carefully chosen diet meal (*Krankenmahlzeit*) had been served on a small table. And at this moment the Hunger Artist always resisted. . . . Then came the food, from which the Impresario fed a little to the Hunger Artist during a faint-like half-sleep. . . .

His refusal to stop fasting is typical of the anorexic's obsessive insistence. The Hunger Artist is deeply disappointed at the forced break of his fast at the end of forty days: "Why did one want to rob him of the fame, to go on fasting, not only to become the greatest Hunger Artist of all times, which he probably already was, but also to surpass himself up to incomprehensibility, since he felt no limits to his capacity to fast."

The Hunger Artist's marginality is evident both in his being the object of a freak show and in his placement within a cage. The latter, with its suggestion of a subhuman existence, becomes even more pressing as the Hunger Artist's value as an attraction diminishes and he is forced to join a circus, his cage located at the entrance to the stables, where he is finally replaced by a panther. Yet the diminished attention of the public, which never understood him or his intent, is also what allows the Hunger Artist to pursue his goal of unlimited fasting. The Hunger Artist's absolute desire to refuse consumption is characterized best, in Gerhard Neumann's terms, as an "autarchic play of self-consumption": society ceases to matter as a force to resist or from which to draw attention and admiration. Ultimately, the Hunger Artist can be seen not as subhuman and monstrous, and also not as superhuman in his resistance to hunger, but rather simply as extrahuman. His attempt to place himself outside the boundaries of society is also an attempt to surpass even his own boundary—literally, because by starving he reduces his own body so that he actually seems to have disappeared into the straw lining the bottom of his cage. Consequently, and taking into consideration how the Hunger Artist in his uninterrupted fast becomes the sole audience for his art, Neumann concludes that the meaning brought about by such an "absolute sign," independent of any outside referent, is that of the "paradox of identity itself."

Frank Vulpi (essay date 1993)

SOURCE: "Kafka's A Hunger Artist: A Cautionary Tale for Faustian Man Caught Between Creativity and Communion," in *Germanic Notes and Reviews,* Vol. 24, No. 1, Spring, 1993, pp. 9-12.

[In the following essay, Vulpi views Kafka's hunger artist as a representation of the Faustian man, one who "pursues an idea or creates something primarily to please himself, gain power, or satisy his ego."]

Whether or not Kafka's **"A Hunger Artist"** (**"Ein Hungerkünstler"**) is about the fate of the artist in twentieth-century society has been a much-discussed question. Critic Meno Spann [in *Franz Kafka,* 1976] comments as follows:

> The word *Hungerkünstler* is misunderstood. The word *Künstler* by itself means artist, but in compounds it designates performers in the circus or in a variety show like *Trapezkünstler* ("trapeze artist") or *Entkleidungskünstler* ("stripper"), both of whom display skills but are not artists. Besides, Kafka never concerned himself with the artist and his relation to society.

Allen Thiher [in *Franz Kafka: A Study of the Short Fiction,* 1990], on the other hand, states: "The question of the artist and the function of art underlies nearly all of Kafka's work. . . ." Thiher also says that in **"A Hunger Artist"** Kafka is giving a literal representation of the cliche about the "misunderstood artist."

W. C. Rubenstein [in "A Hunger Artist," in *Monatshefte* XLIV, No. 1, January 1952] insists that "the hunger artist is the painter, musician, poet or what you will, who devotes himself ascetically to his art." But H. Steinhauer [in "Hungering Artist or Artist in Hungering: Kafka's *A Hunger Artist*," in *Criticism* IV, No. 1, 1962] believes that "Kafka is not writing about an artist but about an ascetic saint."

It seems abundantly clear, to the present writer at least, that the hunger artist (artist in the conventional sense or not) is a representation of the Faustian man. He is a relentless striver after something out of the ordinary. As Spengler has noted in his *The Decline of the West,* our entire culture is Faustian. He claims that the "body" of the Faustian soul "is the Western Culture that blossomed forth with the birth of the Romanesque style in the 10th century in the Northern plain between the Elbe and the Tagus."

We in the West hold it good to ceaselessly strive and to be dissatisfied with any particular past achievement. As he strikes his bargain with Mephistopheles, Goethe has his Faust say: "If ever I lay me on a bed of sloth in peace, / That instant let for me existence cease!" Artist, religious ascetic, business entrepreneur, craftsman, politician—any profession can inspire a monomaniacal devotion. The devotee may be willing to forgo many of the usual familial and social responsibilities or pleasures in order to pursue his goal.

Nietzsche's "will to power" aptly describes the Faustian striver. Michael E. Zimmerman, speaking of Nietzsche [in *Heidegger's Confrontation with Modernity, Technology, Politics, and Art,* 1990] claims that

> For him, Will was the unconditioned subjectivity of life which strives to become ever stronger: the Will to Power was essentially the Will to Will, the aimless striving for ever more striving. This ever-expanding circle never opens up beyond the self-contained limits of blind striving. Humanity, stamped by this Will, is reduced to a clever animal striving for more power.

If an individual pursues an idea or creates something primarily to please himself, gain power, or satisfy his ego, then the originator of that idea or creation can properly be termed a Faustian man.

Does Kafka call into question the wisdom of the Faustian man? I think he does. Kafka's hunger artist is a powerful example of a Faustian man who, in his preoccupation with his ego and personal objectives has become irrevocably estranged from his community and the life around him.

The alternative to working primarily for oneself and towards goals which are established by the individual (and consequently often valuable or relevant only to that individual) is to work in community with others towards a common goal.

In his book, *Between Man and Man,* Martin Buber outlines this dichotomy between working towards creativity and working towards community. Calling the creative instinct the originative instinct, he says:

> There are two forms, indispensable for the building of true human life, to which the originative instinct, left

to itself, does not lead and cannot lead: to sharing in an undertaking and to entering into mutuality.

Sharing in an undertaking and entering into mutuality are clearly aspects of community. Buber comments upon the isolating effect of individual achievement as follows:

> Action leading to an individual achievement is a "one-sided" event. There is a force within the person, which goes out, impresses itself on the material, and the achievement arises objectively . . . so long as he is engaged in his work spirit goes out from him and does not enter him, he replies to the world but he does not meet it any more.

Buber finally concludes: "Yes; as an originator man is solitary."

In order to build "true human life" (or, in Buber's parlance, to enter into an *I-Thou* relationship with others), the instinct for communion must override the originative instinct: "What teaches us the saying of *Thou* is not the originative instinct but the instinct for communion."

For Buber "to be conditioned in a common job, with the unconcious humility of being a part, of participation and partaking, is the true food of earthly immortality." And only if the originator has another person grasp his hand "not as a 'creator' but as someone lost in the world . . . does he have an awareness and a share of mutuality."

Even Goethe's Faust ultimately recognized the validity of working towards the common good. G.M. Priest has written the following [in "An Outline and Interpretation of Goethe's 'Faust'," in *Faust: Parts One and Two,* 1941]:

> As long as Faust was striving toward the goal of an ambitious egoist, he found no satisfying moment. To no moment could he say: "Ah, linger on, thou art so fair!" Now, as one of many free and active men, he knows that there can be such a moment . . . Faust has affirmed life; he has done what he never thought he would do. He sees that life can be worth living . . .

According to Buber, even if the Faustian man does seek communion and "strives" to attain it, he will not succeed. For communion means "being opened up and drawn in." The individual, no matter how driven and intent upon it, cannot "produce" communion with others by willing it. The "other" has to readily cooperate, and both must put aside their personal agendas, preconceived ideas, and any previous decisions made about what the nature of the relationship will be and how it will satisfy their own needs.

Communion occurs only when mutual respect is felt and the awareness of the other's autonomy is acknowledged. Communion happens "between" two people—two people who are opened up to it and are willing to be drawn in to it. Communion stands over and against the compulsive yet "aimless" striving described by Zimmerman as Nietzsche's Will to Power. Buber says that

At the opposite pole from compulsion there stands not freedom but communion . . . At the opposite pole of being compelled by destiny or nature or men there does not stand being free of destiny or nature or men but to commune and to covenant with them.

The hunger artist is a most extreme illustration of the Faustian man: as he reaches perfection in his work (that is, as he starves himself longer and longer) he naturally approaches death and thus, not only figuratively, but literally dies to the possibility of communion.

The hunger artist is a most extreme illustration of the Faustian man: as he reaches perfection in his work (that is, as he starves himself longer and longer) he naturally approaches death and thus, not only figuratively, but literally dies to the possibility of communion.

—Frank Vulpi

Kafka strongly delineates the discrepancy between the objectives of the Faustian man (with his originator instinct) and the Buberian man (who longs to enter into communion with others) by bestowing upon his title character an activity which (despite all the dedication and gravity the hunger artist lavishes on it) cannot possibly be of any use to his community. Of course this polarizes the two opposing instincts—creation and communion—and eliminates the confusion of ideals, motives, and fears out of which most of us act in the real world.

Many real-world Faustian strivers do produce work from which others benefit. They are undoubtedly motivated by concern for others as well as by ego gratification, and their activities and the vigor with which they pursue them are not inevitably detrimental to their physical or emotional well-being, or incompatible with the instinct towards communion. Nontheless, an unhealthy obsession with their work usually results not in a literal death but in a spiritual stagnation, an atrophed emotional growth, or in the cessation of some process vital to their psychic health.

The hunger artist helps no one through his activity: his work is useless, self-destructive, and arbitrarily determined upon. He acts alone and he alone understands his motives. He is a simplified, schematized version of the Faustian man, untroubled by any vestigial notions of tribal solidarity, self-preservation, or love. In the hunger artist, the striving towards his goal as an end in itself leads to death. He is an extreme example of the originator instinct, unadulterated by even the meagerest appetite for communion. Consequently, he has what would be for most of us the severest penalty imposed upon him.

It is a measure of the maleficent nature of his self-centered striving that the man living solely by this principle must die. And it is a measure of the hunger artist's aberrant temperament that he chooses an activity necessarily inimical to life itself and therefore incompatible with the notion of communion. The very nature of his activity (fasting) prevents him from partaking of life, and from participating with others. To fast as long as possible is to consume life in order to reach a goal. Thus life is merely the means of attaining a desired end, and this particular end is attained only when life is completely consumed. To apply this attitude to any activity necessarily glorifies the end and holds the means valuable only in its function as a method of obtaining that end. Thus the originator instinct places priority upon the product of its endeavors, which is, inescapably, a non-human entity. The instinct towards communion, however, finds value in the process that generates the product. Since this process is inevitably a part of the life of the people involved in the undertaking, holding this process to be valuable is fundamentally a life-affirming attitude.

At the story's end, the hunger artist insists that he should not be admired for fasting. When asked why, he exclaims: "Because I have to fast, I can't help it . . . I couldn't find the food I liked." This indicates, as Ronald Gray has noted [in *Franz Kafka,* 1973], that the hunger artist "makes somes spiritual progress, in that, at his dying moment, he is no longer proud of his achievement." For the hunger artist, success was fatal. The pride and the egotistical satisfaction that he felt from his accomplishment prevented the hunger artist from seeking communion with others. At the end of the story, he has so habituated himself to his isolation that had he desired to reenter the community of men, one must doubt that he could have "found the food he liked."

Accustomed to finding his self validation in his ego-centered activities (self-destructive as they were) his desires and needs (growing increasingly perverse with time) would possibly not have been gratified by entering into communion with others. But at least the hunger artist ultimately realizes that his efforts were fruitless and meaningless, and that his energy has been misplaced. For other Faustian strivers, too, pride in the success of their individual achievements reinforces their destructive behavior and moves them further from the idea of working in community with others. They, like the hunger artist, can only progress spiritually if they recognize the futility of finding lasting fulfillment in the originator instinct.

The hunger artist's activity is built on an alienation of a most radical nature. By refusing to partake of food (an activity which when conducted with others symbolizes community perhaps more effectively than any other activity) he implicitly tries to deny his need for community and his humanity itself. Striving towards his goal, that of fasting ever longer, the hunger artist courts death. Attaining his goal inevitably means embracing death. Goethe's Faust, upon attaining his final goal (a goal which results from harnessing his originator instinct to the service of the community and which, consequently, gives him enough satisfaction to be momentarily content) also finds death.

Perhaps **"A Hunger Artist"** is Kafka's commentary on the Faust legend, a fragmentary twentieth-century annotation, an ironic extraction of its conceptual kernel. The originator man discovers the extremity of his isolation in the moment of supreme achievement: his triumph has been a personal one, a victory wrested from the intransigent world through willpower, persistence, and sometimes heroic effort. He imposes his achievement upon the world, whether it will or no, and expects recognition or compensation. The Faustian striver has no one to share his triumph with, no one who truly shared in it and with whom he can now go on to other joint ventures. He must arbitrarily assign himself another task and stave off desolation by immersing himself in it. Otherwise he risks experiencing a kind of spiritual or psychological death, unless he can redirect his energy towards communion.

At the end of his story, Kafka contrasts a life-affirming leopard, which replaces the hunger artist in his cage, to the death-desiring hunger artist. The leopard, however, submerged in his animal nature, is no viable alternative to the hunger artist. We can, upon reading this cautionary tale, perhaps prevent ourselves from going the way of the hunger artist, but we cannot, in our attempt to administer Kafka's prescription, turn ourselves into leopards. We can turn away from the originator instinct, not from creation itself, but from the impulse that leads us to create primarily in order to glorify the ego. That impulse leads us to find ultimate satisfaction in the contemplation of the creation itself, which is no more than a mirror brilliantly reflecting the ego which engendered it. We can, in other words, seek communion with others first and foremost. We can create, together, a community that would profit from all of our talents, one in which our individual efforts would prove more meaningful than we could anticipate.

Perhaps Kafka, in **"A Hunger Artist,"** means to have us look closely at what he considers to be the inevitable evolution of the Faustian striver: a man imbued exclusively with the originator instinct, and one who therefore awards highest priority to his own desires and needs; one who finds the utmost significance in the pleasure he derives from his own ideas, creations, and the completion of self-imposed tasks. Obviously, this man is already with us, and has been since time immemorial: the armaments manufacturer who takes ultimate satisfaction in the sophistication of his weaponry, eschewing thoughts of the havoc it will wreak on humanity; the great industrialist or business entrepreneur content in the size of his financial empire, oblivious to the fate of his employees; the lawyer preoccupied with the quality of his legal work and in obtaining a favorable verdict for his client, inured to the amoral climate in which he works, habitually exercising immoral options because they produce the desired results and fall within the law.

Even the self-centered work of the artist, hungry or not, is usually embarked upon not in a spirit of community but in one of self-aggrandizement and unspoken competition with others. The competitive spirit and the need to satisfy our desires are basic to our survival, but by acting solely on these principles we court extinction. We must always remain open to the possibility of communion and take that possibility with us into every encounter with our fellow creatures. It must be the fundamental motivation in all of our undertakings and must infuse all of our hopes for ourselves and for the world.

Buber says this on the possibility of communion:

> . . . it cannot be dispensed with and it cannot be made use of in itself; without it nothing succeeds, but neither does anything succeed by means of it: it is the run before the jump, the tuning of the violin, the confirmation of that primal and mighty potentiality which it cannot even begin to actualize.

FURTHER READING

Arbuckle, Donald E. and James B. Misenheimer, Jr. "Personal Failure in 'The Egg' and 'A Hunger Artist'." *The Winesburg Eagle: The Official Publication of the Sherwood Anderson Society* 8, No. 2 (April 1983): 1-3.

Compares the fates of the protagonists in Sherwood Anderson's "The Egg" and Kafka's "A Hunger Artist." In both cases, the critics note, "the protagonists try to make their bleak existences important to others and fail miserably."

Foulkes, A. P. "The Cage Image in *Ein Bericht für Eine Akademie* and *Ein Hungerkünstler*." In *The Reluctant Pessimist: A Study of Franz Kafka*, pp. 90-7. The Hague: Mouton, 1967.

Examines the cage image in "A Hunger Artist" and "A Report to an Academy," and contrasts the outlooks on life offered by these stories.

Garrison, Joseph, Jr. "Getting into the Cage: A Note on Kafka's 'A Hunger Artist'." *The International Fiction Review* 8, No. 1 (Winter 1981): 61-3.

Views the narrator rather than the hunger artist as the central figure of Kafka's short story.

Honig, Edwin. "The Expanding Analogy." *In Dark Conceit: The Making of Allegory*, pp. 115-28. Evanston, Ill.: Northwestern University Press, 1959.

Views Kafka as an allegorist who identifies his hunger artist with Christ.

Kaplan, Morton and Robert Kloss. "Fantasy of the Devouring Killer: Kafka's *A Hunger Artist*." In *The Unspoken Motive: A Guide to Psychoanalytic Criticism*, p. 80. New York: Free Press, 1973.

Asserts that "A Hunger Artist" "is perhaps one of the most powerful, perfectly told tales ever written."

McFarland, Ronald E. "Community and Interpretive Communities in Stories by Hawthorne, Kafka and García Márquez." *Studies in Short Fiction* 29, No. 4 (Fall 1992): 551-59.

> Holds that at least three communities are involved in Kafka's "A Hunger Artist," Gabriel García Márquez's "A Very Old Man with Enormous Wings," and Nathaniel Hawthorne's "The Minister's Black Veil": that represented by the spectators, the "interpretive community" of readers, and the "real-life communities" in which the readers participate.

Michaelson, L. W. "Kafka's Hunger Artist and Baudelaire's Old Clown." *Studies in Short Fiction* 5 (1968): 293.

> Asserts that the old clown in Baudelaire's *Le Vieux Saltimbanque* "has many points in sympathy with the hunger artist."

Mitchell, Breon. "Kafka and the Hunger Artists." In *Kafka and the Contemporary Critical Performance: Centenary Readings,* edited by Alan Udoff, pp. 236-52. Bloomington: Indiana University Press, 1987.

> Examines the possible historical sources for "A Hunger Artist," including actual hunger artists of the nineteenth century.

Moyer, Patricia. "Time and the Artist in Kafka and Hawthorne." *Modern Fiction Studies* 4, No. 4 (Winter 1958-59): 295-306.

> Asserts that "in 'The Artist of the Beautiful' and 'The Hunger Artist' Hawthorne and Kafka make their most definitive poetic statements about the position of the artist in the modern world."

Neumarkt, Paul. "Kafka's *A Hunger Artist:* The Ego in Isolation." *American Imago* 27, No. 2 (Summer 1970): 109-21.

> Analyzes the stories collected in *A Hunger Artist* from a psychoanalytic perspective.

Norris, Margot. "Sadism and Masochism in Two Kafka Stories: 'In der Strafkolonie' and 'Ein Hungerkünstler'." *Modern Language Notes* 93, No. 3 (April 1978): 430-47.

> Points out the "striking structural symmetry" of *In the Penal Colony* and "A Hunger Artist," noting that "in each, a fanatical believer in meaningful suffering reenacts a spectacle that in an earlier age drew huge, festival crowds, but now results only in sordid death and burial."

Pasley, J. M. S. "Asceticism and Cannibalism: Notes on an Unpublished Kafka Text." *Oxford German Studies* 1 (1966): 102-13.

> Views the fanatical characters of Kafka's works, including the hunger artist, as representing an aspect of Kafka himself.

Satz, Martha and Zsuzsanna Ozsvath. *"A Hunger Artist* and *In the Penal Colony* in the Light of Schopenhauerian Metaphysics." *German Studies Review* 1, No. 2 (May 1978): 200-10.

> Considers Kafka's short stories "A Hunger Artist" and "In the Penal Colony" in the context of the views of German philosopher Arthur Schopenhauer. The critics observe: "The heroic Artist and Saint figures of Schopenhauer, men who have attained insight by annihilating their will to live, have become the distorted and dubious figures of the Hunger Artist and the Officer in the 'Penal Colony'."

Spann, Meno. "Don't Hurt the Jackdaw." *The Germanic Review* XXXVII, No. 1 (January 1962): 68-78.

> Insists that "A Hunger Artist" is autobiographical rather than allegorical and denies that the central figure represents "the suffering artist or saint in modern society." The story, Meno declares, "is Kafka's swan-song and that evasive ironist's affirmation of nature and life."

——. "The Last Metamorphoses." In *Franz Kafka,* pp. 164-73. Boston: Twayne Publishers, 1976.

> Surveys the prevailing critical interpretations of "A Hunger Artist."

Wood, Cecil. "On the Tendency of Nature to Imitate Art." *The Minnesota Review* VI, No. 2 (1966): 133-48.

> Examines "A Hunger Artist" and Ernest Hemingway's *The Old Man and the Sea* and their treatment of the idealist in a materialistic society.

Additional coverage of Kafka's life and career is contained in the following sources published by Gale Research: *Contemporary Authors,* Vols. 105, 126; *Dictionary of Literary Biography,* Vol. 81; *Discovering Authors; Discovering Authors: British; Discovering Authors: Canadian; Discovering Authors: Modules—Most-Studied Authors Module* and *Novelists Module; Major Twentieth-Century Writers; Short Story Criticism,* Vol. 5; *Twentieth-Century Literary Criticism,* Vols. 2, 6, 13, 29, 47, 53; *World Literature Criticism.*

Appendix:

Select Bibliography of General Sources on Short Fiction

BOOKS OF CRITICISM

Allen, Walter. *The Short Story in English.* New York: Oxford University Press, 1981, 413 p.

Aycock, Wendell M., ed. *The Teller and the Tale: Aspects of the Short Story* (Proceedings of the Comparative Literature Symposium, Texas Tech University, Volume XIII). Lubbock: Texas Tech Press, 1982, 156 p.

Averill, Deborah. *The Irish Short Story from George Moore to Frank O'Connor.* Washington, D.C.: University Press of America, 1982, 329 p.

Bates, H. E. *The Modern Short Story: A Critical Survey.* Boston: Writer, 1941, 231 p.

Bayley, John. *The Short Story: Henry James to Elizabeth Bowen.* Great Britain: The Harvester Press Limited, 1988, 197 p.

Bennett, E. K. *A History of the German Novelle: From Goethe to Thomas Mann.* Cambridge: At the University Press, 1934, 296 p.

Bone, Robert. *Down Home: A History of Afro-American Short Fiction from Its Beginning to the End of the Harlem Renaissance.* Rev. ed. New York: Columbia University Press, 1988, 350 p.

Bruck, Peter. *The Black American Short Story in the Twentieth Century: A Collection of Critical Essays.* Amsterdam: B. R. Grüner Publishing Co., 1977, 209 p.

Burnett, Whit, and Burnett, Hallie. *The Modern Short Story in the Making.* New York: Hawthorn Books, 1964, 405 p.

Canby, Henry Seidel. *The Short Story in English.* New York: Henry Holt and Co., 1909, 386 p.

Current-García, Eugene. *The American Short Story before 1850: A Critical History.* Twayne's Critical History of the Short Story, edited by William Peden. Boston: Twayne Publishers, 1985, 168 p.

Flora, Joseph M., ed. *The English Short Story, 1880-1945: A Critical History.* Twayne's Critical History of the Short Story, edited by William Peden. Boston: Twayne Publishers, 1985, 215 p.

Foster, David William. *Studies in the Contemporary Spanish-American Short Story.* Columbia, Mo.: University of Missouri Press, 1979, 126 p.

George, Albert J. *Short Fiction in France, 1800-1850.* Syracuse, N.Y.: Syracuse University Press, 1964, 245 p.

Gerlach, John. *Toward an End: Closure and Structure in the American Short Story.* University, Ala.: The University of Alabama Press, 1985, 193 p.

Hankin, Cherry, ed. *Critical Essays on the New Zealand Short Story.* Auckland: Heinemann Publishers, 1982, 186 p.

Hanson, Clare, ed. *Re-Reading the Short Story.* London: MacMillan Press, 1989, 137 p.

Harris, Wendell V. *British Short Fiction in the Nineteenth Century.* Detroit: Wayne State University Press, 1979, 209 p.

Huntington, John. *Rationalizing Genius: Ideological Strategies in the Classic American Science Fiction Short Story*. New Brunswick: Rutgers University Press, 1989, 216 p.

Kilroy, James F., ed. *The Irish Short Story: A Critical History*. Twayne's Critical History of the Short Story, edited by William Peden. Boston: Twayne Publishers, 1984, 251 p.

Lee, A. Robert. *The Nineteenth-Century American Short Story*. Totowa, N. J.: Vision / Barnes & Noble, 1986, 196 p.

Leibowitz, Judith. *Narrative Purpose in the Novella*. The Hague: Mouton, 1974, 137 p.

Lohafer, Susan. *Coming to Terms with the Short Story*. Baton Rouge: Louisiana State University Press, 1983, 171 p.

Lohafer, Susan, and Clarey, Jo Ellyn. *Short Story Theory at a Crossroads*. Baton Rouge: Louisiana State University Press, 1989, 352 p.

Mann, Susan Garland. *The Short Story Cycle: A Genre Companion and Reference Guide*. New York: Greenwood Press, 1989, 228 p.

Matthews, Brander. *The Philosophy of the Short Story*. New York, N.Y.: Longmans, Green and Co., 1901, 83 p.

May, Charles E., ed. *Short Story Theories*. Athens, Oh.: Ohio University Press, 1976, 251 p.

McClave, Heather, ed. *Women Writers of the Short Story: A Collection of Critical Essays*. Englewood Cliffs, N. J.: Prentice-Hall, 1980, 171 p.

Moser, Charles, ed. *The Russian Short Story: A Critical History*. Twayne's Critical History of the Short Story, edited by William Peden. Boston: Twayne Publishers, 1986, 232 p.

New, W. H. *Dreams of Speech and Violence: The Art of the Short Story in Canada and New Zealand*. Toronto: The University of Toronto Press, 1987, 302 p.

Newman, Frances. *The Short Story's Mutations: From Petronius to Paul Morand*. New York: B. W. Huebsch, 1925, 332 p.

O'Connor, Frank. *The Lonely Voice: A Study of the Short Story*. Cleveland: World Publishing Co., 1963, 220 p.

O'Faolain, Sean. *The Short Story*. New York: Devin-Adair Co., 1951, 370 p.

Orel, Harold. *The Victorian Short Story: Development and Triumph of a Literary Genre*. Cambridge: Cambridge University Press, 1986, 213 p.

O'Toole, L. Michael. *Structure, Style and Interpretation in the Russian Short Story*. New Haven: Yale University Press, 1982, 272 p.

Pattee, Fred Lewis. *The Development of the American Short Story: An Historical Survey*. New York: Harper and Brothers Publishers, 1923, 388 p.

Peden, Margaret Sayers, ed. *The Latin American Short Story: A Critical History*. Twayne's Critical History of the Short Story, edited by William Peden. Boston: Twayne Publishers, 1983, 160 p.

Peden, William. *The American Short Story: Continuity and Change, 1940-1975*. Rev. ed. Boston: Houghton Mifflin Co., 1975, 215 p.

Reid, Ian. *The Short Story*. The Critical Idiom, edited by John D. Jump. London: Methuen and Co., 1977, 76 p.

Rhode, Robert D. *Setting in the American Short Story of Local Color, 1865-1900*. The Hague: Mouton, 1975, 189 p.

Rohrberger, Mary. *Hawthorne and the Modern Short Story: A Study in Genre*. The Hague: Mouton and Co., 1966, 148 p.

Shaw, Valerie. *The Short Story: A Critical Introduction*. London: Longman, 1983, 294 p.

Stephens, Michael. *The Dramaturgy of Style: Voice in Short Fiction*. Carbondale, Ill.: Southern Illinois University Press, 1986, 281 p.

Stevick, Philip, ed. *The American Short Story, 1900-1945: A Critical History*. Twayne's Critical History of the Short Story, edited by William Peden. Boston: Twayne Publishers, 1984, 209 p.

Summers, Hollis, ed. *Discussion of the Short Story*. Boston: D. C. Heath and Co., 1963, 118 p.

Vannatta, Dennis, ed. *The English Short Story, 1945-1980: A Critical History*. Twayne's Critical History of the Short Story, edited by William Peden. Boston: Twayne Publishers, 1985, 206 p.

Voss, Arthur. *The American Short Story: A Critical Survey*. Norman, Okla.: University of Oklahoma Press, 1973, 399 p.

Walker, Warren S. *Twentieth-Century Short Story Explication: New Series, Vol. 1: 1989-1990*. Hamden, Conn.: Shoe String, 1993, 366 p.

Ward, Alfred C. *Aspects of the Modern Short Story: English and American*. London: University of London Press, 1924, 307 p.

Weaver, Gordon, ed. *The American Short Story, 1945-1980: A Critical History*. Twayne's Critical History of the Short Story, edited by William Peden. Boston: Twayne Publishers, 1983, 150 p.

West, Ray B., Jr. *The Short Story in America, 1900-1950*. Chicago: Henry Regnery Co., 1952, 147 p.

Williams, Blanche Colton. *Our Short Story Writers*. New York: Moffat, Yard and Co., 1920, 357 p.

Wright, Austin McGiffert. *The American Short Story in the Twenties*. Chicago: University of Chicago Press, 1961, 425 p.

CRITICAL ANTHOLOGIES

Atkinson, W. Patterson, ed. *The Short-Story*. Boston: Allyn and Bacon, 1923, 317 p.

Baldwin, Charles Sears, ed. *American Short Stories*. New York, N.Y.: Longmans, Green and Co., 1904, 333 p.

Charters, Ann, ed. *The Story and Its Writer: An Introduction to Short Fiction*. New York: St. Martin's Press, 1983, 1239 p.

Current-García, Eugene, and Patrick, Walton R., eds. *American Short Stories: 1820 to the Present*. Key Editions, edited by John C. Gerber. Chicago: Scott, Foresman and Co., 1952, 633 p.

Fagin, N. Bryllion, ed. *America through the Short Story*. Boston: Little, Brown, and Co., 1936, 508 p.

Frakes, James R., and Traschen, Isadore, eds. *Short Fiction: A Critical Collection*. Prentice-Hall English Literature Series, edited by Maynard Mack. Englewood Cliffs, N.J.: Prentice-Hall, 1959, 459 p.

Gifford, Douglas, ed. *Scottish Short Stories, 1800-1900*. The Scottish Library, edited by Alexander Scott. London: Calder and Boyars, 1971, 350 p.

Gordon, Caroline, and Tate, Allen, eds. *The House of Fiction: An Anthology of the Short Story withCommentary*. Rev. ed. New York: Charles Scribner's Sons, 1960, 469 p.

Greet, T. Y., et. al. *The Worlds of Fiction: Stories in Context*. Boston, Mass.: Houghton Mifflin Co., 1964, 429 p.

Gullason, Thomas A., and Caspar, Leonard, eds. *The World of Short Fiction: An International Collection*. New York: Harper and Row, 1962, 548 p.

Havighurst, Walter, ed. *Masters of the Modern Short Story*. New York: Harcourt, Brace and Co., 1945, 538 p.

Litz, A. Walton, ed. *Major American Short Stories*. New York: Oxford University Press, 1975, 823 p.

Matthews, Brander, ed. *The Short-Story: Specimens Illustrating Its Development*. New York: American Book Co., 1907, 399 p.

Menton, Seymour, ed. *The Spanish American Short Story: A Critical Anthology*. Berkeley and Los Angeles: University of California Press, 1980, 496 p.

Mzamane, Mbulelo Vizikhungo, ed. *Hungry Flames, and Other Black South African Short Stories*. Longman African Classics. Essex: Longman, 1986, 162 p.

Schorer, Mark, ed. *The Short Story: A Critical Anthology*. Rev. ed. Prentice-Hall English Literature Series, edited by Maynard Mack. Englewood Cliffs, N. J.: Prentice-Hall, 1967, 459 p.

Simpson, Claude M., ed. *The Local Colorists: American Short Stories, 1857-1900*. New York: Harper and Brothers Publishers, 1960, 340 p.

Stanton, Robert, ed. *The Short Story and the Reader*. New York: Henry Holt and Co., 1960, 557 p.

West, Ray B., Jr., ed. *American Short Stories*. New York: Thomas Y. Crowell Co., 1959, 267 p.

Short Story Criticism Indexes

Literary Criticism Series
Cumulative Author Index

SSC Cumulative Nationality Index
SSC Cumulative Title Index

How to Use This Index

The main references

Calvino, Italo
1923–1985 .... CLC 5, 8, 11, 22, 33, 39,
73; SSC 3

list all author entries in the following Gale Literary Criticism series:

BLC = Black Literature Criticism
CLC = Contemporary Literary Criticism
CLR = Children's Literature Review
CMLC = Classical and Medieval Literature Criticism
DA = DISCovering Authors
DAB = DISCovering Authors: British
DAC = DISCovering Authors: Canadian
DAM = DISCovering Authors: Modules
    DRAM: Dramatists Module; MST: Most-Studied Authors Module;
    MULT: Multicultural Authors Module; NOV: Novelists Module;
    POET: Poets Module; POP: Popular Fiction and Genre Authors Module
DC = Drama Criticism
HLC = Hispanic Literature Criticism
LC = Literature Criticism from 1400 to 1800
NCLC = Nineteenth-Century Literature Criticism
PC = Poetry Criticism
SSC = Short Story Criticism
TCLC = Twentieth-Century Literary Criticism
WLC = World Literature Criticism, 1500 to the Present

The cross-references

See also CANR 23; CA 85-88;
obituary CA116

list all author entries in the following Gale biographical and literary sources:

AAYA = Authors & Artists for Young Adults
AITN = Authors in the News
BEST = Bestsellers
BW = Black Writers
CA = Contemporary Authors
CAAS = Contemporary Authors Autobiography Series
CABS = Contemporary Authors Bibliographical Series
CANR = Contemporary Authors New Revision Series
CAP = Contemporary Authors Permanent Series
CDALB = Concise Dictionary of American Literary Biography
CDBLB = Concise Dictionary of British Literary Biography
DLB = Dictionary of Literary Biography
DLBD = Dictionary of Literary Biography Documentary Series
DLBY = Dictionary of Literary Biography Yearbook
HW = Hispanic Writers
JRDA = Junior DISCovering Authors
MAICYA = Major Authors and Illustrators for Children and Young Adults
MTCW = Major 20th-Century Writers
NNAL = Native North American Literature
SAAS = Something about the Author Autobiography Series
SATA = Something about the Author
YABC = Yesterday's Authors of Books for Children

Literary Criticism Series
Cumulative Author Index

Abasiyanik, Sait Faik 1906-1954
See Sait Faik
See also CA 123

Abbey, Edward 1927-1989 .... CLC **36, 59**
See also CA 45-48; 128; CANR 2, 41

Abbott, Lee K(ittredge) 1947- .... CLC **48**
See also CA 124; CANR 51; DLB 130

Abe, Kobo 1924-1993 .... CLC **8, 22, 53, 81;**
DAM NOV
See also CA 65-68; 140; CANR 24, 60; DLB
182; MTCW

Abelard, Peter c. 1079-c. 1142 ...... CMLC **11**
See also DLB 115

Abell, Kjeld 1901-1961 .... CLC **15**
See also CA 111

Abish, Walter 1931- .... CLC **22**
See also CA 101; CANR 37; DLB 130

Abrahams, Peter (Henry) 1919- .... CLC **4**
See also BW 1; CA 57-60; CANR 26; DLB
117; MTCW

Abrams, M(eyer) H(oward)
1912- .... CLC **24**
See also CA 57-60; CANR 13, 33; DLB 67

Abse, Dannie
1923- ..... CLC **7, 29; DAB; DAM POET**
See also CA 53-56; CAAS 1; CANR 4, 46;
DLB 27

Achebe, (Albert) Chinua(lumogu)
1930- .... CLC **1, 3, 5, 7, 11, 26, 51, 75;**
BLC; DA; DAB; DAC; DAM MST,
MULT, NOV; WLC
See also AAYA 15; BW 2; CA 1-4R;
CANR 6, 26, 47; CLR 20; DLB 117;
MAICYA; MTCW; SATA 40; SATA-
Brief 38

Acker, Kathy 1948- .... CLC **45**
See also CA 117; 122; CANR 55

Ackroyd, Peter 1949- .... CLC **34, 52**
See also CA 123; 127; CANR 51; DLB 155;
INT 127

Acorn, Milton 1923- .... CLC **15; DAC**
See also CA 103; DLB 53; INT 103

Adamov, Arthur
1908-1970 .... CLC **4, 25; DAM DRAM**
See also CA 17-18; 25-28R; CAP 2; MTCW

Adams, Alice (Boyd)
1926- .... CLC **6, 13, 46; SSC 24**
See also CA 81-84; CANR 26, 53; DLBY 86;
INT CANR-26; MTCW

Adams, Andy 1859-1935 .... TCLC **56**
See also YABC 1

Adams, Douglas (Noel) 1952- .... CLC **27, 60;**
DAM POP
See also AAYA 4; BEST 89:3; CA 106; CANR
34; DLBY 83; JRDA

Adams, Francis 1862-1893 .... NCLC **33**

Adams, Henry (Brooks)
1838-1918 .... TCLC **4, 52; DA; DAB;**
DAC; DAM MST
See also CA 104; 133; DLB 12, 47

Adams, Richard (George)
1920- .... CLC **4, 5, 18; DAM NOV**
See also AAYA 16; AITN 1, 2; CA 49-52;
CANR 3, 35; CLR 20; JRDA; MAICYA;
MTCW; SATA 7, 69

Adamson, Joy(-Friederike Victoria)
1910-1980 .... CLC **17**
See also CA 69-72; 93-96; CANR 22; MTCW;
SATA 11; SATA-Obit 22

Adcock, Fleur 1934- .... CLC **41**
See also CA 25-28R; CAAS 23; CANR 11, 34;
DLB 40

Addams, Charles (Samuel)
1912-1988 .... CLC **30**
See also CA 61-64; 126; CANR 12

Addams, Jane 1860-1935 .... TCLC **76**

Addison, Joseph 1672-1719 .... LC **18**
See also CDBLB 1660-1789; DLB 101

Adler, Alfred (F.) 1870-1937 .... TCLC **61**
See also CA 119; 159

Adler, C(arole) S(chwerdtfeger)
1932- .... CLC **35**
See also AAYA 4; CA 89-92; CANR 19,
40; JRDA; MAICYA; SAAS 15; SATA
26, 63

Adler, Renata 1938- .... CLC **8, 31**
See also CA 49-52; CANR 5, 22, 52;
MTCW

Ady, Endre 1877-1919 .... TCLC **11**
See also CA 107

A.E. 1867-1935 .... TCLC **3, 10**
See also Russell, George William

Aeschylus 525B.C.-456B.C. CMLC **11; DA;**
DAB; DAC; DAM DRAM, MST; WLCS
See also DLB 176

Africa, Ben
See Bosman, Herman Charles

Afton, Effie
See Harper, Frances Ellen Watkins

Agapida, Fray Antonio
See Irving, Washington

Agee, James (Rufus)
1909-1955 .... TCLC **1, 19; DAM NOV**
See also AITN 1; CA 108; 148; CDALB 1941-
1968; DLB 2, 26, 152

Aghill, Gordon
See Silverberg, Robert

Agnon, S(hmuel) Y(osef Halevi)
1888-1970 .... CLC **4, 8, 14; SSC 29**
See also CA 17-18; 25-28R; CANR 60; CAP
2; MTCW

Agrippa von Nettesheim, Henry Cornelius
1486-1535 .... LC **27**

Aherne, Owen
See Cassill, R(onald) V(erlin)

Ai 1947- .... CLC **4, 14, 69**
See also CA 85-88; CAAS 13; DLB 120

Aickman, Robert (Fordyce)
1914-1981 .... CLC **57**
See also CA 5-8R; CANR 3

Aiken, Conrad (Potter)
1889-1973 ...... CLC **1, 3, 5, 10, 52; DAM**
NOV, POET; SSC 9
See also CA 5-8R; 45-48; CANR 4, 60;
CDALB 1929-1941; DLB 9, 45, 102;
MTCW; SATA 3, 30

Aiken, Joan (Delano) 1924- .... CLC **35**
See also AAYA 1; CA 9-12R; CANR 4, 23,
34; CLR 1, 19; DLB 161; JRDA; MAICYA;
MTCW; SAAS 1; SATA 2, 30, 73

Ainsworth, William Harrison
1805-1882 .... NCLC **13**
See also DLB 21; SATA 24

Aitmatov, Chingiz (Torekulovich)
1928- .... CLC **71**
See also CA 103; CANR 38; MTCW; SATA 56

Akers, Floyd
See Baum, L(yman) Frank

Akhmadulina, Bella Akhatovna
1937- .... CLC **53; DAM POET**
See also CA 65-68

Akhmatova, Anna
1888-1966 .... CLC **11, 25, 64; DAM**
POET; PC 2
See also CA 19-20; 25-28R; CANR 35; CAP
1; MTCW

Ambler, Eric 1909- .... CLC **4, 6, 9**
  See also CA 9-12R; CANR 7, 38; DLB 77;
  MTCW

Amichai, Yehuda 1924- .... CLC **9, 22, 57**
  See also CA 85-88; CANR 46, 60; MTCW

Amichai, Yehudah
  See Amichai, Yehuda

Amiel, Henri Frederic 1821-1881 .... NCLC **4**

Amis, Kingsley (William)
    1922-1995 ....   CLC **1, 2, 3, 5, 8, 13, 40,
    44; DA; DAB; DAC; DAM MST, NOV**
  See also AITN 2; CA 9-12R; 150; CANR 8,
    28, 54; CDBLB 1945-1960; DLB 15, 27,
    100, 139; DLBY 96; INT CANR-8; MTCW

Amis, Martin (Louis)
    1949- .... CLC **4, 9, 38, 62, 101**
  See also BEST 90:3; CA 65-68; CANR 8, 27,
    54; DLB 14; INT CANR-27

Ammons, A(rchie) R(andolph)
    1926- ...... CLC **2, 3, 5, 8, 9, 25, 57; DAM
    POET; PC 16**
  See also AITN 1; CA 9-12R; CANR 6, 36, 51;
    DLB 5, 165; MTCW

Amo, Tauraatua i
  See Adams, Henry (Brooks)

Anand, Mulk Raj 1905- .. CLC **23, 93; DAM
    NOV**
  See also CA 65-68; CANR 32; MTCW

Anatol
  See Schnitzler, Arthur

Anaximander
    c. 610B.C.-c. 546B.C. .... CMLC **22**

Anaya, Rudolfo A(lfonso)
    1937- ...... CLC **23; DAM MULT, NOV;
    HLC**
  See also AAYA 20; CA 45-48; CAAS 4;
    CANR 1, 32, 51; DLB 82; HW 1; MTCW

Andersen, Hans Christian
    1805-1875 .... NCLC **7; DA; DAB; DAC;
    DAM MST, POP; SSC 6; WLC**
  See also CLR 6; MAICYA; YABC 1

Anderson, C. Farley
  See Mencken, H(enry) L(ouis); Nathan, George
    Jean

Anderson, Jessica (Margaret) Queale
    1916- .... CLC **37**
  See also CA 9-12R; CANR 4, 62

Anderson, Jon (Victor)
    1940- .... CLC **9; DAM POET**
  See also CA 25-28R; CANR 20

Anderson, Lindsay (Gordon)
    1923-1994 .... CLC **20**
  See also CA 125; 128; 146

Anderson, Maxwell
    1888-1959 .... TCLC **2; DAM DRAM**
  See also CA 105; 152; DLB 7

Anderson, Poul (William) 1926- .... CLC **15**
  See also AAYA 5; CA 1-4R; CAAS 2; CANR
    2, 15, 34; DLB 8; INT CANR-15; MTCW;
    SATA 90; SATA-Brief 39

Anderson, Robert (Woodruff)
    1917- .... CLC **23; DAM DRAM**
  See also AITN 1; CA 21-24R; CANR 32; DLB
    7

Anderson, Sherwood
    1876-1941 ... TCLC **1, 10, 24; DA; DAB;
    DAC; DAM MST, NOV; SSC 1; WLC**
  See also CA 104; 121; CANR 61; CDALB
    1917-1929; DLB 4, 9, 86; DLBD 1; MTCW

Andier, Pierre
  See Desnos, Robert

Andouard
  See Giraudoux, (Hippolyte) Jean

Andrade, Carlos Drummond de .... CLC **18**
  See also Drummond de Andrade, Carlos

Andrade, Mario de 1893-1945 .... TCLC **43**

Andreae, Johann V(alentin)
    1586-1654 .... LC **32**
  See also DLB 164

Andreas-Salome, Lou
    1861-1937 .... TCLC **56**
  See also DLB 66

Andress, Lesley
  See Sanders, Lawrence

Andrewes, Lancelot 1555-1626 .... LC **5**
  See also DLB 151, 172

Andrews, Cicily Fairfield
  See West, Rebecca

Andrews, Elton V.
  See Pohl, Frederik

Andreyev, Leonid (Nikolaevich)
    1871-1919 .... TCLC **3**
  See also CA 104

Andric, Ivo 1892-1975 .... CLC **8**
  See also CA 81-84; 57-60; CANR 43, 60; DLB
    147; MTCW

Androvar
  See Prado (Calvo), Pedro

Angelique, Pierre
  See Bataille, Georges

Angell, Roger 1920- .... CLC **26**
  See also CA 57-60; CANR 13, 44; DLB 171

Angelou, Maya 1928- .... CLC **12, 35, 64, 77;
    BLC; DA; DAB; DAC; DAM MST,
    MULT, POET, POP; WLCS**
  See also AAYA 7, 20; BW 2; CA 65-68; CANR
    19, 42; DLB 38; MTCW; SATA 49

Annensky, Innokenty (Fyodorovich)
    1856-1909 .... TCLC **14**
  See also CA 110; 155

Annunzio, Gabriele d'
  See D'Annunzio, Gabriele

Anodos
  See Coleridge, Mary E(lizabeth)

Anon, Charles Robert
  See Pessoa, Fernando (Antonio Nogueira)

Anouilh, Jean (Marie Lucien Pierre)
    1910-1987 .... CLC **1, 3, 8, 13, 40, 50;
    DAM DRAM**
  See also CA 17-20R; 123; CANR 32; MTCW

Anthony, Florence
  See Ai

Anthony, John
  See Ciardi, John (Anthony)

Anthony, Peter
  See Shaffer, Anthony (Joshua); Shaffer, Peter
    (Levin)

Anthony, Piers 1934- .... CLC **35; DAM POP**
  See also AAYA 11; CA 21-24R; CANR 28, 56;
    DLB 8; MTCW; SAAS 22; SATA 84

Antoine, Marc
  See Proust, (Valentin-Louis-George-Eugene-)
    Marcel

Antoninus, Brother
  See Everson, William (Oliver)

Antonioni, Michelangelo 1912- .... CLC **20**
  See also CA 73-76; CANR 45

Antschel, Paul 1920-1970
  See Celan, Paul
  See also CA 85-88; CANR 33, 61; MTCW

Anwar, Chairil 1922-1949 .... TCLC **22**
  See also CA 121

Apollinaire, Guillaume
    1880-1918 .... TCLC **3, 8, 51; DAM
    POET; PC 7**
  See also Kostrowitzki, Wilhelm Apollinaris de
  See also CA 152

Appelfeld, Aharon 1932- .... CLC **23, 47**
  See also CA 112; 133

Apple, Max (Isaac)
    1941- .... CLC **9, 33**
  See also CA 81-84; CANR 19, 54; DLB 130

Appleman, Philip (Dean) 1926- .... CLC **51**
  See also CA 13-16R; CAAS 18; CANR 6, 29,
    56

Appleton, Lawrence
  See Lovecraft, H(oward) P(hillips)

Apteryx
  See Eliot, T(homas) S(tearns)

Apuleius, (Lucius Madaurensis)
    125(?)-175(?) .... CMLC **1**

Aquin, Hubert 1929-1977 .... CLC **15**
  See also CA 105; DLB 53

Aragon, Louis
1897-1982 .... **CLC 3, 22; DAM NOV, POET**
See also CA 69-72; 108; CANR 28; DLB 72; MTCW

Arany, Janos 1817-1882 .... **NCLC 34**

Arbuthnot, John 1667-1735 .... **LC 1**
See also DLB 101

Archer, Herbert Winslow
See Mencken, H(enry) L(ouis)

Archer, Jeffrey (Howard) 1940- ..... **CLC 28; DAM POP**
See also AAYA 16; BEST 89:3; CA 77-80; CANR 22, 52; INT CANR-22

Archer, Jules 1915- .... **CLC 12**
See also CA 9-12R; CANR 6; SAAS 5; SATA 4, 85

Archer, Lee
See Ellison, Harlan (Jay)

Arden, John 1930- .... **CLC 6, 13, 15; DAM DRAM**
See also CA 13-16R; CAAS 4; CANR 31; DLB 13; MTCW

Arenas, Reinaldo
1943-1990....**CLC 41; DAM MULT; HLC**
See also CA 124; 128; 133; DLB 145; HW

Arendt, Hannah 1906-1975 .... **CLC 66, 98**
See also CA 17-20R; 61-64; CANR 26, 60; MTCW

Aretino, Pietro 1492-1556 .... **LC 12**

Arghezi, Tudor .... **CLC 80**
See also Theodorescu, Ion N.

Arguedas, Jose Maria
1911-1969 .... **CLC 10, 18**
See also CA 89-92; DLB 113; HW

Argueta, Manlio 1936- .... **CLC 31**
See also CA 131; DLB 145; HW

Ariosto, Ludovico 1474-1533 .... **LC 6**

Aristides
See Epstein, Joseph

Aristophanes
450B.C.-385B.C. ... **CMLC 4; DA; DAB; DAC; DAM DRAM, MST; DC 2; WLCS**
See also DLB 176

Arlt, Roberto (Godofredo Christophersen)
1900-1942 .... **TCLC 29; DAM MULT; HLC**
See also CA 123; 131; HW

Armah, Ayi Kwei 1939-..... **CLC 5, 33; BLC; DAM MULT, POET**
See also BW 1; CA 61-64; CANR 21; DLB 117; MTCW

Armatrading, Joan 1950- .... **CLC 17**
See also CA 114

Arnette, Robert
See Silverberg, Robert

Arnim, Achim von (Ludwig Joachim von Arnim) 1781-1831 ...... **NCLC 5; SSC 29**
See also DLB 90

Arnim, Bettina von 1785-1859 .... **NCLC 38**
See also DLB 90

Arnold, Matthew
1822-1888 .... **NCLC 6, 29; DA; DAB; DAC; DAM MST, POET; PC 5; WLC**
See also CDBLB 1832-1890; DLB 32, 57

Arnold, Thomas 1795-1842 .... **NCLC 18**
See also DLB 55

Arnow, Harriette (Louisa) Simpson
1908-1986 .... **CLC 2, 7, 18**
See also CA 9-12R; 118; CANR 14; DLB 6; MTCW; SATA 42; SATA-Obit 47

Arp, Hans
See Arp, Jean

Arp, Jean 1887-1966 .... **CLC 5**
See also CA 81-84; 25-28R; CANR 42

Arrabal
See Arrabal, Fernando

Arrabal, Fernando 1932-.... **CLC 2, 9, 18, 58**
See also CA 9-12R; CANR 15

Arrick, Fran .... **CLC 30**
See also Gaberman, Judie Angell

Artaud, Antonin (Marie Joseph)
1896-1948 .... **TCLC 3, 36; DAM DRAM**
See also CA 104; 149

Arthur, Ruth M(abel) 1905-1979 ...... **CLC 12**
See also CA 9-12R; 85-88; CANR 4; SATA 7, 26

Artsybashev, Mikhail (Petrovich)
1878-1927 .... **TCLC 31**

Arundel, Honor (Morfydd)
1919-1973 .... **CLC 17**
See also CA 21-22; 41-44R; CAP 2; CLR 35; SATA 4; SATA-Obit 24

Arzner, Dorothy 1897-1979 .... **CLC 98**

Asch, Sholem 1880-1957 .... **TCLC 3**
See also CA 105

Ash, Shalom
See Asch, Sholem

Ashbery, John (Lawrence)
1927- .... **CLC 2, 3, 4, 6, 9, 13, 15, 25, 41, 77; DAM POET**
See also CA 5-8R; CANR 9, 37; DLB 5, 165; DLBY 81; INT CANR-9; MTCW

Ashdown, Clifford
See Freeman, R(ichard) Austin

Ashe, Gordon
See Creasey, John

Ashton-Warner, Sylvia (Constance)
1908-1984 .... **CLC 19**
See also CA 69-72; 112; CANR 29; MTCW

Asimov, Isaac
1920-1992 .... **CLC 1, 3, 9, 19, 26, 76, 92; DAM POP**
See also AAYA 13; BEST 90:2; CA 1-4R; 137; CANR 2, 19, 36, 60; CLR 12; DLB 8; DLBY 92; INT CANR-19; JRDA; MAICYA; MTCW; SATA 1, 26, 74

Assis, Joaquim Maria Machado de
See Machado de Assis, Joaquim Maria

Astley, Thea (Beatrice May)
1925- .... **CLC 41**
See also CA 65-68; CANR 11, 43

Aston, James
See White, T(erence) H(anbury)

Asturias, Miguel Angel
1899-1974 ... **CLC 3, 8, 13; DAM MULT, NOV; HLC**
See also CA 25-28; 49-52; CANR 32; CAP 2; DLB 113; HW; MTCW

Atares, Carlos Saura
See Saura (Atares), Carlos

Atheling, William
See Pound, Ezra (Weston Loomis)

Atheling, William, Jr.
See Blish, James (Benjamin)

Atherton, Gertrude (Franklin Horn)
1857-1948 .... **TCLC 2**
See also CA 104; 155; DLB 9, 78

Atherton, Lucius
See Masters, Edgar Lee

Atkins, Jack
See Harris, Mark

Atkinson, Kate .... **CLC 99**

Attaway, William (Alexander)
1911-1986 .... **CLC 92; BLC; DAM MULT**
See also BW 2; CA 143; DLB 76

Atticus
See Fleming, Ian (Lancaster)

Atwood, Margaret (Eleanor)
1939- .... **CLC 2, 3, 4, 8, 13, 15, 25, 44, 84; DA; DAB; DAC; DAM MST, NOV, POET; PC 8; SSC 2; WLC**
See also AAYA 12; BEST 89:2; CA 49-52; CANR 3, 24, 33, 59; DLB 53; INT CANR-24; MTCW; SATA 50

Aubigny, Pierre d'
See Mencken, H(enry) L(ouis)

Aubin, Penelope
1685-1731(?) .... **LC 9**
See also DLB 39

Auchincloss, Louis (Stanton)
1917- ... **CLC 4, 6, 9, 18, 45; DAM NOV; SSC 22**
See also CA 1-4R; CANR 6, 29, 55; DLB 2; DLBY 80; INT CANR-29; MTCW

Auden, W(ystan) H(ugh)
1907-1973 ... **CLC 1, 2, 3, 4, 6, 9, 11, 14, 43; DA; DAB; DAC; DAM DRAM, MST, POET; PC 1; WLC**
See also AAYA 18; CA 9-12R; 45-48; CANR 5, 61; CDBLB 1914-1945; DLB 10, 20; MTCW

Audiberti, Jacques
1900-1965 .... **CLC 38; DAM DRAM**
See also CA 25-28R

Audubon, John James 1785-1851 ... **NCLC 47**

Auel, Jean M(arie)
1936- .... **CLC 31; DAM POP**
See also AAYA 7; BEST 90:4; CA 103; CANR 21; INT CANR-21; SATA 91

Auerbach, Erich 1892-1957 .... **TCLC 43**
See also CA 118; 155

Augier, Emile 1820-1889 .... **NCLC 31**

August, John
See De Voto, Bernard (Augustine)

Augustine, St. 354-430 .... **CMLC 6; DAB**

Aurelius
See Bourne, Randolph S(illiman)

Aurobindo, Sri 1872-1950 .... **TCLC 63**

Austen, Jane
1775-1817 ..... **NCLC 1, 13, 19, 33, 51; DA; DAB; DAC; DAM MST, NOV; WLC**
See also AAYA 19; CDBLB 1789-1832; DLB 116

Auster, Paul 1947- .... **CLC 47**
See also CA 69-72; CANR 23, 52

Austin, Frank
See Faust, Frederick (Schiller)

Austin, Mary (Hunter)
1868-1934 .... **TCLC 25**
See also CA 109; DLB 9, 78

Autran Dourado, Waldomiro
See Dourado, (Waldomiro Freitas) Autran

Averroes 1126-1198 .... **CMLC 7**
See also DLB 115

Avicenna 980-1037 .... **CMLC 16**
See also DLB 115

Avison, Margaret
1918- .... **CLC 2, 4, 97; DAC; DAM POET**
See also CA 17-20R; DLB 53; MTCW

Axton, David
See Koontz, Dean R(ay)

Ayckbourn, Alan
1939- .... **CLC 5, 8, 18, 33, 74; DAB; DAM DRAM**
See also CA 21-24R; CANR 31, 59; DLB 13; MTCW

Aydy, Catherine
See Tennant, Emma (Christina)

Ayme, Marcel (Andre)
1902-1967 .... **CLC 11**
See also CA 89-92; CLR 25; DLB 72; SATA 91

Ayrton, Michael 1921-1975 .... **CLC 7**
See also CA 5-8R; 61-64; CANR 9, 21

Azorin .... **CLC 11**
See also Martinez Ruiz, Jose

Azuela, Mariano
1873-1952 .... **TCLC 3; DAM MULT; HLC**
See also CA 104; 131; HW; MTCW

Baastad, Babbis Friis
See Friis-Baastad, Babbis Ellinor

Bab
See Gilbert, W(illiam) S(chwenck)

Babbis, Eleanor
See Friis-Baastad, Babbis Ellinor

Babel, Isaac
See Babel, Isaak (Emmanuilovich)

Babel, Isaak (Emmanuilovich)
1894-1941(?) .... **TCLC 2, 13; SSC 16**
See also CA 104; 155

Babits, Mihaly 1883-1941 .... **TCLC 14**
See also CA 114

Babur 1483-1530 .... **LC 18**

Bacchelli, Riccardo 1891-1985 .... **CLC 19**
See also CA 29-32R; 117

Bach, Richard (David)
1936- .... **CLC 14; DAM NOV, POP**
See also AITN 1; BEST 89:2; CA 9-12R; CANR 18; MTCW; SATA 13

Bachman, Richard
See King, Stephen (Edwin)

Bachmann, Ingeborg 1926-1973 .... **CLC 69**
See also CA 93-96; 45-48; DLB 85

Bacon, Francis 1561-1626 .... **LC 18, 32**
See also CDBLB Before 1660; DLB 151

Bacon, Roger 1214(?)-1292 .... **CMLC 14**
See also DLB 115

Bacovia, George .... **TCLC 24**
See also Vasiliu, Gheorghe

Badanes, Jerome 1937- .... **CLC 59**

Bagehot, Walter 1826-1877 .... **NCLC 10**
See also DLB 55

Bagnold, Enid 1889-1981 .... **CLC 25; DAM DRAM**
See also CA 5-8R; 103; CANR 5, 40; DLB 13, 160; MAICYA; SATA 1, 25

Bagritsky, Eduard 1895-1934 .... **TCLC 60**

Bagrjana, Elisaveta
See Belcheva, Elisaveta

Bagryana, Elisaveta .... **CLC 10**
See also Belcheva, Elisaveta
See also DLB 147

Bailey, Paul 1937- .... **CLC 45**
See also CA 21-24R; CANR 16, 62; DLB 14

Baillie, Joanna 1762-1851 .... **NCLC 2**
See also DLB 93

Bainbridge, Beryl (Margaret)
1933- ..... **CLC 4, 5, 8, 10, 14, 18, 22, 62; DAM NOV**
See also CA 21-24R; CANR 24, 55; DLB 14; MTCW

Baker, Elliott 1922- .... **CLC 8**
See also CA 45-48; CANR 2

Baker, Jean H. .... **TCLC 3, 10**
See also Russell, George William

Baker, Nicholson
1957- .... **CLC 61; DAM POP**
See also CA 135

Baker, Ray Stannard
1870-1946 .... **TCLC 47**
See also CA 118

Baker, Russell (Wayne) 1925- .... **CLC 31**
See also BEST 89:4; CA 57-60; CANR 11, 41, 59; MTCW

Bakhtin, M.
See Bakhtin, Mikhail Mikhailovich

Bakhtin, M. M.
See Bakhtin, Mikhail Mikhailovich

Bakhtin, Mikhail
See Bakhtin, Mikhail Mikhailovich

Bakhtin, Mikhail Mikhailovich
1895-1975 .... **CLC 83**
See also CA 128; 113

Bakshi, Ralph 1938(?)- .... **CLC 26**
See also CA 112; 138

Bakunin, Mikhail (Alexandrovich)
1814-1876 .... **NCLC 25, 58**

Baldwin, James (Arthur)
1924-1987.... **CLC 1, 2, 3, 4, 5, 8, 13, 15, 17, 42, 50, 67, 90; BLC; DA; DAB; DAC; DAM MST, MULT, NOV, POP; DC 1; SSC 10; WLC**
See also AAYA 4; BW 1; CA 1-4R; 124; CABS 1; CANR 3, 24; CDALB 1941-1968; DLB 2, 7, 33; DLBY 87; MTCW; SATA 9; SATA-Obit 54

Ballard, J(ames) G(raham) 1930-.... **CLC 3, 6, 14, 36; DAM NOV, POP; SSC 1**
See also AAYA 3; CA 5-8R; CANR 15, 39; DLB 14; MTCW; SATA 93

Balmont, Konstantin (Dmitriyevich) 1867-1943 .... **TCLC 11**
See also CA 109; 155

Balzac, Honore de 1799-1850 ... **NCLC 5, 35, 53; DA; DAB; DAC; DAM MST, NOV; SSC 5; WLC**
See also DLB 119

Bambara, Toni Cade 1939-1995 .... **CLC 19, 88; BLC; DA; DAC; DAM MST, MULT; WLCS**
See also AAYA 5; BW 2; CA 29-32R; 150; CANR 24, 49; DLB 38; MTCW

Bamdad, A.
See Shamlu, Ahmad

Banat, D. R.
See Bradbury, Ray (Douglas)

Bancroft, Laura
See Baum, L(yman) Frank

Banim, John 1798-1842 .... **NCLC 13**
See also DLB 116, 158, 159

Banim, Michael 1796-1874 .... **NCLC 13**
See also DLB 158, 159

Banjo, The
See Paterson, A(ndrew) B(arton)

Banks, Iain
See Banks, Iain M(enzies)

Banks, Iain M(enzies) 1954- .... **CLC 34**
See also CA 123; 128; CANR 61; INT 128

Banks, Lynne Reid .... **CLC 23**
See also Reid Banks, Lynne
See also AAYA 6

Banks, Russell 1940- .... **CLC 37, 72**
See also CA 65-68; CAAS 15; CANR 19, 52; DLB 130

Banville, John 1945- .... **CLC 46**
See also CA 117; 128; DLB 14; INT 128

Banville, Theodore (Faullain) de 1832-1891 .... **NCLC 9**

Baraka, Amiri 1934- ... **CLC 1, 2, 3, 5, 10, 14, 33; BLC; DA; DAC; DAM MST, MULT, POET, POP; DC 6; PC 4; WLCS**
See also Jones, LeRoi
See also BW 2; CA 21-24R; CABS 3; CANR 27, 38, 61; CDALB 1941-1968; DLB 5, 7, 16, 38; DLBD 8; MTCW

Barbauld, Anna Laetitia 1743-1825 .... **NCLC 50**
See also DLB 107, 109, 142, 158

Barbellion, W. N. P. .... **TCLC 24**
See also Cummings, Bruce F(rederick)

Barbera, Jack (Vincent) 1945- .... **CLC 44**
See also CA 110; CANR 45

Barbey d'Aurevilly, Jules Amedee 1808-1889 .... **NCLC 1; SSC 17**
See also DLB 119

Barbusse, Henri 1873-1935 .... **TCLC 5**
See also CA 105; 154; DLB 65

Barclay, Bill
See Moorcock, Michael (John)

Barclay, William Ewert
See Moorcock, Michael (John)

Barea, Arturo 1897-1957 .... **TCLC 14**
See also CA 111

Barfoot, Joan 1946- .... **CLC 18**
See also CA 105

Baring, Maurice 1874-1945 .... **TCLC 8**
See also CA 105; DLB 34

Barker, Clive 1952- .... **CLC 52; DAM POP**
See also AAYA 10; BEST 90:3; CA 121; 129; INT 129; MTCW

Barker, George Granville 1913-1991 .... **CLC 8, 48; DAM POET**
See also CA 9-12R; 135; CANR 7, 38; DLB 20; MTCW

Barker, Harley Granville
See Granville-Barker, Harley
See also DLB 10

Barker, Howard 1946- .... **CLC 37**
See also CA 102; DLB 13

Barker, Pat(ricia) 1943- .... **CLC 32, 94**
See also CA 117; 122; CANR 50; INT 122

Barlow, Joel 1754-1812 .... **NCLC 23**
See also DLB 37

Barnard, Mary (Ethel) 1909- .... **CLC 48**
See also CA 21-22; CAP 2

Barnes, Djuna 1892-1982.. **CLC 3, 4, 8, 11, 29; SSC 3**
See also CA 9-12R; 107; CANR 16, 55; DLB 4, 9, 45; MTCW

Barnes, Julian (Patrick) 1946- .... **CLC 42; DAB**
See also CA 102; CANR 19, 54; DLBY 93

Barnes, Peter 1931- .... **CLC 5, 56**
See also CA 65-68; CAAS 12; CANR 33, 34; DLB 13; MTCW

Baroja (y Nessi), Pio 1872-1956 ...... **TCLC 8; HLC**
See also CA 104

Baron, David
See Pinter, Harold

Baron Corvo
See Rolfe, Frederick (William Serafino Austin Lewis Mary)

Barondess, Sue K(aufman) 1926-1977 .... **CLC 8**
See also Kaufman, Sue
See also CA 1-4R; 69-72; CANR 1

Baron de Teive
See Pessoa, Fernando (Antonio Nogueira)

Barres, Maurice 1862-1923 .... **TCLC 47**
See also DLB 123

Barreto, Afonso Henrique de Lima
See Lima Barreto, Afonso Henrique de

Barrett, (Roger) Syd 1946- .... **CLC 35**

Barrett, William (Christopher) 1913-1992 .... **CLC 27**
See also CA 13-16R; 139; CANR 11; INT CANR-11

Barrie, J(ames) M(atthew) 1860-1937 .... **TCLC 2; DAB; DAM DRAM**
See also CA 104; 136; CDBLB 1890-1914; CLR 16; DLB 10, 141, 156; MAICYA; YABC 1

Barrington, Michael
See Moorcock, Michael (John)

Barrol, Grady
See Bograd, Larry

Barry, Mike
See Malzberg, Barry N(athaniel)

Barry, Philip 1896-1949 .... **TCLC 11**
See also CA 109; DLB 7

Bart, Andre Schwarz
See Schwarz-Bart, Andre

Barth, John (Simmons) 1930- ... **CLC 1, 2, 3, 5, 7, 9, 10, 14, 27, 51, 89; DAM NOV; SSC 10**
See also AITN 1, 2; CA 1-4R; CABS 1; CANR 5, 23, 49; DLB 2; MTCW

Barthelme, Donald 1931-1989 ... **CLC 1, 2, 3, 5, 6, 8, 13, 23, 46, 59; DAM NOV; SSC 2**
See also CA 21-24R; 129; CANR 20, 58; DLB 2; DLBY 80, 89; MTCW; SATA 7; SATA-Obit 62

Barthelme, Frederick 1943- .... **CLC 36**
See also CA 114; 122; DLBY 85; INT 122

Barthes, Roland (Gerard) 1915-1980 .... **CLC 24, 83**
See also CA 130; 97-100; MTCW

Barzun, Jacques (Martin) 1907- .... **CLC 51**
See also CA 61-64; CANR 22

Bashevis, Isaac
See Singer, Isaac Bashevis

Bashkirtseff, Marie 1859-1884 ...... **NCLC 27**

Basho
See Matsuo Basho

Bellamy, Atwood C.
See Mencken, H(enry) L(ouis)

Bellamy, Edward 1850-1898 .... NCLC 4
See also DLB 12

Bellin, Edward J.
See Kuttner, Henry

Belloc, (Joseph) Hilaire (Pierre Sebastien Rene Swanton)
1870-1953 ...... TCLC 7, 18; DAM POET
See also CA 106; 152; DLB 19, 100, 141, 174;
YABC 1

Belloc, Joseph Peter Rene Hilaire
See Belloc, (Joseph) Hilaire (Pierre Sebastien Rene Swanton)

Belloc, Joseph Pierre Hilaire
See Belloc, (Joseph) Hilaire (Pierre Sebastien Rene Swanton)

Belloc, M. A.
See Lowndes, Marie Adelaide (Belloc)

Bellow, Saul
1915-.... CLC 1, 2, 3, 6, 8, 10, 13, 15, 25, 33, 34, 63, 79; DA; DAB; DAC; DAM MST, NOV, POP; SSC 14; WLC
See also AITN 2; BEST 89:3; CA 5-8R; CABS 1; CANR 29, 53; CDALB 1941-1968; DLB 2, 28; DLBD 3; DLBY 82; MTCW

Belser, Reimond Karel Maria de 1929-
See Ruyslinck, Ward
See also CA 152

Bely, Andrey .... TCLC 7; PC 11
See also Bugayev, Boris Nikolayevich

Benary, Margot
See Benary-Isbert, Margot

Benary-Isbert, Margot
1889-1979 .... CLC 12
See also CA 5-8R; 89-92; CANR 4; CLR 12;
MAICYA; SATA 2; SATA-Obit 21

Benavente (y Martinez), Jacinto
1866-1954 .... TCLC 3; DAM DRAM, MULT
See also CA 106; 131; HW; MTCW

Benchley, Peter (Bradford)
1940- .... CLC 4, 8; DAM NOV, POP
See also AAYA 14; AITN 2; CA 17-20R;
CANR 12, 35; MTCW; SATA 3, 89

Benchley, Robert (Charles)
1889-1945 .... TCLC 1, 55
See also CA 105; 153; DLB 11

Benda, Julien 1867-1956 .... TCLC 60
See also CA 120; 154

Benedict, Ruth (Fulton)
1887-1948 .... TCLC 60
See also CA 158

Benedikt, Michael 1935- .... CLC 4, 14
See also CA 13-16R; CANR 7; DLB 5

Benet, Juan 1927- .... CLC 28
See also CA 143

Benet, Stephen Vincent
1898-1943 ...... TCLC 7; DAM POET;
SSC 10
See also CA 104; 152; DLB 4, 48, 102; YABC 1

Benet, William Rose 1886-1950 .... TCLC 28;
DAM POET
See also CA 118; 152; DLB 45

Benford, Gregory (Albert) 1941-...... CLC 52
See also CA 69-72; CAAS 27; CANR 12, 24, 49; DLBY 82

Bengtsson, Frans (Gunnar)
1894-1954 .... TCLC 48

Benjamin, David
See Slavitt, David R(ytman)

Benjamin, Lois
See Gould, Lois

Benjamin, Walter 1892-1940 .... TCLC 39

Benn, Gottfried 1886-1956 .... TCLC 3
See also CA 106; 153; DLB 56

Bennett, Alan
1934- ..... CLC 45, 77; DAB; DAM MST
See also CA 103; CANR 35, 55; MTCW

Bennett, (Enoch) Arnold
1867-1931 .... TCLC 5, 20
See also CA 106; 155; CDBLB 1890-1914;
DLB 10, 34, 98, 135

Bennett, Elizabeth
See Mitchell, Margaret (Munnerlyn)

Bennett, George Harold 1930-
See Bennett, Hal
See also BW 1; CA 97-100

Bennett, Hal .... CLC 5
See also Bennett, George Harold
See also DLB 33

Bennett, Jay 1912- .... CLC 35
See also AAYA 10; CA 69-72; CANR 11, 42;
JRDA; SAAS 4; SATA 41, 87; SATA-Brief 27

Bennett, Louise (Simone) 1919- ...... CLC 28;
BLC; DAM MULT
See also BW 2; CA 151; DLB 117

Benson, E(dward) F(rederic)
1867-1940 .... TCLC 27
See also CA 114; 157; DLB 135, 153

Benson, Jackson J. 1930- .... CLC 34
See also CA 25-28R; DLB 111

Benson, Sally 1900-1972 .... CLC 17
See also CA 19-20; 37-40R; CAP 1; SATA 1, 35; SATA-Obit 27

Benson, Stella 1892-1933 .... TCLC 17
See also CA 117; 155; DLB 36, 162

Bentham, Jeremy 1748-1832 .... NCLC 38
See also DLB 107, 158

Bentley, E(dmund) C(lerihew)
1875-1956 .... TCLC 12
See also CA 108; DLB 70

Bentley, Eric (Russell) 1916- .... CLC 24
See also CA 5-8R; CANR 6; INT CANR-6

Beranger, Pierre Jean de
1780-1857 .... NCLC 34

Berdyaev, Nicolas
See Berdyaev, Nikolai (Aleksandrovich)

Berdyaev, Nikolai (Aleksandrovich)
1874-1948 .... TCLC 67
See also CA 120; 157

Berdyayev, Nikolai (Aleksandrovich)
See Berdyaev, Nikolai (Aleksandrovich)

Berendt, John (Lawrence) 1939- ...... CLC 86
See also CA 146

Berger, Colonel
See Malraux, (Georges-)Andre

Berger, John (Peter) 1926- ....CLC 2, 19
See also CA 81-84; CANR 51; DLB 14

Berger, Melvin H. 1927- .... CLC 12
See also CA 5-8R; CANR 4; CLR 32; SAAS 2; SATA 5, 88

Berger, Thomas (Louis)
1924- ... CLC 3, 5, 8, 11, 18, 38; DAM NOV
See also CA 1-4R; CANR 5, 28, 51; DLB 2; DLBY 80; INT CANR-28; MTCW

Bergman, (Ernst) Ingmar
1918- .... CLC 16, 72
See also CA 81-84; CANR 33

Bergson, Henri 1859-1941 .... TCLC 32

Bergstein, Eleanor 1938- .... CLC 4
See also CA 53-56; CANR 5

Berkoff, Steven 1937- .... CLC 56
See also CA 104

Bermant, Chaim (Icyk) 1929- .... CLC 40
See also CA 57-60; CANR 6, 31, 57

Bern, Victoria
See Fisher, M(ary) F(rances) K(ennedy)

Bernanos, (Paul Louis) Georges
1888-1948 .... TCLC 3
See also CA 104; 130; DLB 72

Bernard, April 1956- .... CLC 59
See also CA 131

Berne, Victoria
See Fisher, M(ary) F(rances) K(ennedy)

Bernhard, Thomas
1931-1989 .... CLC 3, 32, 61
See also CA 85-88; 127; CANR 32, 57; DLB 85, 124; MTCW

Brenton, Howard 1942- .... CLC 31
   See also CA 69-72; CANR 33; DLB 13;
   MTCW

Breslin, James 1930-
   See Breslin, Jimmy
   See also CA 73-76; CANR 31; DAM NOV;
   MTCW

Breslin, Jimmy .... CLC 4, 43
   See also Breslin, James
   See also AITN 1

Bresson, Robert 1901- .... CLC 16
   See also CA 110; CANR 49

Breton, Andre
   1896-1966 .... CLC 2, 9, 15, 54; PC 15
   See also CA 19-20; 25-28R; CANR 40, 60;
   CAP 2; DLB 65; MTCW

Breytenbach, Breyten
   1939(?)- .... CLC 23, 37; DAM POET
   See also CA 113; 129; CANR 61

Bridgers, Sue Ellen 1942- .... CLC 26
   See also AAYA 8; CA 65-68; CANR 11, 36;
   CLR 18; DLB 52; JRDA; MAICYA; SAAS
   1; SATA 22, 90

Bridges, Robert (Seymour)
   1844-1930 .... TCLC 1; DAM POET
   See also CA 104; 152; CDBLB 1890-1914;
   DLB 19, 98

Bridie, James .... TCLC 3
   See also Mavor, Osborne Henry
   See also DLB 10

Brin, David 1950- .... CLC 34
   See also AAYA 21; CA 102; CANR 24; INT
   CANR-24; SATA 65

Brink, Andre (Philippus) 1935-...CLC 18, 36
   See also CA 104; CANR 39, 62; INT 103;
   MTCW

Brinsmead, H(esba) F(ay) 1922- .... CLC 21
   See also CA 21-24R; CANR 10; CLR 47;
   MAICYA; SAAS 5; SATA 18, 78

Brittain, Vera (Mary)
   1893(?)-1970 .... CLC 23
   See also CA 13-16; 25-28R; CANR 58; CAP
   1; MTCW

Broch, Hermann 1886-1951 .... TCLC 20
   See also CA 117; DLB 85, 124

Brock, Rose
   See Hansen, Joseph

Brodkey, Harold (Roy) 1930-1996 .... CLC 56
   See also CA 111; 151; DLB 130

Brodsky, Iosif Alexandrovich 1940-1996
   See Brodsky, Joseph
   See also AITN 1; CA 41-44R; 151; CANR 37;
   DAM POET; MTCW

Brodsky, Joseph
   1940-1996 ... CLC 4, 6, 13, 36, 100; PC 9
   See also Brodsky, Iosif Alexandrovich

Brodsky, Michael (Mark) 1948- .... CLC 19
   See also CA 102; CANR 18, 41, 58

Bromell, Henry 1947- .... CLC 5
   See also CA 53-56; CANR 9

Bromfield, Louis (Brucker)
   1896-1956 .... TCLC 11
   See also CA 107; 155; DLB 4, 9, 86

Broner, E(sther) M(asserman)
   1930- .... CLC 19
   See also CA 17-20R; CANR 8, 25; DLB 28

Bronk, William 1918- .... CLC 10
   See also CA 89-92; CANR 23; DLB 165

Bronstein, Lev Davidovich
   See Trotsky, Leon

Bronte, Anne 1820-1849 .... NCLC 4
   See also DLB 21

Bronte, Charlotte
   1816-1855 .... NCLC 3, 8, 33, 58; DA;
   DAB; DAC; DAM MST, NOV; WLC
   See also AAYA 17; CDBLB 1832-1890; DLB
   21, 159

Bronte, Emily (Jane)
   1818-1848 .... NCLC 16, 35; DA; DAB;
   DAC; DAM MST, NOV, POET; PC 8;
   WLC
   See also AAYA 17; CDBLB 1832-1890; DLB
   21, 32

Brooke, Frances 1724-1789 .... LC 6
   See also DLB 39, 99

Brooke, Henry 1703(?)-1783 .... LC 1
   See also DLB 39

Brooke, Rupert (Chawner)
   1887-1915 .... TCLC 2, 7; DA; DAB;
   DAC; DAM MST, POET; WLC
   See also CA 104; 132; CANR 61; CDBLB
   1914-1945; DLB 19; MTCW

Brooke-Haven, P.
   See Wodehouse, P(elham) G(renville)

Brooke-Rose, Christine 1926(?)- .... CLC 40
   See also CA 13-16R; CANR 58; DLB 14

Brookner, Anita
   1928- ...... CLC 32, 34, 51; DAB; DAM
   POP
   See also CA 114; 120; CANR 37, 56; DLBY
   87; MTCW

Brooks, Cleanth 1906-1994 .... CLC 24, 86
   See also CA 17-20R; 145; CANR 33, 35; DLB
   63; DLBY 94; INT CANR-35; MTCW

Brooks, George
   See Baum, L(yman) Frank

Brooks, Gwendolyn 1917- ... CLC 1, 2, 4, 5, 15,
   49; BLC; DA; DAC; DAM MST, MULT,
   POET; PC 7; WLC
   See also AAYA 20; AITN 1; BW 2; CA 1-4R;
   CANR 1, 27, 52; CDALB 1941-1968; CLR
   27; DLB 5, 76, 165; MTCW; SATA 6

Brooks, Mel .... CLC 12
   See also Kaminsky, Melvin
   See also AAYA 13; DLB 26

Brooks, Peter 1938- .... CLC 34
   See also CA 45-48; CANR 1

Brooks, Van Wyck 1886-1963 .... CLC 29
   See also CA 1-4R; CANR 6; DLB 45, 63, 103

Brophy, Brigid (Antonia)
   1929-1995 .... CLC 6, 11, 29, 105
   See also CA 5-8R; 149; CAAS 4; CANR 25,
   53; DLB 14; MTCW

Brosman, Catharine Savage 1934- ..... CLC 9
   See also CA 61-64; CANR 21, 46

Brother Antoninus
   See Everson, William (Oliver)

Broughton, T(homas) Alan 1936- ..... CLC 19
   See also CA 45-48; CANR 2, 23, 48

Broumas, Olga 1949- .... CLC 10, 73
   See also CA 85-88; CANR 20

Brown, Alan 1951- .... CLC 99

Brown, Charles Brockden
   1771-1810 .... NCLC 22
   See also CDALB 1640-1865; DLB 37, 59, 73

Brown, Christy 1932-1981 .... CLC 63
   See also CA 105; 104; DLB 14

Brown, Claude
   1937- .... CLC 30; BLC; DAM MULT
   See also AAYA 7; BW 1; CA 73-76

Brown, Dee (Alexander)
   1908- .... CLC 18, 47; DAM POP
   See also CA 13-16R; CAAS 6; CANR 11, 45,
   60; DLBY 80; MTCW; SATA 5

Brown, George
   See Wertmueller, Lina

Brown, George Douglas 1869-1902...TCLC
   28

Brown, George Mackay
   1921-1996 .... CLC 5, 48, 100
   See also CA 21-24R; 151; CAAS 6; CANR 12,
   37, 62; DLB 14, 27, 139; MTCW; SATA 35

Brown, (William) Larry 1951- .... CLC 73
   See also CA 130; 134; INT 133

Brown, Moses
   See Barrett, William (Christopher)

Brown, Rita Mae
   1944- ...... CLC 18, 43, 79; DAM NOV,
   POP
   See also CA 45-48; CANR 2, 11, 35, 62; INT
   CANR-11; MTCW

Brown, Roderick (Langmere) Haig-
   See Haig-Brown, Roderick (Langmere)

Brown, Rosellen 1939- .... CLC 32
   See also CA 77-80; CAAS 10; CANR 14, 44

Brown, Sterling Allen
1901-1989 ... **CLC 1, 23, 59; BLC; DAM MULT, POET**
See also BW 1; CA 85-88; 127; CANR 26; DLB 48, 51, 63; MTCW

Brown, Will
See Ainsworth, William Harrison

Brown, William Wells
1813-1884 .... **NCLC 2; BLC; DAM MULT; DC 1**
See also DLB 3, 50

Browne, (Clyde) Jackson 1948(?)- .... **CLC 21**
See also CA 120

Browning, Elizabeth Barrett
1806-1861 ... **NCLC 1, 16, 61; DA; DAB; DAC; DAM MST, POET; PC 6; WLC**
See also CDBLB 1832-1890; DLB 32

Browning, Robert
1812-1889 .... **NCLC 19; DA; DAB; DAC; DAM MST, POET; PC 2; WLCS**
See also CDBLB 1832-1890; DLB 32, 163; YABC 1

Browning, Tod 1882-1962 .... **CLC 16**
See also CA 141; 117

Brownson, Orestes (Augustus) 1803-1876
NCLC 50

Bruccoli, Matthew J(oseph) 1931- ... **CLC 34**
See also CA 9-12R; CANR 7; DLB 103

Bruce, Lenny .... **CLC 21**
See also Schneider, Leonard Alfred

Bruin, John
See Brutus, Dennis

Brulard, Henri
See Stendhal

Brulls, Christian
See Simenon, Georges (Jacques Christian)

Brunner, John (Kilian Houston)
1934-1995 .... **CLC 8, 10; DAM POP**
See also CA 1-4R; 149; CAAS 8; CANR 2, 37; MTCW

Bruno, Giordano 1548-1600 .... **LC 27**

Brutus, Dennis 1924- ... **CLC 43; BLC; DAM MULT, POET**
See also BW 2; CA 49-52; CAAS 14; CANR 2, 27, 42; DLB 117

Bryan, C(ourtlandt) D(ixon) B(arnes)
1936- .... **CLC 29**
See also CA 73-76; CANR 13; INT CANR-13

Bryan, Michael
See Moore, Brian

Bryant, William Cullen
1794-1878 .... **NCLC 6, 46; DA; DAB; DAC; DAM MST, POET; PC 20**
See also CDALB 1640-1865; DLB 3, 43, 59

Bryusov, Valery Yakovlevich
1873-1924 .... **TCLC 10**
See also CA 107; 155

Buchan, John 1875-1940 ..... **TCLC 41; DAB; DAM POP**
See also CA 108; 145; DLB 34, 70, 156; YABC 2

Buchanan, George 1506-1582 .... **LC 4**

Buchheim, Lothar-Guenther 1918- .... **CLC 6**
See also CA 85-88

Buchner, (Karl) Georg
1813-1837 .... **NCLC 26**

Buchwald, Art(hur) 1925- .... **CLC 33**
See also AITN 1; CA 5-8R; CANR 21; MTCW; SATA 10

Buck, Pearl S(ydenstricker)
1892-1973 ...... **CLC 7, 11, 18; DA; DAB; DAC; DAM MST, NOV**
See also AITN 1; CA 1-4R; 41-44R; CANR 1, 34; DLB 9, 102; MTCW; SATA 1, 25

Buckler, Ernest
1908-1984 .... **CLC 13; DAC; DAM MST**
See also CA 11-12; 114; CAP 1; DLB 68; SATA 47

Buckley, Vincent (Thomas)
1925-1988 .... **CLC 57**
See also CA 101

Buckley, William F(rank), Jr.
1925- .... **CLC 7, 18, 37; DAM POP**
See also AITN 1; CA 1-4R; CANR 1, 24, 53; DLB 137; DLBY 80; INT CANR-24; MTCW

Buechner, (Carl) Frederick
1926- .... **CLC 2, 4, 6, 9; DAM NOV**
See also CA 13-16R; CANR 11, 39; DLBY 80; INT CANR-11; MTCW

Buell, John (Edward) 1927- .... **CLC 10**
See also CA 1-4R; DLB 53

Buero Vallejo, Antonio 1916- ..... **CLC 15, 46**
See also CA 106; CANR 24, 49; HW; MTCW

Bufalino, Gesualdo 1920(?)- .... **CLC 74**

Bugayev, Boris Nikolayevich 1880-1934
See Bely, Andrey
See also CA 104

Bukowski, Charles
1920-1994 ...... **CLC 2, 5, 9, 41, 82; DAM NOV, POET; PC 18**
See also CA 17-20R; 144; CANR 40, 62; DLB 5, 130, 169; MTCW

Bulgakov, Mikhail (Afanas'evich)
1891-1940 ... **TCLC 2, 16; DAM DRAM, NOV; SSC 18**
See also CA 105; 152

Bulgya, Alexander Alexandrovich
1901-1956 .... **TCLC 53**
See also Fadeyev, Alexander
See also CA 117

Bullins, Ed
1935- .... **CLC 1, 5, 7; BLC; DAM DRAM, MULT; DC 6**
See also BW 2; CA 49-52; CAAS 16; CANR 24, 46; DLB 7, 38; MTCW

Bulwer-Lytton, Edward (George Earle Lytton)
1803-1873 .... **NCLC 1, 45**
See also DLB 21

Bunin, Ivan Alexeyevich
1870-1953 .... **TCLC 6; SSC 5**
See also CA 104

Bunting, Basil
1900-1985 .... **CLC 10, 39, 47; DAM POET**
See also CA 53-56; 115; CANR 7; DLB 20

Bunuel, Luis
1900-1983 .... **CLC 16, 80; DAM MULT; HLC**
See also CA 101; 110; CANR 32; HW

Bunyan, John
1628-1688 .... **LC 4; DA; DAB; DAC; DAM MST; WLC**
See also CDBLB 1660-1789; DLB 39

Burckhardt, Jacob (Christoph)
1818-1897 .... **NCLC 49**

Burford, Eleanor
See Hibbert, Eleanor Alice Burford

Burgess, Anthony ... **CLC 1, 2, 4, 5, 8, 10, 13, 15, 22, 40, 62 , 81, 94; DAB**
See also Wilson, John (Anthony) Burgess
See also AITN 1; CDBLB 1960 to Present; DLB 14

Burke, Edmund
1729(?)-1797 .... **LC 7, 36; DA; DAB; DAC; DAM MST; WLC**
See also DLB 104

Burke, Kenneth (Duva)
1897-1993 .... **CLC 2, 24**
See also CA 5-8R; 143; CANR 39; DLB 45, 63; MTCW

Burke, Leda
See Garnett, David

Burke, Ralph
See Silverberg, Robert

Burke, Thomas 1886-1945 .... **TCLC 63**
See also CA 113; 155

Burney, Fanny 1752-1840 .... **NCLC 12, 54**
See also DLB 39

Burns, Robert 1759-1796 .... **PC 6**
See also CDBLB 1789-1832; DA; DAB; DAC; DAM MST, POET; DLB 109; WLC

Burns, Tex
See L'Amour, Louis (Dearborn)

Burnshaw, Stanley
1906- .... **CLC 3, 13, 44**
See also CA 9-12R; DLB 48

Burr, Anne 1937- .... CLC 6
See also CA 25-28R

Burroughs, Edgar Rice
1875-1950 .... TCLC 2, 32; DAM NOV
See also AAYA 11; CA 104; 132; DLB 8;
MTCW; SATA 41

Burroughs, William S(eward)
1914-1997 .... CLC 1, 2, 5, 15, 22, 42, 75;
DA; DAB; DAC; DAM MST, NOV,
POP; WLC
See also AITN 2; CA 9-12R; 160; CANR 20,
52; DLB 2, 8, 16, 152; DLBY 81; MTCW

Burton, Richard F. 1821-1890 .... NCLC 42
See also DLB 55, 184

Busch, Frederick 1941- ..... CLC 7, 10, 18, 47
See also CA 33-36R; CAAS 1; CANR 45; DLB
6

Bush, Ronald 1946- .... CLC 34
See also CA 136

Bustos, F(rancisco)
See Borges, Jorge Luis

Bustos Domecq, H(onorio)
See Bioy Casares, Adolfo; Borges, Jorge Luis

Butler, Octavia E(stelle)
1947- .... CLC 38; DAM MULT, POP
See also AAYA 18; BW 2; CA 73-76; CANR
12, 24, 38; DLB 33; MTCW; SATA 84

Butler, Robert Olen (Jr.)
1945- .... CLC 81; DAM POP
See also CA 112; DLB 173; INT 112

Butler, Samuel 1612-1680 .... LC 16
See also DLB 101, 126

Butler, Samuel
1835-1902 .... TCLC 1, 33; DA; DAB;
DAC; DAM MST, NOV; WLC
See also CA 143; CDBLB 1890-1914; DLB
18, 57, 174

Butler, Walter C.
See Faust, Frederick (Schiller)

Butor, Michel (Marie Francois)
1926- .... CLC 1, 3, 8, 11, 15
See also CA 9-12R; CANR 33; DLB 83;
MTCW

Buzo, Alexander (John) 1944- .... CLC 61
See also CA 97-100; CANR 17, 39

Buzzati, Dino 1906-1972 .... CLC 36
See also CA 160; 33-36R; DLB 177

Byars, Betsy (Cromer) 1928-............. CLC 35
See also AAYA 19; CA 33-36R; CANR 18, 36,
57; CLR 1, 16; DLB 52; INT CANR-18;
JRDA; MAICYA; MTCW; SAAS 1; SATA
4, 46, 80

Byatt, A(ntonia) S(usan Drabble)
1936- .... CLC 19, 65; DAM NOV, POP
See also CA 13-16R; CANR 13, 33, 50; DLB
14; MTCW

Byrne, David 1952-............................ CLC 26
See also CA 127

Byrne, John Keyes 1926-
See Leonard, Hugh
See also CA 102; INT 102

Byron, George Gordon (Noel)
1788-1824 .... NCLC 2, 12; DA; DAB;
DAC; DAM MST, POET; PC 16; WLC
See also CDBLB 1789-1832; DLB 96, 110

Byron, Robert 1905-1941 .... TCLC 67
See also CA 160

C. 3. 3.
See Wilde, Oscar (Fingal O'Flahertie Wills)

Caballero, Fernan 1796-1877 .... NCLC 10

Cabell, Branch
See Cabell, James Branch

Cabell, James Branch 1879-1958 .... TCLC 6
See also CA 105; 152; DLB 9, 78

Cable, George Washington
1844-1925 .... TCLC 4; SSC 4
See also CA 104; 155; DLB 12, 74; DLBD
13

Cabral de Melo Neto, Joao
1920- .... CLC 76; DAM MULT
See also CA 151

Cabrera Infante, G(uillermo)
1929- ...... CLC 5, 25, 45; DAM MULT;
HLC
See also CA 85-88; CANR 29; DLB 113; HW;
MTCW

Cade, Toni
See Bambara, Toni Cade

Cadmus and Harmonia
See Buchan, John

Caedmon fl. 658-680 .... CMLC 7
See also DLB 146

Caeiro, Alberto
See Pessoa, Fernando (Antonio Nogueira)

Cage, John (Milton, Jr.) 1912- .... CLC 41
See also CA 13-16R; CANR 9; INT CANR-
9

Cahan, Abraham 1860-1951 .... TCLC 71
See also CA 108; 154; DLB 9, 25, 28

Cain, G.
See Cabrera Infante, G(uillermo)

Cain, Guillermo
See Cabrera Infante, G(uillermo)

Cain, James M(allahan)
1892-1977 .... CLC 3, 11, 28
See also AITN 1; CA 17-20R; 73-76; CANR
8, 34, 61; MTCW

Caine, Mark
See Raphael, Frederic (Michael)

Calasso, Roberto 1941- .... CLC 81
See also CA 143

Calderon de la Barca, Pedro
1600-1681 .... LC 23; DC 3

Caldwell, Erskine (Preston)
1903-1987 .... CLC 1, 8, 14, 50, 60; DAM
NOV; SSC 19
See also AITN 1; CA 1-4R; 121; CAAS 1;
CANR 2, 33; DLB 9, 86; MTCW

Caldwell, (Janet Miriam) Taylor (Holland)
1900-1985 .... CLC 2, 28, 39; DAM NOV,
POP
See also CA 5-8R; 116; CANR 5

Calhoun, John Caldwell
1782-1850 .... NCLC 15
See also DLB 3

Calisher, Hortense
1911- ..... CLC 2, 4, 8, 38; DAM NOV;
SSC 15
See also CA 1-4R; CANR 1, 22; DLB 2; INT
CANR-22; MTCW

Callaghan, Morley Edward
1903-1990 .... CLC 3, 14, 41, 65; DAC;
DAM MST
See also CA 9-12R; 132; CANR 33; DLB 68;
MTCW

Callimachus
c. 305B.C.-c. 240B.C. .... CMLC 18
See also DLB 176

Calvin, John 1509-1564 .... LC 37

Calvino, Italo
1923-1985 .... CLC 5, 8, 11, 22, 33, 39,
73; DAM NOV; SSC 3
See also CA 85-88; 116; CANR 23, 61;
MTCW

Cameron, Carey 1952- .... CLC 59
See also CA 135

Cameron, Peter 1959- .... CLC 44
See also CA 125; CANR 50

Campana, Dino 1885-1932 .... TCLC 20
See also CA 117; DLB 114

Campanella, Tommaso 1568-1639 .... LC 32

Campbell, John W(ood, Jr.)
1910-1971 .... CLC 32
See also CA 21-22; 29-32R; CANR 34; CAP
2; DLB 8; MTCW

Campbell, Joseph
1904-1987 .... CLC 69
See also AAYA 3; BEST 89:2; CA 1-4R; 124;
CANR 3, 28, 61; MTCW

Campbell, Maria 1940- .... CLC 85; DAC
See also CA 102; CANR 54; NNAL

Campbell, (John) Ramsey
1946- .... CLC 42; SSC 19
See also CA 57-60; CANR 7; INT CANR-
7

Campbell, (Ignatius) Roy (Dunnachie)
1901-1957 .... TCLC 5
See also CA 104; 155; DLB 20

Campbell, Thomas 1777-1844 .... NCLC 19
See also DLB 93; 144

Campbell, Wilfred .... TCLC 9
See also Campbell, William

Campbell, William 1858(?)-1918
See Campbell, Wilfred
See also CA 106; DLB 92

Campion, Jane .... CLC 95
See also CA 138

Campos, Alvaro de
See Pessoa, Fernando (Antonio Nogueira)

Camus, Albert
1913-1960 ... CLC 1, 2, 4, 9, 11, 14, 32,
63, 69; DA; DAB; DAC; DAM DRAM,
MST, NOV; DC 2; SSC 9; WLC
See also CA 89-92; DLB 72; MTCW

Canby, Vincent 1924- .... CLC 13
See also CA 81-84

Cancale
See Desnos, Robert

Canetti, Elias
1905-1994 .... CLC 3, 14, 25, 75, 86
See also CA 21-24R; 146; CANR 23, 61; DLB
85, 124; MTCW

Canin, Ethan 1960- .... CLC 55
See also CA 131; 135

Cannon, Curt
See Hunter, Evan

Cape, Judith
See Page, P(atricia) K(athleen)

Capek, Karel
1890-1938 .... TCLC 6, 37; DA; DAB;
DAC; DAM DRAM, MST, NOV; DC 1;
WLC
See also CA 104; 140

Capote, Truman
1924-1984 .... CLC 1, 3, 8, 13, 19, 34, 38,
58; DA; DAB; DAC; DAM MST, NOV,
POP; SSC 2; WLC
See also CA 5-8R; 113; CANR 18, 62; CDALB
1941-1968; DLB 2; DLBY 80, 84; MTCW;
SATA 91

Capra, Frank 1897-1991 .... CLC 16
See also CA 61-64; 135

Caputo, Philip 1941- .... CLC 32
See also CA 73-76; CANR 40

Caragiale, Ion Luca 1852-1912 ..... TCLC 76
See also CA 157

Card, Orson Scott 1951- ...... CLC 44, 47, 50;
DAM POP
See also AAYA 11; CA 102; CANR 27, 47;
INT CANR-27; MTCW; SATA 83

Cardenal, Ernesto 1925- .... CLC 31; DAM
MULT, POET; HLC
See also CA 49-52; CANR 2, 32; HW; MTCW

Cardozo, Benjamin N(athan)
1870-1938 .... TCLC 65
See also CA 117

Carducci, Giosue 1835-1907 .... TCLC 32

Carew, Thomas 1595(?)-1640 .... LC 13
See also DLB 126

Carey, Ernestine Gilbreth 1908- .... CLC 17
See also CA 5-8R; SATA 2

Carey, Peter 1943- .... CLC 40, 55, 96
See also CA 123; 127; CANR 53; INT 127;
MTCW; SATA 94

Carleton, William 1794-1869 .... NCLC 3
See also DLB 159

Carlisle, Henry (Coffin) 1926- .... CLC 33
See also CA 13-16R; CANR 15

Carlsen, Chris
See Holdstock, Robert P.

Carlson, Ron(ald F.) 1947- .... CLC 54
See also CA 105; CANR 27

Carlyle, Thomas
1795-1881 .. NCLC 22; DA; DAB; DAC;
DAM MST
See also CDBLB 1789-1832; DLB 55;
144

Carman, (William) Bliss
1861-1929 .... TCLC 7; DAC
See also CA 104; 152; DLB 92

Carnegie, Dale 1888-1955 .... TCLC 53

Carossa, Hans 1878-1956 .... TCLC 48
See also DLB 66

Carpenter, Don(ald Richard)
1931-1995 .... CLC 41
See also CA 45-48; 149; CANR 1

Carpentier (y Valmont), Alejo
1904-1980 .... CLC 8, 11, 38; DAM
MULT; HLC
See also CA 65-68; 97-100; CANR 11; DLB
113; HW

Carr, Caleb 1955(?)- .... CLC 86
See also CA 147

Carr, Emily 1871-1945 .... TCLC 32
See also CA 159; DLB 68

Carr, John Dickson 1906-1977 .... CLC 3
See also Fairbairn, Roger
See also CA 49-52; 69-72; CANR 3, 33, 60;
MTCW

Carr, Philippa
See Hibbert, Eleanor Alice Burford

Carr, Virginia Spencer 1929- .... CLC 34
See also CA 61-64; DLB 111

Carrere, Emmanuel 1957- .... CLC 89

Carrier, Roch
1937- ..... CLC 13, 78; DAC; DAM MST
See also CA 130; CANR 61; DLB 53

Carroll, James P. 1943(?)- .... CLC 38
See also CA 81-84

Carroll, Jim 1951- .... CLC 35
See also AAYA 17; CA 45-48; CANR 42

Carroll, Lewis ..... NCLC 2, 53; PC 18; WLC
See also Dodgson, Charles Lutwidge
See also CDBLB 1832-1890; CLR 2, 18; DLB
18, 163, 178; JRDA

Carroll, Paul Vincent 1900-1968 ...... CLC 10
See also CA 9-12R; 25-28R; DLB 10

Carruth, Hayden
1921- .... CLC 4, 7, 10, 18, 84; PC 10
See also CA 9-12R; CANR 4, 38, 59;
DLB 5, 165; INT CANR-4; MTCW;
SATA 47

Carson, Rachel Louise
1907-1964 .... CLC 71; DAM POP
See also CA 77-80; CANR 35; MTCW; SATA
23

Carter, Angela (Olive)
1940-1992 .... CLC 5, 41, 76; SSC 13
See also CA 53-56; 136; CANR 12, 36, 61;
DLB 14; MTCW; SATA 66; SATA-Obit 70

Carter, Nick
See Smith, Martin Cruz

Carver, Raymond
1938-1988 ...... CLC 22, 36, 53, 55; DAM
NOV; SSC 8
See also CA 33-36R; 126; CANR 17,
34, 61; DLB 130; DLBY 84, 88;
MTCW

Cary, Elizabeth, Lady Falkland
1585-1639 .... LC 30

Cary, (Arthur) Joyce (Lunel)
1888-1957 .... TCLC 1, 29
See also CA 104; CDBLB 1914-1945; DLB
15, 100

Casanova de Seingalt, Giovanni Jacopo
1725-1798 .... LC 13

Casares, Adolfo Bioy
See Bioy Casares, Adolfo

Casely-Hayford, J(oseph) E(phraim)
1866-1930 .... TCLC 24; BLC; DAM
MULT
See also BW 2; CA 123; 152

Casey, John (Dudley) 1939- .... CLC 59
See also BEST 90:2; CA 69-72; CANR 23

Casey, Michael 1947- .... CLC 2
See also CA 65-68; DLB 5

Casey, Patrick
See Thurman, Wallace (Henry)

Casey, Warren (Peter) 1935-1988 ..... CLC 12
   See also CA 101; 127; INT 101

Casona, Alejandro .... CLC 49
   See also Alvarez, Alejandro Rodriguez

Cassavetes, John 1929-1989 .... CLC 20
   See also CA 85-88; 127

Cassian, Nina 1924- .... PC 17

Cassill, R(onald) V(erlin) 1919- .... CLC 4, 23
   See also CA 9-12R; CAAS 1; CANR 7, 45;
   DLB 6

Cassirer, Ernst 1874-1945 .... TCLC 61
   See also CA 157

Cassity, (Allen) Turner 1929- .... CLC 6, 42
   See also CA 17-20R; CAAS 8; CANR 11; DLB
   105

Castaneda, Carlos 1931(?)- .... CLC 12
   See also CA 25-28R; CANR 32; HW; MTCW

Castedo, Elena 1937- .... CLC 65
   See also CA 132

Castedo-Ellerman, Elena
   See Castedo, Elena

Castellanos, Rosario 1925-1974 ...... CLC 66;
   DAM MULT; HLC
   See also CA 131; 53-56; CANR 58; DLB 113;
   HW

Castelvetro, Lodovico 1505-1571 .... LC 12

Castiglione, Baldassare 1478-1529 ...... LC 12

Castle, Robert
   See Hamilton, Edmond

Castro, Guillen de 1569-1631 .... LC 19

Castro, Rosalia de
   1837-1885 .... NCLC 3; DAM MULT

Cather, Willa
   See Cather, Willa Sibert

Cather, Willa Sibert
   1873-1947 ... TCLC 1, 11, 31; DA; DAB;
   DAC; DAM MST, NOV; SSC 2; WLC
   See also CA 104; 128; CDALB 1865-1917;
   DLB 9, 54, 78; DLBD 1; MTCW; SATA 30

Cato, Marcus Porcius
   234B.C.-149B.C. .... CMLC 21

Catton, (Charles) Bruce
   1899-1978 .... CLC 35
   See also AITN 1; CA 5-8R; 81-84; CANR 7;
   DLB 17; SATA 2; SATA-Obit 24

Catullus c. 84B.C.-c. 54B.C. .... CMLC 18

Cauldwell, Frank
   See King, Francis (Henry)

Caunitz, William J. 1933-1996 .... CLC 34
   See also BEST 89:3; CA 125; 130; 152; INT
   130

Causley, Charles (Stanley) 1917- .... CLC 7
   See also CA 9-12R; CANR 5, 35; CLR 30;
   DLB 27; MTCW; SATA 3, 66

Caute, David 1936- .... CLC 29; DAM NOV
   See also CA 1-4R; CAAS 4; CANR 1, 33; DLB 14

Cavafy, C(onstantine) P(eter)
   1863-1933 .... TCLC 2, 7; DAM POET
   See also Kavafis, Konstantinos Petrou
   See also CA 148

Cavallo, Evelyn
   See Spark, Muriel (Sarah)

Cavanna, Betty .... CLC 12
   See also Harrison, Elizabeth Cavanna
   See also JRDA; MAICYA; SAAS 4; SATA 1,
   30

Cavendish, Margaret Lucas
   1623-1673 .... LC 30
   See also DLB 131

Caxton, William 1421(?)-1491(?) .... LC 17
   See also DLB 170

Cayrol, Jean 1911- .... CLC 11
   See also CA 89-92; DLB 83

Cela, Camilo Jose
   1916- ...... CLC 4, 13, 59; DAM MULT;
   HLC
   See also BEST 90:2; CA 21-24R; CAAS 10;
   CANR 21, 32; DLBY 89; HW; MTCW

Celan, Paul .... CLC 10, 19, 53, 82; PC 10
   See also Antschel, Paul
   See also DLB 69

Celine, Louis-Ferdinand .... CLC 1, 3, 4, 7, 9,
   15, 47
   See also Destouches, Louis-Ferdinand
   See also DLB 72

Cellini, Benvenuto 1500-1571 .... LC 7

Cendrars, Blaise .... CLC 18
   See also Sauser-Hall, Frederic

Cernuda (y Bidon), Luis
   1902-1963 .... CLC 54; DAM POET
   See also CA 131; 89-92; DLB 134; HW

Cervantes (Saavedra), Miguel de
   1547-1616 .... LC 6, 23; DA; DAB; DAC;
   DAM MST, NOV; SSC 12; WLC

Cesaire, Aime (Fernand)
   1913- .... CLC 19, 32; BLC; DAM
   MULT, POET
   See also BW 2; CA 65-68; CANR 24, 43; MTCW

Chabon, Michael 1963- .... CLC 55
   See also CA 139; CANR 57

Chabrol, Claude 1930- .... CLC 16
   See also CA 110

Challans, Mary 1905-1983
   See Renault, Mary
   See also CA 81-84; 111; SATA 23; SATA-Obit
   36

Challis, George
   See Faust, Frederick (Schiller)

Chambers, Aidan
   1934- .... CLC 35
   See also CA 25-28R; CANR 12, 31, 58; JRDA;
   MAICYA; SAAS 12; SATA 1, 69

Chambers, James 1948-
   See Cliff, Jimmy
   See also CA 124

Chambers, Jessie
   See Lawrence, D(avid) H(erbert Richards)

Chambers, Robert W.
   1865-1933 .... TCLC 41

Chandler, Raymond (Thornton)
   1888-1959 .... TCLC 1, 7; SSC 23
   See also CA 104; 129; CANR 60; CDALB
   1929-1941; DLBD 6; MTCW

Chang, Eileen 1920- .... SSC 28

Chang, Jung 1952- .... CLC 71
   See also CA 142

Channing, William Ellery
   1780-1842 .... NCLC 17
   See also DLB 1, 59

Chaplin, Charles Spencer
   1889-1977 .... CLC 16
   See also Chaplin, Charlie
   See also CA 81-84; 73-76

Chaplin, Charlie
   See Chaplin, Charles Spencer
   See also DLB 44

Chapman, George
   1559(?)-1634 .... LC 22; DAM DRAM
   See also DLB 62, 121

Chapman, Graham 1941-1989 .... CLC 21
   See also Monty Python
   See also CA 116; 129; CANR 35

Chapman, John Jay 1862-1933 .... TCLC 7
   See also CA 104

Chapman, Lee
   See Bradley, Marion Zimmer

Chapman, Walker
   See Silverberg, Robert

Chappell, Fred (Davis) 1936- ..... CLC 40, 78
   See also CA 5-8R; CAAS 4; CANR 8, 33; DLB
   6, 105

Char, Rene(-Emile)
   1907-1988 .... CLC 9, 11, 14, 55; DAM
   POET
   See also CA 13-16R; 124; CANR 32;
   MTCW

Charby, Jay
   See Ellison, Harlan (Jay)

Chardin, Pierre Teilhard de
   See Teilhard de Chardin, (Marie Joseph) Pierre

Author Index

Charles I 1600-1649 .... **LC 13**

Charyn, Jerome 1937- .... **CLC 5, 8, 18**
See also CA 5-8R; CAAS 1; CANR 7, 61;
DLBY 83; MTCW

Chase, Mary (Coyle) 1907-1981 .... **DC 1**
See also CA 77-80; 105; SATA 17; SATA-Obit
29

Chase, Mary Ellen 1887-1973 .... **CLC 2**
See also CA 13-16; 41-44R; CAP 1; SATA 10

Chase, Nicholas
See Hyde, Anthony

Chateaubriand, Francois Rene de 1768-
1848 .... **NCLC 3**
See also DLB 119

Chatterje, Sarat Chandra 1876-1936(?)
See Chatterji, Saratchandra
See also CA 109

Chatterji, Bankim Chandra 1838-
1894 .... **NCLC 19**

Chatterji, Saratchandra .... **TCLC 13**
See also Chatterje, Sarat Chandra

Chatterton, Thomas 1752-
1770 .... **LC 3; DAM POET**
See also DLB 109

Chatwin, (Charles) Bruce 1940-
1989 .... **CLC 28, 57, 59; DAM POP**
See also AAYA 4; BEST 90:1; CA 85-88; 127

Chaucer, Daniel
See Ford, Ford Madox

Chaucer, Geoffrey 1340(?)-1400 ...... **LC 17;
DA; DAB; DAC; DAM MST, POET; PC
19; WLCS**
See also CDBLB Before 1660; DLB 146

Chaviaras, Strates 1935-
See Haviaras, Stratis
See also CA 105

Chayefsky, Paddy .... **CLC 23**
See also Chayefsky, Sidney
See also DLB 7, 44; DLBY 81

Chayefsky, Sidney 1923-1981
See Chayefsky, Paddy
See also CA 9-12R; 104; CANR 18; DAM
DRAM

Chedid, Andree 1920- .... **CLC 47**
See also CA 145

Cheever, John 1912-1982 .. **CLC 3, 7, 8,
11, 15, 25, 64; DA; DAB; DAC;
DAM MST, NOV, POP; SSC 1;
WLC**
See also CA 5-8R; 106; CABS 1; CANR 5,
27; CDALB 1941-1968; DLB 2, 102; DLBY
80, 82; INT CANR-5; MTCW

Cheever, Susan 1943- .... **CLC 18, 48**
See also CA 103; CANR 27, 51; DLBY 82;
INT CANR-27

Chekhonte, Antosha
See Chekhov, Anton (Pavlovich)

Chekhov, Anton (Pavlovich)
1860-1904 .... **TCLC 3, 10, 31, 55; DA;
DAB; DAC; DAM DRAM, MST; SSC 2,
28; WLC**
See also CA 104; 124; SATA 90

Chernyshevsky, Nikolay Gavrilovich
1828-1889 .... **NCLC 1**

Cherry, Carolyn Janice 1942-
See Cherryh, C. J.
See also CA 65-68; CANR 10

Cherryh, C. J. .... **CLC 35**
See also Cherry, Carolyn Janice
See also DLBY 80; SATA 93

Chesnutt, Charles W(addell)
1858-1932 .... **TCLC 5, 39; BLC; DAM
MULT; SSC 7**
See also BW 1; CA 106; 125; DLB 12, 50, 78;
MTCW

Chester, Alfred
1929(?)-1971 .... **CLC 49**
See also CA 33-36R; DLB 130

Chesterton, G(ilbert) K(eith)
1874-1936 ... **TCLC 1, 6, 64; DAM NOV,
POET; SSC 1**
See also CA 104; 132; CDBLB 1914-1945;
DLB 10, 19, 34, 70, 98, 149, 178; MTCW;
SATA 27

Chiang Pin-chin 1904-1986
See Ding Ling
See also CA 118

Ch'ien Chung-shu 1910- .... **CLC 22**
See also CA 130; MTCW

Child, L. Maria
See Child, Lydia Maria

Child, Lydia Maria 1802-1880 .... **NCLC 6**
See also DLB 1, 74; SATA 67

Child, Mrs.
See Child, Lydia Maria

Child, Philip 1898-1978 .... **CLC 19, 68**
See also CA 13-14; CAP 1; SATA 47

Childers, (Robert) Erskine
1870-1922 .... **TCLC 65**
See also CA 113; 153; DLB 70

Childress, Alice 1920-1994 ..... **CLC 12, 15,
86, 96; BLC; DAM DRAM, MULT,
NOV; DC 4**
See also AAYA 8; BW 2; CA 45-48; 146;
CANR 3, 27, 50; CLR 14; DLB 7, 38;
JRDA; MAICYA; MTCW; SATA 7, 48,
81

Chin, Frank (Chew, Jr.) 1940- .... **DC 7**
See also CA 33-36R; DAM MULT

Chislett, (Margaret) Anne 1943- ...... **CLC 34**
See also CA 151

Chitty, Thomas Willes 1926- .... **CLC 11**
See also Hinde, Thomas
See also CA 5-8R

Chivers, Thomas Holley
1809-1858 .... **NCLC 49**
See also DLB 3

Chomette, Rene Lucien 1898-1981
See Clair, Rene
See also CA 103

Chopin, Kate .... **TCLC 5, 14; DA; DAB;
SSC 8; WLCS**
See also Chopin, Katherine
See also CDALB 1865-1917; DLB 12, 78

Chopin, Katherine 1851-1904
See Chopin, Kate
See also CA 104; 122; DAC; DAM MST, NOV

Chretien de Troyes
c. 12th cent. - .... **CMLC 10**

Christie
See Ichikawa, Kon

Christie, Agatha (Mary Clarissa)
1890-1976 .... **CLC 1, 6, 8, 12, 39, 48;
DAB; DAC; DAM NOV**
See also AAYA 9; AITN 1, 2; CA 17-20R; 61-
64; CANR 10, 37; CDBLB 1914-1945;
DLB 13, 77; MTCW; SATA 36

Christie, (Ann) Philippa
See Pearce, Philippa
See also CA 5-8R; CANR 4

Christine de Pizan 1365(?)-1431(?) .... **LC 9**

Chubb, Elmer
See Masters, Edgar Lee

Chulkov, Mikhail Dmitrievich
1743-1792 .... **LC 2**
See also DLB 150

Churchill, Caryl
1938- .... **CLC 31, 55; DC 5**
See also CA 102; CANR 22, 46; DLB 13;
MTCW

Churchill, Charles 1731-1764 .... **LC 3**
See also DLB 109

Chute, Carolyn 1947- .... **CLC 39**
See also CA 123

Ciardi, John (Anthony) 1916-1986 .. **CLC 10,
40, 44; DAM POET**
See also CA 5-8R; 118; CAAS 2; CANR 5,
33; CLR 19; DLB 5; DLBY 86; INT CANR-
5; MAICYA; MTCW; SATA 1, 65; SATA-
Obit 46

Cicero, Marcus Tullius
106B.C.-43B.C. .... **CMLC 3**

Cimino, Michael 1943- .... **CLC 16**
See also CA 105

Cioran, E(mil) M. 1911-1995 .... **CLC 64**
See also CA 25-28R; 149

Coppee, Francois 1842-1908 .... **TCLC 25**

Coppola, Francis Ford 1939- .... **CLC 16**
See also CA 77-80; CANR 40; DLB 44

Corbiere, Tristan 1845-1875 .... **NCLC 43**

Corcoran, Barbara 1911- .... **CLC 17**
See also AAYA 14; CA 21-24R; CAAS 2;
CANR 11, 28, 48; DLB 52; JRDA; SAAS
20; SATA 3, 77

Cordelier, Maurice
See Giraudoux, (Hippolyte) Jean

Corelli, Marie 1855-1924 .... **TCLC 51**
See also Mackay, Mary
See also DLB 34, 156

Corman, Cid .... **CLC 9**
See also Corman, Sidney
See also CAAS 2; DLB 5

Corman, Sidney 1924-
See Corman, Cid
See also CA 85-88; CANR 44; DAM POET

Cormier, Robert (Edmund)
1925- .... **CLC 12, 30; DA; DAB; DAC;
DAM MST, NOV**
See also AAYA 3, 19; CA 1-4R; CANR 5, 23;
CDALB 1968-1988; CLR 12; DLB 52; INT
CANR-23; JRDA; MAICYA; MTCW;
SATA 10, 45, 83

Corn, Alfred (DeWitt III) 1943- .... **CLC 33**
See also CA 104; CAAS 25; CANR 44; DLB
120; DLBY 80

Corneille, Pierre
1606-1684 .... **LC 28; DAB; DAM MST**

Cornwell, David (John Moore)
1931- .... **CLC 9, 15; DAM POP**
See also le Carre, John
See also CA 5-8R; CANR 13, 33, 59; MTCW

Corso, (Nunzio) Gregory 1930- .... **CLC 1, 11**
See also CA 5-8R; CANR 41; DLB 5, 16;
MTCW

Cortazar, Julio
1914-1984 .... **CLC 2, 3, 5, 10, 13, 15,
33, 34, 92; DAM MULT, NOV; HLC;
SSC 7**
See also CA 21-24R; CANR 12, 32; DLB 113;
HW; MTCW

CORTES, HERNAN 1484-1547 .... **LC 31**

Corwin, Cecil
See Kornbluth, C(yril) M.

Cosic, Dobrica 1921- .... **CLC 14**
See also CA 122; 138; DLB 181

Costain, Thomas B(ertram)
1885-1965 .... **CLC 30**
See also CA 5-8R; 25-28R; DLB 9

Costantini, Humberto
1924(?)-1987 .... **CLC 49**
See also CA 131; 122; HW

Costello, Elvis 1955- .... **CLC 21**

Cotes, Cecil V.
See Duncan, Sara Jeannette

Cotter, Joseph Seamon Sr.
1861-1949 .... **TCLC 28; BLC; DAM
MULT**
See also BW 1; CA 124; DLB 50

Couch, Arthur Thomas Quiller
See Quiller-Couch, Arthur Thomas

Coulton, James
See Hansen, Joseph

Couperus, Louis (Marie Anne)
1863-1923 .... **TCLC 15**
See also CA 115

Coupland, Douglas
1961- .... **CLC 85; DAC; DAM POP**
See also CA 142; CANR 57

Court, Wesli
See Turco, Lewis (Putnam)

Courtenay, Bryce 1933- .... **CLC 59**
See also CA 138

Courtney, Robert
See Ellison, Harlan (Jay)

Cousteau, Jacques-Yves
1910-1997 .... **CLC 30**
See also CA 65-68; 159; CANR 15; MTCW;
SATA 38

Cowan, Peter (Walkinshaw) 1914- .... **SSC 28**
See also CA 21-24R; CANR 9, 25, 50

Coward, Noel (Peirce)
1899-1973 .... **CLC 1, 9, 29, 51; DAM
DRAM**
See also AITN 1; CA 17-18; 41-44R; CANR
35; CAP 2; CDBLB 1914-1945; DLB 10;
MTCW

Cowley, Malcolm 1898-1989 .... **CLC 39**
See also CA 5-8R; 128; CANR 3, 55; DLB 4,
48; DLBY 81, 89; MTCW

Cowper, William
1731-1800 .... **NCLC 8; DAM POET**
See also DLB 104, 109

Cox, William Trevor 1928- .... **CLC 9, 14, 71;
DAM NOV**
See also Trevor, William
See also CA 9-12R; CANR 4, 37, 55; DLB 14;
INT CANR-37; MTCW

Coyne, P. J.
See Masters, Hilary

Cozzens, James Gould
1903-1978 .... **CLC 1, 4, 11, 92**
See also CA 9-12R; 81-84; CANR 19; CDALB
1941-1968; DLB 9; DLBD 2; DLBY 84;
MTCW

Crabbe, George 1754-1832 .... **NCLC 26**
See also DLB 93

Craddock, Charles Egbert
See Murfree, Mary Noailles

Craig, A. A.
See Anderson, Poul (William)

Craik, Dinah Maria (Mulock)
1826-1887 .... **NCLC 38**
See also DLB 35, 163; MAICYA; SATA
34

Cram, Ralph Adams 1863-1942 ..... **TCLC 45**
See also CA 160

Crane, (Harold) Hart
1899-1932... **TCLC 2, 5; DA; DAB;
DAC; DAM MST, POET; PC 3;
WLC**
See also CA 104; 127; CDALB 1917-1929;
DLB 4, 48; MTCW

Crane, R(onald) S(almon)
1886-1967 .... **CLC 27**
See also CA 85-88; DLB 63

Crane, Stephen (Townley)
1871-1900 .... **TCLC 11, 17, 32; DA;
DAB; DAC; DAM MST, NOV, POET;
SSC 7; WLC**
See also AAYA 21; CA 109; 140;
CDALB 1865-1917; DLB 12, 54, 78;
YABC 2

Crase, Douglas 1944- .... **CLC 58**
See also CA 106

Crashaw, Richard 1612(?)-1649 .... **LC 24**
See also DLB 126

Craven, Margaret
1901-1980 .... **CLC 17; DAC**
See also CA 103

Crawford, F(rancis) Marion
1854-1909 .... **TCLC 10**
See also CA 107; DLB 71

Crawford, Isabella Valancy
1850-1887 .... **NCLC 12**
See also DLB 92

Crayon, Geoffrey
See Irving, Washington

Creasey, John
1908-1973 .... **CLC 11**
See also CA 5-8R; 41-44R; CANR 8, 59; DLB
77; MTCW

Crebillon, Claude Prosper Jolyot de (fils)
1707-1777 .... **LC 28**

Credo
See Creasey, John

Credo, Alvaro J. de
See Prado (Calvo), Pedro

Creeley, Robert (White)
1926- .... **CLC 1, 2, 4, 8, 11, 15, 36, 78;
DAM POET**
See also CA 1-4R; CAAS 10; CANR 23,
43; DLB 5, 16, 169; MTCW

Crews, Harry (Eugene)
1935- .... **CLC 6, 23, 49**
See also AITN 1; CA 25-28R; CANR 20, 57;
DLB 6, 143; MTCW

Crichton, (John) Michael
1942- ...... **CLC 2, 6, 54, 90; DAM NOV,
POP**
See also AAYA 10; AITN 2; CA 25-28R;
CANR 13, 40, 54; DLBY 81; INT CANR-
13; JRDA; MTCW; SATA 9, 88

Crispin, Edmund .... **CLC 22**
See also Montgomery, (Robert) Bruce
See also DLB 87

Cristofer, Michael
1945(?)- .... **CLC 28; DAM DRAM**
See also CA 110; 152; DLB 7

Croce, Benedetto 1866-1952 .... **TCLC 37**
See also CA 120; 155

Crockett, David 1786-1836 .... **NCLC 8**
See also DLB 3, 11

Crockett, Davy
See Crockett, David

Crofts, Freeman Wills
1879-1957 .... **TCLC 55**
See also CA 115; DLB 77

Croker, John Wilson
1780-1857 .... **NCLC 10**
See also DLB 110

Crommelynck, Fernand
1885-1970 .... **CLC 75**
See also CA 89-92

Cronin, A(rchibald) J(oseph)
1896-1981 .... **CLC 32**
See also CA 1-4R; 102; CANR 5; SATA 47;
SATA-Obit 25

Cross, Amanda
See Heilbrun, Carolyn G(old)

Crothers, Rachel
1878(?)-1958 .... **TCLC 19**
See also CA 113; DLB 7

Croves, Hal
See Traven, B.

Crow Dog, Mary (Ellen) (?)- .... **CLC 93**
See also Brave Bird, Mary
See also CA 154

Crowfield, Christopher
See Stowe, Harriet (Elizabeth) Beecher

Crowley, Aleister .... **TCLC 7**
See also Crowley, Edward Alexander

Crowley, Edward Alexander 1875-1947
See Crowley, Aleister
See also CA 104

Crowley, John 1942- .... **CLC 57**
See also CA 61-64; CANR 43; DLBY 82;
SATA 65

Crud
See Crumb, R(obert)

Crumarums
See Crumb, R(obert)

Crumb, R(obert) 1943- .... **CLC 17**
See also CA 106

Crumbum
See Crumb, R(obert)

Crumski
See Crumb, R(obert)

Crum the Bum
See Crumb, R(obert)

Crunk
See Crumb, R(obert)

Crustt
See Crumb, R(obert)

Cryer, Gretchen (Kiger) 1935- .... **CLC 21**
See also CA 114; 123

Csath, Geza 1887-1919 .... **TCLC 13**
See also CA 111

Cudlip, David 1933- .... **CLC 34**

Cullen, Countee
1903-1946 .... **TCLC 4, 37; BLC; DA;
DAC; DAM MST, MULT, POET; PC
20; WLCS**
See also BW 1; CA 108; 124; CDALB
1917-1929; DLB 4, 48, 51; MTCW;
SATA 18

Cum, R.
See Crumb, R(obert)

Cummings, Bruce F(rederick) 1889-1919
See Barbellion, W. N. P.
See also CA 123

Cummings, E(dward) E(stlin)
1894-1962 ..... **CLC 1, 3, 8, 12, 15, 68;
DA; DAB; DAC; DAM MST, POET;
PC 5; WLC 2**
See also CA 73-76; CANR 31; CDALB 1929-
1941; DLB 4, 48; MTCW

Cunha, Euclides (Rodrigues Pimenta) da
1866-1909 .... **TCLC 24**
See also CA 123

Cunningham, E. V.
See Fast, Howard (Melvin)

Cunningham, J(ames) V(incent)
1911-1985 .... **CLC 3, 31**
See also CA 1-4R; 115; CANR 1; DLB 5

Cunningham, Julia (Woolfolk)
1916- .... **CLC 12**
See also CA 9-12R; CANR 4, 19, 36;
JRDA; MAICYA; SAAS 2; SATA 1,
26

Cunningham, Michael 1952- .... **CLC 34**
See also CA 136

Cunninghame Graham, R(obert) B(ontine)
1852-1936 .... **TCLC 19**
See also Graham, R(obert) B(ontine)
Cunninghame
See also CA 119; DLB 98

Currie, Ellen 19(?)- .... **CLC 44**

Curtin, Philip
See Lowndes, Marie Adelaide (Belloc)

Curtis, Price
See Ellison, Harlan (Jay)

Cutrate, Joe
See Spiegelman, Art

Cynewulf c. 770-c. 840 .... **CMLC 23**

Czaczkes, Shmuel Yosef
See Agnon, S(hmuel) Y(osef Halevi)

Dabrowska, Maria (Szumska)
1889-1965 .... **CLC 15**
See also CA 106

Dabydeen, David
1955- .... **CLC 34**
See also BW 1; CA 125; CANR 56

Dacey, Philip
1939- .... **CLC 51**
See also CA 37-40R; CAAS 17; CANR 14, 32;
DLB 105

Dagerman, Stig (Halvard)
1923-1954 .... **TCLC 17**
See also CA 117; 155

Dahl, Roald
1916-1990 .... **CLC 1, 6, 18, 79; DAB;
DAC; DAM MST, NOV, POP**
See also AAYA 15; CA 1-4R; 133; CANR 6,
32, 37, 62; CLR 1, 7, 41; DLB 139; JRDA;
MAICYA; MTCW; SATA 1, 26, 73; SATA-
Obit 65

Dahlberg, Edward
1900-1977 .... **CLC 1, 7, 14**
See also CA 9-12R; 69-72; CANR 31, 62; DLB
48; MTCW

Daitch, Susan 1954- .... **CLC 103**

Dale, Colin .... **TCLC 18**
See also Lawrence, T(homas) E(dward)

Dale, George E.
See Asimov, Isaac

Daly, Elizabeth
1878-1967 .... **CLC 52**
See also CA 23-24; 25-28R; CANR 60; CAP
2

Daly, Maureen
1921- .... **CLC 17**
See also AAYA 5; CANR 37; JRDA; MAICYA;
SAAS 1; SATA 2

Damas, Leon-Gontran
1912-1978 .... **CLC 84**
See also BW 1; CA 125; 73-76

Dana, Richard Henry Sr.
    1787-1879 .... **NCLC 53**

Daniel, Samuel 1562(?)-1619 .... **LC 24**
    See also DLB 62

Daniels, Brett
    See Adler, Renata

Dannay, Frederic
    1905-1982 .... **CLC 11; DAM POP**
    See also Queen, Ellery
    See also CA 1-4R; 107; CANR 1, 39; DLB 137;
    MTCW

D'Annunzio, Gabriele
    1863-1938 .... **TCLC 6, 40**
    See also CA 104; 155

Danois, N. le
    See Gourmont, Remy (-Marie-Charles) de

d'Antibes, Germain
    See Simenon, Georges (Jacques Christian)

Danticat, Edwidge 1969- .... **CLC 94**
    See also CA 152

Danvers, Dennis 1947- .... **CLC 70**

Danziger, Paula 1944- .... **CLC 21**
    See also AAYA 4; CA 112; 115; CANR 37;
    CLR 20; JRDA; MAICYA; SATA 36, 63;
    SATA-Brief 30

Da Ponte, Lorenzo 1749-1838 .... **NCLC 50**

Dario, Ruben 1867-1916 .... **TCLC 4; DAM**
    MULT; HLC; PC 15
    See also CA 131; HW; MTCW

Darley, George 1795-1846 .... **NCLC 2**
    See also DLB 96

Darwin, Charles 1809-1882 .... **NCLC 57**
    See also DLB 57, 166

Daryush, Elizabeth 1887-1977 ......**CLC 6, 19**
    See also CA 49-52; CANR 3; DLB 20

Dashwood, Edmee Elizabeth Monica de la Pasture 1890-1943
    See Delafield, E. M.
    See also CA 119; 154

Daudet, (Louis Marie) Alphonse
    1840-1897 .... **NCLC 1**
    See also DLB 123

Daumal, Rene 1908-1944 .... **TCLC 14**
    See also CA 114

Davenport, Guy (Mattison, Jr.)
    1927- .... **CLC 6, 14, 38; SSC 16**
    See also CA 33-36R; CANR 23; DLB 130

Davidson, Avram 1923-
    See Queen, Ellery
    See also CA 101; CANR 26; DLB 8

Davidson, Donald (Grady)
    1893-1968 .... **CLC 2, 13, 19**
    See also CA 5-8R; 25-28R; CANR 4; DLB 45

Davidson, Hugh
    See Hamilton, Edmond

Davidson, John 1857-1909 .... **TCLC 24**
    See also CA 118; DLB 19

Davidson, Sara 1943- .... **CLC 9**
    See also CA 81-84; CANR 44

Davie, Donald (Alfred)
    1922-1995 .... **CLC 5, 8, 10, 31**
    See also CA 1-4R; 149; CAAS 3; CANR 1,
    44; DLB 27; MTCW

Davies, Ray(mond Douglas) 1944- ... **CLC 21**
    See also CA 116; 146

Davies, Rhys 1903-1978 .... **CLC 23**
    See also CA 9-12R; 81-84; CANR 4; DLB 139

Davies, (William) Robertson
    1913-1995 .... **CLC 2, 7, 13, 25, 42, 75,**
    91; DA; DAB; DAC; DAM MST,
    NOV, POP; WLC
    See also BEST 89:2; CA 33-36R; 150;
    CANR 17, 42; DLB 68; INT CANR-17;
    MTCW

Davies, W(illiam) H(enry)
    1871-1940 .... **TCLC 5**
    See also CA 104; DLB 19, 174

Davies, Walter C.
    See Kornbluth, C(yril) M.

Davis, Angela (Yvonne)
    1944- .... **CLC 77; DAM MULT**
    See also BW 2; CA 57-60; CANR 10

Davis, B. Lynch
    See Bioy Casares, Adolfo; Borges, Jorge
    Luis

Davis, Gordon
    See Hunt, E(verette) Howard, (Jr.)

Davis, Harold Lenoir 1896-1960 ...... **CLC 49**
    See also CA 89-92; DLB 9

Davis, Rebecca (Blaine) Harding
    1831-1910 .... **TCLC 6**
    See also CA 104; DLB 74

Davis, Richard Harding
    1864-1916 .... **TCLC 24**
    See also CA 114; DLB 12, 23, 78, 79; DLBD
    13

Davison, Frank Dalby 1893-1970 ..... **CLC 15**
    See also CA 116

Davison, Lawrence H.
    See Lawrence, D(avid) H(erbert Richards)

Davison, Peter (Hubert) 1928- .... **CLC 28**
    See also CA 9-12R; CAAS 4; CANR 3, 43;
    DLB 5

Davys, Mary 1674-1732 .... **LC 1**
    See also DLB 39

Dawson, Fielding 1930- .... **CLC 6**
    See also CA 85-88; DLB 130

Dawson, Peter
    See Faust, Frederick (Schiller)

Day, Clarence (Shepard, Jr.)
    1874-1935 .... **TCLC 25**
    See also CA 108; DLB 11

Day, Thomas 1748-1789 .... **LC 1**
    See also DLB 39; YABC 1

Day Lewis, C(ecil)
    1904-1972 ... **CLC 1, 6, 10; DAM POET;**
    PC 11
    See also Blake, Nicholas
    See also CA 13-16; 33-36R; CANR 34;
    CAP 1; DLB 15, 20; MTCW

Dazai, Osamu .... **TCLC 11**
    See also Tsushima, Shuji
    See also DLB 182

de Andrade, Carlos Drummond
    See Drummond de Andrade, Carlos

Deane, Norman
    See Creasey, John

de Beauvoir, Simone (Lucie Ernestine Marie Bertrand)
    See Beauvoir, Simone (Lucie Ernestine Marie
    Bertrand) de

de Beer, P.
    See Bosman, Herman Charles

de Brissac, Malcolm
    See Dickinson, Peter (Malcolm)

de Chardin, Pierre Teilhard
    See Teilhard de Chardin, (Marie Joseph)
    Pierre

Dee, John 1527-1608 .... **LC 20**

Deer, Sandra 1940- .... **CLC 45**

De Ferrari, Gabriella
    1941- .... **CLC 65**
    See also CA 146

Defoe, Daniel
    1660(?)-1731 .... **LC 1; DA; DAB;**
    DAC; DAM MST, NOV; WLC
    See also CDBLB 1660-1789; DLB 39, 95,
    101; JRDA; MAICYA; SATA 22

de Gourmont, Remy(-Marie-Charles)
    See Gourmont, Remy (-Marie-Charles) de

de Hartog, Jan
    1914- .... **CLC 19**
    See also CA 1-4R; CANR 1

de Hostos, E. M.
    See Hostos (y Bonilla), Eugenio Maria de

de Hostos, Eugenio M.
    See Hostos (y Bonilla), Eugenio Maria de

Deighton, Len .... **CLC 4, 7, 22, 46**
    See also Deighton, Leonard Cyril
    See also AAYA 6; BEST 89:2; CDBLB
    1960 to Present; DLB 87

Deighton, Leonard Cyril 1929-
See Deighton, Len
See also CA 9-12R; CANR 19, 33; DAM NOV,
POP; MTCW

Dekker, Thomas
1572(?)-1632 .... **LC 22; DAM DRAM**
See also CDBLB Before 1660; DLB 62, 172

Delafield, E. M. 1890-1943 .... **TCLC 61**
See also Dashwood, Edmee Elizabeth Monica
de la Pasture
See also DLB 34

de la Mare, Walter (John)
1873-1956 ...... **TCLC 4, 53; DAB; DAC;
DAM MST, POET; SSC 14; WLC**
See also CDBLB 1914-1945; CLR 23; DLB
162; SATA 16

Delaney, Franey
See O'Hara, John (Henry)

Delaney, Shelagh
1939- .... **CLC 29; DAM DRAM**
See also CA 17-20R; CANR 30; CDBLB 1960
to Present; DLB 13; MTCW

Delany, Mary (Granville Pendarves)
1700-1788 .... **LC 12**

Delany, Samuel R(ay, Jr.)
1942- .... **CLC 8, 14, 38; BLC; DAM
MULT**
See also BW 2; CA 81-84; CANR 27, 43; DLB
8, 33; MTCW

De La Ramee, (Marie) Louise 1839-1908
See Ouida
See also SATA 20

de la Roche, Mazo 1879-1961 .... **CLC 14**
See also CA 85-88; CANR 30; DLB 68; SATA
64

De La Salle, Innocent
See Hartmann, Sadakichi

Delbanco, Nicholas (Franklin)
1942- .... **CLC 6, 13**
See also CA 17-20R; CAAS 2; CANR 29, 55;
DLB 6

del Castillo, Michel 1933- .... **CLC 38**
See also CA 109

Deledda, Grazia (Cosima)
1875(?)-1936 .... **TCLC 23**
See also CA 123

Delibes, Miguel .... **CLC 8, 18**
See also Delibes Setien, Miguel

Delibes Setien, Miguel 1920-
See Delibes, Miguel
See also CA 45-48; CANR 1, 32; HW;
MTCW

DeLillo, Don
1936- .... **CLC 8, 10, 13, 27, 39, 54, 76;
DAM NOV, POP**
See also BEST 89:1; CA 81-84; CANR 21;
DLB 6, 173; MTCW

de Lisser, H. G.
See De Lisser, H(erbert) G(eorge)
See also DLB 117

De Lisser, H(erbert) G(eorge)
1878-1944 .... **TCLC 12**
See also de Lisser, H. G.
See also BW 2; CA 109; 152

Deloria, Vine (Victor), Jr. 1933- ..... **CLC 21;
DAM MULT**
See also CA 53-56; CANR 5, 20, 48; DLB 175;
MTCW; NNAL; SATA 21

Del Vecchio, John M(ichael)
1947- .... **CLC 29**
See also CA 110; DLBD 9

de Man, Paul (Adolph Michel)
1919-1983 .... **CLC 55**
See also CA 128; 111; CANR 61; DLB 67;
MTCW

De Marinis, Rick 1934- .... **CLC 54**
See also CA 57-60; CAAS 24; CANR 9, 25,
50

Dembry, R. Emmet
See Murfree, Mary Noailles

Demby, William
1922- .... **CLC 53; BLC; DAM MULT**
See also BW 1; CA 81-84; DLB 33

de Menton, Francisco
See Chin, Frank (Chew, Jr.)

Demijohn, Thom
See Disch, Thomas M(ichael)

de Montherlant, Henry (Milon)
See Montherlant, Henry (Milon) de

Demosthenes 384B.C.-322B.C. ...... **CMLC 13**
See also DLB 176

de Natale, Francine
See Malzberg, Barry N(athaniel)

Denby, Edwin (Orr) 1903-1983 .... **CLC 48**
See also CA 138; 110

Denis, Julio
See Cortazar, Julio

Denmark, Harrison
See Zelazny, Roger (Joseph)

Dennis, John 1658-1734 .... **LC 11**
See also DLB 101

Dennis, Nigel (Forbes) 1912-1989 .... **CLC 8**
See also CA 25-28R; 129; DLB 13, 15;
MTCW

Dent, Lester 1904(?)-1959 .... **TCLC 72**
See also CA 112

De Palma, Brian (Russell) 1940- .... **CLC 20**
See also CA 109

De Quincey, Thomas 1785-1859 ...... **NCLC 4**
See also CDBLB 1789-1832; DLB 110; 144

Deren, Eleanora 1908(?)-1961
See Deren, Maya
See also CA 111

Deren, Maya 1917-1961 .... **CLC 16, 102**
See also Deren, Eleanora

Derleth, August (William)
1909-1971 .... **CLC 31**
See also CA 1-4R; 29-32R; CANR 4; DLB 9;
SATA 5

Der Nister 1884-1950 .... **TCLC 56**

de Routisie, Albert
See Aragon, Louis

Derrida, Jacques 1930- .... **CLC 24, 87**
See also CA 124; 127

Derry Down Derry
See Lear, Edward

Dersonnes, Jacques
See Simenon, Georges (Jacques Christian)

Desai, Anita
1937- .... **CLC 19, 37, 97; DAB; DAM
NOV**
See also CA 81-84; CANR 33, 53; MTCW;
SATA 63

de Saint-Luc, Jean
See Glassco, John

de Saint Roman, Arnaud
See Aragon, Louis

Descartes, Rene 1596-1650 .... **LC 20, 35**

De Sica, Vittorio 1901(?)-1974 .... **CLC 20**
See also CA 117

Desnos, Robert 1900-1945 .... **TCLC 22**
See also CA 121; 151

Destouches, Louis-Ferdinand
1894-1961 .... **CLC 9, 15**
See also Celine, Louis-Ferdinand
See also CA 85-88; CANR 28; MTCW

de Tolignac, Gaston
See Griffith, D(avid Lewelyn) W(ark)

Deutsch, Babette 1895-1982 .... **CLC 18**
See also CA 1-4R; 108; CANR 4; DLB 45;
SATA 1; SATA-Obit 33

Devenant, William 1606-1649 .... **LC 13**

Devkota, Laxmiprasad
1909-1959 .... **TCLC 23**
See also CA 123

De Voto, Bernard (Augustine)
1897-1955 .... **TCLC 29**
See also CA 113; 160; DLB 9

De Vries, Peter
1910-1993 ...... **CLC 1, 2, 3, 7, 10, 28, 46;
DAM NOV**
See also CA 17-20R; 142; CANR 41; DLB 6;
DLBY 82; MTCW

Dexter, John
See Bradley, Marion Zimmer

Dexter, Martin
See Faust, Frederick (Schiller)

Dexter, Pete
1943- .... **CLC 34, 55; DAM POP**
See also BEST 89:2; CA 127; 131; INT 131; MTCW

Diamano, Silmang
See Senghor, Leopold Sedar

Diamond, Neil 1941- .... **CLC 30**
See also CA 108

Diaz del Castillo, Bernal
1496-1584 .... **LC 31**

di Bassetto, Corno
See Shaw, George Bernard

Dick, Philip K(indred)
1928-1982 .... **CLC 10, 30, 72; DAM NOV, POP**
See also CA 49-52; 106; CANR 2, 16; DLB 8; MTCW

Dickens, Charles (John Huffam)
1812-1870 ..... **NCLC 3, 8, 18, 26, 37, 50; DA; DAB; DAC; DAM MST, NOV; SSC 17; WLC**
See also CDBLB 1832-1890; DLB 21, 55, 70, 159, 166; JRDA; MAICYA; SATA 15

Dickey, James (Lafayette)
1923-1997 ...... **CLC 1, 2, 4, 7, 10, 15, 47; DAM NOV, POET, POP**
See also AITN 1, 2; CA 9-12R; 156; CABS 2; CANR 10, 48, 61; CDALB 1968-1988; DLB 5; DLBD 7; DLBY 82, 93, 96; INT CANR-10; MTCW

Dickey, William 1928-1994 .... **CLC 3, 28**
See also CA 9-12R; 145; CANR 24; DLB 5

Dickinson, Charles 1951- .... **CLC 49**
See also CA 128

Dickinson, Emily (Elizabeth)
1830-1886 .... **NCLC 21; DA; DAB; DAC; DAM MST, POET; PC 1; WLC**
See also AAYA 22; CDALB 1865-1917; DLB 1; SATA 29

Dickinson, Peter (Malcolm)
1927- .... **CLC 12, 35**
See also AAYA 9; CA 41-44R; CANR 31, 58; CLR 29; DLB 87, 161; JRDA; MAICYA; SATA 5, 62, 95

Dickson, Carr
See Carr, John Dickson

Dickson, Carter
See Carr, John Dickson

Diderot, Denis 1713-1784 .... **LC 26**

Didion, Joan
1934- .... **CLC 1, 3, 8, 14, 32; DAM NOV**
See also AITN 1; CA 5-8R; CANR 14, 52; CDALB 1968-1988; DLB 2, 173; DLBY 81, 86; MTCW

Dietrich, Robert
See Hunt, E(verette) Howard, (Jr.)

Dillard, Annie
1945- .... **CLC 9, 60; DAM NOV**
See also AAYA 6; CA 49-52; CANR 3, 43, 62; DLBY 80; MTCW; SATA 10

Dillard, R(ichard) H(enry) W(ilde)
1937- .... **CLC 5**
See also CA 21-24R; CAAS 7; CANR 10; DLB 5

Dillon, Eilis 1920-1994 .... **CLC 17**
See also CA 9-12R; 147; CAAS 3; CANR 4, 38; CLR 26; MAICYA; SATA 2, 74; SATA-Obit 83

Dimont, Penelope
See Mortimer, Penelope (Ruth)

Dinesen, Isak .... **CLC 10, 29, 95; SSC 7**
See also Blixen, Karen (Christentze Dinesen)

Ding Ling .... **CLC 68**
See also Chiang Pin-chin

Disch, Thomas M(ichael) 1940- .... **CLC 7, 36**
See also AAYA 17; CA 21-24R; CAAS 4; CANR 17, 36, 54; CLR 18; DLB 8; MAICYA; MTCW; SAAS 15; SATA 92

Disch, Tom
See Disch, Thomas M(ichael)

d'Isly, Georges
See Simenon, Georges (Jacques Christian)

Disraeli, Benjamin 1804-1881 .... **NCLC 2, 39**
See also DLB 21, 55

Ditcum, Steve
See Crumb, R(obert)

Dixon, Paige
See Corcoran, Barbara

Dixon, Stephen 1936- .... **CLC 52; SSC 16**
See also CA 89-92; CANR 17, 40, 54; DLB 130

Doak, Annie
See Dillard, Annie

Dobell, Sydney Thompson
1824-1874 .... **NCLC 43**
See also DLB 32

Doblin, Alfred .... **TCLC 13**
See also Doeblin, Alfred

Dobrolyubov, Nikolai Alexandrovich
1836-1861 .... **NCLC 5**

Dobyns, Stephen 1941- .... **CLC 37**
See also CA 45-48; CANR 2, 18

Doctorow, E(dgar) L(aurence)
1931- .... **CLC 6, 11, 15, 18, 37, 44, 65; DAM NOV, POP**
See also AAYA 22; AITN 2; BEST 89:3; CA 45-48; CANR 2, 33, 51; CDALB 1968-1988; DLB 2, 28, 173; DLBY 80; MTCW

Dodgson, Charles Lutwidge 1832-1898
See Carroll, Lewis
See also CLR 2; DA; DAB; DAC; DAM MST, NOV, POET; MAICYA; YABC 2

Dodson, Owen (Vincent)
1914-1983 . **CLC 79; BLC; DAM MULT**
See also BW 1; CA 65-68; 110; CANR 24; DLB 76

Doeblin, Alfred 1878-1957 .... **TCLC 13**
See also Doblin, Alfred
See also CA 110; 141; DLB 66

Doerr, Harriet 1910- .... **CLC 34**
See also CA 117; 122; CANR 47; INT 122

Domecq, H(onorio) Bustos
See Bioy Casares, Adolfo; Borges, Jorge Luis

Domini, Rey
See Lorde, Audre (Geraldine)

Dominique
See Proust, (Valentin-Louis-George-Eugene-) Marcel

Don, A
See Stephen, Leslie

Donaldson, Stephen R.
1947- .... **CLC 46; DAM POP**
See also CA 89-92; CANR 13, 55; INT CANR-13

Donleavy, J(ames) P(atrick)
1926- .... **CLC 1, 4, 6, 10, 45**
See also AITN 2; CA 9-12R; CANR 24, 49, 62; DLB 6, 173; INT CANR-24; MTCW

Donne, John
1572-1631 .... **LC 10, 24; DA; DAB; DAC; DAM MST, POET; PC 1**
See also CDBLB Before 1660; DLB 121, 151

Donnell, David 1939(?)- .... **CLC 34**

Donoghue, P. S.
See Hunt, E(verette) Howard, (Jr.)

Donoso (Yanez), Jose
1924-1996 .... **CLC 4, 8, 11, 32, 99; DAM MULT; HLC**
See also CA 81-84; 155; CANR 32; DLB 113; HW; MTCW

Donovan, John 1928-1992 .... **CLC 35**
See also AAYA 20; CA 97-100; 137; CLR 3; MAICYA; SATA 72; SATA-Brief 29

Don Roberto
See Cunninghame Graham, R(obert) B(ontine)

Doolittle, Hilda
1886-1961 ..... **CLC 3, 8, 14, 31, 34, 73; DA; DAC; DAM MST, POET; PC 5; WLC**
See also H. D.
See also CA 97-100; CANR 35; DLB 4, 45; MTCW

Dorfman, Ariel 1942- ...... **CLC 48, 77; DAM MULT; HLC**
See also CA 124; 130; HW; INT 130

Dorn, Edward (Merton) 1929- ... **CLC 10, 18**
See also CA 93-96; CANR 42; DLB 5; INT 93-96

Dorsan, Luc
See Simenon, Georges (Jacques Christian)

Dorsange, Jean
See Simenon, Georges (Jacques Christian)

Dos Passos, John (Roderigo)
1896-1970 ... **CLC 1, 4, 8, 11, 15, 25, 34, 82; DA; DAB; DAC; DAM MST, NOV; WLC**
See also CA 1-4R; 29-32R; CANR 3; CDALB 1929-1941; DLB 4, 9; DLBD 1, 15; DLBY 96; MTCW

Dossage, Jean
See Simenon, Georges (Jacques Christian)

Dostoevsky, Fedor Mikhailovich
1821-1881 ... **NCLC 2, 7, 21, 33, 43; DA; DAB; DAC; DAM MST, NOV; SSC 2; WLC**

Doughty, Charles M(ontagu)
1843-1926 .... **TCLC 27**
See also CA 115; DLB 19, 57, 174

Douglas, Ellen .... **CLC 73**
See also Haxton, Josephine Ayres; Williamson, Ellen Douglas

Douglas, Gavin 1475(?)-1522 .... **LC 20**

Douglas, Keith (Castellain)
1920-1944 .... **TCLC 40**
See also CA 160; DLB 27

Douglas, Leonard
See Bradbury, Ray (Douglas)

Douglas, Michael
See Crichton, (John) Michael

Douglas, Norman 1868-1952 .... **TCLC 68**

Douglass, Frederick
1817(?)-1895 .... **NCLC 7, 55; BLC; DA; DAC; DAM MST, MULT; WLC**
See also CDALB 1640-1865; DLB 1, 43, 50, 79; SATA 29

Dourado, (Waldomiro Freitas) Autran
1926- .... **CLC 23, 60**
See also CA 25-28R; CANR 34

Dourado, Waldomiro Autran
See Dourado, (Waldomiro Freitas) Autran

Dove, Rita (Frances)
1952- .... **CLC 50, 81; DAM MULT, POET; PC 6**
See also BW 2; CA 109; CAAS 19; CANR 27, 42; DLB 120

Dowell, Coleman 1925-1985 .... **CLC 60**
See also CA 25-28R; 117; CANR 10; DLB 130

Dowson, Ernest (Christopher)
1867-1900 .... **TCLC 4**
See also CA 105; 150; DLB 19, 135

Doyle, A. Conan
See Doyle, Arthur Conan

Doyle, Arthur Conan
1859-1930 .... **TCLC 7; DA; DAB; DAC; DAM MST, NOV; SSC 12; WLC**
See also AAYA 14; CA 104; 122; CDBLB 1890-1914; DLB 18, 70, 156, 178; MTCW; SATA 24

Doyle, Conan
See Doyle, Arthur Conan

Doyle, John
See Graves, Robert (von Ranke)

Doyle, Roddy 1958(?)- .... **CLC 81**
See also AAYA 14; CA 143

Doyle, Sir A. Conan
See Doyle, Arthur Conan

Doyle, Sir Arthur Conan
See Doyle, Arthur Conan

Dr. A
See Asimov, Isaac; Silverstein, Alvin

Drabble, Margaret
1939- ... **CLC 2, 3, 5, 8, 10, 22, 53; DAB; DAC; DAM MST, NOV, POP**
See also CA 13-16R; CANR 18, 35; CDBLB 1960 to Present; DLB 14, 155; MTCW; SATA 48

Drapier, M. B.
See Swift, Jonathan

Drayham, James
See Mencken, H(enry) L(ouis)

Drayton, Michael 1563-1631 .... **LC 8**

Dreadstone, Carl
See Campbell, (John) Ramsey

Dreiser, Theodore (Herman Albert)
1871-1945 .... **TCLC 10, 18, 35; DA; DAC; DAM MST, NOV; WLC**
See also CA 106; 132; CDALB 1865-1917; DLB 9, 12, 102, 137; DLBD 1; MTCW

Drexler, Rosalyn 1926- .... **CLC 2, 6**
See also CA 81-84

Dreyer, Carl Theodor 1889-1968 ...... **CLC 16**
See also CA 116

Drieu la Rochelle, Pierre(-Eugene)
1893-1945 .... **TCLC 21**
See also CA 117; DLB 72

Drinkwater, John
1882-1937 .... **TCLC 57**
See also CA 109; 149; DLB 10, 19, 149

Drop Shot
See Cable, George Washington

Droste-Hulshoff, Annette Freiin von
1797-1848 .... **NCLC 3**
See also DLB 133

Drummond, Walter
See Silverberg, Robert

Drummond, William Henry
1854-1907 .... **TCLC 25**
See also CA 160; DLB 92

Drummond de Andrade, Carlos
1902-1987 .... **CLC 18**
See also Andrade, Carlos Drummond de
See also CA 132; 123

Drury, Allen (Stuart) 1918- .... **CLC 37**
See also CA 57-60; CANR 18, 52; INT CANR-18

Dryden, John
1631-1700 .... **LC 3, 21; DA; DAB; DAC; DAM DRAM, MST, POET; DC 3; WLC**
See also CDBLB 1660-1789; DLB 80, 101, 131

Duberman, Martin 1930- .... **CLC 8**
See also CA 1-4R; CANR 2

Dubie, Norman (Evans) 1945- .... **CLC 36**
See also CA 69-72; CANR 12; DLB 120

Du Bois, W(illiam) E(dward) B(urghardt)
1868-1963 ... **CLC 1, 2, 13, 64, 96; BLC; DA; DAC; DAM MST, MULT, NOV; WLC**
See also BW 1; CA 85-88; CANR 34; CDALB 1865-1917; DLB 47, 50, 91; MTCW; SATA 42

Dubus, Andre
1936- .... **CLC 13, 36, 97; SSC 15**
See also CA 21-24R; CANR 17; DLB 130; INT CANR-17

Duca Minimo
See D'Annunzio, Gabriele

Ducharme, Rejean 1941- .... **CLC 74**
See also DLB 60

Duclos, Charles Pinot 1704-1772 .... **LC 1**

Dudek, Louis 1918- .... **CLC 11, 19**
See also CA 45-48; CAAS 14; CANR 1; DLB 88

Duerrenmatt, Friedrich
1921-1990 ...... **CLC 1, 4, 8, 11, 15, 43, 102; DAM DRAM**
See also CA 17-20R; CANR 33; DLB 69, 124; MTCW

Duffy, Bruce (?)- .... **CLC 50**

Duffy, Maureen 1933- .... **CLC 37**
See also CA 25-28R; CANR 33; DLB 14; MTCW

Dugan, Alan 1923- .... **CLC 2, 6**
See also CA 81-84; DLB 5

du Gard, Roger Martin
See Martin du Gard, Roger

Duhamel, Georges 1884-1966 .... **CLC 8**
See also CA 81-84; 25-28R; CANR 35; DLB 65; MTCW

Edgerton, Clyde (Carlyle) 1944- ...... **CLC 39**
See also AAYA 17; CA 118; 134; INT 134

Edgeworth, Maria 1768-1849 .... **NCLC 1, 51**
See also DLB 116, 159, 163; SATA 21

Edmonds, Paul
See Kuttner, Henry

Edmonds, Walter D(umaux) 1903- ... **CLC 35**
See also CA 5-8R; CANR 2; DLB 9; MAICYA;
SAAS 4; SATA 1, 27

Edmondson, Wallace
See Ellison, Harlan (Jay)

Edson, Russell .... **CLC 13**
See also CA 33-36R

Edwards, Bronwen Elizabeth
See Rose, Wendy

Edwards, G(erald) B(asil)
1899-1976 .... **CLC 25**
See also CA 110

Edwards, Gus 1939- .... **CLC 43**
See also CA 108; INT 108

Edwards, Jonathan
1703-1758 .... **LC 7; DA; DAC; DAM
MST**
See also DLB 24

Efron, Marina Ivanovna Tsvetaeva
See Tsvetaeva (Efron), Marina (Ivanovna)

Ehle, John (Marsden, Jr.) 1925- .... **CLC 27**
See also CA 9-12R

Ehrenbourg, Ilya (Grigoryevich)
See Ehrenburg, Ilya (Grigoryevich)

Ehrenburg, Ilya (Grigoryevich)
1891-1967 .... **CLC 18, 34, 62**
See also CA 102; 25-28R

Ehrenburg, Ilyo (Grigoryevich)
See Ehrenburg, Ilya (Grigoryevich)

Eich, Guenter 1907-1972 .... **CLC 15**
See also CA 111; 93-96; DLB 69, 124

Eichendorff, Joseph Freiherr von
1788-1857 .... **NCLC 8**
See also DLB 90

Eigner, Larry .... **CLC 9**
See also Eigner, Laurence (Joel)
See also CAAS 23; DLB 5

Eigner, Laurence (Joel) 1927-1996
See Eigner, Larry
See also CA 9-12R; 151; CANR 6

Einstein, Albert 1879-1955 .... **TCLC 65**
See also CA 121; 133; MTCW

Eiseley, Loren Corey 1907-1977 .... **CLC 7**
See also AAYA 5; CA 1-4R; 73-76; CANR 6

Eisenstadt, Jill 1963- .... **CLC 50**
See also CA 140

Eisenstein, Sergei (Mikhailovich)
1898-1948 .... **TCLC 57**
See also CA 114; 149

Eisner, Simon
See Kornbluth, C(yril) M.

Ekeloef, (Bengt) Gunnar
1907-1968 .... **CLC 27; DAM POET**
See also CA 123; 25-28R

Ekelof, (Bengt) Gunnar
See Ekeloef, (Bengt) Gunnar

Ekelund, Vilhelm 1880-1949 .... **TCLC 75**

Ekwensi, C. O. D.
See Ekwensi, Cyprian (Odiatu Duaka)

Ekwensi, Cyprian (Odiatu Duaka)
1921- .... **CLC 4; BLC; DAM MULT**
See also BW 2; CA 29-32R; CANR 18, 42;
DLB 117; MTCW; SATA 66

Elaine .... **TCLC 18**
See also Leverson, Ada

El Crummo
See Crumb, R(obert)

Elia
See Lamb, Charles

Eliade, Mircea 1907-1986 .... **CLC 19**
See also CA 65-68; 119; CANR 30, 62;
MTCW

Eliot, A. D.
See Jewett, (Theodora) Sarah Orne

Eliot, Alice
See Jewett, (Theodora) Sarah Orne

Eliot, Dan
See Silverberg, Robert

Eliot, George
1819-1880 ..... **NCLC 4, 13, 23, 41, 49;
DA; DAB; DAC; DAM MST, NOV; PC
20; WLC**
See also CDBLB 1832-1890; DLB 21, 35,
55

Eliot, John 1604-1690 .... **LC 5**
See also DLB 24

Eliot, T(homas) S(tearns)
1888-1965.... **CLC 1, 2, 3, 6, 9, 10,
13, 15, 24, 34, 41, 55, 57; DA; DAB;
DAC; DAM DRAM, MST, POET; PC
5; WLC 2**
See also CA 5-8R; 25-28R; CANR 41;
CDALB 1929-1941; DLB 7, 10, 45, 63;
DLBY 88; MTCW

Elizabeth 1866-1941 .... **TCLC 41**

Elkin, Stanley L(awrence)
1930-1995..... **CLC 4, 6, 9, 14, 27, 51,
91; DAM NOV, POP; SSC 12**
See also CA 9-12R; 148; CANR 8, 46;
DLB 2, 28; DLBY 80; INT CANR-8;
MTCW

Elledge, Scott .... **CLC 34**

Elliot, Don
See Silverberg, Robert

Elliott, Don
See Silverberg, Robert

Elliott, George P(aul)
1918-1980 .... **CLC 2**
See also CA 1-4R; 97-100; CANR 2

Elliott, Janice 1931- .... **CLC 47**
See also CA 13-16R; CANR 8, 29; DLB 14

Elliott, Sumner Locke
1917-1991 .... **CLC 38**
See also CA 5-8R; 134; CANR 2, 21

Elliott, William
See Bradbury, Ray (Douglas)

Ellis, A. E. .... **CLC 7**

Ellis, Alice Thomas .... **CLC 40**
See also Haycraft, Anna

Ellis, Bret Easton
1964- .... **CLC 39, 71; DAM POP**
See also AAYA 2; CA 118; 123; CANR 51;
INT 123

Ellis, (Henry) Havelock
1859-1939 .... **TCLC 14**
See also CA 109

Ellis, Landon
See Ellison, Harlan (Jay)

Ellis, Trey 1962- .... **CLC 55**
See also CA 146

Ellison, Harlan (Jay)
1934-....... **CLC 1, 13, 42; DAM POP;
SSC 14**
See also CA 5-8R; CANR 5, 46; DLB 8; INT
CANR-5; MTCW

Ellison, Ralph (Waldo)
1914-1994 .... **CLC 1, 3, 11, 54, 86; BLC;
DA; DAB; DAC; DAM MST, MULT,
NOV; SSC 26; WLC**
See also AAYA 19; BW 1; CA 9-12R; 145;
CANR 24, 53; CDALB 1941-1968; DLB 2,
76; DLBY 94; MTCW

Ellmann, Lucy (Elizabeth)
1956- .... **CLC 61**
See also CA 128

Ellmann, Richard (David)
1918-1987 .... **CLC 50**
See also BEST 89:2; CA 1-4R; 122; CANR 2,
28, 61; DLB 103; DLBY 87; MTCW

Elman, Richard 1934- .... **CLC 19**
See also CA 17-20R; CAAS 3; CANR 47

Elron
See Hubbard, L(afayette) Ron(ald)

Eluard, Paul .... **TCLC 7, 41**
See also Grindel, Eugene

Fagen, Donald 1948- .... CLC **26**

Fainzilberg, Ilya Arnoldovich 1897-1937
See Ilf, Ilya
See also CA 120

Fair, Ronald L. 1932- .... CLC **18**
See also BW 1; CA 69-72; CANR 25; DLB 33

Fairbairn, Roger
See Carr, John Dickson

Fairbairns, Zoe (Ann) 1948- .... CLC **32**
See also CA 103; CANR 21

Falco, Gian
See Papini, Giovanni

Falconer, James
See Kirkup, James

Falconer, Kenneth
See Kornbluth, C(yril) M.

Falkland, Samuel
See Heijermans, Herman

Fallaci, Oriana 1930- .... CLC **11**
See also CA 77-80; CANR 15, 58; MTCW

Faludy, George 1913- .... CLC **42**
See also CA 21-24R

Faludy, Gyoergy
See Faludy, George

Fanon, Frantz 1925-1961 .... CLC **74**; **BLC;
DAM MULT**
See also BW 1; CA 116; 89-92

Fanshawe, Ann 1625-1680 .... LC **11**

Fante, John (Thomas)
1911-1983 .... CLC **60**
See also CA 69-72; 109; CANR 23; DLB 130;
DLBY 83

Farah, Nuruddin
1945- .... CLC **53**; **BLC; DAM MULT**
See also BW 2; CA 106; DLB 125

Fargue, Leon-Paul 1876(?)-1947 ... TCLC **11**
See also CA 109

Farigoule, Louis
See Romains, Jules

Farina, Richard 1936(?)-1966 .... CLC **9**
See also CA 81-84; 25-28R

Farley, Walter (Lorimer)
1915-1989 .... CLC **17**
See also CA 17-20R; CANR 8, 29; DLB 22;
JRDA; MAICYA; SATA 2, 43

Farmer, Philip Jose 1918- .... CLC **1, 19**
See also CA 1-4R; CANR 4, 35; DLB 8;
MTCW; SATA 93

Farquhar, George
1677-1707 .... LC **21; DAM DRAM**
See also DLB 84

Farrell, J(ames) G(ordon)
1935-1979 .... CLC **6**
See also CA 73-76; 89-92; CANR 36; DLB
14; MTCW

Farrell, James T(homas)
1904-1979 ... CLC **1, 4, 8, 11, 66; SSC
28**
See also CA 5-8R; 89-92; CANR 9, 61; DLB
4, 9, 86; DLBD 2; MTCW

Farren, Richard J.
See Betjeman, John

Farren, Richard M.
See Betjeman, John

Fassbinder, Rainer Werner
1946-1982 .... CLC **20**
See also CA 93-96; 106; CANR 31

Fast, Howard (Melvin)
1914- ....CLC **23; DAM NOV**
See also AAYA 16; CA 1-4R; CAAS 18;
CANR 1, 33, 54; DLB 9; INT CANR-33;
SATA 7

Faulcon, Robert
See Holdstock, Robert P.

Faulkner, William (Cuthbert)
1897-1962 ... CLC **1, 3, 6, 8, 9, 11, 14,
18, 28, 52, 68; DA; DAB; DAC; DAM
MST, NOV; SSC 1; WLC**
See also AAYA 7; CA 81-84; CANR 33;
CDALB 1929-1941; DLB 9, 11, 44, 102;
DLBD 2; DLBY 86; MTCW

Fauset, Jessie Redmon
1884(?)-1961 ... CLC **19, 54; BLC; DAM
MULT**
See also BW 1; CA 109; DLB 51

Faust, Frederick (Schiller)
1892-1944(?) .... TCLC **49; DAM POP**
See also CA 108; 152

Faust, Irvin 1924- .... CLC **8**
See also CA 33-36R; CANR 28; DLB 2, 28;
DLBY 80

Fawkes, Guy
See Benchley, Robert (Charles)

Fearing, Kenneth (Flexner)
1902-1961 .... CLC **51**
See also CA 93-96; CANR 59; DLB 9

Fecamps, Elise
See Creasey, John

Federman, Raymond 1928- .... CLC **6, 47**
See also CA 17-20R; CAAS 8; CANR 10, 43;
DLBY 80

Federspiel, J(uerg) F. 1931- .... CLC **42**
See also CA 146

Feiffer, Jules (Ralph)
1929- .... CLC **2, 8, 64; DAM DRAM**
See also AAYA 3; CA 17-20R; CANR 30, 59;
DLB 7, 44; INT CANR-30; MTCW; SATA
8, 61

Feige, Hermann Albert Otto Maximilian
See Traven, B.

Feinberg, David B. 1956-1994 .... CLC **59**
See also CA 135; 147

Feinstein, Elaine 1930- .... CLC **36**
See also CA 69-72; CAAS 1; CANR 31; DLB
14, 40; MTCW

Feldman, Irving (Mordecai) 1928- ..... CLC **7**
See also CA 1-4R; CANR 1; DLB 169

Felix-Tchicaya, Gerald
See Tchicaya, Gerald Felix

Fellini, Federico 1920-1993 .... CLC **16, 85**
See also CA 65-68; 143; CANR 33

Felsen, Henry Gregor 1916- .... CLC **17**
See also CA 1-4R; CANR 1; SAAS 2; SATA 1

Fenton, James Martin 1949- .... CLC **32**
See also CA 102; DLB 40

Ferber, Edna 1887-1968 .... CLC **18, 93**
See also AITN 1; CA 5-8R; 25-28R; DLB 9,
28, 86; MTCW; SATA 7

Ferguson, Helen
See Kavan, Anna

Ferguson, Samuel 1810-1886 .... NCLC **33**
See also DLB 32

Fergusson, Robert 1750-1774 .... LC **29**
See also DLB 109

Ferling, Lawrence
See Ferlinghetti, Lawrence (Monsanto)

Ferlinghetti, Lawrence (Monsanto)
1919(?)- .... CLC **2, 6, 10, 27; DAM
POET; PC 1**
See also CA 5-8R; CANR 3, 41; CDALB 1941-
1968; DLB 5, 16; MTCW

Fernandez, Vicente Garcia Huidobro
See Huidobro Fernandez, Vicente Garcia

Ferrer, Gabriel (Francisco Victor) Miro
See Miro (Ferrer), Gabriel (Francisco Victor)

Ferrier, Susan (Edmonstone)
1782-1854 .... NCLC **8**
See also DLB 116

Ferrigno, Robert 1948(?)- .... CLC **65**
See also CA 140

Ferron, Jacques
1921-1985 ....CLC **94; DAC**
See also CA 117; 129; DLB 60

Feuchtwanger, Lion 1884-1958 .... TCLC **3**
See also CA 104; DLB 66

Feuillet, Octave 1821-1890 .... NCLC **45**

Feydeau, Georges (Leon Jules Marie)
1862-1921 .... TCLC **22; DAM DRAM**
See also CA 113; 152

Ford, Richard .... CLC 99

Ford, Richard
1944- .... CLC 46
See also CA 69-72; CANR 11, 47

Ford, Webster
See Masters, Edgar Lee

Foreman, Richard
1937- .... CLC 50
See also CA 65-68; CANR 32

Forester, C(ecil) S(cott)
1899-1966 .... CLC 35
See also CA 73-76; 25-28R; SATA 13

Forez
See Mauriac, Francois (Charles)

Forman, James Douglas 1932- .... CLC 21
See also AAYA 17; CA 9-12R; CANR 4, 19,
42; JRDA; MAICYA; SATA 8, 70

Fornes, Maria Irene
1930- .... CLC 39, 61
See also CA 25-28R; CANR 28; DLB 7; HW;
INT CANR-28; MTCW

Forrest, Leon 1937- .... CLC 4
See also BW 2; CA 89-92; CAAS 7; CANR
25, 52; DLB 33

Forster, E(dward) M(organ)
1879-1970... CLC 1, 2, 3, 4, 9, 10, 13,
15, 22, 45, 77; DA; DAB; DAC;
DAM MST, NOV; SSC 27; WLC
See also AAYA 2; CA 13-14; 25-28R;
CANR 45; CAP 1; CDBLB 1914-1945;
DLB 34, 98, 162, 178; DLBD 10;
MTCW; SATA 57

Forster, John 1812-1876 .... NCLC 11
See also DLB 144, 184

Forsyth, Frederick
1938- .... CLC 2, 5, 36; DAM NOV, POP
See also BEST 89:4; CA 85-88; CANR 38, 62;
DLB 87; MTCW

Forten, Charlotte L. .... TCLC 16; BLC
See also Grimke, Charlotte L(ottie) Forten
See also DLB 50

Foscolo, Ugo 1778-1827 .... NCLC 8

Fosse, Bob .... CLC 20
See also Fosse, Robert Louis

Fosse, Robert Louis 1927-1987
See Fosse, Bob
See also CA 110; 123

Foster, Stephen Collins
1826-1864 .... NCLC 26

Foucault, Michel
1926-1984 .... CLC 31, 34, 69
See also CA 105; 113; CANR 34; MTCW

Fouque, Friedrich (Heinrich Karl) de la Motte
1777-1843 .... NCLC 2
See also DLB 90

Fourier, Charles 1772-1837 .... NCLC 51

Fournier, Henri Alban 1886-1914
See Alain-Fournier
See also CA 104

Fournier, Pierre 1916- .... CLC 11
See also Gascar, Pierre
See also CA 89-92; CANR 16, 40

Fowles, John
1926- ... CLC 1, 2, 3, 4, 6, 9, 10, 15, 33,
87; DAB; DAC; DAM MST
See also CA 5-8R; CANR 25; CDBLB 1960
to Present; DLB 14, 139; MTCW; SATA
22

Fox, Paula 1923- .... CLC 2, 8
See also AAYA 3; CA 73-76; CANR 20, 36,
62; CLR 1, 44; DLB 52; JRDA; MAICYA;
MTCW; SATA 17, 60

Fox, William Price (Jr.)
1926- .... CLC 22
See also CA 17-20R; CAAS 19; CANR 11;
DLB 2; DLBY 81

Foxe, John 1516(?)-1587 .... LC 14

Frame, Janet
1924- .... CLC 2, 3, 6, 22, 66, 96; SSC 29
See also Clutha, Janet Paterson Frame

France, Anatole .... TCLC 9
See also Thibault, Jacques Anatole Francois
See also DLB 123

Francis, Claude 19(?)- .... CLC 50

Francis, Dick
1920- ..... CLC 2, 22, 42, 102; DAM POP
See also AAYA 5, 21; BEST 89:3; CA 5-8R;
CANR 9, 42; CDBLB 1960 to Present; DLB
87; INT CANR-9; MTCW

Francis, Robert (Churchill)
1901-1987 .... CLC 15
See also CA 1-4R; 123; CANR 1

Frank, Anne(lies Marie)
1929-1945 .... TCLC 17; DA; DAB;
DAC; DAM MST; WLC
See also AAYA 12; CA 113; 133; MTCW;
SATA 87; SATA-Brief 42

Frank, Elizabeth 1945- .... CLC 39
See also CA 121; 126; INT 126

Frankl, Viktor E(mil) 1905- .... CLC 93
See also CA 65-68

Franklin, Benjamin
See Hasek, Jaroslav (Matej Frantisek)

Franklin, Benjamin
1706-1790 .... LC 25; DA; DAB; DAC;
DAM MST; WLCS
See also CDALB 1640-1865; DLB 24, 43,
73

Franklin, (Stella Maraia Sarah) Miles
1879-1954 .... TCLC 7
See also CA 104

Fraser, (Lady) Antonia (Pakenham)
1932- .... CLC 32
See also CA 85-88; CANR 44; MTCW; SATA-
Brief 32

Fraser, George MacDonald
1925- .... CLC 7
See also CA 45-48; CANR 2, 48

Fraser, Sylvia 1935- .... CLC 64
See also CA 45-48; CANR 1, 16, 60

Frayn, Michael
1933- ... CLC 3, 7, 31, 47; DAM DRAM,
NOV
See also CA 5-8R; CANR 30; DLB 13, 14;
MTCW

Fraze, Candida (Merrill) 1945- .... CLC 50
See also CA 126

Frazer, J(ames) G(eorge)
1854-1941 .... TCLC 32
See also CA 118

Frazer, Robert Caine
See Creasey, John

Frazer, Sir James George
See Frazer, J(ames) G(eorge)

Frazier, Ian 1951- .... CLC 46
See also CA 130; CANR 54

Frederic, Harold 1856-1898 .... NCLC 10
See also DLB 12, 23; DLBD 13

Frederick, John
See Faust, Frederick (Schiller)

Frederick the Great 1712-1786 .... LC 14

Fredro, Aleksander 1793-1876 .... NCLC 8

Freeling, Nicolas 1927- .... CLC 38
See also CA 49-52; CAAS 12; CANR 1, 17,
50; DLB 87

Freeman, Douglas Southall
1886-1953 .... TCLC 11
See also CA 109; DLB 17

Freeman, Judith 1946- .... CLC 55
See also CA 148

Freeman, Mary Eleanor Wilkins
1852-1930 .... TCLC 9; SSC 1
See also CA 106; DLB 12, 78

Freeman, R(ichard) Austin
1862-1943 .... TCLC 21
See also CA 113; DLB 70

French, Albert 1943- .... CLC 86

French, Marilyn
1929- ..... CLC 10, 18, 60; DAM DRAM,
NOV, POP
See also CA 69-72; CANR 3, 31; INT CANR-
31; MTCW

French, Paul
See Asimov, Isaac

Freneau, Philip Morin
1752-1832 .... NCLC 1
See also DLB 37, 43

Freud, Sigmund 1856-1939 .... TCLC 52
See also CA 115; 133; MTCW

Friedan, Betty (Naomi) 1921- .... CLC 74
See also CA 65-68; CANR 18, 45; MTCW

Friedlander, Saul 1932-...................... CLC 90
See also CA 117; 130

Friedman, B(ernard) H(arper)
1926-.. CLC 7
See also CA 1-4R; CANR 3, 48

Friedman, Bruce Jay 1930- ...... CLC 3, 5, 56
See also CA 9-12R; CANR 25, 52; DLB 2, 28;
INT CANR-25

Friel, Brian 1929- .... CLC 5, 42, 59
See also CA 21-24R; CANR 33; DLB 13;
MTCW

Friis-Baastad, Babbis Ellinor
1921-1970 .... CLC 12
See also CA 17-20R; 134; SATA 7

Frisch, Max (Rudolf)
1911-1991 .... CLC 3, 9, 14, 18, 32, 44;
DAM DRAM, NOV
See also CA 85-88; 134; CANR 32; DLB 69,
124; MTCW

Fromentin, Eugene (Samuel Auguste)
1820-1876 .... NCLC 10
See also DLB 123

Frost, Frederick
See Faust, Frederick (Schiller)

Frost, Robert (Lee)
1874-1963 ...   CLC 1, 3, 4, 9, 10, 13, 15,
26, 34, 44; DA; DAB; DAC; DAM MST,
POET; PC 1; WLC
See also AAYA 21; CA 89-92; CANR 33;
CDALB 1917-1929; DLB 54; DLBD 7;
MTCW; SATA 14

Froude, James Anthony
1818-1894 .... NCLC 43
See also DLB 18, 57, 144

Froy, Herald
See Waterhouse, Keith (Spencer)

Fry, Christopher
1907- .... CLC 2, 10, 14; DAM DRAM
See also CA 17-20R; CAAS 23; CANR 9, 30;
DLB 13; MTCW; SATA 66

Frye, (Herman) Northrop
1912-1991 .... CLC 24, 70
See also CA 5-8R; 133; CANR 8, 37; DLB 67,
68; MTCW

Fuchs, Daniel 1909-1993 .... CLC 8, 22
See also CA 81-84; 142; CAAS 5; CANR 40;
DLB 9, 26, 28; DLBY 93

Fuchs, Daniel 1934- .... CLC 34
See also CA 37-40R; CANR 14, 48

Fuentes, Carlos
1928- ...... CLC 3, 8, 10, 13, 22, 41, 60;
DA; DAB; DAC; DAM MST, MULT,
NOV; HLC; SSC 24; WLC
See also AAYA 4; AITN 2; CA 69-72; CANR
10, 32; DLB 113; HW; MTCW

Fuentes, Gregorio Lopez y
See Lopez y Fuentes, Gregorio

Fugard, (Harold) Athol
1932- ..... CLC 5, 9, 14, 25, 40, 80; DAM
DRAM; DC 3
See also AAYA 17; CA 85-88; CANR 32, 54;
MTCW

Fugard, Sheila 1932- .... CLC 48
See also CA 125

Fuller, Charles (H., Jr.)
1939- .... CLC 25; BLC; DAM DRAM,
MULT; DC 1
See also BW 2; CA 108; 112; DLB 38; INT
112; MTCW

Fuller, John (Leopold) 1937-............. CLC 62
See also CA 21-24R; CANR 9, 44; DLB
40

Fuller, Margaret ....NCLC 5, 50
See also Ossoli, Sarah Margaret (Fuller
marchesa d')

Fuller, Roy (Broadbent)
1912-1991 .... CLC 4, 28
See also CA 5-8R; 135; CAAS 10; CANR 53;
DLB 15, 20; SATA 87

Fulton, Alice 1952- .... CLC 52
See also CA 116; CANR 57

Furphy, Joseph 1843-1912.............. TCLC 25

Fussell, Paul 1924-............................. CLC 74
See also BEST 90:1; CA 17-20R; CANR 8,
21, 35; INT CANR-21; MTCW

Futabatei, Shimei 1864-1909 .... TCLC 44
See also DLB 180

Futrelle, Jacques 1875-1912 .... TCLC 19
See also CA 113; 155

Gaboriau, Emile 1835-1873 .... NCLC 14

Gadda, Carlo Emilio 1893-1973 .... CLC 11
See also CA 89-92; DLB 177

Gaddis, William
1922- .... CLC 1, 3, 6, 8, 10, 19, 43, 86
See also CA 17-20R; CANR 21, 48; DLB 2;
MTCW

Gage, Walter
See Inge, William (Motter)

Gaines, Ernest J(ames)
1933- ..... CLC 3, 11, 18, 86; BLC; DAM
MULT
See also AAYA 18; AITN 1; BW 2; CA 9-
12R; CANR 6, 24, 42; CDALB 1968-
1988; DLB 2, 33, 152; DLBY 80; MTCW;
SATA 86

Gaitskill, Mary 1954- .... CLC 69
See also CA 128; CANR 61

Galdos, Benito Perez
See Perez Galdos, Benito

Gale, Zona
1874-1938 .... TCLC 7; DAM DRAM
See also CA 105; 153; DLB 9, 78

Galeano, Eduardo (Hughes) 1940-... CLC 72
See also CA 29-32R; CANR 13, 32; HW

Galiano, Juan Valera y Alcala
See Valera y Alcala-Galiano, Juan

Gallagher, Tess 1943- ...... CLC 18, 63; DAM
POET; PC 9
See also CA 106; DLB 120

Gallant, Mavis
1922- .... CLC 7, 18, 38; DAC; DAM
MST; SSC 5
See also CA 69-72; CANR 29; DLB 53;
MTCW

Gallant, Roy A(rthur) 1924- .... CLC 17
See also CA 5-8R; CANR 4, 29, 54; CLR 30;
MAICYA; SATA 4, 68

Gallico, Paul (William)
1897-1976 .... CLC 2
See also AITN 1; CA 5-8R; 69-72; CANR 23;
DLB 9, 171; MAICYA; SATA 13

Gallo, Max Louis 1932- .... CLC 95
See also CA 85-88

Gallois, Lucien
See Desnos, Robert

Gallup, Ralph
See Whitemore, Hugh (John)

Galsworthy, John 1867-1933 .... TCLC 1, 45;
DA; DAB; DAC; DAM DRAM, MST,
NOV; SSC 22; WLC 2
See also CA 104; 141; CDBLB 1890-1914;
DLB 10, 34, 98, 162; DLBD 16

Galt, John 1779-1839 .... NCLC 1
See also DLB 99, 116, 159

Galvin, James 1951- .... CLC 38
See also CA 108; CANR 26

Gamboa, Federico 1864-1939 .... TCLC 36

Gandhi, M. K.
See Gandhi, Mohandas Karamchand

Gandhi, Mahatma
See Gandhi, Mohandas Karamchand

Gandhi, Mohandas Karamchand
1869-1948 .... TCLC 59; DAM MULT
See also CA 121; 132; MTCW

Gann, Ernest Kellogg 1910-1991 ...... CLC 23
See also AITN 1; CA 1-4R; 136; CANR 1

Garcia, Cristina 1958- .... CLC 76
See also CA 141

Garcia Lorca, Federico
1898-1936 ..... TCLC 1, 7, 49; DA; DAB;
DAC; DAM DRAM, MST, MULT,
POET; DC 2; HLC; PC 3; WLC
See also CA 104; 131; DLB 108; HW; MTCW

Garcia Marquez, Gabriel (Jose)
1928- .... CLC 2, 3, 8, 10, 15, 27, 47, 55,
68; DA; DAB; DAC; DAM MST, MULT,
NOV, POP; HLC; SSC 8; WLC
See also AAYA 3; BEST 89:1, 90:4; CA 33-
36R; CANR 10, 28, 50; DLB 113; HW;
MTCW

Gard, Janice
See Latham, Jean Lee

Gard, Roger Martin du
See Martin du Gard, Roger

Gardam, Jane 1928- .... CLC 43
See also CA 49-52; CANR 2, 18, 33, 54; CLR
12; DLB 14, 161; MAICYA; MTCW; SAAS
9; SATA 39, 76; SATA-Brief 28

Gardner, Herb(ert) 1934- .... CLC 44
See also CA 149

Gardner, John (Champlin), Jr.
1933-1982 .... CLC 2, 3, 5, 7, 8, 10, 18,
28, 34; DAM NOV, POP; SSC 7
See also AITN 1; CA 65-68; 107; CANR 33;
DLB 2; DLBY 82; MTCW; SATA 40;
SATA-Obit 31

Gardner, John (Edmund) 1926-...... CLC 30;
DAM POP
See also CA 103; CANR 15; MTCW

Gardner, Miriam
See Bradley, Marion Zimmer

Gardner, Noel
See Kuttner, Henry

Gardons, S. S.
See Snodgrass, W(illiam) D(e Witt)

Garfield, Leon 1921-1996 .... CLC 12
See also AAYA 8; CA 17-20R; 152; CANR 38,
41; CLR 21; DLB 161; JRDA; MAICYA;
SATA 1, 32, 76; SATA-Obit 90

Garland, (Hannibal) Hamlin
1860-1940 .... TCLC 3; SSC 18
See also CA 104; DLB 12, 71, 78

Garneau, (Hector de) Saint-Denys
1912-1943 .... TCLC 13
See also CA 111; DLB 88

Garner, Alan
1934- .... CLC 17; DAB; DAM POP
See also AAYA 18; CA 73-76; CANR 15; CLR
20; DLB 161; MAICYA; MTCW; SATA 18,
69

Garner, Hugh 1913-1979 .... CLC 13
See also CA 69-72; CANR 31; DLB 68

Garnett, David 1892-1981 .... CLC 3
See also CA 5-8R; 103; CANR 17; DLB
34

Garos, Stephanie
See Katz, Steve

Garrett, George (Palmer)
1929- .... CLC 3, 11, 51
See also CA 1-4R; CAAS 5; CANR 1, 42; DLB
2, 5, 130, 152; DLBY 83

Garrick, David 1717-1779 .... LC 15; DAM
DRAM
See also DLB 84

Garrigue, Jean 1914-1972 .... CLC 2, 8
See also CA 5-8R; 37-40R; CANR 20

Garrison, Frederick
See Sinclair, Upton (Beall)

Garth, Will
See Hamilton, Edmond; Kuttner, Henry

Garvey, Marcus (Moziah, Jr.)
1887-1940 .... TCLC 41; BLC; DAM
MULT
See also BW 1; CA 120; 124

Gary, Romain .... CLC 25
See also Kacew, Romain
See also DLB 83

Gascar, Pierre .... CLC 11
See also Fournier, Pierre

Gascoyne, David (Emery)
1916- .... CLC 45
See also CA 65-68; CANR 10, 28, 54; DLB
20; MTCW

Gaskell, Elizabeth Cleghorn
1810-1865 .... NCLC 5; DAB; DAM
MST; SSC 25
See also CDBLB 1832-1890; DLB 21, 144,
159

Gass, William H(oward)
1924- ..... CLC 1, 2, 8, 11, 15, 39; SSC 12
See also CA 17-20R; CANR 30; DLB 2;
MTCW

Gasset, Jose Ortega y
See Ortega y Gasset, Jose

Gates, Henry Louis, Jr.
1950- .... CLC 65; DAM MULT
See also BW 2; CA 109; CANR 25, 53; DLB
67

Gautier, Theophile
1811-1872 ... NCLC 1, 59; DAM POET;
PC 18; SSC 20
See also DLB 119

Gawsworth, John
See Bates, H(erbert) E(rnest)

Gay, Oliver
See Gogarty, Oliver St. John

Gaye, Marvin (Penze) 1939-1984 ..... CLC 26
See also CA 112

Gebler, Carlo (Ernest) 1954- .... CLC 39
See also CA 119; 133

Gee, Maggie (Mary) 1948- .... CLC 57
See also CA 130

Gee, Maurice (Gough) 1931-............. CLC 29
See also CA 97-100; SATA 46

Gelbart, Larry (Simon) 1923-.... CLC 21, 61
See also CA 73-76; CANR 45

Gelber, Jack 1932- .... CLC 1, 6, 14, 79
See also CA 1-4R; CANR 2; DLB 7

Gellhorn, Martha (Ellis)
1908- .... CLC 14, 60
See also CA 77-80; CANR 44; DLBY 82

Genet, Jean
1910-1986 .... CLC 1, 2, 5, 10, 14, 44, 46;
DAM DRAM
See also CA 13-16R; CANR 18; DLB 72;
DLBY 86; MTCW

Gent, Peter 1942- .... CLC 29
See also AITN 1; CA 89-92; DLBY 82

Gentlewoman in New England, A
See Bradstreet, Anne

Gentlewoman in Those Parts, A
See Bradstreet, Anne

George, Jean Craighead
1919- .... CLC 35
See also AAYA 8; CA 5-8R; CANR 25; CLR
1; DLB 52; JRDA; MAICYA; SATA 2, 68

George, Stefan (Anton)
1868-1933 .... TCLC 2, 14
See also CA 104

Georges, Georges Martin
See Simenon, Georges (Jacques Christian)

Gerhardi, William Alexander
See Gerhardie, William Alexander

Gerhardie, William Alexander
1895-1977 .... CLC 5
See also CA 25-28R; 73-76; CANR 18; DLB
36

Gerstler, Amy 1956- .... CLC 70
See also CA 146

Gertler, T. .... CLC 34
See also CA 116; 121; INT 121

Ghalib .... NCLC 39
See also Ghalib, Hsadullah Khan

Ghalib, Hsadullah Khan 1797-1869
See Ghalib
See also DAM POET

Ghelderode, Michel de
1898-1962 .... CLC 6, 11; DAM DRAM
See also CA 85-88; CANR 40

Ghiselin, Brewster 1903- .... CLC 23
See also CA 13-16R; CAAS 10; CANR 13

Ghose, Zulfikar 1935- .... CLC 42
See also CA 65-68

Ghosh, Amitav 1956- .... CLC 44
   See also CA 147

Giacosa, Giuseppe 1847-1906 .... TCLC 7
   See also CA 104

Gibb, Lee
   See Waterhouse, Keith (Spencer)

Gibbon, Lewis Grassic .... TCLC 4
   See also Mitchell, James Leslie

Gibbons, Kaye
   1960- .... CLC 50, 88; DAM POP
   See also CA 151

Gibran, Kahlil
   1883-1931 .... TCLC 1, 9; DAM POET,
   POP; PC 9
   See also CA 104; 150

Gibran, Khalil
   See Gibran, Kahlil

Gibson, William
   1914- .... CLC 23; DA; DAB; DAC;
   DAM DRAM, MST
   See also CA 9-12R; CANR 9, 42; DLB 7; SATA
   66

Gibson, William (Ford)
   1948- .... CLC 39, 63; DAM POP
   See also AAYA 12; CA 126; 133; CANR
   52

Gide, Andre (Paul Guillaume)
   1869-1951 ... TCLC 5, 12, 36; DA; DAB;
   DAC; DAM MST, NOV; SSC 13; WLC
   See also CA 104; 124; DLB 65; MTCW

Gifford, Barry (Colby) 1946- .... CLC 34
   See also CA 65-68; CANR 9, 30, 40

Gilbert, Frank
   See De Voto, Bernard (Augustine)

Gilbert, W(illiam) S(chwenck)
   1836-1911 .... TCLC 3; DAM DRAM,
   POET
   See also CA 104; SATA 36

Gilbreth, Frank B., Jr.
   1911- .... CLC 17
   See also CA 9-12R; SATA 2

Gilchrist, Ellen
   1935- .. CLC 34, 48; DAM POP; SSC 14
   See also CA 113; 116; CANR 41, 61; DLB 130;
   MTCW

Giles, Molly 1942- .... CLC 39
   See also CA 126

Gill, Patrick
   See Creasey, John

Gilliam, Terry (Vance) 1940- .... CLC 21
   See also Monty Python
   See also AAYA 19; CA 108; 113; CANR 35;
   INT 113

Gillian, Jerry
   See Gilliam, Terry (Vance)

Gilliatt, Penelope (Ann Douglass)
   1932-1993 .... CLC 2, 10, 13, 53
   See also AITN 2; CA 13-16R; 141; CANR 49;
   DLB 14

Gilman, Charlotte (Anna) Perkins (Stetson)
   1860-1935 .... TCLC 9, 37; SSC 13
   See also CA 106; 150

Gilmour, David
   1949- .... CLC 35
   See also CA 138, 147

Gilpin, William 1724-1804 .... NCLC 30

Gilray, J. D.
   See Mencken, H(enry) L(ouis)

Gilroy, Frank D(aniel)
   1925- .... CLC 2
   See also CA 81-84; CANR 32; DLB 7

Gilstrap, John 1957(?)- .... CLC 99
   See also CA 160

Ginsberg, Allen
   1926-1997 ....   CLC 1, 2, 3, 4, 6, 13, 36,
   69; DA; DAB; DAC; DAM MST, POET;
   PC 4; WLC 3
   See also AITN 1; CA 1-4R; 157; CANR 2, 41;
   CDALB 1941-1968; DLB 5, 16, 169;
   MTCW

Ginzburg, Natalia
   1916-1991 .... CLC 5, 11, 54, 70
   See also CA 85-88; 135; CANR 33; DLB 177;
   MTCW

Giono, Jean
   1895-1970 .... CLC 4, 11
   See also CA 45-48; 29-32R; CANR 2, 35; DLB
   72; MTCW

Giovanni, Nikki
   1943- ....   CLC 2, 4, 19, 64; BLC; DA;
   DAB; DAC; DAM MST, MULT, POET;
   PC 19; WLCS
   See also AAYA 22; AITN 1; BW 2; CA 29-
   32R; CAAS 6; CANR 18, 41, 60; CLR 6;
   DLB 5, 41; INT CANR-18; MAICYA;
   MTCW; SATA 24

Giovene, Andrea
   1904- .... CLC 7
   See also CA 85-88

Gippius, Zinaida (Nikolayevna) 1869-1945
   See Hippius, Zinaida
   See also CA 106

Giraudoux, (Hippolyte) Jean
   1882-1944 ...... TCLC 2, 7; DAM DRAM
   See also CA 104; DLB 65

Gironella, Jose Maria 1917- .... CLC 11
   See also CA 101

Gissing, George (Robert)
   1857-1903 .... TCLC 3, 24, 47
   See also CA 105; DLB 18, 135, 184

Giurlani, Aldo
   See Palazzeschi, Aldo

Gladkov, Fyodor (Vasilyevich)
   1883-1958 .... TCLC 27

Glanville, Brian (Lester) 1931- .... CLC 6
   See also CA 5-8R; CAAS 9; CANR 3; DLB
   15, 139; SATA 42

Glasgow, Ellen (Anderson Gholson)
   1873(?)-1945 .... TCLC 2, 7
   See also CA 104; DLB 9, 12

Glaspell, Susan 1882(?)-1948 .... TCLC 55
   See also CA 110; 154; DLB 7, 9, 78; YABC
   2

Glassco, John 1909-1981 .... CLC 9
   See also CA 13-16R; 102; CANR 15; DLB 68

Glasscock, Amnesia
   See Steinbeck, John (Ernst)

Glasser, Ronald J. 1940(?)- .... CLC 37

Glassman, Joyce
   See Johnson, Joyce

Glendinning, Victoria 1937- .... CLC 50
   See also CA 120; 127; CANR 59; DLB 155

Glissant, Edouard
   1928- .... CLC 10, 68; DAM MULT
   See also CA 153

Gloag, Julian 1930- .... CLC 40
   See also AITN 1; CA 65-68; CANR 10

Glowacki, Aleksander
   See Prus, Boleslaw

Gluck, Louise (Elisabeth)
   1943- ... CLC 7, 22, 44, 81; DAM POET;
   PC 16
   See also CA 33-36R; CANR 40; DLB 5

Glyn, Elinor 1864-1943 .... TCLC 72
   See also DLB 153

Gobineau, Joseph Arthur (Comte) de
   1816-1882 .... NCLC 17
   See also DLB 123

Godard, Jean-Luc 1930- .... CLC 20
   See also CA 93-96

Godden, (Margaret) Rumer
   1907- .... CLC 53
   See also AAYA 6; CA 5-8R; CANR 4, 27, 36,
   55; CLR 20; DLB 161; MAICYA; SAAS 12;
   SATA 3, 36

Godoy Alcayaga, Lucila 1889-1957
   See Mistral, Gabriela
   See also BW 2; CA 104; 131; DAM MULT;
   HW; MTCW

Godwin, Gail (Kathleen)
   1937- .. CLC 5, 8, 22, 31, 69; DAM POP
   See also CA 29-32R; CANR 15, 43; DLB 6;
   INT CANR-15; MTCW

Godwin, William 1756-1836 .... NCLC 14
   See also CDBLB 1789-1832; DLB 39, 104,
   142, 158, 163

Goebbels, Josef
See Goebbels, (Paul) Joseph

Goebbels, (Paul) Joseph
1897-1945 .... **TCLC 68**
See also CA 115; 148

Goebbels, Joseph Paul
See Goebbels, (Paul) Joseph

Goethe, Johann Wolfgang von
1749-1832 ... **NCLC 4, 22, 34; DA; DAB; DAC; DAM DRAM, MST, POET; PC 5; WLC 3**
See also DLB 94

Gogarty, Oliver St. John
1878-1957 .... **TCLC 15**
See also CA 109; 150; DLB 15, 19

Gogol, Nikolai (Vasilyevich)
1809-1852 ... **NCLC 5, 15, 31; DA; DAB; DAC; DAM DRAM, MST; DC 1; SSC 4, 29; WLC**

Goines, Donald
1937(?)-1974 .... **CLC 80; BLC; DAM MULT, POP**
See also AITN 1; BW 1; CA 124; 114; DLB 33

Gold, Herbert
1924- .... **CLC 4, 7, 14, 42**
See also CA 9-12R; CANR 17, 45; DLB 2; DLBY 81

Goldbarth, Albert 1948- .... **CLC 5, 38**
See also CA 53-56; CANR 6, 40; DLB 120

Goldberg, Anatol
1910-1982 .... **CLC 34**
See also CA 131; 117

Goldemberg, Isaac 1945- .... **CLC 52**
See also CA 69-72; CAAS 12; CANR 11, 32; HW

Golding, William (Gerald)
1911-1993 ... **CLC 1, 2, 3, 8, 10, 17, 27, 58, 81; DA; DAB; DAC; DAM MST, NOV; WLC**
See also AAYA 5; CA 5-8R; 141; CANR 13, 33, 54; CDBLB 1945-1960; DLB 15, 100; MTCW

Goldman, Emma 1869-1940 .... **TCLC 13**
See also CA 110; 150

Goldman, Francisco 1955- .... **CLC 76**

Goldman, William (W.)
1931- .... **CLC 1, 48**
See also CA 9-12R; CANR 29; DLB 44

Goldmann, Lucien
1913-1970 .... **CLC 24**
See also CA 25-28; CAP 2

Goldoni, Carlo
1707-1793 .... **LC 4; DAM DRAM**

Goldsberry, Steven 1949- .... **CLC 34**
See also CA 131

Goldsmith, Oliver
1728-1774 .... **LC 2; DA; DAB; DAC; DAM DRAM, MST, NOV, POET; WLC**
See also CDBLB 1660-1789; DLB 39, 89, 104, 109, 142; SATA 26

Goldsmith, Peter
See Priestley, J(ohn) B(oynton)

Gombrowicz, Witold
1904-1969 .... **CLC 4, 7, 11, 49; DAM DRAM**
See also CA 19-20; 25-28R; CAP 2

Gomez de la Serna, Ramon
1888-1963 .... **CLC 9**
See also CA 153; 116; HW

Goncharov, Ivan Alexandrovich
1812-1891 .... **NCLC 1, 63**

Goncourt, Edmond (Louis Antoine Huot) de
1822-1896 .... **NCLC 7**
See also DLB 123

Goncourt, Jules (Alfred Huot) de
1830-1870 .... **NCLC 7**
See also DLB 123

Gontier, Fernande 19(?)- .... **CLC 50**

Gonzalez Martinez, Enrique
1871-1952 .... **TCLC 72**
See also HW

Goodman, Paul 1911-1972 ...... **CLC 1, 2, 4, 7**
See also CA 19-20; 37-40R; CANR 34; CAP 2; DLB 130; MTCW

Gordimer, Nadine
1923- ... **CLC 3, 5, 7, 10, 18, 33, 51, 70; DA; DAB; DAC; DAM MST, NOV; SSC 17; WLCS**
See also CA 5-8R; CANR 3, 28, 56; INT CANR-28; MTCW

Gordon, Adam Lindsay
1833-1870 .... **NCLC 21**

Gordon, Caroline
1895-1981 ..... **CLC 6, 13, 29, 83; SSC 15**
See also CA 11-12; 103; CANR 36; CAP 1; DLB 4, 9, 102; DLBY 81; MTCW

Gordon, Charles William 1860-1937
See Connor, Ralph
See also CA 109

Gordon, Mary (Catherine)
1949- .... **CLC 13, 22**
See also CA 102; CANR 44; DLB 6; DLBY 81; INT 102; MTCW

Gordon, N. J.
See Bosman, Herman Charles

Gordon, Sol 1923- .... **CLC 26**
See also CA 53-56; CANR 4; SATA 11

Gordone, Charles
1925-1995 .... **CLC 1, 4; DAM DRAM**
See also BW 1; CA 93-96; 150; CANR 55; DLB 7; INT 93-96; MTCW

Gore, Catherine 1800-1861 .... **NCLC 65**
See also DLB 116

Gorenko, Anna Andreevna
See Akhmatova, Anna

Gorky, Maxim .... **TCLC 8; DAB; SSC 28; WLC**
See also Peshkov, Alexei Maximovich

Goryan, Sirak
See Saroyan, William

Gosse, Edmund (William)
1849-1928 .... **TCLC 28**
See also CA 117; DLB 57, 144, 184

Gotlieb, Phyllis Fay (Bloom)
1926- .... **CLC 18**
See also CA 13-16R; CANR 7; DLB 88

Gottesman, S. D.
See Kornbluth, C(yril) M.; Pohl, Frederik

Gottfried von Strassburg
fl. c. 1210- .... **CMLC 10**
See also DLB 138

Gould, Lois .... **CLC 4, 10**
See also CA 77-80; CANR 29; MTCW

Gourmont, Remy (-Marie-Charles) de
1858-1915 .... **TCLC 17**
See also CA 109; 150

Govier, Katherine 1948- .... **CLC 51**
See also CA 101; CANR 18, 40

Goyen, (Charles) William
1915-1983 .... **CLC 5, 8, 14, 40**
See also AITN 2; CA 5-8R; 110; CANR 6; DLB 2; DLBY 83; INT CANR-6

Goytisolo, Juan
1931- .... **CLC 5, 10, 23; DAM MULT; HLC**
See also CA 85-88; CANR 32, 61; HW; MTCW

Gozzano, Guido 1883-1916 .... **PC 10**
See also CA 154; DLB 114

Gozzi, (Conte) Carlo
1720-1806 .... **NCLC 23**

Grabbe, Christian Dietrich
1801-1836 .... **NCLC 2**
See also DLB 133

Grace, Patricia 1937- .... **CLC 56**

Gracian y Morales, Baltasar
1601-1658 .... **LC 15**

Gracq, Julien .... **CLC 11, 48**
See also Poirier, Louis
See also DLB 83

Grade, Chaim 1910-1982 .... **CLC 10**
See also CA 93-96; 107

Graduate of Oxford, A
See Ruskin, John

Grafton, Garth
See Duncan, Sara Jeannette

Graham, John
See Phillips, David Graham

Graham, Jorie 1951- .... CLC 48
See also CA 111; DLB 120

Graham, R(obert) B(ontine) Cunninghame
See Cunninghame Graham, R(obert) B(ontine)
See also DLB 98, 135, 174

Graham, Robert
See Haldeman, Joe (William)

Graham, Tom
See Lewis, (Harry) Sinclair

Graham, W(illiam) S(ydney)
1918-1986 .... CLC 29
See also CA 73-76; 118; DLB 20

Graham, Winston (Mawdsley)
1910- .... CLC 23
See also CA 49-52; CANR 2, 22, 45; DLB 77

Grahame, Kenneth 1859-1932 ...... TCLC 64;
DAB
See also CA 108; 136; CLR 5; DLB 34, 141,
178; MAICYA; YABC 1

Grant, Skeeter
See Spiegelman, Art

Granville-Barker, Harley
1877-1946 .... TCLC 2; DAM DRAM
See also Barker, Harley Granville
See also CA 104

Grass, Guenter (Wilhelm)
1927- .... CLC 1, 2, 4, 6, 11, 15, 22, 32,
49, 88; DA; DAB; DAC; DAM MST,
NOV; WLC
See also CA 13-16R; CANR 20; DLB 75, 124;
MTCW

Gratton, Thomas
See Hulme, T(homas) E(rnest)

Grau, Shirley Ann
1929- .... CLC 4, 9; SSC 15
See also CA 89-92; CANR 22; DLB 2; INT
CANR-22; MTCW

Gravel, Fern
See Hall, James Norman

Graver, Elizabeth 1964- .... CLC 70
See also CA 135

Graves, Richard Perceval 1945- .... CLC 44
See also CA 65-68; CANR 9, 26, 51

Graves, Robert (von Ranke)
1895-1985 .... CLC 1, 2, 6, 11, 39, 44,
45; DAB; DAC; DAM MST, POET; PC 6
See also CA 5-8R; 117; CANR 5, 36; CDBLB
1914-1945; DLB 20, 100; DLBY 85;
MTCW; SATA 45

Graves, Valerie
See Bradley, Marion Zimmer

Gray, Alasdair (James) 1934- .... CLC 41
See also CA 126; CANR 47; INT 126;
MTCW

Gray, Amlin 1946- .... CLC 29
See also CA 138

Gray, Francine du Plessix 1930- ..... CLC 22;
DAM NOV
See also BEST 90:3; CA 61-64; CAAS 2;
CANR 11, 33; INT CANR-11; MTCW

Gray, John (Henry) 1866-1934 ...... TCLC 19
See also CA 119

Gray, Simon (James Holliday)
1936- .... CLC 9, 14, 36
See also AITN 1; CA 21-24R; CAAS 3; CANR
32; DLB 13; MTCW

Gray, Spalding
1941- .... CLC 49; DAM POP; DC 7
See also CA 128

Gray, Thomas
1716-1771 .... LC 4, 40; DA; DAB; DAC;
DAM MST; PC 2; WLC
See also CDBLB 1660-1789; DLB 109

Grayson, David
See Baker, Ray Stannard

Grayson, Richard (A.) 1951- .... CLC 38
See also CA 85-88; CANR 14, 31, 57

Greeley, Andrew M(oran) 1928- ..... CLC 28;
DAM POP
See also CA 5-8R; CAAS 7; CANR 7, 43;
MTCW

Green, Anna Katharine
1846-1935 .... TCLC 63
See also CA 112; 159

Green, Brian
See Card, Orson Scott

Green, Hannah
See Greenberg, Joanne (Goldenberg)

Green, Hannah 1927(?)-1996 .... CLC 3
See also CA 73-76; CANR 59

Green, Henry 1905-1973 .... CLC 2, 13, 97
See also Yorke, Henry Vincent
See also DLB 15

Green, Julian (Hartridge) 1900-
See Green, Julien
See also CA 21-24R; CANR 33; DLB 4, 72;
MTCW

Green, Julien .... CLC 3, 11, 77
See also Green, Julian (Hartridge)

Green, Paul (Eliot)
1894-1981 .... CLC 25; DAM DRAM
See also AITN 1; CA 5-8R; 103; CANR 3; DLB
7, 9; DLBY 81

Greenberg, Ivan 1908-1973
See Rahv, Philip
See also CA 85-88

Greenberg, Joanne (Goldenberg)
1932- .... CLC 7, 30
See also AAYA 12; CA 5-8R; CANR 14, 32;
SATA 25

Greenberg, Richard 1959(?)- .... CLC 57
See also CA 138

Greene, Bette 1934- .... CLC 30
See also AAYA 7; CA 53-56; CANR 4; CLR
2; JRDA; MAICYA; SAAS 16; SATA 8

Greene, Gael .... CLC 8
See also CA 13-16R; CANR 10

Greene, Graham (Henry)
1904-1991 ... CLC 1, 3, 6, 9, 14, 18, 27,
37, 70, 72; DA; DAB; DAC; DAM MST,
NOV; SSC 29; WLC
See also AITN 2; CA 13-16R; 133; CANR 35,
61; CDBLB 1945-1960; DLB 13, 15, 77,
100, 162; DLBY 91; MTCW; SATA 20

Greer, Richard
See Silverberg, Robert

Gregor, Arthur 1923- .... CLC 9
See also CA 25-28R; CAAS 10; CANR 11;
SATA 36

Gregor, Lee
See Pohl, Frederik

Gregory, Isabella Augusta (Persse)
1852-1932 .... TCLC 1
See also CA 104; DLB 10

Gregory, J. Dennis
See Williams, John A(lfred)

Grendon, Stephen
See Derleth, August (William)

Grenville, Kate 1950- .... CLC 61
See also CA 118; CANR 53

Grenville, Pelham
See Wodehouse, P(elham) G(renville)

Greve, Felix Paul (Berthold Friedrich)
1879-1948
See Grove, Frederick Philip
See also CA 104; 141; DAC; DAM MST

Grey, Zane
1872-1939 .... TCLC 6; DAM POP
See also CA 104; 132; DLB 9; MTCW

Grieg, (Johan) Nordahl (Brun)
1902-1943 .... TCLC 10
See also CA 107

Grieve, C(hristopher) M(urray)
1892-1978 ...... CLC 11, 19; DAM POET
See also MacDiarmid, Hugh; Pteleon
See also CA 5-8R; 85-88; CANR 33;
MTCW

Griffin, Gerald 1803-1840 .... NCLC 7
See also DLB 159

Griffin, John Howard 1920-1980 ..... CLC 68
See also AITN 1; CA 1-4R; 101; CANR 2

Griffin, Peter 1942- .... CLC 39
See also CA 136

Griffith, D(avid Lewelyn) W(ark)
1875(?)-1948 .... TCLC 68
See also CA 119; 150

Griffith, Lawrence
See Griffith, D(avid Lewelyn) W(ark)

Griffiths, Trevor 1935- .... CLC 13, 52
See also CA 97-100; CANR 45; DLB 13

Grigson, Geoffrey (Edward Harvey)
1905-1985 .... CLC 7, 39
See also CA 25-28R; 118; CANR 20, 33; DLB
27; MTCW

Grillparzer, Franz 1791-1872 .... NCLC 1
See also DLB 133

Grimble, Reverend Charles James
See Eliot, T(homas) S(tearns)

Grimke, Charlotte L(ottie) Forten
1837(?)-1914
See Forten, Charlotte L.
See also BW 1; CA 117; 124; DAM MULT,
POET

Grimm, Jacob Ludwig Karl
1785-1863 .... NCLC 3
See also DLB 90; MAICYA; SATA 22

Grimm, Wilhelm Karl 1786-1859 .... NCLC 3
See also DLB 90; MAICYA; SATA 22

**Grimmelshausen, Johann Jakob Christoffel
von** 1621-1676 .... LC 6
See also DLB 168

Grindel, Eugene 1895-1952
See Eluard, Paul
See also CA 104

Grisham, John
1955- .... CLC 84; DAM POP
See also AAYA 14; CA 138; CANR 47

Grossman, David 1954- .... CLC 67
See also CA 138

Grossman, Vasily (Semenovich)
1905-1964 .... CLC 41
See also CA 124; 130; MTCW

Grove, Frederick Philip .... TCLC 4
See also Greve, Felix Paul (Berthold Friedrich)
See also DLB 92

Grubb
See Crumb, R(obert)

Grumbach, Doris (Isaac)
1918- .... CLC 13, 22, 64
See also CA 5-8R; CAAS 2; CANR 9, 42; INT
CANR-9

Grundtvig, Nicolai Frederik Severin
1783-1872 .... NCLC 1

Grunge
See Crumb, R(obert)

Grunwald, Lisa 1959- .... CLC 44
See also CA 120

Guare, John
1938-............ CLC 8, 14, 29, 67; DAM
DRAM
See also CA 73-76; CANR 21; DLB 7; MTCW

Gudjonsson, Halldor Kiljan 1902-
See Laxness, Halldor
See also CA 103

Guenter, Erich
See Eich, Guenter

Guest, Barbara 1920- .... CLC 34
See also CA 25-28R; CANR 11, 44; DLB 5

Guest, Judith (Ann)
1936- .... CLC 8, 30; DAM NOV, POP
See also AAYA 7; CA 77-80; CANR 15; INT
CANR-15; MTCW

Guevara, Che .... CLC 87; HLC
See also Guevara (Serna), Ernesto

Guevara (Serna), Ernesto 1928-1967
See Guevara, Che
See also CA 127; 111; CANR 56; DAM MULT;
HW

Guild, Nicholas M. 1944- .... CLC 33
See also CA 93-96

Guillemin, Jacques
See Sartre, Jean-Paul

Guillen, Jorge
1893-1984 CLC 11; DAM MULT, POET
See also CA 89-92; 112; DLB 108; HW

Guillen, Nicolas (Cristobal)
1902-1989 .... CLC 48, 79; BLC; DAM
MST, MULT, POET; HLC
See also BW 2; CA 116; 125; 129; HW

Guillevic, (Eugene) 1907- .... CLC 33
See also CA 93-96

Guillois
See Desnos, Robert

Guillois, Valentin
See Desnos, Robert

Guiney, Louise Imogen
1861-1920 .... TCLC 41
See also CA 160; DLB 54

Guiraldes, Ricardo (Guillermo)
1886-1927 .... TCLC 39
See also CA 131; HW; MTCW

Gumilev, Nikolai Stephanovich
1886-1921 .... TCLC 60

Gunesekera, Romesh
1954- .... CLC 91
See also CA 159

Gunn, Bill .... CLC 5
See also Gunn, William Harrison
See also DLB 38

Gunn, Thom(son William)
1929- .... CLC 3, 6, 18, 32, 81; DAM
POET
See also CA 17-20R; CANR 9, 33; CDBLB
1960 to Present; DLB 27; INT CANR-33;
MTCW

Gunn, William Harrison 1934(?)-1989
See Gunn, Bill
See also AITN 1; BW 1; CA 13-16R; 128;
CANR 12, 25

Gunnars, Kristjana 1948- .... CLC 69
See also CA 113; DLB 60

Gurdjieff, G(eorgei) I(vanovich)
1877(?)-1949 .... TCLC 71
See also CA 157

Gurganus, Allan
1947- .... CLC 70; DAM POP
See also BEST 90:1; CA 135

Gurney, A(lbert) R(amsdell), Jr.
1930- ...... CLC 32, 50, 54; DAM DRAM
See also CA 77-80; CANR 32

Gurney, Ivor (Bertie)
1890-1937 .... TCLC 33

Gurney, Peter
See Gurney, A(lbert) R(amsdell), Jr.

Guro, Elena 1877-1913 .... TCLC 56

Gustafson, James M(oody)
1925- .... CLC 100
See also CA 25-28R; CANR 37

Gustafson, Ralph (Barker) 1909- ..... CLC 36
See also CA 21-24R; CANR 8, 45; DLB 88

Gut, Gom
See Simenon, Georges (Jacques Christian)

Guterson, David 1956- .... CLC 91
See also CA 132

Guthrie, A(lfred) B(ertram), Jr.
1901-1991 .... CLC 23
See also CA 57-60; 134; CANR 24; DLB 6;
SATA 62; SATA-Obit 67

Guthrie, Isobel
See Grieve, C(hristopher) M(urray)

Guthrie, Woodrow Wilson 1912-1967
See Guthrie, Woody
See also CA 113; 93-96

Guthrie, Woody .... CLC 35
See also Guthrie, Woodrow Wilson

Guy, Rosa (Cuthbert) 1928- .... CLC 26
See also AAYA 4; BW 2; CA 17-20R; CANR
14, 34; CLR 13; DLB 33; JRDA; MAICYA;
SATA 14, 62

Gwendolyn
See Bennett, (Enoch) Arnold

H. D. .... CLC 3, 8, 14, 31, 34, 73; PC 5
See also Doolittle, Hilda

H. de V.
See Buchan, John

Haavikko, Paavo Juhani
1931- .... **CLC 18, 34**
See also CA 106

Habbema, Koos
See Heijermans, Herman

Habermas, Juergen 1929- .... **CLC 104**
See also CA 109

Habermas, Jurgen
See Habermas, Juergen

Hacker, Marilyn
1942- .... **CLC 5, 9, 23, 72, 91; DAM POET**
See also CA 77-80; DLB 120

Haggard, H(enry) Rider
1856-1925 .... **TCLC 11**
See also CA 108; 148; DLB 70, 156, 174, 178; SATA 16

Hagiosy, L.
See Larbaud, Valery (Nicolas)

Hagiwara Sakutaro
1886-1942 .... **TCLC 60; PC 18**

Haig, Fenil
See Ford, Ford Madox

Haig-Brown, Roderick (Langmere)
1908-1976 .... **CLC 21**
See also CA 5-8R; 69-72; CANR 4, 38; CLR 31; DLB 88; MAICYA; SATA 12

Hailey, Arthur
1920- .... **CLC 5; DAM NOV, POP**
See also AITN 2; BEST 90:3; CA 1-4R; CANR 2, 36; DLB 88; DLBY 82; MTCW

Hailey, Elizabeth Forsythe
1938- .... **CLC 40**
See also CA 93-96; CAAS 1; CANR 15, 48; INT CANR-15

Haines, John (Meade) 1924- .... **CLC 58**
See also CA 17-20R; CANR 13, 34; DLB 5

Hakluyt, Richard 1552-1616 .... **LC 31**

Haldeman, Joe (William) 1943- .... **CLC 61**
See also CA 53-56; CAAS 25; CANR 6; DLB 8; INT CANR-6

Haley, Alex(ander Murray Palmer)
1921-1992 ...... **CLC 8, 12, 76; BLC; DA; DAB; DAC; DAM MST, MULT, POP**
See also BW 2; CA 77-80; 136; CANR 61; DLB 38; MTCW

Haliburton, Thomas Chandler
1796-1865 .... **NCLC 15**
See also DLB 11, 99

Hall, Donald (Andrew, Jr.)
1928- .... **CLC 1, 13, 37, 59; DAM POET**
See also CA 5-8R; CAAS 7; CANR 2, 44; DLB 5; SATA 23

Hall, Frederic Sauser
See Sauser-Hall, Frederic

Hall, James
See Kuttner, Henry

Hall, James Norman 1887-1951 ..... **TCLC 23**
See also CA 123; SATA 21

Hall, (Marguerite) Radclyffe
1886-1943 .... **TCLC 12**
See also CA 110; 150

Hall, Rodney 1935- .... **CLC 51**
See also CA 109

Halleck, Fitz-Greene
1790-1867 .... **NCLC 47**
See also DLB 3

Halliday, Michael
See Creasey, John

Halpern, Daniel 1945- .... **CLC 14**
See also CA 33-36R

Hamburger, Michael (Peter Leopold)
1924- .... **CLC 5, 14**
See also CA 5-8R; CAAS 4; CANR 2, 47; DLB 27

Hamill, Pete 1935- .... **CLC 10**
See also CA 25-28R; CANR 18

Hamilton, Alexander
1755(?)-1804 .... **NCLC 49**
See also DLB 37

Hamilton, Clive
See Lewis, C(live) S(taples)

Hamilton, Edmond 1904-1977 .... **CLC 1**
See also CA 1-4R; CANR 3; DLB 8

Hamilton, Eugene (Jacob) Lee
See Lee-Hamilton, Eugene (Jacob)

Hamilton, Franklin
See Silverberg, Robert

Hamilton, Gail
See Corcoran, Barbara

Hamilton, Mollie
See Kaye, M(ary) M(argaret)

Hamilton, (Anthony Walter) Patrick
1904-1962 .... **CLC 51**
See also CA 113; DLB 10

Hamilton, Virginia
1936- .... **CLC 26; DAM MULT**
See also AAYA 2, 21; BW 2; CA 25-28R; CANR 20, 37; CLR 1, 11, 40; DLB 33, 52; INT CANR-20; JRDA; MAICYA; MTCW; SATA 4, 56, 79

Hammett, (Samuel) Dashiell
1894-1961 ... **CLC 3, 5, 10, 19, 47; SSC 17**
See also AITN 1; CA 81-84; CANR 42; CDALB 1929-1941; DLBD 6; DLBY 96; MTCW

Hammon, Jupiter
1711(?)-1800(?) .... **NCLC 5; BLC; DAM MULT, POET; PC 16**
See also DLB 31, 50

Hammond, Keith
See Kuttner, Henry

Hamner, Earl (Henry), Jr. 1923- ...... **CLC 12**
See also AITN 2; CA 73-76; DLB 6

Hampton, Christopher (James)
1946- .... **CLC 4**
See also CA 25-28R; DLB 13; MTCW

Hamsun, Knut .... **TCLC 2, 14, 49**
See also Pedersen, Knut

Handke, Peter 1942- .... **CLC 5, 8, 10, 15, 38; DAM DRAM, NOV**
See also CA 77-80; CANR 33; DLB 85, 124; MTCW

Hanley, James 1901-1985 ..... **CLC 3, 5, 8, 13**
See also CA 73-76; 117; CANR 36; MTCW

Hannah, Barry 1942- .... **CLC 23, 38, 90**
See also CA 108; 110; CANR 43; DLB 6; INT 110; MTCW

Hannon, Ezra
See Hunter, Evan

Hansberry, Lorraine (Vivian)
1930-1965 .... **CLC 17, 62; BLC; DA; DAB; DAC; DAM DRAM, MST, MULT; DC 2**
See also BW 1; CA 109; 25-28R; CABS 3; CANR 58; CDALB 1941-1968; DLB 7, 38; MTCW

Hansen, Joseph 1923- .... **CLC 38**
See also CA 29-32R; CAAS 17; CANR 16, 44; INT CANR-16

Hansen, Martin A. 1909-1955 .... **TCLC 32**

Hanson, Kenneth O(stlin)
1922- .... **CLC 13**
See also CA 53-56; CANR 7

Hardwick, Elizabeth
1916- .... **CLC 13; DAM NOV**
See also CA 5-8R; CANR 3, 32; DLB 6; MTCW

Hardy, Thomas
1840-1928 ... **TCLC 4, 10, 18, 32, 48, 53, 72; DA; DAB; DAC; DAM MST, NOV, POET; PC 8; SSC 2; WLC**
See also CA 104; 123; CDBLB 1890-1914; DLB 18, 19, 135; MTCW

Hare, David 1947- .... **CLC 29, 58**
See also CA 97-100; CANR 39; DLB 13; MTCW

Harford, Henry
See Hudson, W(illiam) H(enry)

Hargrave, Leonie
See Disch, Thomas M(ichael)

Harjo, Joy 1951- .... **CLC 83; DAM MULT**
See also CA 114; CANR 35; DLB 120, 175;
NNAL

Harlan, Louis R(udolph) 1922- .... **CLC 34**
See also CA 21-24R; CANR 25, 55

Harling, Robert 1951(?)- .... **CLC 53**
See also CA 147

Harmon, William (Ruth) 1938- .... **CLC 38**
See also CA 33-36R; CANR 14, 32, 35; SATA
65

Harper, F. E. W.
See Harper, Frances Ellen Watkins

Harper, Frances E. W.
See Harper, Frances Ellen Watkins

Harper, Frances E. Watkins
See Harper, Frances Ellen Watkins

Harper, Frances Ellen
See Harper, Frances Ellen Watkins

Harper, Frances Ellen Watkins
1825-1911 .... **TCLC 14; BLC; DAM
MULT, POET**
See also BW 1; CA 111; 125; DLB 50

Harper, Michael S(teven)
1938- .... **CLC 7, 22**
See also BW 1; CA 33-36R; CANR 24; DLB
41

Harper, Mrs. F. E. W.
See Harper, Frances Ellen Watkins

Harris, Christie (Lucy) Irwin
1907- .... **CLC 12**
See also CA 5-8R; CANR 6; CLR 47; DLB
88; JRDA; MAICYA; SAAS 10; SATA 6,
74

Harris, Frank 1856-1931 .... **TCLC 24**
See also CA 109; 150; DLB 156

Harris, George Washington
1814-1869 .... **NCLC 23**
See also DLB 3, 11

Harris, Joel Chandler 1848-1908 ... **TCLC 2;
SSC 19**
See also CA 104; 137; DLB 11, 23, 42, 78, 91;
MAICYA; YABC 1

**Harris, John (Wyndham Parkes Lucas)
Beynon** 1903-1969
See Wyndham, John
See also CA 102; 89-92

Harris, MacDonald .... **CLC 9**
See also Heiney, Donald (William)

Harris, Mark 1922- .... **CLC 19**
See also CA 5-8R; CAAS 3; CANR 2, 55; DLB
2; DLBY 80

Harris, (Theodore) Wilson
1921- .... **CLC 25**
See also BW 2; CA 65-68; CAAS 16; CANR
11, 27; DLB 117; MTCW

Harrison, Elizabeth Cavanna 1909-
See Cavanna, Betty
See also CA 9-12R; CANR 6, 27

Harrison, Harry (Max) 1925- .... **CLC 42**
See also CA 1-4R; CANR 5, 21; DLB 8; SATA
4

Harrison, James (Thomas)
1937- .... **CLC 6, 14, 33, 66; SSC 19**
See also CA 13-16R; CANR 8, 51; DLBY 82;
INT CANR-8

Harrison, Jim
See Harrison, James (Thomas)

Harrison, Kathryn 1961- .... **CLC 70**
See also CA 144

Harrison, Tony 1937- .... **CLC 43**
See also CA 65-68; CANR 44; DLB 40;
MTCW

Harriss, Will(ard Irvin) 1922- .... **CLC 34**
See also CA 111

Harson, Sley
See Ellison, Harlan (Jay)

Hart, Ellis
See Ellison, Harlan (Jay)

Hart, Josephine
1942(?)- .... **CLC 70; DAM POP**
See also CA 138

Hart, Moss
1904-1961 .... **CLC 66; DAM DRAM**
See also CA 109; 89-92; DLB 7

Harte, (Francis) Bret(t)
1836(?)-1902 .... **TCLC 1, 25; DA; DAC;
DAM MST; SSC 8; WLC**
See also CA 104; 140; CDALB 1865-1917;
DLB 12, 64, 74, 79; SATA 26

Hartley, L(eslie) P(oles)
1895-1972 .... **CLC 2, 22**
See also CA 45-48; 37-40R; CANR 33; DLB
15, 139; MTCW

Hartman, Geoffrey H. 1929- .... **CLC 27**
See also CA 117; 125; DLB 67

Hartmann, Sadakichi 1867-1944 ... **TCLC 73**
See also CA 157; DLB 54

Hartmann von Aue
c. 1160-c. 1205 .... **CMLC 15**
See also DLB 138

Hartmann von Aue 1170-1210 ...... **CMLC 15**

Haruf, Kent 1943- .... **CLC 34**
See also CA 149

Harwood, Ronald 1934- .... **CLC 32; DAM
DRAM, MST**
See also CA 1-4R; CANR 4, 55; DLB 13

Hasek, Jaroslav (Matej Frantisek)
1883-1923 .... **TCLC 4**
See also CA 104; 129; MTCW

Hass, Robert 1941- ... **CLC 18, 39, 99; PC 16**
See also CA 111; CANR 30, 50; DLB 105;
SATA 94

Hastings, Hudson
See Kuttner, Henry

Hastings, Selina .... **CLC 44**

Hathorne, John 1641-1717 .... **LC 38**

Hatteras, Amelia
See Mencken, H(enry) L(ouis)

Hatteras, Owen .... **TCLC 18**
See also Mencken, H(enry) L(ouis); Nathan,
George Jean

Hauptmann, Gerhart (Johann Robert)
1862-1946 .... **TCLC 4; DAM DRAM**
See also CA 104; 153; DLB 66, 118

Havel, Vaclav 1936- ... **CLC 25, 58, 65; DAM
DRAM; DC 6**
See also CA 104; CANR 36; MTCW

Haviaras, Stratis .... **CLC 33**
See also Chaviaras, Strates

Hawes, Stephen 1475(?)-1523(?) .... **LC 17**

Hawkes, John (Clendennin Burne, Jr.)
1925- **CLC 1, 2, 3, 4, 7, 9, 14, 15, 27, 49**
See also CA 1-4R; CANR 2, 47; DLB 2, 7;
DLBY 80; MTCW

Hawking, Stephen W(illiam)
1942- .... **CLC 63, 105**
See also AAYA 13; BEST 89:1; CA 126; 129;
CANR 48

Hawthorne, Julian 1846-1934 .... **TCLC 25**

Hawthorne, Nathaniel
1804-1864 .... **NCLC 39; DA; DAB;
DAC; DAM MST, NOV; SSC 3, 29;
WLC**
See also AAYA 18; CDALB 1640-1865; DLB
1, 74; YABC 2

Haxton, Josephine Ayres 1921-
See Douglas, Ellen
See also CA 115; CANR 41

Hayaseca y Eizaguirre, Jorge
See Echegaray (y Eizaguirre), Jose (Maria
Waldo)

Hayashi Fumiko 1904-1951 .... **TCLC 27**
See also DLB 180

Haycraft, Anna
See Ellis, Alice Thomas
See also CA 122

Hayden, Robert E(arl)
1913-1980 ...... **CLC 5, 9, 14, 37; BLC;
DA; DAC; DAM MST, MULT, POET;
PC 6**
See also BW 1; CA 69-72; 97-100; CABS
2; CANR 24; CDALB 1941-1968;
DLB 5, 76; MTCW; SATA 19; SATA-
Obit 26

Hayford, J(oseph) E(phraim) Casely
See Casely-Hayford, J(oseph) E(phraim)

Hayman, Ronald 1932- .... **CLC 44**
See also CA 25-28R; CANR 18, 50; DLB 155

Haywood, Eliza (Fowler)
1693(?)-1756 .... **LC 1**

Hazlitt, William 1778-1830 .... **NCLC 29**
See also DLB 110, 158

Hazzard, Shirley 1931- .... **CLC 18**
See also CA 9-12R; CANR 4; DLBY 82;
MTCW

Head, Bessie
1937-1986 .... **CLC 25, 67; BLC; DAM
MULT**
See also BW 2; CA 29-32R; 119; CANR 25;
DLB 117; MTCW

Headon, (Nicky) Topper 1956(?)- ..... **CLC 30**

Heaney, Seamus (Justin)
1939- .... **CLC 5, 7, 14, 25, 37, 74, 91;
DAB; DAM POET; PC 18; WLCS**
See also CA 85-88; CANR 25, 48; CDBLB
1960 to Present; DLB 40; DLBY 95;
MTCW

Hearn, (Patricio) Lafcadio (Tessima Carlos)
1850-1904 .... **TCLC 9**
See also CA 105; DLB 12, 78

Hearne, Vicki 1946- .... **CLC 56**
See also CA 139

Hearon, Shelby 1931- .... **CLC 63**
See also AITN 2; CA 25-28R; CANR 18, 48

Heat-Moon, William Least .... **CLC 29**
See also Trogdon, William (Lewis)
See also AAYA 9

Hebbel, Friedrich
1813-1863 .... **NCLC 43; DAM DRAM**
See also DLB 129

Hebert, Anne 1916- ..... **CLC 4, 13, 29; DAC;
DAM MST, POET**
See also CA 85-88; DLB 68; MTCW

Hecht, Anthony (Evan)
1923- .... **CLC 8, 13, 19; DAM POET**
See also CA 9-12R; CANR 6; DLB 5, 169

Hecht, Ben 1894-1964 .... **CLC 8**
See also CA 85-88; DLB 7, 9, 25, 26, 28, 86

Hedayat, Sadeq 1903-1951 .... **TCLC 21**
See also CA 120

Hegel, Georg Wilhelm Friedrich
1770-1831 .... **NCLC 46**
See also DLB 90

Heidegger, Martin 1889-1976 .... **CLC 24**
See also CA 81-84; 65-68; CANR 34; MTCW

Heidenstam, (Carl Gustaf) Verner von
1859-1940 .... **TCLC 5**
See also CA 104

Heifner, Jack 1946- .... **CLC 11**
See also CA 105; CANR 47

Heijermans, Herman 1864-1924 .... **TCLC 24**
See also CA 123

Heilbrun, Carolyn G(old) 1926- .... **CLC 25**
See also CA 45-48; CANR 1, 28, 58

Heine, Heinrich 1797-1856 .... **NCLC 4, 54**
See also DLB 90

Heinemann, Larry (Curtiss) 1944-... **CLC 50**
See also CA 110; CAAS 21; CANR 31; DLBD
9; INT CANR-31

Heiney, Donald (William) 1921-1993
See Harris, MacDonald
See also CA 1-4R; 142; CANR 3, 58

Heinlein, Robert A(nson)
1907-1988 .... **CLC 1, 3, 8, 14, 26, 55;
DAM POP**
See also AAYA 17; CA 1-4R; 125; CANR 1,
20, 53; DLB 8; JRDA; MAICYA; MTCW;
SATA 9, 69; SATA-Obit 56

Helforth, John
See Doolittle, Hilda

Hellenhofferu, Vojtech Kapristian z
See Hasek, Jaroslav (Matej Frantisek)

Heller, Joseph
1923- ...... **CLC 1, 3, 5, 8, 11, 36, 63; DA;
DAB; DAC; DAM MST, NOV, POP;
WLC**
See also AITN 1; CA 5-8R; CABS 1; CANR
8, 42; DLB 2, 28; DLBY 80; INT CANR-8;
MTCW

Hellman, Lillian (Florence)
1906-1984 .... **CLC 2, 4, 8, 14, 18, 34, 44,
52; DAM DRAM; DC 1**
See also AITN 1, 2; CA 13-16R; 112; CANR
33; DLB 7; DLBY 84; MTCW

Helprin, Mark
1947- ..... **CLC 7, 10, 22, 32; DAM NOV,
POP**
See also CA 81-84; CANR 47; DLBY 85;
MTCW

Helvetius, Claude-Adrien 1715-1771 .. **LC 26**

Helyar, Jane Penelope Josephine 1933-
See Poole, Josephine
See also CA 21-24R; CANR 10, 26; SATA 82

Hemans, Felicia 1793-1835 .... **NCLC 29**
See also DLB 96

Hemingway, Ernest (Miller)
1899-1961.... **CLC 1, 3, 6, 8, 10, 13,
19, 30, 34, 39, 41, 44, 50, 61, 80; DA;
DAB; DAC; DAM MST, NOV; SSC
25; WLC**
See also AAYA 19; CA 77-80; CANR 34;
CDALB 1917-1929; DLB 4, 9, 102; DLBD
1, 15, 16; DLBY 81, 87, 96; MTCW

Hempel, Amy 1951- .... **CLC 39**
See also CA 118; 137

Henderson, F. C.
See Mencken, H(enry) L(ouis)

Henderson, Sylvia
See Ashton-Warner, Sylvia (Constance)

Henderson, Zenna (Chlarson)
1917-1983 .... **SSC 29**
See also CA 1-4R; 133; CANR 1; DLB 8;
SATA 5

Henley, Beth .... **CLC 23; DC 6**
See also Henley, Elizabeth Becker
See also CABS 3; DLBY 86

Henley, Elizabeth Becker 1952-
See Henley, Beth
See also CA 107; CANR 32; DAM DRAM,
MST; MTCW

Henley, William Ernest
1849-1903 .... **TCLC 8**
See also CA 105; DLB 19

Hennissart, Martha
See Lathen, Emma
See also CA 85-88

Henry, O. .... **TCLC 1, 19; SSC 5; WLC**
See also Porter, William Sydney

Henry, Patrick 1736-1799 .... **LC 25**

Henryson, Robert 1430(?)-1506(?) ...... **LC 20**
See also DLB 146

Henry VIII 1491-1547 .... **LC 10**

Henschke, Alfred
See Klabund

Hentoff, Nat(han Irving)
1925- .... **CLC 26**
See also AAYA 4; CA 1-4R; CAAS 6; CANR
5, 25; CLR 1; INT CANR-25; JRDA;
MAICYA; SATA 42, 69; SATA-Brief 27

Heppenstall, (John) Rayner
1911-1981 .... **CLC 10**
See also CA 1-4R; 103; CANR 29

Heraclitus c. 540B.C.-c. 450B.C. ... **CMLC 22**
See also DLB 176

Herbert, Frank (Patrick)
1920-1986 .... **CLC 12, 23, 35, 44, 85;
DAM POP**
See also AAYA 21; CA 53-56; 118; CANR 5,
43; DLB 8; INT CANR-5; MTCW; SATA
9, 37; SATA-Obit 47

Herbert, George
1593-1633 ... **LC 24; DAB; DAM POET;
PC 4**
See also CDBLB Before 1660; DLB 126

Herbert, Zbigniew
1924- .... **CLC 9, 43; DAM POET**
See also CA 89-92; CANR 36; MTCW

Herbst, Josephine (Frey)
1897-1969 .... **CLC 34**
See also CA 5-8R; 25-28R; DLB 9

Hergesheimer, Joseph
1880-1954 .... **TCLC 11**
See also CA 109; DLB 102, 9

Herlihy, James Leo
1927-1993 .... **CLC 6**
See also CA 1-4R; 143; CANR 2

Hermogenes fl. c. 175- .... **CMLC 6**

Hernandez, Jose 1834-1886 .... **NCLC 17**

Herodotus
c. 484B.C.-429B.C. .... **CMLC 17**
See also DLB 176

Herrick, Robert
1591-1674 .... **LC 13; DA; DAB; DAC;
DAM MST, POP; PC 9**
See also DLB 126

Herring, Guilles
See Somerville, Edith

Herriot, James
1916-1995 .... **CLC 12; DAM POP**
See also Wight, James Alfred
See also AAYA 1; CA 148; CANR 40; SATA
86

Herrmann, Dorothy 1941- .... **CLC 44**
See also CA 107

Herrmann, Taffy
See Herrmann, Dorothy

Hersey, John (Richard)
1914-1993 ...... **CLC 1, 2, 7, 9, 40, 81, 97;
DAM POP**
See also CA 17-20R; 140; CANR 33; DLB 6;
MTCW; SATA 25; SATA-Obit 76

Herzen, Aleksandr Ivanovich
1812-1870 .... **NCLC 10, 61**

Herzl, Theodor 1860-1904 .... **TCLC 36**

Herzog, Werner 1942- .... **CLC 16**
See also CA 89-92

Hesiod c. 8th cent. B.C.- .... **CMLC 5**
See also DLB 176

Hesse, Hermann
1877-1962 ... **CLC 1, 2, 3, 6, 11, 17, 25,
69; DA; DAB; DAC; DAM MST, NOV;
SSC 9; WLC**
See also CA 17-18; CAP 2; DLB 66; MTCW;
SATA 50

Hewes, Cady
See De Voto, Bernard (Augustine)

Heyen, William 1940- .... **CLC 13, 18**
See also CA 33-36R; CAAS 9; DLB 5

Heyerdahl, Thor 1914- .... **CLC 26**
See also CA 5-8R; CANR 5, 22; MTCW; SATA
2, 52

Heym, Georg (Theodor Franz Arthur)
1887-1912 .... **TCLC 9**
See also CA 106

Heym, Stefan 1913- .... **CLC 41**
See also CA 9-12R; CANR 4; DLB 69

Heyse, Paul (Johann Ludwig von)
1830-1914 .... **TCLC 8**
See also CA 104; DLB 129

Heyward, (Edwin) DuBose
1885-1940 .... **TCLC 59**
See also CA 108; 157; DLB 7, 9, 45; SATA 21

Hibbert, Eleanor Alice Burford
1906-1993 .... **CLC 7; DAM POP**
See also BEST 90:4; CA 17-20R; 140; CANR
9, 28, 59; SATA 2; SATA-Obit 74

Hichens, Robert S. 1864-1950 .... **TCLC 64**
See also DLB 153

Higgins, George V(incent)
1939- .... **CLC 4, 7, 10, 18**
See also CA 77-80; CAAS 5; CANR 17, 51;
DLB 2; DLBY 81; INT CANR-17; MTCW

Higginson, Thomas Wentworth
1823-1911 .... **TCLC 36**
See also DLB 1, 64

Highet, Helen
See MacInnes, Helen (Clark)

Highsmith, (Mary) Patricia
1921-1995 .... **CLC 2, 4, 14, 42, 102;
DAM NOV, POP**
See also CA 1-4R; 147; CANR 1, 20, 48, 62;
MTCW

Highwater, Jamake (Mamake)
1942(?)- .... **CLC 12**
See also AAYA 7; CA 65-68; CAAS 7; CANR
10, 34; CLR 17; DLB 52; DLBY 85; JRDA;
MAICYA; SATA 32, 69; SATA-Brief 30

Highway, Tomson
1951- .... **CLC 92; DAC; DAM MULT**
See also CA 151; NNAL

Higuchi, Ichiyo 1872-1896 .... **NCLC 49**

Hijuelos, Oscar
1951- ...... **CLC 65; DAM MULT, POP;
HLC**
See also BEST 90:1; CA 123; CANR 50; DLB
145; HW

Hikmet, Nazim 1902(?)-1963 .... **CLC 40**
See also CA 141; 93-96

Hildegard von Bingen
1098-1179 .... **CMLC 20**
See also DLB 148

Hildesheimer, Wolfgang
1916-1991 .... **CLC 49**
See also CA 101; 135; DLB 69, 124

Hill, Geoffrey (William)
1932- ...... **CLC 5, 8, 18, 45; DAM POET**
See also CA 81-84; CANR 21; CDBLB 1960
to Present; DLB 40; MTCW

Hill, George Roy 1921- .... **CLC 26**
See also CA 110; 122

Hill, John
See Koontz, Dean R(ay)

Hill, Susan (Elizabeth)
1942- ... **CLC 4; DAB; DAM MST, NOV**
See also CA 33-36R; CANR 29; DLB 14, 139;
MTCW

Hillerman, Tony
1925- .... **CLC 62; DAM POP**
See also AAYA 6; BEST 89:1; CA 29-32R;
CANR 21, 42; SATA 6

Hillesum, Etty 1914-1943 .... **TCLC 49**
See also CA 137

Hilliard, Noel (Harvey) 1929- .... **CLC 15**
See also CA 9-12R; CANR 7

Hillis, Rick 1956- .... **CLC 66**
See also CA 134

Hilton, James 1900-1954 .... **TCLC 21**
See also CA 108; DLB 34, 77; SATA 34

Himes, Chester (Bomar)
1909-1984 ...... **CLC 2, 4, 7, 18, 58; BLC;
DAM MULT**
See also BW 2; CA 25-28R; 114; CANR 22;
DLB 2, 76, 143; MTCW

Hinde, Thomas .... **CLC 6, 11**
See also Chitty, Thomas Willes

Hindin, Nathan
See Bloch, Robert (Albert)

Hine, (William) Daryl 1936- .... **CLC 15**
See also CA 1-4R; CAAS 15; CANR 1, 20;
DLB 60

Hinkson, Katharine Tynan
See Tynan, Katharine

Hinton, S(usan) E(loise)
1950- .... **CLC 30; DA; DAB; DAC;
DAM MST, NOV**
See also AAYA 2; CA 81-84; CANR 32, 62;
CLR 3, 23; JRDA; MAICYA; MTCW; SATA
19, 58

Hippius, Zinaida .... **TCLC 9**
See also Gippius, Zinaida (Nikolayevna)

Hiraoka, Kimitake 1925-1970
See Mishima, Yukio
See also CA 97-100; 29-32R; DAM DRAM;
MTCW

Hirsch, E(ric) D(onald), Jr. 1928- .... **CLC 79**
See also CA 25-28R; CANR 27, 51; DLB 67;
INT CANR-27; MTCW

Hirsch, Edward 1950- .... **CLC 31, 50**
See also CA 104; CANR 20, 42; DLB 120

Hitchcock, Alfred (Joseph)
1899-1980 .... **CLC 16**
See also AAYA 22; CA 159; 97-100; SATA 27;
SATA-Obit 24

Hitler, Adolf 1889-1945 .... **TCLC 53**
See also CA 117; 147

Hoagland, Edward 1932- .... CLC 28
See also CA 1-4R; CANR 2, 31, 57; DLB 6;
SATA 51

Hoban, Russell (Conwell)
1925- .... CLC 7, 25; DAM NOV
See also CA 5-8R; CANR 23, 37; CLR 3; DLB
52; MAICYA; MTCW; SATA 1, 40, 78

Hobbes, Thomas 1588-1679 .... LC 36
See also DLB 151

Hobbs, Perry
See Blackmur, R(ichard) P(almer)

Hobson, Laura Z(ametkin)
1900-1986 .... CLC 7, 25
See also CA 17-20R; 118; CANR 55; DLB 28;
SATA 52

Hochhuth, Rolf
1931- .... CLC 4, 11, 18; DAM DRAM
See also CA 5-8R; CANR 33; DLB 124;
MTCW

Hochman, Sandra 1936- .... CLC 3, 8
See also CA 5-8R; DLB 5

Hochwaelder, Fritz
1911-1986 .... CLC 36; DAM DRAM
See also CA 29-32R; 120; CANR 42; MTCW

Hochwalder, Fritz
See Hochwaelder, Fritz

Hocking, Mary (Eunice) 1921- .... CLC 13
See also CA 101; CANR 18, 40

Hodgins, Jack 1938- .... CLC 23
See also CA 93-96; DLB 60

Hodgson, William Hope
1877(?)-1918 .... TCLC 13
See also CA 111; DLB 70, 153, 156, 178

Hoeg, Peter 1957- .... CLC 95
See also CA 151

Hoffman, Alice
1952- .... CLC 51; DAM NOV
See also CA 77-80; CANR 34; MTCW

Hoffman, Daniel (Gerard)
1923- .... CLC 6, 13, 23
See also CA 1-4R; CANR 4; DLB 5

Hoffman, Stanley 1944- .... CLC 5
See also CA 77-80

Hoffman, William M(oses) 1939- ...... CLC 40
See also CA 57-60; CANR 11

Hoffmann, E(rnst) T(heodor) A(madeus)
1776-1822 .... NCLC 2; SSC 13
See also DLB 90; SATA 27

Hofmann, Gert 1931- .... CLC 54
See also CA 128

Hofmannsthal, Hugo von
1874-1929 .... TCLC 11; DAM DRAM;
DC 4
See also CA 106; 153; DLB 81, 118

Hogan, Linda
1947- .... CLC 73; DAM MULT
See also CA 120; CANR 45; DLB 175;
NNAL

Hogarth, Charles
See Creasey, John

Hogarth, Emmett
See Polonsky, Abraham (Lincoln)

Hogg, James 1770-1835 .... NCLC 4
See also DLB 93, 116, 159

Holbach, Paul Henri Thiry Baron
1723-1789 .... LC 14

Holberg, Ludvig 1684-1754 .... LC 6

Holden, Ursula 1921- .... CLC 18
See also CA 101; CAAS 8; CANR 22

Holderlin, (Johann Christian) Friedrich
1770-1843 .... NCLC 16; PC 4

Holdstock, Robert
See Holdstock, Robert P.

Holdstock, Robert P. 1948- .... CLC 39
See also CA 131

Holland, Isabelle 1920- .... CLC 21
See also AAYA 11; CA 21-24R; CANR 10, 25,
47; JRDA; MAICYA; SATA 8, 70

Holland, Marcus
See Caldwell, (Janet Miriam) Taylor (Holland)

Hollander, John 1929- .... CLC 2, 5, 8, 14
See also CA 1-4R; CANR 1, 52; DLB 5; SATA
13

Hollander, Paul
See Silverberg, Robert

Holleran, Andrew 1943(?)- .... CLC 38
See also CA 144

Hollinghurst, Alan 1954- .... CLC 55, 91
See also CA 114

Hollis, Jim
See Summers, Hollis (Spurgeon, Jr.)

Holly, Buddy 1936-1959 .... TCLC 65

Holmes, Gordon
See Shiel, M(atthew) P(hipps)

Holmes, John
See Souster, (Holmes) Raymond

Holmes, John Clellon 1926-1988 ...... CLC 56
See also CA 9-12R; 125; CANR 4; DLB
16

Holmes, Oliver Wendell
1809-1894 .... NCLC 14
See also CDALB 1640-1865; DLB 1; SATA
34

Holmes, Raymond
See Souster, (Holmes) Raymond

Holt, Victoria
See Hibbert, Eleanor Alice Burford

Holub, Miroslav 1923- .... CLC 4
See also CA 21-24R; CANR 10

Homer c. 8th cent. B.C.- ... CMLC 1, 16; DA;
DAB; DAC; DAM MST, POET; WLCS
See also DLB 176

Honig, Edwin 1919- .... CLC 33
See also CA 5-8R; CAAS 8; CANR 4, 45; DLB
5

Hood, Hugh (John Blagdon)
1928- .... CLC 15, 28
See also CA 49-52; CAAS 17; CANR 1, 33;
DLB 53

Hood, Thomas 1799-1845 .... NCLC 16
See also DLB 96

Hooker, (Peter) Jeremy 1941- .... CLC 43
See also CA 77-80; CANR 22; DLB 40

hooks, bell .... CLC 94
See also Watkins, Gloria

Hope, A(lec) D(erwent) 1907- .... CLC 3, 51
See also CA 21-24R; CANR 33; MTCW

Hope, Brian
See Creasey, John

Hope, Christopher (David Tully)
1944- .... CLC 52
See also CA 106; CANR 47; SATA 62

Hopkins, Gerard Manley
1844-1889 .... NCLC 17; DA; DAB;
DAC; DAM MST, POET; PC 15; WLC
See also CDBLB 1890-1914; DLB 35, 57

Hopkins, John (Richard) 1931- .... CLC 4
See also CA 85-88

Hopkins, Pauline Elizabeth
1859-1930 .... TCLC 28; BLC; DAM
MULT
See also BW 2; CA 141; DLB 50

Hopkinson, Francis 1737-1791 .... LC 25
See also DLB 31

Hopley-Woolrich, Cornell George 1903-1968
See Woolrich, Cornell
See also CA 13-14; CANR 58; CAP 1

Horatio
See Proust, (Valentin-Louis-George-Eugene-)
Marcel

Horgan, Paul (George Vincent O'Shaughnessy)
1903-1995 .... CLC 9, 53; DAM NOV
See also CA 13-16R; 147; CANR 9, 35; DLB
102; DLBY 85; INT CANR-9; MTCW;
SATA 13; SATA-Obit 84

Horn, Peter
See Kuttner, Henry

Hornem, Horace Esq.
See Byron, George Gordon (Noel)

Horney, Karen (Clementine Theodore Danielsen) 1885-1952 .... **TCLC 71**
See also CA 114

Hornung, E(rnest) W(illiam)
1866-1921 .... **TCLC 59**
See also CA 108; 160; DLB 70

Horovitz, Israel (Arthur) 1939- ...... **CLC 56; DAM DRAM**
See also CA 33-36R; CANR 46, 59; DLB 7

Horvath, Odon von
See Horvath, Oedoen von
See also DLB 85, 124

Horvath, Oedoen von
1901-1938 .... **TCLC 45**
See also Horvath, Odon von
See also CA 118

Horwitz, Julius 1920-1986 .... **CLC 14**
See also CA 9-12R; 119; CANR 12

Hospital, Janette Turner 1942- .... **CLC 42**
See also CA 108; CANR 48

Hostos, E. M. de
See Hostos (y Bonilla), Eugenio Maria de

Hostos, Eugenio M. de
See Hostos (y Bonilla), Eugenio Maria de

Hostos, Eugenio Maria
See Hostos (y Bonilla), Eugenio Maria de

Hostos (y Bonilla), Eugenio Maria de
1839-1903 .... **TCLC 24**
See also CA 123; 131; HW

Houdini
See Lovecraft, H(oward) P(hillips)

Hougan, Carolyn 1943- .... **CLC 34**
See also CA 139

Household, Geoffrey (Edward West) 1900-
1988 .... **CLC 11**
See also CA 77-80; 126; CANR 58; DLB 87; SATA 14; SATA-Obit 59

Housman, A(lfred) E(dward)
1859-1936 .... **TCLC 1, 10; DA; DAB; DAC; DAM MST, POET; PC 2; WLCS**
See also CA 104; 125; DLB 19; MTCW

Housman, Laurence 1865-1959 .... **TCLC 7**
See also CA 106; 155; DLB 10; SATA 25

Howard, Elizabeth Jane 1923- ..... **CLC 7, 29**
See also CA 5-8R; CANR 8, 62

Howard, Maureen 1930- .... **CLC 5, 14, 46**
See also CA 53-56; CANR 31; DLBY 83; INT CANR-31; MTCW

Howard, Richard 1929- .... **CLC 7, 10, 47**
See also AITN 1; CA 85-88; CANR 25; DLB 5; INT CANR-25

Howard, Robert E(rvin)
1906-1936 .... **TCLC 8**
See also CA 105; 157

Howard, Warren F.
See Pohl, Frederik

Howe, Fanny 1940- .... **CLC 47**
See also CA 117; CAAS 27; SATA-Brief 52

Howe, Irving 1920-1993 .... **CLC 85**
See also CA 9-12R; 141; CANR 21, 50; DLB 67; MTCW

Howe, Julia Ward 1819-1910 .... **TCLC 21**
See also CA 117; DLB 1

Howe, Susan 1937- .... **CLC 72**
See also CA 160; DLB 120

Howe, Tina 1937- .... **CLC 48**
See also CA 109

Howell, James 1594(?)-1666 .... **LC 13**
See also DLB 151

Howells, W. D.
See Howells, William Dean

Howells, William D.
See Howells, William Dean

Howells, William Dean
1837-1920 .... **TCLC 7, 17, 41**
See also CA 104; 134; CDALB 1865-1917; DLB 12, 64, 74, 79

Howes, Barbara 1914-1996 .... **CLC 15**
See also CA 9-12R; 151; CAAS 3; CANR 53; SATA 5

Hrabal, Bohumil 1914-1997 .... **CLC 13, 67**
See also CA 106; 156; CAAS 12; CANR 57

Hsun, Lu
See Lu Hsun

Hubbard, L(afayette) Ron(ald)
1911-1986 .... **CLC 43; DAM POP**
See also CA 77-80; 118; CANR 52

Huch, Ricarda (Octavia)
1864-1947 .... **TCLC 13**
See also CA 111; DLB 66

Huddle, David 1942- .... **CLC 49**
See also CA 57-60; CAAS 20; DLB 130

Hudson, Jeffrey
See Crichton, (John) Michael

Hudson, W(illiam) H(enry)
1841-1922 .... **TCLC 29**
See also CA 115; DLB 98, 153, 174; SATA 35

Hueffer, Ford Madox
See Ford, Ford Madox

Hughart, Barry 1934- .... **CLC 39**
See also CA 137

Hughes, Colin
See Creasey, John

Hughes, David (John) 1930- .... **CLC 48**
See also CA 116; 129; DLB 14

Hughes, Edward James
See Hughes, Ted
See also DAM MST, POET

Hughes, (James) Langston
1902-1967 .... **CLC 1, 5, 10, 15, 35, 44; BLC; DA; DAB; DAC; DAM DRAM, MST, MULT, POET; DC 3; PC 1; SSC 6; WLC**
See also AAYA 12; BW 1; CA 1-4R; 25-28R; CANR 1, 34; CDALB 1929-1941; CLR 17; DLB 4, 7, 48, 51, 86; JRDA; MAICYA; MTCW; SATA 4, 33

Hughes, Richard (Arthur Warren)
1900-1976 .... **CLC 1, 11; DAM NOV**
See also CA 5-8R; 65-68; CANR 4; DLB 15, 161; MTCW; SATA 8; SATA-Obit 25

Hughes, Ted
1930- .. **CLC 2, 4, 9, 14, 37; DAB; DAC; PC 7**
See also Hughes, Edward James
See also CA 1-4R; CANR 1, 33; CLR 3; DLB 40, 161; MAICYA; MTCW; SATA 49; SATA-Brief 27

Hugo, Richard F(ranklin)
1923-1982 .. **CLC 6, 18, 32; DAM POET**
See also CA 49-52; 108; CANR 3; DLB 5

Hugo, Victor (Marie)
1802-1885 ... **NCLC 3, 10, 21; DA; DAB; DAC; DAM DRAM, MST, NOV, POET; PC 17; WLC**
See also DLB 119; SATA 47

Huidobro, Vicente
See Huidobro Fernandez, Vicente Garcia

Huidobro Fernandez, Vicente Garcia
1893-1948 .... **TCLC 31**
See also CA 131; HW

Hulme, Keri 1947- .... **CLC 39**
See also CA 125; INT 125

Hulme, T(homas) E(rnest)
1883-1917 .... **TCLC 21**
See also CA 117; DLB 19

Hume, David 1711-1776 .... **LC 7**
See also DLB 104

Humphrey, William 1924-1997 .... **CLC 45**
See also CA 77-80; 160; DLB 6

Humphreys, Emyr Owen 1919- .... **CLC 47**
See also CA 5-8R; CANR 3, 24; DLB 15

Humphreys, Josephine 1945- ..... **CLC 34, 57**
See also CA 121; 127; INT 127

Huneker, James Gibbons
1857-1921 .... **TCLC 65**
See also DLB 71

Hungerford, Pixie
See Brinsmead, H(esba) F(ay)

Hunt, E(verette) Howard, (Jr.)
1918- .... **CLC 3**
See also AITN 1; CA 45-48; CANR 2, 47

Ives, Morgan
See Bradley, Marion Zimmer

J. R. S.
See Gogarty, Oliver St. John

Jabran, Kahlil
See Gibran, Kahlil

Jabran, Khalil
See Gibran, Kahlil

Jackson, Daniel
See Wingrove, David (John)

Jackson, Jesse 1908-1983 .... **CLC 12**
See also BW 1; CA 25-28R; 109; CANR 27;
CLR 28; MAICYA; SATA 2, 29; SATA-Obit
48

Jackson, Laura (Riding) 1901-1991
See Riding, Laura
See also CA 65-68; 135; CANR 28; DLB 48

Jackson, Sam
See Trumbo, Dalton

Jackson, Sara
See Wingrove, David (John)

Jackson, Shirley
1919-1965 .... **CLC 11, 60, 87; DA; DAC;
DAM MST; SSC 9; WLC**
See also AAYA 9; CA 1-4R; 25-28R; CANR
4, 52; CDALB 1941-1968; DLB 6; SATA 2

Jacob, (Cyprien-)Max 1876-1944 .... **TCLC 6**
See also CA 104

Jacobs, Jim 1942- .... **CLC 12**
See also CA 97-100; INT 97-100

Jacobs, W(illiam) W(ymark)
1863-1943 .... **TCLC 22**
See also CA 121; DLB 135

Jacobsen, Jens Peter 1847-1885 .... **NCLC 34**

Jacobsen, Josephine 1908- .... **CLC 48, 102**
See also CA 33-36R; CAAS 18; CANR 23, 48

Jacobson, Dan 1929- .... **CLC 4, 14**
See also CA 1-4R; CANR 2, 25; DLB 14;
MTCW

Jacqueline
See Carpentier (y Valmont), Alejo

Jagger, Mick 1944- .... **CLC 17**

Jakes, John (William)
1932- .... **CLC 29; DAM NOV, POP**
See also BEST 89:4; CA 57-60; CANR 10, 43;
DLBY 83; INT CANR-10; MTCW; SATA
62

James, Andrew
See Kirkup, James

James, C(yril) L(ionel) R(obert)
1901-1989 .... **CLC 33**
See also BW 2; CA 117; 125; 128; CANR 62;
DLB 125; MTCW

James, Daniel (Lewis) 1911-1988
See Santiago, Danny
See also CA 125

James, Dynely
See Mayne, William (James Carter)

James, Henry Sr. 1811-1882 .... **NCLC 53**

James, Henry
1843-1916 ... **TCLC 2, 11, 24, 40, 47, 64;
DA; DAB; DAC; DAM MST, NOV; SSC
8; WLC**
See also CA 104; 132; CDALB 1865-
1917; DLB 12, 71, 74; DLBD 13;
MTCW

James, M. R.
See James, Montague (Rhodes)
See also DLB 156

James, Montague (Rhodes)
1862-1936 .... **TCLC 6; SSC 16**
See also CA 104

James, P. D. .... **CLC 18, 46**
See also White, Phyllis Dorothy James
See also BEST 90:2; CDBLB 1960 to Present;
DLB 87

James, Philip
See Moorcock, Michael (John)

James, William
1842-1910 .... **TCLC 15, 32**
See also CA 109

James I 1394-1437 .... **LC 20**

Jameson, Anna 1794-1860 .... **NCLC 43**
See also DLB 99, 166

Jami, Nur al-Din 'Abd al-Rahman
1414-1492 .... **LC 9**

Jammes, Francis 1868-1938 .... **TCLC 75**

Jandl, Ernst 1925- .... **CLC 34**

Janowitz, Tama 1957- .. **CLC 43; DAM POP**
See also CA 106; CANR 52

Japrisot, Sebastien 1931- .... **CLC 90**

Jarrell, Randall
1914-1965 .... **CLC 1, 2, 6, 9, 13, 49;
DAM POET**
See also CA 5-8R; 25-28R; CABS 2;
CANR 6, 34; CDALB 1941-1968; CLR
6; DLB 48, 52; MAICYA; MTCW;
SATA 7

Jarry, Alfred
1873-1907 ... **TCLC 2, 14; DAM DRAM;
SSC 20**
See also CA 104; 153

Jarvis, E. K.
See Bloch, Robert (Albert); Ellison, Harlan
(Jay); Silverberg, Robert

Jeake, Samuel, Jr.
See Aiken, Conrad (Potter)

Jean Paul 1763-1825 .... **NCLC 7**

Jefferies, (John) Richard
1848-1887 .... **NCLC 47**
See also DLB 98, 141; SATA 16

Jeffers, (John) Robinson
1887-1962 ...... **CLC 2, 3, 11, 15, 54; DA;
DAC; DAM MST, POET; PC 17; WLC**
See also CA 85-88; CANR 35; CDALB 1917-
1929; DLB 45; MTCW

Jefferson, Janet
See Mencken, H(enry) L(ouis)

Jefferson, Thomas 1743-1826 .... **NCLC 11**
See also CDALB 1640-1865; DLB 31

Jeffrey, Francis 1773-1850 .... **NCLC 33**
See also DLB 107

Jelakowitch, Ivan
See Heijermans, Herman

Jellicoe, (Patricia) Ann 1927- .... **CLC 27**
See also CA 85-88; DLB 13

Jen, Gish .... **CLC 70**
See also Jen, Lillian

Jen, Lillian 1956(?)-
See Jen, Gish
See also CA 135

Jenkins, (John) Robin 1912- .... **CLC 52**
See also CA 1-4R; CANR 1; DLB 14

Jennings, Elizabeth (Joan)
1926- .... **CLC 5, 14**
See also CA 61-64; CAAS 5; CANR 8, 39;
DLB 27; MTCW; SATA 66

Jennings, Waylon 1937- .... **CLC 21**

Jensen, Johannes V. 1873-1950 ...... **TCLC 41**

Jensen, Laura (Linnea) 1948- .... **CLC 37**
See also CA 103

Jerome, Jerome K(lapka)
1859-1927 .... **TCLC 23**
See also CA 119; DLB 10, 34, 135

Jerrold, Douglas William
1803-1857 .... **NCLC 2**
See also DLB 158, 159

Jewett, (Theodora) Sarah Orne
1849-1909 .... **TCLC 1, 22; SSC 6**
See also CA 108; 127; DLB 12, 74; SATA 15

Jewsbury, Geraldine (Endsor)
1812-1880 .... **NCLC 22**
See also DLB 21

Jhabvala, Ruth Prawer
1927- .... **CLC 4, 8, 29, 94; DAB; DAM
NOV**
See also CA 1-4R; CANR 2, 29, 51; DLB 139;
INT CANR-29; MTCW

Jibran, Kahlil
See Gibran, Kahlil

Joyce, James (Augustine Aloysius)
1882-1941 ... TCLC 3, 8, 16, 35, 52; DA;
DAB; DAC; DAM MST, NOV, POET;
SSC 26; WLC
See also CA 104; 126; CDBLB 1914-1945;
DLB 10, 19, 36, 162; MTCW

Jozsef, Attila
1905-1937 .... TCLC 22
See also CA 116

Juana Ines de la Cruz 1651(?)-1695 ...... LC 5

Judd, Cyril
See Kornbluth, C(yril) M.; Pohl, Frederik

Julian of Norwich
1342(?)-1416(?) .... LC 6
See also DLB 146

Juniper, Alex
See Hospital, Janette Turner

Junius
See Luxemburg, Rosa

Just, Ward (Swift)
1935- ....CLC 4, 27
See also CA 25-28R; CANR 32; INT CANR-
32

Justice, Donald (Rodney)
1925- .... CLC 6, 19, 102; DAM POET
See also CA 5-8R; CANR 26, 54; DLBY 83;
INT CANR-26

Juvenal c. 55-c. 127 .... CMLC 8

Juvenis
See Bourne, Randolph S(illiman)

Kacew, Romain 1914-1980
See Gary, Romain
See also CA 108; 102

Kadare, Ismail 1936- .... CLC 52

Kadohata, Cynthia .... CLC 59
See also CA 140

Kafka, Franz
1883-1924 ..... TCLC 2, 6, 13, 29, 47, 53;
DA; DAB; DAC; DAM MST, NOV; SSC
5, 29; WLC
See also CA 105; 126; DLB 81; MTCW

Kahanovitsch, Pinkhes
See Der Nister

Kahn, Roger 1927- .... CLC 30
See also CA 25-28R; CANR 44; DLB 171;
SATA 37

Kain, Saul
See Sassoon, Siegfried (Lorraine)

Kaiser, Georg
1878-1945 .... TCLC 9
See also CA 106; DLB 124

Kaletski, Alexander
1946- .... CLC 39
See also CA 118; 143

Kalidasa fl. c. 400- .... CMLC 9

Kallman, Chester (Simon)
1921-1975 .... CLC 2
See also CA 45-48; 53-56; CANR 3

Kaminsky, Melvin 1926-
See Brooks, Mel
See also CA 65-68; CANR 16

Kaminsky, Stuart M(elvin)
1934- .... CLC 59
See also CA 73-76; CANR 29, 53

Kane, Francis
See Robbins, Harold

Kane, Paul
See Simon, Paul (Frederick)

Kane, Wilson
See Bloch, Robert (Albert)

Kanin, Garson 1912- .... CLC 22
See also AITN 1; CA 5-8R; CANR 7; DLB 7

Kaniuk, Yoram 1930- .... CLC 19
See also CA 134

Kant, Immanuel 1724-1804 .... NCLC 27
See also DLB 94

Kantor, MacKinlay 1904-1977............ CLC 7
See also CA 61-64; 73-76; CANR 60; DLB 9,
102

Kaplan, David Michael 1946- .... CLC 50

Kaplan, James 1951- .... CLC 59
See also CA 135

Karageorge, Michael
See Anderson, Poul (William)

Karamzin, Nikolai Mikhailovich
1766-1826 .... NCLC 3
See also DLB 150

Karapanou, Margarita 1946- .... CLC 13
See also CA 101

Karinthy, Frigyes 1887-1938......... TCLC 47

Karl, Frederick R(obert)
1927- .... CLC 34
See also CA 5-8R; CANR 3, 44

Kastel, Warren
See Silverberg, Robert

Kataev, Evgeny Petrovich 1903-1942
See Petrov, Evgeny
See also CA 120

Kataphusin
See Ruskin, John

Katz, Steve 1935- .... CLC 47
See also CA 25-28R; CAAS 14; CANR 12;
DLBY 83

Kauffman, Janet 1945- .... CLC 42
See also CA 117; CANR 43; DLBY 86

Kaufman, Bob (Garnell)
1925-1986 .... CLC 49
See also BW 1; CA 41-44R; 118; CANR 22;
DLB 16, 41

Kaufman, George S. 1889-1961 ...... CLC 38;
DAM DRAM
See also CA 108; 93-96; DLB 7; INT 108

Kaufman, Sue .... CLC 3, 8
See also Barondess, Sue K(aufman)

Kavafis, Konstantinos Petrou 1863-1933
See Cavafy, C(onstantine) P(eter)
See also CA 104

Kavan, Anna 1901-1968......... CLC 5, 13, 82
See also CA 5-8R; CANR 6, 57; MTCW

Kavanagh, Dan
See Barnes, Julian (Patrick)

Kavanagh, Patrick (Joseph)
1904-1967 .... CLC 22
See also CA 123; 25-28R; DLB 15, 20; MTCW

Kawabata, Yasunari
1899-1972 .... CLC 2, 5, 9, 18; DAM
MULT; SSC 17
See also CA 93-96; 33-36R; DLB 180

Kaye, M(ary) M(argaret) 1909- .... CLC 28
See also CA 89-92; CANR 24, 60; MTCW;
SATA 62

Kaye, Mollie
See Kaye, M(ary) M(argaret)

Kaye-Smith, Sheila 1887-1956 .... TCLC 20
See also CA 118; DLB 36

Kaymor, Patrice Maguilene
See Senghor, Leopold Sedar

Kazan, Elia 1909- .... CLC 6, 16, 63
See also CA 21-24R; CANR 32

Kazantzakis, Nikos
1883(?)-1957 .... TCLC 2, 5, 33
See also CA 105; 132; MTCW

Kazin, Alfred 1915- .... CLC 34, 38
See also CA 1-4R; CAAS 7; CANR 1, 45; DLB 67

Keane, Mary Nesta (Skrine) 1904-1996
See Keane, Molly
See also CA 108; 114; 151

Keane, Molly .... CLC 31
See also Keane, Mary Nesta (Skrine)
See also INT 114

Keates, Jonathan 19(?)- .... CLC 34

Keaton, Buster 1895-1966 .... CLC 20

Keats, John
1795-1821 .... NCLC 8; DA; DAB; DAC;
DAM MST, POET; PC 1; WLC
See also CDBLB 1789-1832; DLB 96, 110

Keene, Donald 1922- .... CLC 34
See also CA 1-4R; CANR 5

King, Stephen (Edwin)
1947- ... **CLC 12, 26, 37, 61; DAM NOV, POP; SSC 17**
See also AAYA 1, 17; BEST 90:1; CA 61-64; CANR 1, 30, 52; DLB 143; DLBY 80; JRDA; MTCW; SATA 9, 55

King, Steve
See King, Stephen (Edwin)

King, Thomas
1943- .... **CLC 89; DAC; DAM MULT**
See also CA 144; DLB 175; NNAL

Kingman, Lee .... **CLC 17**
See also Natti, (Mary) Lee
See also SAAS 3; SATA 1, 67

Kingsley, Charles 1819-1875 .... **NCLC 35**
See also DLB 21, 32, 163; YABC 2

Kingsley, Sidney 1906-1995 .... **CLC 44**
See also CA 85-88; 147; DLB 7

Kingsolver, Barbara
1955- .... **CLC 55, 81; DAM POP**
See also AAYA 15; CA 129; 134; CANR 60; INT 134

Kingston, Maxine (Ting Ting) Hong
1940- ...... **CLC 12, 19, 58; DAM MULT, NOV; WLCS**
See also AAYA 8; CA 69-72; CANR 13, 38; DLB 173; DLBY 80; INT CANR-13; MTCW; SATA 53

Kinnell, Galway
1927- .... **CLC 1, 2, 3, 5, 13, 29**
See also CA 9-12R; CANR 10, 34; DLB 5; DLBY 87; INT CANR-34; MTCW

Kinsella, Thomas 1928- .... **CLC 4, 19**
See also CA 17-20R; CANR 15; DLB 27; MTCW

Kinsella, W(illiam) P(atrick)
1935- ..... **CLC 27, 43; DAC; DAM NOV, POP**
See also AAYA 7; CA 97-100; CAAS 7; CANR 21, 35; INT CANR-21; MTCW

Kipling, (Joseph) Rudyard
1865-1936 .... **TCLC 8, 17; DA; DAB; DAC; DAM MST, POET; PC 3; SSC 5; WLC**
See also CA 105; 120; CANR 33; CDBLB 1890-1914; CLR 39; DLB 19, 34, 141, 156; MAICYA; MTCW; YABC 2

Kirkup, James 1918- .... **CLC 1**
See also CA 1-4R; CAAS 4; CANR 2; DLB 27; SATA 12

Kirkwood, James
1930(?)-1989 .... **CLC 9**
See also AITN 2; CA 1-4R; 128; CANR 6, 40

Kirshner, Sidney
See Kingsley, Sidney

Kis, Danilo 1935-1989 .... **CLC 57**
See also CA 109; 118; 129; CANR 61; DLB 181; MTCW

Kivi, Aleksis 1834-1872 .... **NCLC 30**

Kizer, Carolyn (Ashley)
1925- .... **CLC 15, 39, 80; DAM POET**
See also CA 65-68; CAAS 5; CANR 24; DLB 5, 169

Klabund 1890-1928 .... **TCLC 44**
See also DLB 66

Klappert, Peter 1942- .... **CLC 57**
See also CA 33-36R; DLB 5

Klein, A(braham) M(oses)
1909-1972 .... **CLC 19; DAB; DAC; DAM MST**
See also CA 101; 37-40R; DLB 68

Klein, Norma 1938-1989 .... **CLC 30**
See also AAYA 2; CA 41-44R; 128; CANR 15, 37; CLR 2, 19; INT CANR-15; JRDA; MAICYA; SAAS 1; SATA 7, 57

Klein, T(heodore) E(ibon) D(onald)
1947- .... **CLC 34**
See also CA 119; CANR 44

Kleist, Heinrich von
1777-1811 ... **NCLC 2, 37; DAM DRAM; SSC 22**
See also DLB 90

Klima, Ivan 1931- .... **CLC 56; DAM NOV**
See also CA 25-28R; CANR 17, 50

Klimentov, Andrei Platonovich 1899-1951
See Platonov, Andrei
See also CA 108

Klinger, Friedrich Maximilian von
1752-1831 .... **NCLC 1**
See also DLB 94

Klingsor the Magician
See Hartmann, Sadakichi

Klopstock, Friedrich Gottlieb
1724-1803 .... **NCLC 11**
See also DLB 97

Knapp, Caroline 1959- .... **CLC 99**
See also CA 154

Knebel, Fletcher 1911-1993 .... **CLC 14**
See also AITN 1; CA 1-4R; 140; CAAS 3; CANR 1, 36; SATA 36; SATA-Obit 75

Knickerbocker, Diedrich
See Irving, Washington

Knight, Etheridge
1931-1991 .... **CLC 40; BLC; DAM POET; PC 14**
See also BW 1; CA 21-24R; 133; CANR 23; DLB 41

Knight, Sarah Kemble 1666-1727 .... **LC 7**
See also DLB 24

Knister, Raymond 1899-1932 .... **TCLC 56**
See also DLB 68

Knowles, John
1926- .... **CLC 1, 4, 10, 26; DA; DAC; DAM MST, NOV**
See also AAYA 10; CA 17-20R; CANR 40; CDALB 1968-1988; DLB 6; MTCW; SATA 8, 89

Knox, Calvin M.
See Silverberg, Robert

Knox, John c. 1505-1572 .... **LC 37**
See also DLB 132

Knye, Cassandra
See Disch, Thomas M(ichael)

Koch, C(hristopher) J(ohn)
1932- .... **CLC 42**
See also CA 127

Koch, Christopher
See Koch, C(hristopher) J(ohn)

Koch, Kenneth 1925- ..... **CLC 5, 8, 44; DAM POET**
See also CA 1-4R; CANR 6, 36, 57; DLB 5; INT CANR-36; SATA 65

Kochanowski, Jan 1530-1584 .... **LC 10**

Kock, Charles Paul de
1794-1871 .... **NCLC 16**

Koda Shigeyuki 1867-1947
See Rohan, Koda
See also CA 121

Koestler, Arthur
1905-1983 .... **CLC 1, 3, 6, 8, 15, 33**
See also CA 1-4R; 109; CANR 1, 33; CDBLB 1945-1960; DLBY 83; MTCW

Kogawa, Joy Nozomi
1935- .... **CLC 78; DAC; DAM MST, MULT**
See also CA 101; CANR 19, 62

Kohout, Pavel 1928- .... **CLC 13**
See also CA 45-48; CANR 3

Koizumi, Yakumo
See Hearn, (Patricio) Lafcadio (Tessima Carlos)

Kolmar, Gertrud 1894-1943 .... **TCLC 40**

Komunyakaa, Yusef 1947- .... **CLC 86, 94**
See also CA 147; DLB 120

Konrad, George
See Konrad, Gyoergy

Konrad, Gyoergy 1933- .... **CLC 4, 10, 73**
See also CA 85-88

Konwicki, Tadeusz 1926- .... **CLC 8, 28, 54**
See also CA 101; CAAS 9; CANR 39, 59; MTCW

Koontz, Dean R(ay)
1945- .... **CLC 78; DAM NOV, POP**
See also AAYA 9; BEST 89:3, 90:2; CA 108; CANR 19, 36, 52; MTCW; SATA 92

La Fayette, Marie (Madelaine Pioche de la Vergne Comtes 1634-1693 .... **LC 2**

Lafayette, Rene
See Hubbard, L(afayette) Ron(ald)

Laforgue, Jules
1860-1887 .... **NCLC 5, 53; PC 14; SSC 20**

Lagerkvist, Paer (Fabian)
1891-1974 .... **CLC 7, 10, 13, 54; DAM DRAM, NOV**
See also Lagerkvist, Par
See also CA 85-88; 49-52; MTCW

Lagerkvist, Par .... **SSC 12**
See also Lagerkvist, Paer (Fabian)

Lagerloef, Selma (Ottiliana Lovisa)
1858-1940 .... **TCLC 4, 36**
See also Lagerlof, Selma (Ottiliana Lovisa)
See also CA 108; SATA 15

Lagerlof, Selma (Ottiliana Lovisa)
See Lagerloef, Selma (Ottiliana Lovisa)
See also CLR 7; SATA 15

La Guma, (Justin) Alex(ander)
1925-1985 .... **CLC 19; DAM NOV**
See also BW 1; CA 49-52; 118; CANR 25; DLB 117; MTCW

Laidlaw, A. K.
See Grieve, C(hristopher) M(urray)

Lainez, Manuel Mujica
See Mujica Lainez, Manuel
See also HW

Laing, R(onald) D(avid)
1927-1989 .... **CLC 95**
See also CA 107; 129; CANR 34; MTCW

Lamartine, Alphonse (Marie Louis Prat) de
1790-1869 .. **NCLC 11; DAM POET; PC 16**

Lamb, Charles 1775-1834 ..... **NCLC 10; DA; DAB; DAC; DAM MST; WLC**
See also CDBLB 1789-1832; DLB 93, 107, 163; SATA 17

Lamb, Lady Caroline 1785-1828 ... **NCLC 38**
See also DLB 116

Lamming, George (William)
1927- .... **CLC 2, 4, 66; BLC; DAM MULT**
See also BW 2; CA 85-88; CANR 26; DLB 125; MTCW

L'Amour, Louis (Dearborn)
1908-1988 .... **CLC 25, 55; DAM NOV, POP**
See also AAYA 16; AITN 2; BEST 89:2; CA 1-4R; 125; CANR 3, 25, 40; DLBY 80; MTCW

Lampedusa, Giuseppe (Tomasi) di
1896-1957 .... **TCLC 13**
See also Tomasi di Lampedusa, Giuseppe
See also DLB 177

Lampman, Archibald 1861-1899 ... **NCLC 25**
See also DLB 92

Lancaster, Bruce 1896-1963 .... **CLC 36**
See also CA 9-10; CAP 1; SATA 9

Lanchester, John .... **CLC 99**

Landau, Mark Alexandrovich
See Aldanov, Mark (Alexandrovich)

Landau-Aldanov, Mark Alexandrovich
See Aldanov, Mark (Alexandrovich)

Landis, Jerry
See Simon, Paul (Frederick)

Landis, John 1950- .... **CLC 26**
See also CA 112; 122

Landolfi, Tommaso 1908-1979 .... **CLC 11, 49**
See also CA 127; 117; DLB 177

Landon, Letitia Elizabeth
1802-1838 .... **NCLC 15**
See also DLB 96

Landor, Walter Savage
1775-1864 .... **NCLC 14**
See also DLB 93, 107

Landwirth, Heinz 1927-
See Lind, Jakov
See also CA 9-12R; CANR 7

Lane, Patrick
1939- .... **CLC 25; DAM POET**
See also CA 97-100; CANR 54; DLB 53; INT 97-100

Lang, Andrew 1844-1912 .... **TCLC 16**
See also CA 114; 137; DLB 98, 141, 184; MAICYA; SATA 16

Lang, Fritz 1890-1976 .... **CLC 20, 103**
See also CA 77-80; 69-72; CANR 30

Lange, John
See Crichton, (John) Michael

Langer, Elinor 1939- .... **CLC 34**
See also CA 121

Langland, William
1330(?)-1400(?) **LC 19; DA; DAB; DAC; DAM MST, POET**
See also DLB 146

Langstaff, Launcelot
See Irving, Washington

Lanier, Sidney 1842-1881 ..... **NCLC 6; DAM POET**
See also DLB 64; DLBD 13; MAICYA; SATA 18

Lanyer, Aemilia 1569-1645 .... **LC 10, 30**
See also DLB 121

Lao Tzu .... **CMLC 7**

Lapine, James (Elliot) 1949- .... **CLC 39**
See also CA 123; 130; CANR 54; INT 130

Larbaud, Valery (Nicolas)
1881-1957 .... **TCLC 9**
See also CA 106; 152

Lardner, Ring
See Lardner, Ring(gold) W(ilmer)

Lardner, Ring W., Jr.
See Lardner, Ring(gold) W(ilmer)

Lardner, Ring(gold) W(ilmer)
1885-1933 .... **TCLC 2, 14**
See also CA 104; 131; CDALB 1917-1929; DLB 11, 25, 86; DLBD 16; MTCW

Laredo, Betty
See Codrescu, Andrei

Larkin, Maia
See Wojciechowska, Maia (Teresa)

Larkin, Philip (Arthur)
1922-1985 ... **CLC 3, 5, 8, 9, 13, 18, 33, 39, 64; DAB; DAM MST, POET**
See also CA 5-8R; 117; CANR 24, 62; CDBLB 1960 to Present; DLB 27; MTCW

Larra (y Sanchez de Castro), Mariano Jose de
1809-1837 .... **NCLC 17**

Larsen, Eric 1941- .... **CLC 55**
See also CA 132

Larsen, Nella
1891-1964 .... **CLC 37; BLC; DAM MULT**
See also BW 1; CA 125; DLB 51

Larson, Charles R(aymond) 1938- ... **CLC 31**
See also CA 53-56; CANR 4

Larson, Jonathan 1961(?)-1996 .... **CLC 99**

Las Casas, Bartolome de 1474-1566 ... **LC 31**

Lasch, Christopher 1932-1994 .... **CLC 102**
See also CA 73-76; 144; CANR 25; MTCW

Lasker-Schueler, Else 1869-1945 ... **TCLC 57**
See also DLB 66, 124

Latham, Jean Lee 1902- .... **CLC 12**
See also AITN 1; CA 5-8R; CANR 7; MAICYA; SATA 2, 68

Latham, Mavis
See Clark, Mavis Thorpe

Lathen, Emma .... **CLC 2**
See also Hennissart, Martha; Latsis, Mary J(ane)

Lathrop, Francis
See Leiber, Fritz (Reuter, Jr.)

Latsis, Mary J(ane)
See Lathen, Emma
See also CA 85-88

Lattimore, Richmond (Alexander)
1906-1984 .... **CLC 3**
See also CA 1-4R; 112; CANR 1

Leffland, Ella 1931-.............................. CLC 19
    See also CA 29-32R; CANR 35; DLBY 84;
    INT CANR-35; SATA 65

Leger, Alexis
    See Leger, (Marie-Rene Auguste) Alexis Saint-
    Leger

**Leger, (Marie-Rene Auguste) Alexis Saint-
    Leger** 1887-1975 .... CLC 11; DAM
    POET
    See also Perse, St.-John
    See also CA 13-16R; 61-64; CANR 43;
    MTCW

Leger, Saintleger
    See Leger, (Marie-Rene Auguste) Alexis Saint-
    Leger

Le Guin, Ursula K(roeber)
    1929- .... CLC 8, 13, 22, 45, 71; DAB;
    DAC; DAM MST, POP; SSC 12
    See also AAYA 9; AITN 1; CA 21-24R;
    CANR 9, 32, 52; CDALB 1968-1988;
    CLR 3, 28; DLB 8, 52; INT CANR-
    32; JRDA; MAICYA; MTCW; SATA 4,
    52

Lehmann, Rosamond (Nina)
    1901-1990 .... CLC 5
    See also CA 77-80; 131; CANR 8; DLB 15

Leiber, Fritz (Reuter, Jr.)
    1910-1992 .... CLC 25
    See also CA 45-48; 139; CANR 2, 40; DLB 8;
    MTCW; SATA 45; SATA-Obit 73

Leibniz, Gottfried Wilhelm von
    1646-1716 .... LC 35
    See also DLB 168

Leimbach, Martha 1963-
    See Leimbach, Marti
    See also CA 130

Leimbach, Marti .... CLC 65
    See also Leimbach, Martha

Leino, Eino .... TCLC 24
    See also Loennbohm, Armas Eino Leopold

Leiris, Michel (Julien)
    1901-1990 .... CLC 61
    See also CA 119; 128; 132

Leithauser, Brad
    1953- .... CLC 27
    See also CA 107; CANR 27; DLB 120

Lelchuk, Alan 1938- .... CLC 5
    See also CA 45-48; CAAS 20; CANR 1

Lem, Stanislaw
    1921- .... CLC 8, 15, 40
    See also CA 105; CAAS 1; CANR 32;
    MTCW

Lemann, Nancy 1956- .... CLC 39
    See also CA 118; 136

Lemonnier, (Antoine Louis) Camille
    1844-1913 .... TCLC 22
    See also CA 121

Lenau, Nikolaus 1802-1850 .... NCLC 16

L'Engle, Madeleine (Camp Franklin)
    1918- .... CLC 12; DAM POP
    See also AAYA 1; AITN 2; CA 1-4R; CANR
    3, 21, 39; CLR 1, 14; DLB 52; JRDA;
    MAICYA; MTCW; SAAS 15; SATA 1, 27,
    75

Lengyel, Jozsef
    1896-1975 .... CLC 7
    See also CA 85-88; 57-60

Lenin 1870-1924
    See Lenin, V. I.
    See also CA 121

Lenin, V. I. .... TCLC 67
    See also Lenin

Lennon, John (Ono)
    1940-1980 .... CLC 12, 35
    See also CA 102

Lennox, Charlotte Ramsay
    1729(?)-1804 .... NCLC 23
    See also DLB 39

Lentricchia, Frank (Jr.)
    1940- .... CLC 34
    See also CA 25-28R; CANR 19

Lenz, Siegfried
    1926- .... CLC 27
    See also CA 89-92; DLB 75

Leonard, Elmore (John, Jr.)
    1925- .... CLC 28, 34, 71; DAM POP
    See also AAYA 22; AITN 1; BEST
    89:1, 90:4; CA 81-84; CANR 12, 28,
    53; DLB 173; INT CANR-28;
    MTCW

Leonard, Hugh .... CLC 19
    See also Byrne, John Keyes
    See also DLB 13

Leonov, Leonid (Maximovich)
    1899-1994 .... CLC 92; DAM NOV
    See also CA 129; MTCW

Leopardi, (Conte) Giacomo
    1798-1837 .... NCLC 22

Le Reveler
    See Artaud, Antonin (Marie Joseph)

Lerman, Eleanor
    1952- .... CLC 9
    See also CA 85-88

Lerman, Rhoda
    1936- .... CLC 56
    See also CA 49-52

Lermontov, Mikhail Yuryevich
    1814-1841 .... NCLC 47; PC 18

Leroux, Gaston
    1868-1927 .... TCLC 25
    See also CA 108; 136; SATA 65

Lesage, Alain-Rene 1668-1747 .... LC 28

Leskov, Nikolai (Semyonovich)
    1831-1895 .... NCLC 25

Lessing, Doris (May)
    1919-.... CLC 1, 2, 3, 6, 10, 15, 22, 40,
    **94; DA; DAB; DAC; DAM MST,
    NOV; SSC 6; WLCS**
    See also CA 9-12R; CAAS 14; CANR 33, 54;
    CDBLB 1960 to Present; DLB 15, 139;
    DLBY 85; MTCW

Lessing, Gotthold Ephraim
    1729-1781 .... LC 8
    See also DLB 97

Lester, Richard 1932- .... CLC 20

Lever, Charles (James)
    1806-1872 .... NCLC 23
    See also DLB 21

Leverson, Ada 1865(?)-1936(?) ...... TCLC 18
    See also Elaine
    See also CA 117; DLB 153

Levertov, Denise
    1923- .... CLC 1, 2, 3, 5, 8, 15, 28, 66;
    DAM POET; PC 11
    See also CA 1-4R; CAAS 19; CANR 3, 29,
    50; DLB 5, 165; INT CANR-29; MTCW

Levi, Jonathan .... CLC 76

Levi, Peter (Chad Tigar) 1931- .... CLC 41
    See also CA 5-8R; CANR 34; DLB 40

Levi, Primo
    1919-1987 .... CLC 37, 50; SSC 12
    See also CA 13-16R; 122; CANR 12, 33, 61;
    DLB 177; MTCW

Levin, Ira 1929- .... CLC 3, 6; DAM POP
    See also CA 21-24R; CANR 17, 44; MTCW;
    SATA 66

Levin, Meyer
    1905-1981 .... CLC 7; DAM POP
    See also AITN 1; CA 9-12R; 104; CANR 15;
    DLB 9, 28; DLBY 81; SATA 21; SATA-Obit
    27

Levine, Norman 1924-........................ CLC 54
    See also CA 73-76; CAAS 23; CANR 14; DLB
    88

Levine, Philip
    1928- .... CLC 2, 4, 5, 9, 14, 33; DAM
    POET
    See also CA 9-12R; CANR 9, 37, 52; DLB 5

Levinson, Deirdre 1931- .... CLC 49
    See also CA 73-76

Levi-Strauss, Claude 1908- .... CLC 38
    See also CA 1-4R; CANR 6, 32, 57; MTCW

Levitin, Sonia (Wolff) 1934- .... CLC 17
    See also AAYA 13; CA 29-32R; CANR 14,
    32; JRDA; MAICYA; SAAS 2; SATA 4,
    68

Levon, O. U.
    See Kesey, Ken (Elton)

Locke, John 1632-1704 .... **LC 7, 35**
See also DLB 101

Locke-Elliott, Sumner
See Elliott, Sumner Locke

Lockhart, John Gibson
1794-1854 .... **NCLC 6**
See also DLB 110, 116, 144

Lodge, David (John) 1935- .... **CLC 36; DAM POP**
See also BEST 90:1; CA 17-20R; CANR 19, 53; DLB 14; INT CANR-19; MTCW

Loennbohm, Armas Eino Leopold 1878-1926
See Leino, Eino
See also CA 123

Loewinsohn, Ron(ald William)
1937- .... **CLC 52**
See also CA 25-28R

Logan, Jake
See Smith, Martin Cruz

Logan, John (Burton) 1923-1987 .... **CLC 5**
See also CA 77-80; 124; CANR 45; DLB 5

Lo Kuan-chung 1330(?)-1400(?) .... **LC 12**

Lombard, Nap
See Johnson, Pamela Hansford

London, Jack .... **TCLC 9, 15, 39; SSC 4; WLC**
See also London, John Griffith
See also AAYA 13; AITN 2; CDALB 1865-1917; DLB 8, 12, 78; SATA 18

London, John Griffith 1876-1916
See London, Jack
See also CA 110; 119; DA; DAB; DAC; DAM MST, NOV; JRDA; MAICYA; MTCW

Long, Emmett
See Leonard, Elmore (John, Jr.)

Longbaugh, Harry
See Goldman, William (W.)

Longfellow, Henry Wadsworth
1807-1882 .... **NCLC 2, 45; DA; DAB; DAC; DAM MST, POET; WLCS**
See also CDALB 1640-1865; DLB 1, 59; SATA 19

Longley, Michael 1939- .... **CLC 29**
See also CA 102; DLB 40

Longus fl. c. 2nd cent. - .... **CMLC 7**

Longway, A. Hugh
See Lang, Andrew

Lonnrot, Elias 1802-1884 .... **NCLC 53**

Lopate, Phillip 1943- .... **CLC 29**
See also CA 97-100; DLBY 80; INT 97-100

Lopez Portillo (y Pacheco), Jose
1920- .... **CLC 46**
See also CA 129; HW

Lopez y Fuentes, Gregorio
1897(?)-1966 .... **CLC 32**
See also CA 131; HW

Lorca, Federico Garcia
See Garcia Lorca, Federico

Lord, Bette Bao 1938- .... **CLC 23**
See also BEST 90:3; CA 107; CANR 41; INT 107; SATA 58

Lord Auch
See Bataille, Georges

Lord Byron
See Byron, George Gordon (Noel)

Lorde, Audre (Geraldine)
1934-1992 .... **CLC 18, 71; BLC; DAM MULT, POET; PC 12**
See also BW 1; CA 25-28R; 142; CANR 16, 26, 46; DLB 41; MTCW

Lord Houghton
See Milnes, Richard Monckton

Lord Jeffrey
See Jeffrey, Francis

Lorenzini, Carlo 1826-1890
See Collodi, Carlo
See also MAICYA; SATA 29

Lorenzo, Heberto Padilla
See Padilla (Lorenzo), Heberto

Loris
See Hofmannsthal, Hugo von

Loti, Pierre .... **TCLC 11**
See also Viaud, (Louis Marie) Julien
See also DLB 123

Louie, David Wong 1954- .... **CLC 70**
See also CA 139

Louis, Father M.
See Merton, Thomas

Lovecraft, H(oward) P(hillips)
1890-1937 ...... **TCLC 4, 22; DAM POP; SSC 3**
See also AAYA 14; CA 104; 133; MTCW

Lovelace, Earl
1935- .... **CLC 51**
See also BW 2; CA 77-80; CANR 41; DLB 125; MTCW

Lovelace, Richard
1618-1657 .... **LC 24**
See also DLB 131

Lowell, Amy
1874-1925 ... **TCLC 1, 8; DAM POET; PC 13**
See also CA 104; 151; DLB 54, 140

Lowell, James Russell
1819-1891 .... **NCLC 2**
See also CDALB 1640-1865; DLB 1, 11, 64, 79

Lowell, Robert (Traill Spence, Jr.)
1917-1977 ... **CLC 1, 2, 3, 4, 5, 8, 9, 11, 15, 37; DA; DAB; DAC; DAM MST, NOV; PC 3; WLC**
See also CA 9-12R; 73-76; CABS 2; CANR 26, 60; DLB 5, 169; MTCW

Lowndes, Marie Adelaide (Belloc)
1868-1947 .... **TCLC 12**
See also CA 107; DLB 70

Lowry, (Clarence) Malcolm
1909-1957 .... **TCLC 6, 40**
See also CA 105; 131; CANR 62; CDBLB 1945-1960; DLB 15; MTCW

Lowry, Mina Gertrude 1882-1966
See Loy, Mina
See also CA 113

Loxsmith, John
See Brunner, John (Kilian Houston)

Loy, Mina .... **CLC 28; DAM POET; PC 16**
See also Lowry, Mina Gertrude
See also DLB 4, 54

Loyson-Bridet
See Schwob, (Mayer Andre) Marcel

Lucas, Craig 1951- .... **CLC 64**
See also CA 137

Lucas, E(dward) V(errall)
1868-1938 .... **TCLC 73**
See also DLB 98, 149, 153; SATA 20

Lucas, George 1944- .... **CLC 16**
See also AAYA 1; CA 77-80; CANR 30; SATA 56

Lucas, Hans
See Godard, Jean-Luc

Lucas, Victoria
See Plath, Sylvia

Ludlam, Charles 1943-1987 .... **CLC 46, 50**
See also CA 85-88; 122

Ludlum, Robert 1927- ..... **CLC 22, 43; DAM NOV, POP**
See also AAYA 10; BEST 89:1, 90:3; CA 33-36R; CANR 25, 41; DLBY 82; MTCW

Ludwig, Ken .... **CLC 60**

Ludwig, Otto 1813-1865 .... **NCLC 4**
See also DLB 129

Lugones, Leopoldo 1874-1938 .... **TCLC 15**
See also CA 116; 131; HW

Lu Hsun 1881-1936 .... **TCLC 3; SSC 20**
See also Shu-Jen, Chou

Lukacs, George .... **CLC 24**
See also Lukacs, Gyorgy (Szegeny von)

Lukacs, Gyorgy (Szegeny von) 1885-1971
See Lukacs, George
See also CA 101; 29-32R; CANR 62

MacShane, Frank 1927- .... CLC 39
    See also CA 9-12R; CANR 3, 33; DLB
    111

Macumber, Mari
    See Sandoz, Mari(e Susette)

Madach, Imre 1823-1864 .... NCLC 19

Madden, (Jerry) David
    1933- .... CLC 5, 15
    See also CA 1-4R; CAAS 3; CANR 4, 45; DLB
    6; MTCW

Maddern, Al(an)
    See Ellison, Harlan (Jay)

Madhubuti, Haki R.
    1942- .... CLC 6, 73; BLC; DAM MULT,
    POET; PC 5
    See also Lee, Don L.
    See also BW 2; CA 73-76; CANR 24, 51; DLB
    5, 41; DLBD 8

Maepenn, Hugh
    See Kuttner, Henry

Maepenn, K. H.
    See Kuttner, Henry

Maeterlinck, Maurice
    1862-1949 .... TCLC 3; DAM DRAM
    See also CA 104; 136; SATA 66

Maginn, William 1794-1842 .... NCLC 8
    See also DLB 110, 159

Mahapatra, Jayanta 1928- .... CLC 33; DAM
    MULT
    See also CA 73-76; CAAS 9; CANR 15, 33

Mahfouz, Naguib (Abdel Aziz Al-Sabilgi)
    1911(?)-
    See Mahfuz, Najib
    See also BEST 89:2; CA 128; CANR 55; DAM
    NOV; MTCW

Mahfuz, Najib .... CLC 52, 55
    See also Mahfouz, Naguib (Abdel Aziz Al-
    Sabilgi)
    See also DLBY 88

Mahon, Derek 1941- .... CLC 27
    See also CA 113; 128; DLB 40

Mailer, Norman
    1923- ... CLC 1, 2, 3, 4, 5, 8, 11, 14, 28,
    39, 74; DA; DAB; DAC; DAM MST,
    NOV, POP
    See also AITN 2; CA 9-12R; CABS 1;
    CANR 28; CDALB 1968-1988; DLB
    2, 16, 28; DLBD 3; DLBY 80, 83;
    MTCW

Maillet, Antonine
    1929- .... CLC 54; DAC
    See also CA 115; 120; CANR 46; DLB 60;
    INT 120

Mais, Roger
    1905-1955 .... TCLC 8
    See also BW 1; CA 105; 124; DLB 125;
    MTCW

Maistre, Joseph de 1753-1821 .... NCLC 37

Maitland, Frederic 1850-1906 .... TCLC 65

Maitland, Sara (Louise)
    1950- .... CLC 49
    See also CA 69-72; CANR 13, 59

Major, Clarence
    1936- .... CLC 3, 19, 48; BLC; DAM
    MULT
    See also BW 2; CA 21-24R; CAAS 6; CANR
    13, 25, 53; DLB 33

Major, Kevin (Gerald)
    1949- .... CLC 26; DAC
    See also AAYA 16; CA 97-100; CANR 21, 38;
    CLR 11; DLB 60; INT CANR-21; JRDA;
    MAICYA; SATA 32, 82

Maki, James
    See Ozu, Yasujiro

Malabaila, Damiano
    See Levi, Primo

Malamud, Bernard
    1914-1986.... CLC 1, 2, 3, 5, 8, 9, 11,
    18, 27, 44, 78, 85; DA; DAB; DAC;
    DAM MST, NOV, POP; SSC 15;
    WLC
    See also AAYA 16; CA 5-8R; 118; CABS
    1; CANR 28, 62; CDALB 1941-1968;
    DLB 2, 28, 152; DLBY 80, 86; MTCW

Malan, Herman
    See Bosman, Herman Charles; Bosman,
    Herman Charles

Malaparte, Curzio 1898-1957 .... TCLC 52

Malcolm, Dan
    See Silverberg, Robert

Malcolm X .... CLC 82; BLC; WLCS
    See also Little, Malcolm

Malherbe, Francois de 1555-1628 .... LC 5

Mallarme, Stephane
    1842-1898 ... NCLC 4, 41; DAM POET;
    PC 4

Mallet-Joris, Francoise
    1930- .... CLC 11
    See also CA 65-68; CANR 17; DLB
    83

Malley, Ern
    See McAuley, James Phillip

Mallowan, Agatha Christie
    See Christie, Agatha (Mary Clarissa)

Maloff, Saul 1922- .... CLC 5
    See also CA 33-36R

Malone, Louis
    See MacNeice, (Frederick) Louis

Malone, Michael (Christopher)
    1942- .... CLC 43
    See also CA 77-80; CANR 14, 32, 57

Malory, (Sir) Thomas
    1410(?)-1471(?) .... LC 11; DA; DAB;
    DAC; DAM MST; WLCS
    See also CDBLB Before 1660; DLB 146; SATA
    59; SATA-Brief 33

Malouf, (George Joseph) David
    1934- .... CLC 28, 86
    See also CA 124; CANR 50

Malraux, (Georges-)Andre
    1901-1976 .... CLC 1, 4, 9, 13, 15, 57;
    DAM NOV
    See also CA 21-22; 69-72; CANR 34, 58; CAP
    2; DLB 72; MTCW

Malzberg, Barry N(athaniel)
    1939- .... CLC 7
    See also CA 61-64; CAAS 4; CANR 16; DLB
    8

Mamet, David (Alan)
    1947- .... CLC 9, 15, 34, 46, 91; DAM
    DRAM; DC 4
    See also AAYA 3; CA 81-84; CABS 3; CANR
    15, 41; DLB 7; MTCW

Mamoulian, Rouben (Zachary)
    1897-1987 .... CLC 16
    See also CA 25-28R; 124

Mandelstam, Osip (Emilievich)
    1891(?)-1938(?) .... TCLC 2, 6; PC 14
    See also CA 104; 150

Mander, (Mary) Jane 1877-1949 ... TCLC 31

Mandeville, John
    fl. 1350- .... CMLC 19
    See also DLB 146

Mandiargues, Andre Pieyre de .... CLC 41
    See also Pieyre de Mandiargues, Andre
    See also DLB 83

Mandrake, Ethel Belle
    See Thurman, Wallace (Henry)

Mangan, James Clarence
    1803-1849 .... NCLC 27

Maniere, J.-E.
    See Giraudoux, (Hippolyte) Jean

Manley, (Mary) Delariviere
    1672(?)-1724 .... LC 1
    See also DLB 39, 80

Mann, Abel
    See Creasey, John

Mann, Emily 1952- .... DC 7
    See also CA 130; CANR 55

Mann, (Luiz) Heinrich
    1871-1950 .... TCLC 9
    See also CA 106; DLB 66

Mann, (Paul) Thomas
    1875-1955 ..... TCLC 2, 8, 14, 21, 35, 44,
    60; DA; DAB; DAC; DAM MST,
    NOV; SSC 5; WLC
    See also CA 104; 128; DLB 66; MTCW

Mehta, Ved (Parkash) 1934- .... **CLC 37**
See also CA 1-4R; CANR 2, 23; MTCW

Melanter
See Blackmore, R(ichard) D(oddridge)

Melikow, Loris
See Hofmannsthal, Hugo von

Melmoth, Sebastian
See Wilde, Oscar (Fingal O'Flahertie Wills)

Meltzer, Milton 1915- .... **CLC 26**
See also AAYA 8; CA 13-16R; CANR 38; CLR
13; DLB 61; JRDA; MAICYA; SAAS 1;
SATA 1, 50, 80

Melville, Herman
1819-1891 ..... **NCLC 3, 12, 29, 45, 49;
DA; DAB; DAC; DAM MST, NOV; SSC
1, 17; WLC**
See also CDALB 1640-1865; DLB 3, 74; SATA
59

Menander
c. 342B.C.-c. 292B.C. .... **CMLC 9; DAM
DRAM; DC 3**
See also DLB 176

Mencken, H(enry) L(ouis)
1880-1956 .... **TCLC 13**
See also CA 105; 125; CDALB 1917-1929;
DLB 11, 29, 63, 137; MTCW

Mendelsohn, Jane 1965(?)- .... **CLC 99**
See also CA 154

Mercer, David 1928-1980 .... **CLC 5; DAM
DRAM**
See also CA 9-12R; 102; CANR 23; DLB 13;
MTCW

Merchant, Paul
See Ellison, Harlan (Jay)

Meredith, George
1828-1909 ... **TCLC 17, 43; DAM POET**
See also CA 117; 153; CDBLB 1832-1890;
DLB 18, 35, 57, 159

Meredith, William (Morris)
1919- .... **CLC 4, 13, 22, 55; DAM POET**
See also CA 9-12R; CAAS 14; CANR 6, 40;
DLB 5

Merezhkovsky, Dmitry Sergeyevich
1865-1941 .... **TCLC 29**

Merimee, Prosper 1803-1870 ... **NCLC 6, 65;
SSC 7**
See also DLB 119

Merkin, Daphne 1954- .... **CLC 44**
See also CA 123

Merlin, Arthur
See Blish, James (Benjamin)

Merrill, James (Ingram)
1926-1995 ... **CLC 2, 3, 6, 8, 13, 18, 34,
91; DAM POET**
See also CA 13-16R; 147; CANR 10, 49; DLB
5, 165; DLBY 85; INT CANR-10; MTCW

Merriman, Alex
See Silverberg, Robert

Merritt, E. B.
See Waddington, Miriam

Merton, Thomas
1915-1968 ... **CLC 1, 3, 11, 34, 83; PC 10**
See also CA 5-8R; 25-28R; CANR 22, 53; DLB
48; DLBY 81; MTCW

Merwin, W(illiam) S(tanley)
1927- ... **CLC 1, 2, 3, 5, 8, 13, 18, 45, 88;
DAM POET**
See also CA 13-16R; CANR 15, 51; DLB 5,
169; INT CANR-15; MTCW

Metcalf, John 1938- .... **CLC 37**
See also CA 113; DLB 60

Metcalf, Suzanne
See Baum, L(yman) Frank

Mew, Charlotte (Mary)
1870-1928 .... **TCLC 8**
See also CA 105; DLB 19, 135

Mewshaw, Michael 1943- .... **CLC 9**
See also CA 53-56; CANR 7, 47; DLBY
80

Meyer, June
See Jordan, June

Meyer, Lynn
See Slavitt, David R(ytman)

Meyer-Meyrink, Gustav 1868-1932
See Meyrink, Gustav
See also CA 117

Meyers, Jeffrey 1939- .... **CLC 39**
See also CA 73-76; CANR 54; DLB
111

Meynell, Alice (Christina Gertrude Thompson)
1847-1922 .... **TCLC 6**
See also CA 104; DLB 19, 98

Meyrink, Gustav .... **TCLC 21**
See also Meyer-Meyrink, Gustav
See also DLB 81

Michaels, Leonard
1933- .... **CLC 6, 25; SSC 16**
See also CA 61-64; CANR 21, 62; DLB 130;
MTCW

Michaux, Henri 1899-1984 .... **CLC 8, 19**
See also CA 85-88; 114

Micheaux, Oscar 1884-1951 .... **TCLC 76**
See also DLB 50

Michelangelo 1475-1564 .... **LC 12**

Michelet, Jules 1798-1874 .... **NCLC 31**

Michener, James A(lbert)
1907(?)-1997 .... **CLC 1, 5, 11, 29, 60;
DAM NOV, POP**
See also AITN 1; BEST 90:1; CA 5-8R; CANR
21, 45; DLB 6; MTCW

Mickiewicz, Adam 1798-1855 .... **NCLC 3**

Middleton, Christopher 1926- .... **CLC 13**
See also CA 13-16R; CANR 29, 54; DLB 40

Middleton, Richard (Barham)
1882-1911 .... **TCLC 56**
See also DLB 156

Middleton, Stanley 1919- .... **CLC 7, 38**
See also CA 25-28R; CAAS 23; CANR 21, 46;
DLB 14

Middleton, Thomas
1580-1627 .... **LC 33; DAM DRAM,
MST; DC 5**
See also DLB 58

Migueis, Jose Rodrigues 1901- .... **CLC 10**

Mikszath, Kalman 1847-1910 .... **TCLC 31**

Miles, Jack .... **CLC 100**

Miles, Josephine (Louise)
1911-1985 .... **CLC 1, 2, 14, 34, 39; DAM
POET**
See also CA 1-4R; 116; CANR 2, 55; DLB 48

Militant
See Sandburg, Carl (August)

Mill, John Stuart 1806-1873 .... **NCLC 11, 58**
See also CDBLB 1832-1890; DLB 55

Millar, Kenneth 1915-1983 .... **CLC 14; DAM
POP**
See also Macdonald, Ross
See also CA 9-12R; 110; CANR 16; DLB 2;
DLBD 6; DLBY 83; MTCW

Millay, E. Vincent
See Millay, Edna St. Vincent

Millay, Edna St. Vincent
1892-1950 .... **TCLC 4, 49; DA; DAB;
DAC; DAM MST, POET; PC 6; WLCS**
See also CA 104; 130; CDALB 1917-1929;
DLB 45; MTCW

Miller, Arthur
1915- ..... **CLC 1, 2, 6, 10, 15, 26, 47, 78;
DA; DAB; DAC; DAM DRAM, MST;
DC 1; WLC**
See also AAYA 15; AITN 1; CA 1-4R; CABS
3; CANR 2, 30, 54; CDALB 1941-1968;
DLB 7; MTCW

Miller, Henry (Valentine)
1891-1980 ..... **CLC 1, 2, 4, 9, 14, 43, 84;
DA; DAB; DAC; DAM MST, NOV;
WLC**
See also CA 9-12R; 97-100; CANR 33;
CDALB 1929-1941; DLB 4, 9; DLBY 80;
MTCW

Miller, Jason 1939(?)- .... **CLC 2**
See also AITN 1; CA 73-76; DLB 7

Miller, Sue
1943- .... **CLC 44; DAM POP**
See also BEST 90:3; CA 139; CANR 59; DLB
143

Miller, Walter M(ichael, Jr.)
1923- .... CLC 4, 30
See also CA 85-88; DLB 8

Millett, Kate 1934- .... CLC 67
See also AITN 1; CA 73-76; CANR 32, 53;
MTCW

Millhauser, Steven 1943- .... CLC 21, 54
See also CA 110; 111; DLB 2; INT 111

Millin, Sarah Gertrude 1889-1968 ... CLC 49
See also CA 102; 93-96

Milne, A(lan) A(lexander)
1882-1956 .... TCLC 6; DAB; DAC;
DAM MST
See also CA 104; 133; CLR 1, 26; DLB 10,
77, 100, 160; MAICYA; MTCW; YABC 1

Milner, Ron(ald)
1938- .... CLC 56; BLC; DAM MULT
See also AITN 1; BW 1; CA 73-76; CANR 24;
DLB 38; MTCW

Milnes, Richard Monckton
1809-1885 .... NCLC 61
See also DLB 32, 184

Milosz, Czeslaw
1911- ... CLC 5, 11, 22, 31, 56, 82; DAM
MST, POET; PC 8; WLCS
See also CA 81-84; CANR 23, 51; MTCW

Milton, John 1608-1674 ..... LC 9; DA; DAB;
DAC; DAM MST, POET; PC 19; WLC
See also CDBLB 1660-1789; DLB 131, 151

Min, Anchee 1957- .... CLC 86
See also CA 146

Minehaha, Cornelius
See Wedekind, (Benjamin) Frank(lin)

Miner, Valerie 1947- .... CLC 40
See also CA 97-100; CANR 59

Minimo, Duca
See D'Annunzio, Gabriele

Minot, Susan 1956- .... CLC 44
See also CA 134

Minus, Ed 1938- .... CLC 39

Miranda, Javier
See Bioy Casares, Adolfo

Mirbeau, Octave 1848-1917 .... TCLC 55
See also DLB 123

Miro (Ferrer), Gabriel (Francisco Victor)
1879-1930 .... TCLC 5
See also CA 104

Mishima, Yukio
1925-1970 ...... CLC 2, 4, 6, 9, 27; DC 1;
SSC 4
See also Hiraoka, Kimitake
See also DLB 182

Mistral, Frederic 1830-1914 .... TCLC 51
See also CA 122

Mistral, Gabriela .... TCLC 2; HLC
See also Godoy Alcayaga, Lucila

Mistry, Rohinton 1952- .... CLC 71; DAC
See also CA 141

Mitchell, Clyde
See Ellison, Harlan (Jay); Silverberg, Robert

Mitchell, James Leslie 1901-1935
See Gibbon, Lewis Grassic
See also CA 104; DLB 15

Mitchell, Joni 1943- .... CLC 12
See also CA 112

Mitchell, Joseph (Quincy)
1908-1996 .... CLC 98
See also CA 77-80; 152; DLBY 96

Mitchell, Margaret (Munnerlyn)
1900-1949 .. TCLC 11; DAM NOV, POP
See also CA 109; 125; CANR 55; DLB 9;
MTCW

Mitchell, Peggy
See Mitchell, Margaret (Munnerlyn)

Mitchell, S(ilas) Weir
1829-1914 .... TCLC 36

Mitchell, W(illiam) O(rmond)
1914- .... CLC 25; DAC; DAM MST
See also CA 77-80; CANR 15, 43; DLB
88

Mitford, Mary Russell 1787-1855 ... NCLC 4
See also DLB 110, 116

Mitford, Nancy 1904-1973 .... CLC 44
See also CA 9-12R

Miyamoto, Yuriko 1899-1951 .... TCLC 37
See also DLB 180

Miyazawa Kenji 1896-1933 .... TCLC 76
See also CA 157

Mizoguchi, Kenji 1898-1956 .... TCLC 72

Mo, Timothy (Peter) 1950(?)- .... CLC 46
See also CA 117; MTCW

Modarressi, Taghi (M.) 1931- .... CLC 44
See also CA 121; 134; INT 134

Modiano, Patrick (Jean) 1945- .... CLC 18
See also CA 85-88; CANR 17, 40; DLB
83

Moerck, Paal
See Roelvaag, O(le) E(dvart)

Mofolo, Thomas (Mokopu)
1875(?)-1948 ...... TCLC 22; BLC; DAM
MULT
See also CA 121; 153

Mohr, Nicholasa
1935- .... CLC 12; DAM MULT; HLC
See also AAYA 8; CA 49-52; CANR 1, 32;
CLR 22; DLB 145; HW; JRDA; SAAS 8;
SATA 8

Mojtabai, A(nn) G(race)
1938- .... CLC 5, 9, 15, 29
See also CA 85-88

Moliere
1622-1673 .... LC 28; DA; DAB; DAC;
DAM DRAM, MST; WLC

Molin, Charles
See Mayne, William (James Carter)

Molnar, Ferenc
1878-1952 .... TCLC 20; DAM DRAM
See also CA 109; 153

Momaday, N(avarre) Scott
1934- .... CLC 2, 19, 85, 95; DA; DAB;
DAC; DAM MST, MULT, NOV, POP;
WLCS
See also AAYA 11; CA 25-28R; CANR 14, 34;
DLB 143; 175; INT CANR-14; MTCW;
NNAL; SATA 48; SATA-Brief 30

Monette, Paul 1945-1995 .... CLC 82
See also CA 139; 147

Monroe, Harriet 1860-1936 .... TCLC 12
See also CA 109; DLB 54, 91

Monroe, Lyle
See Heinlein, Robert A(nson)

Montagu, Elizabeth 1917- .... NCLC 7
See also CA 9-12R

Montagu, Mary (Pierrepont) Wortley
1689-1762 .... LC 9; PC 16
See also DLB 95, 101

Montagu, W. H.
See Coleridge, Samuel Taylor

Montague, John (Patrick)
1929- .... CLC 13, 46
See also CA 9-12R; CANR 9; DLB 40; MTCW

Montaigne, Michel (Eyquem) de
1533-1592 .... LC 8; DA; DAB; DAC;
DAM MST; WLC

Montale, Eugenio
1896-1981 .... CLC 7, 9, 18; PC 13
See also CA 17-20R; 104; CANR 30; DLB 114;
MTCW

Montesquieu, Charles-Louis de Secondat
1689-1755 .... LC 7

Montgomery, (Robert) Bruce 1921-1978
See Crispin, Edmund
See also CA 104

Montgomery, L(ucy) M(aud)
1874-1942 ...... TCLC 51; DAC; DAM
MST
See also AAYA 12; CA 108; 137; CLR 8; DLB
92; DLBD 14; JRDA; MAICYA; YABC 1

Montgomery, Marion H., Jr. 1925- .... CLC 7
See also AITN 1; CA 1-4R; CANR 3, 48; DLB 6

Montgomery, Max
See Davenport, Guy (Mattison, Jr.)

Montherlant, Henry (Milon) de
1896-1972 .... **CLC 8, 19; DAM DRAM**
See also CA 85-88; 37-40R; DLB 72; MTCW

Monty Python
See Chapman, Graham; Cleese, John
(Marwood); Gilliam, Terry (Vance); Idle,
Eric; Jones, Terence Graham Parry; Palin,
Michael (Edward)
See also AAYA 7

Moodie, Susanna (Strickland)
1803-1885 .... **NCLC 14**
See also DLB 99

Mooney, Edward 1951-
See Mooney, Ted
See also CA 130

Mooney, Ted .... **CLC 25**
See also Mooney, Edward

Moorcock, Michael (John)
1939- .... **CLC 5, 27, 58**
See also CA 45-48; CAAS 5; CANR 2, 17, 38;
DLB 14; MTCW; SATA 93

Moore, Brian
1921- .... **CLC 1, 3, 5, 7, 8, 19, 32, 90;
DAB; DAC; DAM MST**
See also CA 1-4R; CANR 1, 25, 42;
MTCW

Moore, Edward
See Muir, Edwin

Moore, George Augustus
1852-1933 .... **TCLC 7; SSC 19**
See also CA 104; DLB 10, 18, 57, 135

Moore, Lorrie .... **CLC 39, 45, 68**
See also Moore, Marie Lorena

Moore, Marianne (Craig)
1887-1972 .... **CLC 1, 2, 4, 8, 10, 13, 19,
47; DA; DAB; DAC; DAM MST, POET;
PC 4; WLCS**
See also CA 1-4R; 33-36R; CANR 3, 61;
CDALB 1929-1941; DLB 45; DLBD 7;
MTCW; SATA 20

Moore, Marie Lorena 1957-
See Moore, Lorrie
See also CA 116; CANR 39

Moore, Thomas 1779-1852 .... **NCLC 6**
See also DLB 96, 144

Morand, Paul 1888-1976 .... **CLC 41; SSC 22**
See also CA 69-72; DLB 65

Morante, Elsa 1918-1985 .... **CLC 8, 47**
See also CA 85-88; 117; CANR 35; DLB 177;
MTCW

Moravia, Alberto
1907-1990 ... **CLC 2, 7, 11, 27, 46; SSC
26**
See also Pincherle, Alberto
See also DLB 177

More, Hannah 1745-1833 .... **NCLC 27**
See also DLB 107, 109, 116, 158

More, Henry 1614-1687 .... **LC 9**
See also DLB 126

More, Sir Thomas 1478-1535 .... **LC 10, 32**

Moreas, Jean .... **TCLC 18**
See also Papadiamantopoulos, Johannes

Morgan, Berry 1919- .... **CLC 6**
See also CA 49-52; DLB 6

Morgan, Claire
See Highsmith, (Mary) Patricia

Morgan, Edwin (George)
1920- .... **CLC 31**
See also CA 5-8R; CANR 3, 43; DLB
27

Morgan, (George) Frederick
1922- .... **CLC 23**
See also CA 17-20R; CANR 21

Morgan, Harriet
See Mencken, H(enry) L(ouis)

Morgan, Jane
See Cooper, James Fenimore

Morgan, Janet 1945- .... **CLC 39**
See also CA 65-68

Morgan, Lady 1776(?)-1859 .... **NCLC 29**
See also DLB 116, 158

Morgan, Robin 1941- .... **CLC 2**
See also CA 69-72; CANR 29; MTCW; SATA
80

Morgan, Scott
See Kuttner, Henry

Morgan, Seth 1949(?)-1990 .... **CLC 65**
See also CA 132

Morgenstern, Christian
1871-1914 .... **TCLC 8**
See also CA 105

Morgenstern, S.
See Goldman, William (W.)

Moricz, Zsigmond 1879-1942 .... **TCLC 33**

Morike, Eduard (Friedrich)
1804-1875 .... **NCLC 10**
See also DLB 133

Mori Ogai .... **TCLC 14**
See also Mori Rintaro

Mori Rintaro 1862-1922
See Mori Ogai
See also CA 110

Moritz, Karl Philipp 1756-1793 .... **LC 2**
See also DLB 94

Morland, Peter Henry
See Faust, Frederick (Schiller)

Morren, Theophil
See Hofmannsthal, Hugo von

Morris, Bill 1952- .... **CLC 76**

Morris, Julian
See West, Morris L(anglo)

Morris, Steveland Judkins 1950(?)-
See Wonder, Stevie
See also CA 111

Morris, William 1834-1896 .... **NCLC 4**
See also CDBLB 1832-1890; DLB 18, 35, 57,
156, 178, 184

Morris, Wright 1910- ...... **CLC 1, 3, 7, 18, 37**
See also CA 9-12R; CANR 21; DLB 2; DLBY
81; MTCW

Morrison, Arthur 1863-1945 .... **TCLC 72**
See also CA 120; 157; DLB 70, 135

Morrison, Chloe Anthony Wofford
See Morrison, Toni

Morrison, James Douglas 1943-1971
See Morrison, Jim
See also CA 73-76; CANR 40

Morrison, Jim .... **CLC 17**
See also Morrison, James Douglas

Morrison, Toni
1931- ... **CLC 4, 10, 22, 55, 81, 87; BLC;
DA; DAB; DAC; DAM MST, MULT,
NOV, POP**
See also AAYA 1, 22; BW 2; CA 29-32R;
CANR 27, 42; CDALB 1968-1988; DLB 6,
33, 143; DLBY 81; MTCW; SATA 57

Morrison, Van 1945- .... **CLC 21**
See also CA 116

Morrissy, Mary 1958- .... **CLC 99**

Mortimer, John (Clifford)
1923- .. **CLC 28, 43; DAM DRAM, POP**
See also CA 13-16R; CANR 21; CDBLB
1960 to Present; DLB 13; INT CANR-21;
MTCW

Mortimer, Penelope (Ruth) 1918- .... **CLC 5**
See also CA 57-60; CANR 45

Morton, Anthony
See Creasey, John

Mosca, Gaetano 1858-1941 .... **TCLC 75**

Mosher, Howard Frank 1943- .... **CLC 62**
See also CA 139

Mosley, Nicholas 1923- .... **CLC 43, 70**
See also CA 69-72; CANR 41, 60; DLB 14

Mosley, Walter
1952- .... **CLC 97; DAM MULT, POP**
See also AAYA 17; BW 2; CA 142; CANR 57

Moss, Howard 1922-1987 ... **CLC 7, 14, 45,
50; DAM POET**
See also CA 1-4R; 123; CANR 1, 44; DLB 5

Mossgiel, Rab
See Burns, Robert

Nash, (Frediric) Ogden
1902-1971 .... **CLC 23; DAM POET**
See also CA 13-14; 29-32R; CANR 34, 61;
CAP 1; DLB 11; MAICYA; MTCW; SATA
2, 46

Nathan, Daniel
See Dannay, Frederic

Nathan, George Jean 1882-1958 .... **TCLC 18**
See also Hatteras, Owen
See also CA 114; DLB 137

Natsume, Kinnosuke 1867-1916
See Natsume, Soseki
See also CA 104

Natsume, Soseki 1867-1916 .... **TCLC 2, 10**
See also Natsume, Kinnosuke
See also DLB 180

Natti, (Mary) Lee 1919-
See Kingman, Lee
See also CA 5-8R; CANR 2

Naylor, Gloria
1950- .... **CLC 28, 52; BLC; DA; DAC;**
DAM MST, MULT, NOV, POP; WLCS
See also AAYA 6; BW 2; CA 107; CANR 27,
51; DLB 173; MTCW

Neihardt, John Gneisenau
1881-1973 .... **CLC 32**
See also CA 13-14; CAP 1; DLB 9, 54

Nekrasov, Nikolai Alekseevich
1821-1878 .... **NCLC 11**

Nelligan, Emile 1879-1941 .... **TCLC 14**
See also CA 114; DLB 92

Nelson, Willie 1933- .... **CLC 17**
See also CA 107

Nemerov, Howard (Stanley)
1920-1991 .... **CLC 2, 6, 9, 36; DAM**
POET
See also CA 1-4R; 134; CABS 2; CANR 1,
27, 53; DLB 5, 6; DLBY 83; INT CANR-
27; MTCW

Neruda, Pablo
1904-1973 ...... **CLC 1, 2, 5, 7, 9, 28, 62;**
DA; DAB; DAC; DAM MST, MULT,
POET; HLC; PC 4; WLC
See also CA 19-20; 45-48; CAP 2; HW;
MTCW

Nerval, Gerard de
1808-1855 .... **NCLC 1; PC 13; SSC 18**

Nervo, (Jose) Amado (Ruiz de)
1870-1919 .... **TCLC 11**
See also CA 109; 131; HW

Nessi, Pio Baroja y
See Baroja (y Nessi), Pio

Nestroy, Johann 1801-1862 .... **NCLC 42**
See also DLB 133

Netterville, Luke
See O'Grady, Standish (James)

Neufeld, John (Arthur) 1938- .... **CLC 17**
See also AAYA 11; CA 25-28R; CANR 11, 37,
56; MAICYA; SAAS 3; SATA 6, 81

Neville, Emily Cheney 1919- .... **CLC 12**
See also CA 5-8R; CANR 3, 37; JRDA;
MAICYA; SAAS 2; SATA 1

Newbound, Bernard Slade 1930-
See Slade, Bernard
See also CA 81-84; CANR 49; DAM DRAM

Newby, P(ercy) H(oward)
1918- .... **CLC 2, 13; DAM NOV**
See also CA 5-8R; CANR 32; DLB 15;
MTCW

Newlove, Donald 1928- .... **CLC 6**
See also CA 29-32R; CANR 25

Newlove, John (Herbert) 1938- .... **CLC 14**
See also CA 21-24R; CANR 9, 25

Newman, Charles 1938- .... **CLC 2, 8**
See also CA 21-24R

Newman, Edwin (Harold) 1919- .... **CLC 14**
See also AITN 1; CA 69-72; CANR 5

Newman, John Henry
1801-1890 .... **NCLC 38**
See also DLB 18, 32, 55

Newton, Suzanne 1936- .... **CLC 35**
See also CA 41-44R; CANR 14; JRDA; SATA
5, 77

Nexo, Martin Andersen
1869-1954 .... **TCLC 43**

Nezval, Vitezslav 1900-1958 .... **TCLC 44**
See also CA 123

Ng, Fae Myenne 1957(?)- .... **CLC 81**
See also CA 146

Ngema, Mbongeni 1955- .... **CLC 57**
See also BW 2; CA 143

Ngugi, James T(hiong'o) .... **CLC 3, 7, 13**
See also Ngugi wa Thiong'o

Ngugi wa Thiong'o 1938- ...... **CLC 36; BLC;**
DAM MULT, NOV
See also Ngugi, James T(hiong'o)
See also BW 2; CA 81-84; CANR 27, 58; DLB
125; MTCW

Nichol, B(arrie) P(hillip)
1944-1988 .... **CLC 18**
See also CA 53-56; DLB 53; SATA 66

Nichols, John (Treadwell) 1940- .... **CLC 38**
See also CA 9-12R; CAAS 2; CANR 6; DLBY
82

Nichols, Leigh
See Koontz, Dean R(ay)

Nichols, Peter (Richard)
1927- .... **CLC 5, 36, 65**
See also CA 104; CANR 33; DLB 13;
MTCW

Nicolas, F. R. E.
See Freeling, Nicolas

Niedecker, Lorine 1903-1970 .... **CLC 10, 42;**
DAM POET
See also CA 25-28; CAP 2; DLB 48

Nietzsche, Friedrich (Wilhelm)
1844-1900 .... **TCLC 10, 18, 55**
See also CA 107; 121; DLB 129

Nievo, Ippolito 1831-1861 .... **NCLC 22**

Nightingale, Anne Redmon 1943-
See Redmon, Anne
See also CA 103

Nik. T. O.
See Annensky, Innokenty (Fyodorovich)

Nin, Anais
1903-1977 .... **CLC 1, 4, 8, 11, 14, 60;**
DAM NOV, POP; SSC 10
See also AITN 2; CA 13-16R; 69-72;
CANR 22, 53; DLB 2, 4, 152;
MTCW

Nishiwaki, Junzaburo 1894-1982 .... **PC 15**
See also CA 107

Nissenson, Hugh 1933- .... **CLC 4, 9**
See also CA 17-20R; CANR 27; DLB 28

Niven, Larry .... **CLC 8**
See also Niven, Laurence Van Cott
See also DLB 8

Niven, Laurence Van Cott 1938-
See Niven, Larry
See also CA 21-24R; CAAS 12;
CANR 14, 44; DAM POP; MTCW;
SATA 95

Nixon, Agnes Eckhardt 1927- .... **CLC 21**
See also CA 110

Nizan, Paul 1905-1940 .... **TCLC 40**
See also DLB 72

Nkosi, Lewis 1936- .... **CLC 45; BLC; DAM**
MULT
See also BW 1; CA 65-68; CANR 27; DLB
157

Nodier, (Jean) Charles (Emmanuel)
1780-1844 .... **NCLC 19**
See also DLB 119

Nolan, Christopher 1965- .... **CLC 58**
See also CA 111

Noon, Jeff 1957- .... **CLC 91**
See also CA 148

Norden, Charles
See Durrell, Lawrence (George)

Nordhoff, Charles (Bernard)
1887-1947 .... **TCLC 23**
See also CA 108; DLB 9; SATA 23

Norfolk, Lawrence 1963- .... **CLC 76**
See also CA 144

O'Hara, Frank
1926-1966 .... **CLC 2, 5, 13, 78; DAM POET**
See also CA 9-12R; 25-28R; CANR 33; DLB 5, 16; MTCW

O'Hara, John (Henry)
1905-1970 .... **CLC 1, 2, 3, 6, 11, 42; DAM NOV; SSC 15**
See also CA 5-8R; 25-28R; CANR 31, 60; CDALB 1929-1941; DLB 9, 86; DLBD 2; MTCW

O Hehir, Diana 1922- .... **CLC 41**
See also CA 93-96

Okigbo, Christopher (Ifenayichukwu)
1932-1967 .... **CLC 25, 84; BLC; DAM MULT, POET; PC 7**
See also BW 1; CA 77-80; DLB 125; MTCW

Okri, Ben 1959- .... **CLC 87**
See also BW 2; CA 130; 138; DLB 157; INT 138

Olds, Sharon 1942- .... **CLC 32, 39, 85; DAM POET**
See also CA 101; CANR 18, 41; DLB 120

Oldstyle, Jonathan
See Irving, Washington

Olesha, Yuri (Karlovich)
1899-1960 .... **CLC 8**
See also CA 85-88

Oliphant, Laurence
1829(?)-1888 .... **NCLC 47**
See also DLB 18, 166

Oliphant, Margaret (Oliphant Wilson)
1828-1897 .... **NCLC 11, 61; SSC 25**
See also DLB 18, 159

Oliver, Mary 1935- .... **CLC 19, 34, 98**
See also CA 21-24R; CANR 9, 43; DLB 5

Olivier, Laurence (Kerr)
1907-1989 .... **CLC 20**
See also CA 111; 150; 129

Olsen, Tillie 1913- ...... **CLC 4, 13; DA; DAB; DAC; DAM MST; SSC 11**
See also CA 1-4R; CANR 1, 43; DLB 28; DLBY 80; MTCW

Olson, Charles (John)
1910-1970 .... **CLC 1, 2, 5, 6, 9, 11, 29; DAM POET; PC 19**
See also CA 13-16; 25-28R; CABS 2; CANR 35, 61; CAP 1; DLB 5, 16; MTCW

Olson, Toby 1937- .... **CLC 28**
See also CA 65-68; CANR 9, 31

Olyesha, Yuri
See Olesha, Yuri (Karlovich)

Ondaatje, (Philip) Michael
1943- .... **CLC 14, 29, 51, 76; DAB; DAC; DAM MST**
See also CA 77-80; CANR 42; DLB 60

Oneal, Elizabeth 1934-
See Oneal, Zibby
See also CA 106; CANR 28; MAICYA; SATA 30, 82

Oneal, Zibby .... **CLC 30**
See also Oneal, Elizabeth
See also AAYA 5; CLR 13; JRDA

O'Neill, Eugene (Gladstone)
1888-1953.... **TCLC 1, 6, 27, 49; DA; DAB; DAC; DAM DRAM, MST; WLC**
See also AITN 1; CA 110; 132; CDALB 1929-1941; DLB 7; MTCW

Onetti, Juan Carlos 1909-1994 ... **CLC 7, 10; DAM MULT, NOV; SSC 23**
See also CA 85-88; 145; CANR 32; DLB 113; HW; MTCW

O Nuallain, Brian 1911-1966
See O'Brien, Flann
See also CA 21-22; 25-28R; CAP 2

Opie, Amelia 1769-1853 .... **NCLC 65**
See also DLB 116, 159

Oppen, George 1908-1984 ...... **CLC 7, 13, 34**
See also CA 13-16R; 113; CANR 8; DLB 5, 165

Oppenheim, E(dward) Phillips
1866-1946 .... **TCLC 45**
See also CA 111; DLB 70

Origen c. 185-c. 254 .... **CMLC 19**

Orlovitz, Gil 1918-1973 .... **CLC 22**
See also CA 77-80; 45-48; DLB 2, 5

Orris
See Ingelow, Jean

Ortega y Gasset, Jose 1883-1955 .... **TCLC 9; DAM MULT; HLC**
See also CA 106; 130; HW; MTCW

Ortese, Anna Maria 1914- .... **CLC 89**
See also DLB 177

Ortiz, Simon J(oseph)
1941- .... **CLC 45; DAM MULT, POET; PC 17**
See also CA 134; DLB 120, 175; NNAL

Orton, Joe .... **CLC 4, 13, 43; DC 3**
See also Orton, John Kingsley
See also CDBLB 1960 to Present; DLB 13

Orton, John Kingsley 1933-1967
See Orton, Joe
See also CA 85-88; CANR 35; DAM DRAM; MTCW

Orwell, George .... **TCLC 2, 6, 15, 31, 51; DAB; WLC**
See also Blair, Eric (Arthur)
See also CDBLB 1945-1960; DLB 15, 98

Osborne, David
See Silverberg, Robert

Osborne, George
See Silverberg, Robert

Osborne, John (James)
1929-1994 .... **CLC 1, 2, 5, 11, 45; DA; DAB; DAC; DAM DRAM, MST; WLC**
See also CA 13-16R; 147; CANR 21, 56; CDBLB 1945-1960; DLB 13; MTCW

Osborne, Lawrence 1958-................. **CLC 50**

Oshima, Nagisa 1932-......................... **CLC 20**
See also CA 116; 121

Oskison, John Milton
1874-1947 .... **TCLC 35; DAM MULT**
See also CA 144; DLB 175; NNAL

Ossoli, Sarah Margaret (Fuller marchesa d')
1810-1850
See Fuller, Margaret
See also SATA 25

Ostrovsky, Alexander 1823-1886 .. **NCLC 30, 57**

Otero, Blas de 1916-1979 .... **CLC 11**
See also CA 89-92; DLB 134

Otto, Whitney 1955- .... **CLC 70**
See also CA 140

Ouida .... **TCLC 43**
See also De La Ramee, (Marie) Louise
See also DLB 18, 156

Ousmane, Sembene 1923- .... **CLC 66; BLC**
See also BW 1; CA 117; 125; MTCW

Ovid
43B.C.-18(?) .... **CMLC 7; DAM POET PC 2**

Owen, Hugh
See Faust, Frederick (Schiller)

Owen, Wilfred (Edward Salter)
1893-1918... **TCLC 5, 27; DA; DAB; DAC; DAM MST, POET; PC 19; WLC**
See also CA 104; 141; CDBLB 1914-1945; DLB 20

Owens, Rochelle 1936- .... **CLC 8**
See also CA 17-20R; CAAS 2; CANR 39

Oz, Amos
1939- ...... **CLC 5, 8, 11, 27, 33, 54; DAM NOV**
See also CA 53-56; CANR 27, 47; MTCW

Ozick, Cynthia
1928- .... **CLC 3, 7, 28, 62; DAM NOV, POP; SSC 15**
See also BEST 90:1; CA 17-20R; CANR 23, 58; DLB 28, 152; DLBY 82; INT CANR-23; MTCW

Ozu, Yasujiro 1903-1963 .... **CLC 16**
See also CA 112

Pacheco, C.
See Pessoa, Fernando (Antonio Nogueira)

Pa Chin .... CLC 18
See also Li Fei-kan

Pack, Robert 1929- .... CLC 13
See also CA 1-4R; CANR 3, 44; DLB 5

Padgett, Lewis
See Kuttner, Henry

Padilla (Lorenzo), Heberto 1932- ..... CLC 38
See also AITN 1; CA 123; 131; HW

Page, Jimmy 1944- .... CLC 12

Page, Louise 1955- .... CLC 40
See also CA 140

Page, P(atricia) K(athleen)
1916- ... CLC 7, 18; DAC; DAM MST;
PC 12
See also CA 53-56; CANR 4, 22; DLB 68;
MTCW

Page, Thomas Nelson 1853-1922 .... SSC 23
See also CA 118; DLB 12, 78; DLBD 13

Pagels, Elaine Hiesey 1943- .... CLC 104
See also CA 45-48; CANR 2, 24, 51

Paget, Violet 1856-1935
See Lee, Vernon
See also CA 104

Paget-Lowe, Henry
See Lovecraft, H(oward) P(hillips)

Paglia, Camille (Anna) 1947- .... CLC 68
See also CA 140

Paige, Richard
See Koontz, Dean R(ay)

Paine, Thomas 1737-1809 .... NCLC 62
See also CDALB 1640-1865; DLB 31, 43, 73,
158

Pakenham, Antonia
See Fraser, (Lady) Antonia (Pakenham)

Palamas, Kostes 1859-1943 .... TCLC 5
See also CA 105

Palazzeschi, Aldo 1885-1974 .... CLC 11
See also CA 89-92; 53-56; DLB 114

Paley, Grace
1922- ...... CLC 4, 6, 37; DAM POP;
SSC 8
See also CA 25-28R; CANR 13, 46; DLB 28;
INT CANR-13; MTCW

Palin, Michael (Edward) 1943- .... CLC 21
See also Monty Python
See also CA 107; CANR 35; SATA 67

Palliser, Charles 1947- .... CLC 65
See also CA 136

Palma, Ricardo 1833-1919 .... TCLC 29

Pancake, Breece Dexter 1952-1979
See Pancake, Breece D'J
See also CA 123; 109

Pancake, Breece D'J .... CLC 29
See also Pancake, Breece Dexter
See also DLB 130

Panko, Rudy
See Gogol, Nikolai (Vasilyevich)

Papadiamantis, Alexandros
1851-1911 .... TCLC 29

Papadiamantopoulos, Johannes 1856-1910
See Moreas, Jean
See also CA 117

Papini, Giovanni 1881-1956 .... TCLC 22
See also CA 121

Paracelsus 1493-1541 .... LC 14
See also DLB 179

Parasol, Peter
See Stevens, Wallace

Pareto, Vilfredo 1848-1923 .... TCLC 69

Parfenie, Maria
See Codrescu, Andrei

Parini, Jay (Lee) 1948- .... CLC 54
See also CA 97-100; CAAS 16; CANR 32

Park, Jordan
See Kornbluth, C(yril) M.; Pohl, Frederik

Park, Robert E(zra) 1864-1944 ...... TCLC 73
See also CA 122

Parker, Bert
See Ellison, Harlan (Jay)

Parker, Dorothy (Rothschild)
1893-1967 ..... CLC 15, 68; DAM POET;
SSC 2
See also CA 19-20; 25-28R; CAP 2; DLB 11,
45, 86; MTCW

Parker, Robert B(rown)
1932- .... CLC 27; DAM NOV, POP
See also BEST 89:4; CA 49-52; CANR 1, 26,
52; INT CANR-26; MTCW

Parkin, Frank 1940- .... CLC 43
See also CA 147

Parkman, Francis, Jr. 1823-1893 .. NCLC 12
See also DLB 1, 30

Parks, Gordon (Alexander Buchanan)
1912- ..... CLC 1, 16; BLC; DAM MULT
See also AITN 2; BW 2; CA 41-44R; CANR
26; DLB 33; SATA 8

Parmenides
c. 515B.C.-c. 450B.C. .... CMLC 22
See also DLB 176

Parnell, Thomas 1679-1718 .... LC 3
See also DLB 94

Parra, Nicanor
1914- ...CLC 2, 102; DAM MULT; HLC
See also CA 85-88; CANR 32; HW;
MTCW

Parrish, Mary Frances
See Fisher, M(ary) F(rances) K(ennedy)

Parson
See Coleridge, Samuel Taylor

Parson Lot
See Kingsley, Charles

Partridge, Anthony
See Oppenheim, E(dward) Phillips

Pascal, Blaise 1623-1662 .... LC 35

Pascoli, Giovanni 1855-1912 .... TCLC 45

Pasolini, Pier Paolo
1922-1975 .... CLC 20, 37; PC 17
See also CA 93-96; 61-64; DLB 128, 177;
MTCW

Pasquini
See Silone, Ignazio

Pastan, Linda (Olenik)
1932- .... CLC 27; DAM POET
See also CA 61-64; CANR 18, 40, 61; DLB 5

Pasternak, Boris (Leonidovich)
1890-1960 .... CLC 7, 10, 18, 63; DA;
DAB; DAC; DAM MST, NOV, POET;
PC 6; WLC
See also CA 127; 116; MTCW

Patchen, Kenneth 1911-1972 ... CLC 1, 2, 18;
DAM POET
See also CA 1-4R; 33-36R; CANR 3, 35; DLB
16, 48; MTCW

Pater, Walter (Horatio) 1839-1894 .. NCLC 7
See also CDBLB 1832-1890; DLB 57, 156

Paterson, A(ndrew) B(arton) 1864-1941
TCLC 32
See also CA 155

Paterson, Katherine (Womeldorf)
1932- .... CLC 12, 30
See also AAYA 1; CA 21-24R; CANR 28, 59;
CLR 7; DLB 52; JRDA; MAICYA; MTCW;
SATA 13, 53, 92

Patmore, Coventry Kersey Dighton
1823-1896 .... NCLC 9
See also DLB 35, 98

Paton, Alan (Stewart)
1903-1988 .... CLC 4, 10, 25, 55; DA;
DAB; DAC; DAM MST, NOV; WLC
See also CA 13-16; 125; CANR 22; CAP 1;
MTCW; SATA 11; SATA-Obit 56

Paton Walsh, Gillian 1937-
See Walsh, Jill Paton
See also CANR 38; JRDA; MAICYA; SAAS
3; SATA 4, 72

Paulding, James Kirke 1778-1860 ... NCLC 2
See also DLB 3, 59, 74

Paulin, Thomas Neilson 1949-
See Paulin, Tom
See also CA 123; 128

Paulin, Tom .... CLC 37
See also Paulin, Thomas Neilson
See also DLB 40

Paustovsky, Konstantin (Georgievich)
1892-1968 .... CLC 40
See also CA 93-96; 25-28R

Pavese, Cesare
1908-1950 .... TCLC 3; PC 13; SSC 19
See also CA 104; DLB 128, 177

Pavic, Milorad 1929- .... CLC 60
See also CA 136; DLB 181

Payne, Alan
See Jakes, John (William)

Paz, Gil
See Lugones, Leopoldo

Paz, Octavio
1914- .... CLC 3, 4, 6, 10, 19, 51, 65; DA;
DAB; DAC; DAM MST, MULT, POET;
HLC; PC 1; WLC
See also CA 73-76; CANR 32; DLBY 90; HW;
MTCW

p'Bitek, Okot
1931-1982 .... CLC 96; BLC; DAM
MULT
See also BW 2; CA 124; 107; DLB 125;
MTCW

Peacock, Molly 1947- .... CLC 60
See also CA 103; CAAS 21; CANR 52; DLB
120

Peacock, Thomas Love
1785-1866 .... NCLC 22
See also DLB 96, 116

Peake, Mervyn 1911-1968 .... CLC 7, 54
See also CA 5-8R; 25-28R; CANR 3; DLB 15,
160; MTCW; SATA 23

Pearce, Philippa .... CLC 21
See also Christie, (Ann) Philippa
See also CLR 9; DLB 161; MAICYA; SATA 1,
67

Pearl, Eric
See Elman, Richard

Pearson, T(homas) R(eid) 1956- .... CLC 39
See also CA 120; 130; INT 130

Peck, Dale 1967- .... CLC 81
See also CA 146

Peck, John 1941- .... CLC 3
See also CA 49-52; CANR 3

Peck, Richard (Wayne) 1934- .... CLC 21
See also AAYA 1; CA 85-88; CANR 19, 38;
CLR 15; INT CANR-19; JRDA; MAICYA;
SAAS 2; SATA 18, 55

Peck, Robert Newton
1928- ... CLC 17; DA; DAC; DAM MST
See also AAYA 3; CA 81-84; CANR 31; CLR
45; JRDA; MAICYA; SAAS 1; SATA 21,
62

Peckinpah, (David) Sam(uel)
1925-1984 .... CLC 20
See also CA 109; 114

Pedersen, Knut 1859-1952
See Hamsun, Knut
See also CA 104; 119; MTCW

Peeslake, Gaffer
See Durrell, Lawrence (George)

Peguy, Charles Pierre 1873-1914 .. TCLC 10
See also CA 107

Pena, Ramon del Valle y
See Valle-Inclan, Ramon (Maria) del

Pendennis, Arthur Esquir
See Thackeray, William Makepeace

Penn, William 1644-1718 .... LC 25
See also DLB 24

PEPECE
See Prado (Calvo), Pedro

Pepys, Samuel
1633-1703 .... LC 11; DA; DAB; DAC;
DAM MST; WLC
See also CDBLB 1660-1789; DLB 101

Percy, Walker
1916-1990 ... CLC 2, 3, 6, 8, 14, 18, 47,
65; DAM NOV, POP
See also CA 1-4R; 131; CANR 1, 23; DLB 2;
DLBY 80, 90; MTCW

Perec, Georges 1936-1982 .... CLC 56
See also CA 141; DLB 83

Pereda (y Sanchez de Porrua), Jose Maria de
1833-1906 .... TCLC 16
See also CA 117

Pereda y Porrua, Jose Maria de
See Pereda (y Sanchez de Porrua), Jose Maria
de

Peregoy, George Weems
See Mencken, H(enry) L(ouis)

Perelman, S(idney) J(oseph)
1904-1979 .... CLC 3, 5, 9, 15, 23, 44, 49;
DAM DRAM
See also AITN 1, 2; CA 73-76; 89-92; CANR
18; DLB 11, 44; MTCW

Peret, Benjamin 1899-1959 .... TCLC 20
See also CA 117

Peretz, Isaac Loeb
1851(?)-1915 .... TCLC 16; SSC 26
See also CA 109

Peretz, Yitzkhok Leibush
See Peretz, Isaac Loeb

Perez Galdos, Benito
1843-1920 .... TCLC 27
See also CA 125; 153; HW

Perrault, Charles 1628-1703 .... LC 2
See also MAICYA; SATA 25

Perry, Brighton
See Sherwood, Robert E(mmet)

Perse, St.-John .... CLC 4, 11, 46
See also Leger, (Marie-Rene Auguste) Alexis
Saint-Leger

Perutz, Leo 1882-1957 .... TCLC 60
See also DLB 81

Peseenz, Tulio F.
See Lopez y Fuentes, Gregorio

Pesetsky, Bette 1932- .... CLC 28
See also CA 133; DLB 130

Peshkov, Alexei Maximovich 1868-1936
See Gorky, Maxim
See also CA 105; 141; DA; DAC; DAM
DRAM, MST, NOV

Pessoa, Fernando (Antonio Nogueira)
1888-1935 .... TCLC 27; HLC; PC 20
See also CA 125

Peterkin, Julia Mood 1880-1961 .... CLC 31
See also CA 102; DLB 9

Peters, Joan K(aren) 1945- .... CLC 39
See also CA 158

Peters, Robert L(ouis) 1924- .... CLC 7
See also CA 13-16R; CAAS 8; DLB 105

Petofi, Sandor 1823-1849 .... NCLC 21

Petrakis, Harry Mark 1923- .... CLC 3
See also CA 9-12R; CANR 4, 30

Petrarch
1304-1374 ... CMLC 20; DAM POET;
PC 8

Petrov, Evgeny .... TCLC 21
See also Kataev, Evgeny Petrovich

Petry, Ann (Lane)
1908-1997 .... CLC 1, 7, 18
See also BW 1; CA 5-8R; 157; CAAS 6;
CANR 4, 46; CLR 12; DLB 76; JRDA;
MAICYA; MTCW; SATA 5; SATA-Obit
94

Petursson, Halligrimur 1614-1674 .... LC 8

Phaedrus 18(?)B.C.-55(?) .... CMLC 24

Philips, Katherine 1632-1664 .... LC 30
See also DLB 131

Philipson, Morris H. 1926- .... CLC 53
See also CA 1-4R; CANR 4

Phillips, Caryl
1958- .... CLC 96; DAM MULT
See also BW 2; CA 141; DLB 157

Phillips, David Graham
1867-1911 .... TCLC 44
See also CA 108; DLB 9, 12

Phillips, Jack
See Sandburg, Carl (August)

Phillips, Jayne Anne
1952- .... CLC 15, 33; SSC 16
See also CA 101; CANR 24, 50; DLBY 80;
INT CANR-24; MTCW

Phillips, Richard
See Dick, Philip K(indred)

Phillips, Robert (Schaeffer)
1938- .... CLC 28
See also CA 17-20R; CAAS 13; CANR 8; DLB
105

Phillips, Ward
See Lovecraft, H(oward) P(hillips)

Piccolo, Lucio 1901-1969 .... CLC 13
See also CA 97-100; DLB 114

Pickthall, Marjorie L(owry) C(hristie)
1883-1922 .... TCLC 21
See also CA 107; DLB 92

Pico della Mirandola, Giovanni
1463-1494 .... LC 15

Piercy, Marge
1936- .... CLC 3, 6, 14, 18, 27, 62
See also CA 21-24R; CAAS 1; CANR 13, 43;
DLB 120; MTCW

Piers, Robert
See Anthony, Piers

Pieyre de Mandiargues, Andre 1909-1991
See Mandiargues, Andre Pieyre de
See also CA 103; 136; CANR 22

Pilnyak, Boris .... TCLC 23
See also Vogau, Boris Andreyevich

Pincherle, Alberto
1907-1990 .... CLC 11, 18; DAM NOV
See also Moravia, Alberto
See also CA 25-28R; 132; CANR 33;
MTCW

Pinckney, Darryl 1953- .... CLC 76
See also BW 2; CA 143

Pindar
518B.C.-446B.C. .... CMLC 12; PC 19
See also DLB 176

Pineda, Cecile 1942- .... CLC 39
See also CA 118

Pinero, Arthur Wing
1855-1934 .... TCLC 32; DAM DRAM
See also CA 110; 153; DLB 10

Pinero, Miguel (Antonio Gomez)
1946-1988 .... CLC 4, 55
See also CA 61-64; 125; CANR 29; HW

Pinget, Robert
1919-1997 .... CLC 7, 13, 37
See also CA 85-88; 160; DLB 83

Pink Floyd
See Barrett, (Roger) Syd; Gilmour, David;
Mason, Nick; Waters, Roger; Wright,
Rick

Pinkney, Edward 1802-1828 .... NCLC 31

Pinkwater, Daniel Manus
1941- .... CLC 35
See also Pinkwater, Manus
See also AAYA 1; CA 29-32R; CANR 12, 38;
CLR 4; JRDA; MAICYA; SAAS 3; SATA
46, 76

Pinkwater, Manus
See Pinkwater, Daniel Manus
See also SATA 8

Pinsky, Robert
1940- .... CLC 9, 19, 38, 94; DAM
POET
See also CA 29-32R; CAAS 4; CANR 58;
DLBY 82

Pinta, Harold
See Pinter, Harold

Pinter, Harold
1930- ... CLC 1, 3, 6, 9, 11, 15, 27, 58, 73;
DA; DAB; DAC; DAM DRAM, MST;
WLC
See also CA 5-8R; CANR 33; CDBLB
1960 to Present; DLB 13; MTCW

Piozzi, Hester Lynch (Thrale)
1741-1821 .... NCLC 57
See also DLB 104, 142

Pirandello, Luigi
1867-1936 TCLC 4, 29; DA; DAB; DAC;
DAM DRAM, MST; DC 5; SSC 22; WLC
See also CA 104; 153

Pirsig, Robert M(aynard)
1928- .... CLC 4, 6, 73; DAM POP
See also CA 53-56; CANR 42; MTCW; SATA 39

Pisarev, Dmitry Ivanovich
1840-1868 .... NCLC 25

Pix, Mary (Griffith)
1666-1709 .... LC 8
See also DLB 80

Pixerecourt, Guilbert de
1773-1844 .... NCLC 39

Plaatje, Sol(omon) T(shekisho)
1876-1932 .... TCLC 73
See also BW 2; CA 141

Planche, James Robinson
1796-1880 .... NCLC 42

Plant, Robert 1948- .... CLC 12

Plante, David (Robert)
1940- .... CLC 7, 23, 38; DAM NOV
See also CA 37-40R; CANR 12, 36, 58;
DLBY 83; INT CANR-12; MTCW

Plath, Sylvia
1932-1963 ... CLC 1, 2, 3, 5, 9, 11, 14,
17, 50, 51, 62; DA; DAB; DAC; DAM
MST, POET; PC 1; WLC
See also AAYA 13; CA 19-20; CANR 34; CAP
2; CDALB 1941-1968; DLB 5, 6, 152;
MTCW

Plato 428(?)B.C.-348(?)B.C. .... CMLC 8; DA;
DAB; DAC; DAM MST; WLCS
See also DLB 176

Platonov, Andrei .... TCLC 14
See also Klimentov, Andrei Platonovich

Platt, Kin 1911- .... CLC 26
See also AAYA 11; CA 17-20R; CANR 11;
JRDA; SAAS 17; SATA 21, 86

Plautus c. 251B.C.-184B.C. .... DC 6

Plick et Plock
See Simenon, Georges (Jacques Christian)

Plimpton, George (Ames) 1927- .... CLC 36
See also AITN 1; CA 21-24R; CANR 32;
MTCW; SATA 10

Pliny the Elder c. 23-79 .... CMLC 23

Plomer, William Charles Franklin
1903-1973 .... CLC 4, 8
See also CA 21-22; CANR 34; CAP 2; DLB
20, 162; MTCW; SATA 24

Plowman, Piers
See Kavanagh, Patrick (Joseph)

Plum, J.
See Wodehouse, P(elham) G(renville)

Plumly, Stanley (Ross) 1939- .... CLC 33
See also CA 108; 110; DLB 5; INT 110

Plumpe, Friedrich Wilhelm
1888-1931 .... TCLC 53
See also CA 112

Po Chu-i 772-846 .... CMLC 24

Poe, Edgar Allan
1809-1849 ...NCLC 1, 16, 55; DA; DAB;
DAC; DAM MST, POET; PC 1; SSC 1,
22; WLC
See also AAYA 14; CDALB 1640-1865; DLB
3, 59, 73, 74; SATA 23

Poet of Titchfield Street, The
See Pound, Ezra (Weston Loomis)

Pohl, Frederik 1919- .... CLC 18; SSC 25
See also CA 61-64; CAAS 1; CANR 11, 37;
DLB 8; INT CANR-11; MTCW; SATA 24

Poirier, Louis 1910-
See Gracq, Julien
See also CA 122; 126

Poitier, Sidney 1927- .... CLC 26
See also BW 1; CA 117

Polanski, Roman 1933- .... CLC 16
See also CA 77-80

Poliakoff, Stephen 1952- .... CLC 38
See also CA 106; DLB 13

Police, The
See Copeland, Stewart (Armstrong); Sum-
mers, Andrew James; Sumner, Gordon
Matthew

Polidori, John William
  1795-1821 .... NCLC 51
  See also DLB 116

Pollitt, Katha 1949- .... CLC 28
  See also CA 120; 122; MTCW

Pollock, (Mary) Sharon
  1936- .... CLC 50; DAC; DAM DRAM,
    MST
  See also CA 141; DLB 60

Polo, Marco 1254-1324 .... CMLC 15

Polonsky, Abraham (Lincoln)
  1910- .... CLC 92
  See also CA 104; DLB 26; INT 104

Polybius c. 200B.C.-c. 118B.C. ...... CMLC 17
  See also DLB 176

Pomerance, Bernard 1940-.... CLC 13; DAM
    DRAM
  See also CA 101; CANR 49

Ponge, Francis (Jean Gaston Alfred)
  1899-1988 .... CLC 6, 18; DAM POET
  See also CA 85-88; 126; CANR 40

Pontoppidan, Henrik 1857-1943 .... TCLC 29

Poole, Josephine .... CLC 17
  See also Helyar, Jane Penelope Josephine
  See also SAAS 2; SATA 5

Popa, Vasko 1922-1991 .... CLC 19
  See also CA 112; 148; DLB 181

Pope, Alexander
  1688-1744 .... LC 3; DA; DAB; DAC;
    DAM MST, POET; WLC
  See also CDBLB 1660-1789; DLB 95, 101

Porter, Connie (Rose) 1959(?)- .... CLC 70
  See also BW 2; CA 142; SATA 81

Porter, Gene(va Grace) Stratton
  1863(?)-1924 .... TCLC 21
  See also CA 112

Porter, Katherine Anne
  1890-1980 .... CLC 1, 3, 7, 10, 13, 15, 27,
    101; DA; DAB; DAC; DAM MST, NOV;
    SSC 4
  See also AITN 2; CA 1-4R; 101; CANR 1; DLB
    4, 9, 102; DLBD 12; DLBY 80; MTCW;
    SATA 39; SATA-Obit 23

Porter, Peter (Neville Frederick)
  1929- .... CLC 5, 13, 33
  See also CA 85-88; DLB 40

Porter, William Sydney 1862-1910
  See Henry, O.
  See also CA 104; 131; CDALB 1865-1917;
    DA; DAB; DAC; DAM MST; DLB 12, 78,
    79; MTCW; YABC 2

Portillo (y Pacheco), Jose Lopez
  See Lopez Portillo (y Pacheco), Jose

Post, Melville Davisson 1869-1930 . TCLC 39
  See also CA 110

Potok, Chaim
  1929- .... CLC 2, 7, 14, 26; DAM NOV
  See also AAYA 15; AITN 1, 2; CA 17-20R;
    CANR 19, 35; DLB 28, 152; INT CANR-
    19; MTCW; SATA 33

Potter, (Helen) Beatrix 1866-1943
  See Webb, (Martha) Beatrice (Potter)
  See also MAICYA

Potter, Dennis (Christopher George)
  1935-1994 .... CLC 58, 86
  See also CA 107; 145; CANR 33, 61;
    MTCW

Pound, Ezra (Weston Loomis)
  1885-1972 ... CLC 1, 2, 3, 4, 5, 7, 10, 13,
    18, 34, 48, 50; DA; DAB; DAC; DAM
    MST, POET; PC 4; WLC
  See also CA 5-8R; 37-40R; CANR 40; CDALB
    1917-1929; DLB 4, 45, 63; DLBD 15;
    MTCW

Povod, Reinaldo 1959-1994 .... CLC 44
  See also CA 136; 146

Powell, Adam Clayton, Jr.
  1908-1972 .... CLC 89; BLC; DAM
    MULT
  See also BW 1; CA 102; 33-36R

Powell, Anthony (Dymoke)
  1905- .... CLC 1, 3, 7, 9, 10, 31
  See also CA 1-4R; CANR 1, 32, 62; CDBLB
    1945-1960; DLB 15; MTCW

Powell, Dawn 1897-1965 .... CLC 66
  See also CA 5-8R

Powell, Padgett 1952- .... CLC 34
  See also CA 126

Power, Susan 1961- .... CLC 91

Powers, J(ames) F(arl)
  1917- .... CLC 1, 4, 8, 57; SSC 4
  See also CA 1-4R; CANR 2, 61; DLB 130;
    MTCW

Powers, John J(ames) 1945-
  See Powers, John R.
  See also CA 69-72

Powers, John R. .... CLC 66
  See also Powers, John J(ames)

Powers, Richard (S.) 1957- .... CLC 93
  See also CA 148

Pownall, David 1938- .... CLC 10
  See also CA 89-92; CAAS 18; CANR 49; DLB
    14

Powys, John Cowper
  1872-1963 .... CLC 7, 9, 15, 46
  See also CA 85-88; DLB 15; MTCW

Powys, T(heodore) F(rancis)
  1875-1953 .... TCLC 9
  See also CA 106; DLB 36, 162

Prado (Calvo), Pedro 1886-1952 ... TCLC 75
  See also CA 131; HW

Prager, Emily 1952- .... CLC 56

Pratt, E(dwin) J(ohn)
  1883(?)-1964 .... CLC 19; DAC; DAM
    POET
  See also CA 141; 93-96; DLB 92

Premchand .... TCLC 21
  See also Srivastava, Dhanpat Rai

Preussler, Otfried
  1923- .... CLC 17
  See also CA 77-80; SATA 24

Prevert, Jacques (Henri Marie)
  1900-1977 .... CLC 15
  See also CA 77-80; 69-72; CANR 29, 61;
    MTCW; SATA-Obit 30

Prevost, Abbe (Antoine Francois)
  1697-1763 .... LC 1

Price, (Edward) Reynolds
  1933- ..... CLC 3, 6, 13, 43, 50, 63; DAM
    NOV; SSC 22
  See also CA 1-4R; CANR 1, 37, 57; DLB 2;
    INT CANR-37

Price, Richard
  1949- .... CLC 6, 12
  See also CA 49-52; CANR 3; DLBY 81

Prichard, Katharine Susannah
  1883-1969 .... CLC 46
  See also CA 11-12; CANR 33; CAP 1; MTCW;
    SATA 66

Priestley, J(ohn) B(oynton)
  1894-1984 .... CLC 2, 5, 9, 34; DAM
    DRAM, NOV
  See also CA 9-12R; 113; CANR 33; CDBLB
    1914-1945; DLB 10, 34, 77, 100, 139;
    DLBY 84; MTCW

Prince 1958(?)- .... CLC 35

Prince, F(rank) T(empleton)
  1912- .... CLC 22
  See also CA 101; CANR 43; DLB 20

Prince Kropotkin
  See Kropotkin, Peter (Aleksieevich)

Prior, Matthew 1664-1721 .... LC 4
  See also DLB 95

Prishvin, Mikhail 1873-1954 .... TCLC 75

Pritchard, William H(arrison)
  1932- .... CLC 34
  See also CA 65-68; CANR 23; DLB 111

Pritchett, V(ictor) S(awdon)
  1900-1997 .... CLC 5, 13, 15, 41; DAM
    NOV; SSC 14
  See also CA 61-64; 157; CANR 31; DLB 15,
    139; MTCW

Private 19022
  See Manning, Frederic

Probst, Mark 1925- .... CLC 59
  See also CA 130

Raine, Kathleen (Jessie) 1908- ...... **CLC 7, 45**
See also CA 85-88; CANR 46; DLB 20;
MTCW

Rainis, Janis 1865-1929 .... **TCLC 29**

Rakosi, Carl .... **CLC 47**
See also Rawley, Callman
See also CAAS 5

Raleigh, Richard
See Lovecraft, H(oward) P(hillips)

Raleigh, Sir Walter
1554(?)-1618 .... **LC 31, 39**
See also CDBLB Before 1660; DLB 172

Rallentando, H. P.
See Sayers, Dorothy L(eigh)

Ramal, Walter
See de la Mare, Walter (John)

Ramon, Juan
See Jimenez (Mantecon), Juan Ramon

Ramos, Graciliano 1892-1953 .... **TCLC 32**

Rampersad, Arnold 1941- .... **CLC 44**
See also BW 2; CA 127; 133; DLB 111; INT
133

Rampling, Anne
See Rice, Anne

Ramsay, Allan 1684(?)-1758 .... **LC 29**
See also DLB 95

Ramuz, Charles-Ferdinand
1878-1947 .... **TCLC 33**

Rand, Ayn
1905-1982 .... **CLC 3, 30, 44, 79; DA;
DAC; DAM MST, NOV, POP; WLC**
See also AAYA 10; CA 13-16R; 105; CANR
27; MTCW

Randall, Dudley (Felker)
1914- .... **CLC 1; BLC; DAM MULT**
See also BW 1; CA 25-28R; CANR 23; DLB
41

Randall, Robert
See Silverberg, Robert

Ranger, Ken
See Creasey, John

Ransom, John Crowe
1888-1974 ...... **CLC 2, 4, 5, 11, 24; DAM
POET**
See also CA 5-8R; 49-52; CANR 6, 34; DLB
45, 63; MTCW

Rao, Raja 1909- ...... **CLC 25, 56; DAM NOV**
See also CA 73-76; CANR 51; MTCW

Raphael, Frederic (Michael)
1931- .... **CLC 2, 14**
See also CA 1-4R; CANR 1; DLB 14

Ratcliffe, James P.
See Mencken, H(enry) L(ouis)

Rathbone, Julian 1935- .... **CLC 41**
See also CA 101; CANR 34

Rattigan, Terence (Mervyn)
1911-1977 .... **CLC 7; DAM DRAM**
See also CA 85-88; 73-76; CDBLB 1945-1960;
DLB 13; MTCW

Ratushinskaya, Irina 1954- .... **CLC 54**
See also CA 129

Raven, Simon (Arthur Noel)
1927- .... **CLC 14**
See also CA 81-84

Rawley, Callman 1903-
See Rakosi, Carl
See also CA 21-24R; CANR 12, 32

Rawlings, Marjorie Kinnan
1896-1953 .... **TCLC 4**
See also AAYA 20; CA 104; 137; DLB 9, 22,
102; JRDA; MAICYA; YABC 1

Ray, Satyajit
1921-1992 ..... **CLC 16, 76; DAM MULT**
See also CA 114; 137

Read, Herbert Edward 1893-1968 ..... **CLC 4**
See also CA 85-88; 25-28R; DLB 20,
149

Read, Piers Paul 1941- .... **CLC 4, 10, 25**
See also CA 21-24R; CANR 38; DLB 14;
SATA 21

Reade, Charles 1814-1884 .... **NCLC 2**
See also DLB 21

Reade, Hamish
See Gray, Simon (James Holliday)

Reading, Peter 1946- .... **CLC 47**
See also CA 103; CANR 46; DLB 40

Reaney, James
1926- .... **CLC 13; DAC; DAM MST**
See also CA 41-44R; CAAS 15; CANR 42;
DLB 68; SATA 43

Rebreanu, Liviu 1885-1944 .... **TCLC 28**

Rechy, John (Francisco)
1934- .... **CLC 1, 7, 14, 18; DAM MULT;
HLC**
See also CA 5-8R; CAAS 4; CANR 6, 32; DLB
122; DLBY 82; HW; INT CANR-6

Redcam, Tom 1870-1933 .... **TCLC 25**

Reddin, Keith .... **CLC 67**

Redgrove, Peter (William)
1932- .... **CLC 6, 41**
See also CA 1-4R; CANR 3, 39; DLB
40

Redmon, Anne .... **CLC 22**
See also Nightingale, Anne Redmon
See also DLBY 86

Reed, Eliot
See Ambler, Eric

Reed, Ishmael
1938- ... **CLC 2, 3, 5, 6, 13, 32, 60; BLC;
DAM MULT**
See also BW 2; CA 21-24R; CANR 25,
48; DLB 2, 5, 33, 169; DLBD 8;
MTCW

Reed, John (Silas) 1887-1920 .... **TCLC 9**
See also CA 106

Reed, Lou .... **CLC 21**
See also Firbank, Louis

Reeve, Clara 1729-1807 .... **NCLC 19**
See also DLB 39

Reich, Wilhelm 1897-1957 .... **TCLC 57**

Reid, Christopher (John)
1949- .... **CLC 33**
See also CA 140; DLB 40

Reid, Desmond
See Moorcock, Michael (John)

Reid Banks, Lynne 1929-
See Banks, Lynne Reid
See also CA 1-4R; CANR 6, 22, 38; CLR 24;
JRDA; MAICYA; SATA 22, 75

Reilly, William K.
See Creasey, John

Reiner, Max
See Caldwell, (Janet Miriam) Taylor (Holland)

Reis, Ricardo
See Pessoa, Fernando (Antonio Nogueira)

Remarque, Erich Maria
1898-1970 ..... **CLC 21; DA; DAB; DAC;
DAM MST, NOV**
See also CA 77-80; 29-32R; DLB 56;
MTCW

Remizov, A.
See Remizov, Aleksei (Mikhailovich)

Remizov, A. M.
See Remizov, Aleksei (Mikhailovich)

Remizov, Aleksei (Mikhailovich)
1877-1957 .... **TCLC 27**
See also CA 125; 133

Renan, Joseph Ernest
1823-1892 .... **NCLC 26**

Renard, Jules 1864-1910................ **TCLC 17**
See also CA 117

Renault, Mary .... **CLC 3, 11, 17**
See also Challans, Mary
See also DLBY 83

Rendell, Ruth (Barbara)
1930- .... **CLC 28, 48; DAM POP**
See also Vine, Barbara
See also CA 109; CANR 32, 52; DLB 87; INT
CANR-32; MTCW

Renoir, Jean 1894-1979 .... **CLC 20**
See also CA 129; 85-88

S. S.
See Sassoon, Siegfried (Lorraine)

Saba, Umberto 1883-1957 .... **TCLC 33**
See also CA 144; DLB 114

Sabatini, Rafael 1875-1950 .... **TCLC 47**

Sabato, Ernesto (R.)
1911- .... **CLC 10, 23; DAM MULT;**
HLC
See also CA 97-100; CANR 32; DLB 145; HW;
MTCW

Sacastru, Martin
See Bioy Casares, Adolfo

Sacher-Masoch, Leopold von
1836(?)-1895 .... **NCLC 31**

Sachs, Marilyn (Stickle)
1927- .... **CLC 35**
See also AAYA 2; CA 17-20R; CANR 13, 47;
CLR 2; JRDA; MAICYA; SAAS 2; SATA
3, 68

Sachs, Nelly 1891-1970 .... **CLC 14, 98**
See also CA 17-18; 25-28R; CAP 2

Sackler, Howard (Oliver)
1929-1982 .... **CLC 14**
See also CA 61-64; 108; CANR 30; DLB
7

Sacks, Oliver (Wolf) 1933- .... **CLC 67**
See also CA 53-56; CANR 28, 50; INT CANR-
28; MTCW

Sadakichi
See Hartmann, Sadakichi

Sade, Donatien Alphonse Francois, Comte de
1740-1814 .... **NCLC 47**

Sadoff, Ira 1945- .... **CLC 9**
See also CA 53-56; CANR 5, 21; DLB 120

Saetone
See Camus, Albert

Safire, William 1929- .... **CLC 10**
See also CA 17-20R; CANR 31, 54

Sagan, Carl (Edward)
1934-1996 .... **CLC 30**
See also AAYA 2; CA 25-28R; 155; CANR
11, 36; MTCW; SATA 58; SATA-Obit
94

Sagan, Francoise .... **CLC 3, 6, 9, 17, 36**
See also Quoirez, Francoise
See also DLB 83

Sahgal, Nayantara (Pandit)
1927- .... **CLC 41**
See also CA 9-12R; CANR 11

Saint, H(arry) F. 1941- .... **CLC 50**
See also CA 127

St. Aubin de Teran, Lisa 1953-
See Teran, Lisa St. Aubin de
See also CA 118; 126; INT 126

Saint Birgitta of Sweden
c. 1303-1373 .... **CMLC 24**

Sainte-Beuve, Charles Augustin
1804-1869 .... **NCLC 5**

**Saint-Exupery, Antoine (Jean Baptiste
Marie Roger) de**
1900-1944 .... **TCLC 2, 56; DAM
NOV; WLC**
See also CA 108; 132; CLR 10; DLB 72;
MAICYA; MTCW; SATA 20

St. John, David
See Hunt, E(verette) Howard, (Jr.)

Saint-John Perse
See Leger, (Marie-Rene Auguste) Alexis Saint-
Leger

Saintsbury, George (Edward Bateman)
1845-1933 .... **TCLC 31**
See also CA 160; DLB 57, 149

Sait Faik .... **TCLC 23**
See also Abasiyanik, Sait Faik

Saki .... **TCLC 3; SSC 12**
See also Munro, H(ector) H(ugh)

Sala, George Augustus .... **NCLC 46**

Salama, Hannu 1936- .... **CLC 18**

Salamanca, J(ack) R(ichard)
1922- .... **CLC 4, 15**
See also CA 25-28R

Sale, J. Kirkpatrick
See Sale, Kirkpatrick

Sale, Kirkpatrick
1937- .... **CLC 68**
See also CA 13-16R; CANR 10

Salinas, Luis Omar
1937- .... **CLC 90; DAM MULT;
HLC**
See also CA 131; DLB 82; HW

Salinas (y Serrano), Pedro
1891(?)-1951 .... **TCLC 17**
See also CA 117; DLB 134

Salinger, J(erome) D(avid)
1919- .... **CLC 1, 3, 8, 12, 55, 56; DA;
DAB; DAC; DAM MST, NOV, POP;
SSC 2, 28; WLC**
See also AAYA 2; CA 5-8R; CANR 39;
CDALB 1941-1968; CLR 18; DLB 2,
102, 173; MAICYA; MTCW; SATA
67

Salisbury, John
See Caute, David

Salter, James
1925- .... **CLC 7, 52, 59**
See also CA 73-76; DLB 130

Saltus, Edgar (Everton)
1855-1921 .... **TCLC 8**
See also CA 105

Saltykov, Mikhail Evgrafovich
1826-1889 .... **NCLC 16**

Samarakis, Antonis 1919- .... **CLC 5**
See also CA 25-28R; CAAS 16; CANR 36

Sanchez, Florencio 1875-1910 .... **TCLC 37**
See also CA 153; HW

Sanchez, Luis Rafael 1936- .... **CLC 23**
See also CA 128; DLB 145; HW

Sanchez, Sonia 1934- ..... **CLC 5; BLC; DAM
MULT; PC 9**
See also BW 2; CA 33-36R; CANR 24, 49;
CLR 18; DLB 41; DLBD 8; MAICYA;
MTCW; SATA 22

Sand, George
1804-1876 ... **NCLC 2, 42, 57; DA; DAB;
DAC; DAM MST, NOV; WLC**
See also DLB 119

Sandburg, Carl (August)
1878-1967 ...... **CLC 1, 4, 10, 15, 35; DA;
DAB; DAC; DAM MST, POET; PC 2;
WLC**
See also CA 5-8R; 25-28R; CANR 35; CDALB
1865-1917; DLB 17, 54; MAICYA; MTCW;
SATA 8

Sandburg, Charles
See Sandburg, Carl (August)

Sandburg, Charles A.
See Sandburg, Carl (August)

Sanders, (James) Ed(ward) 1939- .... **CLC 53**
See also CA 13-16R; CAAS 21; CANR 13, 44;
DLB 16

Sanders, Lawrence
1920- .... **CLC 41; DAM POP**
See also BEST 89:4; CA 81-84; CANR 33, 62;
MTCW

Sanders, Noah
See Blount, Roy (Alton), Jr.

Sanders, Winston P.
See Anderson, Poul (William)

Sandoz, Mari(e Susette) 1896-1966 .. **CLC 28**
See also CA 1-4R; 25-28R; CANR 17; DLB
9; MTCW; SATA 5

Saner, Reg(inald Anthony) 1931- .... **CLC 9**
See also CA 65-68

Sannazaro, Jacopo 1456(?)-1530 .... **LC 8**

Sansom, William
1912-1976 .... **CLC 2, 6; DAM NOV;
SSC 21**
See also CA 5-8R; 65-68; CANR 42; DLB 139;
MTCW

Santayana, George 1863-1952 .... **TCLC 40**
See also CA 115; DLB 54, 71; DLBD 13

Santiago, Danny .... **CLC 33**
See also James, Daniel (Lewis)
See also DLB 122

Schulz, Charles M(onroe)
1922- .... **CLC 12**
See also CA 9-12R; CANR 6; INT CANR-6;
SATA 10

Schumacher, E(rnst) F(riedrich)
1911-1977 .... **CLC 80**
See also CA 81-84; 73-76; CANR 34

Schuyler, James Marcus
1923-1991 .... **CLC 5, 23; DAM POET**
See also CA 101; 134; DLB 5, 169; INT
101

Schwartz, Delmore (David)
1913-1966 ..... **CLC 2, 4, 10, 45, 87; PC 8**
See also CA 17-18; 25-28R; CANR 35; CAP
2; DLB 28, 48; MTCW

Schwartz, Ernst
See Ozu, Yasujiro

Schwartz, John Burnham 1965- .... **CLC 59**
See also CA 132

Schwartz, Lynne Sharon 1939- .... **CLC 31**
See also CA 103; CANR 44

Schwartz, Muriel A.
See Eliot, T(homas) S(tearns)

Schwarz-Bart, Andre 1928- .... **CLC 2, 4**
See also CA 89-92

Schwarz-Bart, Simone 1938- .... **CLC 7**
See also BW 2; CA 97-100

Schwob, (Mayer Andre) Marcel
1867-1905 .... **TCLC 20**
See also CA 117; DLB 123

Sciascia, Leonardo
1921-1989 .... **CLC 8, 9, 41**
See also CA 85-88; 130; CANR 35; DLB 177;
MTCW

Scoppettone, Sandra 1936- .... **CLC 26**
See also AAYA 11; CA 5-8R; CANR 41; SATA
9, 92

Scorsese, Martin 1942- .... **CLC 20, 89**
See also CA 110; 114; CANR 46

Scotland, Jay
See Jakes, John (William)

Scott, Duncan Campbell
1862-1947 .... **TCLC 6; DAC**
See also CA 104; 153; DLB 92

Scott, Evelyn 1893-1963 .... **CLC 43**
See also CA 104; 112; DLB 9, 48

Scott, F(rancis) R(eginald)
1899-1985 .... **CLC 22**
See also CA 101; 114; DLB 88; INT
101

Scott, Frank
See Scott, F(rancis) R(eginald)

Scott, Joanna 1960- .... **CLC 50**
See also CA 126; CANR 53

Scott, Paul (Mark) 1920-1978 .... **CLC 9, 60**
See also CA 81-84; 77-80; CANR 33; DLB
14; MTCW

Scott, Walter
1771-1832 .. **NCLC 15; DA; DAB; DAC;**
DAM MST, NOV, POET; PC 13; WLC
See also AAYA 22; CDBLB 1789-1832; DLB
93, 107, 116, 144, 159; YABC 2

Scribe, (Augustin) Eugene
1791-1861 .... **NCLC 16; DAM DRAM;**
DC 5

Scrum, R.
See Crumb, R(obert)

Scudery, Madeleine de 1607-1701 .... **LC 2**

Scum
See Crumb, R(obert)

Scumbag, Little Bobby
See Crumb, R(obert)

Seabrook, John
See Hubbard, L(afayette) Ron(ald)

Sealy, I. Allan 1951- .... **CLC 55**

Search, Alexander
See Pessoa, Fernando (Antonio Nogueira)

Sebastian, Lee
See Silverberg, Robert

Sebastian Owl
See Thompson, Hunter S(tockton)

Sebestyen, Ouida 1924- .... **CLC 30**
See also AAYA 8; CA 107; CANR 40; CLR
17; JRDA; MAICYA; SAAS 10; SATA 39

Secundus, H. Scriblerus
See Fielding, Henry

Sedges, John
See Buck, Pearl S(ydenstricker)

Sedgwick, Catharine Maria
1789-1867 .... **NCLC 19**
See also DLB 1, 74

Seelye, John 1931- .... **CLC 7**

Seferiades, Giorgos Stylianou 1900-1971
See Seferis, George
See also CA 5-8R; 33-36R; CANR 5, 36;
MTCW

Seferis, George .... **CLC 5, 11**
See also Seferiades, Giorgos Stylianou

Segal, Erich (Wolf)
1937- .... **CLC 3, 10; DAM POP**
See also BEST 89:1; CA 25-28R; CANR 20,
36; DLBY 86; INT CANR-20; MTCW

Seger, Bob 1945- .... **CLC 35**

Seghers, Anna .... **CLC 7**
See also Radvanyi, Netty
See also DLB 69

Seidel, Frederick (Lewis) 1936- .... **CLC 18**
See also CA 13-16R; CANR 8; DLBY 84

Seifert, Jaroslav 1901-1986 .. **CLC 34, 44, 93**
See also CA 127; MTCW

Sei Shonagon c. 966-1017(?) .... **CMLC 6**

Selby, Hubert, Jr.
1928- .... **CLC 1, 2, 4, 8; SSC 20**
See also CA 13-16R; CANR 33; DLB 2

Selzer, Richard 1928- .... **CLC 74**
See also CA 65-68; CANR 14

Sembene, Ousmane
See Ousmane, Sembene

Senancour, Etienne Pivert de
1770-1846 .... **NCLC 16**
See also DLB 119

Sender, Ramon (Jose)
1902-1982 ... **CLC 8; DAM MULT; HLC**
See also CA 5-8R; 105; CANR 8; HW; MTCW

Seneca, Lucius Annaeus
4B.C.-65 ..... **CMLC 6; DAM DRAM;**
DC 5

Senghor, Leopold Sedar
1906- .... **CLC 54; BLC; DAM MULT,**
POET
See also BW 2; CA 116; 125; CANR 47;
MTCW

Serling, (Edward) Rod(man)
1924-1975 .... **CLC 30**
See also AAYA 14; AITN 1; CA 65-68; 57-60;
DLB 26

Serna, Ramon Gomez de la
See Gomez de la Serna, Ramon

Serpieres
See Guillevic, (Eugene)

Service, Robert
See Service, Robert W(illiam)
See also DAB; DLB 92

Service, Robert W(illiam)
1874(?)-1958 .... **TCLC 15; DA; DAC;**
DAM MST, POET; WLC
See also Service, Robert
See also CA 115; 140; SATA 20

Seth, Vikram
1952- .... **CLC 43, 90; DAM MULT**
See also CA 121; 127; CANR 50; DLB 120;
INT 127

Seton, Cynthia Propper
1926-1982 .... **CLC 27**
See also CA 5-8R; 108; CANR 7

Seton, Ernest (Evan) Thompson
1860-1946 .... **TCLC 31**
See also CA 109; DLB 92; DLBD 13; JRDA;
SATA 18

Seton-Thompson, Ernest
See Seton, Ernest (Evan) Thompson

Settle, Mary Lee
1918- .... **CLC 19, 61**
See also CA 89-92; CAAS 1; CANR 44; DLB
6; INT 89-92

Seuphor, Michel
See Arp, Jean

Sevigne, Marie (de Rabutin-Chantal) Marquise
de 1626-1696 .... **LC 11**

Sewall, Samuel
1652-1730 .... **LC 38**
See also DLB 24

Sexton, Anne (Harvey)
1928-1974 ..... **CLC 2, 4, 6, 8, 10, 15, 53;**
DA; DAB; DAC; DAM MST, POET; PC
2; WLC
See also CA 1-4R; 53-56; CABS 2; CANR 3,
36; CDALB 1941-1968; DLB 5, 169;
MTCW; SATA 10

Shaara, Michael (Joseph, Jr.)
1929-1988 .... **CLC 15; DAM POP**
See also AITN 1; CA 102; 125; CANR 52;
DLBY 83

Shackleton, C. C.
See Aldiss, Brian W(ilson)

Shacochis, Bob .... **CLC 39**
See also Shacochis, Robert G.

Shacochis, Robert G. 1951-
See Shacochis, Bob
See also CA 119; 124; INT 124

Shaffer, Anthony (Joshua) 1926- .... **CLC 19;**
DAM DRAM
See also CA 110; 116; DLB 13

Shaffer, Peter (Levin)
1926- .... **CLC 5, 14, 18, 37, 60; DAB;**
DAM DRAM, MST; DC 7
See also CA 25-28R; CANR 25, 47;
CDBLB 1960 to Present; DLB 13;
MTCW

Shakey, Bernard
See Young, Neil

Shalamov, Varlam (Tikhonovich)
1907(?)-1982 .... **CLC 18**
See also CA 129; 105

Shamlu, Ahmad 1925- .... **CLC 10**

Shammas, Anton 1951- .... **CLC 55**

Shange, Ntozake
1948- ..... **CLC 8, 25, 38, 74; BLC; DAM**
DRAM, MULT; DC 3
See also AAYA 9; BW 2; CA 85-88; CABS 3;
CANR 27, 48; DLB 38; MTCW

Shanley, John Patrick
1950- .... **CLC 75**
See also CA 128; 133

Shapcott, Thomas W(illiam)
1935- .... **CLC 38**
See also CA 69-72; CANR 49

Shapiro, Jane .... **CLC 76**

Shapiro, Karl (Jay) 1913- ... **CLC 4, 8, 15, 53**
See also CA 1-4R; CAAS 6; CANR 1, 36; DLB
48; MTCW

Sharp, William 1855-1905 .... **TCLC 39**
See also CA 160; DLB 156

Sharpe, Thomas Ridley 1928-
See Sharpe, Tom
See also CA 114; 122; INT 122

Sharpe, Tom .... **CLC 36**
See also Sharpe, Thomas Ridley
See also DLB 14

Shaw, Bernard .... **TCLC 45**
See also Shaw, George Bernard
See also BW 1

Shaw, G. Bernard
See Shaw, George Bernard

Shaw, George Bernard
1856-1950 ..... **TCLC 3, 9, 21; DA; DAB;**
DAC; DAM DRAM, MST; WLC
See also Shaw, Bernard
See also CA 104; 128; CDBLB 1914-1945;
DLB 10, 57; MTCW

Shaw, Henry Wheeler
1818-1885 .... **NCLC 15**
See also DLB 11

Shaw, Irwin
1913-1984 .... **CLC 7, 23, 34; DAM**
DRAM, POP
See also AITN 1; CA 13-16R; 112; CANR 21;
CDALB 1941-1968; DLB 6, 102; DLBY 84;
MTCW

Shaw, Robert 1927-1978 .... **CLC 5**
See also AITN 1; CA 1-4R; 81-84; CANR 4;
DLB 13, 14

Shaw, T. E.
See Lawrence, T(homas) E(dward)

Shawn, Wallace 1943- .... **CLC 41**
See also CA 112

Shea, Lisa 1953- .... **CLC 86**
See also CA 147

Sheed, Wilfrid (John Joseph)
1930- .... **CLC 2, 4, 10, 53**
See also CA 65-68; CANR 30; DLB 6;
MTCW

Sheldon, Alice Hastings Bradley 1915(?)-1987
See Tiptree, James, Jr.
See also CA 108; 122; CANR 34; INT 108;
MTCW

Sheldon, John
See Bloch, Robert (Albert)

Shelley, Mary Wollstonecraft (Godwin)
1797-1851 .... **NCLC 14, 59; DA; DAB;**
DAC; DAM MST, NOV; WLC
See also AAYA 20; CDBLB 1789-1832; DLB
110, 116, 159, 178; SATA 29

Shelley, Percy Bysshe
1792-1822 .... **NCLC 18; DA; DAB;**
DAC; DAM MST, POET; PC 14; WLC
See also CDBLB 1789-1832; DLB 96, 110,
158

Shepard, Jim 1956- .... **CLC 36**
See also CA 137; CANR 59; SATA 90

Shepard, Lucius 1947- .... **CLC 34**
See also CA 128; 141

Shepard, Sam
1943- ..... **CLC 4, 6, 17, 34, 41, 44; DAM**
DRAM; DC 5
See also AAYA 1; CA 69-72; CABS 3; CANR
22; DLB 7; MTCW

Shepherd, Michael
See Ludlum, Robert

Sherburne, Zoa (Morin) 1912- .... **CLC 30**
See also AAYA 13; CA 1-4R; CANR 3, 37;
MAICYA; SAAS 18; SATA 3

Sheridan, Frances 1724-1766 .... **LC 7**
See also DLB 39, 84

Sheridan, Richard Brinsley
1751-1816 .... **NCLC 5; DA; DAB; DAC;**
DAM DRAM, MST; DC 1; WLC
See also CDBLB 1660-1789; DLB 89

Sherman, Jonathan Marc .... **CLC 55**

Sherman, Martin 1941(?)- .... **CLC 19**
See also CA 116; 123

Sherwin, Judith Johnson 1936- .... **CLC 7, 15**
See also CA 25-28R; CANR 34

Sherwood, Frances 1940- .... **CLC 81**
See also CA 146

Sherwood, Robert E(mmet)
1896-1955 .... **TCLC 3; DAM DRAM**
See also CA 104; 153; DLB 7, 26

Shestov, Lev 1866-1938 .... **TCLC 56**

Shevchenko, Taras 1814-1861 .... **NCLC 54**

Shiel, M(atthew) P(hipps)
1865-1947 .... **TCLC 8**
See also Holmes, Gordon
See also CA 106; 160; DLB 153

Shields, Carol 1935- .... **CLC 91; DAC**
See also CA 81-84; CANR 51

Shields, David 1956- .... **CLC 97**
See also CA 124; CANR 48

Shiga, Naoya 1883-1971 ...... **CLC 33; SSC 23**
See also CA 101; 33-36R; DLB 180

Shilts, Randy 1951-1994 .... **CLC 85**
See also AAYA 19; CA 115; 127; 144; CANR
45; INT 127

Shimazaki, Haruki 1872-1943
See Shimazaki Toson
See also CA 105; 134

Shimazaki Toson 1872-1943 .... **TCLC 5**
See also Shimazaki, Haruki
See also DLB 180

Sholokhov, Mikhail (Aleksandrovich)
1905-1984 .... **CLC 7, 15**
See also CA 101; 112; MTCW; SATA-Obit 36

Shone, Patric
See Hanley, James

Shreve, Susan Richards 1939- .... **CLC 23**
See also CA 49-52; CAAS 5; CANR 5, 38; MAICYA; SATA 46, 95; SATA-Brief 41

Shue, Larry
1946-1985 .... **CLC 52; DAM DRAM**
See also CA 145; 117

Shu-Jen, Chou 1881-1936
See Lu Hsun
See also CA 104

Shulman, Alix Kates 1932- .... **CLC 2, 10**
See also CA 29-32R; CANR 43; SATA 7

Shuster, Joe 1914- .... **CLC 21**

Shute, Nevil .... **CLC 30**
See also Norway, Nevil Shute

Shuttle, Penelope (Diane) 1947- .... **CLC 7**
See also CA 93-96; CANR 39; DLB 14, 40

Sidney, Mary 1561-1621 .... **LC 19, 39**

Sidney, Sir Philip
1554-1586 .... **LC 19, 39; DA; DAB; DAC; DAM MST, POET**
See also CDBLB Before 1660; DLB 167

Siegel, Jerome 1914-1996 .... **CLC 21**
See also CA 116; 151

Siegel, Jerry
See Siegel, Jerome

Sienkiewicz, Henryk (Adam Alexander Pius)
1846-1916 .... **TCLC 3**
See also CA 104; 134

Sierra, Gregorio Martinez
See Martinez Sierra, Gregorio

Sierra, Maria (de la O'LeJarraga) Martinez
See Martinez Sierra, Maria (de la O'LeJarraga)

Sigal, Clancy 1926- .... **CLC 7**
See also CA 1-4R

Sigourney, Lydia Howard (Huntley)
1791-1865 .... **NCLC 21**
See also DLB 1, 42, 73

Siguenza y Gongora, Carlos de
1645-1700 .... **LC 8**

Sigurjonsson, Johann
1880-1919 .... **TCLC 27**

Sikelianos, Angelos 1884-1951 .... **TCLC 39**

Silkin, Jon 1930- .... **CLC 2, 6, 43**
See also CA 5-8R; CAAS 5; DLB 27

Silko, Leslie (Marmon)
1948- .... **CLC 23, 74; DA; DAC; DAM MST, MULT, POP; WLCS**
See also AAYA 14; CA 115; 122; CANR 45; DLB 143, 175; NNAL

Sillanpaa, Frans Eemil
1888-1964 .... **CLC 19**
See also CA 129; 93-96; MTCW

Sillitoe, Alan
1928- .... **CLC 1, 3, 6, 10, 19, 57**
See also AITN 1; CA 9-12R; CAAS 2; CANR 8, 26, 55; CDBLB 1960 to Present; DLB 14, 139; MTCW; SATA 61

Silone, Ignazio 1900-1978 .... **CLC 4**
See also CA 25-28; 81-84; CANR 34; CAP 2; MTCW

Silver, Joan Micklin 1935- .... **CLC 20**
See also CA 114; 121; INT 121

Silver, Nicholas
See Faust, Frederick (Schiller)

Silverberg, Robert
1935- .... **CLC 7; DAM POP**
See also CA 1-4R; CAAS 3; CANR 1, 20, 36; DLB 8; INT CANR-20; MAICYA; MTCW; SATA 13, 91

Silverstein, Alvin 1933- .... **CLC 17**
See also CA 49-52; CANR 2; CLR 25; JRDA; MAICYA; SATA 8, 69

Silverstein, Virginia B(arbara Opshelor)
1937- .... **CLC 17**
See also CA 49-52; CANR 2; CLR 25; JRDA; MAICYA; SATA 8, 69

Sim, Georges
See Simenon, Georges (Jacques Christian)

Simak, Clifford D(onald)
1904-1988 .... **CLC 1, 55**
See also CA 1-4R; 125; CANR 1, 35; DLB 8; MTCW; SATA-Obit 56

Simenon, Georges (Jacques Christian)
1903-1989 .... **CLC 1, 2, 3, 8, 18, 47; DAM POP**
See also CA 85-88; 129; CANR 35; DLB 72; DLBY 89; MTCW

Simic, Charles
1938- .... **CLC 6, 9, 22, 49, 68; DAM POET**
See also CA 29-32R; CAAS 4; CANR 12, 33, 52, 61; DLB 105

Simmel, Georg 1858-1918 .... **TCLC 64**
See also CA 157

Simmons, Charles (Paul) 1924- .... **CLC 57**
See also CA 89-92; INT 89-92

Simmons, Dan
1948- .... **CLC 44; DAM POP**
See also AAYA 16; CA 138; CANR 53

Simmons, James (Stewart Alexander)
1933- .... **CLC 43**
See also CA 105; CAAS 21; DLB 40

Simms, William Gilmore
1806-1870 .... **NCLC 3**
See also DLB 3, 30, 59, 73

Simon, Carly 1945- .... **CLC 26**
See also CA 105

Simon, Claude
1913- .... **CLC 4, 9, 15, 39; DAM NOV**
See also CA 89-92; CANR 33; DLB 83; MTCW

Simon, (Marvin) Neil
1927- .... **CLC 6, 11, 31, 39, 70; DAM DRAM**
See also AITN 1; CA 21-24R; CANR 26, 54; DLB 7; MTCW

Simon, Paul (Frederick)
1941(?)- .... **CLC 17**
See also CA 116; 153

Simonon, Paul 1956(?)- .... **CLC 30**

Simpson, Harriette
See Arnow, Harriette (Louisa) Simpson

Simpson, Louis (Aston Marantz)
1923- .... **CLC 4, 7, 9, 32; DAM POET**
See also CA 1-4R; CAAS 4; CANR 1, 61; DLB 5; MTCW

Simpson, Mona (Elizabeth)
1957- .... **CLC 44**
See also CA 122; 135

Simpson, N(orman) F(rederick)
1919- .... **CLC 29**
See also CA 13-16R; DLB 13

Sinclair, Andrew (Annandale)
1935- .... **CLC 2, 14**
See also CA 9-12R; CAAS 5; CANR 14, 38; DLB 14; MTCW

Sinclair, Emil
See Hesse, Hermann

Sinclair, Iain 1943- .... **CLC 76**
See also CA 132

Sinclair, Iain MacGregor
See Sinclair, Iain

Sinclair, Irene
See Griffith, D(avid Lewelyn) W(ark)

Sinclair, Mary Amelia St. Clair 1865(?)-1946
See Sinclair, May
See also CA 104

Sinclair, May .... **TCLC 3, 11**
See also Sinclair, Mary Amelia St. Clair
See also DLB 36, 135

Sinclair, Roy
See Griffith, D(avid Lewelyn) W(ark)

Sinclair, Upton (Beall)
1878-1968 ..... **CLC 1, 11, 15, 63; DA; DAB; DAC; DAM MST, NOV; WLC**
See also CA 5-8R; 25-28R; CANR 7; CDALB 1929-1941; DLB 9; INT CANR-7; MTCW; SATA 9

Singer, Isaac
See Singer, Isaac Bashevis

Singer, Isaac Bashevis
1904-1991 ... **CLC 1, 3, 6, 9, 11, 15, 23, 38, 69; DA; DAB; DAC; DAM MST, NOV; SSC 3; WLC**
See also AITN 1, 2; CA 1-4R; 134; CANR 1, 39; CDALB 1941-1968; CLR 1; DLB 6, 28, 52; DLBY 91; JRDA; MAICYA; MTCW; SATA 3, 27; SATA-Obit 68

Singer, Israel Joshua 1893-1944 .... **TCLC 33**

Singh, Khushwant 1915- .... **CLC 11**
See also CA 9-12R; CAAS 9; CANR 6

Singleton, Ann
See Benedict, Ruth (Fulton)

Sinjohn, John
See Galsworthy, John

Sinyavsky, Andrei (Donatevich)
1925-1997 .... **CLC 8**
See also CA 85-88; 159

Sirin, V.
See Nabokov, Vladimir (Vladimirovich)

Sissman, L(ouis) E(dward)
1928-1976 .... **CLC 9, 18**
See also CA 21-24R; 65-68; CANR 13; DLB 5

Sisson, C(harles) H(ubert)
1914- .... **CLC 8**
See also CA 1-4R; CAAS 3; CANR 3, 48; DLB 27

Sitwell, Dame Edith
1887-1964 ... **CLC 2, 9, 67; DAM POET; PC 3**
See also CA 9-12R; CANR 35; CDBLB 1945-1960; DLB 20; MTCW

Siwaarmill, H. P.
See Sharp, William

Sjoewall, Maj 1935- .... **CLC 7**
See also CA 65-68

Sjowall, Maj
See Sjoewall, Maj

Skelton, Robin
1925-1997 .... **CLC 13**
See also AITN 2; CA 5-8R; 160; CAAS 5; CANR 28; DLB 27, 53

Skolimowski, Jerzy 1938- .... **CLC 20**
See also CA 128

Skram, Amalie (Bertha)
1847-1905 .... **TCLC 25**

Skvorecky, Josef (Vaclav)
1924- .... **CLC 15, 39, 69; DAC; DAM NOV**
See also CA 61-64; CAAS 1; CANR 10, 34; MTCW

Slade, Bernard .... **CLC 11, 46**
See also Newbound, Bernard Slade
See also CAAS 9; DLB 53

Slaughter, Carolyn 1946- .... **CLC 56**
See also CA 85-88

Slaughter, Frank G(ill) 1908- .... **CLC 29**
See also AITN 2; CA 5-8R; CANR 5; INT CANR-5

Slavitt, David R(ytman) 1935- ......**CLC 5, 14**
See also CA 21-24R; CAAS 3; CANR 41; DLB 5, 6

Slesinger, Tess 1905-1945 .... **TCLC 10**
See also CA 107; DLB 102

Slessor, Kenneth 1901-1971 .... **CLC 14**
See also CA 102; 89-92

Slowacki, Juliusz 1809-1849 .... **NCLC 15**

Smart, Christopher
1722-1771 ..... **LC 3; DAM POET; PC 13**
See also DLB 109

Smart, Elizabeth 1913-1986 .... **CLC 54**
See also CA 81-84; 118; DLB 88

Smiley, Jane (Graves) 1949- ...... **CLC 53, 76; DAM POP**
See also CA 104; CANR 30, 50; INT CANR-30

Smith, A(rthur) J(ames) M(arshall)
1902-1980 .... **CLC 15; DAC**
See also CA 1-4R; 102; CANR 4; DLB 88

Smith, Adam 1723-1790 .... **LC 36**
See also DLB 104

Smith, Alexander 1829-1867 .... **NCLC 59**
See also DLB 32, 55

Smith, Anna Deavere 1950- .... **CLC 86**
See also CA 133

Smith, Betty (Wehner)
1896-1972 .... **CLC 19**
See also CA 5-8R; 33-36R; DLBY 82; SATA 6

Smith, Charlotte (Turner)
1749-1806 .... **NCLC 23**
See also DLB 39, 109

Smith, Clark Ashton 1893-1961 .... **CLC 43**
See also CA 143

Smith, Dave .... **CLC 22, 42**
See also Smith, David (Jeddie)
See also CAAS 7; DLB 5

Smith, David (Jeddie) 1942-
See Smith, Dave
See also CA 49-52; CANR 1, 59; DAM POET

Smith, Florence Margaret 1902-1971
See Smith, Stevie
See also CA 17-18; 29-32R; CANR 35; CAP 2; DAM POET; MTCW

Smith, Iain Crichton 1928- .... **CLC 64**
See also CA 21-24R; DLB 40, 139

Smith, John 1580(?)-1631 .... **LC 9**

Smith, Johnston
See Crane, Stephen (Townley)

Smith, Joseph, Jr. 1805-1844 .... **NCLC 53**

Smith, Lee 1944- .... **CLC 25, 73**
See also CA 114; 119; CANR 46; DLB 143; DLBY 83; INT 119

Smith, Martin
See Smith, Martin Cruz

Smith, Martin Cruz 1942- ..... **CLC 25; DAM MULT, POP**
See also BEST 89:4; CA 85-88; CANR 6, 23, 43; INT CANR-23; NNAL

Smith, Mary-Ann Tirone 1944- .... **CLC 39**
See also CA 118; 136

Smith, Patti 1946- .... **CLC 12**
See also CA 93-96

Smith, Pauline (Urmson)
1882-1959 .... **TCLC 25**

Smith, Rosamond
See Oates, Joyce Carol

Smith, Sheila Kaye
See Kaye-Smith, Sheila

Smith, Stevie .... **CLC 3, 8, 25, 44; PC 12**
See also Smith, Florence Margaret
See also DLB 20

Smith, Wilbur (Addison) 1933- .... **CLC 33**
See also CA 13-16R; CANR 7, 46; MTCW

Smith, William Jay 1918- .... **CLC 6**
See also CA 5-8R; CANR 44; DLB 5; MAICYA; SAAS 22; SATA 2, 68

Smith, Woodrow Wilson
See Kuttner, Henry

Smolenskin, Peretz 1842-1885 .... **NCLC 30**

Smollett, Tobias (George)
1721-1771 .... **LC 2**
See also CDBLB 1660-1789; DLB 39, 104

Snodgrass, W(illiam) D(e Witt)
1926- .... **CLC 2, 6, 10, 18, 68; DAM POET**
See also CA 1-4R; CANR 6, 36; DLB 5; MTCW

Snow, C(harles) P(ercy)
1905-1980 .... **CLC 1, 4, 6, 9, 13, 19; DAM NOV**
See also CA 5-8R; 101; CANR 28; CDBLB 1945-1960; DLB 15, 77; MTCW

Snow, Frances Compton
See Adams, Henry (Brooks)

Snyder, Gary (Sherman)
1930- .... **CLC 1, 2, 5, 9, 32; DAM POET**
See also CA 17-20R; CANR 30, 60; DLB 5, 16, 165

Snyder, Zilpha Keatley 1927- .... **CLC 17**
See also AAYA 15; CA 9-12R; CANR 38; CLR 31; JRDA; MAICYA; SAAS 2; SATA 1, 28, 75

Soares, Bernardo
See Pessoa, Fernando (Antonio Nogueira)

Sobh, A.
See Shamlu, Ahmad

Sobol, Joshua .... **CLC 60**

Soderberg, Hjalmar 1869-1941 ..... **TCLC 39**

Sodergran, Edith (Irene)
See Soedergran, Edith (Irene)

Soedergran, Edith (Irene)
1892-1923 .... **TCLC 31**

Softly, Edgar
See Lovecraft, H(oward) P(hillips)

Softly, Edward
See Lovecraft, H(oward) P(hillips)

Sokolov, Raymond 1941- .... **CLC 7**
See also CA 85-88

Solo, Jay
See Ellison, Harlan (Jay)

Sologub, Fyodor .... **TCLC 9**
See also Teternikov, Fyodor Kuzmich

Solomons, Ikey Esquir
See Thackeray, William Makepeace

Solomos, Dionysios 1798-1857 .... **NCLC 15**

Solwoska, Mara
See French, Marilyn

Solzhenitsyn, Aleksandr I(sayevich)
1918- .... **CLC 1, 2, 4, 7, 9, 10, 18, 26, 34, 78; DA; DAB; DAC; DAM MST, NOV; WLC**
See also AITN 1; CA 69-72; CANR 40; MTCW

Somers, Jane
See Lessing, Doris (May)

Somerville, Edith 1858-1949 .... **TCLC 51**
See also DLB 135

Somerville & Ross
See Martin, Violet Florence; Somerville, Edith

Sommer, Scott 1951- .... **CLC 25**
See also CA 106

Sondheim, Stephen (Joshua)
1930- .... **CLC 30, 39; DAM DRAM**
See also AAYA 11; CA 103; CANR 47

Sontag, Susan
1933- ... **CLC 1, 2, 10, 13, 31, 105; DAM POP**
See also CA 17-20R; CANR 25, 51; DLB 2, 67; MTCW

Sophocles
496(?)B.C.-406(?)B.C. ..... **CMLC 2; DA; DAB; DAC; DAM DRAM, MST; DC 1; WLCS**
See also DLB 176

Sordello 1189-1269 .... **CMLC 15**

Sorel, Julia
See Drexler, Rosalyn

Sorrentino, Gilbert
1929- .... **CLC 3, 7, 14, 22, 40**
See also CA 77-80; CANR 14, 33; DLB 5, 173; DLBY 80; INT CANR-14

Soto, Gary
1952- ... **CLC 32, 80; DAM MULT; HLC**
See also AAYA 10; CA 119; 125; CANR 50; CLR 38; DLB 82; HW; INT 125; JRDA; SATA 80

Soupault, Philippe 1897-1990 .... **CLC 68**
See also CA 116; 147; 131

Souster, (Holmes) Raymond
1921- ..... **CLC 5, 14; DAC; DAM POET**
See also CA 13-16R; CAAS 14; CANR 13, 29, 53; DLB 88; SATA 63

Southern, Terry 1924(?)-1995 .... **CLC 7**
See also CA 1-4R; 150; CANR 1, 55; DLB 2

Southey, Robert 1774-1843 .... **NCLC 8**
See also DLB 93, 107, 142; SATA 54

Southworth, Emma Dorothy Eliza Nevitte
1819-1899 .... **NCLC 26**

Souza, Ernest
See Scott, Evelyn

Soyinka, Wole 1934- .... **CLC 3, 5, 14, 36, 44; BLC; DA; DAB; DAC; DAM DRAM, MST, MULT; DC 2; WLC**
See also BW 2; CA 13-16R; CANR 27, 39; DLB 125; MTCW

Spackman, W(illiam) M(ode)
1905-1990 .... **CLC 46**
See also CA 81-84; 132

Spacks, Barry (Bernard) 1931- .... **CLC 14**
See also CA 154; CANR 33; DLB 105

Spanidou, Irini 1946- .... **CLC 44**

Spark, Muriel (Sarah)
1918- .... **CLC 2, 3, 5, 8, 13, 18, 40, 94; DAB; DAC; DAM MST, NOV; SSC 10**
See also CA 5-8R; CANR 12, 36; CDBLB 1945-1960; DLB 15, 139; INT CANR-12; MTCW

Spaulding, Douglas
See Bradbury, Ray (Douglas)

Spaulding, Leonard
See Bradbury, Ray (Douglas)

Spence, J. A. D.
See Eliot, T(homas) S(tearns)

Spencer, Elizabeth 1921- .... **CLC 22**
See also CA 13-16R; CANR 32; DLB 6; MTCW; SATA 14

Spencer, Leonard G.
See Silverberg, Robert

Spencer, Scott 1945- .... **CLC 30**
See also CA 113; CANR 51; DLBY 86

Spender, Stephen (Harold)
1909-1995 .... **CLC 1, 2, 5, 10, 41, 91; DAM POET**
See also CA 9-12R; 149; CANR 31, 54; CDBLB 1945-1960; DLB 20; MTCW

Spengler, Oswald (Arnold Gottfried)
1880-1936 .... **TCLC 25**
See also CA 118

Spenser, Edmund
1552(?)-1599 .... **LC 5, 39; DA; DAB; DAC; DAM MST, POET; PC 8; WLC**
See also CDBLB Before 1660; DLB 167

Spicer, Jack
1925-1965 .... **CLC 8, 18, 72; DAM POET**
See also CA 85-88; DLB 5, 16

Spiegelman, Art 1948- .... **CLC 76**
See also AAYA 10; CA 125; CANR 41, 55

Spielberg, Peter 1929- .... **CLC 6**
See also CA 5-8R; CANR 4, 48; DLBY 81

Spielberg, Steven 1947- .... **CLC 20**
See also AAYA 8; CA 77-80; CANR 32; SATA 32

Spillane, Frank Morrison 1918-
See Spillane, Mickey
See also CA 25-28R; CANR 28; MTCW; SATA 66

Spillane, Mickey .... **CLC 3, 13**
See also Spillane, Frank Morrison

Spinoza, Benedictus de 1632-1677 .... **LC 9**

Spinrad, Norman (Richard) 1940- ... **CLC 46**
See also CA 37-40R; CAAS 19; CANR 20; DLB 8; INT CANR-20

Spitteler, Carl (Friedrich Georg)
1845-1924 .... **TCLC 12**
See also CA 109; DLB 129

Spivack, Kathleen (Romola Drucker)
1938- .... **CLC 6**
See also CA 49-52

Spoto, Donald 1941- .... **CLC 39**
See also CA 65-68; CANR 11, 57

Springsteen, Bruce (F.) 1949- .... **CLC 17**
See also CA 111

Still, James 1906- .... CLC **49**
See also CA 65-68; CAAS 17; CANR 10, 26;
DLB 9; SATA 29

Sting
See Sumner, Gordon Matthew

Stirling, Arthur
See Sinclair, Upton (Beall)

Stitt, Milan 1941- .... CLC **29**
See also CA 69-72

Stockton, Francis Richard 1834-1902
See Stockton, Frank R.
See also CA 108; 137; MAICYA; SATA 44

Stockton, Frank R. .... TCLC **47**
See also Stockton, Francis Richard
See also DLB 42, 74; DLBD 13; SATA-Brief
32

Stoddard, Charles
See Kuttner, Henry

Stoker, Abraham 1847-1912
See Stoker, Bram
See also CA 105; DA; DAC; DAM MST, NOV;
SATA 29

Stoker, Bram
1847-1912 .... TCLC **8; DAB; WLC**
See also Stoker, Abraham
See also CA 150; CDBLB 1890-1914; DLB
36, 70, 178

Stolz, Mary (Slattery) 1920- .... CLC **12**
See also AAYA 8; AITN 1; CA 5-8R; CANR
13, 41; JRDA; MAICYA; SAAS 3; SATA
10, 71

Stone, Irving
1903-1989 .... CLC **7; DAM POP**
See also AITN 1; CA 1-4R; 129; CAAS 3;
CANR 1, 23; INT CANR-23; MTCW; SATA
3; SATA-Obit 64

Stone, Oliver (William) 1946- .... CLC **73**
See also AAYA 15; CA 110; CANR 55

Stone, Robert (Anthony)
1937- .... CLC **5, 23, 42**
See also CA 85-88; CANR 23; DLB 152; INT
CANR-23; MTCW

Stone, Zachary
See Follett, Ken(neth Martin)

Stoppard, Tom 1937-.. CLC **1, 3, 4, 5, 8,
15, 29, 34, 63, 91; DA; DAB; DAC;
DAM DRAM, MST; DC 6; WLC**
See also CA 81-84; CANR 39; CDBLB
1960 to Present; DLB 13; DLBY 85;
MTCW

Storey, David (Malcolm)
1933- .... CLC **2, 4, 5, 8; DAM DRAM**
See also CA 81-84; CANR 36; DLB 13, 14;
MTCW

Storm, Hyemeyohsts
1935- .... CLC **3; DAM MULT**
See also CA 81-84; CANR 45; NNAL

Storm, (Hans) Theodor (Woldsen)
1817-1888 .... NCLC **1; SSC 27**

Storni, Alfonsina
1892-1938 .... TCLC **5; DAM MULT;
HLC**
See also CA 104; 131; HW

Stoughton, William 1631-1701 .... LC **38**
See also DLB 24

Stout, Rex (Todhunter)
1886-1975 .... CLC **3**
See also AITN 2; CA 61-64

Stow, (Julian) Randolph
1935- .... CLC **23, 48**
See also CA 13-16R; CANR 33; MTCW

Stowe, Harriet (Elizabeth) Beecher
1811-1896 .... NCLC **3, 50; DA; DAB;
DAC; DAM MST, NOV; WLC**
See also CDALB 1865-1917; DLB 1, 12, 42,
74; JRDA; MAICYA; YABC 1

Strachey, (Giles) Lytton
1880-1932 .... TCLC **12**
See also CA 110; DLB 149; DLBD 10

Strand, Mark
1934- .... CLC **6, 18, 41, 71; DAM
POET**
See also CA 21-24R; CANR 40; DLB 5; SATA
41

Straub, Peter (Francis)
1943- .... CLC **28; DAM POP**
See also BEST 89:1; CA 85-88; CANR 28;
DLBY 84; MTCW

Strauss, Botho 1944-........................... CLC **22**
See also CA 157; DLB 124

Streatfeild, (Mary) Noel
1895(?)-1986 .... CLC **21**
See also CA 81-84; 120; CANR 31; CLR 17;
DLB 160; MAICYA; SATA 20; SATA-Obit
48

Stribling, T(homas) S(igismund)
1881-1965 .... CLC **23**
See also CA 107; DLB 9

Strindberg, (Johan) August
1849-1912 .... TCLC **1, 8, 21, 47; DA;
DAB; DAC; DAM DRAM, MST; WLC**
See also CA 104; 135

Stringer, Arthur 1874-1950 .... TCLC **37**
See also DLB 92

Stringer, David
See Roberts, Keith (John Kingston)

Stroheim, Erich von 1885-1957 ..... TCLC **71**

Strugatskii, Arkadii (Natanovich)
1925-1991 .... CLC **27**
See also CA 106; 135

Strugatskii, Boris (Natanovich)
1933- .... CLC **27**
See also CA 106

Strummer, Joe 1953(?)- .... CLC **30**

Stuart, Don A.
See Campbell, John W(ood, Jr.)

Stuart, Ian
See MacLean, Alistair (Stuart)

Stuart, Jesse (Hilton)
1906-1984 .... CLC **1, 8, 11, 14, 34**
See also CA 5-8R; 112; CANR 31; DLB
9, 48, 102; DLBY 84; SATA 2; SATA-
Obit 36

Sturgeon, Theodore (Hamilton)
1918-1985 .... CLC **22, 39**
See also Queen, Ellery
See also CA 81-84; 116; CANR 32; DLB 8;
DLBY 85; MTCW

Sturges, Preston 1898-1959 .... TCLC **48**
See also CA 114; 149; DLB 26

Styron, William
1925- .... CLC **1, 3, 5, 11, 15, 60; DAM
NOV, POP; SSC 25**
See also BEST 90:4; CA 5-8R; CANR 6, 33;
CDALB 1968-1988; DLB 2, 143; DLBY 80;
INT CANR-6; MTCW

Suarez Lynch, B.
See Bioy Casares, Adolfo; Borges, Jorge Luis

Su Chien 1884-1918
See Su Man-shu
See also CA 123

Suckow, Ruth 1892-1960 .... SSC **18**
See also CA 113; DLB 9, 102

Sudermann, Hermann
1857-1928 .... TCLC **15**
See also CA 107; DLB 118

Sue, Eugene 1804-1857 .... NCLC **1**
See also DLB 119

Sueskind, Patrick 1949- .... CLC **44**
See also Suskind, Patrick

Sukenick, Ronald
1932- .... CLC **3, 4, 6, 48**
See also CA 25-28R; CAAS 8; CANR 32; DLB
173; DLBY 81

Suknaski, Andrew 1942- .... CLC **19**
See also CA 101; DLB 53

Sullivan, Vernon
See Vian, Boris

Sully Prudhomme 1839-1907 .... TCLC **31**

Su Man-shu .... TCLC **24**
See also Su Chien

Summerforest, Ivy B.
See Kirkup, James

Summers, Andrew James 1942- .... CLC **26**

Summers, Andy
See Summers, Andrew James

Taylor, Edward
1642(?)-1729 ... **LC 11; DA; DAB; DAC; DAM MST, POET**
See also DLB 24

Taylor, Eleanor Ross 1920- .... **CLC 5**
See also CA 81-84

Taylor, Elizabeth
1912-1975 .... **CLC 2, 4, 29**
See also CA 13-16R; CANR 9; DLB 139;
MTCW; SATA 13

Taylor, Frederick Winslow
1856-1915 .... **TCLC 76**

Taylor, Henry (Splawn) 1942- .... **CLC 44**
See also CA 33-36R; CAAS 7; CANR 31; DLB
5

Taylor, Kamala (Purnaiya) 1924-
See Markandaya, Kamala
See also CA 77-80

Taylor, Mildred D. .... **CLC 21**
See also AAYA 10; BW 1; CA 85-88; CANR
25; CLR 9; DLB 52; JRDA; MAICYA;
SAAS 5; SATA 15, 70

Taylor, Peter (Hillsman)
1917-1994 .... **CLC 1, 4, 18, 37, 44, 50, 71; SSC 10**
See also CA 13-16R; 147; CANR 9, 50; DLBY
81, 94; INT CANR-9; MTCW

Taylor, Robert Lewis 1912- .... **CLC 14**
See also CA 1-4R; CANR 3; SATA 10

Tchekhov, Anton
See Chekhov, Anton (Pavlovich)

Tchicaya, Gerald Felix
1931-1988 .... **CLC 101**
See also CA 129; 125

Tchicaya U Tam'si
See Tchicaya, Gerald Felix

Teasdale, Sara 1884-1933 .... **TCLC 4**
See also CA 104; DLB 45; SATA 32

Tegner, Esaias 1782-1846 .... **NCLC 2**

Teilhard de Chardin, (Marie Joseph) Pierre
1881-1955 .... **TCLC 9**
See also CA 105

Temple, Ann
See Mortimer, Penelope (Ruth)

Tennant, Emma (Christina)
1937- .... **CLC 13, 52**
See also CA 65-68; CAAS 9; CANR 10, 38,
59; DLB 14

Tenneshaw, S. M.
See Silverberg, Robert

Tennyson, Alfred
1809-1892 .... **NCLC 30, 65; DA; DAB; DAC; DAM MST, POET; PC 6; WLC**
See also CDBLB 1832-1890; DLB 32

Teran, Lisa St. Aubin de .... **CLC 36**
See also St. Aubin de Teran, Lisa

Terence
195(?)B.C.-159B.C. ...... **CMLC 14; DC 7**

Teresa de Jesus, St. 1515-1582 .... **LC 18**

Terkel, Louis 1912-
See Terkel, Studs
See also CA 57-60; CANR 18, 45;
MTCW

Terkel, Studs .... **CLC 38**
See also Terkel, Louis
See also AITN 1

Terry, C. V.
See Slaughter, Frank G(ill)

Terry, Megan 1932- .... **CLC 19**
See also CA 77-80; CABS 3; CANR 43; DLB
7

Tertz, Abram
See Sinyavsky, Andrei (Donatevich)

Tesich, Steve
1943(?)-1996 .... **CLC 40, 69**
See also CA 105; 152; DLBY 83

Teternikov, Fyodor Kuzmich 1863-1927
See Sologub, Fyodor
See also CA 104

Tevis, Walter 1928-1984 .... **CLC 42**
See also CA 113

Tey, Josephine .... **TCLC 14**
See also Mackintosh, Elizabeth
See also DLB 77

Thackeray, William Makepeace
1811-1863 ...... **NCLC 5, 14, 22, 43; DA; DAB; DAC; DAM MST, NOV; WLC**
See also CDBLB 1832-1890; DLB 21, 55, 159,
163; SATA 23

Thakura, Ravindranatha
See Tagore, Rabindranath

Tharoor, Shashi 1956- .... **CLC 70**
See also CA 141

Thelwell, Michael Miles
1939- .... **CLC 22**
See also BW 2; CA 101

Theobald, Lewis, Jr.
See Lovecraft, H(oward) P(hillips)

Theodorescu, Ion N. 1880-1967
See Arghezi, Tudor
See also CA 116

Theriault, Yves
1915-1983 .... **CLC 79; DAC; DAM MST**
See also CA 102; DLB 88

Theroux, Alexander (Louis)
1939- .... **CLC 2, 25**
See also CA 85-88; CANR 20

Theroux, Paul (Edward)
1941- ...... **CLC 5, 8, 11, 15, 28, 46; DAM POP**
See also BEST 89:4; CA 33-36R; CANR 20,
45; DLB 2; MTCW; SATA 44

Thesen, Sharon 1946- .... **CLC 56**

Thevenin, Denis
See Duhamel, Georges

Thibault, Jacques Anatole Francois 1844-1924
See France, Anatole
See also CA 106; 127; DAM NOV; MTCW

Thiele, Colin (Milton) 1920- .... **CLC 17**
See also CA 29-32R; CANR 12, 28, 53; CLR
27; MAICYA; SAAS 2; SATA 14, 72

Thomas, Audrey (Callahan)
1935- .... **CLC 7, 13, 37; SSC 20**
See also AITN 2; CA 21-24R; CAAS 19;
CANR 36, 58; DLB 60; MTCW

Thomas, D(onald) M(ichael)
1935- .... **CLC 13, 22, 31**
See also CA 61-64; CAAS 11; CANR 17, 45;
CDBLB 1960 to Present; DLB 40; INT
CANR-17; MTCW

Thomas, Dylan (Marlais)
1914-1953 ..... **TCLC 1, 8, 45; DA; DAB; DAC; DAM DRAM, MST, POET; PC 2; SSC 3; WLC**
See also CA 104; 120; CDBLB 1945-1960;
DLB 13, 20, 139; MTCW; SATA 60

Thomas, (Philip) Edward
1878-1917 .... **TCLC 10; DAM POET**
See also CA 106; 153; DLB 19

Thomas, Joyce Carol 1938- .... **CLC 35**
See also AAYA 12; BW 2; CA 113; 116;
CANR 48; CLR 19; DLB 33; INT 116;
JRDA; MAICYA; MTCW; SAAS 7; SATA
40, 78

Thomas, Lewis 1913-1993 .... **CLC 35**
See also CA 85-88; 143; CANR 38, 60; MTCW

Thomas, Paul
See Mann, (Paul) Thomas

Thomas, Piri 1928- .... **CLC 17**
See also CA 73-76; HW

Thomas, R(onald) S(tuart)
1913- .... **CLC 6, 13, 48; DAB; DAM POET**
See also CA 89-92; CAAS 4; CANR 30;
CDBLB 1960 to Present; DLB 27;
MTCW

Thomas, Ross (Elmore) 1926-1995 ... **CLC 39**
See also CA 33-36R; 150; CANR 22

Thompson, Francis Clegg
See Mencken, H(enry) L(ouis)

Thompson, Francis Joseph
1859-1907 .... **TCLC 4**
See also CA 104; CDBLB 1890-1914; DLB
19

Upshaw, Margaret Mitchell
  See Mitchell, Margaret (Munnerlyn)

Upton, Mark
  See Sanders, Lawrence

Urdang, Constance (Henriette)
  1922- .... CLC 47
  See also CA 21-24R; CANR 9, 24

Uriel, Henry
  See Faust, Frederick (Schiller)

Uris, Leon (Marcus)
  1924- .... CLC 7, 32; DAM NOV, POP
  See also AITN 1, 2; BEST 89:2; CA 1-4R;
  CANR 1, 40; MTCW; SATA 49

Urmuz
  See Codrescu, Andrei

Urquhart, Jane 1949- .... CLC 90; DAC
  See also CA 113; CANR 32

Ustinov, Peter (Alexander) 1921- .... CLC 1
  See also AITN 1; CA 13-16R; CANR 25, 51;
  DLB 13

U Tam'si, Gerald Felix Tchicaya
  See Tchicaya, Gerald Felix

U Tam'si, Tchicaya
  See Tchicaya, Gerald Felix

Vaculik, Ludvik 1926- .... CLC 7
  See also CA 53-56

Vaihinger, Hans 1852-1933 .... TCLC 71
  See also CA 116

Valdez, Luis (Miguel)
  1940- .... CLC 84; DAM MULT; HLC
  See also CA 101; CANR 32; DLB 122; HW

Valenzuela, Luisa
  1938- .... CLC 31, 104; DAM MULT;
  SSC 14
  See also CA 101; CANR 32; DLB 113; HW

Valera y Alcala-Galiano, Juan
  1824-1905 .... TCLC 10
  See also CA 106

Valery, (Ambroise) Paul (Toussaint Jules)
  1871-1945 ... TCLC 4, 15; DAM POET;
  PC 9
  See also CA 104; 122; MTCW

Valle-Inclan, Ramon (Maria) del
  1866-1936 .... TCLC 5; DAM MULT;
  HLC
  See also CA 106; 153; DLB 134

Vallejo, Antonio Buero
  See Buero Vallejo, Antonio

Vallejo, Cesar (Abraham)
  1892-1938 .... TCLC 3, 56; DAM MULT;
  HLC
  See also CA 105; 153; HW

Vallette, Marguerite Eymery
  See Rachilde

Valle Y Pena, Ramon del
  See Valle-Inclan, Ramon (Maria) del

Van Ash, Cay 1918- .... CLC 34

Vanbrugh, Sir John
  1664-1726 .... LC 21; DAM DRAM
  See also DLB 80

Van Campen, Karl
  See Campbell, John W(ood, Jr.)

Vance, Gerald
  See Silverberg, Robert

Vance, Jack .... CLC 35
  See also Kuttner, Henry; Vance, John Holbrook
  See also DLB 8

Vance, John Holbrook 1916-
  See Queen, Ellery; Vance, Jack
  See also CA 29-32R; CANR 17; MTCW

Van Den Bogarde, Derek Jules Gaspard Ulric
  Niven 1921-
  See Bogarde, Dirk
  See also CA 77-80

Vandenburgh, Jane .... CLC 59

Vanderhaeghe, Guy 1951- .... CLC 41
  See also CA 113

van der Post, Laurens (Jan)
  1906-1996 .... CLC 5
  See also CA 5-8R; 155; CANR 35

van de Wetering, Janwillem
  1931- .... CLC 47
  See also CA 49-52; CANR 4, 62

Van Dine, S. S. .... TCLC 23
  See also Wright, Willard Huntington

Van Doren, Carl (Clinton)
  1885-1950 .... TCLC 18
  See also CA 111

Van Doren, Mark 1894-1972 .... CLC 6, 10
  See also CA 1-4R; 37-40R; CANR 3; DLB 45;
  MTCW

Van Druten, John (William)
  1901-1957 .... TCLC 2
  See also CA 104; DLB 10

Van Duyn, Mona (Jane)
  1921- .... CLC 3, 7, 63; DAM POET
  See also CA 9-12R; CANR 7, 38, 60; DLB
  5

Van Dyne, Edith
  See Baum, L(yman) Frank

van Itallie, Jean-Claude 1936- .... CLC 3
  See also CA 45-48; CAAS 2; CANR 1, 48;
  DLB 7

van Ostaijen, Paul 1896-1928 .... TCLC 33

Van Peebles, Melvin
  1932- .... CLC 2, 20; DAM MULT
  See also BW 2; CA 85-88; CANR 27

Vansittart, Peter 1920- .... CLC 42
  See also CA 1-4R; CANR 3, 49

Van Vechten, Carl 1880-1964 .... CLC 33
  See also CA 89-92; DLB 4, 9, 51

Van Vogt, A(lfred) E(lton) 1912- .... CLC 1
  See also CA 21-24R; CANR 28; DLB 8; SATA
  14

Varda, Agnes 1928- .... CLC 16
  See also CA 116; 122

Vargas Llosa, (Jorge) Mario (Pedro)
  1936- ..... CLC 3, 6, 9, 10, 15, 31, 42, 85;
  DA; DAB; DAC; DAM MST, MULT,
  NOV; HLC
  See also CA 73-76; CANR 18, 32, 42; DLB
  145; HW; MTCW

Vasiliu, Gheorghe 1881-1957
  See Bacovia, George
  See also CA 123

Vassa, Gustavus
  See Equiano, Olaudah

Vassilikos, Vassilis 1933- .... CLC 4, 8
  See also CA 81-84

Vaughan, Henry 1621-1695 .... LC 27
  See also DLB 131

Vaughn, Stephanie .... CLC 62

Vazov, Ivan (Minchov)
  1850-1921 .... TCLC 25
  See also CA 121; DLB 147

Veblen, Thorstein (Bunde)
  1857-1929 .... TCLC 31
  See also CA 115

Vega, Lope de 1562-1635 .... LC 23

Venison, Alfred
  See Pound, Ezra (Weston Loomis)

Verdi, Marie de
  See Mencken, H(enry) L(ouis)

Verdu, Matilde
  See Cela, Camilo Jose

Verga, Giovanni (Carmelo)
  1840-1922 .... TCLC 3; SSC 21
  See also CA 104; 123

Vergil 70B.C.-19B.C. ... CMLC 9; DA; DAB;
  DAC; DAM MST, POET; PC 12; WLCS

Verhaeren, Emile (Adolphe Gustave)
  1855-1916 .... TCLC 12
  See also CA 109

Verlaine, Paul (Marie)
  1844-1896 ... NCLC 2, 51; DAM POET;
  PC 2

Verne, Jules (Gabriel)
  1828-1905 .... TCLC 6, 52
  See also AAYA 16; CA 110; 131; DLB 123;
  JRDA; MAICYA; SATA 21

Very, Jones 1813-1880 .... **NCLC 9**
See also DLB 1

Vesaas, Tarjei 1897-1970 .... **CLC 48**
See also CA 29-32R

Vialis, Gaston
See Simenon, Georges (Jacques Christian)

Vian, Boris 1920-1959 .... **TCLC 9**
See also CA 106; DLB 72

Viaud, (Louis Marie) Julien 1850-1923
See Loti, Pierre
See also CA 107

Vicar, Henry
See Felsen, Henry Gregor

Vicker, Angus
See Felsen, Henry Gregor

Vidal, Gore
1925- .... **CLC 2, 4, 6, 8, 10, 22, 33, 72;
DAM NOV, POP**
See also AITN 1; BEST 90:2; CA 5-8R;
CANR 13, 45; DLB 6, 152; INT CANR-
13; MTCW

Viereck, Peter (Robert Edwin)
1916- .... **CLC 4**
See also CA 1-4R; CANR 1, 47; DLB 5

Vigny, Alfred (Victor) de
1797-1863 .... **NCLC 7; DAM POET**
See also DLB 119

Vilakazi, Benedict Wallet
1906-1947 .... **TCLC 37**

**Villiers de l'Isle Adam, Jean Marie Mathias
Philippe Auguste Comte**
1838-1889 .... **NCLC 3; SSC 14**
See also DLB 123

Villon, Francois 1431-1463(?) .... **PC 13**

Vinci, Leonardo da 1452-1519 .... **LC 12**

Vine, Barbara .... **CLC 50**
See also Rendell, Ruth (Barbara)
See also BEST 90:4

Vinge, Joan D(ennison)
1948- .... **CLC 30; SSC 24**
See also CA 93-96; SATA 36

Violis, G.
See Simenon, Georges (Jacques Christian)

Visconti, Luchino 1906-1976 .... **CLC 16**
See also CA 81-84; 65-68; CANR 39

Vittorini, Elio 1908-1966 .... **CLC 6, 9, 14**
See also CA 133; 25-28R

Vizenor, Gerald Robert 1934- .... **CLC 103;
DAM MULT**
See also CA 13-16R; CAAS 22; CANR 5, 21,
44; DLB 175; NNAL

Vizinczey, Stephen 1933- .... **CLC 40**
See also CA 128; INT 128

Vliet, R(ussell) G(ordon)
1929-1984 .... **CLC 22**
See also CA 37-40R; 112; CANR 18

Vogau, Boris Andreyevich 1894-1937(?)
See Pilnyak, Boris
See also CA 123

Vogel, Paula A(nne) 1951- .... **CLC 76**
See also CA 108

Voight, Ellen Bryant 1943- .... **CLC 54**
See also CA 69-72; CANR 11, 29, 55; DLB
120

Voigt, Cynthia 1942- .... **CLC 30**
See also AAYA 3; CA 106; CANR 18, 37, 40;
CLR 13; INT CANR-18; JRDA; MAICYA;
SATA 48, 79; SATA-Brief 33

Voinovich, Vladimir (Nikolaevich)
1932- .... **CLC 10, 49**
See also CA 81-84; CAAS 12; CANR 33;
MTCW

Vollmann, William T.
1959- .... **CLC 89; DAM NOV, POP**
See also CA 134

Voloshinov, V. N.
See Bakhtin, Mikhail Mikhailovich

Voltaire
1694-1778 .... **LC 14; DA; DAB; DAC;
DAM DRAM, MST; SSC 12; WLC**

von Daeniken, Erich 1935- .... **CLC 30**
See also AITN 1; CA 37-40R; CANR 17,
44

von Daniken, Erich
See von Daeniken, Erich

von Heidenstam, (Carl Gustaf) Verner
See Heidenstam, (Carl Gustaf) Verner von

von Heyse, Paul (Johann Ludwig)
See Heyse, Paul (Johann Ludwig von)

von Hofmannsthal, Hugo
See Hofmannsthal, Hugo von

von Horvath, Odon
See Horvath, Oedoen von

von Horvath, Oedoen
See Horvath, Oedoen von

von Liliencron, (Friedrich Adolf Axel) Detlev
See Liliencron, (Friedrich Adolf Axel) Detlev
von

Vonnegut, Kurt, Jr.
1922- .... **CLC 1, 2, 3, 4, 5, 8, 12, 22, 40,
60; DA; DAB; DAC; DAM MST, NOV,
POP; SSC 8; WLC**
See also AAYA 6; AITN 1; BEST 90:4; CA
1-4R; CANR 1, 25, 49; CDALB 1968-
1988; DLB 2, 8, 152; DLBD 3; DLBY 80;
MTCW

Von Rachen, Kurt
See Hubbard, L(afayette) Ron(ald)

von Rezzori (d'Arezzo), Gregor
See Rezzori (d'Arezzo), Gregor von

von Sternberg, Josef
See Sternberg, Josef von

Vorster, Gordon 1924- .... **CLC 34**
See also CA 133

Vosce, Trudie
See Ozick, Cynthia

Voznesensky, Andrei (Andreievich)
1933- .... **CLC 1, 15, 57; DAM POET**
See also CA 89-92; CANR 37; MTCW

Waddington, Miriam 1917- .... **CLC 28**
See also CA 21-24R; CANR 12, 30; DLB
68

Wagman, Fredrica 1937- .... **CLC 7**
See also CA 97-100; INT 97-100

Wagner, Linda W.
See Wagner-Martin, Linda (C.)

Wagner, Linda Welshimer
See Wagner-Martin, Linda (C.)

Wagner, Richard
1813-1883 .... **NCLC 9**
See also DLB 129

Wagner-Martin, Linda (C.)
1936- .... **CLC 50**
See also CA 159

Wagoner, David (Russell)
1926- .... **CLC 3, 5, 15**
See also CA 1-4R; CAAS 3; CANR 2; DLB 5;
SATA 14

Wah, Fred(erick James)
1939- .... **CLC 44**
See also CA 107; 141; DLB 60

Wahloo, Per
1926-1975 .... **CLC 7**
See also CA 61-64

Wahloo, Peter
See Wahloo, Per

Wain, John (Barrington)
1925-1994 .... **CLC 2, 11, 15, 46**
See also CA 5-8R; 145; CAAS 4; CANR 23,
54; CDBLB 1960 to Present; DLB 15, 27,
139, 155; MTCW

Wajda, Andrzej 1926- .... **CLC 16**
See also CA 102

Wakefield, Dan 1932- .... **CLC 7**
See also CA 21-24R; CAAS 7

Wakoski, Diane
1937- .... **CLC 2, 4, 7, 9, 11, 40; DAM
POET; PC 15**
See also CA 13-16R; CAAS 1; CANR 9, 60;
DLB 5; INT CANR-9

Wakoski-Sherbell, Diane
See Wakoski, Diane

Watkins, Paul 1964- .... **CLC 55**
See also CA 132; CANR 62

Watkins, Vernon Phillips
1906-1967 .... **CLC 43**
See also CA 9-10; 25-28R; CAP 1; DLB
20

Watson, Irving S.
See Mencken, H(enry) L(ouis)

Watson, John H.
See Farmer, Philip Jose

Watson, Richard F.
See Silverberg, Robert

Waugh, Auberon (Alexander)
1939- .... **CLC 7**
See also CA 45-48; CANR 6, 22; DLB 14

Waugh, Evelyn (Arthur St. John)
1903-1966 .... **CLC 1, 3, 8, 13, 19, 27, 44;**
DA; DAB; DAC; DAM MST, NOV,
POP; WLC
See also CA 85-88; 25-28R; CANR 22;
CDBLB 1914-1945; DLB 15, 162;
MTCW

Waugh, Harriet 1944- .... **CLC 6**
See also CA 85-88; CANR 22

Ways, C. R.
See Blount, Roy (Alton), Jr.

Waystaff, Simon
See Swift, Jonathan

Webb, (Martha) Beatrice (Potter)
1858-1943 .... **TCLC 22**
See also Potter, (Helen) Beatrix
See also CA 117

Webb, Charles (Richard) 1939- .... **CLC 7**
See also CA 25-28R

Webb, James H(enry), Jr. 1946- .... **CLC 22**
See also CA 81-84

Webb, Mary (Gladys Meredith)
1881-1927 .... **TCLC 24**
See also CA 123; DLB 34

Webb, Mrs. Sidney
See Webb, (Martha) Beatrice (Potter)

Webb, Phyllis 1927- .... **CLC 18**
See also CA 104; CANR 23; DLB 53

Webb, Sidney (James)
1859-1947 .... **TCLC 22**
See also CA 117

Webber, Andrew Lloyd .... **CLC 21**
See also Lloyd Webber, Andrew

Weber, Lenora Mattingly
1895-1971 .... **CLC 12**
See also CA 19-20; 29-32R; CAP 1; SATA 2;
SATA-Obit 26

Weber, Max 1864-1920 .... **TCLC 69**
See also CA 109

Webster, John
1579(?)-1634(?) .... **LC 33; DA; DAB;**
DAC; DAM DRAM, MST; DC 2; WLC
See also CDBLB Before 1660; DLB 58

Webster, Noah 1758-1843 .... **NCLC 30**

Wedekind, (Benjamin) Frank(lin)
1864-1918 .... **TCLC 7; DAM DRAM**
See also CA 104; 153; DLB 118

Weidman, Jerome 1913- .... **CLC 7**
See also AITN 2; CA 1-4R; CANR 1; DLB 28

Weil, Simone (Adolphine)
1909-1943 .... **TCLC 23**
See also CA 117; 159

Weinstein, Nathan
See West, Nathanael

Weinstein, Nathan von Wallenstein
See West, Nathanael

Weir, Peter (Lindsay) 1944- .... **CLC 20**
See also CA 113; 123

Weiss, Peter (Ulrich)
1916-1982 .... **CLC 3, 15, 51; DAM**
DRAM
See also CA 45-48; 106; CANR 3; DLB 69,
124

Weiss, Theodore (Russell)
1916- .... **CLC 3, 8, 14**
See also CA 9-12R; CAAS 2; CANR 46; DLB
5

Welch, (Maurice) Denton
1915-1948 .... **TCLC 22**
See also CA 121; 148

Welch, James
1940- ...... **CLC 6, 14, 52; DAM MULT,**
POP
See also CA 85-88; CANR 42; DLB 175;
NNAL

Weldon, Fay
1933- ...... **CLC 6, 9, 11, 19, 36, 59; DAM**
POP
See also CA 21-24R; CANR 16, 46; CDBLB
1960 to Present; DLB 14; INT CANR-16;
MTCW

Wellek, Rene
1903-1995 .... **CLC 28**
See also CA 5-8R; 150; CAAS 7; CANR 8;
DLB 63; INT CANR-8

Weller, Michael 1942- .... **CLC 10, 53**
See also CA 85-88

Weller, Paul 1958- .... **CLC 26**

Wellershoff, Dieter 1925- .... **CLC 46**
See also CA 89-92; CANR 16, 37

Welles, (George) Orson
1915-1985 .... **CLC 20, 80**
See also CA 93-96; 117

Wellman, Mac 1945- .... **CLC 65**

Wellman, Manly Wade 1903-1986 .... **CLC 49**
See also CA 1-4R; 118; CANR 6, 16, 44; SATA
6; SATA-Obit 47

Wells, Carolyn 1869(?)-1942 .... **TCLC 35**
See also CA 113; DLB 11

Wells, H(erbert) G(eorge)
1866-1946 ... **TCLC 6, 12, 19; DA; DAB;**
DAC; DAM MST, NOV; SSC 6; WLC
See also AAYA 18; CA 110; 121; CDBLB
1914-1945; DLB 34, 70, 156, 178; MTCW;
SATA 20

Wells, Rosemary 1943- .... **CLC 12**
See also AAYA 13; CA 85-88; CANR 48; CLR
16; MAICYA; SAAS 1; SATA 18, 69

Welty, Eudora
1909- ..... **CLC 1, 2, 5, 14, 22, 33, 105;**
DA; DAB; DAC; DAM MST, NOV; SSC
1, 27; WLC
See also CA 9-12R; CABS 1; CANR 32;
CDALB 1941-1968; DLB 2, 102, 143;
DLBD 12; DLBY 87; MTCW

Wen I-to 1899-1946 .... **TCLC 28**

Wentworth, Robert
See Hamilton, Edmond

Werfel, Franz (V.) 1890-1945 .... **TCLC 8**
See also CA 104; DLB 81, 124

Wergeland, Henrik Arnold
1808-1845 .... **NCLC 5**

Wersba, Barbara 1932- .... **CLC 30**
See also AAYA 2; CA 29-32R; CANR 16, 38;
CLR 3; DLB 52; JRDA; MAICYA; SAAS
2; SATA 1, 58

Wertmueller, Lina 1928- .... **CLC 16**
See also CA 97-100; CANR 39

Wescott, Glenway 1901-1987 .... **CLC 13**
See also CA 13-16R; 121; CANR 23; DLB 4,
9, 102

Wesker, Arnold
1932- .... **CLC 3, 5, 42; DAB; DAM**
DRAM
See also CA 1-4R; CAAS 7; CANR 1, 33;
CDBLB 1960 to Present; DLB 13; MTCW

Wesley, Richard (Errol) 1945- .... **CLC 7**
See also BW 1; CA 57-60; CANR 27; DLB
38

Wessel, Johan Herman 1742-1785 .... **LC 7**

West, Anthony (Panther)
1914-1987 .... **CLC 50**
See also CA 45-48; 124; CANR 3, 19; DLB
15

West, C. P.
See Wodehouse, P(elham) G(renville)

West, (Mary) Jessamyn
1902-1984 .... **CLC 7, 17**
See also CA 9-12R; 112; CANR 27; DLB 6;
DLBY 84; MTCW; SATA-Obit 37

Wilding, Michael 1942- ...... CLC 73
See also CA 104; CANR 24, 49

Wiley, Richard 1944- .... CLC 44
See also CA 121; 129

Wilhelm, Kate .... CLC 7
See also Wilhelm, Katie Gertrude
See also AAYA 20; CAAS 5; DLB 8; INT
CANR-17

Wilhelm, Katie Gertrude 1928-
See Wilhelm, Kate
See also CA 37-40R; CANR 17, 36, 60;
MTCW

Wilkins, Mary
See Freeman, Mary Eleanor Wilkins

Willard, Nancy
1936- .... CLC 7, 37
See also CA 89-92; CANR 10, 39; CLR 5; DLB
5, 52; MAICYA; MTCW; SATA 37, 71;
SATA-Brief 30

Williams, C(harles) K(enneth)
1936- .... CLC 33, 56; DAM POET
See also CA 37-40R; CAAS 26; CANR 57;
DLB 5

Williams, Charles
See Collier, James L(incoln)

Williams, Charles (Walter Stansby) 1
886-1945 .... TCLC 1, 11
See also CA 104; DLB 100, 153

Williams, (George) Emlyn
1905-1987 .... CLC 15; DAM DRAM
See also CA 104; 123; CANR 36; DLB 10,
77; MTCW

Williams, Hugo 1942- .... CLC 42
See also CA 17-20R; CANR 45; DLB
40

Williams, J. Walker
See Wodehouse, P(elham) G(renville)

Williams, John A(lfred)
1925- ..... CLC 5, 13; BLC; DAM MULT
See also BW 2; CA 53-56; CAAS 3; CANR
6, 26, 51; DLB 2, 33; INT CANR-6

Williams, Jonathan (Chamberlain)
1929- .... CLC 13
See also CA 9-12R; CAAS 12; CANR 8; DLB
5

Williams, Joy 1944- .... CLC 31
See also CA 41-44R; CANR 22, 48

Williams, Norman 1952- .... CLC 39
See also CA 118

Williams, Sherley Anne
1944- .... CLC 89; BLC; DAM MULT,
POET
See also BW 2; CA 73-76; CANR 25; DLB
41; INT CANR-25; SATA 78

Williams, Shirley
See Williams, Sherley Anne

Williams, Tennessee
1911-1983 ... CLC 1, 2, 5, 7, 8, 11, 15,
19, 30, 39, 45, 71; DA; DAB; DAC;
DAM DRAM, MST; DC 4; WLC
See also AITN 1, 2; CA 5-8R; 108; CABS 3;
CANR 31; CDALB 1941-1968; DLB 7;
DLBD 4; DLBY 83; MTCW

Williams, Thomas (Alonzo)
1926-1990 .... CLC 14
See also CA 1-4R; 132; CANR 2

Williams, William C.
See Williams, William Carlos

Williams, William Carlos
1883-1963 .... CLC 1, 2, 5, 9, 13, 22, 42,
67; DA; DAB; DAC; DAM MST, POET;
PC 7
See also CA 89-92; CANR 34; CDALB
1917-1929; DLB 4, 16, 54, 86;
MTCW

Williamson, David (Keith) 1942- ...... CLC 56
See also CA 103; CANR 41

Williamson, Ellen Douglas 1905-1984
See Douglas, Ellen
See also CA 17-20R; 114; CANR 39

Williamson, Jack .... CLC 29
See also Williamson, John Stewart
See also CAAS 8; DLB 8

Williamson, John Stewart 1908-
See Williamson, Jack
See also CA 17-20R; CANR 23

Willie, Frederick
See Lovecraft, H(oward) P(hillips)

Willingham, Calder (Baynard, Jr.)
1922-1995 .... CLC 5, 51
See also CA 5-8R; 147; CANR 3; DLB 2, 44;
MTCW

Willis, Charles
See Clarke, Arthur C(harles)

Willy
See Colette, (Sidonie-Gabrielle)

Willy, Colette
See Colette, (Sidonie-Gabrielle)

Wilson, A(ndrew) N(orman)
1950- .... CLC 33
See also CA 112; 122; DLB 14, 155

Wilson, Angus (Frank Johnstone)
1913-1991 ... CLC 2, 3, 5, 25, 34; SSC
21
See also CA 5-8R; 134; CANR 21; DLB 15,
139, 155; MTCW

Wilson, August
1945- .... CLC 39, 50, 63; BLC; DA;
DAB; DAC; DAM DRAM, MST,
MULT; DC 2; WLCS
See also AAYA 16; BW 2; CA 115; 122; CANR
42, 54; MTCW

Wilson, Brian 1942- .... CLC 12

Wilson, Colin 1931- .... CLC 3, 14
See also CA 1-4R; CAAS 5; CANR 1, 22, 33;
DLB 14; MTCW

Wilson, Dirk
See Pohl, Frederik

Wilson, Edmund
1895-1972 .... CLC 1, 2, 3, 8, 24
See also CA 1-4R; 37-40R; CANR 1, 46; DLB
63; MTCW

Wilson, Ethel Davis (Bryant)
1888(?)-1980 .... CLC 13; DAC; DAM
POET
See also CA 102; DLB 68; MTCW

Wilson, John 1785-1854 .... NCLC 5

Wilson, John (Anthony) Burgess 1917-1993
See Burgess, Anthony
See also CA 1-4R; 143; CANR 2, 46; DAC;
DAM NOV; MTCW

Wilson, Lanford
1937- .... CLC 7, 14, 36; DAM DRAM
See also CA 17-20R; CABS 3; CANR45; DLB 7

Wilson, Robert M. 1944- .... CLC 7, 9
See also CA 49-52; CANR 2, 41; MTCW

Wilson, Robert McLiam 1964- .... CLC 59
See also CA 132

Wilson, Sloan 1920- .... CLC 32
See also CA 1-4R; CANR 1, 44

Wilson, Snoo 1948- .... CLC 33
See also CA 69-72

Wilson, William S(mith) 1932- .... CLC 49
See also CA 81-84

Wilson, Woodrow 1856-1924 .... TCLC 73
See also DLB 47

**Winchilsea, Anne (Kingsmill) Finch, Countess
of** 1661-1720 .... LC 3

Windham, Basil
See Wodehouse, P(elham) G(renville)

Wingrove, David (John) 1954- .... CLC 68
See also CA 133

Wintergreen, Jane
See Duncan, Sara Jeannette

Winters, Janet Lewis .... CLC 41
See also Lewis, Janet
See also DLBY 87

Winters, (Arthur) Yvor
1900-1968 .... CLC 4, 8, 32
See also CA 11-12; 25-28R; CAP 1; DLB 48;
MTCW

Winterson, Jeanette
1959- .... CLC 64; DAM POP
See also CA 136; CANR 58

Winthrop, John 1588-1649 .... LC 31
See also DLB 24, 30

Xenophon c. 430B.C.-c. 354B.C. ... **CMLC 17**
See also DLB 176

Yakumo Koizumi
See Hearn, (Patricio) Lafcadio (Tessima Carlos)

Yanez, Jose Donoso
See Donoso (Yanez), Jose

Yanovsky, Basile S.
See Yanovsky, V(assily) S(emenovich)

Yanovsky, V(assily) S(emenovich)
1906-1989 .... **CLC 2, 18**
See also CA 97-100; 129

Yates, Richard 1926-1992 .... **CLC 7, 8, 23**
See also CA 5-8R; 139; CANR 10, 43; DLB 2; DLBY 81, 92; INT CANR-10

Yeats, W. B.
See Yeats, William Butler

Yeats, William Butler
1865-1939 .... **TCLC 1, 11, 18, 31; DA; DAB; DAC; DAM DRAM, MST, POET; PC 20; WLC**
See also CA 104; 127; CANR 45; CDBLB 1890-1914; DLB 10, 19, 98, 156; MTCW

Yehoshua, A(braham) B.
1936- .... **CLC 13, 31**
See also CA 33-36R; CANR 43

Yep, Laurence Michael 1948-............ **CLC 35**
See also AAYA 5; CA 49-52; CANR 1, 46; CLR 3, 17; DLB 52; JRDA; MAICYA; SATA 7, 69

Yerby, Frank G(arvin)
1916-1991 ..... **CLC 1, 7, 22; BLC; DAM MULT**
See also BW 1; CA 9-12R; 136; CANR 16, 52; DLB 76; INT CANR-16; MTCW

Yesenin, Sergei Alexandrovich
See Esenin, Sergei (Alexandrovich)

Yevtushenko, Yevgeny (Alexandrovich)
1933- .... **CLC 1, 3, 13, 26, 51; DAM POET**
See also CA 81-84; CANR 33, 54; MTCW

Yezierska, Anzia 1885(?)-1970 .... **CLC 46**
See also CA 126; 89-92; DLB 28; MTCW

Yglesias, Helen 1915- .... **CLC 7, 22**
See also CA 37-40R; CAAS 20; CANR 15; INT CANR-15; MTCW

Yokomitsu Riichi 1898-1947 .... **TCLC 47**

Yonge, Charlotte (Mary)
1823-1901 .... **TCLC 48**
See also CA 109; DLB 18, 163; SATA 17

York, Jeremy
See Creasey, John

York, Simon
See Heinlein, Robert A(nson)

Yorke, Henry Vincent 1905-1974 ...... **CLC 13**
See also Green, Henry
See also CA 85-88; 49-52

Yosano Akiko 1878-1942 .... **TCLC 59; PC 11**

Yoshimoto, Banana .... **CLC 84**
See also Yoshimoto, Mahoko

Yoshimoto, Mahoko 1964-
See Yoshimoto, Banana
See also CA 144

Young, Al(bert James)
1939- .... **CLC 19; BLC; DAM MULT**
See also BW 2; CA 29-32R; CANR 26; DLB 33

Young, Andrew (John) 1885-1971 ...... **CLC 5**
See also CA 5-8R; CANR 7, 29

Young, Collier
See Bloch, Robert (Albert)

Young, Edward 1683-1765 .... **LC 3, 40**
See also DLB 95

Young, Marguerite (Vivian)
1909-1995 .... **CLC 82**
See also CA 13-16; 150; CAP 1

Young, Neil 1945- .... **CLC 17**
See also CA 110

Young Bear, Ray A. 1950-...... **CLC 94; DAM MULT**
See also CA 146; DLB 175; NNAL

Yourcenar, Marguerite
1903-1987 ...... **CLC 19, 38, 50, 87; DAM NOV**
See also CA 69-72; CANR 23, 60; DLB 72; DLBY 88; MTCW

Yurick, Sol 1925- .... **CLC 6**
See also CA 13-16R; CANR 25

Zabolotskii, Nikolai Alekseevich
1903-1958 .... **TCLC 52**
See also CA 116

Zamiatin, Yevgenii
See Zamyatin, Evgeny Ivanovich

Zamora, Bernice (B. Ortiz)
1938- .... **CLC 89; DAM MULT; HLC**
See also CA 151; DLB 82; HW

Zamyatin, Evgeny Ivanovich
1884-1937 .... **TCLC 8, 37**
See also CA 105

Zangwill, Israel 1864-1926 .... **TCLC 16**
See also CA 109; DLB 10, 135

Zappa, Francis Vincent, Jr. 1940-1993
See Zappa, Frank
See also CA 108; 143; CANR 57

Zappa, Frank .... **CLC 17**
See also Zappa, Francis Vincent, Jr.

Zaturenska, Marya 1902-1982 ...... **CLC 6, 11**
See also CA 13-16R; 105; CANR 22

Zeami 1363-1443 .... **DC 7**

Zelazny, Roger (Joseph)
1937-1995 .... **CLC 21**
See also AAYA 7; CA 21-24R; 148; CANR 26, 60; DLB 8; MTCW; SATA 57; SATA-Brief 39

Zhdanov, Andrei A(lexandrovich)
1896-1948 .... **TCLC 18**
See also CA 117

Zhukovsky, Vasily 1783-1852 .... **NCLC 35**

Ziegenhagen, Eric .... **CLC 55**

Zimmer, Jill Schary
See Robinson, Jill

Zimmerman, Robert
See Dylan, Bob

Zindel, Paul
1936- .... **CLC 6, 26; DA; DAB; DAC; DAM DRAM, MST, NOV; DC 5**
See also AAYA 2; CA 73-76; CANR 31; CLR 3, 45; DLB 7, 52; JRDA; MAICYA; MTCW; SATA 16, 58

Zinov'Ev, A. A.
See Zinoviev, Alexander (Aleksandrovich)

Zinoviev, Alexander (Aleksandrovich)
1922- .... **CLC 19**
See also CA 116; 133; CAAS 10

Zoilus
See Lovecraft, H(oward) P(hillips)

Zola, Emile (Edouard Charles Antoine)
1840-1902 .... **TCLC 1, 6, 21, 41; DA; DAB; DAC; DAM MST, NOV; WLC**
See also CA 104; 138; DLB 123

Zoline, Pamela 1941- .... **CLC 62**

Zorrilla y Moral, Jose 1817-1893 .... **NCLC 6**

Zoshchenko, Mikhail (Mikhailovich)
1895-1958 .... **TCLC 15; SSC 15**
See also CA 115; 160

Zuckmayer, Carl 1896-1977 .... **CLC 18**
See also CA 69-72; DLB 56, 124

Zuk, Georges
See Skelton, Robin

Zukofsky, Louis
1904-1978 .... **CLC 1, 2, 4, 7, 11, 18; DAM POET; PC 11**
See also CA 9-12R; 77-80; CANR 39; DLB 5, 165; MTCW

Zweig, Paul 1935-1984 .... **CLC 34, 42**
See also CA 85-88; 113

Zweig, Stefan 1881-1942 .... **TCLC 17**
See also CA 112; DLB 81, 118

Zwingli, Huldreich 1484-1531 .... **LC 37**
See also DLB 179

Cumulative Nationality Index

Cumulative Title Index

Title Index

Title Index

Title Index

Title Index

Title Index

Title Index

Title Index

Title Index

Title Index

Title Index

"Miss Leonora When Last Seen" (Taylor) **10**:390, 401, 406, 407, 409, 415

Miss Lonelyhearts (West) **16**:345-49, 351-52, 354, 356-57, 359-60, 362, 364, 366-67, 369, 375-81, 383-86, 389-90, 394-402, 404, 407-08, 411, 415, 417

"Miss Manning's Minister" (Jewett) **6**:156, 159

"Miss Mary Pask" (Wharton) **6**:431

"Miss Miller" (de la Mare) **14**:87

"Miss Ophelia Gledd" (Trollope) **28**:319, 323, 348

"Miss Pinkerton's Apocalypse" (Spark) **10**:350, 355, 359, 366

"Miss Plarr" (Ligotti) **16**:280

"Miss Puss's Parasol" (Harris) **19**:183

"Miss Sarah Jack, of Spanish Town, Jamaica" (Trollope) **28**:318, 329

"Miss Smith" (Trevor) **21**:246-47, 262

"Miss Sydney's Flowers" (Jewett) **6**:157, 166, 168

"Miss Tempy's Watcher's" (Jewett) **6**:151, 156

"Miss W." (O'Hara) **15**:258

"Miss Willie Lou and the Swan" (Benet) **10**:148

"Miss Winchelsea's Heart" (Wells) **6**:391

"Miss Witherwell's Mistake" (Chopin) **8**:84, 86

"Miss Yellow Eyes" (Grau) **15**:158, 164

Die Missbrauchten Liebesbriefe (Keller) **26**:107

"Missed Connection" (Campbell) **19**:75

"Missed Vocation" (Pavese)
    See "Mal di mestiere"

"Missing" (Campbell) **19**:74

"Missing" (de la Mare) **14**:70, 80, 83, 87-8, 92

"The Missing Eye" (Bulgakov) **18**:86-7

"The Missing Line" (Singer) **3**:389

"Missing Mail" (Narayan) **25**:138, 140, 153, 155

"The Mission of Jane" (Wharton) **6**:424-25

"The Mission of Mr. Scatters" (Dunbar) **8**:122, 132, 137, 147

"Mrs. Bullfrog" (Hawthorne) **3**:180

"Mrs. Moysey" (Bowen) **3**:30, 33, 40, 42

"Mrs. Windermere" (Bowen) **3**:40, 54

The Mist (King) **17**:265, 268-71, 273-76, 283

"The Mistake" (Gorky) **28**:159

"A Mistake" (Zoshchenko)
    See "A Slight Mistake"

"The Mistake of the Machine" (Chesterton) **1**:131

"The Mistaken Milliner" (Dickens) **17**:135

"Mr. Andrews" (Forster) **27**:69, 75-6, 86, 97, 100, 114, 122, 123

"Mr. Higginbotham's Catastrophe" (Hawthorne) **3**:154

"Mr. Kempe" (de la Mare) **14**:70, 80, 85, 90

"Mr. Lyon" (Carter)
    See "The Courtship of Mr. Lyon"

Mr. (Calvino)
    See *Palomar*

"Mister Palomar in the City" (Calvino) **3**:113, 115

"Mister Palomar's Vacation" (Calvino) **3**:113

"Mister Toussan" (Ellison) **26**:7-9, 11, 21, 28-9

"The Mistletoe Bough" (Sansom) **21**:110, 126

"The Mistletoe Bough" (Trollope) **28**:318, 326, 331, 333, 340, 346, 349, 355

"Mistress into Maid" (Pushkin)
    See "Baryshnia-krest'ianka"

"Mistris Lee" (Arnim) **29**:29-30

"A Misunderstanding (Farrell) **28**:99

"Mitchell on Matrimony" (Lawson) **18**:250-51

"Mitchell on the 'Sex,' and Other 'Problems'" (Lawson) **18**:250

"Mitchell on Women" (Lawson) **18**:250

"Mitosis" (Calvino) **3**:109-10

Mitsou (Colette) **10**:257, 271-74

"A Mixed Bag" (Sansom) **21**:102, 127

"Mixing Cocktails" (Rhys) **21**:68-9

The Mixture as Before (Maugham) **8**:379

"Mizu kara waga namida o nuguitamo hi" (Oe) **20**:220-21, 223, 225, 227-32, 234, 237-44, 246-47, 249-50

"M'liss" (Harte) **8**:210, 219, 222, 224-25, 231-32, 234

"Mlle de Scudèry" (Hoffmann) **13**:202

"The Mnemogogues" (Levi) **12**:279

"Mobile" (Ballard) **1**:68

"Mobiles" (Cowan) **28**:78; 80

Mobiles (Cowan) **28**:80; 83

The Mocassin Ranch (Garland) **18**:182

"The Mock Auction" (Lavin) **4**:183

"The Mocking-Bird" (Bierce) **9**:64, 67-8, 96

"The Model" (Nin) **10**:326

A Model for Death (Bioy Casares)
    See *Un modelo para la muerte*

"A Model Millionaire: A Note of Admiration" (Wilde) **11**:362, 399, 401, 407

Un modelo para la muerte (Bioy Casares) **17**:48, 74; **48**:42

"The Moderate Murderer" (Chesterton) **1**:132

"A Modern Brutus" (Page)
    See "The Outcast"

A Modern Comedy (Galsworthy) **22**:70-1

"Modern Love" (Boyle) **16**:148, 154-56

A Modern Lover (Lawrence) **4**:230

"A Modest Proposal" (Stafford) **26**:274-76, 285, 299, 307, 312

"Moebius Strip" (Cortazar) **7**:69

"Mohammed Fripouille" (Maupassant) **1**:275

"The Mohican" (Nin) **10**:303

"Mojave" (Capote) **2**:79-80

"Molly" (Dubus) **15**:86, 90-1

"Molly Cottontail" (Caldwell) **19**:46

"Molly's Dog" (Adams) **24**:11, 14

"Mom Bi: Her Friends and Enemies" (Harris) **19**:146, 157, 180

"The Moment" (Aiken) **9**:5, 13-14, 41

"The Moment before the Gun Went Off" (Gordimer) **17**:178, 187, 189-90

"The Moment of Truth" (Greene) **29**:223, 228

"Moments of Being: 'Slater's Pins Have No Points'" (Woolf) **7**:375, 388-89, 391-92, 398, 408-10

Moments of Reprieve (Levi)
    See *Lilít e altri racconti*

"Momoku monogatari" (Tanizaki) **21**:181, 188-89, 191, 198, 210-11, 224

"Mon oncle Jules" (Maupassant) **1**:277

"Mon oncle Sosthène" (Maupassant) **1**:263, 272

"A Monday Dream at Alameda Park" (Thomas) **20**:317

"Monday Is Another Day" (Farrell) **28**:120-1

"Monday or Tuesday" (Woolf) **7**:371, 374-75, 390, 392, 397-98, 402

Monday or Tuesday (Woolf) **7**:367-69, 371, 374, 392, 398-401, 404

Monde Comme il va (Voltaire) **12**:340, 393-94

"Money" (Galsworthy) **22**:98

"The Money Diggers" (Irving) **2**:251, 261-62

"The Money Juggler" (Auchincloss) **22**:9, 34, 49-50

"Monk" (Faulkner) **1**:165, 179

"The Monkey" (Dinesen) **7**:163, 167, 170, 173, 200-01, 203

"The Monkey" (King) **17**:274-75, 290-91, 293

"Monkey Nuts" (Lawrence) **4**:231, 234-35

"Monologue of an Old Pitcher" (Farrell) **28**:112

"Monologue of Isabel Watching It Rain in Macondo" (Garcia Marquez) **8**:194

"Monsieur les deux chapeaux" (Munro) **3**:348

"Monsieur Parent" (Maupassant) **1**:259-60, 283

"The Monster" (Moravia)
    See "The Monster"

The Monster (Crane) **7**:103-05, 107, 114, 116, 131, 134, 138, 146-48

The Monster, and Other Stories (Crane) **7**:104

Monte Verità (du Maurier) **18**:126, 137

A Month by the Lake, and Other Stories (Bates) **10**:122, 139-40

"A Monument of French Folly" (Dickens) **17**:124

"The Monumental Arena" (Saroyan) **21**:163

"The Moon and GNAC" (Calvino)
    See "Luna e G N A C"

"The Moon and Six Guineas" (Auchincloss) **22**:49

"The Moon in Letters" (Bierce) **9**:78

"The Moon in the Mill-Pond" (Harris) **19**:173

"The Moon in the Orange Street Skating Rink" (Munro) **3**:348-49

"Moon Lake" (Welty) **1**:474, 486

"The Moon Lens" (Campbell) **19**:72, 81

"Moon-Face" (London) **4**:252, 258-59

Moon-Face, and Other Stories (London) **4**:252

"A Moonlight Fable" (Wells) **6**:376

"Moonlight on the Snow" (Crane) **7**:108

The Moons of Jupiter (Munro) **3**:346-47

"Moonshine Lake" (Bulgakov) **18**:74

"The Moonshiners of Hoho-Hehee Falls" (Murfree) **22**:211

"Moon-Watcher" (Clarke) **3**:127-28

The Moor of Peter the Great (Pushkin)
    See *Arap Petra Velikogo*

Moorland Cottage (Gaskell) **25**:31, 47, 58, 60, 65, 71-2

Moral Tales (Laforgue)
    See *Moralités légendaires*

Moralités légendaires (Laforgue) **20**:85-6, 88-91, 93-5, 97-100, 102, 104-6, 108, 114, 122-23

"A Morality" (Forster)
    See "What Does It Matter? A Morality"

"Mordecai and Cocking" (Coppard) **21**:3

"The Mordivinian Sarafin" (Bunin)
    See "Mordovskiy sarafan"

"Mordovskiy sarafan" (Bunin) **5**:82, 106-08

"More about the Devil" (Gorky)
    See "Eshche o cherte"

"More Alarms at Night" (Thurber) **1**:428

"More Friend Than Lodger" (Wilson) **21**:320-21, 337, 339

More Ghost Stories of an Antiquary (James) **16**:231, 238, 251-52, 255, 258

"More Joy in Heaven" (Warner) **23**:380

"The More Little Mummy in the World" (Thomas) **20**:287, 308, 317

More Pricks than Kicks (Beckett) **16**:64-8, 70-2, 76, 78, 87, 92-4, 106, 108

More Roman Tales (Moravia)
    See *More Roman Tales*

"More Stately Mansions" (Updike) **13**:402, 409

"More Stately Mansions" (Vonnegut) **8**:433

More Stories by Frank O'Connor (O'Connor) **5**:371

"Morella" (Poe) **22**:299, 329

Die Morgenlandfahrt (Hesse) **9**:227-29, 240-41, 244-45

"Morning" (Barthelme) **2**:45, 55

"The Morning" (Updike) **13**:375

"The Morning after the Ball" (Tolstoy)
    See "After the Ball"

"Morning, Noon, Evening" (Shiga) **23**:344, 346, 348

"The Morning of a Landed Proprietor" (Tolstoy)
See *A Landlord's Morning*

"A Morning Walk" (Chopin) **8**:98

Morning-Glories and Other Stories (Alcott) **27**:11, 41-3

"Morphine" (Bulgakov) **18**:86, 89

"Morris in Chains" (Coover) **15**:31, 50-1

"Mort and Mary" (O'Hara) **15**:248

"Une mort héroïque" (Baudelaire) **18**:15-16, 18, 27, 29-30, 34, 60

"The Mortal Coil" (Lawrence) **4**:235

"Mortality and Mercy in Vienna" (Pynchon) **14**:308, 310, 312, 320, 322-25, 328, 342-43, 347-49

"La morte" (Svevo) **25**:330-32, 336-37, 351, 360

"Una morte" (Svevo)
See "La morte"

"La morte addosso" (Pirandello) **22**:281, 283

"La morte amoureuse" (Gautier) **20**:3-4, 6-8, 13, 17-20, 31-2, 38, 41

The Mortgaged Heart (McCullers) **9**:341-44, 355-57, 359

"The Mortification of the Flesh" (Dunbar) **8**:127

"Mortmain" (Greene) **29**:200, 202

"Morton Hall" (Gaskell) **25**:48-9, 59-60, 73

Mosaïque (Merimee) **7**:287-8, 290, 300

"Mosby's Memoirs" (Bellow) **14**:22, 24-5

Mosby's Memoirs, and Other Stories (Bellow) **14**:22-3, 25, 56

"Moscas y arañas" (Bioy Casares) **17**:87-9

"Moscow of the Twenties" (Bulgakov) **18**:92

"The Moslem Wife" (Gallant) **5**:135-38

"The Moss People" (Alcott) **27**:43

Mosses from an Old Manse (Hawthorne) **3**:155, 160, 174, 180, 185

"The Most Extraordinary Thing" (Andersen) **6**:11

"The Most Noble Conquest of Man" (Norris) **28**:205

"The Most Profound Caress" (Cortazar)
See "La caricia más profunda"

"Motel Architecture" (Ballard) **1**:79

"The Moth" (Wells) **6**:383

"Mother" (Anderson) **1**:33, 44

"Mother" (Barnes) **3**:22, 26

"A Mother" (Galsworthy) **22**:59, 98

"A Mother" (Joyce) **3**:205, 210-11, 234, 237, 245, 247, 249; **26**:46, 50

"The Mother" (Pavese) **19**:366, 368, 389

"The Mother" (Saroyan) **21**:134

"The Mother" (Svevo)
See "Le madre"

"Mother and Child" (Hughes) **6**:119, 142

Mother and Child (Vinge) **24**:327-28, 331, 333-35, 337, 345

"Mother and Daughter" (Lawrence) **4**:205, 220; **19**:267

"Mother and Son" (Narayan) **25**:135, 137, 153, 156, 159

"Mother and Son" (O'Flaherty) **6**:262

"The Mother Bit Him" (Narayan) **25**:135

"The Mother Hive" (Kipling) **5**:279

"Mother Matilda's Book" (O'Faolain) **13**:293, 297

"The Mother of a Queen" (Hemingway) **1**:211

The Mother of Captain Shigemoto (Tanizaki)
See *Shosho Shigemoto no haha*

"The Mother Stone" (Galsworthy) **22**:101

"The Mother Trip" (Pohl) **25**:236

"Motherhood" (Anderson) **1**:27

"Mothering Sunday" (Thomas) **20**:321-22

"A Mother-in-Law" (Pirandello) **22**:236

"Mother's Day" (Fuentes) **24**:61, 75-8

"Mother's Death and the New Mother" (Shiga)
See "Haha no shi to atarishi haha"

"Mother's Sense of Fun" (Wilson) **21**:319, 321, 323, 330-31, 333, 337-38, 342-43, 351, 364

"A Mother's Vision" (Peretz) **26**:205

"The Motive" (Cortazar) **7**:69-70

"The Motive" (du Maurier) **18**:125, 138

A Motley (Galsworthy) **22**:58-60, 97-100

"Mouche" (Maupassant) **1**:273, 284

"The Mound" (Lovecraft) **3**:270-71, 274, 279

"The Mountain" (Pavese) **19**:368, 390

"The Mountain Day" (Stafford) **26**:289

"The Mountain Tavern" (O'Flaherty) **6**:277-78, 281, 284

The Mountain Tavern, and Other Stories (O'Flaherty) **6**:262-65, 278, 283

"Mountjoy" (Irving) **2**:242

Mourner at the Door (Lish) **18**:275, 277-78, 280-83

"The Mourners" (Malamud) **15**:203, 205, 214, 217-18, 222-23, 225, 227

"The Mouse" (Lavin) **4**:167, 182

"The Mouse" (Nin) **10**:299-303, 319

"The Mouse and the Woman" (Thomas) **3**:399-402, 408

"La moustache" (Maupassant) **1**:274

"The Moviemaker" (Dixon) **16**:211

"Movies" (Dixon) **16**:206, 208, 214

Movies (Dixon) **16**:205-08, 211, 214-15

"The Moving Finger" (King) **17**:294

"The Moving Finger" (Wharton) **6**:414

"Moving Spirit" (Clarke) **3**:134

"The Mower" (Bates) **10**:124, 131-32

"Mowgli's Brothers" (Kipling) **5**:293

"Moxon's Master" (Bierce) **9**:72, 88

"Mr and Mrs Dove" (Mansfield) **9**:305

"Mr. and Mrs. Elliot" (Hemingway) **1**:208

"Mr. Arcularis" (Aiken) **9**:5-6, 9, 12-13, 15, 18-19, 33-41

"Mr. Austin" (Farrell) **28**:114, 116

"Mr. Bruce" (Jewett) **6**:157, 166

"Mr. Cass and the Ten Thousand Dollars" (O'Hara) **15**:248

"Mr. Coffee and Mr. Fixit" (Carver) **8**:18-19, 32-3, 59-60

"Mr. Cornelius Johnson, Office Seeker" (Dunbar) **8**:122, 125, 128, 131, 141, 144

"Mr. Durant" (Parker) **2**:274

Mr. Featherstone Takes a Ride (Bates) **10**:124

"Mr. Foolfarm's Journal" (Barthelme) **2**:40

"Mr. Fox Gets into Serious Business" (Harris) **19**:171

"Mr. Groby's Slippery Gift" (Dunbar) **8**:122

"Mr. Harrington's Washing" (Maugham) **8**:369, 377, 383

"Mr. Harrison's Confessions" (Gaskell) **25**:32-3, 55, 66-7, 73

"Mr. Humphreys and His Inheritance" (James) **16**:230-32, 234, 245, 252-53, 258

"Mr. Icky" (Fitzgerald) **6**:58

"Mr. Jack Hamlin's Mediation" (Harte) **8**:248-49

"Mr. Jones" (Wharton) **6**:426-27

"Mr. Justice Harbottle" (James) **16**:238

"Mr. Justice Hartbottle" (Le Fanu) **14**:223-25, 232-34, 236-38, 240-41, 248

"Mr. Know-All" (Maugham) **8**:366

"Mr. Lightfoot in the Green Isle" (Coppard) **21**:19

"Mr. McNamara" (Trevor) **21**:247

"Mr. Minns and His Cousin" (Dickens) **17**:121, 125

Mr. Mulliner Speaking (Wodehouse) **2**:338

"Mr. Pale" (Bradbury) **29**:66

"Mr. Peebles' Heart" (Gilman) **13**:126

"Mr. Pietro" (Pavese) **19**:378

"Mr. Potter Takes a Rest Cure" (Wodehouse) **2**:355-56

"Mr. Powers" (Gordon) **15**:143

"Mr. Preble Gets Rid of His Wife" (Thurber) **1**:418

"Mr. Prokharchin" (Dostoevsky) **2**:170, 191-94

"Mr. Rabbit Grossly Deceives Mr. Fox" (Harris) **19**:172, 194

"Mr. Rabbit Nibbles Up the Butter " (Harris) **19**:195

"Mr. Skelmersdale in Fairyland" (Wells) **6**:391-92

"Mr. Smellingscheck" (Lawson) **18**:215

"Mr. U" (Morand) **22**:178-80

"Mr. Wolf Makes a Failure" (Harris) **19**:171

"Mrs. Acland's Ghosts" (Trevor) **21**:262

"Mrs. Bathurst" (Kipling) **5**:266, 278-79, 281

"Mrs. Billingsby's Wine" (Taylor) **10**:392, 401-02

"Mrs. Bonny" (Jewett) **6**:150, 168

"Mrs. Brown" (O'Hara) **15**:248

"Mrs. Brumby" (Trollope) **28**:321, 335, 348, 353

"Mrs. Dalloway in Bond Street" (Woolf) **7**:381-82

Mrs. Dalloway's Party (Woolf) **7**:381-82, 388, 392

"Mrs. Fay Dines on Zebra" (Calisher) **15**:3, 7

"Mrs. Frola and Her Son-in-Law, Mr. Ponza" (Pirandello)
See "La Signora Frola e il signor Ponza, suo genero"

"Mrs. Galt and Edwin" (O'Hara) **15**:248, 266

Mrs. Gaskell's Tales of Mystery and Horror (Frank) **25**:

Mrs. Gaskell's Tales of Mystery and Horror (Gaskell) **25**:37

"Mrs. General Talboys" (Trollope) **28**:317-18, 330, 332, 336, 347, 357

"Mrs. Gunton of Poughkeepsie" (James) **8**:311

"Mrs. Hofstadter on Josephine Street" (Parker) **2**:283

"Mrs. Kemper" (Suckow) **18**:393, 409

"Mrs. Mean" (Gass) **12**:123, 134,138-9

"Mrs. Merrill's Duties" (Gilman) **13**:141

"Mrs. Mobry's Reason" (Chopin) **8**:71

"Mrs. Parkins's Christmas Eve" (Jewett) **6**:156, 159

"Mrs. Partridge Has a Fit" (Harris) **19**:195

"Mrs. Peckover's Sky . . ." (Wilson) **21**:358, 362

"Mrs. Powers' Duty" (Gilman) **13**:141

"Mrs. Reinhardt" (O'Brien) **10**:333

Mrs. Reinhardt, and Other Stories (O'Brien) **10**:333

"Mrs. Rinaldi's Angel" (Ligotti) **16**:280, 292, 294-95, 297

"Mrs. Ripley's Trip" (Garland) **18**:143, 159, 162-63, 165-67, 172, 192

"Mrs. Silly" (Trevor) **21**:233

"Mrs. Skagg's Husbands" (Harte) **8**:234, 244

"Mrs. Stratton of Oak Knoll" (O'Hara) **15**:252, 280

"Mrs. Todd's Shortcut" (King) **17**:275

"Mrs. Vane's Charade" (Alcott) **27**:32, 60

"Mrs. Vincent" (Bates) **10**:117

Title Index

"A Pinch of Salt" (Jewett) **6**:158
"The Pine Tree" (Andersen) **6**:12, 40-1
"The Pines" (Bunin) **5**:100
Ping (Beckett)
    See *Bing*
The Pink and the Green (Stendhal)
    See *Le rose et le vert*
"The Pink Corner Man" (Borges)
    See "Hombre de la esquina rosada"
"Pink May" (Bowen) **3**:31-2, 41; **28**:3-4
"The Pioneer Hep-Cat" (O'Hara) **15**:280
"Pioneers, Oh, Pioneers" (Rhys) **21**:50, 55-6, 65
"The Pious Cat" (Peretz) **26**:201
"La Pipe d'opium" (Gautier) **20**:23-5
Pipe Night (O'Hara) **15**:248-50, 262, 264-65, 267, 269
The Pit (Onetti)
    See *El pozo*
"The Pit and the Pendulum" (Poe) **1**:405-06; **22**:305
"The Pitcher" (Dubus) **15**:83, 100
"The Pixy and the Grocer" (Andersen)
    See "The Goblin at the Grocer's"
"A Place in the Heart" (Bates) **10**:119
"The Place of the Gods" (Benet)
    See "By the Waters of Babylon"
"The Place with No Name" (Ellison) **14**:109, 118, 120, 138
"Les plagiaires de la foudre" (Villiers de l'Isle Adam) **14**:397
"Plagiarized Material" (Oates) **6**:237, 242
"The Plague-Cellar" (Stevenson) **11**:304
"The Plain in Flames" (Rulfo)
    See "El llano en llamas"
The Plain in Flames (Rulfo)
    See *El llano en llamas, y otros cuentos*
"The Plain Man" (Galsworthy) **22**:60, 99
Plain of Fire (Rulfo)
    See *El llano en llamas, y otros cuentos*
Plain Tales (Kipling)
    See *Plain Tales from the Hills*
Plain Tales from the Hills (Kipling) **5**:273-74, 278, 288
"Un plaisant" (Baudelaire) **18**:17-18, 32, 60
Plan de evasión (Bioy Casares) **17**:53-5, 61, 63-4, 94
A Plan for Escape (Bioy Casares)
    See *Plan de evasión*
"Planchette" (London) **4**:265, 294-95
Planet Stories (Bradbury) **29**:90
"The Planets of the Years" (O'Faolain) **13**:291, 318-19
"A Plantation Witch" (Harris) **19**:140, 195
"The Planter of Malata" (Conrad) **9**:147
"Plants and Girls" (Lessing) **6**:217
"The Plattner Story" (Wells) **6**:359, 364-66, 394, 405
The Plattner Story, and Others (Wells) **6**:366-67, 380, 388
The Play, and Other Stories (Dixon) **16**:215
Play Days (Jewett) **6**:165-66
"Playback" (Beattie) **11**:11, 22
"The Playhouse Called Remarkable" (Spark) **10**:359, 361, 370
"A Play-House in the Waste" (Moore)
    See "San n-Diothramh Dubh"
"Playing the Game" (Campbell) **19**:76, 78, 90
"Playing With Fire" (Doyle) **12**:64
"Pleasure" (Lessing) **6**:197
"Pleasure" (O'Hara) **15**:248, 265
"The Pleasure-Cruise" (Kipling) **5**:284
"The Pleasures of Solitude" (Cheever) **1**:88

Plongées (Mauriac) **24**:183-84, 196, 203, 206, 208
"Plots and Counterplots" (Alcott)
    See "V.V.: or Plots and Counterplots"
"The Ploughman" (Dinesen) **7**:177
"Plumbing" (Updike) **13**:348
"A Plunge into Real Estate" (Calvino)
    See "La speculazione edilizia"
"Le plus beau dîner du monde" (Villiers de l'Isle Adam) **14**:377
"Le plus bel amour de Don Juan" (Barbey d'Aurevilly) **17**:7, 11-14, 19-20, 42-4
"Plus Ultra!" (Machado de Assis) **24**:152
"Plutarco Roo" (Warner) **23**:368
"Po' Sandy" (Chesnutt) **7**:5-7, 10, 13, 42
"Pocock Passes" (Pritchett) **14**:271, 285-86, 297
Poems in Prose from Charles Baudelaire (Baudelaire)
    See *Petits poèmes en prose: Le spleen de Paris*
"The Poet" (Dinesen) **7**:167-68, 180, 203, 209
"The Poet" (Hesse) **9**:234
The Poet and the Lunatics (Chesterton) **1**:124-26, 132
"The Poet and the Peasant" (Henry) **5**:194
"The Poet at Home" (Saroyan) **21**:155
"A Poetics for Bullies" (Elkin) **12**:94-7, 99, 117-18
"The Poetry of Modern Life" (Greene) **29**:218
Pohlstars (Pohl) **25**:235
"A Point at Issue" (Chopin) **8**:70, 73
"The Point of It" (Forster) **27**:69, 71, 74, 76-7, 83, 86, 96, 100, 114-15
"A Point of Law" (Faulkner) **1**:177
"Poison" (Mansfield) **9**:310-11
The Poisoned Kiss (Oates) **6**:236, 241-43
"Poker Night" (Updike) **13**:409
"Polar Bears and Others" (Boyle) **5**:54
"Polaris" (Lovecraft) **3**:288
"Polarities" (Atwood) **2**:2-5, 7-8, 10, 13-14
"Poldi" (McCullers) **9**:342, 345, 357
Pole Poppenspäler (Storm) **27**:279, 282, 284
"The Policeman's Ball" (Barthelme) **2**:31, 45
Polikushka (Tolstoy) **9**:376, 389, 393-94, 399, 403
"Polite Conversation" (Stafford) **26**:297, 312
"A Political Boy Is Now Dead" (Oe)
    See "Seiji shonen shisu"
"Political Director of Divine Worship" (Bulgakov) **18**:90
"Pollock and the Porroh Man" (Wells) **6**:388
"Polly: A Christmas Recollection" (Page) **23**:283-84, 297, 303-04
"Polydore" (Chopin) **8**:93
"Polyhymnia Muse of Sacred Song" (Auchincloss) **22**:51
"Polzunkov" (Dostoevsky) **2**:170, 192-93
"Pomegranate Seed" (Wharton) **6**:426-27, 431-32
"The Pomegranate Trees" (Saroyan) **21**:150, 168, 172, 174
"Un pomeriggio Adamo" (Calvino) **3**:97
The Ponder Heart (Welty) **1**:474, 477, 483, 494-95, 497
"Ponto de vista" (Machado de Assis) **24**:151
The Poodle Springs Story (Chandler) **23**:111
"The Pool" (du Maurier) **18**:127-28
"The Pool" (Maugham) **8**:369-71
"The Pool of Narcissus" (Calisher) **15**:15, 17
"The Poor and the Rich" (Saroyan) **21**:166
"The Poor Benefactor" (Stifter)
    See "Der Arme Wohltäter"
"The Poor Bird" (Andersen) **6**:4
"The Poor Boy" (Peretz) **26**:201

"The Poor Child's Toy" (Baudelaire)
    See "Le joujou du pauvre"
"The Poor Clare" (Gaskell) **25**:41, 54-5, 60
"A Poor Girl" (Chopin) **8**:69
"The Poor Heart" (Saroyan) **21**:162
"Poor John" (Andersen) **6**:4
"Poor Little Black Fellow" (Hughes) **6**:118, 121-22, 134
"Poor Little Rich Town" (Vonnegut) **8**:436
"The Poor Man" (Coppard) **21**:3, 15, 17, 27
"Poor Man's Pudding and Rich Man's Crumbs" (Melville) **1**:303, 323
"Poor Mary" (Warner) **23**:370
"Poor People" (O'Flaherty) **6**:262, 264, 280, 283
"The Poor Thing" (Powers) **4**:368, 372-73
"Poor Thumbling" (Andersen) **6**:4, 7
"Pop Goes the Alley Cat" (Stegner) **27**:218, 220
"Pope Zeidlus" (Singer) **3**:364
"Poppy Seed and Sesame Rings" (Jolley) **19**:241
"Popsy" (King) **17**:295
"Popular Mechanics" (Carver) **8**:14, 18, 26, 30, 44-5
"Por boca de los dioses" (Fuentes) **24**:30, 38, 40, 43-4, 54-5
"Por qué ser así?" (Unamuno) **11**:312
"Porcelain and Pink" (Fitzgerald) **6**:59
"Porcupines at the University" (Barthelme) **2**:56
"Porn" (Walker) **5**:412-14
"Le port" (Baudelaire) **18**:6
"Le port" (Maupassant) **1**:264
"Porte cochère" (Taylor) **10**:379, 407
"The Porter's Son" (Andersen) **6**:11-12
"The Portly Gentleman" (O'Hara) **15**:284
"The Portobello Road" (Spark) **10**:350-53, 355, 357-58, 360, 365-66, 368, 370-71
"Portrait" (Boyle) **5**:54
"A Portrait" (Galsworthy) **22**:58, 74-5, 98, 100
"The Portrait" (Gogol)
    See "Portret"
"The Portrait" (Oliphant) **25**:196, 209
"The Portrait" (Wharton) **6**:414
"A Portrait of Shunkin" (Tanizaki)
    See "Shunkin sho"
Portrait of the Artist as a Young Dog (Thomas) **3**:394-97, 399, 402-04, 410-13
"Portrait of the Intellectual as a Yale Man" (McCarthy) **24**:213
"Portraits de maîtresses" (Baudelaire) **18**:18, 25, 37
"Portret" (Gogol) **9**:102-03, 116, 122, 125; **29**:128, 135, 172
Die Portugiesin (Musil) **18**:292-93, 297-303, 322
The Portuguese Lady (Musil)
    See *Die Portugiesin*
"The *Porush* and the Bear" (Peretz) **26**:216
"Poseidon and Company" (Carver) **8**:50-1
"Poseidon's Daughter" (Sansom) **21**:86-7, 124
"Poseshchenie muzeia" (Nabokov)
    See "The Visit to the Museum"
"The Possessed" (Clarke) **3**:132, 135, 143-44, 148
"Possession of Angela Bradshaw" (Collier) **19**:98, 101, 110, 114
"The Possibility of Evil" (Jackson) **9**:256
"Posson Jone'" (Cable) **4**:48, 56, 58, 62, 64-5, 67, 77-80
"The Post" (Chekhov) **2**:130, 156
"The Post Card" (Boell)
    See "Die Postkarte"
"The Post Office" (O'Flaherty)
    See "Oifig an Phoist"

Title Index

Title Index

Title Index